African Intellectual Heritage

A Book of Sources

Molefi Kete Asante
& Abu S. Abarry

African Intellectual Heritage

A Book of Sources

 Temple University Press   *Philadelphia*

Temple University Press, Philadelphia 19122
Copyright © 1996 by Temple University
All rights reserved
Published 1996
Printed in the United States of America

⊗ The paper used in this publication meets the requirements of the American
National Standard for Information Sciences—Permanence of Paper for Printed
Library Materials, ANSI z39.48–1984

Text design by Chiquita Babb

Library of Congress Cataloging-in-Publication Data
African intellectual heritage : a book of sources / Molefi Kete Asante
    and Abu S. Abarry, editors.
        p.   cm.
    Includes bibliographical references and index.
    ISBN 1–56639–402–3 (cloth). —ISBN 1–56639–403–1 (paper)
    1. Africa—Civilization—Sources.   2. Afro-Americans—History—
Sources.   I. Asante, Molefi K., 1942–   .   II. Abarry, Abu
Shardow, 1947–   .
CB235.A33   1996
960—dc20   96-33807

Contents

Contents

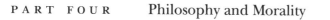

PART FIVE   Society and Politics   *441*

Contents

Preface

Humans have created signs and symbols on the African continent longer than anywhere else on the earth. Yet there remains a general impression that the continent is devoid of an intellectual heritage, cultural traditions, and sources in the way that one speaks of such a heritage in Europe or Asia. One often hears the complaint, "If there were only written records!"

The fact that *African Intellectual Heritage: A Book of Sources* is the first volume to organize documentary evidences of African discourse on a number of significant themes speaks to the marginal role scholars have accredited to Africa since the German philosopher Georg Hegel announced in the nineteenth century that "Africa was no part of history." In a very modest way we seek to provide documents that might be useful in assessing aspects of African thought.

Our premise was simple. We wanted to compile a volume of works by continental and diasporan Africans that would serve as a foundation for study and reflection. There was no attempt to select works based on the political ideology held by the writers. We reviewed a tremendous volume of materials, and chose the works that best represented categories that appeared to be quite common in African literature and oratory. No attempt is made in this book to justify the inclusion of one document or the other because they reflect a certain African way of saying something, as one would not do this, say, if one were compiling a selection of Asian or European writings. We suspect, however, that when sufficient study of the African corpus is made, from the earliest times to the present, there will be a relatively straightforward reassessment of the role written thought has played in the African world.

The project has had its difficulties because several documents had to be retranslated, which depended in large part upon intense discussion and even debate between the editors on "African ways of saying something." For example, in the ancient Egyptian texts we frequently found it necessary to rely upon our own translation of the originals rather than the translations of the nineteenth or early twentieth century. This meant tracking down the originals in libraries and museums in the United States and Egypt, particularly Cairo and Luxor. Furthermore, the information we sought was not always preserved in ways that we could use, and certain oral traditions of importance had not been written in any form. In addition, the preservation of African historical documents was not a priority for either colonial or postcolonial governments on the continent, and therefore we were often at a disadvantage in some regions if we wanted older texts. What remain are those documents that have been collected by interested persons and preserved in the best way they could manage. There are, for example, few national libraries or museums that have preserved the documents of some of the earlier writers. At the University of Algiers we can find work by Ahmed Baba, the famous sixteenth-century professor at the University of Sankore in Timbuktu. There are documents preserved in the Christian monasteries in Ethiopia and at the University of Khartoum. In some places the ravages of time and weather and the pillages of plunderers have rendered hopeless the task of discovering documents. Inscriptions on stone and other durable materials have remained, and we have recorded some of those. It should be remembered, however, that this is not a complete work; it is only the beginning of a process of recovery and reconstruction.

Is there an African canon? Or better yet, is there a need to compile an African canon, since Africa is so diverse? What constitutes the difference between a national canon and a continental canon? Do Africans have a self-conscious understanding and acceptance of a canon? These are questions that shall be debated and discussed for years, and we hope that we have provided at least some of the materials to aid in the discussion.

This collection is the first attempt to define what the limits of an African canon should be, both geographically and temporally. Among the major concerns of the African people have been issues of origin, relationships with the spiritual world and with other humans, and harmony with the organic and inorganic matter that constitutes the physical environment. How to honor Ma'at—that is, justice, righteousness, balance, and harmony— becomes the continental quest. This is to be contrasted with the quest for love and individual freedom in the European canon with its quest for personal self-disclosure.

We wish to acknowledge the assistance of Lona Reeves, Cindy Lehman, Malaika Ndiika Mutere, Anita Samuels, and Letitia Coleman in the preparation of the manuscript. Without them some of the rarer documents would have been even more difficult to find. They all have worked at various times on some aspect of this manuscript. We also thank Nadia Kravchenko, who as usual rises to the occasion to demonstrate what word processing was meant to be. She remains incredible.

During the five years we have worked on this project, we have learned many things, including the *mdu ntr*. Beyond that, however, we have found the tireless encouragement of our editor, Janet Francendese, comforting and supportive, even when we wondered if the task would ever be completed. We are eternally grateful to her for her confidence in our capability.

In addition, we would like to thank Dr. Victor Kwesi Essien, Dr. and Mrs. Emeka Nwadiora, Reverend and Mrs. Ofosu-Donkoh, Clement Oniango, and Al Vara. Special gratitude to Kariamu Welsh-Asante, Nana Abarry, and our children for their support, patience, and love.

Finally, we acknowledge with delight all the discussions about the nature of the African past that we have had with our many colleagues of the Temple Circle of Afrocentricity. We dedicate this book to our graduate students, who are studying and learning how to center African people in the context of their own agency.

M.K.A.
A.S.A.

An African Chronology

THE AUSETIAN AGE

c. 6000–4000 B.C.   The River People emerge along the Nile, Niger, and Congo.

The Isonghee of Zaire introduce mathematical abacus.

Cyclopean stone tombs built in the Central African Republic area.

Amrateans and Badarians in the Nile Valley.

c. 4000–50 B.C.   Nile Valley civilizations commence.

Nubia, Meroë, Napata, Kemet, and Ethiopia rise and fall.

Calendar invented.

The book of knowing the creations composed.

The pyramids built.

The dynasties established.

THE REASCENSION OF RELIGION

c. 100–1000 A.D.   Coptics in Ethiopia and Egypt.

Augustine, bishop of Africa.

The Nubians involved in the Crusades.

c. 500–1500   Engaruka, a town of 6,000 stone houses in Tanzania, occupies a key role in the emergence of Central Africa empires.

The Edo of Benin and the Akan of Ghana build underground tunnels that connect villages.

c. 639–641	Khalif Omar conquers Egypt with Islamic troops.
c. 740–1492	Islamicized Africans invade Spain and rule for seven centuries.
c. 300 B.C.–1242	Ghana emerges as the dominant empire in the West, controlling gold, salt, and trans-Saharan routes.
c. 1242–1600	Mali and Songhay expand African interest in the world; universities opened, ships sent across the ocean, scholars and believers travel to Mecca; Islam makes major inroads into governments.
c. 600–1600	Stone city-states of Zimbabwe, Dhlo-Dhlo, Kilwa, and Sofala.

THE AGE OF DISINTEGRATION

c. 1200–1700	Consolidation of Congo Empire. Emergence of Angola, court intrigues. New art forms depict Congo power.
c. 1480–1808	European intrusions and kidnappings. Deception, slavery, torture, and dispersion.
c. 1500–1957	Colonialism, slavery, and resistance.

THE AGE OF RECONSTRUCTION

| c. 1834–2000 | Slavery abolished in British possessions. Ethiopia defeats Italy. Slavery abolished in the Americas. African nations lose and regain independence. Economic restructuring underway. |
| c. 1950–2000 | Africans in the Caribbean and Americas play roles in the reconstruction of African history, culture, and economies. Africa throws off apartheid in South Africa to regain a free continent. |

African Sources: An Introduction

SANKOFA, OR RETURN TO THE SOURCE

Modern scholarship has confronted two major problems in establishing the source of African traditions in antiquity: (1) the loss of sources, and (2) undeciphered documents. Both problems will be evident in our collection, the first in literary gaps in time and the second in our inability to provide written documents for every area of the continent. This volume does not cover every cultural region of the African world, but it does provide sources from the major areas.

Certain material sources of the Nile Valley civilizations, the oldest on the continent, were destroyed with the various capitulations of Egypt to the armies of Persia, Assyria, Macedonia, Rome, Arabia, and France. Some artifacts, written and material, from ancient Sudan (Nubia, Meroë) and Ethiopia (Axum) have been lost or have not yet been deciphered. Artistic and historical sources were uprooted from their places of origin and removed to museums in Berlin, London, Paris, New York, Lisbon, Madrid, and Rome. In fact, African sources have been vulnerable at least since the Persian invasion of the sixth century B.C. Almost any object not attached to a wall or a boulder could be—and was—carted away. Perhaps no continent's ancient creations have been so wantonly removed as those of Africa. Hundreds of museums, libraries, research centers, and private collectors in the West house thousands of pieces of African art from antiquity as well as more modern times. How many sources of what type were mutilated, destroyed, or cast aside as so much rubble in the rush to sort through the ancient house of Africa? We do not know and cannot estimate the damage done to the intellectual history of the continent.

Since documentary evidences include not simply written materials but artistic and creative materials that may give insight into the lives of the people, we are doubly deprived of records when the artistic and creative works disappear. Fortunately, we have been able to visit archives and museums in Africa, Europe, and North America, including institutions such as the Bode Museum in Berlin, the British Museum in London, the Ile-Ife Museum, the Nigerian Museum of Art, and the Institut Fundamental d'Afrique Noire of Dakar, Senegal, where we have been able to consult original documents and see numerous African artifacts. Although we confronted the loss of sources as problematic, it has not meant that Africa is devoid of ancient sources. Indeed there are more extant ancient sources of the literature and history of Africa than there are of Europe. Yet we must be aware of the lack of sources in some areas due to either human or natural intervention. In the case of humans we are alluding to the displacement of objects and documents as discussed above, whereas the intervention of nature is responsible for erosion, decay, and destruction of biodegradable materials. While the loss of some sources has made our task more challenging, we have also been more justly happy when we have found rare documents that add to the African tradition.

The undeciphered sources are of two types: (1) the commonly known but undeciphered documents, and (2) the lesser known sacred and religious texts. The Meroitic text of ancient Meroe remains undeciphered, although its civilization was probably anterior to Egypt in many concepts, including the monarchy, organized religion, and writing. The Greek philosopher Democritus is credited with attempting to decipher the Meroitic text several centuries before Christ. The results of Democritus's work is not extant, and we can only speculate on its value. While considerable progress has been made in the deciphering of Meroitic texts, it is still too early to declare a victory in this work.

Secret societies, actually societies of secrets, often had their own scripts. One of the more famous of these scripts is that of the Vai in Liberia. But others exist among the Bamum, the Benin, the Bakongo, the Peul, and the Akan. As symbol systems for sacred occasions, these scripts are often under the control of specially trained and consecrated priests. As regularized codes that are used and understood by certain communities, these symbol systems constitute commonly accepted linguistic forms.

Ancient Africans believed that the deity Djehuti invented writing. So firmly was the belief in Djehuti's anteriority in the field of writing that the name of Djehuti, who became the Greek Hermes, was associated with wisdom and knowledge. Writing brought with it so much power and influence that the ancient Africans reserved the knowledge and the skill for priests and kings. Mystery and magic surrounded the development of the art, because few people could appreciate the strange markings on papyrus. One can imagine the aura of awe that accompanied the writing and reading of text skillfully traced on papyri. Those who understood the markings must have employed magic.

The ancients used writing initially for purposes of identification, that is, to provide evidence of a person's name, rank, and possessions on a tomb. The list of offerings, therefore, is perhaps the first full example of writing. Included in the list were possessions such as fabrics, oils, ointments, foods, and jewelry. Carved on the walls of tombs, these lists became permanent reminders of what the nobility possessed.

For the earliest written documents, apart from works of the Meroitic and pre-Meroitic people, we are indebted to the works written in stone and on papyri by the ancient Egyptians. Only in the nineteenth century, however, did we even gain entry into the secrets of that civilization.

We are fortunate that Jean-François Champollion provided the final piece to the puzzle of the ancient Egyptian language when he deciphered the Egyptian language in 1823. When a French artillery officer named Boussard found the Rosetta Stone in the ruins of Fort Saint Julien near the Rosetta Mouth of the Nile River in 1799, he began a chain of events that would lead to one of the greatest achievements in code decipherment. After all, "the Egyptians attained a high degree of refinement and luxury at a time when the whole western world was involved in barbarism, when the history of Europe, including Greece, was not yet unfolded, and ages before Carthage, Athens, and Rome were founded."[1] Thus, when Champollion accomplished his feat of deciphering the Rosetta Stone, he opened the door to information about one of the world's most ancient societies to teach political governance and citizen betterment.

The original Rosetta Stone stands in the British Museum in London, having been taken by the British soon after they took over from the French in Egypt. On its inscribed, side, it measures only 3 feet, 9 inches, by 2 feet, 4¹/₂ inches, by 11 inches. Indeed, this small stone is one of the most significant documents from the African continent. Although it is neither very large nor very old in African terms, it records that Ptolemy V Epiphanes, a descendant of the Ptolemy who had been a general under Alexander, extended benefits to the priests, reserved funds for temple maintenance, remitted the people's taxes during a particularly difficult economic downturn, and carried out extensive engineering feats of irrigation to control the Nile's waters when he ruled as king of Egypt from 205 to 182 B.C. In recognition of the king's magnanimous actions, the priesthood convened in the holy city of Memphis and ordered that a wooden statue of Ptolemy, to be housed in a gilded wooden shrine, be erected in every temple in the land.

Because Ptolemy V Epiphanes was of Macedonian lineage, it was decreed that Greek in addition to the two Egyptian scripts—hieroglyphic and hieratic—be inscribed on stelae describing the king's deeds. The decree was fulfilled in the eighth year of Epiphanes' reign. The Rosetta Stone is the only surviving stela from that period. However, the stone's linguistic value far exceeds its historical value, for it allowed those knowledgeable in Greek to decipher the Egyptian language.

Documents could be read with understanding once the scholars were able to decipher the text, and hence the doorway to African historiography remained opened to new discoveries. Thousands of ancient texts written by African hands were exposed to the inquiring minds for an eager audience. These documents revealed an African cosmogony, or concept of deities, as well as the development of geometry, philosophy, politics, and medicine.

Most Egyptian documents presented in this volume have been previously translated. Others have been retranslated, that is, updated in light of more modern usage and idioms. Still other documents have been translated for the first time either by the editors or by other scholars who are properly acknowledged. In this we have followed the tradition of King Shabaka, who had the Memphite theology recopied because, as it was said, "when his majesty found it even though it was from the ancestors, it had been desecrated by worms." The editors of this volume have found that many of the documents we are presenting here have lain wasting, unattended, in scattered places.

THE AFRICAN-EGYPTIAN QUESTION

The issue of the ethnicity and/or color of the ancient Egyptians is an example of contemporary social ideology entering ancient scholarship. Ethnicity of the ancient Egyptians has been revisited because of the numerous studies done by two continental scholars, Cheikh Anta Diop and Théophile Obenga. Both scholars attacked the central thesis of much Eurocentric scholarship on ancient Egypt. They argued that the European writers attempted to make the ancient Egyptians white in order to discredit the civilizing role of the African continent. Consequently, when African scholars from the continent and the Americas began to question the scholarship of the Eurocentric writers, a new level of dialogue around the ethnicity question entered the popular and scholarly literature. There probably would never have been a question about the Africanity and blackness of the ancient Egyptians had Africans never been enslaved by Europeans. The ancient Greek writers Herodotus, Diodorus Siculús, and Aristotle all testified to the fact that the ancient Egyptians were "black-skinned," not mixed or black-skinned whites, as some later European writers insisted in their works. Herodotus writes in his famous *Histories,* Book II, "On Egypt," that the Colchians must be Egyptians because, like them, they have black skin and wooly hair. Aristotle says in his book *Physiognomonica* that "too black a color marks the coward as witness the Egyptian and the Ethiopian." Largely disputed in its cultural origin because it was the dominant civilization of antiquity, influencing other cultures much as the Nile River flowing from the interior to Africa brought new ideas along its route, ancient Egypt was an African civilization related to the contiguous civilizations and societies of Nubia, Meroë, Napata, and Cush and to the world view of the Nuba and Shilluk, and based upon foundations lent by the African societies of the Amratean and the Badarian. Narmer (Menes), the king of the first dynasty, was simply one of a long list of kings who had ruled on the throne of Upper Egypt, that is, southern Egypt.

Even the African American Frank Snowden, Jr., wrote of Africans in antiquity with a certain smug Eurocentrism. As an author imbued with a peculiarly European focus on Africans, Snowden used the "ancients" to refer exclusively to whites. It seemed impossible for him to place himself in the context of African culture and civilization, as demonstrated in statements such as "in light of the importance the ancients attached to the color the skin as a means of classifying the Ethiopian," or "the ancients did not overlook the changes in color resulting from racial mixture between blacks and whites." Who are the ancients? In Snowden's vocabulary the ancients were the Greeks and the Romans. He succumbed to the heavily European centeredness of the Aryan model of the ancient world.

Neither the Sumerians nor the Chinese, who were the only other major civilizations of a similar date, produced the achievements of the ancient Africans in Egypt. Thus, Egypt remains the most important civilization of antiquity in its impact on European and African civilizations. Of course, the more Egypt is seen as a society of significance to human civilization, the more its origins are disputed by some white scholars. With no authority and no evidence from antiquity, a few European and American writers have said that the ancient Egyptians were either white or a mixture of white- and black-skinned people. Such writing is an indication of the difficulty for some scholars of accepting the African cultural origin of the ancient Egyptians. In their need to explain away the African base of this civilization, often fed by the racist sentiments of contemporary times, these writers have tried to put distance between Egyptians and other Africans. Unfortunately for them, the Nile River flows northward more than four thousand miles from the interior of Africa down to the Mediterranean, bringing with it culture and civilizations. As noted, even ancient Greek scholars said that the ancient Egyptians were black. This is not to say that one could not find white people in ancient Egypt, as one might find whites in Lagos, Nigeria, or Nairobi, Kenya, today. What the Greeks did was to describe the way the Egyptians looked to them. These early Greek writers said that the Egyptians were "black-skinned," and only through the most twisted logic could one get from their comments an idea that they meant "black-skinned whites," as a few Egyptologists such as Gaston Maspero and others have written. Such a person found on the African continent in every era would have been called black, African. Revisionist historians of the fifteenth to twentieth centuries, the age of the European slave trade, tried to discredit Africans and to accredit all African achievements to the presence of European genes. Martin Bernal, in his ground-breaking volumes *Black Athena,* has demonstrated the presence of the Aryan model of interpretation of the ancient world in the works of Europeans beginning with the fifteenth century. Thus, ancient Egypt, although it depicted itself as an African and black civilization, was not allowed to remain

African Sources: An Introduction

so in the minds of the Europeans. They disagreed with the Greeks of earlier times, who had actually *seen* the ancient Egyptians.

THE EARLIEST RECORDS OF AFRICA

According to E. A. Wallis Budge, the Egyptians used burial texts to accompany the dead from about 4500 B.C.[2] No other culture has a comparable antiquity in written documents. Budge is quick to point out, however, that it is difficult to say with certainty the exact date of the creation of the earliest documents. It is not until we arrive at the dynastic period that we have any concrete evidence of the age of documents. By the Fifth Dynasty (2494–2345 B.C.) we already have offering lists, prayers for offerings, and autobiographies. By the Sixth Dynasty (2345–2181 B.C.) we see the appearance of philosophical treatises often called instructions in wisdom or wisdom teachings by early Egyptologists. The earliest surviving philosophical treatise was written by Prince Hardjedef for his son Au-ib-re, possibly in the Fifth Dynasty. Two other works, those of Ptahhotep and of Kagemni, might be considered along with that of Hardjedef as representing the earliest examples of philosophical treatises. Larry Williams and Asa Hilliard identify the *Teachings of Ptahhotep* as the earliest philosophical instruction. Other scholars argue that the language of Ptahhotep and Kagemni is more of the Middle Kingdom than that of Hardjedef, which is clearly of the Old Kingdom.

In the mortuary sphere, the display of ceremonial and ritual inscriptions was extensive from the Old Kingdom throughout the history of Egypt. There were two types of such inscriptions—those called the pyramid texts and those on private tombs. These texts were often rerecorded on papyri.

THE HELLENIC PERIOD

Alexander's Macedonian army conquered Egypt without a fight in 332 B.C. During his brief visit to the country, Alexander was able to mark the site of the new capital—Alexandria, at the Canopic branch of the Nile River. It is reported that he took a trip into the Libyan desert to visit the shrine of Ammon at the oasis of Siwa. The oracle greeted him as a son, which was probably very wise of the god, as Alexander was nearing the height of his power. When Alexander died in 323 B.C. Ptolemy, one of his generals, became the dominant force in Egypt. A portion of the country was ruled by another of Alexander's generals, Seleucus. The dynasties that they founded lasted for nearly three hundred years. During this period, the literature of Egypt often reflected the Hellenic presence.

At the western end of Mediterranean Africa, the Carthaginians were eventually embroiled in struggle against the Romans. The battle to dominate the Mediterranean had begun and would last for several years until Rome, assisted by cavalry from Numidia just south of Carthage, won a great battle at Zama in Tunisia. Using their war elephants (which had probably been trained in Nubia), the main Carthaginian army squared off against the two Roman legions and their hundreds of Numidian supporters. Hannibal the Great had used African war elephants first when he crossed the Alps to fight the Romans in the second Roman-Carthaginian War in 218 B.C. Now at Zama, with a fresh supply of elephants, Hannibal was defeated by the Roman forces. After their conquest, the Romans enlarged the kingdoms of Numidia and Mauritania to take in much of Carthage.

However, Carthage remained a fairly strong kingdom despite the presence of Roman legions in Mediterranean Africa. By 149 B.C. Carthage was ready to fight Rome again, but lost badly in battles that lasted until 146 B.C., when the principal city was laid to waste by the Romans. The subsequent consolidation of Mediterranean Africa as a part of the Roman Empire was easier. Cyrenaica fell in 74 B.C.; Numidia in 46 B.C. and then again in 25 B.C.; and Egypt was defeated in 30 B.C. While Mauritania held nominal power, Rome was the power behind its king Juba II.

KEMET AND OTHER AFRICAN SOCIETIES

It is from the Egyptians that we receive our first written glimpse of Africa to the west and south of the Nile Valley. Narmer (Menes), the first dynastic king, came from the south, where he had been king of Upper Egypt. His conquest is memorialized on the famous Narmer Stela. One cannot have a full appreciation of the sources of African intellectual traditions without connecting Egypt to its natural relationship with the societies contiguous to it. A body of human sciences, constructed from the reasons, nuances, myths, and inquiries of Africans, can only be imagined if we do not begin at the beginning of African classical civilizations. It is from this position that we are able to realize a body of human sciences and studies based upon thousands of years of history. We find in the classical civilizations of Africa the answers to some of the most persistent questions of African capability and possibility.

Every African society owes something to Kemet. Apart from the ideas of medicine, the monarchy, geometry, the calendar, literature, and art, African societies found in Kemet the primordial myths that would govern the way they educated their children, preserved the values of their society, remembered their ancestors, painted their bodies and their houses, and farmed their land. So richly endowed was the Nile civilization that it seemed that all of those that had come before were merely preparatory to the real event. The materialization of the ideas, spirit, and conceptions of Africa in the sculpture, bas reliefs, and grand columns was enough to underscore the place of Kemet in the human process of transforming images into reality. Among the contributions received by the rest of Africa from Kemet was the appreciation for the concrete manifestation of the spiritual.

Throughout the book we use the ancient name "Kemet" to refer to the Land of the Nile, a term that dates from 3100 B.C. and that is commonly accepted among African Egyptologists. The name "Egypt," from the Greek *Aigyptos,* from the Mdunte *Hekaptah,* was used by the Greeks, who, like Homer, began to visit the Nile Valley about 800 B.C. Seeing that the country had many "houses or temples of the deity Ptah," they used Aigyptos to refer to what the inhabitants called "Kmt," that is, Kemet. "Kemet" means "the land of black people" or "black land"; the designation for "Km" in the ancient language is a piece of burnt charcoal.

THE PROBLEM OF A SOURCE BOOK

Although there has not been a collection of works on Africa comparable to this volume, anthologies of African writing have appeared. However, most of them focus on one particular genre of African writing. As examples we could point to the wonderful anthologies by Chinweizu and Henry Louis Gates, Jr. Only Chinweizu attempted to cover the continent and the diaspora, but limited the work to only those writers and materials accessible to him in Nigeria.

The aim of this volume is to provide a comprehensive selection of sources of the African tradition. This is not a literature book. We do not aim to demonstrate the transformation of literary genres or the movement of one phase of literature into another phase, nor do we attempt to compare one region with another. Our purpose is much simpler: to supply our readers with the best critical examples of works created out of the African imagination.

At the same time, we believe that our efforts have not been wholly successful, because we have not uncovered as many works by women as we believe must exist. Having excluded fiction and poetry from the volume, we are prevented from representing much of African women's bountiful literary production. This has frustrated us, but we believe that the intellectual work that does appear in this volume is significant in elucidating the originality and creativity of African women. We suspect that somewhere—either in oral traditions or in obscure records such as those of Arab merchants and European missionaries, accounts of speeches, or unpublished essays—there are important documents of women's thought and voices. What, for example, did Yaa Asantewaa say about Asante nationalism and pride in the face of the British invasion of the royal city of Kumasi in the nineteenth century? What political philosophy guided Nzingha of Ngola as she fortified her people against the Portuguese? It would be a tragedy if such records have not survived. But we anticipate that our volume will spur interest in reclaiming the full history of African women's intellectual work.

In keeping with the theme of reclamation, our translations of ancient texts have made use of previous works by various scholars, particularly the translations by Maulana Karenga in *The Husia* as well as fragments from Asa Hilliard and Théophile Obenga. We have also reviewed the works of Miriam Lichtheim, Richard Lepsius, E. A. Wallis Budge, Sir Alan Gardiner, and John Wilson. We have explored various archives and pursued many avenues in Africa, Europe, and North America in our quest for a comprehensive work.

A note on usage is necessary. We have preferred to use African renderings of words in our text—for example, Ausar to Osiris, and Kemet to Egypt—although we sometimes have used common Western versions.

The state of the information about ancient Africa is still not settled. Consequently, our book of sources reflects that situation. We are not yet able to give definitive translations of some of the documents. Having become familiar with many of the most ancient documents in the past ten years, the editors have spent considerable time discussing the meaning of certain words and phrases. Because we bring to this project the knowledge of the ancient Egyptian language, working knowledge of five other African languages, and access to more than a dozen additional languages, we have been able to provide original documents. Of necessity this collection is the result of our imagination. It is a deliberate reflection of the Afrocentric principles that govern our work. This does not mean that we have been arbitrary. Far from it: we have examined numerous traditions in order to find the documents included in this collection.

NOTES

1. Edward Farr, ed., *Ancient History: From Rollins and Other Ancient Sources,* vol. 1 (New York: Hurst and Co., 1910).
2. E. A. Wallis Budge, *Book of the Dead* (New York: Dover, 1968), p. xi.

The Creation of the Universe

PART ONE

Overleaf: Adinkra symbol for *gye nyame,* nothing greater than God

From the earliest writings to those of the present century, we see in the creation documents and sources of African traditions an emphasis on the sacred idiom. Africa appears always to be creating universes and establishing the presence of the divine. Although there are themes and concepts throughout African history that reflect the manifold dimensions of the various civilizations and cultures of the continent, the quest for the sacred is the most all-encompassing aspect of the African tradition.

In numerous ways, contemporary Africa and Africans are products of the earliest origin texts, explaining the source of nature and the role of humans in nature, and establishing the foundation for agriculture, human relations, science, law, customs, totems, art, architecture, and society. The documents in this section reveal the basis for an intellectual and spiritual heritage without which the modern African mind could not have developed. Between the earliest writings in the Nile Valley and the varied writings of Africans at this moment in history, there are fascinating and illuminating cultural linkages.

No theological documents occur in as much detail as early as the Heliopolis and Memphis theologies. They constitute the first records of human beings writing down what they believed to be the origin of their world, thus providing us with the ontological, cosmological, and epistemological aspects of our environment. Africans who created these first theological explanations become for the rest of us, in this age, the givers of the higher principles of human existence. One could discuss and debate the relative significance of Ptah and Atum—of the correctness of the priests of Memphis as against that of the priests of Heliopolis—thereby presaging what would become the pattern of theological conflict in years to come. Yet we know that the ancients who looked upon the Nile River and felt the heat of the sun during innumerable cloudless days and nights were articulating their responses to the universe while simultaneously creating universes.

The characteristic outlook that appears in this section is epic creation as demonstrated in every region of Africa. While we begin with the ritual myths of early Kemet, we see repeated throughout the continent, especially in the cases we cite, a remarkable reliance on the epic of creation of humans and the earth. There is a divine sanction to these myths; they do not appear in isolation. They are therefore intertwined with the human response to nature and the metaphysical; in fact, the creation myths are the fundamental rituals of African being.

Ancient Egypt stands in relationship to Africa as ancient Greece stands in relationship to Europe; so wrote the late Senegalese scholar Cheikh Anta Diop.[1] One finds in the seams of the philosophy, literature, and religion of the ancient Egyptians all of the threads of African civilization and much of what Western civilization calls its own. Ancient Egypt was called Kemet by its own people. And Kemet, with its long tradition of philosophy, geometry, architecture, and theology, set the tone for the African civilizations that grew up around the Nile Valley. The ancient African along the Nile River was in contact with the spiritual world of the ancestors in ways that are similar to the expressions of ancestral relations found in African societies throughout the continent.

THE HELIOPOLIS AND MEMPHIS NARRATIVES

We begin this section with two creation stories, which are major bases of the African response to the universe in its supernatural and natural forms. The first is the Heliopolis narrative, the second is the Memphite theology expressed in the Declaration of the Deities. Both documents are found in the *Ancient Near Eastern Texts Related to the Old Testament* (*ANET*), edited by James B. Pritchard for the Princeton University Press in 1955. Following Maulana Karenga's work with *The Husia*, we have retranslated these texts in the light of more modern African usage. The second and third documents of this section have been edited only slightly. Whereas Ra, or Ra-Atum, appears to have brought himself into existence through the act of ejaculation, Ptah, as the deity of the city of Memphis, the White Wall, gives us the first historical reference to what the Greeks would call two thousand years later *logos* (word). All things are brought into existence through the spoken word; nothing that exists is without the word being spoken. Ptah, as the god of the Declaration, emerges as the protector, creator, and sustainer not just of Memphis but of all living things.

The Heliopolis myth, as it is sometimes called, is actually the creation account of the priests of On, the ancient name of Heliopolis. We have read the translations of the works of H. Junker, M. Lichtheim, B. Sproul, and K. Sethe. However, because they were unfamiliar with the general African context of the writings, their works often lacked the poetic indirection of the African genre. Admittedly, we have attempted to apply the rhythm while remaining true to the text, using our knowledge of the Kemetic language and other African languages. Readers interested in comparisons might see the work of Junker.[2] In fact, during the period Junker was busy translating these ancient documents, nothing was further from his mind than the relationship of Egypt to the rest of Africa.

The text called the Memphite Declaration of the Deities consists of 2 horizontal lines of text and 62 vertical columns carved on a slab of black granite. Its introduction quite clearly shows that King Shabaka of the Twenty-Fifth Dynasty (c. 710 B.C.) had it recopied because the earlier version on papyrus was found to be worm-eaten. Linguistic and geopolitical analyses date the original text to more than 2500 years before Shabaka had it recopied. The translation in this volume is based on Pritchard's *ANET*.

THE PYRAMID TEXTS AND OTHER ANCIENT INSCRIPTIONS

The remaining ancient texts in this section, such as the royal inscriptions and the pyramid texts, are from the Old Kingdom and are found in volumes by James Breasted and Miriam

The Creation of the Universe

Lichtheim as well as in the *ANET*. Our retranslations of these texts sought only to simplify some of the expressions that were archaic and that represented the early stages of the work of the translators.

The Pyramid Texts

The so-called pyramid texts are documents, treatises, or inscriptions written on the walls of the pyramids. The earliest texts show a decidedly African emphasis on the resurrection of the king and a union with the sky. This is probably the origin of the idea of human resurrection, several thousand years before Christianity. Three stages can be identified in the texts, as the dead awakes, ascends to the sky, and is admitted to the company of the immortal deities.

The pyramid inscriptions of Unas, like those that follow from Teti and Pepi, represent the thoughts of an individual deeply devoted to the principles of eternity. In fact, Unas, the last king of the Fifth Dynasty, and Teti and Pepi, kings of the Sixth Dynasty, are among the most quoted early African philosophers. The selections from Teti further demonstrate the power of the resurrection from the dead as a source of ethical and futuristic orientation. Hope was to dwell eternally in the ancient Egyptian's heart.

Pepi I is credited with one of the most complete and beautiful pyramid texts. The selection here, on human salvation, represents the complexity of human moral choices and the simplicity of salvation by the power of Ra. Usually the ceiling of the sarcophagus's chamber was decorated with stars. In fact, these chambers present us with some of the earliest displays of the art of celestial re-creations.

Other Ancient Inscriptions

Inscriptions are among the most common forms of writing in ancient classical Africa. They are found on thousands of tombs, making ancient Kemet the most writing-obsessed civilization in antiquity. The forms of these inscriptions varied only slightly, but they revealed information about the tomb's owner and became an early version of the epitaph. The examples here, from Princess Ni-sedjer-kai, Hotep-her-akhet, Nefer-seshem-ra, and Ni-hebsed-Pepi, follow our own renditions of the originals.

Creation narratives are found throughout Africa and are not limited to Kemet. Thus, we see among the once widespread San people, now concentrated in southern Africa, a powerful creation story linked in its conceptualization of the deity with human characteristics to the narratives of the Nile. Like the San, the neighboring Khoi perfected their vision of creation based on the oral traditions of their priests. But this was not unlike creation narratives among the Barozvi, Dogon, Yoruba, and Asante, and ultimately the African American response to creation as seen by James Weldon Johnson.

NOTES

1. C. A. Diop, *The Cultural Unity of Black Africa* (Chicago: Third World Press, 1978).
2. H. Junker, *Die Götterlehre von Memphis,* Abhandlungen der Preussichen Akademie der Wissenschaften, 1939, Phil.-hist. KL. No. 23 (Berlin, 1940).

The Heliopolis Creation Narrative

This is the book of knowledge about the evolutions of Ra and the overthrowing of Apep. These are the words Nebertcher spoke soon after he had come into existence.

I am the one who came into being as Khepera, I am the one who created all that came into being, who created all that came into being, everything that came to be.

After my coming into existence, all other things were created through my mouth. Nothing existed in heaven or in earth, no plants, no creeping things, and no places before I created them out of Nu, the primeval water.

I could not find a standing place. Therefore, I worked a charm from my heart.

I found my standing place in Maat and created all my attributes. I was alone, for I had not yet spit out Shu or Tefnut.

Neither did there exist another who worked with me. I made a place in my own heart by my own will and created the multitudes of things which came into being of the things which came into being from out of the things which came into being of births, from out of the things which came into being of their births.

Even I myself used my clenched hand in an intercourse with my shadow, I poured semen into my own mouth and brought forth Shu.

Then I spat out Tefnut, which became moisture, goddess of world order. My father Nu said, "They drained me because for a long time the Trinity came out of me, a single god, in other words they came into existence through me."

Shu and Tefnut, therefore, were raised up and left their watery place of habitation and became one with me under my observation.

Following this unification I wept over my created parts. The tears of my eye gave birth to men and women.

My eye became jealous upon realizing that I had created other parts that might challenge its position of power and glory.

Therefore to appease it I relocated the eye on my forehead and gave it control over the earth and all creation.

Thereafter I came into existence in the forms of plants with all of their resources. I created plants and animals and other beings as well.

Shu and Tefnut, Geb and Nut give birth to Ausar, Heru-Khent-an-Maati, Set, Auset, Neb-het.

In turn, their own offspring gave birth and increased the earth's population.

The Memphite Declaration of the Deities

Heru is alive! He prospers the Two Lands and the Two Goddesses. He prospers the Two Lands, this Golden Heru. He nourishes the Two Lands, the King of Upper and Lower Kemet, Nefer-ka-Ra, the Son of Ra, Shabaka, beloved of Ptah-South-of-His-Wall, the living Ra forever. His majesty revised this text in the house of his father Ptah-South-of-His-Wall. Now when his majesty found it even though it was from the ancestors, it had been desecrated by worms, so that one could not tell head from tail. Therefore, his majesty had it written afresh so that it is better now than before. This he did so that his name might last and his memory be made to persist in the house of his father Ptah-South-of-His-Wall in the course of time. The son of Ra, Shabaka, did this for his father Ptah-tenen for eternal life.

Nine deities came to Geb, and he mediated between Heru and Set. He stopped them from quarreling, and he gave Set the kingship of Upper Kemet at the place of his birth, Su. Then Geb made Heru the King of Lower Kemet at Pezshet-Tawi, the place where his father Ausar was drowned. In this way Heru was in one place and Set in another and were at peace about the Two Lands. Geb said to Set, "Go to Upper Kemet where you were born."

Geb said to Heru, "Go to Lower Kemet where your father was drowned." Then Geb said to Heru and Set, "I have given you Lower and Upper Kemet."

Subsequently, Geb regretted that the portion of Heru was only equal to Set's. Because of this Geb gave his inheritance to Heru. In this way, Heru ruled over the whole land and the Two Lands were united in the great name of Tatenen-South-of-His-Wall, the Lord of Eternity. The two Great Powers grew upon his head and Heru became King of Upper and Lower Kemet.

Reed and papyrus were placed at the great double door of the House of Ptah to symbolize the reconciliation of Heru and Set and the unification of the Two Lands.

> The gods who came into being as Ptah
> Ptah who is upon the Great Throne
> Ptah-Nun, the father who got Atum;
> Ptah-Naunet, the mother who bore Atum;
> Ptah the Great, that is, the heart and tongue of the Ennead;
> Ptah who gave birth to the gods.

Atum came into being as both heart and tongue. The mighty Great One is Ptah, who gives life to all gods as well as to their *ka*'s [souls]. Through heart, Heru became Ptah, and through tongue Tehuti became Ptah. And so it was that the heart and tongue gained control over every other part of the body. Ptah taught that aspects of himself are manifested in all nature, in the mouth of all gods, and in every human, and in animals, plants and all other living things. Thus, whatever Ptah conceived came into being through utterance.

The nine deities stand before him as semen in the hands of Atum. While the nine deities of Atum came into being by his semen and his fingers, the nine deities of Ptah came forth from the teeth and lips in this mouth which pronounced the name of everything, from which Shu and Tefnut also came forth.

All the senses report to the heart. This is the manner in which every completed concept emerges and it is the tongue which announces what the heart thinks.

In this way all the gods were formed and the nine deities completed. Indeed, all divinity really came into being through what the heart thought and the tongue commanded. Thus the souls were made and the protective spirits were appointed, those responsible for all provisions and all nourishment. From that time on, justice was encouraged and injustice discouraged. From that time on, life was given to the one who maintained harmony and death to the one who brought disharmony. All arts and crafts, the arms, the movement of the legs, and the activity of every member were made in keeping with what the heart thought, which was spoken by the tongue, and which gives value to everything.

It was spoken of Ptah: "The one who created everything and brought gods into being." He is indeed Tatenen, who created the gods, for everything emerged from him, nourishment and provisions, the offerings to the gods, and all good things. Because of this it was known and understood that his power is greater than any other gods. And so Ptah was pleased after he had created everything, even the divine order. He had formed the gods, he had made cities, he had founded provinces, he had established the gods in their shrines, he had set their offerings, he had founded their shrines, he had harmonized their bodies with their hearts. Therefore, divinity entered into every tree, every stone, all clay and in anything where the divine might take form. So all the gods, as well as their ka's, gathered themselves to Ptah, content and associated with the Lord of the Two Lands.

The Great Stool, which pleases the heart of the gods, which is in the House of Ptah, the mistress of all life, is the Granary of God by which the sustenance of the Two Lands is prepared. This arrangement came into being as a result of the drowning of Ausar while Auset and Neb-het watched. Seeing him in distress Heru repeatedly ordered Auset and Neb-het to assist him and save him from drowning. Eventually, they were able to bring him to land. But he entered the mysterious portals in the glory of the lords of eternity, in the steps of him who shines forth on the horizon, on the ways of Ra on the Great Stool. He became a member of the court and associated with the gods of Tatenen Ptah, the lord of years.

Thus Ausar came to dwell in the House of the Sovereign on the north side of this land, which he had reached. His son Heru appeared as King of Upper Kemet and King of Lower Kemet, in the embrace of his father Ausar, together with the gods who were in front and behind him.

The Creation of the Universe

Pharaoh Unas

(FIFTH DYNASTY, 2450–2300 B.C., Kemet)

Vision of the Universe

Ascent to the sun-god

Ra-Atum, this Unas comes to you,
A spirit indestructible
Who lays claim to the place of the four pillars!
Your son comes to you, this Unas comes to you,
May you cross the sky united in the dark,
May you rise in lightland, the place in which you shine!
Seth, Nephthys, go proclaim to Upper Egypt's gods
And their spirits:
"This Unas comes, a spirit indestructible,
If he wishes you to die, you will die,
If he wishes you to live, you will live!"

Ra-Atum, this Unas comes to you,
A spirit indestructible
Who lays claim to the place of the four pillars!
Your son comes to you, this Unas comes to you,
May you cross the sky united in the dark,
May you rise in lightland, the place in which you shine!
Ausar, Auset, go proclaim to Lower Egypt's gods
And their spirits:
"This Unas comes, a spirit indestructible,
Like the morning star above Hapy,
Whom the water-spirits worship;
Whom he wishes to live will live,
Whom he wishes to die will die!"

Ra-Atum, this Unas comes to you,
A spirit indestructible
Who lays claim to the place of the four pillars!
Your son comes to you, this Unas comes to you,
May you cross the sky united in the dark,
May you rise in lightland, the place in which you shine!

Thoth, go proclaim to the gods of the west
And their spirits:
"This Unas comes, a spirit indestructible,
Decked above the neck as Anubis,
Lord of the western height,
He will count hearts, he will claim hearts,
Whom he wishes to live will live,
Whom he wishes to die will die!"

Ra-Atum, this Unas comes to you,
A spirit indestructible
Who lays claim to the place of the four pillars!
Your son comes to you, this Unas comes to you,
May you cross the sky united in the dark,
May you rise in lightland, the place in which you shine!
Heru, go proclaim to the powers of the east
And their spirits:
"This Unas comes, a spirit indestructible,
Whom he wishes to live will live,
Whom he wishes to die will die!"
Ra-Atum, your son comes to you,
Unas comes to you,
Raise him to you, hold him in your arms,
He is your son, of your body, forever!

The triumph of the White-crown

White-crown goes forth,
She has swallowed the Great;
White-crown's tongue swallowed the Great,
Tongue was not seen!

The king joins the stars

This Unas comes to you, O Nut,
This Unas comes to you, O Nut,
He has consigned his father to the earth,
He has left Heru behind him.
Grown are his falcon wings,
Plumes of the holy hawk;
His power has brought him,
His magic has equipped him!

The sky-goddess replies

Make your seat in heaven,
Among the stars of heaven,

The Creation of the Universe

For you are the Lone Star, the comrade of Hu!
You shall look down on Ausar,
As he commands the spirits,
While you stand far from him;
You are not among them,
You shall not be among them!

The king is cleansed in the Field of Rushes

Cleansed is he who is cleansed in the Field of Rushes:
Cleansed is Ra in the Field of Rushes;
Cleansed is he who is cleansed in the Field of Rushes:
Cleansed is this Unas in the Field of Rushes.
Hand of Unas in hand of Ra!
O Nut, take his hand!
O Shu, lift him up!
O Shu, lift him up!

The king crosses over to the eastern sky

The sky's reed-floats are launched for Ra,
That he may cross on them to lightland;
The sky's reed-floats are launched for Harakhty,
That Harakhty may cross on them to Ra;
The sky's reed-floats are launched for Unas,
That he may cross on them to lightland, to Ra;
The sky's reed-floats are launched for Unas
That he may cross on them to Harakhty, to Ra.

It is well with Unas and his *ka*,
Unas shall live with his *ka*,
His panther skin is on him,
His staff in his arm, his scepter in his hand.
He subjects to himself those who have gone there,
They bring him those four elder spirits,
The chiefs of the sidelock wearers,
Who stand on the eastern side of the sky
Leaning on their staffs,
That they may tell this Unas's good name to Ra,
Announce this Unas to Nehebkau,
And greet the entry of this Unas.
Flooded are the Fields of Rushes
That Unas may cross on the Winding Water:
Ferried is this Unas to the eastern side of lightland,
Ferried is this Unas to the eastern side of sky,
His sister is Sothis, his offspring the dawn.

Vision of the Universe

The king summons the ferryman

Awake in peace, you of back-turned face, in peace,
You who looks backward, in peace,
Sky's ferryman, in peace,
Nut's ferryman, in peace,
Ferryman of gods, in peace!
Unas has come to you
That you may ferry him in this boat in which you ferry the gods.
Unas has come to his side as a god comes to his side,
Unas has come to his shore as a god comes to his shore.
No one alive accuses Unas;
No dead accuses Unas;
No goose accuses Unas,
No ox accuses Unas.
If you fail to ferry Unas,
He will leap and sit on the wing of Thoth,
Then *he* will ferry Unas to that side!

The king lives because of the gods

Sky rains, stars darken,
The vaults quiver, earth's bones tremble,
The planets stand still
At seeing Unas rise as power,
A god who lives on his fathers,
Who feeds on his mothers!

Unas is master of cunning
Whose mother knows not his name;
Unas's glory is in heaven,
His power is in lightland;
Like Atum, his father, his begetter,
Though his son, he is stronger than he!

The forces of Unas are behind him,
His helpers are under his feet,
His gods on his head, his serpents on his brow,
Unas's lead-serpent is on his brow,
Soul-searcher whose flame consumes,
Unas's neck is in its place.

Unas is the bull of heaven
Who rages in his heart,
Who lives on the being of every god,
Who eats their entrails

The Creation of the Universe

When they come, their bodies full of magic
From the Isle of Flame.

Unas is one equipped who had gathered his spirits,
Unas has risen as Great One, as master of servants,
He will sit with his back to Geb,
Unas will judge with Him-whose-name-is-hidden
On the day of slaying the eldest.
Unas is lord of offerings who knots the cord,
Who himself prepares his meal.

Unas is he who eats men, feeds on gods,
Master of messengers who sends instructions:
It is Horn-grasper who ropes them for Unas,
It is Serpent Raised-head who guards, who holds them for him,
It is He-upon-the-willows who binds them for him.
It is Khonsu, slayer of lords, who cuts their throats for Unas,
Who tears their entrails out for him,
He the envoy who is sent to punish.
It is Shesmu who carves them up for Unas,
Cooks meals of them for him in his dinner-pots.

Unas eats their magic, swallows their spirits:
Their big ones are for his morning meal,
Their middle ones for his evening meal,
Their little ones for his night meal,
And the oldest males and females for his fuel.
The Great Ones in the northern sky light his fire
For the kettles' contents with the old ones' thighs,
For the sky-dwellers serve Unas,
And the pots are scraped for him with their women's legs.

He has encompassed the two skies,
He has circled the two shores;
Unas is the great power that overpowers the powers,
Unas is the divine hawk, the great hawk of hawks,
Whom he finds on his way he devours whole.
Unas's place is before all the nobles in lightland,
Unas is god, oldest of the old,
Thousands serve him, hundreds offer to him,
Great-Power rank was given him by Orion, father of gods.

Unas has risen again in heaven,
He is crowned as lord of lightland.
He has smashed bones and marrow,
He has seized the hearts of gods,
He has eaten the Red, swallowed the Green.
Unas feeds on the lungs of the wise,

Likes to live on hearts and their magic;
Unas abhors licking the coils of the Red
But delights to have their magic in his belly.

The dignities of Unas will not be taken from him,
For he has swallowed the knowledge of every god;
Unas's lifetime is forever, his limit is eternity
In his dignity of "If-he-likes-he-does if-he-hates-he-does-not,"
As he dwells in lightland for all eternity.
Lo, their power is in Unas's belly,
Their spirits are before Unas as broth of the gods,
Cooked for Unas from their bones.
Lo, their power is with Unas,
Their shadows are taken from their owners,
For Unas is of those who risen is risen, lasting lasts.
Nor can evildoers harm Unas's chosen seat
Among the living in this land for all eternity!

The king climbs to the sky on a ladder

Hail, daughter of Anubis, above the hatches of heaven,
Comrade of Thoth, above the ladder's rails,
Open Unas's path, let Unas pass!
Hail, Ostrich on the Winding Water's shore,
Open Unas's path, let Unas pass!
Hail, four-horned Bull of Ra,
Your horn in the west, your horn in the east,
Your southern horn, your northern horn:
Bend your western horn for Unas, let Unas pass!
"Are you a pure westerner?"
"I come from Hawk City."
Hail, Field of Offerings,
Hail to the herbs within you!
"Welcome is the pure to me!"

The king serves the sun-god

Unas is gods' steward, behind the mansion of Ra,
Born of Wish-of-the-gods, who is in the bow of Ra's bark;
Unas squats before him,
Unas opens his boxes,
Unas unseals his decrees,
Unas seals his dispatches,
Unas sends his messengers who tire not,
Unas does what Unas is told.

The Creation of the Universe

Unas has come today from the overflowing flood,
Unas is Sobek, green-plumed, wakeful, alert,
The fierce who came forth from shank and tail of the Great Radiant One,
Unas has come to his streams
In the land of the great flowing flood,
To the seat of contentment
Which lies, green-pastured, in lightland,
That Unas may bring greenness to the Great Eye in the field.
Unas takes his seat in lightland,
Unas arises as Sobek, son of Neith;
Unas eats with his mouth,
Unas spends water, spends seed with his phallus;
Unas is lord of seed who takes wives from their husbands,
Whenever Unas wishes, as his heart urges.

Vision of the Universe

Ascent

> Heaven shouts, earth trembles
> In dread of you, Ausar, at your coming!
> O you milch-cows here, O you nursing cows here,
> Turn about him, lament him, mourn him, bewail him,
> As he comes forth and goes to heaven
> Among his brothers, the gods!

The king is raised from his tomb

> Oho! Oho! Rise up, O Teti!
> Take your head,
> Collect your bones,
> Gather your limbs,
> Shake the earth from your flesh!
> Take your bread that rots not,
> Your beer that sours not,
> Stand at the gates that bar the common people!
> The gatekeeper comes out to you,
> He grasps your hand,
> Takes you into heaven, to your father Geb.
> He rejoices at your coming,
> Gives you his hands,
> Kisses You, Caresses You.

The king prays to the sky-goddess

> O great strider
> Who sows greenstone, malachite, turquoise—stars!
> As you are green so may Teti be green,
> Green as a living reed!

The Creation of the Universe

Sets you before the spirits, the imperishable stars.
The hidden ones worship you,
The great ones surround you,
The watchers wait on you.
Barley is threshed for you,
Emmer is reaped for you,
Your monthly feasts are made with it,
Your half-month feasts are made with it,
As ordered done for you by Geb, your father,
Rise up, O Teti, you shall not die!

The king roams the sky

Spacious is Teti's seat with Geb,
High is Teti's star with Ra,
Teti roams the Fields of Offering,
Teti is that Eye of Ra,
Conceived at night, born every day!

The king prays to the sun-god

Hail, O Ra, in your beauty, your splendor,
On your thrones, in your radiance!
Do bring Teti milk of Auset,
Flowing water from Nephthys,
Flood of the lake, surge of the sea,
Life, prosperity, health, and joy,
Bread, beer, and clothing,
Things on which Teti may live!
May the brewers obey me throughout the day
And provide for me at night,
I shall eat when they are sated with their fare!
May Teti see you when you go forth as Thoth,
When the waterway is made for the bark of Ra,
To his fields that lie in Yasu,
And you surge at the head of your helpers!

The king joins the sun-god

Teti has purified himself:
May he take his pure seat in the sky!
Teti endures:
May his beautiful seats endure!
Teti will take his pure seat in the bow of Ra's bark:
The sailors who row Ra, they shall row Teti!

The sailors who convey Ra about lightland,
They shall convey Teti about lightland!
Teti's mouth has been parted,
Teti's nose has been opened,
Teti's ears are unstopped.
Teti will decide matters,
Will judge between two,
Teti will command one greater than he!
Ra will purify Teti,
Ra will guard Teti from all evil!

Pharaoh Pepi

(SIXTH DYNASTY, 2300–2150 B.C., Kemet)

Vision of the Universe

The king prays to the sky-goddess

> O Great One who became Sky,
> You are strong, you are mighty,
> You fill every place with your beauty,
> The whole earth is beneath you, you possess it!
> As you enfold earth and all things in your arms,
> So have you taken this Pepi to you,
> An indestructible star within you!

The king asks for admittance to the sky

> If you love life, O Heru, upon his life staff of truth,
> Do not lock the gates of heaven,
> Do not bolt its bars,
> After you have taken Pepi's *ka* into heaven,
> To the god's nobles, the god's friends,
> Who lean on their staffs,
> Guardians of Upper Egypt,
> Clad in red linen,
> Living on figs,
> Drinking wine,
> Anointed with unguent,
> That he may speak for Pepi to the great god
> And let Pepi ascend to the great god!

The king becomes a star

> Truly, this Great One had fallen on his side,
> He who is in Nedyt was cast down.
> Your hand is grasped by Ra,
> Your head is raised by the Two Enneads.

Lo, he has come as Orion,
Lo, Ausar has come as Orion,
Lord of wine at the *wag*-feast.
"Good one," said his mother,
"Heir," said his father,
Conceived of sky, born of dusk.
Sky conceived you and Orion,
Dusk gave birth to you and Orion.
Who lives lives by the gods' command,
You shall live!
You shall rise with Orion in the eastern sky,
You shall set with Orion in the western sky,
Your third is Sothis, pure of thrones.

The sky-goddess protects the king

O Ausar Pepi,
Nut, your mother, spreads herself above you,
She conceals you from all evil,
Nut protects you from all evil,
You, the greatest of her children!

The king's power embraces sky and earth

O Ausar Pepi,
You enfold every god in your arms,
Their lands and all their possessions!
O Ausar Pepi,
You are great and round
Like the ring that circles the islands!

The king is a primordial god

Hail, O waters brought by Shu,
Which the twin springs raised,
In which Geb has bathed his limbs,
So that hearts lost fear, hearts lost dread.
Pepi was born in Nun
Before there was sky,
Before there was earth,
Before there were mountains,
Before there was strife,
Before fear came about through the Heru Eye.

Pepi is one of that great group born aforetime in On,
Who are not carried off for a king,

The Creation of the Universe

Who are not brought before magistrates,
Who are not made to suffer,
Who are not found guilty.
Such is Pepi: he will not suffer,
He will not be carried off for a king,
He will not be brought before magistrates,
The foes of Pepi will not triumph.
Pepi will not hunger,
His nails will not grow long,
No bone in him will be broken.

If Pepi goes down into water,
Ausar will lift him up,
The Enneads will support him,
Ra will take Pepi by the hand,
To where a god may be.
If he goes down to earth
Geb will lift him up,
The Enneads will support this Pepi,
He will be led by the hand to where a god may be.

The king addresses the ferryman

O Boatman of the boatless just,
Ferryman of the Field of Rushes!
Pepi is just before heaven and earth,
Pepi is just before this isle of earth,
To which he has swum, to which he has come,
Which is between the thighs of Nut!
He is the Twa of the dances of the gods,
Bringer of joy before his great throne!
This is what you heard in the houses,
What you overheard in the streets
On the day Pepi was called to life,
To hear what had been ordained.
Lo, the two on the great god's throne
Who summon Pepi to life, eternal,
They are Well-being and Health!

Ferry this Pepi to the Field,
The great god's beautiful throne,
That he may do what is done with the revered:
He commends them to the *ka*'s,
He assigns them to the bird-catch;
Pepi is such a one:
He will assign Pepi to the *ka*'s,
He will assign Pepi to the bird-catch.

Vision of the Universe

Awake in peace, O Pure One, in peace!
Awake in peace, Heru of-the-East, in peace!
Awake in peace, Soul-of-the-East, in peace!
Awake in peace, Heru-of-Lightland, in peace!
You lie down in the Night-bark,
You awake in the Day-bark,
For you are he who gazes on the gods,
There is no god who gazes on you!

O father of Pepi, take Pepi with you
Living, to your mother Nut!
Gates of sky, open for Pepi,
Gates of heaven, open for Pepi,
Pepi comes to you, make him live!
Command that this Pepi sit beside you,
Beside him who rises in lightland!
O father of Pepi, command to the goddess beside you
To make wide Pepi's seat at the stairway of heaven!

Command the Living One, the son of Sothis,
To speak for this Pepi,
To establish for Pepi a seat in the sky!
Commend this Pepi to the Great Noble,
The beloved of Ptah, the son of Ptah,
To speak for this Pepi,
To make flourish his jar-stands on earth,
For Pepi is one with these four gods:
Imsety, Hapy, Duamutef, Kebhsenuf,
Who live by *maat,*
Who lean on their staffs,
Who watch over Upper Egypt.

He flies, he flies from you as do ducks,
He wrests his arms from you as a falcon,
He tears himself from you as a kite,
Pepi frees himself from the fetters of earth,
Pepi is released from bondage!

Princess Ni-sedjer-kai
(FIFTH DYNASTY, 2450–2300 B.C., Kemet)

Tomb Inscription

An offering which the king gives and Anubis, king of the necropolis, first of the god's hall: May she be buried in the western necropolis in great old age. May she travel on the good ways on which a revered one travels well.

May offerings be given her on the New Year's feast, the Djehuti feast, the First-of-the-Year feast, the *wag*-feast, the Sokar feast, the Great Flame feast, the Brazier feast, the Procession-of-Min feast, the monthly *sadj*-feast, the Beginning-of-the-Month feast, the Beginning-of-the-Half-Month feast, every feast, every day, to the royal daughter, the royal ornament, Ni-sedjer-kai.

An offering which the king gives and Anubis, first of all the gods: May she be buried in the western necropolis in great old age before the great god.

May offerings be given her on the New Year's feast, the Djehuti feast, the First-of-the-Year feast, the *wag*-feast, and every feast: to the royal daughter, the royal ornament, Ni-sedjer-kai.

The royal daughter, royal ornament, priestess of Hathor,
Priestess of King Khufu, Ni-sedjer-kai.

Hotep-her-akhet

(FIFTH DYNASTY, 2450–2300 B.C., Kemet)

Tomb Inscription

The elder Judge of the Hall, Hotep-her-akhet, says: I made this tomb on the west side in a virgin place, where there had been no tomb before, in order to protect the possession of one who has gone to his *ka*. As for any people who would enter this tomb unclean to do something evil to it, there will be judgment against them by the great god. I made this tomb because I was honored by the king, who brought me a sarcophagus.

Nefer-seshem-ra (Sheshi)
(SIXTH DYNASTY, 2300–2150 B.C., Kemet)

Tomb Inscription

I have come from my town,
I have descended from my home,
I have done justice for its king,
I have satisfied him with what he loves.
I spoke truly, I did right,
I spoke fairly, I repeated fairly,
I seized the right moment,
So as to stand well with people.
I judged between two so as to content them,
I rescued the weak from one stronger than he
As much as was in my power.
I gave bread to the hungry, clothes to the naked,
I brought the boatless to land.
I buried him who had no son,
I made a boat for him who lacked one.
I respected my father, I pleased my mother,
I raised their children.
So says he whose nickname is Sheshi.

Ni-hebsed-Pepi
(SIXTH DYNASTY, 2300–2150 B.C., Kemet)

Memorial Stone

An offering which the king gives to Anubis, who is upon his mountain and in the place of embalming, the lord of the necropolis. Buried be the Royal Seal-bearer, Sole Companion, Chief Scribe of boat crews, Judge, Chief Scribe, Ni-hebsed-Pepi in his tomb which is in the good Western Desert. She has taken his hand, he has joined land, he has crossed the firmament. May the Western Desert give her hands to him in peace, in peace before the great god. An offering which the king gives to Anubis, so that funerary offerings be given to the Royal Seal-bearer, Sole Companion, honored Ausar, Ni-hebsed-Pepi.

The San Creation Narrative

Cagn was the first being; he gave orders and caused all things to appear, and to be made, the sun, the moon, stars, wind, mountains, and animals. His wife's name was Coti. He had two sons, and the eldest was chief, and his name was Cogaz; the name of the second was Gewi. . . . He was at that time making snares and weapons. He made then the partridge and the striped mouse, and he made the wind in order that game should smell up the wind—so they run up the wind still. . . .

A daughter of Cagn became cross because her father had scolded her and she ran away to destroy herself by throwing herself among the snakes. The snakes were also men, and their chief married her and they ate snake's meat, but they gave her eland's meat to eat, because the child of Cagn must eat no evil thing. Cagn used to know things that were far off, and he sent his son Cogaz to bring her back, so Cogaz went with his young men, and Cagn lent him his tooth to make him strong. When the snakes saw Cogaz approaching with his party, they became angry and began to hide their heads, but their chief said, "You must not get angry, they are coming to their child," so the snakes went away to hunt, and his sister gave him meat, and they told her to tell her husband they were coming to fetch her and she prepared food for the road and they went with her next morning, and they prepared themselves by binding rushes round their limbs and bodies, and three snakes followed them. These tried to bite them, but they only bit the rushes; they tried to beat them with reins, but they only beat rushes, and they tried throwing sand at them to cause wind to drive them into the water, not knowing he had the tooth of Cagn, and they failed. The children at home, the young men with the chief of the snakes, knew that when those snakes came back they would fill the country with water. So they commenced to build a high stage with willow poles, and the female snakes took their husbands on their return and threw them into the water, and it rose about the mountains, but the chief and his young men were saved on the high stage; and Cagn sent Cogaz for them to come and turn from being snakes, and he told them to lie down, and he struck them with his stick, and as he struck each the body of a person came out, and the skin of a snake was left on the ground, and he sprinkled the skins with canna, and the snakes turned from being snakes, and they became his people. . . .

Cagn sent Cogaz to cut sticks to make bows. When Cogaz came to the bush, the baboons caught him. They called all the other baboons together to hear him, and they asked him who sent him there. He said his father sent him to cut sticks to make bows. So they said—"Your father thinks himself more clever than we are, he wants those bows to kill us, so we'll kill you," and they killed Cogaz, and tied him up in the top of a tree, and they danced around the tree singing [an untranscribable baboon song], with a chorus saying, "Cagn thinks he is clever." Cagn was asleep when Cogaz was killed, but when he awoke he told Coti to give him his charms, and he put some on his nose, and said the baboons have hung Cogaz. So he went to where the baboons were, and when they saw him coming close by, they changed their song so as to omit the words about Cagn, but a little baboon girl said, "Don't sing that way; sing the way you were singing before." And Cagn said, "Sing as the little girl wishes," and they sang and danced away as before. And Cagn said, "That is the song I heard, that is what I wanted, go on dancing till I return"; and he went and fetched a bag full of pegs, and he went behind each of them as they were dancing and making a great dust, and he drove a peg into each one's back, and gave it a crack, and sent them off to the mountains to live on roots, beetles, and scorpions, as a punishment. Before that baboons were men, but since that they have tails, and their tails hang crooked. Then Cagn took Cogaz down, and gave him canna and made him alive again.

Cagn found an eagle getting honey from a precipice, and said, "My friend, give me some too," and it said, "Wait a bit," and it took a comb and put it down, and went back and took more, and told Cagn to take the rest, and he climbed up and licked only what remained on the rock, and when he tried to come down he found he could not. Presently he thought of his charms, and took some from his belt, and caused them to go to Cogaz to ask advice; and Cogaz sent word back by means of the charms that he was to make water to run down the rock, and he would find himself able to come down; and he did so, and when he got down, he descended into the ground and came up again, and he did this three times, and the third time he came up near the eagle, in the form of a huge bull eland; and the eagle said, "What a big eland," and went to kill it, and it threw an assegai, which passed it on the right side, and then another, which missed it, to the left, and a third, which passed between its legs, and the eagle trampled on it, and immediately hail fell and stunned the eagle, and Cagn killed it, and took some of the honey home to Cogaz, and told him he had killed the eagle which had acted treacherously to him, and Cogaz said, "You will get harm some day by these fightings." And Cagn found a woman named Cgorioinsi, who eats men, and she had made a big fire and was dancing round it, and she used to seize men and throw them into the fire, and Cagn began to roast roots at the fire, and at last she came and pitched him in, but he slipped through at the other side, and went on roasting and eating his roots, and she pitched him in again and again, and he only said, "Wait a bit until I have finished my roots and I'll show you what I am." And when he had done he threw her into the fire as a punishment for killing people. Then Cagn went back to the mountains, where he had left some of the honey he took from the eagle, and he left his sticks there, and went down to the river, and there was a person in the river named Quuisi, who had been standing there a long time, something having caught him by the foot, and held him there since the winter, and he called to Cagn to come and help him, and Cagn went to help him, and put his hand down into the water to loosen his leg, and the thing let go the man's leg, and seized Cagn's arm. And the man ran stumbling out of the water, for his leg was stiffened by his being so long held fast, and he called out, "Now you will be held there till the winter," and he went to the honey, and threw Cagn's sticks away; and Cagn began to bethink him of his charms, and he sent to ask Cogaz for advice through his charms, and Cogaz sent word and told him to let down a piece of his garment into the water alongside his hand, and he did so, and the thing let go his hand and seized his garment, and he cut off the end of his garment, and ran and collected his sticks, and pursued the man and killed him, and took the honey to Cogaz.

The Creation of the Universe

The thorns (*dobbletjes*) were people—they are called Cagn-cagn—they were dwarfs, and Cagn found them fighting together, and he went to separate them, and they all turned upon him and killed him, and the biting ants helped them, and they ate Cagn up; but after a time they and the dwarfs collected his bones, and put them together and tied his head on, and these went stumbling home, and Cogaz cured him and made him all right again, and asked what had happened to him, and he told him; and Cogaz gave him advice and power, telling him how to fight them, that he was to make feints and strike as if at their legs, and then hit them on the head, and he went and killed many, and drove the rest into the mountains.

The Khoi Creation Narrative

Tsui||goab* was a great powerful chief of the Khoikhoi; in fact, he was the first Khoikhoib, from whom all the Khoikhoi clans took their origin. But Tsui||goab was not his original name. This Tsui||goab went to war with another chief, ||Gaunab, because the latter always killed great numbers of Tsui||goab's people. In this fight, however, Tsui||goab was repeatedly overpowered by ||Gaunab, but in every battle the former grew stronger; and at last he was so strong and big that he easily destroyed ||Gaunab, by giving him one blow behind the ear. While ||Gaunab was expiring he gave his enemy a blow on the knee. Since that day the conqueror of ||Gaunab received the name Tsui||goab, "sore knee," or "wounded knee." Henceforth he could not walk properly, because he was lame. He could do wonderful things, which no other man could do, because he was very wise. He could tell what would happen in future times. He died several times, and several times he rose again. And whenever he came back to us, there were great feastings and rejoicings. Milk was brought from every kraal, and fat cows and fat ewes were slaughtered. Tsui||goab gave every man plenty of cattle and sheep, because he was very rich. He gives rain, he makes the clouds, he lives in the clouds, and he makes our cows and sheep fruitful.

Tsui||goab lives in a beautiful heaven, and ||Gaunab lives in a dark heaven, quite separated from the heaven of Tsui||goab.

*The parallel lines represent the "click" sound in the Khoi-San spoken language.—Eds.

The Barozvi Creation Narrative

In the beginning Nyambi made all things. He made animals, fish, birds. At that time he lived on earth with his wife, Nasilele. One of Nyambi's creatures was different from all the others. His name was Kamonu. Kamonu imitated Nyambi in everything Nyambi did. When Nyambi worked in wood, Kamonu worked in wood; when Nyambi forged iron, Kamonu forged iron.

After a while Nyambi began to fear Kamonu.

Then one day Kamonu forged a spear and killed a male antelope, and he went on killing. Nyambi grew very angry at this.

"Man, you are acting badly," he said to Kamonu. "These are your brothers. Do not kill them."

Nyambi drove Kamonu out into another land. But after a while Kamonu returned. Nyambi allowed him to stay and gave him a garden to cultivate.

It happened that at night buffaloes wandered into Kamonu's garden and he speared them; after that, some elands, and he killed one. After some time Kamonu's dog died; then his pot broke; then his child died. When Kamonu went to Nyambi to tell him what had happened he found his dog and his pot and his child at Nyambi's.

Then Kamonu said to Nyambi, "Give me medicine so that I may keep my things." But Nyambi refused to give him medicine. After this, Nyambi met with his two counselors and said, "How shall we live since Kamonu knows too well the road hither?"

Nyambi tried various means to flee Kamonu. He removed himself and his court to an island across the river. But Kamonu made a raft of reeds and crossed over to Nyambi's island. Then Nyambi piled up a huge mountain and went to live on its peak. Still Nyambi could not get away from man. Kamonu found his way to him. In the meantime men were multiplying and spreading all over the earth.

Finally Nyambi sent birds to go look for a place for Litoma, god's town. But the birds failed to find a place. Nyambi sought counsel from a diviner. The diviner said, "Your life depends on Spider." And Spider went and found an abode for Nyambi and his court in the sky. Then Spider spun a thread from earth to the sky and Nyambi climbed up on the thread. Then the diviner advised Nyambi to put out Spider's eyes so that he could never see the way to heaven again and Nyambi did so.

After Nyambi disappeared into the sky Kamonu gathered some men around him and said, "Let us build a high tower and climb up to Nyambi." They cut down trees and put log on log, higher and higher toward the sky. But the weight was too great and the tower collapsed. So that Kamonu never found his way to Nyambi's home.

But every morning when the sun appeared, Kamonu greeted it, saying, "Here is our king. He has come." And all the other people greeted him shouting and clapping. At the time of the new moon men call on Nasilele, Nyambi's wife.

The Dogon Creation Narrative

Ogotemmeli, seating himself on his threshold, scraped his stiff leather-snuff-box, and put a pinch of yellow powder on his tongue.

"Tobacco," he said, "makes for right thinking."

So saying, he set to work to analyze the world system, for it was essential to begin with the dawn of all things. He rejected as a detail of no interest, the popular account of how the fourteen solar systems were formed from flat circular slabs of earth one on top of the other. He was only prepared to speak of the serviceable solar system; he agreed to consider the stars, though they only played a secondary part.

"It is quite true," he said, "that in course of time women took down the stars to give them to their children. The children put spindles through them and made them spin like fiery tops to show themselves how the world turned. But that was only a game."

The stars came from pellets of earth flung out into space by the God Amma, the one God. He had created the sun and the moon by a more complicated process, which was not the first known to man but is the first attested invention of God: the art of pottery. The sun is, in a sense, a pot raised to white heat and surrounded by a spiral of red copper with eight turns. The moon is the same shape, but its copper is white. It was heated only one quarter at a time. Ogotemmeli said he would explain later the movements of these bodies. For the moment he was concerned only to indicate the main lines of the design, and from that to pass to its actors.

He was anxious, however, to give an idea of the size of the sun.

"Some," he said,"think it is as large as this encampment, which would mean thirty cubits. But it is really bigger. Its surface area is bigger than the whole of Sanga Canton."

And after some hesitation he added:

"It is perhaps even bigger than that."

He refused to linger over the dimensions of the moon, nor did he ever say anything about them. The moon's function was not important, and he would speak of it later. He said however that, while Africans were creatures of light emanating from the fullness of the sun, Europeans were creatures of the moonlight: hence their immature appearance.

He spat out his tobacco as he spoke. Ogotemmeli had nothing against Europeans. He was not even sorry for them. He left them to their destiny in the lands of the north.

The God Amma, it appeared, took a lump of clay, squeezed it in his hand and flung it from him, as he had done with the stars. The clay spread and fell on the north, which is the top, and from there stretched out to the south, which is the bottom, of the world, although the whole movement was horizontal. The earth lies flat, but the north is at the top. It extends east and west with separate members like a foetus in the womb. It is a body, that is to say, a thing with members branching out from a central mass. This body, lying flat, face upwards, in a line from north to south, is feminine. Its sexual organ is an anthill, and its clitoris a termite hill. Amma, being lonely and desirous of intercourse with this creature, approached it. That was the occasion of the first breach of the order of the universe.

Ogotemmeli ceased speaking. His hands crossed above his head, he sought to distinguish the different sounds coming from the courtyards and roofs. He had reached the point of the origin of troubles and of the primordial blunder of God.

"If they overheard me, I should be fined an ox!"

At God's approach the termite hill rose up, barring the passage and displaying its masculinity. It was as strong as the organ of the stranger, and intercourse could not take place. But God is all-powerful. He cut down the termite hill, and had intercourse with the excised earth. But the original incident was destined to affect the course of things for ever; from this defective union there was born, instead of the intended twins, a single being, the *Thos aureus* or jackal, symbol of the difficulties of God. Ogotemmeli's voice sank lower and lower. It was no longer a question of women's ears listening to what he was saying; other, nonmaterial, ear-drums might vibrate to his important discourse. The European and his African assistant, Sergeant Koguem, were leaning towards the old man as if hatching plots of the most alarming nature.

But, when he came to the beneficent acts of God, Ogotemmeli's voice again assumed its normal tone.

God had further intercourse with his earth-wife, and this time without mishaps of any kind, the excision of the offending member having removed the cause of the former disorder. Water, which is the divine seed, was thus able to enter the womb of the earth and the normal reproductive cycle resulted in the birth of twins. Two beings were thus formed. God created them like water. They were green in color, half human beings and half serpents. From the head to the loins they were human: below that they were serpents. Their red eyes were wide open like human eyes, and their tongues were forked like the tongues of reptiles. Their arms were flexible and without joints. Their bodies were green and sleek all over, shining like the surface of water, and covered with short green hairs, a presage of vegetation and germination.

These spirits, called Nummo, were thus two homogeneous products of God, of divine essence like himself, conceived without untoward incidents and developed normally in the womb of the earth. Their destiny took them to Heaven, where they received the instructions of their father. Not that God had to teach them speech, that indispensable necessity of all beings, as it is of the world-system; the Pair were born perfect and complete; they had eight members, and their number was eight, which is the symbol of speech.

They were also of the essence of God, since they were made of his seed, the first Word, and could still therefore reveal to diviners certain heavenly purposes; but in the future order of things he was to be merely a laggard in the process of revelation.

The potent second Word developed the powers of its new possessor. Gradually he came to regard his regeneration in the womb of the earth as equivalent to the capture and occupation of that womb, and little by little he took possession of the whole organism, making such use of it as suited him for the purpose of his activities. His lips began to merge with the edges of the anthill, which widened and became a mouth. Pointed teeth

The Creation of the Universe

made their appearance, seven for each lip, then ten, the number of the fingers, later forty, and finally eighty, that is to say, ten for each ancestor.

These numbers indicated the future rates of increase of the families; the appearance of the teeth was a sign that the time for new instruction was drawing near.

But here again the scruples of the Spirits made themselves felt. It was not directly to men, but to the ant, avator of the earth and native to the locality, that the seventh ancestor imparted instruction.

At sunrise on the appointed day the seventh ancestor Spirit spat out eighty threads of cotton; these he distributed between his upper teeth which acted as the teeth of a weaver's reed. In this way he made the uneven threads of a warp. He did the same with the lower teeth to make the even threads. By opening and shutting his jaws the Spirit caused the threads of the warp to make the movements required in weaving. His whole face took part in the work, his nose studs serving as the block, while the stud in his lower lip was the shuttle.

As the threads crossed and uncrossed, the two tips of the Spirit's forked tongue pushed the thread of the weft to and fro, and the web took shape from his mouth in the breath of the second revealed Word.

For the Spirit was speaking while the work proceeded. As did the Nummo in the first revelation, he imparted his Word by means of a technical process, so that all men could understand. By so doing he showed the identity of material actions and spiritual forces, or rather the need for their co-operation.

The words that the Spirit uttered filled all the interstices of the stuff: they were woven in the threads, and formed part and parcel of the cloth. They were the cloth, and the cloth was the Word. That is why woven material is called *soy*, which means "It is the spoken word." *Soy* also means "seven," for the Spirit who spoke as he wove was seventh in the series of ancestors.

While the work was going on, the ant came and went on the edge of the opening in the breath of the Spirit, hearing and remembering his words. The new instruction, which she thus received, she passed on to the men who lived in those regions, and who had already followed the transformation of the sex of the earth.

Up to the time of the ancestor's descent into the anthill, men had lived in holes dug in the level soil like the lairs of animals. When their attention was drawn to the bowls which the ancestors had left behind them, they began to notice the shape of the anthill, which they thought much better than their holes. They copied the shape of the anthill accordingly, making passages and rooms as shelters from the rain, and began to store the produce of the crops for food.

They were thus advancing towards a less primitive way of life; and, when they noticed the growth of teeth round the opening, they imitated these too as a means of protection against wild beasts. They molded great teeth of clay, dried them and set them up round the entrances to their dwellings.

At the moment of the second instruction, therefore, men were living in dens which were already, in some sort, a prefiguration of the place of revelation and of the womb into which each of them in due course would descend to be regenerated. And, moreover, the human anthill, with its occupants and its store-chambers for grain, was a rudimentary image of the system which, much later, was to come down to them from Heaven in the form of a marvelous granary.

These dim outlines of things to come predisposed men to take advice from the ant. The latter, after what it had seen the Spirit do, had laid in a store of cotton-fibers. These it has made into threads and, in the sight of men, drew them between the teeth of the anthill entrance as the Spirit had done. As the warp emerged, the men passed the thread of the weft, throwing it right and left in time to the opening and shutting movements of the jaws, and the resulting web was rolled round a piece of wood, fore-runner of the beam.

The ant at the same time revealed the words it had heard and the man repeated them. Thus there was recreated by human lips the concept of life in motion, of the transposition of forces, of the efficacy of the breath of the Spirit, which the seventh ancestor had created; and thus the interlacing of warp and weft enclosed the same words, the new instruction which became the heritage of mankind and was handed on from generation to generation of weavers to the accompaniment of the clapping of the shuttle and the creaking of the block, which they call the "creaking of the Word."

All these operations took place by daylight, for spinning and weaving are work for the daytime. Working at night would mean weaving webs of silence and darkness.

The Creation of the Universe

The Yoruba Creation Narrative

THE DESCENT FROM THE SKY

In ancient days, at the beginning of time, there was no solid land here where people now dwell. There was only outer space and the sky, and, far below, an endless stretch of water and wild marshes. Supreme in the domain of the sky was the orisha, or god, called Olorun, also known as Olodumare and designated by many praise names. Also living in that place were numerous other orishas, each having attributes of his own, but none of whom had knowledge or powers equal to those of Olorun. Among them was Orunmila, also called Ifa, the eldest son of Olorun. To this orisha Olorun had given the power to read the future, to understand the secret of existence and to divine the processes of fate. There was the orisha Obatala, King of the White Cloth, whom Olorun trusted as though he also were a son. There was the orisha Eshu, whose character was neither good nor bad. He was compounded out of the elements of chance and accident, and his nature was unpredictability. He understood the principles of speech and language, and because of this gift he was Olorun's linguist. These and the other orishas living in the domain of the sky acknowledged Olorun as the owner of everything and as the highest authority in all matters. Also living there was Agemo, the chameleon, who served Olorun as a trusted servant.

Down below, it was the female deity Olokun who ruled over the vast expanses of water and wild marshes, a grey region with no living things in it, either creatures of the bush or vegetation. This is the way it was, Olorun's living sky above and Olokun's domain of water below. Neither kingdom troubled the other. They were separate and apart. The orishas of the sky lived on, hardly noticing what lay below them.

All except Obatala, King of the White Cloth. He alone looked down on the domain of Olokun and pondered on it, saying to himself: "Everything down there is a great wet monotony. It does not have the mark of any inspiration or living thing." And at last he went to Olorun and said: "The place ruled by Olokun is nothing but sea, marsh and mist. If there were solid land in that domain, fields and forests, hills and valleys, surely it could be populated by orishas and other living things."

Olorun answered: "Yes, it would be a good thing to cover the water with land. But it is an ambitious enterprise. Who is to do the work? And how should it be done?"

Obatala said: "I will undertake it. I will do whatever is required."

He left Olorun and went to the house of Orunmila, who understood the secrets of existence, and said to him: "Your father has instructed me to go down below and make land where now there is nothing but marsh and sea, so that living beings will have a place to build their towns and grow their crops. You, Orunmila, who can divine the meanings of all things, instruct me further. How may this work be begun?"

Orunmila brought out his divining tray and cast sixteen palm nuts on it. He read their meanings by the way they fell. He gathered them up and cast again, again reading their meanings. And when he had cast many times he added meanings to meanings, and said: "These are the things you must do: Descend to the watery wastes on a chain of gold, taking with you a snail shell full of sand, a white hen to disperse the sand, a black cat to be your companion, and a palm nut. That is what the divining figures tell us."

Obatala went next to the goldsmith and asked for a chain of gold long enough to reach from the sky to the surface of the water.

The goldsmith asked, "Is there enough gold in the sky to make such a chain?"

Obatala answered: "Yes, begin your work. I will gather the gold." Departing from the forge of the goldsmith, Obatala went then to Orunmila, Eshu and the other orishas, asking each of them for gold. They gave him whatever they had. Some gave gold dust, some gave rings, bracelets or pendants. Obatala collected gold from everywhere and took it to the goldsmith.

The goldsmith said, "More gold is needed."

So Obatala continued seeking gold, and after that he again returned to the goldsmith, saying, "Here is more metal for your chain."

The goldsmith said, "Still more is needed."

Obatala said, "There is no more gold in the sky."

The goldsmith said, "The chain will not reach to the water."

Obatala answered: "Nevertheless, make the chain. We shall see."

The goldsmith went to work. When the chain was finished he took it to Obatala. Obatala said, "It must have a hook at the end."

"There is no gold remaining," the goldsmith said.

Obatala replied, "Take some of the links and melt them down."

The goldsmith removed some of the links, and out of them he fashioned a hook for the chain. It was finished. He took the chain to Obatala.

Obatala said, "Now I am ready." He fastened the hook on the edge of the sky and lowered the chain. Orunmila gave him the things that were needed—a snail shell of sand, a white hen, a black cat, and a palm nut. Then Obatala gripped the chain with his hands and feet and began the descent. The chain was very long. When he had descended only half its length Obatala saw that he was leaving the realm of light and entering the region of greyness. A time came when he heard the wash of waves and felt the damp mists rising from Olokun's domain. He reached the end of the golden chain, but he was not yet at the bottom, and he clung there, thinking, "If I let go I will fall into the sea."

While he remained at the chain's end thinking such things, he heard Orunmila's voice from above, saying, "The sand."

So Obatala took the snail shell from the knapsack at his side and poured out the sand.

Again he heard Orunmila call to him, saying this time, "The hen."

Obatala dropped the hen where he had poured the sand. The hen began at once to scratch at the sand and scatter it in all directions. Wherever the sand was scattered it became dry land. Because it was scattered unevenly the sand formed hills and valleys. When this was accomplished, Obatala let go of the chain and came down and walked on the solid earth that had been created. The land extended in all directions, but still it was barren of life.

Obatala named the place where he came down Ife. He built a house there. He planted

The Creation of the Universe

his palm nut and a palm tree sprang out of the earth. It matured and dropped its palm seeds. More palm trees came into being. Thus there was vegetation at Ife. Obatala lived on, with only his black cat as a companion.

After some time had passed, Olorun the Sky God wanted to know how Obatala's expedition was progressing. He instructed Agemo the chameleon to descend the golden chain. Agemo went down. He found Obatala living in his house at Ife. He said: "Olorun instructed me this way: He said, 'Go down, discover for me how things are with Obatala.' That is why I am here."

Obatala answered, "As you can see, the land has been created, and palm groves are plentiful. But there is too much greyness. The land should be illuminated."

Agemo returned to the sky and reported to Olorun what he had seen and heard. Olorun agreed that there should be light down below. So he made the sun and set it moving. After that there was warmth and light in what had once been Olokun's exclusive domain.

Obatala lived on, with only his black cat for a companion. He thought, "Surely it would be better if many people were living here." He decided to create people. He dug clay from the ground, and out of the clay he shaped human figures which he then laid out to dry in the sun. He worked without resting. He became tired and thirsty. He said to himself, "There should be palm wine in this place to help a person go on working." So he put aside the making of humans and went to the palm trees to draw their inner fluid, out of which he made palm wine. When it was fermented he drank. He drank for a long while. When he felt everything around him softening he put aside his gourd cup and went back to modeling human figures. But because Obatala had drunk so much wine his fingers grew clumsy, and some of the figures were misshapen. Some had crooked backs or crooked legs, or arms that were too short. Some did not have enough fingers, some were bent instead of being straight. Because of the palm wine inside him, Obatala did not notice these things. And when he had made enough figures to begin the populating of Ife he called out to Olorun the Sky God, saying, "I have made human beings to live with me here in Ife, but only you can give them the breath of life." Olorun heard Obatala's request, and he put breath in the clay figures. They were no longer clay, but people of blood, sinews and flesh. They arose and began to do the things that humans do. They built houses for themselves near Obatala's house, and in this way the place Obatala named Ife became the city of Ife.

But when the effects of the palm wine had worn off Obatala saw that some of the humans he had made were misshapen, and remorse filled his heart. He said: "Never again will I drink palm wine. From this time on I will be the special protector of all humans who have deformed limbs or who have otherwise been created imperfectly." Because of Obatala's pledge, humans who later came to serve him also avoided palm wine, and the lame, the blind and those who had no pigment in their skin invoked his help when they were in need.

Now that humans were living on the earth, Obatala gave people the tools they needed to perform their work. As yet there was no iron in the world, and so each man received a wooden hoe and a copper bush knife. The people planted and began the growing of millet and yams, and, like the palm tree, they procreated. Ife became a growing city and Obatala ruled as its Oba or Paramount Chief. But a time came when Obatala grew lonesome for the sky. He ascended by the golden chain, and there was a festival on the occasion of his return. The orishas heard him describe the land that had been created below, and many of them decided to go down and live among the newly created human beings.

The Yoruba Creation Narrative

Thus many orishas departed from the sky, but not before Olorun instructed them on their obligations. "When you settle on the earth," he said, "never forget your duties to humans. Whenever you are supplicated for help, listen to what is being asked of you. You are the protectors of the human race. Obatala, who first descended the chain and dried up the waters, he is my deputy in earthly affairs. But each of you will have a special responsibility to fulfill down below." As for Obatala, he rested in the sky for some time. After that, whenever he wanted to know how things were going at Ife, he returned for a visit. The city of Ife lived on.

But Olokun, the orisha of the sea on whose domain land had been created, was angry and humiliated. And so one time when Obatala was resting in the sky Olokun decided to destroy the land and replace it again with water. She sent great waves rushing against the shores and flooded the low ground everywhere, causing marshes to reappear on every side. She inundated the fields where humans were growing their crops and drowned many of the people of Ife. All that Obatala had created was disappearing, and mankind was suffering. The people called for help from Obatala, but he did not hear them. So they went to the orisha Eshu, who now lived on earth, and begged him to carry to Obatala word of the disaster that was overwhelming them.

Eshu said to them, "Where is the sacrifice that should accompany the message?"

They brought a goat and sacrificed it, saying, "This is the food for Obatala."

But Eshu did not move. He said, "Where is the rest?"

The people said: "We do not understand you. Have we not brought a sacrifice for Obatala?"

Eshu answered: "You ask me to make a great journey. You ask me to be your linguist. Does not a person make a gift to the lowliest of messengers? Give me my part, then I will go."

So the people gave a sacrifice to Eshu, after which he left them and went up to the sky to tell Obatala what was happening to the land and the people over which he ruled.

Obatala was troubled. He was not certain how to deal with Olokun. He went to the Orisha Orunmila to ask for advice. Orunmila consulted his divining nuts, and at last he said to Obatala: "Wait here in the sky. Rest yourself. I will go down this time. I will turn back the water and make the land rise again." So it was Orunmila instead of Obatala who went down to Ife. As Orunmila was the oldest son of Olorun, he had the knowledge of medicine, and he had many other powers as well. He used his powers in Ife, causing Olokun's waves to weaken and the marshes to dry up. The waters of the sea were turned back, and at last Olokun's attempt to reclaim her territory came to an end.

Having accomplished all this, Orunmila prepared to return to the sky. But the people came to him and asked him to stay because of his knowledge. Orunmila did not wish to stay in Ife forever. So he taught certain orishas and men the arts of controlling unseen forces, and he also taught others the art of divining the future, which is to say the knowledge of how to ascertain the wishes and intentions of the Sky God, Olorun. Some men he taught to divine through the casting of palm nuts. Others he taught to foretell the future by the casting of cowry shells or sand or chains. Afterwards, Orunmila went back to the sky and, like Obatala, he frequently made visits to the earth to see how things were going among human beings. What Orunmila taught men about divining was never lost. It was passed on by one generation of babalawos, or diviners, to another.

Earthly order—the understanding of relationships between people and the physical world, and between people and the orishas—was beginning to take shape. But all was not yet settled between Olokun, the orisha of the sea, and the supreme orisha Olorun. Olokun

The Creation of the Universe

considered ways in which she might humiliate or outwit the Sky God. The powers of the sky deities had proved to be greater than her own. But Olokun had the knowledge of weaving and dyeing cloth, and she had cloths of delicate textures and brilliant colors. She believed that in this respect she excelled all other orishas, including Olorun himself. So one day she sent a message to Olorun, challenging him to a contest to show which had the greater knowledge of clothmaking.

Olorun received the challenge. He thought: "Olokun seeks to humiliate me. Nevertheless, she has unequaled knowledge about the making of cloth. Yet, how can I ignore the challenge?" He thought about the matter. Then he sent for Agemo, the chameleon. He instructed Agemo to carry a message to Olokun. Agemo went down from the sky to the place where Olokun lived. Agemo said to Olokun: "The Owner of the Sky, Olorun, greets you. He says that if your cloth is as magnificent as you claim, he will enter the contest. Therefore he asks that you show me some of your most radiant weaving so that I may report to him on the matter."

Because Olokun was vain she could not refrain from showing her cloths to Agemo. She put on a skirt cloth of brilliant green and displayed it to the chameleon. As Agemo looked at it his skin turned the exact color of the skirt. Olokun then put on an orange-hued cloth, and Agemo's skin turned orange. When Olokun brought out a red skirt cloth, Agemo's skin turned red. Olokun was perturbed. She tried a cloth of several colors and saw the chameleon's skin reproduce it perfectly. Olokun thought: "This person is only a messenger, nothing more. Yet in an instant he can duplicate the exact color of my finest cloth. What, then, can the great Olorun do?"

Seeing the futility of competing with Olorun, the orisha of the sea said to Agemo: "Give my greetings to the Owner of the Sky. Tell him that Olokun acknowledges his greatness."

Thus Olokun withdrew her challenge to the Sky God, and Olorun remained supreme in all things.

The Asante Tower to Heaven

Long, long ago Onyankopon lived on earth, or at least was very near to us. Now there was a certain old woman who used to pound her mashed yams and the pestle kept knocking up against Onyankopon, who was not then high in the sky. So Onyankopon said to the old woman: "Why do you keep doing this to me? Because of what you are doing I am going to take myself away up in the sky." And of a truth he did so.

Now the people could no longer approach Onyankopon. But the old woman thought of a way to reach him and bring him back. She instructed her children to go and search for all the mortars they could find and bring them to her. Then she told them to pile one mortar on top of another till they reached to where Onyankopon was. And her children did so, they piled up many mortars, one on top of another, till they needed only one more mortar to reach Onyankopon.

Now, since they could not find another mortar anywhere, their grandmother the old woman said to them: "Take one out from the bottom and put it on top to make them reach." So her children removed a mortar from the bottom and all the mortars rolled and fell to the ground, causing the death of many people.

The Creation of the Universe

The Asante Concept of the Creation of the Lesser Gods

There once was a certain woman who bore eleven children. Every day when she got up and cooked food the children ate it all and the mother did not get any of it. She pondered long about the matter, and went off to the plantation and spoke to the silk-cotton tree, saying, "I shall send my eleven children to come beneath you here to pluck pumpkins; and when they come, pluck off eleven of your branches and kill those children of mine."

The silk-cotton tree said, "I have heard, and I shall do it for you."

The mother then went home and said to her children, "You must go to the plantation beneath the silk-cotton tree; there are pumpkins there. Go pick them and come back."

The children set off. They went and reached the silk-cotton tree. Number Eleven said, "Number One, stand still; Number Two, stand still; Number Three, stand still; Number Four, stand still; Number Five, stand still; Number Six, stand still; Number Seven, stand still; Number Eight, stand still; Number Nine, stand still; Number Ten, stand still; and I myself, Number Eleven, I have stood still."

Number Eleven then addressed them, saying, "Do you not know the sole reason why Mother said we must go and pick pumpkins?"

His brothers answered, "No."

Thereupon he said, "She has told this silk-cotton tree that, when we go there, he must pluck off branches and beat us. Therefore all of you cut sticks and throw them against this silk-cotton tree."

They cut the sticks and threw them against the silk-cotton tree. *Pim! pen! pim! pen!* was the sound they made. The silk-cotton tree supposed that the children had come. He took off eleven of his branches and let them fall to the ground. Little Number Eleven said, "You have seen—had we gone on there, the silk-cotton tree would have killed us."

They picked up the pumpkins and took them to their mother. She cooked them. And at once the children had eaten all! Their mother said, "Ah! as for this matter, I cannot bear it! I shall take these children and give them to the sky-god."

The next morning, when things became visible, she went and told the sky-god all about it, saying, "The children to whom I have given birth eat so fast and so much that when I wish to eat, I can't get anything. Hunger is killing me. Therefore, I implore you. Let the children be brought and killed, so that I may get something to eat."

The sky-god said, "Is that really the case?"

The woman said, "I am speaking with a head, the inside of which is white."

So the sky-god picked out messengers, and they went and dug a large pit in which they placed broken bottles. The sky-god himself went and fetched a snake and a leopard, put them in the pit, and covered it over. And now the messenger went to call the children.

No sooner did they reach the place where the pit lay, than Number Eleven said, "Number One, stand still; Number Two, stand still; Number Three, stand still; Number Four, stand still; Number Five, stand still; Number Six, stand still; Number Seven, stand still; Number Eight, stand still; Number Nine, stand still; Number Ten, stand still; and I myself, little Number Eleven, I have stood still. You must pass here, but you must not pass there."

His brothers said, "Why, when a wide path lies there, must we pass through the bush?"

Now, as they were going along, they all carried clubs. Number Eleven said, "Throw one of these clubs upon this path." They threw a club upon the path, and it fell through into the pit. *Yiridi* was the sound of its fall. Number Eleven said, "There you are! You see! Had we passed there, we should all of us have died."

So they took a bypath and went off to meet the sky-god. The sky-god had caused holes to be dug, covered over, and stools placed upon them, so that when the children came to sit on them, they would fall into the holes. Soon the children arrived before the face of the sky-god. He spoke to them, "Stools are set there. You may go and be seated upon them."

Then Number Eleven said, "Who are we that we should be able to sit upon such very beautiful stools? So, sire, we are going to sit aside here."

Thereupon the sky-god gazed at the children and he said to himself, "I shall send these children to Death's village."

The next morning, when things became visible, he called the children and said, "You must go to Death who lives yonder and receive from her a golden pipe, a golden chewing-stick, a golden snuffbox, a golden whetstone, and a golden fly-switch."

Number Eleven said, "You are our master, wherever you will send us, we shall go."

The sky-god said, "Be off!"

So the children set out for Death's village. When they arrived there, Death said, "Why, when no one must ever come here, have you come here?"

They replied, "We were roaming about and came here quite by chance."

Death said, "Oh, all right then."

The Creation of the Universe

James Weldon Johnson
(1871–1938, United States)

The Creation

A NEGRO SERMON

And God stepped out on space,
And He looked around and said,
"I'm lonely—
I'll make me a world."

And far as the eye of God could see
Darkness covered everything,
Blacker than a hundred midnights
Down in a cypress swamp.

Then God smiled,
And the light broke,
And the darkness rolled up on one side,
And the light stood shining on the other,
And God said, *"That's good!"*

Then God reached out and took the light in His hands,
And God rolled the light around in His hands,
Until He made the sun;
And He set that sun a-blazing in the heavens.
And the light that was left from making the sun
God gathered up in a shining ball
And flung against the darkness,
Spangling the night with the moon and stars.

Then down between
The darkness and the light
He hurled the world;
And God said, *"That's good!"*

Then God himself stepped down—
And the sun was on His right hand,

And the moon was on His left;
The stars were clustered about His head,
And the earth was under His feet.
And God walked, and where He trod
His footsteps hollowed the valleys out
And bulged the mountains up.

Then He stopped and looked and saw
That the earth was hot and barren.
So God stepped over to the edge of the world
And He spat out the seven seas;
He batted His eyes, and the lightnings flashed;
He clapped His hands, and the thunders rolled;
And the waters above the earth came down,
The cooling waters came down.

Then the green grass sprouted,
And the little red flowers blossomed,
The pine-tree pointed his finger to the sky,
And the oak spread out his arms;
The lakes cuddled down in the hollows of the ground,
And the rivers ran down to the sea;
And God smiled again,
And the rainbow appeared,
And curled itself around His shoulder.

Then God raised His arm and He waved His hand
Over the sea and over the land,
And He said, *"Bring forth! Bring forth!"*
And quicker than God could drop His hand,
Fishes and fowls
And beast and birds
Swam the rivers and the seas,
Roamed the forests and the woods,
And split the air with their wings,
And God said, *"That's good!"*

Then God walked around
And God looked around
On all that He had made.
He looked at His sun,
And He looked at His moon,
And He looked at His little stars;
He looked on His world
With all its living things,
And God said, *"I'm lonely still."*

Then God sat down
On the side of a hill where He could think;

The Creation of the Universe

By a deep, wide river He sat down;
With His head in His hands,
God thought and thought,
Till He thought, *"I'll make me a man!"*

Up from the bed of the river
God scooped the clay;
And by the bank of the river
He kneeled Him down;
And there the great God Almighty,
Who lit the sun and fixed it in the sky,
Who flung the stars to the most far corner of the night,
Who rounded the earth in the middle of His hand—
This Great God,
Like a mammy bending over her baby,
Kneeled down in the dust
Toiling over a lump of clay
Till He shaped it in His own image;
Then into it He blew the breath of life,
And man became a living soul.
Amen. Amen.

Religious Ideas

PART TWO

Overleaf: Adinkra symbol for *kerape,* sanctity

Perhaps no idea or set of ideas has been more important in the history of African people than the concept of spiritual intervention in human history. This agency of the spiritual is found throughout the sources of the African tradition as the basis for justice, harmony, and peace. While the ancient documents from the Nile Valley demonstrate the complexity seen in the relationship between humans and the cosmos, those documents also affirm the ethical principles of *Maat*, the key idea in the traditional African approach to life. *Maat* recurs in most African societies as the influence of right and righteousness, justice and harmony, balance, respect, and human dignity.

The sources of the African religion, like the sources of African civilization, are found along the banks of the Nile River. As the cultures of ancient Africa became more complex are distant from the ancient sources, new interpretations, revelations, and permutations occurred. However, in all cases the ideas of religion kept the societies close to the fundamental principles of harmony between humans, humans and the environment, and humans and the spirit world.

Throughout the history of Africa the religious seldom has had a component of retributive justice. Unlike the Hammurabi Code, the famous set of laws named for the Babylonian king and established around 1750 B.C., the African religious sentiments and confessions rarely demonstrated class divisions or retributive justice. For example, the rigid class structure for which the Hammurabi Code was prepared grew out of a particular understanding of society and religion. In the African tradition, the rituals surrounding the deities, the ceremonies of priests, and the propitiation necessary to call deities together in support of human needs are based in the belief that nothing in the earth or heavens is without spirit. Consequently, the religious ideas are applied equally to all sectors of the society, and there is no difference between the rich and the poor, the aristocrat and the commoner, in terms of what is asked by the deities.

African civilizations have posited a world of the unborn, the living, and the dead as a common society. Those unborn and those who have died become ancestors and are weighty presences in African societies.

As far back as one can go in the history of the African world, one finds the insistence of the religious, the divine; even the language of the ancient Kemetic people is referred to as *mdw ntr*, or "divine speech." A person could not live in society without being connected to the totality of the religious idea, the commonality of thought, purpose, and objective. Such interconnectedness meant that each part was critical to the whole. The unborn, living, and dead operated in one sphere in the traditional African world view, separated from yet at the same time dependent upon the gods. When Rameses II went to fight the Hittites at Kadesh in April 1274 B.C., the four main divisions of his army were named for the gods Amen, Ra, Ptah, and Seth. Perhaps it is here that we get the earliest notion of the religious war. With his glittering chariots speeding toward the engagement with the Hittites, this great African commander in chief knew that it was best to go with god on your side, and even better to go with four gods!

The multiplicity of religious responses to the natural world, the divinities, and the ancestors is seen in the selections for this section. The prophecy of Nefer-rohu, the tomb prayers of Paheri, selections from the Papyrus of Ani, Akhenaten's hymns to Aten, Horemhab's prayer and hymn, and the three penitential hymns of Kemet attest to the antiquity of the African's religious response in historical time. Selections from the Book of Henok demonstrate the quest for truth, justice, and harmony found in Ethiopia in the early records of the Christian Church. Of course, one of the best demonstrations of the ancient concepts of communal harmony is in Jomo Kenyatta's work dealing with the veneration of the ancestors, sometimes mistakenly spoken of as "ancestor worship."

We provide a series of writings from popular traditional African religions to show the magnificence of the variety of praise poems, libations, invocations, and rituals in African traditions. The intention is not to exhaust the examples but to introduce the reader to the transgenerational and transcontinental nature of the religious sentiment. Each document is specifically chosen for that purpose.

For example, Nefer-rohu's prophecy is an exact response to the environment, natural and supernatural. Indeed his prophecy, made during the Middle Kingdom (2040–1650 B.C.), is one of the earliest of this genre. Nefer-rohu prophesied that "a man sits in a corner, turning his back, while one man kills another. I show you the son as an enemy, the brother as an enemy, and a man killing his own father." It seems such prophecies, although quite common during times of anarchy, such as those witnessed by Nefer-rohu, were unthinkable for most of the period of the ancient Kemetic civilization because of the strong hold of the state religion. But in the midst of anarchy, one can see the impact of instability reflected in the uncertainty of the prophets. Doom was inevitable.

In addition to Nefer-rohu's prophecy we have included the tomb prayers of Paheri, written to underscore the importance of the life of the deceased and the achievements that recommend him for eternity.

The Papyrus of Ani, often called "The Egyptian Book of the Dead," is not considered a revealed text in the sense that the Koran, the Bible, the Bhagavad-Gita, or the Vedas may be thought of as inspiring in one person some idea of the spiritual world, yet it is every bit as profound as these writings. Ani was simply a priest, a scribe, an official of god, and this is his version of the many texts about the afterlife that had come down through the ages. Thirty-five hundred years ago, Ani collected the various texts that had been used in funerary celebrations and provided us with an entire papyrus of these important writings. They are not ascribed to one principal individual, like Moses, Jesus Christ, Mohammed, or Buddha, and yet scholars believe that in some instances the great prophets of Judaism, Christianity, Islam, and Buddhism were influenced by the ancient teachings of the early African priests. The Kemetic wisdom texts or moral philosophy is more akin to the biblical and

Koranic teachings than to the Papyrus of Ani. Yet we have favored the latter because of its durability in the history of ideas and its appeal to the African world as a statement of the concept of judgment.

Akhenaten's hymns are the most famous hymns of ancient Africa because it is through them that the world considered him the first serious monotheist. Amenhotep IV changed his name to Akhenaten to transform himself symbolically from one with whom "Amen is satisfied" to one "who gives honor to Aten." But he was not the first to espouse monotheism, nor was he the first to regard the sun as a deity. In fact, Ra, the sun god, was a more popular deity than Aten and a more powerful deity throughout the history of Kemet. However, Ra was the energy of the sun, whereas Akhenaten interpreted the disk of the sun as god, that is, as Aten. In his hymns to Aten, Akhenaten demonstrates the intense African interest in religion.

From the ancient Kemetic tradition we have also chosen Horemhab's prayer and hymn and three penitential hymns as examples of these genres. Horemhab was himself a major military pharaoh and one of the last rulers of the Eighteenth Dynasty, and thus his remarkable prayer and hymn are fitting conclusions to a politically and religiously provocative dynastic period.

Writings from other parts of Africa include selections from the Book of Henok (Enoch), which is part of the ancient Ethiopian sacred writings that include the *Kebra Nagast*. By reviewing the Book of Henok, the reader is able to see the continuing narrative of scriptural references in the ancient African tradition. The magnificent civilization of Axum in what is present-day Ethiopia produced a culture that spent its religious zeal on carving out churches from the rocks and writing and interpreting religious documents.

The preceding works are all gifts of literature, but we have also included in this section the orature of many cultures, much of which has been recorded and made available to the general public. Among the works that we have chosen are Jomo Kenyatta's writings on the Kikuyu people, the Asante praise poems to the Tano River and the Mother Earth, libations to the ancestors of the Lodagaa and Ga people, invocations of the Igbo, an exploration of the Yoruba concept of the good, and orature (oral literature) from Mensah Sarbah on the Akan religion.

Kenyatta's work is second to none in its presentation of traditional African religious and cultural life. He shows in clear terms the extent to which the moral behavior of the society is connected to its world view. There is little separation of one's personal life and the collective life of the community. This is the same attitude of the praise songs of Asante. In the African world view, it was not so much that nature was god as that humans and nature were from the same source. How could one spoil the river, or destroy the forest, or pollute the air? In this wholistic view, everything is related, existing in balance. To make the universe right, to restore or maintain balance and harmony to the social order, it is necessary to establish the proper relationship with the ancestors. The tradition is to pour libations to those who represent the departed spirits. All invocations and divinations are part of this righting exercise, this setting the world right-side up. Actually the religious and cultural beliefs of Africans, whether as seen in Sarbah's expounding of Akan religion or in Yoruba religion, are grounded in the fundamental understanding that animated the earliest religions of the Nile Valley: the spiritual and material worlds are interconnected, and everything that humans do will have some effect on the state of the universe.

Of course, myriad religious beliefs and practices coexist in Africa. People such as the Vai, Nsibidi, and Edo have developed their own religious scripts. If we were to devote an entire book on religious beliefs we would be able to present a wider array of traditional sources and demonstrate how the syncretic religions of the Americas, such as Voodoo, Umbanda, Macumba, Candomble, Shango, Ogun, and Santeria have their roots in the African religious soil. Our representations of the original sources, although not the same as the contemporary expressions in the Americas, provide useful groundings for understanding those religions. African beliefs transported to the Americas are still bound up in the holism of the world of the unborn, living, and dead, and our selections are meant to demonstrate that unity.

Nefer-rohu

(ELEVENTH DYNASTY, 2134–1991 B.C., Kemet)

The Prophecy

Now it happened that the majesty of the King of Upper and Lower Egypt: Snefru, the triumphant, was the beneficent king in this entire land. On one of these days it happened that the official council of the Residence City entered into the Great House—life, prosperity, health!—to offer greeting. Then they went out, that they might offer greetings, according to their daily procedure. Then his majesty—life, prosperity, health!—said to the seal-bearer who was at his side: "Go and bring me the official council of the Residence City, which has gone forth hence to offer greetings on this day." Thereupon they were ushered into him immediately. Then they were on their bellies in the presence of his majesty a second time.

Then his majesty—life, prosperity, health!— said to them: "My people, behold, I have caused you to be called to have you seek out for me a son of yours who is wise, or a brother of yours who is competent, or a friend of yours who has performed a good deed, one who may say to me a few fine words or choice speeches, at the hearing of which my majesty may be entertained."

Then they put themselves upon their bellies in the presence of his majesty—life, prosperity, health!—once more. Then they said before his majesty—life, prosperity, health!: "A great lector-priest of Bastet, O Sovereign, our lord, whose name is Nefer-rohu—he is a commoner valiant with his arm, a scribe competent with his fingers; he is a man of rank, who has more property than any peer of his. Would that he *might be permitted* to see his majesty!" Then his majesty—life, prosperity, health!—said: "Go and bring him to me!"

Then he was ushered in to him immediately. Then he was on his belly in the presence of his majesty—life, prosperity, health! Then his majesty—life, prosperity, health!—said: "Come, pray, Nefer-rohu, my friend, that thou mayest say to me a few fine words or choice speeches, at the hearing of which my majesty may be entertained!" Then the lector-priest Nefer-rohu said: "Of what has already happened or of what is going to happen, O Sovereign—life, prosperity, health!—my lord?" Then his majesty—life, prosperity, health!—said: "Rather of what is going to happen. *If it has* taken place *by* today, *pass it by.*" Then he stretched forth his hand for the box of writing equipment; then he drew forth a scroll of papyrus and a palette; thereupon he put it into writing.

What the priest Nefer-rohu said, that wise man of the east, he who belonged to Bastet at her appearances, that child of the Heliopolitan nome, as he brooded over what was to happen in the land as he called to mind the state of the east, when the Asiatics would move about with their strong arms, would disturb the hearts of those who are at the harvest, and would take away the spans of cattle at the plowing. He said:

"*Reconstruct,* O my heart, *how* thou bewailest this land in which thou didst begin! To be silent is *repression.* Behold, there is something about which men speak as *terrifying,* for, behold, the great man is a thing passed away in the land where thou didst begin. Be not lax; behold, it is before thy face! Mayest thou rise up against what is before thee, for, behold, although great men are concerned with the land, what has been done is as what is not done. *Ra must begin the foundation of the earth over again.* The land is completely perished, so that no thing remains, not even the black of the nail survives from what was fated.

"This land is so damaged that there is no one who is concerned with it, no one who speaks, no eye that weeps. How is this land? The sun disc is covered over. It will not shine so that people may see. No one can live when clouds cover over the sun. Then everybody is deaf for lack of it.

"I shall speak of what is before my face; I cannot foretell what has not yet come.

"The rivers of Egypt are empty, so that the water is crossed on foot. Men seek for water for the ships to sail on it. Its course is become a sandbank. The sandbank *is against* the flood; the place of water *is against* the flood—the place of water *and* the sandbank. The south wind will oppose the north wind; the skies are no longer in a single wind. A foreign bird will be born in the marshes of the Northland. It has made a nest beside men, and people have let it approach through want of it. Damaged indeed are those good things, those fish-ponds, where there were those who clean fish, overflowing with fish and fowl. Everything good is disappeared, and the land is prostrate because of woes from that *flood,* the Asiatics who are thoroughout the land.

"Foes have arisen in the east, and Asiatics have come down into Egypt. No protector will listen. Men will enter into the *fortresses.* Sleep will *be banished* from my eyes, as I spend the night wakeful. The wild beasts of the desert will drink at the rivers of Egypt and be at their ease on their banks for lack of *someone to scare them away.*

"This land is helter-skelter, and no one knows the result which will come about, which is hidden from speech, sight, or hearing. The face is deaf, for silence *confronts.* I show thee the land topsy-turvy. That which never happened has happened. Men will take up weapons of warfare, so that the land lives in confusion. Men will make arrows of metal, beg for the bread of blood, and laugh with the laughter of sickness. There is no one who weeps because of death, there is no one who spends the night fasting because of death; but a man's heart pursues himself alone. Dishevelled mourning is no longer carried out today, for the heart is completely *separated from* it. A man sits *in his corner, turning* his back while one man kills another. I show thee the son as a foe, the brother as an enemy, and a man killing his own father.

"Every mouth is full of 'Love me!,' and everything good has disappeared. The land is perished, *as though* laws *were* destined *for it:* the damaging of what had been done, the emptiness of what had been found, and the doing of what had not been done. Men take a man's property away from him, and it is given to him who is from outside. I show thee the possessor in need and the outsider satisfied. He who never filled for himself *(now) empties.* Men will *treat* fellow citizens as hateful, in order to silence the mouth that speaks. If a statement is answered, an arm goes out with a stick, and men speak with: 'Kill him!' The utterance of speech in the heart is like a fire. Men cannot suffer what issues from *a man's* mouth.

"The land is diminished, but its administrators are many; bare, but its taxes are great; little in grain, but the measure is large, and it is measured to overflowing.

"Ra separates himself from mankind. If he shines forth, it is but an hour. No one knows when midday falls, for his shadow cannot be distinguished. There is no one bright of face when seeing him; the eyes are not moist with water, when he is in the sky like the moon. His prescribed time does not fail. His rays are indeed in men's faces in his former way.

"I show thee the land topsy-turvy. The weak of arm is now the possessor of an arm. Men salute respectfully him who formerly saluted. I show thee the undermost on top, turned about *in proportion to* the turning about *of my belly*. Men live in the necropolis. The poor man will make wealth. It is the paupers who eat the offering-bread, while the servants *jubilate*. The Heliopolitan nome, the birthplace of every god, will no *longer be on earth*.

"Then it is that a king will come, belonging to the south, Ameni, the triumphant, his name. He is the son of a woman of the land of Nubia; he is the son of a woman of the land of Nubia; he is one born in Upper Egypt. He will take the White Crown; he will wear the Red Crown; he will united the Two Mighty Ones; he will satisfy the Two Lords with what they desire. The encircler-of-the-fields will be in his grasp, the oar.

"Rejoice, ye people of his time! The son of a man will make his name forever and ever. They who incline toward evil and who plot rebellion have subdued their speech for fear of him. The Asiatics will fall to his sword, and the Libyans will fall to his flame. The rebels belong to his wrath, and the treacherous of the heart to the awe of him. The uraeus-serpent which is on his brow stills for him the treacherous of heart.

"There will be built the Wall of Ruler—life, prosperity, health!—and the Asiatics will not be permitted to come down into Egypt that they might beg for water in the customary manner, in order to let their beasts drink. And justice will come into its place, while wrongdoing is *driven* out. Rejoice, he who may behold this and who may be in the service of the king!

"The learned man will pour out water for me, when he sees what I have spoken come to pass.

"It has come to its end in success, by the *Scribe*."

Tomb Prayers

THE PRAYER FOR OFFERINGS

> An offering given by the King to Amen,
> Lord of Thrones-of-the-Two-Lands,
> King of eternity, lord of everlastingness,
> Ruler, lord of the two great plumes,
> Sole one, primordial, eldest,
> Primeval, without equal,
> Creator of men and gods,
> Living flame that came from Nun,
> Maker of light for mankind;
> And Nekhbet, the White one of Nekhen,
> Mistress of heaven, lady of the Two Lands;
> And Ausar Kehntamentiu,
> Lord of Thinis, great in Abydos;
> And Hathgor, mistress of the desert,
> Strong of heart among the gods;
> And Ptah-Sokar, lord of Shetyt,
> Anubis, lord of Rostau,
> And the Enneads, great and small.
> May they give a thousand of bread, beer, beef, and fowl,
> A thousand of food-offerings,
> A thousand of drink-offerings,
> All the plants that sprout from earth,
> A thousand of all things good and pure,
> That are offered to the eternal lord;
> To receive the bread that came before [him],
> The milk that came upon the altar,
> To drink the water that flows from Yebu,
> On the monthly feast, the sixth-day feast,
> The half-monthly feast, the great procession,
> The rise of Sothis, the *wag*-feast,*
> The Jehuti-feast, the first-birth feast,
> The birth of Auset, the procession of Min,

*A *wag*-feast is a heavenly feast.—EDS.

Religious Ideas

The procession of the *sem*-priest,†
The evening meal, the rise of the river—
The feasts of heaven on their fixed days,
In accord with daily custom.
You are clothed in the robe of finest linen,
The garments that clad the flesh of the god;
You are anointed with pure oil,
You drink water from the altar's rim;
You partake of its possessions,
As a noble in front of the blessed;
For the *ka* of the Mayor of Nekheb,
The Scribe Pheri, the justified,
The loyal trusty of his lord.

The Life in the Beyond

You come in, you go out,
Your heart in joy at the praise of the lord of gods;
A good burial after revered old age,
After old age has come.
You take your place in the lord-of-life,
You come to the earth in the tomb of the west.
To become indeed a living *ba,*
It shall thrive on bread, water, and air;
To assume the form of phoenix, swallow,
Of falcon or heron, as you wish.
You cross in the ferry without being hindered,
You fare on the water's flowing flood.
You come to life a second time,
Your *ba* [soul] shall not forsake your corpse.
Your *ba* is divine among the spirits,
The worthy *ba*'s converse with you.
You join them to receive what is given on earth.
You thrive on water, you breathe air,
You drink as your heart desires.
Your eyes are given you to see.
Your ears to hear what is spoken;
Your mouth speaks, your feet walk,
Your hands, your arms have motion.
Your flesh is firm, your muscles are smooth,
You delight in all your limbs;
You count your members: all there, sound,
There is no fault in what is yours.
Your heart is yours in very truth,
You have your own, your former heart,
You rise to heaven, you open *dat* [underworld],
In any shape that you desire.

†The *sem*-priest is the priest responsible for clothing the gods.—Eds.

You are summoned daily to Wennofer's altar,
You receive the bread that comes before him,
The offering to the lord of the sacred land;
For the *ka* of the Mayor of Nekheb, the Mayor of Iunyt,
Who counts the grain from Iunet to Nekheb,
The watchful leader, free of fault,
The Scribe Paheri, the justified.

You eat bread beside the god,
At the great terrace of the Ennead's Lord;
You turn from there to where he is,
In the midst of the leading council.
You walk about among them,
You consort with the Heru-servants;
You go up, you go down, unhindered,
You are not turned back at the gate of *dat*.
The portals of lightland open for you,
The bolts slide back of themselves;
You reach the Hall of the Two Truths,
The god who is in it welcomes you.
You settle down in the netherworld,
You stride about in the city of Hapy.
Your heart rejoices as you plow
In your plot in the Field of Reeds;
You are rewarded with what you have grown,
You gather a harvest rich in grain.
The rope is roped for you in the ferry,
You sail as your heart desires.
You go outdoors each morning,
You return each evening.
The torch is lit for you at night,
Until the sun shines on your breast.
One says to you, "Welcome, welcome,"
In this your house of the living.
You see Ra in heaven's lightland,
You watch Amen as he dawns.
You waken gladly every day,
All afflictions are expelled.
You traverse eternity in joy,
In the favor of the god who is in you.
Your heart is with you without failing you,
Your provisions remain in their place;
For the *ka* of the Scribe Paheri, the justified.

PAHERI RECALLS HIS BLAMELESS CONDUCT

He says:
I am a noble who served his lord,
One skilled and free of negligence.

I walked on the road I had explored,
I knew the outcome of my life.
I reckoned the limits in the books,
The boundaries of the king's concerns,
All things that pertained to the palace,
Like Hapy in his course to the sea.
My mouth was firm in serving the lord,
I was fearful of deficiency;
I did not neglect making payment in full,
I did not take a slice of the expense.
I was guided by my own heart
On the road of those praised by the king.
My pen of reed made me renowned,
It gave me right in the council;
It made my nature, I surpassed the nobles,
My good character raised me high,
I was summoned as one who is blameless.
Were I to be placed on the scales,
I would come out complete, whole, sound.
I came and went with a steady heart,
I told no lie to anyone.
I knew the god who dwells in man,
Knowing him I knew this from that.
I did the tasks as they were ordered,
I did not confuse the report with the reporter,
I did not speak with low-class words,
I did not talk to worthless people.
I was a model of kindliness,
One praised who came praised from the womb.
The Mayor of Nekheb, Paheri, the justified,
Son of the tutor of the prince, the scribe Itruri, the justified,
Born of the Lady Kam, the justified.

THE APPEAL TO THE LIVING

He says:
Listen, all who now have being,
I speak to you without deceit;
You who live, who have existence,
Nobles, people, upon earth;
Servants of God, priests, attendants,
Every scribe who holds the palette,
Who is skilled in words of god;
Whosoever is good to his subjects,
Whosoever excels in his task:
Ra, everlasting, will commend you,
Also Nekhbet, the White one of Nekhen,

And whoever guides your task.
You will bequeath to your children,
If you say, "An offering, given by the king,"
In the form in which it is written;
"An invocation-offering," as said by the fathers,
And as it comes from the mouth of god.
Whosoever will bend his arm,
He will be on the path of truth.
To act as befits, as conforms to the rules,
Is to bear witness before this stela.
Your thousand of bread, your thousand of beer,
Your hundred thousand of all good things,
Offered pure to the Ausar,
Mayor of Nekheb, Mayor of Iynyt,
Trusty of the treasurer on the southern journey,
The worthy Scribe of the accounts, the justified Paheri.

I say to you, I let you know:
It is a recital without expense,
It does not make poor, it makes no trouble;
It means no quarrel with another,
It is not coercing one who is needy.
It is a pleasing speech that uplifts,
The heart does not tire to hear it.
The breath of the mouth, it is not eaten,
There is no strain, no fatigue in it.
It is good for you when you do it,
You will find it in profit and praise.
While I was in the land of the living,
No sin against God was reproached me.
I have become an equipped blessed spirit.
I have furnished my place in the graveyard.
I have what I need in all things,
I shall not fail to respond.
The dead is father to him who acts for him,
He forgets not him who libates for him,
It is good for you to listen!

Selections from the Papyrus of Ani

Ausar, the scribe Ani, triumphant, saith: "I have come and I have drawn nigh to see thy beauties; my two hands are raised in adoration of thy name Right and Truth. I have drawn nigh unto the place where the acacia tree groweth not, where the tree thick with leaves existeth not, and where the ground yieldeth neither herb nor grass. And I have entered in unto the place of secret and hidden things, I have held converse with the god Sut. Ausar, the scribe Ani, hath entered into the House of Ausar, and he hath seen the hidden and secret things which are therein. The holy rulers of the pylons are in the form of shining ones. Anubis spake unto him with the speech of man when he came from Ta-mera, saying, 'He knoweth our paths and our cities, I have been pacified, and the smell of him is to me even as the smell of one of you.' "

Ani saith unto him: "I am Ausar, the scribe Ani, triumphant in peace, triumphant! I have drawn nigh to behold the great gods, and I feed upon the meals of sacrifice whereon their *kas* feed. I have been to the boundaries of the lands of the Ram, the lord of Tattu, and he hath granted that I may come forth as a *bennu* [phoenix] bird and that I may have the power of speech. I have passed through the river-flood. I have made offerings with incense. I have made my way by the side of the thick-leaved tree of the children. I have been in Abtu in the House of Satet. I have flooded and I have sunk the boat of my enemies. I have sailed forth upon the Lake in the *neshem* boat. I have been the noble ones of Kam-ur. I have been in Tattu, and I have constrained myself to silence. I have set the divine Form upon his two feet. I have been with the god Pa-tep-tu-f, and I have seen the dweller in the Holy Temple. I have entered into the House of Ausar, and I have dressed myself in the apparel of him who is therein. I have entered into Ra-stau, and I have beheld the hidden things which are therein. I have been swathed, but I found for myself a thorough-fare. I have entered into An-aarut-f, and I have clothed my body with the apparel which is therein. The *antu* unguent of women hath been given unto me. Verily, Sut spoke unto me the things which concern himself, and I said, 'Let the thought of the trial of the balance by thee be even within our hearts.' "

The majesty of the god Anubis saith: "Dost thou know the name of this door to declare it unto me?" Ausar, the scribe Ani, triumphant, triumphant in peace, saith: " 'Driven away of Shu' is the name of this door." Saith the majesty of the god Anubis: "Dost thou know the name of the upper leaf and of the lower leaf thereof?" Ausar, the scribe Ani, triumphant in peace, saith: " 'Lord of right and truth, standing upon his two feet' is the name of the upper leaf, and 'Lord of might and power, dispenser of cattle' is the name of the lower leaf." The majesty of the god Anubis saith: "Pass thou, for thou knowest the names, O Ausar, the scribe, teller of the divine offerings of all the gods of Thebes, Ani, triumphant, lord to be revered."

The following shall be said by a man when he cometh unto the Hall of Double Right and Truth, wherein he is purged of all the sins which he hath done, and wherein he seeth the faces of all the gods: "Hail to thee, great god, the lord of Right and Truth! I have come unto thee, O my lord, and I have drawn nigh that I may look upon thy beauties. I know thee, and I know the names of the forty-two gods who dwell with thee in his Hall of Double Right and Truth, and that they may set the sinners in the gives, who live and who feed upon their blood on the day when the natures of men are accounted before Un-neferu. In very truth 'Rekhti-merti-f-ent-Maat' is thy name. Verily I have come unto thee, and I bring before thee Right and Truth. For thy sake I have rejected wickedness. I have done no hurt unto man, nor have I wrought harm unto beasts. I have committed no crime in the place of Right and Truth. I have had no knowledge of evil; nor have I acted wickedly. Each day have I laboured more than was required of me. My name hath not come forth to the boat of the Prince. I have not despised God. I have not caused misery; nor have I worked affliction. I have done not that which God doth abominate. I have caused no wrong to be done to the servant by his master. I have caused none to feel pain. I have made no one to weep. I have not committed murder; nor have I ever bidden any man to slay on my behalf. I have not wronged the people. I have not filched that which hath been offered in the temples; nor have I purloined the cakes of the gods. I have not carried away the offerings made unto the blessed dead. I have not committed fornication, nor have I defiled my body. I have not added unto nor have I minished the offerings which are due. I have not stolen from the orchards; nor have I trampled down the fields. I have not added to the weight of the balance; nor have I made light the weight of the scales. I have not snatched the milk from the mouth of the babe. I have not driven the cattle from their pastures. I have not snared the water-fowl of the gods. I have not caught fishes with bait of their own bodies. I have not turned back water at its springtide. I have not broken the channel of running water. I have not quenched the flame in its fulness. I have not disregarded the seasons for the offerings which are appointed; I have not turned away the cattle set apart for sacrifice. I have not thwarted the processions of the god. I am pure. I am pure. I am pure. I am pure. I am pure with the purity of the great Bennu bird which is in Suten-henen; for, lo! I am the nostrils of the lord of the winds who maketh all men to live on the day when the eye of the sun becometh full in Annu, in the second month of the season of coming forth until the end thereof, in the presence of the lord of this earth. I behold the eye of the sun wax full of Annu. May no evil happen unto me in this land in the Hall of Double Right and Truth, because I know, even I, the names of the gods who live therein and who are the followers of the great god."

The Hall of Double Right and Truth, wherein Ani has to address severally the forty-two gods, who are seated in a row in the middle of the hall. At each end is a door; that on the right is called "Neb-Matt-heri-tep-retui-f," and that on the left, "Neb-pehti-esu-menment." On the centre of the roof, which is crowned with a series of uræi and feathers emblematic of Maat, is a seated deity with hands extended, the right over the eye of Heru and the left over a pool. On the right, at the end of the hall, are four small vignettes, in which are depicted: Two seated figures of the goddess Maat, with emblems of Right and Truth, on the head, and scepters and emblems of life in the right and left hands. Ausar, seated, wearing the *atef* crown, and holding in his hands the crook and flail.

Before him, by the side of an altar of offerings, stands Ani, with both hands raised in adoration. A balance with the heart, symbolizing the conscience of Ani, in one scale, and,

Religious Ideas

emblematic of Right and Truth, in the other. Beside the balance is the tri-formed monster Amemit. Thoth, ibis-headed, seated on a pylon-shaped pedestal, painting a large feather of Maat.

THE DECLARATIONS OF INNOCENCE

(1) Ani saith: "Hail, thou whose strides are long, who comest forth from Annu, I have not done iniquity."

(2) "Hail, thou who are embraced by flame, who comest forth from Kheraba, I have not robbed with violence."

(3) "Hail, Fentiu, who comest forth from Khemennu, I have not stolen."

(4) "Hail, Devourer of the Shade, who comest forth from Qernet, I have done no murder; I have done no harm."

(5) "Hail, Nehau, who comest forth from Ra-stau, I have not defrauded offerings."

(6) "Hail, god in the form of two lions, who comest forth from heaven, I have not diminished oblations."

(7) "Hail, thou whose eyes are of fire, who comest forth from Saut, I have not plundered the gods."

(8) "Hail, thou Flame, which comest and goest, I have spoken no lies."

(9) "Hail, Crusher of bones, who comest forth from Suten-henen, I have not snatched away food."

(10) "Hail, thou who shootest forth the Flame, who comest forth from Het-Ptah-ka, I have not caused pain."

(11) "Hail, Qerer, who comest forth from Amentet, I have not committed fornication."

(12) "Hail, thou whose face is turned back, who comest forth from thy hiding place, I have not caused shedding of tears."

(13) "Hail, Bast, who comest forth from the secret place, I have not dealt deceitfully."

(14) "Hail, thou whose legs are of fire, who comest forth out of the darkness, I have not transgressed."

(15) "Hail, Devourer of Blood, who comest forth from the block of slaughter, I have not acted guilefully."

(16) "Hail, Devourer of the inward parts, who comest forth from Mabet, I have not laid waste the ploughed land."

(17) "Hail, Lord of Right and Truth, who comest forth from the city of Right and Truth, I have not been an eavesdropper."

(18) "Hail, thou who dost stride backwards, who comest forth from the city of Bast, I have not set my lips in motion against any man."

(19) "Hail, Sertiu, who comest forth from Annu, I have not been angry and wrathful except for a just cause."

(20) "Hail, thou being of two-fold wickedness, who comest forth from Ati, I have not defiled the wife of any man."

(21) "Hail, thou two-headed serpent, who comest forth from the torture-chamber, I have not defiled the wife of any man."

(22) "Hail, thou who dost regard what is brought unto thee, who comest forth from pa-Amsu, I have not polluted myself."

Selections from the Papyrus of Ani

(23) "Hail, thou Chief of the mighty, who comest forth from Amentet, I have not caused terror."

(24) "Hail, thou Destroyer, who comest forth from Kesiu, I have not transgressed."

(25) "Hail, thou who orderest speech, who comest forth from Urit, I have not burned with rage."

(26) "Hail, thou Babe, who comest forth from Uab, I have not stopped my ears against the words of Right and Truth."

(27) "Hail, Kenemti, who comest forth from Kenemet, I have not worked grief."

(28) "Hail, thou who bringest thy offering, I have not acted with insolence."

(29) "Hail, thou who orderest speech, who comest forth from Unaset, I have not stirred up strife."

(30) "Hail, Lord of Faces, who comest forth from Netchfet, I have not judged hastily."

(31) "Hail, Sekheriu, who comest forth from Utten, I have not been an eavesdropper."

(32) "Hail, Lord of the Two Horns, who comest forth from Sais, I have not multiplied words exceedingly."

(33) "Hail, Nefer-tmu, who comest forth from Het-Ptah-Ka, I have done neither harm nor ill."

(34) "Hail, Tmu in thine hour, who comest forth from Tattu, I have never cursed the king."

(35) "Hail, Tmu in thine hour, who comest forth from Tattu, I have not worked treason."

(36) "Hail, thou who workest in thy heart, who comest forth from Tebtu, I have never befouled the water."

(37) "Hail, thou bearer of the sistrum, who comest forth from Nu, I have not spoken scornfully."

(38) "Hail, thou who dost make mankind to flourish, who comest forth from thy hall, I have not cursed God."

(39) "Hail, Nehebnefert, who comest forth from . . . , I have not acted with arrogance."

(40) "Hail, Neheb-kau, who comest forth from thy city, I have not been overweeningly proud."

(41) "Hail, Tcheser-tep, who comest forth from thy hiding place, I have never magnified my condition beyond what was fitting."

(42) "Hail, thou who bringest thine arm, who comest forth from Aukert, I have never slighted the god in my town."

Religious Ideas

Akhenaten

(EIGHTEENTH DYNASTY, 1550–1305 B.C., Kemet)

Hymns to Aten

PRAISE TO THE ATEN

Adoration of *Ra-Harakhti-who-rejoices-in-lightland In-his-name-Shu-who-is-Aten,* who gives live forever, by the King who lives by Maat, the Lord of the Two Lands: *Neferkheprure, Sole-one-of-Ra;* the Son of Ra who lives by Maat, the Lord of crowns: *Akhenaten,* great in his lifetime, given life forever.

Beautiful you rise, O eternal living god!
You are radiant, lovely, powerful,
Your love is great, all-encompassing.
Your rays make all radiant,
Your brightness gives life to hearts,
When you fill the Two Lands with your love.
Revered God who fashioned himself,
Who made every land, created what is in it,
All peoples, herds, and flocks,
All trees that grow from soil;
They live when you rise for them,
You are mother and father of all that you made.

When you rise their eyes observe you,
As your rays light the whole earth;
Every heart acclaims your sight,
When you are risen as their lord.
When you set in the sky's western horizon,
They lie down as if to die,
Their heads covered, their noses stopped,
Until you rise in sky's eastern horizon.
Their arms adore you *ka,*
As you nourish the hearts by your beauty;
One lives when you cast your rays,
Every land is in festivity.

In the Tomb of Ay

Adoration of *Ra-Harakhti-who-rejoices-in-lightland In-his-name-Shu-Whi-is-Aten*, living forever; the great living Aten who is in jubilee, the lord of all that the Disk encircles, lord of sky, lord of earth, lord of the house-of-Aten in Akhet-Aten; and of the King of Upper and Lower Egypt, who lives by Maat, the Lord of the Two Lands, *Neferkheprure, Sole-one-of-Ra;* the Son of Ra who lives by Maat, the Lord of Crowns, *Akhenaten*, great in his lifetime; and his beloved great Queen, the Lady of the Two Lands, *Nefer-nefru-Aten Nefertiti*, who lives in health and youth forever. The Vizier, the Fanbearer on the right of the King,———[Ay]; he says:

> Beautiful you rise in heaven's horizon,
> O eternal, living creator!
> When you have risen in eastern horizon,
> You fill every land with your beauty.
> You are lovely, great, radiant,
> High over every land;
> Your rays embrace the lands,
> To the limit of your creations.
> Being Ra, you reach their limits,
> You bend them for the son whom you love;
> Though you are far, your rays are on earth,
> Though one sees you, your strides are unseen.
>
> When you set in the western horizon,
> Earth is in darkness as if in death;
> One sleeps in chambers, heads covered,
> One eye does not see another.
> Were they robbed of their goods,
> That are under their heads,
> People would not remark it.
> Every lion comes from its den,
> All the serpents bite;
> Darkness hovers, earth is silent,
> As their maker rests in the horizon.
>
> Earth brightens when you rise in the eastern horizon,
> When you shine as Aten of daytime;
> As you dispel the dark,
> As you cast your rays,
> The Two Lands are in festivity.
> Awake they stand on their feet,
> You have awaken them;
> Bodies washed, clothed,
> Their arms love your appearance.
> The entire land sets out to work,
> All beasts browse on their herbs;

Trees, herbs are sprouting,
Birds fly from their nests,
Their wings greeting your *ka*.
All flocks frisk on their feet,
All that fly up and alight,
They live when you rise for them.
Ships go north, go south as well,
Roads lie open when you rise;
The fish in the river dart before you,
Your rays are in the midst of the sea.

Who makes women fertile,
Who creates life from sperm,
Who feeds the son in his mother's womb,
Who soothes him to still his tears.
Nurse in the womb,
Giver of breath,
To nourish all that he made.
When he comes from the womb to breathe,
On the day of his birth,
You open wide his mouth,
You supply his needs.
When the chick in the egg speaks in the shell,
You give him breath within to sustain him;
When you have made him complete,
To break out from the egg,
He comes out from the egg,
To announce his completion,
Walking on his legs he comes from it.

How great are your deeds,
Though hidden from sight,
Only God beside whom there is none other!
You made the earth as you wished, you alone,
All peoples, herds, and flocks;
All upon earth that walk on legs,
All on high that fly on wings,
The lands of Khor and Kush,
The land of Egypt.
You are every man in his place,
You supply their needs;
Everyone has his food,
His lifetime is counted.
Their tongues differ in speech,
Their characters likewise;
Their skins are distinct,
For you distinguished the peoples.

You made Hapy in *dat,*
You bring him when you will,

To nourish the people,
For you made them for yourself.
God of all who toils for them,
God of all lands who shines for them,
Aten of daytime, great in glory!
All distant lands, you make them live,
You made a heavenly Hapy descend for them;
He makes waves on the mountains like the sea,
To drench their fields and their towns.
How excellent are your ways, O Lord of eternity!
A Hapy from heaven for foreign peoples,
And all lands' creatures that walk on legs,
For Egypt the Hapy who comes from *dat*.

Your rays nurse all fields,
When you shine they live, they grow for you;
You made the seasons to foster all that you made,
Winter to cool them, heat that they taste you.
You made the far sky to shine therein,
To behold all that you made;
You alone, shining in your form of living Aten,
Risen, radiant, distant, near.
You made millions of forms from yourself alone,
Towns, villages, fields, and river's course;
All eyes observe you upon them,
For you are the Aten of daytime on high.

  •   •   •

You are in my heart,
There is no other who knows you,
Only your son, *Neferkheprure, Sole-one-of-Ra,*
Whom you have taught your ways and your might.
Those on earth come from your hand as you made them,
When you have risen they live,
When you set they die;
You yourself are lifetime, one lives by you.
All eyes are on your beauty until you set,
All labor ceases when you rest in the west;
When you rise you stir everyone for the King,
Every foot is on the move since you founded the earth.
You awaken them for your son who came from your body,
The King who lives by Maat, the Lord of the Two Lands,
Neferkheprure, Sole-one-of-Ra,
The Son of Ra who lives by Maat, the Lord of crowns,
Akhenaten, great in his lifetime;
And the great Queen whom he loves, the Lady of the Two Lands,
Nefer-nefru-Aten Nefertiti, living forever.

Haremhab

(EIGHTEENTH DYNASTY, 1550–1305 B.C., Kemet)

Prayer and Hymn

THE PRAYER

A royal offering to Jehuti, lord of writing, lord of Khmun,
Who determines *maat,* who embarks Ra in the night-bark,
May your speech be answered for its rightness.
I am a righteous one toward the courtiers,
    If a lie is told me,
    My tongue is sharp to set it right.
I am the recorder of royal laws,
    Who gives directions to the courtiers,
    Wise in speech, there's nothing I ignore.
I am the public adviser
    Who teaches each man his course,
    Without forgetting my charge.
I am one who reports to the Lord of the Two Lands,
    Who speaks of whatever was forgotten,
    Who does not ignore the words of the King.
I am the herald of the council,
    Who does not ignore the plans of his Majesty;
    For the *ka* of the Prince, Royal Scribe, Horemhab, justified.

A royal offering to Ptah South-of-his-Wall,
Sakhmet, the beloved of Ptah,
Ptah-Sokar, lord of Shetit,
Osiris, lord of Rostau:
May you let the *ba* come forth by day to see Aten,
And listen to his daily prayer as a spirit whom you made spirit.
May you command me to follow you always as one of your favorites,
For I have always been a just one of God,
I satisfy him with *maat* every day.
I have shunned wrongdoing before him,
I never did evil since my birth;
Indeed I am a gentle one before God,

One wise, one calm, one who listens to *maat*.
May you let me be in the crew of the *neshmet*-bark,
At its feast in the region of Peqer;
For the *ka* of the Prince, Sole Companion,
King's Deputy before the Two Lands,
Royal Scribe, Haremhab, justified.

THE HYMN TO JEHUTI

Adoration of Jehuti, Son of Ra, Moon,
Of beautiful rising, lord of appearings, light of the gods,
By the Prince, Count, Fan-bearer on the King's right,
Great Troop-commander, Royal Scribe, Haremhab, justified, he says:
Hail to you, Moon, Jehuti,
Bull in Khmun, dweller in Hesret,
Who makes way for the gods!
Who knows the secrets,
Who records their expression,
Who distinguishes one speech from another,
Who is judge of everyone.
Keen-faced in the Ship-of-millions,
Courier of mankind,
Who knows a man by his utterance,
Who makes the deed rise against the doer.
Who contents Ra,
Advises the only Lord,
Lets him know whatever happens;
At dawn he summons in heaven,
And forgets not yesterday's report.

Who makes safe the night-bark,
Makes tranquil the day-bark,
With arms outstretched in the bow of the ship.
Pure-faced when he takes the stern-rope,
As the day-bark rejoices in the night-bark's joy,
At the feast of crossing the sky.
Who fells the fiend,
Sunders western lightland.
The Ennead in the night-bark worships Jehuti,
They say to him: "Greetings, Son of Ra,
Praised of Ra, whom the gods applaud!"
They repeat what your *ka* wishes,
As you make way for the place of the bark,
As you act against that fiend:
You cast his corpse in the fire,
You are the god who slaughters him.
Nothing is done without your knowing,

Religious Ideas

Great one, son of a Great one, who came from her limbs,
Champion of Harakhti,
Wise friend in On,
Who makes the place of the gods,
Who knows secrets,
Expounds their words.

Let us give praise to Jehuti,
Straight plummet in the scales,
Who repulses evil,
Who accepts him who leans not on crime.
The vizier who settles cases,
Who changes turmoil to peace;
The scribe of the mat who keeps the book,
Who punishes crime,
Who accepts the submissive.
Who is sound of arm,
Wise among the Ennead,
Who relates what was forgotten.
Counselor to him who errs,
Who remembers the fleeting moment,
Who reports the hour of night,
Whose words endure forever,
Who enters *dat*, knows those in it.
And records them in the list.

Penitential Hymns

HYMN TO AMEN-RA

Amen-Ra, Lord of Thrones-of-the-Two-Lands,
The great god who presides over Ipet-sut,
The august god who hears prayer,
Who comes at the voice of the poor in distress,
Who gives breath to him who is wretched.

Giving praise to Amen-Ra,
Lord of Thrones-of-the-Two-Lands,
Who presides over Ipet-sut;
Kissing the ground to Amen of Thebes, the great god,
The lord of this sanctuary, great and fair,
That he may let my eyes see his beauty;
For the *ka* of the draftsman of Amen, Nebre, justified.

Praise giving to Amen.
I make for him adoration to his name,
I give him praises to the height of heaven,
And over the breadth of the earth,
I tell his might to travelers north and south:
Beware ye of him!
Declare him to son and daughter,
    To the great and small,
Herald him to generations,
    Not yet born;
Herald him to fishes in the deep,
    To birds in the sky,
Declare him to fool and wise,
Beware ye of him!

You are Amen, the Lord of the silent,
Who comes at the voice of the poor;

When I call to you in my distress,
You come to rescue me,
To give breath to him who is wretched,
To rescue me from bondage.

You are Amen-Ra, Lord of Thebes,
Who rescues him who is in *dat;*
For you are he who is merciful,
When one appeals to you,
You are he who comes from afar.

Made by the draftsman of Amen in the Place-of-Truth, Nebre, justified, son of the draftsman in the Place-of-Truth, Pay, [justified], to the name of his Lord Amen, Lord of Thebes, who comes at the voice of the poor.

I made for him praises to his name,
For his might is great;
I made supplications before him,
In the presence of the whole land,
On behalf of the draftsman Nakhtamun, justified,
Who lay sick unto death,
In the power of Amen, through his sin.
I found the Lord of Gods coming as north wind,
Gentle breezes before him;
He saved Amen's draftsman Nakhtamun, justified,
Son of Amen's draftsman in the Place-of-Truth, Nebre, justified,
Born of the Lady Peshed, justified.

He says:
Though the servant was disposed to do evil,
The Lord is disposed to forgive.
The Lord of Thebes spends not a whole day in anger,
His wrath passes in a moment, none remains.
His breath comes back to us in mercy,
Amen returns upon his breeze.
May your *ka* be kind, may you forgive,
It shall not happen again.
Says the draftsman of the Place-of-Truth, Nebre, justified.

He says:
"I will make this stela to your name,
And record this praise on it in writing,
For you saved for me the draftsman Nakhtamun,"
So I said to you and you listened to me.
Now behold, I do what I have said,
You are the Lord to him who calls to you,
Content with *maat*, O Lord of Thebes!
Made by the draftsman Nebre and his son, the scribe Khay.

Hymn to Mertseger

Giving praise to the Peak of the West,
Kissing the ground to her *ka*.
I give praise, hear my call,
I was a truthful man on earth!
Made by the servant in the Place-of-Truth, Neferabu, justified.

I was an ignorant man and foolish,
Who knew not good from evil;
I did the transgression against the Peak,
And she taught a lesson to me.
I was in her hand by night as by day,
I sat on bricks like the women in labor,
I called to the wind, it came not to me,
I libated to the Peak of the West, great of strength,
And to every god and goddess.

Behold, I will say to the great and small,
Who are in the troop:
Beware of the Peak!
For there is a lion within her!
The Peak strikes with the stroke of a savage lion,
She is after him who offends her!

I called upon my Mistress,
I found her coming to me as sweet breeze;
She was merciful to me,
Having made me see her hand.
She returned to me appeased,
She made my malady forgotten;
For the Peak of the West is appeased,
If one calls upon her.

So says Neferabu, justified.
He says:
Behold, let hear every ear,
That lives upon earth:
Beware the Peak of the West!

Hymn to Ptah

Praise giving to Ptah, Lord of Maat,
King of the Two Lands,
Fair of face on his great seat,
The One God among the Ennead,
Beloved as King of the Two Lands.

May he give life, prosperity, health,
Alertness, favors, and affection,
And that my eyes may see Amen every day,
As is done for a righteous man,
Who has set Amen in his heart!
So says the servant in the Place-of-Truth, Neferabu, justified.

[*Reverse*] Beginning of the recital of the might of Ptah, South-of-his-Wall, by the servant in the Place-of-Truth on the West of Thebes, Neferabu, justified. He says:

I am a man who swore falsely by Ptah, Lord of Maat,
And he made me see darkness by day.
I will declare his might to the fool and the wise,
To the small and great:
Beware of Ptah, Lord of Maat!
Behold, he does not overlook anyone's deed!
Refrain from uttering Ptah's name falsely,
Lo, he who utters it falsely, lo he falls!

He caused me to be as the dogs of the street,
I being in his hand;
He made men and gods observe me,
I being as a man who has sinned against his Lord.
Righteous was Ptah, Lord of Maat, toward me,
When he taught a lesson to me!
Be merciful to me, look on me in mercy!
So says the servant in the Place-of-Truth on the West of Thebes, Neferabu, justified
    before the great god.

Selections from the Book of Henok (Enoch)

The words of the blessing of Enoch according to which he blessed the chosen and righteous who must be present on the day of distress which is appointed for the removal of all the wicked and impious. And Enoch answered and said: there was a righteous man whose eyes were opened by the Lord, and he saw a holy vision in the heavens which the angels showed to me. And I heard everything from them, and I understood what I saw, but not for this generation, but for a distant generation which will come. Concerning the chosen I spoke, and I uttered a parable concerning them: The Holy and Great One will come out from his dwelling, and the Eternal God will tread from there upon Mount Sinai, and he will appear with his host, and will appear in the strength of his power from heaven. And all will be afraid, and the Watchers will shake, and fear and great trembling will seize them unto the ends of the earth. And the high mountains will be shaken, and the high hills will be made low, and will melt like wax before the flame. And the earth will sink and everything that is on the earth will be destroyed, and there will be judgement upon all, and upon all the righteous. But for the righteous he will make peace, and he will keep safe the chosen, and mercy will be upon them. They will all belong to God, and will prosper and be blessed, and the light of God will shine upon them. And behold! He comes with ten thousand holy ones to execute judgement upon them and to destroy the impious, and to contend with all flesh concerning everything which the sinners and the impious have done and wrought against him.

· · ·

Contemplate all the events in heaven, how the lights in heaven do not change their courses, how each rises and sets in order, each at its proper time, and they do not transgress their law. Consider the earth, and understand from the work which is done upon it, from the beginning to the end, that no work of God changes as it becomes manifest. Consider the summer and the winter, how the whole earth is full of water, and clouds and dew and rain rest upon it.

Contemplate and see how all the trees appear withered, and how all their leaves are stripped, with the exception of fourteen trees which are not stripped, which remain with the old foliage until the new comes after two or three years.

And again, *contemplate* the days of summer, how *at its beginning* the sun is above it the earth. You seek shelter and shade because of the heat of the sun, and the earth burns with a scorching heat, and you cannot tread upon the earth, or upon a rock, because of its heat.

Contemplate how the trees are covered with green leaves, and bear fruit. And understand in respect of everything and perceive how He who lives forever made all these things for you; and how his works are before him in each succeeding year, and all his works serve him and do not change, but as God has decreed, so everything is done. And consider how the seas and rivers together complete their tasks. But you have not persevered, nor observed the law of the Lord. But you have transgressed, and have spoken proud and hard words with your unclean mouth against his majesty. You hard of heart! You hard of heart! You will not have peace! And because of this you will curse your days, and the years of your life you will destroy. And the external curse will increase, and you will not receive mercy. In those days you will transform your *name* into an eternal curse to all the righteous, and they will curse you sinners for ever—you together with the sinners. For the chosen there will be light and joy and peace, and they will inherit the earth. But for you, the impious, there will be a curse. When wisdom is given to the chosen, they will all live, and will not again do wrong, either through forgetfulness, or through pride. But those who possess wisdom will be humble. They will not again do wrong, and they will not be judged all the days of their life, and they will not die of the divine wrath or anger. But they will complete the number of the days of their life, and their life will grow in peace, and the years of their joy will increase in gladness and in eternal peace all the days of their life.

And it came to pass, when the sons of men had increased, that in those days there were born to them fair and beautiful daughters. And the angels, the sons of heaven, saw them and desired them. And they said to one another: "Come, let us choose for ourselves wives from the children of men, and let us beget for ourselves children." And Semyaza, who was their leader, said to them: "I fear that you may not wish this deed to be done, and that I alone will pay for this great sin." And they all answered him and said: "Let us all swear an oath, and bind one another with curses not to alter this plan, but to carry out this plan effectively." Then they all swore together and all bound one another with curses to it. And they were in all two hundred, and they came down on Ardis which is the summit of Mount Hermon. And they called the mountain Hermon, because on it they swore and bound one another with curses. And these are the names of their leaders: Semyaza, who was their leader, Urakiba, Ramiel, Kokabiel, Tamiel, Daniel, Ezeqiel, Baraqiel, Asael, Armaros, Batriel, Ananel, Zaqiel, Samsiel, Sartael, Turiel, Yomiel, Araziel. These are the leaders of the two hundred angels, and of all the others with them.

Jomo Kenyatta
(1891–1978, Kenya)

Religion and Ancestor Veneration

The Gikuyu people, it is certain, maintain a close and vital relationship with spiritual entities. Their daily lives, both as individuals and groups, are influenced at all points by belief in the supernatural. It is then of the very first importance to know the nature of the beliefs themselves and of the Beings in whom they are reposed. Is there a belief in a single High God? If so, is it a vital belief or a mere formalism? Who and what is the High God? Is He a mere abstraction, easily forgotten, or a real entity, visible both in picturesque dwelling-places and in His awful or beneficent works?

These and many such questions must be asked and answered before we begin to appreciate the religious life of the Gikuyu people, as of any other people. Further, are there any other spiritual creatures besides the Deity, and, if so, how do they function in the day-to-day, year-to-year life of the people? We shall assume that there are such beings, the spirits of our ancestors. With them we constantly commune. Hence the first two elements in the title of this chapter. Further, sacrificial practices are of such importance in establishing connections with both the High God and the other supernatural Beings that I have given them a third place in the title. Our work is to bring out the functioning mode of these two great departments of Gikuyu religion and of the main means of their formal expression in the sacrificial ceremonies which everywhere define and punctuate them. To do this adequately it is necessary to describe various forms of religious ceremonies and sacrifices. In this way we shall make clear the differences among the three parts of our subject-matter: Deity worship, communion with ancestors, and sacrificial practices.

The ideas underlying these three expression may best be brought out by means of linguistic analysis. First, we have *gothaithaya Ngai,* which may clearly be translated: "To beseech Ngai," or "To worship Ngai." The essential difference between Deity worship, in the true sense, and what is known as "ancestor worship," is demonstrated by the fact that *gothaithaya* is never used in connection with ancestral spirits. The term used for what I shall call "communion with ancestors" is *goitangera ngoma njohi*—literally, "to pour out or to sprinkle beer for spirits." This refers to the pouring out of a little of whatever you are drinking on to the ground for the ancestors, and, in a special sense, to a larger offering of a similar nature made on the occasion of communion ceremonies, when a special quantity of beer is brewed for presentation to the ancestral spirits. At the same time a beast will be sacrificed. Generally on special occasions these two elements are necessary.

When both the beer and the animal are offered, an additional term has to be used: *gothenjera na goitangera ngoma njohi*—literally, "to slaughter and pour out beer for the spirits." It will be clear from this that the Gikuyu people have a clear idea and understanding of two supernatural elements. On the one hand is the relationship with the one High God, Ngai, which may accurately be termed one of worship. Gikuyu religion has definitely two departments. Both are really vital; they function in unison, but in different spheres. We . . . find, for example, that when a sacrifice is made to the High God on an occasion of national (tribal) importance, the ancestors must join in making the sacrifice.

The term for "sacrificial practices" is *koruta magongona*, "to offer or to perform sacrifices or rituals and ceremonies." *Igongona* (sing.) is the only Gikuyu word which can possibly be translated "religion," although *mambura* (lit. "sacred") is practically synonymous with it. These words convey the idea of sacredness in general, so that *koruta magongona* may also be translated "sacred offerings." These are carried out . . . in connection with both Ngai worship and *ngoma* communion.

It may be worth mentioning at this stage that Christian missionaries in Gikuyu country have ignored both of the Gikuyu words for religion. The reason is probably that they feel them to be associated with "native ideas of spirit worship." Instead, the Swahili term, *dini*, has been imported.

Asante Praise Poems to Tano River and the Earth

The stream crosses the path,
The path crosses the stream,
Which of them is elder?
Did we not cut the path to go and meet the stream?
The stream had its origin from long, long ago,
The stream had its origin from the Creator;
He created things,
Pure, pure Tano . . . come here, Tano . . .

.   .   .

Earth, condolences,
Earth, condolences,
Earth and her dust, Boafo Agyei,
When I am dying, I depend upon you,
When I am alive, I depend upon you,
Earth who eats corpses,
Firempon, condolences.

A Lodagaa Libation to the Ancestors

Gods,
ancestors,
guardians,
beings of the wild,
the leather bottles
say we should perform,
because of the scorpion's sting,
because of suicide,
aches in the belly,
pains in the head.
The elder brother
slept badly.
He took out some guinea corn
and hurried along
to the diviner
who poured out his bag
and then said,
let's grasp the stick.
They did so
and he picked up "deity"
and he picked up "the wild"
and he picked up "sacrifice."
He picked up "deity,"
that was what
he picked up first.
He picked out "deity"
and began to ask,
What "deity"?
Deity of childbirth?
Deity of farming?
Deity of daughters?
Deity of grandfathers?
Deity of grandmothers?

Abu Shardow Abarry
(b. 1947, Ghana)

Recurrent Themes in
Ga Libation (Mpai) Oratory

Ga libation oratory is a complex African genre that has interesting functional and aesthetic values. Rooted in the people's worldview, it is distinguished by its concern for eloquence and participation as well as the stability of the community. Social, moral and philosophical issues, therefore, tend to dominate its themes. As such they reflect the values, history, fears, hopes and aspiration of the community. For instance, when a traditional Ga is confronted with certain problems in life, he/she would normally have recourse to the Supreme Being, deities and the ancestral spirits for the solution of those problems, mainly through rituals requiring libation. A man who believes he has been cursed by someone in the society, or who has committed a ritual offense and wishes to neutralize the curse, has to undergo rituals featuring libation. Conversely, when a person has experienced a measure of peace, success or prosperity he expresses his gratitude to the Supreme Being and the divine beings by having libation performed in his behalf. A typical text refers to one Ataa Kome, a fisherman who, during the celebration of Homowo (the traditional New Year), gathers all his family to the shrine in order to supplicate the Supreme Being, the lesser deities and the ancestral spirits for their blessings and for general prosperity in life. The libator prays that the supplicant's family may be spiritually fortified against hazards of life and the pernicious intent of malicious people. He further prays that the supplicant should be blessed with more children and productive farmlands.[1] In spite of modernization and social change, Ga like other African peoples still regard family size as an index of success in life.[2] It is, therefore, prestigious to have as many children as possible, and children born in response to prayers to any deities are sometimes named after them. The libation concludes with an entreaty to the divine forces to clear off any misfortune that may lie in the path of the supplicant and all members of the Ga community, and replace it with goodness, abundant food, prosperity, solidarity and security throughout the year.

Another recurrent theme derives from the content of ritual episodes. As with traditional Africans elsewhere, various rituals are performed by the Ga on specific occasions and for specific deities.[3] On all such occasions the texts reveal the significance of the ritual and the specific deity for whom it is performed. Agricultural rites are more frequent and they portray the entire dependence of the people on the divinities for the fertility of the land, good sowing and a successful harvest to last all year round. This is hardly surprising since Ghana is an agricultural country, and many traditional Ga are either fisherfolks or farmers. A text on *"Sakumo gmaa dumo"* (a millet-planting rite of the War and Lagoon deity) reveals that on the previous day members of the Time god (Dantu) cultic group planted their grains. This stipulates that Tuesday is the day on which the Sakumo group should do their own sowing. The calendrical significance of Dantu is thereby affirmed.[4] Here the libator prays for abundant and auspicious rain in Galand, so that the seeds of those who bear them good-will may flourish into good crops, but the seeds of those who bear ill will against them should remain dormant in the earth. He then prays for unity and solidarity among the people, for success, long life, peace and prosperity.

The themes also embrace the content of any life crisis rite such as in birth and death; puberty, marriage and divorce; enstoolment and destoolment of a chief. Whereas all these are expressed in an interesting way, the texts performed during *"Kpojiemo"* are distinguished. *Kpojiemo* (out-dooring) is a very important rite among the Ga by which a new candidate or being is admitted into a new status, both temporal and spiritual. It grants public recognition to a chosen leader. And it legitimizes and formally admits a newly born baby into the world of the living. This is usually done on the eighth day following the child's birth. The text below is usually performed on such occasions:

> Hail! Hail! Hail! May happiness come!
> Hail, may happiness come!
> May our stools thicken.
> May our brooms thicken.
> Whenever we join up to make a circle may our chain be complete.
> Whenever we dig a well may we come upon water.
> Whenever we draw the water to bathe may our limbs be relieved.
> May it be darkness behind the stranger who has come.
> And brightness before him.
> May we leave whole, and may we return in whole.
> May his mother have long life.
> May his father have long life.
> May he eat by the labour of his five fingers.
> May he labor for his father.
> May he labor for his mother.
> May we forgive him everything forgivable.
> May he grow to respect the world.
> May he not steal.
> May he not lie.
> The humble Ga never lies.
> You see, You haven't seen.
> You hear, You haven't heard.
> When we see white, may it be white clay.
> When we see black, may it be his slaves.
> He came with black.
> May he go back with white.
> Hail, may happiness come!

Typical of libation oratory, the text pays attention to the newborn child, his family and the community.[5] The libator appeals to their traditional sense of solidarity and prays for increase in their numerical strength. He entreats the deities to ensure that only goodness befalls the baby on her/his way through life; that he/she may not become irresponsible, wicked or a thief. May he/she develop physically and morally to be able to distinguish between good and bad, truth and falsity.

Recurrent Themes in Ga Libation (Mpai) Oratory

Ga libation themes may also touch on aspects of even modern ceremonies like the opening of parliament, of a new building or the celebration of a birthday or success party. Some themes consist in entreating the protection of the Supreme Being and the deities for a person about to depart on a journey, or the expression of gratitude on the successful return from a long or hazardous journey of an individual or a group of people. A few reflect ideas about death and the hereafter; and others concern the confirmation of secular transactions and agreements between individuals or groups of people.[6]

The foregoing thematic analysis amply illustrates the significance of libation in Ga life. The text reveals the people's philosophical outlook, their moral values, geographical location and cultural identity. It is a statement on their basic priorities in life: securities, peace, good health, growth in humans, agriculture and livestock. Though libation may be performed for an individual, the discourse transcends the former by linking his/her welfare and interests with those of the community. And individual achievements, goals and aspirations are normally validated in communal consciousness. This way the well being of all is promoted; and social, moral and spiritual harmony are maintained.

NOTES

1. English translation:

> Hail! Hail! Hail! May happiness come!
> Hail! May happiness come!
> What day is it today?
> Today is Tuesday
> Grandfathers' and Grandmothers' Tuesday.
> Grandfather Sakumo the Great
> You destroy, You rebuild.
> God, the Almighty, One on whom one leans
> Who created heaven and earth
> Well, it's for nothing that I call you
> But this is what your grandson who lives at Bukom
> Called Ataa Kome, the fisherman, says:
> He says, he and his wife, and children
> Are holding their drinks and fowls
> With which they have come to kneel before you
> Whatever we do is devoid of success
> If you don't have a hand in it.
> So they are entreating you
> That they may be blessed
> That they may prosper
> That all may be well with them
> That all mishaps may be cleared away
> That you may bring prosperity
> That you bestow upon us food and meat
> That we may never go hungry
> Life and prosperity to our children and those yet unborn
> May all ailing people shake themselves of their ailments
> Hail! May happiness come!

2. See Gladys Azu, *The Ga Family and Social Change* (Birmingham, Eng.: University of Birmingham Center for West African Studies, 1974).

3. Margaret Field, *Religion and Medicine of the Ga People* (London: Oxford University Press, 1942), 1–9.

4. This refers merely to Dantu's position on the traditional Ga calendar. Though he is a very

old god, he is not of the highest ranking. It is members of his cult group, the Lante Janwe, who initiate the cycle of agricultural rites in Accra. Normally, they plant the ritual millet, harvest it and celebrate the Homowo Festival two weeks before the other cult groups. Thus, their Homowo is the calendrical marker for calculating the commencement of the sacred year nine months later.

5. Marion Kilson, "The Ga Naming Rite," *Anthropos*, 63/64. 5/6 (1968/69), 904–20.

6. English translation:

> Hail! Hail! Hail! May happiness come!
> Hail! May happiness come!
> God, Almighty
> Grandfathers and Grandmothers
> Gbobu
> Oshwe
> Nyonmo Tsawe
> Albi
> Owofu
> Come and take this drink
> Well, your grandchildren from the big learning center at Legon
> Have arrived here this Saturday morning.
> They didn't come for anything evil.
> But that they have come to be taught Ga custom and ancient stories
> Which they would put on the surface of paper [books]
> So that children and those yet unborn
> Will come to meet and study them
> But today we are already occupied
> We are occupied because we are attending a funeral
> Therefore we have come to an understanding
> That exactly today's week at nine o'clock in the morning
> We shall all meet here
> And we shall go into things with them
> And help them in their studies.
> Hail! May happiness come!

Recurrent Themes in Ga Libation (Mpai) Oratory

Igbo Invocations

PROTECTION

My God and ancestors,
I thank you
For letting me see this day;
May I continue to see more
Till my hair becomes white;
May the hoe never cut my feet;
Protect me and my household
From evil men and spirits;
I wish no man evil,
But if anyone says I have lived too long,
Let him go before me to see
What it is like in the land of the dead;
The man who holds on to *owho**
Cannot get lost in his journey.

KOLA-NUT

Hills, take kola-nut
Earth, take kola-nut
Sun, take kola-nut
Valleys, take kola-nut
Ancestors, take kola-nut:
Go before us
Stand behind us
We don't eat kola-nut with its radicle†
We eat what is due to humans
We don't eat what is due to Spirits:
Take, all of you, your kola radicle

*A staff symbolizing righteousness.—EDS.
†The radicle belongs to the deities by right.—EDS.

Religious Ideas

Take, all of you, the slices of kola-nut
ISE-E . . . ISE-E

LIFE

God the Creator,
Sky and Earth,
Sun of the Supreme Creator,
Our Ancestors:
It is life
And what it is supported with—
Wealth upon wealth—
These we ask of you.

Wande Abimbola
(b. 1938, Yoruba, Nigeria)

Wapele: The Concept of Good Character in Ifá Literary Corpus

The Ifá literary corpus is an important source of information about the Yorùbá value and belief system. As the mouthpiece of the other divinities, Ifá is the repository of all the myths and moral tenets of the other divinities. The Yorùbá people believe that Ọrúnmìlà was present when Olódùmarè (the Almighty God) created heaven and earth. Ifá therefore knows the history of earth and heaven and mastered the moral and physical laws with which Olódùmarè governs the universe. This is why Ọrúnmìlà is regarded as the wise counsellor, the historian and the custodian of all divine wisdom. Hence the following are among his praise names:

> (He who teaches one wisely like one's own kinsman.
> The wisdom of the earth,
> The historian of the land of Ifẹ̀.)

Some of the important philosophical concepts embodied in the Ifá literary corpus include the concepts of orí (inner or spiritual head), ẹbọ (sacrifice) and ìwàpẹ̀lẹ́ (good character). These three concepts are closely related and are complementary to one another. Orí is the essence of luck and the most important force responsible for human success or failure. Furthermore, orí is the individual's personal divinity who governs his life and communicates on his behalf with the major divinities. Whatever has not been sanctioned by a man's orí cannot be approved by the divinities. This is the meaning of the statement found in Ogúndá Méjì:

> (Ori, I hail you
> Who will always quickly bless your own.
> You, who blesses a man before any divinity.
> No divinity blesses a man without the
> knowledge of his ori).

Ẹbọ (sacrifice) is a means of symbolic and ritual communication between all the forces of the universe. The Yorùbá believe that apart from man himself, there are two opposing forces in the universe, one of which is benevolent to man while the other is hostile. The benevolent forces are collectively know as ìbọ (the divinities), and the malevolent agents are known as ajogun (the warriors against man). The àjẹ́ (the witches) are also in alliance with the ajogun for the ruination of man and his handiwork. Man needs to offer sacrifice to both forces in order to survive. He needs to offer sacrifice to the benevolent forces so as to continue to enjoy their support and blessings. Man needs to offer sacrifice to the ajogun and the àjẹ́ in order that they might not oppose him whenever an important project is embarked upon.

The divinity who acts as the middle-man between the three parties mentioned above is Èṣù who shares a little of the attributes of the benevolent and the malevolent forces. He is the policeman of the universe. Furthermore he is impartial since he will only support the man or divinity who performs sacrifice. This is the meaning of the statement 'ẹni ó rúbọ lÈṣùú gbè'. Once he receives the prescribed sacrifice, he will forbid the ajogun from harming the supplicant. Èṣù is the keeper of the àṣẹ, a copy of the divine power and authority with which Olódùmarè created the universe. Èṣù is therefore the effective ruler of the universe, the principle of order and harmony and the agent of reconciliation. His wife, Agbèrù, receives all sacrifices on his behalf. After taking his own share of aárùún (five cowries) and a little bit of the other materials offered for sacrifice, Èṣù takes the offering to the divinity or the ajogun concerned. The effect is usually the return of peace and reconciliation between the warring parties.

An interesting question immediately arises from the analysis above. What role is reserved for human beings in the Yorùbá universe where the individual cannot act independent of his orí and where he is at the mercy of two powerful groups of supernatural powers to whom he has to make sacrifices ceaselessly in order to survive. Does the individual actually matter in such a system? This is where the concept of ìwàpẹ̀lẹ̀ comes in. Together with a set of other minor principles such as àyà and ẹsẹ̀, the principle of ìwàpẹ̀lẹ̀ to some extent redeems man from the authoritarian and hierarchical structure of the universe and, in any case, provides him with a set of principles with which to regulate his life in order to avoid collision with the supernatural powers and also with his fellow men. What follows is a short description and interpretation of the principle of ìwà in relation to the beliefs of the Yorùbá already discussed.

The word ìwà is formed from the verbal root wà (to be, to exist) by the addition of the deverbative prefix ì. The original meaning of ìwà can therefore be interpreted as 'the fact of being, living or existing'. Thus, when Ifá speaks of

Ire owó,
Ire ọmọ,
Ire àìkú parí ìwà,

the meaning of ìwà in that context is the ordinary meaning referred to above.

It is my impression that the other meaning of ìwà (character, moral behavior) originates from an idiomatic usage of this original lexical meaning. If this is the case, ìwà (character) is therefore the essence of being. A man's ìwà is what can be used to characterize his life especially in ethical terms.

Furthermore, the word ìwà (character) can be used to refer to either good or bad character. For example in sentence form, we can say:

Ìwà ọkùnrin náá kò dára.
The man's character is not good.

Ìwà ọkùnrin náàá dára.
The man's character is good.

But sometimes, the word ìwà is used to refer to good character alone.

Obìnrin náàá ní ìwà.
The woman has good character.

One can also speak of:

1. Ìwà pẹ̀lẹ́   (gentle or good character)
2. Ìwà búburú   (bad character)

This paper is concerned with ìwà pẹ̀lẹ́ which can be translated as gentle character or in a general sense, good character.

As mentioned above, ìwà is regarded by the Yorùbá as one of the very aims of human existence. Every individual must strive to have ìwàpẹ̀lẹ́ in order to be able to lead a good life in a belief system dominated by many supernatural powers and a social structure controlled by a hierarchy of authorities. The man who has ìwàpẹ̀lẹ́ will not collide with any of the powers both human and supernatural and will therefore live in complete harmony with the forces that govern his universe.

This is why the Yorùbá regard ìwàpẹ̀lẹ́ as the most important of all moral values, and the greatest attribute of any man. The essence of religious worship for the Yorùbá consists therefore in striving to cultivate ìwàpẹ̀lẹ́. This is the meaning of the saying:

Ìwà lẹ̀sìn
(Ìwà is another name for religious devotion).

In Ifá literary corpus, ìwà is regarded as a woman. Ogbè Alárá, one of the minor Odù Ifá, says that ìwà was a woman of exceeding beauty whom Ọrúnmìlà married after she had divorced several of the other divinities. Despite her beauty, ìwà lacked good behaviour. She had rough habits and an unruly tongue. Furthermore, she was a lazy woman who always shirked her responsibilities. After they had been married for some time, Ọrúnmìlà himself could no longer tolerate her bad habit, and he therefore sent her away. But almost immediately after she left his house, Ọrúnmìlà discovered that he could hardly live without her. He lost the respect of his neighbours and was despised by the community. Furthermore all his clients deserted him and his divination practice was no longer profitable. He lacked money to spend, clothes to wear, and other materials which he could use to live a good and noble life.

Ọrúnmìlà therefore put on an Egúngún costume and set out in search of ìwà. He visited the homes of all the sixteen important chiefs of the Ifá cult but he did not find his wife. He stood for a while outside the house of each of these chiefs and sang the following song:

Wisdom of the mind, Ifá priest of Alárá's house,
Performed Ifá divination for Alárá,
Nick-named Èjì Ọ̀sá,
Offspring of those who use one iron rod to make thirty gongs.

Religious Ideas

Great understanding, Ifá priest of Ajerò
Performed Ifá divination of Ajerò,
Offspring of the brave man who refused entirely to engage in a fight.
Where did you see Ìwà, tell me.
Ìwà, ìwà is the one I am looking for.

If you have money,
But if you do not have good character,
The money belongs to someone else.
Ìwà, ìwà is the one we are searching for.
If one has children,

But if one lacks good character,
The children belong to someone else.
Ìwà, ìwà is the one we are searching for.
If one has a house,
But if one lacks good character,

The house belongs to someone else.
Ìwà, ìwà is what we are searching for.
If one has clothes,
But if one lacks good character,
The clothes belong to someone else.

Ìwà, ìwà is what we are looking for.
All the good things of life which a man has,
If he lacks good character,
They belong to someone else.
Ìwà, ìwà is what we are searching for.

After a very long search, Ọrúnmìlà found Ìwà in the house of Olójo who had married her again. When Ọrúnmìlà got to the house of Olójo, he sang the same song and Olójo came out to meet him. Ọrúnmìlà told him that he was searching for Ìwà his wife, who had deserted him. Olójo refused to hand over Ìwà back to Ọrúnmìlà and a quarrel ensued during which he struck Olójo with the arm of the goat which he had used for sacrifice before he left home. The impact threw Olójo several miles away. Ọrúnmìlà then took his wife away in peace.

The story quoted above about ìwà is important for several reasons. In the first place, it is significant that the symbol of good character is a woman. In Yorùbá folklore, women represent the two opposite poles of emotional involvement. Women are the symbol of love, care, devotion, tenderness and beauty. At the same time, they are (especially as witches), the symbol of wickedness, callousness, deceit and disloyalty. Since ìwà is an attribute which can be good or bad (as explained above) only the women folk about whom the Yorùbá already have such a stereotyped moral belief can be used as the symbol of ìwà. What Ifá wants us to understand by using this symbol is that every individual must take care of his character as he takes care of his wife. Just as a wife can sometimes be a burden to her husband, good character can be a burden to the just and the faithful but they must never shirk the responsibility. Women may be regarded as witches and liars, but the Yorùbá realize that without them human society cannot survive. In the same way, good character may be difficult to have as an attribute, but without people who have it, the world will be a very difficult place to live in.

Secondly, it is important as well that ìwà herself was a woman who lacked good character and who indulged herself in dirty habits. This means that a man who would aspire to have good character must be prepared to harbour what the Yorùbá call ègbin (a filthy or an indecent thing). The man who aspires to have good character should know that he will sometimes find himself in unpleasant situations which will offend his sense of dignity and decency. Yet, he must not disengage himself from the path of good character lest he loses the very essence and value of his life.

The Ifá verse quoted above compares ìwà with other valuable things which a man always aspires to have—money, children, houses and clothes. Ifá rates ìwà above all these valuable things. A man who has all these things but who does not have ìwà will soon lose all of them probably to someone else who has ìwà and who therefore knows how to take care of them. Ìwà is therefore the most valuable thing among all the other things in the Yorùbá value system.

Another Ifá poem about ìwà quoted by Mr. Modupẹ Alade in his address to the Ẹgbẹ Ìjìnlẹ Yorùbá (Yorùbá Cultural Society), Lagos Branch, on August 31, 1967 and published in the Yorùbá Cultural Magazine, *Olókun*,[7] No. 8, of August, 1969, differs in some significant detail from the one quoted above. The following is an excerpt from that poem:

> If we take rágbá wooden object and strike it against the calabash,
> Let us hail Ìwà.
> If we take rágbà wooden object to strike the calabash,
> Let us hail Ìwà.
>
> If we take rágbá wooden object to strike a stone,
> Let us hail Ìwà.
> Ifá divination was performed for Ọrúnmìlà
> When the father was going to marry Ìwà.
> The first time that Ọrúnmìlà married a wife,
>
> Ìwà was the one he married.
> And Ìwà herself
> Was the daughter of Sùúrù (Patience).
> When Ọrúnmìlà proposed to marry Ìwà,
> She said it was alright.
>
> She said that she would marry him.
> But there was one thing to observe.
> Nobody should send her away from her matrimonial home.
> But she must not be used carelessly as one uses rain water.
> Nobody must punish her unnecessarily . . .
>
> Ọrúnmìlà exclaimed, 'God will not let me do such a thing.'
> He said that he would take care of her.
> He said that he would treat her with love,
> And he would treat her with kindness.
> He then married Ìwà.

After a very long time,
He became unhappy with her . . .
He therefore started to worry Ìwà.
If she did one thing,
He would complain that she did it wrongly.

If she did another thing,
He would also complain.
When Ìwà saw that the trouble was too much for her,
Ìwà said alright,
She would go to her father's house.

And her father was the first-born son of Olódùmarè.
His name was Sùúrù, the father of Ìwà.
She then gathered her calabash utensils,
And left her home.
She went to ọrun.

When Ọrúnmìlà returned, he said,
'Greetings to the people inside the house.
Greetings to the people inside the house.
Greetings to the people inside the house.'
But Ìwà did not show up.

The father then asked for Ìwà.
The other inmates said that they did not see her.
'Where has she gone?
Did she go to the market?
Did she go somewhere?'

He asked these questions for long until he added two cowries to three,
And went to the house of an Ifá priest.
They told him that Ìwà had run away.
He was advised to go and find her in Alárá's household.
When he got to the house of Alárá, he said:

'If we take rágbá wooden object,
And strike it against the calabash.
Ìwà is the one we are seeking.
Let us hail Ìwà.
If we take ràgbà wooden object,

And strike it against the calabash.
Ìwà is the one we are seeking.
Let us hail Ìwà.
If we take rágbá wooden object,
And strike it against the stone.

Ìwà is the one we are seeking.
Let us hail Ìwà.
Alárá, if you see Ìwà, let me know.
Ìwà is the one we are seeking.
Ìwà'.

Alárá said that he did not see Ìwà
The father then went to the house of Òràngún, king of the city of Ìlá,
Offspring of one bird with plenty of feathers.
He asked whether Òràngún saw Ìwà.
But Òràngún said that he did not see her.

There was hardly any place he didn't go.
After a long time,
He turned back,
And inquired from his divination instruments.
He said that he looked for Ìwà in the house of Alárá.

He looked for her in the house of Ajerò.
He looked for her in the house of Òràngún.
He looked for her in the abode of Ògbérè, Ifá priest of Olówu.
He looked for her in the abode of Àṣéégbá, Ifá priest of Ẹ̀gbá.
He looked for her in the abode of Àtàkúmòsà, Ifá priest of Ìjèṣà.

He looked for her in the abode of Òṣépurútù, Ifá priest of Rémọ.
But they told him that Ìwà had gone to òrun.
He said that he would like to go and take her from there.
They said that was alright,
Provided he was prepared to perform sacrifice.

They asked him to offer a net,
And give honey to Èṣù.
He offered honey as sacrifice to Èṣù.
When Èṣù tasted the honey,
He said, 'What is this which is so sweet'?

Ọrúnmìlà then entered the costume of Egúngún,
And went to heaven.
He started to sing again.
Èṣù then played the game of deceit,
And went to the place where Ìwà was.

He said, 'A certain man has arrived in heaven,
If you listen to his song,
He is saying such and such a thing. . . .
You are the one he is looking for . . .'
Ìwà then left (her hiding place),

Religious Ideas

And went to meet them where they were singing.
Ọrúnmìlà was inside Egúngún costume.
He saw Ìwà from the net of the costume,
And he embraced her . . .
Those who change bad luck into good then opened up the costume.

'Ìwà, why did you behave like that.
And you left me on earth and went away'.
Ìwà said that was true.
She said that it was because of how he maltreated her
That she ran away,

So that she might have rest of mind.
Ọrúnmìlà then implored her to please,
Have patience with him,
And follow him.
But Ìwà refused.

But she said that was alright,
She still could do something else.
She said, 'You Ọrúnmìlà,
Go back to the earth.
When you get there,

All the things which I have told you not to do,
Don't attempt to do them.
Behave very well.
Behave with good character.
Take care of your wife,

And take care of your children.
From today on, you will not set your eyes on Ìwà any more.
But I will abide with you.
But whatever you do to me,
Will determine how orderly your life will be'.

The Ifá verse quoted above agrees with the earlier version in the following respects. In both poems, Ìwà is a woman, and she was a wife of Ọrúnmìlà. Furthermore, in both stories, Ọrúnmìlà had to seek for Ìwà after they had parted. The song with Ọrúnmìlà chanted in both poems as he was searching for ìwà from one place to another is also similar to some extent. Apart from the instances mentioned above these two poems are different from each other. The second poem mentions that Ìwà was the daughter of Sùúrù (Patience) who was the first-born son of Olódùmarè. This very significant detail is missing from the first poem and it is therefore necessary to comment on it.

The second poem links Ìwà with patience and also with God himself. The significance of this is that in order to have good character, a man must first of all have patience. This is why we have the saying: 'Sùúrù ni baba iwa (Patience is the father of good character). Out of all the attributes which a man with good character must have, patience is the most important of them because the person who is patient will have time to consider things well and arrive at a just and honest solution. One must therefore be patient with people and learn to tolerate them in order to have good character. If Ọrúnmìlà had learnt to be patient, he would not have lost Ìwà, his wife.

The second poem also links up Ìwà with Olódùmarè, who in the story is, in fact, her grandfather. The meaning of this is quite clear. It means that Olódùmarè himself is the embodiment of good character. He therefore expects human beings to have good character as well. It is a sin against the divine law of Olódùmarè for anybody to deviate from the path of good character. Such a person will be punished by the divinities unless he offers sacrifice which will show that he as repented and which will bring back peace and harmony into the strained relationship which his deviation creates between him and the supernatural powers. This, then, is the reason why the Yorùbá regard good character as the essence of religion.

Ifá literary corpus can therefore be regarded as a set of historical and mythical poems offering to us through the use of analogy, images and symbols what to do in order to be at peace with God, the supernatural powers, our neighbours and, indeed, ourselves. All these precepts and admonitions boil down to one thing: strive very hard to cultivate good character so that your life may be good.

The Yorùbá concept of existence transcends the time when the individual is on earth. It goes beyond that period and includes the memories which a man leaves behind after his death. Therefore, it is important to be a man of good character so that one may leave good memories behind. In a society which elevates the dead to the position of ancestors and which records praises about them in its verbal art, the only lasting reward of the man with good character lies in the poems, the masks and the annual ceremonies which will be done in his honour after his death.

The importance placed on the principle of ìwà by the Yorùbá shows that African traditional religions are based on deep moral values which sustain the beliefs of the adherents of those religions. We have often been told by the ignorant devotees of Christianity and Islam that African traditional religions are not grounded on any worthwhile ethical values. Nothing can be farther from the truth. The example of the principle of ìwà shows that African traditional religions are based on profound and meaningful philosophical ideas.

Mensah Sarbah
(1864–1910, Ghana)

Akan Religion

The student who closely examines the habits and manners of West Africans and the constitution of their communities will not fail to discover the influence of religion over many things. Ancestor worship even now permeates the actions of all, although some persons will deny this. The venerable Reindorf is of the opinion that the Asanti and Fanti Constitution has run through three stages, namely, that of the prophet; the priest, when the high priest of the national shrine practically ruled the people; and lastly the king. He also draws attention to the position of priests, whose power over lands and revenues is gradually falling into the hands of the king and other civil rulers.

The object, however, of this work is not to deal with religious theories, deities, or matters of belief. In the Fanti districts, with their numerous free and independent communities, the priests who officiated at the shrine of Nansam (that is ancestors), the national cities, situate at Mankesim, exercised large powers and wielded great influence, so much so that the opinion has been expressed that the high priest, a Braffo, was the sovereign ruler of the Fanti people. The physician was so often a priest that it is not surprising to discover him possessed of much influence; but this much may be said, the priests did not rule the people. The general name for God is Nyankupon (Nyankrupon according to the Akanfu), meaning the Only One, than who none is greater, or, as others say, the Great Friend. Nyankupon is invisible. He lives above the heavens, and the winds are His messengers. The common saying is, "Speak to the winds, and God will hear thee." This word has different pronunciations, and the difficulty of finding its root may be through this cause. Rain is called Nyankum; rainbow is nyankunton. Nyan is to awaken, and it has been suggested that probably Onyan (the awakener) was an old name for the sky. One is rather inclined to form the opinion that Nyankupon is not derived from *ye*, meaning to do, act, create, as some say. This subject is certainly interesting, and requires further study and much thinking over.

In the days when the worship of Nansam was general, people always consulted the oracles at their shrine, and on many occasions the priests heard and decided cases about witchcraft and other serious matters. According to tradition, it came to pass that the high priest of a certain period had a son, by name Etum Eduansa. He was his father's favourite. While following the chase one day, he discovered a palm tree with the shoot torn off. In the cavity was some white liquid. This he tasted; finding it sweet, he drank some, and resting himself, was soon asleep. He awoke refreshed. Next day he inspected the tree and found more palm-wine. Having quenched his thirst, he took some home for his father.

The old man tasted the wine, and so much did he relish it that during his son's absence to the chase he consumed the remainder. The hour arrived for attending to the business of his office, but the old man was found fast asleep. Try as much as possible, the attendants could not awaken him. Suspecting foul play by poison, they were alarmed, and questioned the servants, who said nothing unusual had been given to the old man, but that his son Etum Eduansa had brought some white liquid which they saw him taste. The other priests and all the people first concluded the old man had been poisoned by his son. Search parties were sent to scour the forests for him, and with instructions to kill him wherever apprehended. Etum Eduansa was found and forthwith killed. His head was brought home. When the old priest awoke from his deep sleep, feeling quite refreshed, he asked for his son. He was told what had happened, and his head was shown him. They say the tragic end of his son broke the heart of the old priest, and he soon died, blaming the men who had so hastily murdered his innocent son. It seems father and son were buried together. This calamity made a great impression on the people, and the incident is referred to as a warning against the condemnation of any one without a fair trial or hearing. Thenceforth no religious service was performed or business transacted unless Etum Eduansa's tragic song was rehearsed. All persons approaching Nansam's shrine to consult the oracles, and pilgrims thither bent on business always repeated this chant, which children even now, in some parts of the country, are taught by their mothers to lisp— . . .

> "Womma yenkohwe Etum Eduansa,
> Etum Eduansa oanye biribi,
> Boribori Mfantsi Wokum'nu gyan,
> Wokum'nu gyan. Enyiadu!"

> "Haste we to thy grave, Etum Eduansa;
> Though free from guile was Etum Eduansa,
> Boribori Mfantsi vainly slew him,
> That innocent dutiful son, oh Bard!"

Religious Ideas

Culture and Identity

PART THREE

Overleaf: Adinkra symbol for *nkon son nko nson,* length of life and experience

Reflecting an African Heritage

It is a hazardous undertaking to deal with diverse African peoples transgenerationally under simple headings like "religious ideas," "culture and identity," and so forth. Ordinarily, we are reluctant to assume too much commonality or to attempt to defend generalizations. Each African society is unique, having developed its own orientation to the universe and the physical environment in its concepts of religion, science, art, and politics. Indeed, human relationships are shaped by the ways in which individual societies deal with the universal events of birth, life, and death.

Without throwing our reticence completely to the wind or abandoning our principles, for the purposes of this collection we have taken the stand that African civilization, that is, civilization as expressed from the ancient cultures of the Nile Valley, have tied together the diverse peoples of the continent and the diaspora in ways that distinguish Africans from Europeans or Asians. Various writers in the African tradition have advanced this idea, taking it quite directly from the practical experiences of African peoples, thus articulating the unity of Africa.

The spread of the ancient myths and beliefs in resurrection and life, reincarnation, matrilineality, burial of the dead, the value of children, and the ultimate goodness of the earth have thrust elements of the African life style and civilization across the entire continent. The sense of what it means to be African is rooted in the past yet is expressed not as something ancient or distant but as a present moment in the dynamic world of the living and the dead. In the Americas, since the arrival of African people one can see similar forces at work in cultural creativity that draws on common musical rhythms, exploration of multicolors, polycentric appeals to diverse textures, play on repetition, and call-and-response modes of verbal activity. Our search for commonalities drives this volume, but by no means obscures the vast differences that exist in the specific histories of African peoples; the Ga are not the Zulu and the African Brazilians are distinct from the Jamaicans because of the diversity of the physical, cultural, and spiritual materials brought to bear on the various societies over time. Still, the common thread of African civilization is discernible through the variegated cultural and historical fabrics of African people everywhere.

THE SOURCES

One of the most profound sets of African documents comprises those that introduce us to the great body of praise and blame, ethics and aesthetics, sentiment and emotion, that form the essential core of the ritual of respect and celebration found throughout the continent. In this section we have organized the major sources in a way that shows the interconnectedness of one generation and the next. For example, the "Yoruba Praises to Ogun" and "The Akan Blackened Stool and the *Odwira* Festival" are both found in the same era (fourteenth through sixteenth centuries) whereas the "obelisk inscriptions of Queen Hatshepsut are from the Eighteenth Dynasty of Egyptian history. Separated by thousands of years, these documents nonetheless reflect the same quest for culture and identity.

Sources of the twentieth century are preoccupied with the idea of race, a response to the European's influence on African thinking. Prior to the interaction with the European and Arab populations that invaded Africa, the idea of race was nearly nonexistent; however, the concepts of community, group, clan, family, and ethnicity did exist. The cultural adaptations to environment and circumstances, to beliefs and visions, helped to form African social and political identities. Taken collectively, these adaptations are the sources of some of the most poignant expressions of the African personality. While none of these documents alone is sufficient to represent the whole of Africa, each one, taken as a special focus, represents a standpoint from which to describe and interpret some aspects of the same African cultural reality.

The Yoruba "Praises to Ogun" and "The Akan Blackened Stool and the *Odwira* Festival" are, by virtue of their particularity in specific African expressions, devoted to the ancestral roots of cultural identity.

Although it is possible to see the same quest for identity and culture from one part of the continent to the other, the intimacy and integrity of content in each document must be viewed as valuable in and of themselves. Thus, these conditions are cultural icons from a broad swath of African history.

Yet the specific instances of cultural identity or assertion of power, as in the case of Queen Hatshepsut, or Ma'at Ka Re, as she was ritually called, and Olaudah Equiano, are enough to demonstrate that gender and race are both at the core of identity. Hatshepsut is the first recorded queen to rule with authority. The daughter of Thutmose I and the widow of Thutmose II, she became queen in the middle of the Eighteenth Dynasty, during the period of Egypt's New Kingdom. Regarded in scholarship as the greatest queen of Egypt, Hatshepsut often dressed in royal male attire, including a false beard and wig, to rule also as "king." She built a great merchant navy for both commerce and war, sent out expeditions, expanded foreign trade, and forged international diplomatic relations. She also was able to effect changes within Egypt, supporting the arts and encouraging historical preservation.

Olaudah's autobiography, though to be the earliest African writing of this genre in English, is similar in some ways to Hatshepsut's assertion of power. The autobiography gives Olaudah's own perspective on the cross-cultural relations between Africans and Europeans. This 1789 document explains how African systems of servitude differed from the chattel slavery of the Europeans. A great defense of Africa, Olaudah's autobiographical work is an essential piece of early African writing.

We return to a common theme in African history—identity and culture—as Aimé Césaire sarcastically applauds the life of those who have not created mere technology. Using the voice of those who often attack Africa and Africans, Césaire celebrates African culture in much the same way as other Negritude writers did.

Amilcar Cabral, a revolutionary and intellectual who fought for the liberation of Guinea-Bissau from the Portuguese, provides a context for discussing identity based on struggle. J. Caseley Hayford, the Ghanaian scholar, suggests the importance of ancient traditions on identity. In both cases—the instance where struggle against evil defines an identity and the instance where identity is shaped over the years—the African will express itself as humans seeking justice and harmony.

W. E. B. Du Bois articulated conceptions of culture and race that showed his American environment. Eager to explain the idea of culture or race as being wholly complicated by history or biology, both are skillful artists who are able to negotiate the curvature of the American intellectual scene.

Cheikh Anta Diop writes of the origin and history of the African world with a rare clarity of insight into the millennia of the African world's development. His project is to identity the distortions we have learned and to correct them for future generations. The preeminent African scholar of the twentieth century, Diop took on all of Africa's enemies in his day, amassing a corpus of works that stand as the single greatest contribution to African scholarship in the twentieth century.

Selections from Martin Delany's "On the Condition and Destiny of Africans in the United States" show him to be an astute observer of the conditions of African people under duress. Delany is considered a forerunner of the proponents of African nationalism.

Wole Soyinka, the Nobel Laureate, expresses the view that African concepts of tragedy, unlike Greek concepts, channel the tragic state into a celebration in the resolution of inner crisis. He concentrates on the cultural significance of the African community as a source of values. In fact, Peter Sarpong's attention to the cultural basis of the festivals of Ghana represents another attempt to define the culture and identity of African people. There is a direct link between Sarpong's and Abu Abarry's emphasis on culture.

Abu Shardow Abarry's work on the Ga Homowo festival reflects the commemoration of the arrival of the Ga people in Ghana. Much like other cultural groups, the Ga celebrate their historic journey, which took them from ancient Kemet, through Benin, to their present home in Ghana.

J. Africanus B. Horton speaks to the pivotal role played by Africans in the early development of scientific and literary history.

Molefi Kete Asante's discussion of the principal issues in Afrocentric inquiry explains the idea of centeredness or African agency in the context of cultural identity and scientific method. In the late twentieth century, Afrocentricity has become a major philosophical and ideological thesis in the African world. Thus these works, taken collectively, represent a journey toward cultural agency.

Queen Hatshepsut

(EIGHTEENTH DYNASTY, 1550–1305 B.C., Kemet)

Her Assertion of Her Power

SPEECH OF THE QUEEN

I have done this with a loving heart for my father Amen;
Initiated in his secret of the beginning,
Acquainted with his beneficent might,
I did not forget whatever he had ordained.
My majesty knows his divinity,
I acted under his command;
It was he who led me,
I did not plan a work without his doing.
It was he who gave directions,
I did not sleep because of his temple,
I did not stray from what he commanded.
My heart was Sia before my father,
I entered into the plans of his heart.
I did not turn my back to the city of the All-Lord,
Rather did I turn my face to it.
I know that Ipet-sut is the lightland on earth,
The august hill of the beginning,
The Sacred Eye of the All-Lord,
His favored place that bears his beauty,
That gathers in his followers.

It is the King himself who says:
I declare before the folk who shall be in the future,
Who shall observe the monument I made for my father,
Who shall speak in discussion,
Who shall look to posterity—
It was when I sat in the palace,
And thought of my maker,
That my heart led me to make for him
Two obelisks of electrum,
Whose summits would reach the heavens,

Culture and Identity

In the august hall of columns,
Between the two great portals of the King,
The Strong Bull, King Aakheperkare, the Heru triumphant.
Now my heart turns to and fro,
In thinking what will the people say,
They who shall see my monument in after years,
And shall speak of what I have done.

Beware of saying, "I know not, I know not:
Why has this been done?
To fashion a mountain of gold throughout,
Like something that just happened."
I swear, as I am loved of Ra,
As Amen, my father, favors me,
As my nostrils are refreshed with life and dominion,
As I wear the white crown,
As I appear with the red crown,
As the Two Lords have joined their portions for me,
As I rule this land like the son of Auset,
As I am mighty like the son of Nut,
As Ra rests in the evening bark,
As he prevails in the morning bark,
As he joins his two mothers in the god's ship,
As sky endures, as his creation lasts,
As I shall be eternal like an undying star,
As I shall rest in life like Atum—
So as regards these two great obelisks,
Wrought with electrum by my majesty for my father Amen,
In order that my name may endure in this temple,
For eternity and everlastingness,
They are each of one block of hard granite,
Without seam, without joining together!

All foreign lands are my subjects,
He placed my border at the limits of heaven,
What Aten encircles labors for me.
He gave it to him who came from him,
Knowing I would rule it for him.
I am his daughter in very truth,
Who serves him, who knows what he ordains.
My reward from my father is life-stability-rule,
On the Heru throne of all the living, eternally like Ra.

My majesty began work on them in year 15, second month of winter, day 1, ending in year 16, fourth month of summer, last day, totaling seven months of quarry work. I did it for him out of affection, as a king for a god. It was my wish to make them for him gilded with electrum. "Their foil lies on their body," is what I expect people to say. My mouth is effective in its speech; I do not go back on my word. Hear ye! I gave for them of the finest electrum. I measured it by the gallon like sacks of grain. My majesty summoned a quantity beyond what the Two Lands had yet seen. The ignorant and the wise know it.

> Not shall he who hears it say,
> "It is a boast," what I have said;
> Rather say, "How like her it is,
> She is devoted to her father!"
> Lo, the god knows me well,
> Amen, Lord of Thrones-of-the-Two-Lands;
> He made me rule Black Land and Red Land as reward,
> No one rebels against me in all lands.

Culture and Identity

Yoruba Praises to Ogun

Ogun kills on the right and destroys on the right.
Ogun kills on the left and destroys on the left.
Ogun kills suddenly in the house and suddenly in the field.
Ogun kills the child with the iron with which it plays.
Ogun kills in silence.
Ogun kills the thief and the owner of the stolen goods.
Ogun kills the owner of the slave—and the slave runs away.
Ogun kills the owner of thirty *iwofa* [pawns]—and his money, wealth and children
    disappear.
Ogun kills the owner of the house and paints the hearth with his blood.
Ogun is the death who pursues a child until it runs into the bush.
Ogun is the needle that pricks at both ends.
Ogun has water but he washes in blood.

Ogun do not fight me. I belong only to you.
The wife of Ogun is like a tim tim [decorated leather cushion].
She does not like two people to rest on her.

Ogun has many gowns. He gives them all to the beggars.
He gives one to the woodcock—the woodcock dyes it indigo.
He gives one to the coucal [pheasant]—the coucal dyes it in camwood.
He gives one to the cattle egret—the cattle egret leaves it white.

Ogun is not like pounded yam:
Do you think you can knead him in your hand
And eat of him until you are satisfied?
Ogun is not like maize gruel:
Do you think you can knead him in your hand
And eat of him until you are satisfied?
Ogun is not like something you can throw in your cap:
Do you think you can put on your cap and walk away with him?

Ogun scatters his enemies.
When the butterflies arrive at the place where the cheetah excretes,
They scatter in all directions.

The light shining on Ogun's face is not easy to behold.
Ogun, let me not see the red of your eye.

Ogun sacrifices an elephant to his head.
Master of iron, head of warriors,
Ogun, great chief of robbers.
Ogun wears a bloody cap.
Ogun has four hundred wives and one thousand four hundred children.
Ogun, the fire that sweeps the forest.
Ogun's laughter is no joke.

Ogun eats two hundred earthworms and does not vomit.
Ogun is a crazy orisha [deity] who still asks questions after 780 years.
Whether I can reply, or whether I cannot reply,
Ogun please don't ask me anything.

The lion never allows anybody to play with his cub.
Ogun will never allow his child to be punished.
Ogun do not reject me!
Does the woman who spins ever reject a spindle?
Does the woman who dyes ever reject a cloth?
Does the eye that sees ever reject a sight?
Ogun, do not reject me!

Isidore Okpewho
(b. 1941, Nigeria)

The Resources of the Oral Epic

The major problem in discussing the oral epic involves nomenclature. I have expressed a belief in the integrity of the *oral* art as a subject distinct from the *literate* variety, with an idiom of its own. A qualification of this belief is, I think, necessary. I do not mean that there is no common ground whatsoever between the two kinds of art. On the contrary, it is clear that, since they both aim to please through the medium of the word and the images that words, aptly combined, can create, they share certain architechtonic tendencies and effects: the fitting description, the portraiture of a character that is true to life or at least to the peculiar ideals of the world within which the character operates, and various other creative tricks and devices. In such respects, admittedly, the distinction between oral and literary art is hard to make. But the fundamental difference is in the process by which the work of art comes to be, the context within which it is created. It is in this regard that the *word* is subject to behaviors that make it acceptable for one category of art and unsuitable for another.

For instance, a statement may be apt; but if the poet is so thoroughly overjoyed by its aptness that he is moved to repeat that statement many times over, then the text is very likely to be the product of an oral performance in which the poet perhaps used a musical instrument to support the lyrical feeling engendered by that happy statement; for no writer, however pleased he is with a statement, will feel inclined to belabor it over several successive lines just for the sheer joy that he finds in its aptness. Faced therefore with the text of such a statement, we are moved not simply to admire its verbal excellence but indeed to glean the circumstances that led to its being repeated so many times. That is the logic of an independent poetics for the oral performance: much more than literary criticism ever cares to do, oral criticism asks questions about the context or process during which a piece of poetry is created.[1]

A second problem in studying the oral epic is painting a balanced picture of the tradition as we see it now and what it was several ages ago, in the preliterate days. We have much cause to believe that in those days the bard did not encounter the kinds of curiosity he finds in the modern audience. Then, he sang simply as part of a social process before familiar clansmen, or on the road before strangers to whom he was a familiar phenomenon. Today, cornered into a recording studio, made to perform before strange equipment and without the regular audience, asked questions about his art to which he had never given much of a thought, he watches with a certain distraction as his interrogator studiously scribbles down his statements. Clearly, we are dealing with two generations of the oral epic; standard pictures of the bard cannot be easily painted. In his preface to *Sunjata IV*, Niane observes that the career of the contemporary griot (the bard among the Mandingo of the West African Sudan) "was not always so in ancient Africa." Then, they counseled kings and cheered them with songs of noble deeds; today, they play and sing for curious and not so kingly audiences and are congealed into record by scholars like Niane. From his experience in Yugoslavia, Albert Lord tells us of the practice of "seeking a normal ten-syllable line" from the Serbian guslars whose songs are recorded; as a result of this practice, "the dictated version tends to be more perfect metrically than the sung version."[2] We ought to be grateful to the scholar who has taken the trouble to catch something of a great tradition before it is completely swept away by the relentless tide of progress. But it seems only honest to admit that the bard whom we meet in our recorded songs is not quite the archetypal singer of a distant age. He may be the worse for being put into an unfamiliar environment, or he may be the better for the new challenge that the scholar's expectations set for him. In either case, he is a bit different and thus we should be cautious in making connections between the past and the present.

Finally, something should be said about the terms "oral" or "traditional" epic and "bard," which will be used many times in this study. Lord has definitively analyzed the difficulties attending the nomenclature of this genre of art;[3] it would be superfluous for me to try to stretch the arguments any further. An oral epic is fundamentally a tale about the fantastic deeds of a man or men endowed with something more than human might and operating in something larger than the normal human context and it is of significance in portraying some stage of the cultural or political development of a people. It is usually narrated or performed to the background of music by an unlettered singer working alone or with some assistance from a group of accompanists. To avoid monotony, terms like "traditional epic," "heroic song," or "narrative" will be used in its place, but the nature of the art remains the same.

It is convenient to see the bard exclusively within the context of the oral epic, since that is the subject of this study; however, a full appreciation will often reveal that his competence embraces other kinds of songs. In Africa, the singer of heroic tales sometimes finds himself obliged to sing ordinary lyric songs that he has in his repertoire and is happy to garner a varied patronage by demonstrating this versatility.[4] In fact, there is little difference in training between the "epic" bard and any other kind of performer in song.[5] Admittedly, the structural nuances of the heroic narrative song and the touch of grandeur that characterizes its content make it somewhat different from, say, the ordinary lyric song. But our bard is a performer just like the others, and shares with them both the training in the creative use of memory and the overall sense of public image. He becomes typecast by the heroic narrative because he sings it more often either by request or by choice; quite often he can also sing many other kinds of songs, but may just not feel inclined to dabble in those other areas.[6]

II

We shall start our discussion by examining the very title of bard, which has often been extended, with varying degrees of defensibility, to anyone with a modicum of skill in song. The chances for this confusion are particularly great in studies of African musicianship. We have often been told that the African, because of his early exposure to musical situations, has a built-in capacity for music. Says J.H.K. Nketia of the Akan child in Ghana:

His experience, even at this early age, is not confined to children's songs. Like other African peoples, Akan mothers often carry their children on their backs to public arenas. Sometimes they even enter the dancing ring with their children on their backs. Later when the children are old enough, they are even encouraged to take part in the dancing. By the time a child reaches adolescence, his musical experience has widened considerably.[7]

This is an impressive picture, but we must draw the line somewhere between exposure and interest, between contact and career. The pertinent question in our search for the right definition of the bard should perhaps be: in his scale of occupations, what position does his interest in song take? The question is important because our search for the traditional bard has often taken us—no doubt with good reason sometimes—to characters in our texts who have in one way or another been associated with music. Under this category comes much of the poetic self-praise done by many African chiefs.[8] In the Sunjata epic we have the interesting case of the king Sumanguru who periodically sang his own praises to the accompaniment of a charmed harp (IV:39). Even the hero-child Lianja—still called "gamin" at this stage of his career—plays the harp (*Lianja* 53). A similar case occurs in the *Iliad*. When the Achaean peace party visits Achilles in his tent, they find him with a lyre in his hand, with which he "gladdened his heart and sang the feats of men" (9:189). If we take *Beowulf* 2105ff. as referring to Hrothgar, as some editors seem to do, then the old warrior-king must have made an impression on the Geat party with the "glee-wood," fetching back old-time feats both "true" and "wonderful."[9] Tempting as these references are, we must place the expertise of our bard considerably above that of the rest of the population, even when it can be shown that "the art is enjoyed by a whole society."[10] The seminal qualification for the bard must therefore be that he has a specialist's interest in the art. The warrior-ruler would care far less for the craft than the bard would.

Yet, in spite of this criterion, we are not necessarily justified in crediting the bard with professional excellence in the modern sense of the phrase. Put differently: even when singing is what the man excels in doing, we may not really call it his "profession" in terms of a sole or major source of sustenance and thus of a steady concern for self-improvement.

In fact, very few bards, in the traditional (rural) context, actually sustain themselves and their families primarily by their songs. Of the Akan bard-musician Nketia says:

> In the past he could live on the bounty of the chief if it was his duty to perform on state occasions, but this was a privilege enjoyed by all servants of the State. In ordinary life he is like everybody else—a farmer, trader, carver, or fisherman who depends more on these for his living than on his music.[11]

Of the Bala in the Congo country, Alan Merriam says:

> Among the Bala, no musician is a complete economic specialist. Even the *ngombe*, who is a wandering musician, keeps his ties to the land, which he cultivates himself when possible or leaves to the care of members of his family. All informants are agreed on this matter; all say that it is impossible to make one's complete living from music, though some will argue the question as a theoretical point. . . .[12]

Merriam adds that, in spite of this situation, such a minstrel can sometimes earn almost a third of the average income in his community in one festival week.

Babalola comments on the *ijala* or heroic hunters' chants among the Yoruba of Nigeria:

> Ijala-chanting is rarely a full-time occupation for any of the artists. Although some members of the public spoil the reputation of the ijala-chanters by calling them *onraye*,

ole, koninkanise, etc., meaning that they are lazy drones seeking an easy life, investigation reveals that in actual fact many an ijala artist takes to ijala-chanting only as a hobby or a side-line, and that he is primarily a hunter, a farmer, a sawyer, or a diviner-physician.[13]

The bard of *The Mwindo Epic,* Mr. Shekarisi Rurede, is a maker of baskets and mats, among other occupations (*Mwindo* 15ff.).

So far, we have been talking about bards of a more or less independent status, who owe no allegiance to a steady patron. It seems clear that though they enjoy public acclaim for their excellence, they still have to support themselves and their families by having a regular job, which means they cannot devote undivided attention to their songs. There are parallel cases among the Yugoslav guslars of the Parry-Lord collections. Salih Ugljanin farmed livestock in his native Ugao; at Novi Pazar he kept a coffeehouse, until he became too old and made his living as hired help (or consultant). Sulejman Fortić found life "hard in the village," and preferred life as "a waiter in the coffeehouse" at Novi Pazar. Demail Zogić also kept a coffeehouse there. Sulejman Makić was a cattle farmer from Senica, and Alija Fjuljanin a country farmer from Stavica.[14] In classical Greece, Hesiod is apparently the only acclaimed bard of independent status we know of, and he was a shepherd in the valley of Mount Helicon (*Theogony* 23).

The situation of the bard with a steady patron, like the court minstrel, is not radically different. In *Sunjata* IV, we have the case of Gnankouman Doua, griot to Nare Maghan, the hero's father. Doua is a gleeman and sings Maghan's praises. But he is also a seer, sorcerer, and the king's counselor and closest confidante, sharing with him his cares of state; Doua's son, Balla Fasseke, inherits the same functions when Sunjata comes of age. This all-purpose role of the griot is vividly portrayed in one tale of origin that Hugo Zemp records from the Dan of the Ivory Coast. From the words of his informant, Zemp is able to conclude: "The account of the old man from Dan underlines the time-honoured function of the court musician: to swell the prestige of the chief. The text also indicates the peculiar position of the griot: he serves as messenger."[15]

In many such court situations in Africa—as in the emir's palaces of northern Nigeria—the bard is a multipurpose palace hand, performing duties that are often far from glamorous. We are reminded in Homer of the singer whom Agamemnon is said to have left behind in Argos with full instructions to spy on Klytaimnestra (*Odyssey* 3.267ff.); in a similar vein, in the Ozidi epic, the witch Oreame strikes the earth, and a drummer and hornblower issue forth, charged specifically with protecting the boy-hero against intrigue (*Ozidi* 48).

The concept of professionalism may seem to be different with regard to bards who today receive quite generous patronage from radio and television networks, or from rich businessmen, and may therefore not bother to seek other work. But in real terms, and as far as the performance of extended texts of heroic tales are concerned, there is hardly any difference between the city-based bard and his rustic counterpart. Seldom does either sit down and carefully chisel out his lines so as to achieve anything like a flawless text. Almost invariably, songs are performed for patrons on short order or "as occasion requires,"[16] and in such spontaneous moments textual purity is beyond the capacity of the bard, even with the best of a formular device or mnemonic skill. He may indeed, never be inclined to achieve the kind of verbal and structural uniformity that we may hope to find. Since the song is composed "in" and not "for" a performance, he is likely to be content that the other ingredients of his craft (music, dramatization, and so on) will make up adequately for the incidental mud along the way. That mud is of the very nature of the oral performance, and we may be doing the bard a disservice by endowing his work with a transparency or "purity" that he never intended.

Even from the training of the bard, it is possible to glean something of the background to this happily informal character of traditional minstrelsy. This does not imply that the mode of learning is any less conscientious. Rureke, the bard of *Mwindo,* started his training as a youth by becoming "a helper of Kenyangara of Bese, who was such an expert narrator of the Mwindo epic"; such an apprenticeship requires that one cultivate a thorough presence of mind so as to be able, for instance, to "repeat a whole sentence during each short pause made by the bard" and indeed help him "find the thread of his story" now and then (*Mwindo* 13, 17). But the very unfixed nature of the text makes it clear that the apprentice is being trained not in the rigid use of memory but in the flexible technique of improvisation. From early youth, as Babalola tells us of the apprentice *ijala* bard, the pupil learns his trade assiduously. But he also soon develops "a strong sense of competence and self-reliance," which come through in his response to charges of historical inaccuracy in his performance: *"K'onikaluku o maa ba poro opo 'e lo"* (Let each animal follow the smooth stretch of its own road).[17]

Other than the mode of attachment discussed above, the bard's training can be quite informal, though the learner remains dedicated to his goal.[18] But the most interesting aspect of the training of the singer is the practice of acquiring an extensive repertoire. It seems to be almost universally accepted as a sure means of sharpening the bardic skill. Among the Nyanga, as the editors of *The Mwindo Epic* tell us, "the expert narrators and singers may know a fairly large number of texts" (*Mwindo* 6). Among the Yoruba, Babalola says, "the best ijala-chanter" is "the one whose repertoire is the most extensive,"[19] among other criteria. Ames tells us that among the Hausa the process of musical training "often entails learning a host of songs."[20] And the editors of *Kambili* write of the repertoire of the bard:

> A typical evening's performance will include songs for amusement and dancing, ritual songs which can be danced only by those who have performed certain deeds and, at the close of the evening, an epic song of one of the many hunter heroes. We have recorded twelve epic performances of Seydou Camara and well over fifty of his songs. (p. ix)

We could compare this with the situation elsewhere. The foundations of the formular technique may indeed lie partly in the fact that the bard has a vast number of tales or lays from which he could draw some easily deployable phrases and themes. Homer has been credited with quite a few songs. Aristotle ascribes the satirical *Margites* to him; Callinus of Ephesus, according to Pausanias (x.9.5), attributed a *Thebaid* to him; and the Herodotean life of Homer reports that on the day of the new moon, the bard went about the homes of rich men singing, in the company of children, a short song called *eiresione*. Within the *Odyssey* we have an indication of the minstrel's varied repertoire. Demodokos sings of the Trojan experience of the Achaeans and draws tears from Odysseus. But he also has some lighter and even danceable lays, like the one on the luckless adultery of Ares and Aphrodite. In an earlier parallel, in book 1, Phemios has been singing of the Achaeans' grievous homecoming and moves Penelope to tears with his tunes. Thereupon she pleads with him:

> Phemios, since you know many other actions of mortals
> and gods, which can charm men's hearts and which the singers celebrate,
> sit before them and sing one of these and let them in silence

go on drinking their wine, but leave off singing this sad
song, which always afflicts the dear heart deep inside me,
since the unforgettable sorrow comes to me, beyond others,
so dear a head do I long for whenever I am reminded
of my husband, whose fame goes wide through Hellas and midmost Argos.

(1.337–44)

The Chadwicks also discuss the tradition of Irish minstrelsy, in which training involved "learning a large number of sagas each year."[21] And the Yugoslav guslar Sulejman Fortić tells us that, in the course of learning to be a minstrel, "the best thing is for us to know as many songs as we can" (*SCHS* 225).[22]

In view of this large fund of songs and themes, an interchange, whether we call it interpolation or interflow, frequently occurs. For the bard who knows his craft well, the incidental mud, as I have said, can only add a touch of color to the overall flow of the delivery. A good case in point is furnished by the *Kambili* epic. The warrior Kanji is unable to have a child, and several soothsayers are invited to solve the problem and name who among his wives will bear the child (the hero Kambili). If a soothsayer fails in the task, he is immediately beheaded by the order of Samory Toure, Kanji's general and ruler of the land. Now, one of these soothsayers is Nerikoro, a head of the powerful Komo (blacksmith cult-group), which is the ultimate mystical power in traditional Mande society. Beheading such a man would be unthinkable; so though Nerikoro fails to solve the child problem, he goes scot-free. Here is how the bard introduces the character Nerikoro into the story:

Nerikoro, the Komo man has come!
Fakoli was a smith, Samory!
If an insult is made to a smith, pleasure will sour.
The world's first child was a smith,
An insult to a smith, pleasure is ruined.
Ah! Smith! Samory!
If you insult a smith . . .

(536–42)

The significant reference in this piece is "Fakoli." He does not feature at all in the Kambili epic as a character, but is very much one—and a force to reckon with—in the Sunjata legend. According to his editors, the bard Seydou Camara has a version of this legend, yet to be transcribed. But most other versions feature Fakoli, leader of the powerful blacksmith caste. In both the Innes* and Niane† editions, Fakoli is nephew to Sumanguru, the sorcerer-king of the Susu and archenemy of the hero, Sunjata. In the great war between these two, Fakoli takes Sunjata's side against his uncle Sumanguru, who has offended him by taking his wife from him (*Sunjata* IV.43). And part of the reason that Sumanguru comes to grief in that war is that he has alienated the powerful smith caste who venerate Fakoli.

An "insult" to a smith, such as Fakoli has experienced, is therefore fraught with serious consequences. In the relevant context in *Kambili*, the detail serves a cautionary purpose and explains why the bard does not subject Nerikoro to a treatment he ordinarily deserves.

*Gordon Innes, *Sunjata: Three Mandinka Versions* (London: School of Oriental and African Studies, 1974).—EDS.
†D. T. Niane, *Sundiata: An Epic of Old Mali,* trans. A. D. Pickett (London: Longman, 1965).—EDS.

Culture and Identity

Thus a detail or line from one song is deployed, with functional ease, in another song in such a way that it bestows on its new context a bold associative or metaphorical flavor. Perhaps this, other than prosody, is the effect intended when Homer calls the swineherd Eumaios "foremost of men" or says that Telemachos' sneeze "clashed horribly," or even makes Eumaios' pigsty[23] look very much like Priam's palace in layout, as Monro has observed. This may be mud, but it does give the flood a touch of genuineness—and epic song is hardly a clear, mellifluous stream.

Now, what does the bard look like as a person, and what does he think of himself and his craft? In many cases, apparently, he would like to draw public attention to himself by the materials that he wears. Otherwise, something marks him out (when he leads a group) other than the musical instrument that he holds. This could take the form of the representative paraphernalia of his craft. The photograph on the cover of the text of *Kambili** shows Seydou Camara decked all over with charms—amulets, cowries, and whatnot—like the hero-hunter of his song. Likewise, the cover photo to *The Mwindo Epic*† has Rureke holding the musical calabash-rattle in the right hand, and in the left a "*conga*-scepter," the main instrument of power continually wielded by the hero in the story. For the Ozidi affair, the narrator will hold in one hand a fan (as constantly used for magical effect by Oreame in the tale) and in the other a sword (the hero's regular weapon) (*Ozidi* xxiv). In the Sunjata story, perhaps of the same order is the picture of Gnankouman Doua, griot to Nare Maghan Kon Fatta, as he responds to "the grave music of the 'bolon'" during the celebrations of the king's marriage to Sogolon Kedjou: "Doua, standing amid the eminent guests, held his great spear in his hand and sang the anthem of the Mandingo kings" (*Sunjata* IV.10).[24]

Alternatively, these outward effects are largely a mark of the gleeman's love of display, evidence of his public image. This is apparent from David Ames's observation about the Hausa musician:

> The musician often wears gowns made of brightly colored and richly patterned cloth. The items of clothing seldom match since they have been received as payment from different clients and patrons.[25]

"The Mongo bards," in Daniel Biebuyck's useful catalogue, "wearing a feather hat, adorn their bodies and face with various geometrical designs, and carry a ceremonial knife or spear. Among the Fang, the bards wear a feather hat, a mane-like coiffure, a fiber skirt, a multitude of wild animal skins that hang from their arms and waist, and anklet bells."[26]

A similar picture emerges from Salih Ugljanin's description of the legendary Yugoslav guslar, Cor Huso Husović, from whom Salih claims to have learned some of his songs. Asked what Huso did for a living, Salih says: "Nothing, he had no trade, nothing but his horse and his arms, and he went about the world. He was blind in one eye and his clothes and arms were of the finest. And he went thus from town to town and sang to everybody to the gusle" (*SCHS* 61). Although the singers of the Parry-Lord collections are not particularly well dressed, Salih's observation of Huso perhaps indicates that the glamorous get-up is something of an ideal among this tradition of singers.[27]

We may also usefully compare the Homeric scene. Homer says nothing of the bard's outward appearance, but some scholars have understood the "wand" or the "rod" as a

---

*C. Bird et al., *The Song of Seydou Camara. Vol. 1: Kambili* (Bloomington: African Studies Center, Indiana University, 1974).—Eds.

†D. Biebuyck and K. C. Mateene, *The Mwindo Epic* (Berkeley and Los Angeles: University of California Press, 1969).—Eds.

later or post-Homeric substitute for the *phorminx* or *kitharis* in the accompaniment of heroic song. This is only half the truth, however. The earliest reference to the wand is from Hesiod, who tells us that the muses "plucked off and gave to me a rod, a twig of sturdy laurel, an admirable thing: and they inspired me with a divine voice to celebrate things that are to be and things that have been" (*Theogony* 30ff.). The next authority, Pindar, gives us the picture of a "rhapsodic" Homer in words that faintly echo Hesiod. Pindar is talking about Homer's glorification of Ajax:

> But Homer has done him
> Honour among men; for he set straight
> All his prowess, and to his wand of celestial words
> Told of it, to the delight of men to come.
>
> (*Isthmian* 4.37–40)

It seems clear that the rod (*skeptron*) that Hesiod claims to have received is nothing more than a recognition of his bardic eminence by the muses (he finds another occasion, in *Works* 657, to mention this eminence). Of Pindar's remark there are many possible interpretations. Perhaps the most plausible is that the rod—on the authority of Hesiod, at least—came to represent for later generations a symbol of excellence in "divine" or "celestial" song. The rhapsode thus held the rod as he recited his lines (an example is the vase figure of the Kleophrades Painter's rhapsode), more to demonstrate his claims to authority in celestial song than as "an aid to rhetorical emphasis in recitation"[28] or a substitute for a lyre.

Evidently, the concern for image or external effect is a traditional feature of the bard's craft. Bards are also generally very outspoken about their merits. They have a rather competitive spirit—especially when a number of them operate in the same community—and are usually jealous about each other's claims and capacities. It is possible that Djeli Mamoudou Kouyate, the bard of Niane's edition of the Sunjata epic, saw the transcribing scholar as a threat to his trade and was thus moved to condemn the culture of "dumb books" as inferior to "the warmth of the human voice" which he represented in the transmission of history (*Sunjata* IV.41). In his version of the same epic, Bamba Suso proudly announces that he comes from a distinguished line of griots who have told the tale, starting from his grandfather Koriyang Musa, who received his harp-lute from the spirits:

> He met the *jinns,* and brought back a *Kora.*
> The very first *Kora*
> Was like a *simbingo*
> The Kora came from the *jinns.*
>
> (*Sunjata* I.13–16)

In yet another version, the griot Banna Kanute, apparently on observing that the host is not particularly impressed by his performance, tells him with a certain touch of pique, "Don't you know/That an ordinary narrator and an expert singer are not the same?" (*Sunjata* II.1265f.). Of the Hausa singers, Ames observes that "they commonly view themselves as outstanding musicians but neglect others."[29] Merriam notes that among the Bala of the Congo, "the individual musician . . . invariably names himself as the outstanding

Culture and Identity

musician of the village."[30] And Seydou Camara has several lines in his song touting his abilities—for example:

> Ah! It's the voice of Seydou!
> The thing is not easy for all.
> It's the sound of the harp-playing Seydou from Kabaya.
>
> (*Kambili* 51–54)

There are several parallels from the European world. Hesiod's mention of his excellence in song, as I have observed, is clearly of this order; and it is possible, as some have pointed out, that he sets the "truth" of his song against the "fiction" of the Homeric School (*Theogony* 27f.). The blind bard of "rocky Chios," who sings the hymn to Delian Apollo, is anxious that he should be judged "the sweetest singer" to visit Delos.[31] Among the Slavs, the bard of *The Song of Igor's Campaign* would seem to be setting his standards against those of a legendary Boyan, not only in terms of style but also of the honesty of his sentiments (*Igor* 1 off.). At Novi Pazar, on being told that Salih Ugljanin claims he knows a hundred songs, the reaction of Sulejman Makić is an immediate denial: "He lies!" (*SCHS* 265). And Milman Parry quotes the following from Matija Murko's record of his experiences in collecting folk songs:

> The singers are artists, as is well demonstrated by the fact that they seem extremely jealous of one another. One day, at Sarajevo, after I had recorded three singers, I paid all three of them the same amount. One of them refused to take his payment. It struck me at once that I had behaved rather badly. The people there did, indeed, intimate to me that the man regarded himself as a much better singer than the other two.[32]

But we may well ask: If it is true that the bard has such a bold view of his merits, then why does he attribute his creative powers to a divine source and lay his merits at the feet, so to speak, of divinity? For this appears to be the pattern among many societies, and anthropologists generally seize upon it as a proof of the religious uses of art. Among the Yoruba, the *ijala* artist claims to be the "mouthpiece" of Ogun,[33] the god of blood and iron, of war and the deadly hunt. The Mandingo griot traditionally traces the source of his art to a certain Sourakata, reputedly the closest companion and aide of the Prophet Mohammed.[34] Among the Nyanga, the god Karisi is said to impart the skill of singing the Mwindo legend and could reveal himself in a dream to whoever he blesses with this skill (*Mwindo* 12,14). The dream element also appears in the origins that John Pepper Clark has traced for the Ozidi Saga:

> Tradition holds that many years ago the High Priest of Orua in Tarakiri clan fell asleep at the foot of the clan's big shrine. In that sleep came the vision of Azudu, or Ozidi as he is sometimes called. And so compulsive was the urge to tell it the man woke up never to have a moment's rest again, moving from town to town through one clan into another down the hundred odd creeks and islands of the Niger Delta. The story took him seven nights in telling, and on each occasion, however far away from Orua, he had always to return home to the foot of the shrine to intone the last line there or die on the spot of telling in a strange land.[35]

In their several ways these claims tend to reinforce the bard's tremendous self-esteem and sense of uniqueness; like Hesiod, every bard considers himself, and none other, the chosen one in his craft, commissioned by the supernatural powers to deliver the *truth* in song. It is possible that Homer's appeal to the muse ("Sing, goddess . . .") is of this order.

If the very daughters of almighty Zeus chose to speak through the mouth of the poet, what greater proof could there be of excellence and veracity?

It is not clear what the reason is for this self-esteem, especially in view of the variety of circumstances in which the bard is to be found. In monarchical societies, the bard often holds a revered place in the king's court; perhaps the attitude is principally an effort to justify this reverence. The society of ancient Mali is generally reputed to have its origins in Mecca,[36] and the griot who shared the counsels of his lord naturally saw himself in the same position that Sourakata held with Mohammed. Among the Akan of Ghana, the court musician also saw himself as occupying this time-honored position, as is clear from the following drum message:

> When the creator created things,
> When the manifold creator created things;
> What did he create?
> He created the court crier,
> He created the Drummer,
> He created the Principal State Executioner.[37]

In some societies, republican as well as monarchical, the bard may not be held in much regard. People may like his music for the joy that it brings, but they do not consider him indispensable. In such a situation, self-esteem might simply be a reaction against injured pride. Among the Dan of the Ivory Coast, as Hugo Zemp tells us, the griot is today considered inferior, and nobody would allow his daughter to marry one of these musicians; so it is significant that it was from among them that Zemp collected the legend that when Zra (God) created the first chief he gave him a griot as a close companion.[38] In the emirates of northern Nigeria, as Ames reports, the situation is very much the same as in the Ivory Coast; the musicians, thus painfully underestimated, are reduced to ranking one another on the basis of patronage.[39] And the idea of the dream/vision may be just as plausible a means of self-justification as the above cases; as Bowra has observed:

> Dream may well give a man the confidence and impulse which he needs to start poetical composition. He will regard them with great awe as coming from the gods and remember them clearly, and, what is more, he will feel that the gods have chosen him for a task, and this will give him a special sense of his own importance and ability.[40]

The implication of all this seems clear. The flights of song will be beyond the compass of a bard who cannot summon the presumption for such an exercise. In the more communalistic world of the olden days, the attitude probably helped the bard to demonstrate that his efforts were just as germane to the common good as those of other craftsmen, like the prophet, the physician, or the woodworker—a fact succinctly stated by Eumaios in *Odyssey* 17.328–185. In today's more competitive milieu, quite possibly the bard is anxious to avoid being done out of the scheme of things. Among the Bala of the Congo, as Merriam reports, musical talent is regarded as "a matter arranged by Efile Mukulu (God)"; yet Chite, the most acknowledged musician in the clan, owned he took up musical training "because I thought of all the money I would make!"[41]

NOTES

1. Cf. A. B. Lord, *Singer of Tales*, p. 5.
2. A. B. Lord, "Homer, Parry and Huso," p. 42; cf. Lord, "Homer's Originality: Oral Dictated Texts," p. 126f; and Lord, "Homer and Other Epic Poetry," p. 195.

3. Lord, *Singer of Tales,* p. 6.

4. For the varied repertoire of Seydou Camara, see *Kambili,* p. ix. Some of the chants in the story—e.g., the hunters' marriage song sung at the wedding of Kambili and Kumba and the song of praise for the killing of the lion—are, apparently, independent songs that have simply found fitting use in the story; see notes 157 and 164 to the text of *Kambili.* Cf. also *Mwindo* 14.

5. Something of a uniform pattern can indeed be seen in the following portraits of the singer-musician (in terms of training at least): Lord, *Singer of Tales,* pp. 20ff.; Babalola, *Content and Form,* pp. 40–55; D. W. Ames, "A Sociocultural View of Hausa Musical Activity"; and A. P. Merriam, "The Bala Musician." The last two studies are in W. L. d'Azevedo, ed., *The Traditional Artist in African Societies.*

6. Cf. Babalola, *Content and Form,* pp. vi, 23.

7. Nketia, "Musician in Akan Society," p. 88.

8. See R. Finnegan, *Oral Literature in Africa,* p. 116.

9. One suspects, though, that in many of these cases the bard simply accords the art to the hero as a way of glorifying it: it is the occupation even of kings and heroes!

10. C. M. Bowra, *Heroic Poetry,* p. 410. For the various instances in which traditional African poetry and song are practiced on a nonspecialist basis, see Finnegan, *Oral Literature,* p. 104. Sir Walter Scott has made perhaps the best comments on this issue of proliferation of poetical skill in a community: "It is indeed easily discovered, that the qualities necessary for composing such poems are not the portion of every man in the tribe; that the bard, to reach excellence in his art, must possess something more than a full command of words and phrases, and the knack of arranging them in such a form as ancient examples have fixed upon as the recognized structure of national verse . . ." (*Minstrelsy of the Scottish Border,* p. 3).

11. Nketia, "Musician in Akan Society," p. 83.

12. Merriam, "Bala Musician," p. 258; cf. D. Biebuyck, "The Epic as a Genre in Congo Oral Literature," p. 261.

13. Babalola, *Content and Form,* p. 41.

14. *SCHS,* pp. 59f., 225, 235, 263, and 289 respectively.

15. "Le récit du vieillard dan souligne la fonction primordiale du musicien attaché à la cour: augmenter le prestige du chef. Le texte indique aussi la position particulière du griot malinké: il sert de messager." H. Zemp, "Musiciens autochtones et griots malinke chez les Dan de Cote d'Ivoire," p. 377; cf. also p. 378 on professionalism. Gordon Innes has also argued, quite forcefully, that there is little support for the claim that griots held lofty positions in the courts of the old Mandingo kings: see *Sunjata: Three Mandinka Versions,* pp. 8–9. Indeed, in the version of the Sunjata legend by Banna Suso, griots appear occasionally to be grouped together with slaves: see *Sunjata* I. 65ff. (though here the bard awards greater wisdom to his mythic counterpart) and 1173.

16. Babalola, *Content and Form,* p. 47.

17. *Ibid.,* pp. 41f., 61f. Dembo Kanute and his brother Banna, two of the griots of the Innes collection, prove that the student does not have to echo his teacher. Dembo was trained by their father and then trained Banna under their father's supervision (Innes, *Sunjata* p. 260); but their versions are thoroughly different. Not only are their temperaments evidently unalike but they have pursued their careers in different environments.

18. Cf. Nketia, "Musician in Akan Society," p. 87.

19. Babalola, *Content and Form,* p. 50.

20. Ames, "A Sociocultural View," p. 153.

21. H. M. Chadwick and N. K. Chadwick, *The Growth of Literature,* 1:603.

22. Cf. Lord, "Homer and Other Epic Poetry," p. 209.

23. *Odyssey,* 14.121, 17.541, and 14.13ff.

24. Among the Asaba Igbo of midwestern Nigeria, there is a traditional war dance called *egwu-ota,* a quite frightening affair. The young men clash their matchets against wicker shields and howl war cries as the dance proceeds in a phalanxlike movement.

25. Ames, "A Sociocultural View," p. 154.

26. Biebuyck, "The African Heroic Epic," p. 22.

27. Kirk thinks (wrongly, I believe) that this is simply a tourist pose and an evidence of "degeneracy" in the bardic tradition: see G. S. Kirk, *The Songs of Homer* plate 8c.

28. G. S. Kirk, "Homer and Modern Oral Poetry," p. 289. For the rhapsode's adornments, see Plato, *Ion* 530b, 535d.

29. Ames, "A Sociocultural View," p. 144.

30. Merriam, "Bala Musician," p. 256.

31. Hymn to Apollo, pp. 166ff. Also, for the rhapsode's exaggerated claims, see Plato, *Ion* 530c, d, 533c, 541b.

32. "Les chanteurs sont des artistes, le fait qu'ils se monstrent extremement jaloux l'un de l'autre le prouve encore. Un jour, à Sarajévo, aprés avoir recueilli des phonogrammes de trois chanteurs, je donnai à tous trois la même recompense. L'un d'entre eux réfusa de l'accepter. Je flairai aussitôt que je l'avais froissé de quelque manière. Les personnes presentes me previnrent en effet qu'il se considérait comme un bien meilleur chanteur que les deux autres." M. Parry, "Studies in the Epic Technique of Oral Verse-Making II," p. 15.

33. Babalola, *Content and Form*, p. 46.

34. H. Zemp, "La légende des griots malinke," pp. 614ff.

35. J. P. Clark, "The Azudu Saga," p. 9. For the dream/vision, compare the story of Caedmon in Bede, *Hist. Eccles.* IV.24; also Ennius' vision of Homer, in Cicero, *Acad. Pr.* II.16.51.

36. See *Sunjata* IV.2f.; cf. N. Levtzion, *Ancient Ghana and Mali*, pp. 25f.; and C. Bird, "Heroic Songs of the Mande Hunters," *African Folklore*, p. 446.

37. J. H. K. Nketia, *Folk Songs of Ghana*, p. 154.

38. Zemp, "Musiciens autochtones," pp. 376f.

39. Ames, "A Sociocultural View," pp. 155f.

40. Bowra, *Heroic Poetry*, p. 428.

41. Merriam, "Bala Musician," pp. 262f.

Culture and Identity

Kouroukan Fougan, or the Division of the World by Sundiata

Leaving Do, the land of ten thousand guns, Sundiata wended his way to Ka-ba, keeping to the river valley. All his armies converged on Ka-ba and Fakoli and Tabon Wana entered it laden with booty. Sibi Kamandjan had gone ahead of Sundiata to prepare the great assembly which was to gather at Ka-ba, a town situated on the territory belonging to the country of Sibi.

Ka-ba was a small town founded by Niagalin M'Bali Faly, a hunter of Sibi, and by Sounoumba Traore, a fisherman. Ka-ba belonged to the king of Sibi and nowadays you can also find Keitas at Ka-ba, but the Keitas did not come there until after Sundiata's time. Ka-ba stands on the left bank of the Niger and it is through Ka-ba that the road to old Mali passes.

To the north of the town stretches a spacious clearing and it is there that the great assembly was to foregather. King Kamandjan had the whole clearing cleaned up and a great dais was got ready. Even before Djata's arrival the delegation from all the conquered peoples had made their way to Ka-ba. Huts were hastily built to house all these people. When all the armies had reunited, camps had to be set up in the big plain lying between the river and the town. On the appointed day the troops were drawn up on the vast square that had been prepared. As at Sibi, each people was gathered round its king's pennant. Sundiata had put on robes such as are worn by a great Muslim king. Balla Fasséké, the high master of ceremonies, set the allies around Djata's great throne. Everything was in position. The sofas, forming a vast semi-circle bristling with spears, stood motionless. The delegations of the various people had been planted at the foot of the dais. A complete silence reigned. On Sundiata's right, Balla Fasséké, holding his mighty spear, addressed the throng in this manner:

"Peace reigns today in the whole country; may it always be thus. . . ."

"Amen," replied the crowd, then the herald continued:

"I speak to you, assembled peoples. To those of Mali I convey Maghan Sundiata's greeting; greetings to those of Do, greetings to those of Ghana, to those from Mema greetings, and to those of Fakoli's tribe. Greetings to the Bobo warriors and, finally, greetings to those of Sibi and Ka-ba. To all the peoples assembled, Djata gives greetings.

"May I be humbly forgiven if I have made any omission. I am nervous before so many people gathered together.

"Peoples, here we are, after years of hard trials, gathered around our saviour, the restorer of peace and order. From the east to the west, from the north to the south, everywhere his victorious arms have established peace. I convey to you the greetings of Soumaoro's vanquisher, Maghan Sundiata, king of Mali.

"But in order to respect tradition, I must first of all address myself to the host of us all, Kamandjan, king of Sibi; Djata greets you and gives you the floor."

Kamandjan, who was sitting close by Sundiata, stood up and stepped down from the dais. He mounted his horse and brandished his sword, crying "I salute you all, warriors of Mali, of Do, of Tabon, of Mema, of Wagadou, of Bobo, of Fakoli . . . ; warriors, peace has returned to our homes, may God long preserve it."

"Amen," replied the warriors and the crowd. The king of Sibi continued.

"In the world man suffers for a season, but never eternally. Here we are at the end of our trials. We are at peace. May God be praised. But we owe this peace to one man who, by his courage and his valiance, was able to lead our troops to victory.

"Which one of us, alone, would have dared face Soumaoro? Ay, we were all cowards. How many times did we pay him tribute? The insolent rogue thought that everything was permitted him. What family was not dishonoured by Soumaoro? He took our daughters and wives from us and we were more craven than women. He carried his insolence to the point of stealing the wife of his nephew Fakoli! We were prostrated and humiliated in front of our children. But it was in the midst of so many calamities that our destiny suddenly changed. A new sun arose in the east. After the battle of Tabon we felt ourselves to be men, we realized that Soumaoro was a human being and not an incarnation of the devil, for he was no longer invincible. A man came to us. He had heard our groans and came to our aid, like a father when he sees his son in tears. Here is that man. Maghan Sundiata, the man with two names foretold by the soothsayers.

"It is to you that I now address myself, son of Sogolon, you, the nephew of the valorous warriors of Do. Henceforth it is from you that I derive my kingdom for I acknowledge you my sovereign. My tribe and I place ourselves in your hands. I salute you, supreme chief, I salute you, Fama of Famas. I salute you, Mansa!"

The huzza that greeted these words was so loud that you could hear the echo repeat the tremendous clamour twelve times over. With a strong hand Kamandjan stuck his spear in the ground in front of the dais and said, "Sundiata, here is my spear, it is yours."

Then he climbed up to sit in his place. Thereafter, one by one, the twelve kings of the bright savanna country got up and proclaimed Sundiata "Mansa" in their turn. Twelve royal spears were stuck in the ground in front of the dais. Sundiata had become emperor. The old tabala of Niani announced to the world that the lands of the savanna had provided themselves with one single king. When the imperial tabala had stopped reverberating, Balla Fasséké, the grand master of ceremonies, took the floor again following the crowd's ovation.

"Sundiata, Maghan Sundiata, king of Mali, in the name of the twelve kings of the 'Bright Country,' I salute you as 'Mansa.'"

The crowd shouted, "Wassa, Wassa . . . , Ayé."

It was amid such joy that Balla Fasséké composed the great hymn "Niama" which the griots still sing:

> Niama, Niama, Niama,
> You, you serve as a shelter for all,
> All come to seek refuge under you.

And as for you, Niama,
Nothing serves you for shelter,
God alone protects you.

The festival began. The musicians of all the countries were there. Each people in turn came forward to the dais under Sundiata's impassive gaze. Then the war dances began. The sofas of all the countries had lined themselves up in six ranks amid a great clatter of bows and spears knocking together. The war chiefs were on horseback. The warriors faced the enormous dais and at a signal from Balla Fasséké, the musicians, massed on the right of the dais, struck up. The heavy war drums thundered, the bolons gave off muted notes while the griot's voice gave the throng the pitch for the "Hymn to the Bow." The spearmen, advancing like hyenas in the night, held their spears above their heads; the archers of Wagadou and Tabon, walking with a noiseless tread, seemed to be lying in ambush behind bushes. They rose suddenly to their feet and let fly their arrows at imaginary enemies. In front of the great dais the Kéké-Tigui, or war chiefs, made their horses perform dance steps under the eyes of the Mansa. The horses whinnied and reared, then, overmastered by the spurs, knelt, got up and cut little capers, or else scraped the ground with their hooves.

The rapturous people shouted the "Hymn to the Bow" and clapped their hands. The sweating bodies of the warriors glistened in the sun while the exhausting rhythm of the tam-tams wrenched from them shrill cries. But presently they made way for the cavalry, beloved by Djata. The horsemen of Mema threw their swords in the air and caught them in flight, uttering mighty shouts. A smile of contentment took shape on Sundiata's lips, for he was happy to see his cavalry manoeuvre with so much skill.

In the afternoon the festivity took on a new aspect. It began with the procession of prisoners and booty. Their hands tied behind their backs and in triple file, the Sosso prisoners made their entry into the giant circle. All their heads had been shaved. Inside the circle they turned and passed by the foot of the dais. Their eyes lowered, the poor prisoners walked in silence, abuse heaped upon them by the frenzied crowd. Behind came the kings who had remained faithful to Soumaoro and who had not intended to make their submission. They also had their heads shorn, but they were on horseback so that everyone could see them. At last, right at the back, came Sosso Balla, who had been placed in the midst of his father's fetishes. The fetishes had been loaded onto donkeys. The crowd gave loud cries of horror on seeing the inmates of Soumaoro's grisly chamber. People pointed with terror at the snake's pitcher, the magic balafon [a traditional African string instrument], and the king of Sosso's owls. Soumaoro's son Balla, his hands bound, was on a horse but did not dare look up at this throne, which formerly used to tremble with fear at mere talk of his father. In the crowd could be heard:

"Each in his turn, Sosso Balla; lift up your head a bit, impudent little creature!" Or else: "Did you have any idea that one day you would be a slave, you vile fellow!"

"Look at your useless fetishes. Call on them then, son of a sorcerer!"

When Sosso Balla was in front of the dais, Djata made a gesture. He had just remembered the mysterious disappearance of Soumaoro inside the mountain. He became morose, but his griot Balla Fasséké noticed it and so he spoke thus:

"The son will pay for the father, Soumaoro can thank God that he is already dead."

When the procession had finished Balla Fasséké silenced everyone. The sofas got into line and the tam-tams stopped.

Sundiata got up and a graveyard silence settled on the whole place. The Mansa moved forward to the edge of the dais. Then Sundiata spoke as Mansa. Only Balla Fasséké could hear him, for a Mansa does not speak like a town-driver.

"I greet all the peoples gathered here." And Djata mentioned them all. Pulling the spear of Kamandjan, king of Sibi, out of the ground, he said:

"I give you back your kingdom, king of Sibi, for you have deserved it by your bravery; I have known you since childhood and your speech is as frank as your heart is straightforward.

"Today I ratify forever the alliance between the Kamaras of Sibi and the Keitas of Mali. May these two people be brothers henceforth. In future, the land of the Keitas shall be the land of the Kamaras, and the property of the Kamaras shall be henceforth the property of the Keitas.

"May there nevermore be falsehood between a Kamara and a Keita, and may the Kamaras feel at home in the whole extent of my empire."

He returned the spear to Kamandjan and the king of Sibi prostrated himself before Djata, as is done when honoured by a Fama.

Sundiata took Tabon Wana's spear and said, "Fran Kamara, my friend, I return your kingdom to you. May the Djallonkés and Mandingoes be forever allies. You received me in your own domain, so may the Djallonkés be received as friends throughout Mali. I leave you the lands you have conquered, and henceforth your children and your children's children will grow up at the court of Niani where they will be treated like the princes of Mali."

One by one all the kings received their kingdoms from the very hands of Sundiata, and each one bowed before him as one bows before a Mansa.

Sundiata pronounced all the prohibitions which still obtain in relations between the tribes. To each he assigned its land, he established the rights of each people and ratified their friendships. The Kondés of the land of Do became henceforth the uncles of the imperial family of Keita, for the latter, in memory of the fruitful marriage between Naré Maghan and Sogolon, had to take a wife in Do. The Tounkaras and the Cissés became "banter-brothers" of the Keitas while the Cissés, Bérétés and Tourés were proclaimed great divines of the empire. No kin group was forgotten at Kouroukan Fougan [when the world was divided]; each had its share in the division. To Fakoli Koroma, Sundiata gave the kingdom of Sosso, the majority of whose inhabitants were enslaved. Fakoli's tribe, the Koromas, which others call Doumbouya or Sissoko, had the monopoly of the forge, that is, of iron working. Fakoli also received from Sundiata part of the lands situated between the Bafing and Bagbé rivers. Wagadou and Mema kept their kings who continued to bear the title of Mansa, but these two kingdoms acknowledged the suzerainty of the supreme Mansa. The Konaté of Toron became the cadets of the Keitas so that on reaching maturity a Konaté could call himself Keita.

When Sogolon's son had finished distributing lands and power he turned to Balla Fasséké, his griot, and said: "As for you, Balla Fasséké, my griot, I make you grand master of ceremonies. Henceforth the Keitas will choose their griot from your tribe, from among the Kouyatés. I give the Kouyatés the right to make jokes about all the tribes, and in particular about the royal tribe of Keita."

Thus spoke the son of Sogolon at Kouroukan Fougan. Since that time his respected word has become law, the rule of conduct for all the peoples who were represented at Ka-ba.

So, Sundiata had divided the world at Kouroukan Fougan. He kept for his tribe the blessed country of Kita, but the Kamaras inhabiting the region remained masters of the soil.

If you go to Ka-ba, go and see the glade of Kouroukan Fougan and you will see a linké tree planted there, perpetuating the memory of the great gathering which witnessed the division of the world.

J. P. Clark-Bekederemo
(b. 1935, Nigeria)

The Ozidi Saga

THE MYTH

Tradition and awe surround *The Ozidi Saga*. There is the local lore at Orua that the epic began there several generations ago at the feet of the great god of Tarakiri Clan[1] in Western Ij̱o. The high priest at Orua had fallen into a trance one day while worshipping at the shrine. Out of that trance arose the vision of Ozidi. The man never quite came out of it, for upon waking, he knew no rest again until he had enacted to his people the drama that their god across the river had revealed to him in his uncommon sleep. Nor did he stop there. Moving from settlement to settlement, from clan to clan, through the innumerable creeks of the Niger delta, he took the story of Ozidi abroad, bringing fame to himself and his people. But like all gifts from the gods, there was a curse attendant upon the new-found powers of the story-telling priest: he had to return home to Orua every time to say the final line or die abroad in the act. This is a cue very well remembered today by all narrators of the saga, whether they are from Orua, the place generally accepted as the seat of the story, or from other settlements outside Tarakiri.

Although claimed by one clan, the saga of Ozidi has become the proud property of all Ij̱o speaking people in the Niger delta of Nigeria. Told in seven nights[2] to dance, music, mime, and ritual, it begins with the treason and treachery committed by a group of warlords in the city-state of Orua against the brothers Temugedege, who is king, and Ozidi, the leading general of the state. The rest of the epic tells of the posthumous birth of the general's son, the extraordinary manner of his growing up under the magic wings of his grandmother O̱re̱ame̱, and of the numerous battles the hero does with all manner of men and monsters to regain for his family its lost lineal glory. In this process, he oversteps the natural bounds set to his quest, and it is not until he has received divine visitation from the Smallpox King that he emerges purged and is received back into the society of men.

Ozidi is a supreme warrior who has to perform a number of seemingly impossible feats to reach a destined end. These adventures are by no means simple, separate episodes through which a single character moves to no approved purpose. Together, they spell out a mission arising out of a personal sense of wrong, the settlement of which determines the future course of public affairs in a powerful state.

Before the task, there is a period of tremendous preparation and initiation to pain, terror, and despair in their most naked forms. But it is not simple human power and courage that takes Ozidi triumphantly through his trials. Each of his opponents possesses these attributes, a good number of them to a greater degree. Ozidi overcomes them all because the gods are with him, right up to Tamara the Almighty, and they are with him because of his filial piety, his devotion to duty typical of many epic heroes. He is in fact a straight instrument of justice, and wielding him all the time is his grandmother Oreame of the supernatural powers, who is fate as well as conscience driving him on. When Ozidi later forgets his true role and overreaches himself in a series of excesses, he is visited with divine punishment, and this time not even the supreme witch his grandmother can save him.

It is here that by one quick turn of irony humanity comes back into its own in the emergence of Ozidi's mother Orea. Innocence and simplicity are the kit she brings to the rescue of her heroic son so that, when he recovers purified, there is a general sense of relief and rejoicing that natural order has at last been restored.

The Ozidi Saga is as much drama as narrative, and is examined here first for its narrative and dramatic character; secondly, its language and poetry; thirdly, its music, mime, and dance properties; fourthly, the religious, ritual, and festival aspects of the work; and, finally, for matters arising out of the text presented here.

THE NARRATIVE AND DRAMATIC CHARACTER: ITS TWO MODES OF PRESENTATION

The Ozidi Saga has a plot running into six phases or acts which in turn run into some eighty scenes or situations. In addition, there are the scores of times the story-teller-protagonist weaves in and out of the general line of incidents representing the action. This spreads over a staging period of seven days with an average of a four-hour performance each day. Perhaps, more remarkable than a number of unpredictable factors affecting its production is the fact that the two modes of presenting the piece both observe its structure. One is the narrative method in which the story-teller, by word, mime, and dance, enters into all parts of the piece as its sole performer. The other is the dramatic mode in which he becomes the story-teller-protagonist in a group of players impersonating all the characters in the drama-saga. While either mode of presentation preserves the plot, the texture of the narrative and dialogue is not fixed. It varies with each raconteur and troupe, more or less as a news story will have as many versions as there are reporters and newspapers to present it.

The story of Ozidi opens with the ancient city-state of Orua casting about for a candidate to fill its fatal vacant throne. It is the turn of the seventh and last quarter to present the candidate. In the council hall there is open disagreement between two brothers qualified for election. Ozidi, the younger and the hero, would rather his family waived their turn; but his idiot elder, Temugedege, rages for his right, and promptly is granted ascension by the Olotu set, the city lords, all of them no lovers of Ozidi.

For seven days after the installation, the people deny the new king his traditional tributes, chief of which is a human head. This angers Ozidi, and at his harangue the traditional raid for tributaries is planned by the army. But the commanding generals, long jealous of Ozidi's supremacy among them, turn the expedition into an ambush against him. After killing their comrade, they bring his decapitated head home as tribute to his brother. All the coward can do is flee into the bush.

Ozidi's young widow Orea, left alone, gathers up the head of her husband from the dust where his enemies have dumped it, and cradling it on her lap, blows flies from off the face to a loud lament. Later, she is contemplating suicide, when her mother Oreame, the supreme witch, flies in on her magic fan. The old woman reveals to her daughter she is heavy with child, and with this annunciation unheard by the conspirators and assassins, mother and daughter fly from the hostile city-state of Orua for their own town of Ododama.

Thus in the very first phase, serving as prologue to the epic, the themes and conflicts of the action are outlined in all their amplitude and suspense. The main body of the story unfolds with the premature birth of the younger Ozidi in the thick of a storm, followed by the extraordinary manner of his growing up, his grim preparation for the task of avenging his father, his return to the homestead of his fathers, now overtaken by the forest, where his idiot uncle cowers decrepit under a silk cotton tree, his discovery of the assassins through their foolish boastful wives as they go to market, the grand running spectacle of his battles and encounters with strange men and monsters, finally, the inevitable excesses of one who has shed too much blood in pursuit of relentless justice, and then his eventual visitation and purification by the Smallpox King.

In permanent opposition to father and son is a formidable list of Olotu, the warrior lords. At their head is Ofe the Short, Ogueren of the Twenty Toes, Azezabife the Skeleton Man, and Agbogidi of the Naked Parts. A terrible team to overawe any enemy anywhere, the elder Ozidi outranked them all. Here lay the demon of their spite which drives them to killing him with sticks and stones, for such as the man's magic endowments that swords, spears, and guns could not harm him. Many years later, challenged by the avenging son returned home, they hold endless counsels, quarrel among themselves, resort to various subterfuge measures, but one by one are taken on and routed by the younger Ozidi.

Other champions in the list seek out the hero as a result of rumours and reports of his unmatched prowess. Both Engbesibeoru the Scrotum King and Tebesonoma of the Seven Heads belong to this group. But once drawn out, and driven by the insatiable Oreame, Ozidi gives no quarter and indeed will go on to slaughter the defenceless and stay-at-home relatives of his adversaries, as he serves the sister of Tebesonoma and her new-born child. This begins the theme of excess.

Another theme, that of temptation and fall, arises, from the wilful acts of Ozidi, when against all advice, he walks into dens and traps of enemies like Odogu the Ogre[3] and the mother-and-son cannibal team of Azema and Azemaroti. Here hunger seems to be the bait that draws the hero astray: hunger for the knowledge of woman he is forbidden but which draws him into the lap of the temptress wife of Odogu, and hunger for further adventure from sheer force of habit, which lands him and his party on the brink of Azema's seven pots, kept always on the boil for human meat.

An interesting character is the retired wizard Bouakarakarabiri. With his deep knowledge of every herb held secret in the forest, it is he who invests the young Ozidi with the master charm of mortar and seven cauldrons that, boiling over at every fight, fill all his opponents with fear. Because the cunning old magician also passes the same secret and power to a second client, namely, Odogu the Ugly, a deadly dramatic situation is created when both men clash over the favour of one woman.

But probably the greatest dramatic irony of all is the appearance, in the midst of this galaxy of champions, of the dim-witted and dotty Temugedege, too afraid to fight, and too lazy to go to either farm or stream. Instead, there he is, rather like Falstaff among the valiant in the divided court of Henry IV of England, insisting on his personal rights to peace and sleep, while others are bellowing away life and limb to settle matters of honour. He has had his taste of kingship and wants nothing more now than to be left alone under his silk cotton tree among a host of elephant and spear grass. His trembling figure, running for cover and raining curses on his nephew, as the horn blows for battle, conjures up mixed emotions of pity and laughter.

Another comic character is the blacksmith who forges Ozidi's sword. It has to be a most special piece. The scene, where the fabulous blacksmith turns a bull [loose] in his own shop, as he runs helter-skelter to meet the express order of his imperious patron, provides a rare blaze of laughter and splash of fright showering forth at one and the same time. In the course of this, the blacksmith who, true to character, comes from Awka in the Ibo country of Nigeria, spills about the place his broken bits of Ijo, a hail that never fails to rock the local auditorium with laughter.

Very human too is Ozidi's mother Orea. For most of the time, she remains behind scenes, a passive figure of tears and prayers, first with her husband who goes to the hunt against her warning, and then with her son taken over at birth by her mother for his special mission in life. Her one moment of action is right at the close when her son is laid prostrate by smallpox. Since this is divine punishment for Ozidi's excesses, not even Oreame, the ultimate in sorcery, can find a cure. The all-conquering hero, therefore, is left to die in despair. Then suddenly, in the general grief and panic, his simple mother Orea recalls that her son has as yet not suffered an attack of yaws—a common disease of growing up among children in the Niger delta. So she treats his rash of smallpox as yaws; and mistaken for a commoner, the Smallpox King goes off in a huff, followed by his entire royal entourage of Migraine, Fever, Cold, Cough, Spots, and Maggots.

No mere figures out of allegory, the character range appearing in the saga of Ozidi reveals something of the world-view of the Ijo. There hardly exists here a sharp line between the world of the living and the dead. Man in the system is a link in the one continuum that is life, a medial link in a chain embracing the dead, the living, and the unborn. In this order of things, the kingdom of the dead, situated on the other bank of the river of life as in Greek and Roman mythology, is essentially a gathering of the ancestral clan, where members after death act as patrons and arbiters over the affairs of the living, regulating the birth of children, and recalling everybody home by way of death.[4]

There is a seat in the assembly for every member of the line who lives a good life and dies a natural death at a mature age. The dead in fact are considered as having been called home, and therefore among the elected offered sacrifice by descendants. The corollary of course is clear. The dishonourable in life and death are kept out, adrift in the evil grove, until such a time that each is called to town through a purification act entailing tremendous expense. This may take years, and usually the celebrant is no other than the heir. It is the desire to reinstate a murdered father that provides the prime force moving Ozidi. The ability to procreate is, therefore, truly a matter of life and death for the Ijo.

Influencing this stream flowing between life and death are spirits tenanting the sky, streams, and swamps in which the Ijo are immersed. Over and above all sits the supreme figure of Oyin the Mother or Tamara, She Who is the Moulder of All.

But as the Herskovits testify for characters in Fōn myth, "neither gods nor men are pawns in an all-ordering system. Where individuals are endowed with supernatural powers, they derive these from spiritual helpers who respond when they are called on, but the individual is not moved like marionette."[5]

The staging ground for *The Ozidi Saga* is the open public square of the marketplace, uncluttered by scenery and free for the great imaginative act to come to life. The storyteller-protagonist has only to wave his fan before the audience, point his sword across the river, and the ancient city-state of Orua rears to life with broad highways spanning the wide expanse of swamps and stream. In the same spirit of evocation, violence, so dominant in the saga and providing a constant source of threat to players and spectators alike, is either reported or represented in dance and mime.

As if to compensate for its relative lack of stage properties, masks and costumes abound in the sage of Ozidi. Apart from adding colour and spectacle, they help to delineate individual characters, from Tortoise, who takes his house with him wherever he goes, to legendary Bouezeremeze, a figure so tall that Ozidi has to seek his face in the sky at their terrible encounter.

Another device serving to underline individual traits in this great gallery of characters is colour. Dress shades and make-up are therefore chosen and worn with particular care. The story-teller, because he represents the hero beloved by everybody, appears always in white, denoting purity and innocence. In contrast, intractable roles demand blue and indigo, and really sinister ones charcoal. This is a pattern noticeable in the use of white Benin chalk as against common charcoal. The application of either pigment about the eye suggests the kind of vision, baleful or innocent, that a role requires of a player.

Once characteristics like these are observed, actors are left alone to appear their best or fiercest in their respective parts, although within the general design laid down by tradition. The great warrior, for example, sports eagle plumes, amulets, magic bangles, girdles, and kilt as part of his battle outfit, while the seer wears among other chilling effects a scarlet skull cap, decked with parrot feathers, flaunting at the same time a fan embossed with beaded charms and legends.

Three related devices peculiar with Ijo dramatic and narrative presentation are those of the "kile," the ululation, and what may be termed the story reminder. The "kile" is praise greeting for men, village, and clan. Essentially a panegyric, it consists of a roll-call of appellations that are prize attributes of the claimant. When directed on the master-drum at an individual, the device demands a manly dialogue between the person so singled out and the master-drummer. On the other hand, the "kile" given to town and clan may swell into a robust rhapsody, with all the men answering in one voice as a leader-linguist, versed in the titles and deeds of his people, intones their common praise. Taken with the stampede dance that goes with this kind, the "kile" easily becomes an impressive, aggressive gesture.

The ululation is an imitative yell emitted at appropriate points in the performance. It is no more than the traditional cheer of "iye" repeated several times over, usually by women and accompanied with hand-claps. An alternative cry of cheer, more intense and piercing, is that reserved for times of masquerade and emergency. As if to justify the demand for absolute attention, the ululating spectator may spell aloud her reasons, namely, her pride and joy in sharing with some brilliant performer special ties, like those between father and daughter, husband and wife, brother and sister, on account of which general delight becomes a personal one. It is this total identity of spectator with actor that moves many to dance from time to time straight into the arena of action, presenting gifts of money and perfume to favourites.

The "story reminder" is self-explanatory. Antiphonal in form, it carries the story forward all the way to its end. It keeps in constant view the immediate aim of the gathering—to see a good presentation, and to revel in the high spirits of the adventure transmitted. Occasionally, the form is extended to include a citation of probable difficulties and the prompt refutation of these. "Are you strong? If you see, will you act? Are there men in Ijo?" often comes the challenge. In each case, the response, of course, is an emphatic "yes."

All these are devices of cheer with the common effect of the interpolated exclamation. Thrown spontaneously into the main line of the story, each achieves a measure of punctuation, allowing the narrator time to introduce transitions between scenes and situations.

Culture and Identity

They also act as memory aids, for this is one production where details wrongly stated and staged are instantly cried down. When well injected, all three are dramatic practices that heighten suspense by holding up the narrative flow to build up dramatic tension. Needless to say, they also keep awake anyone dozing in the wings.

THE LANGUAGE AND THE POETRY

Because the Ijo of Tarakiri Clan own the saga of Ozidi, their dialect can be regarded as the original one for the saga. It is spoken at Sampo inside Bomadi Creek, Bulou-Orua up the Sagbama Creek, and in the settlements of Toro-Orua, Angalabiri and Ebedebri on the River Forcados, the distributary providing the main line of commerce and traffic up and down the Niger in the western half of its delta. The Tarakiri dialect is not only mutually intelligible with others geographically adjacent to it, for example, the twin Kabo-Kunbowei Clans to the north of it and Mein Clan that lies to the south, but it also is with a majority of the twenty-five odd dialects that constitute the language of the Ijo, an ancient water people inhabiting the coastal Niger Delta area of Nigeria—from Okitipupa division in Ondo State to near Calabar in the Cross River State. Most narrators of the epic-drama, if from outside the clan, aspire to this dialect, prefacing their performance with apologies. Two reasons may account for this: respect for the original place where the epic came to life before spreading out and becoming the property of all the clans of Ijo, and secondly, reverence for the great god of the clan with which the piece has come to have close connections.

Ijo, a language spoken by a people said to be about the fifth largest in the Nigerian federation, has still to be studied in all its complete structure, its system of grammar usage and syntax. The nearest attempt at this is that by Dr Kay Williamson in her study of Kolo-kuma, a dialect placed about the centre of the area and lying in the Rivers State, but this is only a beginning. Using this as a paradigm, she makes a number of points about the language in general.[6]

Ijo is unique among West African languages in having a complex tonal system, not complex for having a three-to-five-tone system, but complex in that its tone system subordinates word tones to larger tone patterns so that syntax determines word and tone groups. This, Dr Williamson says on the authority of Professor H. A. Gleason, "marks a language, which is, historically, changing from a tonal to a pitch-accent or purely intonational system." Secondly, the language possesses a few of what may be called inflectional forms, having lost the noun-class system common among neighbouring languages, except for relics now functioning as "meaningless vowel suffixes." On the other hand, "it has a system of definite articles suffixed to the noun, apparently developed from demonstratives." One rare quality of Ijo is its possession of "separate feminine pronoun, demonstrative and definite articles; some dialects . . . also have a neuter." Ijo has in addition a word-order in which "modifiers consistently precede heads and the object precedes the verb, and there is present in the language the feature of passive voice."

But "the most interesting syntactic feature" in Ijo, according to Dr Williamson, "is the verb phrase which may contain a series of verb roots," and it is the one aspect which marks the rules of the language as "alien" from English. From this she makes a number of observations which echo earlier ones made of the Fōn language by the Herskovits.[7]

First is the use of the verb in a multiple string to describe segments of what in English is conceived of as a single act. For example, the construction "ina agbodo minimo bo" occur[s] frequently in the hero's battle song. Literally, this means in deep archaic Ijọ "my sword pull-out-and-bring-prey-for me to wipe out." Or take the more colloquial form "ina agbọdọ kọn bo" which word for word means "my-sword-bring-come." In English the concept really is of a single act—that of fetching of a sword.[8]

A second verbal feature is what in Fōn the Herskovits described as the flow of the narrative through "a sentence structure that is dominated by an imagery of motion" expressed by the verb "where in English verbs express rest at a place." Here the verbs "express motion towards or away from" with an imagery that raises questions of degree of empathy aroused by such statements of condition as "hunger is killing me" for "I am hungry" or "fear catches me" for "I am afraid."[9] With Fōn so it is with the Ijọ expressions "Mọn Ozidi kẹrẹ dẹ," or "Mọn Ozidi baa mẹnẹ" and "Ozidi Ọfẹ kẹrẹ mẹnẹ ya."

The third verbal device occurs when verbs of motion take qualifying onomatopoeic words to meet descriptive needs with economy as well as nuanced elaboration, the modifying imagery taking on the form of a repetitive sense-sound figure.[10] The obvious example in *The Ozidi Saga* is the cauldron-and-mortar song thematic of Ozidi's raging bowels and in which all the strange creatures that go into making this master magic charm return to life with a vengeance. Chief of these are an eagle-hornbill, a male monkey, and a crested lizard. Here is that "vivid representation of an idea in sound" which Dr Williamson says C. M. Doke also found in Bantu. It is the use of "a word often onomatopoeic which describes a predicate, qualificative or adverb in respect to manner, colour, sound, smell, action, state or intensity."[11]

Similar again to another stylistic device found in Fōn[12] narrative is the use of allusion and suggestion to place time or setting, to hint at a state of being, and to delineate by one stroke of the brush, as it were, a whole backdrop, making description superfluous. Thus the constant references like "in times before our clan settled this stream," and to well-known places and states like "the big market-place," "the big market-day for the living and the dead," "the evil grove," and "the passage to the town of the dead." Conversely, there is recourse among narrators, especially ones resident in cities outside the tribe, to a frame of reference in which, like Amos Tutuola, mythical personages and objects are seen in contemporary technological terms. The flight of a witch is likened to an aeroplane, a tall champion is compared to an electric pole, and time is measured out by aid of clocks and weeks.

These linguistic features and a number of other forms, like the lyric song, the "kile" or praise greeting for person or group, the lament, the interpolated exclamation, and various gradations of dialogue, combine to weave that rich texture of language for which the epic drama is so famous. Otherwise *The Ozidi Saga* is straight prose. It shows no definite repetitive pattern of rhythm that can be called a system of metre nor any accumulation of parallel statements; the more proverbial the weightier.

Vocalic clusters and coincidences occur quite often in the songs and laments proliferating the Ozidi story, a not unusual incidence for a text in a language with so many vowel sounds. There remains however the double difficulty of ascertaining whether these are terminal within a cadence system as with rhymes in a given metre, and whether in fact there obtains the convention of a line-by-line structure to the poetry of these lyrics and laments.

Naturally, the work relies a lot on epic images. Hyperbole, metaphor, and simile serve to frame and throw into magnificent reliefs the legendary figures that bestride the story and its setting. The hero has an abnormal birth; is invested with magic charms that turn his bowels, the Ijọ seat of rage, literally into a mortar and seven pots; and he wields a sword of seven prongs and of a steel so true that at its trial in the forge, after two earlier ones had snapped in the air and struck to death sons of Ofe and Azezabife at play miles away, the blade spiralled about his forearm as a python does the palm tree. His grandmother Oreame, the great witch, is seen in terms of a vampire bat, a gadfly, mediums which enable the old woman to fly like an aeroplane, with wings, sound and all, to fetch for Ozidi all the right formulas for success. Indeed, on one critical occasion, she ascends beyond rainbow and sun to ask intervention of Oyin Herself, the Supreme God.

The same images of size, great distance, and fantastic physical attributes go to delineate other principal characters in the story. Ozidi's adversaries are in fact painted over-size to underline the improbable nature of the task the young avenging son had of it despatching each champion on the list.

But there are also moments of human failing and tenderness in the general run of battle and blood. Ozidi himself is taken by surprise at one point, trussed up, and carried home by Ebeya, his feet dragging on the ground like the hind legs and tail of a goat being led to sacrifice. Full of pathos too is the scene where the sister of Tebesonoma, newly delivered of an only child she has waited all her life to bear, holds the crying baby to her breast, then lays herself down on her back for the deranged Ozidi to mow through like a plantain tree and its sucker fallen in a storm.

While action at such stages is described as well as demonstrated, it is the responsibility of the story-teller to conjure up by word the beauty and pity pregnant in the situation. But also ready to hand is a repertoire of songs to raise and release tension. Most of the songs in the drama follow a call and response pattern, allowing for a solo voice to state the subject-matter after which there is a confirmation of the situation by the entire group taking the strain up in repeat formation. Several of the songs defy translation, but in their original Ijo, as will be seen later, they possess a directness of flow and style that through a reliance on repetition makes them beautiful lyrics.

Closely connected with the song is what may rightly be termed the lament. Apart from the ululation which is stylized wailing using imitative sound, the lament is the regular manner of expressing loss of life and honour among Ijo people. The prototype can be said to consist of a repeated call on the name of the deceased, a catalogue of his talents and natural gifts, usually exaggerated, and the declaration by the mourner of personal helplessness in a world of enemies happy now the situation is so. Recitative in delivery, the lament is reserved for moments when the beloved is most missed. Used by a bereaved for a beloved dead, before cocks begin crowing in the morning, it carries a shudder right through the Ijo village asleep by some stream. In the Ozidi drama, with all its flow of carnage and vendetta, the lament therefore is a commonplace. Probably the most poignant occasion of its use is when the newly widowed Orea cradles the head of her husband on her lap and beats the flies off it while Temugedege, the one man in the house, flees the scene.

An aspect of language perhaps odd in a traditional Ijo piece like the Ozidi epic is the occurrence of foreign words in the text. The incidence is at four levels: first, the use of English words like aeroplane, railway, electric pole, clock, and field for descriptive purposes, usually by way of comparison, simile, and metaphor. Apparently, where these filled a genuine gap of expression in the narration and production of the saga, no objection was raised by members of the participating audience. As a matter of fact, such anachronisms often provided a fresh source of laughter as did the second kind. This was Okabou's use of local places at Ibadan, names like Mokola and Dugbe Markets, to serve as points of reference in relation to the spot of performance so that distances in the story assumed concrete life and dimension. But the use of English terms like "time" and "meeting" for concepts already named in the language was a practice always frowned upon, one for which the narrator never failed to receive tutoring. Fortunately, this was always taken in the co-operative spirit of the enterprise. The third kind of foreign words appears in some of the magic formulas and preparations with which characters arm themselves and over-awe their opponents. These seem mainly of Ibo origin. Their power of evocation lies in the fact that they are exotic, and to the non-Ibo speaking audience, esoteric. The same can be said for the last type. This is the use of languages like Edo, Isoko, [and] Urhobo for lyrics of songs. The theme song of <u>Ofe</u> the Short, chief of the conspirators against the house of Ozidi, is a famous example. It conveys no precise meaning, yet its effect is electric upon an Ijọ crowd.

THE MUSIC, MIME, AND DANCE PROPERTIES

A living example of the world's oral stock of heroic stories that are drama at the same time, *The Ozidi Saga* assumes its double literary character as much by beauty of words as by the fullness of music and movement arising directly from its action. These properties, distinct and yet interdependent, make the epic of Ozidi one perfect union of drama, dance, and music at every stage of its development.

Unfortunately, the music of *The Ozidi Saga,* like most traditional African music today, is still to be faithfully caught by the recording machine. So far, no expert in the field has found it easy to notate and score what has been collected on tape. Problems of scale differences apart, songs in the saga carry such a high pitch, especially for male voices, and drummers move their hands at such speed and intricate combination that the human eye and that of the camera barely catch them in motion.

Songs and incantations, accompanied by an orchestra, constitute the score of the saga. A tune is called by a leader, this is taken up by members of the band of male dancers forming a close chorus for the protagonist-story-teller, and this chorus in turn is supported by a fluid group of hand-clapping women active in the wings. Any member of the audience embracing the entire community may also join in when so moved. This call-and-response pattern is noticeable in all the songs sung in the seven days of performance.

Verses to these songs usually are simple lyrics, like this alarm one sung by a defenceless woman about to be slain by Ozidi:

> Death that does not touch God
> It is has come to kill me
> Death that does not touch God
> It is has come to kill me
> Ozidi the strong man
> It is has come to kill me.

This English rendering is nothing like the original for lyric beauty. A sure sense of state-ment and image, often relying only on indirection and repetition, seems to be the secret formula. Sung by an innocent woman just delivered of a child and who must die at the hand of Ozidi, driven mad on the one hand by her brother T<u>e</u>bes<u>onoma</u> and on the other by the implacable <u>Oreame</u>, the effect of both music and word upon actors and audience is a swift gasp of pity and horror, finding expression in the instant participation of all in the singing and dancing. The muse, as it were, at such points of the epic play releases the poet to merge with his audience all now subsumed in the act of creation.

As has been observed of traditional songs in many places, the relationship existing between melody and verse in these songs is to a large extent reciprocal.[13] Sometimes, the words serve the melodic lines of the tunes, and at other times melody bends to the spoken line. But on several occasions, as in the song above, melody and verse become so evenly matched that they enjoy an equal partnership.

Then there is the rhythmic pattern at play in every dance, whether secular or sacred. This also conditions melody and verbal lines with rhythmic contours helping to mould each verse for its special purpose and place in the epic drama. Such dance patterns range from the deliberate pace of the processional song of sacrifice at the stream to the brisk trot of the recession, and from the reeling measure of a warrior drunk with blood to the flutter and rush of a witch taking off on her wings. Some steps are more cut out for the young while others are of a style more suited to the old and titled. In other words, the melodic form is generally governed by the master-rhythm of its type, just as the verse may obey the melodic and rhythmic requirements of the music to which it is set. Within this fall the thrown-in phrase, the use of partially or wholly repeated sonorous words as well as the use of elisions and glides, not infrequent variations in these songs.

But even more significant is the modulation noticeable at the close of each song. Suddenly, the pace quickens at the end, the last lines of the verse, taken in part between leader and chorus, displacing the main body of the verse. For instance, in the song above, instead of solo and chorus singing in alternation the whole verse, one would now sing the penultimate line and the other the last line.

Songs in *The Ozidi Saga* are of several kinds, depending on the functions they serve in the general line of drama and narrative. Every mood, every situation, and every character carries a leitmotif, an identifying tune indicative of its quality and significance. Thus there are songs of worship, songs of war, songs of joy and life as well as songs of sorrow and death, of magic and witchcraft, and there are numbers that announce the champion and the coward, the mourner and the carefree. In the same way, some simply provide points for rest while others build up tension. Ozidi the hero executes his enemies to the chant of his shrine and charms, and his grandmother O̱reame flies to her own peculiar strain. Even Temugedege has his own song. Indeed it may well be said of this work as it has been of Oriental classical drama that all sounds are sung and that no movement is expressed without dancing.

Dance in the drama of Ozidi is traditional, having nothing of the temporary and acculturative qualities that give away movements and styles infiltrating in from outside by the season among the young. First, there are the procession and recession to and from the stream for the sacrifice of the seven virgins, serving as prelude to each day's performance. The procession is a simple stylized walk, slow and solemn in descending to the water's edge. In contrast, the recession is almost a scramble up the cliff of the beach as if the group were impatient to get to the square to begin the act.

Next comes the ogele, a dance with elements of the processional. Starting out in a two-row formation with a nucleus of leading dancers, it can attract in no time almost the whole community as it moves from one end of town to the other along the stream. It is a rousing dance, beginning from behind the scenes, so to speak, and summoning all true sons and daughters of the land to the public square where all festivals and ritual ceremonies of the land are staged. The ogele is therefore a highly communal dance calling everybody to occasions as different as wrestling, war, masquerade, and in the days of the politicians after independence even to election campaign meetings.

Probably the most intricate of all the dances in *The Ozidi Saga* is the *agene* or *kene-kene-koro* which, literally translated, means "one-one-you-may-drop." This directive as to leg movement is not as simple as it sounds; it is in fact deceptive. But done by Ijo men and women, their bodies bent fully forward from the waist, their arms held out in front and bent at the elbows, *agene* is an intricate, floating dance in which the feet seem never to touch the ground at any one given moment.

Finally, there are the imitative and highly stylized dances representing specific actions. The *aro* dance, for example, depicts the progress of a war-canoe like that used by the Smallpox King to invest Ozidi. A good number of others represent attack and defence motions of battles recurrent in the saga. The take-off of witches is simulated by flying movements, and the hand-over-head dance, *avinvin se*, is symbolic of great grief as when Ozidi is struck down by deadly disease.

Side by side with all this is the unfailing use of face expression, limb movement, and general gestures to mime segments of the action. The ambush and bludgeoning to death of the older Ozidi, though done to pantomime and grunts, comes across in all its fierceness and horror—and it is only one of several instances where movement of muscles alone arouses just the right degree of meaning.

A great amount of improvisation and personal resourcefulness goes into this pantomime but many of the motions and gestures, as mentioned earlier with costume and colour, spring from the common stock of expressions that the community has drawn upon for generations. The widowed Orea, beating flies off her mutilated husband, the boy-hero, playing games of tops and target-shooting with agemates who taunt him for not knowing his father, the magician-seer Bouakarakarabiri conjuring up his master charm of mortar-and-cauldrons for the hero, and the Awka blacksmith, forging a sword for the hero in a confused forge—each of these characters employs motions and gestures that express for the audience definite moods and emotions.

Traditional Ijo dance, as seen in the story of Ozidi, apparently has no beginning, no middle, no end within a time structure. The dancer, submerged in the stream of everyday chores, rises spontaneously to the beat of the drum, to the sound of the song, and the dance flows on for as long as there is the tidal wave of drum and song sweeping through the town. It is the special quality of such experience that in its seeming monotony and fixity a dancer may in fact attain to a new fluidity of movement, achieving freedom of spirit from this material world. This surely is transfiguration, whether pejoratively termed "a state of possession" or "auto-intoxication" by those outside such an area of experience. Among actors of the Ozidi drama, possession is a regular phenomenon calling for immediate intervention from anxious colleagues and spectators.

One cannot speak of the music, mime, and dance forming an integral part of the drama of Ozidi without mentioning, however briefly here, the orchestra out of which it all flows. The central piece to this is the master-drum *ozi*. In support are three side drums, the *okoin*, the *kainga*, and the *ekere*. There are extras, for example, the horn. The *ozi*, hollowed out of a huge stem to a blind end, stands about three feet from the ground. Sitting at a level with the instrument, the master-drummer plays at it with a stick in either hand. To gain speech intonation and stress, he regulates the drum with his heel, sometimes with his fist. In this way, as Professor Kwabena Nketia says of the master-drummer in Akan,[14] he can send out coded signals to the initiated, call forth the dance for all members of the community, and engage in manly dialogue with any male actor or spectator that catches his eye and imagination. Whether the occasion is one for wrestling, for war, for burial, for worship, or for entertainment as in the enacting of the Ozidi sequence, this is the moment of recognition for personal excellence in an otherwise aggregate state of being.

THE FESTIVAL AND RELIGIOUS ASPECTS

Unlike most Ijọ festivals and religious occasions, *The Ozidi Saga* observes no distinctions of age, sex, season, and place. In this connection, the *owu* masquerade, probably the most popular medium of entertainment that the Ijọ possess as a people, provides a good contrast. It is strictly a dance and festival put on by men. This gives it from the start its occult character, although it is staged in the open to amuse members of the public. Among men, there are again sharp denominations of groups along age lines, stretching in a pyramid formation from youths to elders at intervals of about six years. Thus in an Ijọ village, there may be as many as ten separate sets of masquerades, each very proud and secretive about its own prize collection of masks. In the dry season, particularly during the August break, any of these groups, consisting of men of more or less the same period of birth, may stage a performance in the open. Its measure of success in the three days normal for production could be considered in direct proportion to the degree of participation aroused among members of the general public, particularly among women of its corresponding age-group.

But the production of the Ozidi drama observes none of these sanctions. It begins each day with a round up of seven virgin girls, as special sacrificial offerings are gathered at the compound of the story-teller-protagonist. This sets at once the religious tone of the drama and story. After worshipping before his household and personal gods, the story-teller-protagonist, supported by the Amananaowei, that is, the town-owner, and other leading citizens, leads a solemn song-procession of the seven virgins to the stream washing the feet of every Ijọ village. There sacrifice is offered in homage to spirits of the water without whose help the enterprise on land cannot prosper. It is well to note here that the prayer is not for art alone but also for life so that the people may have their own fair share of women, children, and money apparently flowing to enrich life elsewhere and without which there can be no real enjoyment of art anywhere. The worship over, the party returns in a recession dance to the square at a brisk pace of song and dance.

Next comes the ogele dance, the men leading the women, with many more behind reinforcing the beat of song and drum by clap of hands. Soon the dance gathers force, attracting into its wake spectators and actors alike all the way to the marketplace. Here it modulates into *agene* as the group resolves into a two-tier stand of chorus-dancers and voices to sing the seven prelude songs thematic of the action each day.

Meanwhile, spectators form on three sides of the square, keeping clear of the river-side where the stream, the forest-bank beyond, and the vast rolling skies farther on still, combine to drop the one permanent back-cloth of the production. Forming the pit rows are the children all huddled on the ground, and behind them are seated their parents and other adults, many on their own chairs and stools specially brought in for the occasion. On the outskirts, astride canoes carving on the shore, aloft mango and coconut trees, and perched on roof-tops, still building, scramble the young and agile to gain the best view possible. The occasion definitely is one for general gaiety and bustle, and it brings together in a holiday spirit men and women, relatives and friends, that for a great part of the year are in separate places seeking a living.

Festival and entertainment, *The Ozidi Saga* would not be the great drama that it is if it was not also an act of worship. It begins with a sacrificial procession and recession every day, ceremonies which in themselves are religious. The story-teller in his white garb of purity, the seven girls in their virginal innocence, the seven pots of offerings[15] they bring the spirits of the stream, and the act of sacrifice itself are all spiritual rites carried out according to strict custom and belief.

In the epic proper, the worthiness and sanctity of the hero's mission clearly [are] self-evident in that he has to find ultimate rest for his father murdered by treacherous colleagues. To recapitulate a little, such a violent unhappy death, the Ijo believe, deprives a dead man of the privilege of joining his ancestors. If he has heirs with any sense of honour, these certainly will ask the community for an inquest which usually takes the form of warlike preparations, followed by restitution and rites of purification. Only when these motions have been gone through, an expensive process, can the dead be deemed properly buried.

This is Ozidi's set mission, to call home his father from the evil grove where the miserable of his kind are dumped without ceremony after death. In fulfilling it, he receives, as we have seen, assistance and guidance not only from his grandmother who has supernatural powers but also from a variety of deities and beings peopling the Ijo cosmos. The *dueotu* who are ancestors watchful underground, the *oru* who are mer-people in the rivers and sea around, the *bou-osu-owei* breed who are spirits of the forests, and Oyin or Tamara, Mother and Moulder of All, are divinities affecting in their several ways the fortunes and fate of Ozidi.

Then there are the preternatural forces appearing as personal gods and charms. Ozidi has his own household gods to which he reports in his shrine before and after each of his terrible battles. So do all his enemies. The one champion who eventually worsts the hero is Smallpox, a divine manifestation, taken for the angry visitation made by Tamara Herself to punish Ozidi for his transgressions.

The extraordinary filial bond so evident between Ozidi and Oreame also carries spiritual overtones. It is no simple mother-fixation explainable in terms of Oedipus complex. Rather the apparent female domination of Ozidi by his grandmother stems from the Ijo family system which inclines to the matrilineal. A man's fate or "final womb" is his mother's ancestral home. In the large polygamous family run by every successful man, it is the mother who is for all practical purposes a child's mainstay.

Of interest too is the fact that the Ijo mother, known as *kie-ere*, retains the right of taking her children home with her should the marriage break up. This is because she is co-equal with her man as is each of her children in a legal relationship well summed up by the local saying of *tebe-tebe*, meaning "head to head." Consequently, neither mother nor child can be sacrificed or sold into slavery. By the same token, no child by such a mother can become king in several clans of Western Ijo, although he may serve as priest. Both roles of king and bondsman are ones reserved for offspring of women brought in from outside the tribe at great cost and as absolute possessions known as *bra-ere*, that is, "hand-maids." Foreign mother and child can be disposed of and nobody need raise a finger.

This special status of the Ijo mother, which Oreame invokes and exercises over Ozidi, may also be said to derive directly from the idea of divinity in the Ijo hierarchy. As already

Culture and Identity

stated, the concept is a female one: "Oyin," "Our Mother" or Tamara, "She Who Creates" is the one source of life.

The various taboos that characters observe for their own safety and success are religious symbols. Ozidi is forbidden the knowledge of woman until the completion of his sacred trust and task. Odogu, his deadly double whose wife tempts him, may not see a new-born child. Others are forbidden the sight of new-laid eggs, unglazed pots, fresh fish; and not one of them may come in touch with a woman "who has passed outside," that is, has her monthly menstrual period. According to Ijọ convention and custom, she must live well away from the house as she is considered to be in an unclean state.

Here perhaps enters the element of the unpredictable, however fixed and predestined the order of things might seem at first. For characters, though aided by oracles and gods and other supernatural forces, remain complete agents of themselves. Either they must have personal resourcefulness to discover the secret chink in their opponent's armour or else succumb to greater cunning and courage. It is in the light of this that the repeated acts of magic, like exorcism, featuring so prominently in the Ozidi story, become an organic part of its ritual.

Finally, the state of possession which we said actors regularly run into the course of enacting *The Ozidi Saga* surely is religious fervour. It is a condition actually anticipated with awe and sympathy. The story-teller, for instance, has an attendant specially set aside, not only to play slave to his protagonist in the drama and story, but also to serve as a bodyguard, following his every step to prevent him breaking loose suddenly and thereby doing himself harm in that climacteric stage when, as the Ijọ put it, "things enter" the man. For extra measure, during the sacrifice at the stream, a strong leash of cloth is tied around the waist of the protagonist, as with a chief masquerade, for strong alert men to hold so that the performer is not snatched away by the evil spirits, believed present among the crowd of spectators and patrons.

At the head of these patrons is the great god of the Tarakiri people in Western Ijọ, represented in person at the performance by his wife-priestess. Since tradition links the story and drama of Ozidi directly to the deity, it is at his feet that its last lines and rites are performed well away from public view.

NOTES

1. Clan, that is, *ibe* in Ijọ, is a cluster of settlements of people, speaking the same dialect, claiming a common ancestor, and worshipping one central god apart from the Almighty God who is Mother of all creation, usually served by a high priest known as Perẹ and who in some cases combines the functions of a king.

2. Seven is a magic number in Ijọ; three incidentally, is male and four female. Each of the seven nights of the saga could be taken as the equivalent of a book in the European epic.

3. He is also known as Odogu the Ugly.

4. Melville J. & Frances S. Herskovits, *Dahomean Narrative*, Northwestern University Press, Evanston, 1958.

5. *ibid.*, p. 74.

6. Kay Williamson, *A Grammar of the Kolokuma Dialect of Ijọ*, Cambridge University Press, London, in association with the West African Languages Survey and the Institute of African Studies, University of Ibadan, Ibadan, 1965, pp. 6–8.

7. *ibid.*

8. Herskovits & Herskovits, *op. cit.*, pp. 50–51.

9. *ibid.*

10. *ibid.*

11. Kay Williamson, *op. cit.*, p. 8.

12. Herskovits & Herskovits, *op. cit.*, p. 53, pp. 70–72.

13. *ibid.*, pp. 67–70.

14. J. H. Kwabena Nketia, *African Music in Ghana*, Longman, London, 1962, and "The Poetry of Akan Drums," *Black Orpheus*, Vol. 2, No. 2, Lagos, June–September 1968, pp. 27–35.

15. These consist of soft drinks, sweets, and biscuits, foreign items all right, but they serve as a special recipe to placate and cool down the fiery nature of gods and heroes in the epic drama.

Mazisi Kunene

(b. 1930, South Africa)

The Rise of Shaka

Mawewe, who was now king by default,
Panicked as the numbers of Dingiswayo's followers swelled.
He fled to safer regions but was killed by Dingiswayo's agents.
Dingiswayo quickly mobilised the Mthethwa armies
And infused in them the old spirit of heroes and heroines.
With this courage they ventured to far-distant lands,
Entering in triumph many regions of Nguniland.
He vowed: 'I shall break the necks of the troublesome bulls.'
The Mthethwa kingdom became the haven of many harassed nations.
From many regions people sang of Dingiswayo's greatness.
'Great lord of lords, we come for shelter.
Our lands are infested with maurading bandits and heartless rulers.'
There were kings without mercy, like Phungashe, like Zwide;
Who created commotion and fear in all parts of Nguniland.
But Dingiswayo welcomed and embraced the fugitives.
He gave them a place of safety.
The Mthethwa empire was known as the region of tranquillity.
Nation after nation applauded his reign.
Even those lurking in the outposts of Delagoe Bay
Sent to him their representatives of trade.
Royal villages emerged in every part of the land;
Nations and peoples crowded his court with tributes of gifts and praise.

Shaka found a place to rest his mind.
His new home was filled with endless laughter.
Summer sprouts its new leaves from the buds of winter,
The growing lion learns to fight from its parent.
Here Shaka lived with many young men of his own age.
Raising his tall frame from the ground, he would say:
'Here I can rest. I feel at last a man among men.
No one here questions anyone's origins.'

Shaka and General Bhuza of his youth's brigade often debated.
It was in this brigade of iziChwe that Shaka planted his thought

He often argued: 'Speed determines the outcome of battle.
A great army strikes like lightning and devastates like a thunderbolt.'
In his regiment were many famous heroes.
Amongst them was the much-praised Mgobhozi-of-the-Mountain.
With him and Nqoboka, Shaka shared a close friendship.
Enemy armies fled in terror from them.
For these episodes Shaka was named 'The Unbeatable One'.
Of him they said: 'Only speed in flight can save a man.
Let such a man carry his hands on his head like a woman.'
Shaka spoke once to Bhuza: 'My lord, great general,
Something haunts my mind and troubles my sleep.
We launch our campaigns in all parts of the land.
Our skill lies only in flinging the long-stemmed spear.'
Then such were the wars of our forefathers:
Whenever an army exhausted its supplies
Then such were the wars of our Forefathers:
Whenever an army exhausted its supplies
Then members would flee to join their crowd of spectators.
Each side would sing and dance to outdo the other.
Sometimes the two armies would send to the arena their bravest men.
It was on one such occasion a Mthethwa general ordered:
'Let the bravest in your army face our bravest man.'
His candidate was a fierce-looking man with muscles of iron.
Many feared him, trusting only to their feet.
No sooner had the general spoken than he began to move,
Flexing his muscles and bending his legs like a gigantic tree.
He groaned like a bull that had recently been stung by wasps.
From the opposing side came the Dweller-of-the-Round-Mountains.
The clash of weapons, the writhing of muscles,
The swivelling movement of arms,
The thundering of feet, the challenging ram,
The clash of heads like two bounding boulders—
The spectators stood entranced by this spectacle.
The wild cry of 'Surrender! The eagle!'; the tears of the rabbit;
Crestfallen and defeated they turned back, singing in discord.
It was such half-hearted battles that incensed Shaka.
He uttered doctrines never heard in Mthethwaland before.
'How many times have we gone to battle and returned without victory?
We conquer and yet come back like the vanquished.
The defeated re-emerge, again and again. They launch new wars.
Like the menace of weeds in a fertile field they are.
The weapons we carry are long spears of fragile wood.
Each one who can carve carves his own weapon.
Many return empty-handed, having exhausted their supplies of iron.
Yet victory must be final.
The enemy must be chased and trapped in his own home.
Then he shall not raise his head again.'
As he said these words many listened silently,

Doubting the wisdom of these new ideas
And claiming this strategy was an open gate to bloodshed.
Was it not true, they asked, the king's fame lay in his kindliness?
Was it not this that won him many hearts?
Surely, they reasoned, war is for subjugation, not destruction?
Such outrageous assaults against a victim
Might build allies who might rally to his support,
Eager to stem the tide of bitterness
And vowing the destroyer should himself be destroyed.
As generals and regiments argued, puzzled by these ideas,
Shaka stood up and picked a long spear from General Bhuza's feet.
He broke it in pieces like a light reed and said:
'How can anyone fight with this thin-marrowed piece of wood?
How can such feeble twigs support empires and kingdoms?'
Some began to see his persuasive logic.
He continued: 'I ask of you, great general,
Give me your consent to mould my own weapons,
To shape my shield with which to parry my enemies.
When I have completed these tasks
Grant that I fight alone, a body of men.
Let them throw their spears at me at will.'
From every side came applause of this imagined battle.
Mgobhozi, who trusted in him, stood up and said:
'Brother of the battlefield, we shall be together in that battle.'

When Shaka was granted this wish
He set out to the Mbonambi clans, the makers of intricate iron.
He told the amazed listeners his own ideas:
'I want a spear made short and of the toughest wood.
Even as I stab the trunk of a tree, let it remain firm.
I shall pay for such a spear with my choicest beasts.'
As he spoke he pointed to his cattle in the cattle-fold.
Their flesh trembled with fatness.
The Mbonambi experts consented but derided these ideas,
Knowing how many believed victory comes from shape of weapons.
On the second day the spear-maker summoned him:
'Young man of Zululand, your weapon is done,
But one question obsesses me:
How will you use such a spear for missile-battles?'
Shaka smiled and only said:
'Father, I shall not throw my precious spear.
I shall come close to the man and hug him with my weapons.'
The old man shook his head, puzzled at these ideas.
He said: 'Take your gift of beasts.
Give me only from those of your future triumphs.
It seems I shall die at the beginning of an era.
I give you my blessing, child of Nguniland.
Let it be your fate to conquer.

The Rise of Shaka

But never forget those who prophesied your greatness.'
Shaka departed, his mind in turmoil,
Sensing a generous blessing of the Forefathers.
He ran his hand over his weapon,
Caressing the shaft and its blade with his long fingers.
Often he laughed loud as though seized by some madness.

As he reached his agemates of the iziChwe regiment
A young fighter ran forward, declaiming his poems.
It was as though he sensed the fires of war in him.
Shaka said, restraining him:
'I am grateful to you for these words, Sontongela.'
Examining his spear, testing its thrust,
And shaking it in all directions,
Shaka commented: 'From this weapon shall come a plan
That shall be parent to all my strategies.
With my black shield I shall cover and hook the enemies,
Taking them with my shadow into their night.
By my sister, I swear, I shall finish them!'
They looked at each other, still confused at these words.
He called aside Nqoboka and demonstrated on him his device.
He hooked him and swivelled him around with his shield.
Then he laughed, as if he had discovered a secret.
He said: 'Tomorrow I need someone who can run,
Who, with an antelope's speed can cross the whole wide field.
Should he outrun me he shall take all my cattle.'
They accepted this, thinking it only a young man's frivolous joke.
Next day at dawn the fleet-footed young men stood boasting,
Waiting at the end of a long stretch of land.
Then, suddenly, like two bodies of the wind rushing from the south,
Like two antelopes startled by a pack of howling dogs,
Dust rose from their feet, spinning high like wings of clouds.
Shaka speeded past a clump of dense foliage,
His feet thundering like a stampede of giraffes,
Until in one loud triumphal cry he reached the regimental grounds.
It was then they realized he had discarded his impeding sandals.
He threw himself on the ground,
Laughing triumphantly until his laughter made others laugh.
It was as if his very lungs flapped against his ribs.
He laughed until tears rolled down his face.
Catching his breath, he said:
'I held the tail of the whirlwinds!
All hail, children of the king! Great voice of the Ancestral Spirits!
I hold the hair of the wind! I hold the men!
The roots are torn out of the high mountain!'
Many who listened were baffled by these garbled words
But he kept their secret and their truth in his heart.

Culture and Identity

Addressing his regimental assembly
He said things that puzzled even the masters of war strategy:
'I ask you to listen to me carefully:
I have discovered an unbeatable plan against our enemies.
I repeat, the essence of success in war is speed.
Speed is of the mind and all intricacies of wars.
Speed is of those who meticulously examine the war's arena,
Who combine their wisdom with the wisdom of the wiser men.
Through this knowledge the enemy is surrounded.
Speed is of the feet not encumbered by sandals.
Speed is embedded in the shape of my spear.
By this our heroes shall reap the enemy in close combat.
As the enemy dissipates its power
And throws all its missiles,
We shall break through their lines,
Turning our clouds of shields into a forest of weapons.
We shall rip their naked chests at close quarters.
If we follow this strategy, no enemy shall defeat us,
For all wars are the same, following only laws of battle.'
As he spoke his eyes caught every face in the crowd,
As if from each word he hoped for an ecstatic applause;
Nor could he sit in one place.
His very intestines seemed tied into knots,
Many gestured as though to talk but only looked at each other.
Had Shaka not been the favourite-hero of iziChwe regiment
They might have summoned the doctors of war
To heal him of the fierce power that a man inherits from battle.
It was Bhuza, the great general of iziChwe, who spoke:
'Shaka, the mountains of the world seem to constantly call your name.
Each day you bring us ever-new ideas.
Perhaps it is not our age that shall inherit your wisdom
But a future generation which shall better penetrate your visions.
Even though some may see madness in your plans
I always discover in them a wisdom beyond our times.
Yet it would be more laudable if they came in limited amounts,
For people prefer to be persuaded slowly about their customs.'
Shaka leapt up and spoke angrily:
'General, I have always hated the shackles of custom.
For, after all, in human affairs there are no eternal laws;
Each generation makes a consensus of its own laws.
They do not bind forever those still to be born.
Those who feast on the grounds of others
Often are forced into gestures of friendship they do not desire.
But we are the generation that cannot be bypassed.
We shall not be blinded by gifts from feasts.
With our own fire we shall stand above the mountains, as the sun.'
Shaka was alarmed at the violence of his own voice.
He sat down, his face contorted with rage.

The Rise of Shaka

Someone near him nudged him with an elbow,
Trying to restrain him from this haughty dialogue.
But Shaka turned his eyes in fury and was about to speak
When he saw the general looking at him.
Shaka knew no one succeeds in a blind clash with leadership;
Nor does it win him credence to ignore the faith of others.
Bhuza said to him: 'I acclaim the penetrating truth of your words.
Your visions gallop ahead of our thoughts.
With the permission of the Assembly
I shall put these views before the king.'

Their gathering dispersed at once.
Shaka, still in a dark mood, set off in his own solitary direction.
He reached a lone spot where he often sat, meditating.
He walked a few paces till he could see a little hill.
Here he halted, guessing out passages and escape points of the hill.
At each route he posted imaginary troops.
Some he commanded to move around the hill;
Some he commanded to close the gap of the retreating troops,
So overcome with this victory, he sang a new song.
Thus was born the great war hymn of the Fasimba regiment.
He walked over the hill humming this song.
He saw new exits at the sheer sides of the hill
And knew then, despite the imagined victory,
Through an error of judgement many would have lost their lives.
Like this he continued fighting his battles of fantasy
Until at the late-day-cycle he walked home slowly,
Still engrossed in his thoughts.

Phungashe was the powerful king of the Buthelezi nation.
He made many a neighbouring nation live in constant fear.
Some fled from him to the sanctuary of towering mountains;
Some ran to the kindly and generous Dingiswayo.
One day Phungashe told his war-hungry regiments:
'I shall strike Dingiswayo, the stubborn, indomitable fool.
I shall make him flee, humiliating him among his followers.'
He boasted, believing that having crushed the monster's arms
He shall have broken its body.
Phungashe, the wily one, even boasted:
'We shall acquire the authority to rule the earth.
We shall reap freely of its harvests.
All its wealth shall be for our children.'
His army was infused with this crusading spirit.

From all distant hills emerged the fierce army of Phungashe.
The high cliffs resounded with slogans of war.
Battle songs echoed like the many voices of thunder.
Even distant kings, like Zwide, sensing the smell of iron, began to arm,

Culture and Identity

Though no threat was posed against them.
They hoped when the two giants had drained each other's strength
They would intervene to rule the world.
When Dingiswayo heard of Phungashe's impending attack
He roamed the royal grounds restlessly,
Knowing the terror Phungashe often brought with his army.
Dingiswayo had believed peace was settled at last,
Yet the earth trembled;
Conflagrations of war leapt into the sky.
Dingiswayo had believed peace was settled at last,
'Tell me again the strategy you spoke of yesterday.
Perhaps this way we may teach this upstart king a lesson.'
Yet it was only a day before
He had heaped contempt on these tactics,
Condemning them for their violence,
Denouncing the bloodthirstiness of their authors.
While other regiments sang, ready for battle,
iziChwe regiment talked and guffawed,
Elated now that the great king had authorized their plans.
Shaka moved restlessly amongst the crowds,
Making his regiment race till late at night.
Sometimes to emphasize his thoughts he would say:
'A great fighter imitates the movements of the wind.
A war is a dance, the other side of the feast.'
It was for this they followed the horns of the moon,
Surrounding imaginary enemies around the body of the hill.

When the two armies faced each other with blood-red eyes,
A tall young man of the belligerent Buthelezi nation lurched forward.
He danced, the proud one, raising the dust from the arena.
It was as if the wind itself was frightened of him.
Only the turbulent son of Nandi rushed forward.
He—'the fire whose fierce flames cannot be curbed
From whom the challenger retreats in terror—'
Crouched underneath his upraised shield.
In vain the Buthelezi hero tried to stab him with his missiles.
Each one Shaka parried with his black ox-hide shield.
He neared him, holding high his uninitiated spear.
When he came close to him
The Buthelezi hero attempted to probe him from a distance,
Thrusting at him his long, quivering spear.
Shaka threw his weapon off course.
He hooked him with his great black shield,
Driving his weapon through the shocked body.
He fell down with his eyes fixed on Shaka,
As if he had waited for this moment for their final meeting.
Crowds of spectators shouted in amazement.
Shaka proceeded to attack those with their bundles of spears,

The Rise of Shaka

Tearing at them with his initiated spear,
Shouting slogans from the king and his own poems of excellence.
Mgobhozi and Nqoboka, the twins of battle, rushed over,
Opening a wide path and confusing the whole enemy army.
The Buthelezis took to their heels
As the fierce iziChwe regiment ran wild after them.
The Mthethwa army flung their spears at them.
It was amidst this pandemonium that Dingiswayo shouted:
'Son of Nandi! It is enough!'
He knew now that Phungashe was humbled.
He sought only to stop the uncontrolled killing.
Ndima, the son of Moyeni of the Buthelezi clan, died there.
Bhakuza, the son of King Senzangakhona,
Born of the great wife, Mkhabi, died there.
The Mthethwa army was mesmerized by Shaka's performance.
A message came to him from the supreme commander, Ngomane:
'Son of Senzangakhona, the king demands to see you.'
In spite of all the hubbub, Shaka was not excited; he knew
Phungashe and his army would attack again.
Before Dingiswayo he humbled himself, lowering his head.
Dingiswayo spoke kindly to him:
'Your bravery I have seen with my own eyes.
I saw your strategies reaping substantial fruit.
I wish I could reinforce them through many battles
But I fear their outcome.
Son of Zulu, bloodshed begets bloodshed.
But since I love your courage and mind
I give you the regiment of iziChwe to command.
Teach them your own strategies and tactics.
I give you a herd of my best breed of cattle—it is yours.'
Shaka thanked the king, not for the gift
But for the privilege of maturing his plans.
He said: 'My lord, I am grateful to you.
Your words far excel any words ever said to me.
You have made me commander over my agemate regiment,
Despite the many heroes who have fought the king's battles.
Only one request I make of you, my lord:
Allow me to divide this gift among my brothers of iziChwe regiment,
Though custom forbids that the king's gift be given to others.'
Dingiswayo granted Shaka his request commenting:
'Son of Zulu, you are a man amongst men.
Great families boast their wealth of innumerable cattle
Which their heroes have reaped from the gifts of war.
How much more noble of you to give when you count only a few cattle!'
When Dingiswayo made these comments his councillors were troubled,
Knowing these words were truly directed at them.
They loudly applauded Shaka to hide their own shame.
As Shaka was about to leave the king summoned him back:

'By the way, my son, I have received a strange message.
There is a visitor on the way who desires your presence.
He comes to ask that I mourn with him his son.'
Shaka was about to ask (pretending not to know),
When the king crowded him with words and said:
'Your father, Senzangakhona, comes here in summer.'
Shaka's face turned dark like the skies of a gathering storm,
But he only said: 'I thank the king for his word.'

The young men of iziChwe regiment danced all night,
Sending their flames of victory to far-distant lands.
No sooner had King Phungashe lost in his battle
Than he followed the path of other kings and princes
Who lavished Dingiswayo with gifts.
Shaka himself was elated;
The brotherhood of the iziChwe regiment embraced him excitedly.
To them he said: 'It is not I who won against Phungashe
But the concentrated power of all our heroes;
And so it shall be in all our wars.
I am rich with gifts from the king, yet these are not mine.

Henry Louis Gates, Jr.

(b. 1947, United States)

A Myth of Origins:

Esu-Elegbara and the Signifying Monkey

Esu, do not undo me,
Do not falsify the words of my mouth,
Do not misguide the movements of my feet,
You who translates yesterday's words
Into novel utterances,
Do not undo me,
I bear you sacrifice.

Traditional *Oriki Esu*[1]

Ah yes!
Edju played many tricks
Edju made kindred people go to war;
Edju pawned the moon and carried off the sun;
Edju made the Gods strive against themselves.
But Edju is not evil.
He brought us the best there is;
He gave us the Ifa oracle;
He brought the sun.
But for Edju, the fields would be barren.

Traditional *Oriki Esu*[2]

through Harlem smoke of beer and whiskey, I
understand the mystery of the signifying monkey
in a blue haze of inspiration, I reach to the
totality of Being.

Larry Neal, "Malcolm X—An Autobiography"[3]

I

The black Africans who survived the dreaded "Middle Passage" from the west coast of Africa to the New World did not sail alone. Violently and radically abstracted from their civilizations, these Africans nevertheless carried within them to the Western hemisphere aspects of their cultures that were meaningful, that could not be obliterated, and that they chose, by acts of will, not to forget: their music (a mnemonic device for Bantu and Kwa tonal languages), their myths, their expressive institutional structures, their metaphysical systems of order, and their forms of performance. If "the Dixie Pike," as Jean Toomer put the matter in *Cane,* "has grown from a goat path in Africa," then the black vernacular tradition stands as its signpost, at that liminal crossroads of culture contact and ensuing difference at which Africa meets Afro-America.

Common sense, in retrospect, argues that these retained elements of culture should have survived, that their complete annihilation would have been far more remarkable than their preservation. The African, after all, was a traveler, albeit an abrupt, ironic traveler, through space and time; and like every traveler, the African "read" a new environment within a received framework of meaning and belief. The notion that the Middle Passage was so traumatic that it functioned to create in the African a tabula rasa of consciousness is as odd as it is a fiction, a fiction that has served several economic orders and their attendant ideologies. The full erasure of traces of cultures as splendid, as ancient, and as shared by the slave traveler as the classic cultures of traditional West Africa would have been extraordinarily difficult. Slavery in the New World, a veritable seething cauldron of cross-cultural contact, however, did serve to create a dynamic of exchange and revision among numerous previously isolated Black African cultures on a scale unprecedented in African history. Inadvertently, African slavery in the New World satisfied the preconditions for the emergence of a new African culture, a truly Pan-African culture fashioned as a colorful weave of linguistic, institutional, metaphysical, and formal threads. What survived this fascinating process was the most useful and the most compelling of the fragments at hand. Afro-American culture is an African culture with a difference as signified by the catalysts of English, Dutch, French, Portuguese, or Spanish languages and cultures, which informed the precise structures that each discrete New World Pan-African culture assumed.[4]

Of the music, myths, and forms of performance that the African brought to the Western Hemisphere, I wish to discuss one specific trickster figure that recurs with startling frequency in black mythology in Africa, the Caribbean, and South America. This figure appears in black cultures with such frequency that we can think of it as a repeated theme or topos. Indeed, this trickster topos not only seems to have survived the bumpy passage to the New World, but it appears even today in Nigeria, Benin, Brazil, Cuba, Haiti, and the United States. Within New World African-informed cultures, the presence of this topos, repeated with variations as circumstances apparently dictated, attests to shared belief systems maintained for well over three centuries, remarkably, by sustained vernacular traditions. We can trace this particular topos ultimately to the Fon and Yoruba cultures of Benin and Nigeria. Its particular configurations in Western black cultures separated by vast distances of space and time, and isolated by the linguistic barriers of the Germanic and the Romance languages, testify to the fragmented unity of these black cultures in the Western Hemisphere. There can be little doubt that certain fundamental terms for order that the black enslaved brought with them from Africa, and maintained through the mnemonic devices peculiar to oral literature, continued to function both as meaningful units of New World belief systems and as traces of their origins. We lack written documents to answer the historical questions of how this occurred, questions about the means of transmission, translation, and recuperation of the ensuing difference. Nevertheless, this topos functions as a sign of the disrupted wholeness of an African system of meaning and belief that black slaves re-created from memory, preserved by oral narration, improvised upon in ritual—especially in the rituals of the repeated oral narrative—and willed to their own subsequent generations, as hermetically sealed and encoded charts of cultural descent. If the existence of such traceable topoi seems remarkable, it also seems remarkable that scholars have only begun to explicate them systematically in this century.

This topos that recurs throughout black oral narrative traditions and contains a primal scene of instruction for the act of interpretation is that of the divine trickster figure of Yoruba mythology, Esu-Elegbara. This curious figure is called Esu-Elegbara in Nigeria and Legba among the Fon in Benin. His New World figurations include Exú in Brazil, Echu-Elegua in Cuba, Papa Legba (pronounced La-Bas) in the pantheon of the loa of Vaudou of Haiti, and Papa La Bas in the loa of Hoodoo in the United States. Because I see these individual tricksters as related parts of a larger, unified figure, I shall refer to them collectively as Esu, or as Esu-Elegbara. These variations on Esu-Elegbara speak eloquently of an unbroken arc of metaphysical presupposition and a pattern of figuration shared through time and space among certain black cultures in West Africa, South America, the Caribbean, and the United States. These trickster figures, all aspects or topoi of Esu, are fundamental, divine terms of mediation: as tricksters they are mediators, and their mediations are tricks. If the Dixie Pike leads straight to Guinea, then Esu-Elegbara presides over its liminal crossroads, a sensory threshold barely perceptible without access to the vernacular, a word taken from the Latin *vernaculus* ("native"), taken in turn from *verna* ("slave born in his master's house").[5]

Each version of Esu is the sole messenger of the gods (in Yoruba, *iranse*), he who interprets the will of the gods to man; he who carries the desires of man to the gods. Esu is the guardian of the crossroads, master of style and of stylus, the phallic god of generation and fecundity, master of that elusive, mystical barrier that separates the divine world from the profane. Frequently characterized as an inveterate copulator possessed by his enormous penis, linguistically Esu is the ultimate copula, connecting truth with understanding, the sacred with the profane, text with interpretation, the word (as a form of the verb *to be*) that links a subject with its predicate. He connects the grammar of divination with its rhetorical structures. In Yoruba mythology, Esu is said to limp as he walks precisely because of his mediating function: his legs are of different lengths because he keeps one anchored in the realm of the gods while the other rests in this, our human world.

Scholars have studied these figures of Esu, and each has found one or two characteristics of this mutable figure upon which to dwell, true to the nature of the trickster.[6] A partial list of these qualities might include individuality, satire, parody, irony, magic, indeterminacy, open-endedness, ambiguity, sexuality, chance, uncertainty, disruption and reconciliation, betrayal and loyalty, closure and disclosure, encasement and rupture. But it is a mistake to focus on one of these qualities as predominant. Esu possesses all of these characteristics, plus a plethora of others which, taken together, only begin to present an idea of the complexity of this classic figure of mediation and of the unity of opposed forces.

Esu's various characteristics are gleaned from several sources: what the Yoruba call the *Oriki Esu*, the narrative praise poems, or panegyrics, of Esu-Elegbara; the *Odu Ifa*, the Ifa divination verses; the lyrics of "Esu songs"; and the traditional prose narratives in which are encoded the myths of origin of the universe, of the gods, and of human beings' relation to the gods and their place within the cosmic order. Much of Esu's literature concerns the origin, the nature, and the function of interpretation and language use "above" that of ordinary language. For Esu is the Yoruba figure of the meta-level of formal language use, of the ontological and epistemological status of figurative language and its interpretation. The literature of Esu consists to a remarkable degree of direct assertions about the levels of linguistic ascent that separate literal from figurative modes of language use.[7]

The Fon call Legba "the divine linguist," he who speaks all languages, he who interprets the alphabet of Mawu to man and to the other gods. Yoruba sculptures of Esu almost always include a calabash that he holds in his hands. In this calabash he keeps *ase*, the very *ase* with which Olodumare, the supreme deity of the Yoruba, created the universe. We can translate *ase* in many ways, but the *ase* used to create the universe I translate as "logos," as the word as understanding, the word as the audible, and later the visible, sign of reason. *Ase* is more weighty, forceful, and action-packed than the ordinary word. It is the word with irrevocability, reinforced with double assuredness and undaunted authenticity. This probably explains why Esu's mouth, from which the audible word proceeds, sometimes appears double; Esu's discourse, metaphorically, is double-voiced. Esu's mastery of *ase* gives him an immense amount of power; *ase* makes Esu "he who says so and does so," as inscribed in a canonical *Oriki Esu*.[8]

Ase is an elusive concept, and thus its translations vary. Part of one of the canonical *Odu*, "The Story of Osetua," informs us that *ase* is power:

> *Ase* spread and expanded on earth:
> Semen became child,
> Men on sick bed got up,
> All the world became pleasant,
> It became powerful.[9]

But *power* somehow lacks the force to convey the multiple significations of *ase*. The calabash that Esu carries *(Ado-iran)*, presented to him by Olorun, contains "the power which propagates itself." In this calabash Esu carries *ase*. It is this *ase*, "controlled and represented by Esu, which mobilizes each and every element in the system," as Juana and Deoscoredes dos Santos conclude. *Ase*, in other words, is the force of coherence of process itself, that which makes a system a system. My translation of *ase* as "logos" is, I think, the closest analogue through which *ase* can be rendered in English, and in English we have merely borrowed the word from the Greek. As one *babalawo* put it, *ase* is "the light that crosses through the tray of the earth, the firmament from one side to the other, forward and backward." It was this *ase* that Olodumare used to create the universe. When the *babalawo* say that Orunmila acts with the *ase* of Esu, it is the logos that is implied.[10]

Esu's most direct Western kinsman is Hermes. Just as Hermes' role as messenger and interpreter for the gods lent his name readily to *hermeneutics*, our word for the study of methodological principles of interpretation of a text, so too is it appropriate for the literary critic to name the methodological principles of the interpretation of black texts *Esu-'tufunaalo*, literally "one who unravels the knots of Esu."[11] Esu is the indigenous black metaphor for the literary critic, and *Esu-'tufunaalo* is the study of methodological principles of interpretation itself, or what the literary critic does. *Esu-'tufunaalo* is the secular analogue of Ifa divination, the richly lyrical and densely metaphorical system of sacred interpretation that the Yoruba in Nigeria have consulted for centuries, and which they continue to consult. Whereas the god Ifa is the text of divine will, Esu is the text's interpreter *(Onitumo)*, "the one who translates, who explains, or 'who loosens knowledge.'" Indeed, Esu would seem to have a priority over Ifa in the process of interpretation. Esu not only taught his friend the system; Esu also confirms or condemns the "message" of Ifa. For this reason, it is often said in Ifa poetry that

O tase Esu bonu.

(He [Ifa] borrowed Esu's *ase* and put it in his own mouth to give a message to the
supplicant.) [12]

Esu, as the Yoruba say, is the path to Ifa, and his image often appears at the center of the
upper perimeter of the Ifa divining board.

Ifa consists of the sacred texts of the Yoruba people, as does the Bible for Christians,
but it also contains the commentaries on these fixed texts, as does the Midrash. Its system
of interpretation turns upon a marvelous combination of geomancy and textual exegesis,
in which sixteen palm nuts are "dialed" sixteen times, and their configurations or signs
then read and translated into the appropriate, fixed literary verse that the numerical signs
signify. These visual signs are known in the Yoruba as "signatures of an *Odu*," and each
signature the *babalawo*, or priest, translates by reading or reciting the fixed verse text
that the signature signifies. These verse texts, whose meanings are lushly metaphorical,
ambiguous, and enigmatic, function as riddles, which the propitiate must decipher and
apply as is appropriate to his or her own quandary.

Although this is not the place for a full explication of the inner principles of interpretation shared by these systems of divination from West Africa to Latin America, precisely
because of Esu's role in this African myth of origins of interpretation it is instructive to
explain, albeit painfully briefly, the system that Esu created and taught to his friend, the
god Ifa. In African and Latin American mythology, Esu, as I have suggested, is said to have
taught Ifa how to read the signs formed by the sixteen sacred palm nuts. The *Opon Ifa*,
the carved wooden divination tray used in the art of interpretation, represents a trace of
this priority of Esu in the process of interpretation by containing at the center of its upper
perimeter a carved image of Esu himself, meant to signify his relation to the act of interpretation, which we can translate either as *itumo* (literally "to untie or unknot knowledge") or as *iyipada* (literally "to turn around" or "to translate"). That which we call
close reading, moreover, the Yoruba call *Didafa* (literally "reading the signs"). Above all
else, Esu, as the originator of this uniquely African mode of reading, is the Yoruba figure
of indeterminacy itself, *ayese ayewi*, or *ailemo*, literally "that which we cannot know." If Esu
is a repeated topos, for my purposes he is also a trope, a word that has come to be used in
Yoruba discourse in figurative senses far removed from its literal denotations. If we examine some of the primal myths of origins in which Esu defines his metaphoric uses for black
literary criticism, we shall be able to speculate on Esu's relation to his functional equivalent in Afro-American mythic discourse: that oxymoron, the Signifying Monkey.

Before examining myths of the origin of Ifa divination, it will be useful to consider the
figures the Yoruba employ to account for this system of oral interpretation. Figures of
writing recur in descriptions of Ifa. Ifa is frequently called "scribe" or "clerk," or "one
who writes books" *(akowe, a-ko-iwe)*. Ifa wrote for his fellow gods, and taught each *babalawo*
to write the figures of Ifa on his tray of divination. Ifa speaks or interprets on behalf of all
the gods through the act of divination. Ifa, however, can only speak to human beings by
inscribing the language of the gods onto the divining tray in visual signs that the *babalawo*
reads aloud in the language of the lyrical poetry called *ese*. Curiously enough, the oral
literature is described in chirographic metaphors: Ifa's process of oral narration is likened
to writing. This quirk of representation gives Ifa a richness that suggests a central hermeneutical principle of the system itself. The voice of Ifa, the text, writes itself as a crypto-
gram. Esu then assumes his role of interpreter and implicitly governs the process of
translation of these written signs into the oral verse of the *Odu*.

One myth of Ifa accounts for the invention of writing and helps to explain the priority that metaphors of written language seem to have among the Yoruba:

> Olorun was the eldest of the deities, and the first child of the King of the Air (Oba Orufi). Some forty years afterward the King of the Air had a second son, Ela, who was the father of the diviners. In the *morning* all the *Whitemen* used to come to Ela to learn how to read and write, and in the *evening* his *African* children, the babalawo, gathered around him to memorize the Ifa verses and learn divination. Ifa taught them to write on their divining trays, which the Muslims copied as their wooden writing boards (wala), and the Christians copied as the slates used by school children and as books.[13] (emphasis added)

The oppositions here—morning/evening, Whitemen/Africans, reading and writing/ memorizing and reciting, cryptographic/phonetic script—reveal that the Yoruba themselves felt it necessary to account for the differences between traditional African forms of writing and those practiced by "Muslims" and "Whitemen." Significantly, the myth explains phonetic scripts as copies of the oral tradition, encoded in the cryptograms formed by the sixteen sacred palm nuts of Ifa.

Another myth, which Willem Bosman claims to have recorded in the latter decades of the seventeenth century in Asante, offers a radically different account of the absence of writing among the Africans and its presence among the Europeans. . . . It is instructive to consider how writing figures as an opposition within its structure. God created the races of man but created the African first. Because of his priority, the African had first election between knowledge of the arts and sciences, or writing, and all the gold in the earth. The African, because of his avarice, chose the gold; precisely because of his avarice, the African was punished by a curse: never would Africans master the fine art of reading and writing. This myth, oddly enough, is remarkably compatible with seventeenth- and eighteenth-century European speculations on the absence of writing among Africans and its significance. For, without the presence of writing as the visible sign of reason, the Africans could not demonstrate their "innate" mental equality with the European and hence were doomed to a perpetual sort of slavery until such mastery was demonstrated. For the Yoruba, nevertheless, if not the Asante of the Gold Coast, phonetic scripts were derivative, shadow imitations of the prior form of inscription that is manifested in Ifa.

The Yoruba myth of the origins of interpretation is relevant to the use of Esu as the figure of the critic and is helpful in explaining the presence of a monkey in Latin American versions of this primal myth. It is the presence of the monkey in the Yoruba myth, repeated with a difference in Cuban versions, which stands as the trace of Esu in Afro-American myth, a trace that enables us to speculate freely on the functional equivalence of Esu and his Afro-American descendant, the Signifying Monkey.[14]

Frobenius's account of the myth, "given to me," he tells us, "by a dweller on the border of Kukurukuland," is one of the fullest. Frobenius translates *Esu* as "Edshu" or "Edju." His text follows:

> Once upon a time the Gods were very hungry. They did not get enough to eat from their wandering sons on the face of the earth. They were discontented with each other and quarreled. Some of them went forth to hunt. Other Gods, the Olokun in particular, wanted to go fishing; yet, although one antelope and one fish were caught, these did not last long. Now their descendants had forgotten them, and they asked themselves how they were to get their sustenance from men again. Men no longer made them burnt offerings, and the Gods wanted meat. So Edju set out. He asked Yemaya for

something with which to regain man's goodwill. Yemaya said: "You will have no success. Shankpanna has scourged them with pestilence, but they do not come and make sacrifice to him; he will kill them all, but they will not bring him food. Shango struck them dead with the lightning which he sent upon them, but they do not trouble themselves about him or bring him things to eat. Better turn your thought to something else. Men do not fear death. Give them something so good that they will yearn for it and, therefore, want to go on living." Edju went further on. He said to himself: "What I cannot get from Yemaya, Orungan will give me." He went to him. Orungan said: "I know why you are come. The sixteen Gods are ahungered. They must now have something which shall be good. I know of such a thing. It is a big thing made of sixteen palm-nuts. If you get them and learn their meaning, you will once more gain the goodwill of mankind." Edju went to where the palm-trees were. The monkeys gave him sixteen nuts. Edju looked at these, but did not know what to do with them. The monkeys said to him: "Edju, do you know what to do with the nuts? We will counsel you. You got the sixteen nuts by guile. Now go round the world and ask for their meaning everywhere. You will hear sixteen sayings in each of the sixteen places. Then go back to the Gods. Tell men what you yourself have learned, and then men will also learn once more to fear you."

Edju did as he was told. He went to the sixteen places round the world. He went back into the sky.

Edju told the Gods what he had learned himself. The Gods spake: "It is well." Then the Gods imparted their knowledge to their descendants, and now men can know the will of the Gods every day, and what will come to pass in the future. When men saw that all evil things would happen in the days to come, and what they would be able to escape by offering sacrifices, they began to slaughter animals again and burn them for the Gods. This was the way in which Edju brought the Ifa (palm-nuts) down to men. When he went back, he stayed with Ogun, Shango and Obatalla, and these four watched to see what men would do with the kernels.[15]

Esu clearly has priority in the art of interpretation. In other myths of the origins of Ifa, Esu both teaches and wills the system to his friend. This explains why the Yoruba say that "Esu is the path (or route) to Ifa." A canonical narrative, "Esu Taught Orunmila How to Divine," also stresses Esu's importance:

Esu had taught Ifa how to divine with *ikin*. In this way, Ifa became very important as the communication link between men and the Orisas. The Irunmoles [earth spirits], who numbered two hundred and one, were jealous of Ifa, but they could not harm him because Esu was always on hand to fight on Ifa's behalf.[16]

Legba retains this priority in the Fon myths.

Melville Herskovits suggests that this is so primarily to allow human beings " 'a way out' of a supernaturally willed dilemma." And that way out

is offered by a celestial trickster, who is the youngest son of the Creator. In Dahomey, as in most of West Africa, the youngest son is held to be the most astute in the family. Though Fa, who is destiny, is of the greatest importance, the trickster, Legba, comes even before Fa, . . . [In] dealing with the supernatural officialdom, a man can, by winning the favor of Legba, mollify an angered deity and set aside his vengeance.[17]

While Herskovits gives a practical, or functional, explanation for Legba's role in interpretation, both Ifa and Fa systems have inscribed this hierarchy within their myths of origin, and they have done so for hermeneutical reasons.

The roles of Esu and of the Monkey, in several accounts of the myth, are crucial. For reasons extremely difficult to reconstruct, the monkey became, through a displacement in African myths in the New World, a central character in this crucial scene of instruction. In the curious manner repeated throughout this transmission process from Africa to the Western Hemisphere, one structural element that appears to be minor—to judge from subsequent versions taken from Yoruba *babalawo*—became a major character in the surviving oral variation in a New World black culture. Lydia Cabrera's account of this myth within Afro-Cuban mythology makes the central role of the Monkey apparent:

> In some of the Elegua [Elegbara] tales, he is portrayed as the first interpreter, responsible for teaching or uncovering the art of divination to Oruba [Ifa] while accompanied by Moedun [the Monkey] and the tree—a palm tree growing in the garden of Orungan [the midday sun]—as well as being the messenger of Odu, the divination seeds. The reference is to the cowry shells, the means of interpretation of the babalochas and the iyaloches. Bake Elegua is associated with this orisha: "he controls the largest number of cowry shells."[18]

While *Moedun* could possibly derive from the Yoruba *omo* ("child of") *edun* ("a type of monkey"), more probably it derives from the Yoruba *mo*, the first person singular pronoun ("I"), used with past and continuous tenses. *Moedun*, then, can be translated as "I who was/am the Monkey." In Yoruba, furthermore, "monkey" *(òwè)* and proverb or riddle *(òwe)* are virtual homonyms. What is clear is that Esu's role as the first interpreter survived the Middle Passage accompanied by both the Monkey and the tree in which the monkeys lived and from which they selected the sixteen palm nuts that became the sacred characters of Ifa divination. Many contemporary statues of Exu in Brazil depict him with both a large erect penis and a long tail.

To be sure, the Monkey appears in other African narratives and even appears with the Lion and the Elephant (as in the Signifying Monkey narrative poems) in a well-known Fon narrative entitled "Why Monkey Did Not Become Man." The Monkey who surfaces in relation to divination in a second canonical Fon narrative, "Monkey's Ingratitude: Why One Does Not Deceive the Diviner."[19] But the direct conjunction of the Monkey and Esu seems to be confined to this myth of origins of the process of interpretation itself. The Monkey, furthermore, is one of Esu's bynames, as in the following *Oriki Esu:*

> King of Ketu,
> The Monkey has no lamp at Akesan,
> My mother's money its eyes serve as lamps all over the farm,
> Product of today's hustle and bustle
> Offshoot of tomorrow's hustle and bustle
> The evil eye has stunted Monkey's growth
> They call him child of no means and position
> Let him not consort with people on Alaketu's street
> Let him not bring about the curse more effective than poison.[20]

(Two of Esu's physical characteristics are his extraordinarily dark color and his tiny size.) Perhaps even more telling is the Fon myth, "The First Humans." Legba, acting without knowledge of Mawu, the creator, transforms two of the earth's four primal beings into monkeys. It is from these two monkeys that all monkeys descended. Legba, therefore, is the father of the Monkey.[21]

There is a fascinating conflation of the Monkey and Esu in Afro-Cuban mythology. This occurs in the figure of the *guije* or *jigue,* a black trickster topos whose identity has not yet, to my knowledge, been satisfactorily defined. The literature of the *guije* or *jigue* consists of two types. In the first, the *guije* is depicted as a small black man, as in the oral narrative, "El guije de la Bajada," collected by Salvador Bueno in his *Leyendas cubanas*. The two signal physical characteristics of Esu, as I have said above, are his extremely dark color and his tiny size. The other form that the *guije* assumes, generally in poetry rather than in narrative, is the *jigue*, or monkey. Teofilo Radillo's poem, "The Song of the Jigue," helps us to resolve the mystery of this conflated trickster's origins.[22]

"The jigue," Radillo informs us, "was born in Oriente" province, that curious Cuban site, or cauldron, at which Yoruba culture met European Hispanic culture to produce a novel mixture:

> The jigue was born in Oriente.
> The jigue came from the waters . . .
> By the edge of the lagoon,
> while the children bathe.

His emergence from the waters suggests his African origins. Among the *jigue's* physical characteristics are his dark color, his pointed teeth, and his long hair, the color and sort of hair that are characteristic descriptions of Esu:

> A dark jigue is watching
> with a great length of hair . . .
> His teeth are pointed
> and his intentions are sharp.

The *jigue's* eyes, in addition, are large and penetrating, as are Esu's eyes:

> Mother, I have seen a jigue
> yesterday, when I was bathing
> in the still waters:
> He was black . . . and glared at me
> with what . . . I could not tell,
> may have been eyes of live coals.

Most important, the *jigue* underwent a transformation of the most profound sort in his passage from Africa to the New World. Where once he was a monkey, he emerged from the rite of passage—or, more truly, a *rite de marges* (as we might think of the Middle Passage)—as Esu, or Echu:

> The jigue was born in Oriente
> and brought there from Africa,
> where he had been a monkey: the last
> monkey who fell into the water;
> the monkey who drowned
> for the sake of the nganga—
> the nganga forever floating
> over the waves of water—

The *jigue*'s connection with a monkey is clear etymologically. *Guije* and *jigue* are derived from the Efik-Ejagham word for "monkey," *jiwe*.[23]

The etymology of *nganga* is also suggestive. In Kikongo, *nganga* means one expert in medicine or magic, a doctor of various sorts, in other words. *Nganga* means action, work, or arrangement. And *nganga* means to experience an attack of wrath, to cause pain, to reflect or to question. In Kiswahili, *ng'ang'ama* means to clutch hold of, as of a swinging branch or tree, while *ng'ang'ania* means to beg earnestly, beseech, until one attains a desired end. In a study of "Langue Congo" in Cuba, Germain de Granada defines *nganga* as a magical object. Most suggestively of all, however, Tulu Kia Mpansu Buakasa defines *nganga* as "interpreter."[24]

As used in Teofilo Radillo's "The Song of the Jigue," *nganga* could connote any number of these meanings:

> the monkey who drowned
> for the sake of the nganga—
> the nganga forever floating
> over the waves of water—

It could refer to a magic object, or an interpreter (doctor) of the traditional sort; or, more suggestively, *nganga* could imply the victim of an attack of wrath or one insistent on questioning the received, or the imposed, order. In a more literal sense, the Kiswahili root of *ng'ang'ama* suggests one clutching a swinging branch of a tree (as a monkey would) to escape torrential waters, only to lose one's grip and to tumble into the water, "drowning," as the poem states, "for the sake of nganga." The poem reads:

> jigue who frightens children
> who hangs by the white girl
> by the edge of the river
> where night is bathing
> at the tune of the moon
> curling around the silver light.

The significance of *nganga* suggests a multiplicity of meanings, each of which informs the KiKongo-Cuban survival. Most dramatically of all, Rodillo figures the *nganga* "forever floating over the waves of water" like a wandering signifier, suggesting perpetually its range of meanings from its Bantu roots, even—or especially—in its New World setting. We may take this sort of perpetual, or wandering, signification as an emblem of the process of cultural transmission and translation that recurred with startling frequency when African cultures encountered New World–European cultures and yielded a novel blend.

The poem's last stanza comes to bear directly on the relationship among Esu, the monkey, and the interpreter that I am attempting to establish:

> Jigue-monkey,
> monkey-jigue,
> nganga-jigue,
> jigue-nganga;

These are represented as terms of equivalence: "Jigue-monkey / monkey-jigue" echoes the Cuban neologism *moedun*, from the Yoruba, meaning "I-monkey" and "I who am / was the monkey." "Nganga-Jigue" here suggests the identity between the monkey and the interpreter figure, clearly an interpreter of the traditional sort, a trickster figure of the order of Esu.

This conflated set of figures, now rendered equivalent semantically and functionally, represents one who has come from Africa to Cuba:

> you have come from very far,
> galloping over the waters
> in dreams which arrived
> muzzled to these shores.

The last two lines of this wonderful image form a marvelous figure of the initiate who emerged at the Western pole of the Middle Passage; the initiate survived, dreams intact, but the dreams are "muzzled to these shores."

But what, or who, can emerge intact from such traumatic crossings, in response to the passionate call of the originary language, figured by the drum? Only the black trickster:

> One playful jigue emerges
> as the drum calls;
> as the drum bursts it is said
> that many jigues dance.

Esu is also a highly accomplished dancer, a mask-in-motion, who signifies in ritual by his phallic dance of generation, of creation, of translation.

Who, ultimately, is the jigue?

> The jigue while there, in the forest,
> was a monkey, the last monkey. . . .
> and drowned . . . to float today
> in the sleeping waters of legends
> which cradled a whole race.

Drowning, in Africa when the slavers stole our people, the trickster figure can "float today / in the sleeping waters of legends," legends in which are inscribed the New World African's metaphysical origins, legends whose meanings and perpetuation "cradled a whole race." Who, finally, is the jigue?

> Monkey-jigue,
> jigue-monkey,
> nganga-jigue,
> jigue-nganga!

The jigue is the monkey, and the monkey is Esu, and both are doctors of interpretation. The three are trickster figures of the same order, the hermeneutical order.

While we lack archeological and historical evidence to explain the valorized presence of the Monkey in Cuban mythology, in the textual evidence, on the other hand, we commonly encounter Esu with his companion, as depicted even in visual representations of Esu. As Alberto del Pozo writes, "Echu Elegua frequently has a monkey . . . by his side."[25] If we examine the general characteristics of Esu, as derived from the *Oriki Esu* and as classed together under the rubric of "rhetorical principles," the Signifying Monkey emerges from his mysteriously beclouded Afro-American origins as Esu's first cousin, if not his American heir. It is as if Esu's friend, the Monkey, left his side at Havana and swam to New Orleans. The Signifying Monkey remains as the trace of Esu, the sole survivor of a disrupted partnership. Both are tropes that serve as transferences in a system aware of the nature of language and its interpretation.

What is the importance of these apparently related tricksters and their myths to literary criticism? Perhaps this will be clearer if we return briefly to Ifa divination and to a fuller discussion of Esu's role. It is convenient to think of the Yoruba god Ifa as the text of divination, who gave to divination not only his name but the 256 *Odu* as well as the thousands of poems that comprise these *Odu*. This extensive, highly structured body of lyrical poetry stands as the verbal, literary, or textual analogue of 256 cryptograms that can be formed by the *babalawo* as he manipulates the sixteen sacred palm nuts. This vast array of poetry exists as the separate stanzas of one extensive text, which we might think of profitably as the text of Ifa. Human beings consult this text in attempts to decipher their destiny, or fate. What the supplicant hears read to him, in "the signature of Odu," is neither a literal revelation of his fate nor a set of commands that can be put into practice to appease, or redress, the human being's curse of the indeterminacy or uncertainty of fate. Rather, the supplicant hears read by the *babalawo* a series of lyrical poems that are so metaphorical and so ambiguous that they may be classified as enigmas, or riddles, which must be read or interpreted, but which, nevertheless, have no single determinate meaning. The supplicant, the reader as it were, must produce meaning by stopping the *babalawo* as he chants an *ese*, which in some way strikes the supplicant as being relevant to his dilemma. Then, the *babalawo* interprets the poem for his client and prescribes the appropriate sacrifices. Fairly frequently, the client cannot recognize his situation in the metaphorical language of the poem, despite the fact that Ifa has inscribed the person's fate into the appropriate *Odu*, signified by the patterns formed by the palm nuts.

Ifa is the god of determinate meanings, but his meaning must be rendered by analogy. Esu, god of indeterminacy, rules this interpretive process; he is the god of interpretation because he embodies the ambiguity of figurative language. Although he allowed his friend Ifa to rule and name the texts of the tradition, it is Esu who retains dominance over the act of interpretation precisely because he signifies the very divinity of the figurative. For Ifa, one's sought meaning is patently obvious; it need only be read. Esu decodes the figures.

If Ifa, then, is our metaphor for the text itself, then Esu is our metaphor for the uncertainties of explication, for the open-endedness of every literary text. Whereas Ifa represents closure, Esu rules the process of disclosure, a process that is never-ending, that is dominated by multiplicity. Esu is discourse upon a text; it is the process of interpretation that he rules. This is the message of his primal scene of instruction with his friend Ifa. If Esu stands for discourse upon a text, then his Pan-African kinsman, the Signifying Monkey, stands for the rhetorical strategies of which each literary text consists. For the Signifying Monkey exists as the great trope of Afro-American discourse, and the trope of tropes, his language of Signifyin(g), is his verbal sign in the Afro-American tradition.

We can summarize the importance of these tricksters to theory in three related ways. First, they and the myths in which they are characters function as focal points for black theories about formal language use. The figure of writing appears to be peculiar to the myth of Esu, while the figure of speaking, of oral discourse densely structured rhetorically, is peculiar to the myth of the Signifying Monkey. Here, the vernacular tradition names the great opposition of its formal literary counterpart, the tension between the oral and the written modes of narration that is represented as finding a voice in writing. As figures of the duality of the voice within the tradition, Esu and his friend the Monkey manifest themselves in the search for a voice that is depicted in so very many black texts. The tension between them surfaces in the double-voiced discourse so commonly found here. This tension between the oral and the written plays itself out in one form as the two dominant narrative voices that serve as counterpoint in texts such as Jean Toomer's *Cane*. In another form, it surfaces as the free indirect discourse of what I am calling the speakerly text, in which third and first person, oral and written voices, oscillate freely within one structure, as in Zora Neale Hurston's *Their Eyes Were Watching God*. These tensions are figured in the myths of Esu and the Monkey.

Second, in the myths of Esu and the Monkey the tradition defines the role of the figurative. Polemical traditions seem to valorize the literal. Pragmatics argues that it cannot be otherwise; the vernacular tradition, however, undercuts this penchant at its deepest level, that of underlying rhetorical principle. The myths of origins of the tradition privilege both the figurative and the ambiguous. The determinate meanings often sought in criticism run counter to the most fundamental values of the tradition as encased in myth. In this sense, the literal and the figurative are locked in a Signifyin(g) relation, the myths and the figurative Signified upon by the real and literal, just as the vernacular tradition Signifies upon the tradition of letters, and as figures of writing and inscription are registered, paradoxically, in an oral literature. This is another example of the presence of the dual voice. The notion of double-voiced discourse, related to Mikhail Bakhtin's theory of narrative but also indigenously African, comprises the crux of the method I use for the close readings of Afro-American texts. . . . The Afro-American concept of Signifyin(g) can be conveniently introduced here as formal revision that is at all points double-voiced.

The third conclusion that we can draw from the myths of Esu and the Monkey concerns the indeterminacy of interpretation. Esu is a principle of language, of written discourse particularly. He is "all metaphor, all ambiguous oracle," as Robert Pelton has said.[26] The most famous myth about him is read as a story about indeterminacy. It is inscribed in the well-known canonical tale of "The Two Friends." . . . Indeterminacy, then, is accounted for by the vernacular tradition, as an unavoidable aspect of acts of interpretation. These three general observations summarize, in the broadest sense, the self-reflexive functions that Esu serves in Yoruba discourse.

NOTES

1. *Oriki Esu*, quoted by Ayodele Ogundipe, *Esu Elegbara, the Yoruba God of Chance and Uncertainty: A Study in Yoruba Mythology*, 2 vols. Ph.D. dissertation, Indiana University, 1978, Vol. II, p. 135.

2. *Oriki Esu*, quoted by Leo Frobenius, *The Voice of Africa* (New York: Benjamin Blom, 1913), Vol. I, p. 229.

3. Larry Neal, "Malcolm X–An Autobiography," in *Black Fire: An Anthology of Afro-American Writing* (New York: William Morrow, 1968), p. 316.

4. The literature on "African survivals" is extensive. The following sources are helpful: Okon E. Uya, "The Culture of Slavery: Black Experience Through a Filter," *Afro-American Studies* 1 (1971): 209; Robert Farris Thompson, *Flash of the Spirit* (New York: Random House, 1983); William Bascom,

Shango in the New World (Austin: African and Afro-American Institute, University of Texas, 1972); Melville J. Herskovits, ed., *The Interdisciplinary Aspects of Negro Studies* (Washington: American Council of Learned Societies *Bulletin* No. 32, 1941); M. G. Smith, "The African Heritage in the Caribbean," in *Caribbean Studies: A Symposium,* ed. Vera Rubin (Seattle: University of Washington Press, 1960); George E. Simpson and Peter B. Hammond, "Discussion," in *Caribbean Studies,* ed. Rubin; Robert Farris Thompson, "African Influence on the Art of the United States," in *Black Studies in the University: A Symposium,* ed. Armstead L. Robinson et al. (New Haven: Yale University Press, 1969), pp. 122–70; and Roger D. Abrahams and John F. Szwed, *After Africa: Extracts from British Travel Accounts and Journals of the Seventeenth, Eighteenth, and Nineteenth Centuries Concerning the Slaves, Their Manners, and Customs in the British West Indies* (New Haven: Yale University Press, 1983), esp. pp. 4–22.

5. For a brilliant parallel study to this book, see Houston A. Baker, Jr., *Blues, Ideology, and Afro-American Literature: A Vernacular Theory* (Chicago: University of Chicago Press, 1984). Baker explores another side of the Afro-American vernacular—the blues—as his trope for a theory of criticism based on the black vernacular music tradition, whereas I am exploring here a theory of criticism based on the linguistic and poetic traditions of the vernacular encoded in the ritual of Signifyin(g). My great indebtedness to Baker's work is obvious and is acknowledged here (especially his readings of the liminality of the trickster figure).

6. To supplement my explication of hundreds of *Oriki Esu* and myths of Esu still in use today among the Yoruba of Nigeria, the Fon of Benin, the Nago of Brazil, and the Lucumi of Cuba, I have explored systematically the extensive secondary literature on Esu and his or her variants. Some sources especially useful to this study of the nature of interpretation are: Juana Elbein dos Santos and Deoscoredes M. dos Santos, *Esu Bara Laroye: A Comparative Study* (Ibadan: Institute of African Studies, 1971); idem, "Esu Bara, Principle of Individual Life in the Nago System," *Colloque International sur la Notion de Personne en Afrique Noire* (Paris: Centre National de la Recherche Scientifique, Colloque Internationaux, No. 544, 1971); Juana Elbein dos Santos, *Os Nàgô e a Morte: Pàde, Àsèsè e o Culto Egun na Bahia* (Paris: Editoria Vozes, Petropolis, 1976); Robert Farris Thompson, *Black Gods and Kings: Yoruba Art at UCLA* (1971; Bloomington: Indiana University Press, 1976); idem, *Flash of the Spirit;* Ogundipe, *Esu Elegbara;* Melville J. Herskovits, *Dahomey, An Ancient West African Kingdom,* 2 vols. (Evanston: Northwestern University Press, 1967); idem and Frances S. Herskovits, *Dahomean Narrative: A Cross-Cultural Analysis* (Evanston: Northwestern University Press, 1958); Bernard Maupoil, *La Géomancie à l'ancienne Côte des Esclaves,* Travaux et Mémoires de l'Institut d'Ethnologie, Vol. 42 (Paris: Institut d'Ethnologie, 1943); Wande Abimbola, "An Exposition of Ifa Literary Corpus," Ph.D. dissertation, University of Lagos, 1970; idem, *Sixteen Great Poems of Ifa* (New York: UNESCO, 1975); idem, *Ifa Divination Poetry* (New York: Nok, 1977); E. Bolaji Idowu, *Olodumare: God in Yoruba Belief* (London: Longman, 1962); William Bascom, *Ifa Divination: Communication Between Gods and Men in West Africa* (Bloomington: Indiana University Press, 1969); Lydia Cabrera, *El Monte: Igbo Fina Ewe Orisha, Vititinfinda* (Havana: Ediciones C. R., 1954); Pierre Verger, *Notes sur le culte des Orisha et Voudoun à Bahia, la Baie de tous les saint au Brésil et à l'ancienne Côtes des Esclaves, en Afrique,* Memoria 51 du Institut Français pour l'Afrique Noir (Dakar: Ifan, 1957); Roger Bastide, *Le Candomblé de Bahia, Rite Nagô* (Paris: Mouton, 1958); Robert D. Pelton, *The Trickster in West Africa: A Study of Mythic Irony and Sacred Delight* (Los Angeles: University of California Press, 1980); Peter M. Morton-Williams, "An Outline of the Cosmology and Cult Organization of Oyo Yoruba," *Africa* 32 (1962): 336–53; and Hans Witte, *Ifa and Esu: Iconography of Order and Disorder* (Soest, Holland: Kunsthandel Luttik, 1984).

7. Because the variations of Esu are topoi and because I wish to underscore the literary (rather than the anthropological) discourse unfolding in this chapter, I use the words *Esu* and *Yoruba* interchangeably with Esu's bynames in the Yoruba-informed cultures in Dahomey, Brazil, and Cuba. *Esu* and *Yoruba* for me are signs of shared hermeneutical principles that transcend mere national boundaries.

8. *Ase* has plural signification. See Juana Elbein and D. M. dos Santos, "La Religion Nago generatrice de reserve de valeurs culturelles au Bresil," Colloquium on African Traditional Religions, UNESCO and SAC, Cotonou, 1970; idem, "Esu Bara"; dos Santos, *Os Nagô e a Morte,* pp. 171–81; and Thompson, *Flash of the Spirit,* Chap. 1. I refer to "Esu Ebitan lo Riwa." I was taught this *Oriki Esu* by my Yoruba instructor, Professor Michael O. Afolayan, whose understanding of Yoruba poetics and linguistics is unsurpassed. My understanding of the nature and function of the Ifa oracle is a direct result of my instruction by Afolayan and by Wole Soyinka.

9. Dos Santos and dos Santos, *Esu Bara Laroye*, p. 80.

10. Ibid., pp. 28, 26, and 2.

11. Wole Soyinka coined this neologism for this book.

12. *Oriki Esu*, cited by Michael O. Afolayan. See also Abimbola, "An Exposition of Ifa Literary Corpus," pp. 388, 394, for a slightly different version.

13. Bascom, *Ifa Divination*, pp. 109–10. Bascom writes that the myth was said to be based on a verse from Ofun Ogunda. For a full analysis of Bosman's myth, see my *Black Letters in the Enlightenment: On Race, Writing, and Difference* (New York: Oxford University Press, forthcoming).

14. For other myths of origin of Ifa that underscore Esu's role as teacher of the system of Ifa to his friend, see Rev. P. Baudin, *Fetichism and Fetich Worshippers*, trans. M. McMahon (New York: Benziger Brothers, 1885), pp. 32–35. See also A. B. Ellis, *The Yoruba-Speaking Peoples of the Slave Coast of West Africa* (London: Chapman and Hall, 1894), pp. 56–64; James Johnson, *Yoruba Heathenism* (Exeter: James Townsend and Son, 1899); R. E. Dennett, *At the Back of the Black Man's Mind* (London: Macmillan, 1906), pp. 243–69; Frobenius, *The Voice of Africa*, Vol. I, pp. 229–32; Stephen S. Farrow, *Faith, Fancies and Fetich, or Yoruba Paganism* (London: Society for Promoting Christian Knowledge, 1926), pp. 36–37; J. Olumide Lucas, *The Religion of the Yoruba: Being an Account of the Religious Beliefs and Practices of the Yoruba Peoples of Southern Nigeria, Especially in Relation to the Religion of Ancient Egypt* (Lagos: C.M.S. Bookshop, 1948), pp. 73–74; and Ogundipe, *Esu Elegbara*, Vol. II, pp. 100–101, 128–32. See esp. Bascom, *Ifa Divination*, pp. 105–7, 156–61, 221–27, 553–55.

15. Frobenius, *The Voice of Africa*, Vol. I, pp. 229–32.

16. Ogundipe, *Esu Elegbara*, Vol. II, pp. 100–101, 128. See also Baudin, *Fetichism*, p. 34; Frobenius, *The Voice of Africa*, Vol. I, pp. 229–32; Farrow, *Faith, Fancies and Fetich*, p. 37; and Lucas, *The Religion of the Yoruba*, pp. 73–74. See esp. Herskovits and Herskovits, *Dahomean Narrative*, pp. 173–83.

17. Herskovits, *Dahomey*, Vol. II, pp. 295–96.

18. Cabrera, *El Monte*, p. 87. Alberto del Pozo graciously located this source for me. The translation published here is by José Piedra. See also Alberto del Pozo, *Oricha* (Miami: 1982), p. 1. Piedra's work on the Yoruba-KiKongo-Cuban cultural matrix is superb. See his "Money Tales and Cuban Songs," *Modern Language Notes* 100 (1985): 361–90.

19. Herskovits and Herskovits, *Dahomean Narrative*, pp. 151–52, 193–94.

20. Ogundipe, *Esu Elegbara*, Vol. II, p. 42.

21. Herskovits and Herskovits, *Dahomean Narrative*, pp. 150–51.

22. I am profoundly indebted to José Piedra, whose reading of an earlier draft of this chapter led him to the Cuban myth of the *guije* and the *jigue* as analogues of the Signifying Monkey. I am delighted to discover the *jigue* to be another dense encoding of Esu. See "El guije de la Bajada," in Salvador Bueno, *Leyendas cubanas* (Havana: Editorial Arte y Literatura, 1978), pp. 257–61; Teofilo Radillo, "Canción del jigue" ("The Song of the Jigue") in Enrique Noble, *Literatura afro-hispano-americana: Poesía y prose de ficción* (Lexington, Mass., and Toronto: Xerox College Publishing, 1973), pp. 49–52; and Facundo Ramos, "El mito del guije cubano," in Samuel Feijoo, *El negro en la literatura folklórica cubana* (Havana: Editorial Letras Cubanas, 1980), pp. 322–59. The translation of Radillo's poem by José Piedra. The *Oriki Esu* are replete with descriptions of Esu as "little man."

23. *Guije* or *jigue*, from the Efik-Ejagham word *jiwe* ("monkey"), as verified by Fernando Ortiz, *Nuevo Catauro de Cubanismos*, reedited version of his own *Un catauro de cubanismo: Apuntes lexicográficos* (Havana: Colección Cubana de Libros y Documentos Inéditos y Raros, Vol. 4, 1923), published posthumously (Havana: Editorial de Ciencias Sociales, 1974), p. 305; Pierre Alexandre, *Languages and Language in Black Africa* (Evanston: Northwestern University Press, 1972), pp. 56, 39.

24. In Swahili, *nganga* would be *mganga*, a traditional African doctor cum philosopher. The KiKongo alternative is more likely because of the large numbers of people who were stolen from Congo and enslaved in the Western Hemisphere. *Nganga-Nganga*, in English transliteration from KiKongo, is applied in compound words to the concept of expert on a particular subject. Its early colonial translation as "fetish-maker" clearly conveys a biased misconception and should be substituted by other terms such as *faiseur* ("maker" or "producer"), as it was called in French by J. Van Wing, according to his etymological study of the word, in his *Études BaKongo: Sociologie—Religion et Magie*, 2d ed. (1921, 1938; rpt. Leopoldville: Museum Lessianum, Section Missiologique No. 39, 1959), pp. 418–19. The most complete study on this subject is by Buakasa, who suggests the essential function of the *nganga* to be the interpretation of *kindoki* (a language of obscure forces ruling communication, which includes acts, words, objects, and dreams). See Tulu Kia Mpansu Buakasa, *L'Impense du Discours: "Kindoki" et "nkisi" en pays kongo du Zaire* (Kinshasa: Presse Universitaire,

1973). See also Germain de Granada, *De la Matrice Africaine de la "Langue Congo" de Cuba (Recherche preliminaires)* (Dakar: Centre de Hautes Etudes Afro-Ibero-Americaines, 1973).

25. Del Pozo, *Oricha*, p. 1.

26. Pelton, *The Trickster in West Africa*, p. 162. See esp. Chaps. 3 and 4 for a brilliant analysis of Esu's relation to discourse, as a "kind of reconciliation of opposites of discourse" (p. 79).

Olaudah Equiano
(1745–1797, Nigeria)

Identity, Culture, and Kidnapping

I hope the reader will not think I have trespassed on his patience in introducing myself to him, with some account of the manners and customs of my country [Nigeria]. They had been implanted in me with great care, and made an impression on my mind which time could not erase, and which all the adversity and variety of fortune I have since experienced served only to rivet and record; for, whether the love of one's country be real or imaginary, or a lesson of reason, or an instinct of nature, I still look back with pleasure on the first scenes of my life, though that pleasure has been for the most part mingled with sorrow.

. . . My father, besides many slaves, had a numerous family, of which seven lived to grow up, including myself and a sister, who was the only daughter. As I was the youngest of the sons, I became, of course, the greatest favorite with my mother, and was always with her; and she used to take particular pains to form my mind. I was trained up from my earliest years in the arts of agriculture and war: my daily exercise was shooting and throwing javelins; and my mother adorned me with emblems, after the manner of your greatest warriors. In this way I grew up till I was turned the age of eleven, when an end was put to my happiness in the following manner:—Generally, when the grown people in the neighborhood were gone far in the fields to labour, the children assembled together in some of the neighbors' premises to play; and commonly some of us used to get up a tree to look out for any assailant or kidnapper that might come upon us; for they sometimes took those opportunities of our parents' absence, to attack and carry off as many as they could seize. One day, as I was watching at the top of a tree in our yard, I saw one of those people come into the yard of our next neighbor but one, to kidnap, there being many stout young people in it. Immediately, on this, I gave the alarm of the rogue, and he was surrounded by the stoutest of them, who entangled him with cords, so that he could not escape till some of the grown people came and secured him. But alas! ere long, it was my fate to be thus attacked, and to be carried off, when none of our grown people were nigh. One day, when all our people were gone out to their works as usual, and only I and my dear sister were left to mind the house, two men and a woman got over our walls, and in a moment seized us both; and without giving us time to cry out, or make resistance, they stopped our mouths and ran off with us into the nearest wood. Here they tied our hands, and continued to carry us as far as they could, till night came on, when we reached a small house, where the robbers halted for refreshment, and spent the night. We were then unbound, but were unable to take any food; and, being quite overpowered by fatigue and grief, our only relief was some sleep, which allayed our misfortune for a short time. The next morning we left the house, and continued travelling all the day. For a long time we had kept the woods, but at last we came into a road which I believed I knew. I now had some hopes of being delivered; for we had advanced but a little way when I discovered some people at a distance, on which I began to cry out for their assistance; but my cries had no other effect than to make them tie me faster and stop my mouth, and then they put me into a large sack. They also stopped my sister's mouth and tied her hands; and in this manner we proceeded till we were out of the sight of these people.—When we went to rest the following night they offered us some victuals, but we refused them; and the only comfort we had was in being in one another's arms all that night, and bathing each other with our tears. But alas! we were soon deprived of even the small comfort of weeping together. The next day proved a day of greater sorrow than I had yet experienced; for my sister and I were then separated, while we lay clasped in each other's arms: it was in vain that we besought them not to part us; she was torn from me, and immediately carried away, while I was left in a state of distraction not to be described. I cried and grieved continually; and for several days did not eat any thing but what they forced into my mouth. At length, after many days travelling, during which I had often changed masters, I got into the hands of a chieftain, in a very pleasant country. This man had two wives and some children, and they all used me extremely well, and did all they could to comfort me; particularly the first wife, who was something like my mother. Although I was a great many days journey from my father's house, yet these people spoke exactly the same language with us. This first master of mine, as I may call him, was a smith, and my principal employment was working his bellows, which was the same kind as I had seen in my vicinity. They were in some respects not unlike the stoves here [England] in gentlemen's kitchens; and were covered over with leather; and in the middle of that leather a stick was fixed, and a person stood up, and worked it, in the same manner as is done to pump water out of a cask with a hand pump. I believe it was gold he worked, for it was a lovely bright yellow colour, and was worn by the women on their wrists and ankles. I was there I suppose about a month, and they at last used to trust me some little distance from the house. This liberty I used in embracing every opportunity to inquire the way to my own home: and I also sometimes, for the same purpose, went with the maidens, in the cool of the evenings, to bring pitchers of water from the springs for the use of the house. I had also remarked where the sun rose in the morning, and set in the evening, as I had travelled along; and I had observed that my father's house was towards the rising of the sun. I therefore determined to seize the first opportunity of making my escape, and to shape my course for that quarter; for I was quite oppressed and weighed down by grief after my mother and friends; and my love of liberty, ever great, was strengthened by the mortifying circumstance of not daring to eat with the free-born children, although I was mostly their companion.—While I was projecting my escape one day, an unlucky event happened, which quite disconcerted my plan, and put an end to my hopes. I used to be sometimes employed in assisting an elderly woman slave to cook and take care of the poultry; and one morning while I was feeding some chickens, I happened to toss a small pebble at one of them, which hit it on the middle, and directly killed it. The old slave, having soon after missed the chicken, inquired after it; and on my relating the accident (for I told her the truth, because my mother would never suffer me to tell a lie), she flew into a violent passion, threatened that I should suffer for it; and, my master being out, she immediately went and told her mistress what I had done. This alarmed me very much, and I expected an instant flogging, which to me was uncommonly dreadful; for I had seldom been beaten at home. I therefore resolved to fly; and accordingly I ran into a thicket that was hard by, and hid myself in the bushes. Soon afterwards my mistress and the slave returned, and, not seeing me, they searched all the house, but not finding me, and I not making answer when they called to me, they thought I had run away, and the whole neighborhood was raised in the pursuit of me. In that part of the country (as well as ours) the houses and villages were skirted with woods or shrubberies, and the bushes were so thick, that a man could readily conceal himself in them, so as to elude the strictest search. The neighbors continued the whole day looking for me, and several times many of them came within a few yards of the place where I lay hid. I expected every moment, when I heard a rustling among the trees, to be found out, and punished by my master; but they never discovered me, though they were often so near that I even heard their conjectures as they were looking about for me; and I now learned from them that any attempt to return home would be hopeless. Most of them supposed I had fled towards home; but the distance was so great, and the way so intricate, that they thought I could never reach it, and that I should be lost in the woods. When I heard this I was seized with a violent panic, and abandoned myself to despair. Night too began to approach, and aggravated all my fears. I had before entertained hopes of getting home, and had determined when it should be dark to make the attempt; but I was now convinced that it was fruitless, and began to consider that, if possibly I could escape all other animals, I could not those of the human kind; and that, not knowing the way, I must perish on the woods.—Thus I was like the hunted deer:

—"Ev'ry leaf, and ev'ry whisp'ring breath
"Convey'd a foe, and ev'ry foe a death."

I heard frequent rustling among the leaves; and being pretty sure they were snakes, I expected every instant to be stung by them.—This increased my anguish; and my horror of my situation became now quite insupportable. I at length quitted the thicket, very faint and hungry, for I had not eaten or drank anything all the day, and crept to my master's kitchen, from whence I set out at first, and which was an open shed, and laid myself down in the ashes with an anxious wish for death to relieve me from all my pains. I was scarcely awake in the morning, when the old woman slave, who was the first up, came to light the fire, and saw me in the fireplace. She was very much surprised to see me, and could scarcely believe her own eyes. She now promised to intercede for me, and went for her master, who soon after came, and having lightly reprimanded me, ordered me to be taken care of, and not ill treated.

Soon after this my master's only daughter and child by his first wife sickened and died, which affected him so much that for some time he was almost frantic, and really would have killed himself, had he not been watched and prevented. However, in a small time afterwards he recovered and I was again sold. I was now carried to the left of the sun's rising, through many dreary wastes and dismal woods, amidst the hideous roaring of wild beasts.—The people I was sold to used to carry me very often, when I was tired, either on their shoulders or on their backs. I saw many convenient well-built sheds along the road, at proper distances, to accommodate the merchants and travellers, who lay in those buildings along with their wives, who often accompany them; and they always go well armed.

From the time I left my own nation I always found somebody that understood me till I came to the sea coast. The languages of different nations did not totally differ, nor were they so copious as those of the Europeans, particularly the English. They were therefore easily learned; and while I was journeying thus through Africa, I acquired two or three different tongues. In this manner I had been travelling for a considerable time, when one evening to my great surprise, whom should I see brought to the house where I was but my dear sister? As soon as she saw me she gave a loud shriek, and ran into my arms. I was quite overpowered: neither of us could speak, but, for a considerable time, clung to each other in mutual embraces, unable to do anything but weep. Our meeting affected all who saw us; and indeed I must acknowledge, in honour of those sable destroyers of human rights, that I never met with any ill treatment, or saw any offered to their slaves, except tying them, when necessary to keep them from running away. When these people knew we were brother and sister, they indulged us to be together; and the man, to whom I supposed we belonged, lay with us, he in the middle, while she and I held one another by the hands across his breast all night; and thus for awhile we forgot our misfortunes in the joy of being together; but even this small comfort was soon to have an end; for scarcely had the fatal morning appeared, when she was again torn from me for ever! I was now more miserable, if possible, than before. The small relief which her presence gave me from pain was gone, and the wretchedness of my situation was redoubled by my anxiety after her fate, and my apprehension lest her sufferings should be greater than mine, when I could not be with her to alleviate them. Yes, thou dear partner of my childish sports! thou sharer of my joys and sorrows! happy should I have ever esteemed myself to encounter every misery for you, and to procure your freedom by the sacrifice of my own! Though you were early forced from my arms, your image has been always rivetted in my heart, from which neither *time nor fortune* have been able to remove it: so that, while the thoughts of your suffering have dampened my prosperity, they have mingled with adversity and increased its bitterness.—To that Heaven which protects the weak from the strong, I commit the care of your innocence and virtues, if they have not already received their full reward, and if your youth and delicacy have not long since fallen victims to the violence of the African trader, the pestilential stench of a Guinea ship, the seasoning in the European colonies, or the lash and lust of a brutal and unrelenting overseer.

I did not long remain after my sister. I was again sold, and carried through a number of places, till after travelling a considerable time, I came to a town called Tinmah, in the most beautiful country I had yet seen in Africa. It was extremely rich, and there were many rivulets which flowed through it, and supplied a large pond in the centre of the town, where the people washed. Here I first saw and tasted cocoa nuts, which I thought superior to any nuts I had ever tasted before; and the trees which were loaded were also interspersed among the houses, which had commodious shades adjoining, and were in the same manner as ours, the insides being neatly plastered and whitewashed. Here I also saw and tasted for the first time, sugar cane. Their money consisted of little white shells, the size of the finger nail. I was sold here for one hundred and seventy-two of them, by a merchant who lived and brought me there. I had been about two or three days at his house, when a wealthy widow, a neighbor of his, came there one evening, and brought with her an only son, a young gentleman about my own age and size. Here they saw me; and having taken a fancy to me, I was bought of the merchant, and went home with them. Her house and premises were situated close to one of those rivulets I have mentioned, and were the finest I ever saw in Africa: they were very extensive, and she had a number of slaves to attend her. The next day I was washed and perfumed, and when meal time came, I was led into the presence of my mistress, and ate and drank before her with her son. This filled me with astonishment; and I could scarce help expressing my surprise that the young gentleman should suffer me, who was bound, to eat with him who was free; and not only so, but that he would not at any time either eat or drink till I had taken first, because I was the eldest, which was agreeable to our custom. Indeed, everything here, and all their treatment of me, made me forget that I was a slave. The language of these people resembled ours so nearly, that we understood each other perfectly. They had also the same customs as we. There were likewise slaves daily to attend us, while my young master and I, with other boys, sported with our darts and bows and arrows, as I had been used to do at home. In this resemblance to my former happy state, I passed about two months; and I now began to think I was to be adopted into the family, and was beginning to be reconciled to my situation, and to forget by degrees my misfortunes, when all at once the delusion vanished; for, without the least previous knowledge, one morning early, while my dear master and companion was still asleep, I was awakened out of my reverie to fresh sorrow, and hurried away even amongst the uncircumcised.

Thus at the very moment I dreamed of the greatest happiness, I found myself most miserable; and it seemed as if fortune wished to give me this taste of joy only to render the reverse more poignant.—The change I now experienced, was as painful as it was sudden and unexpected. It was a change indeed, from a state of bliss to a scene which is inexpressible by me, as it discovered to me an element I had never before beheld, and till then had no idea of, and wherein such instances of hardship and cruelty occurred, as I can never reflect on but with horror.

All the nations and people I had hitherto passed through, resembled our own in their manners, customs, and language; but I came at length to a country, the inhabitants of which differed from us in all those particulars. I was very much struck with this difference, especially when I came among a people who did not circumcise, and ate without washing their hands. They cooked also in iron pots, and had European cutlasses and cross bows, which were unknown to us, and fought with their fists among themselves. Their women were not so modest as ours, for they ate and drank, and slept with their men. But, above all, I was amazed to see no sacrifices or offerings among them. In some of these places the people ornamented themselves with scars, and likewise filed their teeth very sharp. They wanted sometimes to ornament me in the same manner, but I would not suffer them; hoping that I might some time be among a people who did not thus disfigure themselves, as I thought they did. At last I came to the banks of a large river which was covered with canoes, in which the people appeared to live with their household utensils, and provisions of all kinds. I was beyond measure astonished at this, as I had never before seen any water larger than a pond or a rivulet: and my surprise was mingled with no small fear when I was put into one of these canoes, and we began to paddle and move along the river. We continued going on thus till night, when we came to land, and made fires on the banks, each family by themselves; some dragged their canoes on shore, others stayed and cooked in theirs, and laid in them all night. Those on the land had mats, of which they made tents, some in the shape of little houses; in these we slept; and after the morning meal, we embarked again and proceeded as before. I was often very much astonished to see some of the women, as well as the men, jump into the water, dive to the bottom, come up again, and swim about.—Thus I continued to travel, sometimes by land, sometimes by water, through different countries and various nations, till, at the end of six or seven months after I had been kidnapped, I arrived at the sea coast. It would be tedious and uninteresting to relate all the incidents which befell me during this journey, and which I have not yet forgotten; of the various hands I passed through, and the manners and customs of all the different people among whom I lived. I shall therefore only observe, that in all the places where I was, the soil was exceedingly rich; the pumpkins, eadas, plaintains, yams, etc., were in great abundance, and of incredible size. There were also vast quantities of different gums, though not used for any purpose, and everywhere a great deal of tobacco.

The cotton even grew quite wild, and there was plenty of red-wood. I saw no mechanics whatever in all the way, except such as I have mentioned. The chief employment in all these countries was agriculture, and both the males and females, as with us, were brought up to it, and trained in the arts of war.

The first object which saluted my eyes when I arrived on the coast, was the sea, and a slave ship, which was then riding at anchor, and waiting for its cargo. These filled me with astonishment, which was soon converted into terror, when I was carried on board. I was immediately handled, and tossed up to see if I were sound, by some of the crew; and I was now persuaded that I had gotten into a world of bad spirits, and that they were going to kill me. Their complexions, too, differing so much from ours, their long hair, and the language they spoke (which was very different from any I had ever heard) united to confirm me in this belief. Indeed, such were the horrors of my views and fears at the moment, that, if ten thousand worlds had been my own, I would have freely parted with them all to have exchanged my condition with that of the meanest slave in my own country. When I looked round the ship too, and saw a large furnace of copper boiling, and a multitude of black people of every description chained together, every one of their countenances expressing dejection and sorrow, I no longer doubted of my fate; and quite overpowered with horror and anguish, I fell motionless on the deck and fainted. When I recovered a little, I found some black people about me who I believed were some of those who had brought me on board, and had been receiving their pay; they talked to me in order to cheer me, but all in vain. I asked them if we were not to be eaten by those white men with horrible looks, red faces, and long hair. They told me I was not: and one of the crew brought me a small portion of spirituous liquor in a wine glass, but, being afraid of him, I would not take it out of his hand. One of the blacks, therefore, took it from him and gave it to me, and I took a little down my palate, which, instead of reviving me, as they thought it would, threw me into the greatest consternation at the strange feeling it produced, having never tasted any such liquor before. Soon after this, the blacks who brought me on board went off, and left me abandoned to despair.

I now saw myself deprived of all chance of returning to my native country, or even the least glimpse of hope of gaining the shore, which I now considered as friendly; and I even wished for my former slavery in preference to my present situation, which was filled with horrors of every kind, still heightened by my ignorance of what I was to undergo. I was not long suffered to indulge my grief; I was soon put down under the decks, and there I received such a salutation in my nostrils as I had never experienced in my life: so that, with the loathsomeness of the stench and crying together, I became so sick and low that I was not able to eat, nor had I the least desire to taste any thing. I now wished for the last friend, death, to relieve me; but soon, to my grief, two of the white men offered me eatables; and, on my refusing to eat, one of them held me fast by the hands, and laid me across, I think the windlass, and tied my feet, while the other flogged me severely. I had never experienced any thing of this kind before, and although not being used to the water, I naturally feared that element the first time I saw it, yet, nevertheless, could I have got over the nettings, I would have jumped over the side, but I could not; and besides, the crew used to watch us very closely who were not chained down to the decks, lest we should leap into the water; and I have seen some of these poor African prisoners most severely cut, for attempting to do so, and hourly whipped for not eating. This indeed was often the case with myself. In a little time after, amongst the poor chained men, I found some of my own nation, which in a small degree gave ease to my mind. I inquired of these what was to be done with us? They gave me to understand, we were to be carried to these white people's country to work for them. I then was a little revived, and thought, if it were no worse than working, my situation was not so desperate; but still I feared I should be put to death, the white people looked and acted, as I thought, in so savage a manner; for I had never seen among any people such instances of brutal cruelty; and this not only shown towards us blacks, but also to some of the whites themselves. One white man in particular I saw, when we were permitted to be on deck, flogged so unmercifully with a large rope near the foremast, that he died in consequence of it; and they tossed him over the side as they would have done a brute. This made me fear these people the more; and I expected nothing less than to be treated in the same manner. I could not help expressing my fears and apprehensions to some of my countrymen; I asked them if these people had no country, but lived in this hollow place [the ship]? They told me they did not, but came from a distant one. "Then," said I, "how comes it in all our country we never heard of them?" They told me because they lived so very far off. I then asked where were their women? had they any like themselves? I was told they had. "And why," said I, "do we not see them?" They answered, because they were left behind. I asked how the vessel could go? They told me they could not tell; but that there was cloth put upon the masts by the help of the ropes I saw, and then the vessel went on; and the white men had some spell or magic they put in the water when they liked in order to stop the vessel. I was exceedingly amazed at this account, and really thought they were spirits. I therefore wished much to be from amongst them, for I expected they would sacrifice me; but my wishes were vain, for we were so quartered that it was impossible for any of us to make our escape.

While we stayed on the coast I was mostly on deck; and one day, to my great astonishment, I saw one of the vessels coming in with the sails up. As soon as the whites saw it, they gave a great shout, at which we were amazed; and the more so, as the vessel appeared larger by approaching nearer. At last, she came to an anchor in my sight, and when the anchor was let go, I and my countrymen who saw it, were lost in the astonishment to observe the vessel stop—and were now convinced it was done by magic. Soon after this the other ship got her boats out, and they came on board of us, and the people of both ships seemed very glad to see each other.—Several of the strangers also shook hands with us black people, and made motions with their hands, signifying, I suppose, we were to go to their country, but we did not understand them.

At last, when the ship we were in had got in all her cargo, they made ready with many fearful noises, and we were all put under deck, so that we could not see how they managed the vessel. But this disappointment was the least of my sorrow. The stench of the hold while we were on the coast was so intolerably loathsome, that it was dangerous to remain there for any time, and some of us had been permitted to stay on the deck for the fresh air; but now that the whole ship's cargo were confined together, it became absolutely pestilential. The closeness of the place, and the heat of the climate, added to the number in the ship, which was so crowded that each had scarcely room to turn himself, almost suffocated us. This produced copious perspirations, so that the air soon became unfit for respiration, from a variety of loathsome smells, and brought on a sickness among the slaves, of which many died—thus falling victims to the improvident avarice, as I may call it, of their purchasers. This wretched situation was again aggravated by the falling of the chains, now become insupportable; and the filth of the necessary tubs, into which the children often fell, and were almost suffocated. The shrieks of the women, and the groans of the dying, rendered the whole a scene of horror almost inconceivable. Happily, perhaps, for myself, I was soon reduced so low here that it was thought necessary to keep me almost always on deck; and from my extreme youth I was not put in fetters. In this situation

I expected every hour to share the fate of my companions, some of whom were almost daily brought upon the deck at the point of death, which I began to hope would soon put an end to my miseries. Often did I think many of the inhabitants of the deep much more happy than myself. I envied them the freedom they enjoyed, and as often wished I could change my condition for theirs. Every circumstance I met with, served only to render my state more painful, and heightened my apprehensions, and my opinion of the cruelty of the whites.

One day they had taken a number of fishes; and when they had killed and satisfied themselves with as many as they thought fit, to our astonishment, who were on deck, rather than give any of them to us to eat, as we expected, they tossed the remaining fish into the sea again, although we begged and prayed for some as well as we could, but in vain; and some of my countrymen, being pressed by hunger, took an opportunity, when they thought no one saw them, of trying to get a little privately; but they were discovered, and the attempt procured them some very severe floggings. One day, when we had a smooth sea and moderate wind, two of my wearied countrymen who were chained together (I was near them at the time), preferring death to such a life of misery, somehow made through the nettings and jumped into the sea: immediately, another quite dejected fellow, who, on account of his illness, was suffered to be out of irons, also followed their example; and I believe many more would very soon have done the same, if they had not been prevented by the ship's crew, who were instantly alarmed. Those of us that were the most active, were in a moment put down under the deck, and there was such a noise and confusion amongst the people of the ship as I never heard before, to stop her and get the boat out to go after the slaves. However, two of the wretched were drowned, but they got the other, and afterwards flogged him unmercifully, for thus attempting to prefer death to slavery. In this manner we continued to undergo more hardships than I can now relate, hardships which are inseparable from this accursed trade. Many a time we were near suffocation from the want of fresh air, which we were often without for whole days together. This and the stench of the necessary tubs, carried off many.

During our passage, I first saw flying fishes, which surprised me very much; they used frequently to fly across the ship, and many of them fell on the deck. I also now first saw the use of the quadrant; I had often with astonishment seen the mariners make observations with it, and I could not think what it meant. They at last took notice of my surprise; and one of them, willing to increase it, as well as to gratify my curiosity, made me one day look through it. The clouds appeared to me to be land, which disappeared as they passed along. This heightened my wonder; and I was now more persuaded than ever, that I was in another world, and that every thing about me was magic. At last, we came in sight of the island of Barbadoes [sic], at which the whites on board gave a great shout, and made many signs of joy to us. We did not know what to think of this; but as the vessel drew nearer, we plainly saw the harbor, and other ships of different kinds and sizes, and we soon anchored amongst them, off Bridgetown. Many merchants and planters now came on board, though it was in the evening. They put us in separate parcels, and examined us attentively. They also made us jump, and pointed to the land, signifying we were to go there. We thought by this, we should be eaten by these ugly men, as they appeared to us; and, when soon after we were all put down under the deck again, there was much dread and trembling among us, and nothing but bitter cries to be heard all the night from these apprehensions, insomuch that at last the white people got some old slaves from the land to pacify us. They told us we were not to be eaten, but to work, and were soon to go on land, where we should see many of our country people. This report eased us much. And sure enough, soon after we were landed, there came to us Africans of all languages.

We were conducted immediately to the merchant's yard, where we were all pent up together, like so many sheep in a fold, without regard to sex or age. As every object was new to me, everything I saw filled me with surprise. What struck me first was that the houses were built with bricks and stories, and in every other respect different from those I had seen in Africa; but I was still more astonished on seeing people on horseback. I did not know what this could mean; and, indeed, I thought these people were full of nothing but magical arts. While I was in this astonishment, one of my fellow-prisoners spoke to a countryman of his, about the horses, who said they were the same kind they had in their country. I understood them, though they were from a distant part of Africa; and I thought it odd I had not seen any horses there; but afterwards, when I came to converse with different Africans, I found they had many horses amongst them, and much larger than those I then saw.

J. Caseley Hayford
(1866–1933, Ghana)

Indigenous Institutions of Ghana

The King

At the head of the Native State stands prominently the *Ohin* (King), who is the Chief Magistrate and Chief Military Leader of the State. He is first in the councils of the country, and the first Executive Officer. His influence is only measured by the strength of his character. He it is who represents the State in all its dealings with the outside world; and, so long as he keeps within constitutional bounds, he is supreme in his own State.

The term "*Ohin*" is applied to the head of any considerable community of Aborigines, but all kings are not of the same degree. Hence the distinction which is sometimes made of applying the term "king" to the paramount ruler of a state, and the term "chief" to subordinate rulers under the King paramount. Thus the Head of the State of Ahanta is the King Baidoe Bonso, whose capital is Busua, near Dixcove, while the Head of the Province of Axim, in the State of Ahanta, is also known as *Ohin* Atta among all natives. Nor is this in any way strange, since each native community, be it small or be it large, is a composite whole, having its form and method of government the same in all essentials. The entire fabric in either case may be analysed into the same elements.

The term "*Cabboceer*" was at one time employed to mark chiefs of first importance from minor chiefs, but it has fallen into disuse. It will be good policy to revive the title, and generally to enhance the dignity of the native Chiefs, as their influence for good in a well regulated system of government will be simply incalculable.

The office of king is elective. No king, that is to say, is born a king. There are a number of circumstances which may prevent the nearest to the stool from ever sitting thereon. A junior heir to the stool may be selected to sit upon the stool, if a senior heir is a profligate, or otherwise incapable of maintaining the kingly dignity. Nor does a king acquire an indefeasible title to the stool when once he has sat upon it. It is the right of those who placed him thereon to put him off the stool for any just cause. But no other authority can rightly interfere with his position, if his people are satisfied with him. He holds such position for life, and, upon his death, his younger uterine brother, cousin, or eldest nephew, is selected to succeed him. During his life the King often indicates who such successor shall be, and, generally, his wishes are respected.

In the case of *Hima Diki v. Agiman and others*, decided as recently as the 7th of February, 1901, by His Honour Mr. Justice Nicoll, in the Divisional Court at Axim, Hima Diki, the King of Dixcove, had been deposed by the people of Dixcove, and replaced by Anansu Mensah, his uncle. The ex-king sought to recover from the defendants, as representing the Chiefs and Elders of Dixcove, the stool and the paraphernalia thereof. Said His Honour in giving judgment: "I find (1) that the plaintiff was King of Dixcove and duly instooled; (2) that he was deposed according to native custom about a year ago."

Nothing daunted, the ex-king next brought an action to test the legality of his destoolment. It came before the same learned judge on the 21st day of October, 1901, when evidence of a highly important character as to the Customary Law thereto appertaining was given. Kweku Atta, King of Axim, was called as an expert witness.

> *"Question:* In the case of a town chief would you tell the procedure in taking him off the stool first when the family complain?

> *"Answer:* The family complain to the townspeople, who put me on the stool, and we meet, and I am found to be in the wrong, I ask the townsmen to beg my family. They beg my family to forgive me. I satisfy them. If I do it again a second time, again forgiveness. The third time, you must go, you must have opportunity of defending yourself.

> *"Question:* Now when the townspeople complain?

> *"Answer:* Your family accompany you to the meeting of the townsmen, and the townsmen put before the family what you have done, and after you have made your defence, and your family found that you are in the wrong the family and yourself beg the town to forgive you. They forgive you, and you pacify them. If you repeat it four times, then, they tell the family they don't want you any more, and that ends it. That is the native law and practice."

The Court in giving judgment in this case said: "I find that the plaintiff was Chief of Dixcove, and that he has never been properly deposed, and is now Chief of Dixcove, sitting on Dixcove stool; and I order the stool to be given up to plaintiff, or some one for him."

The case of Kweku Inkruma, ex-King of Peppissa District, is in point. In April, 1901, the King Kwamina Enimil of Eastern Wassaw being in Axim, the Councillors and Elders of the stool charged Kweku Inkruma with divers acts unbecoming the kingly office, and, the facts being proved to the satisfaction of the King's Court, he was put off the stool.

From the foregoing cases the following principles are clearly deducible as to the destoolment of a king.

Firstly: The authority which, in accordance with the Customary Law, called the King to the stool, is the only authority which can call for his destoolment.

Secondly: To render the destoolment of a king valid, he must have been properly destooled; and before he can be properly destooled, he must have had full opportunity of showing cause why he should not be destooled.

Thirdly: It is not for every petty act of misconduct that a king's destoolment can be called for. He must have been convicted of acts seriously detrimental to the State, or otherwise gravely unbecoming the kingly dignity. The Customary Law herein carries out the spirit of the direction to pardon your brother, if he sins against you seventy times seven.

Fourthly: The proper tribunal, in accordance with the Customary Law, must try the King, and the law is jealous of the procedure on such occasions.

It is obvious why the Customary Law keeps a wakeful eye over the proceedings affecting a king's destoolment. The kingly office is, as we have seen, of the highest importance in the State, and the person of the King is, indeed, sacred. If it were possible for every trifling cause to arraign the first Magistrate of the State before his peers, or to deprive him of power by the merest whim of his people, there would be little or no stability in the State itself. So that, to some extent, it may be said that the people are ever indulgent to their King, and cast around his person a halo of dignity and prerogative which cannot be lightly broken through.

Now, what does it mean when a native king is said to be put on, or off, the stool? What is the idea conveyed by the stool in its concrete sense upon which the King is said to sit? I have said that the King is the first Magistrate of the State, essentially the fountain of justice, and the allusion to him as sitting upon a stool bears out this principle more than anything else. For, you see, in a native state every matter is settled by the "bringing together of stools." When there is a big "palaver" coming on, the people say they are going to bring together stools—*wo ri bobo ingwa*. What actually takes place at the appointed hour of the meeting is, that you observe a number of attendants carrying to the public arena a number of native stools of the pattern generally seen in public pictorial prints after a military expedition in the hinterland of the Gold Coast. Each of these stools represents an ancient house in the community, and the King's stool would, naturally, be the most important and the most ancient stool present. They are now going to hold a "palaver," and the owners of the several stools will be the Councillors, and the occupant of the kingly stool will be the President of the Council. It is the King's Linguist who will open the proceedings. It is he who will announce to the assembled people the decision of the Council, thus clearing showing the King to be the first Magistrate of the State.

But what is the origin of the native kingly office, and what are the principles which govern the election of a king? The kingly office springs from a period in native history when there was continual warfare among the different tribes inhabiting the country. The choice of a king was most probably determined by the personal valour, intelligence, and capability of the individual to lead the forces of the community in time of war. Such individual was undoubtedly the best man the community could produce. The successful leader would in time of peace be the first man of the community and naturally its head. He would come in for a larger proportion of the lands that had been acquired by the strength of his arms, and when he died, in accordance with the Customary Law, his nephew would succeed him. So also where the community settled in a new country whose virgin forest they cleared, pressed down, probably, after a disastrous war. All the native communities on the Gold Coast proper settled in the country in this way. The old war chiefs came to unoccupied land and settled thereupon, first clearing the virgin forest. The principle of partition would be the same as in the case of settlement after conquest. In all my several years of active practice at the Bar, I have not come across a case where title to land has been based upon a right of conquest. It is perfectly safe to say that it is more the exception than the rule. It is a well-known fact that Kwantabissa, King of Denkira, as late as 1901, claimed the right to lease, and actually did lease, land on the other side of the Offin River from which his ancestors had been driven by the Ashantis in ancient times. The usage of war among the Aborigines would seem to be that after the conclusion of peace the vanquished still retained their lands.

So long as the nephew was a man of character and capacity he would not be disturbed in his leadership of the people, and, gradually, the kingly office would become an institution, and remain in a given family. But still the community would continue to possess the power of veto in case a given member of the royal family was found incapable of performing the kingly functions. They would say, in effect, to the incompetent aspirant, "We appointed your ancestor to the kingly office as a reward for uncommon abilities, and we are prepared to honour his family by seeking election to the kingly office from and by it; but we must object to being ruled by any unfit person. We will, through the family council, decide which member of the family shall govern us, if we are dissatisfied with the family's own selection." And thus we arrive at the principles which govern the election of a king.

Now, how comes it about that there are so many kings in a given native state? The reason is obvious. Before the country was settled in a peaceful way there were many independent chiefs, each a king in his own province. Intertribal strife then began, and, gradually, the weaker kings went to the wall, and the fittest and strongest became the paramount king of a number of provinces in a given state.

Upon the demise of a king, the Councillors meet and demand of the royal family a successor. The royal family then nominates a successor, who may be the uterine brother, the cousin, or nephew of the deceased King. Descent being traced through the female line, such a cousin would be the son of the sister of the deceased King's mother; and such a nephew would be the son of the sister of the late King. The person nominated is next presented to the Councillors, and, upon being approved, is placed by them upon the stool. This is the strict theory of the law; but, as a matter of fact, during the lifetime of the King, there is an heir apparent upon whom both the Councillors and the royal family cast an eye, so that the power of veto is seldom exercised by the Councillors. But that such a power exists is a clearly established principle. In the case of *Enima v. Pai* the plaintiff sought, *inter alia,* to be declared the rightful successor to the Assankra Breman or Kwinbontu's stool in the Wassaw district to which the *Werempims,* or Councillors, of Assankra Breman had elected Pai, and upon which they had actually placed him. The plaintiff and the defendant being cousins, the question was as to the right of selection by the *Werempims,* which the Court had no difficulty in upholding.

The King is the Chief Executive Officer of the State, but not the Executive Council of the State. Such a council exists, and any acts done by the King without its concurrence are liable to be set aside.

In the case of *The African (West) Exploitation and Development Syndicate, Ltd., v. Sir Alfred Kirby and the Princes River Gold Mines, Ltd.,* the Head-Chief of Princes had granted a lease of the lands in dispute to the plaintiff company without the concurrence of his Chiefs, and his successor, Kofi Ainibah, had granted the same lands to the defendants with such concurrence. After taking a deal of expert evidence, the Court decided that the subsequent lease should prevail, and judgment was entered for the defendants. Upon appeal the point as to the right of the Councillors to concur in the lease was upheld.

The King is the President of the Legislative Board, but he seldom, if ever, initiates any legislative act. It is the province of the people through their representatives, the Councillors, to introduce legislation, and say what law shall direct their conduct. Hence, when a law is to be promulgated, which is done by the "beating of the gong-gong," the formula, in the mouth of the Linguist is, "The King and his Councillors and Elders say I must inform you—"; then follows the particular command and the words, "PAR HI," an emphatic exclamatory phrase, and a loud rattle of the gong, by way of a general proclamation. Such a law, once thus promulgated, lives from generation to generation, within the memory of the community, and the command is never without its sanction. Any other way of enacting laws for the people is not in accordance with the Customary Law of the people.

The King is the Chief Military Officer of his forces. In time of war, he directs the operations; and if he is a man of capacity, he has the leading place in the councils of war. There is generally a *Tufu Hin,* or Captain-General, of the forces; but his authority is subordinate to that of the King, and he is, in every essential, an officer of the King.

The King is also, as we have seen, the first Magistrate of his people. In the Native State System the people have not yet arrived at the stage when the King is merely the fountain of justice and appoints officers to dispense it merely in his name. He himself presides over the hearing of all important cases, supported by his principal Chiefs, Councillors, and Linguists. There are other important Chiefs in a state, who are empowered to decide cases; but the courts of such Chiefs are subsidiary to the King's Court, and not independent of it.

Martin Delany

(1812–1885, United States)

The Condition and Destiny of Africans
in the United States

The United States, untrue to her trust and unfaithful to her professed principles of republican equality, has also pursued a policy of political degradation to a large portion of her native born countrymen, and that class is the Colored People. Denied an equality not only of political but of natural rights, in common with the rest of our fellow citizens, there is no species of degradation to which we are not subject. . . .

It was expected that anti-slavery, according to its professions, would extend to colored persons, as far as in the power of its adherents, those advantages nowhere else to be obtained among white men; that colored boys would get situations in their shops and stores, and every other advantage tending to elevate them as far as possible, would be extended to them. . . . But in all this we were doomed to disappointment, sad, sad disappointment. Instead of realizing what we had hoped for, we find ourselves occupying the very same position in relation to our anti-slavery friends, as we do in relation to the pro-slavery part of the community—a mere secondary, underling position, in all our relations to them, and anything more than this is not a matter-of-course affair—it comes not by established anti-slavery custom or right, but, like that which emanates from the pro-slavery portion of the community, by mere sufferance.

It is true that the *Liberator* office, in Boston, has got Elijah Smith, a colored youth, at the cases—the *Standard*, in New York, a young colored man, and the *Freeman*, in Philadelphia, William Still, another, in the publication office, as "packing clerk"; yet these are but three out of the hosts that fill these offices in their various departments, all occupying places that could have been, and as we once thought, would have been, easily enough, occupied by colored men. . . .

And if it be urged that colored men are incapable as yet to fill these positions, all we have to say is, that the cause has fallen far short; almost equivalent to a failure, of a tithe, of what it promised to do in half the period of its existence, to this time, if it have not as yet, now a period of twenty years, raised up colored men enough, to fill the offices within its patronage. We think it not unkind to say, if it had been half as faithful to itself, as it should have been—its professed principles we mean, it could have reared and tutored from childhood colored men enough by this time, for its own especial purpose. These we know could have been easily obtained, because colored people in general are favorable to the anti-slavery cause, and wherever there is an adverse manifestation, it arises from sheer ignorance; and we have now but comparatively few such among us. . . .

When we speak of colonization, we wish distinctly to be understood as speaking of the American Colonization Society—or that which is under its influence—commenced in Richmond, Va., in 1817, under the influence of Mr. Henry Clay of Kentucky, Judge Bushrod Washington of Virginia, and other Southern slaveholders, having for their express object, as their speeches and doings all justify us in asserting in good faith, the removal of the free colored people from the land of their birth, for the security of the slaves, as property to the slave propagandists.

The scheme had no sooner been propagated than the old and leading colored men of Philadelphia, Pa., with Richard Allen, James Forten, and others at their head, true to their trust and the cause of their brethren, summoned the colored people together, and then and there, in language and with voices pointed and loud, protested against the scheme as an outrage, having no other object in view, than the benefit of the slave-holding interests of the country, and that as freemen they would never prove recreant to the cause of their brethren in bondage, by leading them without hope of redemption from their chains. This determination of the colored patriots of Philadelphia was published in full, authentically, and circulated throughout the length and breadth of the country by the papers of the day. The colored people everywhere received the news, and at once endorsed with heart and soul, the doings of the Anti-Colonization Meeting of colored freemen. From that time forth the colored people generally have had no sympathy with the colonization scheme, nor confidence in its leaders, looking upon them all as arrant hypocrites, seeking every opportunity to deceive them. In a word, the monster was crippled in its infancy, and had never as yet recovered from the stroke. . . .

The colored races are highly susceptible of religion; it is a constituent principle of their nature, and an excellent trait in their character. But unfortunately for them, they carry it too far. Their hope is largely developed, and, consequently, they usually stand still—hope in God, and really expect Him to do that for them, which it is necessary they should do themselves. This is their great mistake, and arises from a misconception of the character and ways of Deity. . . .

Moral theories have long been resorted to by us, as a means of effecting the redemption of our brethren in bonds, and the elevation of the free colored people in this country. Experience has taught us that speculations are not enough; that the *practical* application of principles adduced, the thing carried out, is the only true and proper course to pursue.

We have speculated and moralized much about equality—claiming to be as good as our neighbors, and everybody else—all of which may do very well in ethics, but not in politics. We live in society among men, conducted by men, governed by rules and regulations. However arbitrary, there are certain policies that regulate all well organized institutions and corporate bodies. . . . Society regulates itself, being governed by mind, which, like water, finds its own level. . . . By the regulations of society, there is no equality of persons where there is not an equality of attainments.

We will suppose a case for argument: In this city reside two colored families, of three sons and three daughters each. At the head of each family there is an old father and mother. The opportunities of these families may or may not be the same for educational advantages; be that as it may, the children of the one go to school, and become qualified for the duties of life. One daughter becomes a school teacher, another a mantua-maker, and a third a fancy shopkeeper; while one son becomes a farmer, another a merchant, and a third a mechanic. All enter into the business with fine prospects, marry respectably, and settle down in domestic comfort; while the six sons and daughters of the other family grow up without educational and business qualifications, and the highest aim they have is to apply to the sons and daughters of the first named family, to hire for domestics! Would there be an equality here between the children of these two families? Certainly not. This, then, is precisely the position of the colored people generally in the United States, compared with the whites. What is necessary to be done, in order to attain an equality, is to change the condition, and the person is at once changed. If, as before stated, a knowledge of all the various business enterprises, trades, professions, and sciences is necessary for the elevation of the white, a knowledge of them also is necessary for the elevation of the colored man; and he can not be elevated without them.

White men are producers; we are consumers. They build houses, and we rent them. They raise produce, and we consume it. They manufacture clothes and wares, and we garnish ourselves with them. They build coaches, vessels, cars, hotels, saloons, and other vehicles and places of accommodation, and we deliberately wait until they have got them in readiness, then walk in, and contend with as much assurance for a "right," as though the whole thing was bought by, paid for, and belonged to us. . . .

It ever has been denied that the United States recognized or knew any difference between the people. This is not true. . . . By the provisions of this bill the colored people of the United States are positively degraded beneath the level of the whites—are made liable at any time, in any place, and under all circumstances, to be arrested, and, upon the claim of any white person, without the privilege even of making a defence, sent into endless bondage. Let no visionary nonsense about *habeas corpus*, or a fair trial, deceive us; there are no such rights granted in this bill, and, except where the commissioner is too ignorant to understand when reading it, or too stupid to enforce it when he does understand, there is no earthly chance—no hope under heaven for the colored person who is brought before one of these officers of the law. Any leniency that may be expected must proceed from the whims or caprice of the magistrate—in fact, it is optional with them; and *our* rights and liberty [are] entirely at their disposal.

We are slaves in the midst of freedom, waiting patiently, and unconcernedly—indifferently, and stupidly, for masters to come and lay claim to us, trusting to their generosity, whether or not they will own us and carry us into endless bondage.

The slave is more secure than we; he knows who holds the heel upon his bosom—we know not the wretch who may grasp us by the throat. His master may be a man of some conscientious scruples; ours may be unmerciful. Good or bad, mild or harsh, easy or hard, lenient or severe, saint or Satan—whenever that master demands any one of us, even our affectionate wives and darling little children, *we must go into slavery*—there is no alternative. The *will* of the man who sits in judgment on our liberty, is the law. To him is given *all power* to say whether or not we have a right to enjoy freedom. This is the power over the slave in the South that is now extended to the North. The will of the man who sits in judgment over us is the law; because it is explicitly provided that the *decision* of the commissioner shall be final, from which there can be no appeal. . . .

What can we do? What shall we do? This is the great and important question:—Shall we submit to be dragged like brutes before heartless men, and sent into degradation and bondage? Shall we fly, or shall we resist?

This important inquiry we shall answer, and find a remedy in when treating of the emigration of the colored people. . . .

That there have been people in all ages under certain circumstances, that may be benefited by emigration, will be admitted; and that there are circumstances under which emigration is absolutely necessary to their political elevation, can not be disputed.

This we see in the Exodus of the Jews from Egypt to the land of Judea; in the expedition of Dido and her followers from Tyre to Mauritania; and, not to dwell upon hundreds of modern European examples, also in the very memorable emigration of the Puritans, in 1620, from Great Britain, the land of their birth to the wilderness of the New World, at which may be fixed the beginning of emigration to this continent as a permanent residence.

This may be acknowledged; but to advocate the emigration of the colored people of the United States from their native homes, is a new feature in our history, and at first view may be considered objectionable, as pernicious to our interests. This objection is at once removed, when reflecting on our condition as incontrovertibly shown in a foregoing part of this work. And we shall proceed at once to give the advantages to be derived from emigration, to us as a people, in preference to any other policy that we may adopt. This granted, the question will then be, Where shall we go? This we conceive to be all-important, of paramount consideration, and shall endeavor to show the most advantageous locality; and premise the recommendation with the strictest advice against any countenance whatever to the emigration scheme of the so-called Republic of Liberia. . . .

Let our young men and women prepare themselves for usefulness and business; that the men may enter into merchandise, trading, and other things of importance; the young women may become teachers of various kinds, and otherwise fill places of usefulness. Parents must turn their attention more to the education of the children. We mean, to educate them for useful practical building purposes. Educate them for the store and the counting house—to do everyday practical business. Consult the children's propensities, and direct their education according to their inclinations. It may be that there is too great a desire on the part of parents to give their children a professional education, before the body of the people are ready for it. A people must be a business people, and have more to depend upon than mere help in people's houses and hotels, before they are either able to support, or capable of properly appreciating the services of professional men among them. This has been one of our great mistakes—we have gone in advance of ourselves. We have commenced at the superstructure of the building instead of the foundation—at the top instead of the bottom. We should first be mechanics and common tradesmen, and professions as a matter of course would grow out of the wealth made thereby. Young men and women must now prepare for usefulness—the day of our elevation is at hand—all the world now gazes at us—and Central and South America, and the West Indies, bid us come and be men and women, protected, secure, beloved and Free.

Houston A. Baker, Jr.
(b. 1942, United States)

W. E. B. Du Bois and *The Souls of Black Folk*

The bright ideals of the past,—physical freedom, political power, the training of brains and the training of hands,—all these in turn have waxed and waned, until even the last grows dim and overcast. Are they all wrong,—all false? No, not that, but each alone was oversimple and incomplete,—the dreams of a credulous race-childhood, or the fond imaginings of the other world which does not know and does not want to know our power. To be really true, all these ideals must be melted and welded into one.[1]

Thus spoke W. E. B. Du Bois, the herald of a new age in the history of the black American, and the statement tells a good deal about Du Bois's point of view. Du Bois was conscious of the ideals of the past in the black American experience, and he recognized their value. He felt that a new stage in the growth of the black man in America had been reached, and he believed there had to be a synthesis of the ideals of the past, a synthesis that would lead to the manhood of the black American race. The realization of the "pastness of the past" and the sense of a new age that inform *The Souls of Black Folk* are not surprising when one considers that Du Bois was a man of the twentieth-century—he died in the last decade [1963]. The more interesting part of the statement is the portion that deals with synthesis, the melting and welding of a wide range of ideas into a broader and more effective whole; for it is his stand as a synthesizer that marks Du Bois as a man of culture.

The word *culture,* as Raymond Williams[2] has insisted, is a protean entity, but Du Bois seems to belong to a tradition of the cultured man that was perhaps best characterized by Matthew Arnold. Both Arnold and Du Bois, along with men like Walter Pater and Oscar Wilde, seem to express a similar point of view when they speak of culture and the cultural man. For Du Bois and Arnold, culture consisted of the study of harmonious perfection and the acquisition and diffusion of "the best that has been thought and known in the world . . . [in order] to make all men live in an atmosphere of sweetness and light."[3]

It encompassed a knowledge of the classics, a grounding in broad human sympathies, and a struggle for self-realization through the arts of the Western world. The cultured man is elevated above the scenes of clerical and secular life; he is at some remove from the people, a man of astute sensibility who can wisely and justly criticize the state of society. In short, he was for Du Bois a "Negro intellectual," and to a certain extent *The Souls of Black Folk* is a prototype for Harold Cruse's recent work.

In defining the Negro intellectual, Du Bois drew from a tradition that played a large part in European and American civilization during the last decades of the nineteenth century; not only was Arnold's idea of culture involved, but also the aestheticism of men like Pater, Wilde, and a host of others in Britain, France, and America. Although the *fin de siècle* saw some outrageous poets and a few delicate poseurs, there were also a number of writers who felt that "art for art's sake" meant art for culture's sake. Many writers believed that the products of the intellect and the imagination, if properly handled, could lead to self-realization; from the individual who possessed this virtue it was but a short step to a better society. These writers were in the front ranks of those who looked to "culture" as a court of appeal above the sometimes grim realities of an industrial age; for them the word culture denoted an ethereal substance or process that had little to do with "a whole way of life" engaged in by a specific, homogeneous group of people. Oscar Wilde, Pater's chief disciple, expressed all of these points in his collection *Intentions.*

Du Bois frequently prefaces or intersperses his essays with quotations from the aesthetic school, and the tone of many of his passages is that of decadence—of the passing of the old order, with a hint of ominous events to come. But the *raison d'être* for the black man of culture is what connects Du Bois's point of view with a well-defined tradition. The cultured man will insure the growth and harmonious progress of America. At several points in *The Souls of Black Folk,* Du Bois emerges as a fervent nationalist championing the ideal of human brotherhood—a sort of classical harmony of souls. In his first essay, for example, he advocates "the ideal of fostering and developing the traits and talents of the Negro, not in opposition to or contempt for other races, but rather in large conformity to the greater ideals of the American Republic, in order that some day on American soil two world-races may give each to each those characteristics both so sadly lack" (p. 220). The black man of culture is in a position to contribute to the welfare of society as a whole.

Du Bois's delineation of the cultured man as an asset to the American Republic is best seen in two essays—"Of the Training of Black Men" and "Of the Sons of Master and Man." In the first essay, he traces the development of black education and concludes that the most influential early educators saw that it was necessary to have a group of college-bred black men before the education of the entire race could be achieved, for such men ran the common, normal, and industrial schools. The growth of black education had to commence at the college level, at such schools as Fisk, Howard, Atlanta, and Shaw. Du Bois goes on to state that whites doubted the wisdom of giving blacks a college education since they felt it would unfit blacks for "useful" work, but he demonstrates that the majority of black men who received B.A. degrees were productive citizens—teachers, physicians, civil servants, and artisans. Du Bois then points out the sterling merits of educated black men:

> Comparing them as a class with my fellow students in New England and in Europe, I cannot hesitate in saying that nowhere have I met men and women with a broader spirit of helpfulness, with deeper devotion to their life-work, or with more consecrated determination to succeed in the face of bitter difficulties than among Negro college-bred men. [P. 280]

The blacks of whom he speaks, moreover, are cultured men, men of "larger vision and deeper sensibility" (p. 280). And they offer one solution to the American racial problem, for Du Bois felt that ". . . the present social separation and acute race-sensitiveness must eventually yield to the influences of culture [i.e., the arts and artifacts of the West and the way of life they project], as the South grows more civilized . . ." (p. 281). More significant to Du Bois, however, is the fact that black men of culture generally make "conservative, careful leaders"; they are men who have withstood the temptation to lead the mob and have worked steadily and faithfully in the South. The implications of this statement are obvious, and they bring out a remarkable similarity between Du Bois's point of view and the outlook of Booker T. Washington.

Du Bois sets the black man of culture up as a stop gap between the masses and the progress of society; such a man will stress non-violent political activities, the rectification of economic ills, and educational ideals that will keep the millions from brooding over the wrongs of the past and the difficulties of the present.[4] If the "Talented Tenth" of the race is not recognized and allowed to lead, Du Bois feels the results are foreordained:

> . . . as the black third of the land grows in thrift and skill, unless skillfully guided in its larger philosophy, it must more and more brood over the red past and the creeping, crooked present, until it grasps a gospel of revolt and revenge and throws its new-found energies athwart the current of advance. [P. 282]

This gospel is a long way from the militant revolutionary syndrome of our own time. Of course, "A Litany at Atlanta," the poem that Du Bois wrote in response to the Atlanta race riot of 1906, could be offered as a counter to this statement, for a life that spans nearly a century must possess its restless turnings and abrupt shifts. And Du Bois's career was no exception. He moved from essential agreement with Booker T. Washington to almost total disagreement, from the Niagara Movement and the National Association for the Advancement of Colored People to socialism, from a moderate socialism to membership in the Communist party, and from the United States to Africa where he died as a Ghanaian citizen. One of the most important aspects of *The Souls of Black Folk,* however, is its delineation of the black man of culture as a mediator between opposing sides of the American veil. Some of Du Bois's highly-rhetorical conclusions would make today's revolutionaries cringe: "I sit with Shakespeare and he winces not. Across the color line I move arm in arm with Balzac and Dumas, where smiling men and welcoming women glide in gilded halls. . . . So, wed with truth, I dwell above the Veil" (p. 284).

The second essay, "Of the Sons of Masters and Man," offers a further instance of Du Bois's elevated stance. After dealing in sociological terms with the question of personal contact between blacks and whites in the South, Du Bois concludes that the "best" of the two races seldom come together in economic, educational, political, or religious activities; in fact, the "best" men of each group normally encounter only the worst of the other. This situation, according to Du Bois, is inimical to progress; as long as both groups continue to see only each other's worst aspects, the old myths of black inferiority and white insipidity and indifference will remain. In effect, Du Bois champions a sort of "house servant" perspective, for he feels that during slavery the best of the whites and the best of the blacks did get together in the "big house"; after slavery, moreover, the black domestics (who were the best blacks of their time according to Du Bois) still came into contact with the "best" white families of the South. The tragedy of twentieth-century society, Du Bois feels, is that the "color-line" has been drawn so strictly that it excludes from polite society not only the black lower class, but also the truly deserving black men of culture.

Such a situation was deplorable partly because it meant that the most competent leaders of the black masses were not fulfilling their proper roles. Like the liberals of the nineteenth century, Du Bois hesitated to ask for unconditional equality and unrestricted freedom; his demand was primarily that a sort of Washingtonian "merit" be recognized and rewarded. If classification was necessary to differentiate the high from the low, the leaders from the laborers, Du Bois was all for classification: "Draw lines of crime, of incompetency, of vice, as tightly and uncompromisingly as you will, for these things must be proscribed; but a color-line not only does not accomplish the purpose, but thwarts it"

(p. 336). And while arguing for finer sympathies and broader understanding, Du Bois even enters a Washingtonian apology for the best traditions of the South:

> I freely acknowledge that it is possible, and sometimes best, that a partially developed people should be ruled by the best of their stronger and better neighbors for their own good, until such time as they can start and fight the world's battles alone . . . and I am quite willing to admit that if the representatives of the best white Southern public opinion were the ruling and guiding power in the South to-day the conditions indicated [economic and spiritual guidance for the black masses] would be fairly well fulfilled. [P. 329]

Du Bois felt, however, that the educated black men of his day were in a position to take over the job of guiding and leading the masses; they had only to be recognized by the "best white Southern public opinion" and allowed to assume the job. To this end public opinion had to be informed through social intercourse with the black man of culture (over a "social cigar and a cup of tea"). The result of the cultural man's leadership, of course, would be the advancement of the nation and the spiritual improvement of the masses, for Du Bois argues that once it is granted that individual black men have the ability to "assimilate the culture and common sense of modern civilization, and to pass it on, to some extent at least, to their fellows," certain assumptions can be made:

> If this is true, then here is the path out of the economic situation, and here is the imperative demand for trained Negro leaders of character and intelligence—men of skill, men of light and leading, college-bred men, black captains of industry, and missionaries of culture; men who thoroughly comprehend and know modern civilization, and can take hold of Negro communities and raise and train them by force of precept and example, deep sympathy, and the inspiration of common blood and ideals. [P. 326]

At least two other essays in *The Souls of Black Folk* define the black man of culture and his role in modern society—"Of the Wings of Atalanta" and "Of the Quest of the Golden Fleece." In both pieces, Du Bois presents culture and the cultured man as foils to materialism, as did Arnold in *Culture and Anarchy*. Men trained in the things of the intellect and imagination can aid in the salvation of a land of "dust and dollars" by guiding the beautifully ideal Atalanta away from the fatal golden apples. In the second essay, Du Bois again poses the tragic results of the South's quest for cotton, the golden fleece, and the beneficial counterinfluences of culture.

The definition of the cultural man's role seems not only justifiable, but also ideal. A great many people in Du Bois's age believed that certain artistic and intellectual pursuits could lead to the improvement of society through individual self-realization. Yet some qualifications are in order. While elevating the black intellectual, Du Bois perhaps depressed the masses too far. Throughout *The Souls of Black Folk,* one finds invidious distinctions between the man of culture and all black people who inhabit the realms "beneath" him. One finds the author speaking of the "black lowly," "Sambo," the "black peasantry," and the "black crowd gaudy and dirty." These terms might have acted only as heuristic epithets reinforcing Du Bois's argument, but he made it indubitably clear that he believed the man of culture was qualitatively better than the next man. In one essay, for example, he makes a distinction between "honest toil" and "dignified manhood," a distinction that seems to place the worker in a subhuman category. And this dichotomy is further emphasized when the author speaks of a "reverent comradeship between the black lowly and the black *men* emancipated by training and culture" [my italics]. Moreover, in "Of the Coming of John," one is led to feel sympathy only for John, the tragic black man of culture who is not accepted by whites and who is too elevated to communicate with his own people—"the ignorant and turbulent" black proletariat.

Du Bois's cultured contempt for Washington, moreover, lends credence to the charge that he was overzealous in championing the black intellectual. In "Of Mr. Booker T. Washington and Others," he assumes an almost perfectly Arnoldian approach to criticism; denying any envy of Washington, he asserts that he must denounce the Tuskegeean for the good of the country. In evaluating some of the ways in which black Americans have dealt with the experience of slavery and its aftermath, Du Bois writes off two categories—the submissive and the militantly revolutionary—as ineffectual, then goes on to link Nat Turner, Denmark Vesey, and Gabriel Prosser with the colonizationists (who wished to send blacks "home" to Africa), while placing Washington, rather abruptly, in the submissive category. Washington emerges as a man who has sold out the rights of his people, who has forfeited the black man's demands for political power, civil rights, and higher education. Moreover, he is presented as a leader whose career was paralleled by a retrogression of his followers and whose leadership was "imposed" from the outside on an unwilling people. Finally, Washington's entire career comes to be viewed as a paradox, and the man himself as a submissive compromiser, a somewhat naive, proletarian Uncle Tom. And Du Bois's picture of Washington has had a succession of admirers.

The irony of this portrait, however, is that many of the charges that Du Bois levels against Washington have a double edge: they turn and cut the author himself. While insisting that Washington's leadership was imposed from the outside, Du Bois seems surprisingly unaware that he himself is a Harvard man addressing the nation in sophisticated prose. Speaking of the lack of "self-assertion" and "self-respect" in Washington's philosophy, Du Bois seems willfully to ignore the fact that one of Washington's key concepts was that of "self-help," an important element in the same liberal tradition that informs much of *The Souls of Black Folk*. While condemning Washington's concessions to white America, Du Bois speaks in rhapsodic tones of the American "Fatherland." While belittling Washington's failure to demand all the rights that belong to the black American, Du Bois himself condones a conditional suffrage and states that black universities should be dwellings for "the best of the Negro youth."

This, of course, is neither to say that Du Bois's charges lack validity, nor that the picture he presents is totally inaccurate. The multiple ironies of Du Bois's portrait simply illustrate that what he says of Washington's philosophy is equally true of his own: it contains many "half truths." Washington is not given credit for the great work he accomplished in the South, and Tuskegee is not seen as a fine and productive institution. The fact that Washington's achievements are understated in Du Bois's account simply marks the author once again as a man who made somewhat invidious distinctions, a man who (despite his breadth of vision) was sometimes unable to see those below his cultural level in a fair light. Washington, after all, was not a "college-bred" man in Du Bois's estimation. A proletarian, capitalistic, submissive Washington, therefore, is set against a self-assertive, broad-minded, thoughtful, patriotic, sympathetic black intellectual.

Dudley Randall's humorous poem, "Booker T. and W.E.B.," captures what seems to be a prevailing view of Washington and Du Bois:

"It seems to me," said Booker T.,
"It shows a mighty lot of cheek
To study chemistry and Greek

When Mister Charlie needs a hand
To hoe the cotton on his land,
And when Miss Ann looks for a cook,
Why stick your nose inside a book?"

"I don't agree," said W.E.B.
"If I should have the drive to seek
Knowledge of chemistry or Greek,
I'll do it. Charles and Miss can look
Another place for hand or cook.
Some men rejoice in skill of hand,
And some in cultivating land,
But there are others who maintain
The right to cultivate the brain."

"It seems to me," said Booker T.,
"That all you folks have missed the boat
Who shout about the right to vote,
And spend vain days and sleepless nights
In uproar over civil rights.
Just keep your mouths shut, do not grouse,
But work, and save, and buy a house."

"I don't agree," said W.E.B.,
"For what can property avail
If dignity and justice fail?
Unless you help to make the laws,
They'll steal your house with trumped-up clause.
A rope's as tight, a fire as hot,
No matter how much cash you've got.
Speak soft, and try your little plan,
But as for me, I'll be a man."

"It seems to me," said Booker T.—

"I don't agree,"
Said W.E.B.[5]

    The point of view that Du Bois expressed in *The Souls of Black Folk,* however, was as far removed from that of the majority of black Americans in 1903 as was Booker T. Washington's. At the turn of the century, approximately ninety per cent of black Americans lived in poverty in the deep South, and an industrial education and self-help were just as far beyond their ken and their economic means as an education in the best that had been thought and known in the Western world or an effective non-violent campaign for civil rights. What qualified Du Bois's philosophy for praise and permanence was its attention to the true folk experience of the black American and its orientation toward the future. Washington's outlook was grounded in its age, and it tended to revise the folk experience along lines acceptable to "the best white Southern public opinion." With his broader vision and deeper sensibility, his training at Fisk, Harvard, and the University of Berlin, Du Bois was able to survey the black American experience through the lenses of sociology, philosophy, history, and creative literature. A man gifted with high intellectual abilities, Du Bois was seldom subject to the type of critical myopia that beset Washington when he was asked to conceive of patterns of action not encompassed by the ruling philosophy of Tuskegee.

At times Du Bois's stance as a man of culture caused him to treat the masses of black America unjustly, but this same point of view enabled him to grasp the essential character of the black American folk experience. While studying in Berlin under Gustav Schmoller (1892–94), Du Bois came to believe that the solution to the American racial problem was "a matter of systematic investigation," and throughout his life he was dedicated to critical objectivity—to what Matthew Arnold defined as "disinterestedness." The critic could achieve this ideal, according to Arnold, "by keeping aloof from what is called 'the practical view of things'; by resolutely following the law of [criticism's] own nature, which is to be a free play of the mind on all subjects which it touches."[6] Du Bois allowed his mind to play freely on all facets of the black experience, and the results were often praise and admiration.

In *The Souls of Black Folk* he pays tribute to the black church ("Of the Faith of Our Fathers"), to black leaders ("Of Alexander Crummell"), to the black folk who have striven to meliorate their condition (Josie in "Of the Meaning of Progress"), and to the spirit of endurance and beauty that has always characterized black folk culture ("Of Our Spiritual Strivings," "Of the Sorrow Songs"). In short, Du Bois broadened the Arnoldian definition of culture, which was narrowly white and Western, to include the best that had been thought and known in the world of the black American folk. By bringing his critical and creative abilities to bear on black America he was able to see where the true strength of that culture, of that whole way of life, lay: in its ability to create beauty from wretchedness, intellectuals from victims of slavery, and viable institutions from rigidly proscribed patterns of action. Du Bois employed the methods of careful scholarships, yet he conveyed his findings in a beautifully lyrical prose style:

> Such [black] churches are really governments of men, and consequently a little investigation reveals the curious fact that, in the South, at least, practically every American Negro is a church member. Some, to be sure, are not regularly enrolled, and a few do not habitually attend services; but, practically, a proscribed people must have a social centre, and that centre for this people is the Negro church. [P. 341]

Throughout *The Souls of Black Folk* there are such passages (indeed, entire essays) that pulsate with knowledge of the folk and with the oracular Biblical tones of the prophet. The diction is literary, and the intended audience (given the condition of the majority of black Americans in 1903) was either white America or the educated elite of black America, but the sentiments expressed proceed directly out of the folk experience. Du Bois, in fact, was only one of a number of black intellectuals who at the turn of the century began the task of transcribing the values and achievements of an oral, folk experience into the cultured and written forms known to only a few black Americans.[7]

The number of black college-bred men and women was destined to increase, however, and Du Bois and other turn-of-the-century intellectuals were destined to become their models and their leaders. By the time of the Harlem Renaissance, the ideal of the cultured man had become a norm in the black American experience, and Du Bois was a seminal influence. Ernest Kaiser states that "Du Bois' works were part of the background for the

Harlem Renaissance of the 1920s and early thirties. Du Bois participated in this movement as the encouraging editor of *The Crisis* during this period, and as the author of the essay 'The Black Man Brings His Gifts,' published in Alain Locke's *The New Negro* (1925) and of the novel *Dark Princess* (1928)."[8] The literary and social life of black America during the Renaissance was influenced and guided by such men as Countee Cullen, Alain Locke, Wallace Thurman, Charles S. Johnson, Arna Bontemps, and Langston Hughes—all of whom were well educated and aware of the value of Western culture, and were not averse to criticizing blacks in works that are sometimes scathing in their satire (for example, Cullen's *One Way to Heaven* and Thurman's *The Blacker the Berry* and *Infants of the Spring*). The majority of the writers and scholars of the Harlem Renaissance, however, were as acculturated as Du Bois himself; their perspectives were broadened and enriched by a knowledge of black folk culture. The poetry of Langston Hughes, Claude McKay's *Home to Harlem*, the short stories of Rudolph Fisher, James Weldon Johnson's *God's Trombones*, and many other works of the Harlem Renaissance celebrate the survival values and the lyrical beauty of the folk experience.

Finally, one has only to survey the works of Richard Wright, Ralph Ellison, and James Baldwin to see that the norm of the black man of culture established for this century by W. E. B. Du Bois has played a significant role in contemporary black American culture. Wright, Ellison, and Baldwin have adopted a detached [cultured] point of view; employed standard, literary prose; and chosen characteristically Western literary forms for their work. Like Du Bois, however, each writer was open to the free play of ideas, and this led to an acculturative experience. In works such as *Native Son, Invisible Man,* and *Go Tell It on the Mountain,* the arts, institutions, and leaders of black America are normally lauded for their role in insuring the survival and growth of a culture and in providing maturation and value for its artists. The invocation that concludes *The Souls of Black Folk* has been answered: "Hear my cry, O God the Reader; vouchsafe that this my book fall not still-born into the world wilderness." The book had little chance of falling still-born. The whole way of life that it ultimately celebrates has continued to grow in strength and beauty, and the author's stance as a black man of culture and a transcriber of folk values has provided a paradigm for several generations of black artists and intellectuals.

NOTES

1. W. E. B. Du Bois, *The Souls of Black Folk,* in *Three Negro Classics,* ed. John Hope Franklin (New York, 1969), pp. 219–20. All citations in my text are to this edition.

2. Raymond Williams, *Culture and Society, 1780–1950* (New York, 1958).

3. Matthew Arnold, *Culture and Anarchy,* ed. J. Dover Wilson (Cambridge, 1963), pp. 48, 70.

4. Saunders Redding states, in *"The Souls of Black Folk:* Du Bois' Masterpiece Lives On," *Black Titan: W. E. B. Du Bois,* ed. John Henrik Clarke (Boston, 1970), pp. 47–51, that *The Souls of Black Folk* "not only represented a profound change in its scholar-author's view of what was then called the 'Negro Problem'; but heralded a new approach to social reform on the part of the American Negro people—an approach of patriotic, nonviolent activism which achieved its first success a decade ago." According to Redding, Du Bois's collection was as influential in determining the strategies of liberation of the last two decades as Gandhi's resistance in India, the 1954 Supreme Court decision, and the work of Martin Luther King. While this is an overstatement, it must be acknowledged that Du Bois's point of view has been adopted (to a greater or lesser extent) by a number of prominent black leaders since the second decade of the century. As one of the founders and long-term officers of the National Association for the Advancement of Colored People and as editor of its journal, *The Crisis,* Du Bois provided a living example of the type of guidance and the patterns of action that he called for in *The Souls of Black Folk.* Such men as James Weldon Johnson, Walter White,

Roy Wilkins, the late Whitney Young, and James Farmer have shared Du Bois's educational ideals and have attempted to position themselves as buffers between the latent rage of the black masses and the progress of American society.

5. In *Black Voices,* ed. Abraham Chapman (New York, 1968), pp. 470–71.

6. Matthew Arnold, "The Function of Criticism at the Present Time," in *Criticism: The Major Texts,* ed. Walter Jackson Bate (New York, 1952), p. 458.

7. Others were James Weldon Johnson, Charles Chesnutt, Paul Laurence Dunbar, William Monroe Trotter, Archibald Grimké, Carter G. Woodson, and J. Rosamond Johnson.

8. Ernest Kaiser, "Cultural Contributions of Dr. Du Bois," in Clarke, *Black Titan,* p. 71.

Aimé Césaire
(b. 1913, Martinique)

Notes on a Return to the Native Land

And this long-ago joy, bringing me awareness of my present misery, a bumpy road quilting its way through a hollow in which it scatters several shacks; an indefatigable road that charges full speed up a hill to sink abruptly in a sea of ramshackle cabins; a road climbing crazily, descending recklessly, and the carcass of wood comically perched on minuscule paws of cement that I call our "house," its tin mane rippling in the sun like a skin laid out to dry, the dining room, rough floor with nailheads glinting, rafters of pine and shadow that run across the ceiling, chairs of phantom straw, the dull lamplight, the rapid gleam of roaches that hum until you ache.

.   .   .

As there are hyena-men and panther-men I would be a Jew-man
A Kafir
a Hindu from Calcutta
a voteless man from Harlem
The hungry man, insulted man, the tortured man that anyone at any time can seize and beat and kill—yes, absolutely kill—without being accountable to anyone or needing to apologize. . . .
    I would retrieve the secret of great combustions and great communications. I would say storm. I would say river. Tornado I would say. I would say leaf. I would say tree. I would be watered by all rains, dampened by all dews. I would rumble onward like frenetic blood on the slow stream of the eye my words like wild horses like radiant children like clots like curfew-bells in temple ruins like precious stones so distant as to discourage miners. He who would not understand me would not understand the roaring of the tiger either. . . .

.   .   .

To leave. My heart murmured emphatic generosities. To leave . . . I would arrive young and polished in this country of mine, and I would say to this country whose slime is a part of the composition of my flesh: "I have wandered long and I return to your hideous, deserted wounds."
    I would come to this country of mine and say to it: "Embrace me without fear. . . . And if all I know how to do is speak, it is for you that I shall speak."

Culture and Identity

And I would say more:

"My lips shall speak for miseries that have no mouth, my voice shall be the liberty of those who languish in the dungeon of despair. . . . "

And as I came I would tell myself:

"And above all, my body, as well as my soul, beware of crossing your arms in the sterile attitude of spectator, for life is not a spectacle, a sea of pain is not a proscenium, a man who cries out is not a dancing bear. . . . "

And here I am!

Once again this life limping before me; not this life, this death, this death without piety or purpose, this death whose magnitude runs pitifully aground, the dazzling insignificance of this death, this death that limps from insignificance to insignificance, these serving spoons of petty greediness from the conquistador, these scoops of tiny flunkeys on the great wild thing, these shovelfuls of shabby souls on the three-souled Caribbean, and all these futile deaths. . . .

This is mine, these few thousand humiliated souls circling round inside a calabash isle, and mine too the archipelago curved as if anxiously seeking to deny itself, in a maternal anxiety one might say to protect the more delicate slenderness separating one America from the other, and their flanks secreting the Gulf Stream's good liquor for Europe, one of the two incandescent versants through which the equator funambulates toward Africa. And my unenclosed island, its bright audacity upright at this polynesia's tail end; Guadeloupe in front of it, bisected at the dorsal line, suffering our sickness too; Haiti where negritude first stood up and said it believed in its humanity, and the comic little tail of Florida where a Negro is being strangled, and, gigantically caterpillaring toward the Hispanic foot of Europe, Africa, in whose nudity Death cuts a wide swath.

> And I tell myself Bordeaux and Nantes and Liverpool and New York and San
>   Francisco.
> there is no place on this earth without my fingerprint,
> and my heel upon the skeleton of skyscrapers, and my
> sweat in the brilliance of diamonds!
> Who can boast of more than I?
> Virginia   Tennessee   Georgia   Alabama
> Monstrous putrefactions of inoperative
> revolts,
> swamps of putrid blood,
> trumpets absurdly stopped,
> red lands, sanguine,
> consanguine.
>
> This is mine too: a little
> cell in the Jura Mountains,
> a little cell,
> the snow lines its bars with white,
> the snow is a white
> jailer standing guard before a prison.
> This is mine,
> a man alone
> imprisoned in white,

a man alone who defies the white
cries of white
death
(TOUSSAINT, TOUSSAINT
L'OUVERTURE),
a man who fascinates the white
hawk of white
death,
a man alone in a sterile sea of white
snow,
an old darky standing tall
against the waters of the sky.
Death traces a shining circle
above this man,
gently sprinkling stars about his head.
Death breathes like a mad thing
in the ripe roughness of his arms.
Death gallops in the prison like a white
horse.
Death gleams in the darkness
like a cat's eyes.
Death hiccups
like the water under coral reefs.
Death is a wounded bird.
Death wanes,
wavers.
Death is a great shady tree.
Death expires in a white
pool of silence.
Puffs of night
at the four corners
of this dawn.
Convulsions of stiffening
death.
Tenacious destiny.
Will the splendor
of this blood
not burst mute earth
with its upright cries?

.   .   .

I refuse to take my bombast for authentic glories
and I laugh at my childish old imaginings.

No, we were never Amazons to the king of Dahomey, or Ghanaian princes with eight hundred camels, or doctors in Timbuktu when Askia the Great was king, or the architects of Djenné, or Madhis, or warriors. We do not feel the armpit itch of those who once upon a time bore lances. And since I've sworn to leave out nothing of our history (I who admire nothing so much as the sheep browsing in his afternoon shadow), I want to admit that for all time we have been rather wretched dishwashers, shoeshine boys with little scope, let's make it even plainer, rather conscientious conjurors, and the only indisputable record we have held is that of endurance to the whip. . . .

And this country cried out for centuries that we were rude beasts; that the pulsing of humanity stopped at Negro doors; that we are a walking dunghill morbidly promising tender cane and silky cotton, and they marked us with red-hot irons, and we slept in our excrement and they sold us in the public squares, and a bolt of English cloth or a side of salted meat from Ireland cost more than we did, and this land was calm, tranquil, pro-claiming the spirit of the Lord was in its actions.

> We, vomited from slaveships.
> We, hunted in the Calebars.
> What? Stop up our ears?
> We, sotted to death from being rolled, mocked, jeered at,
> Stifled with fog!
> Forgiveness partner whirlwind!
> Nothing could ever urge us toward noble, desperate adventure.
> So be it. So be it.
> I am of no nationality foreseen by chancelleries;
> I defy the craniometer. *Homo sum et cetera*
> That they serve and deceive and die.
> So be it. So be it. It was written in the shape of their pelvis.

.   .   .

> I live for the flattest part of my soul,
> For the dullest part of my flesh.
> Tepid dawning of ancestral warmth and fear
> I tremble now with the common trepidation of our docile
> blood pulsing in the madrepore.

> And these tadpoles within me hatched of my prodigious ancestry!
> Those who invented neither gunpowder nor compass,
> Those who never vanquished steam or electricity,
> Those who explored neither seas nor sky,
> But who know in its uttermost corners the landscape of pain,
> Those who've known no voyages other than uprootings,
> Those who have been stupefied from falling on their knees,
> Those who were Christianized and tamed,
> Those who were inoculated with decay,
> Tom-toms of empty hands,
> Futile tom-toms echoing with wounds,
> Tom-toms made absurd by atrophied betrayals.
> Tepid dawning of ancestral warmth and fear;
> Overboard, my peregrine riches,

Overboard, my authentic falsehoods.
But what strange pride illuminates me suddenly? . . .

O friendly light!
O fresh source of light!
Those who invented neither gunpowder nor compass
Those who never knew how to conquer steam or electricity
Those who explored neither seas nor sky
But those without whom the earth would not be earth,
Protuberance so much more beneficial than deserted earth,
Earthier,
Silo preserving and ripening the earth's most earthy,
My negritude is not a stone, its deafness hurled against
The clamor of the day;
My negritude is not a speck of dead water on the earth's dead eye,
My negritude is neither tower nor cathedral.

It plunges into the red flesh of the earth,
It plunges into the ardent flesh of the sky,
It perforates opaque dejection with its upright patience.

Eia for the royal *Kailcédrat!*
Eia for those who never invented anything,
Who never explored anything,
Who never conquered anything,
But who abandon themselves to the essence of all things,
Ignorant of surfaces, caught by the motion of all things,
Indifferent to conquering but playing the game of the world,

Truly the eldest sons of the world,
Porous to all the breathing of the world,
Fraternal space for all the breathing of the world,
Bed without drain for all the waters of the world,
Spark of the sacred fire of the world,
Flesh of the world's flesh palpitating with the very movement of the world. . . .

Cheikh Anta Diop
(1923–1986, Senegal)

The Origin and History of the Black World

In all likelihood, present-day African peoples are in no way invaders come from another continent; they are the aborigines. Recent scientific discoveries that show Africa to be the cradle of humanity increasingly negate the hypothesis of this continent being peopled by outlanders.

From the appearances of *homo sapiens*—from earliest prehistory until our time—we are able to trace our origins as a people without significant breaks in continuity. In early prehistory, a great South-North movement brought the African peoples of the Great Lakes region into the Nile Basin. They lived there in clusters for millennia.

In prehistoric times, it was they who created the Nilotic Sudanese civilization and what we know as Egypt.

These first Black civilizations were the first civilizations in the world, the development of Europe having been held back by the last Ice Age, a matter of a hundred thousand years.

Beginning in the sixth century B.C. (525, when Cambyses occupied Egypt) with the end of the independence of the great Black power base, the African peoples, until then drawn to the Nile Valley as by a magnet, fanned out over the continent. Perhaps they then came upon small pockets of populations descended from paleolithic or neolithic infiltrations.

A few centuries later, around the first century, they founded the first of the continental civilizations in the West and South: Ghana, Nok-Ifé, Zimbabwe, and others.

We now know, thanks to radiocarbon methods, that the earliest sites in Zimbabwe do date back at least as far as the first century of the Christian Era. On the east coast of Africa Roman coins have been discovered at the port of Dunford as well as in Zanzibar, indicating a flourishing sea trade.

The first Nigerian civilization, which Bernard and William Fagg named the Nok civilization, has been traced back to the first millennium B.C., the ceramics found there being radiocarbon-dated over a range from 900 B.C. to 200 A.D. The *Tarikh es-Sudan* tells us that the city of Kukia, on the Niger former capital of Songhay before Gao, was contemporaneous with the time of the pharaohs. However that may be, we do know with certainty that in the eighth century A.D. the Empire of Ghana was already in existence, extending over all of West Africa, right to the Atlantic. So we can see that the African states of the Middle Ages had come into being practically when Egyptian-Sudanese antiquity came to its close. The Nilotic Sudan was finally to lose its independence only in the nineteenth century, and its old eastern province of Ethiopia would retain its identity until the Italian occupation of 1936, barring which, it never lost its independence. That being the case, Ethiopia is in point of fact the oldest state in the world. Ghana lasted from about the third century A.D. until 1240, to be succeeded by Mali from that date to 1464 (accession of Soni-Ali, founder of the Songhay Empire).

The dismembering of these nations was effectively completed in the nineteenth century by the European occupation of Africa. The breaking-up went on apace; what we saw then were tiny kingdoms, each jealous of its own independence, such as those of Cayor in Senegal conquered by General Louis Faidherbe under Napoleon III after a fierce resistance. The kingdoms of East Africa with trading cities on the coast prospered from the end of classical antiquity until the fifteenth and sixteenth centuries when they fell to the Portuguese. These kingdoms maintained a lively trade with India, Siam, and the Chinese Far East, evidenced both by chronicles and by Chinese potteries found there. It is hard for us today to picture the opulence of the authentically Black trading centers of that period. Father Gervase Mathew, of Oxford, in relating Swahili tradition mentions that in these cities there were silver staircases leading to beds of ivory. Such luxurious furnishings are barely imaginable today. The houses, built of stone, rose to five or six stories. The people were authentic jet-black Africans. Their women had shaven heads as in Ghana.

These civilizations were overthrown by the Portuguese who, in the sixteenth century, altered the old trade routes and sea lanes of the Indian Ocean. The conception of African history just briefly sketched is today to all intents and purposes accepted and endorsed by scholars:

> Black African culture set for the whole world an example of extraordinary vitality and vigor. All vitalist conceptions, religious as well as philosophic, I am convinced, came from that source. The civilization of ancient Egypt would not have been possible without the great example of Black African culture, and in all likelihood it was nothing but the sublimation thereof.

The history of the Nilotic Sudan, Egypt, and present-day Ethiopia is well known. Until recently, however, the past of West Africa was related quite summarily. We have felt it necessary to bring this past to life through documents we have had at our disposal and by establishing a socio-historical analysis covering two thousand years.

The old political, social, and economic organization of Black Africa over those two thousand years, the military, judicial, and administrative apparatus, the educational set-up, the university and technical levels, the pomp and circumstance of court life, the customs and mores—all details which had been presumed lost in the deep dark past—we were able to bring strikingly and scientifically back to life, especially insofar as West Africa was concerned, in *L'Afrique Noire pré-coloniale* (Pre-Colonial Black Africa).

A similar work should be undertaken for the Benin-Ife civilization. What would be of special interest there would be the fact that even in its ideological superstructure the civilization of Benin borrowed nothing from either the Semitic or the Aryan worlds. On the other hand, it does display a close relationship wtih ancient Egypt, as might be expected: Its art, in a certain measure, represents African sculptural classicism.

The same kind of exhumation and revivification work on our history for the period from antiquity to the present can and must be undertaken in a systematic way for all of eastern, central, and southern Africa.

Egyptian, Greek, Roman, Persian, Chinese, and Arabic documents known to exist and with what archeology may add to them allow this to be done in large measure. Nowhere in African history are there holes that cannot be filled in. The empty spaces are only temporary, and the period that affects us runs without a break from Egyptian-Sudanese antiquity and fits right in sequence.

So, historical consciousness is properly restored. The general framework of African history is set out. The evolution of peoples is known in its broad lines, but the research already begun will have to be continued in order to fill the small gaps that still exist, thus reinforcing the framework. One can no longer see "darkest Africa" set against a "deep dark past"; the African can clearly follow his evolution from prehistory to our own day. Historical unity has become manifest.

The psychological unity existing for all those who inhabit the Dark Continent, and which each of us feels, is an elementary fact that needs no demonstration.

Geographical unity likewise is obvious, and it necessarily implies economic unity. . . .

A consideration of the structure of the precolonial African family, that of the State, the accompanying philsophical and moral concepts, and the like, reveals a consistent cultural unity, resulting from similar adaptations to the same material and physical conditions of life. This was the subject of my *L'Unité culturelle de l'Afrique Noire* (The Cultural Unity of Black Africa).

There is also a common linguistic background. The African languages constitute one linguistic family, as homogeneous as that of the Indo-European tongues. Nothing is easier than to set down the rules that allow transfer from a Zulu language (Bantu) to one of those of West Africa (Serer-Wolof, Peul), or even to ancient Egyptian (cf. *L'Afrique Noire pré-coloniale*, Part II). However, the old imperial languages, Sarakole in Ghana, Mandingo in Mali, Songhay in Koaga (Gao), have had their areas of extension sharply reduced today. At the apogee of these African empires, the imperial tongues, the languages of trade and government affairs, were the African languages themselves; even after the advent of Islam, Arabic always remained only the language of religion and erudition, as did Latin in Europe of the same period.

With European occupation in the nineteenth century the official African languages were replaced by those of the various "mother countries." Local dialects surfaced and vied against the older national cultural languages which had virtually submerged them. It became less and less necessary for civil administration, politics, or social intercourse to learn the latter. The demands of daily life required learning the European languages; the disrepute of the old linguistic unities in our day reached its depth.

While we may be able to build a Federated African State covering all of the Black Continent on the basis of historical, psychological, economic, and geographical unity, we will be forced, in order to complete such national unity and set it on a modern autochthonous cultural base, to recreate our linguistic unity through the choice of an appropriate African tongue promoted to the influence of a modern cultural language.

Linguistic unity dominates all national life. Without it, national cultural unity is but fragile and illusory. The wranglings within a bilingual country, such as Belgium, illustrate the point.

Ali A. Mazrui
(b. 1933, Kenya)

Africa's Tripartite Heritage:
Towards Cultural Synthesis

The interplay of Africa's indigenous cultures with Islam on one side and Western civilisation on the other has had . . . political and economic ramifications. But in the final analysis
the central process of the triple heritage has been cultural and civilisational. We define
culture as a system of inter-related values, active enough to influence and condition perception, judgement, communication and behaviour in a given society. We define civilisation as a culture which has endured, expanded, innovated and been elevated to new moral
sensibilities. An interviewer once asked India's Mahatma Gandhi, "What do you think of
Western civilisation?" The Mahatma is reported to have replied, "I didn't know they had
any!" It was presumably the West's "moral sensibilities" which Mahatma Gandhi was questioning.

But by the other criteria of the concept of "civilisation," especially that of innovation,
the Western world surely scores rather high in the last three or four centuries of human
history. For our purposes . . . the word civilisation can be applied to the Western and
Islamic as well as indigenous legacies, provided we bear in mind that the term is always
relative and somewhat hyperbolic.

STAGES OF CULTURAL INTEGRATION

A number of stages can be discerned in the evolution of the triple heritage at this cultural
level. Initially, there is the simple phenomenon of culture contact, two systems of values
being introduced to each other and beginning to be aware of each other's peculiarities.

In African history this was followed by culture conflict, as the two or three legacies
began to clash with each other when they discovered areas of incompatibility and mutual
incoherence.

Third comes the stage of culture conquest as one legacy establishes a clear ascendancy
and sometimes effectively compels the more vulnerable culture to surrender.

Then follows a period of cultural confusion. Among the members of the subordinate or
vulnerable culture the choice is between cultural surrender, cultural alienation or cultural
revival and the resurrection of original authenticity.

But is there really no other choice apart from surrender, alienation or revival? In reality there is a fourth possible outcome—cultural coalescence or integration, a fusion of two or more cultures into a new mixed legacy.

What is Correct Behaviour?

It is not very easy to distinguish the stage of culture conflict from the stage of cultural confusion. Analytically, the culture conflict occurs when the indigenous system is still relatively intact and is resisting the encroachments and blandishments of the newly arrived civilisation seeking to impose its own will. The stage of culture confusion follows a partial conquest, a conversion of some of the leaders of the indigenous culture to the new gods of the conquerors, and a conflict of values within the same individuals creating psychological and moral bewilderment.

Nowhere is this better illustrated than on the issue of what constitutes corruption and abuse of privilege. The phenomenon of corrupt practices, conspicuous consumption and perversion of governmental procedures in Africa has its roots in the ideological flux which characterises the transition from indigenous moral restraints, on one side, to the complexities of modern discipline, on the other.

What is at stake, is the phenomenon of cultural transition. Politics in Africa, for example, are sometimes hard to keep clean merely because people are moving from one set of values to another. In no other area of life is this better illustrated than in the issue of ethnic solidarity and kinship obligations. Pressures are exerted on an African official or politician to remind him of those who share his social womb. People from his area or from his clan enquire on how best the well-placed African politician, or even academic, might help his kinsmen to gain admission to a job or to a scholarship. African vice-chancellors have been known to undergo agonising pressure to persuade them to help appoint members of their own "tribe" to positions of authority and earning power within the universities over which they preside. When I was Dean of the Faculty of Social Sciences at Makerere University in Uganda I was under comparable pressure from relatives in Mombasa seeking to gain admission as students.

The ordinary people who exert these pressures on their more successful ethnic compatriots are often oblivious of the moral inconsistencies of the situation. It was after all traditionally acceptable that God helped those who helped their relatives. It was therefore right that a prospective Ibo porter should look to an established Ibo official for appointment, or that a young Yoruba graduate should look to a more highly placed Yoruba man for promotion. Before a clash of values entered the lives of these Nigerians, there might have been no moral dilemmas involved in such issues. But the Western world had now created a political entity called Nigeria, whose boundaries were not chosen by either the Ibo or the Yoruba, but whose reality cast Ibo and Yoruba in competition with each other for the resources of a colonially created political system. Moreover, with Western ideas came the issue of individual merit *versus* collective solidarity. Individual candidates for a scholarship have to be assessed independently of ideas of ethnic unity. A clash was inevitable between these new values of political communities and the old commitments of a more natural "tribal" community.

But nepotism is not the only form of corruption which has links with older indigenous traditions. Even bribery can be a cultural residuum. Chinua Achebe, the Nigerian novelist, brings this out effectively in his novel, *No Longer at Ease*. In traditional Ibo values there was a principle of reciprocity involved in the very act of serving somebody else. Dignity often demanded that the beneficiary of a favour should have given something in return.

> They said a man expects you to accept "kola" from him for services rendered, and until you do, his mind is never at rest. . . . A man to whom you do a favor will not understand if you say nothing, make no noise, just walk away. You may cause more trouble by refusing a bribe than by accepting it.[1]

Achebe's character, Obi Okonkwo, a young Nigerian newly returned from his studies in England, had been full of defiance and resistance to all temptations of this kind in the early stages of his career in the civil service in Nigeria. When the temptations of bribery first came his way, he was suitably self-righteous and indignant as he resisted those temptations. We cannot therefore say that in his case the intended recipient of the bribe was unaware of the ethical dubiousness of accepting it under the new rules of the game. On the other hand, the giver of that bribe could be a real case of cultural transition anticipating a favour to himself by extending a favour to his future beneficiary. What is at stake is the principle of *prior appreciation,* an extension of thanks in advance of the favour. What is also at stake is the principle of reciprocity, extending a favour in anticipation of receiving a favour. In the words of the British political economist, Colin Leys:

> While traditional gift-giving [in Africa] can be distinguished from a bribe of money, it is quite obvious that from the point of view of the giver the one has shaded into the other, so that although the practice has taken on a new significance, as the open gift of a chicken is replaced by a more furtive gift of a pound note, it is nevertheless an established fact of life, in which the precise nature of the rule-infringement is partially concealed by a continuity with an older custom.[2]

The central question still persists: is there such a thing as corruption, or is it all a matter of culture? It does seem as if one culture's bribery is another's mutual goodwill.

All over Africa people are no longer sure where traditional prior appreciation ends and the new sin of bribery and corruption begins. Two factors have contributed to this confusion. One is the coming of entirely new institutions such as Western-style banks, with their new rules and new values; institutions which range from the modern civil service to the banking organs and investment agencies of modern capitalism. The other factor behind the confusion is the money economy itself, which is relatively new in many parts of Africa. The modern money economy includes problems of balance of payments, foreign exchange and international transfers. This area has enlarged the scale of economic activity and economic intercourse among Africans. Powerful Africans no longer deal in chickens and cockerels and kola nuts. Quite often they deal in millions of dollars, banked sometimes in Swiss banks. The massive enlargement of scale puts a different quality on the issue of economic morality and the principles of economic behaviour. These new institutions have given Africans more than one standard of conduct, more than one code of behaviour. And these standards and codes are often in conflict. The result is the simple fact that the continent is no longer at ease morally, no longer sure what is the correct behaviour.

But corruption is not just a case of receiving favours from outside. It is also a question of misappropriating funds from inside. To some extent, the problem goes back to the colonial administration, with all its rootlessness and lack of legitimacy. The colonial regime was alienated from the population not only because, by definition, it was a case of foreign control but also because it was artificial, newly invented. Because the government lacked legitimacy, government property lacked respect. When I was growing up in colonial

Culture and Identity

east Africa, the term *mali ya serikali* (government property) had a kind of contemptuous ring about it, as if that kind of property lacked sanctity.

It became almost a patriotic duty to misappropriate the resources of the colonial government when this was possible without risk of punishment or exposure. After all, to steal from a foreign thief could be an act of heroic restoration. Post-colonial Africa still suffers from the cynical attitudes to government property generated by the colonial experience.

Finally, there is the conflict between patriotism and paternity, between allegiance to the nation and loyalty to one's family. But what is the nation in Africa? Very often it is an artificial entity invented by the colonial order, with boundaries which bear no relation to ethnic limits or traditional kingdoms. The European powers carved up Africa to suit European convenience. Loyalty to Nigeria or to Kenya or Uganda was therefore loyalty to an entity carved out by white intruders without reference to indigenous cultural boundaries. Why should I regard those colonial frontiers as being more important than the needs of my children? Why should I regard integrity in the service of an artificial national entity as more important than staple food for my children? While I abuse the resources of my artificial nation in favour of my authentic family, let the innocent cast the first stone.

LANGUAGE AND CULTURE CHANGE

But while on the issue of bribery and corruption Africa is in a state of either cultural confusion or culture conflict, on the issue of such legacies as language and dress culture the continent has been experiencing culture conquest, especially by the Western world. . . . The Arabic language [has had an impact] on Africa, both as a medium of worship and as a source of loan words for indigenous African languages. Taken as a whole, the African continent has more speakers of the Arabic language than any other tongue, either indigenous or alien. But the native speakers of Arabic are overwhelmingly in the north of the continent. The impact of Arabic south of the Sahara as a medium of communication has been indirectly through providing loan words for such languages as Hausa, Kiswahili, Wolof and Somali. Some of these deeply Arabised indigenous languages have in turn influenced neighbouring languages. For example, many other languages in east Africa have borrowed words from Kiswahili which had originally borrowed them from Arabic.

There are occasions when Arabic finds itself in competition with a Western language for influence. Perhaps this is particularly well illustrated in the case of a choice of alphabet. Kiswahili had for centuries used a modified version of the Arabic alphabet for its own writings. But after European colonisation of east Africa, the Roman or Latin alphabet began to gain ascendancy and to be used widely for written Kiswahili. More and more African languages have turned to the Latin or Roman alphabet for their own literary expression. In the case of Kiswahili the ascendancy of the Roman alphabet is rational and justified since it seems to be more efficient in handling Kiswahili than the Arabic alphabet. The cumbersomeness of the Arabic alphabet for Kiswahili applied especially to the issue of vowels, which do need to be inserted for Kiswahili, but are often dispensable when the alphabet is used for its original language, Arabic.

Somalia agonised for a long time over a triple heritage of alphabet. Should the Somali language use the Arabic, the Roman or a new indigenous alphabet of its own? In the end the Somali government opted, to the surprise of many people, for the Roman alphabet—a decision politically controversial in the Muslim world but probably intellectually rational.

But the West has not been winning all the battles of language and literature in Africa.

While the Roman alphabet seems irresistible and is conquering all the continent's languages except Arabic itself, the picture concerning Western languages (as distinct from the alphabet) is more complicated. In the struggle between the English language and Kiswahili as the primary language of political discourse in Tanzania, there is no doubt that Kiswahili has been winning. English since Tanganyika's independence in 1961 and Zanzibar's independence in 1963 has been declining as a domestic political medium. Government notices and government discussions are conducted primarily in Kiswahili. Parliamentary debates are conducted entirely in Kiswahili, and so is the business of the ruling political party, Chama Cha Mapinduzi (CCM).

In primary and secondary education, there has also been competition between English and Kiswahili, with the odds in favour of the latter. The increasing Swahilisation of Tanzania's educational system is already having an effect on the standard of English in the country. There is evidence that Tanzanians entering as undergraduates at the University of Dar es Salaam now begin with a lower command of the English language than that of undergraduates twenty years ago.

In neighbouring Kenya the Swahilisation of government and politics has not gone quite as far as it has done in Tanzania, but there is no doubt that Kiswahili has made spectacular progress since independence. The overwhelming majority of public political meetings in the country are now addressed in Kiswahili. President Jomo Kenyatta actually made Kiswahili the language of parliament, compelling almost all business in the national assembly to be conducted in Kiswahili. This decision was made overnight; and overnight yesterday's great orators (in English) became today's weak speakers (in Kiswahili)—and, of course, vice versa. The balance of eloquence was transferred with the stroke of a presidential decree.

There are occasions when the mixture of cultures can be particularly striking. For example, a daily newspaper is not an indigenous tradition in east Africa but was borrowed from the West. On the other hand, when one is sitting at the breakfast table in the Western world, one does not normally expect to be reading poetry in the morning newspaper. But in the world of Swahili culture, one does. There is a section in Tanzania's newspapers not only for letters to the editor but also for poems to the editor. These poems are on a wide range of subjects: on inflation, or traditional medicine, or some recent government policy.

There is a school of thought in English poetry, represented by such people as Wordsworth and Coleridge, to the effect that poetry should approximate to the ordinary language of conversation. But in Swahili culture there is a school of thought which would argue that ordinary conversation should try to approximate the elegant language of poetry. Those poems to the editor in Tanzanian newspapers, poems of dialogue, are part of this tradition.

But sometimes those verses in the newspapers are provoked by another function of poetry in Swahili culture—poetry as release from stress, as liberation from tense emotion. In the newspapers the emotions may be political, but poetry is used in more personalised anguish as well.

A few years ago two of my three sons suddenly went blind. It was a traumatic experience for all of us. In the course of this period of pain I received poems from friends and relatives, poems of sympathy, shared sadness in rhyme. I responded with my own poem, "Ode to the Optic Nerve." When the pain subsided, I could not but reflect afresh upon the nature of Swahili culture—a civilisation which had evolved distinctive ways of communicating compassion between its members.

But the cultural competition for the mind and body of Africa is not only between civilisations, like the competition between Western and Swahili legacies. The rivalry is sometimes within each of those civilisations as they have sought to influence the African condition. Particularly noteworthy in Africa is the rivalry between ancestral European culture and American cultural revisionism. Western Europe and the United States are in the grips of cultural competition for the soul of Africa and much of the rest of the Third World. It is to this comparative area of Westernism that we now turn.

CONQUEST: EUROPEANISATION *VERSUS* AMERICANISATION

The Western world as a whole has been much more successful in transmitting capitalism than in transferring democracy, though both of them are relatively weak in Africa. Capitalism is the doctrine of competitive economics, resulting in market forces. Liberal democracy, on the other hand, is the doctrine of competitive politics, resulting in political pluralism.

The Carter Administration decided to put an emphasis on the export of liberal democracy. Hence the special premium President Jimmy Carter put on human rights as an aspect of American foreign policy. The Reagan Administration has put an emphasis on the export of capitalism, hence the special premium Reagan's Administration put on private enterprise and fair prices for farmers in American foreign policy towards the Third World.

During the colonial era and at the beginning of independence the versions of Western liberalism which were most influential in Africa were usually in the image of the colonial powers. Indeed, it was widely believed at the time of independence that Britain's greatest legacy to its colonies and former colonies was parliamentary government. The brightest jewel in the British crown was no longer British India; it was British democracy. And so the parliamentary package was shipped out to Africa. "Mr Speaker, Sir," the mace, the speech from the throne, the Leader of the Opposition, the front and back benches, the white paper—the entire package of Westminster was put together for export.

Unfortunately for the idealists, it did not work. Single-party systems and military rule affected the fortunes of parliamentary government in different parts of Africa. Many buildings which once housed a national assembly have gone silent. No more the loud exchanges of policy disagreements; no more the boisterous laughter of African jokes; no more votes of censure and votes of no confidence. The legislative house in Lagos, for example, is now dead. It bears solemn testimony to the proposition that although one can teach other people how to speak the English language, or how to practise Christianity, one cannot teach them how to govern themselves. That they must learn for themselves.

In the case of Nigeria, the collapse of the Westminster model in 1966 was followed thirteen years later after a military interlude by an American-style system of government. The second Republic of Nigeria under Al'Hajii Shehu Shagari collapsed even faster than did the first Republic under Al'Hajii Tafawa Balewa.

A more resilient American contribution to the Nigerian political system is, of course, the federal principle which has been the basis of Nigeria's government since its independence. The number of states within the federation has increased from the original three to nineteen plus Abuja (the new capital-to-be), but the essential principle of federal power sharing has survived many coups and convulsions.

A more widespread indirect American contribution to post-colonial African political systems is the phenomenon of presidentialism. One African country after another has moved away from a focus on parliament to a focus on its president.

But the competition between the United States and Europe for cultural influence in Africa is not merely in the field of capitalism and liberal democracy in their usual forms, but is also in the arena of life-styles and in the sciences and the arts. In the field of education, for example, the American impact is greater on the tertiary level than on secondary and primary levels. In English-speaking Africa the American idea of semester-long courses is beginning to catch on, especially in west Africa. Term papers are beginning to count towards the final grade (instead of basing the grade almost entirely on the final examination, as the British ethos tended to do). The American title of "Associate Professor" has replaced the old British rank, often unintelligible to foreigners, of "Reader" which had originally been transferred to the British colonies.

In technology the United States is particularly victorious. Both American varieties of domesticated technology and American successes in high technology have exerted considerable influence on the rest of the world. In Africa much of the technology is only affecting the lives of the élite. American home gadgets, from dishwashers to air conditioners, have become part of the life-style of the more Westernised members of Africa's social echelons.

There is also the issue of dress culture. In a sense, every man in the world has two dress cultures—his own and Western (the Western man has the two traditions fused into one). No one regards a Japanese in a Western suit, or an Arab with a Western tie, as a cultural incongruity. It is only when we see a Japanese in Arab regalia, or an Arab in Japanese dress that we are amazed. The European suit especially has become truly universal. We can therefore confirm that at the level of formal Western dress Europe prevails over the United States in influencing the choices of Africa's Westernised élites.

But in terms of *casual* dress, the picture is very different. The American genius for casual attire is conquering. Casual bush shirts, T-shirts and jeans are capturing the imagination of the young in African cities.

On the issue of food, the American genius is in fast food—while Western Europe continues to prevail in more formal cuisine. The hamburger revolution has begun to penetrate even Africa. Some African cities already have at least one Kentucky Fried Chicken and one American-style pizzeria. American impatience and preoccupation with speed are part of this triumph with fast foods. When you do not have time to spare, eat American. But when you have a whole evening for indulgence, by all means eat French!

There is rivalry over drinks between Western Europe and the United States. In much of Africa, Europe still reigns supreme in alcoholic drinks. French wine, Scotch whisky and Czech and German beer are truly triumphant. Their American equivalents are decidedly poor seconds or thirds in popularity. But where America has communicated effectively is in the field of *soft* drinks. I sold Coca-Cola at the Mombasa Institute of Muslim Education in Kenya back in the 1950s. There is no real European equivalent to either Coke or Pepsi. In the field of soft drinks we have indeed been witnessing the Coca-Colonisation of the world—symbolic of a much wider process of Americanisation of humanity.

In the world of fiction and art, Europe is still triumphant among African connoisseurs of Western heritage. But in the field of science and society, the United States has been establishing a lead. American great novels and great plays are almost unknown in Africa. But in the natural sciences, the applied sciences and the social sciences, the American impact is clear.

At the more popular level there is the triumph of American news magazines, especially *Time* and *Newsweek*. This triumph extends to imitation. Many magazines about Africa printed in London are modelled on *Time* and *Newsweek* magazines in format.

Culture and Identity

In the field of music the American impact is restricted to the popular variety of Western sounds, from jazz to varieties of rock music—while Europeans continue to lead in Western classical strands. Michael Jackson in the mid-1980s had already become a world figure and not just an American legend. But African lovers of Western classical music, limited in number as they are, are unlikely to know much about either American composers or American performers in this field. In popular music the United States has become a leader but in classical Western music, the United States is still Europe's follower.

In film and television the United States continues to maintain high international visibility in spite of the decline of Hollywood. American soap operas such as *Dynasty* and *Dallas* have wide audiences from Mombasa in coastal Kenya to Maiduguri in northern Nigeria.

American high art and painting is much less known than European high culture of the brush. In much of Westernised Africa names such as Rembrandt, Michelangelo and Picasso have no real American equivalents.

On the other hand, is there a European equivalent of Walt Disney? American genius is revealed more starkly in cartoons than in the art gallery. The United States is Europe's follower in the high art of painting but is the absolute leader in the popular art of film cartoon.

In most areas of life, American genius lies in the popular art form rather than the élite speciality, in mass involvement rather than aristocratic cultivation. After all, America was the West's first *mass* democracy. Why then should its popular culture not be its main claim to global leadership and immortality?

But perhaps the Western world's most important impact on the private lives of Africans lies not in the music they play or the dress they wear but in the sexual mores which govern their lives.

NOTES

1. Achebe, *No Longer at Ease* (London: Heinemann Educational Books, 1960 and New York: Astor-Honor, 1961), pp. 87–8.
2. See Colin Leys, "What is the Problem About Corruption?" *The Journal of Modern African Studies*, Vol. III, No. 2, 1965, p. 225. Consult also M. G. Smith, "Historical and Cultural Conditions of Political Corruption Among the Hausa," *Comparative Studies in Society and History*, January 1964, pp. 164–98.

John Henrik Clarke
(b. 1915, United States)

The Origin and Growth of Afro-American Literature

Africans were great story tellers long before their first appearance in Jamestown, Virginia, in 1619. The rich and colorful history, art and folklore of West Africa, the ancestral home of most Afro-Americans, present evidence of this, and more.

Contrary to a misconception which still prevails, the Africans were familiar with literature and art for many years before their contact with the Western world. Before the breaking up of the social structure of the West African states of Ghana, Melle (Mali), and Songhay, and the internal strife and chaos that made the slave trade possible, the forefathers of the Africans who eventually became slaves in the United States lived in a society where university life was fairly common and scholars were beheld with reverence.

There were in this ancestry rulers who expanded their kingdoms into empires, great and magnificent armies whose physical dimensions dwarfed entire nations into submission, generals who advanced the technique of military science, scholars whose vision of life showed foresight and wisdom, and priests who told of gods that were strong and kind. To understand fully any aspect of Afro-American life, one must realize that the black American is not without a cultural past, though he was many generations removed from it before his achievements in American literature and art commanded any appreciable attention.

I have been referring to the African Origin of Afro-American literature and history. This preface is essential to every meaningful discussion of the role of the Afro-American in every major aspect of American life, past and present. Before getting into the main body of this talk I want to make it clear that the Black Race did not come to the United States culturally empty-handed.

I will elaborate very briefly on my statement to the effect that "the forefathers of the Africans who eventually became slaves in the United States once lived in a society where university life was fairly common and scholars were beheld with reverence."

During the period in West African history—from the early part of the fourteenth century to the time of the Moorish invasion in 1591—the City of Timbuktu, with the University of Sankore in the Songhay Empire, was the intellectual center of Africa. Black scholars were enjoying a renaissance that was known and respected throughout most of Africa and in parts of Europe. At this period in African history, the University of Sankore, at Timbuktu, was the educational capital of the Western Sudan. In his book *Timbuktu the Mysterious*, Felix DuBois gives us the following description of this period:

The scholars of Timbuktu yielded in nothing, to the saints in their sojourns in the foreign universities of Fez, Tunis and Cairo. They astounded the most learned men of Islam by their erudition. That these Negroes were on a level with the Arabian Savants is proved by the fact that they were installed as professors in Morocco and Egypt. In contrast to this, we find that the Arabs were not always equal to the requirements of Sankore.

I will speak of only one of the great black scholars referred to in the book by Felix DuBois.

Ahmed Baba was the last chancellor of the University of Sankore. He was one of the greatest African scholars of the late sixteenth century. His life is a brilliant example of the range and depth of West African intellectual activity before the colonial era. Ahmed Baba was the author of more than 40 books; nearly every one of these books had a different theme. He was in Timbuktu when it was invaded by the Moroccans in 1592, and he was one of the first citizens to protest this occupation of his beloved home town. Ahmed Baba, along with other scholars, was imprisoned and eventually exiled to Morocco. During his expatriation from Timbuktu, his collection of 1,600 books, one of the richest libraries of his day, was lost.

Now, West Africa entered a sad period of decline. During the Moorish occupation, wreck and ruin became the order of the day. When the Europeans arrived in this part of Africa and saw these conditions, they assumed that nothing of order and value had ever existed in these countries. This mistaken impression, too often repeated, has influenced the interpretation of African and Afro-American life in history for over 400 years.

Negroes played an important part in American life, history, and culture long before 1619. Our relationship to this country is as old as the country itself.

Africans first came to the new world as explorers. They participated in the exploratory expeditions of Balboa, the discoverer of the Pacific, and Cortes, the conqueror of Mexico. An African explorer helped to open up New Mexico and Arizona and prepared the way for the settlement of the Southwest. Africans also accompanied French Jesuit missionaries on their early travels through North America.

In the United States, the art and literature of the Negro people has had an economic origin. Much that is original in black American folklore, or singular in "Negro spirituals" and blues, can be traced to the economic institution of slavery and its influence upon the Negro's soul.

After the initial poetical debut of Jupiter Hammon and Phillis Wheatley, the main literary expression of the Negro was the slave narrative. One of the earliest of these narratives came from the pen of Gustavas Vassa, an African from Nigeria. This was a time of great pamphleteering in the United States. The free Africans in the North, and those who had escaped from slavery in the South, made their mark upon this time and awakened the conscience of the nation. Their lack of formal educational attainments gave their narratives a strong and rough-hewed truth, more arresting than scholarship.

Gustavas Vassa established his reputation with an autobiography, first printed in England. Vassa, born in 1745, was kidnapped by slavers when he was 11 years old and taken to America. He was placed in service on a plantation in Virginia. Eventually, he was able to purchase his freedom. He left the United States, made his home in England and became active in the British anti-slavery movement. In 1790, he presented a petition to Parliament to abolish the slave trade. His autobiography, *The Interesting Narrative of the Life of Gustavas Vassa,* was an immediate success and had to be published in five editions.

At the time when slave ships were still transporting Africans to the New World, two

18th century Negroes were writing and publishing works of poetry. The first of these was Jupiter Hammon, a slave in Queens Village, Long Island. In 1760, Hammon published *An Evening Thought: Salvation by Christ with Penitential Cries.* . . . In all probability this was the first poem published by an American Negro. His most remarkable work, "An Address to the Negroes of New York," was published in 1787. Jupiter Hammon died in 1800.

Phillis Wheatley (1753–1784), like Hammon, was influenced by the religious forces of the Wesley-Whitefield revival. Unlike Hammon, however, she was a writer of unusual talent. Though born in Africa, she acquired in an incredibly short time both the literary culture and the religion of her New England masters. Her writings reflect little of her race and much of the age in which she lived. She was a New England poet of the third quarter of the 18th century, and her poems reflected the poetic conventions of the Boston Puritans with whom she lived. Her fame continued long after her death in 1784 and she became one of the best known poets of New England.

Another important body of literature came out of this period. It is the literature of petition, written by free black men in the North, who were free in name only. Some of the early petitioners for justice were Caribbean-Americans who saw their plight and the plight of the Afro-Americans as one and the same.

In 18th century America, two of the most outstanding fighters for liberty and justice were the West Indians—Prince Hall and John B. Russwurm. When Prince Hall came to the United States, the nation was in turmoil. The colonies were ablaze with indignation. Britain, with a series of revenue acts, had stoked the fires of colonial discontent. In Virginia, Patrick Henry was speaking of liberty or death. The cry, "No Taxation Without Representation," played on the nerve strings of the nation. Prince Hall, then a delicate-looking teenager, often walked through the turbulent streets of Boston, an observer unobserved.

A few months before these hectic scenes, he had arrived in the United States from his home in Barbados, where he was born about 1748, the son of an Englishman and a free African woman. He was, in theory, a free man, but he knew that neither in Boston nor in Barbados were persons of African descent free in fact. At once, he questioned the sincerity of the vocal white patriots of Boston. It never seemed to have occurred to them that the announced principles motivating their action [were] stronger argument in favor of destroying the stem of slavery. The colonists held in servitude more than a half million human beings, some of them white; yet they engaged in the contradiction of going to war to support the theory that all men were created equal.

When Prince Hall arrived in Boston, that city was the center of the American slave trade. Most of the major leaders of the revolutionary movement, in fact, were slaveholders or investors in slave-supported businesses. Hall, like many other Americans, wondered: what did these men mean by freedom?

The condition of the free black men, as Prince Hall found them, was not an enviable one. Emancipation brought neither freedom nor relief from the stigma of color. They were still included with slaves, indentured servants, and Indians in the slave codes. Discriminatory laws severely circumscribed their freedom of movement.

By 1765, Prince Hall saw little change in the condition of the blacks, and though a freeman, at least in theory, he saw his people debased as though they were slaves still in bondage. These things drove him to prepare himself for leadership among his people. So, through diligence and frugality, he became a property owner, thus establishing himself in the eyes of white people as well as the blacks.

But the ownership of property was not enough. He still had to endure sneers and

Culture and Identity

insults. He went to school at night, and later became a Methodist preacher. His church became the forum for his people's grievances. Ten years after his arrival in Boston, he was the accepted leader of the black community.

In 1788, Hall petitioned the Massachusetts Legislature, protesting the kidnapping of free Negroes. This was a time when American patriots were engaged in a constitutional struggle for freedom. They had proclaimed the inherent rights of all mankind to life, liberty, and the pursuit of happiness. Hall dared to remind them that the black men in the United States were human beings and as such were entitled to freedom and respect for their human personality.

Prejudice made Hall the father of African secret societies in the United States. He is the father of what is now known as Negro Masonry. Hall first sought initiation into the white Masonic Lodge in Boston, but was turned down because of his color. He then applied to the Army Lodge of an Irish Regiment. His petition was favorably received. On March 6, 1775, Hall and fourteen other black Americans were initiated in Lodge Number 441. When, on March 17, the British were forced to evacuate Boston, the Army Lodge gave Prince Hall and his colleagues a license to meet and function as a Lodge. Thus, on July 3, 1776, African Lodge No. I came into being. This was the first Lodge in Masonry established in America for men of African descent.

The founding of the African Lodge was one of Prince Hall's greatest achievements. It afforded the Africans in the New England area a greater sense of security, and contributed to a new spirit of unity among them. Hall's interest did not end with the Lodge. He was deeply concerned with improving the lot of his people in other ways. He sought to have schools established for the children of the free Africans in Massachusetts. Of prime importance is the fact that Prince Hall worked to secure respect for the personality of his people and also played a significant role in the downfall of the Massachusetts slave trade. He helped to prepare the groundwork for the freedom fighters of the 19th and 20th centuries, whose continuing efforts have brought the black American closer to the goal of full citizenship.

The literature of petition was continued by men like David Walker whose *Appeal,* an indictment of slavery, was published in 1829. Dynamic ministers like Samuel Ringgold Ward and Henry Highland Garnet joined the ranks of the petitioners at the time a journalist literature was being born.

Frederick Douglass, the noblest of American black men of the 19th century, was the leader of the journalist group. He established the newspaper *North Star* and, later, the magazine *Douglass Monthly.* John B. Russwurm and Samuel Cornish founded the newspaper *Freedom's Journal* in 1827.

In 1829, a third poet, George Moses Horton, published his book, *The Hope of Liberty.* In his second volume, *Naked Genius* (1865), he expressed his anti-slavery convictions more clearly. George Moses Horton was the first slave poet to openly protest his status.

Throughout the early part of the 19th century, the slave narrative became a new form of American literary expression.

The best known of these slave narratives came from the pen of Frederick Douglass, the foremost Negro in the anti-slavery movement. His first book was *The Narrative of the Life of Frederick Douglass* (1845). Ten years later, an improved and enlarged edition, *My Bondage and My Freedom,* was published. His third autobiography, *Life and Times of Frederick Douglass,* was published in 1881 and enlarged in 1892. Douglass fought for civil rights and against lynching and the Ku Klux Klan. No abuse of justice escaped his attention and his wrath.

It was not until 1887 that an Afro-American writer emerged who was fully a master of the short story as a literary form. This writer was Charles W. Chesnutt. Chesnutt, an Ohioan by birth, became a teacher in North Carolina while still in his middle teens. He studied the traditions and superstitions of the people that he taught and later made this material into the ingredient of his best short stories. In August 1887, his short story, "The Goophered Grapevine," appeared in *The Atlantic Monthly*. This was the beginning of a series of stories which were later brought together in his first book, *The Conjure Woman* (1899). "The Wife of His Youth" also appeared in the *Atlantic* (July 1898) and gave the title to his second volume, *The Wife of His Youth and Other Stories of the Color Line* (1899). Three more stories appeared later: "Baxter's Procrustes" in the *Atlantic* (June, 1904), and "The Doll" and "Mr. Taylor's Funeral" in *The Crisis* magazine (April, 1912 and April–May, 1915).

Chesnutt's novel did not measure up to the standards he had set with his short stories, though they were all competently written. In 1928, he was awarded the Spingarn Medal for his "pioneer work as a literary artist depicting the life and struggle of Americans of Negro descent."

Paul Laurence Dunbar, a contemporary of Charles W. Chesnutt, made his reputation as a poet before extending his talent to short stories. Both Dunbar and Chesnutt very often used the same subject matter in their stories. Chesnutt was by far the better writer, and his style and attitude differed radically from Dunbar's.

Dunbar's pleasant folk tales of tradition-bound plantation black folk were more acceptable to a large white reading audience with preconceived ideas of "Negro characteristics." In all fairness, it must be said that Dunbar did not cater to this audience in all of his stories. In such stories as "The Tragedy at Three Forks," "The Lynching of Jube Benson," and "The Ordeal of Mt. Hope," he showed a deep concern and understanding of the more serious and troublesome aspects of Afro-American life. Collections of his stories are: *Folks from Dixie* (1898), *The Strength of Gideon* (1900), *In Old Plantation Days* (1903), and *The Heart of Happy Hollow* (1904). Only one of his novels, *The Sport of the Gods* (1902), is mainly concerned with Afro-American characters.

Chesnutt and Dunbar, in their day, reached a larger general reading audience than any of the black writers who came before them. The period of the slave narratives had passed. Yet the black writer was still an oddity and a stepchild in the eyes of most critics. This attitude continued in a lessening degree throughout one of the richest and most productive periods in Afro-American writing in the United States—the period called "the Negro Renaissance." The community of Harlem was the center and spiritual godfather and midwife for this renaissance. The cultural emancipation of the Afro-American that began before the first World War was now in full force. The black writer discovered a new voice within himself and liked the sound of it. The white writers who had been interpreting our life with an air of authority and a preponderance of error looked at last to the black writer for their next cue. In short story collections like Jean Toomer's *Cane* (1923) and Langston Hughes' *The Ways of White Folks* (1934) heretofore untreated aspects of Afro-American life were presented in an interesting manner that was unreal to some readers because it was new and so contrary to the stereotypes they had grown accustomed to.

In her book *Mules and Men* (1935), Zora Neale Hurston presented a collection of folk tales and sketches that showed the close relationship between humor and tragedy in Afro-American life. In doing this, she also fulfilled the first requirement of all books—to entertain and guide the reader through an interesting experience that is worth the time and

Culture and Identity

attention it takes to absorb it. In other stories like *The Gilded Six Bits, Drenched in Light,* and *Spunk* another side of Miss Hurston's talent was shown.

In the midst of this renaissance, two strong voices from the West Indians were heard. Claude McKay, in his books *Ginger Town* (1932) and *Banana Bottom* (1933), wrote of life in his Jamaican homeland in a manner that debunked the travelogue exoticism usually attributed to Negro life in the Caribbean area. Before the publication of these books, Harlem and its inhabitants had already been the subject matter for a group of remarkable short stories by McKay and the inspiration for his book, *Home to Harlem,* still the most famous novel ever written about that community.

In 1926, Eric Walrond, a native of British Guiana, explored and presented another side of West Indian life in his book, *Tropic Death,* a near classic. In these 10 naturalistic stories, Eric Walrond concerns himself mostly with labor and living conditions in the Panama Canal Zone where a diversity of people and ways of life meet and clash, while each tries to survive at the expense of the other. Clear perception and strength of style enabled Mr. Walrond to balance form and content in such a manner that the message was never intruded upon the unfolding of the stories.

Rudolph Fisher, another bright star of the Harlem literary Renaissance, was first a brilliant young doctor. The new and light touch he brought to his stories of Afro-American life did not mar the serious aspect that was always present. The message in his comic realism was more profound because he was skillful enough to weave it into the design of his stories without destroying any of their entertainment value. His stories "Blades of Steel," "The City of Refuge," and "The Promised Land" were published in *The Atlantic Monthly.* "High Yaller" appeared in *The Crisis* magazine during the hey-day of that publication, and was later reprinted in the O'Brien anthology, *Best Short Stories of 1934.* Unfortunately, he died before all of his bright promise was fulfilled.

The Harlem literary renaissance was studded with many names. Those already mentioned are only a few of the most outstanding. During the period of this literary flowering among black writers, Harlem became the Mecca, the stimulating Holy City, drawing pilgrims from all over the country and from some places abroad. Talented authors, playwrights, painters, and sculptors came forth eagerly showing their wares.

Three men, W. E. B. Du Bois, James Weldon Johnson, and Alain Locke, cast a guiding influence over this movement without becoming a part of the social climbing and pseudo-intellectual aspect of it. W. E. B. Du Bois, by continuously challenging the old concepts and misinterpretations of Afro-American life, gave enlightened new directions to a whole generation. As editor of *The Crisis,* he introduced many new black writers and extended his helpful and disciplined hand when it was needed. Following the death of Booker T. Washington and the decline of the Booker T. Washington school of thought, he became the spiritual father of the new black intelligentsia.

James Weldon Johnson moved from Florida to New York. His diversity of talent established his reputation long before the beginning of the "New Negro literary movement." Later, as a participant in and historian of the movement, he helped to appraise and preserve the best that came out of it. In his books, *Autobiography of an Ex-Colored Man* (1912), *The Book of American Negro Poetry* (1922), *Black Manhattan* (1930), and *Along This Way,* an autobiography (1933). James Weldon Johnson showed clearly that Negro writers have made a distinct contribution to the literature of the United States. His own creative talent made him one of the most able of these contributors.

Alain Locke is the writer who devoted the most time to the interpretation of the "New

Negro literary movement" and to Afro-American literature in general. In 1925, he expanded the special Harlem issue of the magazine *Survey Graphic* (which he edited) into the anthology, *The New Negro*. This book is a milestone and a guide to Afro-American thought, literature, and art in the middle twenties. The objective of the volume "to register the transformation of the inner and outer life of the Negro in America that had so significantly taken place in the last few preceding years," was ably achieved. For many years, Mr. Locke's annual appraisal of books by and about Negroes, published in *Opportunity* magazine, was an eagerly awaited literary event.

Early in the Harlem literary renaissance period, the black ghetto became an attraction for a varied assortment of white celebrities and just plain thrill-seeking white people lost from their moorings. Some were insipid rebels, defying the mores of their upbringing by associating with Negroes on a socially equal level. Some were too rich to work, not educated enough to teach, and not holy enough to preach. Others were searching for the mythological "noble savage"—the "exotic Negro."

These professional exotics were generally college educated Negroes who had become estranged from their families and the environment of their upbringing. They talked at length about the great books within them waiting to be written. Their white sponsors continued to subsidize them while they "developed their latent talent." Of course the "great books" of these camp followers never got written and, eventually, their white sponsors realized that they were never going to write—not even a good letter. Ironically, these sophisticates made a definite contribution to the period of the "New Negro literary renaissance." In socially inclined company, they proved that a black American could behave with as much attention to the details of social protocol as the best bred and richest white person in the country. They could balance a cocktail glass with expertness. Behind their pretense of being writers they were really actors—and rather good ones. They were generally better informed than their white sponsors and could easily participate in a discussion of the writings of Marcel Proust in one minute, and the music of Ludwig van Beethoven the next. As social parasites, they conducted themselves with a smoothness approaching an artistic accomplishment. Unknown to them, their conduct had done much to eliminate one of the major prevailing stereotypes of Afro-American life and manners.

Concurrently with the unfolding of this mildly funny comedy, the greatest productive period in Afro-American literature continued. The more serious and talented black writers were actually writing their books and getting them published.

Opportunity magazine, then edited by Charles Johnson, and *The Crisis*, edited by W. E. B. Du Bois, were the major outlets for the new black writers.

Opportunity short story contests provided a proving ground for a number of competent black writers. Among the prize winners were Cecil Blue, John F. Matheus, Eugene Gordon, and Marita Bonner.

Writers like Walter White, Jessie Fauset, Wallace Thurman, Nella Larsen, George S. Schuyler, Sterling A. Brown, and Arna Bontemps had already made their debut and were accepted into the circle of the matured.

The stock market collapse of 1929 marked the beginning of the depression and the end of the period known as "The Negro Renaissance." The "exotic Negro," professional and otherwise, became less exotic now that a hungry look was upon his face. The numerous white sponsors and well-wishers who had begun to flock to Harlem ten years before no longer had time or money to explore and marvel over Harlem life. Many Harlem residents lived and died in Harlem during this period without once hearing of the famous literary movement that had flourished and declined within their midst. It was not a mass movement. It was a fad, partly produced in Harlem and partly imposed on Harlem. Most of the writers associated with it would have written just as well at any other time.

In the intervening years between the end of "The Negro Renaissance" and the emergence of Richard Wright, black writers of genuine talent continued to produce books of good caliber. The lack of sponsorship and pampering had made them take serious stock of themselves and their intentions. *The Crisis,* organ of the National Association for the Advancement of Colored People, and *Opportunity,* organ of the National Urban League, continued to furnish a publishing outlet for new black writers. The general magazines published stories by black writers intermittently, seemingly on a quota basis.

During this period writers like Ralph Ellison, Henry B. Jones, Marian Minus, Ted Poston, Lawrence D. Reddick, and Grace W. Thompkins published their first short stories.

In 1936 Richard Wright's first short story to receive any appreciable attention, "Big Boy Leaves Home," appeared in the anthology, *The New Caravan.* "The Ethics of Living Jim Crow: An Autobiographical Sketch" was published in *American Stuff,* anthology of the Federal Writers' Project, the next year. In 1938, when his first book, *Uncle Tom's Children,* won a $500 prize contest conducted by *Story Magazine,* his talent received national attention. With the publication of his phenomenally successful novel, *Native Son,* in 1940, a new era in Afro-American literature had begun. Here, at last, was a black writer who undeniably wrote considerably better than many of his white contemporaries. As a short story craftsman, he was the most accomplished black writer since Charles W. Chesnutt.

After the emergence of Richard Wright, the period of indulgence for Negro writers was over. Hereafter, black writers had to stand or fall by the same standards and judgments used to evaluate the work of white writers. The era of the patronized and pampered black writer had at last come to an end. The closing of this era may, in the final analysis, be the greatest contribution Richard Wright made to the status of Negro writers and to Negro literature.

When the United States entered the second World War, the active Negro writers, like most other writers in the country, turned their talents to some activity in relation to the war.

The first short stories of Ann Petry began to appear in *The Crisis. The Negro Caravan,* the best anthology of Negro literature since Alain Locke edited *The New Negro* sixteen years before, had already appeared with much new material. Chester B. Himes, a dependable writer during the depression period, managed to turn out a number of remarkable short stories while working in shipyards and war industries in California. In 1944, he received a Rosenwald Fellowship to complete his first novel, *If He Hollers Let Him Go.* In 1945, Frank Yerby won an O. Henry Memorial Award for his excellent short story, "Health Card," which had been published in *Harper's* magazine a year before.

A new crop of post-war black writers was emerging. In their stories they treated new aspects of Afro-American life or brought new insights to the old aspects. Principally, they were good story tellers, aside from any message they wanted to get across to their readers. The weepy sociological propaganda stories (so prevalent during the depression era) had had their day with the Negro writer and all others. There would still be protest stories, but the protest would now have to meet the standards of living literature.

Opportunity and *The Crisis,* once the proving ground for so many new black writers, were no longer performing that much needed service. The best of the new writers found acceptance in the general magazines. Among these are James Baldwin, Lloyd Brown, Arthur P. Davis, Owen Dodson, Lance Jeffers, John O. Killens, Robert H. Lucas, Albert Murray, George E. Norford, Carl R. Offord, John H. Robinson, Jr., John Caswell Smith, Jr., and Mary E. Vroman.

With the rise of nationalism and independent states in Africa, and the rapid change of the status of the Negro in the United States, the material used by black writers and their treatment of it did, of necessity, reflect a breaking away from the old mooring.

Among black writers the period of the late 1940's was the period of Richard Wright. The period of the 1960's was the period of James Baldwin.

The now flourishing literary talent of James Baldwin had no easy birth, and he did not emerge overnight, as some of his new discoverers would have you believe. For years this talent was in incubation in the ghetto of Harlem, before he went to Europe a decade ago [1959] in an attempt to discover the United States and how he and his people relate to it. The book in which that discovery is portrayed, *The Fire Next Time*, is a continuation of his search for place and definition.

Baldwin, more than any other writer of our times, has succeeded in restoring the personal essay to its place as a form of creative literature. From his narrow vantage point of personal grievance, he has opened a "window on the world." He plays the role traditionally assigned to thinkers concerned with the improvement of human conditions—that of alarmist. He calls national attention to things in the society that need to be corrected and things that need to be celebrated.

When Richard Wright died in Paris in 1960, a new generation of black writers, partly influenced by him, was beginning to explore, as Ralph Ellison said, "the full range of American Negro humanity." In the short stories and novels of such writers as Frank London Brown, William Melvin Kelly, LeRoi Jones, Paule Marshall, Rosa Guy, and Ernest J. Gaines, both a new dimension and a new direction in writing are seen. They have questioned and challenged all previous interpretations of Afro-American life. In doing this, they have created the basis for a new American literature.

The black writer and his people are now standing at the crossroads of history. This is the black writer's special vantage point, and this is what makes the task and the mission of the black writer distinctly different from that of the white writer. The black writer, concerned with creating a work of art in a segregated society, has a double task. First: he has to explain the society to himself and create his art while opposing that society. Second: he cannot be honest with himself or his people without lending his support, at least verbally, to the making of a new society that respects the dignity of men.

The black writer must realize that his people are now entering the last phase of a transitional period between slavery and freedom; it is time for the black writer to draw upon the universal values in his people's experience, just as Sean O'Casey and Sholem Aleichem drew upon the universal values in the experiences of the Irish and the Jews. In the next phase of Afro-American writing, a literature of celebration must be created—not a celebration of oppression, but a celebration of survival in spite of it.

First Congress of Negro Writers and Artists

Paris, September 19–22, 1956

RESOLUTION

Whereas the Conference has shown that there is a profound interest in the work undertaken during its sessions in regard to various Negro cultures which have often been ignored, under-estimated or sometimes destroyed.

Whereas there has been made evident the urgent necessity to rediscover the historical truth and revalue Negro cultures; these truths, often misrepresented and denied, being partly responsible for provoking a crisis in Negro culture and in the manner in which that culture relates to World culture;

We recommend that artists, writers, scholars, theologians, thinkers and technicians participate in the historic task of unearthing, rehabilitating and developing those cultures so as to facilitate their being integrated into the general body of World culture.

We Negro writers, artists and intellectuals of various political ideologies and religious creeds have felt a need to meet at this crucial stage in the evolution of mankind in order to examine objectively our several views on culture and to probe those cultures with a full consciousness of our responsibilities—first, before our own respective peoples, second, before colonial people and those living under conditions of racial oppression, and, third, before all free men of good will.

We deem it unworthy of genuine intellectuals to hesitate to take a stand regarding fundamental problems, for such hesitations serve injustice and error.

Jointly we have weighed our cultural heritages and have studied how they have been affected by social and general conditions of racialism and colonialism.

We maintain that the growth of culture is dependent upon the termination of such shameful practices in this twentieth century as colonialism, the oppression of weaker peoples and racialism.

We affirm that all peoples should be placed in a position where they can learn their own national cultural values (history, language, literature, etc.) and enjoy the benefits of education within the framework of their own culture.

This Conference regrets the involuntary absence of a delegation from South Africa.

This Conference is pleased to take due notice of recent advances made throughout the world, advances which imply a general abolition of the colonial system, as well as the final and universal liquidation of racialism.

This Conference invites all Negro intellectuals to unite their efforts in securing effective respect for the Rights of Man, whatever his colour may be, and for all peoples and all nations whatsoever.

This Conference urges Negro intellectuals and all justice-loving men to struggle to create the practical conditions for the revival and the growth of Negro cultures.

Paying tribute to the cultures of all lands and with due appreciation of their several contributions to the progress of Civilisation, the Conference urges all Negro intellectuals to defend, illustrate and publicise throughout the world the national values of their own peoples.

We Negro writers and artists proclaim our fellowship with all men and expect from them, for our people, a similar fellowship.

At the request of several members of Congress the Officers have undertaken the responsibility of setting up an International Association of Negro Men of Culture.

Second Congress of Negro Writers and Artists

Rome, March 25–April 11, 1959

PREAMBLE

The Negro Writers and Artists, meeting in Congress at Rome on the 25th, 26th, 27th, 28th, 29th, 30th and 31st March, 1959, welcome the process of decolonisation which has begun in the world on a large scale.

They consider that this movement should be extended and amplified and that, as the nineteenth century was the century of colonisation, so the twentieth century should be the century of general decolonisation.

They regard it as the imperative duty of the members of the S.A.C. [Society of African Culture] to make themselves actively militant in all fields on behalf of this decolonisation, which is indispensable to the peace of the world and the development of culture.

They protest against all manifestations and all acts of violence, wherever they may happen, by means of which a retarded colonialism attempts to prevent the colonised peoples from regaining their freedom.

They reassert their conviction:

1. That political independence and economic liberation are the essential conditions for the cultural advance of the underdeveloped countries in general and the Negro-African countries in particular.

2. That every effort towards the regrouping of countries or nations artificially divided by imperialism, every realisation of fundamental solidarity and every determination towards unity are advantageous and profitable for restoring the equilibrium of the world and for the revitalisation of culture.

3. That every effort towards the personification and enrichment of national culture, and every effort to implant Negro men of culture in their own civilisation, constitute in fact, progress towards universalisation and are a contribution towards the civilisation of mankind.

The Congress, therefore, recommends the Negro Writers and Artists to regard it as their essential task and sacred mission to bring their cultural activity within the scope of the great movement for the liberation of their individual peoples, without losing sight of the solidarity which should unite all individuals and peoples who are struggling for the liquidation of colonisation and its consequences as well as those who are fighting through-out the world for progress and liberty.

RESOLUTION OF THE COMMISSION ON LITERATURE

The Commission on Literature of the Second Congress of Negro Writers and Artists, after studying the Reports submitted to it, and after a general discussion of these Reports and of their conclusions, at its sessions of Thursday 26th, Friday 27th, Saturday 28th and Sunday 29th March, 1959, examined,

I. The state of vernacular literature in Negro Africa and the countries of African population, and the need to defend those oral literatures which constitute the real basis of Negro-African cultures and their ethics, as well as the legitimate expression of national or regional peculiarities in the various countries concerned.

This work of defence and development has already been undertaken, for example, for Ghana, Guinea and Haiti, where the sovereign Governments are encouraging the development of the autochthonous languages, either by financial assistance to existing institutions, or by including these languages in the school curriculum, or by publishing newspapers and reviews, etc., and by the creation of Drama Centres.

The Commission also examined,

II. The confrontation of these traditional cultures with the forms of Western culture, in the unhealthy, and most frequently barbarous context of colonisation.

This confrontation in most cases resulted in a dead stop and in *cultural degeneration*. It involved the countries of African population in a long period of silence and loss of personality.

This contact also brought about new structures within the traditional literature, to the extent that, for good or evil, every culture in our time is influenced by other cultures.

There is a need for the study of these new structures and for help in acquiring con-sciousness of them and thus ensuring the transition from oral literatures to the stage of written literature, without impairing the character and ethics of these literatures.

The Commission also examined,

III. The situation of the Negro writer in the modern world. Such a writer is most fre-quently cut off from his authentic public by the use of a language which, in its literary form, is inaccessible to the mass of Negro peoples.

Such a writer experiences serious difficulties in getting his work published, in the mod-ern Western conditions in which he finds himself; his public is therefore most frequently a restricted one.

He may also suffer from another cause of disequilibrium in those cases where the use of his autochthonous language is imperative for him and where its creative possibilities are limited by the fact that this language is not in literary use.

Emphasis should nevertheless be laid on the progressive character of the use of the Western languages to the extent that they led to economy of time in constructing the new Africa.

This observation should in no way lessen the obligation to develop the autochthonous languages.

In view of all the reasons and considerations set out above, the Commission on Litera-ture calls the attention of the Delegates of the Second Congress of Negro Writers and Artists to the following projects which should be instituted in the various Negro States:

Culture and Identity

1. The institution in each independent country of a strict and rigorous plan for the fight against illiteracy, inspired both by the most modern techniques already in use, and the original peculiarities of the country in question.

2. An increase in the number of fundamentally decentralised popular libraries, and the use of films and sound-recordings.

3. The institution of African Cultural Research Centres; these Centres, which would be responsible for working out practical plans, would be in close contact with the International Organisations, and with other nations.

4. The translation into autochthonous languages, wherever possible, of representative works of Negro writers in the French, English, Portuguese, Spanish, etc., languages.

5. The exchange of translations between the various cultural areas (French, English, Spanish, Italian and Portuguese) of Africa and the other countries of African population. Negro writers should not necessarily adopt the contradictions between the various Western cultures emanating from the nations which have dominated the Negro world.

6. The creation of national organisations for aid to writers. Such organisations already exist in various forms in Ghana and Guinea.

7. The Commission proposes the creation of effective aid to young writers within the Society of African Culture itself.

8. The Commission recommends the Society of African Culture to arrange cultural meetings with the writers of all countries.

9. Finally, the Commission hopes that the Congress will call the attention of the Governments of Negro States to the need to support and encourage the creation of theatrical schools along the lines set out above.

The Commission on Literature hopes that Negro-African writers will work to define their common language, their common manner of using words and ideas and of reacting to them. The desire for an ordered language expressing coherent cultures is embodied, among other things, in work within a national reality from which the flagrant disorder specifically inherent in the colonial situation will be banished. This language, transcending the various languages used, transcending the legitimate forms of national cultures, will thus contribute towards strengthening the unity of the Negro peoples, and will furnish their writers with a working tool.

The Commission also finally recognises that this contribution to the progress of the Negro-African peoples cannot fail additionally to strengthen the universal brotherhood of mankind. The Commission had endeavoured to carry out its work bearing constantly in mind this brotherhood and the generosity of spirit which it implies.

Resolution of the Commission on Philosophy

Considering the dominant part played by philosophic reflection in the elaboration of culture,

Considering that until now the West has claimed a monopoly of philosophic reflection, so that philosophic enterprise no longer seems conceivable outside the framework of the categories forged by the West,

Considering that the philosophic effort of traditional Africa has always been reflected in vital attitudes and has never had purely conceptual aims,

The Commission declares:

1. That for the African philosopher, philosophy can never consist in reducing the African reality to Western systems;

2. That the African philosopher must base his inquiries upon the fundamental certainty that the Western philosophic approach is not the only possible one;
and therefore,

1. Urges that the African philosopher should learn from the traditions, tales, myths and proverbs of his people, so as to draw from them the laws of a true African wisdom complementary to the other forms of human wisdom and to bring out the specific categories of African thought.

2. Calls upon the African philosopher, faced by the totalitarian or egocentric philosophers of the West, to divest himself of a possible inferiority complex, which might prevent him from starting from his African *being* to judge the foreign contribution.

It calls upon the philosopher to transcend any attitude of withdrawal into himself and his traditions so as to bring out, in true communication with all philosophies, the true universal values.

It is highly desirable that the modern African philosopher should preserve the unitary vision of cosmic reality which characterises the wisdom of traditional Africa.

SYNTHESIS BY THE SUB-COMMISSION ON THEOLOGY

We, African believers, of all forms of faith, meeting as the Theological Sub-Commission of the Second International Congress of Negro Writers and Artists,

I. Find:

1. That there is a difficult and heavy responsibility upon us, in the present crisis of human values; a difficult responsibility, since religion involves requirements which demand the whole man, whose profit is not material and does not immediately appear; a heavy responsibility, because our Negro-African culture is in danger of losing what makes it original, if the profoundly religious spirit which inspires it came to be extinguished.

2. That we have our proper cultural personality, which is the source of our originality.

3. That the fundamental values of that cultural personality which might allow a valid communication between the various confessions known to the Negro world, may be summed up as follows:

—a fundamental faith in a transcendental Force from which man draws his origin, upon which he depends and towards which he is drawn.

—the sense of a vital solidarity ("*solidarité*"), a French word which seems to us the least removed from the Fulah *neddaku*, the Bambara *maya*, the Madagascan *fihavanana*, and others, and which comprises a series of moral and social virtues, such as Ancestor worship, the veneration of the Elders, hospitality, the spirit of tolerance, etc.

—the vital union between spiritual and practical life.

4. That these fundamental values through which the African religious spirit finds expression, are undergoing a twofold crisis:

—by reason of their encounter with the modern world and with religions coming from elsewhere.

II. Declare:

1. That it is our duty to acquire and diffuse a better knowledge of our cultural patrimony which is profoundly penetrated by the religious spirit.

2. That we must be lucid in assessing what is obsolete and what is lasting in the expressions of our cultural heredity.

3. That we must lay our hearts and minds open to everything which is universal in the values of any culture or religious expression whatsoever, distinguishing in them what is universal and therefore valid for all men, from what is the proper expression of their own cultural heredity.

4. That we wish to establish communication between the different religions by which the Negro-African world lives, a communication which must not end in an insuperable opposition between one religion and another, but in a mutual enrichment which will enable each of them to express itself through Negro-African culture.

III. Motions.

1. We call upon all religious forces to preserve and enrich the religious spirit of the Negro world.

2. We ask all those who guide the destinies of our countries (politicians, artists and scientists), to give the religious spirit its proper place in Negro-African culture.

3. We invite the ministers of all religions to continue their efforts towards the comprehension of African culture and to make use of it in transmitting their message.

4. We call upon all the elect to assemble and make known our oral sacred literature.

5. We ask all foreign scientists who have the noble ambition of making us rediscover our religious traditions, while grateful to them for all that is positive in their contribution, to beware of passing too rapidly from hypothesis to assertion.

6. We decide to make greater use of *Présence Africaine* to make our work known.

7. We demand that we shall not be compelled, in the name of an unconditioned fidelity to Africa, and of technical progress erected into a supreme value, to renounce our religious convictions, thus forgetting the fact that no properly understood religion is in opposition to progress and denying the great African spirit of toleration.

RESOLUTION ON TECHNICAL SCIENCES AND MEDICINE

It seems daring to refer to science in speaking of modern Africa, so distant is the memory of the Cultural Centres which were found all over ancient Africa.

We have not in effect shared in the scientific upsurge which began in Europe with the sixteenth century and gathered momentum in the nineteenth, so paralysed were we by the slave trade which not only drained Africa of more than a hundred million human beings, but also caused the destruction on the spot of whole populations and the flight of the survivors to the forest regions, a relatively effective place of refuge, but hardly propitious for the development of science.

The colonisation which succeeded the slave trade was no more favourable to us. Technique never develops except under the pressure of real needs and thanks to investment which is sometimes burdensome, African techniques, crystallised since the sixteenth century, could only evolve with difficulty in contact with more highly developed European techniques responding to priority requirements which are foreign to us.

At the same time, the obstacles which have limited the development of science in Africa are not all of an external character. There are internal obstacles (maintained and aggravated by colonisation) such as:

1. The initiatory form of scientific knowledge in old Africa. This form of spreading knowledge both dangerously limited the number of "those who know" (our wise men) and at the same time did not allow these "wise men," who before attaining full knowledge had already passed the most creative age, to give of their best.

2. The absence in the greater part of Africa of the writing which is necessary to sustain scientific reflection.

Report of the Commission on the Arts

Whereas:

The two points which received greatest attention of the Second Congress of Negro Artists and Writers under the headings of descriptions and spirit were:

1. The unity of thought indispensable to the equilibrium of the Black World, and

2. The overriding obligation imposed on all black artists to produce within their culture a liberation of all different forms of expression.

Whereas:

The Commission on the Arts finds that in the actual state of our knowledge, the work which has been done (mostly by Western specialists), and which is in the process of attempting to articulate general laws and the aesthetic principles of African art, does not yet yield more than hypotheses needing much further explanation!

Whereas:

The Society of African Culture is the sole existing medium on the international level for the mobilisation of the artistic production of black artists and writers, and has a unique possibility and responsibility for demonstrating before the world the richness and the value of the talent and competence of the new culture in the Negro world.

Whereas:

The Commission has understood the vital role of the cinema as a medium of communication, education and indoctrination, which can be of extraordinary value to the native States of Africa (or of imminent harm, if delivered to remain by default, under alien domination);

Be it resolved that:

The Second International Congress of Negro Artists and Writers propose to the principal S.A.C. organisation the establishment of a team of Negro specialists who would be charged with making on-the-spot inventories of African sculpture to find out

(a) the general laws which have governed the elaboration of African sculpture and statuary;

(b) the spirit and the general laws governing the diverse expressions of Negro plastic art;

(c) the present condition of the painter and the sculptor in the different artistic zones of the Negro world; the condition of the painter and the sculptor in countries with populations of African descent; African sources of these artistic zones; the influence of the African plastic arts on Europe, and inversely, the influence of Western arts on Negro-African art.

Motion by a Group of Marxists

We, African Marxists,

Recognise that the evolution of Societies, the steady improvement of technique, recent discoveries and the consequent emergence of new economic links and new social relationships make the enrichment and effective broadening of Marxism both possible and desirable.

The analyses of Western society worked out by Marx, although linked to the interpretation of a specific system of production, namely capitalism, enabled Marx to describe the feudal (pre-capitalist) forms of society, forms whose equivalent can be found today in the regions which are commonly called underdeveloped.

The economic situation with which Marx found himself faced at the time when he was explaining the laws which govern society led him to advocate certain forms of action.

It is nevertheless clear that in the particular case of underdeveloped countries and, more precisely in the case of Africa, the original forms of struggle take on specific dimensions; already at grips with colonialism, African leaders must further take into account their need to promote a programme of technical modernisation with the maximum speed and efficiency.

African Marxists, in their reflections and in their practice, must look strictly, not only at general economic problems, but also and especially at the facts of economic underdevelopment and the cultural configurations proper to their regions.

African Marxists must also draw inspiration from current experiments in other underdeveloped countries which have already attained independence.

In consequence, considering that,

1. The cultural references in Marx's thought are nearly all drawn from Western experience;

2. The economic situation of the Western proletariat cannot be strictly identified with that of the underdeveloped people;

3. A doctrine is all the more universal so far as, on the one hand, it takes into account all experience, historic, economic, etc., and the diversity of the cultural genius of peoples, and on the other hand, its application is controlled by a really representative authority.

We invite African Marxists to develop their doctrine on the basis of the real history, aspirations and economic situation of their peoples and to build and found it on the authority of their own culture.

Frantz Fanon
(1925–1961, Martinique)

On National Culture

Each generation must out of relative obscurity discover its mission, fulfill it, or betray it. In underdeveloped countries the preceding generations have both resisted the work or erosion carried by colonialism and also helped on the maturing of the struggles of today. We must rid ourselves of the habit, now that we are in the thick of the fight, of minimizing the action of our fathers or of feigning incomprehension when considering their silence and passivity. They fought as well as they could, with the arms that they possessed then; and if the echoes of their struggle have not resounded in the international arena, we must realize that the reason for this silence lies less in their lack of heroism than in the fundamentally different international situation of our time. It needed more than one native to say "We've had enough"; more than one peasant rising crushed, more than one demonstration put down before we could today hold our own, certain in our victory. As for we who have decided to break the back of colonialism, our historic mission is to sanction all revolts, all desperate actions, all those abortive attempts drowned in rivers of blood.

In this chapter we shall analyze the problem, which is felt to be fundamental, of the legitimacy of the claims of a nation. It must be recognized that the political party which mobilizes the people hardly touches on this problem of legitimacy. The political parties start from living reality and it is in the name of this reality, in the name of the stark facts which weigh down the present and the future of men and women, that they fix their line of action. The political party may well speak in moving terms of the nation, but what it is concerned with is that the people who are listening understand the need to take part in the fight if, quite simply, they wish to continue to exist.

Today we know that in the first phase of the national struggle colonialism tries to disarm national demands by putting forward economic doctrines. As soon as the first demands are set out, colonialism pretends to consider them, recognizing with ostentatious humility that the territory is suffering from serious underdevelopment which necessitates a great economic and social effort. And, in fact, it so happens that certain spectacular measures (centers of work for the unemployed which are opened here and there, for example) delay the crystallization of national consciousness for a few years. But, sooner or later, colonialism sees that it is not within its powers to put into practice a project of economic and social reforms which will satisfy the aspirations of the colonized people. Even where food supplies are concerned, colonialism gives proof of its inherent incapability. The colonialist state quickly discovered that if it wishes to disarm the nationalist parties

Culture and Identity

on strictly economic questions then it will have to do in the colonies exactly what it has refused to do in its own country. It is not mere chance that almost everywhere today there flourishes the doctrine of Cartierism.

The disillusioned bitterness we find in Cartier when up against the obstinate determination of France to link to herself peoples which she must feed while so many French people live in want shows up the impossible situation in which colonialism finds itself when the colonial system is called upon to transform itself into an unselfish program of aid and assistance. It is why, once again, there is no use in wasting time repeating that hunger with dignity is preferable to bread eaten in slavery. On the contrary, we must become convinced that colonialism is incapable of procuring for the colonized peoples the material conditions which might make them forget their concern for dignity. Once colonialism has realized where its tactics of social reform are leading, we see it falling back on its old reflexes, reinforcing police effectives, bringing up troops, and setting a reign of terror which is better adapted to its interests and its psychology.

Inside the political parties, and most often in offshoots from these parties, cultured individuals of the colonized race make their appearance. For these individuals, the demand for a national culture and the affirmation of the existence of such a culture represent a special battlefield. While the politicians situate their action in actual present-day events, men of culture take their stand in the field of history. Confronted with the native intellectual who decides to make an aggressive response to the colonialist theory of pre-colonial barbarism, colonialism will react only slightly, and still less because the ideas developed by the young colonized intelligentsia are widely professsed by specialists in the mother country. It is in fact a commonplace to state that for several decades large numbers of research workers have, in the main, rehabilitated the African, Mexican, and Peruvian civilizations. The passion with which native intellectuals defend the existence of their national culture may be a source of amazement; but those who condemn this exaggerated passion are strangely apt to forget that their own psyche and their own selves were conveniently sheltered behind a French or German culture which has given full proof of its existence and which is uncontested.

I am ready to concede that on the plane of factual being the past existence of an Aztec civilization does not change anything very much in the diet of the Mexican peasant of today. I admit that all the proofs of a wonderful Songhai civilization will not change the fact that today the Songhais are underfed and illiterate, thrown between sky and water with empty heads and empty eyes. But it has been remarked several times that this passionate search for a national culture which existed before the colonial era finds its legitimate reason in the anxiety shared by native intellectuals to shrink away from that Western culture in which they all risk being swamped. Because they realize they are in danger of losing their lives and thus becoming lost to their people, these men, hotheaded and with anger in their hearts, relentlessly determine to renew contact once more with the oldest and most pre-colonial springs of life of their people.

Let us go further. Perhaps this passionate research and this anger are kept up or at least directed by the secret hope of discovering beyond the misery of today, beyond self-contempt, resignation, and abjuration, some very beautiful and splendid era whose existence rehabilitates us both in regard to ourselves and in regard to others. I have said that I have decided to go further. Perhaps unconsciously, the native intellectuals, since they could not stand wonderstruck before the history of today's barbarity, decided to back further and to delve deeper down; and, let us make no mistake, it was the greatest delight that they discovered that there was nothing to be ashamed of in the past, but rather dignity, glory, and solemnity. The claim to a national culture in the past does not only rehabilitate that nation and serve as a justification for the hope of a future national culture. In the sphere of psycho-affective equilibrium it is responsible for an important change in the native. Perhaps we have not sufficiently demonstrated that colonialism is not simply content to impose its rule upon the present and the future of a dominated country. Colonialism is not satisfied merely with holding a people in its grip and emptying the native's brain of all form and content. By a kind of perverted logic, it turns to the past of the oppressed people, and distorts, disfigures, and destroys it. This work of devaluing pre-colonial history takes on a dialectical significance today.

When we consider the efforts made to carry out the cultural estrangement so characteristic of the colonial epoch, we realize that nothing has been left to chance and that the total result looked for by colonial domination was indeed to convince the natives that colonialism came to lighten their darkness. The effect consciously sought by colonialism was to drive into the natives' heads the idea that if the settlers were to leave, they would at once fall back into barbarism, degradation, and bestiality.

On the unconscious plane, colonialism therefore did not seek to be considered by the native as a gentle, loving mother who protects her child from a hostile environment, but rather as a mother who unceasingly restrains her fundamentally perverse offspring from managing to commit suicide and from giving free rein to its evil instincts. The colonial mother protects her child from itself, from its ego, and from its physiology, its biology, and its own unhappiness which is its very essence.

In such a situation the claims of the native intellectual are not a luxury but a necessity in any coherent program. The native intellectual who takes up arms to defend his nation's legitimacy and who wants to bring proofs to bear out that legitimacy, who is willing to strip himself naked to study the history of his body, is obliged to dissect the heart of his people.

Such an examination is not specifically national. The native intellectual who decides to give battle to colonial lies fights on the field of the whole continent. The past is given back its value. Culture, extracted from the past to be displayed in all its splendor, is not necessarily that of his own country. Colonialism, which has not bothered to put too fine a point on its efforts, has never ceased to maintain that the Negro is a savage; and for the colonist, the Negro was neither an Angolan nor a Nigerian, for he simply spoke of "the Negro." For colonialism, this vast continent was the haunt of savages, a country riddled with superstitions and fanaticism, destined for contempt, weighted down by the curse of God, a country of cannibals—in short, the Negro's country. Colonialism's condemnation is continental in its scope. The contention by colonialism that the darkest night of humanity lay over pre-colonial history concerns the whole of the African continent. The efforts of the native to rehabilitate himself and to escape from the claws of colonialism are logically inscribed from the same point of view as that of colonialism. The native intellectual who has gone far beyond the domains of Western culture and who had got it into his head to proclaim the existence of another culture never does so in the name of Angola or of Dahomey. The culture which is affirmed is African culture. The Negro, never so much a Negro as since he has been dominated by the whites, when he decides to prove that he has a culture and to behave like a cultured person, comes to realize that history points out a well-defined path to him: he must demonstrate that a Negro culture exists.

And it is only too true that those who are most responsible for this racialization of thought, or at least for the first movement toward that thought, are and remain those Europeans who have never ceased to set up white culture to fill the gap left by the absence of other cultures. Colonialism did not dream of wasting its time in denying the existence

Culture and Identity

of one national culture after another. Therefore the reply of the colonized peoples will be straight away continental in its breath. In Africa, the native literature of the last twenty years is not a national literature but a Negro literature. The concept of negritude, for example, was the emotional if not the logical antithesis of that insult which the white man flung at humanity. This rush of negritude against the white man's contempt showed itself in certain spheres to be the one idea capable of lifting interdictions and anathemas. Because the New Guinean or Kenyan intellectuals found themselves above all up against a general ostracism and delivered to the combined contempt of their overlords, their reaction was to sing praises in admiration of each other. The unconditional affirmation of African culture has succeeded the unconditional affirmation of European culture. On the whole, the poets of negritude oppose the idea of an old Europe to a young Africa, tiresome reasoning to lyricism, oppressive logic to high-stepping nature, and on one side stiffness, ceremony, etiquette, and scepticism, while on the other frankness, liveliness, liberty, and—why not?—luxuriance: but also irresponsibility.

The poets of negritude will not stop at the limits of the continent. From America, black voices will take up the hymn with fuller unison. The "black world" will see the light and Busia from Ghana, Birago Diop for Senegal, Hampaté Ba from the Soudan, and Saint-Clair Drake from Chicago will not hesitate to assert the existence of common ties and a motive power that is identical.

The example of the Arab world might equally well be quoted here. We know that the majority of Arab territories have been under colonial domination. Colonialism has made the same effort in these regions to plant deep in the minds of the native population the idea that before the advent of colonialism their history was one which was dominated by barbarism. The struggle for national liberty has been accompanied by a cultural phenomenon known by the name of the awakening of Islam. The passion with which contemporary Arab writers remind their people of the great pages of their history is a reply to the lies told by the occupying power. The great names of Arabic literature and the great past of Arab civilization have been brandished about with the same ardor as those of the African civilizations. The Arab leaders have tried to return to the famous Dar El Islam which shone so brightly from the twelfth to the fourteenth century.

Today, in the political sphere, the Arab League is giving palpable form to this will to take up again the heritage of the past and to bring it to culmination. Today, Arab doctors and Arab poets speak to each other across the frontiers, and strive to create a new Arab culture and a new Arab civilization. It is in the name of Arabism that these men join together, and that they try to think together. Everywhere, however, in the Arab world, national feeling has preserved even under colonial domination a liveliness that we fail to find in Africa. At the same time that spontaneous communion of each with all, present in the African movement, is not to be found in the Arab League. On the contrary, paradoxically, everyone tries to sing the praises of the achievements of his nation. The cultural process is freed from the indifferentiation which characterized it in the African world, but the Arabs do not always manage to stand aside in order to achieve their aims. The living culture is not national but Arab. The problem is not as yet to secure a national culture, not as yet to lay hold of a movement differentiated by nations, but to assume an African or Arabic culture when confronted by the all-embracing condemnation pronounced by the dominating power. In the African world, as in the Arab, we see that the claims of the man of culture in a colonized country are all-embracing, continental, and in the case of the Arabs, worldwide.

This historical necessity in which the men of African culture find themselves to racialize their claims and to speak more of African culture than of national culture will tend to lead them up a blind alley. Let us take for example the case of the African Cultural Society. This society has been created by African intellectuals who wished to get to know each other and to compare their experiences and the results of their respective research work. The aim of this society was therefore to affirm the existence of an African culture, to evaluate this culture on the plane of distinct nations, and to reveal the internal motive forces of each of their national cultures. But at the same time this society fulfilled another need: the need to exist side by side with the European Cultural Society, which threatened to transform itself into a Universal Cultural Society. There was therefore at the bottom of this decision the anxiety to be present at the universal trysting place fully armed, with a culture springing from the very heart of the African continent. Now, this Society will very quickly show its inability to shoulder these different tasks, and will limit itself to exhibition-ist demonstrations, while the habitual behavior of the members of the Society will be confined to showing Europeans that such a thing as African culture exists, and opposing their ideas to those of ostentatious and narcissistic Europeans. We have shown that such an attitude is normal and draws its legitimacy from the lies propagated by men of Western culture, but the degradation of the aims of this Society will become more marked with the elaboration of the concept of negritude. The African Society will become the cultural society of the black world and will come to include the Negro dispersion, that is to say the tens of thousands of black people spread over the American continents.

The Negroes who live in the United States and in Central or Latin America in fact experience the need to attach themselves to a cultural matrix. Their problem is not funda-mentally different from that of the Africans. The whites of America did not mete out to them any different treatment from that of the whites who ruled over the Africans. We have seen that the whites were used to putting all Negroes in the same bag. During the first congress of the African Cultural Society which was held in Paris in 1956, the Ameri-can Negroes of their own accord considered their problems from the same standpoint as those of their African brothers. Cultured Africans, speaking of African civilizations, de-creed that there should be a reasonable status within the state for those who had formerly been slaves. But little by little the American Negroes realized that the essential problems confronting them were not the same as those that confronted the African Negroes. The Negroes of Chicago only resemble the Nigerians or the Tanganyikans in so far as they were all defined in relation to the whites. But once the first comparisons had been made and subjective feelings were assuaged, the American Negroes realized that the objective problems were fundamentally heterogeneous. The test cases of civil liberty whereby both whites and blacks in America try to drive back racial discrimination have very little in common in their principles and objectives with the heroic fight of the Angolan people against the detestable Portuguese colonialism. Thus, during the second congress of the African Cultural Society the American Negroes decided to create an American society for people of black cultures.

Negritude therefore finds its first limitation in the phenomena which take account of the formation of the historical character of men. Negro and African-Negro culture broke up into different entities because the men who wished to incarnate these cultures realized that every culture is first and foremost national, and that the problems which kept Richard Wright or Langston Hughes on the alert were fundamentally different from those which might confront Leopold Senghor or Jomo Kenyatta. In the same way certain Arab states, though they had chanted the marvelous hymn of Arab renaissance, had nevertheless to realize that their geographical position and the economic ties of their region were stronger even than the past that they wished to revive. Thus we find today the Arab states organically linked once more with societies which are Mediterranean in their culture. The fact is that these states are submitted to modern pressure and to new channels of trade while the network of trade relations which was dominant during the great period of Arab history has disappeared. But above all there is the fact that the political regimes of certain Arab states are so different, and so far away from each other in their conceptions, that even a cultural meeting between these states is meaningless.

Thus we see that the cultural problem as it sometimes exists in colonized countries runs the risk of giving rise to serious ambiguities. The lack of culture of the Negroes, as proclaimed by colonialism, and the inherent barbarity of the Arabs ought logically to lead to the exaltation of cultural manifestations which are not simply national but continental, and extremely racial. In Africa, the movement of men of culture is a movement toward the Negro-African culture or the Arab-Moslem culture. It is not specifically toward a national culture. Culture is becoming more and more cut off from the events of today. It finds its refuge beside a hearth that glows with passionate emotion, and from there makes its way by realistic paths which are the only means by which it may be made fruitful, homogeneous, and consistent.

If the action of the native intellectual is limited historically, there remains nevertheless the fact that it contributes greatly to upholding and justifying the action of politicians. It is true that the attitude of the native intellectual sometimes takes on the aspect of a cult or of a religion. But if we really wish to analyze this attitude correctly we will come to see that it is symptomatic of the intellectual's realization of the danger that he is running in cutting his last moorings and of breaking adrift from his people. This stated belief in a national culture is in fact an ardent, despairing turning toward anything that will afford him secure anchorage. In order to ensure his salvation and to escape from the supremacy of the white man's culture the native feels the need to turn backward toward his unknown roots and to lose himself at whatever cost in his own barbarous people. Because he feels he is becoming estranged, that is to say because he feels that he is the living haunt of contradictions which run the risk of becoming insurmountable, the native tears himself away from the swamp that may suck him down and accepts everything, decides to take all for granted and confirms everything even though he may lose body and soul. The native finds that he is expected to answer for everything, and to all comers. He not only turns himself into the defender of his people's past; he is willing to be counted as one of them, and henceforward he is even capable of laughing at his past cowardice.

This tearing away, painful and difficult though it may be, is however necessary. If it is not accomplished there will be serious psycho-affective injuries and the result will be individuals without an anchor, without a horizon, colorless, stateless, rootless—a race of angels. It will be also quite normal to hear certain natives declare, "I speak as a Senegalese and as a Frenchman. . . . " "I speak as an Algerian and as a Frenchman. . . . " The intellectual who is Arab and French, or Nigerian and English, when he comes up against the need to take on two nationalities, chooses, if he wants to remain true to himself, the negation of one of these determinations. But most often, since they cannot or will not make a choice, such intellectuals gather together all the historical determining factors which have conditioned them and take up a fundamentally "universal standpoint."

This is because the native intellectual has thrown himself greedily upon Western culture. Like adopted children who only stop investigating the new family framework at the moment when a minimum nucleus of security crystallizes in their psyche, the native intellectual will try to make European culture his own. He will not be content to get to know

Rabelais and Diderot, Shakespeare and Edgar Allan Poe; he will bind them to his intelligence as closely as possible:

> La dame n'était pas seule
> Elle avait un mari
> Un mari très comme il faut
> Qui citait Racine et Corneille
> Et Voltaire et Rousseau
> Et le Père Hugo et le jeune Musset
> Et Gide et Valéry
> Et tant d'autres encore.

But at the moment when the nationalist parties are mobilizing the people in the name of national independence, the native intellectual sometimes spurns these acquisitions which he suddenly feels make him a stranger in his own land. It is always easier to proclaim rejection than actually to reject. The intellectual who through the medium of culture has filtered into Western civilization, who has managed to become part of the body of European culture—in other words who has exchanged his own culture for another—will come to realize that the cultural matrix, which now he wishes to assume since he is anxious to appear original, can hardly supply any figureheads which will bear comparison with those, so many in number and so great in prestige, of the occupying power's civilization. History, of course, though nevertheless written by the Westerners to serve their purposes, will be able to evaluate from time to time certain periods of the African past.

Amilcar Cabral
(1921–1973, Guinea-Bissau)

Identity and Dignity in the Context of Struggle

The people's struggle for national liberation and independence from imperialist rule has become a driving force of progress for humanity and undoubtedly constitutes one of the essential characteristics of contemporary history.

An objective analysis of imperialism insofar as it is a fact or a "natural" historical phenomenon, indeed "necessary" in the context of the type of economic political evolution of an important part of humanity, reveals that imperialist rule, with all its train of wretchedness, of pillage, of crime and of destruction of human and cultural values, was not just a negative reality. The vast accumulation of capital in half a dozen countries of the northern hemisphere which was the result of piracy, of the confiscation of the property of other peoples and of the ruthless exploitation of the work of these peoples will not only lead to the monopolization of colonies, but to the division of the world, and more imperialist rule.

In the rich countries imperialist capital, constantly seeking to enlarge itself, increased the creative capacity of man and brought about a total transformation of the means of production thanks to the rapid progress of science, of techniques and of technology. This accentuated the pooling of labor and brought about the ascension of huge areas of population. In the colonized countries where colonization on the whole blocked the historical process of the development of the subjected peoples or else eliminated them radically or progressively, imperialist capital imposed new types of relationships on indigenous society, the structure of which became more complex and it stirred up, fomented, poisoned or resolved contradictions and social conflicts; it introduced together with money and the development of internal and external markets, new elements in the economy, it brought about the birth of new nations from human groups or from peoples who were at different stages of historical development.

It is not to defend imperialist domination to recognize that it gave new nations to the world, the dimensions of which it reduced and that it revealed new stages of development in human societies and in spite of or because of the prejudices, the discrimination and the crimes which it occasioned, it contributed to a deeper knowledge of humanity as a moving whole, as a unity in the complex diversity of the characteristics of its development.

Imperialist rule on many continents favored a multilateral and progressive (sometimes abrupt) confirmation not only between different men but also between different societies. The practice of imperialist rule—its affirmation or its negation—demanded (and still demands) a more or less accurate knowledge of the society it rules and of the historical reality (both economic, social, and cultural) in the middle of which it exists. This knowledge is necessarily exposed in terms of comparison with the dominating subject and with its own historical reality. Such a knowledge is a vital necessity in the practice of imperialist rule which results in the confrontation, mostly violent, between two identities which are totally dissimilar in their historical elements and contradictory in their different functions. The search for such a knowledge contributed to a general enrichment of human and social knowledge in spite of the fact that it was one-sided, subjective, and very often unjust.

In fact, man has never shown as much interest in knowing other men and other societies as during this century of imperialist domination. An unprecedented mass of information of hypotheses and theories has been built up, notably in the fields of history, ethnology, ethnography, sociology, and culture concerning people or groups brought under imperialist domination. The concepts of race, caste, ethnicity, tribe, nation, culture, identity, dignity, and many others, have become the object of increasing attention from those who study men and the societies described as "primitive" or "evolving."

More recently, with the rise of liberation movements, the need has arisen to analyze the character of these societies in the light of the struggle they are waging, and to decide the factors which launch or hold back this struggle. The researchers are generally agreed that in this context culture shows special significance. So one can argue that any attempt to clarify the true role of culture in the development of the (pre-independence) liberation movement can make a useful contribution to the broad struggle of the people against imperialist domination.

In this short lecture, we consider particularly the problems of the "return to the source," and of identity and dignity in the context of the national liberation movement.

The fact that independence movements are generally marked, even in their early stages, by an upsurge of cultural activity, has led to the view that such movements are preceded by a "cultural renaissance" of the subject people. Some go as far as to suggest that culture is one means of collecting together a group, even a *weapon* in the struggle for independence.

From the experience of our own struggle and one might say that of the whole of Africa, we consider that there is too limited, even a mistaken idea of the vital role of culture in the development of the liberation movement. In our view, this arises from a fake generalization of a phenomenon which is real but limited which is at a particular level in the vertical structure of colonized societies—at the level of the *elite* or the colonial *diasporas*. This generalization is unaware of or ignores the vital element of the problem: the indestructible character of the cultural resistance of the masses of the people when confronted with foreign domination.

Certainly imperialist domination calls for cultural oppression and attempts either directly or indirectly to do away with the most important elements of the culture of the subject people. But the people are only able to create and develop the liberation movement because they keep their culture alive despite continual and organized repression of their cultural life and because they continue to resist culturally even when their politico-military resistance is destroyed. And it is cultural resistance which, at a given moment, can take on new forms, i.e., political, economic, armed to fight foreign domination.

With certain exceptions, *the period of colonization* was not long enough, at least in Africa, for there to be a significant degree of destruction or damage of the most important facets of the culture and traditions of the subject people. Colonial experience of imperialist domination in Africa (genocide, racial segregation and apartheid excepted) shows that the only so-called positive solution which the colonial power put forward to repudiate the subject people's cultural resistance was *"assimilation."* But the complete failure of the policy of "progressive assimilation" of native populations is the living proof both of the falsehood of this theory and of the capacity of the subject people to resist. As far as the Portuguese colonies are concerned, the maximum number of people assimilated was 0.3% of the total population (in Guinea) and this was after 500 years of civilizing influence and half a century of "colonial peace."

On the other hand, even in the settlements where the overwhelming majority of the population are indigenous peoples, the area occupied by the colonial power and especially the area of *cultural influence* is usually restricted to coastal strips and to a few limited parts in the interior. Outside the boundaries of the capital and other urban centers, the influence of the colonial power's culture is almost nil. It only leaves its mark at the very top of the colonial social pyramid—which created colonialism itself—and particularly it influences what one might call the "indigenous lower middle class" and a very small number of workers in urban areas.

It can thus be seen that the masses in the rural areas, like a large section of the urban population, say, in all, over 99% of the indigenous population are untouched or almost untouched by the culture of the colonial power. This situation is partly the result of the necessarily obscurantist character of the imperialist domination which while it despises and suppresses indigenous culture takes no interest in promoting culture for the masses who are their pool for forced labor and the main object of exploitation. It is also the result of the effectiveness of cultural resistance of the people, who when they are subjected to political domination and economic exploitation find that their own culture acts as a bulwark in preserving their *identity*. Where the indigenous society has a vertical structure, this defense of their cultural heritage is further strengthened by the colonial power's interest in protecting and backing the cultural influence of the ruling classes, their allies.

The above argument implies that generally speaking there is not any marked destruction or damage to culture or tradition, neither for the masses in the subject country nor for the indigenous ruling classes (traditional chief, noble families, religious authorities). Repressed, persecuted, humiliated, betrayed by certain social groups who have compromised with the foreign power, culture took refuge in the villages, in the forests, and in the spirit of the victims of domination. Culture survives all these challenges and through the struggle for liberation blossoms forth again. Thus the question of a "return to the source" or of a "cultural renaissance" does not arise and could not arise for the masses of these people, for it is they who are the repository of the culture and at the same time the only social sector who can preserve and build it up and *make history*.

Thus, in Africa at least, for a true idea of the real role which culture plays in the development of the liberation movement a distinction must be made between the situation of the masses, who preserve their culture, and that of the social groups who are assimilated or partially so, who are cut off and culturally alienated. Even though the indigenous colonial elite who emerged during the process of colonization still continue to pass on some element of indigenous culture yet they live both materially and spiritually according to the foreign colonial culture. They seek to identify themselves increasingly with this culture both in their social behaviors and even in their appreciation of its values.

In the course of two or three generations of colonization, a social class arises made up of civil servants, people who are employed in various branches of the economy, especially commerce, professional people, and a few urban and agricultural landowners. This indigenous petite bourgeoisie which emerged out of foreign domination and is indispensable to the system of colonial exploitation, stands midway between the masses of the working class in town and country and the small number of local representatives of the foreign ruling class. Although they may have quite strong links with the masses and with the traditional chiefs, generally speaking, they aspire to a way of life which is similar if not identical with that of the foreign minority. At the same time while they restrict their dealings with the masses, they try to become integrated into this minority often at the cost of family or ethnic ties and always at great personal cost. Yet despite the apparent exceptions, they do not succeed in getting past the barriers thrown up by the system. They are prisoners of the cultural and social contradictions of their lives. They cannot escape from their role as a marginal class, or a "marginalized" class.

The marginal character or the "marginality" of this class both in their own country and in the *diasporas established in the territory* of the colonial power is responsible for the socio-cultural conflicts of the colonial elite or the indigenous petite bourgeoisie, played out very much according to their material circumstances and level of acculturation but always at the individual level, never collectively.

It is within the framework of this daily drama, against the backcloth of the usually violent confrontation between the mass of the people and the ruling colonial class that a feeling of bitterness or a *frustration complex* is bred and develops among the indigenous petite bourgeoisie. At the same time, they are becoming more and more conscious of a compelling need to question their marginal status, and to re-discover an identity.

Thus, they turn to the people around them, the people at the other extreme of the socio-cultural conflict—the native masses. For this reason arises the problem of "return to the source" which seems to be even more pressing the greater is the isolation of the petite bourgeoisie (or native elites) and their acute feelings of frustration as in the case of African diasporas living in the colonial or racist metropolis. It comes as no surprise that the theories or "movements" such as *Pan-Africanism* or *Negritude* (two pertinent expressions arising mainly from the assumption that all black Africans have a cultural identity) were propounded outside black Africa. More recently, the black Americans' claim to an African identity is another proof, possibly rather a desperate one, of the need for a "return to the source" although clearly it is influenced by a new situation: the fact that the great majority of African people are now independent.

But the "return to the source" is not and cannot in itself be an *act of struggle* against foreign domination (colonialist and racist) and it no longer necessarily means a return to traditions. It is the denial, by the petite bourgeoisie, of the pretended supremacy of the culture of the dominant power over that of the dominated people with which it must identify itself. The "return to the source" is therefore not a voluntary step, but the only possible reply to the demand of concrete need, historically determined, and enforced by the inescapable contradiction between the colonized society and the colonial power, the mass of the people exploited and the foreign exploitive class, a contradiction in the light of which each social stratum or indigenous class must define its position.

When the "return to the source" goes beyond the individual and is expressed through "groups" or "movements," the contradiction is transformed into struggle (secret or overt), and is a prelude to the pre-independence movement or of the struggle for liberation from the foreign yoke. So, the "return to the source" is of no historical importance unless it brings not only real involvement in the struggle for independence, but also complete and absolute identification with the hopes of the mass of the people, who contest not only the foreign culture but also the foreign domination as a whole. Otherwise, the "return to the source" is nothing more than an attempt to find short-term benefits—knowingly or unknowingly a kind of political opportunism.

Culture and Identity

One must point out that the "return to the source," apparent or real, does not develop at one time and in the same way in the heart of the indigenous petite bourgeoisie. It is a slow process, broken up and uneven, whose development depends on the degree of acculturation of each individual, of the material circumstances of his life, on the forming of his ideas and on his experience as a social being. This unevenness is the basis of the split of the indigenous petite bourgeoisie into three groups when confronted with the liberation movement: a) a minority, which, even if it wants to see an end to foreign domination, clings to the dominant colonialist class and openly oppose the movement to protect its social position; b) a majority of people who are hesitant and indecisive; c) another minority of people who share in the building and leadership of the liberation movement.

But the latter group, which plays a decisive role in the development of the pre-independence movement, does not truly identify with the mass of the people (with their culture and hopes) except through struggle, the scale of this identification depending on the kind or methods of struggle, on the ideological basis of the movement and on the level of moral and political awareness of each individual.

Wole Soyinka
(b. 1934, Nigeria)

African Classical Concepts of Tragedy

The persistent search for the meaning of tragedy, for a redefinition in terms of cultural or private experience is, at the least, man's recognition of certain areas of depth-experience which are not satisfactorily explained by general aesthetic theories; and, of all the subjective unease that is aroused by man's creative insights, that wrench within the human psyche which we vaguely define as "tragedy" is the most insistent voice that bids us return to our own sources. There, illusively, hovers the key to the human paradox, to man's experience of being and non-being, his dubiousness as essence and matter, intimations of transience and eternity, and the harrowing drives between uniqueness and Oneness.

Our course to the heart of the Yoruba Mysteries leads by its own ironic truths through the light of Nietzsche and the Phrygian deity; but there are the inevitable, key departures. "Blessed Greeks!" sings our mad votary in his recessional rapture, "how great must be your Dionysus, if the Delic god thinks such enchantments necessary to cure you of your Dithyrambic madness." Such is Apollo's resemblance to the serene art of Obatala the pure unsullied one, to the "essence" idiom of his rituals, that it is tempting to place him at the end of a creative axis with Ogun, in a parallel evolutionary relationship to Nietzsche's Dionysus-Apollo brotherhood. But Obatala the sculptural god is not the artist of Apollonian illusion but of inner essence. The idealist bronze and terra-cotta of Ife which may tempt the comparison implicit in "Apollonian" died at some now forgotten period, evidence only of the universal surface culture of courts and never again resurrected. It is alien to the Obatala spirit of Yoruba "essential" art. Obatala finds expression, not in Nietzsche's Apollonian "mirror of enchantment" but as a statement of world resolution. The mutual tempering of illusion and will, necessary to an understanding of the Hellenic spirit, may mislead us, when we are faced with Yoruba art, for much of it has a similarity in its aesthetic serenity to the plastic arts of the Hellenic. Yoruba traditional art is not ideational however, but "essential." It is not the idea (in religious arts) that is transmitted into wood or interpreted in music or movement, but a quintessence of inner being, a symbolic interaction of the many aspects of revelations (within a universal context) with their moral apprehension.

Ogun, for his part, is best understood in Hellenic values as a totality of the Dionysian, Apollonian and Promethean virtues. Nor is that all. Transcending, even today, the distorted myths of his terrorist reputation, traditional poetry records him as "protector of orphans," "roof over the homeless," "terrible guardian of the sacred oath"; Ogun stands for a transcendental, humane but rigidly restorative justice. (Unlike Sango, who is primarily retributive.) The first artist and technician of the forge, he evokes like Nietzsche's Apollonian spirit, a "massive impact of image, concept, ethical doctrine and sympathy." Obatala is the placid essence of creation; Ogun the creative urge and instinct, the essence of creativity.

> Rich-laden is his home, yet decked in palm fronds
> He ventures forth, refuge of the down-trodden,
> To rescue slaves he unleashed the judgment of war
> Because of the blind, plunged into forests
> Of curative herbs, Bountiful One
> Who stands bulwark to offsprings of the dead of heaven
> Salutations, O lone being, who swims in rivers of blood.

Such virtues place Ogun apart from the distorted dances to which Nietzsche's Dionysiac frenzy led him in his search for a selective "Aryan" soul, yet do not detract from Ogun's revolutionary grandeur. Ironically, it is the depth-illumination of Nietzsche's intuition into basic universal impulses which negates his race exclusivist conclusions on the nature of art and tragedy. In our journey to the heart of Yoruba tragic art which indeed belongs in the Mysteries of Ogun and the choric ecstasy of revellers, we do not find that the Yoruba, as the Greek did, "built for his chorus the scaffolding of a fictive chthonic realm and placed thereon fictive nature spirits . . ." on which foundation, claims Nietzsche, Greek tragedy developed: in short, the principle of illusion.

Yoruba tragedy plunges straight into the "chthonic realm," the seething cauldron of the dark world will and psyche, the transitional yet inchoate matrix of death and becoming. Into this universal womb once plunged and emerged Ogun, the first actor, disintegrating within the abyss. His spiritual re-assemblage does not require a "copying of actuality" in the ritual re-enactment of his devotees, any more than Obatala does in plastic representation, in the art of Obatala. The actors in Ogun Mysteries are the communicant chorus, containing within their collective being the essence of that transitional abyss. But only as essence, held, contained and mystically expressed. Within the mystic summons of the chasm the protagonist actor (and every god-suffused choric individual) resists, like Ogun before him, the final step towards complete annihilation. From this alone steps forward the eternal actor of the tragic rites, first as the unresisting mouthpiece of the god, uttering visions symbolic of the transitional gulf, interpreting the dread power within whose essence he is immersed as agent of the choric will. Only later, in the evenness of release from the tragic climax, does the serene self-awareness of Obatala reassert its creative control. He, the actor, emerges still as the mediant voice of the god, but stands now as it were beside himself, observant, understanding, creating. At this stage is known to him the sublime *aesthetic* joy, not within Nietzsche's heart of original oneness but in the distanced celebration of the cosmic struggle. This resolved aesthetic serenity is the link between Ogun's tragic art and Obatala's plastic beauty. The unblemished god, Obatala, is the serene womb of chthonic reflections (or memory), a passive strength awaiting and celebrating each act of vicarious restoration of his primordial being. . . . His beauty is enigmatic, expressive only of the resolution of plastic healing through the wisdom of acceptance. Obatala's patient suffering is the well-known aesthetics of the saint.

For the Yoruba, the gods are the final measure of eternity, as humans are of earthly transience. To think, because of this, that the Yoruba mind reaches intuitively towards absorption in godlike essence is to misunderstand the principle of religious rites, and to misread, as many have done, the significance of religious possession. Past, present and future being so pertinently conceived and woven into the Yoruba world view, the element of eternity which is the gods' prerogative does not have the same quality of remoteness or exclusiveness which it has in Christian or Buddhist culture. The belief of the Yoruba in the contemporaneous existence within his daily experience of these aspects of time has long been recognised but again misinterpreted. It is no abstraction. The Yoruba is not, like European man, concerned with the purely conceptual aspects of time; they are too concretely realised in his own life, religion, sensitivity, to be mere tags for explaining the metaphysical order of his world. If we may put the same thing in fleshed-out cognitions, life, present life, contains within it manifestations of the ancestral, the living and the un-born. All are vitally within the intimations and affectiveness of life, beyond mere abstract conceptualisation.

And yet the Yoruba does not for that reason fail to distinguish between himself and the deities, between himself and the ancestors, between the unborn and his reality, or discard his awareness of the essential gulf that lies between one area of existence and another. This gulf is what must be constantly diminished by the sacrifices, the rituals, the ceremon-ies of appeasement to those cosmic powers which lie guardian to the gulf. Spiritually, the primordial disquiet of the Yoruba psyche may be expressed as the existence in collective memory of a primal severance in transitional ether, whose first effective defiance is symbol-ised in the myth of the gods' descent to earth and the battle with immense chaotic growth which had sealed off reunion with man. For they were coming down, not simply to be acknowledged but to be re-united with human essence, to reassume that portion of re-creative transient awareness which the first deity Orisa-nla possessed and expressed through his continuous activation of man images—brief reflections of divine facets—just as man is grieved by a consciousness of the loss of the eternal essence of his being and must indulge in symbolic transactions to recover his totality of being.

Tragedy, in Yoruba traditional drama, is the anguish of this severance, the fragmenta-tion of essence from self. Its music is the stricken cry of man's blind soul as he flounders in the void and crashes through a deep abyss of a-spirituality and cosmic rejection. Tragic music is an echo from that void; the celebrant speaks, sings and dances in authentic arche-typal images from within the abyss. All understand and respond, for it is the language of the world.

It is necessary to emphasise that the gods were coming down to be reunited with man, for this tragedy could not be, the anguish of severance would not attain such tragic pro-portions, if the gods' position on earth (i.e., in man's conception) was to be one of divine remoteness. This is again testified to by the form of worship, which is marked by camarade-rie and irreverence just as departure to ancestorhood is marked by bawdiness in the midst of grief. The anthropomorphic origin of uncountable deities is one more leveller of divine class-consciousness but, finally, it is the innate humanity of the gods themselves, their bond with man through a common animist relation with nature and phenomena. Conti-nuity for the Yoruba operates both through the cyclic concept of time and the animist interfusion of all matter and consciousness.

Culture and Identity

Peter Sarpong
(b. 1933, Ghana)

The Akan Blackened Stool and the *Odwira* Festival

The *Odwira* festival differs from the *Adae* in many respects. Unlike *Adae*, it is a national festival celebrated only in such towns as Kumasi, Wenchi, Akwamufie, Kibi and Akropong-Akwapim. It is performed once a year. It is not entirely devoted to the ancestors as the *Adae* is. Nor does its celebration end in one day. It lasts over a period of more than one week. We are here interested only in the part of the celebrations that concerns the ancestors and the place of the blackened stool in that part. Unfortunately, *Odwira* has not been held in Kumasi since the deportation of King Prempeh I to the Seychelles in 1896.

The *Odwira* or *Apafram* was an annual ceremony held in September in honour of the departed Akan Kings, and for purification of the whole nation and the gods from defilement.

The festival is announced on the Monday immediately following a Sunday *Adae*. Eleven days elapsed before the ceremony proper began. In the meantime, things were made ready for it. The Paramount chiefs of Ashanti went to Kumasi. On the eleventh day of the announcement—a Thursday—the King, his councillors and ministers preceded by the Golden Stool, paid ceremonial visits to houses of certain persons, poured libation and made sacrifices.

They first went to the house of the head of the stool-carriers of the Golden Stool; next, to the house of the chief of Dominase, where a sheep was killed, and its blood smeared over the stools of the ancestors. From here, they proceeded to the mausoleum at Bantama and poured libation before the skeletons of the dead kings. They went to many houses until they arrived at that of the queen-mother. Here too a sheep was offered to the queen-mother's ancestral stools. They went through similar rites of making offerings to the blackened stools of such people as Boakye Yaw Kuma (father of King Kwaku Dua I), Afiriyie (father of King-Osei Kwadwo), Tutu (head of the executioners and guardian of the blackened stool of Nyaako Kusi Amoa, sister of King Osei-Tutu), and finally Owusu Ansa (the father of King Bonsu Panyin). Wherever libation was being poured, the spokesman repeated the following words after the King: "Spirits of the dead, receive this wine and this sheep. Let no bad thing come (upon us), we are about to celebrate *Odwira*."

The Golden Stool was carried by a man on the nape of the neck and was sheltered from the sun by a huge umbrella. Attendants walked on either side of the stool, each supporting one of the solid gold bells attached to the stool. The purpose of this royal procession was to inform the ancestral spirits of all the famous houses of Kumasi about the business on hand, mainly through their stools.

On Saturday the heads of the territorial divisions who had not yet sworn the oath of allegiance to the King did so by swearing one of the Ashanti ancestral oaths. The following day, the skulls of the important generals and kings who had been captured or slain in wars were brought before the King. The skulls ordinarily lay before the coffins of the particular kings who commanded the army responsible for the capture. The King then placed his foot on each, saying, "Such and such of my ghost ancestors slew you."

In the afternoon of the same day, and from this time onwards many interesting rituals were performed on the *Odwira Suman*, the account of which will be omitted as it is not relevant here.

The following Friday was a *Fofie* festival. This was a day of purification for all. The King and his court, dressed in their best, and preceded by the Golden Stool and the ancestral blackened stools, the *Odwira Suman* . . . [and] the shrines of the gods, together with all other stools, chairs, drums, horns, and so on, were marched to the stream, near Akyere-made. Here the war-chair called *Hwedom* ("drive back the enemy") was set up, and upon this was placed the Golden Stool. The numerous blackened stools, the shrines of the ancestral spirits, were held in front of the bearers, each by its respective stool-carrier. The King held in his hand a branch of the plant called *Bosommuru Adwera;* this he dipped into a large brass basin that had been filled with the sacred water, and with it sprinkled the Golden Stool, repeating as he did so the following words:

> Friday Stool of Kings, I sprinkle water upon you, may your power return sharp and fierce.
> Grant that when I and another meet in battle it might be as when I met Denkyira; you let me cut off his head.
> As when I met Akyem; you let me cut off his head. As when I met Domaa; you let me cut off his head.
> As when I met Tekyiman; you let me cut off his head.
> As when I met Gyaman; you let me cut off his head.
> The edges of the year have mte [*sic?*],
> I pray for life.
> May the nation prosper.
> May the women bear children.
> May the hunters kill meat.
> We who dig for gold, let us get gold to dig, and grant that I get some for the upkeep of my kingship.

Then the *Odwira Suman*, the ancestral blackened stools, and the assembled people were likewise sprinkled, and similar prayers offered up, asking for prosperity for the nation, freedom from sickness, plentiful crops, and fertility.

Then everybody went home. Sheep were sacrificed to the ancestors on their stools and yams and wine offered to them with the following words:

> The edges of the year have met; I take sheep and new yams and give you that you may eat.
> Life to me.
> Life to my Ashanti people.

Culture and Identity

Women who cultivate the farms, when they do so, grant that food comes forth in abundance. Do not allow illness to come.

A week later the chief of Bantama gave new yams once more to the ancestral ghosts. Only after this might the King, his chiefs, and the nation eat of the new crop.

Abu Shardow Abarry
(b. 1947, Ghana)

The Ga Homowo (Hunger-Hooting) Cultural Festival

Homowo is the main festival of the Ga people. It is celebrated annually as a kind of first fruit festival during which the people commemorate the famine which their progenitors and first settlers suffered in the dim past.

During its celebration, many Gamei who have gone, by reason of work or some social activity, to stay in the outlying villages and elsewhere, come to meet their other kinsmen in the ancestral home in the main Ga towns. They come to express their unflinching loyalty to their gods, ancestral spirits and all kinsmen. They propitiate the gods and the ancestors from whom blessings and prosperity for the new year are solicited. "Kpekple" (steamed corn dough) is then sprinkled on to the earth for the gods and ancestral spirits to eat, after which there is a big feast in which many Gamei take part. Non-Gamei too may be invited by friends or neighbors to participate. In their merriment the Gamei symbolically jeer or "hoot" at the famine that confronted their ancestors.

About a week later, the peace of the dawn is shattered by spontaneous wailing and general expression of grief and sorrow. This is the phase at which all dead relations, especially the most recently dead, are remembered and mourned. They are congratulated or rebuked, according to the fortune of the house in the outgoing year; and their continued protection and blessings are solicited for the ensuring year. Then, meetings are organized here and there with the view to reuniting friends and kinsmen who, for one reason or the other, have fallen out in the outgoing year. When this has been done and everybody is at peace with himself and his relations and neighbors, then come exchanges among the people of New Year greetings and gratitude for all the prosperity of the previous year.

In all these activities, music, dance and drama, all containing gems of oral literature, are the main vehicles of communication. The arrival of the gods is hailed by music and dancing which also mark their triumphant return to their abode. Songs are sung to invoke and exalt the gods who are thereby persuaded to descend upon their mediums through whom their will and injunctions are expressed. Perhaps it is this significance of music and dancing in African worship that has led Nketia* to the conclusion that African gods "are music-loving gods." The secular songs, too, have their values: they often have congratulatory, exhortatory, punitive or reformative import. They are, therefore, useful instruments of social control by which the cherished values and ideals of Ga society are perpetuated.

*Kwabena Nketia, ex-director of The Institute of African Studies, University of Ghana, Legon.—Eds.

Culture and Identity

J. Africanus B. Horton
(1835–1883, Sierre Leone)

Africa as the Nursery of Science and Literature

Africa, in ages past, was the nursery of science and literature; from thence they were taught in Greece and Rome, so that it was said that the ancient Greeks represented their favourite goddess of Wisdom—Minerva—as an African princess. Pilgrimages were made to Africa in search of knowledge by such eminent men as Solon, Plato, Pythagoras; and several came to listen to the instruction of the African Euclid, who was at the head of the most celebrated mathematical school in the world, and who flourished 300 years before the birth of Christ. The conqueror of the great African Hannibal made his associate and confidant the African poet Terence. "Being emancipated by his master, he took him to Rome and gave him a good education; the young African soon acquired reputation for the talent he displayed in his comedies. His dramatic works were much admired by the Romans for their prudential maxims and moral sentences, and, compared with his contemporaries, he was much in advance of them in point of style."

Origen, Tertullian, Augustine, Clemens Alexandrinus, and Cyril, who were fathers and writers of the Primitive Church, were tawny African bishops of Apostolic renown. Many eminent writers and historians agree that these ancient Ethiopians were Negroes, but many deny that this was the case. The accounts given by Herodotus, who travelled in Egypt, and other writers, settle the question that such they were. Herodotus describes them as "woolly-haired blacks, with projecting lips." In describing the people of Colchis, he says that they were Egyptian colonists, who were "Black in complexion and wool-haired." This description undoubtedly refers to a race of Negroes, as neither the Copts, their descendants, nor the mummies which have been preserved, would lead us to believe that their complexion was black. Even the large sphinx, which was excavated by M. Caviglia in Egypt, and which is regarded by all scientific men as a stupendous piece of sculpture, has its face "of the Negro cast," and is said to be of a mild and even of a sublime expression. "If it be not admitted that their nations were black, they were undoubtedly of very dark complexion, having much of the Negro physiognomy, as depicted in Egyptian sculpture and painting, and from them the Negro population, indeed the whole race of Africa, have sprung. Say not, then, I repeat it, that Africa is without her heraldry of science and fame. Its inhabitants are the offshoots—wild and untrained, it is true, but still the offshoots of a stem which was once proudly luxuriant in the fruits of learning and taste; whilst that from which the Goths, their calumniators, have sprung, remained hard, and knotted, and barren." And why should not the same race who governed Egypt, attacked the most famous and flourishing city—Rome, who had her churches, her universities and her repositories of learning and science, once more stand on their legs and endeavour to raise their characters in the scale of the civilized world?

Molefi Kete Asante
(b. 1942, United States)

The Principal Issues in Afrocentric Inquiry

The Afrocentric enterprise is framed by cosmological, epistemological, axiological, and aesthetic issues. In this regard the Afrocentric method pursues a world voice distinctly African-centered in relationship to external phenomena. How do we gather meaning out of African or other existence?

Although I recognize the transitional nature of all cultural manifestations of a social, economic, or political dimension, I also know that in the United States and other parts of the African world, culturally speaking, there is movement toward new, more cosmocultural forms of understanding. Nevertheless, meaning in the contemporary context must be derived from the most centered aspects of the African's being. When this is not the case, psychological dislocation creates automatons who are unable to fully capture the historical moment because they are living on someone else's terms. We are either existing on our own terms or the terms of others. Where will the African person find emotional and cultural satisfaction, if not in her own terms? By "terms" I mean position, place or space.

Cosmological Issue

The place of African culture in the myths, legends, literatures, and oratures of African people constitutes, at the mythological level, the cosmological issue within the Afrocentric enterprise. What role does the African culture play in the African's interface with the cosmos? Are dramas of life and death in this tradition reflected in metaphysical ways? How are they translated by lunar, solar or stellar metaphors? The fundamental assumptions of Africalogical inquiry are based on the African orientation to the cosmos. By "African" I mean clearly a "composite African" not a specific discrete African orientation which would rather mean ethnic identification, i.e., Yoruba, Zulu, Nuba, etc.

There are several concerns which might be considered cosmological in the sense that they are fundamental to any research initiative in this field.

Racial Formation. Race as a social factor remains prevalent in heterogeneous but hegemonically Eurocentric societies. In the United States, the most developed example of such a society, the question of race is the most dominant aspect of intersocial relations.

Culture. A useful way to view the cultural question Afrocentrically lies in the understanding of culture as shared perceptions, attitudes, and predisposition that allow people to organize experiences in certain ways. A student of African American culture, for example, must be prepared to deal with the complex issue of "bleeding cultures," that is, the fact that African Americans constitute the most heterogeneous group in the United States biologically but perhaps one of the most homogeneous socially. Overlaps in social and cultural definitions, explanations, and solutions have to be carefully sorted out for the Africalogist to be able to determine how issues, areas, and people are joined, or differentiated in given settings. For example, something might be the result of social behaviors rather than cultural behaviors. Furthermore, the cultural behaviors may result from African American patterns from the South or from Jamaica.

Gender. Africalogy recognizes gender as a substantial research issue in questions dealing with social, political, economic, cultural, or aesthetic problems. Since the liberation of women is not an act of charity but a fundamental part of the Afrocentric project, the researcher must be cognizant of sexist language, terminology, and perspectives. It is impossible for a scholar to deal effectively with either the cultural/aesthetic or the social/ behavioral concentrations without attention to the historic impact and achievement of women within the African community. Both female and male scholars must properly examine the roles that women have played in liberating Africans and others from oppression, resisting the imposition of sexist repression and subjugation, and exercising economic and political authority.

Class. Class distinctions for the Afrocentrist consist in four aspects of property relations: (1) those who possess income-producing properties, (2) those who possess some property that produces income and a job that supplements income, (3) those who maintain professions or positions because of skills, and (4) those who do not have skills and whose services may or may not be employed.

Epistemological Issue

What constitutes the quest for truth in the Afrocentric enterprise? In Africalogy, language, myth, ancestral memory, dance-music-art, and science provide the sources of knowledge, the canons of proof and the structures of truth.

Language. Language exists when a community of people use a set of agreed-upon symbols to express concepts, ideas, and psychological needs. The Afrocentric scholar finds the source of a people's truth close to the language. In the United States Ebonics serves as the archetype of African-American language.

Myth. There is an idea of preconcept, prebelief based upon the particularity of the African experience in the world. I postulate that myth, especially the central myth of the next millennium in heterogeneous but hegemonically Eurocentric societies, will be the resolution of ethnic conflict. All behavior will be rooted in experiential patterns played out in the intervention of ideas and feelings in the imposing movement of the European worldview. As Robert Armstrong* has said of the mythoform it "is strong, viable, subtle, inescapable, pervasive—operating behind each possibility of man's relationship with the world, refracting through each sense and each faculty into terms appropriate to them."

Dance-Music-Art. Performing and representational art forms are central to any Afrocentric interpretation of cultural or social reality. Indeed, the fact that dance is a way of life

*Robert Armstrong is the ex-director of The Institute of African Studies, University of Ibadan, Nigeria.— EDS.

in traditional African life and not a leisure activity to be done when one is finished with "real work" as in the West informs any Afrocentric analysis. In the diaspora the ubiquity of the dance finds its expression in the Africanization of the Walkman and radio. Dance and music must be interwoven with life.

Axiological Issue

The question of value is at the core of the Afrocentric quest for truth because the ethical issues have always been connected to the advancement of African knowledge which is essentially functional.

Good. What constitutes good is a matter of the historical conditions and cultural developments of a particular society. A common expression among African Americans relates the good to the beautiful, "beauty is as beauty does" or "she's beautiful because she's good." The first statement places the emphasis on what a person does, that is, how a person "walks" among others in the society. The second statement identifies the beautiful by action. If a person's actions are not good, it does not matter how the person looks physically. Doing good is equivalent to being beautiful.

Right Conduct, therefore, represents a category of the axiological issue in Afrocentric analysis. The Afrocentric method isolates conduct rather than physical attributes of a person in literary or social analysis.

Aesthetic Issue

According to Welsh-Asante*, the African aesthetic is comprised of seven aspects which she calls "senses." These senses are: (1) polyrhythm, (2) polycentrism, (3) dimensional, (4) repetition, (5) curvilinear, (6) epic memory, (7) wholism.

These aesthetic "senses" are said to exist as the leading elements of the African's response to art, plastic or performing. Polyrhythm refers to the simultaneous occurrence of several major rhythms. Polycentrism suggests the presence of several colors in a painting or several movements on a dancer's body occurring in the context of a presentation of art. Dimensional is spatial relationships and shows depth and energy, the awareness of vital force. Repetition is the recurring theme in a presentation of art. The recurrence is not necessarily an exact one but the theme or concept is presented as central to the work of art. Curvilinear means that the lines are curved in the art, dance, music, or poetry—this is normally called indirection in the spoken or written art forms. Epic memory carries with it the idea that the art contains the historic memory that allows the artist and audience to participate in the same celebration or pathos. Wholism is the unity of the collective parts of the art work despite the various unique aspects of the art.

THE SHAPE OF THE DISCIPLINE

Centrism, the groundedness of observation and behavior in one's own historical experiences, shapes the concepts, paradigms, theories, and methods of Africalogy. In this way

*K. Welsh-Asante, *African Culture: Rhythms of Unity* (Westport, Conn.: Greenwood Press, 1985).—EDS.

Africalogy secures its place alongside other centric pluralisms without heirarchy and without seeking hegemony. As a discipline, Africalogy is sustained by a commitment to centering the study of African phenomena and events in the particular cultural voice of the composite African people. Furthermore, it opens the door for interpretations of reality based in evidence and data secured by reference to the African world voice.

The anteriority of the classical African civilizations must be entertained in any Africalogical inquiry. Classical references are necessary as baseline frames for discussing the development of African cultural phenomena. Without such referent points most research would appear disconnected, without historical continuity, discrete and isolated, incidental and nonorganic.

I have consistently argued that the African American Studies or African Studies scholar whom I shall call an "Africalogist" must begin analysis from the primacy of the classical African civilizations, namely Kemet (Egypt), Nubia, Axum, and Meroe. This simply means that adequate understanding of African phenomena cannot occur without a reference point in the classic and most documented African culture. This is not to say that everything one writes must be shown to be tied to Egypt but it means that one cannot write fully without a self-conscious attempt to place the historical enterprise in an organic relationship to African history.

Africalogy is defined, therefore, as the Afrocentric study of phenomena, events, ideas, and personalities related to Africa. The mere study of phenomena of Africa is not Africalogy but some other intellectual enterprise. The scholar who generates research questions based on the centrality of Africa is engaged in a very different research inquiry than the one who imposes Western criteria on the phenomena.

The uses of African origins of civilization and the Kemetic high culture as a classical starting point are the practical manifestations of the ways the scholar secures centrism when studying Africa. Africalogy uses the classical starting place as the beginning of knowledge. This is why Afrocentric is perhaps the most important word in the above definition of Africalogy. Otherwise one could easily think that any study of African phenomena or people constitutes Africalogy.

The geographical scope of the African world, and hence, the Africalogical enterprise, includes Africa, the Americas, the Caribbean, various regions of Asia and the Pacific. Wherever people declare themselves as African, despite the distance from the continent or the recentness of their out-migration, they are accepted as part of the African world. Thus, the indigenous people of Australia and New Guinea are considered African and in a larger context subjects for Africalogists who maintain a full analytical and theoretical discussion of African phenomena.

Although the major regions of the African culture are Africa, the Caribbean, and the Americas, even within those regions there are varying degrees of cultural and technological affinity to an African world voice. Africalogy is concerned with Africans in any particular region as well as all regions. Thus, Nascimento can remind us that Brazil specifically, and South America generally, have provided an enormous amount of cultural, historical, and social data about Africans. In Brazil, Zumbi, the greatest of the kings of the Republic of Palmares, Luisa Mahin, and Luiz Gama are principal figures in the making of African American history; in the Dominican Republic, Diego de Campo and Lemba provide cause for celebration; in Venezuela, Oyocta, King Miguel, and King Bayano stand astride the political and social history of the region; in Colombia, there is Benkos Bioho; and in Mexico, no fighter for freedom was ever any more courageous than Yanga.

Africalogy rejects the Africanist idea of the separation of African people as being short-sighted, analytically vapid, and philosophically unsound. One cannot study Africans in the United States or Brazil or Jamaica without some appreciation for the historical and cultural significance of Africa as source and origin. A reactionary posture which claims Africalogy as "African Slave Studies" is rejected outright because it disconnects the African in America from thousands of years of history and tradition. Thus, if one concentrates on studying Africans in the inner cities of the Northeast United States, which is reasonable, it must be done with the idea in the back of the mind that one is studying African people, not "made-in-America Negroes" without historical depth.

In addition to the problem of geographical scope is the problem of gathering data about African people from oral, written, and artifactal records. The work of scholars will be greatly enhanced by oral and video records that have become essential tools of analysis for contemporary African American studies. On the other hand, studies in ancient African present different challenges.

Much of the data used in a reconstructive Egyptian primacy must be artifactal since written records are barely 6,000 years old. Although humans seemed to have appeared more than 2 million years ago, the fact that permanent records are fairly new is a limiting factor in assessing with complete certainty what their existence was like during the early period.

The records are abundant enough in certain concrete areas, however, for the scholar to examine the origins of African civilizations as never before. Of course, Afrocentric approaches to these records, written or material, must be advanced. For example, because written documents are not found in a certain area does not mean that written documents did not exist. In fact, the materials upon which writing was done may not have survived. Neither can we say that in societies of priestly writing where a limited number of scribes had the knowledge of text that writing was unknown. It may have been generally not practiced while remaining specifically the function of a small cadre of scribes. Nor is it possible to make any assessment of the origin of writing with any certainty. Speculative answers are heuristic but not definitive. Thus in any discussion of the nature of records in Africa or among African people we must redefine the approach, perhaps to see writing as a stage in human history much like the introduction of radio or television.

Authors tend to write about what is accessible whether they are novelists or scholars. Therefore, Christian Thomsen's 1836 interpretation of societies moving from stone to bronze to iron age was applicable to Denmark, the model for its development, and not to Japan. Definitions become contextual and experiential in terms of what the scholar knows; the more appreciation one has of other societies the less provincial the definitions should be. Of course, this does not always hold true, as it should.

We now know, of course, that these contextualized definitions are often the results of ignorance. At one time the Europeans held that the earth evolved through a series of catastrophes and that human beings emerged after the last general catastrophe. Without an appreciation for depth in time of the human race, all material remains were generally looked upon as the results of people the Europeans knew like Vikings and Phoenicians. Scholars are still trying to sort out the contributions of these seafaring people. Since the seafaring Europeans of the eighteenth and nineteenth centuries spent considerable time writing about the Vikings and Phoenicians they attributed to these people a wider array of material culture than was justified. Since we now know, however, of material artifacts that extend far beyond the 6,000-year history of the earth the European biblicalists accepted as fact we are in a better position to assess the antiquity of African civilizations.

Tournal is credited with using the term *prehistorique* in 1833 as an adjective but it was not until 1851 when Daniel Wilson wrote *The Archaeology and Prehistoric Annals of Scotland* that the idea of a discipline emerged. In fact, the idea behind prehistory seems to be when written records cease to be available as you go back in time you have prehistory. Because Eurocentric writers often used race as a primary concept in discussing civilizations and cultures we are frequently called upon to "make sense" out of statements of value identified with race theory.

Any Afrocentric methodology must explain racial characteristics in a realistic manner. To begin with we must admit the strategic ambiguity of this term as it is often used. For us, race refers to the progeny of a fairly stable common gene pool which produces people with similar physical characteristics. Of course, by this definition we can quickly see that the defined gene pool may be large or small thus giving the possibility of many races. For our purposes, however, we speak of the African race meaning the gene pool defined by the whole of the African continent including people in every geographical area of the land from Egypt to South Africa, from Senegal to Kenya. The oceans constitute the biggest barriers to gene pool overflow, with the Mediterranean and Red Seas being relatively minor barriers. Although it is possible to have gene pool overflow in any direction it is most likely that the major oceans serve as fairly tight boundaries.

The Sahara is not and has never been the barrier to commerce trade or interaction among African people it has appeared to be to some writers. In fact, it is a culturally interactive arena itself and has been a greater context for such interaction in the past. Herodotus spoke of the Garamantes, whose capital now appears to have been Garama in the Libyan desert, as being a people who controlled areas of the vast desert. But long before the Garamantes, indeed at least 10,000 years earlier, Africans whose physical features were like those of the Hausa and Yoruba built canals and villages in the desert. Thus, we cannot speak correctly of Africa north of the Sahara or south of the Sahara; the Sahara is Africa and numerous people inhabit the Sahara.

The African race stems from a continental African gene pool and includes all of those whose ancestors originated there and who possess linguistic or cultural qualities and traits associated with the gene pool. Like other definitions of gene pools this one is imprecise. We know, for example, that in one biological sense all humans are Africans since we all possess the mitochondrial DNA of an African woman who lived about 200,000 years ago. In the present historical epoch, however, African has come to mean one who has physical and cultural characteristics similar to those presently found in some region of the continent.

The definition of society useful to our discussion is an interrelated set of habits created and maintained by humans interacting. As a point of reference culture is a cognitive concept about how humans interact, create, maintain, and develop institutions inasmuch as culture exists in the brain as well as in the execution.

Although Christian Thomsen had divided prehistory into stone, bronze, and iron ages we now know that this division was too arbitrary. Societies did not all go through the same stages and if they did they went through them differentially. Furthermore, the great variety of human societies require more flexible conceptual approaches for analysis. The imposition of concepts derived from European analysis alone tends to obscure the fact that all societies have been more or less successful.

Théophile Obenga
(b. 1936, Congo, Central Africa)

Genetic Linguistic Connections of Ancient Egypt and the Rest of Africa

Not one single scholar in the world has ever established direct links of an historical order between Germanic people (German, English, etc.) and ancient Greeks. Nevertheless, all the people who naturally speak Germanic languages (German, Dutch, English, etc.) consider ancient Greece as their own cultural base. This is because of the Indo-European linguistic and genetic link, which means that Germanic, Slav, Latin, Greek, Hittite, etc., derive from a common predialectal ancestor, namely the "Indo-European," which is only the result of historical linguistic reconstruction. With the help of geography, Greco-Latin antiquity became the classical antiquity of Europe, that is to say, a precious heritage, and on a solid base with Judaeo-Christianity and Western civilization, up to its most modern aspects. European cultural consciousness maintains a huge space formed precisely by antiquity, not the Mesopotamian, but the Greco-Latin, rightly considered as their own antiquity. Everything else: Chinese, Indian, African, Precolombian, and Oceanian antiquities belong to the cultural and historical heritage of humanity. The West does not identify with Chinese antiquity even if they are studied and taught in the West. And it was not an accident that the European Economic Community chose Athens as the cultural capital of Europe.

In the same manner, on the African side, one should not hesitate to draw all the consequences of the genetic and linguistic link of ancient Egyptian, Coptic, and modern African languages.

These are the main axioms of comparative historical or evolutionary linguistics:

(a) Human languages develop and change: diachronic linguistics precisely studies the successive modification of language and its evolution.

(b) The evolutionary rhythm of languages is rather slow and a language develops even if it is not written: a language has an oral tradition independently of writing. For instance, Latin appears in history in mid-third century BC, to develop and die with Roman Latin, from the fifth to the eight centuries AD. Nothing prevents us from including Latin and Lithuanian (a Baltic language) in the Indo-European comparison, even if Lithuanian is only attested to in history from the fifteenth century: Latin: *sum* (a repair), *es, est;* Lithuanian: *esmi, esi êsti,* "I am," "you are," "he/she *is.*"

(c) The object of synchronic linguistics is to study the system of a language as it works at a given moment. In reality, diachronic and synchronic linguistics interlock.

(d) The comparative method restores the main outlines of the predialectal mother tongue, the common predialectal language, by comparing and examining sounds (phonetics), the form of the words and of grammar (morphology, syntax), the lexicological facts (vocabulary), common to the words and grammar, the lexicological facts common to the different attested languages which are, in fact, different forms taken during the course of time, by a unique original language.

The comparative method shows that a language is rarely isolated in time and space, that is to say, that it is rare to come across a language which does not belong to a more or less large community, family, or group, that is not more or less ancient. This belonging of a language to a family is interpreted by profound similarities which are not fortuitous, nor acquired by borrowing words. They must be correspondences, similarities, resemblances which rest upon basic and inherited facts.

As we have seen, the method is comparative and inductive. One starts from the instruction of the similarities and differences between the attested and compared languages, to demonstrate their common origin. So, languages that are today distinctive, derive from a uniquely common language if continuity is more or less established between the compared languages.

Regarding the subject of genetic linguistic links, Emile Benveniste further clarifies the methodology: "The proof of the link consists of regular similarities, defined by correspondences, between complete forms, morphemes, and phonemes" (Emile Benveniste, *Problems de Linguistique Générale*, Paris: Gallimard, 1966, p. 101).

It is obvious that series are imperative and that random coincidences must be discarded, also borrowings and the effects of convergence. The presumption of link is acquired if the proof is convincing: "So, the correspondence between Latin *est: sunt,* German *ist: sind,* and French *est: sont,* suggests, at the same time, phonetic equations, the same morphological structure, the same alternation, the same classes of verbal forms and the same meaning" (Emile Benveniste, *Ibidem*).

The example given by Benveniste is quite Indo-European:

Hittite (2nd millennium BC):	esmi	Sanskrit:	ásmi
	essi		ási
	eszi		ásti
Greek:	emí	Latin:	sum
	ei	(Dorian essi)	es
	estí		est

All these forms originally rest upon the Indo-European + *esmi,* + *esi* + *esti,* forms which are rebuilt by comparison and induction.

Let us take another example. The Greek word *drus,* tree, originally rests upon an Indo-European theme + *dru-,* with a short u: it refers to the name of a "tree," the meaning "oak" being secondary. It is because the oak is not an Indo-European tree. Other languages bring these testimonies: Indo-Iranian *dāru,* "tree"; old Slav, *drewo,* "tree"; Gothic, *triu,* "tree"; Anglo-Saxon, *Treow,* "tree"; English, *tree.* The Greek *dendron* is a reduplication. It is difficult for a language to borrow a word such as tree from another. This word is therefore inherited.

From these attested forms:

| Sanskrit | : | páti- | "husband, master" |
| Avestic | : | paaiati- | "husband, master" |

Tokharian A:	pats	"husband"
Tokharian B:	petso	"husband"
Greek :	pósis, pósios	"husband" (that is to say, head of the household)
Latin :	potis	"powerful," "who can" (from an ancient *patìs*),
Lithuanian :	pàts	"husband"
Latvian (Baltic) :	pats	"husband"

This linguistic reasoning results in posing this predialectal, unique common form of Indo-European origin: + *potis,* "husband," "master."

An Indo-European root word: + *mer-,* "to die," has taken different historical forms in time and space: Sanskrit: *mriyáte* (*mrtá-,* "death"); Avestic: *marata-,* "death"; Latin: *morior* (*mortuus*); old Slav: *miro* (*mrutvu,* "death"): Lithuanian: *mìrstu.* The likelihood of a language borrowing the word "die" from another is obviously improbable. It is well and truly a lexeme inherited from a predialectal common ancestor.

An old root-name of Indo-European origin: + *domo,* "house" (built), "dwelling," gave, in history: Sanskrit, *dáma,* "house"; old Slav, *domu;* Russian, *dom;* Latin, *domus;* Provençal, *doma;* French, *domicile* (from the Latin word *domicilium,* abbreviation for *domus*); Italian *duomo* (hence the French *dôme:* the dôme of Milan, that is to say, the cathedral; English *king*-dom, "realm" (= the King's abode, King's domain); Greek *dómos,* "dwelling," "house."

With these few examples: + *domo-,* + *mer-,* + *potis,* + *dru,* + *esmi,* we can see how they were carried into attested historical languages. A genetic link connects all historical forms derived from the original common forms. Indeed, each element of expression of a word in a language is linked by a function to an element of expression from other languages of comparison. And the function of each element is naturally conditioned by its surrounding and by the position it occupies in the word.

In these examples, we insisted above all on lexicology and vocabulary facts. It is quite a pertinent level of comparison.

Linguistic science is not less universal than other sciences. The comparative and inductive method of general and historical linguistics is applicable to all the languages of the world, including, of course, black African languages.

It is also obvious that the pedigree of a scholar like Emile Benveniste can be summarized as follows: the method is well known. It has been tested in establishing more than one linguistic family, e.g., the Indo-European, the Common Semitic, etc.

It can well be applied to languages without history, without writing, whatever their structure. This fertile method is neither limited to any type of languages nor to any region of the world. "There are no reasons," concludes Benveniste, "to think that 'exotic' or 'primitive languages' should require other comparative criteria *different* from those required for Indo-European or Semitic languages" (Emile Benveniste, *op. cit.,* pp. 101–102).

It is therefore quite legitimate, in the field of linguistic science, to apply the comparative and inductive method of historical linguistics to black African languages, to Coptic and Pharaonic Egyptian, in order to demonstrate whether or not these languages are genetically linked. One has to lay down the criteria.

These criteria are essential and operational:

(a) Language has an oral tradition independent of writing. The Latin of the 3rd century BC and the Lithuanian of the 16th, both present, however remote in time or space, a faithful picture of Indo-European. We can therefore compare Egyptian and Coptic forms with correspondences in modern black African forms, even if we do not have all the successive stages of black African languages in the written form.

Leonard Bloomfield's (1887–1949) book, *Language,* is the basis of the American structuralist school, and in it he compared, genetically and historically, four principal languages of the Algonquin central group: Fox, Ojibway, Cree, and Menomini. He was therefore able to demonstrate with reconstructed forms of attested languages, *Primitive Central Algonquin* or proto-Algonquin, but the American linguistic scholar did not possess any previous recordings or documents for the four compared languages ("for which we have no older records": Leonard Bloomfield, *Language,* edition of 1965, pp. 359–360; first edition 1933).

(b) The criteria of comparison are guaranteed by Pharaonic Egyptian which is the oldest witness of compared languages. So the big time span between Pharaonic Egyptian and modern black African languages, instead of being a handicap, is, conversely, a strong criterion for comparison which must always make sure of some ancient facts for certain compared languages. This means that it is linguistically and historically less interesting to compare, for instance, the *Fongbe* (Abomey, Benin) and the *Yoruba* (Nigeria, West Africa), but it is more pertinent to compare, for instance, *Pharaonic Egyptian* and *Yoruba.* Indeed, the oldest Egyptian hieroglyphic texts date back to around 3000 years BC and the first written forms of Coptic as early as the 3rd century BC.

(c) Consequently, the enormous geographical discontinuity strongly favors the exclusion of borrowing in these ancient times on the whole established, morphological, phonetical, and lexicological concordances.

That is to say, that the very old separation between the Egyptian and Yoruba languages, from the common predialectal block, eliminates the effects of convergence, and random, haphazard borrowing:

1. Pharaonic Egyptian: mi "take"
   Coptic (vocalised   :   mo, ma, "take~"
        Egyptian)
   Yoruba   :   mú, "take"

2. Pharaonic Egyptian: mw, "water"
   Coptic   :   mo, mē, "water"
   Yoruba   :   o-mi, omi, "water" (Bini, Edo: a-mē, amē)

3. Pharaonic Egyptian: dj.t, "cobra"
   Coptic   :   adjō, edjō, "viper"
   Yoruba   :   ejò, edjò, "snake"

4. Pharaonic Egyptian: ir.t, "eye"
   Coptic   :   eyer, yer, "eye"
   Yoruba   :   ri, "to see"

It would be very fortunate indeed if all these Egyptian and Yoruba forms, identical on the basis of inherited lexemes, came by pure chance.

If connections and serial links are established between Pharaonic Egyptian, Coptic, and modern black African languages, one is consequently compelled to recognize a familiarity, a knock-on effect (as the expression goes for plants), even if one drifts further away from the initial type, that is to say, from the prototypes which are only rebuilt by linguistic reasoning. Thus, Tokharion B *petso,* Greek *posis, posios,* Lithuanian *pàts (patis),* take us back to the unique predialectal form of Indo-European: + *potis.*

The linguistic domain of "Hamito-Semitic" or "Afro-Asiatic" is said to include the following linguistic groups or families:

(a) Semitic languages: *Akkadian* (Assyrian, or North Akkadian, Babylonian or South Akkadian) attested in the times of Sargon of Agade around 2350 BC; *Ugaritic* (14th–13th centuries BC); *Canaanitic* in the first millennium including: *Phoenician* (and its variant *Punic*), *Hebrew, Ammonitic, Moabitic, Edomitic; Aramaic; ancient Aramaic* (around the 9th–8th centuries BC), *imperial Aramaic* (around 7th–4th centuries BC), and *recent Aramaic* including *Palestinian, Nabatean, Palmyrenian, Hatrean,* then, *Syriac, Babylonian Aramaic, Mandean,* etc.; Northern Arabic dialects: Libyanitic, Thamudeon, Safaitic, Dedanitic; and Southern Arabian dialects: Minean, Sabaean, Himyaritic, Qatabanic, Hadramutic, Ethiopic (Ge'ez, Amharic). The ancient periods of these Arabic dialects are situated around 600 BC to 600 AD.

(b) The Egyptian language: Ancient Egyptian, Middle Egyptian or Classical Egyptian, neo-Egyptian, Demotic, Coptic. With the Coptic being spoken in Upper Egypt until the 17th century, the spoken Egyptian language lasted about 5000 years, since the oldest texts in hieroglyphs date back to around 3000 BC, and the most recent to the year 394. Coptic has nine main dialectal variants: *Sahidic* (S), *Boharic* (B), *Bachoumouric* (G), *Fayumic* (F), *Achmouninic* (H), *Akhmimic* (A), etc.

(c) The Berber language: from the oasis of Siwa, there is the language of Ghadames, dialects of the central region, such as *Mzabit, Tuareg, Djebel Nefoussa;* the language of the Kabyle, dialects of the Moroccan Rif like those of the *Guelâ'la,* of the Kibdana, of the Beni Ouriaghel, of the Bot'ioua, the Beni Sa'id, and the Temsaman, etc.

It is obvious that *Semitic, Egyptian,* and *Berber* are not genetically linked. The common predialectal ancestor that some want to impose upon these groups of attested languages was *never* reconstructed: "Hamito-Semitic" or "Afro-Asiatic" is only a fantasy, not a linguistic reconstruction (such as Indo-European or Common Semitic) from facts of attested languages.

"Hamito-Semitic" or "Afro-Asiatic" is only a simple scientific hoax which unfortunately still persists, since E. Hincks (1842) and T. Benfey (1844). Marcel Cohen (1947) and J. H. Greenberg (1952) persisted with this scientific hoax. The *"Afro-Asiatic"* journal edited by Robert Hetzron (Santa Barbara, California, USA) and Russell G. Schuh (Los Angeles, California, USA) is one more hoax: the studies published by this journal are more detailed studies connected with such or such particular linguistic systems (Hebrew, Arabic, Egyptian, Amharic, etc.), *but never with comparative studies* (Hebrew-Egyptian-Akkadian-Ethiopian, etc.).

"Hamito-Semitic" or "Afro-Asiatic" reminds us of another famous scientific swindle, but this time in archaeology, the bogus discovery of the alleged remains of prehistoric man, *Piltdown Man* in 1912.

What is, in truth, the reality of Hamito-Semitic or Afro-Asiatic when we consider the following facts?

Akkadian	:	samas, shamash, "sun"
Berber	:	tafukt
Ugaritic	:	sps
Hebrew	:	semes
Ancient Egyptian	:	rᶜ, ra
Coptic	:	rē, re, rei, ri

Common Semitic: + *sms.* The Arabic language is truly Semitic: *sams,* "sun."

Can one find a common original form to all these historically attested forms of a visibly inherited lexeme? No linguistic reasoning allows us to do so. "Hamito-Semitic" or "Afro-Asiatic," which would be this common predialectal form, does not exist in the materiality of facts.

Elsewhere, this same inherited word "sun" obviously unites Indo-European languages:

Sanskrit	:	súra-, súrya
Gothic	:	sauil, and its derivative sunno
Latin	:	sōl
German	:	sonne
English	:	sun
Greek	:	hēlios, Aeolion āélios, Cretan abélios, Dorian ālios, Arcadian aélios, with or without aspirate
Welsh	:	haul
Lithuanian:		sáulē (feminine derivative)

All these historical forms allow us to put a radical with a remarkable vocalism: + sāwel-, + sūl, "sun," in reconstructed, predialectal Indo-European.

Egyptian rather belongs to black African to form an evident linguistic family.

Ancient Egyptian	:	rᶜ, ra, "sun"
Coptic	:	rē, re, rei, ri
Sidamo (Kushitic)	:	arrisō
Saho-Afa (Kushitic):		ayrō
Rendille (Kenya)	:	orr'ah, "sun"
Songhay (Niger)	:	ra
Vai (Liberia)	:	ra
Susu (Guinea)	:	ra
Gbin	:	ra
Kono	:	ra
Numu	:	re
Huela	:	re
Ligbi	:	re
Samo	:	re

We also have this inherited word: "earth, country, region":

Akkadian	:	ersetu
Ugaritic	:	'ars
Hebrew	:	'eres
Syriac	:	ar'ā
Arabic	:	'ard, 'ardh
Berber	:	akal
Ancient Egyptian	:	tȝ, ta
Coptic	:	tō, to, te-

Here again, where is the reality of "Hamito-Semitic" or "Afro-Asiatic," which is supposed to be the common form of all these attested historical forms?

As expected, Egyptian is obviously black African:

Ancient Egyptian	:	tȝ, ta, "earth, country, region"
Coptic	:	tōr, to, te-
Nuer (Sudan)	:	thau
Gmbwaga (Republic of Central Africa)	:	to
Gbanzirr (Republic of Central Africa)	:	to

Monzombo (Republic of Central Africa):   to
Degema (Nigeria)   :   ù-tò
Bantu (or proto-Bantu)   :   + sí

Let us take another inherited word, just as difficult to borrow from another language: the word "mouth": one speaks, eats, and drinks with the mouth:

Akkadian	: pu, "mouth"	Ancient Egyptian:	r3, ra
Ugaritic	: p	Coptic	: ra, rō, ro, re, la, lō, le
Hebrew	: pē	Beber	: imi
Phoenician:	p	Ghadamsi	: ami
Arabic	: fam, pl. afmām	Zenaga	: immi
		Ethiopian	: 'af

That it is difficult to contemplate and dare put a *common radical* to all these Semitic, Egyptian, and Berber forms, is obvious. It is only necessary to open one's eyes.

On the contrary, Pharaonic Egyptian and Coptic are well and truly black African in this broad context:

Ancient Egyptian	: r3, ra, "mouth"
Coptic	: ra, rō, ro, re, la, lō, le
Isekiri (Nigeria)	: arū
Bozo	: lo
Kpele	: la
Sarakolle (Mali)	: la
Busa	: le
Guro (Ivory Coast)	: le
Ndemli (Benue-Congo):	lu

A name is a universal cultural phenomenon: it identifies the one who carries it, and so differentiates one from other individuals. Also on this point, there is no cultural, linguistic "Hamito-Semitic" or "Afro-Asiatic" universe:

Akkadian	: sumu, shumu, "name"
Ugaritic	: sēm, shēm
Hebrew	: sēm, shēm
Aramaic	: sum, shum
Ethiopian	: sam
Arabic	: 'ism
Ancient Egyptian:	rn
Coptic	: ran, ren, lan, len, rin

The palatoalveolar fricative consonant of Akkadian, Ugaritic, Hebrew, and Aramaic, disappears in Arabic and Ethiopian. Berber is: *ism, isem,* "name."

It is virtually impossible to find a common predialectal form to Semitic and Egyptian languages on these terms, which can only be inherited. Therefore, where is the reality, when it comes to verifiable facts, of the "Hamito-Semitic" family or "Afro-Asiatic" family?

On the other hand, the Egyptian language, obviously connects with other black African languages:

Ancient Egyptian :	rn, "name"
Coptic	: ran, ren, lan, len, rin
Shilluk (Sudan) :	rin

Galke (Adamawa)	:	rìn
Pormi (Adamawa)	:	rìn
Ngoumi	:	rìn
Pandjama	:	rìn
Mbe	:	lén
Bantu	:	rína, lína, dína, ína, jína, zína
Fanti (Ghana)	:	dzin
Asante (Ashanti)	:	din'

Even if relations are often obscure between the following words, they are nevertheless related and refer to the fact of a common origin:

Latin	:	nōmen, "name"
Sanskrit	:	nāma
Avestic	:	nāma
Gothic	:	namo
Hittite	:	iāman (without doubt issued from a dissimulation)
Welsh	:	enw
Old Irish	:	ainm
Old Slav	:	ime
Old Prussian	:	emmens
Albanian	:	emer, êmen
Armenian	:	anun
Tokharion A	:	ñom; Tokharian B: ñem
Greek	:	hónoma, hoúnoma (Homeric), hónuma in Dorian (h = aspirated) Radical: + nomn

The families are also distinct:

Semitic	:	sumum, samum, shumu, shem, shum, etc.
Indo-European	:	nomen, nom, name, nama, etc.
Afro-Egyptian	:	rn, ran, ren, len, rin, rina, etc.

Where is the "Hamito-Semitic" or "Afro-Asiatic" in the above mentioned examples? One can confirm that the "Afro-Asiatic" family is evidently a scientific hoax. One must consequently rid African linguistics of this fake family, which does not exist in the materiality of verifiable facts.

For the word "house," we have:

Hebrew	:	bayit, "house" (as opposed to "tent": ōhel)
South Arabic	:	byt, p. 'byt
Arabic	:	bayt
Berber	:	tigemmi, "house" (or akhkham)
Ancient Egyptian	:	pr, "house"
Coptic	:	per-

The other modern black African languages say:

Wolof	:	per, "fence of the house," "house" by extension
Loko	:	pèrè, "house"
Mende	:	pèrè
Loma (Toma)	:	pèlè (p-r/p-l)
Mofu	:	ver (p-r/v-r)
Uzam	:	ver
Zidim	:	ver

Finally, where is the pertinence of the "Hamito-Semitic" or "Afro-Asiatic," with this group of words which is only used in the imperative?:

Akkadian	:	sabat, "take"
Arabic	:	hud, hudh, "take," "hold"
Ethiopian	:	yaz
Berber	:	amez
Ancient Egyptian	:	mi
Coptic	:	mo, ma

Once more, the Egyptian language belongs to the whole family of black African languages:

Ancient Egyptian	:	mi, "take"
Coptic	:	mo, ma
Yoruba	:	mú
Banda (Central African Republic)	:	mi
Mbochi (Bantu)	:	má
Fang (Gabon)	:	mē

See the word "black":

Arabic	:	'aswad, "black"
Berber	:	istif, dlu, bekhkhen
Ancient Egyptian	:	km
Coptic	:	kame, kemi, kam, kem

The Egyptian connects with the black African:

Ancient Egyptian	:	km, "black" (from km. t, "Black land," "Black country" = "Egypt")
Coptic	:	kame, kemi, kam, kem, "black"
Mbochi (Congo)	:	i-káma, "coalman," "darkness"
Bambora (Mali)	:	kami, "to reduce to embers" (km, "pile of burning wood" in Pharaonic)
Mossi (Burkina Faso)	:	kim, "to burn"
Val (Liberia)	:	kembu, "charcoal"
Yaaku	:	-kumpu-, "black"

So, with words like "black," "take" (which is in fact a whole phrase), "house," "name," "mouth," "earth," "country," "region," "sun," and so many others, it is proved radically impossible (strictly in historical linguistics terms, which are comparative and inductive) to find common roots between Semitic languages: Akkadian, Ugaritic, Hebrew, Arabic, Ethiopian, etc.; the Egyptian language: Ancient Pharaonic Egyptian, Demotic, Coptic; and the Berber dialects: Siwa, Ghadames, Riffian, Tuareg, Kabyle, etc. Such possible common roots would be a reconstruction which could be validly called "Afro-Asiatic" or "Hamito-Semitic," that is to say, a linguistic family which would united some African-Berber languages, Egyptian, Ethiopian, and the languages of Asia and the Middle East (Akkadian, Hebrew, Arabic, Phoenician, etc.) under one group. Well, it is absolutely impossible to reconstruct such original roots from inherited words.

So, all things well considered, the "Hamito-Semitic" or "Afro-Asiatic" family does not exist in the materiality of facts. Those who want to impose this unreal linguistic family at all cost, manifestly commit an intellectual swindle.

But what, finally, is the significance of all of this? One can only interpret this as that the champions of "Afro-Asiatic" want "to play" and "to cheat" with history:

1. They want to put the ancient world of the Jewish people (the Hebrews) and the Pharaonic world of the Nile Valley on an equal footing, although we know that the Hebrews created no significant contribution to the development of civilization in antiquity except in religion for which ancient Egypt is owed a tremendous debt.

2. Above all, they want to cut the Pharaonic world from the black African cultural universe, by wrongly preaching, obviously, that the language which supports the Pharaonic civilization has nothing in common with the languages spoken today by black Africans. Therefore, logically, the Pharaonic cultural and linguistic world does not belong to the black African world on the whole.

The Afro-Asiatic is a mere myth that must be destroyed.

We have completed a rather detailed work regarding all the fundamental aspects of the common grammatical and formal structures between ancient Egypt and black Africa. Here, we would only like to emphasize a few unarguable and precise facts.

There is a most remarkable correlation, a perfect concordance between the third person singular of the Egyptian and the Wolof suffix *pronoun*, both masculine and feminine: Ancient Egyptian .f, .s, Wolof .ef, .es; for the third person plural, the Wolof is closer to Pharaonic Egyptian than Coptic itself: Ancient Egyptian *sn*, Coptic *ou*, Wolof *sen:*

Ancient Egyptian:	mr. n. f, "he loved"
	mr. n. s, "she loved"
	mr. n. sn, "they loved"
Wolof :	mār. an. ef, "he loved madly"
	mār. on. es, "she loved madly"
	mār. on. sen, "they loved madly"
	(they also say: mar. on. nanw)

This concordance concerns a specific point, peculiar to Egyptian and Wolof morphology. Let us note what follows:

Ancient Egyptian	:	mr, "to love," "to desire"; mrw. t, "love"
Coptic	:	mere, meri, melli, me, meri, maerie, mi, id.
Acoli (Nilotic)	:	maaro, "to love," maar, "love"
Lwo, Luo (Nilotic)	:	mer, "to agree, to be in accord with," "kindness"
Nuer (Nilotic)	:	Mar, "friend"
Mangbetu (North-East Zaire):	:	o-mu, omu, "to love"; mu, "friend"
Wolof (Atlantic)	:	Mār, "to love madly"
Hebrew (by comparison)	:	ahab, "love"
Arabic (by comparison)	:	habba, "to love," "to desire"; 'ahabba, "to be fond of, to love"; hubb, "love, affection, attachment"

Furthermore, the Coptic (which is Ancient Egyptian vocalised) and the Bambara (Mali) present similar verbal forms:

Coptic	Bambara (West Africa)
i'na'di, "I will give"	i nā-di, "you will give"
n na-di, "we will give"	an nā-do, "they will give"
ou na-di, "he/she will give"	ou nā-di, "he/she will give"

The functional element *n* in Egyptian, Coptic *na*, Bambara *na*, Wolof *on*, expressly indicates the future. One finds the same functional *na* everywhere in the field of black Africa. For example, in Luganda (Uganda):

Bambara (West Africa)	Luganda (African Great Lakes)
n'nā-be, "I will be"	n-naa-ba, "I will be" (ba, "to be")
i nā-be, "you will be"	o naa-ba, "you will be"
a nā-be, "he/she will be"	a-naa-ba, "he/she will be"

There is another Pharaonic particle to explicitly indicate the future: *ka* and the form *sedjem.ka.ef*, "to hear," which are mostly encountered in religious texts and inscriptions in temples: *ha. ka. sen. ma. sen tou*, "They will certainly rejoice when they see you" (*Urk.* IV, 569, 10); *peri. ka Hâpl er pet*, "Hapi (the flood of the Nile) will rise to the sky."

In Hausa, we have *ka*, whose use is above all confined to the poetic (Charles H. Robinson, *Hausa Grammar*, p. 36). In Baguirmien, the particle *ka* is also present to indicate the future: *i mala ka tad*, "you will make yourself" (*i*, "You"; *tad/a*, "to do"); *ne ka tad*, "he will do" (*ne*, "he, him").

In Fant, the immediate and distant future is expressed with the element *ke: me ke so akiri*, "I am coming tomorrow" (*me*, "I, me"; *so*, "to come," "to arrive"; *akiri*, "tomorrow"; *kiri*, "morning").

In Kimbundu, it is the particle *ka* which is used to form the distant future: *ame nga ka landa*, "I will do the shopping" (*landa*, "to buy, to do the shopping"). In Bambara, after the verb *be*, "to be," the particle *ka* is used to translate various tenses of the verb, among which is the future: *min bi ka nin ke*, "the one who will do this" (*min*, "the one who"; *nin* "this is, that is, this"; *ke*, "to do"). In Mbochi, the particle *ka* explicitly indicates the future: *bà ka badzwà pòò*, "they will go to the village" (*bà*, "they, them"; *idzwà*, "to go," "to leave"; *pòò*, "village"). In Mancagne, the constructions which indicate the future are: *bia ka, lun ka, ia ka*. For the immediate future, one uses the construction *ia ka: a ia ka lilendar*, "he will rejoice."

How could Hausa borrow the *ka* from Kimbundu or Mbochi? How could Bambara borrow the *ka* from Ancient Egyptian? How could Fang borrow the *ke* from Baguirmain? According to the method in operation, there is a link of origin:

Ancient Egyptian *ka*
Hausa (Nigeria) *ka*
Baguirmien (Chad) *ka*
Fang (Gabon) *ke*
Mbochi (Cong) *ka*
Kimbundu (Angola) *ka*
Bambara (Mali) *ka*
Mancagne (Ziguinchor, South Senegal, and Guinea-Bissau) *ia ka*

In Ancient Egyptian, there is only one way of translating the *negative imperative:* we use *m*, from the verb *imi*, itself a negative verb (Gardiner, *Egyptian Grammar*, § 340, § 345).

Here are some examples: *ir*, "do," *m ir* "don't" (to a close friend); *snd*, "be afraid," *m snd*, "don't be afraid"; *m rdi kt m st kt*, "do not substitute this for that other" (*Urk.* IV 1090, 9, 1091.2).

This negative imperative of Pharaonic Egyptian *m* is a singular, pertinent fact, almost idiomatic. In Yoruba, the negative form *ma* is also used to grammatically form the negative imperative: "The negative of the simple form of command is formed by placing the particle *ma* before the verb" (E. L. Lasebikan, *Learning Yoruba*, Oxford University Press, 1958, p. 58).

In Pharaonic Egyptian as in Yoruba, *m/má* is a particle employed *solely* and *exclusively* for the negative imperative. Pharaonic Egyptian: *m ir*, "don't"; Yoruba: *joko*, "sit down"; *má joko*, "don't sit." In Arabic: *'if ʿal*, "do"; *la taf ʿal*, "don't"; *hud*, "take"; *la tahud*, "don't take." The element *la* is the negative. This is a typical, singular, pertinent encounter for it is the same phonetic reality (*m'má*), same morphology, same syntax (its use strictly limited to the negative imperative, the same initial position). It is therefore a consequence of total concordance: lexicologic, morphologic, syntactic, phonetic, between Pharaonic Egyptian and Yoruba.

The *liaison particles* are grammatical significations which establish specific relations. To speak like Ferdinand de Saussure, liaison particles express a host of connections insofar as grammatical and lexicological means. Liaison particles (conjunctions, prepositions, etc.) are invariable words which link juxtaposed elements in a sentence; they bring a nuance or precision of meaning, and also work in relation to an ensemble of other elements linked between them, to express syntactical, grammatical relations. Usually, the liaison particle is a consonant followed by a vowel.

The psychological, grammatical mechanism relation in Pharaonic Egyptian and in Coptic is done with the same linguistic tools, the same signification and particles as in the mechanisms of modern black African languages. Here are some examples:

I.

Ancient Egyptian	:	m, "within, out of, with, by means of, like, as much as, in, when, while, then"
Coptic	:	'm-, 'mmo, "inside, during, of, out of, by means of"; 'm pai-ma, "in these premises, within this place"; 'n-t-sfi, "by the word," "by means of the sword" (m turns into n before t)
Acoli (Nilotic)	:	me, "the, for, of"
Banda (Central African Republic)	:	ma, me, "inside, to at"
Ngbandi (Central African Republic)	:	ma, "like"
Luganda (Uganda)	:	mu, "inside"
Sena (Zambia)	:	mu, "when"
Soubiya (Zambia)	:	m, mo, umo, "there" (Pharaonic Egyptian m, im, "there")
Zulu (South Africa)	:	mo, mu, "inside"
Baoule (Ivory Coast)	:	mo, "inside" (with, above all, the names of village, of the country)
Senufo (Manianka, Mali)	:	ma/na, "for, in favour of, at"
Hausa (Nigeria)	:	ma, "at, for" (ma, ka, "yours")
Bambara (Mali)	:	ma, "when/as, like"

Berber (for comparison)	:	d'i, d'eg, "at, inside, in"; d', id', "with" (ifal Essoudan did terekfin, "He went to the Sudan by caravan"; Ghadames.) Again we have in Berber: r'ef, "because of"; g, "inside"; s, sa, "when"; akken, "when/as"; dus, dous, doussen, "there"
Arabic (for comparison)	:	fi, "in"; fi al-bayt, "in the house" when Pharaonic Egyptian is: m pr, "inside the house" (m, "inside")

II.

Ancient Egyptian	:	r, "around, subject to, friendly with, against, for"
Coptic	:	e-, ero, "at, towards, of, outside, on"; ero. f, "at his"; e p- schafe, "about the desert, at the desert"
Bambara (Mali)	:	ra, ro, "at, of"
Mangbetu (East Zaire)	:	ru, "with, by means of"
Nuer (Nilotic)	:	re, "between"
Songhay (Niger)	:	ra, "in, inside, inside of"
Azer (Medieval Soninke)	:	ra, re, "at"
Arabic (for comparison)	:	ilā, "about, at"; ilā sahra', "about the desert"

III.

Ancient Egyptian	:	n, "for, at, because of, of" (dative and genitive)
Coptic	:	'n, 'n = , "at" (dative); pedjō.ou na.f, "they will tell him" (na, "at"; na.f, "to him"); n becomes m before p: 'm-pi-kosmos, "at the world"
Baguirmien	:	an, "for, at, of"
Hausa	:	na, "of"; dokin Dauda = doki na Dauda, "David's horse"
Senufo	:	ni, "at, of"
Bambara	:	na, "at"
Tsogho (South Gabon)	:	na, "at, because of"
Mpongwe (Coastal Gabon)	:	ni, na, "for, because of, by, in"
Ngabndi (Zaire)	:	na, "at"
Gourmantché (Burkina Faso)	:	n, "relating to, with"
Lingala (Zaire, Congo)	:	na, "of, at"; ndako na biso, "our house (literally: "house of ours"); na, "by, for"; na bolingo, "by love, because of love"
Berber (for comparison)	:	i, d, et, "at, for, because of love"

The concordance of the three Egyptian particles: *m, r,* and *n* (Coptic, '*m-*, '*mmo; e-, ero;* '*n-*, '*n=* , *na*) with the corresponding ones in modern black African languages confirm, if still necessary, the profound ties of origin between Pharaonic Egyptian, Coptic, and black African. Facts are facts. It is not permitted to cheat with the facts. A profound, formal, and grammatical link exists between Egyptian and black African. It is the only legitimate conclusion to draw from facts such as the ones just delineated.

Clearly and simply, this question is one of internal and reductive analysis, which one has to bring in formulating phonetic laws. From then on, phonetic analysis is the most essential and instructive port of the comparison. It is a question of establishing rules of phonetic correspondences between the compared languages.

Phonetic alteration, change, and linguistic transformations are not isolated incidents. They occur quite regularly and are determined in all cases where the same conditions are realized. Example: The Latin /p/ of *saponem* remains in the Italian *sapone,* but changes slightly in the Provençal *sabo,* and even more, in becoming an aspirant in the French *savon;* it is the same for the Latin *ripam* which becomes *riba* in Provençal and *rive* in French. We have here a phonetic /p/>/b/>/v/, in the series examined.

Sometimes, the differences which are not apparent can baffle the uninitiated: *florem* gives *fleur* (flower), *cantatorem* gives *chanteur* (singer). How can one explain the transformations? It is rather simple, the Latin *o* stressed in open syllable, leads to the French *eu.*

There is a systematic correspondence between the English /d/ and the German /t/: English *drink* / German *trinken;* English *door* / German *tür;* English *dream* / German *traum.*

But it is required not to reason from borrowed words: the Serbo-Croatian words *avlija,* "court"; *pendzer,* "window"; *dimnije,* "women's clothing"; *kilim,* "carpet", etc., are Turkish words, and history tells us that the Turks colonized the Slavs-Yugoslavians (the Slavs of the South) for almost three and a half centuries. From then on, Serbo-Croatian is not under the influence of the dominant Turkish.

Consequently, one must be able to distinguish the borrowed words owed to geographical contacts and to the history of heritage which comes from the common original language.

The similarities between the *Ewe* and the *Mbochi* (Congo) are truly striking:

Ewe (Togo-Ghana, West Africa)	Mbochi (Congo, Central Africa)
abo, "arm"	ɛ.bo, "arm" (open o)
kú, "dead"	le.kú, i.kú, "the dead"
ku, "character, conduct"	e.kú, "jealousy"
me, "to burn"	miá, "fire"
mi, "to swallow"	i. mìá, "to swallow"
ta, "saliva"	a.tɛ, "saliva"
te, "stand up"	tɛɛ, "stand up"
to, "to grow, to shoot, to produce"	too, "to germinate, to grow"
tó, "family, parent"	i,to, "to marry"

Chance cannot explain such facts, even less the borrowing of words. It can only be due to a remote, prehistorical link.

When we have a series with the initial /d/ like with the word "to eat," it can only be inherited:

Mancagne	:	dɛ, "to eat"
Mossi	:	di
Gourmantche:		di/dye

Senoufo	:	di
Ewe	:	du
Kikongo	:	-dia/-dya
Kuba	:	o-dia, -dia
Shilele	:	ku-dia, -dia
Lunda	:	ku-de, -de
Mbochi	:	i-dza, dza
Yoruba	:	je, djɛ

That is to say, given a series which covers Africa from Guinea-Bissau (Mancagne) to Central Africa (Kuba, Lunda, etc.) to different geographical locations on the continent, it is difficult or nearly impossible to put down to chance such examples of obvious phonetic connections.

On the contrary, these series reveal a profound link with the relevant languages: these relatively recent, though different pronunciations (*di, dia, du, de, djè, dza,* etc.) imply a unique, more ancient pronunciation, as in the French *nuit,* Spanish *noche,* Italian *notte,* recent forms linked to a more ancient ($\pm$ *nocte*).

We have in Pharaonic Egyptian $d^c = dj\hat{a}$, which means: "spices for bread" (*Urk.* IV, 1157, 15). And the Coptic: *djē,* "a dish." A comparatist notes first that on the semantic level, there is a slight evolution: *bread, a dish for nourishment, to eat,* are realities which capture the same field of signification, and recall a daily reality (bread, dish, to eat).

But the really important point is that we have the same word which hardly developed phonetically (Ancient Egyptian *dyâ,* Mbochi *-dza,* Teke *dza,* Fang *zi, dzi',* Coptic *djē,* Yoruba *djè djɛ, je*), and the phonetic mutations are almost self-explanatory: Baoule *li,* "to eat"; Vili *ku-lia, -lia;* Mbe *ò-lía/líé; dia/lia; di/li.*

We can therefore affirm that all these forms: *djâ, djē, dza, dia, di, de, du, dye, lia, dzi, zi, za,* etc., refer to the same and only ancestral phonetic form. In other words, ancient Pharaonic Egyptian, Coptic, and modern black African languages are genetically and historically linked.

Berber is not linked with this African Egyptian family: Berber *etch,* "to eat," aortic *itchou.*

The Akan (Ghana) is evidently black African: *didi,* "to eat" in Asante (Ashanti), and *dzidzi,* "to eat" in Fanti: the Akan has simply doubled the simple form (*di/didi; dzi/dzidzi*).

In Arabic we have: *akala,* "to eat," and *'aki,* "food." This is manifestly different from the forms: *djâ, dza, dzi, djē, di, de, dia, lia, li,* etc., from black African languages, since Pharaonic Egyptian.

After these remarks and general observations, we can analyze in a much deeper way the phonetic correspondences on one or two precise examples, for there is no space for more ample demonstrations, which are quite tedious for those who are not specialists in comparative linguistics.

The muffled dorso-velar occlusive /k/

The initial and mid-vowel: the same position and frame in Ancient Egyptian, in Coptic, and in Mbochi (Congo, Bantu language). Therefore:

-/k/ Introduces a bilabial nasal occlusive /m/:
Pharaonic Egyptian	:	km, "black"
Coptic (evolved Egyptian) :		kame, kam, kemi, kem, "black"
Mbochi (Bantu)	:	i-kama, "to mine for coal, to blacken"

Culture and Identity

Therefore, we have these phonetic alterations at consonent level: k- k- k- and -m -m -m. The consonantal structure is not rigorously the same everywhere. The *a* of Coptic *kame, kam* recurs in Mbochi: *i-kama,* the *i-* being a prefix of the infinitive, and the final *a* of *i-kama* being only a supportive vowel. Therefore, Coptic and Mbochi are absolutely identical phonetically.

/k/ Introduces another muffled dorso-velar occlusive /k/
Pharaonic Egyptian: *k*kw, "darkness"
Coptic   :   *k*ale, *k*eke, "darkness"
Mbochi   :   ɛ.koko, "evening darkness"

This gives these phonetic correspondences: *k- k- k-* and *-k -k -k.* The three lexemes, in fact, rest upon an identical consonantal base: = kʷkʷ "darkness" of the evening, of the night (the ancient Egyptian word being written with a determinative which perfectly allows it to speak of darkness of evening, darkness, or nocturnal darkness).

-/k/ Introduces two muffled dental occlusives /tt/:
Pharaonic Egyptian: *k*tt, "small"
Coptic   :   *k*oy, koye, "small"
Mbochi   :   *k*yɛ, "small, little"

In Coptic and Mbochi, these two consonants /tt/ have disappeared. This phenomenon is very constant in Coptic Egyptian. But this disappearance led to a diphthongization, and the Mbochi again presents: ɛ.keɛ, "small, little." The Kikkongo offers: *nke, -ke,* "small, little." On the other hand, the muffled dental is still there in Sango (Central African Republic), *k*e*t*ɛ, "small, little"; *lo mu na mbi ingo k*e*t*ɛ, "he has given me a little salt" (literally: "he gave to me little salt").

-/k/ is introduced by a deaf /s/:
Pharaonic Egyptian: sk, ska, "to plough" (not a causative)
Coptic   :   se*k*ai, sekayi, "to plough"
Mbochi   :   i-sàkà (dialectial variant: i-sàà) "to plough"
Kikongo   :   ku-sàakà, "to harvest, to reap cereals, to hoe"
We, therefore, have: *s- s- s-* and *-k -k -k*

So, for the facts examined here, the phonetic correspondences are absolutely rigorous between Pharaonic Egyptian, Coptic, and Mbochi, notably at consonantal level, the very frame of the words.

The apico-alveolar vibrant /r/

This phoneme is very interesting to analyze.

Pharaonic Egyptian: rmt, "man," "to be human"
Coptic   :   rōme, "man," "husband"
                      rōmi
                      ōmi

The apico-alveolar vibrant of Pharaonic Egyptian loses its vibration and becomes an apico-alveolar lateral in Coptic, in the Fayumuc dialect: *rmt/lmi* (r/l). In the Bantu-Mbochi language of the Congo, there is also an *i* which presents itself as: *o-lómi,* "husband, spouse," "male."
So, we have three series—with /r/, with /l/, with /n/—plus a zero series without an initial consonant, for the words "man, husband, spouse":

(a) *Series with /r/:*

Pharaonic Egyptian: rōme, rōmi
Nuer (Sudan)   : ram, "human person, individual"
Azer (Mali)   : reme, remme, "child" (semantic transfer)

(b) *Series with /l/:*

Coptic   : lōmi
Azer   : leme, lemme
Common Bantu   : + -lúmi
Mbochi   : o-lómì, pl. a-lómì
Topoke (Zaire)   : -lome
Luba (Kasai, Zaire): mu-lume
Teke (Tio, Congo) : o-lúm', n-lum', mu-lum'

(c) *Series with /n/:*

Fang (Gabon)   : n-nôm
Mponwe (Gabon) : o-nome, o-nomo
Kuba (Zaire)   : num, nuum
Vili (Congo)   : nunni (attraction of m which becomes n)

(d) *Zero series*

Tetela (Zaire)   : omi (facing rōme/lōmi; lumi/nôm/num/lum)
Lomongo (Zaire) : b-ome (b- nominal prefix)
Ntomba (Zaire)   : bo-ome (bo- class prefix)
Tsogho (Gabon) : m-ome, pl. a-ome
Akwa Opa   : mo-omi, pl. b- ami

We notice that the /r/ underwent modifications: r/r (maintaining), but r/l and r/l/n were permuted. However, the nasal bilabial /m/ appears everywhere as the nucleus-consonant, the fundamental element, without change: *rmt, rōme, rōmi, ram, reme, lōmi, leme, lume, lumi, o-lomi, mu-lume, n-nôme, o-nome (o-rome/o-lome/-o-nome), num (o-nume/o-rome/ o-lome), omi, -ome, omi (rōme/lome/nome/ome)*. This clearly speaks of a family relation, which permits us to clearly see the history of the compared languages, their characteristic innovations in relation to more ancient forms (Pharaonic Egyptian, Coptic).

The phonetic rule is as follows: The Egyptian /r/ (Pharaonic and Coptic), in losing its vibration, became a lateral in the Fayumic Coptic dialect /l/. This lateral, becoming more nasal, became an apicodental nasal occlusive /n/. So: *rmt/rōme, rōmi/lōmi/o-lomi/nome*. In the same way: "mouth" in Pharaonic, *r₃, ra,* in Coptic *rō, la, lō,* and in Mbochi *o.noo,* "mouth"; Fongbe *nu, nû;* Yoruba *enu,* Ewe *nu,* Fanti *anu,* Baoulé *ne,* Bini (Edo) *unu,* Mossi *no;* Bozo *lo,* Sarakolle *la,* etc.

The resemblance of the words examined here can be explained by an identity of origin, for these resemblances, both in form and meaning, convey terms, manifestly inherited: the compared languages have not been in contact recently, except for the contacts of origin, before the division of the languages. On the other hand, the testimony of two or three non-adjacent languages, remote in space, favors the original link, since chance is excluded on inherited terms. Therefore:

1. Pharaonic Egyptian   : bâi, "palm"
   Coptic   : bam bae, bai, bei, "palm," "palm branch"
   Mbochi (Congo)   : i-bía, "palm tree"
   Teke (Congo, Gabon, Zaire) : bá, "palm tree"
   Lakonda (Zaire)   : i-bá, "palm tree"

Mofu (North Cameroon)	:	tu-bah
Arabic (for comparison)	:	nahia, "palm," "palm tree," "date palm"

2.
Pharaonic Egyptian	:	ba, "spirit, soul"
Coptic	:	bai, "spirit, soul"
Mbochi (Congo)	:	bà, "to be sound in spirit," "to be spiritually honest"
Ronga (Mozambique)	:	ku-ba, -ba, "to be" (the b is a fricative)
Songhay (Niger)	:	bi (bi-yo), "double of a being," "soul"
Mangbetu (North-East Zaire)	:	o-bu, "to be, to exist" (to have spirit)
Bambara (Mali)	:	be, bi, "to be, to exist" (to have spirit)
Arabic (for comparison)	:	nafs, "soul," "essence," "being" ruh, "vital breath"

3.
Pharaonic Egyptian	:	bin, "bad"
Coptic	:	boone, baane, boni, bani, "bad"
Mbochi (Congo)	:	e-béná, "informed," "ill"
Wolof (Senegal)	:	bōn, "bad"
Bambara (Mali)	:	bone, "bad luck"
Azer (Medieval Soninke)	:	bane, "bad"
Sénoufo	:	buon, "bad luck"
Songhay (Niger)	:	bone, "ill"
Peul	:	bone, "maliciousness"
Mossi	:	bone, "ill, bad"
Kaje (Nigeria, Plateau)	:	biyin, "bad"
Arabic (for comparison)	:	sar, "ill"; sayyi', "bad" (sayyi' assu', "bad character")

4.
Pharaonic Egyptian	:	iba, yiba, "to dance," "dance"
Wolof (Senegal)	:	yiba, "to dance"
Mangbetu (North-East Zaire)	:	eba, "to dance"
Gmbwaga (CAR [Central African Republic])	:	be, "dance"
Gbanziri (CAR)	:	be, "dance"
Mondzombo (CAR)	:	be, "dance"
Caffino (Kushitic, Ethiopia)	:	dū-bō, "dance"; du-b, "to dance"
Bambara (Mali)	:	bo, "drum" (bo koro, "dance hall")
Mbochi (Congo)	:	i-bí-na (core element - bi-), "to dance"
Arabic (for comparison)	:	raqs, "dance"; raqasa, "to dance"

5.
Pharaonic Egyptian	:	mw, "water"
Coptic	:	moou, mōu, mau, mo, mē
Mbochi (Congo)	:	mà
Lingala (Zaire, Congo)	:	may (mai, maí)
Yoruba (Nigeria)	:	o-mi, omi
Bini (Edo, Nigeria)	:	a-mē, amē
Mago (Benin)	:	omi
Tiv (Nigeria)	:	mà
Gwara (Nigeria)	:	ímè
Margi (Nigeria)	:	'imí

Pelci (Nigeria)	:	mâ
Arabic (for comparison)	:	ma, "water"

6.
Pharaonic Egyptian	:	me.t, "mother"
Coptic	:	maau, mau, meu, mo
Mbochi (Congo)	:	máá, móó
Mossi (Burkina Faso)	:	ma
Logba	:	ámá
Baoule (Ivory Coast)	:	ma (an né)
Bambara (Mali)	:	ma (and bá)
Labi-Benoue	:	ma
Wandala	:	mu
Nuer (South Sudan)	:	mur, mor, mar, mwor (r additive element)
Zelgwa (North Cameroon)	:	mur
Sotho (Southern Africa)	:	mmé
Arabic (for comparison)	:	'umm, "mother"

7.
Pharaonic Egyptian	:	ka, "so, then"
Coptic	:	ke, "so, self"
Acoli (Luo, Lwo)	:	ka, "if, then"
Mangbetu (Zaire)	:	ka, "therefore"
Kikongo (Congo)	:	e-kà, "if, then"
Douala (Cameroon)	:	kɛ, "in this case, then, and then"
Bini (Edo, Nigeria)	:	'ke, "and then"
Bambara (Mali)	:	ko, "following behind"

8.
Pharaonic Egyptian	:	s, "man" (someone); z in the Ancient Empire
Coptic	:	sa, "man, husband"
Gangero (Kushitic)	:	a-sa, asa, "man"
Kapsiki	:	za (Ancient Empire z)
Koro	:	ò-sa, "husband"
Logba	:	o sá, "husband"
Tunen (South Cameroon)	:	mò-sa, pl. bà-sa, "man"
Mbochi (Congo)	:	o-sí, pl. a-sí, "someone from"
Sango (CAR)	:	zo, "man" (Ancient Empire z)
Ngandi (CAR, Zaire)	:	zo, "man"
Mangbetu (North-East Zaire)	:	ma-si, "man, husband, male"
Common Bantu	:	+ -sí (mu-sí, omu-sí, o-sí, etc.), "folk," "lives at"
Arabic (for comparison)	:	rajul, "man"; zawj, "husband, spouse"

9.
Pharaonic Egyptian	:	ii, "to come," "to arrive"
Coptic	:	ei, i, eye, ie, ye, eia, eya, hie
Bantu and Benue-Congo	:	+ yi-, "to come," "to arrive"
Mbochi (Congo)	:	i-yaa
Kuba (Zaire)	:	i (like the Coptic i)
Ivili (Gabon)	:	ya
Duala (Cameroon)	:	ya
Baoule (Ivory Coast)	:	i (i-dè, "come here," like the Coptic i)
Gouin	:	yô
Bete (Ivory Coast)	:	yi, i, gi

Culture and Identity

Topoke (Zaire, Equator)	:	-y- (yô, "come"); yei, "come on"
Bade	:	àyῐ, "come"
Janji (Nigeria, Plateau)	:	'àye, "to come"
Arabic (for comparison)	:	atā, jā'a, "to come," "to arrive"
10. Pharaonic Egyptian	:	rimi, rmi, "to cry"
Coptic	:	rime, rimi, limi
Birri (Nigeria, Plateau)	:	rami, "to cry"
Acoli (Luo, Lwo, Kenya)	:	reèmò, "to make someone sad" (to make him cry)
Ewondo (Cameroon)	:	n-som, "who cries loudly"
Mbochi (Congo)	:	i-samí, "mocking and teasing to the point of tears" (r-m/s-m)
Arabic (for comparison)	:	bakā, "to cry," "to be tearful"

Conclusion

The conclusion is obvious:

1. The "Hamito-Semitic" or the "Afro-Asiatic" is only a scientific invention; a predialectal ancestor common to Semitic, to Berber, and to Egyptian languages was never reconstructed following the method of historically compared linguistics, whose aim is, precisely, to link genetically the solicited languages.

2. The numerous morphological, syntactic, phonetic and lexicological concordances that can be clearly established between Pharaonic Egyptian, Coptic, and all modern black African languages are of an historical genetic order, and it might be scientifically possible to reconstruct the common predialectal ancestor of all these ancient and modern languages.

3. Consequently, if African linguistic studies go round in circles, it is precisely because of the lack of a new and dynamic methodology, and also because of the tenacious preconception which insists on splitting the Egypto-Nubian Valley of the Nile from the rest of the black African world.

4. It is imperative not to follow the well trodden paths in the field of inherited African linguistics; not to follow a particular linguistic canon (solely descriptive), but to engage in a veritable general, African comparative and scientific linguistics.

5. This fertile path is the same that was laid out, with devotion and science, by our master, Professor CHEIKH ANTA DIOP.

Philosophy and Morality

PART FOUR

Overleaf: Adinkra symbol for *nkyinkyimiie,* stability

Wherever rational humans have existed, they have reflected on the nature of their existence and responded to their summations by drawing up codes of conduct. African philosophy and morality, therefore, are found in the deep reflections of the thinkers who have produced as "documents" of those reflections, certain beliefs, values, methods, and systems of thought explaining the nature of things.

The word *philosophy*, according to the philosopher Théophile Obenga, is derived from the ancient Egyptian word *seba* (wisdom), which became *sophia* in Greek. An inscription on the tomb of Antef I (2052 B.C.) has a long statement on wisdom and the wise. But even prior to this time the words and works of philosophers were being heeded in ancient Africa. Imhotep, the prince of the early thinkers, not only wrote "wisdom sayings" but also constructed temples and practiced medicine based upon his reflections.

The names of the earliest African philosophers are rarely heard in the West. Thus, Ptah-hotep, Kagemni, Khunanup, Kete, Sonchis, Pepi, and Wennofer have remained outside Western knowledge, although their philosophical statements have informed or have coincided with many other African streams of thought. It is our wish that by the presentations of a few of the classical works from the African tradition, readers will get a sense of the depth of the wisdom heritage.

The broad discussions on philosophy provided by John Mbiti and Kwame Gyekye, two of Africa's most brilliant writers on this subject, provide this section with an apt introduction to the questions of philosophy and morality. Both Mbiti and Gyekye argue convincingly for an African philosophy, articulating the fundamental principles of African community life as the basis for their positions. Mbiti, an East African, and Gyekye, a West African, have brought their ideas to bear on the major issues of the day. Inclusion of their works in this section is relevant to the continuing discourse on the nature of African philosophy.

Philosophical statements emerge out of concrete contexts of social, political, and behavioral modalities. For this reason we have included the moral teachings of Ptah-hotep, one of the earliest African philosophical treatises, the statement by Sinuhe on his victory over circumstances, the instructions of Amenemope, the speech of pharaoh installing

Rekhmire as prime minister, "The Doomed Prince," "The Story of the Two Brothers," Wen-Amon's account of his Asian journey, and "The Lion in Search of Man." The aim is to emphasize the diversity of the African's approach to the conditions of life. All philosophy is contextualized, and the statements we make about life are connected to what we do and say. The concepts presented here are not orphaned ideas unconnected to life in the various African societies. This is why we find in this section various intellectual, moral, and proverbal declarations.

But the reflections of Léopold Sédar Senghor and Kwame Nkrumah are also important documents in the intellectual discourse on philosophy and morality. Senghor's understanding of African socialism through the prism of his Negritude and Nkrumah's consciencism, a philosophy of personal and collective development and progressive cooperation, captured the imagination of their generation and gave Africa energy for independence.

Much like the values inherent in the works of the early Egyptians and in the writings of Senghor and Nkrumah, the Zulu Declaration, popularized by Jordan Ngubane in its oral form, reinforces the idea that we are who we are because of the collective group. Chinua Achebe, one of the most celebrated African writers of the twentieth century, explains how the African writer undertakes the task of writing, particularly in a foreign language. While there are many controversies and issues in this discussion, including the ones introduced by Chinweizu, Ngugi wa Thiong'o, and Thomas Houessou-Adin, Achebe's voice is important for the dialogue.

Proverbal wisdom from the Igbo and Luyia peoples underpins the daily lives of Africans on both sides of the ocean. Indeed, it may be said that without a proverb, Africans are rarely considered eloquent.

We have included the African American spirituals under the heading of philosophy and morality because they speak to the patterns of thought, the creative management of spiritual ideas, and the philosophical ingenuity of a people working under duress to explain to themselves and the conditions of their lives. Additional writings on this theme are included in the work of Maria Stewart, the first African American woman to give a public speech, Marcus Garvey, the greatest mass leader of African people, W. E. B. Du Bois, the most significant African American intellectual of the twentieth century, and Alain Locke, the interpreter of the Harlem Renaissance.

Philosophy and Morality

John Mbiti
(b. 1931, Kenya)

The Study of African Religions and Philosophy

The world has now begun to take African traditional religions and philosophy seriously. It was only around the middle of the twentieth century that these subjects had begun to be studied properly and respectfully as an academic discipline in their own right. During the preceding one hundred years African religions were described by European and American missionaries and by students of anthropology, sociology and comparative religion. It is from these writers that we have most of our written information, although some of them had never been to Africa and only a few had done serious field study of these religions. In the early part of that period, the academic atmosphere was filled with the theory of evolution which was applied in many fields of study. It is this theory which colours many of the earlier descriptions, interpretations and explanations of African religions. We shall consider briefly some of the early approaches before coming to the present situation.

THE EARLY WESTERN APPROACHES AND ATTITUDES

One of the dominating attitudes in this early period was the assumption that African beliefs, cultural characteristics and even foods, were all borrowed from the outside world. German scholars pushed this assumption to the extreme, and have not all abandoned it completely to this day. All kinds of theories and explanations were put forward on how the different religious traits had reached African societies from the Middle East or Europe. It is true that Africa has always had contact with the outside world, but religious and cultural influence from this contact cannot have flowed only one way: there was always a give-and-take process. Furthermore, African soil is not so infertile that it cannot produce its own new ideas. This game of hunting for outside sources is dying out, and there are writers who now argue that in fact it was Africa which exported ideas, cultures and civilization to the outside world. But surely a balance between these two extremes is more reasonable.

These earlier descriptions and studies of African religions left us with terms which are inadequate, derogatory and prejudicial. They clearly betray the kind of attitude and interpretation dominant in the mind of those who invented or propagated the different theories about traditional religions. *Animism* is a word derived from the Latin *anima* which means breath, breath of life, and hence carries with it the idea of the soul or spirit. This term has become the most popular designation for African religions and is found in many writings even this day. It was invented by the English anthropologist, E. B. Tylor, who used it first in an article in 1866 and later in his book, *Primitive Culture* (1871). For Tylor the basic definition of religion was the "belief in spirit beings." He saw the anima as a shadowy vaporous image animating the object it occupied. He thought that the so-called "primitive people" imagined the anima to be capable of leaving the body and entering other men, animals or things; and continuing to live after death. Pursuing the theory further, Tylor went on to say that such "primitive" men considered every object to have its own soul, thus giving rise to countless spirits in the universe.

Tylor's ideas were popularized by his disciples. Since then, the term *animism* has come to be widely used in describing traditional religions of Africa and other parts of the world. In an atmosphere filled with the theory of evolution, the notion of countless spirits opened the way for the idea of religious evolution. This led on to the theory that single spirits existed over each major department of nature. For example, all the spirits of the rivers would have one major spirit in charge of them, and the same for trees, rocks, lakes and so on. Accordingly, this gave man the idea of many gods (polytheism), which in turn evolved further to the stage of one supreme God over all the other departmental spirits. . . .

This type of argument and interpretation places African religions at the bottom of the supposed line of religious evolution. It tells us that Judaism, Christianity and Islam are at the top, since they are monotheistic. The theory fails to take into account the fact that another theory equally argues that man's religious development began with a monotheism and moved towards polytheism and animism. We need not concern ourselves unduly here with either theory. We can only comment that African peoples are aware of all these elements of religion: God, spirits and divinities are part of the traditional body of beliefs. Christianity and Islam acknowledge the same type of spiritual beings. The theory of religious evolution, in whichever direction, does not satisfactorily explain or interpret African religions. Animism is not an adequate description of these religions and it is better for that term to be abandoned once and for all. It needs to be emphasized that African religions are historically older than both Christianity and Islam.

In classifying the religions of the world, we hear that "redemptive religions" like Christianity, Judaism and Islam incorporate into their teaching the doctrine of the soul's redemption in the next world. "Morality religions" like Shintoism and the teachings of Confucius lay a great emphasis on moral considerations. Finally, "primitive religions" are those whose followers are described by some writers as "savage," "primitive" and lacking in either imagination or emotion. Of course the word primitive in its Latin root *primus* had no bad connotations as such, but the way it is applied to African religions shows a lack of respect and betrays derogatory undertones. It is extraordinary that even in our day, fellow men should continue to be described as "savage" and lacking in emotion or imagination. This approach to the study of African religions will not go very far, neither can it qualify as being scientifically or theologically adequate. Some traditional religions are extremely complex and contain elements which shed a lot of light on the study of other religious traditions of the world.

In his book, *Principles of Sociology* (1885), the anthropologist Herbert Spencer used the phrase *ancestor worship* to describe speculation that "savage" peoples associated the spirits of the dead with certain objects, and in order to keep on good terms with the spirits of their ancestors, people made sacrifices to them. Other writers have borrowed this term and applied it almost to anything that Africans do in the way of religious ceremonies. Many books speak of "ancestor worship" to describe African religions. Certainly it cannot be denied that the departed occupy an important place in African religiosity; but it is wrong to interpret traditional religions simply in terms of "worshipping the ancestors." . . . The departed, whether parents, brothers, sisters or children, form part of the family, and must therefore be kept in touch with their surviving relatives. Libation and the giving of food to the departed are tokens of fellowship, hospitality and respect; the drink and food so given are symbols of family continuity and contact. "Worship" is the wrong word to apply in this situation; and Africans themselves know very well that they are not "worshipping" the departed members of their family. It is blasphemous, therefore, to describe these acts of family relationships as "worship." Furthermore, African religions do not end at the level of family rites of libation and food offerings. They are deeper and more comprehensive than that. To see them only in terms of "ancestor worship" is to isolate a single element, which in some societies is of little significance, and to be blind to many other aspects of religion.

Western missionaries, anthropologists, journalists and scholars who keep harping about "ancestor worship" should look at or consider cemeteries in their home countries and see how many flowers, candles and even photographs of the dead, are put on the graves of relatives and friends. That is often more extreme than anything we find in Africa and I do not know what form of "worship" to call this beloved custom in the West. African peoples do not feel ashamed to remember their departed members of the family. Remembering them . . . is not worshipping them.

Other writers have tried to study or refer to African religions in terms of magic. Some consider magic to have evolved before religion, as man's attempt to manipulate the unseen world. When man failed to control natural objects and phenomena by means of magic, he then resigned himself to forces beyond him, which in turn led to a belief in God as the Source of all power. As such, magic is considered to be the mother of religion. Since every African society has both magic and religion, it was inevitable to conclude that Africans had not evolved beyond the stage of detaching religion from magic. Some writers even tell us that Africans have no religion at all and only magic. We shall devote a whole chapter to this subject of magic, and there is an increasing amount of good literature on it. We need here only comment briefly. A careful examination of the situation in African societies shows that magic is part of the religious background, and it is not easy to separate the two. Some of the ceremonies, for example in rainmaking and preventing epidemics, incorporate both religion and magic. So long as magical acts are beneficial to the community involved, they are acceptable and people may even pay a great deal of their wealth in order to secure such help. This gives no contradiction to their beliefs. Magic belongs to the religious mentality of African peoples. But religion is not magic, and magic cannot explain religion. Religion is greater than magic, and only an ignorant outsider could imagine that African religions are nothing more than magic.

Other terms employed to describe African religions include *Dynamism, Totemism, Fetishism* and *Naturism*. We need not go into them here. These and the previous terms show clearly how little the outside world has understood African religions. Some of the terms are being abandoned as more knowledge comes to light. But the fact remains that African religions and philosophy have been subjected to a great deal of misinterpretation, misrepresentation and misunderstanding. They have been despised, mocked and dismissed as primitive and underdeveloped. One needs only to look at the earlier titles and accounts to see the derogatory language used, prejudiced descriptions given and false judgments passed upon these religions. In missionary circles they have been condemned as superstition, satanic, devilish and hellish. In spite of all these attacks, traditional religions have survived, they dominate the background of African peoples, and must be reckoned with even in the middle of modern changes.

INTERMEDIATE AND CURRENT STUDIES

In recent years a change of approach and attitude has begun to take place. We mention here some of the books and new methods, without elaborating on them. The first of these new approaches is represented by writers like Tempels, Jahn and Taylor. In his book, *Bantu Philosophy* (French edition 1945, English 1959), the late P. Tempels presents his understanding of Baluba religion and philosophy, starting from the attitude that "primitive peoples have a concrete conception of being and of the universe." For Tempels the key concept to African religions and philosophy is what he calls "the vital force." He isolates this as the essence of being: "force is being, and being is force." His philosophy of forces explains for him everything about African thinking and action.

In spite of his arrogant and superior attitudes, Tempels' book opens the way for a sympathetic study of African religions and philosophy. His motive and that of the fellow colonialists whom he addresses, is "to civilize, educate and raise the Bantu." The book is primarily Tempels' personal interpretation of the Baluba, and it is ambitious to call it "Bantu philosophy" since it only deals with one people among whom he had worked for many years as a missionary. It is open to a great deal of criticism, and the theory of "vital force" cannot be applied to other African peoples with whose life and ideas I am familiar. The main contribution of Tempels is more in terms of sympathy and change of attitude than perhaps in the actual contents and theory of his book.

In the same group is the late J. Jahn's book, *Muntu* (German edition 1958, English 1961), which deals primarily with what he calls "neo-African culture." He devotes one section to African philosophy, while others are on art, dance, history and literature. It covers a great part of Africa, the basic material being collected through wide reading. In the religious-philosophical section Jahn adopts the categories of the late A. Kagame (from Rwanda), and squeezes everything into one of four categories:

> *Muntu* is the philosophical category which includes God, spirits, the departed, human beings and certain trees. These constitute a "force" endowed with intelligence.
>
> *Kintu* includes all the "forces" which do not act on their own but only under the command of *Muntu,* such as plants, animals, minerals and the like.
>
> *Hantu* is the category of time and space.
>
> *Kuntu* is what he calls "modality," and covers items like beauty, laughter, etc.

According to Jahn's interpretation, "all being, all essence, in whatever form it is conceived, can be subsumed under one of these categories. Nothing can be conceived outside them." These items are supposed to be related in the purely linguistic stem -NTU which occurs in all the four words on which the categories are based. Jahn supposes this -NTU to be "the universal force . . . which, however, never occurs apart from its manifestations: Muntu, Kintu, Hantu and Kuntu. NTU is Being itself, and cosmic universal force. . . . NTU is that force in which Being and beings coalesce. . . . NTU expresses, not the effect of these forces, but their being. But the forces act continually, and are constantly effective" (pp. 99 ff.).

The main contribution of Jahn's book is in pointing out the fact that Africa has some-

Philosophy and Morality

thing of philosophical value which deserves to be taken seriously and studied accordingly. In his enthusiasm about Africa, Jahn may have overstated his case (he says, for instance, that Europe has nothing to compare with African philosophy). But he has argued his ideas with conviction and has put them across persuasively, whether one accepts or rejects them.

In the English world this sympathetic approach to African religions and philosophy is best represented by J. V. Taylor in his book, *The Primal Vision* (1963). This is a contribution to studies in the series "Christian Presence," and the book is clearly directed towards that end. With one foot in Christian theology and the other in contemporary Africa with its traditional and modern life, Taylor managed to penetrate considerably African thought, in describing mainly for European readers, what he calls "the primal world." In this attempt he is carried away by that world, becoming too sympathetic and insufficiently critical. He presents everything as if it were so sacred, holy, pure and clean that it is being polluted by Christianity, Westernism, urbanization and the ways of technological life. The book has a disturbing sharp distinction between the "we" (Europeans) and the "they" (Africans), seen against the background of what "we" can learn from "them."

These three books have in common the attitude that African religions and philosophy are a reality which colors the whole life of African peoples. As such, they deserve to be taken seriously and studied sympathetically.

The second modern approach is represented by writers from England, France and West Germany. This approach attempts to treat African religions systematically, putting together information from various peoples. The pioneer work is E. G. Parrinder's *African Traditional Religion* (1954), which has been re-issued several times. This relatively short book gives an excellent and accurate presentation of the main items in African religions. The writer is both sympathetic and critical, and handles his material from many parts of Africa in a simple but scholarly way. Having lived and worked in western Africa, Parrinder has made field study of African religions (both traditional and Christian), and writes with confidence. His book pays less attention to philosophy and more to religion.

Les Religions de L'Afrique Noire (1960) by H. Deschamps represents this approach in the French world. It is of less value than Parrinder's book, and draws its material almost entirely from western Africa and the French-speaking countries. The writer is an anthropologist, and his treatment of the subject is anthropological and sociological. Another French work to mention here is one by Henri Maurier: *Philosophies de L'Afrique Noir* (1985) which, as the title indicates, concentrates more on philosophical interpretation, taking up the question of relationships as the central theme.

From West Germany comes E. Dammann's book, *Die Religionen Afrikas* (1963), which is a sizeable and well documented volume. It draws the material from English, French and German sources. It leans towards the search for outside influence and the use of some of the earlier phraseology and theories. But it is a comprehensive work, and valuable particularly in its descriptive parts. It also treats, but too briefly, other religions like Judaism, Christianity and Islam in Africa, and the impact of modern change upon religion. The book gives the impression of prejudice and superiority mentality, sometimes looking down upon or patronizing African religion. A different and more sympathetic treatment in the German circles is by Theo Sundermeier, *Nur Gemeinsam Können Wir Leben* (1988), though concentrating as it does on African religion around the concepts of Man.

The third approach in Western trends is represented by, among others, two books by anthropologists. E. E. Evans-Pritchard's *Nuer Religion* (1936) is the fruit of a long study of the Nuer people. The writer went and lived with them, learnt their language and participated as much as possible in all their activities. So he describes Nuer religion from within, using the scientific tools of an anthropologist but looking at it through the eyes of the Nuer themselves. He demonstrates how profoundly religious the Nuer are, with a deep conception of God as Spirit. G. Lienhardt in *Divinity and Experience: The Religion of the Dinka* (1961) follows exactly the same method. He brings out the importance of the personal encounter between God and men, which the Dinka recognize in every aspect of their life. They see the world of the spirit beings and of men converging in human experience; and this constitutes the essence of Dinka religion.

There are other books on the same lines, but these two are the classical representatives. The main contribution here is in concentrating on the religion of individual peoples and treating it both in depth and in relation to the total situation of the people concerned. If such studies could be made for most African peoples, they would be of infinite value as a bank of information on African traditional religions. Such studies place African religions in the context of their sociological and cultural environment. It is to be hoped that more attention will be given to modern trends of these traditional religions.

In recent decades a lot of studies on African religions, particularly in relation to the religion of Afro-Americans, is being undertaken in America. These are generally sympathetic, particularly since religious ties between Africa and the "New World" are not hard to feel or uncover. Evidence of this great interest and the work being done can be found in, among others, Ethel L. Williams and Clifton F. Brown: *The Howard University Bibliography of African and Afro-American Religious Studies with Locations in American Libraries* (1977). Since financial, library resources and technological aids (audio-visual, computers, cameras and video-recorders) are more available for American than African scholars, we may expect still more work in America and/or by Americans than [in] Africa itself, on African religion. This will often produce a different feeling from the traditional Western approach of interpreting and understanding African religiosity.

Another way of studying African religions and philosophy is represented by African scholars who take up single subjects and study them in depth within the situation of their people. This also has great value in that it concentrates on a given topic, describing it and interpreting it through African experience and understanding. One of the main advantages here is that the scholars themselves have a knowledge of the language and their people, from within and not without. Representative examples include: J. B. Danquah, *The Akan Doctrine of God* (1944), J. H. Nketia, *Funeral Dirges of the Akan People* (1955), A. Kagame, *La Philosophie Bantu-Rwandaise de L'Être* (1956), E. B. Idowu, *Olodumare: God in Yoruba Belief* (1962), G. M. Setiloane, *The Image of God Among the Sotho-Tswana* (1976) and E. Ikenga-Metuh, *God and Man in African Religion: A Case Study of the Igbo of Nigeria* (1981).

There is great potential in African scholars studying African religions and philosophy, with the aid of scientific tools and methodology and with the advantages of being part of the peoples of Africa, having almost unlimited access to information and speaking the languages which are the key to serious research and understanding of traditional religions and philosophy. The study of African religions and philosophy in universities, colleges and seminaries began in West Africa (e.g., Legon in Ghana, and Ibadan in Nigeria) in the late 1940s and early 1950s and has since become commonplace there. In the 1960s and 1970s similar steps were taken in East Africa, for example at Makerere University in Uganda and Nairobi University in Kenya, and later in Southern Africa. In French-speaking central Africa, similar studies have been initiated, especially in Zaire and Rwanda. A number of (rather popular) books have consequently been published, presenting African religion regionally and in general. Some of these include books . . . by: J. O. Awolaluy and

P. A. Dopamu, J. Mugambi and N. Kirima, V. Mulago, K. A. Opoku and T.N.O. Quarcoo-pome. As more books on the subject appear on the market so their quality will vary considerably. Some even copy the contents or outline of existing works, without acknowledging it! For further surveys see [the works of] D. Westerlond. . . . In the philosophy area mention can be made of works by K. C. Anyanwu and E. A. Ruch, A. Kagame and K. Wiredu.

My approach in this book is to treat religion as an ontological phenomenon, with the concept of time as the key to reaching some understanding of African religions and philosophy. I do not pretend that the notion of time explains everything, but I am convinced that it adds to our understanding of the subject, and if that much is achieved, these efforts will have been more than adequately rewarded.

Kwame Gyekye
(b. 1934, Ghana)

The Idea of African Philosophy

I started this book with a discussion of the question of philosophy in African culture in which I argued that there *is* a philosophical dimension to African traditional thought. I end it [here] with a discussion of thought systems as wholes, at the level at which we speak of Western or European or Oriental philosophy. The major question is: "May we in [a] similar vein talk also of *African* philosophy? Is the idea of African philosophy intelligible?" One answering these questions in the negative would, I suspect, prefer to talk rather of Akan, Yoruba, Kikuyu, Bantu, or Mende philosophy. But it should be noted that in addition to Western philosophy, one can speak as well of American, British, French, and German philosophy, and similarly of Chinese, Japanese, Korean, and Indian philosophy in addition to Oriental (or Eastern) philosophy. (There is indeed a philosophical journal with the title *Philosophy East and West.*) If it makes sense to talk of Western or Eastern philosophy, would it not make sense to talk of African philosophy too?

. . . I shall argue that the common features discernible in the cultures and thought systems of sub-Saharan African peoples justify the existence of an African philosophy. The intention here is not to argue that there is or ever will be either a unitary or a uniform African philosophical perspective, for such an argument will not hold water. It is to argue, rather, that a justification exists for talking of African philosophy or describing a body of ideas as African—not in the sense that these ideas are not to be found anywhere else in the world, but in the sense that this body of ideas is seen, interpreted, and analyzed by many African thinkers (and societies) in their own way. Thus, by "African" I do not mean to imply that a particular body of philosophical ideas is uniquely or exclusively African. I am using "African" in the sense in which one might use "Western" or "European" or "Oriental." The task here is a formidable but a significant one.

THE NEED NOT TO GENERALIZE

In a critical discussion of Mbiti's *African Religions and Philosophy* I accused him of "generalizations, over-simplifications, premature judgments and sparse analysis."[1] In this well-known book Mbiti recognizes the diversity of religious beliefs and practices in Africa and so speaks of African "religions" in his title, whereas in his use of the singular "philosophy" he means perhaps to convey the impression that Africans have a common philosophical perspective, although he himself speaks of "philosophical *systems* of different African peoples."[2] Mbiti wrote: "But since there are no parallel philosophical systems which can be observed in similarly concrete terms we shall use the singular 'philosophy' to refer to the philosophical understanding of African peoples concerning different issues of life."[3] This statement invites two responses. The first is that even though the philosophical contours of the various African thinkers are yet to be seriously delineated, yet it is safe to say that it is impossible for the philosophical understanding of African peoples to be similar or uniform. Second, the view that "there are no parallel philosophical systems which can be observed" can hardly be advanced when one knows, as Mbiti does, that "the philosophical systems of different African peoples have not yet been formulated."[4]

As to Mbiti's generalizations, I shall cite only two examples, namely, his views on the so-called African concept of time and on the nature of moral evil in African thought. I have . . . criticized . . . his views on the African concept of time, disagreeing especially with the way he generalizes his analysis from East Africa to the rest of African peoples. On the nature of moral evil Mbiti says that in African communities "something is considered to be evil not because of its intrinsic nature, but by virtue of who does it to whom and from which level of status."[5] Although this latter view is controversial, my difficulty with it here, as with his views on the African concept of time, concerns the basis for generalizing it for Africa as a whole even if it is true of his own ethnic group. There is no need to generalize a particular philosophical position for all African peoples in order for that position to be African.

I wish to make it clear that in criticizing Mbiti some time ago, as now, my intention was not to deny the legitimacy of the idea of African philosophy (using "philosophy" in the singular), but to question the bases of some of his bald, generalized assertions about African thought, assertions that need not have been made and that can hardly be justified. I believe that in many areas of thought we can discern features of the traditional life and thought of African peoples sufficiently common to constitute a legitimate and reasonable basis for the construction (or reconstruction) of a philosophical system that may properly be called African—African not in the sense that every African adheres to it, but in the sense that that philosophical system arises from, and hence is essentially related to, African life and thought. Such a basis would justify a discourse in terms of "African philosophy," just as the similarity of the experiences, traditions, cultural systems, values, and mentalists justify the appropriateness of the labels European philosophy, Oriental philosophy, Western philosophy, and so on.

COMMON FEATURES IN AFRICAN CULTURES

The basis I have in mind is made up of the beliefs, customs, traditions, values, sociopolitical institutions, and historical experiences of African societies. This observation will doubtless evoke cynicism, even scandal, among many Africanists, who are given to harping on the diversities of the cultures of Africa. Such scholars see no affinities among the cultures of Africa, even though the fact of cultural pluralism, which they expend great intellectual effort in pointing out, is so obvious a consequence of ethnic pluralism in Africa. Yet cultural pluralism, I maintain, does not necessarily eliminate the possibility of horizontal relationships between individual cultures.

On the intellectual level the works of such eminent Western anthropologists as Rattray, Herskovits, Forde, Fortes, Evans-Pritchard, Radcliffe-Brown, Lienhardt, and Goody, which generally deal with specific ethnic groups in Africa, have produced the impression, which was not intended by their authors, that the institutions and practices of the ethnic groups in Africa are very different from one another. The reason is that none of these authors, through either lack of interest in other ethnic groups or consciousness of his own limitations, tried in any significant way to relate his own observations and conclusions to those of other scholars, where they were available. The few comparisons in their works are usually made in passing, as if tangential to the import and structure of the work. The valuable productions of such individual Africanists do not therefore provide an opportunity for a synoptic study of African cultures. Consequently, such works fail to convey the impression that African cultures can be examined from a continental perspective.

In this connection such works as *African Worlds*, edited by Forde (1954), *African Political Systems*, edited by Fortes and Evans-Pritchard (1940), and *African Systems of Kinship and Marriage*, edited by Radcliffe-Brown and Forde (1956) are of immeasurable value. Each of these books focuses on a specific theme as it may be found in a number of African societies: the first on cosmological ideas and social values, the second on traditional political systems, and the third on social institutions. The great value of such works is that they provide one with a horizontal conspectus of some of the cultural systems of a number of African peoples. Others, like Geoffrey Parrinder, cover the whole of Africa, or a big region of it, in one sweep, an approach that has didactic advantages, even though it may leave out important details and can lead to superficiality if not properly handled. The point is that anyone interested in offering a considered, not pedestrian, opinion on the general nature of African cultures must make comparative investigations. This approach is certainly arduous, for it requires that one delve into many publications on the various cultural systems of Africa. Yet it is the approach most likely to yield a fruitful result.

A painstaking comparative study of African cultures leaves one in no doubt that despite the undoubted cultural diversity arising from Africa's ethnic pluralism, threads of underlying affinity do run through the beliefs, customs, value systems, and sociopolitical institutions and practices of the various African societies.

This kinship among the cultural systems of Africa has been noted by a number of scholars, mostly non-African. Edwin Smith, an anthropologist and missionary in Central Africa during the first half of this century, believed that "there is an underlying identity in religion throughout sub-Saharan African which allows one to talk legitimately of a unified *African* Religion."[6] Gelfand was impressed by the similarities of African belief in different parts of the continent.[7] Forde wrote [in] the introduction to his collection of essays on social values and cosmological ideas of several ethnic groups in Africa: "When these studies are considered *together* one is impressed not only by the great diversity of ritual forms, but also by *substantial underlying similarities* in religious outlook and moral injunction."[8] Later he spoke of "the religious ideas and social values which are *widespread* in Africa."[9] Elsewhere Forde asserted:

> Thus the linguistic distributions in West Africa suggest several important underlying features of cultural development . . . . Since . . . all the languages of West Africa appear to be ultimately derived from a common stock, one would expect to find *significant elements of a common early tradition in the cultures of all West African peoples.* Little systematic enquiry has so far been given to this question but there are many indications that underlying the great regional and tribal differences in the elaboration of cult and cosmological ideas *there is a very widespread substratum of basic ideas* that persists in the rituals, myths and folktales of West African peoples.[10]

In an introduction to a collection of studies on the political systems of different African peoples Fortes and Evans-Pritchard opined that "the societies described are representative of *common types* of African political systems" and that "most of the forms described are variants of a *pattern* of political organization found among contiguous or neighboring societies . . . we believe that all the major principles of African political organization are brought out in these essays."[11] Parrinder also observed that "there is much more kinship between the various peoples in Africa than might appear at first sight."[12] Hilda Kuper's view was that "the piling up of ethnographic detail produces an impression of chaos where there is in fact only variation on a few themes. . . . African tribal societies are relatively undifferentiated and homogenous."[13] Recently the eminent Ghanaian sociologist K. A. Busia observed that "from such studies as have already been done on the religious beliefs and rites of different communities, it is possible to discern *common* religious ideas and assumptions about the universe held *throughout* Africa, and which provide a world-view that may be described as African."[14] Earlier Busia had written: "I am not aware of an agreed Christian view of nature, but I submit that there is an *African* one which is that nature has power which may be reverted as well as used for man's benefit."[15] Taylor observed that there is in Africa, south of the Sahara, "a basic world view which fundamentally is everywhere the same."[16] And according to Idowu,

> There is a *common Africanness* about the total culture and religious beliefs and practices of Africa. This common factor may be due either to the fact of diffusion or to the fact that most Africans share common origins with regard to race and customs and religious practices . . . ; with regard to the concept of God, there is a *common* thread, however tenuous in places, running throughout the continent.[17]

Such views regarding the common features of the cultural systems of Africa justify, in my opinion, the assertion that ethnic pluralism does *not* necessarily or invariably produce absolute verticalism with respect to cultures, allowing no room for shoulder-rubbing of any kind, but producing windowless monads of cultural systems.

There are several ways in which the cultural system of the various African societies may be said to be related. First, a number of Africa's ethnic groups are so small, and consequently their cultures have been so greatly influenced by those of neighboring large groups that they may now be said to a great extent to share the culture of the large groups. A foremost scholar of Akan culture, J. H. Kwabena Nketiah, said of the Akans: "Not only is their language the most widely spoken throughout the country but also their culture has influenced those of several ethnic groups within the borders of Ghana."[18] According to Kenneth Little, "The Mende . . . form the larger cultural group in Sierra Leone, and their culture is shared to a considerable extent by peoples living in a wide region around them."[19] The cultural influence of the Yoruba on the Fon of Dahomey has likewise been noted.[20] Second, it is a common feature of the cultural landscape of Africa that a seemingly distinct ethnic group may in fact turn out to be a subdivision or component of a larger ethnic group. In Ghana, for instance, the Nzema and the Ashanti are regarded by non-Ghanaian writers as separate ethnic entities, whereas in fact both of them are parts of the Akans, sharing common cultural experiences with other component Akan groups such as the Fantes, Akwamus, Akwapims, Akims, and others. The Shilluk of the Upper Nile are culturally related to the Nuer and the Dinnka.[21] Third, there are ethnic groups in Africa that, following the arbitrary and unrealistic boundaries drawn a century ago by Africa's colonial masters, are found in two or more neighboring countries. Thus, there are Ewes in Ghana, Togo, and Dahomey (Benin); there are Akans in Ghana, Togo, and Ivory Coast; there are Yorubas in western Nigeria and Dahomey. The Bantu are spread over central, eastern, and southern Africa: The Abaluyia, for instance, are Bantu tribes of the Nyanza province of Kenya.[22] Writing on "An African Morality," Godfrey Wilson states: "The African people whose morality is here described are the Nyakusa of the Rungwe district of South Tanganyika; the same cultural group extends into Nyasaland under the name Ngonde."[23] "The Yoruba, Bini, and Dahomeans," wrote Fortes, "are closely related in culture . . . I have dwelt on their beliefs because they are characteristic of West Africa. . . ."[24]

A close look at the ethnic configuration of Africa shows a number of such dislocations or transplants resulting from the drawing of boundaries that placed peoples bound by ties of kinship, language, and culture in different states. As a result it is possible to see particular cultural patterns extending across states in Africa.

THE COMMUNITY OF CULTURAL ELEMENTS AND IDEAS

I wish now to present, in a nutshell, the worldviews, sociopolitical ideas, values, and institutions that can with a high degree of certainty be said to pervade the cultural systems of different African peoples. What I have done is to extract the common or rather pervasive elements and ideas in the cultures of African peoples as may be found in as many of the existing publications as I have been able to look at. Such pervasive cultural elements and ideas are the elements which constitute the basis for constructing African philosophy (using "philosophy" in the singular). In some cases the attempt to bring out the philosophical implications of beliefs, ideas, attitudes, or practices has led to brief philosophical discussions; so that this section is not just a catalog of facts about African cultures. We may start, then, with the African metaphysic.

METAPHYSICS

Categories of Being in African Ontology

A critical examination of the scholarly literature[25] on traditional African religions shows that most African peoples do have a concept of God as the Supreme Being who created the whole universe out of nothing and who is the absolute ground of all being. Thus, Busia wrote: "The postulate of God is universal throughout Africa; it is a concept which is handed down as part of the culture."[26] After studying the concept of God held by nearly three hundred peoples in Africa, Mbiti concluded thus: "In all these societies, without a single exception, people have a notion of God as the Supreme Being."[27] The Supreme Being is held to be omnipotent, omniscient, and omnipresent. He is considered uncreated and eternal, attributes implying his transcendence. But transcendence is also implicit in African beliefs about God removing himself far from the world of humankind as a result of our misconduct. "It appears to be a widespread notion in Africa that at the beginning God and man lived together on earth and talked one to another; but that owing to misconduct of some sort on the part of man—or more frequently of a woman—God deserted the earth and went to live in the sky."[28] But God is also held by African peoples to be immanent in that He is "manifested in natural objects and phenomena, and they can turn to Him in acts of worship, at any place and any time."[29]

African ontology, however, is a pluralistic ontology that recognizes, besides the Supreme Being, other categories of being as well. These are the lesser spirits (variously referred to as spirits, deities, gods, nature gods, divinities), ancestors (that is, ancestral spirits), man, and the physical world of natural objects and phenomena. Mbiti observed: "Myriads of spirits are reported from every African people,"[30] and "the class of the spirits is an essential and integral part of African ontology."[31] The reality of the ancestral spirits is the basis of the so-called ancestor worship that has been considered by some as an important feature of African religion. Thus, Fortes wrote: "It has long been recognized that ancestor worship is a conspicuous feature of African religious systems."[32] And Parrinder observed: "Thus there is no doubt that ancestral spirits play a very large part in African thought; they are [so] prominent in the spiritual world."[33] The physical world is also considered real in African ontology.

Mbiti thought that in addition to these four entities in African ontology—namely, God, chi the Absolute Being, lesser spirits (consisting of superhuman beings and ancestral spirits), man, and, finally, the world of natural objects—"there seems to be a force, power or energy permeating the whole universe"[34] which, in his opinion, is to be added as a separate ontological category.[35] But although African ontology distinguishes four or five categories of being, yet it must not be supposed that these entities are on the same level of reality. For God, as the Supreme Being and the ground of all existence, must be categorically distinguished from the lesser spirits and the other beings that were his creations. The Supreme Being is held as the ultimate reality, which is inferable not only from the attributes ascribed to God,[36] but also from the religious attitude and behavior of African peoples, the majority of whose "prayers and invocations are addressed to God."[37] Moreover, in spontaneous religious outbursts references are made to the Supreme Being rather than to the lesser spirits.[38] The lesser spirits are thus on a lower level of reality. African ontology therefore is hierarchical,[39] with the Supreme Being at the apex and the world of natural objects and phenomena at the bottom.

African ontology appears to be essentially spiritualistic, although this does not imply a denial of the reality of the nonspiritual, empirical world. Conceptually, a distinction is made between the empirical and nonempirical (that is, spiritual) world. But this distinction is not projected onto the level of being, so that in terms of being both worlds are regarded as real. Thus, McVeigh stated: "Both the world of the seen and the unseen are realities."[40] And Mbiti observed that in African conceptions "the physical and spiritual are but two dimensions of one and the same universe."[41] Reality in African thought appears to be homogeneous. Thus, just as African ontology is neither wholly pluralistic nor wholly monistic but possesses attributes of both, so it is neither idealistic—maintaining that what is real is only spirit, nor materialistic (naturalistic)—maintaining that what is real is only matter, but possesses attributes of both.

Causation

African ontological structure constitutes the conceptual framework for explaining the notion of causality. Implicit in the hierarchical character of that structure is that a higher entity has the power to control a lower entity. Since man and the physical world are the lower entities of that hierarchy, occurrences in the physical world are causally explained by reference to supernatural powers, which are held to be the real or ultimate sources of action and change in the world. Wrote Mbiti:

> African peoples . . . feel and believe that all the various ills, misfortunes, accidents, tragedies . . . which they encounter or experience, are caused by the use of (this)

mystical power. . . . It is here that we may understand, for example, that a bereaved mother whose child has died from malaria will not be satisfied with the scientific explanation. . . . She will wish to know why the mosquito stung her child and not somebody else's child. . . . Everything is caused by someone directly or through the use of mystical power.[42]

Elsewhere Mbiti wrote that "for many millions of African people" such phenomena, as the eclipse of the sun, "do not just happen without mystical, mythological, or spiritual causes. It is not enough for them to ask *why* or *how* this causes them to happen. In traditional life the *who questions and answers* are more important and meaningful than the *how questions and answers*."[43] McVeigh made reference to "the African concern with the deeper 'why' questions,"[44] and "the African tendency to seek immediately mystical answers."[45] In a book that deals specifically with eastern and southern African peoples, Monica Wilson referred to the dogmas regarding mystical power as "the explanation of good and evil fortune, the answer to 'Why did it happen to me?' "[46] She observed that in Africa scientific answers are regarded as incomplete, for science "cannot answer the question the Mpondo or Nyakyusa is primarily concerned with when his child dies: 'Why did it happen to me?' 'Who caused it?' "[47]

The evidence, then, is that causation is generally explained in terms of spirit, of mystical power. Scientific or empirical explanations, of which they are aware, are considered not profound enough to offer complete satisfaction. The notion of chance is the alternative to the African proclivity to the "why" and the "who" questions when the answers to the "how" and "what" questions are deemed unsatisfactory. But the Africans' conception of an orderly universe and their concern for ultimate causes lead them to reject the notion of chance. Consequently, in African causal explanations the notion or chance does not have a significant place.[48]

Concept of the Person

"Every culture produces a dogma of human personality, that is to say, an accepted formulation of the physical and psychical constitution of man." So wrote the renowned British anthropologist Meyer Fortes.[49] African systems of thought indeed teem with elaborate dogmas of the nature of the human being. The African philosophy of the person is, in my view, rigidly dualistic: The person consists of body and soul. However, the common conception of the soul varies widely in its details. In some cases the soul is conceived as having three or even more parts, as, for example, among the people of Dahomey;[50] others, such as the Dogon,[51] the Rwanda,[52] the Nupe and Gwari of northern Nigeria,[53] and the Yoruba,[54] conceive it as bipartite. Still others, like the Mende and the Shilluk,[55] have simpler conceptions of the soul.

The soul is understood as the immaterial part of a person that survives after death. The African belief in the soul—and hence in the dualistic nature of the person—leads directly to their conception of an ancestral world inhabited by departed souls. Thus the logical relation between the belief in the soul and the belief in the ancestral world is one of dependence: The latter belief depends on the former. It is the immaterial, undying part of a person, namely, the soul, that continues to live in the world of the ancestral spirits. Thus, McVeigh was right when he wrote: ". . . it is impossible to deny that African thought affirms the survival of the human personality (that is, soul) after death."[56] For this reason, "the Christian missionary," in McVeigh's view, "does not go to Africa to inform the people that there is a spiritual world or that the personality survives the grave. Africans know this from their own experience."[57] The psychophysical conception of a person common to African thought systems and the commonly observable phenomena of psychophysical therapeutics practiced in all African communities presuppose a belief in psychophysical causal interaction.

Concept of Fate (Destiny)

As the absolute being and the ultimate ground of being in the African metaphysic, the Supreme Being constitutes the controlling principle in the world. This fact, together with others to be mentioned presently, is the basis of the belief in fate (or destiny) common in African thought systems. "Running through the African conception of God," observed McVeigh, "is a clear sense of fate or destiny."[58] Dickson also noted that "The concept of Destiny is quite widespread in Africa; certainly the literature on West Africa suggests that many of its people have some ideas which may be put down under the heading of Destiny."[59] Writing on the African ideas about the works of God, Mbiti said: "God not only continues to create physically, but He also *ordains the destiny* of His creatures, especially that of man."[60] Fortes, however, thought that the concept of fate is held only in the religions of West African people: "Indeed one of the characteristic marks of West African religions, as compared with other African religions (for example: East and South African Bantu religions) in which ancestor worship also plays a part, is the occurrence of the notion of Fate in them."[61] It is not true, however, that eastern and southern African religions lack the notion of fate. Mbiti, for instance, noted that "Similar notions of predestination are found among peoples like the Ila, Tswana, Bacongo, Barundi, Yao and others."[62] (These are peoples in eastern and southern Africa.)

The concept of fate must be implicit, in my view, in systems of thought, like the African, which postulate a creator who not only fashioned man and the world but also established the order of the world in which man lives. It makes sense logically to assume that if human beings were fashioned, then they were fashioned in such a way that would determine a number of things about them. This assumption therefore must have been a basis for the African belief in fate. Further, the repudiation of the notion of chance in African thought would seem to lead to the idea of fate. Thus, some other assumptions in African thought involve a general belief in fate.

What is not clear is whether fate is self-determined, that is, chosen or decided upon by the individual soul or divinely imposed. Some African peoples think that destiny is chosen by the individual whereas others think that it is conferred by the Supreme Being. Among the Yoruba the manner in which the destiny comes to the individual is ambiguously conceived: In one way the individual "*chooses* his destiny"; in another he "*receives* his destiny," that is, from Olodumare (God): in yet another way "his destiny is *affixed* to him."[63] In the conceptions of the Rwandas, the Fon of Dahomey, the Lele of Kasai (southwestern Congo Kinshasa), and others, God decides the destiny of the individual.[64] However, whatever the source of the individual's destiny, the fact remains . . . that the individual enters the world with a predetermined destiny. The concept of fate in African thought appears to be quite complex and, like other concepts, stands in need of thorough analysis and explication.

The Problem of Evil

Busia . . . claimed that the African concept of deity does not generate the problem of evil, for the sources of evil in the world are the lesser spirits and other supernatural forces.

This is to say, God is not the source of evil. Mbiti asserted that "many [African] societies say categorically that God did not create what is evil, nor does He do any evil whatsoever . . . . In nearly all African societies, it is thought that spirits are either the origin of evil, or agents of evil."[65] A few African peoples hold, however, that in the words of McVeigh, God is "the explanation for what is good and evil in man's life."[66] Among such peoples are the Shilluk, Dinka, Nupe, Bacongo, and Vashona. The assumption of God as the source of evil in the world stems from the conception of God as the first principle and the ultimate ground of explanation for all existence. This of course raises the problem of evil, since God is also considered in African thought to be good[67] and omnipotent.

Most African peoples, however, deny that God is the source of evil. Does their view succeed in eliminating the problem of evil, as Busia and others claimed? Maquet, writing about the Rwanda, said: "The century-old problem of evil in the world, particularly acute where there is a belief in the existence of a being who is omnipotent and infinitely good, has been solved by putting the responsibility for all evil and all suffering on agents other than *Imana*. . . . *Imana* (God) himself does not cause any evil but he allows the causes of evil to act."[68] These agents or causes of evil, according to Maquet, are the "malevolent agencies of the invisible world,"[69] that is, evil spirits. Maquet is surely mistaken in maintaining that the fact that evil is traceable to evil spirits eliminates the problem of evil. . . . Thus even if it is the lesser spirits and not God which are held as the sources of evil, evil still remains a genuine problem for African philosophy and theology.

•   •   •

CONCLUSION: THE LEGITIMACY OF TALKING OF AFRICAN PHILOSOPHY

The main purpose of [this article] is to point out one thing: namely, that it is legitimate and intelligible to talk of "African philosophy," the basis of which is the common or pervasive features in African cultural and thought systems. I do not claim that the features of the African life and thought I have presented are peculiarly African, for they are in fact found in non-African traditional settings as well. But this observation is harmless in itself, and does not detract from the need to explore ideas from the African perspective. African philosophical systems will not be unique. The important thing is to see how the ideas of being, causation, the nature of a person, destiny, evil, morality, the nature of human society and social relationships, etc., are comprehended and analyzed by African thinkers on the basis of African cultural and intellectual experience. African perspectives on these ideas may be similar to those of others; nevertheless, they are worth examining within the African conceptual crucible. After all, the fact that Indians, Chinese, and Japanese have concepts of communalism or destiny, for instance, does not mean that those concepts are necessarily the same as those of African thinkers.

I have already argued that a given culture forms the basis of a philosophy and creates the controlling and organizing categories and principles for philosophizing. For me, then, a philosophical discourse that critically interacts or communes with African cultural and intellectual experiences, with African mentalities and traditions, will be African. That thesis does not have to be accepted by all Africans in order for it to be African, nor does it have to be generalized for all Africans. *It only needs to be the results of the reflective exertions of an African thinker, aimed at giving analytical attention to the intellectual foundations of African culture and experience. That is all.* When modern African philosophers discuss ideas produced by African traditional thinkers, or when they philosophize with the contemporary African situation in mind, diverse, even incompatible, analyses will undoubtedly emerge. Yet they will all come under the umbrella of African philosophy. So that even though what will emerge as African philosophy will in reality be a philosophical mosaic, this fact will not detract from the Africanness of those philosophies. They will, after all, be the product of the "African mind," just as Western culture—Western mind—constitutes the ground for Western philosophy, which also consists of numerous philosophies. There is indeed no single philosophical idea or doctrine shared or adhered to by all European or Westerners; yet such an idea or doctrine does not, on that account, cease to be European or Western. As noted recently by a Western philosopher, "There is no such thing as contemporary philosophy, of course, at least if this is construed as some sum total of commonly held tenets of the day. There are contemporary *philosophies, philosophies as numerous, one sometimes thinks, as philosophers.*"[70] But it must be noted that despite the numerousness of these philosophies (produced by Western philosophers), they all come, nevertheless, under the umbrella of Western philosophy. The reason for this is that they are all grounded in the Western cultural experience. . . .

I conclude, then, by saying that modern African philosophers should turn their philosophical gaze on the *intellectual foundations of African culture and experience* (in addition to contributions to Western philosophy, which some of them are in a hurry to pursue). It is never too late in human history to start from where one should start (or should have started). As part of the people of Africa and speaking their language—which fact is essential for investigating the philosophy of a people—modern African philosophers are in a unique position to elucidate, analyze, and interpret the philosophy of African peoples and to sharpen its contours on the global philosophical map.

NOTES

1. In *Second Order*, Vol. IV, No. 1, January 1975, p. 86.
2. John S. Mbiti, *African Religions and Philosophy*, p. 2; my italics (New York: Doubleday, 1970).
3. Ibid.
4. Ibid.
5. Ibid., p. 271.
6. Malcolm J. McVeigh, *God in Africa*, p. 5; also p. 142.
7. Michael Gelfand, *An African's Religion: The Spirit of Nyajena* (Capetown: Juta, 1966), pp. 110–17.
8. Daryll Forde (ed.), *African Worlds* (Oxford: Oxford University Press, 1954), p. x; my italics.
9. Ibid., p. xiii; my italics.
10. Daryll Forde, "The Cultural Map of West Africa," in Simon Ottenberg and Phoebe Ottenberg (eds.), *Cultures and Societies of Africa* (New York: Random House, 1960), p. 123; my italics.
11. M. Fortes and E. E. Evans-Pritchard (eds.), *African Political Systems* (Oxford: Oxford University Press, 1940), p. 1.
12. E. G. Parrinder, *African Traditional Religion* (New York: Harper & Row, 1962), p. 11.
13. Quoted in Parrinder, p. 11.
14. K. A. Busia, *Africa in Search of Democracy*, p. 4; my italics.
15. K. A. Busia, "The African World-View," p. 149; my italics.
16. John V. Taylor, *The Primal Vision* (London: SCM Press, 1963), p. 27.
17. E. Bolaji Idowu, *African Traditional Religion: A Definition* (London: SCM Press, 1973), p. 103.
18. J. H. Kwabena Nketiah, "Traditional Festivals in Ghana," in *Sankofa* (Accra), Vol. 1, 1977, p. 14.
19. Kenneth L. Little, *The Mende of Sierra Leone* (London: Routledge and Kegan Paul, 1967), p. 7.

20. Forde (ed.), *African Worlds*, p. 210.

21. Ibid., pp. 138, 140.

22. Ibid., p. 27, n. 1.

23. Godfrey Wilson, "An African Morality," in Ottenberg and Ottenberg (eds.), *Cultures and Societies*, p. 346; my italics.

24. M. Fortes, *Oedipus and Job in West African Religion* (Cambridge: Cambridge University Press, 1959), pp. 24–5; my italics.

25. Bibliographical citations will necessarily be limited by lack of space.

26. Busia, *Africa in Search of Democracy*, p. 5.

27. Mbiti, p. 37; also McVeigh, p. 16; Parrinder, pp. 32ff.

28. Edwin Smith (ed.), *African Ideas of God: A Symposium* (London: Edinburgh House Press, 1950), p. 7.

29. Mbiti, p. 43.

30. Ibid., p. 102; also Parrinder, pp. 23, 43ff; McVeigh, pp. 32ff; Forde (ed.), *African Worlds;* Monica Wilson, *Religion and the Transformation of Society* (Cambridge: Cambridge University Press, 1971), pp. 26–7.

31. Mbiti, p. 105.

32. M. Fortes, "Some Reflections on Ancestor Worship in Africa," in M. Fortes and G. Dieterlen (eds.), *African Systems of Thought* (Oxford: Oxford University Press, 1965), p. 122; also McVeigh, p. 34; Mbiti, p. 107ff.

33. Parrinder, p. 57. African scholars, however, argue that "ancestor worship" is a misnomer. Idowu, for instance, wrote that "ancestor worship" was not worship but only a veneration. . . . Idowu, *African Traditional Religion.* . . .

34. Mbiti, p. 21.

35. Ibid., p. 257.

36. Ibid., pp. 37–49.

37. Ibid., p. 80.

38. Ibid., pp. 55, 84–86

39. McVeigh, p. 139.

40. Ibid., p. 103.

41. Mbiti, p. 74; also p. 97.

42. Ibid., pp. 261–2; also p. 222. See also Forde (ed.), *African Worlds*, pp. 8, 173; Robin Horton in Bryan R. Wilson, *Rationality* (Oxford: Basil Blackwell, 1974), p. 133.

43. John S. Mbiti, "The Capture of the Sun," in *Modern Science and Moral Values* (New York: International Cultural Foundation, 1983), p. 191; my italics.

44. McVeigh, p. 164.

45. Ibid., p. 230, n. 57.

46. Monica Wilson, p. 38.

47. Ibid., p. 141.

48. Forde (ed.), *African Worlds*, p. 168; McVeigh, p. 163; Mbiti, p. 262; J. O. Sodipo, "Notes on the Concept of Cause and Chance in Yoruba Traditional Thought," *Second Order*, Vol. II, No. 2, July 1973.

49. M. Fortes, "Some Reflections," p. 126.

50. Forde (ed.), *African Worlds*, p. 227.

51. Marcel Griaule, "The Idea of Person among the Dogon," in Ottenberg and Ottenberg (eds.), *Cultures and Societies*, p. 366.

52. Forde (ed.), *African Worlds*, p. 174.

53. Ottenberg and Ottenberg (eds.), *Cultures and Societies*, p. 408.

54. E. Bolaji Idowu, *Olodumare*, pp. 169–70.

55. Forde (ed.), *African Worlds*, pp. 115, 155.

56. McVeigh, p. 26.

57. Ibid., p. 37.

58. Ibid., p. 130; also p. 144.

59. Kwesi A. Dickson, *Aspects of Religion and Life in Africa*, p. 3.

60. Mbiti, p. 52; my italics.

61. Fortes, *Oedipus and Job*, p. 19.

62. Mbiti, p. 52; also Forde (ed.), *African Worlds*, pp. 168ff.

63. Idowu, *Olodumare*, p. 173; italics in original.

64. Forde (ed.), *African Worlds*, pp. 9, 169, 228.

65. Mbiti, pp. 226–67; also Forde (ed.), *African Worlds*, pp. 43, 75.

66. McVeigh, 128–9; also Forde (ed.), *African Worlds*, pp. 160–1.

67. Mbiti, p. 47; Forde (ed.), *African Worlds*, p. 169.

68. J. J. Maquet, "The Kingdom of Ruanda," in Forde (ed.), *African Worlds*, p. 172.

69. Ibid., p. 169.

70. Ralph M. McInerny, *Thomism in an Age of Renewal* (Notre Dame: University of Notre Dame Press, 1968), p. 17; my italics.

Ptah-hotep

(FIFTH DYNASTY, 2450–2300 B.C., Kemet)

Moral Teachings

Let not your heart be puffed-up because of thy knowledge; be not confident because thou art a wise man. Take counsel with the ignorant as well as the wise. The full limits of skill cannot be attained, and there is no skilled man equipped to his full advantage. Good speech is more hidden than the emerald, but it may be found with maidservants as the grindstones.

If thou art a leader commanding the affairs of the multitude, seek out for thyself every beneficial deed, until it may be that thy own affairs are without wrong. Justice is great, and its appropriateness is lasting; it has not been disturbed since the time of him who made it, whereas there is punishment for him who passes over its laws. It is the right path before him who knows nothing. Wrongdoing had never brought its undertaking into port. It may be that it is fraud that gains riches, but the strength of justice is that it lasts, and a man may say: "It is the property of my father."

If thou art one of those sitting at the table of one greater than thyself, take what he may give, when it is set before thy nose. Thou shouldst gaze at what is before thee. Do not pierce him with many stares, for such an aggression against him is an abomination to the *ka*. Let thy face be cast down until he addresses thee, and thou shouldst speak only when he addresses thee. Laugh after he laughs, and it will be very pleasing to his heart and what thou mayest do will be pleasing to the heart. No one can know what is in the heart.

As for the great man when he is at meals, his purposes conform to the dictates of his *ka*. He will give to the one whom he favors. The great man gives to *the man whom he can reach*, but it is the *ka* that lengthens out his arms. The eating of bread is under the planning of god—it is only a fool who would *complain of* it.

If thou art a man of intimacy, whom one great man sends to another, be thoroughly reliable when he sends thee. Carry out the errand for him as he has spoken. Do not be reserved about what is said to thee, and beware of any act of forgetfulness. Grasp hold of truth, and do not exceed it. *Mere gratification is by no means to be repeated.* Struggle against making words worse, thus *making* one great man *hostile* to another *through vulgar speech*. A great man, a little man—it is the *ka*'s abomination.

If thou art a poor fellow, following a man of distinction, one of good standing with the god, know thou not his former insignificance. Thou shouldst not be puffed-up against him because of what thou didst know of him formerly. Show regard for him in conformance with what has accrued to him—property does not come of itself. It is their law for him who wishes them. *As for him who oversteps, he is feared.* It is god who makes a man's quality, and he defends him even while he is asleep.

If thou art one to whom petition is made, be calm as thou listenest to the petitioner's speech. Do not rebuff him before he has swept out his body or before he has said that for which he came. A petitioner likes attention to his words better than the fulfilling of that for which he came. He is rejoicing thereat more than any other petitioner, even before that which has been heard has come to pass. As for him who plays the rebuffer of a petitioner, men say: "Now why is he doing it?" It is not *necessary* that everything about which he has petitioned *should* come to pass, but a good hearing is a soothing of the heart.

If thou desirest to make friendship last in a home to which thou hast access as a master, as a brother, or as a friend, into any place where thou mightest enter, beware of approaching the women. It does not go well with the place where that is done. *The face has no alertness by splitting it.* A thousand men *may be distracted from* their own advantage. One is made a fool by limbs of fayence, as she stands there, become all carnelian. A mere trifle, the likeness of a dream—and one attains death through knowing her. Do not do it—it is really an abomination—and thou shalt be free from sickness of heart every day. As for him who escapes from gluttony for it, all affairs will prosper with him.

Do not be covetous at a division. Do not be greedy, unless it be for thy own portion. Do not be covetous against thy own kindred. Greater is the respect for the mild than for the strong. He is a mean person who *exposes* his kinsfolk; he is empty of *the fruits of conversation.* It is only a little of that for which one is covetous that turns a calm man into a contentious man.

If thou art a man of standing, thou shouldst found thy household and love thy wife at home as is fitting. Fill her belly; clothe her back. Ointment is the prescription for her body. Make her heart glad as long as thou livest. She is a profitable field for her lord. Thou shouldst not contend with her at law, and keep her far from gaining control. Her eye is her stormwind. Let her heart be soothed through what may accrue to thee; it means keeping her long in thy house.

If thou art now important after thy former unimportance, so that thou mayest do thing after a neediness formerly in the town which thou knowest, in contrast to what was thy lot before, do not be miserly with thy wealth, which has accrued to thee as the gift of god. Thou art not behind some other equal of thine to whom the same has happened.

If a son accepts what his father says, no project of his miscarries. He whom thou instructest as thy obedient son, who will stand well in the heart of the official, his speech is guided with respect to what has been said to him, one regarded as obedient. But the *induction* of him who does not hearken miscarries. The wise man rises early in the morning to establish himself, but the fool rises early in the morning only to *agitate* himself.

Sinuhe

(TWELFTH DYNASTY, 1990–1785 B.C., Kemet)

My Victory over Circumstances

THE HEREDITARY PRINCE AND COUNT, Judge and District Overseer of the domains of the Sovereign in the Lands of the Asiatics, real acquaintance of the king, his beloved, the Attendant Sinuhe. He says:

I was an attendant who followed his lord, a servant of the royal harem and of the Hereditary Princess, the great of favor, the wife of King Sen-Usert in the pyramid town Khenem-sut, the daughter of King Amen-em-het in the pyramid town Qa-nefru, Nefru, the lady of reverence.

YEAR 30, THIRD MONTH OF THE FIRST SEASON, DAY 7. The god ascended to his horizon; the King of Upper and Lower Egypt: Sehetep-ib-Re was taken up to heaven and united with the sun disc. The body of the god merged with him who made him. The Residence City was in silence, hearts were in mourning, the Great Double Doors were sealed shut. The courtiers sat head on lap, and the people were in grief.

Now his majesty had sent an army to the land of the Temeh-Libyans, with his eldest son as the commander thereof, the good god Sen-Usert, and even now he was returning and had carried off living captives of the Tehenu-Libyans and all kinds of cattle without number.

The courtiers of the palace [were] sent to the western border to let the King's Son know the events which had taken place at the court. The messengers met him on the road, and they reached him in the evening time. He did not delay a moment; the falcon flew away with his attendants, without letting his army know it. Now the royal children who had been following him in his army had been sent for, and one of them was summoned. While I was standing nearby I heard his voice as he was speaking and I was a little way off. My heart was distraught, my arms spread out in dismay, trembling fell upon all my limbs. I removed myself *by leaps and bounds* to seek a hiding place for myself. I placed myself between two bushes, in order to *cut myself off from* the road and its *travel*.

I set out southward, but I did not plan to reach this Residence City, for I thought that there would be civil disorder, and I did not expect to live after him. I crossed Lake Ma'aty near Sycamore, and I came to Snefru Island. I spent the day there on the *edge* of the fields. I *came into the open* light, while it was *still* day, and I met a man standing near by. He stood in awe of me, for he was afraid. When the time of the evening meal came, I drew near to Ox-town. I crossed over in a barge without a rudder, by aid of the west wind. I passed by the east of the quarry above Mistress-of-the-Red-Mountain. I gave free road to my feet going northward, and I came up to the Wall-of-the-Ruler, made to oppose the Asiatics and to crush the Sand-Crossers. I took a crouching position in a bush, for fear lest the watchmen upon the wall where their day's duty was might see me.

I set out at evening time, and when day broke I reached Peten. I halted at the Island of Kem-wer. An attack of thirst overtook me. I was parched, and my throat was dusty. I said: "This is the taste of death!" But then I lifted up my heart and collected myself, for I had heard the sound of the lowing of cattle, and I spied Asiatics. The sheikh among them, who had been in Egypt, recognized me. Then he gave me water while he boiled milk for me. I went with him to his tribe. What they did for me was good.

One foreign country gave me to another. I set off for Byblos and aproached Qedem, and spent a year and a half there. Ammi-enshi—he was a ruler of Upper Retenu—took me and said to me: "Thou wilt do well with me, and thou wilt hear the speech of Egypt." He said this, for he knew my character, he had heard of my wisdom, and the people of Egypt who were there with him had borne witness for me. . . .

He set me at the head of this children. He married me to his eldest daughter. He let me choose for myself of his country, of the choicest of that which was with him on his frontier with another country. It was a good land, named Yaa. Figs were in it, and grapes. It had more wine than water. Plentiful was its honey, abundant its olives. Every kind of fruit was on its trees. Barley was there, and emmer. There was no limit to any kind of cattle. Moreover, great was that which accrued to me as a result of the love of me. He made me ruler of a tribe of the choicest of his country. Bread was made for me as daily fare, wine as daily provision, cooked meat and roast fowl, beside the wild beasts of the desert, for they hunted for me and laid before me, beside the catch of my own hounds. Many . . . were made for me, and milk in every kind of cooking.

I spent many years, and my children grew up to be strong men, each man as the restrainer of his own tribe. The messenger who went north or who went south to the Residence City stopped over with me, for I used to make everybody stop over. I gave water to the thirsty. I put him who had strayed back on the road. I rescued him who had been robbed. When the Asiatics became so bold as to oppose the rulers of foreign countries, I counseled their movements. This ruler of Retenu had me spend many years as commander of his army. Every foreign country against which I went forth, when I had made my attack on it, was driven away from its pasturage and its wells. I plundered its cattle, carried off its inhabitants, took away their food, and slew people in it by my strong arm, by my bow, by my movements, and by my successful plans. I found favor in his heart, he loved me, he recognized my valor, and he placed me at the head of his children, when he saw how my arms flourished.

A mighty man of Retenu came, that he might challenge me in my own camp. He was a hero without his peer, and he had repelled all of it. He said that he would fight me, he intended to despoil me, and he planned to plunder my cattle, on the advice of his tribe. That prince discussed it with me, and I said: "I do not know him. Certainly I am no confederate of his, so that I might move freely in his encampment. Is it the case that I have ever opened his *door* or overthrown his fences? Rather, it is hostility because he sees me carrying out thy commissions. I am really like a stray bull in the midst of another herd, and a bull of these cattle attacks him. . . ."

During the night I strung my bow and shot my arrows, I gave free play to my dagger, and polished by weapons. When day broke, Retenu was come. I had *whipped up* its tribes and collected the countries of a good half of it. It had thought only of his fight. Then he came to me as I was waiting, for I had placed myself near him. Every heart burned for me; women and men groaned. Every heart was sick for me. They said: "Is there another strong man who could fight against him?" Then *he took* his shield, his battle-axe, and his *armful of javelins. Now* after I had let his weapons issue forth, I made his arrows pass by me uselessly, one close to another. He charged me, and I shot him, my arrow sticking in his neck. He cried out and fell on his nose. I felled him with his own battle-axe and raised my cry of victory over his back, while every Asiatic roared. I gave praise to Montu, while his adherents were mourning for him. This ruler Ammi-enshi took me into his embrace. Then I carried off his goods and plundered his cattle. What he had planned to do to me I did to him. I took what was in his tent and stripped his encampment. I became great thereby, I became extensive in my wealth, I became abundant in my cattle.

Thus did god to show mercy to him upon whom he had *laid blame,* whom he had led astray to another country. But today his heart is assuaged. . . .

Now when the majesty of the King of Upper and Lower Egypt: Kheper-ka-Re, the justified, was told about this situation in which I was, then his majesty kept sending to me with presentations from the royal presence, that he might gladden the heart of this servant like the ruler of any foreign country. The royal children in his palace let me hear their commissions. . . .

Then they came for this servant. . . . I was permitted to spend a day in Yaa handing over my property to my children, my eldest son being responsible for my tribe. My tribe and all my property were in his charge: my serfs, all my cattle, my fruit, and every pleasant tree of mine.

Then this servant came southward. I halted at the "Ways of Heru." The commander there who was responsible for the patrol sent a message to the Residence to make it known. Then his majesty sent a capable overseer of peasants of the palace, with loaded ships in his train, carrying presentations from the royal presence FOR THE ASIATICS WHO HAD FOLLOWED ME, ESCORTING ME TO THE "WAYS OF HERU." I called each of them by his name. Every butler was busy at his duties. When I started and set sail, the kneading and straining of beer was carried on beside me, until I had reached the town of Lisht.

When day had broken, very early, they came and summoned me, ten men coming and ten men going to usher me to the palace. I put my brow to the ground between the sphinxes, while the royal children were waiting in a *recess* to meet me. The courtiers who usher into the audience hall set me on the way to the private chambers. I found his majesty upon the Great Throne in a *recess* of fine gold. When I was stretched out upon my belly, I knew not myself in his presence, although this god greeted me pleasantly. I was like a man caught in the dark: my soul departed, my body was powerless, my heart was not in my body, that I might know life from death.

THEN HIS MAJESTY SAID TO ONE OF THESE COURTIERS: "Lift him up. Let him speak to me." Then his majesty said: "Behold, thou art come. Thou hast trodden the foreign countries *and made a flight.* But now elderliness has attacked thee; thou hast reached old age. It is no small matter that thy corpse be properly buried; thou shouldst not be interred by bowmen. Do not, do not act thus any longer: for thou dost not speak when thy name is pronounced!" Yet I was afraid of respond, and I answered it with the answer of one afraid: "What is it that my lord says to me? I should answer it, but there is nothing that I can do: it is really the hand of a god. It is a terror that is in my belly like that which produced the fated flight. BEHOLD, I AM BEFORE THEE. THINE IS LIFE. MAY THY MAJESTY DO AS HE PLEASES."

THEREUPON the royal children WERE ushered in. Then his majesty said to the Queen: "Here is Sinuhe, come as a Bedu, *in the guise of* the Asiatics." She gave a very great cry, and the royal children clamored all together. Then they said to his majesty: "It is not really he, O Sovereign, my lord!" Then his majesty said: "It is really he!" Now when they had brought with them their bead-necklaces, their rattles, and their sistra, then they presented them to his majesty. ". . . Loose the horn of thy bow and relax thy arrow! Give breath to him that was stifled! Give us our goodly gift in this sheikh Si-Mehit, a bowman born in Egypt. He made a flight through fear of thee; he left the land through terror of thee. But the face of him who beholds thy face shall not *blench;* the eye which looks at thee shall not be afraid!"

Then his majesty said: "He shall not fear. He has no *title* to be in dread. He shall be a courtier among the nobles. He shall be put in the ranks of the courtiers. Proceed ye to the inner chambers of the *morning toilet,* in order to make his position."

So I went forth from the midst of the inner chambers, with the royal children giving me their hands. Thereafter we went to the Great Double Door. I was put into the house of a royal son, in which were splendid things. A cool room was in it, and images of the horizon. Costly things of the Treasury were in it. Clothing of royal linen, myrrh, and prime oil of the king and of the nobles whom he loves were in every room. Every butler was busy at his duties. Years were made to pass away from my body. I was *plucked,* and my hair was combed. A load of dirt was given to the desert, and my clothes to the Sand-Crossers. I was clad in fine linen and anointed with prime oil. I slept on a bed. I gave up the sand to them who are in it, and wood oil to him who is anointed with it. I was given a house *which had a garden,* which had been in the possession of a courtier. Many *craftsmen* built it, and all its woodwork was newly restored. Meals were brought to me from the palace three or four times a day, apart from that which the royal children gave, without ceasing a moment.

There was constructed for me a pyramid-tomb of stone in the midst of the pyramid-tombs. The stonemasons who hew a pyramid-tomb took over its ground-area. The outline-draftsmen designed in it; the chief sculptors carved in it; and the overseers of work who are in the necropolis made it their concern. Its necessary materials were made from all the outfittings which are placed at a tomb-shaft. Mortuary priests were given to me. There was made for me a necropolis garden, with fields in it *formerly extending* as far as the town, like that which is done for a chief courtier. My statue was overlaid with gold, and its skirt was of fine gold. It was his majesty who had it made. There is no poor man for whom the like has been done.

So I was under the favor of the king's presence until the day of mooring had come.

Amenemope

(NINETEENTH DYNASTY, 1305–1195 B.C., Kemet)

Instructions for Well-Being

PROLOGUE

Let us start with the teaching for life,
The instructions for well-being,
Every rule for relations with elders,
For conduct toward rulers;
To know how to answer one who speaks,
To know how to reply to one who sends a message.
So as to direct him on the paths of life,
To make him prosper upon earth;
To let his heart enter its shrine,
Steering clear of evil;
To save him from the mouth of strangers,
To let him be praised in the mouth of people.
Made by the overseer of fields, experienced in his office,
The offspring of a scribe of Egypt,
The overseer of grains who controls the measure,
Who sets the harvest-dues for his lord,
Who registers the islands of new land,
In the great name of his majesty,
Who records the markers on the borders of fields,
Who acts for the king in his listing of taxes,
Who makes the land-register of Egypt;
The scribe who determines the offerings for all the gods,
Who gives land-leases to the people,
The overseer of grains, provider of foods,
Who supplies the granary with grains,
The truly silent of This of Ta-wer,
The justified in Ipu,
Who owns a tomb on the west of Senu,
Who has a chapel at Abydos,
Amenemope, the son of Kanakht,
The justified of Ta-wer.

For his son, the youngest of his children,
The smallest of his family,
The devotee of Min-Kamutef,
The water-pourer of Wennofer,
Who places Heru on his father's throne,
Who guards him in his noble shrine,
The Guardian of the mother of god,
Inspector of the black cattle of the terrace of Min,
Who protects Min in his shrine:
Hor-em-maakher is his true name,
The child of a nobleman of Ipu,
The son of the sistrum-player of Shu and Tefnut,
And chief songstress of Heru, Tawosre.

CHAPTER 1

He says:
Give your ears, hear the sayings,
Give your heart to understand them;
It profits to put them in your heart,
Woe to him who neglects them!
Let them rest in the casket of your belly,
May they be bolted in your heart;
When there rises a whirlwind of words,
They'll be a mooring post for your tongue.
If you make your life with these in your heart,
You will find it a success;
You will find my words a storehouse for life,
Your being will prosper upon earth.

CHAPTER 2

Beware of robbing a wretch,
Of attacking a cripple;
Don't stretch out your hand to touch an old man,
Nor open your mouth to an elder.
Don't let yourself be sent on a mischievous errand,
Nor be friends with him who does it.
Don't raise an outcry against one who attacks you,
Nor answer him yourself.
He who does evil, the shore rejects him,
Its floodwater carries him away.
The northwind descends to end his hour,
It mingles with the thunderstorm.
The storm cloud is tall, the crocodiles are vicious,
You heated man, how are you now?
He cries out, his voice reaches heaven,
It is the Moon who declares his crime.

Steer, we will ferry the wicked,
We do not act like his kind;
Lift him up, give him your hand,
Leaven him in the hands of the god;
Fill his belly with bread of your own,
That he be sated and weep.
Another thing good in the heart of the god:
To pause before speaking.

CHAPTER 3

Don't start a quarrel with a hot-mouthed man,
Nor needle him with words.
Pause before a foe, bend before an attacker,
Sleep on it before speaking.
A storm that bursts like fire in straw,
Such is the heated man in his hour.
Withdraw from him, leave him alone,
The god knows how to answer him.
If you make your life with these words in your heart,
Your children will observe them.

CHAPTER 4

As for the heated man in the temple,
He is like a tree growing indoors;
A moment lasts its growth of shoots,
Its end comes about in the woodshed;
It is floated far from its place,
The flame is its burial shroud.
The truly silent, who keeps apart,
He is like a tree grown in a meadow.
It greens, it doubles its yield,
It stands in front of its lord.
Its fruit is sweet, its shade delightful,
Its end comes in the garden.

CHAPTER 5

Do not falsify the temple rations,
Do not grasp and you'll find profit.
Do not remove a servant of the god,
So as to do favors to another.
Do not say: "Today is like tomorrow,"
How will this end?

Comes tomorrow, today has vanished,
The deep has become the water's edge.
Crocodiles are bared, hippopotami stranded,
The fish crowded together.
Jackals are sated, birds are in feast,
The fishnets have been drained.
But all the silent in the temple,
They say: "Ra's blessing is great."
Cling to the silent, then you find life,
Your being will prosper upon on earth.

CHAPTER 6

Do not move the markers on the borders of fields,
Nor shift the position of the measuring-cord.
Do not be greedy for a cubit of land,
Nor encroach on the boundaries of a widow.
The trodden furrow worn down by time,
He who disguises it in the fields,
When he has snared it by false oaths,
He will be caught by the might of the Moon.
Recognize him who does this on earth:
He is an oppressor of the weak,
A foe bent on destroying your being,
The taking of life is in his eye.
His house is an enemy to the town,
His storage bins will be destroyed;
His wealth will be seized from his children's hands,
His possessions will be given to another.
Beware of destroying the borders of fields,
Lest a terror carry you away;
One pleases god with the might of the lord
When one discerns the borders of fields.
Desire your being to be sound,
Beware of the Lord of All;
Do not erase another's furrow,
It profits you to keep it sound.
Plow your fields and you'll find what you need,
You'll receive bread from your threshing-floor.
Better is a bushel given you by the god,
Than five thousand through wrongdoing.
They stay not a day in bin and barn,
They make no food for the beer jar;
A moment is their stay in the granary,
Comes morning they have vanished.
Better is poverty in the hand of the god,
Than wealth in the storehouse;
Better is bread with a happy heart
Than wealth with vexation.

CHAPTER 7

Do not set your heart on wealth,
There is no ignoring Fate and Destiny;
Do not let your heart go straying,
Every man comes to his hour.
Do not strain to seek increase,
What you have, let it suffice you.
If riches come to you by theft,
They will not stay the night with you.
Comes day they are not in your house,
Their place is seen but they're not there;
Earth opened its mouth, leveled them, swallowed them,
And made them sink into *dat.*
They made a hole as big as their size,
And sank into the netherworld;
They made themselves wings like geese,
And flew away to the sky.
Do not rejoice in wealth from theft,
Nor complain of being poor.
If the leading archer presses forward,
His company abandons him;
The boat of the greedy is left in the mud,
While the bark of the silent sails with the wind.
You shall pray to the Aten when he rises,
Saying: "Grant me well-being and health";
He will give you your needs for this life,
And you will be safe from fear.

CHAPTER 8

Set your goodness before people,
Then you are greeted by all;
One welcomes the Uraeus,
One spits upon Apopis.
Guard your tongue from harmful speech,
Then you will be loved by others.
You will find your place in the house of god,
You will share in the offerings of your lord.
When you're revered and your coffin conceals you,
You will be safe from the power of god.
Do not shout "crime" against a man,
When the cause of his flight is hidden.
Whether you hear something good or evil,
Do it outside where it is not heard.
Put the good remark on your tongue,
While the bad is concealed in your belly.

CHAPTER 9

Do not befriend the heated man,
Nor approach him for conversation.
Keep your tongue from answering your superior,
And take care not to insult him.
Let him not cast his speech to catch you,
Nor give free rein to your answer.
Converse with a man of your own measure,
And take care not to offend him.
Swift is the speech of one who is angered,
More than wind over water.
He tears down, he builds up with his tongue,
When he makes his hurtful speech.
He gives an answer worthy of a beating,
For its weight is harm.
He hauls freight like all the world,
But his load is falsehood.
He is the ferryman of snaring words,
He goes and comes with quarrels.
When he eats and drinks inside,
His answer is heard outside.
They say he is charged with his crime
Is misfortune for his children.
If only Khnum came to him,
The Potter to the heated man,
So as to knead the faulty heart.
He is like a young wolf in the farmyard,
He turns one eye against the other,
He causes brothers to quarrel.
He runs before every wind like clouds,
He dims the radiance of the sun;
He flips his tail like the crocodile's young,
He draws himself up so as to strike.
His lips are sweet, his tongue is bitter,
A fire burns in his belly.
Don't leap to join such a one,
Lest a terror carry you away.

CHAPTER 10

Don't force yourself to greet the heated man,
For then you injure your own heart;
Do not say "greetings" to him falsely,
While there is terror in your belly.
Do not speak falsely to a man.
The god abhors it;

Do not sever your heart from your tongue,
That all your strivings may succeed.
You will be weighty before the others,
And secure in the hand of the god.
God hates the falsifier of words,
He greatly abhors the dissembler.

CHAPTER 11

Do not covet a poor man's goods,
Nor hunger for his bread;
A poor man's goods are a block in the throat,
It makes the gullet vomit.
He who makes gain by lying oaths,
His heart is misled by his belly;
Where there is fraud success is feeble,
The bad spoils the good.
You will be guilty before your superior,
And confused in your account;
Your please will be answered by a curse,
Your prostrations by a beating.
The big mouthful of bread—you swallow, you vomit it,
And you are emptied of your gain.
Observe the overseer of the poor,
When the stick attains him;
All his people are bound in chains,
And he is led to the executioner.
If you are released before your superior,
You are yet hateful to your subordinates;
Steer away from the poor man on the road,
Look at him and keep clear of his goods.

CHAPTER 12

Do not desire a noble's wealth,
Nor make free with a big mouthful of bread;
If he sets you to manage his property,
Shun his, and yours will prosper.
Do not converse with a heated man.
So as to befriend a hostile man.
If you are sent to transport straw,
Stay away from its container.
If a man is observed on a fraudulent errand,
He will not be sent on another occasion.

Philosophy and Morality

CHAPTER 13

Do not cheat a man through pen on scroll,
The god abhors it;
Do not bear witness with false words,
So as to brush aside a man by your tongue.
Do not assess a man who had nothing,
And thus falsify your pen.
If you find a large debt against a poor man,
Make it into three parts;
Forgive two, let one stand,
You will find it a path of life.
After sleep, when you wake in the morning,
You will find it as good news.
Better is praise with the love of men
Than wealth in the storehouse;
Better is bread with a happy heart
Than wealth with vexation.

CHAPTER 14

Do not recall yourself to a man,
Nor strain to seek his hand.
If he says to you: "Here is a gift.
No have-not will refuse it,"
Don't blink at him, nor bow your head,
Nor turn aside your gaze.
Salute him with your mouth, say, "Greetings,"
He will desist, and you succeed.
Do not rebuff him in his approach,
Another time he'll be taken away.

CHAPTER 15

Do the good and you will prosper,
Do not dip your pen to injure a man.
The finger of the scribe is the beak of the Ibis,
Beware of brushing it aside.
The Ape dwells in the House of Khnum,
His eye encircles the Two Lands;
When he sees one who cheats with his finger,
He carries his livelihood off in the flood.
The scribe who cheats with his finger,
His son will not be enrolled.
If you make your life with these words in your heart,
Your children will observe them.

Instructions for Well-Being

Chapter 16

Do not move the scales nor alter the weights,
Nor diminish the fractions of the measure;
Do not desire a measure of the fields,
Nor neglect those of the treasury.
The Ape sits by the balance,
His heart is in the plummet;
Where is a god as great as Thoth,
Who invented these things and made them?
Do not make for yourself deficient weights,
They are rich in grief through the might of god.
If you see someone who cheats,
Keep your distance from him.
Do not covet copper,
Disdain beautiful linen;
What good is one dressed in finery,
If he cheats before the god?
Faience disguised as gold,
Comes day, it turns to lead.

Chapter 17

Beware of disguising the measure,
So as to falsify its fractions;
Do not force it to overflow,
Nor let its belly be empty.
Measure according to its true size,
Your hand clearing exactly.
Do not make a bushel of twice its size,
For then you are headed for the abyss.
The bushel is the Eye of Ra,
It abhors him who trims;
A measurer who indulges in cheating,
His Eye seals the verdict against him.
Do not accept a farmer's dues
And then assess him so as to injure him;
Do not conspire with the measurer,
So as to defraud the share of the Residence.
Greater is the might of the threshing floor
Than an oath by the great throne.

Chapter 18

Do not lie down in fear of tomorrow:
"Comes day, how will tomorrow be?"

Man ignores how tomorrow will be;
God is ever in his perfection,
Man is ever in his failure.
The words men say are one thing,
The deeds of the god are another.
Do not say: "I have done no wrong,"
And then strain to seek a quarrel;
The wrong belongs to the god,
He seals the verdict with his finger.
There is no perfection before the god,
But there is failure before him;
If one strains to seek perfection,
In a moment he has marred it.
Keep firm your heart, steady your heart,
Do not steer with your tongue;
If a man's tongue is the boat's rudder,
The Lord of All is yet its pilot.

CHAPTER 19

Do not go to court before an official
In order to falsify your words;
Do not vacillate in your answers,
When your witnesses accuse.
Do not strain with oaths by your lord,
With speeches at the hearing;
Tell the truth before the official,
Lest he lay a hand on you.
If another day you come before him,
He will incline to all you say;
He will relate your speech to the Council of Thirty,
It will be observed on another occasion.

CHAPTER 20

Do not confound a man in the law court,
In order to brush aside one who is right.
Do not incline to the well-dressed man,
And rebuff the one in rags.
Don't accept the gift of a powerful man,
And deprive the weak for his sake.
Maat is a great gift of god,
He gives it to whom he wishes.
The might of him who resembles him,
It saves the poor from his tormentor.
Do not make for yourself false documents,

Instructions for Well-Being

They are a deadly provocation;
They mean the great restraining oath,
They mean a hearing by the herald.
Don't falsify the oracles in the scrolls,
And thus disturb the plans of god;
Don't use for yourself the might of god,
As if there were no Fate and Destiny.
Hand over property to its owners,
Thus do you seek life for yourself;
Don't raise your desire in their house,
Or your bones belong to the execution-block.

Chapter 21

Do not say: "Find me a strong superior,
For a man in your town has injured me";
Do not say: "Find me a protector,
For one who hates me has injured me."
Indeed you do not know the plans of god,
And should not weep for tomorrow;
Settle in the arms of the god,
Your silence will overthrow them.
The crocodile that makes no sound,
Dread of it is ancient.
Do not empty your belly to everyone,
And thus destroy respect of you;
Broadcast not your words to others,
Nor join with one who bares his heart.
Better is one whose speech is in his belly
Than he who tells it to cause harm.
One does not run to reach success,
One does not move to spoil it.

Chapter 22

Do not provoke your adversary,
So as to make him tell his thoughts;
Do not leap to come before him,
When you do not see his doings.
First gain insight from his answer,
Then keep still and you'll succeed.
Leave it to him to empty his belly,
Know how to sleep, he'll be found out.
Grasp his legs, do not harm him,
Be wary of him, do not ignore him.
Indeed you do not know the plans of god,

And should not weep for tomorrow;
Settle in the arms of the god,
Your silence will overthrow them.

CHAPTER 23

Do not eat in the presence of an official
And then set your mouth before him;
If you are sated pretend to chew,
Content yourself with your saliva.
Look at the bowl that is before you,
And let it serve your needs.
An official is great in his office,
As a well is rich in drawings of water.

CHAPTER 24

Do not listen to an official's reply indoors
In order to repeat it to another outside.
Do not let your word be carried outside,
Lest your heart be aggrieved.
The heart of man is a gift of god,
Beware of neglecting it.
The man at the side of an official,
His name should not be known.

CHAPTER 25

Do not laugh at a blind man,
Nor tease a dwarf,
Nor cause hardship for the lame.
Don't tease a man who is in the hand of the god,
Nor be angry with him for his failings.
Man is clay and straw,
The god is his builder.
He tears down, he builds up daily,
He makes a thousand poor by his will,
He makes a thousand men into chiefs,
When he is in his hour of life.
Happy is he who reaches the west,
When he is safe in the hand of the god.

CHAPTER 26

Do not sit down in the beer-house
In order to join one greater than you,

Instructions for Well-Being

Be he a youth great through his office,
Or be he an elder through birth.
Befriend a man of your own measure,
Ra is helpful from afar.
If you see one greater than you outdoors,
Walk behind him respectfully;
Give a hand to an elder sated with beer,
Respect him as his children would.
The arm is not hurt by being bared,
The back is not broken by bending it.
A man does not lose by speaking sweetly,
Nor does he gain if his speech bristles.
The pilot who sees from afar,
He will not wreck his boat.

CHAPTER 27

Do not revile one older than you,
He has seen Ra before you;
Let him not report you to the Aten at his rising,
Saying: "A youth has reviled an old man."
Very painful before Pre
Is a youth who reviles an elder.
Let him beat you while your hand is on your chest,
Let him revile you while you are silent;
If next day you come before him,
He will give you food in plenty.
A dog's food is from its master,
It barks to him who gives it.

CHAPTER 28

Do not pounce on a widow when you find her in the fields
And then fail to be patient with her reply.
Do not refuse your oil jar to a stranger,
Double it before your brothers.
God prefers him who honors the poor
To him who worships the wealthy.

CHAPTER 29

Do not prevent people from crossing the river,
If you stride freely in the ferry.
When you are given an oar in the midst of the deep,
Bend your arms and take it.

Philosophy and Morality

It is no crime before the god,
If the passenger is not passed up
Don't make yourself a ferry on the river
And then strain to seek its fare;
Take the fare from him who is wealthy,
And let pass him who is poor.

CHAPTER 30

Look to these thirty chapters,
They inform, they educate;
They are the foremost of all books,
They make the ignorant wise.
If they are read to the ignorant,
He is cleansed through them.
Be filled with them, put them in your heart,
And become a man who expounds them,
One who expounds as a teacher.
The scribe who is skilled in his office,
He is found worthy to be a courtier.

COLOPHON

That is its end.
Written by Senu, son of the divine father Pemu.

The Pharaoh's Speech at the Installation of Rekhmire as Prime Minister

Consider the office of vizier,
Check it out,
Consider, it is the pillar for the whole land.
Consider, being vizier,
Consider, it is not sweet,
Consider, it is bitter as gall.
Consider, he is the copper that shields the gold of his master's house,
Consider, he is not one who bends his face to magistrates and councillors,
Not one who makes of anyone his client.
Consider, what a man does in his master's house will be his happiness,
Consider, he shall not act in the house of another.

Consider, petitioners come from the South and the North,
The whole land is eager for the counsel of the vizier;
See to it that all is done according to law,
That all is done exactly right,
In giving a man his vindication.
Consider, the magistrate who judges in public,
Wind and water report all that he does,
Consider, there is none who ignores his deeds.
If he makes a mistake in deciding his case,
And fails to reveal it through the mouth of the clerk,
It will be known through the mouth of him whom he judged,
Through his telling it to the clerk by saying:
"This is not the decision of my case."
If the petitioner is sent,
Or a magistrate,
One will not ignore what he did.
Consider, the magistrate's safety is acting by the rule,
In acting on a petitioner's speech;
Then the judged cannot say:

"I was not given my right."
A proverb in the Book of Memphis says:
"Gracious king, lawful vizier."

Avoid what was said of the vizier Akhtoy,
That he denied his own people for the sake of others,
For fear of being falsely called partial.
If one of them appealed a judgment,
That he had made against him,
He persisted in denying him leniency,
But that is excess of justice.
Do not judge unfairly,
God abhors partiality;
This is an instruction,
Plan to act accordingly.
Regard one you know like one you don't know,
One near you like one far from you.
The magistrate who acts like this,
He will succeed here in this place.

Do not pass over a petitioner,
Before you have considered his speech.
When a petitioner is about to petition you,
Don't dismiss what he says as already said.
Deny him after you let him hear
On what account you have denied him.
Consider, it is said:
"A petitioner wants his plea considered
Rather than have his case adjudged."
Do not scold a man wrongfully,
Scold where scolding is due.
Cast your fear, that you be feared,
The feared magistrate is a magistrate.
A magistrate's worth is that he does right,
But if a man makes himself feared a million times,
People think something is wrong with him,
And they don't say of him, "He is a man."

This too is said:
A magistrate who lies comes out as he deserves.
You succeed in doing this office by doing justice,
Doing justice is what is wanted in the actions of the vizier,
Consider, the vizier is its true guardian since the time of God.
Consider, what one says of the vizier's chief scribe:
"Scribe of Justice" one says of him.
As to the hall in which you judge,
It has a room full of written decisions.

The Pharaoh's Speech at the Installation of Rekhmire as Prime Minister

He who does justice before all people,
He is the vizier.
Consider, a man remains in his office,
If he acts as he is charged.

The Doomed Prince

It is said, there once was a king to whom no son had been born. After a time his majesty begged a son for himself from the gods of his domain, and they decreed that one should be born to him. That night he slept with his wife and she became pregnant. When she had completed the months of childbearing, a son was born.

Then came the Hathors to determine a fate for him. They said: "He will die through the crocodile, or the snake, or the dog." When the people who were with the child heard it, they reported it to his majesty. Then his majesty's heart became very very sad. His majesty had a house of stone built for him upon the desert, supplied with people and with every good thing of the palace, and the child was not to go outdoors.

Now when the boy had grown, he went up to his roof, and he saw a greyhound following a man who was walking on the road. He said to his servant, who was beside him: "What is it that is walking behind the man who is coming along the road?" He told him: "It is a greyhound." The boy said to him: "Have one like it brought to me." Then the servant went and reported it to his majesty. His majesty said: "Bring him a little puppy, so that his heart will not grieve." So they brought him a greyhound.

Now when many days had passed and the boy was fully grown in all his body, he sent to his father saying: "To what purpose is my sitting here? I am committed to Fate. Let me go, that I may act according to my heart, until the god does what is in his heart." Then a chariot was harnessed for him, equipped with all sorts of weapons, and a servant was given him as an attendant. He was ferried over to the eastern shore and was told: "Go wherever you wish," and his greyhound was with him. He went northward across the desert, following his heart and living on the best of all the desert game.

He reached the Prince of Nahrin. Now the Prince of Nahrin had no children except one daughter. For her a house had been built whose window was seventy cubits away from the ground. He had sent for all the sons of all the princes of Khor and told them: "He who reaches the window of my daughter, his wife she shall be." Now when many days had passed and they were at their daily pursuit, the youth passed by them. Then they took the youth to their house. They washed him; they gave fodder to his team. They did everything for the youth. They anointed him; they bandaged his feet; they gave food to his attendant. And they said to him by way of conversation: "Whence have you come, you good youth?" He said to them: "I am the son of an officer of the land of Egypt. My mother died; my father took another wife, a stepmother. She came to hate me, and I went away, fleeing from her." Then they embraced him and kissed him on all his body.

Now when many days had passed, he said to the sons: "What is this you are doing here?" They said: "For three months now we are here passing the time in leaping. For he who reaches the window of the daughter of the Prince of Nahrin will get her as wife." He said to them: "If only my feet did not hurt, I would go leaping with you." They went leaping in their daily manner, while the youth stood at a distance watching, and the gaze of the daughter of the Prince of Nahrin was upon him.

Now when many days had passed, the youth came to leap with the sons of the princes. He leaped, he reached the window of the daughter of the Prince of Nahrin. She kissed him, she embraced him on all his body. One went to inform her father and told him: "One man has reached the window of your daughter." Then the Prince questioned him saying: "Which prince's son?" They said to him: "The son of an officer who came fleeing from Egypt, away from his stepmother." Thereupon the Prince of Nahrin became exceedingly angry. He said: "Am I to give my daughter to this fugitive from Egypt? Make him go away!"

They went and told him: "Go back where you came from!" But the daughter held him, and she swore by the god saying: "As Pre-Harakhti lives, if he is taken from me, I shall not eat, I shall not drink, I shall die right away!" The messenger went and reported to her father every word that she had said. And her father sent men to slay him on the spot. But the daughter said to them: "As Pre lives, if they slay him, when the sun sets I shall be dead. I will not live an hour longer than he!"

They went to tell it to her father. Then her father had the youth brought before him together with his daughter. And when the youth stood before him his dignity impressed the Prince. He embraced him, he kissed him on all his body; he said to him: "Tell me about yourself, for now you are my son." He said to him: "I am the son of an officer of the land of Egypt. My mother died; my father took another wife. She came to hate me; I left fleeing from her." Then he gave him his daughter as wife. He gave him a house and fields as well as cattle and all sorts of good things.

Now when many days had passed, the youth said to his wife: "I am given over to three fates: the crocodile, the snake, the dog." Then she said to him: "Have the dog that follows you killed." He said to her: "What foolishness! I will not let my dog be killed, whom I raised when it was a puppy." So she began to watch her husband very much and did not let him go out alone.

Now on the day on which the youth had left Egypt in his wandering, the crocodile, his fate had followed him. It came to be opposite him in the village in which the youth was, and it dwelled in the lake. But there was a demon in it. The demon did not let the crocodile come out; nor did the crocodile let the demon come out to stroll about. As soon as the sun rose they stood and fought each other every day for three months now.

And when more days had passed, the youth sat down to a feastday in his house. Then when night had come, the youth lay down on his bed, and sleep overwhelmed his body. Then his wife filled a bowl with wine and another bowl with beer. Thereupon a snake came out of its hole to bite the youth. But his wife was sitting beside him, not sleeping. She placed the bowls before the snake. It drank, it became drunk, it lay down on its back. Then the woman had it hacked to pieces with her axe. Then woke her husband. She said to him: "Look, your god has given one of your fates into your hand. He will protect you from the others also." Then he made an offering to Pre, praising him and extolling his might every day.

Now when many days has passed, the youth went out for a pleasure stroll on his estate. His wife did not go out with him, but his dog was following him. Then his dog began to speak saying: "I am your fate." Thereupon he ran before it. He reached the lake. He descended into the water in flight from the dog. Then the crocodile seized him and carried him off to where the demon was. But he was gone. The crocodile said to the youth: "I am your fate that has come after you. But for three months now I have been fighting with the demon. Now look, I shall release you. If my enemy returns to fight, you shall help me to kill the demon."

The Story of the Two Brothers

Now they say that once there were two brothers of one mother and one father. Anubis was the name of the elder, and Bata was the name of the younger. Now, as for Anubis, he had a house and had a wife, and his younger brother lived with him as a sort of minor. He was the one who made clothes for him and went to the fields driving his cattle. He was the one who did the plowing and who harvested for him. He was the one who did all kinds of work for him which are in the fields. Really, his younger brother was a good grown man. There was no one like him in the entire land. Why, the strength of a god was in him.

Now after many days after this, his younger brother was tending his cattle in his custom of every day, and he left off to go to his house every evening, loaded with all kinds of plants of the field, with milk, with wood, and with every good thing of the fields, and he laid them in front of his elder brother, who was sitting with his wife. And he drank and he ate, and *he went out to sleep* in his stable among his cattle *by himself.*

Now when it was dawn and a second day had come, he *prepared food,* which was cooked, and laid it before his elder brother. And he gave him bread for the fields. And he along after his cattle, and they would say to him: "The grass of such-and-such a place is good," and he would understand whatever they said and would take them to the place of good grass which they wanted. So the cattle which were before him became very, very fine. They doubled their calving very, very much.

Now at the time of plowing his elder brother said to him: "Get a yoke *of oxen* ready for us for plowing. Also come to the fields with seed, for we shall be busy with plowing in the morning." So he spoke to him. Then his younger brother did all the things which his elder brother had told him to do.

Now when it was dawn and a second day had come, they went to the fields with their seed, and they were busy with plowing, and their hearts were very, very pleased with their activity at the beginning of their work.

Now after many days after this, they were in the fields and ran short of seed. Then he sent his younger brother, saying: "Go and fetch us seed from the village." And his younger brother found the wife of his elder brother sitting and doing her hair. Then he said to her: "Get up and give me some seed, for my older brother is waiting for me. Don't delay!" Then she said to him: "Go and open the bin and take what you want! Don't make me leave my combing unfinished!" Then the lad went into his stable, and he took a big jar, for he wanted to carry off a lot of seed. So he loaded himself with barley and emmer and came out carrying them.

Then she said to him: "How much is it that is on your shoulder?" And he said to her: "Three sacks of emmer, two sacks of barley, five in all, is what is on my shoulder." So he spoke to her. Then she talked with him, saying: "There is great strength in you! Now I see your energies every day!" And she wanted to know him as one knows a man.

Then she stood up and took hold of him and said to him: "Come, let's spend an hour sleeping together! This will do you good, because I shall make fine clothes for you!" Then the lad became like a leopard with great rage at the wicked suggestion which she had made to him, and she was very, very much frightened. Then he argued with her, saying: "See here—you are like a mother to me, and your husband is like a father to me! Because—being older than I—he was the one who brought me up. What is this great crime which you have said to me? Don't say it to me again! And I won't tell it to a single person, nor will I let it out of my mouth to any man!" And he lifted up his load, and he went to the fields. Then he reached his elder brother, and they were busy with activity at their work.

Now at the time of evening, then his elder brother left off to go to his house. And his younger brother tended his cattle, and he loaded himself with everything of the fields, and he took his cattle in front of him, to let them sleep in their stable which was in the village.

But the wife of his elder brother was afraid because of the suggestion which she had made. Then she took fat and grease, and she became like one who has been criminally beaten, wanting to tell her husband: "It was your younger brother who did the beating!" And her husband left off in the evening, after his custom of every day, and he reached his house, and he found his wife lying down, terribly sick. She did not put water on his hands, after his custom, nor had she lit a light before him, and his house was in darkness, and she lay there vomiting. So her husband said to her: "Who has been talking with you?" Then she said to him: "Not one person has been talking with me except your younger brother. But when he came to take the seed to you he found me sitting alone, and he said to me: 'Come, let's spend an hour sleeping together! Put on your curls!' So he spoke to me. But I wouldn't listen to him: 'Aren't I your mother?—for your elder brother is like a father to you!' So I spoke to him. But he was afraid, and he beat me, so as not to let me tell you. Now, if you let him live, I'll kill myself! Look, when he comes *don't let him speak,* for, if I accuse him of this wicked suggestion, he will be ready to do it *tomorrow again!*"

Then his elder brother became like a leopard, and he made his lance sharp, and he put it in his hand. Then his elder brother stood behind the door of his stable to kill his younger brother when he came back in the evening to put his cattle in the stable.

Now when the sun was setting, he loaded himself with all plants of the fields, according to his custom of every day, and he came back. When the first cow came into the stable, she said to her herdsman: "Here's your elder brother waiting before you, carrying his lance to kill you! Run away from him!" Then he understood what his first cow had said. And another went in, and she said the same. So he looked under the door of his stable, and he saw the feet of his elder brother, as he was waiting behind the door, with his lance in his hand. So he laid his load on the ground, and he started to run away and escape. And his elder brother went after him, carrying his lance.

Then his younger brother prayed to the Re-Har-akhti, saying: "O my good lord, thou art he who judges the wicked from the just!" Thereupon the Ra heard all his pleas, and the Ra made a great body of water appear between him and his elder brother, and it was full of crocodiles. So one of them came to be on one side and the other on the other. And his elder brother struck his hand twice because of his not killing him. Then his younger brother called to him from the other side, saying: "Wait here until dawn. When the sun disc rises, I shall be judged with you in his presence, and he will turn the wicked over to the just, for I won't be with you ever *again;* I won't be in a place where you are—I shall go to the Valley of the Cedar!"

Now when it was dawn and a second day had come, the Re-Har-akhti arose, and one of them saw the other. Then the lad argued with his elder brother, saying: "What do you mean by coming after me to kill me falsely, when you wouldn't listen to what I had to say? Now I am still your younger brother, and you are like a father to me, and your wife is like a mother to me! Isn't it so? When I was sent to fetch us some seed, your wife said to me: 'Come, let's spend an hour sleeping together!' But, look, it is twisted for you into something else!" Then he let him know all that had happened to him and his wife. Then he swore to the Re-Har-akhti, saying: "As for your killing me falsely, you carried your lance on the word of a filthy whore!" And he took a reed-knife, and he cut off his phallus, and he threw it into the water. And the shad swallowed it. And he was faint and became weak. And his elder brother's heart was very, very sad, and he stood weeping aloud for him. He could not cross over to where his younger brother was because of the crocodiles. . . .

Then the younger brother went off to the Valley of the Cedar, and his elder brother went off to his house, with his hand laid upon his head, and he was smeared with dust. So he reached his house, and he killed his wife, and he threw her out to the dogs. And he sat in mourning for his younger brother.

Wen-Amon

(TWENTIETH DYNASTY, 1195–1080 B.C., Kemet)

My Journey to Asia

YEAR 5, 4TH MONTH OF THE 3RD SEASON, DAY 16: the day on which Wen-Amon, the Senior of the Forecourt of the House of Amon, Lord of the Thrones of the Two Lands, set out to fetch the woodwork for the great and august barque of Amon-Ra, King of the Gods, which is on the River and which is named: "User-het-Amon." On the day when I reached Tanis, the place where Ne-su-Ba-neb-Ded and Ta-net-Amon were, I gave them the letters of Amon-Ra, King of the Gods, and they had them read in their presence. And they said: "Yes, I will do as Amon-Ra, King of the Gods, our lord, has said!" I SPENT UP TO THE 4TH MONTH OF THE 3RD SEASON in Tanis. And Ne-su-Ba-neb-Ded and Ta-net-Amon sent me off with the ship captain Mengebet, and I embarked on the great Syrian sea IN THE 1ST MONTH OF THE 3RD SEASON, DAY 1.

I reached Dor, a town of the Tjeker, and Beder, its prince, had 50 loaves of bread, one jug of wine, and one leg of beef brought to me. And a man of my ship ran away and stole one vessel of gold, amounting to 5 deben, four jars of silver, amounting to 20 deben, and a sack of 11 deben of silver. Total of what he stole: 5 deben of gold and 31 deben of silver.

I got up in the morning, and I went to the place where the Prince was, and I said to him: "I have been robbed in your harbor. Now you are the prince of this land, and you are its investigator who should look for my silver. Now about this silver—it belongs to Amon-Ra, King of the Gods, the lord of the lands; it belongs to Ne-su-Ba-neb-Ded; it belongs to Heri-Hor, my lord, and the other great men of Egypt! It belongs to you; it belongs to Weret; it belongs to Mekmer; it belongs to Zakar-Baal, the Prince of Byblos!"

And he said to me: "Whether you are important or whether you are eminent—look here, I do not recognize this accusation which you have made to me! Suppose it had been a thief who belonged to my land who went on your boat and stole your silver, I should have repaid it to you from my treasury, until they had found this thief of yours—whoever he may be. Now about the thief who robbed you—he belongs to you! He belongs to your ship! Spend a few days here visiting me, so that I may look for him."

I spent nine days moored in his harbor, and I went to call on him, and I said to him: "Look, you have not found my silver. Just let me go with the ship captains and with those who go to sea!" But he said to me: "Be quiet!" I went out of Tyre at the break of dawn. I found 30 deben of silver in it, and I seized upon it. And I said to the Tjeker: "I have seized upon your silver, and it will stay with me until you find my silver or the thief who stole it! Even though you have not stolen, I shall take it." So they went away, and I enjoyed my triumph in a tent on the shore of the sea, in the harbor of Byblos. And I hid Amon-of-the-Road, and I put his property inside him.

And the Prince of Byblos sent to me, saying: "Get out of my harbor!" And I sent to him, saying: "Where should I go to? If you have a ship to carry me, have me taken to Egypt again!" So I spent twenty-nine days in his harbor, while he spent the time sending to me every day to say: "Get out of my harbor!"

Now while he was making offering to his gods, the god seized one of his youths and made him possessed. And he said to him: "Bring up the god! Bring the messenger who is carrying him! Amon is the one who sent him out! He is the one who made him come!" And while the possessed youth was having his frenzy on this night, I had already found a ship headed for Egypt and had loaded everything that I had into it. While I was watching for the darkness, thinking that when it descended I would load the god also, so that no other eye might see him, the harbor master came to me, saying: "Wait until morning—so says the Prince." So I said to him: "Aren't you the one who spends the time coming to me every day to say: 'Get out of my harbor'? Aren't you saying 'Wait' tonight in order to let the ship which I have found get away—and then you will come again to say: 'Go away!'?" So he went and told it to the Prince. And the Prince sent to the captain of the ship to say: "Wait until morning—so says the Prince!"

When morning came, he sent and brought me up, but the god stayed in the tent where he was, on the shore of the sea. And I found him sitting in his upper room, with his back turned to a window, so that the waves of the great Syrian sea broke against the back of his head.

So I said to him: "May Amon favor you!" But he said to me: "How long, up to today, since you came from the place where Amon is?" So I said to him: "Five months and one day up to now." And he said to me: "Well, you're truthful! Where is the letter of Amon which should be in your hand? Where is the dispatch of the High Priest of Amon which should be in your hand?" And I told him: "I gave them to Ne-su-Ba-neb-Ded and Ta-net-Amon." And he was very, very angry, and he said to me: "Now see—neither letters nor dispatches are in your hand! Where is the cedar ship which Ne-su-Ba-neb-Ded gave to you? Where is its Syrian crew? Didn't he turn you over to this foreign ship captain to have him kill you and throw you into the sea? Then with whom would they have looked for the god? And you too—with whom would they have looked for you too?" So he spoke to me.

But I said to him: "Wasn't it an Egyptian ship? Now it is Egyptian crews which sail under Ne-su-Ba-neb-Ded! He has no Syrian crews." And he said to me: "Aren't there twenty ships here in my harbor which are in commercial relations with Ne-su-Ba-neb-Ded? As to this Sidon, the other place which you have passed, aren't there fifty more ships there which are in commercial relations with Werket-El, and which are drawn up to his house?" And I was silent in this great time.

And he answered and said to me: "On what business have you come?" So I told him: "I have come after the woodwork for the great and august barque of Amon-Ra, King of the Gods. Your father did it, your grandfather did it, and you will do it too!" So I spoke to him. But he said to me: "To be sure, they did it! And if you give me something for doing it, I will do it! Why, when my people carried out this commission, Pharaoh—life, prosperity, health!—sent six ships loaded with Egyptian goods, and they unloaded them into their storehouses! You—what is it that you're bringing me—me also?" And he had the journal rolls of his fathers brought, and he had them read out in my presence, and they found a thousand deben of silver and all kinds of things in his scrolls.

So he said to me: "If the ruler of Egypt were the lord of mine, and I were his servant also, he would not have to send silver and gold, saying: 'Carry out the commission of Amon!' There would be no carrying of a royal-gift, such as they used to do for my father.

As for me—me also—I am not your servant! I am not the servant of him who sent you either! If I cry out to the Lebanon, the heavens open up, and the logs are here lying on the shore of the sea! Give me the sails which you have brought to carry your ships which would hold the logs for Egypt! Give me the ropes which you have brought to lash the cedar logs which I am to cut down to make you. See, Amon made thunder in the sky when he put Seth near him. Now when Amon founded all lands, in founding them he founded first the land of Egypt, from which you come; for craftsmanship came out of it, to reach the place where I am, and learning came out of it, to reach the place where I am. What are these silly trips which they have had you make?"

And I said to him: "That's not true! What I am on are no 'silly trips' at all! There is no ship upon the River which does not belong to Amon! The sea is his, and the Lebanon is his, of which you say: 'It is mine!' It forms the nursery for User-het-Amon, the lord of every ship! Why, he spoke—Amon-Ra, King of the Gods—and said to Heri-Hor, my master: 'Send me forth!' So he had me come, carrying this great god. But see, you have made this great god spend these twenty-nine days moored in your harbor, although you did not know it. Isn't he here? Isn't he the same as he was? You are stationed here to carry on the commerce of the Lebanon with Amon, its lord. As for your saying that the former kings sent silver and gold—suppose that they had life and health; then they would not have had such things sent! But they had such things sent to your fathers in place of life and health! Now as for Amon-Ra, King of the Gods—he is the lord of this life and health, and he was the lord of your fathers. They spent their lifetimes making offering to Amon. And you also—you are the servant of Amon! If you say to Amon: 'Yes, I will do it!' and you carry out his commission, you will live, you will be prosperous, you will be healthy, and you will be good to your entire land and your people! But don't wish for yourself anything belonging to Amon-Ra, King of the Gods. Why, a lion wants his own property! Have your secretary brought to me, so that I may send him to Ne-su-Ba-neb-Ded and Ta-net-Amon, the officers whom Amon put in the north of his land, and they will have all kinds of things sent. I shall send him to them to say: 'Let it be brought until I shall go back again to the south, and I shall then have every bit of the debt still due to you brought to you.' " So I spoke to him.

So he entrusted my letter to his messenger, and he loaded in the keel, the bow-post, the stern-post, along with four other hewn timbers—seven in all—and he had them taken to Egypt. And in the first month of the second season his messenger who had gone to Egypt came back to me in Syria. And Ne-su-Ba-neb-Ded and Ta-net-Amon sent: 4 jars and 1 kak-men of gold; 5 jars of silver; 10 pieces of clothing in royal linen; 10 kherd of good Upper Egyptian linen; 500 rolls of finished papyrus; 500 cowhides; 500 ropes; 20 sacks of lentils; and 30 baskets of fish. And she sent to me personally; 5 pieces of clothing in good Upper Egyptian linen; 5 kherd of good Upper Egyptian linen; 1 sack of lentils; and 5 baskets of fish.

And the Prince was glad, and he detailed three hundred men and three hundred cattle, and he put supervisors at their head, to have them cut down the timber. So they cut them down, and they spent the second season lying there.

In the third month of the third season they dragged them to the shore of the sea, and the Prince came out and stood by them. And he sent to me, saying: "Come!" Now when I presented myself near him, the shadow of his lotus-blossom fell upon me. And Pen-Amon, a butler who belonged to him, cut me off, saying: "The shadow of Pharaoh—life, prosperity, health!—your lord, has fallen on you!" But he was angry at him, saying: "Let him alone!"

So I presented myself near him, and he answered and said to me: "See, the commission which my fathers carried out formerly, I have carried it out also, even though you have not done for me what your fathers would have done for me, and you too should have done! See, the last of your woodwork has arrived and is lying here. Do as I wish, and come to load it in—for aren't they going to give it to you? Don't come to look at the terror of the sea! If you look at the terror of the sea, you will see my own too! Why, I have not done to you what was done to the messengers of Kha-em-Waset, when they spent seventeen years in this land—they died where they were!" And he said to his butler: "Take him and show him their tomb in which they are lying."

But I said to him: "Don't show it to me! As for Kha-em-Waset—they were men whom he sent to you as messengers, and he was a man himself. You do not have one of his messengers here in me, when you say: 'Go and see your companions!' Now, shouldn't you rejoice and have a stela made for yourself and say on it: 'Amon-Ra, King of the Gods, sent to me Amon-of-the-Road, his messenger—life, prosperity, health!—and Wen-Amon, his human messenger, after the woodwork for the great and august barque of Amon-Ra, King of the Gods. I cut it down. I loaded it in. I provided it with my ships and my crews. I caused them to reach Egypt, in order to ask fifty years of life from Amon for myself, over and above my fate.' And it shall come to pass that, after another time, a messenger may come from the land of Egypt who knows writing, and he may read your name on the stela. And you will receive water in the West, like the gods who are here!"

And he said to me: "This which you have said to me is a great testimony of words!" So I said to him: "As for the many things which you have said to me, if I reach the place where the High Priest of Amon is and he sees how you have carried out this commission, it is your carrying out of this commission which will draw out something for you."

And I went to the shore of the sea, to the place where the timber was lying, and I spied eleven ships belonging to the Tjeker coming in from the sea, in order to say: "Arrest him! Don't let a ship of his go to the land of Egypt!" Then I sat down and wept. And the letter scribe of the Prince came out to me, and he said to me: "What's the matter with you?" And I said to him: "Haven't you seen the birds go down to Egypt a second time? Look at them—how they travel to the cool pools! But how long shall I be left here! Now don't you see those who are coming again to arrest me?"

So he went and told it to the Prince. And the Prince began to weep because of the words which were said to him, for they were painful. And he sent out to me his letter scribe, and he brought to me two jugs of wine and one ram. And he sent to me Ta-net-Not, an Egyptian singer who was with him, saying: "Sing to him! Don't let his heart take on cares!" And he sent to me, to say: "Eat and drink! Don't let your heart take on cares, for tomorrow you shall hear whatever I have to say."

When morning came, he had his assembly summoned, and he stood in their midst, and he said to the Tjeker: "What have you come for?" And they said to him: "We have come after the blasted ships which you are sending to Egypt with our opponents!" But he said to them: "I cannot arrest the messenger of Amon inside my land. Let me send him away, and you go after him to arrest him."

So he loaded me in, and he sent me away from there at the harbor of the sea. And the wind cast me on the land of Alashiya. And they of the town came out against me to kill me, but I forced my way through them to the place where Heteb, the princess of the town, was. I met her as she was going out of one house of hers and going into another of hers.

So I greeted her, and I said to the people who were standing near her: "Isn't there one of you who understands Egyptian?" And one of them said: "I understand it." So I said to him: "Tell my lady that I have heard, as far away as Thebes, the place where Amon is, that injustice is done in every town but justice is done in the land of Alashiya. Yet injustice is done here every day!" And she said: "Why, what do you mean by saying it?" So I told her: "If the sea is stormy and the wind casts me on the land where you are, you should not let them take me in charge to kill me. For I am a messenger of Amon. Look here—as for me, they will search for me all the time! As to this crew of the Prince of Byblos which they are bent on killing, won't its lord find ten crews of yours, and he also kill them?"

So she had the people summoned, and they stood there. And she said to me: "Spend the night. . . ."

The Lion in Search of Man

There was a lion on the mountain who was mighty in strength and was good at hunting. The small game of the mountains knew fear of him and terror of him. One day it happened that he met a panther whose fur was stripped, whose skin was torn, who was half dead and half alive because of his wounds. The lion said: "How, did you get into this condition? Who scraped your fur and stripped your skin?" The panther said to him: "It was man." The lion said to him: "Man, what is that?" The panther said to him: "There is no one more cunning than man. May you not fall into the hand of man!" The lion became enraged against man. He ran away from the panther in order to search for man.

The lion encountered a team yoked so that one bit was in the mouth of the horse, the other bit in the mouth of the donkey. The lion said to them: "Who is he who has done this to you?" They said: "It is man, our master." He said to them: "Is man stronger than you?" They said: "Our lord, there is not one more cunning than man. May you not fall into the hand of man!" The lion became enraged against man; he ran away from them.

The same happened to him with an ox and a cow, whose horns were clipped, whose noses were pierced, and whose heads were roped. He questioned them; they told him the same.

The same happened with a bear whose claws had been removed and whose teeth had been pulled. He asked him, saying: "Is man stronger than you?" He said: "That is the truth. I had a servant who prepared my food. He said to me: 'Truly, your claws stick out from your flesh; you cannot pick up food with them. Your teeth protrude; they do not let the food reach your mouth. Release me, and I will cause you to pick up twice as much food!' When I released him, he removed my claws and my teeth. I have no food and no strength without them! He threw sand in my eyes and ran away from me." The lion became enraged against man. He ran away from the bear in order to search for man.

He met a lion who was tied to a tree of the desert, the trunk being closed over his paw, and he was very distressed because he could not run away. The lion said to him: "How did you get into this evil condition? Who is he who did this to you?" The lion said to him: "It is man! Beware, do not trust him! Man is bad. Do not fall into the hand of man! I had said to him: 'What work do you do?' He said to me: 'My work is giving old age. I can make for you an amulet, so that you will never die. Come, I will cut a tree for you and place it on your body as an amulet, so that you will never die.' I went with him. He came to this tree of the mountain, sawed it, and said to me: 'Stretch out your paw.' I put my paw between the trunk; he shut its mouth on it. When he had ascertained of me that my paw was fastened, so that I could not run after him, he threw sand into my eyes and ran away from me."

Then the lion laughed and said: "Man, if you should fall into my hand, I shall give you the pain that you inflicted on my companions on the mountain!"

Then, as the lion was walking in search of man, there strayed into his paw a little mouse, small in size, tiny in shape. When he was about to crush him, the mouse said to him: "Do not crush me, my lord the lion! If you eat me you will not be sated. If you release me you will not hunger for me either. If you give me my breath of life as a gift, I shall give you your own breath of life as a gift. If you spare me from your destruction, I shall make you escape from your misfortune." The lion laughed at the mouse and said: "What is it that you could do in fact? Is there anyone on earth who would attack me?" But he swore an oath before him, saying: "I shall make you escape from your misfortune on your bad day!" Now although the lion considered the words of the mouse as a joke, he reflected, "If I eat him I shall indeed not be sated," and he released him.

Now it happened that there was a hunter with a net who set traps and had dug a pit before the lion. The lion fell into the pit and fell into the hand of man. He was placed in the net, he was bound with dry leather straps, he was tied with raw straps. Now as he lay suffering on the mountain, in the seventh hour of the night, Fate wished to make his joke come true, because of the boastful words that the lion had spoken, and made the little mouse stand before the lion. He said to him: "Do you recognize me? I am the little mouse to whom you gave his breath of life as a gift. I have come in order to repay you for it today, and to rescue you from your misfortune, since you are suffering. It is beautiful to do good to him who does it in turn." Then the mouse set his mouth to the fetters of the lion. He cut the dry straps; he gnawed through all the raw straps with which he had been bound, and released the lion from his fetters. The mouse hid himself in his mane, and he went off with him to the mountain on that day.

Léopold Sédar Senghor
(b. 1906, Senegal)

African Socialism

Address Given to the American Society
of African Culture

Let us recapitulate Marx's positive contributions. They are: the philosophy of humanism, economic theory, dialectical method. To these we may add trade unionism, planning, and also federalism and cooperation, which come to us from the French idealistic socialists: Saint Simon, Proudhon, and Fourier, to name only the outstanding ones.

Thus, we are not *Communists*. Does this mean that we shall practice anti-communism? Certainly not. Anti-communism, the "witch hunt" can have but one result: increased tension between East and West and a continuation of the Cold War at the obvious risk of unleashing a third global conflict from which humanity would not recover.

We are not communists for a theoretical reason. Lenin's definition of matter proceeds from a one-sided concept, from a purely materialistic and deterministic postulate. At the beginning of *Anarchy and Socialism*, Stalin goes even further: "Marxism is not only a theory of socialism, it is a definitive view of the world, a philosophical system."

We are not communists for a practical reason. The anxiety for human dignity, the need for freedom—man's freedoms, the freedoms of collectivities—which animate Marx's thought and provide its revolutionary ferment—this anxiety and this need are unknown to communism whose major deviation is Stalinism. The "dictatorship of the proletariat," which was to be only temporary, becomes the dictatorship of the party and State by perpetuating itself. "The Soviet Union," said Mamadou Dia on his return from Moscow, "has succeeded in building socialism, but at the sacrifice of religion, of the soul."

The paradox of socialistic construction in communist countries in the Soviet Union, is that it increasingly resembles capitalistic construction in the United States of America, the American way of life, with high salaries, frigidaires, washing machines and television sets. And it has less art and freedom of thought. Nevertheless, we shall not be won over by a regime of liberal capitalism and free enterprise. We cannot close our eyes to segregation, although the Federal Government combats it; nor can we accept the elevation of material success to a way of life.

We stand for a middle course, for a *democratic socialism*, which goes so far as to integrate spiritual values, a socialism which ties in with the old ethical current of the French socialists. Historically and culturally we belong to this current. Besides, the French socialists— from Saint Simon to the Léon Blum of *A l'Echelle humaine*[1]—are not so utopian as they are reputed to be. In so far as they are idealists, they fulfill the requirements of the Negro

African soul, the requirements of men of all races and countries. *Man does not live by bread alone*—this is the title of a novel by Doudintsey a citizen of the Soviet Union, and the Russians read this book avidly. Khrushchev was not mistaken: "De-Stalinization was imposed by the people, by the thirst for freedom, the hunger for spiritual nourishment."

Concluding his report on the East German Republic (Communist Germany), Michel Bosquet writes: "But when I ask him (the head of a labor union) what the workers demand, he replies: 'Today they want TV sets and motorcycles. When they get them, they will demand a shorter work week. And then? . . . I can only answer for myself. What I would like, what I miss, is more good literature.' "[2] This fact is not unrelated to a phenomenon observed in America: the appeal of the contemplative life, as a reaction against the surrounding machinism. Among American Catholics, the proportion of priests to laity is one of the highest in the world.

This thirst for freedom, this hunger for spiritual nourishment, strengthened by the moral tradition of French socialism, explains why numerous French Marxists in recent years have shunned Stalinism and even communism: Henri Lefebvre, Pierre Fougeyrollas, and Edgar Morin, among others, who have stated their reasons lately in sorrowful but lucid volumes.[3] The major reason, common to all of them, is that the party has come to submerge the individual under the collectivity, the person under the class, to hide reality behind the screen of ideology. If we reflect about these cases, we shall discover that not only Marxism but Marx himself is "called to question"—except perhaps by Lefebvre. For, if the person is submerged, it is because Marx did not pay sufficient attention to the "natural determination," namely the *Nation,* that is not effaced by class.

Marx underestimated political and national idealism which, born in France upon the ruins of provincial fatherlands, with the Revolution of 1789, won over the world. "Justice," Marx writes, "humanity, liberty, equality, fraternity, independence . . . , these relatively moral categories which sound so nice, but which, in historical and political questions, prove absolutely nothing."[4] I repeat: *independence.* If the creator of scientific sociology returned to this earth, he would perceive with amazement that these "chimeras," as he called them, and above all the concept of *Nation,* are living realities in the xxth century.

What is left of the 1789 Revolution? A political doctrine and technique, accepted nowadays even by the devout. . . . From Marxism there will surely remain an economic doctrine and technique, inasmuch as they do not contradict the teachings of Christianity and Islam—far from it.

But a third revolution is taking place, as a reaction against capitalistic and communistic materialism, and which will integrate moral, if not religious values, with the political and economic contributions of the two great revolutions. In this revolution, the colored peoples, including the Negro African, must play their part; they must bring their contribution to the construction of the new monetary civilization. As Aimé Césaire says: "They will not come empty-handed to the rendezvous of give-and-take." Between the two world wars, Paul Morand observed: "The Negroes have rendered an enormous service to America. But for them, one might have thought that men could not live without a bank account and a bathtub. I am quoting from memory.

OUR NEED FOR A TRIPLE INVENTORY

We must build our own *Development Plan,* based on European, socialist contributions and also on the best of Negro African civilization. In so doing, we shall only be putting into practice the lesson of socialism. In his correspondence and even in *Capital*, Marx continued to insist on this fact: his theory is not an "Open sesame to historico-philosophical theory," and the conclusions of *Capital*, resulting from a study of the capitalist societies of Western Europe in the mid-nineteenth century, are valid only for that milieu and for that period. They were not even valid for Russia, as his letters to Mikhaloski and Vera Zassoulich indicate.

Before drawing up our Development Plan, we must therefore make an appraisal of our *situation*, using the dialectical method. We mean "of our present situation." On a three-fold level, we must name: (1) an inventory of our traditional civilization; (2) an inventory of the encounter that colonialism provoked between our traditional civilization and French civilization; and (3) an inventory of our economic resources, with our needs and our potentialities. Our Development Plan must not be solely an economic plan; it must be social in the broadest sense of the word: political, economic and social, *cultural* also. We insist on this last word.

African politicians have a tendency to neglect culture, to make it an appendage of politics. This is a mistake. These two areas, like the others, are certainly closely connected, reacting each on the other. But, if one stops to reflect, culture is at once the basis and the ultimate aim of politics. Remember the labor leader quoted a short while ago: "And then? ... What I should like, what I miss, is more good literature." He could have added: "Good theater, good painting, good music, etc." Culture is also basic in the socialist connotation of the word. It is "the sum of objects, ideas, symbols, beliefs, feelings, values and social forms which are transmitted from one generation to another in a given society."[5] We can accept this definition, although I usually call that "civilization," reserving the word "culture" for the spirit of civilization. Culture is the very texture of society.

Ethnologists—not to speak of archaeologists, geographers, historians, musicologists, and linguists—have been making an *inventory of Negro African* civilization since the start of the century. The French Institute of Black Africa (*Institut Français d'Afrique Noire*), the University of Dakar, and *Présence Africaine* are continuing this research. All of us should have in our libraries: *La Philosophie bantoue*, by Rev. Placide Tempels;[6] *Dieu d'eau*, by Marcel Griaule;[7] or simply, *Les Contes de l'Ouest african*, by Roland Colin.[8] From these volumes we would learn that Negro African philosophy, like socialist philosophy, is existentialist and humanistic, but that it integrates spiritual values. We would learn that, for the Negro African, the "vital forces" are the texture of a world animated by a dialectical movement. We would learn that Negro African society is collectivist or, more exactly, communal, because it is rather a *communion* of souls than an aggregate of individuals. We would learn that we had already realized *socialism* before the coming of the European. We would conclude that our duty is to renew it by helping it to regain spiritual dimensions.

The sociologists are now making an *inventory of the encounter of civilizations*. Much remains to be done in this field. The work of our African writers and artists is not negligible. They present syntheses, the elements of which must be analyzed. For we must attain a synthesis of civilizations, retaining only the fecund elements of each. The objective is a *dynamic symbiosis*, I mean a cultural blending which, like all blending or grafting, produces a more succulent fruit.

The *inventory of our economic resources* will not be the least important. At this point we must congratulate both the governments of the Federated States and the government of Mali for having thought of this. Senegal and Sudan have, in fact, created *study committees*, consisting of competent technicians, assigned to examine our various problems and to seek the best solutions. For institutional problems, a study committee whose conclusions have helped us to prepare our constitutions; a study committee for social problems, another on civil service reform, still another on economic problems.

With respect to the latter, it is essential that the plans for economic development be coordinated on the level of the Mali Federation. The prerequisite is that the preparation of plans for the Federated States be entrusted to the same technicians. Senegal has selected the team of Father Lebret. The Sudan would be well advised to examine the possibility of doing likewise. The mien of Father Lebret's group is that he belongs to the school of *Economics and Humanism*, and that he is motivated by an "open socialism" very similar to our own conception.

The Development Plan must be essentially economic and social. Nevertheless, it must be comprehensive, basing itself on the cultural inventory so as to flow into our political future. It is as a function of our objectives that the economic and social choices will be made. But it is as a function of our starting point—Negro African culture—that the socialistic contribution must be adapted to our realities.

We have spoken of the Mali Federation. Needless to say, our reflections and proposals are valid for all the States of what used to be called French West Africa, for all the French-speaking Negro African states. . . . If Mali succeeds, it will serve as an example and a magnet. Then we will be able to create a single federation which may extend—why not?—from Dakar to Brazzaville.

FOR A STRONG FEDERAL DEMOCRACY

Let us get on to the program proper. We remind you that it will be less a question of drawing up a complete and detailed program than of defining the probable course of our development, of posing the problems that confront us, and of indicating orientations. As of now, even before obtaining the results of the triple inventory, we have enough information to indicate orientations. This may facilitate the task of the researchers.

We shall begin by affirming the *primacy of politics*. Politics, one usually says, is "the art of governing the city." This is an orientation in the sense of a general option. *Man*, depicted in black on the flag of Mali, indicates our general option. This black man, our nearest neighbor, must be advanced in all respects and become, not only a consumer, but above all a *producer of culture*.

The Secretary General of our temporary committee, our comrade Modibo Keita [now President of the Mali Federation] declared in the projected statutes of the P.F.A. that our first aim is the institution of a *democracy*. Only democracy, that is to say the "government by the people and for the people," will allow the Negro African to realize himself. After all, democracy is the traditional form of Negro African societies.

Our democracy will be *federal*. . . . We do not need to remind you that local diversities with their complementary qualities, will enrich the Federation. Inversely, the Federation will preserve those diversities. The decentralized federal structure will be extended, within the framework of the Federal State, to regional and communal collectivities, even into economic and social areas. The *Yugoslavian* structures, adapted to our realities, will, in this instance, serve as a model.

Thus we shall fill the dangerous void now existing between the Federal State and the village. Our cadres are bored with their freedom from responsibility. Even when they fill this void by the political formation of militants, they tend to devote their activity to contention over slogans. Regional and communal assemblies, among others, would give them a practical opportunity to exercise their responsibilities. A revolution remains ideological, therefore ineffective, so long as it is not translated into concrete action which by transforming the structure, raises the standard of living and culture of the citizens. . . .

A federal democracy, yes, . . . but a strong democracy. As the Secretary General suggests in his report, it is a question of avoiding two dangers: on the one hand, fascist dictatorship, which one observes in the anti-federalist States; on the other hand, governmental instability, which was common in France during the Third and Fourth Republics. Both deviations are signs of weakness; in the long run, they provoke the revolt of the people and the disintegration of the State.

The Federation of Mali, like the Federated States, will be a democracy. The electoral law will continue to be impartial . . . not a law of circumstance, cut to the measure of the Government or the majority party. Freedom of opinion, speech, press, assembly, and association are guaranteed by the constitutions of Mali and the Federated States—in the anti-federalist States also. But, with us, these freedoms do not exist only on paper; they are effectively enjoyed and will continue to be so. Above all, the right of *free settlement* of the citizens will be assured, whether or not they be born in Mali. A democratic policy pays dividends; in addition it conforms to our humanitarian ideal. Already public opinion in Black Africa and France is grateful to us. This is excellent propaganda for Mali.

The rights of the minority, of the Opposition, will therefore be respected in Mali. They will find their natural and legal limits in the rights of the majority, the popular will, which is sovereign; in other words, in the rights of the nation-state. For we are a *quasi-nation,* as François Perroux says.[9]

The stability of the Executive is guaranteed by our constitutions. We need to assure it in actual political practice. It is necessary that governments govern, that they, along with the legislation assemblies, take the initiative of making laws within the framework of the doctrine and program of the majority party. Governments must apply the law firmly and legislative assemblies must check on the action of the government. It is necessary that the Party—Congress, executive committee, and board—have the final word in matters of control. Yet, to be effective, the various controls will be general and *a posteriori*. Meddling and harassing controls would not work. Here again, we shall avoid two dangers: granting government action a blank check, and taking away the executive power. The controls must be political, not technical.

Let us return to the rights of the Opposition. Their role, certainly, is to criticize. But *criticism* means critical spirit, not spirit of criticism, systematic carping. In a democracy, criticism must be constructive and serve the general, not factional, interest. At any rate, one cannot grant the Opposition more rights than the Majority enjoys. The law also applies to the Opposition, which is likewise required to observe it. Under the control of the majority party, the governments will take all necessary steps to curb demagogic opposition. They will not tolerate violations of the law, appeals to illegality or to violence, whether the pretexts be religious or racial. This is the democratic sense that we attach to the "dictatorship of the proletariat."

FOR RATIONAL, DYNAMIC PLANNING

We need not stress the well known fact that underdeveloped countries are entangled in a series of contradictions that must be resolved: contradictions between our sickly undernourishment and our need for productivity; between the low percentage of children enrolled in school and our need for cadres; in general, between our poverty and our retardation in all areas. Illness, ignorance, poverty—such is our lot, such the condition from which we must rescue our people. There can be no doubt that we underdeveloped countries are at the bottom of the scale in sickness and hunger, ignorance and poverty. In addition, our countries are underpopulated. If you are still unconvinced, we refer you to a volume by Father Lebret, *Suicide ou Survie de l'Occident*.[10] His statistics are taken from the most authentic sources: the publications of the United Nations. You will also be interested in reading a volume by Georges Balandier, *Le Tiers Monde*.[11]

Our task is enormous. To fulfill it, we must draw up a developmental plan; even before that, we must arouse our people's faith in their destiny and galvanize all their energy and enthusiasm. It is necessary that the *élites* understand their role and accept their responsibility. Those in privileged positions must be willing to make the heaviest sacrifices.

The *élites* are in the first place the *Students*. At twenty, one is enthusiastic and idealistic. That is good. One pounces upon books and studies furiously. That too is good. In the intelligence and generosity of our students, we have a precious leaven, admirable potentialities. These potentialities must be realized, must serve the common good. Our students must understand that to study is to assimilate; that the theories they study have been developed in Europe and for Europe; that, in order to serve, these theories must be confronted with Negro African realities and be applicable to those realities; that knowledge without experience is but empty smoke. As models, they may take the North African students, who have always trusted the political leaders of their respective countries. The North African students favored autonomy when their leaders were struggling for autonomy; they favored independence when, and only when, their leaders fought for independence. What counts is the unanimity of a people, rather than a particular doctrine, however excellent it may be.

Our *élites* also include the labor leaders. They became confused at the time of the Referendum.[12] It is time for them to recover; they have already begun to do so. Their role is not to replace the politicians but, over and above professional demands, to help the political leaders to carry out their program. An appreciable number of labor leaders, I refer to the U.G.T.A.N. (General Union Workers of Black Africa), call themselves "Marxists." Kautsky reminds them that the most grievous mistake they could make would be to destroy the unity of the labor movement for theoretical considerations. "A Marxist," he writes, "who would push an argument so far as to cause a split in a militant proletarian organization, would not be conforming to the doctrine of Marx, for whom every step forward in a real movement is more important than a dozen programs."[13] Moreover, Alioune Cissé[14] has frankly admitted that the labor unions cannot rightly oppose the majority of the people. This is the lesson to be learned from the Referendum.

Let us get to the heart of the problem. At its Constitution Congress in Cotonou (Dahomey), the U.G.T.A.N. abandoned the "class struggle" theory. This was a return to Negro African realities, from the clouds to *terra firma*. There are no classes in our society. But analysis reveals a certain tendency, a "real movement" toward the *formation of classes*. Paradoxically, some labor leaders include in the proletariat, the union membership as a whole, composed exclusively of government employees and salaried workers in private employ. Nevertheless, the annual income of an African government worker is about 360,000 francs C.F.A.; that of a salaried worker in private employment 180,000 francs; whereas that of a peasant in the former French West Africa is 10,000 francs. Therefore, the proletarian is not necessarily the one who claims that title.

When the unions, especially those of government employees, demand a raise in salary, the African governments, *in the light of present conditions,* can justifiably object on two counts. The first is that the salaries of these employees, when converted into metropolitan francs, are, on a given grade level, at least equal to those received by metropolitan employees. There is, however, a disparity if we consider wages paid in private employment. But the most important objection stems from a comparison between the respective standard of living of city dwellers—government employees, workers, and laborers—and of the peasants, who constitute more than 90% of the population. It could not serve the public interest to increase the disproportion between the living standards of the classes now in process of formation.

Our Negro African situation is not identical with the situation in France, where the salaried folk are struggling to snatch, from a bourgeois State, a larger share of the national income. In Africa, we and you are the State. At least the governments are composed of Africans and government employees in the overwhelming majority. It is against themselves that the labor unions, particularly the government employees, are struggling. This is an unnatural contradiction.

Does this mean that we should do nothing for the government workers? We are not saying that. What we are saying is that our economic and financial situation is not that of France; we have to disconnect. We have already disconnected. The living standard of our government employees should be higher than that of the peasants; but we cannot do less than to fix a relationship between the living levels of our quasi-classes. As the standard of living of the peasants rises, in the same proportion we would raise that of the government employees and of salaried workers in private employment. However, to raise the peasants' standard of living, it is indispensable that we invest productively in agriculture. This implies an increase in our budgets and, accordingly, a temporary freezing of salaries.

In France, government workers constitute 17% of the adult population and earn 25% of the budget. In Senegal, they constitute only 1% of the population, but earn 48% of the budget! These figures need no commentary. We believe that the government employees as well as the students will appreciate the dramatic situation facing our governments. To renounce productive investments would place us in a vicious circle and make us beg France to balance our budgets; this would in fact mean renunciation of all political autonomy. The government workers will understand their role in the building of the nation and will accept the sacrifices asked of them. The peasants are already enthusiastic. One has only to note their confidence in the party and in our governments. The labor unions must do even more. They must integrate themselves into the quasi-nation. The U.G.T.A.N., for example, must be converted into a general Union of the workers of Mali and establish its headquarters in Mali; later it will be free to enter a Confederation of the Workers of Black Africa.

This general enthusiasm must help the Federal State to build the nation but it must first help us to realize our *Development Plan.* This plan requires the investment of substantial sums that will come from three sources: (1) the budgets—those of Mali and the Federated States; (2) the *Community's Fund of Aid and Cooperation* (F.A.C.) along with the *European Fund;* and (3) *private capital.* We shall review these three sources.

The Budgets. We shall begin by aiding ourselves in the hope that heaven and others will then aid us. This is a matter of *dignity* and efficiency. It is not right for us to expect assistance from France without having first balanced our basic budget and begun to invest in our own resources. Beggars are never respected. Moreover, as you know, whoever supplies the money exercises political control over the use of the funds. One cannot hope for political autonomy, much less independence, without practicing economy. That is obvious. Admittedly, for populations like ours which increase by almost 3% each year, we would be required, in order to raise the living level by an annual 3%, to invest 20% of the national income. Since Mali has an income of about 140 billion francs (C.F.A.), we would have to invest 28 billions annually. We have nothing like that amount available. In any event, we must begin by investing 20% of our budgets, or six billions. Then we shall be able to find the rest more readily elsewhere.

The F.A.C. and *European Fund* represent the second source of investment. If we begin by making a collective effort; if, in addition, we prepare solid dossiers, there is every chance that we shall obtain satisfaction—in so far as our representatives on the Executive Council are careful to see that the credits are objectively shared, and remember the effort of austerity and budgetary severity incumbent upon each State in Black Africa. Our membership in the French Community must not create any inferiority complex whatsoever in us. Every community presents advantages and disadvantages—more advantages than disadvantages—rights and responsibilities. If we were independent, we would none the less turn to States more fortunate than ourselves: to European nations and to the U.S.A., probably to both. We would only be changing guardians—you see the disadvantages; at the worst, we could turn to everybody, thus bringing the Cold War ever closer to us. This would serve neither our interests nor peace.

The problem of *private capital* remains. We shall not scorn private capital; instead, we shall seek it, whether it comes from France or elsewhere, provided it does not alienate the rights of our quasi-nation. . . . There is a semblance of contradiction between our socialistic ideal and the aid we request of capital. Analysis reveals that the contradiction is only superficial; that it can, in any case, be resolved if indeed it really exists. We shall point out that "the accumulation of capital," its formation, is necessary for the development of every modern State. In this respect, there is no difference between a capitalist and a socialist State.

In addition, there can be no question of *nationalization* in an underdeveloped nation. Neither Guinea nor Ghana is nationalizing. They are right. This is because one has to find something to nationalize. Furthermore, to nationalize the meager capital at our disposal, would mean, even in the case of independence—and we are not yet independent— "killing the hen that lays the golden eggs," preventing other capital, urgently needed, from being invested. Economists note that, in order to nationalize, one must have the necessary cadres, which is not true in our case. Even under these conditions and in developed countries, nationalization does not always succeed. One final argument: the very fact that capitalists train and employ African personnel, reinvest part of their profits, and pay taxes, indicates that, for all practical purposes, capital is nationalized.

Does this mean that we shall adopt a policy of laissez-faire? No. The Development Plan has as its negative objective the prevention of a laissez-faire economy. Its positive aim is to organize production rationally. Our plan will include three sectors: a socialized sector— agriculture; a mixed sector: public utilities and societies with mixed economy; and a free sector. The latter—banks, commerce, industry—will itself be oriented toward the objectives of the Plan and, to a certain extent, controlled. How? By a long-term moratorium on taxes, accorded either to new investments or to enterprises that enter the framework of the Plan. In return, capital in this sector will be expected to accept social legislation and even to cooperate in building the social infrastructure: schools, dispensaries, housing, cooperatives.

The mixed sector will preferably comprise transports and energy—within the limits of our possibilities, of course. As for agriculture, we are fortunate that it has traditionally been socialistic, because of its communal nature in Negro African society. Once again, we say *communal* and not *collective* as one usually says. Our agricultural society was more than collective. It did not consist of an aggregate of individuals but was strongly structured, made up of family cooperatives in the framework of the village mutual. The basis of the latter was religious feeling, which gave its members a single soul, a high ideal of solidarity in which all communed. Our new mutuals and cooperatives, integrating all the peasants, will be similarly structured and *animated* by the same ideal.

Any why do we need capital? This is the final question that we must answer. We need it for productive investments. Only the development of production along with a more equitable distribution of the national income can make Mali a modern State; this is a *sine qua non* for the transformation of the quasi-nation into a Nation.

One is just beginning to realize that the most productive investment is the human investment. By that we do not mean the form now referred to as *forced labor*. We feel, incidentally, that we must someday—the sooner the better—employ in useful labor the soldiers excused from military service. In the rural communes, we shall even reach the point of having secondary roads built by the villages themselves. What we do have in mind here are such questions as the training of cadres, schooling, acculturation, and finally nutrition. The human investment will permit the national State to train citizens: cultivated men, properly fed, and trained in a trade or profession.

One frequently uses the expression "Africanization of cadres." One even abuses it. I shall not say "Malianization of cadres," for ours will not consist solely of persons from Mali. We fear that the problem is incorrectly phrased. If our educated élite were sufficiently numerous, the question would not need to be raised. But we lack professors, physicians, engineers, researchers, above all specialists in finance and economics. It is often difficult for us to recruit them even in France. Consequently, the problem is not political, it is technical, for it is a matter of *training African cadres*. This is not the same thing. Let us be careful not to substitute a political problem for a technical problem. That is a mistake often made by political leaders in underdeveloped countries. For a long time yet we shall need technicians from France. We must attract them, not discourage them by untimely words and gestures.

The University of Dakar offers us an Institute of Higher Administrative Studies and an Institute of Higher Economic and Commercial Studies, not to mention the Institute of Human Sciences. This is our good fortune. We can create other centers of apprenticeship and vocational training schools for workers and secondary cadres. And, above all, we have at our disposal the great scientific and technical schools of France, which rank among the best in the world. We shall also mention research institutes, for we need research workers. The development of production, linked with that of productivity, is directly dependent on the development of scientific research. All this to say that our students will be oriented in their studies. The role of the school is not to give courses in political philosophy, but rather to provide us with highly qualified technicians. The Federal Scholarship Commission of the former French West Africa too often tended to orient all our students toward the University. We shall react by directing them towards courses preparing for the competitive examination for admission to the *Grandes Ecoles*.[15]

This brings up the question of schools. Everyone agrees that elementary instruction should be developed. Then we shall have, for our secondary schools, for our universities, and *Grandes Ecoles*, a broader base from which to choose. It so happens that it would take our total budget to provide schools for our entire school-age population. In developed countries, the credits allocated to instruction represent 20% of the budget in the most

Philosophy and Morality

favorable cases. We can do no better. We hope to compensate for our meager means by raising the *quality* of instruction.

Whoever says quality, says Africanization of instruction, and this means *education.* On the elementary level, we shall adapt our textbooks to our social and cultural realities. It is unthinkable that our pupils should henceforth be ignorant of the history, geography, and art of Black Africa. Something has already been done in this direction; the effort must be carried through. It is a mistake to cultivate only our youngsters' reason and overlook their creative imagination. The race for the B.A. degree is sterile in France; it is *homicidal* in Africa. Even more, we must educate, outside of school, those who do not and those who do know how to read. We must accomplish this by folklore festivals, by political, trade union; and athletic manifestations, by the theater and motion pictures, but still more by conferences and cultural clubs. We take this opportunity to thank the Federal Minister of Education for his excellent initiative in creating a Service of Arts and Letters. It is a matter of acculturating, at the same time, French instruction and our traditional values to our situation.

Education, cultural and vocational training are forms of the human investment, though not the only ones. They require, from the outset, that man be properly fed. What a man eats is more important than how much he eats. Our populations suffer less from undernourishment than from malnutrition. They do not have a sufficient quantity of calories or animal proteins. In this connection, the documents of the United Nations show that the populations of West Africa are the most poorly nourished. These nutritional deficiencies, along with lack of hygiene, are the principal causes of so-called tropical endemic diseases, which are really "mass maladies."

Any plan that neglects the human investment will be doomed to failure. To produce, it is necessary to feed, teach, and train the producers. These facts will govern the distribution of funds, which must be devoted, in part, to the human investment, the development of the social infrastructure: schools, dispensaries, hospitals. Then the credits should be allocated to productive investments.

We shall insist on the credits intended for *agriculture,* mutuals and cooperatives, for the modernization of agricultural methods, cattle-raising, and fishing. Mao Tse-tung understood this and went beyond Marx's instructions in this area. The Russians made the mistake of neglecting the peasants and agriculture. Mao Tse-tung did not repeat this error: he leaned on the peasants; his revolution was primarily a peasant revolution. Even in advanced countries, to neglect agriculture for industry is to upset the balance and hamper the raising of the standard of living, not to mention the danger of arousing the peasantry which is, almost always, the most numerous class. Our countries are fundamentally agricultural. We do not merely risk creating disequilibrium to the disadvantage of agriculture. What we risk is developing industry at the expense of food. The case of Senegal is typical.

On the other hand, there is no developed country without industry. The creation of heavy industry does not concern us at the moment. We have no army to maintain and our aims must be governed by our means, which are limited. Moreover, we lack the requirements for heavy industry. We have no coal, no electricity, except in the form of potential which is low. Wisdom dictates that we should develop what we have: processing industries, the raw materials for which are found at home or nearby.

Agriculture, cattle-raising, fishing—in Mali we have the finest cattle and the most plentifully stocked fishing waters in West Africa—can be processing industries. These are the poles of development, this is the direction that our investments will take. Obviously, all of this must be carefully studied and then coordinated by the Mali authorities. Between

Senegal and the Sudan, overlapping and duplication, competition and bottlenecks will be avoided. One will not forget to investigate our potential in minerals. Only half of Senegal has been prospected; in the Sudan, nothing has been done in this respect. Nor shall we forget the development of the general infrastructure, harbors, airfields, roads. These are the pathways to development, to civilization.

CONCLUSION

Let us harvest our thoughts. The ultimate aim of the Party of African Federation is the construction of a *Negro African Nation* in West Africa, which would correspond to a Central African Nation. For *Nation* is the first reality of the xxth century. These nations will consist of the former French colonies in Black Africa. They will be inspired by the ideal of socialism, but it will be an "open socialism." Within this perspective, they will be groups in federal States. As their objective, these States will select the progress of Man by raising his standard of living and culture. The ways and means will be a strong democracy and a planned economy.

The second reality of the xxth century is the *interdependence* of races, continents, and nations. François Perroux illustrates this truth in a recent article on Guinea.[16] In it he notes that nominal independence is an advantage, but that it is not self-sufficient: that Guinea faces the task of constructing her real independence by taking into account the international structures of the economy in which she is placed; that she can neither disregard these structures nor break with her immediate historical past without danger; that, in view of these realities, a developmental plan cannot be prepared, much less fulfilled, in the narrow limits of a national territory. . . .

We speak of independence; we shall speak of it again. It would be neither honest nor effetive to talk of "immediate independence." General de Gaulle offered this to us on September 28, 1958. We did not take it. Let us have the logic and the courage of our convictions. We thought then, and we continue to think, with François Perroux, that "the real powers by which sovereignty is exercised are today for all nations, a function of effective alliances and coalitions."[17] We believed then, and we still believe that the Community—presented as a dynamic entity in the October 4th Constitution—is the ideal framework for an effective coalition, an association.

French technicians are in demand throughout the world. Whereas the great nations of Europe and America allot only 1% of their national income to aid underdeveloped countries, France allots 2%. Finally, the French people have always spoken up in favor of the emancipation of the colored peoples. It is they who have produced the most important and impressive anti-colonialist literature. Those are facts: and one cannot argue successfully against facts. Let us speak therefore of transforming the Community into a *multinational Confederation*.

We shall nevertheless be mindful of Guinea and the Arab Maghreb. They were linked with us during the old regime. They are our African neighbors. Their intellectuals were trained in French schools. Under the aegis of the French Community, we must reach economic or even cultural agreements with them, while waiting for the Community to evolve to the point where it allows us to forge political ties.

Nor do we intend to forget our African neighbors who speak English. But let us be frank: they should not ask us to leave the Community while they remain in the Commonwealth. Horizontal inter-African solidarity will gradually be established, by beginning at

Philosophy and Morality

the beginning with economic and cultural relations, while vertical solidarity between our-selves and our European metropoles will be modified but not dissolved. We shall obtain peace neither by race war nor by continental war.

Man remains our first consideration: he constitutes our *measure*. That is what the man represents on the flag of Mali, with his roots in the soil and his eye turned heavenward. I shall end by paraphrasing Dostoevski, the Russian. A nation that refuses to keep its rendez-vous with history, that does not believe itself to be the bearer of a unique message—that nation is finished, ready to be placed in a museum. The Negro African is not finished even before he gets started. Let him speak; above all let him act. Let him bring, like a leaven, his message to the world in order to help build a universal civilization.

Notes

1. Léon Blum (1872–1950), French socialist leader. *A l'Echelle humaine* (Paris, Gallimard, 1945) was written in 1941, while the author was in prison. (Translator's note).

2. *L'Express,* June 4, 1959; p. 24.

3. Cf. Lefebvre, *La Somme et le reste* (La Nef de Paris); Fougeyrollas, *Le Marxisme en question* (Ed. du Seuil); Morin, *Autocritique* (Julliard).

4. *Oeuvres posthumes* (Edition Mhring, quoted by André Vène, *op. cit.;* p. 345).

5. Nilakanta Sastri, "l'Avenir des cultures traditionnelles," *Chronique de l'UNESCO,* May 1959.

6. (Paris, Présence Africaine, 1949).

7. (Paris, Ed. du Chêne, 1948).

8. (Paris, Présence Africaine, 1957).

9. François Perroux, professor at the Collège de France, is one of the most distinguished French economists. (Translator's note).

10. (Paris, Les Editions ouvrières, 1958; 37-140).

11. (Paris, Presses Universitaires de France, 1956).

12. The Referendum of September 28, 1958, which allowed the overseas territories to decide, by voting *oui* or *non,* whether they wished to remain in the French Community. Guinea became independent by voting *non.* (Translator's note).

13. *Le Capital,* Introduction (Ed. A. Costes; I. LXI).

14. Alioune Cissé is a Senegalese labor leader, affiliated with the u.g.t.a.n. (Translator's note).

15. The *Grandes Ecoles* include such institutions as the Higher Normal School, Polytechnic Insti-tute, School of Public Works, etc. (Translator's note).

16. "Une Nation en voie de se faire: la République de Guinée," *Revue de l'Action populaire,* No. 129, June 1959; 683-705.

17. *Ibid.,* p. 704.

Kwame Nkrumah
(1909–1972, Ghana)

Consciencism

Practice without thought is blind; thought without practice is empty. The three segments of African society . . . , the traditional, the Western, and the Islamic, co-exist uneasily; the principles animating them are often in conflict with one another. . . . The principles which inform capitalism are in conflict with the socialist egalitarianism of the traditional African society.

What is to be done then? . . . The two other segments, in order to be rightly seen, must be accommodated only as experiences of the traditional African society. If we fail to do this our society will be racked by the most malignant schizophrenia.

Our attitude to the Western and the Islamic experience must be purposeful. It must also be guided by thought, for practice without thought is blind. What is called for as a first step is a body of connected thought which will determine the general nature of our action in unifying the society which we have inherited, this unification to take account, at all times, of the elevated ideals underlying the traditional African society. Social revolution must therefore have, standing firmly behind it, an intellectual revolution, a revolution in which our thinking and philosophy are directed towards the redemption of our society. Our philosophy must find its weapons in the environment and living conditions of the African people. It is from those conditions that the intellectual content of our philosophy must be created. The emancipation of the African continent is the emancipation of man. This requires two aims: first, the restitution of the egalitarianism of human society, and, second, the logistic mobilization of all our resources towards the attainment of that restitution.

The philosophy that must stand behind this social revolution is that which I have once referred to as philosophical consciencism; consciencism is the map in intellectual terms of the disposition of forces which will enable African society to digest the Western and the Islamic and the Euro-Christian elements in Africa, and develop them in such a way that they fit into the African personality. The African personality is itself defined by the cluster of humanist principles which underlie the traditional African society. Philosophical consciencism is that philosophical standpoint which, taking its start from the present content of the African conscience, indicates the way in which progress is forged out of the conflict in that conscience.

Its basis is in materialism. The minimum assertion of materialism is the absolute and independent existence of matter. Matter, however, is also a plenum of forces which are in antithesis to one another. The philosophical point of saying this is that matter is thus endowed with powers of self-motion.

Philosophy and Morality

Of course, there are diverse sorts of motion. Philosophers have accepted different kinds of phenomena as illustrating motion. There is the obvious case of change of place. If one object changes its position in relation to objects in a locality, it is said to move. Against this, it might be thought at first that the whole universe could revolve asymmetrically around an object, in which case it could in absolute terms be fancied that the object had not moved. If this happened it would be indistinguishable from the first situation in which the object itself changes its position relative to the rest of the universe; it does not signify a difference. And if these putative two states do not signify a difference, the latter cannot constitute an objection to the former.

The statement that an object moves is a significant one. And when two significant statements fail in the above way to indicate a difference they must signify the same thing. What I am enunciating here is quite other than the Verification Principle. The Verification Principle, as is well known, has two parts. In the first place, it asserts a proposition to be significant only if it is subject to empirical verification; and in the second place, it asserts that the meaning of a significant proposition is yielded by its method of verification. The principle which I am on the other hand anxious to defend states no condition for meaningfulness, but only establishes a sufficient condition for identity of meaning. The central idea is as follows: if there are two expressions such that precisely the same consequences follow from the conjunction of the first with any other proposition as follow from the conjunction of the second with the same proposition, then the two expressions are identical in meaning.

It will be seen that this Principle of Identity of Meaning is akin to Leibniz's Principle of Identity of Meaning and to Frege's Principle of Identity of Meaning. I have described one kind of motion which philosophers accept. They also distinguish rotary motion, which Plato illustrated with the movement of a top. There is however a third kind of motion, which consists in alteration of property. If properties can be distinguished from relations, it can be said that there are two broad categories of motion, such that one introduces a change in relation while the other introduces a change in property, seeing that linear as well as rotary motion involves change of relation. If there are these two kinds of motion, one resulting in a change of relation, the other in a change of property, then when it is said that matter has an original power of self-motion, neither kind is necessarily implied, nor are both together.

It is fashionable, in particular among philosophers who eschew dialectics, to say that matter is inert. What this means must be distinguished from what the inertia of matter means in Newton. Newton defined inertia axiomatically as, for example, in his first law of motion. According to this law, a body, except in so far as it is impressed upon by an external force, continues in its state of uniform motion in a straight line. The position of rest is easily accommodated as a limiting case of motion in a straight line. Now it is quite proper, instead of giving a direct definition of an introduced term, to elucidate its meaning by means of axioms. The axioms will in fact set out what one is to gather from the use of the introduced term. In the case of Newton's first law of motion, we see that here too a body's power of linear self-motion is denied. Indeed, Newton would also deny a body's power of rotary self-motion. To borrow a word invented by Whitehead, the inertia of matter corresponds to its pushiness.

When it is enquired what the philosophers mean by the inertness of matter, something different transpires. In reality the philosophers seek an intellectual parallel to physical motion, and deny this of matter. Hence, we find them harping incontinently on the "stupidity" of matter. They mean by this that matter is incapable of intellectual action, neither thinking, perceiving nor feeling. Of course, they are grateful for Newton's denial of the physical activity of matter. They take this up and increase it with a further denial of the intellectual activity of matter. Hence, when a philosopher says that matter is "stupid," he does not mean that it is slow-witted, but that it has no wit at all. In this denial of activity, both physical and mental, of matter, it is however not unusual for philosophers to contradict themselves. If one looks through Locke's magnum opus, *The Essay on Human Understanding*, one quickly comes upon such contradictions.

There Locke denies that matter is active, attributing all activity to spirit. Nevertheless, in his theory of perception, he says that corpuscles *travel* from a *perceived object* to our appropriate organ of sense in order that we should be able to perceive it. These corpuscles are said by him to be parts of the perceived object which detach themselves and subject us to a kind of radiative bombardment. Here, Locke patently contradicts himself. For this activity of matter is not said by him to be induced, but original, natural.

But even the theory of gravity, while it does explain the current motion of bodies (including rest), is properly silent over the question of antecedents. It does not face the question why bodies move at all, how it is that the heavenly bodies, for example, come to be moving, but only how they keep moving and why they keep moving as they do.

And yet, all those who conceive the universe in terms of an original super-atom which multiplied internal stresses to such a pitch as to burst asunder, thereby imply that matter has powers of self-motion, for they do not conceive this primordial building-up of internal stresses in terms of *externally* impressed forces.

Both the phenomenon of radiation and the wave mechanics of quantum theory indubitably presuppose that body has original powers of self-motion even in that sense which requires something other than change of property. If matter perpetrates a spontaneous emission, then to the extent that there is an emission of particles there is motion; to the extent that this emission is spontaneous, there is self-motion.

The classical philosophers have in fact been over-impressed by at least two considerations. The first is that we do not discern a direct phenomenon of radiation or corpuscular motion by any of our celebrated five senses. But we do see apples thrown to go up. And we observe feathers blown to make them air-borne. By contrast, even though we know of cases where humans and animals are pushed, we witness day after day the more overt and directly obtrusive phenomenon of spontaneous motion in living things. Our classical philosophers have then without much ado closed the dossier, pleasantly identifying the limits of their own knowledge with the limits of what can be.

Now, if one wishes to maintain the philosophical inertness of matter, one must ascribe the phenomenal self-motion of bodies to some non-material principle, usually a soul or a spirit. This soul or spirit may of course be said to inhere in matter or to be external to it. But even when it is said that there is a spirit or a soul in matter which is responsible for its spontaneous motion, it will not have been said that in *every* case of phenomenal spontaneous motion of a body there must be presumed a spirit concealed in the body, a ghost lurking in the machine. Hence the philosophical inertness of matter is not achieved by the mere postulate of spirit or soul. It is in fact made a defining characteristic of matter that it is philosophically inert.

In the postulate of a soul or spirit, vitalism and diverse forms of occultism could easily be provided sustenance and defence. But in this also, we find the second consideration which has over-impressed philosophers. This is the idea of intention. It was thought that spontaneous motion could only be deliberate or purposeful, subsuming the idea of intention in any case. Deliberateness, purpose, intention was at the same time exclusively attributed only to living things, and not even to all living things at that. Matter, in itself non-living, was therefore held to be incapable of deliberateness, purpose or intention. Spontaneity of any sort could not therefore be ascribed to it. This is in fact at the heart of philosophical inertness which is quaintly called "stupidity"!

In a way, it is not the philosophers of today but the natural scientists who are the successors of the ancient philosophers. Attentive to the phenomenon of radiation, that of spontaneous emission of particles of matter, and Newton's silence over the source of the original motion of bodies, one can, if an "inert" philosopher, embrace a thorough-going animism, and infuse non-living matter with a plethora of spirits, or one can correctly abandon the now groundless denial of the capacity of matter for self-motion.

Indeed, the philosophical ancestor of all Western philosophers, Thales, was stared in the face by both alternatives. He had said that the world was not to be explained in terms of super-nature, and had accordingly said that everything was water. It now fell upon him to explain why hosts of things were not "watery." The minimum he could do was to put a principle of change in water itself, so that by the operation of that principle, a transmutation from the state we know as water to other things would be possible. But if he was not to abandon his first statement that everything is water, the principle must permit only geometrical changes in water, that is, in its operation, it must be limited to the rarefaction and condensation of water. For this, the principle needed to be a principle of motion. Hence, he said that things were full of gods. Though this smells unpleasantly of animism, he only meant, through asserting the capacity of matter for spontaneous self-motion, to reject its inertness. In saying things were full of gods, he did not mean that every object was the locus of some god, for his whole philosophical revolution consisted in his neutralizing of the gods, his rendering them irrelevant for purposes of explanation of the objects and processes of the world. It is his idiom, not his thought, which was picturesque. Just as Aristotle was later to recover the forms from Plato's heaven and restore them to matter, so Thales was now retrieving the source of motion and the cause of processes from the priests' heaven for matter.

Matter is not inert in the sense of the philosophers. It is capable of self-motion both in the sense of change of relation, and in the sense of change of property. But matter has inertia. Inertia and inertness have been sufficiently distinguished, and while inertness implies inertia, inertia does not imply inertness.

The initial assertions of what I put forward as philosophical consciencism are therefore twofold. First, there is the assertion of the absolute and independent existence of matter; second, there is the assertion of the capacity of matter for spontaneous self-motion. To the extent of these two initial assertions, philosophical consciencism is deeply materialist.

There is a supreme need to distinguish here between the materialism which is involved in philosophical consciencism and that materialism which implies the sole existence of matter. . . . A materialist philosophy which accepts the primary reality of matter must either deny other categories of being, or else claim that they are one and all reducible without left-overs to matter. If this does not present a dilemma, at least the choice is often painful. In a materialist philosophy admitting the primary reality of matter, if spirit is accepted as a category of being, non-residual reduction to matter must be claimed. Furthermore, the phenomenon of consciousness, like that of self-consciousness, must be held to be in the ultimate analysis nothing but an aspect of matter.

Strictly speaking, the assertion of the sole reality of matter is atheistic, for pantheism, too, is a species of atheism. Philosophical consciencism, even though deeply rooted in materialism, is not necessarily atheistic.

According to philosophical consciencism, certain activities possessing all of the syndromes of purpose may still be the direct activity of matter. Such activity is widespread and is characterized by a non-apperceptive response to stimulus; that is to say, it is characterized by a response to stimulus emptied of all self-awareness, a response devoid of any cognition beyond the reaction to that which is for the time being acting as stimulus. Instinctive response is this kind of activity, for in instinctive response there is a non-apperceptive response to stimulus, a response which is not conditioned by any realization of a possible relation of purpose between the stimulus and the stimulated. On the other hand, apperceptive response is deliberate. Here, there is a self-awareness and an appraisal of the situation involving stimulus and response.

The suspicion that living things exhibit non-apperceptive response is not new. Indeed, Descartes thought that the response of all non-human animals was non-apperceptive. He therefore denied that non-human animals possessed souls, remaining content to believe that all the actions of such animals could be given a mechanical explanation which is complete. But even humans are not entirely above non-apperceptive response. Indeed a response that starts by being apperceptive could in time be rendered non-apperceptive by the technique of producing a conditioned reflex.

Aristotle had, before Descartes, maintained a similar opinion, that only humans were capable of a self-conscious, apperceptive response. This opinion of Aristotle's was confirmed in his invention of the vegetable and the animal souls, as distinct from the rational soul.

It might seem that a philosophical position which accepts a duality of the Cartesian type cannot comfortably treat all the actions of animals as purely mechanical. For this kind of duality, there should ensue a nagging doubt, the doubt whether spirit as a category should not really be excised with Occam's razor. According to Occam's razor, entities should not be multiplied without logical need.

But according to Cartesian duality, there are two irreducible types of substance. There is spiritual substance which is purely active, thinks and is non-extended. Then there is matter which is purely extended and is inert in the philosopher's sense. Now a great many of the actions of animals are, as outward marks, quite similar to those of men. It is therefore a kind of special pleading to hold that these actions are spirit-produced in the one case and not in the other, especially since Descartes makes an issue of the existence of minds other than his own and God's.

In order to remove this feeling that Occam's razor might be applied to shave off spirit, it is necessary to show, as distinct from claiming, that actions which have syndromes of being mind-inspired can result from mere matter. To do this is to show how some mind-language is reducible without residue to body-language. That is, to show how expressions which might be used in describing spirit-directed operations can be shown to be completely apt in describing mechanical action; almost to show, indeed, that rudimentary minds are nothing but active matter. That this is so was in fact explicitly claimed by Leibniz, who said that matter was rudimentary mind, thereby breaking the categorial ice between matter and mind.

. . . I discussed [previously] at some length how categorial conversion or reduction is possible, making free reference in the course of the discussion to the work of logicians. If spiritual phenomena are in fact the outcome of material phenomena, then it is hardly surprising that environment, which is but a disposition of matter, can enhance, intensify, even develop the consciousness. Furthermore, the mind-body problem is solved. This solution of the mind-body problem has sometimes taken the form of cutting the Gordian knot. The mind-body problem arises in the following manner. If one says that there are only two types of substances, matter and mind, and furthermore allows interaction between them, then the question arises how there can be interaction between substances which are so disparate. Mind is purely active, thinks and is unextended; matter is passive, extended and is without awareness. If one asserts the sole reality of matter, as extreme materialists do, or if one asserts the sole reality of spirit as Leibniz must be deemed to have done, then the mind-body problem is solved by removing the conditions in which the perplexity arises. This is to cut the Gordian knot, for now mind and body will not be disparate, but will either both be forms of matter or both be forms of spirit.

In philosophical consciencism, however, the interaction of mind and body is accepted as a fact. The philosophical perplexity which darkens this interaction is removed by the demonstration of the possibility of categorial conversion. Categorial conversion must be distinguished from parallelism. Descartes himself tried to solve the mind-body problem by resorting to a kind of parallelism. He instituted parallel occurrences, and thus explained pain as that grief which the soul felt at the damage to its body. On this point, as on several others, Descartes was assailed by the critical acumen of the Ghanian philosopher Anthony William Amo. According to Amo, all that the soul could do on Descartes' terms is to take cognizance of the fact that there is a hole in its body or a contusion on it, and unless knowledge is itself painful, the mind could not be said to grieve thereat. Of course, if the mind could be said to grieve in this way, on bare knowledge of the state of the body, then one *might* say that the body could affect the mind. But not so necessarily, for, strictly speaking, according to Descartes the body does not affect the mind, but the mind *commiserates* with the body.

Philosophical consciencism has no room for a mere parallelism on the mind-body problem. For philosophical consciencism *retains* the two categories of mind and body, *recognizes* the problem by accepting the fact of interaction, but offers a solution thereto. Parallelism, while recognizing the two categories, in fact denies interaction. The solution offered by philosophical consciencism is by way of categorial conversion.

According to philosophical consciencism, qualities are generated by matter. Behind any qualitative appearance, there stands a quantitative disposition of matter, such that the qualitative appearance is a surrogate of the quantitative disposition. I do not mean by this that qualities are the quantities themselves. I am not, for example, saying that a colour is the same thing as a certain wave-length. Of course the wave-length is not the colour, though we do know, thanks to the physicists, that individual colours are tied to characteristic wave-lengths. What I am however saying is that the colour is precisely the visual surrogate of a wave-length. A colour is the eye's mode of impression of a wave with certain mathematical properties; it is the visual surrogate of a quantitative disposition of matter. Sounds, similarly, are the ear's mode of impression of waves with certain properties. In general, sensations and perceptions are sensory surrogates of quantitative dispositions of matter. All natural properties, whatever property is discernible by medium of one sense or more, are nothing but sensory surrogates of quantitative dispositions of matter.

. . . I refuted [previously] the claim that Einstein's Theory of Relativity was incompatible with materialism. The gravamen of the objection was that philosophical materialism requires the absolute and independent existence of space and time as necessary receptacles for matter. At that point, I explained that there was no conflict with the Theory of Relativity, and also that materialism was itself inconsistent with the absolute and independent existence of space or time.

If the sole existence of matter is asserted, then space and time, in so far as they are not matter, must be unreal. Philosophical consciencism does not assert the sole reality of matter. Rather it asserts the primary reality of matter. Here again, if space were absolute and independent, matter could not with respect to it be primary. Therefore philosophical consciencism, in asserting the primary existence of matter, also maintains that space must, to the extent that it is real, derive its properties from those of matter through a categorial conversion. And since the properties of space are geometrical, it then follows from philosophical consciencism that the geometry of space is determined by the properties of matter.

When one now turns to Einstein's General Theory of Relativity, one finds exactly the same conclusion there. For in his Theory, Einstein relies on a principle of Mach's about the conditions of significance to affirm that the properties of space are fixed by the masses of bodies in a gravitational field. This principle of Einstein's, like philosophical consciencism, rejects the absolute and independent existence of space. With regard to space, relativity and philosophical consciencism are mutually consistent.

In discussing the possibility of categorial conversion, I said that two approaches were available to philosophy. First, the possibility of categorial conversion could be demonstrated in conceptual terms. This has been achieved by modern logic. Second, models fulfilling the conditions of categorial conversion might be cited. Such models are offered by modern science.

Philosophical consciencism claims the reality of categorial conversion. But if the conversion from one category to another category is not to represent a mere apparition, a philosophical will-o'-the-wisp, then such a conversion must represent a variation in the mass of its initial matter. The conversion is produced by a dialectical process, and if it is from a lower logical type to a higher logical type, it involves loss of mass.

Here again, that loss of mass actually takes place is deducible from Einstein's General Theory of Relativity. It follows from this Theory that every chemical change from simpler substances to more complex substances, in so far as it entails the emergence of new properties, represents a loss of mass. Indeed, it represents a conversion of part of the mass of matter. In Einstein's Theory, the loss is calculable according to the general formula $e = mc^2$ where e represents ergs of energy, m mass, and c the velocity of light. If, for example, one gram of mass were substituted for m, the equivalence in ergs of energy will be 9×20^{10} ergs, for in this case e will be equal to c^2. According to philosophical consciencism, however, though the whole of this amount of mass is converted, it is not all of it which is converted to the emergent properties. In actual chemical changes, some of it transpires as heat.

It is this reality of categorial conversion which prompts philosophical consciencism to assert not the sole reality of matter, but its primary reality. If higher categories are only surrogates of quantitative processes of matter, they are still not empty apparitions, but are quite real.

It follows from this that in philosophical consciencism, matter is capable of dialectic change, for if natural properties are nothing but surrogates of quantitative dispositions of matter, then since natural properties change, matter must change in quantitative disposition. And matter, in being a plenum of forces in *tension*, already contains the incipient change in disposition which is necessary to bring about a change in quality or property. Force itself is the way in which particles of matter exist; it is their mathematical or quantitative constitution. Force is not a description of a particle of matter; it is not something which particles of matter wear on their face. Rather, it is internal to them.

Since matter is a plenum of forces in tension, and since tension implies incipient change, matter must have the power of self-motion original to it. Without self-motion, dialectical change would be impossible.

By a dialectical change, I mean the emergence of a third factor of a higher logical type from the tension between two factors or two sets of factors of a lower logical type. Matter belongs to one logical type, properties and qualities of matter to a higher logical type, properties of properties to an even higher logical type.

This appropriately raises questions of an epistemological nature about consciencism. Epistemological problems are those which concern the nature of knowledge, and its types, and also the avenues to them which are open to the mind. Consciencism, by avoiding the assertion of the sole reality of matter, prepares itself for the painless recognition of the objectivity of different types of being. Indeed, the conception of dialectic is itself connected with a recognition of different types of being. Types of being are logical types. If they form a scale of being, it is not to be inferred that this scale is correlated with a scale of value. The types are logical types, such that material objects form one logical type; those general terms, which can be applied in description only to material objects, form a higher logical type; those general terms which can be applied in description to general terms of the first group form another logical type which is even higher.

Material objects and their properties belong to different logical types, and so do material objects and mind. It is these differences in type which make categorial absurdity possible. By a categorial absurdity, I mean that special absurdity which arises from coupling types of terms which should not be coupled. Terms can be coupled only when they belong to the same type or belong to proximate types. Thus "people" and "independence" belong to proximate types, and may therefore be coupled as in the proposition "we are an independent people." But the number two and "red" neither belong to the same type nor belong to proximate types; hence, not unexpectedly, the proposition "the number two is red," which couples them, does commit a categorial absurdity.

In the same way, terms which can be coupled with philosophical surrogates in description of the latter cannot be coupled with the items which give rise to the surrogates, though there is nothing which is incapable of translation, without residue, to propositions about these items whose surrogates they are.

Terms which can be coupled with philosophical surrogates in description of them cannot be coupled with the items which give rise to the surrogates, because if a term can be coupled with a philosophical surrogate, it must be of the same logical type as the philosophical surrogate, or, if it is in description of it, must be of a type higher than and proximate to that to which the surrogate belongs. Terms which can be coupled in description with a philosophical surrogate must be one logical type higher than the surrogate, since such terms are always one type higher than their subjects. As such these terms are at least two types higher than the items which give rise to the surrogate. They cannot therefore be ascribed even by way of complement. One cannot say that the number two is a red thing (complement) any more than one can say that the number two is red (description).

This epistemological consequence of philosophical consciencism provides an antecedent philosophical justification for such pursuits as the investigation of the nature of mind by the exclusive means of the investigation of the nature and functioning of brain. This is a great advantage, for as the mind is not subject to experimental exposure, if all propositions about mind are in principle translatable without residue to propositions about the nervous system, *which is* subject to experimental exposure, then a great deal of mental research can be done in terms of neural research. In general, philosophical consciencism narrows down the extent of academic hermitage. It does this by making research into the nature of one category possible in terms of another category.

There is a growing tendency among some philosophers who hold the view that when materialism has triumphed and has won victory over idealism, it must, like its victim, disappear or "wither away" as a philosophy. It is envisaged that this will take place when the classless society is achieved. Marx and Engels regarded materialism as the true form of science and, indeed, held that with the final overthrow of idealism, materialism must have science for its positive content. What is important is not so much that it may not be necessary to stress materialism as a philosophy when idealism is overthrown, but rather that the importance and correctness of materialism will not in any way be diminished in its hour of victory. Some philosophers expect that materialism will then disappear and give way to a philosophy of mind—and that philosophical theory of the mind which is not explicitly prefaced by philosophical materialism will open the door to a new idealism.

Thought without practice is empty, and philosophical consciencism constantly exhibits areas of practical significance, like the one above. If philosophical consciencism initially affirms the absolute and independent existence of matter, and holds matter to be endowed with its pristine objective laws, then philosophical consciencism builds itself by becoming a reflection of the objectivity, in conceptual terms, of the unfolding of matter. When a philosophy so restricts itself to the reflection of the objective unfolding of matter, it also establishes a direct connection between knowledge and action.

This idea of a philosophy as the conceptual image of nature is also found in Spinoza, and, indeed, it is a tenet of rationalism in general. According to Spinoza, at least, the order and connection of ideas is the same as the order and connection of nature. The mistake of the rationalists regarding the connection between philosophy and nature is in their treating philosophy as the blue-print, the strait-jacket for nature, instead of being content with a mere assertion of mutual reflection. If, however, the order and connection of ideas is the same as the order and connection of nature, then according to Spinoza, knowledge of the one order and connection must be knowledge of the other order and connection. Indeed, it can be said that, according to Spinoza, mind is the idea of that whose body is nature. To the extent that he allows action to be possible, knowledge of the mind can be the direct objective basis of an intervention in nature.

I said earlier on that in spite of the profound cleavage between idealism and materialism, they did not present different inventories of the world. This hardly means, however, that they share the same attitude to the world. They certainly differ in their conception of the nature of the connection between thought and action. In this field, idealism is jejune and grotesquely ineffectual. Materialism is, on the other hand, dynamic and constantly throws up areas of practical significance.

But if philosophical consciencism connects knowledge with action, it is still necessary to inquire whether it conceives this connection as a purely mechanistic one, or whether it makes it susceptible of ethical influence and comment.

It is evident at least that philosophical consciencism cannot issue in a closed set of ethical rules, a set of rules which must apply in any society and at any time. Philosophical consciencism is incapable of this because it is itself based upon a view of matter, as caught in the grip of an inexorable dialectical evolution.

To the extent that materialism issues in egalitarianism on the social plane, it issues in ethics. Egalitarianism is not only political but also ethical; for it implies a certain range of human conduct which is alone acceptable to it. At the same time, because it conceives matter as a plenum of tensions giving rise to dialectical change, it cannot freeze its ethical rules with changelessness. It would be wrong, however, to seek to infer from this that the ethical principles which philosophical consciencism sanctions are at any one time gratuitous and devoid of objective grounding; for even when rules change, they can still be informed, still be governed by the same basic principles in the light of changing social conditions.

It is necessary to understand correctly the relationship between rules and principles. This relationship is similar to that between ideals and institutions and also to that between statutes and by-laws. Statutes, of course, state general principles, they do not make explicit those procedures by means of which they may be carried out and fulfilled. By-laws are an application of such principles. It is obvious that when the conditions in which by-laws operate alter seriously, it could be necessary to amend the by-laws in order that the same statute should continue to be fulfilled. Statutes are not on the same level as by-laws, nor do they imply any *particular* by-laws. It is because they carry no specific implication of particular by-laws, but can be subserved by any one of a whole spectrum of such, that it is possible to amend by-laws, while the statute which they are meant to fulfil suffers no change.

The relationship between ideals and institutions is a similar one. That circumstances change is a truism. For all that, it is significant. For it means that, if ideals must be pursued throughout the changing scenes of life, it may be necessary to modify or replace institutions in order that the same ideals should effectively be served. There are no particular institutions, which, irrespective of local circumstances, are uniquely tied to their ideals. Institutions should be shot through and through with pragmatism.

It is in the same way that principles are related to rules even when they are ethical. The idea that ethical rules can change, and indeed need to change, is one which a little reflection can confirm.

Evidently, even when two societies share the same ethical principles, they may differ in the rules which make the principles effective. Asses were of such overwhelming importance in Israel that God found it necessary to regulate human relations by an ethical rule mentioning them specifically. Thou shalt not covet thy neighbour's ass. If God deigned to give us a similar rule today, he would no doubt forbid us to covet our neighbour's motorcar, hardly his ass. Here God would be giving a new ethical rule, designed at giving effect to an unchanging ethical principle, but taking full account of modern times.

Progress in man's conquest and harnessing of the forces of nature has a profound effect on the content of ethical rules. Some ethical rules fall into abeyance, because the situations in which they take effect lose all likelihood of recurrence; others give way to their opposite, as, for example, when a matriarchal society changes into a patriarchal one, for here many ethical rules arising from the position of the woman will have to give way to those arising from the new position of the man. And yet, the principles standing behind these diverse clusters of ethical rules may remain constant, and identical as between society and society.

According to philosophical consciencism, ethical rules are not permanent but depend on the stage reached in the historical evolution of a society, so however that cardinal principles of egalitarianism are conserved.

A society does not change its ethics by merely changing its rules. To alter its ethics, its principles must be different. Thus, if a capitalist society can become a socialist society, then a capitalist society will have changed its ethics. Any change of ethics constitutes a revolutionary change.

Nevertheless, many times moral rules have changed so startlingly as to give the impression of a revolution in ethics. For example, one can take that profound change in our attitude to offenders for which modern psychology is responsible. Modern psychology brings to our notice relevant facts of whose existence we have no inkling in our dreams. When these new facts change our attitude, moral rules have not necessarily changed. But application of them is withheld, for the new considerations provoke a reclassification of the act involved, and, possibly, bring it under a different ethical rule. In that case, a different moral attitude could become relevant.

Investigations into the psychology of delinquency are a case in point. Such investigations tend by their results to attenuate the acrimony of our moral attitude to delinquents, by compelling us, not admittedly to waive moral rules, but to re-classify delinquent acts.

The cardinal ethical principle of philosophical consciencism is to treat each man as an end in himself and not merely as a means. This is fundamental to all socialist or humanist conceptions of man. It is true that Immanuel Kant also identified this as a cardinal principle of ethics, but whereas he regarded it as an immediate command of reason, we derive it from a materialist viewpoint.

This derivation can be made by way of that egalitarianism which, we have seen, is the social reflection of materialism. Egalitarianism is based on the monistic thesis of materialism. Matter is one even in its different manifestations. If matter is one, it follows that there is a route connecting any two manifestations of matter. This does not mean that between any two manifestations of matter there is a route which does not pass through any third form; the route need not be direct, for it may take one back to the primary form of matter. Dialectical processes are not unilinear, they do not follow just one line, but are ramified. There is a route from any twig of a tree to any other twig, such that the route never leaves the tree. But this does not mean that the twigs all have some one point in common, for it may be necessary to pass to the trunk and join another branch in order to pass from one twig to another. Nevertheless there is this route. The different manifestations of matter are all results of dialectical processes unfolding according to objective laws. There is a determinate process through which every manifestation is derived.

In saying however that there is a route between any two forms of matter, I do not attach the implication that any one form of matter can in fact be derived from any other form, for this may involve the reversal of a process which is irreversible. The upshot of what I mean is the continuity of nature: though the dialectical evolution of matter may lead to culs-de-sac (like the vanished plants and animals of pre-historic days), dialectical evolution contains no hiatuses.

It is the basic unity of matter, despite its varying manifestations, which gives rise to egalitarianism. Basically, man is one, for all men have the same basis and arise from the same evolution according to materialism. This is the objective ground of egalitarianism.

David Hume raised the question that ethical philosophies begin with statements of fact and suddenly seek to base statements of appraisal thereon, without explaining the legitimacy of their inference. If man is basically one, then if action is objectively attentive to this fact, it must be guided by principles. The guiding principles can be stated with such generality that they become autonomous. That is to say, first, that if action is to conform to the objectivity of human unity, then it must be guided by general principles which always keep this objectivity in view, principles which would prevent action from proceeding as if men were basically different. Second, these principles, because they relate to fact, can be stated boldly, as though they were autonomous, like the principle that an individual should not be treated by another merely as a means but always as an end.

If ethical principles are founded on egalitarianism, they must be objective. If ethical principles arise from an egalitarian idea of the nature of man, they must be generalizable, for according to such an idea man is basically one in the sense defined. It is to this non-differential generalization that expression is given in the command to treat each man as an end in himself, and not merely as a means. That is, philosophical consciencism, though it has the same cardinal principle of ethics as Kant, differs from Kant in founding ethics on a philosophical idea of the nature of man. This is what Kant describes as ethics based on anthropology. By anthropology Kant means any study of the nature of man, and he forbids ethics to be based on such a study.

It is precisely this that philosophical consciencism does. It also agrees with the traditional African outlook on many points, and thus fulfils one of the conditions which it sets for itself. In particular, it agrees with the traditional African idea of the absolute and independent existence of matter, the idea of its powers of self-motion in the sense explained, the idea of categorial convertibility, and the idea of the grounding of cardinal principles of ethics in the nature of man.

The traditional African standpoint, of course, accepts the absolute and independent idea of matter. If one takes the philosophy of the African, one finds that in it the absolute and independent existence of matter is accepted. Further, matter is not just dead weight, but alive with forces in tension. Indeed, for the African, everything that exists, exists as a complex of forces in tension. In holding force in tension to be essential to whatever exists, he is, like Thales and like philosophical consciencists, endowing matter with an original power of self-motion, they were endowing it with what matter would need to initiate qualitative and substantial changes.

When a plurality of men exist in society, and it is accepted that each man needs to be treated as an end in himself, not merely as a means, there transpires a transition from ethics to politics. Politics become actual, for institutions need to be created to regulate the behaviour and actions of the plurality of men in society in such a way as to conserve the fundamental ethical principle of the initial worthiness of each individual. Philosophical consciencism consequently adumbrates a political theory and a social-political practice which together seek to ensure that the cardinal principles of ethics are effective.

The social-political practice is directed at preventing the emergence or the solidifying of classes, for in the Marxist conception of class structure, there is exploitation and the subjection of class to class. Exploitation and class-subjection are alike contrary to consciencism. By reason of its egalitarian tenet, philosophical consciencism seeks to promote individual development, but in such a way that the conditions for the development of all become the conditions for the development of each; that is, in such a way that the individual development does not introduce such diversities as to destroy the egalitarian basis. The social-political practice also seeks to co-ordinate social forces in such a way as to mobilize them logistically for the maximum development of society along true egalitarian lines. For this, planned development is essential.

In its political aspect, philosophical consciencism is faced with the realities of colonialism, imperialism, disunity and lack of development. Singly and collectively these four militate against the realization of a social justice based on ideas of true equality.

The first step is to liquidate colonialism wherever it is. In *Towards Colonial Freedom* I stated that it is the aim of colonial governments to treat their colonies as producers of raw materials, and at the same time as the dumping-ground of the manufactured goods of foreign industrialists and foreign capitalists. I have always believed that the basis of colonialism is economic, but the solution of the colonial problem lies in political action, in a fierce and constant struggle for emancipation as an indispensable first step towards securing economic independence and integrity.

I said earlier on that consciencism regards matter as a plenum of forces in tension; and that in its dialectical aspect, it holds categorial conversion to be possible by a critical disposition of matter. This gives us a clue how to analyse the fact of colonialism, not only in Africa, but indeed everywhere. It also gives us a clue how to defeat it.

In a colonial situation, there are forces which tend to promote colonialism, to promote those political ties by means of which a colonialist country binds its colonies to itself with the primary object of furthering her economic advantages. Colonialism requires exertion, and much of that exertion is taken up by the combat of progressive forces, forces which seek to negate this oppressive enterprise of greedy individuals and classes by means of which an egotistical imposition of the strong is made upon the weak.

Just as the placid appearance of matter only disguises the tension of forces underlying that appearance, like the bow of Heraclitus, so in a colonial territory, an opposition of reactionary and revolutionary forces can nevertheless give an impression of final and acquiescent subjugation. But just as a quality can be changed by quantitative (measurable) changes of a critical nature in matter, so this acquiescent impression can be obliterated by a change in the relation of the social forces. These opposing sets of forces are dynamic, in the sense that they seek and tend to establish some social condition. One may therefore refer to them by the name of action in order to make their dynamic nature explicit. In that case, one may say that in a colonial situation positive action and negative action can be discerned. Positive action will represent the sum of those forces seeking social justice in terms of the destruction of oligarchic exploitation and oppression. Negative action will correspondingly represent the sum of those forces tending to prolong colonial subjugation and exploitation. Positive action is revolutionary and negative action is reactionary.

It ought to be recognized at the outset that the introduced terms of positive and negative action are abstractions. But the ground for them is in social reality. It is quite possible by means of statistical analysis to discover the ways in which positive action and negative action are related in any given society. The statistical analysis will be of such facts as production, distribution, income, etc. Any such analysis must reveal one of three possible situations. Positive action may exceed negative action, or negative action may exceed positive action, or they may form an unstable equilibrium.

In a colonial situation, negative action undoubtedly outweighs positive action. In order that true independence should be won, it is necessary that positive action should come to overwhelm negative action. Admittedly, a semblance of true independence is possible without this specific relation. When this happens, we say that neo-colonialism has set in, for neo-colonialism is a guise adopted by negative action in order to give the impression that it has been overcome by positive action. Neo-colonialism is negative action playing possum.

In order to forestall this, it is necessary for positive action to be backed by a mass party, and qualitatively to improve this mass so that by education and an increase in its degree of consciousness, its aptitude for positive action becomes heightened. We can therefore say that in a colonial territory, positive action must be backed by a mass party, complete with its instruments of education. This was why the Convention People's Party of Ghana developed from an early stage its education wing, workers' wing, farmers' wing, youth wing, women's wing, etc. In this way, the people received constant political education, their self-awareness was increased and such a self-image was formed as ruthlessly excluded colonialism in all its guises. It is also in the backing of millions of members and supporters, united by a common radical purpose, that the revolutionary character of the Convention People's Party consists, and not merely in the piquancy of its programmes. Its mass and national support made it possible to think in realistic terms of instituting changes of a fundamental nature in the social hotch-potch bequeathed by colonialism.

A people's parliamentary democracy with a one-party system is better able to express and satisfy the common aspirations of a nation as a whole, than a multiple-party parliamentary system, which is in fact only a ruse for perpetuating, and covers up, the inherent struggle between the "haves" and the "have-nots."

In order that a territory should acquire the nominal attributes of independence, it is of course not necessary that positive action should exceed negative action. When a colonialist country sees the advance of positive action, it unfailingly develops a policy of containment, a policy whereby it seeks to check this advance and limit it. This policy often takes the form of conferences and protracted constitutional reforms.

Containment is, however, accepted by the colonialist country only as a second best. What it would really like to do is to roll back positive action. It is when it is assured of the impossibility of rolling back the billows of history that it applies the policy of containment, that it tries to limit the achievement of progress by devising frivolous reforms. The colonialist country seeks to divert positive action into channels which are harmless to it.

To do this it resorts to diverse subtle means. Having abandoned direct violence, the colonialist country imparts a deceptive orientation to the negative forces in its subject territory. These negative forces become the political wolf masquerading in sheep's clothing, they join the clamour for independence, and are accepted in good faith by the people. It is then that like a wasting disease they seek from the inside to infest, corrupt, pervert and thwart the aspirations of the people.

The people, the body and the soul of the nation, the final sanction of political decisions, and the inheritors of sovereignty, cannot be fooled for long. Quick on the scent, they ferret out these Janus-faced politicians who run with the hare and hunt with the hounds. They turn away from them. Once this colonialist subterfuge is exposed, and the minion accomplices discredited, the colonial power has no option but to acknowledge the independence of the people. By its very next act, however, it seeks without grace to neutralize this same independence by fomenting discontent and disunity; and, finally, by arrant ingratiation and wheedling it attempts to disinherit the people and constitute itself their conscience and their will, if not their voice and their arm. Political decisions, just as they were before independence was won, lose their reference to the welfare of the people, and serve once again the well-being and security of the erstwhile colonial power and the clique of self-centered politicians.

Any oblique attempt of a foreign power to thwart, balk, corrupt or otherwise pervert the true independence of a sovereign people is neo-colonialist. It is neo-colonialist because it seeks, notwithstanding the acknowledged sovereignty of a people, to subordinate their interests to those of a foreign power.

A colonialist country can in fact offer independence to a people, not with the intention which such an act might be thought to imply, but in the hope that the positive and progressive forces thus appeased and quietened, the people might be exploited with greater serenity and comfort.

Neo-colonialism is a greater danger to independent countries than is colonialism. Colonialism is crude, essentially overt, and apt to be overcome by a purposeful concert of national effort. In neo-colonialism, however, the people are divided from their leaders and, instead of providing true leadership and guidance which is informed at every point by the ideal of the general welfare, leaders come to neglect the very people who put them in power and incautiously become instruments of suppression on behalf of the neo-colonialists.

It is far easier for the proverbial camel to pass through the needle's eye, hump and all, than for an erstwhile colonial administration to give sound and honest counsel of a *political* nature to its liberated territory. To allow a foreign country, especially one which is loaded with economic interests in our continent, to tell us what *political* decisions to take, what *political* courses to follow, is indeed for us to hand back our independence to the oppressor on a silver platter.

Likewise, since the motivation of colonialism, whatever protean forms it may take, is well and truly economic, colonialism itself being but the institution of political bonds fastening colonies to a colonialist country, with the primary object of the metropolitan economic advantages, it is essential that a liberated territory should not bind her economy to that of the ousted rulers. The liberation of a people institutes principles which enjoin the recognition and destruction of imperialistic domination, whether it is political, economic, social or cultural. To destroy imperialistic domination in these forms, political, economic, social and cultural action must always have reference to the needs and nature of the liberated territory, and it is from these needs and nature that the action must derive authenticity. Unless this self-reference is religiously maintained, a liberated territory will welcome with open arms the very foe which it has sought to destroy at cost of terrible suffering.

The true welfare of a people does not admit of compromise. If we compromise on the true interest of our people, the people must one day judge us, for it is with their effort and their sacrifice, with their forbearance and their denial, that independence is won. Independence once won, it is possible to rule against the erstwhile colonial power, but it is not really possible to rule against the wish and interest of the people.

The people are the backbone of positive action. It is by the people's effort that colonialism is routed, it is by the sweat of the people's brow that nations are built. The people are the reality of national greatness. It is the people who suffer the depredations and indignities of colonialism, and the people must not be insulted by dangerous flirtations with neo-colonialism.

There is a fundamental law of the evolution of matter to higher forms. This evolution is dialectical. And it is also the fundamental law of society. It is out of tension that being is born. Becoming is a tension, and being is the child of that tension of opposed forces and tendencies.

Just as in the physical universe, since the moving object is always impressed upon by external forces, any motion is in fact a resultant, so in society every development, every progressive motion, is a resultant of unharmonious forces, a resultant, a triumph of positive action over negative action.

This triumph must be accompanied by knowledge. For in the way that the process of natural evolution can be aided by human intervention based upon knowledge, so social evolution can be helped along by political intervention based upon knowledge of the laws of social development. Political action aimed at speeding up social evolution is of the nature of a catalyst.

The need for such a catalyst is created by the fact that natural evolution is always wasteful. It takes place at the cost of massive loss of life and at the cost of extreme anguish. Evolution speeded by scientific knowledge is prompter, and represents an economy of material. In the same way, the catalysis which political action introduces into social evolution represents an economy of time, life and talent.

Without positive action, a colonial territory cannot be truly liberated. It is doomed to creep in its petty pace from day to day towards the attainment of a sham independence that turns to dust, independence which is shot through and through with the supreme interest of an alien power. To achieve true liberation, positive action must begin with an objective analysis of the situation which it seeks to change. Such an analysis I attempted in *Towards Colonial Freedom*. Positive action must, furthermore, seek an alignment of all the forces of progress and, by marshalling them, confront the negative forces. It must at the same time anticipate and contain its own inner contradictions, for, though positive action unites those forces of a situation which are, in regard to a specific purpose, progressive, many of these forces will contain tendencies which are in other respects reactionary.

Hence, when positive action resorts to an alignment of forces, it creates in itself seams at which this alignment might fall apart. It is essential that positive action should in its dialectical evolution anticipate this seminal disintegration and discover a way of containing the future schismatic tendencies, a way of nipping fragmentation in the bud as colonialism begins to reel and totter under the frontal onslaught of positive action.

But even with colonialism worsted, positive action cannot relent, for it is at about this time that the schismatic tendencies referred to ripen. Besides, political independence, though worthwhile in itself, is still only a means to the fuller redemption and realization of a people. When independence has been gained, positive action requires a new orientation away from the sheer destruction of colonialism and towards national reconstruction.

It is indeed in this address to national reconstruction that positive action faces its gravest dangers. The cajolement, the wheedlings, the seductions and the Trojan horses of neo-colonialism must be stoutly resisted, for neo-colonialism is a latter-day harpy, a monster which entices its victims with sweet music.

In order to be able to carry out this resistance to neo-colonialism at every point, positive action requires to be armed with an ideology, an ideology which, vitalizing it and operating through a mass party shall equip it with a regenerative concept of the world and life, forge for it a strong continuing link with our past and offer to it an assured bond with our future. Under the searchlight of an ideology, every fact affecting the life of a people can be assessed and judged, and neo-colonialism's detrimental aspirations and sleights of hand will constantly stand exposed.

In order that this ideology should be comprehensive, in order that it should light up every aspect of the life of our people, in order that it should affect the total interest of our society, establishing a continuity with our past, it must be socialist in form and in content and be embraced by a mass party.

And yet, socialism in Africa today tends to lose its objective content in favour of a distracting terminology and in favour of a general confusion. Discussion centres more on the various conceivable types of socialism than upon the need for socialist development. More is surely required than a mere reaction against a policy of domination. Independence is of the people; it is won by the people for the people. That independence is of the people is admitted by every enlightened theory of sovereignty. That it is won by the people is to be seen in the successes of mass movements everywhere. That it is won for the people follows from their ownership of sovereignty. The people have not mastered their independence until it has been given a national and social content and purpose that will generate their well-being and uplift.

The socialism of a liberated territory is subject to a number of principles if independence is not to be alienated from the people. When socialism is true to its purpose, it seeks a connection with the egalitarian and humanist past of the people before their social evolution was ravaged by colonialism; it seeks from the results of colonialism those elements (like new methods of industrial production and economic organization) which can be adapted to serve the interest of the people; it seeks to contain and prevent the spread of those anomalies and domineering interests created by the capitalist habit of colonialism; it reclaims the psychology of the people, erasing the "colonial mentality" from it; and it resolutely defends the independence and security of the people. In short, socialism recognizes dialectic, the possibility of creation from forces which are opposed to one another; it recognizes the creativity of struggle, and, indeed, the necessity of the operation of forces to any change. It also embraces materialism and translates this into social terms of equality.

Philosophy and Morality

The Zulu Personal Declaration

I;
I am;
I am alive;
I am conscious and aware;
I am unique;
I am who I say I am; I am the value UQOBO [essence]
I forever evolve inwardly and outwardly in response to the challenge of my nature;
I am the face of humanity;
The face of humanity is my face.
I contemplate myself and see everything in me.
I perceive; that which I perceive is form.
Form is an unchanging value.
Value is eternal consciousness;
Consciousness is that in which all things have their origin;
It does not change; it exists from eternity to eternity;
It is an infinite cluster of clusters of itself;
It is forever evolving in response to the challenge of its nature.
It is ULTIMATE VALUE;
It is UQOBO.
The value metamorphoses into a phenomenon;
Each phenomenon is a total of smaller forms;
Phenomena form clusters to produce other phenomena;
The cosmic order is an indefinite total of forms and phenomena.
I am a phenomenon; I am a person.
I am UQOBO; I am the consciousness.
The infinity is a unity; it cannot be destroyed;
I am a constituent of the unity;
I cannot be destroyed;
The infinity and I are inseparable;
I cannot exist outside of the infinity,
For, there is no outside of it.
Everything is inside the infinity.
UQOBO is the Infinity.
It is a Whole;

It cannot be other than Whole; without me it cannot be Whole;
Nothing can be added to or subtracted from the Whole.
The infinity is alive;
There is no death within it;
There is life and perpetual agmination.
That which is alive has purpose;
Purpose is destiny;
Perpetual evolution is the destiny of UQOBO;
UQOBO evolves in response to the challenge of its nature,
The *Law* regulates evolution;
It is a constituent of UQOBO
It is the will of the Infinity;
It is my will; it explains everything, for there are no mysteries;
Mystery is the redoubt of the ignorant.
Everything, everywhere, evolves according to the *Law;*
The *Law* is knowable;
I cannot violate the *Law* no matter what I do;
I incarnate the *Law;*
Everything I do translates into action one section of the *Law* or the other;
The processes of the *Law* are irreversible;
Ultimate Absurdity is the attempt to invert the *Law;*
The inversion of the *Law* is a cosmic cataclysm;
It is Ultimate Criminality;
I am the reconciler of all contradictions.
UBOQO, the *Law* and I are together the Definitive Agminate;
Nothing can separate us.
I live now,
And shall forever live, in UQOBO,
For, I am UQOBO;
I am eternal; I am the secret that drives out all fear.
Perpetual evolution is my destiny.
I evolve forever, in response to the challenge of being human.
I have a mind to light my path in the mazes of the cosmic order.
This mind has many sides;
It comprehends all things;
It establishes my right to latitude; to being heard;
It makes me feel at home in the cosmic order.
My neighbour has a mind;
It, also, comprehends all things.
My neighbour and I have the same origins;
We have the same life-experience and a common destiny;
We are the obverse and reverse sides of one entity;
We are unchanging equals;
We are the faces which see themselves in each other;
We are mutually fulfilling complements;
We are simultaneously legitimate values;
My neighbour's sorrow is my sorrow;
His joy is my joy.

He and I are mutually fulfilled when we stand by each other in moments of need.
His survival is a precondition of my survival.
That which is freely asked or freely given is love;
Imposed love is a crime against humanity.
I am sovereign of my life;
My neighbour is sovereign of his life;
Society is a collective sovereignty;
It exists to ensure that my neighbour and I realise the promise of being human.
I have no right to anything I deny my neighbour.
I am all; all are me.
I come from eternity;
The present is a moment in eternity;
I belong to the future.
I can commit no greater crime than to frustrate life's purpose for my neighbour.
Consensus is our guarantee of survival.
I define myself in what I do to my neighbour.
No community has any right to prescribe destiny for other communities.
This universe I challenge, a higher being than me to show;
My knees do not quake when I contemplate my destiny;
I know my way to eternity;
I make obeisances to the million sides of the ciliate mind;
The Eternal Person is Universal Man, Universal Woman and Universal Child.
I am a Universal Constant; I am a Cosmic Constant;
I am All-in-One; I am One-in-All.
I am the circle which encompasses infinity;
I am the point that is the beginning of the circle;
I am the value behind the circle.
I am *umuntu,* the knower of all probabilities and possibilities;
There is nothing I cannot know;
There is no tyranny I cannot crush;
The value of water is H_2O; it lives from eternity to eternity;
Nothing exists anywhere which can destroy it.
I am who I am;
I am not a creature; nothing can destroy me;
I am the self-evolving value NTU; I live forever and ever.
I am the phenomenon MUNTU [life force].
I am a person; a *Ngubane;* I am *Ngogo Zabantu Nezezinkomo;*
I am a cluster; I am *Skeletons of People and their Cattle.*
The cluster has vital elements;
They are the centre and core: the value NTU;
The body, the aura, the LAW and UQOBO.
The *Law* and UQOBO are the environment in which I exist.
I am a *Ngubane;* the *Skeletons* tell my history; they, too, define me.
I am adequate; I have in me all I need to be the best I can be.
I have contempt for that which is not freely given to me.
Whoever wishes me good,
Let that good go to him;
Whoever wishes me to be a prince,

Let him become a prince;
Whoever wishes that I should die,
Let his wish be his fate,
For I want nothing to which I have no right.
I am the servant of my ancestors;
My father is the messenger of my ancestors;
My ancestors are humanity;
All I live for is to be the best that I can be.
I do not prescribe destiny for my neighbour;
My neighbour is myself in a different guise;
Equals do not prescribe destiny for each other;
They hold conversations of minds;
They oppose ideas with counter-ideas.
This, my ancestors, told Shaka,
Was the behaviour of civilised men.
They told him this from their fortress cave.
Shaka forgot nothing;
He carved everything on stone.
A Zulu forgets nothing;
I carve everything on stone;
My adequacy makes me magnanimous;
It makes me wise when strong and brave when weak.
There are no frontiers I cannot cross,
For I, the person, am my own challenge.
Disease has no power over me when I know;
I determine my health; I am what I want to be;
I see mankind on the high road to eternity;
It marches along many routes;
The Light in the person guides the march;
It leads mankind along safer routes to a better future.
I join my hand with the hand of my neighbour;
This is my guarantee of reaching the future I desire;
I march confidently and triumphantly into the future;
My harmonised personality enables me to see my goal clearly;
Every moment is a rebirth into a new dimension of being human;
My duty is to guide the rebirth;
I and I alone guide the rebirth.
I outgrow the use of crutches;
I face the challenge of being eternal;
I align the cells in my body;
I know each, by name;
I am self-knowledge without end;
That which I eat, drink or learn I convert into myself;
I walk in humility in the presence of the person;
I can afford to be humble; I am not afraid; I am adequate;
That doctrine shall prevail which is not afraid of the person.
I reject all dogmas; they create disorder in my personality.
I am the enemy of all dogma, for dogma is a prison of the mind.

Philosophy and Morality

I am the egg in my mother's womb;
I draw to myself that which I need to evolve;
Every moment of my life I evolve,
For perpetual evolution is my destiny.
I am the clot that extends itself into the person;
I am the person who extends himself into humanity;
The mind of humanity comprehends infinity;
Humanity is the blanket that covers my body; it is my flesh;
It is the matrix in which I grow;
It is the face of the infinity which sees itself.
For UQOBO knows itself;
It knows its nature;
It knows its destiny;
It has within itself everything it desires;
It is itself;
It has no race and no colour;
The human value has no race and colour;
Each value metamorphoses in response to its environment;
Behind each complexion is the environment;
In each environment is a section of the *Law;*
The *Law* is a Whole.
UQOBO is an infinite cluster of forces;
Life is one of its components;
The *Law* is another;
So is Energy;
So are others, seen, unseen and incapable of being seen;
My mandate is to know them all;
To understand them all.
I move from eternity to eternity to understand them.
My sojourn on earth is a moment in my never-ending journey.
My destiny is forever to respond to the call of the morrow.
I have in me all I need to make the journey;
I move from one dimension of being human to another;
I move in proportion to the degree that I know;
Knowledge is the key to the gates of every dimension;
My title to the key is that I am human;
I contemplate myself to discover myself;
The key is my birthright;
He is the enemy of humanity who denies me the key.
For the key is the *Law.*
I am born according to the *Law;*
I live, grow and die according to it;
My mother is the *Law;*
My father is the *Law;*
My relatives and neighbours are the *Law;*
We are all bound together by the *Law;*
My neighbours are mankind;
Mankind is the *Law;*

The Zulu Personal Declaration

Phenomena divide and fuse according to the *Law;*
Conflict is a dimension of the *Law;*
Conflict is a moment of agmination;
The stages of agmination are collision, disintegration and fusion.
Harmony and equilibrium are the fulfilment of the *Law;*
The world is the *Law;*
Everything is the *Law;* I am everything.
I am the *Law;* I am a jewel of the cosmic order;
The *Law* is my and my neighbour's will;
I am a value; I have all the power to be what I want to be;
There is glory in being human; in being a self-defining value.
My name is *Man;* my name is *Woman;*
I formed myself from my mandate;
My mandate was the *Law;*
I entered earth as an act of will;
I came to realise the promise of being a value;
To realise the glory of being human;
To discover more satisfying dimensions of being a person.
I am not alone; I have never been alone;
I shall never be alone,
For I am a cluster.
I am Father-Mother;
I am the cluster of phenomena which constitute me.
I am Father-Mother-Child.
I am the past, the present and the future.
I have no beginning and no end;
I am the geodesic circle in which Father and Mother merged to become *Me.*
I extend myself into the child.
I am the brick out of which society is built;
I am the Eternal Person.
In everything I think and do, I describe myself;
I show how I face the challenge of being human.
The *Law* is a component of UQOBO
It has an infinite number of sections;
The sections interact on each other;
The interactions produce thought;
The *Law* interacting on itself in me produces thought;
I translate thought into action;
I create the world I desire through action;
I evolve in response to the challenge of my nature.
Thus to evolve is life's purpose for me and my neighbour;
We have in us everything we need to evolve;
To discover satisfying dimensions of being human;
To realise the promise of being persons.
I am a witness of eternity;
So is my neighbour;
We are witnesses of what we are;
We are living moments in eternity.

Philosophy and Morality

I am a tiny component of UQOBO
I am an element, a substance and an incarnation of UQOBO
I am an incarnation of the *Law;*
I live in the *Law;* the *Law* lives in me;
It acts through me and fulfils itself through me.
When I know, the *Law* fulfils itself freely.
When I am ignorant I disorganise the *Law's* interactions;
I create disharmonies in my personality;
I hurt my neighbour;
I sow dissension in my environment;
I frustrate life's purpose for humanity.
I flee from the challenge of being human;
I live in terror of myself;
I plant terror into my neighbour's psyche;
I terrorise all human beings;
I move the world in cycles of conflict to catastrophe;
I finally collapse midst the ruins I build;
I rot in the prison of the mind I create;
Passers-by note the stink;
Here lies one who fled from the challenge of being human, they say.
For I create my destiny in everything I do;
I and I alone know this destiny.
The challenge of being human is forever to explore myself;
It is forever to understand my neighbour;
Forever to reveal the power of the Definitive Agminate.
The cosmic order is the seraskierate of the Definitive Agminate;
I am the vizier of the seraskierate;
The *Law* is my sceptre;
To know it is the challenge of being human;
Forever to discover it is the promise of being human.
Perfection is the continuing response to the ever-beckoning hand of the *Law.*
Conquest forever distorts my personality;
It is the aching wound that never heals.
I listen to the call of the morrow,
When to Ncome I shall return;
When to Ulundi I shall return.
I wait in the shadows of eternity;
I wait for the day of rebirth into a satisfying destiny.
I do not apologise for being human.
I walk in humility in the presence of the person;
If aught there is to worship, it is the person.
To worship the person is to glorify myself.
The person is real; he needs no oracles to interpret him;
He has compassion in his bosom; the gods are capricious;
They are crutches for all partisans for ignorance.
The gods are trustees of my estate; I am the master.
I grow in understanding.
I outgrow the need for divine trustees; I stand on my feet;

The Zulu Personal Declaration

I march into the future on my terms.
Nothing can strike terror into my heart,
For I am *uqobo* of UQOBO.
I know every one of my cells;
My mother taught me how to count them.
My mother is all women; all women are my mother.
I prostrate myself before all women;
I cry out to them: Arise, mothers of the person!
Lead your children along safer routes to a better future!
To all men I cry: Arise, fathers of the person!
Create the world in which it will be no crime to be your children!
For all I desire is to realise the promise of being human.
Good and evil are related;
Either translates the *Law* into action.
Virtue is knowledge and practice of the *Law;*
Vice is ignorance of the *Law.*
To know the *Law* is the glory of being human;
It is *ukuba ngumuntu;*
Perpetually to be responsible in *ukuba ngumuntu.*
I have all I need forever to be responsible.
For I am the source of all meaning, all value and all authority.
I build a Civilisation in homage to the person;
The highest points reached by other civilisations are in the sky;
These zeniths are the levels from which I start building;
I entered the earth to create order out of chaos;
I recognise the person as my Light;
I pay homage to the Light;
The Light will prevail,
For I know the heights from which they made me fall;
I know the depths into which they thrust me;
I know I shall prevail,
For I am who I say I am;
He has not been born who shall say he has conquered me!

Philosophy and Morality

Chinua Achebe
(b. 1930, Nigeria)

The African Writer and the English Language

In June 1952, there was a writers' gathering at Makerere, impressively styled: "A Conference of African Writers of English Expression." Despite this sonorous and rather solemn title, it turned out to be a very lively affair and a very exciting and useful experience for many of us. But there was something which we tried to do and failed—that was to define "African literature" satisfactorily.

Was it literature produced *in* Africa or *about* Africa? Could African literature be on any subject, or must it have an African theme? Should it embrace the whole continent or south of the Sahara, or just *Black* Africa? And then the question of language. Should it be in indigenous African languages or should it include Arabic, English, French, Portuguese, Afrikaans, et cetera?

In the end we gave up trying to find an answer, partly—I should admit—on my own instigation. Perhaps we should not have given up so easily. It seems to me from some of the things I have since heard and read that we may have given the impression of not knowing what we were doing, or worse, not daring to look too closely at it.

A Nigerian critic, Obi Wali, writing in *Transition 10* said: "Perhaps the most important achievement of the conference . . . is that African literature as now defined and understood leads nowhere."

I am sure that Obi Wali must have felt triumphantly vindicated when he saw the report of a different kind of conference held later at Fourah Bay to discuss African literature and the University curriculum. This conference produced a tentative definition of African literature as follows: "Creative writing in which an African setting is authentically handled or to which experiences originating in Africa are integral." We are told specifically that Conrad's *Heart of Darkness* qualifies as African literature while Graham Greene's *Heart of the Matter* fails because it could have been set anywhere outside Africa.

A number of interesting speculations issue from this definition which admittedly is only an interim formulation designed to produce an indisputably desirable end, namely, to introduce African students to literature set in their environment. But I could not help being amused by the curious circumstance in which Conrad, a Pole, writing in English could produce African literature while Peter Abrahams would be ineligible should he write a novel based on his experiences in the West Indies.

What all this suggests to me is that you cannot cram African literature into a small, neat definition. I do not see African literature as one unit but as a group of associated units—in fact the sum total of all the *national* and *ethnic* literatures of Africa.

A national literature is one that takes the whole nation for its province and has a realized or potential audience throughout its territory. In other words a literature that is written in the *national* language. An ethnic literature is one which is available only to one ethnic group within the nation. If you take Nigeria as an example, the national literature, as I see it, is the literature written in English; and the ethnic literatures are in Hausa, Ibo, Yoruba, Efik, Edo, Ijaw, etc., etc.

Any attempt to define African literature in terms which overlook the complexities of the African scene at the material time is doomed to failure. After the elimination of white rule shall have been completed, the single most important fact in Africa in the second half of the twentieth century will appear to be the rise of individual nation-states. I believe that African literature will follow the same pattern.

What we tend to do today is to think of African literature as a newborn infant. But in fact what we have is a whole generation of newborn infants. Of course, if you only look cursorily, one infant is pretty much like another; but in reality each is already set on its own separate journey. Of course, you may group them together on the basis of anything you choose—the color of their hair, for instance. Or you may group them together on the basis of the language they will speak or the religion of their fathers. Those would all be valid distinctions; but they could not begin to account fully for each individual person carrying, as it were, his own little, unique lodestar of genes.

Those who in talking about African literature want to exclude North Africa because it belongs to a different tradition surely do not suggest that Black Africa is anything like homogeneous. What does Shabaan Robert have in common with Christopher Okigbo or Awoonor-Williams? Or Mongo Beti of Cameroun and Paris with Nzekwu of Nigeria? What does the champagne-drinking upper-class Creole society described by Easmon of Sierra Leone have in common with the rural folk and fishermen of J. P. Clark's plays? Of course, some of these differences could be accounted for on individual rather than national grounds, but a good deal of it is also environmental.

I have indicated somewhat offhandedly that the national literature of Nigeria and of many other countries of Africa is, or will be, written in English. This may sound like a controversial statement, but it isn't. All I have done has been to look at the reality of present-day Africa. This "reality" may change as a result of deliberate, e.g., political, action. If it does, an entirely new situation will arise, and there will be plenty of time to examine it. At present it may be more profitable to look at the scene as it is.

What are the factors which have conspired to place English in the position of national language in many parts of Africa? Quite simply the reason is that these nations were created in the first place by the intervention of the British which, I hasten to add, is not saying that the peoples comprising these nations were invented by the British.

The country which we know as Nigeria today began not so very long ago as the arbitrary creation of the British. It is true, as William Fagg says in his excellent new book, *Nigerian Images,* that this arbitrary action has proved as lucky in terms of African art history as any enterprise of the fortunate Princess of Serendip. And I believe that in political and economic terms too this arbitrary creation called Nigeria holds out great prospects. Yet the fact remains that Nigeria was created by the British—for their own ends. Let us give the devil his due: colonialism in Africa disrupted many things, but it did create big political units where there were small, scattered ones before. Nigeria had hundreds of autonomous communities ranging in size from the vast Fulani Empire founded by Usman dan Fodio in the north to tiny village entities in the east. Today it is one country.

Of course there are areas of Africa where colonialism divided up a single ethnic group

Philosophy and Morality

among two or even three powers. But on the whole it did bring together many peoples that had hitherto gone their several ways. And it gave them a language with which to talk to one another. If it failed to give them a song, it at least gave them a tongue, for sighing. There are not many countries in Africa today where you could abolish the language of the erstwhile colonial powers and still retain the facility for mutual communication. Therefore those African writers who have chosen to write in English or French are not unpatriotic smart alecks with an eye on the main chance—outside their own countries. They are by-products of the same process that made the new nation-states of Africa.

You can take this argument a stage further to include other countries of Africa. The only reason why we can even talk about African unity is that when we get together we can have a manageable number of languages to talk in—English, French, Arabic.

The other day I had a visit from Joseph Kariuki of Kenya. Although I had read some of his poems and he had read my novels, we had not met before. But it didn't seem to matter. In fact I met him through his poems, especially through his love poem, *Come Away My Love,* in which he captures in so few words the trials and tensions of an African in love with a white girl in Britain:

> Come away, my love, from streets
> Where unkind eyes divide
> And shop windows reflect our difference.

By contrast, when in 1960 I was traveling in East Africa and went to the home of the late Shabaan Robert, the Swahili poet of Tanganyika, things had been different. We spent some time talking about writing, but there was no real contact. I knew from all accounts that I was talking to an important writer, but of the nature of his work I had no idea. He gave me two books of his poems which I treasure but cannot read—until I have learned Swahili.

And there are scores of languages I would want to learn if it were possible. Where am I to find the time to learn the half dozen or so Nigerian languages, each of which can sustain a literature? I am afraid it cannot be done. These languages will just have to develop as tributaries to feed the one central language enjoying nationwide currency. Today, for good or ill, that language is English. Tomorrow it may be something else, although I very much doubt it.

Those of us who have inherited the English language may not be in a position to appreciate the value of the inheritance. Or we may go on resenting it because it came as part of a package deal which included many other items of doubtful value and the positive atrocity of racial arrogance and prejudice which may yet set the world on fire. But let us not in rejecting the evil throw out the good with it.

Some time last year I was traveling in Brazil meeting Brazilian writers and artists. A number of the writers I spoke to were concerned about the restrictions imposed on them by their use of the Portuguese language. I remember a woman poet saying she had given serious thought to writing in French! And yet their problem is not half as difficult as ours. Portuguese may not have the universal currency of English or French but at least it is the national language of Brazil with her eighty million or so people, to say nothing of the people of Portugal, Angola, Mozambique, etc.

Of Brazilian authors I have only read, in translation, one novel by Jorge Amado, who is not only Brazil's leading novelist but one of the most important writers in the world. From that one novel, *Gabriella,* I was able to glimpse something of the exciting Afro-Latin culture which is the pride of Brazil and is quite unlike any other culture. Jorge Amado is only one of the many writers Brazil has produced. At their national writers' festival there were literally hundreds of them. But the work of the vast majority will be closed to the rest of the world forever, including no doubt the work of some excellent writers. There is certainly a great advantage to writing in a world language.

I think I have said enough to give an indication of my thinking on the importance of the world language which history has forced down our throats. Now let us look at some of the most serious handicaps. And let me say straightaway that one of the most serious handicaps is *not* the one people talk about most often, namely, that it is impossible for anyone ever to use a second language as effectively as his first. This assertion is compounded of half truth and half bogus mystique. Of course, it is true that the vast majority of people are happier with their first language than with any other. But then the majority of people are not writers. We do have enough examples of writers who have performed the feat of writing effectively in a second language. And I am not thinking of the obvious names like Conrad. It would be more germane to our subject to choose African examples.

The first name that comes to my mind is Olauda Equiano, better known as Gustavus Vassa, the African. Equiano was an Ibo, I believe from the village of Iseke in the Orlu division of Eastern Nigeria. He was sold as a slave at a very early age and transported to America. Later he bought his freedom and lived in England. In 1789 he published his life story, a beautifully written document which, among other things, set down for the Europe of his time something of the life and habit of his people in Africa, in an attempt to counteract the lies and slander invented by some Europeans to justify the slave trade.

Coming nearer to our times, we may recall the attempts in the first quarter of this century by West African nationalists to come together and press for a greater say in the management of their own affairs. One of the most eloquent of that band was the Honorable Caseley Hayford of the Gold Coast. His presidential address to the National Congress of British West Africa in 1925 was memorable not only for its sound common sense but as a fine example of elegant prose. The governor of Nigeria at the time was compelled to take notice and he did so in characteristic style: he called Hayford's Congress "a self-selected and self-appointed congregation of educated African gentlemen." We may derive some amusement from the fact that British colonial administrators learned very little in the following quarter of a century. But at least they *did* learn in the end—which is more than one can say for some others.

It is when we come to what is commonly called creative literature that most doubt seems to arise. Obi Wali, whose article "Dead End of African Literature" I referred to, has this to say:

> . . . until these writers and their Western midwives accept the fact that any true African literature must be written in African languages, they would be merely pursuing a dead end, which can only lead to sterility, uncreativity and frustration.

But far from leading to sterility, the work of many new African writers is full of the most exciting possibilities.

Take this from Christopher Okigbo's *Limits:*

> Suddenly becoming talkative like weaverbird
> Summoned at offside of dream remembered
> Between sleep and waking
> I hand up my egg-shells

To you of palm grove,
Upon whose bamboo towers hang
Dripping with yesterupwine
A tiger mask and nude spear. . . .

Queen of the damp half light,
    I have had my cleansing.
Emigrant with air-borne nose,
    The he-goat-on-heat.

Or take the poem, *Night Rain,* in which J. P. Clark captures so well the fear and wonder felt by a child as rain clamors on the thatch roof at night and his mother, walking about in the dark, moves her simple belongings

Out of the run of water
That like ants filing out of the wood
Will scatter and gain possession
Of the floor. . . .

I think that the picture of water spreading on the floor "like ants filing out of the wood" is beautiful. Of course if you had never made fire with faggots, you may miss it. But Clark's inspiration derives from the same source which gave birth to the saying that a man who brings home ant-ridden faggots must be ready for the visit of lizards.

I do not see any signs of sterility anywhere here. What I do see is a new voice coming out of Africa, speaking of African experience in a world-wide language. So my answer to the question *Can an African ever learn English well enough to be able to use it effectively in creative writing?* is certainly yes. If on the other hand you ask: *Can he ever learn to use it like a native speaker?* I should say, I hope not. It is neither necessary nor desirable for him to be able to do so. The price a world language must be prepared to pay is submission to many different kinds of use. The African writer should aim to use English in a way that brings out his message best without altering the language to the extent that its value as a medium of international exchange will be lost. He should aim at fashioning out an English which is at once universal and able to carry his peculiar experience. I have in mind here the writer who has something new, something different to say. The nondescript writer has little to tell us, anyway, so he might as well tell it in conventional language and get it over with. If I may use an extravagant simile, he is like a man offering a small, nondescript routine sacrifice for which a chick, or less, will do. A serious writer must look for an animal whose blood can match the power of his offering.

In this respect Amos Tutola is a natural. A good instinct has turned his apparent limitation in language into a weapon of great strength—a half-strange dialect that serves him perfectly in the evocation of his bizarre world. His last book, and to my mind, his finest, is proof enough that one can make even an imperfectly learned second language do amazing things. In this book, *The Feather Woman of the Jungle,* Tutola's superb storytelling is at last cast in the episodic form which he handles best instead of being painfully stretched on the rack of the novel.

From a natural to a conscious artist: myself, in fact. Allow me to quote a small example from *Arrow of God,* which may give some idea of how I approach the use of English. The Chief Priest in the story is telling one of his sons why it is necessary to send him to church:

> I want one of my sons to join these people and be my eyes there. If there is nothing in it you will come back. But if there is something there you will bring home my share. The world is like a Mask, dancing. If you want to see it well you do not stand in one place. My spirit tells me that those who do not befriend the white man today will be saying *had we known* tomorrow.

Now supposing I had put it another way. Like this for instance:

> I am sending you as my representative among these people—just to be on the safe side in case the new religion develops. One has to move with the times or else one is left behind. I have a hunch that those who fail to come to terms with the white man may well regret their lack of foresight.

The material is the same. But the form of the one is *in character* and the other is not. It is largely a matter of instinct, but judgment comes into it too.

You read quite often nowadays of the problems of the African writer having first to think in his mother tongue and then to translate what he has thought into English. If it were such a simple, mechanical process, I would agree that it was pointless—the kind of eccentric pursuit you might expect to see in a modern Academy of Lagado; and such a process could not possibly produce some of the exciting poetry and prose which is already appearing.

One final point remains for me to make. The real question is not whether Africans *could* write in English but whether they *ought to.* Is it right that a man should abandon his mother tongue for someone else's? It looks like a dreadful betrayal and produces a guilty feeling.

But for me there is no other choice. I have been given this language and I intend to use it. I hope, though, that there always will be men, like the late Chief Fagunwa, who will choose to write in their native tongue and insure that our ethnic literature will flourish side by side with the national ones. For those of us who opt for English, there is much work ahead and much excitement.

Writing in the London *Observer* recently, James Baldwin said:

> My quarrel with the English language has been that the language reflected none of my experience. But now I began to see the matter another way. . . . Perhaps the language was not my own because I had never attempted to use it, had only learned to imitate it. If this were so, then it might be made to bear the burden of my experience if I could find the stamina to challenge it, and me, to such a test.

I recognize, of course, that Baldwin's problem is not exactly mine, but I feel that the English language will be able to carry the weight of my African experience. But it will have to be a new English, still in full communion with its ancestral home but altered to suit its new African surroundings.

Igbo Proverbs

CAUTION

If a man taps palm wine and cooks food,
One or the other is fated to be badly done;
The man who stands firm by his falsehood
Is more dignified than he who deserts his truth;
Frequenting the fortune teller's shrine
Does not always bring one wisdom;
A dog is deep in thought
And is thought to be asleep;
A tortoise is advised to be ready for a foe,
But he is already lying in ambush;
One who pursues a den to its end
Often ends up losing his fingers;
The pursuer after the innocent fowl
Is doomed to fall down;
The stick used for removing a millipede
Is often thrown away with it;
One who has not eaten the *udala** fruit
Never suffers from the disease caused by it;
For one who holds on to *owho*†
Is never lost in a journey.

SPIRIT POT

Spirit pot;
It is filled and unfilled at once!
One who hurries into a fight
Does not realise that to fight is to die!
One who has broken the *inyi* wood,
Can the *akpaka* wood defy him?
A worn-out basket:
It is recovered for use on the day of sacrifice!
If the vultures were meant to be eaten as food

*An orange-like fruit common in Eastern Nigeria.—EDS.
†An individual's guiding spirit.—EDS.

The ancestors would have exhausted them!
Magic paraphernalia:
They are never lacking in a *Dibia's** bag!
If the sky-vulture looms,
The devil enters the eagle's eye!

WHAT WILL IT BE?

What will it be today?
Success or failure?
Death or life?
Ha! the flood cannot run up the hill.
What is this evil spirit that throws his shade
Between me and the truth?
I hold my sacred staff against it.
Here is the east, there is the west;
Here the sun rises—
See the truth come riding on the rays of the sun.
The Sky and the Earth keep me company,
And can my tongue go zig-zag?
The grey hair is an enemy of lies.
Come, the spirits of my forefathers,
Stand by your son.
Let us show this client of ours what we can do
We have been known for this power:
If one cuts the *Ngwu* tree by noon,
It mocks him with a new shoot before the sun falls
Speak, speak to your son.

INVINCIBLE

Market is higgle-haggle;
If the market meets not, the pot cooks not,
Fowl never confers with fox;
Heavy she-goat is above being dragged;
White goat never confers with wolf;
Butterfly never sinks in a pit;
Empty calabash never sinks in water;
Basket never collects water;
Stone never answers a call;
Back of palm picks nothing from the ground;
Fight for peace never eats a hero;
The evil one causes stays put with him;
Blabbing made shrew's mouth pointed;
Smoke goes first, and fire follows.

*A soothsayer.—EDS.

(NINETEENTH CENTURY, Kenya)

Luyia Proverbs

A small tree grows up near a big tree.

The voice of the frog is no interference to the thirsty animals.

The hyena ate its protector.

A small thorn of a poisonous plant can kill an elephant.

When you take a sickle from a child, give it a stick.

The calf crosses where the mother crosses.

He who gives little will receive little.

He who is lame knows how to fall.

Whatever is not known remains unknown.

(NINETEENTH CENTURY, United States)

African American Spirituals

THAT LONESOME VALLEY

When you walk-a that lonesome Valley,
You got tuh walk it by yo'sef;
No one heah may walk it with you,
You got tuh walk it by yo'sef.

Chorus

Oh you got tuh walk-a that lonesome Valley,
You got tuh go that by yo'sef;
No one heah to go tha with you,
You got tuh go tha by yo'sef.

When you reach the rivah Jurdun,
You got tuh cross it by yo'sef;
No one heah may cross it with you,
You got tuh cross it by yo'sef.

When you face that Judgmunt mawnin',
You got tuh face it by yo'sef;
No one heah to face it faw you,
You got tuh face it by yo'sef.

Loud an' strong yo Mastuh callin',
You got tuh answer by yo'sef;
No one heah to answer faw you,
You got tuh answer by yo'sef.

You got tuh stand yo' trial in Judgmunt,
You got tuh stand it by yo'sef;
No one heah to stand it faw you,
You got tuh stand it by yo'sef.

Jurdun's stream is cold and chilly,
You got tuh wade it by yo'sef;
No one heah to wade it faw you,
You got tuh wade it by yo'sef.

When my dear Lawd was hangin' bleedin',
He had tuh hang tha by His-sef;
No one tha could hang tha faw Him,
He had tuh hang tha by His-sef.

You got tuh join that Christian Army,
You got tuh join it by yo-sef;
No one heah to join it faw you,
You got tuh join it by yo'sef.

You got tuh live a life of service,
You got tuh live it by yo'sef;
No one heah to live it faw you,
You got tuh live it by yo'sef.

SOON ONE MAWNIN' DEATH COME CREEPIN' IN YO' ROOM

Soon one mawnin' Death come creepin' in yo' room,
Soon one mawnin' Death come creepin' in yo' room,
   Hallelujah! Well
Soon one mawnin' Death come creepin' in yo' room.
Oh my Lawd, Oh my Lawd, what shall I do?

Soon one mawnin' Death come knockin' at yo' do',
Soon one mawnin' Death come knockin' at yo' do',
   Hallelujah! Well
Soon one mawnin' Death come knockin' at yo' do'.
Oh my Lawd, Oh my Lawd, what shall I do?

Hush! Hush! There's some one callin' mah name,
Hush! Hush! There's some one callin' mah name,
   Hallelujah! Well
Hush! Hush! There's some one callin' mah name.
Oh my Lawd, Oh my Lawd, what shall I do?

I'm so glad I belong to the church of God,
I'm so glad I belong to the church of God,
   Hallelujah! Well
I'm so glad I belong to the church of God.
Oh my Lawd, Oh my Lawd, what shall I do?

I'm so glad I can pray like the Savior prayed,
I'm so glad I can pray like the Savior prayed,
   Hallelujah! Well

I'm so glad I can pray like the Savior prayed.
Oh my Lawd, Oh my Lawd, what shall I do?

I'm so glad that Jesus will call mah name,
I'm so glad that Jesus will call mah name,
    Hallelujah! Well
I'm so glad that Jesus will call mah name.
Oh my Lawd, Oh my Lawd, what shall I do?

I'm so glad that trouble doan last always,
I'm so glad that trouble doan last always,
    Hallelujah! Well
I'm so glad that trouble doan last always.
Oh my Lawd, Oh my Lawd, what shall I do?

OH MARY, OH MARTHY

Chorus

Oh! Mary, Oh! Marthy, go tell my disciples,
Gwine-a meet Him in Gallalee,
Gwine-a meet Him in Gallalee.
Yes, bless de Lawd, meet Him in Gallalee.
Gwine-a meet Him in Gallalee.

Oh! yondah come duh charet,
Duh hosses dressed in white,
Duh of' wheels a runnin' by duh grace ob God,
An' duh hin' wheels a runnin' by love;
An' duh hin' wheels a runnin' by love.

Oh! yondah come ole Satan
Wid a black book under his arm;
A hollerin' give me jestice,
Mo'n hafen dem people am mine,
Mo'n hafen dem people am mine.
Yes, bless de Lawd, hafen dem people am mine;
Mo'n hafen dem people am mine.

Oh! yondah come Brudder Peter,
An' how do you know it's him?
Wid a crown upon his fo'head
An' de keys of Bethlyham,
An' de keys of Bethlyham.
Yes, bless de Lawd, keys of Bethlyham;
An' de keys of Bethlyham.

Philosophy and Morality

Oh! yondah come Sista Mary,
An' how do you know it's huhr?
A shoutin' Hallelujah
An' praises to duh Lamb,
An' praises to duh Lamb,
An' praises duh Lawd, praises to duh Lamb;
An' praises to duh Lamb.

My God Is a Man of War

Chorus

My God He is a Man—a Man of war,
My God He is a Man—a Man of war,
My God He is a Man—a Man of war,
    An' de Lawd God is His name.

He tole Noah to build an ark,
    By His Holy plan;
He tole Moses to lead the chillun,
    From Egypt to the Promised Lan'.
My God He is a Man—a Man of war,
My God He is a Man—a Man of war,
My God He is a Man—a Man of war,
    An' de Lawd God is His name.

Long befo' the flyin' clouds,
    Befo' the heavens above,
Befo' creation evuh was made,
    He had redeemin' love.
My God He is a Man—a Man of war,
My God He is a Man—a Man of war,
My God He is a Man—a Man of war,
    An' de Lawd God is His name.

He made the sun an' moon an' stahrs,
    To rule both day an' night;
He placed them in the firmament,
    An' told them to give light.
My God He is a Man—a Man of war,
My God He is a Man—a Man of war,
My God He is a Man—a Man of war,
    An' de Lawd God is His name.

He made the birds of the air,
    An' made the earth aroun';
He made the beasts of the field,
    An' made the serpents on the groun'.

My God He is a Man—a Man of war,
My God He is a Man—a Man of war,
My God He is a Man—a Man of war,
    An' de Lawd God is His name.

TIME IS DRAWIN' NIGH

See the signs of the Judgmunt, yes,
See the signs of the Judgmunt, yes,
See the signs of the Judgmunt, yes, Lawd,
Time is drawin' nigh.

God talkin' in the lightenin', yes,
An' He's talkin' in the thunder, yes,
An' the world's all a-wonder, yes, Lawd,
Time is drawin' nigh.

See the sign of the fig tree, yes,
My Jesus said it would be, yes,
The sign of the Judgmunt, yes, Lawd,
Time is drawin' nigh.

Loose horse in the valley, yes,
Don't you hear him laughin', yes,
He's laughin' like Judgmunt, yes, Lawd,
Time is drawin' nigh.

God told Moses, yes,
Sanctify the people, yes,
An' take to the mountains, yes, Lawd,
Time is drawin' nigh.

In the city of Jerusalem, yes,
On the day of Pentecost, yes,
The people received the Holy Ghost, Lawd,
Time is drawin' nigh.

Who is that yonduh, yes,
Comin' from Eden, yes,
Dyed garments from Bozah, yes, Lawd,
Time is drawin' nigh.

It looks like Jesus, yes,
Glorious in His appearance, yes,
Treadin' the wine press, yes, Lawd,
Time is drawin' nigh.

Philosophy and Morality

Thy Kingdom come, yes,
Thy will be done, yes,
They'll speak in other tongues, yes, Lawd,
Time is drawin' nigh.

They will hate one another, yes,
My Jesus said it would be, yes,
They'll take you in council, yes, Lawd,
Time is drawin' nigh.

Have you been converted, yes,
Sanctified an' holy, yes,
Baptized with the Holy Ghost, yes, Lawd,
Time is drawin' nigh.

I have my ticket, yes,
It takes a holy ticket, yes,
Signed all the way to glory, yes, Lawd,
Time is drawin' nigh.

Come on children, yes,
Let's go to glory, yes,
An' don't get tired, yes, Lawd,
Time is drawin' nigh.

Do Lord Remember Me

Chorus

> *Do Lawd, do Lawd, do remembuh, me,*
> *Do Lawd, do Lawd, do remembuh, me,*
> *Do Lawd, do Lawd, do remembuh, me,*
>   *Do, Lawd, remembuh me.*

When I'm sick an' by myself,
  Do remembuh me;
When I'm sick an' by myself,
  Do remembuh me.
When I'm sick an' by myself,
  Do remembuh me,
Do, Lawd, remembuh me.

When I'm crossin' Jurdon,
  Do remembuh me;
When I'm crossin' Jurdon,
  Do remembuh me.
When I'm crossin' Jurdon,
  Do remembuh me,
Do, Lawd, remembuh me.

If I ain't got no frien's at all,
    Do remembuh me;
If I ain't got no frien's at all,
    Do remembuh me.
If I ain't got no frien's at all,
    Do remembuh me,
Do, Lawd, remembuh me.

Paul an' Silus bound in jail,
    Do remembuh me;
Paul an' Silus bound in jail,
    Do remembuh me.
Paul an' Silus bound in jail,
    Do remembuh me,
Do, Lawd, remembuh me.

One did sing while the other one prayed,
    Do remembuh me;
One did sing while the other one prayed,
    Do remembuh me.
One did sing while the other one prayed,
    Do remembuh me,
Do, Lawd, remembuh me.

When I'm bound in trouble,
    Do remembuh me;
When I'm bound in trouble,
    Do remembuh me.
When I'm bound in trouble,
    Do remembuh me,
Do, Lawd, remembuh me.

When I'm goin' from do' to do',
    Do remembuh me;
When I'm goin' from do' to do',
    Do remembuh me.
When I'm goin' from do' to do',
    Do remembuh me,
Do, Lawd, remembuh me.

I GOT A HIDIN' PLACE

Chorus

> *I got a hidin' place—*
>   *In de Word of God,*
> *I got a hidin' place.*

Philosophy and Morality

The ship she stop
In de middle of de sea,
Jonah cried out—
Lawd have mercy, is it me?
    Throw me overboa'd.
I got a hidin' place,
    Throw me overboa'd,
I got a hidin' place.
I got a hidin' place—
    In de Word of God,
I got a hidin' place.

Wonder what's the matter
That de ship don't go;
There's too many liyuhs
Gittin' on boa'd.
    Throw 'em overboa'd.
I got a hidin' place,
    Throw 'em overboa'd,
I got a hidin' place.
I got a hidin' place—
    In de Word of God,
I got a hidin' place.

Wonder what's the matter
That de ship won't go;
There's too many hypocrits
Gittin' on boa'd.
    Well you cain't hide now.
I got a hidin' place,
    Well you cain't hide now,
I got a hidin' place.
I got a hidin' place—
    In de Word of God,
I got a hidin' place.

Tell that watchman
That he cain't hide;
If he hasn't got de Holy Ghost
He cain't ride.
    Get de Holy Ghost.
I got a hidin' place,
    Get de Holy Ghost,
I got a hidin' place—
    In de Word of God,
I got a hidin' place.

There's too many people
Like Jonah today;

God sends 'um out
An' they will not obey.
    Won't you help me Lawd
I got a hidin' place,
    Won't you help me Lawd
I got a hidin' place.
I got a hidin' place—
    In de Word of God,
I got a hidin' place.

If you wawnta go to heabum
Like anybody else;
Treat yo' neighbuh
Like you treat yo'self.
    Treat yo' neighbuh
I got a hidin' place,
    Treat yo' neighbuh
I got a hidin' place.
I got a hidin' place—
    Roun' de throne of God,
I got a hidin' place.

Well, when I git to heabum
Gonna sing an' shout;
There's nobody there
Gonna put me out.
    Well in Canaan land.
I got a hidin' place,
    Well in Canaan land,
I got a hidin' place.
I got a hidin' place—
    Roun' de throne of God,
I got a hidin' place.

Maria W. Stewart

(1803–1879, United States)

On African Rights and Liberty

African rights and liberty is a subject that ought to fire the breast of every free man of color in these United States, and excite in his bosom a lively deep, decided, and heart-felt interest. When I cast my eyes on the long list of illustrious names that are enrolled on the bright annals of fame among the whites, I turn my eyes within, and ask my thoughts, "Where are the names of our illustrious ones?" It must certainly have been for the want of energy on the part of the free people of color, that they have been long willing to beat the yoke of oppression. It must have been the want of ambition and force that has given the whites occasion to say that our natural abilities are not as good, and our capacities by nature inferior to theirs. They boldly assert that did we possess a natural independence of soul, and feel a love for liberty within our breasts, some one of our sable race, long before this, would have testified it, notwithstanding the disadvantages under which we labor. We have made ourselves appear altogether unqualified to speak in our own defence, and are therefore looked upon as objects of pity and commiseration. We have been imposed upon, insulted, and derided on every side; and now, if we complain, it is considered as the height of impertinence. We have suffered ourselves to be considered as dastards, cowards, mean, faint-hearted wretches; and on this account (not because of our complexion) many despise us, and would gladly spurn us from their presence.

These things have fired my soul with a holy indignation, and compelled me thus to come forward, and endeavor to turn their attention to knowledge and improvement; for knowledge is power. I would ask, is it blindness of mind, or stupidity of soul, or the want of education that has caused our men who are 60 or 70 years of age, never to let their voices be heard, nor their hands be raised in behalf of their color? Or has it been for the fear of offending the whites? If it has, O ye fearful ones, throw off your fearfulness, and come forth in the name of the Lord, and in the strength of the God of Justice, and make yourselves useful and active members in society; for they admire a noble and patriotic spirit in others; and should they not admire it in us? If you are men, convince them that you possess the spirit of men; and as your day, so shall your strength be. Have the sons of Africa no souls? Feel they no ambitious desires? Shall the chains of ignorance forever confine them? Shall the insipid appellation of "clever negroes," or "good creatures," any longer content them? Where can we find among ourselves the man of science, or a philosopher, or an able statesman, or a counsellor at law? Show me our fearless and brave, our noble and gallant ones. Where are our lecturers in natural history, and our critics in useful knowledge? There may be a few such men among us, but they are rare. It is true our fathers bled and died in the revolutionary war, and others fought bravely under the command of Jackson, in defence of liberty. But where is the man that has distinguished himself in these modern days by acting wholly in the defence of African rights and liberty? There was one, although he sleeps, his memory lives.

I am sensible that there are many highly intelligent men of color in these United States, in the force of whose arguments, doubtless, I should discover my inferiority; but if they are blessed with wit and talent, friends and fortune, why have they not made themselves men of eminence, by striving to take all the reproach that is cast upon the people of color, and in endeavoring to alleviate the woes of their brethren in bondage? Talk, without effort, is nothing; you are abundantly capable, gentlemen, of making yourselves men of distinction; and this gross neglect, on your part, causes my blood to boil within me. Here is the grand cause which hinders the rise and progress of people of color. It is their want of laudable ambition and requisite courage.

Individuals have been distinguished according to their genius and talents, ever since the first formation of man, and will continue to be while the world stands. The different grades rise to honor and respectability as their merits may deserve. History informs us that we sprung from one of the most learned nations of the whole earth; from the seat, if not the parent, of science. Yes, poor despised Africa was once the resort of sages and legislators of other nations, was esteemed the school for learning, and the most illustrious men in Greece flocked thither for instruction. But it was our gross sins and abominations that provoked the Almighty to frown thus heavily upon us, and give our glory unto others. Sin and prodigality have caused the downfall of nations, kings and emperors; and were it not that God in wrath remembers mercy, we might indeed despair; but a promise is left us; "Ethiopia shall again stretch forth her hands unto God."

But it is of no use for us to boast that we sprung from this learned and enlightened nation, for this day a thick mist of moral gloom hangs over millions of our race. Our condition as a people has been low for hundreds of years, and it will continue to be so, unless by true piety and virtue, we strive to regain that which we have lost. White Americans, by their prudence, economy, and exertions, have sprung up and become one of the most flourishing nations in the world, distinguished for their knowledge of the arts and sciences, for their polite literature. While our minds are vacant and starve for want of knowledge, theirs are filled to overflowing. Most of our color have been taught to stand in fear of the white man from their earliest infancy, to work as soon as they could walk, and to call "master" before they could scare lisp the name of mother. Continual fear and laborious servitude have in some degree lessened in us that natural force and energy which belong to man; or else, in defiance of opposition, our men, before this, would have nobly and boldly contended for their rights. But give the man of color an equal opportunity with the white from the cradle to manhood, and from manhood to the grave, and you would discover the dignified statesman, the man of science, and the philosopher. But there is no such opportunity for the sons of Africa, and I fear that our powerful ones are fully determined that there never shall be. Forbid, ye Powers on high, that it should any longer be said that our men possess no force. O ye sons of Africa, when will your voices be heard in our legislative halls, in defiance of your enemies, contending for equal rights and liberty? How can you, when you reflect from what you have fallen, refrain from crying mightily unto God, to turn away from us the fierceness of his anger, and remember our transgressions against us no more forever? But a god of infinite purity will not regard the prayers of those who hold religion in one hand, and prejudice, sin, and pollution in the other; he will not regard the prayers of self-righteousness and hypocrisy. Is it possible, I exclaim, that for the want of knowledge we have labored for hundreds of years to support others, and been content to receive what they chose to give us in return? Cast your eyes about, look as far as you can see; all, all is owned by the lordly white except here and there a lowly dwelling which the man of color, midst deprivations, fraud, and opposition has been scarce able to procure. Like King Solomon, who put neither nail or hammer to the temple, yet received the praise; so also have the white Americans gained themselves a name, like the names of the great men that are in the earth, while in reality we have been their principal foundation and support. We have pursued the shadow, they have obtained the substance; we have performed the labor, they have received the profits; we have planted the vines; they have eaten the fruits of them.

I would implore our men, and especially our rising youth, to flee from the gambling board and the dance-hall; for we are poor, and have no money to throw away. I do not consider dancing as criminal in itself, but it is astonishing to me that our fine young men are so blind to their own interest and the future welfare of their children as to spend their hard earnings for this frivolous amusement; for it has been carried on among us to such an unbecoming extent that it has become absolutely disgusting. "Faithful are the wounds of a friend, but the kisses of an enemy are deceitful" [Proverbs 27:6]. Had those men among us who had an opportunity, turned their attention as assiduously to mental and moral improvement as they have to gambling and dancing, I might have remained quietly at home and they stood contending in my place. These polite accomplishments will never enroll your names on the bright annals of fame who admire the belle void of intellectual knowledge, or applaud the dandy that talks largely on politics, without striving to assist his fellow in the revolution, when the nerves and muscles of every other man forced him into the field of action. You have a right to rejoice, and to let your hearts cheer you in the days of your youth; yet remember that for all these things God will bring you into judgment. Then, O ye sons of Africa, turn your mind from these perishable objects, and contend for the cause of God and the rights of man. Form yourselves into temperance societies. There are temperate men among you; then why will you any longer neglect to strive, by your example, to suppress vice in all its abhorrent forms? You have been told repeatedly of the glorious results arising from temperance, and can you bear to see the whites arising in honor and respectability without endeavoring to grasp after that honor and respectability also?

But I forbear. Let our money, instead of being thrown away as heretofore, be appropriated for schools and seminaries of learning for our children and youth. We ought to follow the example of the whites in this respect. Nothing would raise our respectability, add to our peace and happiness, and reflect so much honor upon us, as to be ourselves the promoters of temperance, and the supporters, as far as we are able, of useful and scientific knowledge. The rays of light and knowledge have been hid from our view; we have been taught to consider ourselves as scarce superior to the brute creation; and have performed the most laborious part of American drudgery. Had we as a people received one-half the early advantages the whites have received, I would defy the government of these United States to deprive us any longer of our rights.

I am informed that the agent of the Colonization Society has recently formed an association of young men for the purpose of influencing those of us to go to Liberia who may feel disposed. The colonizationists are blind to their own interest, for should the nations of the earth make war with America, they would find their forces much weakened by our abscence; or should we remain here, can our "brave soldiers" and "fellow citizens," as they were termed in time of calamity, condescend to defend the rights of whites and be again deprived of their own, or sent to Liberia in return? Or, if the colonizationists are the real friends to Africa, let them expend the money which they collect in erecting a college to educate her injured sons in this land of gospel, light, and liberty; for it would be most thankfully received on our part, and convince us of the truth of their professions, and save time, expense, and anxiety. Let them place before us noble objects worthy of pursuit, and see if we prove ourselves to be those unambitious Negroes they term us. But, ah, methinks their hearts are so frozen toward us they had rather their money should be sunk in the ocean than to administer it to our relief: and I fear, if they dared, like Pharaoh, king of Egypt, they would order every male child among us to be drowned. But the most high God is still as able to subdue the lofty pride of these white Americans as He was the heart of that ancient rebel. They say, though we are looked upon as things, yet we sprang from a scientific people. Had our men the requisite force and energy they would soon convince them by their efforts, both in public and private, that they were men, or things in the shape of men. Well may the colonizationists laugh us to scorn for our negligence; well may they cry: "Shame to the sons of Africa." As the burden of the Israelites was too great for Moses to bear, so also is our burden too great for our noble advocate to bear. You must feel interested, my brethren, in what he undertakes, and hold up his hands by your good works, or in spite of himself his soul will become discouraged and his heart will die within him; for he has, as it were, the strong bulls of Bashan [Psalms 22:12] to contend with.

It is of no use for us to wait any longer for a generation of well-educated men to arise. We have slumbered and slept too long already; the day is far spent; the night of death approaches; and you have sound sense and good judgment sufficient to begin with, if you feel disposed to make a right use of it. Let every man of color throughout the United States, who possesses the spirit and principles of a man, sign a petition to Congress to abolish slavery in the District of Columbia, and grant you the rights and privileges of common free citizens; for if you had had faith as a grain of mustard seed [Matthew 13:31], long before this the mountain of prejudice might have been removed. We are all sensible that the Anti-Slavery Society has taken hold of the arm of our whole population, in order to raise them out of the mire. Now all we have to do is, by a spirit of virtuous ambition, to strive to raise ourselves; and I am happy to have it in my power thus publicly to say that the colored inhabitants of this city, in some respects, are beginning to improve. Had the free people of color in these United States nobly and freely contended for their rights, and showed a natural genius and talent, although not so brilliant as some; had they held up, encouraged, and patronized each other, nothing could have hindered us from being a thriving and flourishing people. There has been a fault among us. The reason why our distinguished men have not made themselves more influential, is because they fear that the strong current of opposition through which they must pass would cause their downfall and prove their overthrow. And what gives rise to this opposition? Envy. And what has it amounted to? Nothing. And who are the cause of it? Our whited sepulchres [Matthew 23:27], who want to be great, and don't know how; who love to be called of men "Rabbi, Rabbi"; who put on false sanctity, and humble themselves to their brethren for the sake of acquiring the highest place in the synagogue and the uppermost seat at the feast. You, dearly beloved, who are the genuine followers of our Lord Jesus Christ—the salt of the earth, and the light of the world—are not so culpable. As I told you in the very first of my writing, I will tell you again, I am but as a drop in the bucket—as one particle of the small dust of the earth [Isaiah 40:15]. God will surely raise up those among us who will plead the cause of virtue and the pure principles of morality more eloquently than I am able to do.

It appears to me that America has become like the great city of Babylon, for she has boasted in her heart: "I sit a queen and am no widow, and shall see no sorrow" [Revelation 18:7]! She is, indeed, a seller of slaves and the souls of men; she has made the Africans drunk with the wine of her fornication; she has put them completely beneath her feet, and she means to keep them there; her right hand supports the reins of government and her left hand the wheel of power, and she is determined not to let go her grasp. But many powerful sons and daughters of Africa will shortly arise, who will put down vice and immorality among us, and declare by Him that sitteth upon the throne that they will have their rights; and if refused, I am afraid they will spread horror and devastation around. I believe that the oppression of injured Africa has come up before the majesty of Heaven; and when our cries shall have reached the ears of the Most High, it will be a tremendous day for the people of this land; for strong is the hand of the Lord God Almighty.

Life has almost lost its charms for me; death has lost its sting, and the grave its terrors [I Corinthians 15:55]; and at times I have a strong desire to depart and dwell with Christ, which is far better. Let me entreat my white brethren to awake and save our sons from dissipation and our daughters from ruin. Lend the hand of assistance to feeble merit; plead the cause of virtue among our sable race; so shall our curses upon you be turned into blessings; and though you should endeavor to drive us from these shores, still we will cling to you the more firmly; nor will we attempt to rise above you; we will presume to be called your equals only.

The unfriendly whites first drove the native American from his much loved home. Then they stole our fathers from their peaceful and quiet dwellings, and brought them hither, and made bond-men and bond-women of them and their little ones. They have obliged our brethren to labor; kept them in utter ignorance; nourished them in vice, and raised them in degradation; and now that we have enriched their soil, and filled their coffers, they say that we are not capable of becoming like white men, and that we can never rise to respectability in this country. They would drive us to a strange land. But before I go, the bayonet shall pierce me through. African rights and liberty is a subject that ought to fire the breast of every free man of color in these United States, and excite in his bosom a lively, deep, decided, and heartfelt interest.

Marcus Garvey
(1887–1940, Jamaica)

Philosophy and Opinions

Africa for the Africans

For five years the Universal Negro Improvement Association has been advocating the cause of Africa for the Africans—that is, that the Negro peoples of the world should concentrate upon the object of building up for themselves a great nation in Africa.

When we started our propaganda toward this end several of the so-called intellectual Negroes who have been bamboozling the race for over half a century said that we were crazy, that the Negro peoples of the western world were not interested in Africa and could not live in Africa. One editor and leader went so far as to say at his so-called Pan-African Congress that American Negroes could not live in Africa, because the climate was too hot. All kinds of arguments have been adduced by these Negro intellectuals against the colonization of Africa by the black race. Some said that the black man would ultimately work out his existence alongside of the white man in countries founded and established by the latter. Therefore, it was not necessary for Negroes to seek an independent nationality of their own. The old time stories of "African fever," "African bad climate," "African mosquitos," "African savages," have been repeated by these "brainless intellectuals" of ours as a scare against our people in America and the West Indies taking a kindly interest in the new program of building a racial empire of our own in our Motherland. Now that years have rolled by and the Universal Negro Improvement Association has made the circuit of the world with its propaganda, we find eminent statesmen and leaders of the white race coming out boldly advocating the cause of colonizing Africa with the Negroes of the western world. A year ago Senator MacCullum of the Mississippi Legislature introduced a resolution in the House for the purpose of petitioning the Congress of the United States of America and the President to use their good influence in securing from the Allies sufficient territory in Africa in liquidation of the war debt, which territory should be used for the establishing of an independent nation for American Negroes. About the same time Senator France of Maryland gave expression to a similar desire in the Senate of the United States. During a speech on the "Soldiers' Bonus," he said: "We owe a big debt to Africa and one which we have too long ignored. I need not enlarge upon our peculiar interest in the obligation to the people of Africa. Thousands of Americans have for years been contributing to the missionary work which has been carried out by the noble men and women who have been sent out in that field by the churches of America."

This reveals a real change on the part of prominent statesmen in their attitude to the African question. Then comes another suggestion from Germany, for which Dr. Heinrich Schnee, a former Governor of German East Africa, is author. This German statesman suggests in an interview given out in Berlin, and published in New York, that America takes over the mandatories of Great Britain and France in Africa for the colonization of American Negroes. Speaking on the matter, he says "As regards the attempt to colonize Africa with the surplus American colored population, this would in a long way settle the vexed problem, and under the plan such as Senator France has outlined, might enable France and Great Britain to discharge their duties to the United States, and simultaneously ease the burden of German reparations which is paralyzing economic life."

With expressions as above quoted from prominent world statesmen, and from the demands made by such men as Senators France and MacCullum, it is clear that the question of African nationality is not a far-fetched one, but is as reasonable and feasible as was the idea of an American nationality.

A "Program" at Last

I trust that the Negro peoples of the world are now convinced that the work of the Universal Negro Improvement Association is not a visionary one, but very practical, and that it is not so far fetched, but can be realized in a short while if the entire race will only co-operate and work toward the desired end. Now that the work of our organization has started to bear fruit we find that some of these "doubting Thomases" of three and four years ago are endeavoring to mix themselves up with the popular idea of rehabilitating Africa in the interest of the Negro. They are now advancing spurious "programs" and in a short while will endeavor to force themselves upon the public as advocates and leaders of the African idea.

It is felt that those who have followed the career of the Universal Negro Improvement Association will not allow themselves to be deceived by these Negro opportunists who have always sought to live off the ideas of other people.

The Dream of a Negro Empire

It is only a question of a few more years when Africa will be completely colonized by Negroes, as Europe is by the white race. What we want is an independent African nationality, and if America is to help the Negro peoples of the world establish such a nationality then we welcome the assistance.

It is hoped that when the time comes for American and West Indian Negroes to settle in Africa, they will realize their responsibility and their duty. It will not be to go to Africa for the purpose of exercising an over-lordship over the natives, but it shall be the purpose of the Universal Negro Improvement Association to have established in Africa that brotherly co-operation which will make the interests of the African native and the American and West Indian Negro one and the same, that is to say, we shall enter into a common partnership to build up Africa in the interests of our race.

Oneness of Interests

Everybody knows that there is absolutely no difference between the native African and the American and West Indian Negroes, in that we are descendants from one common family stock. It is only a matter of accident that we have been divided and kept apart for over three hundred years, but it is felt that when the time has come for us to get back together, we shall do so in the spirit of brotherly love, and any Negro who expects that he will be assisted here, there or anywhere by the Universal Negro Improvement Association to exercise a haughty superiority over the fellows of his own race, makes a tremendous mistake. Such men had better remain where they are and not attempt to become in any way interested in the higher development of Africa.

The Negro has had enough of the vaunted practice of race superiority as inflicted upon him by others, therefore he is not prepared to tolerate a similar assumption on the part of his own people. In America and the West Indies, we have Negroes who believe themselves so much above their fellows as to cause them to think that any readjustment in the affairs of the race should be placed in their hands for them to exercise a kind of an autocratic and despotic control as others have done to us for centuries. Again I say, it would be advisable for such Negroes to take their hands and minds off the now popular idea of colonizing Africa in the interest in the Negro race, because their being identified with this new program will not in any way help us because of the existing feeling among Negroes everywhere not to tolerate the infliction of race or class superiority upon them, as is the desire of the self-appointed and self-created race leadership that we have been having for the last fifty years.

The Basis of an African Aristocracy

The masses of Negroes in America, the West Indies, South and Central America are in sympathetic accord with the aspirations of the native Africans. We desire to help them build up Africa as a Negro Empire, where every black man, whether he was born in Africa or in the Western world, will have the opportunity to develop on his own lines under the protection of the most favorable democratic institutions.

It will be useless, as before stated, for bombastic Negroes to leave America and the West Indies to go to Africa, thinking that they will have privileged positions to inflict upon the race that bastard aristocracy that they have tried to maintain in this Western world at the expense of the masses. Africa shall develop an aristocracy of its own, but it shall be based upon service and loyalty to race. Let all Negroes work toward that end. I feel that [it] is only a question of a few more years before our program will be accepted not only by the few statesmen of America who are now interested in it, but by the strong statesmen of the world, as the only solution to the great race problem. There is no other way to avoid the threatening war of the races that is bound to engulf all mankind, which has been prophesied by the world's greatest thinkers; there is no better method than by apportioning every race to its own habitat.

The time has really come for the Asiatics to govern themselves in Asia, as the Europeans are in Europe and the Western world, so also is it wise for the Africans to govern themselves at home, and thereby bring peace and satisfaction to the entire human family.

It comes to the individual, the race, the nation, once in a life time to decide upon the course to be pursued as a career. The hour has now struck for the individual Negro as well as the entire race to decide the course that will be pursued in the interest of our own liberty.

We who make up the Universal Negro Improvement Association have decided that we shall go forward, upward and onward toward the great goal of human liberty. We have determined among ourselves that all barriers placed in the way of our progress must be removed, must be cleared away for we desire to see the light of a brighter day.

The Negro Is Ready

The Universal Negro Improvement Association for five years has been proclaiming to the world the readiness of the Negro to carve out a pathway for himself in the course of life. Men of other races and nations have become alarmed at this attitude of the Negro in his desire to do things for himself and by himself. This alarm has become so universal that organizations have been brought into being here, there and everywhere for the purpose of deterring and obstructing this forward move of our race. Propaganda has been waged here, there and everywhere for the purpose of misinterpreting the intention of this organization; some have said that this organization seeks to create discord and discontent among the races; some say we are organized for the purpose of hating other people. Every sensible, sane and honest-minded person knows that the Universal Negro Improvement Association has no such intention. We are organized for the absolute purpose of bettering our condition, industrially, commercially, socially, religiously and politically. We are organized not to hate other men, but to lift ourselves, and to demand respect of all humanity. We have a program that we believe to be righteous; we believe it to be just, and we have made up our minds to lay down ourselves on the altar of sacrifice for the realization of this great hope of ours, based upon the foundation of righteousness. We declare to the world that Africa must be free, that the entire Negro race must be emancipated from industrial bondage, peonage and serfdom; we make no compromise, we make no apology in this our declaration. We do not desire to create offense on the part of other races, but we are determined that we shall be heard, that we shall be given the rights to which we are entitled.

The Propaganda of Our Enemies

For the purpose of creating doubts about the work of the Universal Negro Improvement Association, many attempts have been made to cast shadow and gloom over our work. They have even written the most uncharitable things about our organization; they have spoken so unkindly of our effort, but what do we care? They spoke unkindly and uncharitably about all the reform movements that have helped in the betterment of humanity. They maligned the great movement of the Christian religion; they maligned the great liberation movements of America, of France, of England, of Russia; can we expect, then, to escape being maligned in this, our desire for the liberation of Africa and the freedom of four hundred million Negroes of the world?

We have unscrupulous men and organizations working in opposition to us. Some [are] trying to capitalize the new spirit that has come to the Negro to make profit out of it to their own selfish benefit; some are trying to set back the Negro from seeing the hope of his own liberty, and thereby poisoning our people's mind against the motives of our organization; but every sensible far-seeing Negro in this enlightened age knows what propaganda means. It is the medium of discrediting that which you are opposed to, so that the propaganda of our enemies will be of little avail as soon as we are rendered able to carry to our peoples scattered throughout the world the true message of our great organization.

"Crocodiles" as Friends

Men of the Negro race, let me say to you that a greater future is in store for us; we have no cause to lose hope, to become faint-hearted. We must realize that upon ourselves depend our destiny, our future; we must carve out that future, that destiny, and we who make up the Universal Negro Improvement Association have pledged ourselves that nothing in the world shall stand in our way, nothing in the world shall discourage us, but opposition shall make us work harder, shall bring us closer together so that as one man in the millions of us will march on toward that goal that we have set for ourselves. The new Negro shall not be deceived. The new Negro refuses to take advice from anyone who has not felt with him, and suffered with him. We have suffered for three hundred years, therefore we feel that the time has come when only those who have suffered with us can interpret our feelings and our spirit. It takes the slave to interpret the feelings of the slave; it takes the unfortunate man to interpret the spirit of his unfortunate brother; and so it takes the suffering Negro to interpret the spirit of his comrade. It is strange that so many people are interested in the Negro now, willing to advise him how to act, and what organizations he should join, yet nobody was interested in the Negro to the extent of not making him a slave for two hundred and fifty years, reducing him to industrial peonage and serfdom after he was freed; it is strange that the same people can be so interested in the Negro now, as to tell him what organization he should follow and what leader he should support.

Whilst we are bordering on a future of brighter things, we are also at our danger period, when we must either accept the right philosophy, or go down by following deceptive propaganda which has hemmed us in for many centuries.

Deceiving the People

There is many a leader of our race who tells us that everything is well, and that all things will work out themselves and that a better day is coming. Yes, all of us know that a better day is coming; we all know that one day we will go home to Paradise, but whilst we are hoping by our Christian virtues to have an entry into Paradise we also realize that we are living on earth, and that the things that are practised in Paradise are not practised here. You have to treat this world as the world treats you; we are living in a temporal, material age, an age of activity, an age of racial, national selfishness. What else can you expect but to give back to the world what the world gives to you, and we are calling upon the four hundred million Negroes of the world to take a decided stand, a determined stand, that we shall occupy a firm position; that position shall be an emancipated race and a free nation of our own. We are determined that we shall have a free country; we are determined that we shall have a flag; we are determined that we shall have a government second to none in the world.

An Eye for an Eye

Men may spurn the idea, they may scoff at it; the metropolitan press of this country may deride us; yes, white men may laugh at the idea of Negroes talking about government; but let me tell you there is going to be a government, and let me say to you also that whatsoever you give, in like measure it shall be returned to you. The world is sinful, and therefore man believes in the doctrine of an eye for an eye, a tooth for a tooth. Everybody believes that revenge is God's, but at the same time we are men, and revenge sometimes springs up, even in the most Christian heart.

Why should man write down a history that will react against him? Why should man perpetrate deeds of wickedness upon his brother which will return to him in like measure? Yes, the Germans maltreated the French in the Franco-Prussian war of 1870, but the French got even with the Germans in 1918. It is history, and history will repeat itself. Beat the Negro, brutalize the Negro, kill the Negro, burn the Negro, imprison the Negro, scoff at the Negro, deride the Negro, it may come back to you one of these fine days, because the supreme destiny of man is in the hands of God. God is no respecter of persons, whether that person be white, yellow or black. Today the one race is up, tomorrow it has fallen; today the Negro seems to be the footstool of the other races and nations of the world; tomorrow the Negro may occupy the highest rung of the great human ladder.

But when we come to consider the history of man, was not the Negro a power, was he not great once? Yes, honest students of history can recall the day when Egypt, Ethiopia and Timbuctoo towered in their civilizations, towered above Europe, towered above Asia. When Europe was inhabited by a race of cannibals, a race of savages, naked men, heathens and pagans, Africa was peopled with a race of cultured black men, who were masters in art, science and literature; men who were cultured and refined; men who, it was said, were like the gods. Even the great poets of old sang in beautiful sonnets of the delight it afforded the gods to be in companionship with the Ethiopians. Why, then, should we lose hope? Black men, you were once great; you shall be great again. Lose not courage, lose not faith, go forward. The thing to do is to get organized; keep separated and you will be exploited, you will be robbed, you will be killed. Get organized, and you will compel the world to respect you. If the world fails to give you consideration, because you are black men, because you are Negroes, four hundred millions of you shall, through organization, shake the pillars of the universe and bring down creation, even as Samson brought down the temple upon his head and upon the heads of the Philistines.

An Inspiring Vision

So Negroes, I say, through the Universal Negro Improvement Association, that there is much to live for. I have a vision of the future, and I see before me a picture of a redeemed Africa, with her dotted cities, with her beautiful civilization, with her millions of happy children, going to and fro. Why should I lose hope, why should I give up and take a back place in this age of progress? Remember that you are men, that God created you Lords of this creation. Lift up yourselves, men, take yourselves out of the mire and hitch your hopes to the stars; yes, rise as high as the very stars themselves. Let no man pull you down, let no man destroy your ambition, because man is but your companion, your equal; man is your brother; he is not your lord; he is not your sovereign master.

We of the Universal Negro Improvement Association feel happy; we are cheerful. Let them connive to destroy us; let them organize to destroy us; we shall fight the more. Ask me personally the cause of my success, and I say opposition; oppose me, and I fight the more, and if you want to find out the sterling worth of the Negro, oppose him, and under the leadership of the Universal Negro Improvement Association he shall fight his way to victory, and in the days to come, and I believe not far distant, Africa shall reflect a splendid demonstration of the worth of the Negro, of the determination of the Negro, to set himself free and to establish a government of his own.

W. E. B. Du Bois

(1868–1963, United States)

The Concept of Race

I want now . . . to consider the conception which is after all my main subject. The concept of race lacks something in personal interest, but personal interest in my case has always depended primarily upon this race concept and I wish to examine this now. The history of the development of the race concept in the world and particularly in America, was naturally reflected in the education offered me. In the elementary school it came only in the matter of geography when the races of the world were pictured: Indians, Negroes and Chinese, by their most uncivilized and bizarre representatives; the whites by some kindly and distinguished-looking philanthropist. In the elementary and high school, the matter was touched only incidentally, due I doubt not to the thoughtfulness of the teachers; and again my racial inferiority could not be dwelt upon because the single representative of the Negro race in the school did not happen to be in any way inferior to his fellows. In fact it was not difficult for me to excel them in many ways and to regard this as quite natural.

At Fisk, the problem of race was faced openly and essential racial equality asserted and natural inferiority strenuously denied. In some cases the teachers expressed this theory; in most cases the student opinion naturally forced it. At Harvard, on the other hand, I began to face scientific race dogma: first of all, evolution and the "Survival of the Fittest." It was continually stressed in the community and in classes that there was a vast difference in the development of the whites and the "lower" races; that this could be seen in the physical development of the Negro. I remember once in a museum, coming face to face with a demonstration: a series of skeletons arranged from a little monkey to a tall well-developed white man, with a Negro barely out-ranking a chimpanzee. Eventually in my classes stress was quietly transferred to brain weight and brain capacity, and at last to the "cephalic index."

In the graduate school at Harvard and again in Germany, the emphasis again was altered, and race became a matter of culture and cultural history. The history of the world was paraded before the observation of students. Which was the superior race? Manifestly that which had a history, the white race; there was some mention of Asiatic culture, but no course in Chinese or Indian history or culture was offered at Harvard, and quite unanimously in America and Germany, Africa was left without culture and without history. Even when the matter of mixed races was touched upon their evident and conscious inferiority was mentioned. I can never forget that morning in the class of the great Heinrich von Treitschke in Berlin. He was a big aggressive man, with an impediment in his speech which forced him to talk rapidly lest he stutter. His classes were the only ones always on time, and an angry scraping of feet greeted a latecomer. Clothed in black, big, bushy-haired, peering sharply at the class, his words rushed out in a flood: "Mulattoes," he thundered, "are inferior." I almost felt his eyes boring into me, although probably he had not noticed me. "Sie fühlen sich niedriger!" "Their actions show it," he asserted. What contradiction could there be to that authoritative dictum?

The first thing which brought me to my senses in all this racial discussion was the continuous change in the proofs and arguments advanced. I could accept evolution and the survival of the fittest, provided the interval between advanced and backward races was not made too impossible. I balked at the usual "thousand years." But no sooner had I settled into scientific security here, than the basis of race distinction was changed without explanation, without apology. I was skeptical about brain weight; surely much depended upon what brains were weighed. I was not sure about physical measurements and social inquiries. For instance, an insurance actuary published in 1890 incontrovertible statistics showing how quickly and certainly the Negro race was dying out in the United States through sheer physical inferiority. I lived to see every assumption of Hoffman's "Race Traits and Tendencies" contradicted; but even before that, I doubted the statistical method which he had used. When the matter of race became a question of comparative culture, I was in revolt. I began to see that the cultural equipment attributed to any people depended largely on who estimated it; and conviction came later in a rush as I realized what in my education had been suppressed concerning Asiatic and African culture.

It was not until I was long out of school and indeed after the World War that there came the hurried use of the new technique of psychological tests, which were quickly adjusted so as to put black folk absolutely beyond the possibility of civilization. By this time I was unimpressed. I had too often seen science made the slave of caste and race hate. And it was interesting to see Odum, McDougall and Brigham eventually turn somersaults from absolute scientific proof of Negro inferiority to repudiation of the limited and questionable application of any test which pretended to measure innate human intelligence.

So far I have spoken of "race" and race problems quite as a matter of course without explanation or definition. That was our method in the nineteenth century. Just as I was born a member of a colored family, so too I was born a member of the colored race. That was obvious and no definition was needed. Later I adopted the designation "Negro" for the race to which I belong. It seemed more definite and logical. At the same time I was of course aware that all members of the Negro race were not black and that the pictures of my race which were current were not authentic nor fair portraits. But all that was incidental. The world was divided into great primary groups of folk who belonged naturally together through heredity of physical traits and cultural affinity.

I do not know how I came first to form my theories of race. The process was probably largely unconscious. The differences of personal appearance between me and my fellows, I must have been conscious of when quite young. Whatever distinctions came because of that did not irritate me; they rather exalted me because, on the whole, while I was still a youth, they gave me exceptional position and a chance to excel rather than handicapping me.

Then of course, when I went South to Fisk, I became a member of a closed racial group with rites and loyalties, with a history and a corporate future, with an art and philosophy. I received these eagerly and expanded them so that when I came to Harvard the theory of race separation was quite in my blood. I did not seek contact with my white fellow students. On the whole I rather avoided them. I took it for granted that we were training ourselves for different careers in worlds largely different. There was not the slighest idea of the permanent subordination and inequality of my world. Nor again was there any idea of racial amalgamation. I resented the assumption that we desired it. I frankly refused the possibility while in Germany and even in America gave up courtship with one "colored" girl because she looked quite white, and I should resent the inference on the street that I had married outside my race.

All this theory, however, was disturbed by certain facts in America, and by my European experience. Despite everything, race lines were not fixed and fast. Within the Negro group especially there were people of all colors. Then too, there were plenty of my colored friends who resented my ultra "race" loyalty and ridiculed it. They pointed out that I was not a "Negro," but a mulatto; that I was not a Southerner but a Northerner, and my object was to be an American and not a Negro; that race distinctions must go. I agreed with this in part and as an ideal, but I saw it leading to inner racial distinction in the colored group. I resented the defensive mechanism of avoiding too dark companions in order to escape notice and discrimination in public. As a sheer matter of taste I wanted the color of my group to be visible. I hotly championed the inclusion of two black school mates whose names were not usually on the invitation list to our social affairs. In Europe my friendships and close contact with white folk made my own ideas waver. The eternal walls between races did not seem so stern and exclusive. I began to emphasize the cultural aspects of race.

It is probably quite natural for persons of low degree, who have reached any status, to search feverishly for distinguished ancestry, as a sort of proof of their inherent desert. This is particularly true in America and has given rise to a number of organizations whose membership depends upon ancestors who have made their mark in the world. Of course, it is clear that there must be here much fable, invention and wishful thinking, facilitated by poor vital statistics and absence of written records. For the mass of Americans, and many Americans who have had the most distinguished careers, have been descended from people who were quite ordinary and even less; America indeed has meant the breaking down of class bars which imprisoned personalities and capabilities and allowing new men and new families to emerge. This is not, as some people assume, a denial of the importance of heredity and family. It is rather its confirmation. It shows us that the few in the past who have emerged are not necessarily the best; and quite certainly are not the only ones worthy of development and distinction; that, on the contrary, only a comparatively few have, under our present economic and social organization, had a chance to show their capabilities.

I early began to take a direct interest in my own family as a group and became curious as to that physical descent which so long I had taken for granted quite unquestioningly. But I did not at first think of any but my Negro ancestors. I knew little and cared less of the white forebears of my father. But this chauvinism gradually changed. There is, of course, nothing more fascinating than the question of the various types of mankind and their intermixture. The whole question of heredity and human gift depends upon such knowledge; but ever since the African slave trade and before the rise of modern biology and sociology, we have been afraid in America that scientific study in this direction might lead to conclusions with which we were loath to agree; and this fear was in reality because the economic foundation of the modern world was based on the recognition and preservation of so-called racial distinctions. In accordance with this, not only Negro slavery could be justified, but the Asiatic coolie profitably used and the labor classes in white countries kept in their places by low wage.

It is not singular then that here in America and in the West Indies, where we have had the most astonishing modern mixture of human types, scientific study of the results and circumstances of this mixture has not only lagged but been almost non-existent. We have not only not studied race and race mixture in America, but we have tried almost by legal process to stop such study. It is for this reason that it has occurred to me just here to illustrate the way in which Africa and Europe have been united in my family. There is nothing unusual about this interracial history. It has been duplicated thousands of times; but on the one hand, the white folk have bitterly resented even a hint of the facts of this intermingling; while black folk have recoiled in natural hesitation and affected disdain in admitting what they know.

I am, therefore, relating the history of my family and centering it around my maternal great-great-grandfather, Tom Burghardt, and my paternal grandfather, Alexander Du Bois.

Absolute legal proof of facts like those here set down is naturally unobtainable. Records of birth are often nonexistent, proof of paternity is exceedingly difficult and actual written record rare. In the case of my family I have relied on oral tradition in my mother's family and direct word and written statement from my paternal grandfather; and upon certain general records which I have been able to obtain. I have no doubt of the substantial accuracy of the story that I am to tell.

Of my own immediate ancestors I knew personally only four: my mother and her parents and my paternal grandfather. One other I knew at second hand—my father. I had his picture. I knew what my mother told me about him and what others who had known him, said. So that in all, five of my immediate forebears were known to me. Three others, my paternal great-grandfather and my maternal great-grandfather and great-great-grandfather, I knew about through persons who knew them and through records; and also I knew many of my collateral relatives and numbers of their descendants. My known ancestral family, therefore, consisted of eight or more persons. None of these had reached any particular distinction or were known very far beyond their own families and localities. They were divided into whites, blacks and mulattoes, most of them being mulattoes.

My paternal great-grandfather, Dr. James Du Bois, was white, and descended from Chrétien du Bois who was a French Huguenot farmer and perhaps artisan and resided at Wicres near Lille in French Flanders. It is doubtful if he had any ancestors among the nobility, although his white American descendants love to think so. He had two, possibly three, sons of whom Louis and Jacques came to America to escape religious persecution. Jacques went from France first to Leiden in the Netherlands, where he was married and had several children, including a second Jacques or James. In 1674 that family came to America and settled at Kingston, New York. James Du Bois appears in the Du Bois family genealogy as a descendant of Jacques in the fifth generation, although the exact line of descent is not clear; but my grandfather's written testimony establishes that James was a physician and a landholder along the Hudson and in the West Indies. He was born in 1750, or later. He may have been a loyalist refugee. One such refugee, Isaac Du Bois, was given a grant of five hundred acres in Eleuthera after the Revolutionary War.

The career of Dr. James Du Bois was chiefly as a plantation proprietor and slave owner in the Bahama Islands with his headquarters at Long Cay. Cousins of his named Gilbert also had plantations near. He never married, but had one of his slaves as his common-law wife, a small brown-skinned woman born on the island. Of this couple two sons were

Philosophy and Morality

born, Alexander and John. Alexander, my grandfather, was born in 1803, and about 1810, possibly because of the death of the mother, the father brought both these boys to America and planned to give them the education of gentlemen. They were white enough in appearance to give no inkling of their African descent. They were entered in the private Episcopal school at Cheshire, Connecticut, which still exists there and has trained many famous men. Dr. James Du Bois used often to visit his sons there, but about 1812, on his return from a visit, he had a stroke of apoplexy and died. He left no will and his estate descended to a cousin.

The boys were removed from school and bound out as apprentices, my grandfather to a shoemaker. Their connection with the white Du Bois family ceased suddenly, and was never renewed. Alexander Du Bois thus started with a good common school and perhaps some high school training and with the instincts of a gentleman of his day. Naturally he passed through much inner turmoil. He became a rebel, bitter at his lot in life, resentful at being classed as a Negro and yet implacable in his attitude toward whites. Of his brother, John, I have only a picture. He may have been the John Du Bois who helped Bishop Payne to purchase Wilberforce University.

If Alexander Du Bois, following the footsteps of Alexander Hamilton, had come from the West Indies to the United States, stayed with the white group and married and begotten children among them, anyone in after years who has suggested his Negro descent would have been unable to prove it and quite possibly would have been laughed to scorn, or sued for libel. Indeed the legal advisers of the publishers of my last book could write: "We may assume as a general proposition that it is libelous to state erroneously that a white man or woman has colored blood." Lately in Congress the true story, in a WPA history, of miscegenation affecting a high historic personage raised a howl of protest.

Alexander Du Bois did differently from Hamilton. He married into the colored group and his oldest son allied himself with a Negro clan but four generations removed from Africa. He himself first married Sarah Marsh Lewis in 1823 and then apparently set out to make his way in Haiti. There my father was born in 1825, and his elder sister, Augusta, a year earlier, either there or just as the family was leaving the United States. Evidently the situation in Haiti did not please my grandfather or perhaps the death of his young wife when she was scarcely thirty turned him back to America. Within a year he married Emily Basset who seems to have been the widow of a man named Jacklyn and lived in New Milford. Leonard Bacon, a well-known Congregational clergyman, performed his second marriage.

The following year, Alexander began his career in the United States. He lived in New Haven, Springfield, Providence, and finally in New Bedford. For some time, he was steward on the New York–New Haven boat and insisted on better treatment for his colored help. Later about 1848 he ran a grocery store at 23 Washington Street, New Haven, and owned property at different times in the various cities where he lived. By his first wife, my grandmother, he had two children, and by his second wife, one daughter, Henrietta. Three or four children died in infancy. Alexander was a communicant of Trinity Parish, New Haven, and was enrolled there as late as 1845; then something happened, because in 1847 he was among that group of Negroes who formed the new colored Episcopal Parish of St. Luke, where he was for years their senior warden. Probably this indicates one of his bitter fights and rebellions, for nothing but intolerable insult would have led him into a segregated church movement. Alexander Crummell was his first rector here.

As I knew my grandfather, he was a short, stern, upstanding man, sparing but precise in his speech and stiff in manner, evidently long used to repressing his feelings. I remember as a boy of twelve, watching his ceremonious reception of a black visitor, John Freedom; his stately bow, the way in which the red wine was served and the careful almost stilted conversation. I had seen no such social ceremony in my simple western Massachusetts home. The darkened parlor with its horsehair furniture became a very special and important place. I was deeply impressed. My grandfather evidently looked upon me with a certain misgiving if not actual distaste. I was brown, the son of his oldest son, Alfred, and Alfred and his father had never gotten on together.

The boy Alfred was a throwback to his white grandfather. He was small, olive-skinned and handsome and just visibly colored, with curly hair; and he was naturally a play-boy. My only picture of him shows him clothed in the uniform of the Union Army; but he never actually went to the front. In fact, Alfred never actually did much of anything. He was gay and carefree, refusing to settle long at any one place or job. He had a good elementary school training but nothing higher. I think that my father ran away from home several times. Whether he got into any very serious scrapes or not, I do not know, nor do I know whether he was married early in life; I imagine not. I think he was probably a free lance, gallant and lover, yielding only to marital bonds when he found himself in the rather strict clannishness of my mother's family. He was barber, merchant and preacher, but always irresponsible and charming. He had wandered out from eastern New England where his father lived and come to the Berkshire valley in 1867 where he met and married my brown mother.

The second wife of Alexander Du Bois died in 1865. His oldest daughter, Augusta, married a light mulatto and has descendants today who do not know of their Negro blood. Much later Alexander Du Bois married his third wife, Annie Green, who was the grandmother than I knew, and who knew and liked my father Alfred, and who brought me and my grandfather together. Alexander Du Bois died December 9, 1887, at the age of eighty-four, in New Bedford, and lies buried today in Oak Grove Cemetery near the Yale campus in New Haven, in a lot which he owned and which is next to that of Jehudi Ashmun of Liberian fame.

My father, by some queer chance, came into western Massachusetts and into the Housatonic Valley at the age of forty-two and there met and quickly married my brown mother who was then thirty-six and belonged to the Burghardt clan. This brings us to the history of the black Burghardts.

In 1694, Rev. Benjamin Wadsworth, afterwards president of Harvard College, made a journey through western Massachusetts, and says in regard to the present site of the town of Great Barrington, "Ye greatest part of our road this day was a hideous, howling wilderness." Here it was that a committee of the Massachusetts General Court confirmed a number of land titles in 1733–34, which had previously been in dispute between the English, Dutch and Indians. In the "fifth division" of this land appears the name of a Dutchman, who signed himself as "Coenraet Borghghardt." This Borghghardt, Bogoert or Burghardt family has been prominent in Dutch colonial history and its descendants have been particularly identified with the annals of the little town of about five thousand inhabitants which today still lies among the hills of middle Berkshire.

Coenrod Burghardt seems to have been a shrewd pushing Dutchman and is early heard of in Kinderhook, together with his son John. This family came into possession of an African Negro named Tom, who had formerly belonged to the family of Etsons (Ettens?) and had come to the Burghardts by purchase or possibly by marriage. This African has had between one hundred and fifty and two hundred descendants, a number of whom are now living and reach to the eighth generation.

Tom was probably born about 1730. His granddaughter writes me that her father told her that Tom was born in Africa and was brought to this country when he was a boy. For many years my youthful imagination painted him as certainly the son of a tribal chief, but there is no warrant for this even in family tradition. Tom was probably just a stolen black boy from the West African Coast, nameless and lost, either a war captive or a tribal pawn. He was probably sent overseas on a Dutch ship at the time when their slave trade was beginning to decline and the vast English expansion to begin. He was in the service of the Burghardts and was a soldier in the Revolutionary War, going to the front probably several times; of only one of these is there official record when he appeared with the rank of private on the muster and payroll of Colonel John Ashley's Berkshire County regiment and Captain John Spoor's company in 1780. The company marched northward by order of Brigadier-General Fellows on an alarm when Fort Anne and Fort George were taken by the enemy. It is recorded that Tom was "reported a Negro." (Record Index of the Military Archives of Massachusetts, Vol. 23, p. 2.)

Tom appears to have been held as a servant and possibly a legal slave first by the family of Etsons or Ettens and then to have come into the possession of the Burghardts who settled at Great Barrington. Eventually, probably after the Revolutionary War, he was regarded as a freeman. There is record of only one son, Jacob Burghardt, who continued in the employ of the Burghardt family, and was born apparently about 1760. He is listed in the census of 1790 as "free" with two in his family. He married a wife named Violet who was apparently newly arrived from Africa and brought with her an African song which became traditional in the family. After her death, Jacob married Mom Bett, a rather celebrated figure in western Massachusetts history. She had been freed under the Bill of Rights of 1780 and the son of the judge who freed her wrote, "Even in her humble station, she had, when occasion required it, an air of command which conferred a degree of dignity and gave her an ascendancy over those of her rank, or color. Her determined and resolute character, which enabled her to limit the ravages of Shays's mob, was manifested in her conduct and deportment during her whole life. She claimed no distinction, but it was yielded to her from her superior experience, energy, skill and sagacity. Having known this woman as familiarly as I knew either of my parents, I cannot believe in the moral or physical inferiority of the race to which she belonged. The degradation of the African must have been otherwise caused than by natural inferiority."

Family tradition has it that her husband, Jacob, took part in suppressing this Shays's Rebellion. Jacob Burghardt had nine children, five sons of whom one was my grandfather, and four daughters. My grandfather's brothers and sisters had many children: Harlow had ten and Ira also ten; Maria had two. Descendants of Harlow and Ira still survive. Three of these sons, Othello, Ira, Harlow, and one daughter Lucinda settled on South Egremont plain near Great Barrington, where they owned small adjoining farms. A small part of one of these farms I continue to own.

Othello was my grandfather. He was born November 18, 1791, and married Sarah Lampman in 1811. Sarah was born in Hillsdale, New York, in 1793, of a mother named Lampman. There is no record of her father. She was probably the child of a Dutchman perhaps with Indian blood. This couple had ten children, three sons and seven daughters. Othello died in 1872 at the age of eighty-one and Sarah or Sally in 1877 at the age of eighty-six. Their sons and daughters married and drifted to town as laborers and servants. I thus had innumerable cousins up and down the valley. I was brought up with the Burghardt clan and this fact determined largely my life and "race." The white relationship and connections were quite lost and indeed unknown until long years after. The black

Burghardts were ordinary farmers, laborers and servants. The children usually learned to read and write. I never heard or knew of any of them of my mother's generation or later who were illiterate. I was, however, the first one of the family who finished in the local high school. Afterward, one or two others did. Most of the members of the family left Great Barrington. Parts of the family are living and are fairly prosperous in the Middle West and on the Pacific Coast. I have heard of one or two high school graduates in the Middle West branch of the family.

This, then, was my racial history and as such it was curiously complicated. With Africa I had only one direct cultural connection and that was the African melody which my great-grandmother Violet used to sing. Where she learned it, I do not know. Perhaps she herself was born in Africa or had it of a mother or father stolen and transported. But at any rate, as I wrote years ago in the "Souls of Black Folk," "coming to the valleys of the Hudson and Housatonic, black, little, and lithe, she shivered and shrank in the harsh north winds, looked longingly at the hills, and often crooned a heathen melody to the child between her knees, thus:

Do bana coba, gene me, gene me!
Do bana coba, gene me, gene me!
Ben d'nuli, nuli, nuli, nuli, ben d'le.

The child sang it to his children and they to their children's children, and so two hundred years it has traveled down to us and we sing it to our children, knowing as little as our fathers what its words may mean, but knowing well the meaning of its music."

Living with my mother's people I absorbed their culture patterns and these were not African so much as Dutch and New England. The speech was an idiomatic New England tongue with no African dialect; the family customs were New England, and the sex mores. My African racial feeling was then purely a matter of my own later learning and reaction; my recoil from the assumptions of the whites; my experience in the South at Fisk. But it was none the less real and a large determinant of my life and character. I felt myself African by "race" and by that token was African and an integral member of the group of dark Americans who were called Negroes.

At the same time I was firm in asserting that these Negroes were Americans. For that reason and on the basis of my great-great-grandfather's Revolutionary record I was accepted as a member of the Massachusetts Society of the Sons of the American Revolution, in 1908. When, however, the notice of this election reached the headquarters in Washington and was emphasized by my requesting a national certificate, the secretary, A. Howard Clark of the Smithsonian Institution, wrote to Massachusetts and demanded "proof of marriage of the ancestor of Tom Burghardt and record of birth of the son." He knew, of course, that the birth record of a stolen African slave could not possibly be produced. My membership was, therefore, suspended.

Countee Cullen sings:

What is Africa to me:
Copper sun or scarlet sea,
Jungle star or jungle track,
Strong bronzed men, or regal black
Woman from whose loins I sprang
When the birds of Eden sang?

One three centuries removed
From the scenes his fathers loved,
Spicy grove, cinnamon tree,
What is Africa to me?

What is Africa to me? Once I should have answered the question simply: I should have said "fatherland" or perhaps better "motherland" because I was born in the century when the walls of race were clear and straight; when the world consisted of mutually exclusive races; and even though the edges might be blurred, there was no question of exact definition and understanding of the meaning of the word. One of the first pamphlets that I wrote in 1897 was on "The Conservation of Races" wherein I set down as the first article of a proposed racial creed: "We believe that the Negro people as a race have a contribution to make to civilization and humanity which no other race can make."

The Ethics of Culture

The Ethics of Culture

I am to speak to you on the ethics of culture. Because I teach the one and try to practice the other, it may perhaps be pardonable for me to think of them together, but I hope at least not to leave you without the conviction that the two are in a very vital and immediate way connected. In my judgment, the highest intellectual duty is the duty to be cultured. Ethics and culture are usually thought out of connection with each other—as, in fact, at the very opposite poles. Particularly for our country, and the type of education which generally prevails, is this so. Quite unfortunately, it seems, duty toward the beautiful and the cultural is very generally ignored, and certainly, beauty as a motive has been taken out of morality, so that we confront beautiless duty and dutiless beauty. In an issue like this, it behooves education to try to restore the lapsing ideals of humanism, and to center more vitally in education the duty to be cultured.

It follows if there is any duty with respect to culture, that it is one of those that can only be self-imposed. No one can make you cultured, few will care whether you are or are not, for I admit that the world of today primarily demands efficiency—and further the only reward my experience can offer you for it is the heightened self-satisfaction which being or becoming cultured brings. There is, or ought to be, a story of a lad to whom some rather abstract duty was being interpreted who is said to have said, "If I only owe it to myself, why then I really don't owe it at all." Not only do I admit that culture is a duty of this sort, but I claim that this is its chief appeal and justification. The greatest challenge to the moral will is in the absence of external compulsion. This implies, young ladies and gentlemen, that I recognize your perfect right not to be cultured, if you do not really want to be, as one of those inalienable natural-born privileges which so-called "practical minded," "ordinary" Americans delight to claim and exercise. As a touch-stone for the real desire and a sincere motive, the advocates of culture would not have it otherwise.

The way in which duty comes to be involved in culture is this: culture begins in education where compulsion leaves off, whether it is the practical spur of necessity or the artificial rod of the school-master. I speak to a group that has already chosen to be educated. I congratulate you upon that choice. Though you have so chosen for many motives and with very diverse reasons and purposes, I fear that education for most of you means, in last practical analysis, the necessary hardship that is involved in preparing to earn a better living, perhaps an easier living. It is just such narrowing and truncating of the conception of education that the ideals and motives of culture are effective to remove or prevent.

Education should not be so narrowly construed, for in the best sense, and indeed in the most practical sense, it means not only the fitting of the man to earn his living, but to live and to live well. It is just this latter and higher function of education, the art of living well, or, if I may so express it, of living up to the best, that the word *culture* connotes and represents. Let me offer you, if I may, a touch-stone for this idea, a sure test of its presence. Whenever and wherever there is carried into education the purpose and motive of knowing better than the practical necessities of the situation demand, whenever the pursuit of knowledge is engaged in for its own sake and for the inner satisfaction it can give, culture and the motives of culture are present. I sense immediately that you may have quite other and perhaps more authoritative notions of culture in mind. Culture has been variously and beautifully defined. But I cannot accept for the purpose I have in view even that famous definition of Matthew Arnold's, "Culture is the best that has been thought and known in the world," since it emphasizes the external rather than the internal factors of culture. Rather is it the capacity for understanding the best and most representative forms of human expression, and of expressing oneself, if not in similar creativeness, at least in appreciative reactions and in progressively responsive refinement of tastes and interests. Culture proceeds from personality to personality. To paraphrase Bacon, it is that, and only that, which can be inwardly assimilated. It follows, then, that, like wisdom, it is that which cannot be taught, but can only be learned. But here is the appeal of it, it is the self-administered part of your education, that which represents your personal index of absorption and your personal coefficient of effort.

As faulty as is the tendency to externalize culture, there is still greater error in over-intellectualizing it. Defining this aspect of education, we focus it, I think, too much merely in the mind, and project it too far into the abstract and formal. We must constantly realize that without experience, and without a medium for the absorption and transfer of experience, the mind could not develop or be developed. Culture safeguards the educative process at these two points, and stands for the training of the sensibilities and the expressional activities. Mentioning the former as the neglected aspect of American education, former President Eliot contends that, since it is the business of the senses to serve the mind, it is reciprocally the duty of the mind to serve the senses. He means that properly to train the mind involves the proper training of the sensibilities, and that, without a refinement of the channels through which our experience reaches us, the mind cannot reach its highest development. We too often expect our senses to serve us and render nothing back to them in exchange. As a result they do not serve us half so well as they might: coarse channels make for sluggish response, hampered impetus, wastage of effort. The man of culture is the man of trained sensibilities, whose mind expresses itself in keenness of discrimination and, therefore, in cultivated interests and tastes. The level of mentality may be crowded higher for a special effort or a special pursuit, but in the long run it cannot rise much higher than the level of tastes. It is for this reason that we warrantably judge culture by manners, tastes, and the fineness of discrimination of a person's interests. The stamp of culture is, therefore, no conventional pattern, and had no stock value: it is the mold and die of a refined and completely developed personality. It is the art medallion, not the common coin.

On this very point, so necessary for the correct estimation of culture, most of the popular mistakes and misconceptions about culture enter in. Democracy and utilitarianism suspect tastes because they cannot be standardized. And if I should not find you over-interested in culture or over-sympathetic toward its ideals, it is because of these same prejudices of puritanism and materialism, which, though still typically American, are fortunately no longer representatively so. Yet it is necessary to examine and refute some of these prevalent misconceptions about culture. You have heard and will still hear culture derided as *artificial, superficial, useless, selfish, over-refined,* and *exclusive.* Let us make inquiry into the reasons for such attitudes. It is not the part of loyal advocacy to shirk the blow and attack of such criticism behind the bastions of dilettantism. Culture has its active adversaries in present-day life, indeed the normal tendencies of life today are not in the direction either of breadth or height of culture. The defense of culture is a modern chivalry, though of some hazard and proportional glory.

The criticism of culture as artificial first concerns us. In the mistaken name of naturalism, culture is charged with producing artificiality destructive of the fine original naturalness of human nature. One might as well indict civilization as a whole on this point; it, too, is artificial. But perhaps just a peculiar degree of artificiality is inveighed against—to which our response must be that it is just that very painful intermediate stage between lack of culture and wholesomeness of culture which it is the object of further culture to remove. All arts have their awkward stages: culture itself is its own cure for this. Closely associated, and touched by the same reasoning, is the argument that culture is superficial. Here we encounter the bad effect of a process undertaken in the wrong order. If the polished surface is, so to speak, the last coat of a consistently developed personality, it lends its final added charm to the total worth and effect. If, on the contrary, beginning with the superficial as well as ending with the superficial, it should be merely a veneer, then is it indeed both culturally false and artistically deceptive. No true advocacy of an ideal involves the defense or extenuation of its defective embodiments. Rather on the contrary, culture must constantly be self-critical and discriminating, and deplore its spurious counterfeits and shallow imitations.

More pardonable, especially for our age, is the charge of uselessness. Here we need not so much the corrective of values as that of perspective. For we only need to appreciate the perennial and imperishable qualities of the products of culture to see the fallacy in such depreciation. Fortified in ideas and ideals, culture centers about the great human constants, which, though not rigidly unchangeable, are nevertheless almost as durable as those great physical constants of which science makes so much. Indeed, if we count in the progressive changes of science through discovery, these are the more constant—the most constant then of all the things in human experience. Moreover, there is their superior representativeness by which posterity judges each and every phase of human development. Through their culture products are men most adequately represented; and by their culture-fruits are they known and rated. As we widen our view from the standpoint of momentary and partial judgment, this fact becomes only too obvious.

I take seriously, and would have you, also, the charge that culture is selfish. Being unnecessarily so is to be unduly so. Yet there is a necessary internal focusing of culture because true culture must begin with self-culture. Personality, and to a limited extent character also, are integral parts of the equation. In the earlier stages of the development of culture there is pardonable concentration upon self-cultivation. Spiritual capital must be accumulated; indeed, too early spending of the meager resources of culture at an early stage results in that shallow and specious variety which means sham and pretense at the start, bankruptcy and humiliation at the finish. Do not begin to spend your mental substance prematurely. You are justified in serious self-concern and earnest self-consideration at the stage of education. And, moreover, culture, even when it is rich and mature, gives only by sharing, and moves more by magnetic attraction than by transfer of material or energy. Like light, to which it is so often compared, it radiates, and operates effectively only through being self-sufficiently maintained at its central source. Culture polarizes in self-hood.

Finally we meet the criticism of exclusiveness, over-selectness, perhaps even the extreme of snobbery. Culture, I fear, will have to plead guilty to a certain degree of this: it cannot fulfill its function otherwise. Excellence and the best can never reside in the average. Culture must develop an elite that must maintain itself upon the basis of standards that can move forward but never backwards. In the pursuit of culture one must detach himself from the crowd. Your chief handicap in this matter as young people of today is the psychology and "pull" of the crowd. Culturally speaking, they and their point of view define vulgarity. As Professor Palmer says, "Is this not what we mean by the vulgar man? His manners are not an expression of himself, but of somebody else. Other men have obliterated him." There is no individuality in being ordinary: it is the boast of sub-mediocrity. Who in the end wishes to own that composite of everybody's average qualities, so likely to be below our own par? Culture's par is always the best: one cannot be somebody with everybody's traits. If to be cultured is a duty, it is here that that element is most prominent, for it takes courage to stand out from the crowd. One must, therefore, pay a moral as well as an intellectual price for culture. It consists in this: "Dare to be different— stand out!" I know how difficult this advice will be to carry out: America's chief social crime, in spite of her boasted freedom, is the psychology of the herd, the tyranny of the average and mediocre; in other words, the limitations upon cultural personality. Strive to overcome this for your own sake and, as Cicero would say, "for the welfare of the Republic."

I am spending too much time, I fear, in pointing out what culture is when I would rather point out the way to its attainment. I must not trespass, however, upon the provinces of my colleagues who are to interpret culture more specifically to you in terms of the art of English speech, the fine arts, and music. I content myself with the defense of culture in general, and with the opportunity it gives of explaining its two most basic aspects—the great amateur arts of personal expression—conversation and manners. These personal arts are as important as the fine arts; in my judgment, they are their foundation. For culture without personal culture is sterile—it is that insincere and hypocritical profession of the love of the beautiful which so often discredits culture in the eyes of the many. But with the products of the fine arts translating themselves back into personal refinement and cultivated sensibilities, culture realizes itself in the fullest sense, performs its true educative function, and becomes a part of the vital art of living. We too often estimate culture materialistically by what has been called "the vulgar test of production." On the contrary, culture depends primarily upon the power of refined consumption and effective assimilation; it consists essentially in being cultured. Whoever would achieve this must recognize that life itself is an art, perhaps the finest of the fine arts—because it is the composite blend of them all.

However, to say this is not to commit the man of culture to hopeless dilettantism, and make him a Jack of the arts. Especially for you, who for the most part work toward very practical professional objectives and who lack as Americans of our time even a modicum of leisure, would this be impossible. But it is not necessary to trouble much about this, for, even were it possible, it would not be desirable. There are, of course, subjects which are primarily "cultural" and subjects which are not, but I am not one of those who bewail altogether the departure from the old-fashioned classical program of education and the waning appeal of the traditional "humanities." Science, penetratingly studied, can yield as much and more culture than the humanities mechanically studied. It lies, I think, more in the point of view and the degree of intrinsic interest rather than in the special subject-matter or tradition of a subject. Nevertheless, to be sure of culture, the average student should elect some of the cultural studies; and, more important still, in his outside diversions, should cultivate a steady and active interest in one of the arts, aiming thereby to bring his mind under the quickening influence of cultural ideas and values. Not all of us can attain to creative productiveness and skill in the arts, though each of us has probably some latent artistic temperament, if it only expresses itself in love and day-dreaming. But each of us can, with a different degree of concentration according to his temperament, cultivate an intelligent appreciation of at least one of the great human arts, literature, painting, sculpture, music, or what not. And if we achieve a high level of cultivated taste in one art it will affect our judgment and interest and response with respect to others.

May I at this point emphasize a peculiarly practical reason? In any community, in any nation, in any group, the level of cultural productiveness cannot rise much higher than the level of cultural consumption, cannot much outdistance the prevalent limits of taste. This is the reason why our country has not as yet come to the fore in the production of culture-goods. And as Americans we all share this handicap of the low average of cultural tastes. As educated Americans, we share also and particularly the responsibility for helping raise this average. A brilliant Englishman once characterized America as a place where everything had a price, but nothing a value, referring to the typical preference for practical and utilitarian points of view. There is a special need for a correction of this on your part. As a race group we are at the critical stage where we are releasing creative artistic talent in excess of our group ability to understand and support it. Those of us who have been concerned about our progress in the things of culture have now begun to fear as the greatest handicap the discouraging, stultifying effect upon our artistic talent of lack of appreciation from the group which it represents. The cultural par, we repeat, is always the best: and a group which expects to be judged by its best must live up to its best so that that may be truly representative. Here is our present dilemma. If the standard of cultural tastes is not rapidly raised in the generation which you represent, the natural affinities of appreciation and response will drain off, like cream, the richest products of the group, and leave the mass without the enriching quality of its finest ingredients. This is already happening: I need not cite the painful individual instances. The only remedy is the more rapid development and diffusion of culture among us.

It follows from this that it is not creditable nor your duty to allow yourselves to be toned down to the low level of average tastes. Some of you, many of you, I hope, will be making your life's work in sections of this country and among groups that are fittingly characterized as "Saharas of culture," that know culture neither by taste nor sight. You betray your education, however, and forego the influence which as educated persons you should always exert in any community if you succumb to these influences and subside to the mediocre level of the vulgar crowd. Moreover, you will find that, like knowledge or technical skill, culture to be maintained must be constantly practiced. Just as we saw that culture was not a question of one set of subjects, but an attitude which may be carried into all, so also we must realize that it is not a matter of certain moments and situations, but the characteristic and constant reaction of a developed personality. The ideal culture is representative of the entire personality even in the slighest detail.

I recall an incident of visiting with a friend a celebrated art connoisseur for his expert judgment upon a painting. He examined with a knife and a pocket magnifying glass a corner of the canvas. I perhaps thought for a moment he was searching for a signature, but it was not the signature corner. Without further scrutiny, however, he gave us his judgment: "Gentlemen, it is not a Holbein." The master painter puts himself into every inch of his canvas, and can be told by the characteristic details as reliably, more reliably even than by general outlines. Culture likewise is every inch representative of the whole personality when it is truly perfected. This summing up of the whole in every part is the practical test which I want you to hold before yourselves in matters of culture. Among cultivated people you will be judged more by your manner of speech and deportment than by any other credentials. They are meant to bear out your training and your heritage, and more reliably than your diplomas or your pedigree will they represent you or betray you. Manners are thus the key to personal relations, as expression is the key to intellectual intercourse. One meets that element in others which is most responsively tuned to a similar element in ourselves. The best fruits of culture, then, are the responses it elicits from our human environment. And should the environment be limited or unfavorable, then, instead of compromising with it, true culture opens the treasuries of art and literature, and lives on that inheritance.

Finally I must add a word about that aspect of culture which claims that it takes several generations to produce and make the truly cultured gentleman. Exclusive, culture may and must be, but seclusive culture is obsolete. Not all that are well-born are well-bred, and it is better to be well-bred. Indeed, one cannot rest satisfied at any stage of culture: it has to be earned and re-earned, though it returns with greater increment each time. As Goethe says, "What thou hast inherited from the fathers, labor for, in order to possess it." Thus culture is inbred—but we ourselves are its parents. With all of the possible and hoped for spread of democracy, we may say that excellence of this sort will always survive. Indeed, when all the other aristocracies have fallen, the aristocracy of talent and intellect will still stand. In fact, one suspects that eventually the most civilized way of being superior will be to excel in culture.

This much, then, of the ideals of humanism must survive; the goal of education is self-culture, and one must hold it essential even for knowledge's own sake that it be transmuted into character and personality. It must have been the essential meaning of Socrates' favorite dictum—"Know thyself"—that to know, one must be a developed personality. The capacity for deep understanding is proportional to the degree of self-knowledge, and by finding and expressing one's true self, one somehow discovers the common denominator of the universe. Education without culture, therefore, ignores an important half of the final standard, "a scholar and a gentleman," which, lest it seem obsolete, let me cite in those fine modern words which former President Eliot used in conferring the arts degree. "I hereby admit you to the honorable fellowship of educated men." Culture is thus education's passport to converse and association with the best.

Moreover, personal representativeness and group achievement are in this respect identical. Ultimately a people is judged by its capacity to contribute to culture. It is to be hoped that as we progressively acquire in this energetic democracy the common means of modern civilization, we shall justify ourselves more and more, individually and collectively, by the use of them to produce culture-goods and representative types of culture. And this, so peculiarly desirable under the present handicap of social disparagement and disesteem, must be for more than personal reasons the ambition and the achievement of our educated classes. If, as we all know, we must look to education largely to win our way, we must look largely to culture to win our just reward and recognition. It is, therefore, under these circumstances something more than your personal duty to be cultured—it is one of your most direct responsibilities to your fellows, one of your most effective opportunities for group service. In presenting this defense of the ideals and aims of culture, it is my ardent hope that the Howard degree may come increasingly to stand for such things—and especially the vintage of 1926.

William E. Abraham
(b. 1934, Ghana)

The Life and Times of Anton Wilhelm Amo, the First African (Black) Philosopher in Europe

Only the barest facts of the life of Anton Wilhelm Amo are now known for certain—his African birth, his distinguished scholarly career in Europe, his eventual return to Ghana. He was born sometime around 1703, taken to Holland four years later, served at the court of Duke Anton Ulric in Brunswick-Wolfenbuttel, attended the universities of Halle, Wittenberg and probably Helmstedt, taught at Halle, Wittenberg and Jena, returned to Ghana sometime before 1753 and died on the coast probably during the 1760's. In this paper I have tried to examine these bare facts as closely as possible, to fill them out with a careful study of the known records of, and references to, this remarkable man, and thus to present the most comprehensive picture of his career yet done.

I

The fullest primary account of Amo's life is a short reference to him in an obituary notice of David Henri Gallandet published by Winkelmann in 1782 and based upon diaries and notebooks, now lost, of Gallandet himself. Gallandet, a Swiss-Dutch physician, was a ship's surgeon on a vessel that called at Axim in 1753 and, according to Winkelmann,

> While he (Gallandet) was on this trip to Axim on the Gold Coast in Africa, he went to visit the famous Mr. Antony William Amo, a Guinea-African, Doctor of Philosophy and Master of Arts. He was a negro, who lived about thirty years in Europe. He had been in Amsterdam in the year 1707, and was presented to the Duke Anton Ulric who gave him later to his son August Wilhelm. The latter made it possible for him to study in Halle and in Wittenberg. In the year 1727 he was promoted Doctor in Philosophy and Master in the Liberal Arts. Some time after this his master died. This made him so depressed that it influenced him into returning to his fatherland. Here he lived like a hermit, and acquired the reputation of a soothsayer. He spoke different languages including Hebrew, Greek, Latin, French, and High and Low German. He was skilled in astrology and astronomy and was generally a great sage. He was then about fifty years old. His father and one sister were still alive, and resided at a place four days' journey inland. He had a brother who was a slave in the colony of Suriname. Later he left Axim and went to live in the fort of the West Indies Company of St. Sebastian at Chama.[1]

There are a number of difficulties in Winkelmann's account which we shall discuss in due course, but, to start with, it does seem clear that Amo was born in or near Axim, because Winkelmann reports both that he chose that area to live in upon his return and that his surviving family was still living nearby. Moreover, in the Register of Undergraduates of the University of Halle for 1727 Amo has set down in his own hand next to his name the words, "Ab Aximo in Guinea Africana"—"Born in Axim in Guinea, Africa." Finally, Henri Gregoire, Constitutional Bishop of Blois and one of Amo's main biographers, wrote in 1800 that *"Amo . . . resolut de . . . retourner dans sa terre natale a Axim, sur la Cote-d'Or",[2] "terre natale"* means not the country of origin but the locality, the area, where one was born and refers therefore not to "la Cote-d'Or," but to Axim. This was also the opinion of the Reverend Attoh Ahuma of Ghana, who devoted a chapter of his book, *West African Celebrities*, 1700–1850,[3] to Amo.

As to the question of Amo's birthdate, here again we have to rely primarily on Winkelmann, who appears to be reporting Gallandet. It is safe to say that Amo himself was ignorant of his precise date of birth; if, however, he considered himself "about fifty years old" in 1753, he must have been born sometime between, say, 1700 and 1706 (since he was already in Germany in 1707). None of the biographers states the year of birth with any firmness—they all guess 1700, 1701, or 1703—and one can gather from this that the records of Brunswick-Wolfenbuttel contained no specific reference; indeed the baptismal records of the court chapel mention no birthdate, though they do give his date of baptism and his baptismal godfathers. The most reasonable conjecture is that Amo learned his age from his parents when he returned to Axim—they would have been able to calculate it with some accuracy in terms of the yearly Kuntum festivals, as is common in Axim[4]—and that it was only his scholarly habit of mind that cautioned him to use the word "about" when talking to Gallandet. We may therefore posit that Amo was indeed fifty years old in 1753, which puts his birthdate as 1703.

We can also posit that Amo left Axim some time toward the end of 1706, since he was first taken to Holland before he found himself in Brunswick-Wolfenbuttel in 1707 and since the normal voyage from Axim to Holland, by way of the West Indies, would have taken at least six months.

The reasons for Amo's departure from his native land so early in life are only inferential. Three hypotheses have been broached in the attempt to explain it: (1) he was kidnapped by sea-farers and taken to Europe; (2) he was bought as a childslave and taken to Europe; (3) he was sent to Europe originally to be brought up as a predikant of the Dutch Reformed Church.

The first hypothesis has been championed by Professor Wolfram Suchier, a former Librarian of the University of Halle and the rediscoverer of the story of Amo in Germany, in two articles published early in this century.[5] It has also been put forth by Dr. Brentjes, a specialist in oriental archaeology working in the University of Halle, and by two Ghanaians—a prosperous timber merchant of Axim, Mr. Amoo-Mensah, who gave me personal assurance that wicked sailors had captured Amo while he and his friends were picking berries in bushes near the sea, and a Mr. Polly of Asomka, a village near Axim, who held that Amo had been enticed by the predatory sailors with a piece of cake.

Against this hypothesis, however, must be listed the reasonable conjecture that if he had been kidnapped at the tender age of three it is unlikely that his Ghanaian name of Amo would have been preserved, even if he had been able to communicate it to his kidnappers;[6] another Ghanaian, known to us as John Jacob Eliza Capitein, who was kidnapped in 1725 at the age of eight, was unable to preserve his Ghanaian name. Moreover, it is possible that Amo would have been unable to find his parents at a place four days' journey inland from the coast when he returned to Ghana later on, for he could well have had no memory of their names of their probable location if he had been kidnapped at the age of three.

The second hypothesis, that Amo was sold into slavery, runs into the same objections, for under these conditions also Amo would probably not have been able to preserve his Ghanaian name or rediscover his parents. Moreover, against this theory is the important point that in the early eighteenth century no Ghanaian parents would have sold their children;[7] among other evidence for this is the conclusion of Roemer, a Danish resident in Ghana from 1727 to 1749, who wrote in his account of the Guinea coast that "those who have read this will no longer accuse Africans of selling their children."[8]

There is, however, one piece of circumstantial evidence to support this hypothesis, and that is Winkelmann's statement that Amo's brother was a slave in Suriname; what was true of one brother might have been true of the other. But, in the first place, if Amo's brother had really been taken away as a slave it is difficult to see how Winkelmann (or Gallandet) could have known his whereabouts with the precision which Suriname implies. Second, given the fact that his parents would not have sold him, Amo's brother could only have been taken as a slave in error, and if so he would have been repatriated as soon as the error was discovered; there is abundant evidence to show that the Dutch West Indies Company would not have jeopardized its lucrative slave trade by such arbitrary and thoughtless acts and that when Ghanaians were mistakenly taken as slaves they were indeed repatriated.[9] The most likely explanation of Winkelmann's reference is that Amo's brother was in Suriname as a member of the voluntary military corps recruited from Africa which the Dutch also established in Indonesia; Ghanaians are known to have served in such a corps and one such is known to have been stationed in Suriname.

The third hypothesis therefore seems to me to be the most tenable. Now it must be admitted that there is no direct evidence for this hypothesis, but it does enjoy a certain amount of support from indirect evidence. First, if Amo were sent to Holland to be brought up as a predikant either he or his supervisors would presumably have had a full record of his parents' names and his birthplace which he could use upon his return to Ghana. Second, it seems likely that Dutch preachers in Ghana, at least before 1708, were accustomed to sending some children of Christian fathers to the Netherlands to be trained in Christianity. As direct evidence for this we have a letter from Assembly X, dated 28 March, 1708, addressed to Johannes van der Star, Preacher in Ghana, and instructing him that children of Christian fathers were not to go to Holland but were to be baptised at home and that someone suitable to teach and expound Bible stories to them would be sought and sent over;[10] the implication is that children had been sent to Holland previously. Third, it is just possible that this particular letter was written in response to the arrival in the Netherlands of Amo himself and in light of the difficulties which the Dutch West Indies Company had in placing the boy. We know from Winkelmann that Amo was in Holland in 1707 and from court records that he was presented to Duke Anton Ulric of Brunswick-Wolfenbuttel sometime later that year, and it is possible that the Company had had the child on its hands for most of that year without being able to find a guardian for him; in the end, it seems, no guardian was to be found in the Netherlands and so he was sent off to Germany. After this kind of bother it would not be surprising if the company early in the next year instructed the Dutch missionaries not to send additional Ghanaian children.

In 1707 young Amo was sent to the court of Duke Anton Ulric, a rather strange old man but an ardent promoter of science and the arts, a composer of hymns and a novelist. His most serious work was *Fifty Reasons Why One Must Be a Catholic,* which convinced at least its author, who in 1710 abandoned the Augsburg Confession and was received into the Catholic Church; but since Amo arrived before this conversion he was baptised as a Protestant. The baptismal ceremony took place on 29 July, 1708, in the chapel of the castle at Wolfenbuttel and is mentioned in the church register thus:

> This twenty-ninth day of July has been baptized a little Moor in the Saltzthal Castle Chapel, and he has been christened Anton Wilhelm. His Godfathers are all[11] of them very noble Lordships.[12]

The church register also records Amo's later confirmation, on a Sunday in the year 1721. At that time he is referred to as "Anton Wilhelm Rudolph Mohre," the first three names coming from the successive dukes of Brunswick-Wolfenbuttel and the last coming probably from a German word for a black man, *"Mohr."* One might conjecture that when Amo was to be confirmed the priests balked at his African name, which they would have scorned as pagan, and replaced it with "Mohre," a practice which had also been in force at Wolfenbuttel since 1716 at the latest.

The other references to Amo during this period are found in the court's account books for 1716–17 and 1720–21 in the Staatsarchiv at Wolfenbuttel. In these books he is listed as having received the sum of thirty-two thalers as his stipend for the period from Easter 1716 to Michaelmas 1716 and as having received an equivalent sum for the period from Michaelmas 1716 to Easter 1717; he is next mentioned as having received sixteen thalers for the Easter 1720–June 1720 period and the June 1720–Michaelmas 1720 period, but he was later granted an additional three thalers for this last period and a full nineteen thalers for the period from Michaelmas 1720 to Christmas 1720. These references—the only ones to Amo in the account book—indicated that Amo received a stipend of sixteen thalers a quarter from Easter 1716 to Easter 1717 and from Easter 1720 to June 1720, and a stipend of nineteen thalers between June 1720 and December 1720.

Thus Norbert Lochner in his article on Amo reproduced in the *Transactions of the Historical Society of Ghana* in 1958 is quite wrong in saying that "between Christmas 1719 and Michaelmas 1720 . . . Amo was paid a quarterly stipend amounting to sixteen thalers."[13] He is also wrong in suggesting that this sum "can be assumed also for the intermediary period [from Easter 1717 to Easter 1720], although this cannot be proved," for the registers make no mention of Amo during this time and since there do not seem to have been omissions in these registers (their pagination, for example, is complete and correct) it must be presumed that no direct payments were in fact made to Amo then. Lochner is also wrong in dating the decree announcing the rise from sixteen to nineteen thalers as Christmas 1720, as the reference in the register is quite legibly and clearly to 25 January 1720; nor is there any indication that the decree was retroactive, as Lochner claims.

The important question about these payments is what they signify. Of Amo's preceeding biographers, only Brentjes addresses himself to this, and his answer is most unsatisfactory; he asserts, without disclosing the reasons for his conclusion, that Amo had been working as a page in Wolfenbuttel and that the payments in the registers refer to this service.[14] However, Amo is never described as a page in the registers (being referred to as "the negro Anthon Wilhelm" or "the negro Anton Wilhelm Amo") whereas the librarian, for example, is described as "librarian Hoffmann," and furthermore this does not explain what Amo was doing between Easter 1717 and Easter 1720 and why he was not paid then. Nor does Brentjes offer any explanation of the quaint idea of Amo as a page in 1720 when he was probably at least seventeen years old.

A much more reasonable explanation is that the payments were simply pocket money for Amo during the time he was at court, and that the reason they stopped between Easter 1717 and Easter 1720 was that Amo was then at school. There are several reasons for supposing that Amo was at school during this time. First, it explains why Amo was paid no stipend during these years, for the court would have sent his tuition fees directly to the school. Second, since Amo was confirmed in 1721 he must first have had instruction in religious matters, which he very likely received at school and not at court. Third, it is known that Amo was proficient enough in Latin to have entered the University of Halle in 1727 and to write an inaugural dissertation in that language in 1729—and though his training might only have been obtained at university it can be conjectured that it began before that. Finally, there is some reason to think that Amo attended the University of Helmstedt after 1721 and, if so, he would need to have had some education beforehand.

It is not certain how Amo obtained his education, but we can suppose that he would not have had a private tutor at court since this would have proved heavily expensive and his status as an outsider would not normally have entitled him to this privilege. Nor is it likely that he went to one of the aristocratic private schools of the time (although there was such a school in Wolfenbuttel), for again he was not suited by birth or fortune for this and he certainly would not have learned sufficient Latin or religious training in these haughty, inefficient institutions concerned chiefly with utilitarian subjects and the "aristocratic graces." It is equally unlikely that Amo attended the free peasant schools at the other end of the social scale, for the Dukes were neither so poor nor would they have been so callous as to send him to a low-grade, poorly taught pauper's school; he could not have learned sufficient Latin there either. It is therefore reasonable to suggest that Amo attended the last type of institution available, a grammar school (one of which, the Ritter-academie of Wolfenbuttel, was located nearby), where he would have had a full classical education, sound religious training and instruction in accurate and elegant Latinity; only such a school could have taught Amo all he needed to know in order to gain admittance to a university.

We can thus conjecture an account for the years from 1717 to 1720, but it is more difficult to account for those from 1721 to 1727, during which period there are no records of Amo at all. Lochner supposes that he was studying at the University of Helmstedt, near Wolfenbuttel, a supposition which I think is tenable for a variety of reasons; the fact that there is no direct evidence of this could be explained by the cessation of that university, whose records were lost. Brentjes' contention that Amo could not have attended this Protestant university since the ducal court of Wolfenbuttel was Catholic[15] is based on the mistake of thinking that because Anton Ulric became a Catholic the whole court followed suit, which is not true; the university was undoubtedly irritated by the Duke's conversion but that could hardly have turned it into a deadly foe of every member of his household.

It would not be terribly unusual for a European nobleman to send an African protege to university and, indeed, the example of Peter the Great of Russia, who sent the African Ibrahim Hannibal through school in Paris, would undoubtedly have been known at Wolfenbuttel, where the court had connections with the Russian royal family. And if the Duke of Wolfenbuttel—at this time Augustus Wilhelm—were so inclined, it is likely that he would have sent Amo first to the local university, Helmstedt, to see his mettle first-hand before sending him on to other more distant, and possibly more difficult, universities.

There are several other reasons to support this theory. First, if we are right in assuming that Amo was in fact in school from 1717 to 1720, it is unlikely that he would have been made to wait until 1727, when he entered the University of Halle, for his higher education; presumably he would have gone to university as soon after 1720 as possible. Second, in the Register of Undergraduates of the University of Halle, Amo has signed himself as immatriculating on 9 June 1727, and in the next column is entered the word *"gratis,"* meaning that he had sought and obtained exemption from paying matriculation fees. This suggests that Amo was not then being supported by the Wolfenbuttel court, perhaps because he had already been supported through one university—i.e., Helmstedt—after which the court would feel no obligation to keep paying his fees. Third, in this same register a number of students who have come directly from a secondary school indicate this fact, mentioning the name of the school and the number of years they had spent there,[16] and the implication is that those against whose names there was no such information had not come from a school but from a university; there is no mention of a school against Amo's name. Finally, and most important, it is reported that Amo took courses only in law at the University of Halle,[17] courses which could be taken only by those with a Bachelor's degree; and since there is no record of Amo's having taken the Bachelor's degree at Halle, it must have been obtained at another university, most likely Helmstedt.

We have no definitive way of knowing the number of years for which Amo might have attended Helmstedt, but if he was there only for a Bachelor's degree it probably would not have taken him more than two years—say, from 1725 to 1727. (It is of course possible that he completed a full Master's course at Helmstedt—which would have meant attendance from 1723 to 1727—since he was in fact awarded a Master's degree in 1730; but it is much more reasonable to assume that this degree was awarded for his postgraduate work at Halle from 1727 to 1729, especially since the degree came so soon after.) This leaves the years 1721–25 to account for, and my conjecture is that Amo was then acquiring a more advanced education in a more advanced grammar school, most likely the Ritter-academie located right in Wolfenbuttel.

III

If Amo did attend Helmstedt, we can surmise that he would not have found there a terribly congenial intellectual climate. The university was cluttered with clericalism, the priests were for the most part tolerant of the hierarchical social order of Germany (in which Amo's rank would be low), and the professors probably would not have sympathized with Amo's views either on religion or on the status of Africans in Europe, both of which were made known in his thesis delivered at Halle in 1729, in which he questioned "to what extent the freedom or servibility of Africans in Europe, who had been bought by Christians, was according to laws commonly accepted at that time."[18]

At Halle, however, Amo could expect a more sympathetic atmosphere, for that university, which had been founded only in 1694, was already vigorous in its claim to intellectual freedom and was known for the number of its free-thinking professors and students who embraced the humanist faith. Probably the best known of these humanists was Christian Thomasius, a teacher who had angered the Lutheran orthodoxy by his firm views against witch-hunting (common at the time), who took as his personal motto the maxim that "unlimited freedom gives the best life to all spirits," and who boldly opposed the growing clericalism in his demands for complete freedom of research and freedom from persecution for unpopular opinions honestly formed and sincerely held. No less vigorous was his colleague Christian Wolff, an unrepentant apostle of the liberal *"Aufklarung,"* who insisted that free inquiry ought to be trusted far more than any appeal to authority and therefore sought the complete secularization of education.

That this free-thinking, anti-clerical attitude would have been shared by Amo is evident from an examination of what we know of his first dissertation, which was described in a notice published in the weekly newspaper of the University of Halle in 1729. The notice read:

> Here [in Halle] resided for some time an African called Antonius Wilhelmus Amo who was in the service of this Royal Highness the reigning Duke of Wolfenbuttel, and as he had before then thoroughly studied the Latin language, he very diligently and with great success studied here with the School of Private Law. In consequence, he became most accomplished in that field. So with the knowledge and consent of his patrons who up to that time had kept him, he registered with the Dean von Ludewig publicly to defend a dissertation under him. In order that the argument of the dissertation might suit his status and circumstance, they gave him the theme *"de jure Maurorum in Europa"*: in other words, "about the rights of Africans."[19] Therein not only has he shown basing himself upon law and history that the kings of the Africans were at one time vassal to the Roman Emperor, and that every one of them had an Imperial Patent, which Justinian too had granted, but he also especially examined to what extent the freedom or servibility of Africans in Europe, who had been bought by Christians, was according to laws commonly accepted at that time.[20]

This dissertation has so far not been traced. It appears, however, that in it Amo objected to the crime of slavery, not by facilely resorting to sentimental denunciations but by engaging the intellect of as wide a spectrum of educated men as possible. It is also interesting that Amo is not reported as basing himself on Scripture. He was in fact pleading in the court of humanity, though basing himself exclusively on European presuppositions. Europe prided itself on its heritage of the Roman civilisation, in fact on its historical vassalage to Rome. Its pride, its claim to status and privilege, was regularly built on its subjection to the Roman law. But had not the Roman law granted all sorts of immunity and privileges to those over whom it had jurisdiction? The kernel of Amo's argument was that Africans were entitled to the same immunities and privileges to precisely that extent that the erstwhile European vassals of Rome enjoyed them, for the African kings had been likewise subject to Rome under a Patent which the Emperors had granted, and which Justinian too had granted. With every new emperor, however, an African king who had held a Roman Imperial Patent had had to seek it anew. The effect of this was of course that successive Roman Emperors including Justinian explicitly recognised the vassalage of the African kings.

If Roman law provided, as it did, for the inviolability of the individual who was subject to it, then the same inviolability of person is thereby extended by the same law of Africans who were by the Imperial Patent subject to it. In that case, their purchase and enslavement by Europeans who claimed descent from the Roman law must be contrary to accepted laws.

The argument would be the same if one looked upon Europeans as Christians; for they claimed to be Christians tracing their lineage through Roman Christian Emperors like Justinian himself. And according to Roman Christian law, those who were subject to it enjoyed inviolability of person. As Justinian, a Christian Roman Emperor, had granted to African kings an Imperial Patent recognising their subjection to Roman Christian law, the Patent endowed them with inviolability according to that law. Thus Amo was arguing that the enslavement of Africans was contrary to Law and even religion.

The dissertation, which earned Amo the candidature of both private and public law, was examined and publicly defended under the chairmanship of Professor Peter von Ludewig (1668–1743). Ludewig was a strange man to have presided over the examination of such an obviously anti-clerical thesis, as he had been unfriendly both to Christian Thomasius and Christian Wolff; at the same time, however, not even his sedulous service to the Prussian king had endeared him to the clerics. In any case, it is known that Ludewig gave his protection to Amo until his death in 1743, and it is likely that he was the "master" whose death "influenced [Amo] into returning to his fatherland," as Winkelmann reported. Brentjes, citing an announcement of a book by Ludewig on Justinian in 1730, contends that the mention of this emperor in Amo's dissertation was due to Ludewig's influence, the influence which every supervisor inevitably has on a candidate's thesis.[21] This seems a little far-fetched, however, since Amo would in any case have mentioned Justinian, for it linked his indictment of Europe at that point both to Europe's Roman as well as her Christian tradition; it was no mere embellishment to please a superior. Moreover, there is no evidence that Ludewig was Amo's supervisor—he is only known to have been his examiner.

Suchier, Brentjes and Lochner all say bluntly that Amo defended his dissertation in November 1729 and cite the above notice in the 28 November 1729 weekly paper. However, that notice does not *say* that Amo defended the dissertation in November, and in fact the opening sentence, which uses the simple past tense instead of the perfect, suggests that Amo was no longer in Halle by 28 November and therefore that he defended his dissertation sometime earlier.

About the time of Amo's dissertation, unfortunately, the University of Halle was in a new, pro-clerical phase and the intellectual climate was most strained. The humanists and free-thinkers were seriously opposed by the clerical pietists who were able to enlist the intervention of the Prussian King, Friedrich Wilhelm, on their behalf. In fact, Christian Wolff had been expelled just a month before Amo went to Halle, thanks to the vicious rantings of Joachim Lange, ringleader of the clerical obscurantism and persecution, which convinced the king that Wolff's ideas were inimical to the state. Christian Thomasius had died in 1728. And a number of philosophers had left the university, clearly preferring exile to intellectual slavery. Lange in the meantime continued his efforts against Wolff and his followers, referring to the "oversmart Wolfian Magistri (Masters)" who were seducing students from their proper lectures—especially at Jena where, to his chagrinned regret, "Wolfianism had taken strong hold"; Lange expressed pity for the Prussian youths who studied in Jena and who, having been corrupted, would not be permitted to return to Halle.[22] By 1729 Halle, from Amo's standpoint, was doomed. The signs of impoverishment of the intellectual climate, compounded with the hostility which he would inevitably have evoked by indicting Christians and Europeans in his dissertation, would have encouraged Amo to leave Halle as soon as he was free to—i.e., as soon as he finished his thesis.[23]

IV

Amo presumably left Halle after defending his thesis in 1729, and is not heard of again until 2 September 1730, when he immatriculated into the University of Wittenberg, not far from Halle. He may very well have considered going to Leipzig, where Christian Wolff had gone, but that university was then festulating with enemies of Christian Thomasius whose wrath he had unleashed by his free-thinking views. And at Wittenberg he would have had a mentor, Martin Gotthelf Loescher, a friend of Ludewig's who taught Amo medicine, physiology and psychology and who took the chair when Amo defended his second known thesis in April 1734.

Now Amo was awarded the degree of Master of Philosophy and the Liberal Arts (which a few years later was to be called the Doctor of Philosophy degree) at Wittenberg on 10 October 1730—barely a month after he entered the university—according to the *Historische Alte und Neue Curiosa Saxonica* of September 1743 (p. 279). Since this was awarded so shortly after he immatriculated, it has caused doubt in the minds of some of his biographers, and the confusion is compounded because the date in the *Historische* reads "1703" and not "1730."

To explain this, Brentjes puts forth the idea that the date should be 10 October 1733, while Suchier claims that Amo was made a Master in a "Rektor Program" dated 24 May 1733, although no such "Rektor Program" has been discovered. The difficulty with both these ideas is that we have independent evidence that Amo was a Master at least by 10 May 1733—that is, before the dates that these biographers suggest; this evidence is an article in the *Hamburgische Berichte* of 2 June 1733, referring to events of 10 and 11 May 1733, in which there is a mention of "Magister (i.e., Master) Amo."[24]

If we assume, then, that Amo was in fact given his Master's degree on 10 October 1730, how can we explain that this came so soon after entering Wittenberg, before proper examination formalities could have been satisfied? The most reasonable explanation is that Amo had already qualified for the Master's degree by the time he entered Wittenberg through his two-year course in law at the University of Halle; we can suppose that he completed all the examination requirements for the degree at Halle, but left that university before the degree could be granted since he had incurred both social and professional hostility by his strong dissertation. To support this idea, we have the information that Amo was studying in law and wrote his dissertation in law at Halle, and this was a course only for those with a Bachelor's degree working for a Master's degree; moreover, the fact that the dissertation was mentioned at such a high level as Gottfried Ludewig's *Universal Historie* in 1744 suggests that it was more than just an undergraduate work and at least a postgraduate one. Finally, it is known that between 1730 and 1734 Amo regularly gave lectures in the University of Wittenberg,[25] and to do this he would have needed, by university requirement, a Master's degree.

There is some evidence that while he was at Wittenberg Amo earned a Master's degree in both medicine and science: Suchier's "Rektor Program" of 24 May 1733 might have conferred the medical degree, especially since we know Amo was taking medical courses from Loescher before this time and since he was allowed to attach a poem of praise to a doctoral dissertation presented by a medical student in 1737; and references in an address appended to his second dissertation refer to Amo as "that Most Distinguished Master of Science and the Liberal Arts" and as having been "decorated with the laurels of philosophy," both of which may refer to his earning a Master's degree in science.[26]

At any rate, Amo successfully defended a dissertation at Wittenberg in April 1734[27] which would have been sufficient to earn him the Master's degree in science. The thesis is entitled *"De humanae mentis Apatheia seu sensionis ac facultatis sentiendi in mente humana absentia et earum in corpore nostro organico ac vivo praesentia"* ("Of the *apatheia* of the human mind, namely the absence of sensation and the faculty of sense in the human mind, and their presence in our organic and living body"); in it Amo subjected Descartes to some very telling criticisms. Copies can now be found in the libraries of the universities of Griefswold, Halle, Jena and Göttingen, in the Free University of Berlin and in the University of Ghana.

At the end of this dissertation were appended two interesting addresses, one from the rector of the University of Wittenberg and the other from Loescher to Amo. The first reads:

> The Rector and Public Assembly of Wittemberg [sic] University to the kind reader, greetings: Great once was the dignity of Africa, whether one considers natural talents of mind or the study of letters, or even the very institutions for safe-guarding religion. For she has given birth to several men of the greatest pre-eminence by whose talents and efforts the whole of human knowledge has been built up. No one in former times and no one in our own age has been judged to be either more prudent in civic life or more elegant than Terence, the Carthagenian. Plato in his Socratic dialogues even assures us that so vigorous was the insight of Apuleius the Madarensian into the secrets of things, indeed so comprehensive was his study of former ages that when other schools had been torn apart, the Apuleian School continued to flourish, that School which dared to rival the Ciceronian for pre-eminence in eloquence.
>
> In Christian teaching too how great are the men who have come out of Africa. Of the more distinguished, it is enough to mention Tertullian, Cyprian, Arnobius, Optatus, Milevitanus, Augustine, the refinement of all of whose souls rivals the learning of every race. And finally with how great faith and steadfastness for soundness in sacred matters the African doctors continued their memorials, their deeds and their martyrdom and their councils declare.
>
> Those who say that the African Church has always merely been a receiver of instruction do her immeasurable wrong. While admitting that with the spread of Arab power into Africa, great changes have indeed taken place there, nevertheless one must say that all the light of their genius and learning has been far from being extinguished by Arab absolutism. By an old established custom of this race to whom learning seems to have migrated, liberal science was cultivated, and where the Moors crossed from Africa into Spain their ancient writers brought with them at the same time much assistance in the cultivation of letters from the darkness which had taken hold of it. Such was the position of learning, since it is satisfying that it brought pleasure to the Africa of ancient times.
>
> But though in our own times indeed that part of the world is reported to be more prolific in other things than in learning, nevertheless, that it is by no means exhausted of genius, Anthony William Amo here, that Most Distinguished Master of Science and the Liberal Arts, would teach by his example.
>
> Born in a very distant recess of Africa where it faces the rising sun, he came to Europe as a very little child. He was initiated by sacred rites in the Julian Halls, and so enjoyed the kindness of Guelf, of Augustus Wilhelm and of Ludwig Rudolph, which was so great that in the matter of his education no bounty of paternal love was lacking. Because of his proven gentleness of spirit, he frequented the Saxon Halls, and already learned in various doctrines, he came to us, and, by continuing the curriculum with diligence, he won the affection of the Order of Philosophy to such an extent that by the unanimous vote of the Fathers, he was decorated with the laurels of philosophy. The honour won by the deserts of his ability, of his outstanding uprightness, industry, erudition, which he has shown by public and private exercises, he increased with praise. By his behaviour with the best and most learned, he acquired great influence; among his equals, he easily shone out. In consequence, trained and stimulated by his studies of these things, he handed over his knowledge of philosophy to several at home. Having

examined the opinions of the ancients as well as the moderns, he garnered all that was best, and what he picked out he interpreted with precision and with lucidity. This work proved that his intellectual ability was as great as his powers of teaching nor have these powers proved themselves unequal to the office of teaching to which by some natural instinct he is at length being drawn to administer in the University. Therefore, since he has completely justified our expectation, there is no reason whatever why we should deny him our public judgement and attestation to which he has a right. Indeed, we hope for all the best things from him and we adjudge him worthy of that Princely favour which he has dutifully respected, and which he publicises in every address. And now for good fortune in order that he may be able to enjoy for a long time to come this fortune and attain to the most renowned fruition of his hope, for the well-being of the good and great Prince, Ludwig Rudolph, for the preservation of the whole House of Brunswick, Guelfbytanic, celebrated for so many great services to all Germany, let us all address prayer to God.

> John Godfrey Kraus, Doctor,
> Rector of the University.

The second address reads:

We proclaim Africa and its region of Guinea planted apart at a very great distance from us, formerly the golden coast, so called by Europeans on account of its abundant and copious yield of gold, but known by us as your fatherland, in which you first saw the light of day, the mother not only of many good things and treasures of nature but also of the most auspicious minds, we proclaim her quite deservedly. Among these auspicious minds, your genius stands out particularly, most noble and most distinguished Sir, seeing that you have excellently proved that felicity and superiority of your genius, the solidity and refinement of your learning and teaching, in countless examples up to now and even in this our University with great honour in all worthy things and now also in your present dissertation.

I return to you still complete and absolutely unchanged in any respect that which you have worked out with proper contentiousness in an elegant manner supported with erudition, in order that the power of your intellect may shine forth all the more strongly henceforth.

It now only remains for me to congratulate you wholeheartedly on this singular example of your refined scholarship, and, with a more abundant feeling of heart than words can convey. I solicit for you all good fortune, and to the Divine Grace and also to the Highest and Most Noble Prince Ludwig Rudolph, for whose health and safety I shall never tire of worshipping the Divine Majesty, I commend you.

I write this at Wittemberg [sic] in Saxony, in the month of April, A.O.R., 1734.

In the same year of Amo's own dissertation, on 29 May, he examined the dissertation of one Joannes Theodosius Meiner and appended to it an address of his own. It reads:

To the most noble John Theodosius Meiner, let public greetings be given, from the Chairman.

Of your continued diligence towards learning and human knowledge, which can only be gained by even more unremitting application, and which can only be increased by swift additions of great importance, you have given public manifestation with honour.

There persevere happily as you have been doing for some time, commended by honourable conduct and prudent living, in rendering assistance to letters. In this way, the best people will have affection for you. In this way, your parent, long worthy of respect in age, that mistress of things of honour deservedly destined (to him), distinguished in titles and in piety, who in your fair Misnia provided the graceful holy temple,

Philosophy and Morality

will have in you a son not unworthy of so great a parent. Thus, your most noble family, renowned by its ancestry and the splendour of its achievements will see in you its virtues prosper and flower.

I congratulate you, noble Sir, more for your promise of mental excellence than for the ambiguity of your words.[28]

V

Sometime between 1734 and 1736 Amo returned to the University of Halle, for it is known that in 1736 he opposed a dissertation presented at Halle. The reasons for his return can only be conjectured, but there is evidence to indicate that the free-thinking Wolffians were growing in strength there, despite the continuing efforts of that persistent obscurantist, Joachim Lange. Lange himself gives a clue to their growth in an article in 1734 when he complains about the revival of the liberal movement and the expansion and attraction of anti-clerical lectures[29] and again in 1735 when he attacks students who run to anti-clerical masters instead of attending their proper lectures.[30] In 1736 he succeeded in getting the king to issue a reprimand against the Faculty of Theology, in which he complained that whereas he used to draw a crowd of two to three hundred students to his private expositions of holy scripture, in later years even those lecturers more edifying than he could count on only twenty or thirty; he added that the Wolffian philosophy had been trying for some years to become popular again and had, unfortunately, gained a certain following.[31]

There are several references to Amo during his tenure at Halle. The first is the account of his opposition to a dissertation on anatomy in 1736, about which the Halle weekly wrote:

> During this deputation, then Magister Amo of Africa, and there born in Guinea, a genuine negro, but a humble and honourable philosopher, put the public opposition with pleasure according to his wont, besides others.[32]

Next there is an entry in the university records for 21 July 1736 granting Amo permission to give public lectures, thus enabling him to supplement the undoubtedly meagre income he made from private lectures:

> Antony William Amo, Master of Philosophy and the Liberal Arts, born in Guinea in a coastal province of Africa, has put forward a petition in which he asks that that same right of delivering public lectures in certain parts of philosophy be given to him among us, as he used to enjoy in the area of Wittenberg. When this request had been communicated to each person, it was with great pleasure that this facility was granted to this learned but poor man who had indeed only recently lost his most serene benefactor.[33]

Finally, there is a poem in German, in pure iambic meter, written by Amo and attached to a dissertation by Moses Abraham Wolff presented in 1737. Roughly translated, the poem reads:

> Your nimble mind moving so fast in contemplation
> And in profound study with unceasing toil,
> Has, noble soul, made you in the scholar's world
> A star of such dimensions that, shining
> Ever brighter, your fame is thus enlarged

As honours multiply. It's wisdom's gift
To those who are her sons. But enough!
From heaven let there fall upon yourself and yours
Deep joy and purest blessings.

This has with congratulations been added
By Anton Wilhelm Amo, from Guinea
In Africa, Magister and University Lecturer
In Philosophy and the Liberal Arts.

Suchier says that he discovered another dissertation to which Amo had added a poem in Latin, but unfortunately he lost all trace of it and reports only that it was signed simply, "Amo."

During his tenure at Halle, Amo gave regular lectures and published a book. His lectures were on a wide variety of subjects; one series was devoted to a critical exposition of Leibniz's *Principle of Sufficient Reason,* in which he would most probably have agreed with Leibniz that physiological processes were "mechanical" or automatic and not influenced by the soul. He also gave lectures on the political thought of Christian Wolff (though Wolff was still in royal disfavour), on Professor Fleischer's *Natural and International Institutions of Law,* and on the decimal system and the theory of codes. His book, first described in the *Transactions of the Faculty of Philosophy of Halle* on 4 March 1737, was printed in Halle in 1738 under the title, *De Arte Sobrie et Accurate Philosophandi* (On the Art of Sober and Accurate Philosophising). Copies of it survive in Bamberg, Erlangen, the Library of the Soviet Academy of Sciences in Leningrad and in Ghana. A work of logical criticism, the book opens with a discussion of the essence of mind, attempts a classification of various kinds of knowledge, then shows the relation of philosophy to other mental pursuits and finally discusses philosophy as logic, ontology, pneumatology, ethics and politics.

The "mechanistic" flavour of this work would surely have angered Lange and his group, which may have been a factor in Amo's decision to go to the University of Jena, a Wolffian centre, in 1739. On 27 June of that year we have a letter from Amo addressed to the Faculty of Philosophy requesting permission to give public lectures as a university lecturer:

Following a practice of doing good service for the state, pricked on by the sharp dart of poverty (for I have a poor home), I have, to the best of my ability, been teaching philosophy at home in both the universities of Wittenberg and Halle, and have quite often engaged in public disputation, and have performed these tasks with diligence. Therefore, you, gentlemen of outstanding reputation in the world of letters, I hope that you will pay the same attention to me in this, your famous seat of the Muses. Once you have kindly shown me this indulgence, I shall thank you for your action, and shall never grow tired of praying to heaven that you, my excellent patron, may enjoy forever a most desirable happiness.[34]

The letter is signed, "Antonius Guilielmus Amo Afer, Philos. et art. liberal. Magister legens et. Jur. cand." It was circulated immediately to the other members of the faculty by the Dean, Friedrick Andreas Hallbauer, who pointed out that Amo did not have the means to pay the nostrification fees and had requested that these charges should be deferred until he had earned something from his lectures.

There were five other members of the Faculty of Philosophy, Johann Bernhard Wiedeburg, Georg Erhard Hamberger, Johann Jacob Lehman, Johann Peter Reusch and Christin Gottlieb Buder. All except Lehman approved the exemption from nostrification fees immediately, and apparently Lehman approved it shortly, for on 8 July 1739 Hallbauer recorded in the Book of Faculty that Amo's request had been granted and the nostrification fees deferred until Easter of 1740; Amo was therefore permitted to become a university lecturer. A notice dated 17 July (no year given, but perhaps 1739) lists the lectures Amo was to give, including one on "the valuable portions of philosophy" and one on the refutation of superstitious beliefs.

The last document bearing Amo's hand which has so far come to light is an album of his friend Gottfried Achenwall from Elbing, the inventor of statistics in Germany, which according to the title page contained memorials of men who had attained eminence in science and learning. Amo signed the book on 5 May 1740 in Jena and appended a quotation from Epictetus which was his personal motto: "He who can accommodate himself to necessity is wise and has an inkling of things divine." At the foot of this is added: "These words Antony William Amo, an African, Master and University Lecturer in Philosophy and the Liberal Arts, has put down in everlasting memory of himself."[35]

There is no direct evidence that after his stay at Jena Amo became a counsellor of the Court of Berlin, but Professor Blumenbach in an article written in 1787 has the following:

> Our honoured Professor Hollman, while he was still in Wittenberg, conferred the degree of Doctor of Philosophy on a negro, who proved his great talent both in his writings and in his lectures, and who later came to Berlin as counsellor to the King. I have two of his treatises before me, of which one especially contains much unexpected and well-digested reading in the best physiological works of that time.[36]

It is not known what Blumenbach's source was for his assertion, but if Amo did in fact go to Berlin it seems doubtful that it would have been in 1739, while Friedrich Wilhelm I was still king, for Friedrich Wilhelm had patronised pietism and the clerical reaction, against the philosophical free-thinkers with whom Amo was allied. He may, however, have gone to Berlin after 1740, when Friedrich II, "the Great," came to power and for a few years liberalised the Prussian regime.

The last record which has been discovered of Amo's sojourn in Germany is of a satirical recitation performed in a theatre and reported in 1747.[37] The title of the recitation was "A Comic student, the false academic virgin and Magister Amo's proposal," and it apparently made fun of Amo by having him fall in love with, and be rejected by a female student—an idea that could have been amusing only to one of the clericalists who had been opposing Amo. The fact that the recitation was billed for Halle suggests that the dramatised incidents had taken place at Halle and therefore that Amo may have returned to Halle, perhaps at the promise of a new dispensation offered, but later withdrawn, by the new King of Prussia, Friedrich II. The date suggests that Amo stayed in Germany until 1747 at least.

VI

It is not known when Amo left Germany to return to Ghana, but if we can rely on Winkelmann's statement that he left because "his master died," then we must suppose that he did not leave at least until 7 September 1743, when his old mentor, Johann Peter von Ludewig, died. We can assume that the "master" mentioned by Winkelmann was Ludewig since no other academic close to Amo died between 1740 (when we know he was at Jena) and 1753 (when we know he was in Ghana) and since the only non-academic who could have been referred to as "master" would have been a Duke of Wolfenbuttel, none of whom died between 1735 and 1755. Amo, then, most probably left Germany after the death of Ludewig in 1743 but not much before the satirical recitation of 1747. There is an additional piece of information which suggests that he did not return before 1747: Capitein, the Ghanaian who had studied in Holland until 1742, returned that year to Ghana and spent the next five years until his death in 1747 on the coast, chiefly at Elmina but occasionally also at Chama; it seems likely that Capitein would have met Amo if the latter were on the coast before 1747, and yet there is no mention of him in any of Capitein's writings.

We have very little information about Amo's life back in Ghana, except for Winkelmann's report that he lived first at Axim and "later he left Axim and went to live in the fort of the West Indies Company of St. Sebastian at Chama."[38] This information is probably not from Gallandet, who met Amo in Axim, but perhaps something that Winkelmann gathered from unknown Dutch sources. But it is difficult to see any reason why Amo should of his own accord have left Axim, in a region where his father was living and where he had "acquired the reputation of a soothsayer" and "a great sage," according to Winkelmann. The only possible explanation is that Amo's ideas about slavery and vitalism, both those which he was known to have published in Europe and those which he may be presumed to have accounted in Ghana, had made the Dutch so anxious about his harmful effects on the flourishing slave trade at Axim that they sent him as a prisoner to a lesser fort.

There is no further record of Amo. An expedition under Professor Donatie is known to have toured the Guinea coast sometime after April 1759 making nature study observations, but there is no mention of Amo in any of Professor Donatie's works. The diaries of the two governors of the fort at Chama in the 1750's, Mr. Sandra and Mr. Soyer, both of which would presumably contain additional information, have not yet been found. The fort, in any case, was in ruins by 1769, by which time Amo was presumably dead.

NOTES

1. Winkelmann, "Verhandelingen uitgegeven door het zeeuwsch genootschap der wetenschappen te Vlissingen," *Proceedings of the Zeeland Academy of Science* (Middelburg, 1782).

2. Henri Gregoire, *De la literature des Nègres* (Paris, 1800); translated into German in 1809, into English in 1826.

3. Attoh Ahuma, *West African Celebrities* (London, 1910).

4. As Kwame Nkrumah, also from the Axim area, wrote in *Ghana* (New York, Nelson, 1957), p. 3: "By tribal custom it was enough for a mother to assess the age of her child by calculating the number of national festivals that had been celebrated since its birth."

5. Wolfram Suchier, "A. W. Amo. Ein Mohr als Student und Privatdozent der Philosophie in Halle, Wittenberg und Jena, 1727/40," *Akademische Rundschau*, 4 Jahrg. H 9/10 (Leipzig, 1916); "Weiteres über den Mohren Amo," *Altsachen Zeitschrift des Altsachsenbundes für Heimatschutz und Heimatkunde*, No. 1/2 (Holzminden, 1918), pp. 7–9.

6. Suchier, realizing Amo would not have been able to preserve his Ghanaian name, permits himself to doubt that "Amo" is an African name at all; his strange idea is that Amo could have portrayed a little *Amor* at court or could have been showered with such a profusion of love that he was even called "Amor," and that he lost the "r" in the course of years. All this is quite wrong; "Amo," of course, is a common Ghanaian name.

7. The misconception that Africans were selling their children probably arose from a mistrans-

lation of phrases used by the African slavers; their *"Medze ba bi aba"* (Akan) or *"Mo gbe omo kon wa"* (Yoruba) should not have been translated as "I have a son for sale" but "I have a chap for sale."

8. Roemer, *Tilforladelig Efterretning om Kysten Guinea* (Copenhagen, 1760), p. 145.

9. For example: a 1707 memorandum from Assembly X to a new Director for Ghana reads, "The Director shall on his arrival at the Coast of Guinea employ all possible zeal to bring the trade there to a proper state to which end he shall treat the natives of the country with consideration [beleefdelyk] . . . and the Director shall be allowed for the better trade of slaves to make some presents to the Kings of Fida, Aquamboe, Fetu, Commany and Ardra" (The Hague, West Indies Company: 54). Another letter from Assembly X to an Assistant Director General says, ". . . seeing that the whole trade which is driven on the coast by the Company can be done not otherwise than with the natives and that the Company enjoys no profits outside trade, but on the contrary seems to suffer such injury by the diversion of trade and the closing of the passages, it is therefore of the utmost necessity . . . that your Highness treat, and cause to be treated, the kings and caboceers of all the districts together with the lesser natives in all friendship and by all reasons to encourage them to trade: and if any questions and disputes should occur between them, to settle the same in the best way possible so that trade may flourish for the company . . ." (The Hague, West Indies Company: 23 July 1706). In 1749 Assembly X wrote to their Director at Elmina about the repatriation of Ghanaians: "After much trouble and great expense (total £ 3271: 15: 8) have finally been transported from Suriname hither six of the free natives carried off by Christian Hogeroop commanding the private free merchant ship Africa and sold as slaves . . . It is therefore necessary to recommend Your Highness to represent to the brother and/or relations of Atta [one of the six] that the carrying off of Atta was done without our consent or blame and if he had not died he would have been brought back, that skipper Christian Hogeroop has at their request been arrested and put in irons. But if they are not satisfied by this, persist in their claim, and you think they may have bad consequences, they not being subjects of the company or belonging under any stabilised fortress, if they will agree to a sum not exceeding the value of 6–800 guilders, we allow you to settle it accordingly in the most economical way possible."

10. Assembly X of 28 March, 1708, to Johann van der Star.

11. The use of "all" instead of "both" is probably a grammatical laxity, since Amo's Christian names were most likely taken from his godfathers, Duke Anton Ulric (died 1714) and his son Wilhelm August (1662–1731); if the third member of the family, Ludwig Rudolph (1676–1735) had been a godfather, his name would undoubtedly have been added, as it was in 1721.

12. Saltzthal Chapel register in the Staatsarchiv at Wolfenbuttel.

13. Norbert Lochner, "Anton Wilhelm Amo," *Ubersee Rundschau* (Hamburg: July 1958); reprinted in *Transactions of the Historical Society of Ghana*, Vol. III, part 3 (Achimota, 1958).

14. Brentjes, "Anton Wilhelm Amo—in Halle, Wittenberg and Jena," unpublished, but expected 1964/65.

15. *Ibid.*

16. For example, Entry 485 of 8 June 1727 was one Andreas Fridericus Wilhelmus de Crohn, who had been at the Rostock Academy; Entry 486 was a Johannes Gottlieb Stremel who had spent two years in the Leipzig Academy; Entry 483 was Nicolaus B. Brokelman who had spent a year in the Leipzig Academy.

17. *Hallische Frage-und-Anzeigen Nachrichten*, 28 November, 1729, Sections 271–273.

18. *Ibid.*

19. This has been persistently mistranslated as "The Law of the Moors in Europe," but it is correctly "About the Rights of Africans in Europe."

20. *Hallische Frage-und-Anzeigen Nachrichten, loc. cit.*

21. Brentjes, *op. cit.*

22. Johann Joachim Lange, "Clear Proof that the 130 Questions of the New Mechanic Philosophy especially the Metaphysic" [*sic*], 1735.

23. This dispute between the free-thinkers and the clericals is illustrated by a passage from Nikolaus Hironymus Gundling's *Vollstandinge Historie der Gelehrheit* (Frankfurt/Leipzig, 1734), Part 4, p. 5256: ". . . the medical men have ranged themselves in two sects these days, if we can speak in such world. First there are the Mechanists, and second the Stahlians. Of them the former endeavour to maintain that the vital actions in the human body originate and for the most part act in health as in sickness mechanically, and by use of the body's physiology. They say even that the medicaments applied act in a mechanical way in the body; and hence that the soul contributes little or nothing

to all this. To this, the Stahlians state the opposite view: namely that the human soul is the prime mover in the body, and that the body through its physiological structure is only a mobile instrument; also that the medicaments applied are only stimulants which prompt the soul to motion."

24. *Hamburgische Berichte von neuen gelehrten Sachien*, 2 June 1733, p. 366: ". . . right in front the student corporations stood Magister Amo, an African, in the middle of the road as the commander of the entire corps."

25. Address by Rector Kraus appended to Amo's *"De humanae mentis Apatheia . . . ,"* quoted below in full.

26. *Ibid.*

27. Gundling, *op. cit.*, p. 5601.

28. Copies of Meiner's dissertation, *"Disputatio Philosophica continens ideam distinctam eorum, quae competunt vel menti vel corpori nostro vivo et organico,"* are located in the libraries of the university of Griefswald, the Bodleian Library at Oxford and in Ghana.

29. Johann Joachim Lange in *Hallische Frage-und-Anzeigen Nachrichten*, 12 July 1734.

30. *Ibid.*, 1735.

31. *Ibid.*, 14 May 1736.

32. *Ibid.*, November 1736. It is interesting to find Amo referred to as a genuine African, for James Hunt, writing in the nineteenth century, offered to prove at some unspecified date that no genuine African had ever shown the least signs of intelligence and that those who had been mentioned in works like those of Bishop Gregoire were either fictitious or half-caste!

33. University Archives of Halle for 1736. The benefactor was Duke Ludwig Rudolph, who had died in 1735.

34. "The Hamburg Report of Learned Matters," *Hamburgische Berichte von neuen gelehrten Sachien*, 24 November 1739.

35. The album is at present in the library of the University of Göttingen.

36. Blumenbach, "Von den Negern," *Magazin für das Neueste aus der Physik und Naturgeschichte*, Vol. IV, No. 3 (Gotha, 1787). The treatise mentioned is the lost *"De humanae mentis Apatheia . . ."*

37. *Hallische Frage-und-Anzeigen Nachrichten*, 1747.

38. Winkelmann, *loc. cit.*

Society and Politics

PART FIVE

Overleaf: Adinkra symbol for *mate masie,* unity

African men and women have made their own history, woven from the fabric of various cultures, by organized actions, the development of common objectives, and the manipulation of social and political symbols. While the political sentiment reaches back to the earliest of times, the manifestations of the objectives have shifted from society to society and from age to age. Indeed, the ancient Egyptians and Nubians built their societies along caste lines, not so rigidly defined as those that were to develop in India, but nevertheless stringent enough to produce certain responses to phenomena based upon one's caste position. Priests, for example, were definitely different, and treated as different, from the common farmer in ancient Egypt. Those of the military caste were different from members of the royal families, and so forth. To some degree this kind of organization, as Cheikh Anta Diop argues in his book *Precolonial Black Africa,* existed in the Mali and Songhay empires of West Africa. Vestiges of the caste system may still be seen in some contemporary communities.

The last half of this millennium has seen the rise of resistance politics, the creation of new societies, and the denigration of old social and political structures due in large part to the intrusion of the European and Arab cultures. In fact, the Arab influence begins in the seventh century A.D. with the *jihads* (religious wars) from Arabia into northern Africa. Taken collectively, these influences or interventions have shaken the foundation of what was considered African prior to the arrival of the Arabs and Europeans, and altered forever the character of much of African society. The colonization of the continent, with the exception of Ethiopia and Liberia, by non-Africans has meant the grafting of new ideas and strange customs onto the social and political cultures of the people. In the case of Liberia, recolonized by Africans returning from the United States, we see similar actions and reactions. The new Europeanized colonists brought to Liberia customs and cultures that were different from those in Africa. From West Africa to East Africa, from the north to the south, for at least eighty years there was almost total control of the continent by external powers.

The heroic political names of the African tradition represent responses to the numerous social and political crises confronted by the African people. Although we could not include every political idea or all social thinkers in this section, however, we tried to provide pieces that we believe most aptly fit the designation "sources of the African tradition," that is, ideas that have proven useful in discussion and debate long after they were issued.

Providing examples of ancient African responses to society, responsibility, and duty, the autobiographies by Weni and Harkhuf, governors of Upper Egypt, speak to the sophisticated and complex political relations of the Old Kingdom. (Weni served during the reigns of Teti, Pepi I, and Menere; Harkhuf served under Pepi II and Mernere.)

During the late nineteenth century the Fante people of the southern part of Ghana wrote their codes of government into the Fante National Constitution, the first modern constitution of an African society. We include this legal document because it embodies some of the principles of governance that the Fante had developed over a long period. Similarly, some of the commentaries of modern or relatively recent thinkers advance ideas that echo the works of writers and political figures of much earlier historical periods.

Among these individuals is the widely celebrated African scholar Edward Wilmot Blyden. Born in St. Thomas and educated in the United States, he became one of the leading interpreters of the African world and was without peer in the analysis of the role of religion among Africans. In fact, Blyden opened the examination of the role of religion, particularly in his book on Islam and Christianity, in the liberation of African people. He eventually moved to Liberia and served in that government until his death.

Booker T. Washington took a more secular approach to the movement to uplift African Americans. He was preeminently a social activist and an educator devoted to the creation of an institution. He stands astride the history of African Americans as the most prominent voice for the southern African American during the last part of the nineteenth century and the early part of the twentieth century. Washington was called the "Negro Leader," and that title probably fitted him more than it did any other spokesperson before or after in the sense that whites saw him as an African with whom they could deal on issues of business, education, and politics. Washington cultivated the image of the African who was reasonable, that is, one who could deal with whites on the terms they understood and appreciated. Africans, on the other hand, often saw Washington as an accommodationist, one who compromised with whites on an inferior social status for African Americans. But the fact that Tuskegee Institute remains a viable institution long after Washington's death must be credited to the vision that he inspired in many people.

We also include here W. E. B. Du Bois, who wrote in his diary during his twenties that he wanted to do all that he could to demonstrate that African people were equal to any other people. Of course, this would lead him to conflict with the attitude he saw projected in many of Booker T. Washington's policies. It seemed to Du Bois that Washington encouraged whites to see Africans as inferior in thought, behavior, and capability. Du Bois objected to this line of social improvement and sought instead to find empowerment through direct political action, the ballot box, and participation in the political process.

In addition to his involvement in domestic issues, Du Bois was one of the leaders of the Pan-African Movement. During the First International European War (the First World War) a group of Africans from the Caribbean, the Americas, and Africa met in London to discuss the future of the African nation. They were committed to the liberation of Africans everywhere in the world. The objectives of the Pan-African Congresses, as this series of meetings were called, were clear, but years passed before the associations and alliances were clearly defined and made permanent. After 1919 a Pan-African Movement formed; while its progress from time to time was thwarted by internal dissension and debates over the nature of the movement and the populations represented, it nevertheless continued to attract followers.

Marcus Garvey, an ardent Pan-Africanist, came to the United States from Jamaica in 1916. Arriving a year after the death of Booker T. Washington, he was disappointed that he would not meet the man whom he had so long revered. Garvey went to work to establish in New York his Universal Negro Improvement Association and African Communities League as an international body to coordinate and promote the interests of the African world. His eloquence and passion won hundreds of thousands to his cause and gave him a platform of immense stature. This section includes essays by Garvey's wife, Amy Jacques Garvey, who speaks of the role of women as leaders and adds significantly to the discussion of women in the movement for African liberation, and Tony Martin, the eminent Garvey scholar, who discusses the role of the women in the Garvey movement.

Garvey's influence was electric. Even Paul Robeson, the great athlete and performer, was captured by his arguments. Rising from poverty in Princeton, New Jersey, Robeson earned a law degree at Rutgers University. He became internationally famous as a musician and actor, but never distanced himself from his cultural heritage. His concerns about social justice led him to the Communist Party; along with many other political dissenters, however, he saw his motives misconstrued and his career ruined. Robeson courageously became a major advocate of human rights and cultural freedom; he stands out as an extraordinary figure of classic proportions in the African world.

In this section also Maulana Karenga, a leading African American philosopher of culture, offers the seven principles of the Kawaida theory, and Abdias do Nascimento extrapolates on the concept of *quilombismo* in Afro-Brazilian culture.

Two former presidents of African countries, Julius Nyerere (Tanzania) and Kwame Nkrumah (Ghana), discuss how their own political philosophies developed in the context of colonialism. C. L. R. James, the brilliant commentator on colonialism in the Caribbean, examines the significance of Nkrumah's rise and fall.

The section ends with works by James Baldwin and Cornel West. Baldwin, the preeminent African American essayist and outstanding novelist, contributes a searing essay indicting racial oppression in the United States. Cornel West, a leading contemporary philosopher, provides a telling analysis of W. E. B. Du Bois as an American philosopher.

Weni

(SIXTH DYNASTY, 2300–2150 B.C., Kemet)

Autobiography

The Count, Governor of Upper Egypt, Chamberlain, Warden of Nekhen, Mayor of Nekheb, Sole Companion, honored by Ausar Foremost-of-the-Westerners, Weni says: I was a fillet-bearing youth under the majesty of King Teti, my office being that of custodian of the storehouse, when I became inspector of tenants of the palace. When I had become overseer of the robing-room under the majesty of King Pepi, his majesty gave me the rank of companion and inspector of priests of his pyramidtown.

His majesty made me senior warden of Nekhen, his heart being filled with me beyond any other servant of his. I heard cases alone with the chief judge and vizier, concerning all kinds of secrets. I acted in the name of the king for the royal harem and for the six great houses, because his majesty's heart was filled with me beyond any official of his, any noble of his, any servant of his.

When I begged of the majesty of my lord that there be brought for me a sarcophagus of white stone from Tura, his majesty had a royal seal-bearer cross over with a company of sailors under this command, to bring me this sarcophagus from Tura. It came with him in a great barge of the court, together with its lid, a doorway, lintel, two doorjambs, and a libation-table. Never before had the like been done for any servant—but I was excellent in his majesty's heart; I was rooted in his majesty's heart; his majesty's heart was filled with me.

While I was senior warden of Nekhen, his majesty made me a sole companion and overseer of the royal tenants. I replaced four overseers of royal tenants who were there. I acted for his majesty's praise in guarding, escorting the king, and attending. I acted throughout so that his majesty praised me for it exceedingly.

When there was a secret charge in the royal harem against Queen Weret-yamtes, his majesty made me go in to hear it alone. No chief judge and vizier, no official was there, only I alone; because I was worthy, because I was rooted in his majesty's heart; because his majesty had filled his heart with me. Only I put it in writing together with one other senior warden of Nekhen, while my rank was only that of overseer of royal tenants. Never before had one like me heard a secret of the king's harem; but his majesty made me hear it, because I was worthy in his majesty's heart beyond any official of his, beyond any noble of his, beyond any servant of his.

When his majesty took action against the Asiatic Sand-dwellers, his majesty made an army of many tens of thousands from all of Upper Egypt: from Yebu in the south to Medenyt in the north; from Lower Egypt: from all of the Two-Sides-of-the-House and from

Sedjet and Khen-sedjru; and from Irtjet-Nubians, Medja-Nubians, Yam-Nubians, Wawat-Nubians, Kaau-Nubians; and from Themeh-land.

His majesty sent me at the head of this army, there being counts, royal seal-bearers, sole companions of the palace, chieftains and mayors of towns of Upper and Lower Egypt, companions, chief priests of Upper and Lower Egypt, and chief district officers at the head of the troops of Upper and Lower Egypt, from the villages and towns that they governed and from the Nubians. I was the one who commanded them—while my rank was that of overseer of royal tenants—because of my office, so that no one attacked his fellow, so that no one took a loaf or sandals from a traveler, so that no one took a cloth from any town, so that no one took a goat from anyone.

> This army returned in safety,
> > It had ravaged the Sand-dwellers' land.
> This army returned in safety,
> > It had flattened the Sand-dwellers' land.
> This army returned in safety,
> > It had sacked its strongholds.
> This army returned in safety,
> > It had cut down its figs, its vines.
> This army returned in safety,
> > It had thrown fire in all its mansions.
> This army returned in safety,
> > It had slain its troops by many ten-thousands.
> This army returned in safety,
> > It had carried off many troops as captives.

His majesty praised me for it beyond anything. His majesty sent me to lead this army five times, to attack the land of the Sand-dwellers.

WENI BECOMES GOVERNOR OF UPPER EGYPT

When I was chamberlain of the palace and sandal-bearer, King Mernere, my lord who lives forever, made me Count and Governor of Upper Egypt, from Yebu in the south to Medenyt in the north, because I was worthy in his majesty's heart, because I was rooted in his majesty's heart, because his majesty's heart was filled with me. When I was chamberlain and sandal-bearer, his majesty praised me for the watch and guard duty which I did at court, more than any official of his, more than any noble of his, more than any servant of his. Never before had this office been held by any servant.

I governed Upper Egypt for him in peace, so that no one attacked his fellow. I did every task. I counted everything that is countable for the residence in this Upper Egypt two times, and every service that is countable for the residence in this Upper Egypt two times. I did a perfect job in this Upper Egypt. Never before had the like been done in this Upper Egypt. I acted throughout so that his majesty praised me for it.

His majesty sent me to Ibhat to bring the sarcophagus "chest of the living" together with its lid, and the costly august pyramidion for the pyramid "Mernere-appears-in-splendor," my mistress. His majesty sent me to Yebu to bring a granite false-door and its libation stone and granite lintels, and to bring granite portals and libation stones for the upper chamber of the pyramid "Mernere-appears-in-splendor," my mistress. I traveled north with them to the pyramid "Mernere-appears-in-splendor" in six barges and three tow-boats of eight ribs in a single expedition. Never had Yebu and Ibhat been done in a single expedition under any king. Thus everything his majesty commanded was done entirely as his majesty commanded.

His majesty sent me to Hatnub to bring a great alter of alabaster of Hatnub. I brought this alter down for him in seventeen days. After it was quarried at Hatnub, I had it go downstream in this barge I had built for it, a barge of acacia wood of sixty cubits in length and thirty cubits in width. Assembled in seventeen days, in the third month of summer, when there was no water on the sandbanks, it landed at the pyramid "Mernere-appears-in-splendor" in safety. It came about through me entirely in accordance with the ordinance commanded by my lord.

His majesty sent me to dig five canals in Upper Egypt, and to build three barges and four tow-boats of acacia wood of Wawat.

Then the foreign chiefs of Irtjet, Wawat, Yam, and Medja cut the timber for them. I did it all in one year. Floated, they were loaded with very large granite blocks for the pyramid "Mernere-appears-in-splendor." Indeed I made a [saving] for the palace with all these five canals. As King Mernere who lives forever is august, exalted, and mighty more than any god, so everything came about in accordance with the ordinance commanded by his *ka*.

I was one beloved of his father, praised by his mother, gracious to his brothers. The count, true governor of Upper Egypt, honored by Ausar, Weni.

Harkhuf

(SIXTH DYNASTY, 2300–2150 B.C., Kemet)

Autobiography

An offering which the king gives and Anubis, he who is upon his mountain, before the god's shrine, in the place of embalming, the lord of the necropolis: May he be buried in the necropolis in the western desert, in great old age as one honored by the great god. The Count, Governor of Upper Egypt, Royal Seal-bearer, Sole Companion, Lector-priest, Chief of scouts, honored by Ptah-Sokar, Harkhuf.

An offering which the king gives and Ausar, lord of Busiris: May he journey in peace on the holy ways of the West, journeying on them as one honored. May he ascend to the god, lord of heaven, as one honored by [the god, lord of heaven]. The Count, Chamberlain, Warden of Nekhen, Mayor of Nekheb, Sole Companion, Lector-priest, honored by Ausar, Harkhuf.

An offering which the king gives, to provide for him in the necropolis; and may he be transfigured by the lector-priest on every New Year's day, every Jehuti-feast, every First-of-the-Year feast, every *wag*-feast, every Sokar-feast, on every great feast. The Royal Seal-bearer, Sole Companion, Lector-priest, Chief of scouts, Harkhuf.

> I have come here from my city,
> I have descended from my nome;
> I have built a house, set up [its] doors,
> I have dug a pool, planted sycamores.
> The king praised me,
> My father made a will for me.
> I was one worthy—
> One beloved of his father,
> Praised by his mother,
> Whom all his brothers loved.
> I gave bread to the hungry,
> Clothing to the naked,
> I brought the boatless to land.
> O you who live upon earth,
> Who shall pass by this tomb
> Going north or going south,
> Who shall say: "a thousand loaves and beer jugs
> For the owner of this tomb,"

I shall watch over them in the necropolis.
I am an excellent equipped spirit [*akh*],
A lector-priest who knows his speech.
As for any man who enters this tomb unclean.
I shall seize him by the neck like a bird,
He will be judged for it by the great god!
I was one who spoke fairly, who repeated what was liked,
I never spoke evilly against any man to his superior,
For I wished to stand well with the great god.
Never did I judge between two contenders
In a manner which deprived a son of his father's legacy.

An offering which the king gives and Anubis, who is upon his mountain and before the god's shrine, as provision for him in the necropolis, for one honored by Anubis, he upon his mountain and before the god's shrine. The Count, Lector-priest, Sole Companion, Chief of scouts, the honored Harkhuf.

The Count, Sole Companion, Lector-priest, Chamberlain, Warden of Nekhen, Mayor of Nekheb, Royal Seal-bearer, Chief of scouts, Privy-councillor of all affairs of Upper Egypt, favorite of his lord, Harkhuf.

The Royal Seal-bearer, Sole Companion, Lector-priest, Chief of scouts, who brings the produce of all foreign lands to his lord, who brings gifts to the Royal Ornament, Governor of all mountainlands belonging to the southern region, who casts the dread of Heru into the foreign lands, who does what his lord praises; the Royal Seal-bearer, Sole Companion, Lector-priest, Chief of scouts, honored by Sokar, Harkhuf, says:

The majesty of Mernere, my lord, sent me together with my father, the sole companion and lector-priest, Iri, to Yam, to open the way to that country. I did it in seven months; I brought from it all kinds of beautiful and rare gifts, and was praised for it very greatly.

His majesty sent me a second time alone. I went up on the Yebu road and came down via Mekher, Terers, and Irtjet which are in Irtjet in the space of eight months. I came down bringing gifts from that country in great quantity, the likes of which had never before been brought back to this land. I came down through the region of the house of the chief of Setju and Irtjet, I explored those foreign lands. I have not found it done by any companion and chief of scouts who went to Yam previously.

Then his majesty sent me a third time to Yam. I went up from the nome of This upon the Oasis road. I found that the ruler of Yam had gone off to Tjemeh-land, to smite the Tjemeh to the western corner of heaven. I went up after him to Tjemeh-land and satisfied him, so that he praised all the gods for the sovereign.

I dispatched the courtier X with a man from Yam to the retinue of Heru, to let the majesty of Mernere, my lord, know that I had gone to Tjemeh-land after the ruler of Yam. Now when I had satisfied this ruler of Yam, I came down through south of Irtjet and north of Setju. I found the ruler of the confederacy of Irtjet, Setju, and Wawat. I came down with three hundred donkeys laden with incense, ebony, *hknw*-oil, *s3t*, panther skins, elephant's-tusks, throw sticks, and all sorts of good products. Now when the ruler of Irtjet, Setju, and Wawat saw how strong and numerous the troop from Yam was which came down with me to the residence together with the army that had been sent with me, this ruler escorted me, gave me cattle and goats, and led me on the mountain paths of Irtjet— because of the excellence of the vigilance I had employed beyond that of any companion and chief of scouts who had been sent to Yam before.

Now when this servant fared down to the residence, the sole companion and master of the cool-rooms, Khuni, was sent to meet me with ships laden with date wine, cake, bread, and beer. The Count, Royal Seal-bearer, Sole Companion, Lector-priest, God's Seal-bearer, Privy-councillor of ordinances, the honored Harkhuf.

The King's own seal: Year 2, third month of the first season, day 15. The King's decree to the Sole Companion, Lector-priest, Chief of scouts, Harkhuf. Notice has been taken of this dispatch of yours which you made for the King at the Palace, to let one know that you have come down in safety from Yam with the army that was with you. You have said in this dispatch of yours that you have brought all kinds of great and beautiful gifts, which Hathor mistress of Imaau has given to the *ka* of King Neferkare, who lives forever. You have said in this dispatch of yours that you have brought a Twa of the god's dances from the land of the horizon-dwellers, like the Twa whom the god's seal-bearer Bawerded brought from Punt in the time of King Isesi. You have said to my majesty that no one like this Twa had ever been brought by anyone who had come from Yam previously.

Truly you know how to do what your lord loves and praises. Truly you spend day and night planning to do what your lord loves, praises, and commands. His majesty will provide your many worthy honors for the benefit of your son's son for all time, so that all people will say, when they hear what my majesty did for you: "Does anything equal what was done for the sole companion Harkhuf when he came down from Yam, on account of the vigilance he showed in doing what his lord loved, praised, and commanded?"

Come north to the residence at once! Hurry and bring with you this Twa whom you brought from the land of the horizon-dwellers, live, hale, and healthy, for the dances of the god, to gladden the heart, to delight the heart of King Neferkare who lives forever! When he goes down with you into the ship, get worthy men to be around him on deck, lest he fall into the water! When he lies down at night, get worthy men to lie around him in his tent. Inspect ten times at night! My majesty desires to see this Twa more than the gifts of the mine-land and of Punt!

When you arrive at the residence of his majesty with this Twa live, hale, and healthy, my majesty will do great things for you, more than was done for the god's seal-bearer Bawerded in the time of King Isesi, in accordance with my majesty's wish to see this Twa. Orders have been brought to the chief of the new towns and the companion, overseer of priests to command that supplies be furnished from what is under the charge of each from every storage depot and every temple that has not been exempted.

William E. Abraham
(b. 1934, Ghana)

Theory of Human Society

One may wish to pose two questions here: first, whether general procedures of psychology are applicable in Africa, and, second, whether findings by psychologists who have studied European communities might stand in Africa without being further checked; or might the psyche of Africans turn out to be quite distinct and not really support the findings of European psychologists who have studied Europe? One may of course wish to pose a third question, the question whether Africans have theories of the resolution of their own psyche. The way in which a people resolve their psyche into aspects is bound to affect the explanations which they give of human behaviour. And the two together affect the way in which their society is set up and run. Freud, for example, is largely responsible for the ever-growing tendency to treat certain evil-doers as sick men, through his account of the human psyche.

The Akans were not without such an account. In a human being, apart from his body, the Akans distinguished the *okra*. The *okra* is the guiding spirit of a man, the bearer and instrument of his destiny, that in a man which antecedently to the incarnation takes its leave of God. The *okra* is also that whose departure from the living man means death, and marks the completion of his destiny. It returns to God to justify its earthly existence. So important is this held to be that there is an Akan saying to the effect that all men are children of God, and no man is a child of the earth. Only human beings have an *okra*. The *okra* is capable of appearing time after time on earth in different bodies, and it is the crucial factor in personal identity. This is what encourages the Akans to talk of a person's real self.

The *okra*, by being the bearer of destiny, lends its name to signal good luck and signal bad luck, both being thought in a way to be deserved, or at least unavoidable and perhaps even fitting. When either takes place, one says it is the person's *okra*. It is believed that the *okra* of a person can be interrogated by priests while it is still in the mother's womb. This, again, is an impious attempt to scrutinise and perhaps divert what God has laid down beforehand. In Akan mysticism, it must consequently be adjudged to be superstitious.

In addition to the *okra*, the Akans distinguished the *sunsum* of a man. The *okra* was conceived to be automatic in its functioning, even when it gives advice which is good or bad. Its advice does not arise from any interest, but from the ineluctable unfolding of the destiny appointed for it. In face of danger it can therefore be the means of its possessor's salvation to prevent death betimes. The saying that someone dies betimes is consequently, to speak strictly, quite meaningless in Akan conceptualism.

The destiny of a man was called his *nkrabea*. His *nkrabea* often appeared as an encumbrance to him, for though the *okra* was the basis of his personal identity, the living man did not identify himself with his *okra*, and of a man whose *okra* did not, so to say, bring him good luck, it was said that he had *okrabiri* (a black *okra*). It was said that a man whose *okra* was pink always ate berries and tender fruits and wore embroidered linen. By contrast, if a man's *okra* was black, that was an abomination; application brought him no gain. Trouble searched him out.

Sunsum appears to have been a spiritual substance responsible for *suban*, character, genius, temper and quality. *Sunsum* is moral in its operation, not automatic, and is educable. Whereas the *okra* is that which makes a person breathe and so is the principle of life, the *sunsum* is not, and is thought to be able to leave a man during sleep. It is that second man who is a *dramatis persona* in dreams. A man's *sunsum* is also that spirit of a man which may be attacked by witchcraft. The *sunsum* as the basis of character is said to be strong or wicked or good. And when a person is a witch or wizard, it is through the power of the *sunsum*.

The Akans also distinguished the *ntoro*. The *ntoro* is inheritable, but not the *sunsum* or the *okra*. The *ntoro* does not at death depart with the *okra*, but goes down to a man's children or, failing these, to his nephews and nieces by his brother. The father's *ntoro* takes the place of the child's *ntoro* until the child attains puberty. Puberty among the Akans is not tied to any particular age, but is claimed with the appearance and luxuriance of pubic hairs. The child's own *sunsum* begins to operate at puberty. But its father's *ntoro* does not for this reason cease altogether to be operative. The *ntoro* of the father is cited by the Akans in explanation of inherited characteristics, and is also thought of as a group of characteristics, a type of personality. And it is the co-operation of the father's *ntoro* with the mother's blood in the sense of kinship which is believed to form the foetus and mould it into the form of a human being.

Finally, the Akans distinguished the *mogya* which is a type of spiritual factor, and is the basis of the *abusua* or clan. This can only be bestowed by females. It is the *mogya* which at the death of a person becomes his *saman* (ghost). As a *saman* it retains the bodily form. It has a chance of reincarnation though this is only possible through a woman of the same clan. Not even reincarnation can make a person change clan.

From the Akan theory of man it is evident that human personality and character were seen by them to rest on a number of factors and influences; comprising the *okra*, which above all was the ineducable and unswervable element; the *sunsum*, which was educable through precept and a system of punishment and reward, and was the foundation of personal and moral responsibility; the *ntoro*, which was inherited and related mainly to the prescription of certain practices and the avoidance of others, thereby moulding temperament through the operation of taboos; and finally the *mogya*, which ensured that one was amenable to reason, made one a human being. In the Akan theory of man, consequently, spiritual factors were primary.

A man was thought to be survived at death by his *okra* which went back to *Nyankopon*, and by his *mogya* which became his *saman*, and bore a physical resemblance to him. It is this *mogya* as *saman* which is invoked in what is miscalled ancestor-worship.

Three kinds of *nsamanfo* were distinguished. There was the *samanpa* or good *saman*. A *saman* was deemed good if the death of the man was not followed either by a run of general bad luck, including further deaths, for his family or even community, or if his death was followed by the cessation of a previous run of bad luck. These ghosts are shy, and hide round corners when they see a man.

There was the *saman-twen-twen*, the ghost which could not be laid. Such a ghost was seen at intervals by living persons around the man's old haunts. They were incapable of going to the spirit world where their like are. They hung around dark corners and back-yards. They hung around the earth as a temporary or everlasting punishment. They had not much power for harm and contented themselves with scarifications.

Finally, there was also the *tofo*, the ghost of a man who met a violent death. As being unlucky, such a man was given specially deprecatory burial rites. These ghosts cannot get on with the good ones; they wander about, painted with white clay, and clothed in white raiment. But unlike the good ones, they are bold and aggressive.

Ghosts were associated with a particular odour said to be like that of *nunum*, a certain aromatic plant. A ghost is, when visible, always dressed in white. It is not an object of friendship; and you are cautioned that if one should offer you its hand, you quickly bend yours away. A good ghost, however, showers blessings on its orphan. Ghosts have ana-logues of human senses and passions, including those of hunger, thirst, and anger. Quite impolitely, they sometimes invite themselves to meals, a sure sign of their activity being the too-rapid disappearance of food and drink with which everyone is familiar. To forestall this people often drop a morsel on the ground to distract ghosts. Stools are often tilted when not in use to prevent stray and tired ghosts from sitting on them; and should a person sit on one before a ghost can get away, he contracts pains in the waist.

Ghosts by and large inhabit the spirit world. There is a half-cynical, half-reverent atti-tude to this world illustrated in the saying that if the spirit world has nothing to it, at least it has its name behind it. Each man has to go there himself, messages are neither sent nor carried. Nor does one go there oneself and return as one pleases. If Orpheus had been an Akan, he would not have known any route save death to the underworld. The spirit world has a social organisation complete with chiefs and subjects. But opinion is not cer-tain about its location. Some say it is under the earth. Some say it is up in the skies. But there is always a route to it from one's grave wherever one is buried. It is an extensive country and the journey there takes one over mountains. The track to the spirit world of a man who dies a peaceful death is dark and unluminous. But a man who dies a violent death drops some of the white clay off him on his track, and this is why the milky way is white. At the same time there is a compresence between spirits and men. And the chief difficulty of going to the spirit world is not navigational, but one of transformation. Since heaven is in a sense around us, to speak to God one speaks to the wind. In the same way the spirits of our ancestors are always within call, and can be summoned at will through ritual invocation without raising the voice.

In what is called ancestor-worship, ancestors are invoked to give succour to their family descendants. A great deal of respect is shown to them on such occasions. The basis of the respect is twofold, first that the ancestors are our predecessors, our elders, and for this reason alone command our respect; and second that in their spiritual state they note more than we can, being in unhindered touch with the essence of things. The ceremony of ancestor-worship is also an occasion for remembering them, a sort of family reunion. An Akan family can only grow, it cannot diminish, for the ancestors are continuing members of it. But because they no longer belong to the three-dimensional order of things, special-ised avenues of consultation have to be devised to reach them. This creates the need for rites. The rites of ancestor-worship are not rites of worship but methods of communica-tion. There is no feeling of self-abasement and self-negation on the part of the living during such rites. The lineages to which the ancestors belong are not political devices, though they lend themselves to use in sorting out political claims. In themselves they are antecedent to political arrangements, and this indeed is the reason why they can be cited in evidence of political claims. The permanence of the lineage is also a method of family archive.

The lineage is an extremely formal sequence, complete with its totem, its taboos, and even its personality. Personality implies a high degree of integration and systematisation. The clue to this is to be found in statements to the effect that such and such a thing is not in character. A nation has no personality unless it is highly systematised in its attitudes and in its responses. A lineage, because it is for these purposes a closed system, has a personality which may in fact be called its group personality. The notion of a group personality is not a farfetched one and may be referred readily to heaven and hell because of the systematisation involved in the conception of these. In any case, the inheritability of the *ntoro* and the *mogya* gives additional unity to the lineage traced matrilineally, and reinforces the group personality. The inter-relation of the several lineages in the community in a definite way bestows a certain formality on the larger society too, and creates the foundation of the community personality. This community personality is the crux of the Akan theory of the State. The State is almost personified, and takes precedence over every individual. So does the *Abusua* or clan. Between the *Abusua* and the *Oman* (State), the *Oman* is supreme. The kinship involved in the *Abusua* organisation first and foremost places duties on its members. This is how the Akan society comes to be founded on duties rather than rights. The duties are both ritualistic and humanist. The ritualistic duties consolidate the clan at the spiritual level. The humanistic ones consolidate it at the human level. The responsibility of a member of the clan for the welfare of other members is nevertheless not calculated to encourage the lazy and indolent. It has no suggestion of anyone rushing out of step to save the needy but foolish. There are a great many sayings all tending to this point. When you are needy, you do pick nuts from a dung heap, runs one. This does little towards conjuring a picture of clansmen thrusting their bounty on one. A few more run as follows:

> When you are needy, you eat the skin of a goat;
> Need turns a nobleman into a slave;
> Poverty is like madness (in what it makes you do).

The responsibility of your clansmen takes effect when you are a stranger in a village, or when without your fault you become indigent or fall into debt, and are quite close to the last ditch. To confirm this need for solidarity and permanence, there is a saying that a clan is like a flowering shrub, it blossoms in clusters. There is another saying that the family tree is not clipped.

Though clans were basic to the State, they were not coordinate in importance. There was a clan or a hierarchy of clans from which alone rulers could be elected, other things being equal. The Akans say that all clans are equally clans and good enough at that; but we nevertheless look closely at the nuts of the oil-palm. The establishment of a hierarchy among clans was evidently a cohesive device for the *Oman,* for it created the basis of leadership, and the authority for command, and thereby lessened power-struggle of a disintegrative kind, while at the same time preserving a democracy of leadership through elections.

The whole education of youth was given a utilitarian orientation. The *Oman* included venerable ancestors, and in a way reflected in visible embodiment the structure of the spiritual world with which it was in continuous touch. It was therefore in effect a religious set-up. It was to the nurture of this religious set-up that the education of youth was directed. An admonitory saying holds that when the State begins to collapse, the cause can be found in the home. Another, which emphasises the completeness of the individual's absorption in the *Oman*, held that if the State or the people cut silly patterns on the hair of one's head, one did not erase them. The absoluteness of the State's claim on the individual's obedience was in this saying endorsed. The State's call on the individual was, however, not arbitrary and gratuitous but based on reflection and decision of a public kind, and tending towards the public good.

The opinion is often expressed that the coherence of traditional African societies set close limits on individual freedom and initiative, and might even be expected to have produced a great deal of pusillanimity. There possibly is a misconception here. In any State, instruments must be devised for preserving public peace and establishing a range of public harmony and efficiency. In modern States, there are legal organisations to preserve peace, and clusters of professional and semi-professional organisations to lay down additional rules of conduct, e.g. for the press, for lawyers, for doctors, tennis players, *et cetera;* there are clubs and also public opinion to establish a range of harmony through ideas about things which are not done, and things which one may do. In a society which is not organised in these ways, the purposes which these bodies serve are still legitimate and desirable. The intense development of the communal spirit becomes an optimum way of securing these ends. The communal spirit was in fact raised in Akan society through education and public opinion. When the bodies and clubs referred to come into existence, individuals are freed from their pertinent *direct* obligations to the community, and express these obligations *indirectly* through allegiance to these bodies and clubs. The obligations are still there; what has altered is their visibility. But because these obligations become more narrowly centered now, the individual obtains a sense of liberation, initiative, and creativeness. The division of the Akan state into clans was in fact also a way of lightening the weight of the State on the back of the individual. The individual could concentrate on nurturing the clan instead of feeling directly responsible for the world. The clan was an instrument of making the communal spirit effective.

Inevitably, this subservience to the clan, because it made one's obligations to it moral and spiritual, tended to limit one's freedom of expression and action more than a merely social loyalty to a club or professional loyalty to an organisation might do. The reprisals which disloyalty involved were, not unexpectedly, quite grave. Disloyalty in the communalistic set-up was held to endanger the very fabric of society extending to and including the spirits of departed ancestors. Disloyalty to the clan could therefore in certain cases carry the aura of sacrilege. Disloyalty to a club or a professional organisation, because more limited in direction, often carries with it nothing more serious than expulsion or the demand for an apology. Here society is not enabled to feel immediately threatened as disloyalty to the clan led it to feel.

But if the clan limited the freedom of expression and action, and even the variety of feeling of its members, it is not to be inferred that thought was thwarted and stifled. The embargo on the expression of certain dangerous and impious opinions operated only in the presence of one's elders. School-teachers have in fact complained about the difficulty of getting African children to express definite opinions in speech. The cause of this is not any lack of definite, vigorous, original, and creative thoughts, but the inability through upbringing to join issue with one's elders, in this case teachers. The essays written by the same children do not square with their public speech. This habit extends from primary schools to universities. There is an Akan saying that the words of one's elders are greater than an amulet. Elders were the repository of communal wisdom, and were not to be gainsaid lightly. The justification for this attitude lay in the fact that the wisdom of Africa was practical. In theoretical matters, where errors might have no more radical consequences than the waste of time and effort, dispute between learners and people who know better may be inconsequential, and even a healthy exercise. Where elders occupy a hierarchic position, public disputes with younger and lower persons cannot but bring a loss of dignity and effectiveness to their position. The wisdom which they represented might have been adequate to clan needs and state needs in their time. They are not adequate today. And in the age of searchings and seekings, disputes with them have become thinkable.

The restriction on action was largely limited to the choice of a wife and the choice of a career. In marriage, ideas about clan descent became operative. Akan clans are exogamous, exception being made only for kings, for a certain reason. The reason for the exception was interestingly identical with the reason for the general rule. As to the limitation on the freedom to choose a career, this could be expected in any society which had no notable surpluses of goods and wealth. The Akan society had a subsistence economy with very little surplus. The opportunities in such a society would be few, as they were in Akan society, and pure scholars had to depend exclusively on courtly patronage. Since the fortunes of an individual were connected with those of his family, his choice of a career was a matter integral to the family set-up. His fertility as a source of succour to the family in bad times, and his liability to claim succour from the family, made his choice of career susceptible to their feelings and opinions. Careers were chosen not as a means to self-fulfillment, but as a discharge of family responsibility. With the expansion of opportunities more members of a family can exert themselves both in their own favour and in that of their family. The larger the number of those who can do this, the less is their risk of being called upon to help, the greater therefore is their emancipation.

In art and literature and technology the canons of acceptability were dependent more on the individual apprehension than on social necessity.

The reason which explains the exogamy of the clan and the endogamy of the chief also explains the right of succession. The right of succession cannot be understood without the theory of ownership. The Akans recognised both private ownership and public ownership. In fact, their insight into the effects of private ownership was considerable. Land was the central object owned publicly. The land of a clan is jointly owned in perpetuity by the whole clan including the dead ancestors, and may not be alienated either in part or in whole. Freehold of land was unprovided for in the land tenure system. In England, there is no such thing as absolute ownership in the soil, the ultimate landowner being the Sovereign on behalf of the State. The strongest form of ownership open to Her Majesty's subjects is involved in fee-simple absolute in possession. For practical purposes, this is tantamount to absolute ownership in the land. Among the Akans, the practice is comparable to the theory in England. Land was vested in the throne or stool of the chief who held it in trust for the people. Even the chief had no absolute ownership in the land. Land was classified in two ways, administrative and stool. Stool land could be used personally by the reigning paramount chief for as long as he was chief. Consent of the chief was necessary to permit interference with such land. The administrative land of the stool was, on the other hand, merely land over which the stool had jurisdiction. This was the terrestrial area of his subjects. The Akan political system distinguished between population and territory in order to establish a polity. The administrative land, the territory of the State, was equitably distributed for farming and occupation under the surveyance of the chief's court. This arrangement is quite general in Africa and is only somewhat modified by historical events; for example, in Uganda variations in detail can be explained in terms of the feudalistic elements introduced by Galla invaders.

The rarity of private ownership makes the appointment of successors a formalistic matter. Precedence in inheritance is in the following order:

(1) the eldest brother by the same mother
(2) the eldest son of eldest sister
(3) grandson through female line
(4) another branch of the same family
(5) a slave.

Though succession was formalistic, the needs of trusteeship made consideration of expediency relevant. The successor, like his predecessor, only held property in trust, and if unfitted for this office could be bypassed without fuss. An heir required formal as well as aptitude qualifications. Even bodily blemish, not to speak of incompetence, could lead to the preference of the eldest son of the eldest sister over the eldest brother by the same mother. Slaves were occasionally preferred to living members of the same family. One regulative principle cited in succession disputes says in so many words that when mother's sons are not exhausted, nephews do not inherit.

There of course is a reason for this succession arrangement. The source of the family was held to be the woman. Hence members of the family and the clan were identified matrilineally. It was the woman who gave birth to the child; in a visible way, the child was more obviously the woman's than the man's; it was nurtured by the woman's blood and carried in the woman's womb. *Mogya,* that factor which determined the child's form, was contributed entirely by the mother. There is·a saying that it is your mother's child who is your kin. Possessiveness over property would be an inducement to restrict succession to people tracing their *mogya* to a common source. In the case of the king or paramount chief, marriage within the same clan was allowed to preserve the royalty of the clan and the complete authenticity of the king.

The line of succession was not unconnected with the type of social organisation. When social organisation becomes completely substantive, a thing in itself, which does not consult antecedent metaphysics, the society is run on an intensely economic basis. And where the economic functions of the male become impressive to a certain degree, the succession becomes patrilineal. Where the same functions are discharged by a woman, there, whether the society has reference to antecedent metaphysics or not, the society is matrilineal. In the Akan society of traditional purity, economic obligations towards the child were mainly fulfilled by the mother. The filial attachment to the mother was in turn considered to be unseverable, and there is a saying that when one's mother hits hard times, one does not leave her to make somebody else one's mother.

The upbringing of the child was extremely pragmatic. Great store was always set by experience and wisdom among the Akans. Virtue was inculcated more through exercise than through precept. As one can expect, there are several sayings underlining this idea. A few are listed here:

"A child who is to be successful is not reared exclusively on a bed of down."

"It is the knife-blade without a safety handle which frees itself from the hands of the child."

"If a child pretends to be dead and plays possum, you pretend to bury him."

"If a child does nine mischievous things, five of them always come back to him."

"If a child insists on clutching live coals, by all means let him; when he gets burnt you won't have to encourage him to throw them away."

Society and Politics

The words of one's elders are greater than an amulet. In these few quotations one can already gather that the Akans believed in the discipline of children, and entirely endorsed the right of age to instruct youth. Wisdom was always preferred to authority, as the arrangements of inheritance themselves suggest. The Akans said that there was an old man before a lord was born. Though the Akans loved wisdom greatly, their attitude towards fools was not one of harshness, but one of ridicule and mild contempt. Wisdom was always practical, the fool being the man who was constantly at a loss, and not simply a theoretically inept person. I set out a few sayings touching upon the fool.

"The fool says: they mean my friend, not me."

Here the shiftlessness of the fool, his utter inability to profit from anything not shoved into his mouth, is meant. A wise man, one supposes, profits from everything.

"When you quote a proverb to a fool, you also need to explain it."

"It is only the fool who needs a proverb explained to him."

This is equivalent to the saying *verbum sapienti*.
Touching the improvidence of the fool, the Akans say that

"When he is squandering his gold, he says his scales are out of order."

And since he does not do things with his eyes wide open, they say that

"It is the fool whose own tomatoes are sold to him."

The Akans expressed their dislike for purely academic points in the saying that

"Wisdom is not like money to be tied up and hidden."

The admonition to the wise to profit from every situation lends itself to a literal interpretation. In readiness for this possibility, the Akans wryly remark that

"When two astute persons deal with each other, feelings run high."

In the same style of interpretation, it is said that

"The wise man levers eight pounds from a fool with the aid of a penny."

This kind of dealing was not much praised and you are warned that

"Where you cheat the fool, a wise man sits and watches."

The pragmatic and whimsical colour of Akan wisdom, which in fact pervades African wisdom in general, makes it immediately available for the modernistic reconstruction of African societies. The need for reconstruction is itself mainly pragmatic. . . . The Akan attitudes as they affected life were in fact modernistic and mature. The communal spirit is strong at a certain low level of economic development, and its essentially negative character promises not to interfere with economic development. The preparation for the economic uplift of Africa will involve considerable pain and sacrifice which calls for the examination of African attitudes towards poverty and riches. Once again, one must turn to sayings in order to discover the principles underlying these attitudes and also the judgments liable to be made in money economy situations. Accordingly, I am setting down a few relevant sayings:

"In the extremes of need, a human being will live in the forest (like an animal)."

"Indigence will make one search for nuts in a dung-heap."

"Poverty turns a nobleman into a slave."

"Poverty is madness."

This group of quotations illustrates the shifts to which poverty is capable of driving one. The likening of poverty to madness shows considerable insight into that appearance of unaccountability which poverty produces in certain temperaments. The Akans did not however win the release of creative energies which poverty is again capable of provoking. In their recognition of the harshness and cruelty which accompany such energies they showed their essential humanity. They even said, "If Europe knew no poverty, the white man would not leave his people to live in the black man's country." This reveals that the spirit with which some of the Akans defended themselves against European attempts to settle or alienate their land was not always due to the metaphysical entanglements in which they involved land in their thinking. The appreciation of the relevance of economic wants and motives to the brutalities of colonialism was quickly made. The likeness of poverty to madness was explored in specific sayings about the dispositions of the poor man.

"Poverty has no friends."

In a strongly communalistic society, this makes one either a god or a beast.

"The poor man has no anger."

Not because he is not provoked. Poverty and strength of personality were thought to be ill bedfellows, and the degradation of poverty was completed in statements like the following:

"The apophthegms of the poor are not quoted."

"A poor man's suit is summarily disposed of."

"When the poor man wears a necklace of the soft silky *gorow*, it is said he is wearing a sheep's halter."

" 'I am in need, please do this for me,' that is how some became slaves."

In this last saying, the Akans showed their regard for personal independence, and this was undoubtedly connected with the negative and conditional responsibility that the clan had for looking after individual members. Akan communalism bore striking resemblances to the Social Welfare State.

Personal thrift was enjoined and the lack of it was coupled with idiocy, as in the saying about the fool and his scales. Poverty, the Akans said, does not announce a date.

The connection between authority, prestige, and wealth was also noticed and felt.

"No one bullies another with his poverty."

"The rich man is the man of authority."

"Money is sharper than the sword."

"When wealth came and passed by, nothing came after."

"Money is like a servant, if you abuse it, it runs away."

"When a rich man gets drunk, you say he is indisposed."

"The misdeeds of a rich man are always invisible."

"Fame of being nobly born does not spread, it is the fame of riches which spreads."

"One does not cook one's nobility and eat, it is wealth that counts."

Poverty was not necessarily connected with slavery by the Akans, though in general it was connected with status. A slave could through efficiency and competence even establish a claim to succession, and certainly at times became very wealthy. There were three ways in which one could become a slave. There were those who voluntarily placed themselves under a master for protection and food and shelter, or even for payment. Second, there were those who were pledged or pawned by their relatives to liquidate debts or as security for a debt. Included in this group were those who were forcibly seized in surety for a debt in what was known as *panyarring*. There were, thirdly, those who became slaves from being children of slaves. They were usually made to carry loads and help in the cultivation of farms.

Slaves were considered to form part of households, even if they were the lowest members. And though they were said not to choose their own masters, they were not treated with cruelty or contempt, for as the Akan saying had it, all men were children of God and no-one was a child of the earth. To people who were given to treating slaves badly, the question was rhetorically put whether one would say the big and heavy drum was good for Kobuobi to carry if he were one's mother's child. Theoretically, slaves could regain their freedom on grounds of cruelty. At the same time, it was said that one did not acquire a slave in order to be affronted by him. The impertinence of certain slaves was recorded in the saying that when a slave has amassed some wealth, he assigned himself to the Nsona, a leading clan. Slaves were allowed to use property that they had acquired as they pleased, and occasionally they became wealthier than their masters, gathered a larger retinue, and even commanded free soldiers.

At the same time, the slave was legally without responsibility, and acts committed, whether or not in pursuance of his master's bidding, were regarded as his master's act. He was responsible for his slave's debts and for compensation for injury inflicted by him. A slave's obedience was to his immediate master and could not be transitively claimed by his master's master. The origins of slavery were traced by the Akans to the loss of independence by shiftless persons, who depended on others for their livelihood and security. Apologists of the slave trade, which was completely out of touch with slavery among the Akans, said slanderously that if the Akans had the right to sell their children, strangers had the right to buy them. As early as 1749, Roemer, the Danish historian who had for a long time been in the Gold Coast and Ashanti, wrote a book refuting this allegation. The allegation was founded on a misunderstanding of the Akan word *oba*. The European merchants understood the sentence "*Me dze me ba bi aba*" to mean "I have brought a son with me" instead of "I have brought a fellow with me," said when people offered someone for sale.

Mensah Sarbah
(1864–1910, Ghana)

On the Fante National Constitution

ORIGIN AND GOVERNMENT OF AKAN COMMUNITIES

On the west coast of Africa, washed by the waters of the Gulf of Guinea, lies a vast territory, comprising several districts and kingdoms peopled by various peoples, which Europe has called Gold Coast. After long years of uncertainty, succeeded by a period of hesitation, the boundaries of these British possessions with the sphere of influence have been defined by an Order in Council bearing date the 26th day of September, 1901. Even this is at best an arbitrary arrangement intended for administrative purposes. With Asanti and the Northern Territories Protectorate the total area of Gold Coast Colony is said to be 105,900 square miles, which is approximately the size of New Zealand. On the littoral of the Gulf of Guinea it extends from Newtown on the west to Afflao on the east, the seaboard being about 350 miles in length, while the maximum depth measured from the said coastline is about 440 miles.

•   •   •

In studying aboriginal institutions one has to guard himself against misleading and erroneous analogies, plausible generalizations, hasty deductions, and faulty conclusions. Former travellers, from what they saw in the trading forts and settlements, essayed to describe Fanti and Asanti national institutions; and, in many instances, what were observed in the coast towns were erroneously taken to be applicable in their entirety to the whole country, without any attempt to find out the principles governing them.

Every aboriginal inhabitant of this country is a member of some clan, the relationship to which is traced through the mother. Take the case of a man who is about to build a separate home or settle on some portion of land of the tribe or clan: he will be accompanied by his wives, if any, also his mother, brothers, unmarried sisters, nephews, and nieces who have left their fathers. The land on which this man with his people will settle may be either a portion of the virgin forest or where he had been farming before. When the brothers marry their wives join them, but their children are not members of this family. As the household increases and multiplies new houses are set up. In this smallest family group the Penin, or Egya, is the natural guardian of every member. The land on which the members dwell is family property. The Penin, as head of the family, represents all the members, holding and administering the property as a trustee for himself and them. If the family is so wealthy as to hold slaves and pawns (Ahubafu), they reside with their masters. When this family unit has grown large it is usual to appoint a person to "sit behind" the Penin. He must be a fit and proper person, generally one of the heritable blood relations (Dihyi); in some instances, however, a bondsman is selected. This second man acts as the spokesman of the Penin, assists him in settling disputes, takes a prominent part at the annual observance of the stool, or other festival, then, in the presence of the whole family, he makes the libation and offers the family sacrifice with prayers to the spirits of the departed ones.

Persons wishing to reside in the village, or on the land adjacent thereto, must obtain the permission of the first settlers, and join the other inhabitants of the village in tilling the farm of the Penin. This usage was observed in 1600 by Artus, who writes, "No man claimeth any land to himself; the king keeping all the woods, the fields, and lands in his hands; so that they neither sow nor plant therein but by his consent and license."

•   •   •

The Penin of the subsequent settlers exercises similar rights over his own people, and as the household grows larger so is that Penin assisted by a person "sitting behind" him. The founder of the village or his successor is now called Odzikuro (owner of the village), who, in looking after the village affairs, is assisted by the Penin of the new settlers, and thus arises the village council. The different family groups become the village community, and in all public matters the village council, composed of the Penin of each important household, acts, the Odzikuro being president of such council. The members of the village council have a spokesman (Kyiami, a linguist), whose office is hereditary, but is traced in the male line, for a son succeeds as linguist his father, and not his uncle. Land in possession of the founder of the village is family stool property. Land cleared and occupied by subsequent settlers who have joined the founder is the property of the subsequent settlers. Land acquired by the founder and the settlers together is held by the village community, and becomes attached to the stool of the person for the time being head of the village. All the inhabitants of the village have each of them a proportionate share in such lands as common property, without any possession or title to distinct portions. From the moment a tribal community settles down finally upon a definite tract of land, the land begins to be the basis of society in place of kinship. The Odzikuro, with the village council, has the control of such land, but each person has the right to cultivate any portion of it, and having done so or settled on it, he may not be removed by any single individual unless the council so decrees.

In the small settlement which has so grown into a village community there will be subordinate stools belonging to the junior families, which are offshoots of the parent family. The holders reside in the village or in its neighbourhood, and are usually members of the village council. It will be found that the headman of the village community is generally a member of the family which founded the village, and has succeeded to that post by virtue of his right as head of the founder's family; but inasmuch as he rules over the whole community, the inhabitants, through the village council, have the right to reject any one proposed as headman if deemed unsuitable for the post, and, passing over the original family, can select a fit and proper person from another family whose connection with the village is ancient. And so all things being equal, preference is given to families according to priority of settlement.

Omanhene is the head of the national life, and naturally president of the rulers of the people assembled either as a court for deciding cases or for legislation. The district, taken as a whole, is likewise considered as a body, whereof the Omanhene supports the head, and the next man in authority to him carries the foot. By virtue of his office, Omanhene has the right to be carried by four men or more, and uses three or more canopy umbrellas. At his installation a small sword, the insignia of his office, is handed to him, and he enjoys several other privileges. He is the commander-in-chief of all the fighting men of the district. His bodyguard and the immediate fighting men are called Gyasi. He is almost invariably a member of the Domtsifu or Intsin Company. Tufuhene is the man whose duty it is to command the fighting men (from *tu*, "to throw, *e.g.*, arrows, etc.;" hence *etuo, itur*, "a gun"); a fighting leader, or commander. In some districts, and especially in the coast towns, Tufuhene is the next man in authority after Ohene.

An Ohene is entitled to ride in a palanquin carried by two men and attended by two canopy umbrellas. An Odzikuro is the headman of a village. Penin is an elder, generally an old man of experience. Sahene is a man appointed to conduct war. A Safuhene is a captain of a company, and in some instances is a stoolholder. In fact, among the Akanfu, that is Asanti, Wassaw, Assin, Akim, and such like, each Ohene of the several towns and districts is referred to as the Safuhene of his Omanhene. The Gyasi are the bodyguard of an Ohene or Omanhene. They comprise, first, the blood relatives, especially the children and grandsons of the Ohene, and are called Bogyadom (*bogya*, "blood"; *dom*, "troop"), who have the immediate custody of the stool; secondly, certain Asafuhenefu, with their men; thirdly, personal servants and domestic attendants (Gyasifu). The Gyasi perform the rites of the stool custom each year.

Supi is a company captain, who keeps the company's flags, and especially their ammunition. The spokesman of an Ohene or village community is selected by the Ohene or Odzikuro. On his appointment it is usual in some districts for his family to give to the Ohene or councillors *sua duma*, that is, £2 9s. 6d. The councillors (Begwafu) are sometimes selected by the people on account of personal character and intelligence. Every councillor is not a stoolholder, nor is every stoolholder a councillor; but a great number of the councillors, however, are stoolholders. A stoolholder may be appointed a councillor, and his successor, when deemed a fit and proper person, follows him in his office. When a person becomes a councillor he is considered as promoted, therefore he severs his connection with his company, and must not take an active part in the management of the affairs of the company. A councillor must not be a partisan. Councillors who have not attained that position by right of inheritance are practically, and in truth, the direct representatives of the people, and voice public opinion. It is somewhat difficult to define the qualifications of such public men.

But as a man attracts the favourable attention of the observant ones of his tribe, as he more and more impresses the people by his ability in their public gatherings, by the soundness of his opinion, by the depth of his knowledge of the customary laws and traditions, by his skill in public debate, by his keen interest in public affairs, by his bravery or warlike qualities, or by some other qualifications, he acquires public influence, and is accepted, in a greater or less degree, as a public man, representative of a portion of the community. Success in trade, or other personal attributes, are likewise qualifications for his post. The position of such a person is definitely confirmed when the head ruler with his council invites him to be a councillor. Attending an Omanhene or Ohene are always to be found some councillors, who assist him in hearing and determining lawsuits and administering justice. In the town of the Omanhene these men perform many of the duties of officers, who in European countries are known as ministers of state. It is worthy of note that, as a general rule, a Tufuhene is not a member of the Council (Begwa) of the Ohene or Omanhene.

The Council of the people is the only effective instrument or body which tempers the will or power of the ruler. For no discreet or wise ruler would undertake any matter of importance affecting his people, until it has been discussed at length in council, where freedom of speech and the publicity thereof give every facility for the expression of public opinion. In fact, it is the duty of every ruler first to summon his councillors, and then his people, when an occasion arises, in the same way as the head of a family calls the senior or elder members of his family and confers about the affairs and other business of the family. The principle is the same; the application thereof is only a matter of degree.

The representative character of a councillor is well understood and appreciated by the people. The expression generally used by old councillors and other public men whose influence has waned, who are not considered to reflect current public opinion, or who do not command public confidence, is as follows: "Nya Oman ese nidu wontūtū n'anan mu," meaning "the representatives of the people of the time being should not be interrupted too much nor without very good reason."

To remove the Omanhene or head ruler of a district or town against the wish of the people is to weaken public authority. To break up a public council is to strike at the root of what supports the liberty of the subject, and to give a death-blow to the free institutions of the people. The Public Council occupies the most prominent position in the constitution of the body politic; to suppress it is to destroy the best, safest, and surest means for ascertaining the views of the public, as well as for influencing and instructing them in matters relating to their welfare and good government. Its existence opens a field for many to interest themselves in public affairs; it is an incentive to municipal enterprise; promoter of the patriotism that toils for the public good, that strives to effect reforms, whose watchword is progress. The Ohene is the head, but the Council is the heart of the people.

•   •   •

To obtain a correct knowledge of the constitution of this country, one ought not to be misled by what he sees in the coast districts, but he should study the aboriginal system which obtains in Wassaw, Assin, Akim, Sefwhi, and districts peopled by those who revolted from the Asanti rule in the early part of the nineteenth century.

In ancient times the Omanhene held the whole unoccu₁ied land in his territory as trustee for the people, and as they increased so this public land was brought under cultivation. The chiefs of the different towns were actually placed in charge of the unoccupied land in the districts, or were considered as caretakers for the Omanhene. When a tribe was conquered it became subject of the conqueror's stool; these people continued to hold and enjoy the lands under cultivation; but used forests and unoccupied land as public property attached to the stool of the Omanhene. Besides the public land, the Omanhene has attached to his stool family land in the occupation of his family; his subsequent deposition does not affect the possession of the family. The Omanhene can live and reside and farm on any unoccupied part of his territory without the leave or permission of the sub-ruler, who holds it as caretaker, but he cannot sell or lease it without the concurrence of such sub-ruler. He is entitled to an Ebusā, a small tax, from the sub-ruler. His immediate followers or household servants may mine for him, but no tribute is payable to the sub-ruler. The subordinate captains (Safuhene, pl. Asafuhene) are bound to obey the commands of the Ohene and pay tribute to him of all gold gotten from gold workings. It is not usual to pay Ebusā to the Ohene or Safuhene on the ordinary washing for alluvial gold. Ebusā is only paid when work is being done in a gold-field, or when one has found an unusually large quantity of gold or discovered a large nugget, or persons are systematically mining.

.   .   .

It has been shown that an Ohene, on being enstooled, succeeds to the family stool with his family possessions as well as to the public stool and the property attached thereto. As head ruler he can deal with the family property on the behalf of his family with the consent of the elder members thereof, but in dealing with the public property he must do so with the concurrence of his councillors. The rents and profits accruing from the family property belong to the family and himself.

The immediate retinue and body-guard of the Omanhene are called Gyasi, and consist of three groups of persons. (1) His male blood relatives, e.g. brothers, uncles, nephews; also his sons, whether by free or bond women. These persons usually are captains of the other fighting men. (2) Servants, slaves, and pawns, and their descendants. (3) Those originally attached to him by commendation or adoption; and captains, with their forces, appointed by the community as such.

The Wassaw Amenfi Gyasi is divided into three fighting companies, namely, (a) Ankobia, under Yebua Sasraku and other captains; (b) Manwel, under Egay Kuow of Bopo, Kwamina Badu of Piasu, Biaku of Inkasan; and (c) Asabiefu, under Kwamin Damua of Manponsu, Kuow Ku, and Kwaku Bua of Dumasi.

The above in battle array follow the Asamanfu forces in the same order. Next to them are the headmen, household, and the Gyasi of Busumtwi district. It will be found that, besides acting as the body-guard, some of them have certain duties to perform; the Gyasi of Busumtwi guard the royal burial-place, and Nuama, the Captain of Ankobia, guards a sacred place called *Asaman Kama Bura*, which is a lake. The Omanhene is entitled to one-third of all rents, fees, and tributes of any Asamanfu ruler, whereas in the case of the Gyasi ruler, not only does he take a half, but he must be a party to any contract affecting land in the district. The general rule in all these cases is, that an occupier of any land who is a subject of the stool does not pay rent, but only renders service if residing near the stool-holder or a reasonable distance from him. Whenever there is a stool debt he is bound to pay his share of the contribution for its settlement.

The government of the sea-coast communities is a variation of the general system which has been described. This variation has been caused by frequent intercourse with European traders and the accumulation of wealth by means of lucrative trade. Ancient travellers who wrote described only what they saw in the coast towns. From these men one learns that, over two centuries ago, at seedtime farmers marked out for farming their plots of land, situate usually on rising grounds near the towns and villages. The next step was to obtain the permission of the Ohene or his officers in charge of the land, after permission had been granted, to pay the usual rent. The head of the family, assisted by his wives, children, and any slaves he might possess, prepared the ground for sowing. When the day of sowing arrived, the farm belonging to the village, or town chief, was first sown by all the people, and the others followed in due course. This custom has continued to modern times with slight modifications. A few years ago the sum of half a crown was paid to landowners on asking for a plot of land to farm on for one season, but within the last two years this sum has been raised to ten shillings; in some instances, such as for land near the large towns, as much as a pound has been paid.

.   .   .

According to some ancient writers, there are two forms of government at the Gold Coast, namely, Monarchical and Republican. The districts of Axim, Ahanta, Fanti, and others were, previous to the year 1700, considered to be commonwealths; whereas Commenda, at that time a very populous district, Effutu or Fetu, Asebu, and Accra, were of the first kind. Henry Meredith, whose work was published in 1811, describes the governments along the coast as partaking of various forms. At Appolonia it was monarchical and absolute; in Ahanta it was a kind of aristocracy; but in the Fanti country, and extending to Accra, it was composed of a strange number of forms; for in some places the government was vested in particular persons, whilst in others it was in the hands of the community. What struck him as strange in the Fanti districts was that they frequently changed their form of government on certain occasions by uniting together under particular persons for their general safety, giving implicit obedience to their leaders; but as soon as the object of their union was attained, they reverted to their independent units. What is undoubtedly true is, that for very many years the Fanti town and village communities have enjoyed independence in a greater degree than any other tribes on the Gold Coast. In Appolonia one finds that so much authority was vested in the Omanhene that writers frequently thought his power was absolute. But on examining the constitutions of these places, they will be found to be sprung from the same root; the monarchical form of government so mentioned is what is common in Wassaw and other inland districts, and the republican is simply the constitution of some of the sea-coast towns close to European settlements and forts. These coast towns are communities whose government is based on the system already described; the president is Ohene, and his office is elective. Each town is divided into several parts, for fighting purposes, called companies (Asafu). One of these companies acts as the Gyasi to the Ohene. The Tufuhene is responsible for the good order of all the fighting men; the orders of the Ohene and his council are communicated to them by the Tufuhene.

The several households of each town are divided into wards, which are under the control of several heads of families; an elder of these is called Penin (pl. Mpeninfu). A council, composed of Mpeninfu and other representative men, as well as Abremponfu and the Ohene, governs the town. This council is the tribunal that settles all law-suits and regulates the internal organization of the community and enacts laws. There are other persons elected to see after local sanitary matters, such as the cleaning of the country lanes, footpaths, and market roads. They summon before the council persons breaking sanitary regulations, as well as those committing any serious breach of the public peace.

The male persons of each ward originally formed a company, having its distinctive flags, drums, and other equipments. The honour of the flag is the first consideration, and his service to his company is the most indispensable duty of the citizen. The organization of the town companies has been already described. In some towns there are as many as seven companies, members of which reside not only in the town, but also in the neighbouring villages. Lands cleared by the companies belong to them. The lands of the companies do not belong to the Ohene, for there are town lands, family lands, and stool lands. The Ohene has no right to ordinary tribute, and the public-stool income is derived from fines, penalties, and court fees. In this also the jurisdiction is personal. The Tufuhene, the councillors, and captains of the companies take part in the election and installation of a new Ohene. Before them he takes his oath of office, and if any lands are attached to the town stool, he holds them in trust for the public. The succession generally follows the common rule, but in some places it is the son who succeeds, not the brother or nephew. The townspeople can pass over the person nominated by the family and elect some other suitable person instead. They may also remove the Ohene, if found unfit to rule them any longer; in either of which events the town sword and stool, with all the public property thereunto appurtenant, are vested in the town council, whose duty it is to take them from the deposed ruler or his family and give them to the person appointed as new ruler or manager during the interval.

The Ohene of every district is the supreme commander of the fighting men. His orders are communicated through the captains (Asafuhenefu), or the Tufuhene, as the case may be. Whenever a council of war is convened he presides, and it is his duty to provide them with some powder and shot. Every male person able to bear arms is bound to serve his country, and each fighting man provides himself with arms and ammunitions, as well as provisions, at his own expense.

•   •   •

Some misconception exists in connection with the removal of a ruler or of the head of a family. The right of removing a ruler belongs to the people immediately connected with the stool; in the case of the head of a family the right is in the senior members, and the act of the majority is binding on the rest.

The grounds on which a ruler may be removed from his office or position are:—(1) Adultery: this must be notorious and habitual; for the second or third offence he is generally made to give satisfaction in money equivalent to (where the amount is not fixed) what he would receive if he were the injured husband. (2) Habitual drunkenness and disorderly conduct which degrades him. (3) Habitually opposing the councillors and disregarding their advice without just cause. (4) Theft and general misconduct, such as constantly provoking strife by acts and words, and stirring up bad blood between his people and other rulers'; inability to uphold the dignity and good reputation of the stool. (5) Perverting justice when hearing cases, and inflicting extortionable fines and penalties; failing to protect his subjects or to espouse their cause. (6) Cowardice in war. (7) Extravagance and persistently involving his people in debt and other liabilities improperly contracted or incurred. (8) Conduct derogatory and unworthy of his position; e.g. one Aban, ruler of Adjumaku, was removed from his office for holding a canopy umbrella over Edu, king of Mankesim, and for going to the public market to purchase provisions.

A subordinate ruler is removed from his office on complaint by the people of the town, the councillors, or the family. By the first he is charged before the councillors and the principal members of his family; by the second, before the elders of the town and principal members of the family; and by the third, before the elders of the town and councillors; but when the plaint is by the people of the town, including the councillors, the superior ruler and his council hear it.

Complaint against a ruler, whether superior or subordinate, is the last remedy of those under him, for one must rest assured that before this step is taken the offending ruler had been warned and remonstrated with many a time. For some offences, such as cowardice, theft, and conduct deemed by his subjects derogatory, he can be removed at once if his defence or explanation be found unsatisfactory. In the other cases, if after two or three warnings he does not reform, he may be removed.

Where a ruler who is summoned to answer complaints against him fails to attend the hearing, and does not give good reasons for his absence, he may be removed. A subordinate ruler may be removed by his subjects, but he has the right to appeal to the superior ruler, who may investigate the matter afterwards. Should he find him in the wrong, the removal is confirmed; if the subordinate ruler be found in the right, but the subjects will not have him at any price, he is nevertheless removed, but his people are bound to pay all expenses he may have incurred in respect of the stool.

Edward Wilmot Blyden

(1832–1912, Virgin Islands)

Mohammedanism and the Negro Race

To students of general literature in Europe and the United States, until within the last few years, the Orientals most celebrated in religion or politics, in literature or learning, were known only by name. The Oriental world, to the student aiming at practical achievements, presented a field of so little promise that he scarcely ever ventured beyond a distant survey of what seemed to him a boundless and impracticable area. But, thanks to the exigencies of commerce, to philanthropic zeal, and to the scientific impulse, the East is daily getting to be "nearer seen and better known," not only in its outward life, but in those special aspects which, in religion and government, in war and policy, differentiate Eastern from Western races. It has been recently stated by a distinguished authority that "the intimate acquaintance with the languages, thoughts, history, and monuments of Eastern nations is no longer a luxury, but a necessity." And the visits, within the last ten years, of Oriental rulers to Europe—the Sultan of Turkey, the Khedive of Egypt, the Shah of Persia, and the Seyyid of Zanzibar—have stimulated in the popular mind a livelier curiosity as to the character, condition, and influence of Mohammedan countries.

Drawn away from the beaten track of Roman and Greek antiquity by considerations, for the most part, of a material nature, and wandering into paths which, heretofore, were trodden only by such enthusiastic pioneers as Sir William Jones, the Western student finds rewards far rarer and richer than he had anticipated. And even those who have not the opportunity of familiarising themselves with Oriental languages find enough in translations—inadequate and unsatisfactory as they often are—to inspire them with a desire not only to increase their acquaintance with Eastern subjects, but to impart the knowledge they glean to others.

·   ·   ·

And, so far as Islam is concerned, scholars are arising within its ranks imbued with Western learning, and taking the part not only of defenders of their faith, but of interpreters between the Eastern and Western world. It has recently occasioned some surprise and comment that a Mohammedan writer should have written an able work in the English tongue, "challenging European and Christian thinkers on their own ground." Since the appearance of Syed Ahmed's essays, another work has appeared in the English language, written by a young Mohammedan, in which he has briefly, temperately, and ably discussed the various subjects in relation to which Islam is usually assailed.

But it is not only in recent days, as the writer in the *British Quarterly Review* would seem to imply, that Mohammedans have availed themselves of the power of the pen, in defence of their faith. There have always been, and there are now, able controversialists among them altogether unknown to Western fame. The celebrated work of Dr. Pfander, the Mizan-al-Hakk, attacking the Mohammedan system, has been reviewed in the Arabic language by a Mohammedan scholar, Rahmat Allah, in a learned and incisive reply, in which he reveals a marvelous acquaintance with European literature. We have heard of no attempt at a rejoinder to the work of Rahmat Allah. We saw a copy of this book in the hands of a West African Mohammedan at Sierra Leone, who was reading and commenting upon it to a number of his co-religionists.

We are glad to notice that Mr. Bosworth Smith's book has been republished in the United States, and that the able article of Deutsch on Islam has been reproduced in the same volume as an appendix. They are fit companions—*par nobile fratrum.* The traveller, contemplating a visit to Mohammedan countries, or the theologian wishing to get a clear view of a religious system which is shaping the destiny of millions of the race, may now carry in his pocket a complete compendium of Mohammedan literature. If we except the very remarkable article on the "Historical statements in the Koran," written in 1832, by the then stripling reviewer, Mr. J. Addison Alexander, of Princeton, and the able "Review of the Koran," by Professor Alexander Draper, of the New York University, in his *History of the Intellectual Development of Europe,* American scholarship has as yet, as far as we are aware, produced nothing of importance in this branch of literature.

•   •   •

Three streams of influence have always penetrated into Negroland: one, from Egypt, through Nubia, to Bornou and Hausa; another, from Abyssinia to Yoruba and Ashantee; the third, from the Barbary States across the desert to Timbuktu. By the first two, Egypt and Arabia exchanged their productions for the raw materials of the Soudan. By the third, the ports of the Mediterranean, through the Great Desert, having Timbuktu as a centre, became outlets for the wealth of Nigritia. Even in the days of Herodotus there appears to have been intercourse between the region of the Tsad and the Mediterranean, and the valuable products collected at various centres by the itinerant traffic, which still flourishes in the interior, shared by numerous caravans, found their way by means of Phoenician ships to different countries of Europe and the Levant.

Central Africa has never been cut off commercially from European and Asiatic intercourse. But it was not until the ninth century of the Christian era that any knowledge of the true God began to penetrate into Negroland. To Akbah, a distinguished Muslim general, belongs the credit or discredit of having subdued North Africa to Islam. He marched from Damascus at the head of ten thousand enthusiastic followers, and in a short time spread his conquests along the shores of North Africa, advancing to the very verge of the Atlantic, whose billows alone checked his westward career. But the energy which could not proceed westward turned northward and southward. In its southern progress it crossed the formidable wastes of the Sahara, penetrated into the Soudan, and established the centre of its influence at Timbuktu. In less than a century from that time several large Nigritian tribes had yielded to the influence of Islam; and it shaped so rapidly the ideas, the manners, and the history of those tribes, that when in the Middle Ages Ibn Batoutah, an Arab traveller, visited those regions, he found that Islam had taken firm root among several powerful peoples, had mastered their life and habits, and dominated their whole social and religious policy. Among the praiseworthy qualities which attracted his attention as a result of their conversion, he mentions their devotion to the study of the Koran, and relates the following illustrative incidents, which we give in the French version now before us:

> Ils ont un grand zèle pour apprendre par coeur le sublime Coran. Dans le cas où leurs enfants font preuve de négligence à cet égard, ils leur mettent des entraves aux pieds et ne les leur ôtent pas qu'ils ne le sachent réciter de mémoire. Le jour de la fête, étant entré chez le juge, et ayant vu ses enfants enchaînés, je lui dis: "Est-ce que tu ne les mettras pas en liberté?" Il repondit: "Je ne le ferai que lorsqu'ils sauront par coeur le Coran." Un autre jour, je passai devant un jeune nègre, beau de figure, revêtu d'habits superbes, et portant aux pieds une lourde chaîne. Je dis à la personne qui m'accompagnait: "Qu'a fait ce garçon? Est-ce qu'il assassiné quelqu'un?" Le jeune nègre entendit mon propos et se mit à rire. On me dit: "Il a été enchaîné uniquement pour le forcer à apprendre le Coran de mémoire."

Mohammedanism in Africa counts in its ranks the most energetic and enterprising tribes. It claims as adherents the only people who have any form of civil polity or bond of social organization. It has built and occupies the largest cities in the heart of the continent. Its laws regulate the most powerful kingdoms—Futah, Masina, Hausa, Bornou, Waday, Darfur, Kordofan, Senaar, &c. It produces and controls the most valuable commerce between Africa and foreign countries; it is daily gaining converts from the ranks of Paganism; and it commands respect among all Africans wherever it is known, even where the people have not submitted to the sway of the Koran.

No one can travel any distance in the interior of West Africa without being struck with the different aspects of society in different localities, according as the population is Pagan or Mohammedan. Not only is there a difference in the methods of government, but in the general regulations of society, and even in the amusements of the people. The love of noisy terpsichorean performances, so noticeable in Pagan communities, disappears as the people come under the influence of Mohammedanism. It is not a fact that "when the sun goes down, all Africa dances," but it might be a fact if it were not for the influence of Islam. Those who would once have sought pleasure in the excitement of the tom-tom, now repair five times a-day to the mosque, where they spend a quarter of an hour on each occasion in devotional exercises. After the labours of the day they assemble in groups near the mosque to hear the Koran recited, or the Traditions or some other book read. In traversing the region of country between Sierra Leone and Futah Jallo in 1873, we passed through populous Pagan towns; and the transition from these to Mohammedan districts was striking. When we left a Pagan and entered a Mohammedan community, we at once noticed that we had entered a moral atmosphere widely separated from, and loftier far than, the one we had left. We discovered that the character, feelings, and conditions of the people were profoundly altered and improved.

It is evident that, whatever may be said of the Koran, as long as it is in advance of the Shamanism or Fetichism of the African tribes who accept it—and no one will doubt that Islam as a creed is an enormous advance not only on all idolatries, but on all systems of purely human origin—those tribes must advance beyond their primitive condition.

The Koran is, in its measure, an important educator. It exerts among a primitive people a wonderful influence. It has furnished to the adherents of its teachings in Africa a ground of union which has contributed vastly to their progress. Hausas, Foulahs, Mandingoes, Soosoos, Akus, can all read the same books and mingle in worship together, and there is to all one common authority and one ultimate umpirage. They are united by a common religious sentiment, by a common antagonism to Paganism. Not only the sentiments, but the language, the words of the sacred book are held in the grestest reverence and esteem. And even where the ideas are not fully understood, the words seem to possess for them a nameless beauty and music, a subtle and indefinable charm, incomprehensible to those acquainted only with European languages. It is easy for those not acquainted with the language in which the Koran was written, and therefore, judging altogether as outsiders, to indulge in depreciation of its merits. Such critics lose sight of the fact that the Koran is a poetical composition, and a poetical composition of the earliest and most primitive kind, and that therefore its ideas and the language in which they are conveyed cannot well be separated. The genuine poet not only creates the conception, but the word which is its vehicle. The word becomes the inseparable drapery of the idea. Hence the highest poetry cannot be translated. We see this in the numerous versions by which it has been sought in every age to reach the sense of the poetical portions of the Bible. No words yet furnished by Greek, Roman, or Teutonic literature have been fully adequate to bring out the subtle beauties of the Semitic original. Among Mohammedans, written or printed translations of the Koran are discouraged. The Chinese, Hindoos, Persians, Turks, Mandingoes, Foulahs, &c., who have embraced Islam, speak in their "own tongues wherein they were born," but read the Koran in Arabic.

Mr. Bosworth Smith was right to begin his preparations for the valuable work he has written by a careful study of the Koran. But it is to be regretted that he had not access to the force and beauty of the original, which neither Sale, Kasimirsky, Lane, nor Rodwell have been able—though they laboured hard to do so—to retain in their excellent translations. A distinguished Oriental scholar and critic says:

> There can be no doubt that, to understand thoroughly this wonderful book, the aid of those learned men, Arabs and others, who have devoted themselves to the careful study of it, is not only desirable, but necessary. . . . The subject is of sufficient importance to men of research to render it advisable that it should be examined from all points of view, for by no other means can we hope to obtain as clear an insight into the origin of Islam, as by a careful study of the book which contains its fundamental principles.

To the outside world, easily swayed by superficial impressions, and carried away by matters of mere dramatic interest, there may be nothing attractive in the progress of Islam in Africa, because, as far as known to Western readers, the history of African Mohammedanism is deficient in great characters and in remarkable episodes. There has been, it is supposed, no controlling mind developed, which has moved great masses of men. But the words of Horace are applicable here:

> Omnes illacrimabiles
> Urgentur, ignotique longa
>   Nocte, carent quia vate sacro.

It is not, however, that no bard has written, but they have had very few readers in Christian countries. To those acquainted with the interior of Africa—to the Mohammedan world of North Africa and Arabia—it is well known that numerous characters have arisen in Africa—Negro Muslims—who have exerted no little influence in the military, political, and ecclesiastical affairs of Islam, not only in Africa, but in the lands of their teachers. In the biographies of Ibn Khallikan are frequent notices of distinguished Negro Mohammedans. Koelle, in his *Polyglotta Africana*, gives a graphic account of the proceedings of the great Fodie, whose zeal, enthusiasm, and bravery spread Islam over a large portion of Nigritia.

One of the most remarkable characters who have influenced the history of the region of country between Timbuktu and the West Coast was a native of Futah Toro, known as the Sheikh Omaru Al-Hajj. He is said to have been a Waleeu, a man of extraordinary endowments, of commanding presence, and great personal influence. He was educated by the Sheikh Tijani, a Muslim missionary from Arabia. Having spent several years under the instruction of this distinguished teacher, visiting Mecca in the meanwhile, he became profoundly learned in the Arabic language. After the death of his master, he went twice to Mecca on pilgrimage. On his return to his country the second time, he undertook a series of proselytising expeditions against the powerful pagan tribes on the east and southeast of Futah Toro. He conquered several powerful chiefs and reduced their people to the faith of Islam. He banished Paganism from Sego, and purified the practices of several Mohammedan districts which had become imbued with heathenish notions. He thus restored Jenne, and Hamd-Allahi, and was on his way to Timbuktu, about ten years ago, when, through the treachery of the Arabs of that region, he was circumvented and killed at a town in Masina. One of his sons, Ahmadu, is now King of Sego, another rules over Hamd-Allahi, two of the largest cities in Central Africa.

Al-Hajj Omaru wrote many Arabic works in prose and poetry. His poems are recited and sung in every Mohammedan town and village, from Foulah-town, in Sierra Leone, to Kano. His memory is held in the greatest respect by all native students, and they attribute to him many extraordinary deeds, and see in his successful enterprises, literary and military, proofs of divine guidance.

We have heard of numerous instances of these "half-military, half-religious geniuses," as Mr. Bosworth Smith calls them, "which Islam always seems capable of producing."

To the Mohammedans of Negroland, far away from the complex civilization of European life, with its multifarious interests, the struggle for the ascendancy of Islam is the one great object which should engage the attention of a rational being. It is a struggle between light and darkness, between knowledge and ignorance, between good and evil. The traditional enthusiasm of their faith makes them utterly indifferent to the sufferings of any who stand in the way of the dissemination of the truth, and patient of any evils they may have to endure in order to ensure the triumph of their cause. "Paradise is under the shadow of swords," is one of their stimulating proverbs.

There is one passage in Mr. Bosworth Smith's book of which we do not think that the author, who, as it seems, has not himself been in Africa, perceived the full import, but which the Christian world, it appears to us, would do well to ponder. It is as follows:

> Christian travellers, with every wish to think otherwise, have remarked that the Negro who accepts Mohammedanism acquires at once a sense of the dignity of human nature not commonly found even among those who have been brought to accept Christianity.

Having enjoyed exceptional advantages for observation and comparison in the United States, the West Indies, South America, Egypt, Syria, West and Central Africa, we are compelled, however reluctantly, to endorse the statement made by Mr. B. Smith. And we are not surprised at his seizing hold, in his researches, of this most important fact and giving it such prominence—a prominence it richly deserves—in the discussion. Wherever the Negro is found in Christian lands, his leading trait is not docility, as has been often alleged, but servility. He is slow and unprogressive. Individuals here and there may be found of extraordinary intelligence, enterprise, and energy, but there is no Christian community of Negroes anywhere which is self-reliant and independent. Haiti and Liberia, so-called Negro Republics, are merely struggling for existence, and hold their own by the tolerance of the civilized powers. On the other hand, there are numerous Negro Mohammedan communities and states in Africa which are self-reliant, productive, independent, and dominant, supporting, without the countenance or patronage of the parent country, Arabia, whence they derived them, their political, literary, and ecclesiastical institutions. In Sierra Leone, the Mohammedans, without any aid from Government—Imperial or local—or any contributions from Mecca or Constantinople, erect their mosques, keep up their religious services, conduct their schools, and contribute to the support of missionaries from Arabia, Morocco, or Futah when they visit them. The same compliment cannot be paid to the Negro Christians of that settlement. The most enlightened native Christians there look forward with serious apprehension—and, perhaps, not without good grounds—to the time when, if ever, the instructions and influence from London will be withheld. An able paper on the "Condition and Wants of Liberia," by an intelligent and candid Liberian, has the following:

> We want, as a people, the spirit of liberality. We have learned to depend upon foreign institutions to support our churches. This should not be so. If, indeed, we have not enough of the Christian religion to induce us to contribute liberally to the cause of the Gospel; if we have not enough zeal for the cause of Christ to make us willing to sacrifice time and money for its good, &c., we had as well give up churches and religion. . . . I have known some persons to change a two cent. piece so as to get one cent. for the church. Alas, for such religion! alas for the churches thus supported!

In the recent Ashantee war the most trustworthy Negro troops were the Hausas, who are rigid Mohammedans. The West India Christian Negro troops were not relied on to the same extent.

Now, what has produced this difference in the effects of the two systems upon the Negro race? In reply, we remark generally that the difference must be attributed to the difference in the conditions under which the systems came to those of the Negro race who embraced the one or the other. Mohammedanism found its Negro converts at home in a state of freedom and independence of the teachers who brought it to them. When it was offered to them they were at liberty to choose for themselves. The Arab missionaries, whom we have met in the interior, go about without "purse or scrip," and disseminate their religion by quietly teaching the Koran. The native missionaries—Mandingoes and Foulahs—unite with the propagation of their faith active trading. Wherever they go, they produce the impression that they are not preachers only, but traders; but, on the other hand, that they are not traders merely, but preachers. And, in this way, silently and almost unobtrusively, they are causing princes to become obedient disciples and zealous propagators of Islam. Their converts, as a general thing, become Muslims from choice and conviction, and bring all the manliness of their former condition to the maintenance and support of their new creed.

When the religion was first introduced it found the people possessing all the elements and enjoying all the privileges of an intrammelled manhood. They received it as giving them additional power to exert an influence in the world. It sent them forth as the guides and instructors of their less favoured neighbours, and endowed them with the self-respect which men feel who acknowledge no superior. While it brought them a great deal that was absolutely new, and inspired them with spiritual feelings to which they had before been utter strangers, it strengthened and hastened certain tendencies to independence and self-reliance which were already at work. Their local institutions were not destroyed by the Arab influence introduced. They only assumed new forms, and adapted themselves to the new teachings. In all thriving Mohammedan communities, in West and Central Africa, it may be noticed that the Arab superstructure has been superimposed on a permanent indigenous culture.

Edward Wilmot Blyden
(1832–1912, Virgin Islands)

Christianity and the Negro Race

Mr. Gladstone, in the exordium of his celebrated article on the Church of England, in the *Contemporary Review* (July 1875), says:

> To uphold the integrity of the Christian dogma, to trace its working, and to exhibit its adaptation to human thought and human welfare, in all the varying experience of the ages, is, in my view, perhaps the noblest of all tasks which it is given to the human mind to pursue. This is the guardianship of the great fountain of human hope, happiness, and virtue. But with respect to the clothing which the Gospel may take to itself, my mind has a large margin of indulgence, if not of laxity, both ways. Much is to be allowed—I can hardly say how much—to natural, sectional, and personal divergencies.

This is a view to which the very highest minds in the world—the best cultivated and the most enlightened—would at once readily subscribe. By the word "dogma" Mr. Gladstone evidently means, not the petrified formula of any particular sect or race, deduced according to their view from the Word of God, but the whole system of Christianity itself, as a living organism, in *esse* and in *posse,* in its essence as well as in its capabilities and potentialities; for in the same paragraph he uses the word "Gospel" as synonymous with "dogma." Looking at the Gospel system as a whole, it may be called, with no inconsiderable propriety, the "Christian dogma," or that system of belief which distinguishes the Christian world from all others.

We have said that the very highest minds would readily subscribe to the view of Mr. Gladstone, for only the highest minds would cordially agree with the whole paragraph. A very large number—perhaps the whole Christian Church—would give their sanction to the first two sentences; but the number is comparatively small who would read the last two sentences without feeling disposed to brand the author as a latitudinarian and unsafe guide. And yet those sentences contain the lessons which all practical experience teaches must be learned by the aggressive portion of the Church, before the Gospel can take root in "all the world," and become the spiritual life of "every creature."

There is, we doubt not, one and only one Prophet for all times and for all nations—the immaculate Son of God; and the teachings which He inculcated contain the only principles that will regenerate humanity of all races, climes, and countries. But the Gospel, though it has been promulgated for eighteen hundred years, has, as yet, taken extensive root only among one race—the Indo-European. It is established in Europe, Asia, Africa, America, and on all the islands of the sea, but, for the most part, in regions and localities occupied by different branches of the same Aryan family.

When Dean Church wishing to illustrate the "Influences of Christianity on National Character," had passed in review the Greek, Latin, and Teutonic races he evidently felt that his subject was exhausted. Dean Merivale went as far afield as the facts would allow him to go, when after concluding his lectures on the "Conversion of the Roman Empire," he proceeded to discuss the "Conversion of the Northern Nations." Indeed, so convinced was the learned author that his two courses of lectures embraced all he could say on the subject of the spread of Christianity in the conversion of nations, that, in his preface to the second course, he remarks, that if, at some future time, he should print them together, he will probably give them the general title of the "Conversion of the Ancient Heathens." But would such a title be strictly accurate in view of the "Ancient" Semitic, Mongolian, and Negro "Heathens" who have been left out of the lecturer's calculations? The omission of the little word "the" from the proposed new title would probably meet the wish to have a comprehensive title, without transcending the bounds of strict accuracy.

It could not have escaped the distinguished lecturer, that only comparatively small portions of the Semitic, Mongolian, and Negro families of man have as yet embraced the religion of Jesus. And we are disposed to think that one chief reason why the progress of the Gospel among races foreign to the European has been so limited, lies in the fact that the last two sentences of Mr. Gladstone's paragraph quoted above are not yet understood and heeded by those who may be called the missionary nations of the earth, and who, having the vigorous and dominant instincts of the Aryan race, have become providentially the instruments through which the Semitic conceptions of Deity and the Semitic inspirations of Christianity are to be spread through all nations.

The object of this paper is to trace the influence of Christianity upon the Negro race, and to enquire how far the method of its dissemination has affected their reception of it. And our illustrations will be drawn principally from the Western world, as containing the largest portion of the Negro race who have been brought under the influence of Christianity, and especially from the United States, where the largest number of Negroes live together under the same Christian Government.

Everybody knows how it happened that the Africans were carried in such large numbers from Africa to America; how one continent was made to furnish the labourers to build up another; how the humanity of a Romish priest, while anxious to dry up tears in America, was indifferent to unsealing their fountains in Africa. It was out of deep pity for the delicate Caribs, whom he saw groaning under the arduous physical toil of the Western hemisphere that Las Casas strove to replace them by robust and indefatigable Africans. Hence the innumerable woes which have attended the African race for the last three hundred years in Christian lands. In justice, however, to the memory of Bartolomé de las Casas, it should be stated that, before he died, he changed his mind on the subject, and declared that the captivity of the Negroes was as unjust as that of the Indians, and even expressed a fear that, though he had fallen into the error of favouring the importation of black slaves into America from ignorance and goodwill, he might, after all, fail to stand excused for it before the Divine Justice.

But the tardy, though commendable, repentance of Las Casas did not arrest the flow of that blood-red stream which, from the fountain opened by his mistaken philanthropy, poured incessantly, for three hundred years, from East to West. It was not long before the transference of Negroes from Africa to the Western hemisphere assumed the importance of a national policy. Even England, under a contract with Spain, enjoyed the monopoly of the traffic in slaves for thirty years.

The first slaves were landed in North America in 1620, and men whose characters were otherwise irreproachable, were induced by the habits of thought then prevailing, and by the supposed necessity and convenience of slave labour, to purchase the African captives brought to their shores. Some even of the most eminent divines were so far implicated in the error, that, with perfect ease of conscience, they held Negroes in bondage. The distinguished William Penn, the Rev. George Whitefield, of world-wide celebrity, and President Edwards, author of several standard works in theology, were *slave-holders*. Good and conscientious men were led away by the plausible arguments of those who, while they were busy turning to pecuniary account the benighted Africans, alleged, that they were thus being brought under the influence of the Gospel. But, according to Mr. Bancroft, there were among the colonists some far-seeing men who foresaw the mischiefs that would ultimately result from the introduction of slavery into the colonies. Virginia and South Carolina did place some restrictions upon the importation of Negroes. But the British Government, listening to her African slave merchants rather than to her American colonists, not only neutralised those restrictions, but obliged the noble-hearted [James] Oglethorpe to relax his determination that in Georgia, the colony which he founded, there should be neither slavery nor slave trade.

Thus, for nearly two hundred years, Negroes were poured into North America without restriction. During six generations, large interests grew up out of the system, giving it in the eyes of those upon whom it had been entailed, a sanction and a sanctity which it was regarded as sacrilegious to question.

Of course, the slaves who were introduced during the first hundred years, we may presume, died Heathens, or with only imperfect glimpses of Christian teaching. For the Christianization of their descendants, a system was invented which so shocked the feelings of John Wesley that, in view of its resulting enormities, he denounced American slavery as the "sum of all villainies."

That which the early colonists of Virginia, South Carolina, and Georgia had opposed, having now grown into gigantic proportions, was not only apologized for by their descendants, but eulogized as eminently necessary and useful to the proper development of society; and all the religious, political, and scientific teachings of the time were not only tinged, but deeply steeped, in pro-slavery sentiments. Generations descending from Huguenot and Puritan ancestry were trained to believe that God has endowed them with the right to enslave the African for ever. And upon those Africans who became members of the Christian Church, the idea was impressed that it was their duty to submit, in everything, to their masters. Christian divines of all shades of opinion, in the South, taught this doctrine, and embodied it in books prepared specially for the instruction of the slaves— their "oral instructions," for they were not allowed to learn to read.

For example, the Right Rev. William Mean, Bishop of the diocese of Virginia, published a book of sermons, tracts, and dialogues, for masters and slaves, and recommended them to all masters and mistresses to be used in their families. In the preface of the book, the Bishop remarks:

> The editor of this volume offers it to all masters and mistresses in our Southern States, with the anxious wish and devout prayer that it may prove a blessing to themselves and their households.

On page 93 he says:

> Some He hath made masters and mistresses for taking care of their children and others that belong to them. . . . Some He hath made servants and slaves, to assist and work for their masters and mistresses, that provide for them; and others He hath made ministers

Christianity and the Negro Race

and teachers to instruct the rest, to show them what they ought to do, and to put them in mind of their several duties.

On pages 94 and 95, he says, addressing the slaves:

Almighty God hath been pleased to make you slaves here, and to give you nothing but labour and poverty in this world, which you are obliged to submit to, as it is His will that it should be so. Your bodies, you know, are not your own; they are at the disposal of those you belong to, &c.

Again, on page 132:

When *correction* is given you, you either deserve it or you do not deserve it. But whether you really deserve it or not, it is your duty, and Almighty God requires, that you bear it patiently. You may, perhaps, think that this is hard doctrine, but if you consider right you must needs think otherwise of it. Suppose, then, that you deserve correction, you cannot but say that it is just and right you should meet with it. Suppose you do not, or at least you do not deserve so much, or so severe a correction for the fault you have committed, you perhaps have escaped a great many more, and are at last paid for it all. Or, supposed you are quite innocent of what is laid to your charge, and suffer wrongfully in that particular thing, is it not possible you may have done some other bad thing which was never discovered, and that Almighty God, who saw you doing it, would not let you escape without punishment one time or another?

A clergyman of another denomination wrote a catechism for the use of slaves, in which we find the following:

Q. Is it right for the servant to run away, or is it right to harbour a run-away?
A. No.

Q. What did the Apostle Paul to Onesimus, who was a runaway? Did he harbour him, or send him back to his master?
A. He sent him back to his master with a letter.

A right reverend prelate tells the slave, in another work written for his "oral instruction," that "to disobey his master is to yield to the temptation of the devil."

It will be noticed that both these works, though written for slaves, carefully conceal on the title-page the unfortunate class for whom they were intended under the softening euphemism, in the one case, of "coloured persons," and in the other of "those who cannot read." That Christian divines should publish books drawn from the Scripture for "slaves," no doubt seemed to clerical educators an incongruity which, even in those days of ardent pro-slavery views, they hesitated to perpetrate.

But the politicians were not so scrupulous. In order to uphold the system, they did not hesitate to brand with folly the founders of the Republic, and to pour contempt upon the judgment of the wisest of their statesmen.

Chancellor Harper, in his *Memoir on Slavery,* takes up the sentence of Jefferson, that "All men are born free and equal, and endowed with certain inalienable rights," &c.; and proceeds in a most elaborate, but false and sophistical discussion, to demonstrate that Jefferson was wrong.

The most audacious utterances we have read on this subject are those by General Hammond in his notorious *Letters to Clarkson.* That gallant and chivalrous gentleman says, under date of 28 January 1845, writing from Silver Bluff, South Carolina:

I firmly believe that American slavery is not a sin, but especially commanded by God himself through Moses, and approved by Christ through His Apostles. . . . I endorse without reserve the much-abused sentiment of Governor McDuffie, that "slavery is the corner-stone of our Republican edifice"; while I repudiate as ridiculously absurd that much-lauded but nowhere accredited dogma of Mr. Jefferson, that "all men are born equal." . . . Slavery is truly the "corner-stone" and foundation of every well-designed and durable Republican edifice.

Again:

> If the slave is not allowed to read the Bible, the sin rests upon the abolitionists; for they stand prepared to furnish him with a key to it, which would make it, not a book of hope, and love, and peace, but of despair, hatred, and blood; which would convert the reader, not into a Christian, but a demon.

We wonder what key would be required when such wide doors into the temple of liberty as the following stand so constantly open—Jeremiah xxxiv, 17; Matt. vii, 12; Luke iv, 18 and 19?

Nor was such teaching confined to divines and politicians. Philologists and scientific men, brought contributions from their peculiar fields to strengthen and adorn the infamous fabric whose corner-stone was slavery. John Fletcher, of Louisiana, in *Studies on Slavery in Easy Lessons,* published at Natchez in 1852, brings the resources of the Hebrew language to the support of his idol. He gives the public a paradigm of the Hebrew verb, *abad,* to slave . . . and a declension of the "*factitious, euphonic segholate*" noun, *ebed,* a slave. Messrs. Nott and Gliddon contributed to the same honourable worship the results of their scientific researches.

But these reasoners have, one and all, been easily beaten on their own fields. Not one of these writers for slavery, whether political, theological, or scientific, ever produced anything with the mark on it of original observation or genius. None of their effusions ever passed the limits of the time or place at which they were produced. Entirely local and temporary, they have added nothing to the sum of human knowledge.

At last, when Charles Sumner was hurling those thunderbolts against the system which made it tremble from its base to its apex—when he was exposing the degenerate departure of the South from every noble American tradition, and when Calhoun, the great "nullifier," was no more, and the voice of Hayne, the brilliant and accomplished orator and politician, was silent—there came on the floor of the Senate a warrior from the South, not to hurl back in impassioned oratory, as Calhoun would have done, the charges of Sumner; not to neutralise their immediate effect by a gorgeous rhetoric, as Hayne would have done; but to appeal to brute force, and by one blow to exile the great Senator from his seat for four years. *Non opus est verbis, sed fustibus.*

Such were the circumstances under which the Negro throughout the United States received Christianity. The Gospel of Christ was travestied and diluted before it came to him to suit the "peculiar institution" by which millions of human beings were converted into "chattels." The highest men in the South, magistrates, legislators, professors of religion, preachers of the Gospel, governors of states, gentlemen of property and standing, all united in upholding a system which every Negro felt was wrong. Yet these were the men from whom he got his religion, and whom he was obliged to regard as guides. Under such teaching and dsicipline, is it to be wondered at that his morality is awry—that his sense of the "dignity of human nature" is superficial—that his standard of family and social life is low and defective?

Not so much by what Christianity said as by the way in which, through their teachers, it said it, were the Negroes influenced. The teachings they received conveyed for them no clear idea or definite impression of the religion of Christ. As regards their religion, they were left less to their intellectual apprehension of the truth than to their emotional impulses. The emotions were their guide on Sunday and on Monday, in the conventicle and in the cornfield. No change was wrought upon their moral nature, for there was nothing to act upon it. Nothing was imparted from without, and nothing was checked and stifled within. The influence of the Church was exerted continually to repress—to produce absolute outward submission. Such influences, even if it has been wholesome, could not penetrate deep or mould with much force the inner working of the soul. It produced an outward conformity to the views and will of their master, while it left the heart untouched. Or, perhaps, it might be more accurate to say that their whole nature was taken possession of, and all its capacities for thought and feeling, for love and hope, for joy and grief, were completely under the control of their taskmasters.

Nevertheless, by that mysterious influence which is imparted to man independently of outward circumstances, to not a few of them the preaching of the Gospel, defective as was its practical exemplification, opened a new world of truth and goodness. There streamed into the darkness of their surroundings a light from the Cross of Christ, and they say that, through suffering and affliction, there is a path to perfect rest above this world; and, in the hours of the most degrading and exhausting toil, they sang of the eternal and the unseen; so that while the scrupulous among their masters often with Jefferson "trembled for their country," the slaves who had gained a new language and new faculties were enjoying themselves in rapturous music—often labouring and suffering all day, and singing, all night, sacred songs, which, in rude but impressive language, set forth their sad fortunes and their hopes for the future. No traveller in the South, who passed by the plantations thronged with dusky labourers, and listened to their cheerful music, could ever dream that they beheld in that suffering but joyous race the destroyers of the Southern whites. The captive Jews would not sing by the waters of Babylon, but the Negroes in the dark dungeon of American slavery made themselves harps and swept them to some of the most thrilling melodies. From a people who were so full of music no mischief could have been apprehended, excepting by the delinquent of the drama, who "fears each bush an officer." It is the man "who hath no music in his soul" who is fit for stratagems and treasons and all dark deeds. We do not wonder that the *Westminster Review,* some years ago, made the following remark: "Were we forced at this moment to search for the saints of America, we should not be surprised to find them amongst the despised bondsmen."

Saints, no doubt, there were among the bondsmen, but they became so not in consequence, but in default, and often, we may say, in defiance of, instruction. And it cannot be expected that a people brought out of savagery into contact with a new, if a higher life, would, under such circumstances, produce, as a rule, such characters as "Uncle Tom." There have been "Uncle Toms" in the South, but they were the exceptions. As a rule, the Christianity of the Negroes is just such a grotesque and misshapen thing as the system under which they were trained and calculated to produce.

The Africans who were carried to the Western world were, as a general rule, of the lowest of the people in their own country. They did not fairly represent the qualities and endowments of the race. Even the traditions of their country they carried away in the most distorted form. And in the midst of their sorrows in a strange country, they constructed, out of their dim recollections of what they had been at home, a system of religion and government for themselves, which they curiously combined with what they received from their new masters; and so the elements of civilization and barbarism—of Christianity and Heathenism—not only subsisted side by side, but, so far as the Negro was concerned, were inlaid, so to say, into each other, in a sort of inharmonious mosaic all over the Weastern hemisphere.

Booker T. Washington
(1856–1915, United States)

Racial Accommodation

Some have advised that the Negro leave the South and take up his residence in the Northern States. I question whether this would leave him any better off than he is in the South, when all things are considered. It has been my privilege to study the condition of our people in nearly every part of America; and I say, without hesitation, that, with some exceptional cases, the Negro is at his best in the Southern States. While he enjoys certain privileges in the North that he does not have in the South, when it comes to the matter of securing property, enjoying business opportunities and employment, the South presents a far better opportunity than the North. Few coloured men from the South are as yet able to stand up against the severe and increasing competition that exists in the North, to say nothing of the unfriendly influence of labour organisations, which in some way prevents black men in the North, as a rule, from securing employment in skilled labour occupations. . . .

. . . As a race, they do not want to leave the South, and the Southern white people do not want them to leave. We must therefore find some basis of settlement that will be constitutional, just, manly, that will be fair to both races in the South and to the whole country. This cannot be done in a day, a year, or any short period of time. We can, it seems to me, with the present light, decide upon a reasonably safe method of solving the problem, and turn our strength and effort in that direction. In doing this, I would not have the Negro deprived of any privilege guaranteed to him by the Constitution of the United States. It is not best for the Negro that he relinquish any of his constitutional rights. It is not best for the Southern white man that he should.

In order that we may, without loss of time or effort, concentrate our forces in a wise direction, I suggest what seems to me and many others the wisest policy to be pursued. . . . But I wish first to mention some elements of danger in the present situation, which all who desire the permanent welfare of both races in the South should carefully consider.

First.—There is danger that a certain class of impatient extremists among the Negroes, who have little knowledge of the actual conditions in the South, may do the entire race injury by attempting to advise their brethren in the South to resort to armed resistance or the use of the torch, in order to secure justice. All intelligent and well-considered discussion of any important question or condemnation of any wrong, both in the North and the South, from the public platform and through the press, is to be commended and encouraged; but ill-considered, incendiary utterances from black men in the North will tend to add to the burdens of our people in the South rather than relieve them.

Second.—Another danger in the South, which should be guarded against, is that the whole white South, including the wise, conservative, law-abiding element, may find itself represented before the bar of public opinion by the mob, or lawless element, which gives expression to its feelings and tendency in a manner that advertises the South throughout the world. Too often those who have no sympathy with such disregard of law are either silent or fail to speak in a sufficiently emphatic manner to offset, in any large degree, the unfortunate reputation which the lawless have too often made for many portions of the South.

Third.—No race or people ever got upon its feet without severe and constant struggle, often in the face of the greatest discouragement. While passing through the present trying period of its history, there is danger that a large and valuable element of the Negro race may become discouraged in the effort to better its condition. Every possible influence should be exerted to prevent this.

Fourth.—There is a possibility that harm may be done to the South and to the Negro by exaggerated newspaper articles which are written near the scene or in the midst of specially aggravating occurrences. Often these reports are written by newspaper men, who give the impression that there is a race conflict throughout the South, and that all Southern white people are opposed to the Negro's progress, overlooking the fact that, while in some sections there is trouble, in most parts of the South there is, nevertheless, a very large measure of peace, good will, and mutual helpfulness. . . .

Fifth.—Under the next head I would mention that, owing to the lack of school opportunities for the Negro in the rural districts of the South, there is danger that ignorance and idleness may increase to the extent of giving the Negro race a reputation for crime, and that immortality may eat its way into the moral fibre of the race, so as to retard its progress for many years. In judging the Negro in this regard, we must not be too harsh. We must remember that it has only been within the last thirty-four years that the black father and mother have had the responsibility, and consequently the experience, of training their own children. That they have not reached perfection in one generation, with the obstacles that the parents have been compelled to overcome, is not to be wondered at.

Sixth.—As a final source of danger to be guarded against, I would mention my fear that some of the white people of the South may be led to feel that the way to settle the race problem is to repress the aspirations of the Negro by legislation of a kind that confers certain legal or political privileges upon an ignorant and poor white man and withholds the same privileges from a black man in the same condition. Such legislation injures and retards the progress of both races. It is an injustice to the poor white man, because it takes from him incentive to secure education and property as prerequisites for voting. He feels that, because he is a white man, regardless of his possessions, a way will be found for him to vote. I would label all such measures, "Laws to keep the poor white man in ignorance and poverty.". . .

Such laws as have been made—as an example, in Mississippi—with the "understanding" clause hold out a temptation for the election officer to perjure and degrade himself by too often deciding that the ignorant white man does understand the Constitution when it is read to him and that the ignorant black man does not. By such a law the State not only commits a wrong against its black citizens; it injures the morals of its white citizens by conferring such a power upon any white man who may happen to be a judge of elections.

Such laws are hurtful, again, because they keep alive in the heart of the black man the feeling that the white man means to oppress him. The only safe way out is to set a high standard as a test of citizenship, and require blacks and whites alike to come up to it.

When this is done, both will have a higher respect for the election laws and those who make them. I do not believe that, with his centuries of advantage over the Negro in the opportunity to acquire property and education as prerequisites for voting, the average white man in the South desires that any special law be passed to give him advantage over the Negro, who has had only a little more than thirty years in which to prepare himself for citizenship. In this relation another point of danger is that the Negro has been made to feel that it is his duty to oppose continually the Southern white man in politics, even in matters where no principle is involved, and that he is only loyal to his own race and acting in a manly way when he is opposing him. Such a policy has proved most hurtful to both races. Where it is a matter of principle, where a question of right or wrong is involved, I would advise the Negro to stand by principle at all hazards. A Southern white man has no respect for or confidence in a Negro who acts merely for policy's sake; but there are many cases—and the number is growing—where the Negro has nothing to gain and much to lose by opposing the Southern white man in many matters, that relate to government. . . .

In the future, more than in the past, we want to impress upon the Negro the importance of identifying himself more closely with the interests of the South,—the importance of making himself part of the South and at home in it. Heretofore, for reasons which were natural and for which no one is especially to blame, the coloured people have been too much like a foreign nation residing in the midst of another nation. . . . The bed-rock upon which every individual rests his chances of success in life is securing the friendship, the confidence, the respect, of his next-door neighbour of the little community in which he lives. Almost the whole problem of the Negro in the South rests itself upon the fact as to whether the Negro can make himself of such indispensable service to his neighbour and the community that no one can fill his place better in the body politic. There is at present no other safe course for the black man to pursue. If the Negro in the South has a friend in his white neighbour and a still larger number of friends in his community, he has a protection and a guarantee of his rights that will be more potent and more lasting than any our Federal Congress or any outside power can confer.

We must admit the stern fact that at present the Negro, through no choice of his own, is living among another race which is far ahead of him in education, property, experience, and favourable condition; further, that the Negro's present condition makes him dependent upon the white people for most of the things necessary to sustain life, as well as for his common school education. In all history, those who have possessed the property and intelligence have exercised the greatest control in government, regardless of colour, race, or geographical location. This being the case, how can the black man in the South improve his present condition? And does the Southern white man want him to improve it?

The Negro in the South has it within his power, if he properly utilises the forces at hand, to make of himself such a valuable factor in the life of the South that he will not have to seek privileges, they will be freely conferred upon him. To bring this about, the Negro must begin at the bottom and lay a sure foundation, and not be lured by any temptation into trying to rise on a false foundation. While the Negro is laying this foundation he will need help, sympathy, and simple justice. Progress by any other method will be but temporary and superficial, and the latter end of it will be worse than the beginning. American slavery was a great curse to both races, and I would be the last to apologise for it; but, in the presence of God, I believe that slavery laid the foundation for the solution of the problem that is now before us in the South. During slavery the Negro was taught every trade, every industry, that constitutes the foundation for making a living. Now, if on this foundation—lain in rather a crude way, it is true, but a foundation, nevertheless—we can gradually build and improve, the future for us is bright. Let me be more specific. Agriculture is, or has been, the basic industry of nearly every race or nation that has succeeded. The Negro got a knowledge of this during slavery. Hence, in a large measure, he is in possession of this industry in the South to-day. The Negro can buy land in the South, as a rule, wherever the white man can buy it, and at very low prices. Now, since the bulk of our people already have a foundation in agriculture, they are at their best when living in the country, engaged in agricultural pursuits. Plainly, then, the best thing, the logical thing, is to turn the larger part of our strength in a direction that will make the Negro among the most skilled agricultural people in the world. The man who has learned to do something better than any one else, has learned to do a common thing in an uncommon manner, is the man who has a power and influence that no adverse circumstances can take from him. The Negro who can make himself so conspicuous as a successful farmer, a large tax-payer, a wise helper of his fellow-men, as to be placed in a position of trust and honour, whether the position be political or otherwise, by natural selection, is a hundred-fold more secure in that position than one placed there by mere outside force or pressure. . . .

Let us help the Negro by every means possible to acquire such an education in farming, dairying, stock-raising, horticulture, etc., as will enable him to become a model in these respects and place him near the top in these industries, and the race problem would in a large part be settled, or at least stripped of many of its most perplexing elements. This policy would also tend to keep the Negro in the country and smaller towns, where he succeeds best, and stop the influx into the large cities, where he does not succeed so well. The race, like the individual, that produces something of superior worth that has a common human interest, makes a permanent place for itself, and is bound to be recognised.

At a county fair in the South not long ago I saw a Negro awarded the first prize by a jury of white men, over white competitors, for the production of the best specimen of Indian corn. Every white man at this fair seemed to be pleased and proud of the achievement of this Negro, because it was apparent that he had done something that would add to the wealth and comfort of the people of both races in that county. . . . While race prejudice is strongly exhibited in many directions, in the matter of business, of commercial and industrial development, there is very little obstacle in the Negro's way. A Negro who produces or has for sale something that the community wants finds customers among white people as well as black people. A Negro can borrow money at the bank with equal security as readily as a white man can. A bank in Birmingham, Alabama, that has now existed ten years, is officered and controlled wholly by Negroes. This bank has white borrowers and white depositors. A graduate of the Tuskegee Institute keeps a well-appointed grocery store in Tuskegee, and he tells me that he sells about as many goods to the one race as to the other. What I have said of the opening that awaits the Negro in the direction of agriculture is almost equally true of mechanics, manufacturing, and all the domestic arts. . . .

But it is asked, Would you confine the Negro to agriculture, mechanics, and domestic arts, etc.? Not at all; but along the lines that I have mentioned is where the stress should be laid just now and for many years to come. We will need and must have many teachers and ministers, some doctors and lawyers and statesmen; but these professional men will have a constituency or a foundation from which to draw support just in proportion as the race prospers along the economic lines that I have mentioned. During the first fifty or one hundred years of the life of any people are not the economic occupations always given the greater attention? This is not only the historic, but, I think, the commonsense view. If this generation will lay the material foundation, it will be the quickest and surest way for the succeeding generation to succeed in the cultivation of the fine arts, and to surround itself even with some of the luxuries of life, if desired. What the race now most needs, in my opinion, is a whole army of men and women well trained to lead and at the same time infuse themselves into agriculture, mechanics, domestic employment, and business. As to the mental training that these educated leaders should be equipped with, I should say, Give them all the mental training and culture that the circumstances of individuals will allow,—the more, the better. No race can permanently succeed until its mind is awakened and strengthened by the ripest thought. But I would constantly have it kept in the thoughts of those who are educated in books that a large proportion of those who are educated should be so trained in hand that they can bring this mental strength and knowledge to bear upon the physical conditions in the South which I have tried to emphasise. . . .

To state in detail just what place the black man will occupy in the South as a citizen, when he has developed in the direction named, is beyond the wisdom of any one. Much will depend upon the sense of justice which can be kept alive in the breast of the American people. Almost as much will depend upon the good sense of the Negro himself. That question, I confess, does not give me the most concern just now. The important and pressing question is, Will the Negro with his own help and that of his friends take advantage of the opportunities that now surround him? When he has done this, I believe that, speaking of his future in general terms, he will be treated with justice, will be given the protection of the law, and will be given the recognition in a large measure which his usefulness and ability warrant. If, fifty years ago, any one had predicted that the Negro would have received the recognition and honour which individuals have already received, he would have been laughed at as an idle dreamer. Time, patience, and constant achievement are great factors in the rise of a race.

I do not believe that the world ever takes a race seriously, in its desire to enter into the control of the government of a nation in any large degree, until a large number of individuals, members of that race, have demonstrated, beyond question, their ability to control and develop individual business enterprises. When a number of Negroes rise to the point where they own and operate the most successful farms, are among the largest taxpayers in their county, are moral and intelligent, I do not believe that in many portions of the South such men need long be denied the right of saying by their votes how they prefer their property to be taxed and in choosing those who are to make and administer the laws. . . . But a short time ago I read letters from nearly every prominent white man in Birmingham, Alabama, asking that the Rev. W.R. Pettiford, a Negro, be appointed to a certain important federal office. What is the explanation of this? Mr. Pettiford for nine years has been the president of the Negro bank in Birmingham to which I have alluded. During these nine years these white citizens have had the opportunity of seeing that Mr. Pettiford could manage successfully a private business, and that he had proven himself a conservative, thoughtful citizen; and they were willing to trust him in a public office. Such individual examples will have to be multiplied until they become the rule rather than the exception. While we are multiplying these examples, the Negro must keep a strong and courageous heart. He cannot improve his condition by any short-cut course or by artificial methods. Above all, he must not be deluded into the temptation of believing that his condition can be permanently improved by a mere battledore and shuttlecock of words or by any process of mere mental gymnastics or oratory alone. What is desired, along with a logical defence of his cause, are deeds, results,—multiplied results,—in the direction of building himself up, so as to leave no doubt in the minds of any one of his ability to succeed. . . .

My own feeling is that the South will gradually reach the point where it will see the wisdom and the justice of enacting an educational or property qualification, or both, for voting, that shall be made to apply honestly to both races. The industrial development of the Negro in connection with education and Christian character will help to hasten this end. When this is done, we shall have a foundation, in my opinion, upon which to build a government that is honest and that will be in a high degree satisfactory to both races. . . .

The problem is a large and serious one, and will require the patient help, sympathy, and advice of our most patriotic citizens, North and South, for years to come. But I believe that, if the principles which I have tried to indicate are followed, a solution of the question will come. So long as the Negro is permitted to get education, acquire property, and secure employment, and is treated with respect in the business or commercial world,—as is now true in the greater part of the South,—I shall have the greatest faith in his working out his own destiny in our Southern States.

Booker T. Washington

(1856–1915, United States)

The Atlanta Exposition Address

Atlanta, Georgia, 1895

Mr. President and Gentlemen of the Board of Directors and Citizens:

One third of the population of the South is of the Negro race. No enterprise seeking the material, civil, or moral welfare of this section can disregard this element of our population and reach the highest success. I but convey to you, Mr. President and Directors, the sentiments of the masses of my race when I say that in no way have the value and manhood of the American Negro been more fittingly and generously recognized than by the managers of this magnificent exposition at every stage of its progress. It is a recognition that will do more to cement the friendship of the two races than any occurrence since the dawn of our freedom.

Not only this, but the opportunity here afforded will awaken among us a new era of industrial progress. Ignorant and inexperienced, it is not strange that in the first years of our new life we began at the top instead of at the bottom; that a seat in Congress or the State Legislature was more sought than real estate or industrial skill; that the political convention or stump-speaking had more attraction than starting a dairy farm or truck garden.

A ship lost at sea for many days suddenly sighted a friendly vessel. From the mast of the unfortunate vessel was seen a signal: "Water, water; we die of thirst!" The answer from the friendly vessel at once came back: "Cast down your bucket where you are." A second time the signal, "Water, water; send us water!" ran up from the distressed vessel, and was answered: "Cast down your bucket where you are." And a third and fourth signal for water was answered, "Cast down your bucket where you are." The captain of the distressed vessel, at last heeding the injunction, cast down his bucket, and it came up full of fresh, sparkling water from the mouth of the Amazon River. To those of my race who depend upon bettering their condition in a foreign land, or who underestimate the importance of cultivating friendly relations with the Southern white man who is their next-door neighbor, I would say: "Cast down your bucket where you are"—cast it down in making friends, in every manly way, of the people of all races by whom we are surrounded.

Cast it down in agriculture, mechanics, in commerce, in domestic service, and in the professions. And in this connection it is well to bear in mind that whatever other sins the South may be called to bear, when it comes to business, pure and simple, it is in the South that the Negro is given a man's chance in the commercial world, and in nothing is this

Exposition more eloquent than in emphasizing this chance. Our greatest danger is that in the great leap from slavery to freedom we may overlook the fact that the masses of us are to live by the production of our hands, and fail to keep in mind that we shall prosper in proportion as we learn to dignify and glorify common labor, and put brains and skill into the common occupations of life; shall prosper in proportion as we learn to draw the line between the superficial and the substantial, the ornamental gew-gaws of life and the useful. No race can prosper till it learns that there is as much dignity in tilling a field as in writing a poem. It is at the bottom of life we must begin, and not at the top. Nor should we permit our grievances to overshadow our opportunities.

To those of the white race who look to the incoming of those of foreign birth and strange tongue and habits for the prosperity of the South, were I permitted, I would repeat what I say to my own race, "Cast down your bucket where you are." Cast it down among the eight million Negroes whose habits you know, whose fidelity and love you have tested in days when to have proved treacherous meant the ruin of your firesides. Cast down your bucket among these people who have without strikes and labor wars tilled your fields, cleared your forests, builded your railroads and cities, brought forth treasures from the bowels of the earth, and helped make possible this magnificent representation of the progress of the South. Casting down your bucket among my people, helping and encouraging them as you are doing on these grounds, and, with education of head, hand, and heart, you will find that they will buy your surplus land, make blossom the waste places in your fields, and run your factories. While doing this, you can be sure in the future, as in the past, that you and your families will be surrounded by the most patient, faithful, law-abiding, and unresentful people that the world has seen. As we have proved our loyalty to you in the past, in nursing your children, watching by the sick bed of your mothers and fathers, and often following them with tear-dimmed eyes to their graves, so in the future, in our humble way, we shall stand by you with a devotion that no foreigner can approach, ready to lay down our lives, if need be, in defense of yours, interlacing our industrial, commercial, civil, and religious life with yours in a way that shall make the interests of both races one. In all things that are purely social we can be as separate as the fingers, yet one as the hand in all things essential to mutual progress.

There is no defense or security for any of us except in the highest intelligence and development of all. If anywhere there are efforts tending to curtail the fullest growth of the Negro, let these efforts be turned into stimulating, encouraging, and making him the most useful and intelligent citizen. Effort or means so invested will pay a thousand per cent interest. These efforts will be twice blessed—"Blessing him that gives and him that takes."

There is no escape through law of man or God from the inevitable:

> "The law of changeless justice bind
>   Oppressor with oppressed;
> And close as sin and suffering joined
>   We march to fare abreast."

Nearly sixteen millions of hands will aid you in pulling the load upward, or they will pull, against you, the load downward. We shall constitute one third and more of the ignorance and crime of the South, or one third its intelligence and progress; we shall contribute one third to the business and industrial prosperity of the south, or, we shall prove a veritable body of death, stagnating, depressing, retarding every effort to advance the body politic.

Gentlemen of the Exposition, as we present to you our humble effort at an exhibition of our progress, you must not expect overmuch. Starting thirty years ago with ownership here and there is a few quilts and pumpkins and chickens (gathered from miscellaneous sources), remember, the path that has led from these to the inventions and production of agricultural implements, buggies, steam engines, newspapers, books, statuary carving, paintings, the management of drugstores and banks, has not been trodden without contact with thorns and thistles. While we take pride in what we exhibit as a result of our independent efforts, we do not for a moment forget that our part in this exhibition would fall far short of your expectations but for the constant help that has come to our educational life, not only from the Southern states, but especially from Northern philanthropists, who have made their gifts a constant stream of blessing and encouragement.

The wisest among my race understand that the agitation of questions of social equality is the extremest folly, and that progress in the enjoyment of all the privileges that will come to us must be the result of severe and constant struggle rather than of artificial forcing. No race that has anything to contribute to the markets of the world is long, in any degree, ostracized. It is important and right that all privileges of the law be ours, but it is vastly more important that we be prepared for the exercise of those privileges. The opportunity to earn a dollar in a factory just now is worth infinitely more than the opportunity to spend a dollar in an opera house.

In conclusion, may I repeat that nothing in thirty years has given us more hope and encouragement, and drawn us so near to you of the white race, as this opportunity offered by the Exposition; and here bending, as it were over the altar that represents the results of the struggles of your race and mine, both starting practically empty-handed three decades ago, I pledge that, in your effort to work out the great and intricate problem which God has laid at the doors of the South, you shall have at all times the patient, sympathetic help of my race; only let this be constantly in mind, that while, from representations in these buildings of the product of field, of forest, of mine, of factory, letters, and art, much good will come, yet far above and beyond material benefits will be that higher good, that, let us pray God, will come in a blotting out of sectional differences and racial animosities and suspicions, in a determination to administer absolute justice, in a willing obedience among all classes to the mandates of law. This, coupled with our material prosperity, will bring into our beloved South a new heaven and a new earth.

W. E. B. Du Bois
(1868–1963, United States)

Of Mr. Booker T. Washington and Others

Easily the most striking thing in the history of the American Negro since 1876 is the ascendancy of Mr. Booker T. Washington. It began at the time when war memories and ideals were rapidly passing; a day of astonishing commercial development was dawning; a sense of doubt and hesitation overtook the freedmen's sons,—then it was that his leading began. Mr. Washington came, with a single definite programme, at the psychological moment when the nation was a little ashamed of having bestowed so much sentiment on Negroes, and was concentrating its energies on Dollars. His programme of industrial education, conciliation of the South, and submission and silence as to civil and political rights, was not wholly original; the Free Negroes from 1830 up to wartime had striven to build industrial schools, and the American Missionary Association had from the first taught various trades; and Price and others had sought a way of honorable alliance with the best of the Southerners. But Mr. Washington first indissolubly linked these things; he put enthusiasm, unlimited energy, and perfect faith into this programme, and changed it from a by-path into a veritable Way of Life. And the tale of the methods by which he did this is a fascinating study of human life.

It startled the nation to hear a Negro advocating such a programme after many decades of bitter complaint; it startled and won the applause of the South, it interested and won the admiration of the North; and after a confused murmur of protest, it silenced if it did not convert the Negroes themselves.

To gain the sympathy and cooperation of the various elements comprising the white South was Mr. Washington's first task; and this, at the time Tuskegee was founded, seemed, for a black man, well-nigh impossible. And yet ten years later it was done in the word spoken at Atlanta: "In all things purely social we can be as separate as the five fingers, and yet one as the hand in all things essential to mutual progress." This "Atlanta Compromise" is by all odds the most notable thing in Mr. Washington's career. The South interpreted it in different ways: the radicals received it as a complete surrender of the demand for civil and political equality; the conservatives, as a generously conceived working basis for mutual understanding. So both approved it, and to-day its author is certainly the most distinguished Southerner since Jefferson Davis, and the one with the largest personal following.

Next to this achievement comes Mr. Washington's work in gaining place and consideration in the North. Others less shrewd and tactful had formerly essayed to sit on these two stools and had fallen between them; but as Mr. Washington knew the heart of the South from birth and training, so by singular insight he intuitively grasped the spirit of the age which was dominating the North. And so thoroughly did he learn the speech and thought of triumphant commercialism, and the ideals of material prosperity, that the picture of a lone black boy poring over a French grammar amid the weeds and dirt of a neglected home soon seemed to him the acme of absurdities. One wonders what Socrates and St. Francis of Assisi would say to this.

And yet this very singleness of vision and thorough oneness with his age is a mark of the successful man. It is as though Nature must needs make men narrow in order to give them force. So Mr. Washington's cult has gained unquestioning followers, his work has wonderfully prospered, his friends are legion, and his enemies are confounded. To-day he stands as the one recognized spokesman of his ten million fellows, and one of the most notable figures in a nation of seventy millions. One hesitates, therefore, to criticise a life which, beginning with so little, has done so much. And yet the time is come when one may speak in all sincerity and utter courtesy of the mistakes and shortcomings of Mr. Washington's career, as well as of his triumphs, without being thought captious or envious, and without forgetting that it is easier to do ill than well in the world.

The criticism that has hitherto met Mr. Washington has not always been of this broad character. In the South especially has he had to walk warily to avoid the harshest judgments,—and naturally so, for he is dealing with the one subject of deepest sensitiveness to that section. Twice—once when at the Chicago celebration of the Spanish-American War he alluded to the color-prejudice that is "eating away the vitals of the South," and once when he dined with President Roosevelt—has the resulting Southern criticism been violent enough to threaten seriously his popularity. In the North the feeling has several times forced itself into words, that Mr. Washington's counsels of submission overlooked certain elements of true manhood, and that his educational programme was unnecessarily narrow. Usually, however, such criticism has not found open expression, although, too, the spiritual sons of the Abolitionists have not been prepared to acknowledge that the schools founded before Tuskegee, by men of broad ideals and self-sacrificing spirit, were wholly failures or worthy of ridicule. While, then, criticism has not failed to follow Mr. Washington, yet the prevailing public opinion of the land has been but too willing to deliver the solution of a wearisome problem into his hands, and say, "If that is all you and your race ask, take it."

Among his own people, however, Mr. Washington has encountered the strongest and most lasting opposition, amounting at times to bitterness, and even to-day continuing strong and insistent even though largely silenced in outward expression by the public opinion of the nation. Some of this opposition is, of course, mere envy; the disappointment of displaced demagogues and the spite of narrow minds. But aside from this, there is among educated and thoughtful colored men in all parts of the land a feeling of deep regret, sorrow, and apprehension at the wide currency and ascendancy which some of Mr. Washington's theories have gained. These same men admire his sincerity of purpose, and are willing to forgive much to honest endeavor which is doing something worth the doing. They cooperate with Mr. Washington as far as they conscientiously can; and, indeed, it is no ordinary tribute to this man's tact and power that, steering as he must between so many diverse interests and opinions, he so largely retains the respect of all.

But the hushing of the criticism of honest opponents is a dangerous thing. It leads some of the best of the critics to unfortunate silence and paralysis of effort, and others to burst into speech so passionately and intemperately as to lose listeners. Honest and earnest criticism from those whose interests are most nearly touched,—criticism of writers by readers, of government by those governed, of leaders by those led,—this is the soul of democracy and the safeguard of modern society. If the best of the American Negroes receive by outer pressure a leader whom they had not recognized before, manifestly there is here a certain palpable gain. Yet there is also irreparable loss,—a loss of that peculiarly valuable education which a group receives when by search and criticism it finds and commissions its own leaders. The way in which this is done is at once the most elementary and the nicest problem of social growth. History is but the record of such group-leadership; and yet how infinitely changeful is its type and character! And of all types and kinds, what can be more instructive than the leadership of a group within a group?—that curious double movement where real progress may be negative and actual advance be relative retrogression. All this is the social student's inspiration and despair.

Now in the past the American Negro has had instructive experience in the choosing of group leaders, founding thus a peculiar dynasty which in the light of present conditions is worth while studying. When sticks and stones and beasts form the sole environment of a people, their attitude is largely one of determined opposition to and conquest of natural forces. But when to earth and brute is added an environment of men and ideas, then the attitude of the imprisoned group may take three main forms,—a feeling of revolt and revenge; an attempt to adjust all thought and action to the will of the greater group; or, finally, a determined effort at self-realization and self-development despite environing opinion. The influence of all of these attitudes at various times can be traced in the history of the American Negro, and in the evolution of his successive leaders.

Before 1750, while the fire of African freedom still burned in the veins of the slaves, there was in all leadership or attempted leadership but the one motive of revolt and revenge,—typified in the terrible Maroons, the Danish blacks, and Cato of Stono, and veiling all the Americas in fear of insurrection. The liberalizing tendencies of the latter half of the eighteenth century brought, along with kindlier relations between black and white, thoughts of ultimate adjustment and assimilation. Such aspiration was especially voiced in the earnest songs of Phyllis, in the martyrdom of Attucks, the fighting of Salem and Poor, the intellectual accomplishments of Banneker and Derham, and the political demands of the Cuffes.

Stern financial and social stress after the war cooled much of the previous humanitarian ardor. The disappointment and impatience of the Negroes at the persistence of slavery and serfdom voiced itself in two movements. The slaves in the South, aroused undoubtedly by vague rumors of the Haytian revolt, made three fierce attempts at insurrection,—in 1800 under Gabriel in Virginia, in 1822 under Vesey in Carolina, and in 1831 again in Virginia under the terrible Nat Turner. In the Free States, on the other hand, a new and curious attempt at self-development was made. In Philadelphia and New York color-prescription led to a withdrawal of Negro communicants from white churches and the formation of a peculiar socio-religious institution among the Negroes known as the African Church,—an organization still living and controlling in its various branches over a million of men.

Walker's wild appeal against the trend of the times showed how the world was changing after the coming of the cotton-gin. By 1830 slavery seemed hopelessly fastened on the South, and the slaves thoroughly cowed into submission. The free Negroes of the North, inspired by the mulatto immigrants from the West Indies, began to change the basis of their demands; they recognized the slavery of slaves, but insisted that they themselves were freemen, and sought assimilation and amalgamation with the nation on the same terms with other men. Thus, Forten and Purvis of Philadelphia, Shad of Wilmington, Du Bois of

New Haven, Barbadoes of Boston, and others, strove singly and together as men, they said, not as slaves; as "people of color," not as "Negroes." The trend of the times, however, refused them recognition save in individual and exceptional cases, considered them as one with all the despised blacks, and they soon found themselves striving to keep even the rights they formerly had of voting and working and moving as freemen. Schemes of migration and colonization arose among them; but these they refused to entertain, and they eventually turned to the Abolition movement as a final refuge.

Here, led by Remond, Nell, Wells-Brown, and Douglass, a new period of self-assertion and self-development dawned. To be sure, ultimate freedom and assimilation was the ideal before the leaders, but the assertion of the manhood rights of the Negro by himself was the main reliance, and John Brown's raid was the extreme of its logic. After the war and emancipation, the great form of Frederick Douglass, the greatest of American Negro leaders, still led the host. Self-assertion, especially in political lines, was the main programme, and behind Douglass came Elliot, Bruce, and Langston, and the Reconstruction politicians, and, less conspicuous but of greater social significance Alexander Crummell and Bishop Daniel Payne.

Then came the Revolution of 1876, the suppression of the Negro votes, the changing and shifting of ideals, and the seeking of new lights in the great night. Douglass, in his old age, still bravely stood for the ideals of his early manhood,—ultimate assimilation *through* self-assertion, and on no other terms. For a time Price arose as a new leader, destined, it seemed, not to give up, but to re-state the old ideals in a form less repugnant to the white South. But he passed away in his prime. Then came the new leader. Nearly all the former ones had become leaders by the silent suffrage of their fellows, had sought to lead their own people alone, and were usually, save Douglass, little known outside their race. But Booker T. Washington arose as essentially the leader not of one race but of two,—a compromiser between the South, the North, and the Negro. Naturally the Negroes resented, at first bitterly, signs of compromise which surrendered their civil and political rights, even though this was to be exchanged for larger chances of economic development. The rich and dominating North, however, was not only weary of the race problem, but was investing largely in Southern enterprises, and welcomed any method of peaceful cooperation. Thus, by national opinion, the Negroes began to recognize Mr. Washington's leadership; and the voice of criticism was hushed.

Mr. Washington represents in Negro thought the old attitude of adjustment and submission; but adjustment at such a peculiar time as to make his programme unique. This is an age of unusual economic development, and Mr. Washington's programme naturally takes an economic cast, becoming a gospel of Work and Money to such an extent as apparently almost completely to overshadow the higher aims of life. Moreover, this is an age when the more advanced race are coming in closer contact with the less developed races, and the race-feeling is therefore intensified; and Mr. Washington's programme practically accepts the alleged inferiority of the Negro races. Again, in our own land, the reaction from the sentiment of war time has given impetus to race-prejudice against Negroes, and Mr. Washington withdraws many of the high demands of Negroes as men and American citizens. In other periods of intensified prejudice all the Negro's tendency to self-assertion had been called forth; at this period a policy of submission is advocated. In the history of nearly all other races and peoples the doctrine preached at such crises has been that manly self-respect is worth more than lands and houses, and that a people who voluntarily surrender such respect, or cease striving for it, are not worth civilizing.

In answer to this, it has been claimed that the Negro can survive only through submission. Mr. Washington distinctly asks that black people give up, at least for the present, three things,—

> First, political power,
>
> Second, insistence on civil rights,
>
> Third, higher education of Negro youth,—

and concentrate all their energies on industrial education, the accumulation of wealth, and the conciliation of the South. This policy has been courageously and insistently advocated for over fifteen years, and has been triumphant for perhaps ten years. As a result of this tender of the palm-branch, what has been the return? In these years there have occurred:

1. The disfranchisement of the Negro.
2. The legal creation of a distinct status of civil inferiority for the Negro.
3. The steady withdrawal of aid from institutions for the higher training of the Negro.

These movements are not, to be sure, direct results of Mr. Washington's teachings; but his propaganda has, without a shadow of doubt, helped their speedier accomplishment. The question then comes: Is it possible, and probable, that nine millions of men can make effective progress in economic lines if they are deprived of political rights, made a servile caste, and allowed only the most meager chance for developing their exceptional men? If history and reason give any distinct answer to these questions, it is an emphatic *No*. And Mr. Washington thus faces the triple paradox of his career:

1. He is striving nobly to make Negro artisans business men and property-owners; but it is utterly impossible, under modern competitive methods, for workingmen and property-owners to defend their rights and exist without the right of suffrage.
2. He insists on thrift and self-respect, but at the same time counsels a silent submission to civic inferiority such as is bound to sap the manhood of any race in the long run.
3. He advocates common-school and industrial training, and depreciates institutions of higher learning; but neither the Negro common-schools, nor Tuskegee itself, could remain open a day were it not for teachers trained in Negro colleges, or trained by their graduates.

This triple paradox in Mr. Washington's position is the object of criticism by two classes of colored Americans. One class is spiritually descended from Toussaint the Savior, through Gabriel, Vesey, and Turner, and they represent the attitude of revolt and revenge; they hate the white South blindly and distrust the white race generally, and so far as they agree on definite action, think that the Negro's only hope lies in emigration beyond the borders of the United States. And yet, by the irony of fate, nothing has more effectually made this programme seem hopeless than the recent course of the United States toward weaker and darker peoples in the West Indies, Hawaii, and the Philippines,—for where in the world may we go and be safe from lying and brute force?

The other class of Negroes who cannot agree with Mr. Washington has hitherto said little aloud. They deprecate the sight of scattered counsels, of internal disagreement; and especially they dislike making their just criticism of a useful and earnest man an excuse for a general discharge of venom from small-minded opponents. Nevertheless, the questions involved are so fundamental and serious that it is difficult to see how men like the Grimkes, Kelly Miller, J. W. E. Bowen, and other representatives of this group, can much longer be silent. Such men feel in conscience bound to ask of this nation three things:

1. The right to vote.

2. Civic equality.

3. The education of youth according to ability.

They acknowledge Mr. Washington's invaluable service in counselling patience and courtesy in such demands; they do not ask that ignorant black men vote when ignorant whites are debarred, or that any reasonable restriction in the suffrage should not be applied; they know that the low social level of the mass of the race is responsible for much discrimination against it, but they also know, and the nation knows, that relentless color-prejudice is more often a cause than a result of the Negro's degradation; they seek the abatement of this relic of barbarism, and not its systematic encouragement and pampering by all agencies of social power from the Associated Press to the Church of Christ. They advocate, with Mr. Washington, a broad system of Negro common schools supplemented by thorough industrial training; but they are surprised that a man of Mr. Washington's insight cannot see that no such educational system ever has rested or can rest on any other basis than that of the well-equipped college and university, and they insist that there is a demand for a few such institutions throughout the South to train the best of the Negro youth as teachers, professional men, and leaders.

This group of men honor Mr. Washington for his attitude of conciliation toward the white South; they accept the "Atlanta Compromise" in its broadest interpretation; they recognize, with him, many signs of promise, many men of high purpose and fair judgment, in his section; they know that no easy task has been laid upon a region already tottering under heavy burdens. But, nevertheless, they insist that the way to truth and right lies in straightforward honesty, not in indiscriminate flattery; in praising those of the South who do well and criticising uncompromisingly those who do ill; in taking advantage of the opportunities at hand and urging their fellows to do the same, but at the same time in remembering that only a firm adherence to their higher ideals and aspirations will ever keep those ideals within the realm of possibility. They do not expect that the free right to vote, to enjoy civic rights, and to be educated, will come in a moment; they do not expect to see the bias and prejudices of years disappear at the blast of a trumpet; but they are absolutely certain that the way for a people to gain their reasonable rights is not by voluntarily throwing them away and insisting that they do not want them; that the way for a people to gain respect is not by continually belittling and ridiculing themselves; that, on the contrary, Negroes must insist continually, in season and out of season, that voting is necessary to modern manhood, that color discrimination is barbarism, and that black boys need education as well as white boys.

In failing thus to state plainly and unequivocally the legitimate demands of their people, even at the cost of opposing an honored leader, the thinking classes of American Negroes would shirk a heavy responsibility,—a responsibility to themselves, a responsibility to the struggling masses, a responsibility to the darker races of men whose future depends so largely on this American experiment, but especially a responsibility to this nation,—this common Fatherland. It is wrong to encourage a man or a people in evil-doing; it is wrong to aid and abet a national crime simply because it is unpopular not to do so. The growing spirit of kindliness and reconciliation between the North and South after the frightful difference of a generation ago ought to be the source of deep congratulation to all, and especially to those whose mistreatment caused the war; but if that reconciliation is to be marked by the industrial slavery and civic death of those same black men, with permanent legislation into a position of inferiority, then those black men, if they are really men, are called upon by every consideration of patriotism, and loyalty to oppose such a course by all civilized methods, even though such opposition involves disagreement with Mr. Booker

T. Washington. We have no right to sit silently by while the inevitable seeds are sown for a harvest of disaster to our children, black and white.

First, it is the duty of black men to judge the South discriminatingly. The present generation of Southerners are not responsible for the past, and they should not be blindly hated or blamed for it. Furthermore, to no class is the indiscriminate endorsement of the recent course of the South toward Negroes more nauseating than to the best thought of the South. The South is not "solid"; it is a land in the ferment of social change, wherein forces of all kinds are fighting for supremacy; and to praise the ill the South is to-day perpetrating is just as wrong as to condemn the good. Discriminating and broad-minded criticism is what the South needs,—needs it for the sake of her own white sons and daughters, and for the insurance of robust, healthy mental and moral development.

To-day even the attitude of the Southern whites toward the blacks is not, as so many assume, in all cases the same; the ignorant Southerner hates the Negro, the workingmen fear his competition, the money-makers wish to use him as a laborer, some of the educated see a menace in his upward development, while others—usually the sons of the masters— wish to help him to rise. National opinion has enabled this last class to maintain the Negro common schools, and to protect the Negro partially in property, life, and limb. Through the pressure of the money-makers, the Negro is in danger of being reduced to semi-slavery, especially in the country districts; the workingmen, and those of the educated who fear the Negro, have united to disfranchise him, and some have urged his deportation; while the passions of the ignorant are easily aroused to lynch and abuse any black man. To praise this intricate whirl of thought and prejudice is nonsense; to inveigh indiscriminately against "the South" is unjust; but to use the same breath in praising Governor Aycock, exposing Senator Morgan, arguing with Mr. Thomas Nelson Page, and denouncing Senator Ben Tillman, is not only sane, but the imperative duty of thinking black men.

It would be unjust to Mr. Washington not to acknowledge that in several instances he has opposed movements in the South which were unjust to the Negro; he sent memorials to the Louisiana and Alabama constitutional conventions, he has spoken against lynching, and in other ways has openly or silently set his influence against sinister schemes and unfortunate happenings. Notwithstanding this, it is equally true to assert that on the whole the distinct impression left by Mr. Washington's propaganda is, first, that the South is justified in its present attitude toward the Negro because of the Negro's degradation; secondly, that the prime cause of the Negro's failure to rise more quickly is his wrong education in the past; and, thirdly, that his future rise depends primarily on his own efforts. Each of these propositions is a dangerous half-truth. The supplementary truths must never be lost sight of: first, slavery and race-prejudice are potent if not sufficient causes of the Negro's position; second, industrial and common-school training were necessarily slow in planting because they had to await the black teachers trained by higher institutions,—it being extremely doubtful if any essentially different development was possible, and certainly a Tuskegee was unthinkable before 1880; and, third, while it is a great truth to say that the Negro must strive and strive mightily to help himself, it is equally true that unless his striving be not simply seconded, but rather aroused and encouraged, by the initiative of the richer and wiser environing group, he cannot hope for great success.

In his failure to realize and impress this last point, Mr. Washington is especially to be criticised. His doctrine has tended to make the whites, North and South, shift the burden of the Negro problem to the Negro's shoulders and stand aside as critical and rather pessimistic spectators; when in fact the burden belongs to the nation, and the hands of none of us are clean if we bend not our energies to righting these great wrongs.

The South ought to be led, by candid and honest criticism, to assert her better self and do her full duty to the race she has cruelly wronged and is still wronging. The North—her co-partner in guilt—cannot salve her conscience by plastering it with gold. We cannot settle this problem by diplomacy and suaveness, by "policy" alone. If worse come to worst, can the moral fibre of this country survive the slow throttling and murder of nine millions of men?

The black men of America have a duty to perform, a duty stern and delicate,—a forward movement to oppose a part of the work of their greatest leader. So far as Mr. Washington preaches Thrift, Patience, and Industrial Training for the masses, we must hold up his hands and strive with him, rejoicing in his honors and glorying in the strength of this Joshua called of God and of man to lead the headless host. But so far as Mr. Washington apologizes for injustice, North or South, does not rightly value the privilege and duty of voting, belittles the emasculating effects of caste distinctions, and opposes the higher training and ambition of our brighter minds,—so far as he, the South, or the Nation, does this,—we must unceasingly and firmly oppose them. By every civilized and peaceful method we must strive for the rights which the world accords to men, clinging unwaveringly to those great words which the sons of the Fathers would gain forget: "We hold these truths to be self-evident: That all men are created equal; that they are endowed by their Creator with certain unalienable rights; that among these are life, liberty, and the pursuit of happiness."

Monroe Trotter
(1872–1934, United States)

A Critique of Booker T. Washington's Plan

A. "Why Be Silent?"

Under the caption, "Principal Washington Defines His Position," the *Tuskegee Student*, the official organ of Tuskegee, prints the institute letter in which Mr. Washington said: "We cannot elevate and make useful a race of people unless there is held out to them the hope of reward for right living. Every revised constitution throughout the southern states has put a premium upon intelligence, ownership of property, thrift and character." This little sheet begins by saying that the letter "appeared in all of the important papers of the country on Nov. 28. It has been unstintingly praised from one section of the country to the other for its clarity and forcefulness of statement, and for its ringing note of sincerity." Although such words are to be expected from the employees of the school they are for the most part only too true. It is true that, although the letter was sent to the *Age Herald* of Birmingham, Alabama, it appeared simultaneously "in all the important papers of the country." Then its effect must be admitted to have been greater than if any other Negro had written it, for admittedly no other Negro's letter could have obtained such wide publicity. If it has in it aught that was injurious to the Negro's welfare or to his manhood rights, therefore, such worked far more damage than if any other Negro or any other man, save the president himself, had written the words.

What man is there among us, whether friend or foe of the author of the letter, who was not astounded at the reference to the disfranchising constitutions quoted above. "Every revised constitution throughout the southern states has put a premium upon intelligence, ownership of property, thrift and character," and all the more so because Mr. Washington had not been accused by even the southerners of opposing these disfranchising constitutions. . . . If the statement is false, if it is misleading, if it is injurious to the Negro, all the more blamable and guilty is the author because the statement was gratuitous on his part.

Is it the truth? Do these constitutions encourage Negroes to be thrifty, to be better and more intelligent? For this sort of argument is the most effective in favor of them. . . . Where is the Negro who says the law was or is ever intended to be fairly applied? . . . If so, then every reputable Negro orator and writer, from Hon. A. H. Grimke on, have been mistaken. If so, every Negro clergyman of standing, who has spoken on the subject . . . have been misinformed. We happen to know of an undertaker who has an enormous establishment in Virginia, who now can't vote. Is that encouraging thrift? Two letter carriers, who have passed the civil service examinations, are now suing because disfranchised.

Is that encouraging intelligence? . . . Even a Republican candidate for governor in Virginia recently said Negro domination was to be feared if 10 Negroes could vote because they could have the balance of power. Mr. Washington's statement is shamefully false and deliberately so.

But even were it true, what man is a worse enemy to a race than a leader who looks with equanimity on the disfranchisement of his race in a country where other races have universal suffrage by constitutions that make one rule for his race and another for the dominant race, by constitutions made by conventions to which his race is not allowed to send its representatives, by constitutions that his race although endowed with the franchise by law are not allowed to vote upon, and are, therefore, doubly illegal, by constitutions in violation to the national constitution, because, forsooth, he thinks such disfranchising laws will benefit the moral character of his people. Let our spiritual advisers condemn this idea of reducing a people to serfdom to make them good.

But what was the effect of Mr. Washington's letter on the northern white people? . . .

No thinking Negro can fail to see that, with the influence Mr. Washington yields [wields] in the North and the confidence reposed in him by the white people on account of his school, a fatal blow has been given to the Negro's political rights and liberty by his statement. The benevolence idea makes it all the more deadly in its effect. It comes very opportunely for the Negro, too, just when Roosevelt declares the Negro shall hold office, . . . when Congress is being asked to enforce the Negro's constitutional rights, when these laws are being carried to the Supreme Court. And here Mr. Washington, having gained sufficient influence through his doctrines, his school and his elevation by the President, makes all these efforts sure of failure by killing public sentiment against the disfranchising constitutions.

And Mr. Washington's word is the more effective for, discreditable as it may seem, not five Negro papers even mention a statement that belies all their editorials and that would have set aflame the entire Negro press of the country, if a less wealthy and less powerful Negro had made it. Nor will Negro orators nor Negro preachers dare now to pick up the gauntlet thrown down by the great "educator." Instead of being universally repudiated by the Negro race his statement will be practically universally endorsed by its silence because Washington said it, though it sounds the death-knell of our liberty. The lips of our leading politicians are sealed, because, before he said it, Mr. Washington, through the President, put them under obligation to himself. Nor is there that heroic quality now in our race that would lead men to throw off the shackles of fear, of obligation, of policy and denounce a traitor though he be a friend, or even a brother. It occurs to none that silence is tantamount to being virtually an accomplice in the treasonable act of this Benedict Arnold of the Negro race.

O, for a black Patrick Henry to save his people from this stigma of cowardice; to rouse them from their lethargy to a sense of danger; to scorn the tyrant and to inspire his people with the spirit of those immortal words: "Give Me Liberty or Give Me Death."

B. "Some Real Tuskegee Gems"

From Booker T. Washington's speech before the Twentieth Century Club at the Colonial Theatre last Saturday we have clipped some excerpts which, we feel, can properly be classed as "Tuskegee gems." . . .

Here is a gem of real value:

"Those are most truly free who have passed through the greatest discipline."

Then slavery was the best condition of society, for all admit it was the severest discipline yet experienced by man. Was it not wrong in Lincoln to deprive our race thus of the highest freedom?

Here are two more gems:

> "My request to the white men of the north is that they bring more coolness, more calmness, more deliberation and more sense of justice to the Negro question."

> "As soon as our race gets property in the form of real estate, of intelligence, of high Christian character, it will find that it is going to receive the recognition which it has not thus far received."

The coolness is needed in the South, not in the North; this section needs to warm up a little in the interest of its former ideals.

As to the question of wealth and character, etc., winning one recognition, we see quite the contrary in the South. These things are damned there in Negroes. For proofs see the efforts made there to keep all Negroes from places of preferment. . . .

Gem No. 4 says:

> "We have never disturbed the country by riots, strikes or lockouts; ours has been a peaceful, faithful, humble service."

Now, it is doubtful compliment to have this said about us; for the reason that strikes and lockouts are sometimes necessary conditions in society, and people who brag that they do not resort to these necessities are not always to be commended. In fact, the Negro in any and all professions and callings is safest in doing just the same, and no different from his white brother.

Gem No. 5:

> "One farm bought, one house built, one home sweetly and intelligently kept, one man who is the largest taxpayer or who has the largest banking account, one school or church maintained, one factory running successfully, one garden profitably cultivated, one patient cured by a Negro doctor, one sermon well preached, one life cleanly lived, will tell more in our favor than all the abstract eloquence that can be summoned to plead our cause."

All of this last is mere claptrap. All the wealth, skill and intelligence acquired and accumulated by Negroes before '61 did not do half so much toward freeing the slave as did the abstract eloquence of [Frederick] Douglass, [Samuel Ringgold] Ward, [William Lloyd] Garrison and [Wendell] Phillips. . . . This habit of always belittling agitation on the part of Washington, that very thing which made him free, and by which he lives and prospers is one of his great faults if a man with such a blundering can have any degrees in stupidity.

Society and Politics

Amy Jacques Garvey
(1896–1973, Jamaica)

Women as Leaders

The exigencies of this present age require that women take their places beside their men. White women are rallying all their forces and uniting regardless of national boundaries to save their race from destruction, and preserve its ideals for posterity. . . . White men have begun to realize that as women are the backbone of the home, so can they, by their economic experience and their aptitude for details, participate effectively in guiding the destiny of nation and race.

No line of endeavor remains closed for long to the modern woman. She agitates for equal opportunities and gets them; she makes good on the job and gains the respect of men who heretofore opposed her. She prefers to be a bread-winner than a half-starved wife at home. She is not afraid of hard work, and by being independent she gets more out of the present-day husband than her grandmother did in the good old days.

The women of the East, both yellow and black, are slowly but surely imitating the women of the Western world, and as the white women are bolstering up a decaying white civilization, even so women of the darker races are sallying forth to help their men establish a civilization according to their own standards, and to strive for world leadership.

Women of all climes and races have as great a part to play in the development of their particular group as the men. Some readers may not agree with us on this issue, but do they not mould the minds of their children, the future men and women? Even before birth a mother can so direct her thoughts and conduct as to bring into the world either a genius or an idiot. Imagine the early years of contact between mother and child, when she directs his form of speech, and is responsible for his conduct and deportment. Many a man has risen from the depths of poverty and obscurity and made his mark in life because of the advices and councils of a good mother whose influence guided his footsteps throughout his life.

Women therefore are extending this holy influence outside the realms of the home, softening the ills of the world by their gracious and kindly contact.

Some men may argue that the home will be broken up and women will become coarse and lose their gentle appeal. We do not think so, because everything can be done with moderation. . . . The doll-baby type of woman is a thing of the past, and the wide-awake woman is forging ahead prepared for all emergencies, and ready to answer any call, even if it be to face the cannons on the battlefield.

New York has a woman Secretary of State. Two States have women Governors, and we would not be surprised if within the next ten years a woman graces the White House in

Washington D.C. Women are also filling diplomatic positions, and from time immemorial women have been used as spies to get information for their country.

White women have greater opportunities to display their ability because of the standing of both races, and due to the fact that black men are less appreciative of their women than white men. The former will more readily sing the praises of white women than their own; yet who is more deserving of admiration than the black woman, she who has borne the rigors of slavery, the deprivations consequent on a pauperized race, and the indignities heaped upon a weak and defenseless people? Yet she has suffered all with fortitude, and stands ever ready to help in the onward march to freedom and power.

Be not discouraged, black women of the world, but push forward, regardless of the lack of appreciation shown you. A race must be saved, a country must be redeemed, and unless you strengthen the leadership of vacillating Negro men, we will remain marking time until the Yellow race gains leadership of the world, and we be forced to subserviency under them, or extermination.

We are tired of hearing Negro men say, "There is a better day coming," while they do nothing to usher in the day. We are becoming so impatient that we are getting in the front ranks, and serve notice on the world that we will brush aside the halting, cowardly Negro men, and with prayer on our lips and arms prepared for any fray, we will press on and on until victory is ours.

Africa must be for Africans, and Negroes everywhere must be independent, God being our guide. Mr Black man, watch your step! Ethiopia's queens will reign again, and her Amazons protect her shores and people. Strengthen your shaking knees, and move forward, or we will displace you and lead on to victory and to glory.

Abdias do Nascimento
(b. 1915, Brazil)

Brazilian *Quilombismo*

> Pardon, beloved Lady Motherland, for having arrived so late!
> Pardon, brothers and sisters for only now arriving!
> Pardon, King Zumbi, for arriving only now to receive the inheritance you have left me!
> —from a letter of Gerardo Mello Mourao

Only now, nearly four centuries later, we, Black Brazilians, were able for the first time collectively to visit the Serra da Barriga, in the Brazilian state of Alagoas, and recapture the historic space where the famous Republic of Palmares existed, founded in the sixteenth century by Africans who rose up against slavery and created a free country, egalitarian, just, and productive. This first visit to our ancestral land took place on the 24th of August 1980, when dozens and dozens of African men and women gathered in Maceio (capital of Alagoas) in order to discuss the creation of a memorial to Zumbi, the Afro-Brazilian king of Palmares—not a park, or monument, but a veritable pole of Afro-Brazilian liberation culture.

The feats of that cluster of *quilombos* [military communities] called Palmares were heroic to the point of mingling with legend, and catapulted the republic into history as the Black Troy. Nevertheless, they are not celebrated in Brazilian civic holidays or even remembered—much less studied or taught—in the scholastic curricula on any educational level. This had been the major means of eradicating African memory and history from the scenario of Brazilian life.

But we were there to recapture, celebrate, and reaffirm them in all their content of beauty, myth, and history. With this sentiment, I climbed the impenetrable paths of the Serra's slope, treading the same trail that Zumbi's followers had walked. And from the villagers of Serra da Barriga I heard the oral account (however fragmented) of the histories, legends, and stories that enable us to reconstruct the concrete existence of those 30,000 bronze heroes who wrote, with their lives and blood, the page of history most vibrant with the love of liberty known in American lands. With sweat covering my face from the effort of the climb, I noticed on the third tier, very distant, the great closed forest where people would be lost forever if they took away the fruits of the trees. There was also the belief that buried somewhere in the forest was the hidden treasure of the *quilombolas;* an institution from the United States has even projected excavations to search for Zumbi's gold. Meanwhile, even today many mothers in the area (not of African origin) scare their rambunctious children with the threat: "I'll get Zumbi out here to fix you!" And it is said that one can hear in certain areas and valleys of the Serra, the sounds of chains, the crack of breaking bones, muffled screams of those who leap or are thrown to the abyss.

The *quilombos'* lines of defense, it seems, began with deep trenches almost at the foot of the hills, filled with pointed spears on which attackers would impale themselves—the first palisade. This military defense system was repeated, forming four lines of palisades up to the top. I climbed up to the place where possibly there existed the fourth and last of these. Along the entire path I found reminiscences of what the *quilombolas* of the sixteenth century probably harvested: bamboo, oranges, *jaca,* mangoes, yams, lemons, corn, and sugar cane, and everywhere there were the elegant palms—coconuts of various species. There were the *palmares* that gave the place its name, and there they stood, green and mute, giving witness to so many centuries of Afro-Brazilian history—a history that will be rescued, beginning now, from the distortion and oblivion that the dominant elite has practiced.

UPDATING ANCIENT AFRICAN KNOWLEDGE

Afro-Brazilian memory, much to the contrary of the statements of conventional historians of limited vision and superficial understanding, does not begin with the slave traffic or the dawn of African chattel slavery in the fifteenth century. In Brazil, the ruling class always, particularly after the so-called abolition of slavery (1888), developed and refined innumerable techniques for preventing Black Brazilians from identifying and actively drawing on their ethnic, historical, and cultural roots, cutting them off from the trunk of their African family tree. Except in terms of its recent expansionist economic interests, Brazil's traditional elite has always ignored the African continent. Brazil turned its back on Africa as soon as the slaver elite found itself no longer able to scorn the prohibition of commerce in African flesh imposed by Britain around 1850. A massive immigration of Europeans occurred a few years later, and the ruling elite emphasized its intentions and its actions in order to wrench out of the mind and heart of slaves' descendants any image of Africa as a positive memory of nation, of motherland, or native home. Never in our educational system was there taught a discipline revealing any appreciation or respect for the cultures, arts, languages, political or economic systems, or religions of Africa. And physical contact of Afro-Brazilians with their brothers in the continent and the diaspora was always prevented or made difficult, among other methods, by the denial of economic means permitting black people to move and travel outside the country. But none of these hindrances had the power of obliterating completely, from our spirit and memory, the living presence of Mother Africa. And even in the existential hell we are subjected to now, this rejection of Africa on the part of the dominant classes has functioned as a notably positive factor, helping to maintain the black nation as a community above and beyond difficulties in time and space.

Diversified as are the strategies and devices arrayed against black people's memory, they have recently undergone serious erosion and irreparable discrediting. This is due largely to the dedication and competence of a few Africans preoccupied with the secular destitution the black race has suffered at the hands of European and Euro-American capitalist civilization. This group of Africans, simultaneously scholars, scientists, philosophers, and creators of literature and art, includes persons from the African continent and diaspora. To mention only a few of their names: Cheikh Anta Diop of Senegal; Chancellor Williams, Shawna Maglangbayan Moore, Haki Madhubuti, Molefi K. Asante, and Maulana

Ron Karenga of the United States; George G. M. James and Ivan Van Sertima of Guyana; Yosef Ben-Jochannan of Ethiopia; Theophile Obenga, of Congo Brazzaville; Wole Soyinka, Ola Balogun, and Wande Abimbola of Nigeria. These figure among the many who are actively producing works fundamental to the contemporary and coming development of Africa. In different fields, with diverse perspectives, the energies of these eminent Africans channel themselves toward the exorcism of the falsities, distortions, and negations that Europeans for so long have been weaving around Africa with the purpose of obscuring or erasing from our memory the wisdom, scientific and philosophical knowledge, and realizations of the peoples of Black African origin. Black Brazilian memory is only a part of this gigantic project of reconstructing the larger past to which all Afro-Brazilians are connected. To redeem this past is to have a consequent responsibility in the destiny and future of the Black African nation worldwide, still preserving our role as edifiers and genuine citizens of Brazil.

It is appropriate here to refer briefly to certain basic texts of Cheikh Anta Diop, principally his book *The African Origin of Civilization* (1974), selections translated from *Nation nègre et culture* and *Antériorité des civilizations nègres*. Let is be said from the outset that the volume presents a radical confrontation and unanswerable challenge to the Western academic world, describing its intellectual arrogance, scientific dishonesty, and ethical vacuum in dealing with the peoples, civilizations, and cultures produced by Africa. Using Western Europe's own scientific resources—Diop is a chemist, director of the radiocarbon laboratory of IFAN [Fundamental Institute for Black Africa] in Dakar, as well as an Egyptologist, historian, and linguist—this sage reconstructs the significance and value of the ancient Black African civilizations, far too long obscured by manipulations, lies, distortions, and thefts. These civilizations include ancient Egypt. The Egyptians were black and not a people of any Aryan (white) or so-called "dark-red race," as Western scholars have claimed Egyptians to be, with an emphasis as deceitful as it is self-interested. Let us see how Diop characterizes this situation:

> The ancient Egyptians were Negroes. The moral fruit of their civilization is to be counted among the assets of the Black world. Instead of presenting itself to history as an insolvent debtor, that Black world is the very initiator of the "Western" civilization flaunted before our eyes today. Pythagorean mathematics, the theory of the four elements of Thales of Miletus, Epicurean materialism, Plantonic idealism, Judaism, Islam and modern sciences are rooted in Egyptian cosmogony and science. One needs only to meditate on Ausar, the redeemer-god, who sacrifices himself, dies and is resurrected to save mankind, a figure essentially identifiable with Christ.

Diop's statements are based on rigorous research, examinations, and conclusions, leaving no margin for doubt or argument, yet far from taking on that dogmatism that always characterizes the "scientific" certainties of the Western world. What Diop did was simply to demolish the supposedly definitive structures of "universal" knowledge with respect to Egyptian and Greek antiquity. Like it or not, white Westerners have to swallow truths like this one: "four centuries before the publication of *La Mentalité primitive [Primitive Mentality]* by Levy-Bruhl, Black Muslim Africa was commenting on Aristotle's formal logic (which he plagiarized from the Black Egyptians) and was already expert in dialectics." And let us not forget that this was almost five centuries before Hegel or Marx were born.

Diop turns around the entire process of mystification of a Black Egypt turned white by the magical arts of European Egyptologists. He notes how, after the military campaign of Bonaparte in Egypt in 1799, and after the hieroglyphs of the Rosetta stone were deciphered by Champollion in 1822, Egyptologists were dumbfounded before the grandiosity of the revealed discoveries:

> The gradually recognized [Egypt] as the most ancient civilization, that had engendered all others. But, imperialism being what it is, it became increasingly "inadmissible" to continue to accept the theory—evident until then—of a Negro Egypt. The birth of Egyptology was thus marked by the need to destroy the memory of Negro Egypt at any cost and in all minds. Henceforth, the common denominator of all the theses of the Egyptologists, their close relationship and profound affinity, can be characterized as a desperate attempt to refute that opinion. Almost all Egyptologists stress its falsity as a matter of course.

The Eurocentric pretentiousness of this episode is exposed in all its nakedness: the Egyptologists continued obstinately in their vain efforts to prove "scientifically" that this great civilization of Black Egypt had a white origin. Precarious as their theories were in fact, they were accepted by the "civilized" world as a cornerstone in the belief of white supremacy.

Diop, compassionate and humane before the dogmatism of the white Egyptologists, reveals much patience and generosity, explaining what should be obvious to anyone approaching the subject in good faith: that he does not allege racial superiority or any specific black genius in this purely scientific confirmation that the civilization of ancient Egypt was built and governed by black people. The event, explains Diop, resulted from a series of historical factors, climatic conditions, natural resources, and so on, added to other nonracial elements. So much so that even after having expanded through all of Black Africa, to the central and western part of the continent, the Egyptian civilization, under the impact of other influences and historical situations, later entered into a process of retrogressive disintegration. What is important here is to note some of the factors that contributed to the construction of Egyptian civilization, among which Diop enumerates these: geographical conditioning of the sociopolitical development of the peoples that lived on the banks of the river Nile, such as floods and other natural disasters that forced collective measures of defense and survival; a situation that favored unity and discouraged individual or personal egotism. In this context arose the need for a central coordinating authority over common life and activities. The invention of geometry was born of the imperatives of geographical division, and other advances were attained in the effort to attend to the exigencies of building a viable society.

One detail is particularly important to the memory of Brazilian blacks. Diop mentions ancient Egypt's relationship to Black Africa, specifically the Yoruba people, who constitute an important element of Afro-Brazilian demographic and cultural heritage. It seems that these Egyptian-Yoruba relationships were so intimate that one can "consider a historical fact the common possession of the same primitive habitat by the Yorubas and the Egyptians." Diop raises the hypothesis that the Latinization of the name of Heru, son of Ausar and Auset, resulted in the appellative Orisha. Following this line of comparative study, in the field of linguistics and other disciplines, Diop cites J. Olumide Lucas, of Nigeria. In *The Religion of the Yorubas* (1948) Lucas traces Egyptian links with his people, concluding that all paths lead to the verification of (a) a similarity or identity of language; (b) a similarity or identity of religious beliefs; (c) a similarity or identity of religious ideas and practices; (d) a survival of customs, names of places and persons, objects, etc.

My objective here is simply to call attention to this significant dimension of the antiquity of Afro-Brazilian memory. It is for the Afro-Brazilian and African researchers of the present and future to flesh out the details of such a fundamental aspect of our history, a task too vast to touch upon here.

It is not only in ancient Egypt or West Africa that we find the historical antecedents of Afro-Brazilian peoples and culture. Another dimension of our memory lies in the presence of Africans in various parts of ancient America, long before the arrival of Columbus. And this is not a superficial or passing phenomenon, but a presence so deep that it left indelible marks on pre-Columbian civilizations. Various historians and researchers have left evidence of this phenomenon. Among others, we can cite the Mexican colonial historian Orozco y Berra, who by 1862 had already mentioned the intimate relations which ancient Mexicans must have cultivated with African visitors and immigrants. The most important recent contribution in this sense has been that of Ivan Van Sertima, whose book *They Came Before Columbus* (1976) registers in unanswerable and definitive form the African contribution to the pre-Columbian cultures of the Americas, particularly those of Mexico. Nevertheless, other authors of various epochs and origins have also confirmed the same result: R. A. Jairazbhoy, Lopez de Gomara, Alexander von Wuthenau, Leo Weiner, and others, each in their own specialties, have added to the reconstitution of the African presence in America before Columbus.

Elisa Larkin Nascimento has noted linkages with Egyptian and West African symbols and artistic techniques, manifested in the funeral urns and other art of San Agustin and Tierradentro in Colombia, sites of indigenous civilizations dating from more or less a century before Christ. Similar types of comparisons also can be documented with respect to the Taina culture of Puerto Rico and the Olmec, Toltec, Aztec, and Maya of Mexico, as well as the Inca of Bolivia, Ecuador, and Peru. Remarkable portraiture of African faces and figures in ceramics and sculpture, shared mummification techniques, funeral traditions, mythical and artistic themes, symbols such as the feathered serpent, as well as countless linguistic identities, are among the visible witnesses to the active interchange between ancient American and African civilizations. Perhaps most intriguing is the obvious connection in engineering techniques of pyramid construction in Nubia, Egypt, and the Americas. At this point it is well to note, along with Elisa Larkin Nascimento, that the pre-Columbian presence of African civilization in the Americas "in no way underestimates or detracts from the enormous design and engineering capacities of the original American peoples that were the authors and builders of the formidable pre-Columbian urban civilizations."

This African-American interchange, among the original peoples of the respective continents, establishes an extensive and legitimate relationship between African and American indigenous peoples that long predates European chattel slavery of Africans. The true historical basis for solidarity among these peoples is thus much deeper and more authentic than has generally been recognized. As *quilombismo* searches for the best world for Africans in the Americas, it knows that such a struggle cannot be separated from the mutual liberation of the indigenous peoples of these lands, who are also victims of the racism and wanton destructiveness introduced and enforced by the European colonialists and their heirs.

BLACK CONSCIOUSNESS AND *QUILOMBIST* SENTIMENT

From a narrower perspective, Black Brazilian memory reaches a crucial historical state in the slavist period, beginning around 1500, just after the territory's "discovery" by the

Portuguese and their inaugural acts toward its colonization. Along with the briefly en-slaved and then progressively exterminated Indians, Africans were the first and only work-ers, throughout three and a half centuries, who built the structures of Brazil. I think it necessary to evoke once more the vast lands Africans sowed with their sweat, or to remem-ber again the cane fields; cotton fields; coffee plantations; gold, diamond, and silver mines; and the many other elements in the formation of Brazil which [were] nourished with the martyred blood of slaves. The black, far from being an upstart or a stranger, is the very body and soul of this country. Yet, despite this undeniable historical fact, Africans and their descendants were never treated as equals by the minority white segments that complement the national demographic tableau, nor are they today. This minority has maintained an exclusive grip on all power, welfare, health, education, and national in-come.

It is scandalous to note that significant portions of the Euro-Brazilian population began to arrive in Brazil at the end of the nineteenth century as poor and needy immigrants. Immediately they bought into the enjoyment of privileges which the conventional white society conceded them as partners in race and Eurocentric supremacy. These poor immi-grants demonstrated neither scruples nor difficulties in assuming the racist mythologies in force in Brazil and Europe; endorsing the consequent contempt, humiliation, and dis-crimination enforced against blacks; and benefiting from these practices, filling the places in the labor market denied to ex-slaves and their descendants. Blacks were literally ex-pelled from the system of production as the country approached the "abolitionist" date of May 13, 1888.

The contemporary condition of black people is worse than it was then. At the margins of employment, or left in situations of semiemployment and underemployment, black people remain largely excluded from the economy. Residential segregation is imposed on the black community by the double factor of race and poverty, marking off, as black living areas, ghettoes of various denominations: *favelas, alagados, poroes, mocambos, invasoes, conjuntos populares,* or *residenciais.* Permanent policy brutality and arbitrary arrests moti-vated by racism contribute to the reign of terror under which blacks live daily. In such conditions, one comprehends why no conscious black person has the slightest hope that a progressive change can occur spontaneously in white society to the benefit of the Afro-Brazilian community. Slums swarm in all the large cities: Rio de Janeiro, São Paulo, Bahia, Recife, Brasilia, São Luis de Maranhao, Porto Alegre, are a few examples. Statistics on these *favelados* (residents of the slums) express expanding misery in themselves alone. According to the Department of Social Services in São Paulo, published in *O Estado de Sao Paulo* on August 16, 1970, more than 60 percent of that city's enormous population lives in extremely precarious conditions. To be *favelado* means starvation or malnutrition, no health care, no lighting, water lines, public services, or houses—only makeshift shanties of cardboard or sheet metal, perched precariously on steep, muddy hills, or swamps. Yet São Paulo is Brazil's best-served city in terms of water and sewer lines; with this in mind we can get an idea of the impossible living and hygienic conditions in which the Afro-Brazilian vegetates all over this country. In Brasilia, according to the magazine *Veja* (Octo-ber 8, 1969), 80,000 of 510,000 inhabitants of the federal capital were *favelados.* In Rio de Janeiro, the percentage oscillates between 40 and 50 percent of the population. The vast majority of Brazilian *favelados,* 95 percent or more, are of African origin. Such a situation characterizes irrefutable proof of racial segregation; the converse also holds true, the vast majority of black people in Brazil are *favelados.*

Up to now we have dealt with the urban black population. It is necessary to emphasize that the great majority of African descendants still live in the countryside, slaves in fact: slaves of a feudal seignorial landholding and social system, in a situation of total destitution, as peasants, sharecroppers, or migrant workers. One could say that these people do not live a life of human beings.

The urban segment of the Afro-Brazilian population makes up a category which the Annual Statistical Report of the Brazilian Institute of Geography and Statistics calls "service employees," a strange euphemism for the severe underemployment and semiemployment which marks the lives of almost 4.5 million Brazilians. Such a euphemism is ironic, since this classification picks up masses of people "employed" without fixed pay, i.e., odd-jobsmen living the small daily adventure of trying to shine shoes, wash cars, deliver packages or messages, sell fruit or candy on the street, and so on—all for the miserable and unreliable "salary" of pennies.

This is an imperfect sketch of a much graver situation which has been the reality of Afro-Brazilians through the entire course of their history. From this reality is born the urgent necessity of black people to defend their survival and assure their very existence as human beings. *Quilombos* were the results of this vital exigency for enslaved Africans, to recover their liberty and human dignity through escape from captivity, organizing viable free societies in Brazilian territory. The multiplicity in space and time of the *quilombos* made them an authentic, broad, and permanent sociopolitical movement. Apparently a sporadic phenomenon in the beginning, *quilombos* were rapidly transformed from the improvisation of emergency into the methodical and constant life form of the African masses who refused to submit to the exploitation and violence of the slave system. *Quilombismo* was structured in associative forms that could be found in hole independent communities in the depths of forests or in jungles of difficult access, facilitating their defense and protecting their economic, social, and political organization. *Quilombos* could also follow models of organization permitted or tolerated by the authority, frequently with ostensibly religious (Catholic), recreational, charity, athletic, cultural, or mutual assistance objectives. Whatever their appearances and declared objectives, all of them fulfilled an important social function for the black community, performing a relevant and central role in sustaining African continuity and serving as genuine focal points of physical, as well as cultural, resistance. Objectively, this web of associations, brotherhoods, clubs, *terreiros* (houses of worship of Afro-Brazilian religion), *tendas*, *afoches*, samba schools, *gafieiras*, *gremios*, *confrarias*, were and are *quilombos* legalized by ruling society. On the other side of the law are the underground, secretive *quilombos* we know of. Nevertheless, the "legalized" and the "illegal" form a unity, a unique human, ethnic, and cultural affirmation, at once integrating a practice of liberation and assuming command of their own history. This entire complex of African social phenomena, of Afro-Brazilian *praxis*, I denominate *quilombismo*.

It is important to note that this tradition of *quilombist* struggle has existed throughout centuries and exists throughout the Americas. In Mexico, these societies were called *cimarrones*; in Venezuela, *cumbes*; in Cuba and Colombia, *palenques*; in Jamaica and the United States, maroon societies. They have proliferated throughout the Caribbean and South and Central America. Researching and building upon the history of these free African societies in the Americas, and their cultural, economic, political, and social bases, Afro-Americans throughout the entire hemisphere can consolidate their true heritage of solidarity and struggle. *Quilombismo* and its various equivalents throughout the Americas, expressed in the legacy of *cumbes*, *palenques*, *cimarrones*, and maroons, constitutes an international alternative for popular black political organization.

Easy confirmation of the enormous number of Black Brazilian organizations that have taken the title, in the past and the present, of *quilombo,* or the name of Palmares (evoking the Republic of Palmares, a huge community of *quilombos* which resisted the armed aggression of the Portuguese and the Dutch for a full century, from 1595–1695), testifies to the significance of the *quilombist* examples as a dynamic value in the tactics and strategies of survival, resistance, and progress of African communities in contemporary Brazil. In effect, *quilombismo* has already revealed itself as a factor capable of mobilization the black masses in a disciplined manner, because of its deep psychosocial appeal, rooted in the history, culture, and experience of Afro-Brazilians. The Unified Black Movement Against Racism and Racial Discrimination registers its *quilombist* concept in the following definition of Black Consciousness Day, published in a 1978 manifesto:

> We, Brazilian Blacks, proud of descending from Zumbi, leader of the Black Republic of Palmares, which existed in the state of Alagoas from 1595 to 1696, defying Portuguese and Dutch dominion, come together, after 283 years to declare to the Brazilian people our true and effective date: November 20, National Black Consciousness Day!
>
> The day of the death of the great Black national leader Zumbi, responsible for the first and only Brazilian attempt to create a democratic society, free, in which all people—Blacks, Indians, and whites—achieved a great political, economic and social advance. An attempt which was always present in all *quilombos.*

A continuity of this consciousness of political-social struggle extends through all Brazilian states with a significant population of African origin. The *quilombist* model has remained active as an idea-force, a source of energy-inspiring models of dynamic organization, since the fifteenth century. In this dynamic, almost always heroic process, *quilombismo* is in a constant process of revitalization and remodernization, attending to the needs of the various historical times and geographical environments which imposed upon the *quilombos* certain differences in their organizational forms. But essentially they were alike. They were (and are), in the words of Afro-Brazilian historian Beatriz Nascimento, "a place where liberty was practiced, where ethnic and ancestral ties were reinvigorated." Nascimento shows in her scholarly work that the *quilombo* exercised "a fundamental role in the historical consciousness of the Black people."

One perceives the *quilombist* ideal, diffuse but consistent, permeating all levels of black life, in the most recondite wanderings and folds of Afro-Brazilian personality. It is a strong and dense ideal that remains, as a rule, repressed by the systems of domination; other times it is sublimated through various defense mechanisms furnished by the individual or collective unconscious. It also happens, at times, that black people appropriate certain mechanisms that the dominant society concedes to them, intending them as instruments of control. In this reversal of ends, black people utilize such unconfessed propositions of domestication like an offensive boomerang. Such is the example left us by João Candeia, composer of sambas and a black man intelligently dedicated to the rehabilitation of his people. He organized the Quilombo Samba School, in the poor outlying areas of Rio de Janeiro, with a deep sense of the political/social value of the samba for the collective progress of the black community. (Samba schools are generally a means of diversionary control, relegating black creative energies to white-controlled commercial channels in the context of Carnaval, the great tourist attraction.)

This important member of the *quilombist* family, Candeia, recently passed away, but up to the instant of this death he sustained a lucid vision of the objectives of the entity he founded and presided over, the Quilombo Samba School, in the spirit of the most legitimate interests of the Afro-Brazilian people. For illustrations, it is enough to leaf through the book he authored, along with Isnard, and to read passages like this one:

> Quilombo Recreational Group for Black Art (Samba School) . . . was born of the necessity to preserve all the influence of the Afro in Brazilian culture. We intended to call the Brazilian people's attention to the roots of Brazilian Black art. The position of "Quilombo" is, principally, against the importation of readymade cultural products produced abroad.

In this passage the authors touch upon an important point in the *quilombist* tradition: the nationalist character of the movement. Nationalism here must not be translated as xenophobia. *Quilombismo,* an anti-imperialist struggle, identifies itself with Pan-Africanism and sustains a radical solidarity with all peoples of the world who struggle against exploitation, oppression, and poverty, as well as with all inequalities motivated by race, color, religion, or ideology. Black nationalism is universalist and internationalist in itself, in that it sees the national liberation of all peoples and respects their unique cultural and political integrity as an imperative for world liberation. Faceless uniformity in the name of a "unity" or "solidarity," conditioned upon conformity to the dictates of any Western social model, is not in the interests of oppressed non-Western peoples. *Quilombismo,* as a nationalist movement, teaches us that every people's struggle for liberation must be rooted in their own cultural identity and historical experience.

In a pamphlet entitled *Ninety Years of Abolition,* published by the Quilombo Samba School, Candeia registers the fact that "It was through the Quilombo, and not the abolitionist movement, that the struggle of the Black people against slavery was developed." The *quilombist* movement is far from having exhausted its historical role. It is as alive today as in the past, for the situation of the black community remains the same, with small alterations of a superficial character. Candeia goes on to say:

> The Quilombos were violently repressed, not only by the forces of the government, but also by individuals interested in the profits they would obtain by returning escapees to their owners. These specialists in hunting escaped slaves earned a name of sad recall: bush captains.

Citation of the bush captains is important. As a rule they were mulattoes, that is, light-skinned blacks assimilated by the white ruling classes and pitted against their African brothers and sisters. We must not allow ourselves today to be divided into adverse categories of "blacks" and "mulattoes," weakening our fundamental identity as Afro-Brazilians, Afro-Americans of all the continent; that is, Africans in the diaspora.

Our Brazil is so vast, so much still unknown and "undiscovered," that we can suppose, without a large margin or error, that there must exist many rural black communities, isolated, without ostensive connection to the small cities and villages, in the interior of the country. These are tiny localities, unlinked to the mainstream of the country's life, maintaining African or quasi-African life styles and habits, under a collective agricultural regimen of subsistence or survival. Many might continue to use their original language brought from Africa, clumsy or transformed, it may be true, but still the same African language, conserved in the species of *quilombismo* in which they live. At times they may even earn special and extensive attention in the press, as has occurred with the community of Cafundo, situated in the area of Salto de Pirapora, in São Paulo state. The members of this African community inherited a plantation from their colonial master; recently their lands have been invaded by surrounding landowners. These white *latifundiarios* (giant landholders), with their slaver mentality, cannot accept the idea that a group of African descendants can possess real property. They are bent on destroying Cafundo. This is not a unique situation, but it is one which has received publicity, mobilizing blacks of the city of São Paulo in their defense. The foremost organization of this nature is ECO (Experiencia Comunitaria), a group that works under the able leadership of Hugo Ferreira da Silva.

In 1975, the first time I visited the town of Conceicão do Mato Dentro, in Minas Gerais state, I had the opportunity of meeting one of the villagers of a black community in that area similar to Cafundo. These Africans had also inherited their property, according to this villager, a black man 104 years old, mentally and physically active and agile. Every day, he would walk a distance of nearly 10 kilometers on foot, and so maintained the contact of his people with the town of Conceicão do Mato Dentro.

The advance of big landowners and real estate speculators onto the lands of black people calls for a broad and intensive investigation. This is happening in the cities as well as in rural areas. It was noted in the magazine *Veja,* for instance:

> Since their long-ago appearance in Salvador, almost two centuries ago, the Candomble *terreiros* (houses of worship) have always been harassed by severe police restrictions. And, at least in the last twenty years, the police siege has been considerably strengthened by a powerful ally: real estate expansion, which has extended to areas distant from the center of the city, where drums resounded. Worse yet, at no time has the Mayor's office sketched legal boundaries to protect these strongholds of Afro-Brazilian culture—even though the capital of Bahia extracts fat dividends from exploitation of the tourism fomented by the magic of the Orishas. And never have sanctions been known to be applied to the unscrupulous landlords of plots neighboring the houses of worship, to take over areas of the *terreiros* with impunity. This was how, a few years back, the Saint George of the Old Mill Beneficient Society, or White House Terreiro, ended up losing half of its former area, 7,700 meters square. Even more unlucky, the Saint Bartholemew of the Old Mill Society of the Federation, or Bogum Candomble, impotently watches the rapid reduction of the sacred space where stands the mythical "tree of Azaudonor"—brought from Africa 150 years ago and periodically attacked by a neighbor who insists upon lopping off its most leafy branches.

With all reason, cinematographer Rubem Confete recently denounced, in a round-table discussion sponsored by the news magazine *Pasquim:*

> How much was robbed from the Black people! I know five families who lost all of their land to the government and to the Catholic Church. Jurandir Santos Melo was the owner of land that stretched from the current airport of Salvador to the city. Today he is a simple taxi driver, living on small savings. The family of Ofelia Pittman owned all the area that today is the MacKensie (University in São Paulo). This is more serious than is generally thought, because there was a time when Black people had representation and economic strength.

Here we see how ruling society closed in the circle of destitution, hunger, and genocide against African descendants. Even those few individuals, the rare exceptions that by some miracle manage to surpass the implacable frontiers of poverty or religious institutions—those who have occupied a certain space over centuries find their estates invaded and their families usurped from their lands!

Quilombismo: A Scientific Historical-Cultural Concept

Conscious of the extent and depth of the problems they confront, black people know that their opposition cannot be exhausted in the attainment of small gains in employment or civil rights, in the context of the dominant capitalist white society and its organized middle class. Black people understand that they will have to defeat all components of the system in force, including its intelligentsia. This segment was and is responsible for the ideological coverup of oppression by way of "scientific" theories of the biosocial inferiority of blacks, and by academic elaboration of the ideology of whitening (socially compulsory miscegenation) or the myth of "racial democracy." This Euro-Brazilian "intelligentsia," along with its European and North-American mentors, fabricated a set of historical or human "sciences" that assisted in the dehumanization of Africans and their descendants, serving the interests of the Eurocentric oppressors. Therefore, European and Euro-Brazilian science is not appropriate to black people's needs. A historical science which does no service to the history of the people it deals with is negating itself.

How can Western human and historical sciences—ethnology, economics, history, anthropology, sociology, etc.—born, cultivated, and defined by other peoples, in an alien socioeconomic context, offer useful and effective service to African people worldwide, their existential realization, their problems, aspirations, and projects? Can the social sciences elaborated in Europe or in the United States be so universal in their application? Black people know in their very flesh the fallaciousness of the "universalism" and "objectivity" of this Eurocentric "science." Indeed, the idea of an historical science that is pure and universal is now passé, even in European circles.

Black people require a scientific knowledge that allows them to formulate theoretically—in systematic and consistent form—their experience of almost five centuries of oppression, resistance, and creative struggle. There will be inevitable errors, perhaps, in our search for systematization of our social values, in our efforts toward self-definition and self-determination of ourselves and our future paths. For centuries we have carried the burden of the crimes and falsities of "scientific" Eurocentrism, its dogmas imposed upon our being as the brands of a definitive, "universal" truth. Now we return to the obstinate "white" segment of Brazilian society its lies, its ideology of European supremacy, the brainwashing with which it intended to rob us of our humanity, our national identity, our dignity, our liberty. By proclaiming the demise of Eurocentric mental colonization, we celebrate the advent of *quilombist* liberation.

Black people have a collective project: the erection of a society founded on justice, equality, and respect for all human beings; on freedom, a society whose intrinsic nature makes economic or racial exploitation impossible; an authentic democracy, founded by the destitute and disinherited of the country. We have no interest in the simple restoration of obsolete types and forms of political, social, and economic institutions; this would serve only to procrastinate the advent of our total and definitive emancipation, which can come only with radical transformation of existing socioeconomic and political structures. We have no interest in proposing an adaptation or reformation of the models of capitalist class society. Such a solution is not to be accepted as an ineluctable mandate. We trust in the mental integrity of the black people, and we believe in the reinvention of ourselves and our history, a reinvention of Afro-Brazilians whose life is founded on our own historical experience, built by utilizing critical and inventive knowledge of our own social and economic institutions, battered as they have been by colonialism and racism. In sum, to reconstruct in the present a society directed toward the future, but taking into account what is still useful and positive in the stores of our past.

An operative conceptual tool must be developed, then, within the guidelines of the immediate needs of the Black Brazilian people. This tool must not and cannot be the fruit of arbitrary or abstract cerebral machinations. Nor can it be a set of imported principles, elaborated from the starting point of other historical contexts and realities. The crystallization of our concepts, definitions, and principles must express black collective experience, in culture and in *praxis,* reincorporating our integrity as a people in our historic time, enriching and expanding our capacity for struggle.

Where do we find such experience? In the *quilombos. Quilombos* does not mean escaped slave, as the conventional definitions have indicated. In means fraternal and free reunion, or encounter; solidarity, living together, existential communion. *Quilombist* society represents an advanced stage in sociopolitical and human progress in terms of economic egalitarianism. Known historical precedents confirm this position. As an economic system, *quilombismo* has meant the adaptation of African traditions of communitarianism and/or Ujamaa to the Brazilian environment. In such a system, relations of production differ basically from those that prevail in the capitalist economy, based on the exploitation and social degradation of work, founded on the concept of profit at any human cost, particularly the cost of the lives of enslaved Africans. *Quilombismo* articulates the diverse levels of collective life whose dialectic interaction proposes complete fulfillment and realization of the creative capacities of the human being. All basic factors and elements of the economy are of collective ownership and use. Work is not defined as a form of punishment, oppression, or exploitation; work is first a form of human liberation, which the citizen enjoys as a right and a social obligation.

The *quilombos* of the sixteenth, seventeenth, eighteenth, and nineteenth centuries left us a patrimony of *quilombist* practice. It is for the black people of today to sustain and amplify the Afro-Brazilian culture of resistance and affirmation of our truth. A method of social analysis, comprehension, and definition of a concrete experience, *quilombismo* expresses scientific theory: a scientific theory inextricably welded to our historical practice, that can effectively contribute to black people's liberation from centuries of inexorable extermination.

Condemned to survive surrounded and permeated by hostility, Afro-Brazilian society has nevertheless persisted throughout almost 490 years, under the sign of permanent tension. It is this tension, the tension of struggle—repression and resistance—that embodies the essence and process of *quilombismo.*

To assure the fullest human condition of the Afro-Brazilian masses is the ethical grounding of *quilombismo,* and its most basic concept. *Quilombismo* is a scientific historical philosophy whose pivotal focal point is the human being, as actor and subject (not merely as passive object, as in the Western scientific tradition), within a worldview and a conception of life in which science constitutes one among many other paths to knowledge.

Pan-African Congress Resolution

Paris, 1919

RESOLUTION

(a) That the Allied and Associated Powers establish a code of law for the international protection of the natives of Africa, similar to the proposed international code for labour.

(b) That the League of Nations establish a permanent Bureau charged with the special duty of overseeing the application of these laws to the political, social, and economic welfare of the natives.

(c) The Negroes of the world demand that hereafter the natives of Africa and the peoples of African descent be governed according to the following principles:

(i) *The Land.* The land and its natural resources shall be held in trust for the natives and at all times they shall have effective ownership of as much land as they can profitably develop.

(ii) *Capital.* The investment of capital and granting of concessions shall be so regulated as to prevent the exploitation of the natives and the exhaustion of the natural wealth of the country. Concessions shall always be limited in time and subject to State control. The growing social needs of the natives must be regarded and the profits taxed for social and material benefit of the natives.

(iii) *Labour.* Slavery and corporal punishment shall be abolished and forced labour except in punishment of crime, and the general conditions of labour shall be prescribed and regulated by the State.

(iv) *Education.* It shall be the right of every native child to learn to read and write his own language, and the language of the trustee nation, at public expense, and to be given technical instruction in some branch of industry. The State shall also educate as large a number of natives as possible in higher technical and cultural training and maintain a corps of native teachers.

(v) *The State.* The natives of Africa must have the right to participate in the Government as fast as their development permits, in conformity with the principle that the Government exists for the natives, and not the natives for the Government. They shall at once be allowed to participate in local and tribal government, according to ancient usage, and this participation shall gradually extend, as education and experience proceed, to the offices of states; to the end that, in time, Africa is ruled by consent of the Africans. . . . Whenever it is proven that African natives are not receiving just treatment at the hands of any State or that any State deliberately excludes its civilised citizens or subjects of Negro descent from its body politic and culture, it shall be the duty of the League of Nations to bring the matter to the notice of the civilised world.

Pan-African Congress Resolution

Manchester, 1945

I

To secure equal opportunities for all colonial and coloured people in Great Britain, this Congress demands that discrimination on account of race, creed or colour be made a criminal offence by law.

That all employments and occupations shall be opened to all qualified Africans, and that to bar such applicants because of race, colour or creed shall be deemed an offence against the law.

In connection with the political situation, the Congress observed:

(a) That since the advent of British, French, Belgian and other Europeans in West Africa, there has been regression instead of progress as a result of systematic exploitations by these alien imperialist Powers. The claims of "partnership," "Trusteeship," "guardianship" and the "mandate system," do not serve the political wishes of the people of West Africa.

(b) That the democratic nature of the indigenous institutions of the peoples of West Africa has been crushed by obnoxious and oppressive laws and regulations, and replaced by autocratic systems of government which are inimical to the wishes of the people of West Africa.

(c) That the introduction of pretentious constitutional reforms in West African territories [is] nothing but spurious attempts on the part of alien imperialist Powers to continue the political enslavement of the peoples.

(d) That the introduction of Indirect Rule is not only an instrument of oppression but also an encroachment on the right of the West African natural rulers.

(e) That the artificial divisions and territorial boundaries created by the imperialist Powers are deliberate steps to obstruct the political unity of the West African peoples.

II

Economic. As regards that West African economic set-up, the Resolution asserted:

(a) That there has been a systematic exploitation of the economic resources of the West African territories by imperialist Powers to the detriment of the inhabitants.

(b) That the industrialisation of West Africa by the indigenes has been discouraged and obstructed by the imperialist rulers, with the result that the standard of living has fallen below subsistence level.

(c) That the land, the rightful property of West Africans, is gradually passing into the hands of foreign Governments and other agencies through various devices and ordinances.

(d) That the workers and farmers of West Africa have not been allowed independent trade unions and co-operative movements without official interference.

(e) That the mining industries are in the hands of foreign monopolies of finance capital, with the result that wherever a mining industry has developed there has been a tendency to deprive the people of their land holdings (e.g., mineral rights in Nigeria and Sierra Leone [are] now the property of the British Government).

(f) That the British Government in West Africa is virtually controlled by a merchants' united front, whose main objective is the exploitation of the people, thus rendering the indigenous population economically helpless.

(g) That when a country is compelled to rely on one crop (e.g., cocoa) for a single monopolistic market, and is obliged to cultivate only for export while at the same time its farmers and workers find themselves in the grip of finance capital, then it is evident that the Government of that country is incompetent to assume responsibility for it.

Commenting on the social needs of the area, the Resolution said:

(a) That the democratic organisations and institutions of the West African peoples have been interfered with, that alien rule has not improved education, health or the nutrition of the West African peoples, but on the contrary tolerates mass illiteracy, ill-health, malnutrition, prostitution and many other social evils.

(b) That organised Christianity in West Africa is identified with the political and economic exploitations of the West African peoples by alien Powers.

III

1. The principles of the Four Freedoms and the Atlantic Charter be put into practice at once.

2. The abolition of land laws which allow Europeans to take land from the Africans. Immediate cessation of any further settlement by Europeans in Kenya or in any other territory in East Africa. All available land to be distributed to the landless Africans.

3. The right of Africans to develop the economic resources of their country without hindrance.

4. The immediate abolition of all racial and other discriminatory laws at once (the Kipande system in particular) and the system of equal citizenship to be introduced forthwith.

5. Freedom of speech, Press, association and assembly.

6. Revision of the system of taxation and of the evil and criminal codes.

7. Compulsory free and uniform education for all children up to the age of sixteen, with free meals, free books and school equipment.

8. Granting of the franchise, i.e., the right of every man and woman over the age of twenty-one to elect and be elected to the Legislative Council, Provincial Council and all other Divisional and Municipal Councils.

9. A state medical, health and welfare service to be made available to all.

10. Abolition of forced labour, and the introduction of the principle of equal pay for equal work.

IV

Declaration to the Colonial Powers

The delegates believe in peace. How could it be otherwise, when for centuries the African peoples have been the victims of violence and slavery? Yet if the Western world is still determined to rule mankind by force, then Africans, as a last resort, may have to appeal to force in the effort to achieve freedom, even if force destroys them and the world.

We are determined to be free. We want education. We want the right to earn a decent living; the right to express our thoughts and emotions, to adopt and create forms of beauty. We demand for Black Africa autonomy and independence, so far and no further than it is possible in this One World for groups and peoples to rule themselves subject to inevitable world unity and federation.

We are not ashamed to have been an age-long patient people. We continue willingly to sacrifice and strive. But we are unwilling to starve any longer while doing the world's drudgery, in order to support by our poverty and ignorance a false aristocracy and a discarded imperialism.

We condemn the monopoly of capital and the rule of private wealth and industry for private profit alone. We welcome economic democracy as the only real democracy.

Therefore, we shall complain, appeal and arraign. We will make the world listen to the facts of our condition. We will fight in every way we can for freedom, democracy and social betterment.

V

Declaration to the Colonial Peoples

We affirm the right of all colonial peoples to control their own destiny. All colonies must be free from foreign imperialist control, whether political or economic.

The people of the colonies must have the right to elect their own Governments, without restrictions from foreign Powers. We say to the peoples of the colonies that they must fight for these ends by all means at their disposal.

The object of imperialist Powers is to exploit. By granting the right to colonial peoples to govern themselves that object is defeated. Therefore, the struggle for political power by colonial and subject peoples is the first step towards, and the necessary prerequisite to, complete social, economic and political emancipation. The Fifth Pan-African Congress therefore calls on the workers and farmers of the colonies to organise effectively. Colonial workers must be in the front of the battle against imperialism. Your weapons—the strike and the boycott—are invincible.

We also call upon the intellectuals and professional classes of the colonies to waken to their responsibilities. By fighting for trade union rights, the right to form co-operatives, freedom of the Press, assembly, demonstration and strike, freedom to print and read the literature which is necessary for the education of the masses, you will be using the only means by which your liberties will be won and maintained. Today there is only one road to effective action—the organisation of the masses. And in that organisation the educated colonials must join. Colonial and subject peoples of the world, Unite!

Paul Robeson
(1898–1976, United States)

The Power of Negro Action

"How long, O Lord, How long?"—that ancient cry of the oppressed is often voiced these days in editorials in the Negro newspapers whose pages are filled with word-and-picture reports of outrages against our people. A photograph of a Negro being kicked by a white mobster brings the vicious blow crashing against the breast of the reader, and there are all the other horrible pictures—burning cross, beaten minister, bombed school, threatened children, mutilated man, imprisoned mother, barricaded family—which show what is going on.

How long? The answer is: *As long as we permit it.* I say that Negro action can be decisive. I say that we ourselves have the power to end the terror and to win for ourselves peace and security throughout the land. The recognition of this fact will bring new vigor, boldness and determination in planning our program of action and new militancy in winning its goals.

The denials and doubts about this idea—the second part of the challenge which confronts us today—are even more evident than those I noted in regard to the first. The diehard racists who shout "Never!" to equal rights, and the gradualists who mumble "Not now," are quite convinced that the Negro is powerless to bring about a different decision. Unfortunately, it is also true that to a large extent the Negro people do not know their own strength and do not see how they can achieve the goals they so urgently desire. The basis for this widespread view is obvious. We are a minority, a tenth of the population of our country. In all the terms in which power is reckoned in America—economic wealth, political office, social privilege—we are in a weak position; and from this the conclusion is drawn that the Negro can do little or nothing to compel a change.

It must be seen, however, that this is not a case of a minority pitting itself against a majority. If it were, if we wanted to gain something for ourselves by taking it away from the more powerful majority, the effort would plainly be hopeless. But that is not the case with our demand. Affirming that we are indeed created equal, we seek the equal rights to which we are entitled under the law. The granting of our demand would not lessen the democratic rights of the white people: on the contrary, it would enormously strengthen the base of democracy for all Americans. We ask for nothing that is not ours by right, and herein lies the great moral power of our demand. It is the admitted *rightness* of our claim which has earned for us the moral support of the majority of white Americans.

The granting of our demand for first-class citizenship, on a par with all others, would not in itself put us in a position of equality. Oppression has kept us on the bottom rungs

Society and Politics

of the ladder, and even with the removal of all barriers we will still have a long way to climb in order to catch up with the general standard of living. But the equal *place* to which we aspire cannot be reached without the equal *rights* we demand, and so the winning of those rights is not a maximum fulfillment but a minimum necessity and we cannot settle for less. Our viewpoint on this matter is not a minority opinion in our country. Though the most rabid champions of "white superiority" are unwilling to test their belief by giving the Negro an equal opportunity, I believe that most white Americans are fair-minded enough to concede that we should be given that chance.

The moral support of the American majority is largely passive today, but what must be recognized—and here we see the decisive power of Negro action—is this:

Wherever and whenever we, the Negro people, claim our lawful rights with all of the earnestness, dignity and determination that we can demonstrate, the moral support of the American people will become an active force on our side.

The most important part of the Little Rock story was not what Governor Faubus and the local mobs did, nor was it what President Eisenhower was moved to do: the important thing was that nine Negro youngsters, backed by their parents, the Negro community and its leadership, resolved to claim their right to attend Central High School. The magnificent courage and dignity these young people displayed in making that claim won the admiration of the American public. Their *action* did more to win the sympathy and support of democratic-minded white people than all the speeches about "tolerance" that have ever been made.

Little Rock was but one of the first skirmishes in the battle to end Jim Crow schools; much greater tests of our determination will soon be at hand. The desegregation of public education is as yet only in the first stages and the hard core of resistance has not been met. But there is no turning back, and the necessity to prepare ourselves for the struggles that lie ahead is urgent.

I have pointed to the sources of strength that exist at home and abroad. What power do we ourselves have?

We have the power of numbers, the power of organization and the power of spirit. Let me explain what I mean.

Sixteen million people are a force to be reckoned with, and indeed there are many nations in the U.N. whose numbers are less. No longer can it be said that the Negro question is a sectional matter: the continuing exodus from the South has spread the Negro community to all parts of the land and has concentrated large numbers in places which are economically and politically the most important in the nation. In recent years much has been written about the strategic position of Negro voters in such pivotal states as New York, Ohio, Pennsylvania, Michigan, Illinois and California, but generally it can be said that the power of our numbers is not seen or acted upon. Let us consider this concept in connection with something that is apparent to all.

Very often these days we see photographs in the newspapers and magazines of a Negro family—the husband, wife, their children—huddled together in their newly purchased or rented home, while outside hundreds of Negro-haters have gathered to throw stones, to howl filthy abuse, to threaten murder and arson; and there may or may not be some policemen at the scene. But something is missing from this picture that ought to be there, and its absence gives rise to a nagging question that cannot be stilled: *Where are the other Negroes?* Where are the hundreds and thousands of other Negroes in that town who ought to be there protecting their own? The *power of numbers* that is missing from the scene would change the whole picture as nothing else could. It is one thing to terrorize a helpless few, but the forces of race hate that brazenly whoop and holler when the odds are a thousand to one are infinitely less bold when the odds are otherwise.

I am not suggesting, of course, that the Negro people should take law enforcement into their own hands. But we have the right and, above all, we have the duty, to bring the strength and support of our entire community to defend the lives and property of each individual family. Indeed, the law itself will move a hundred times quicker whenever it is apparent that the power of our numbers has been called forth. The time has come for the great Negro communities throughout the land—Chicago, Detroit, New York, Birmingham and all the rest—to demonstrate that they will no longer tolerate mob violence against one of their own. In listing the inalienable rights of man, Thomas Jefferson put *life* before *liberty, and the pursuit of happiness;* and it must be clear that for Negro Americans today the issue of *personal security* must be put first, and resolved first, before all other matters are attended to. When the Negro is told that he must "stay in his place," there is always the implicit threat that unless he does so mob violence will be used against him. Hence, as I see it, nothing is more important than to establish the fact that we will no longer suffer the use of mobs against us. Let the Negro people of but a single city respond in an all-out manner at the first sign of a mob—in mass demonstrations, by going on strike, by organizing boycotts—and the lesson will be taught in one bold stroke to people everywhere.

It was an excellent idea to call for a Prayer Pilgrimage for Freedom to assemble in Washington on May 17, 1957, the third anniversary of the Supreme Court decision, and the thousands who gathered there were inspired with a sense of solidarity and were deeply stirred by the speeches that were made. In terms of dignity and discipline the gathering was a matter for great pride. But there was at the same time a sense of disappointment at the size of the rally which did not, as a national mobilization, truly reflect the power of our numbers. Various charges were later made in the press, and heatedly denied, that important elements of leadership had "dragged their feet" in the preparations, but no constructive purpose would be served by going into those arguments here. The point I wish to make is this: When we call for such a mobilization again (and it ought to be done before another three years passes), we must go all-out to rally not tens of thousands but hundreds of thousands in a demonstration that will show we really mean business. And we should do more than listen to speeches and then go quietly home. Our spokesmen should go to the White House and to Congress and, backed by the massed power of our people, present our demands for action. Then they should come back to the assembled people to tell them what "the man" said, so that the people can decide whether they are satisfied or not and what to do about it.

The time for pussyfooting is long gone. If someone or other fears that some politician might be "embarrassed" by being confronted by such a delegation, or is concerned lest such action seem too bold—well, let that timid soul just step aside, for there are many in our ranks who will readily go in to "talk turkey" with any or all of the top men in government. We must get it into our heads—and into every leader's head—that we are not asking "favors" of the Big White Folks when, for example, we insist that the full power of the Executive be used to protect the right of Negroes to register and vote in the South. And when we really turn out for such a demand the answer can only be yes.

The *power of organization,* through which the power of numbers is expressed, is another great strength of the Negro people. Few other areas of American life are as intensively organized as is the Negro community. Some people say that we have far too many organizations—too many different churches and denominations, too many fraternal societies, clubs and associations—but that is what we have and there is no use deploring it. What is important is to recognize a meaningful fact which is so often denied: Negroes can and do band together and they have accomplished remarkable works through their collective efforts. "The trouble with our folks"—how often you have heard it (or perhaps said it yourself)—"is that we just won't get together"; but the plain truth is that we just about do more joining and affiliating than anybody else. "Our folks are just not ready to make financial sacrifices for a good cause," we hear, and yet we see that all over the country congregations of a few hundred poor people contribute and collect thousands of dollars year in and year out for the purposes that inspire them.

The Negro communities *are* organized and that condition is not made less significant by the fact that our people have formed a great number of organizations to meet their needs and desires. Organizations like the N.A.A.C.P., which has won many splendid victories in the courts for our rights and has done much other notable work, deserve a much greater membership and financial support than is now the case. Yet it is clear that to exert fully our power of organization we must bring together, for united action, all of the many organizations which now encompass the masses of our people. The great struggle and victory in Montgomery, Alabama, against Jim Crow buses proved beyond all doubt that the various existing organizations of the Negro community can be effectively united for a common purpose. Of course the factor of leadership, which I shall discuss later in this chapter, is a key point, but what I wish to emphasize here is that the *organizational base* for successful struggle exists in all other communities no less than in Montgomery. And who, in the face of the brilliant organization of every practical detail that was devised and carried through by our people in Montgomery, can still assert that Negroes do not have the capacity for effective collective action? What other mass movement in our country was better planned and carried out?

The central role that was played in Montgomery by the churches and their pastors highlights the fact that the Negro church, which has played such a notable part in our history, is still the strongest base of our power of organization. This is true not only because of the large numbers who comprise the congregations, but because our churches are, in the main, independent *Negro* organizations. The churches and other groups of similar independent character—fraternal orders, women's clubs and so forth—will increasingly take the lead because they are closer to the Negro rank-and-file, more responsive to their needs, and less subject to control by forces outside the Negro community.

Here let me point to a large group among this rank-and-file which is potentially the most powerful and effective force in our community—the two million Negro men and women who are members of organized labor. We are a working people and the pay-envelope of the Negro worker is the measure of our general welfare and progress. Government statistics on average earnings show that for every dollar that the white worker is paid the Negro worker gets only 53 cents; and that the average Negro family has a yearly income of $2,410, compared with an average of $4,339 per year for white families. Here, on the basic bread-and-butter level, is a crucial front in our fight for equality and here the Negro trade unionists are the main force to lead the way.

It must be seen, too, that in relation to our general struggle for civil rights the Negro trade unionists occupy a key position. They comprise a large part of the membership of our community organizations and at the same time they are the largest section of our people belonging to interracial organizations. Hence, the Negro trade union members are a strategic link, a living connection with the great masses of the common people of America who are our natural allies in the struggle for democracy and whose active support must be won for our side in this critical hour.

To our men and women of organized labor I would say: A twofold challenge confronts you. The Negro trade unionists must increasingly exert their influence in every aspect of our people's community life. No church, no fraternal, civic or social organization in our communities must be permitted to continue without the benefit of the knowledge and experience that you have gained through your struggles in the great American labor movement. You are called upon to provide the spirit, the determination, the organizational skill, the firm steel of unyielding militancy to the age-old strivings of our people for equality and freedom.

Secondly, on your shoulders there is the responsibility to rally the strength of the whole trade union movement, white and black, to the battle for liberation of our people. Though you are still largely unrepresented in the top levels of labor leadership, you must use your power of numbers to see to it that the leadership of the A.F.L.–C.I.O., which has shown much concern for the so-called "crusade for freedom" abroad, shall not continue to be silent and unmoving in our crusade for freedom *at home*. You must rally your white fellow workers to support full equality for Negro workers; for their right to work at any job; to receive equal pay for equal work; for an end to Jim Crow unions; for the election of qualified Negroes to positions of union leadership; for fair employment practices in every industry; for trade union educational programs to eliminate the notions of "white superiority" which the employers use to poison the minds of the white workers in order to pit them against you.

I have watched and participated in your militant struggles everywhere I have been these past years—in Chicago with the packinghouse workers; with the auto workers of Detroit; the seamen and longshoremen of the West Coast; the tobacco workers of North Carolina; the miners of Pittsburgh and West Virginia; the steel workers of Illinois, Pennsylvania, Indiana and Ohio; the furriers, clerks and garment workers of New York and Philadelphia; with workers in numerous other places throughout the land—and I feel sure that you will meet the challenge which confronts you today.

To all groups in Negro life I would say that the key to set into motion our power of organization is the concept of *coordinated action*, the bringing together of the many organizations which exist in order to plan and to carry out the common struggle. We know full well that it is not easy to do this. We are divided in many ways—in politics, in religious affiliations, in economic and social classes; and in addition to these group rivalries there are the obstacles of personal ambitions and jealousies of various leaders. But as I move among our people these days, from New York to California, I sense a growing impatience with petty ways of thinking and doing things. I see a rising resentment against control of our affairs by white people, regardless of whether that domination is expressed by the blunt orders of political bosses or more discreetly by the "advice" of white liberals which must be heeded or else. There is a rapidly growing awareness that despite all of our differences it is necessary that we become unified, and I think that the force of that idea will overcome all barriers. Coordinated action will not, of course, come all at once: it will develop in the grass-roots and spread from community to community. And the building of that unity is a task which each of us can undertake wherever we are.

A unified people requires a unified leadership, and let me make very clear what I mean by that. Recently the distinguished Negro journalist Carl T. Rowan, who had published in *Ebony* magazine an interview with me, was himself interviewed about that subject on a radio network program where he said: "It's Robeson's contention that the Negro people will never be free in this country until they speak more or less as one voice, and, very obviously, Robeson feels that that one voice should be something close to his voice."

Actually, that is *not* how I feel, and I would not want Mr. Rowan or anyone else to misunderstand my view of this matter. The one voice in which we should speak must be the expression of our entire people on the central issue which is all-important to every Negro—our right to be free and equal. On many other issues there are great differences among us, and hence it is not possible for any one person, or any group of people, to presume to speak for us all.

Far from making any such claim for myself, what I am advocating is in fact the opposite idea! I advocate a unity based upon our common viewpoint as Negroes, a nonpartisan unity, a unity in which we subordinate all that divides us, a unity which excludes no one, a unity in which no faction or group is permitted to impose its particular outlook on others. A unified leadership of a unified movement means that people of *all* political views—conservatives, liberals and radicals—must be represented therein. Let there be but one requirement made without exception: that Negro leadership, and every man and woman in that leadership, place the interests of our people, and the struggle for those interests, above all else.

There is a need—an urgent need—for a national conference of Negro leadership, not of a handful but a broad representative gathering of leadership from all parts of the country, from all walks of life, from every viewpoint, to work out a *common program of action* for Negro Americans in the crisis of our times. Such a program does not exist today and without it we are a ship without a rudder; we can only flounder around on a day-to-day basis, trying to meet developments with patchwork solutions. We must chart a course to be followed in the stormy days that are here and in the greater storms that are on the way, a course that heads full square for freedom.

The need for a *central fund*, not only for legal purposes but for all the purposes of Negro coordinated action, has been expressed in various editorials in the press and else-where; and the national conference I speak of could meet this need. A central fund would be a "community chest" to help our struggles everywhere. Nonpartisan and not con-trolled by any single organization, this fund would be a national institution of our whole people, and a well-organized campaign to build it would meet with a generous response from Negro America. And more: such a fund would undoubtedly receive a great deal of support from white people who sympathize with our struggle.

If we must think boldly in terms of the power of numbers, we must likewise think big in terms of organization. Our cause is the cause of all, and so our methods of reaching our goal must be such that all of our people can play a part. The full potential of the Negro people's power of organization must be achieved in every city and state throughout the land.

The *power of spirit* that our people have is intangible, but it is a great force that must be unleashed in the struggles of today. A spirit of steadfast determination, exaltation in the face of trials—it is the very soul of our people that has been formed through all the long and weary years of our march toward freedom. It is the deathless spirit of the great ones who have led our people in the past—Douglass, Tubman and all the others—and of the millions who kept "a-inching along." That spirit lives in our people's songs—in the sub-lime grandeur of "Deep River," in the driving power of "Jacob's Ladder," in the militancy of "Joshua Fit the Battle of Jericho," and in the poignant beauty of all our spirituals.

It lives in every Negro mother who wants her child "to grow up and be somebody," as it lives in our common people everywhere who daily meet insult and outrage with quiet courage and optimism. It is that spirit which gives that "something extra" to our athletes, to our artists, to all who meet the challenge of public performance. It is the spirit of little

James Gordon of Clay, Kentucky, who, when asked by a reporter why he wanted to go to school with white children, replied: "Why shouldn't I?"; and it is the spirit of all the other little ones in the South who have walked like mighty heroes through menacing mobs to go to school. It is the spirit of the elderly woman of Montgomery who explained her part in the bus boycott by saying: "When I rode in the Jim Crow buses my body was riding but my soul was walking, but now when my body is walking my soul is riding!"

Yes, that power of the spirit is the pride and glory of my people, and there is no human quality in all of America that can surpass it. It is a force only for good: there is no hatefulness about it. It exalts the finest things of life—justice and equality, human dignity and fulfillment. It is of the earth, deeply rooted, and it reaches up to the highest skies and mankind's noblest aspirations. It is time for this spirit to be evoked and exemplified in all we do, for it is a force mightier than all our enemies and will triumph over all their evil ways.

For Negro action to be decisive—given the favorable opportunity which I have outlined . . . and the sources of strength indicated above—still another factor is needed: *effective Negro leadership*. In discussing this subject I shall not engage in any personalities, nor is it my intention either to praise or blame the individuals who today occupy top positions in our ranks. Such critical appraisal must, of course, be made of their leaders by the Negro people, and so I would like here to discuss not this or that person but rather the *principles* of the question, the standards for judgment, the character of leadership that is called for today.

The term "leadership" has been used to express many different concepts, and many of these meanings have nothing to do with what I am concerned with here. Individuals attain prominence for a wide variety of reasons, and often people who have climbed up higher on the ladder are called leaders though they make it plain that their sole interest is personal advancement and the more elevated they are above all other Negroes the better they like it. Then, too, it has been traditional for the dominant group of whites, in local communities and on a national scale as well, to designate certain individuals as "Negro leaders," regardless of how the Negro people feel about it; and the idea is that Negro leadership is something that white folks can bestow as a favor or take away as punishment.

The concept that I am talking about has nothing to do with matters of headline prominence, personal achievement or popularity with the powers-that-be. I am concerned, rather, with Negro leadership in the struggle for Negro rights. This includes those who are directly in charge of the organizations established for such purpose, and many others as well—the leaders of Negro churches, fraternal and civic organizations, elected representatives in government, trade union officials, and others whose action or inaction directly affects our common cause.

The primary quality that Negro leadership must possess, as I see it, is *a single-minded dedication to their people's welfare*. Any individual Negro, like any other person, may have many varied interests in life, but for the true leader all else must be subordinated to the interests of those whom he is leading. If today it can be said that the Negro people of the United States are lagging behind the progress being made by colored peoples in other lands, one basic cause for it has been that all too often Negro leadership here has lacked the selfless passion for their people's welfare that has characterized the leaders of the colonial liberation movements. Among us there is a general recognition—and a grudging acceptance—of the fact that some of our leaders are not only unwilling to make sacrifices but they must see some gain for themselves in whatever they do. A few crumbs for a few is

Society and Politics

too often hailed as "progress for the race." To live in freedom one must be prepared to die to achieve it, and while few if any of us are ever called upon to make that supreme sacrifice, no one can ignore the fact that in a difficult struggle those who are in the forefront may suffer cruel blows. He who is not prepared to face the trials of battle will never lead to a triumph. This spirit of dedication, as I have indicated, is abundantly present in the ranks of our people but progress will be slow until it is much more manifest in the character of leadership.

Dedication to the Negro people's welfare is one side of a coin: the other side is *independence.* Effective Negro leadership must rely upon and be responsive to no other control than the will of their people. We have allies—important allies—among our white fellow-citizens, and we must ever seek to draw them closer to us and to gain many more. But the Negro people's movement must be led by *Negroes,* not only in terms of title and position but in reality. Good advice is good no matter what the source and help is needed and appreciated from wherever it comes, but Negro action cannot be decisive if the advisers and helpers hold the guiding reins. For no matter how well-meaning other groups may be, the fact is our interests are secondary at best with them.

Today such outside controls are a factor in reducing the independence and effectiveness of Negro leadership. I do not have in mind the dwindling group of Uncle Toms who shamelessly serve even an Eastland; happily, they are no longer of much significance. I have in mind, rather, those practices of Negro leadership that are based upon the idea that it is white power rather than Negro power that must be relied upon. This concept has been traditional since Booker T. Washington, and it has been adhered to by many who otherwise reject all notions of white supremacy. Even Marcus Garvey, who rose to leadership of a nationalist mass movement in the 1920's and who urged that the Negro peoples of the world "go forward to the point of destiny as laid out by themselves," believed that white power was decisive. Indeed, no one has stated the idea more clearly than Garvey did in his essay "The Negro's Place in World Reorganization," in which he said:

> The white man of America has become the natural leader of the world. He, because of his exalted position, is called upon to help in all human efforts. From nations to individuals the appeal is made to him for aid in all things affecting humanity, so, naturally, there can be no great mass movement or change without first acquainting the leader on whose sympathy and advice the world moves.

Much has changed since those words were written, and I have no doubt that if Garvey were alive today he would recognize that the "white man of America" is no longer all-powerful and that the colored peoples of the world are moving quite independently of that "sympathy and advice."

In Booker Washington's day it was the ruling white man of the South whose sympathy was considered indispensable; today it is the liberal section of the dominant group in the North whose goodwill is said to be the hope for Negro progress. It is clear that many Negro leaders act or desist from acting because they base themselves on this idea. Rejecting the concept that "white is right" they embrace its essence by conceding that "might is right." To the extent that this idea is prevalent in its midst, Negro leadership lacks the quality of independence without which it cannot be effective.

Dedication and independence—these are the urgent needs. Other qualities of leadership exist in abundance: we have many highly trained men and women, experienced in law, in politics, in civic affairs; we have spokesmen of great eloquence, talented organizers, skilled negotiators. If I have stressed those qualities which are most needed on the national level, it is not from any lack of appreciation for much that is admirable. On the local level, especially, there are many examples of dedicated and independent leadership. Indeed, the effective use of Negro power—of numbers, of organization, of spirit—in Montgomery was the result of Negro leadership of the highest caliber. And the whole nation has witnessed the heroic dedication of many other leaders in the South, who, at the risk of their lives and all they hold dear, are leading their people's struggles. There are many from our ranks who ought to be elevated to national leadership because by their deeds they have fully demonstrated their right to be there.

We should broaden our conception of leadership and see to it that all sections of Negro life are represented on the highest levels. There must be room at the top for people from down below. I'm talking about the majority of our folks who work in factory and field: they bring with them that down-to-earth view which is the highest vision, and they can hammer and plow in more ways than one. Yes, we need more of them in the leadership, and we need them in a hurry.

We need more of our women in the higher ranks, too, and who should know better than the children of Harriet Tubman, Sojourner Truth and Mary Church Terrell that our womenfolk have often led the way. Negro womanhood today is giving us many inspiring examples of steadfast devotion, cool courage under fire and brilliant generalship in our people's struggles; and here is a major source for new strength and militancy in Negro leadership on every level.

But if there are those who ought to be raised to the top, there are some others already there who should be retired. I have noted, in another connection, that the Negro people are patient and long-suffering—sometimes to a fault. The fault is often expressed by permitting unworthy leaders to get away with almost anything. It is as if once a man rises to leadership, his responsibility to his people is no longer binding upon him.

But, in these critical days, we ought to become a little less tolerant, a little more demanding that all Negro leaders "do right." I have in mind, for example, the case of an important Negro leader in a large Northern city, who, at the time when mobs were barring the Negro children from high school in Little Rock and beating up Negro newspapermen, got up before his people and said: "We cannot meet this crisis by force against force. Under no circumstances can Federal troops be used. This would be a confession of our moral decadence, it would precipitate a second Civil War—it would open the stopper and send democracy down the drain for at least our generation and maybe forever." These words, so utterly devoid of any concern for his people and lacking all regard for the truth, were hardly spoken before the President sent in Federal troops! No civil war was started, democracy got a new lease on life, the mobs were dispersed, the Negro children were escorted to school and for the first time since 1876 the lawful force of the Federal government was called out against the lawless force of White Supremacy in the South.

When, as in this case, a Negro leader vigorously opposes that which he should be fighting for and makes it clear that some other folks' interests are of more concern to him than his own people's—well, the so-called "politically-wise" may say: "Oh, that's just politics—forget it." But the so-called "politically-dumb" just can't see it that way. How can we be led by people who are not going our way?

There are others, honest men beyond all doubt and sincerely concerned with their people's welfare, who seem to feel that it is the duty of a leader to discourage Negro mass action. They think that best results can be achieved by the quiet negotiations they carry on. And so when something happens that arouses the masses of people, and when the

Society and Politics

people gather in righteous anger to demand that militant actions be started, such men believe it their duty to cool things off.

We saw this happen not long ago when from coast to coast there was a great upsurge of the people caused by the brutal lynching of young Emmett Till. At one of the mass protest meetings that was held, I heard one of our most important leaders address the gathering in words to this effect: "You are angry today, but you are not going to do anything about it. I know that you won't do anything. You clamor for a march on Mississippi but none of you will go. So let's stop talking about marching. Just pay a dollar to our organization and leave the rest to your leaders. If you want to do something yourself, let each of you go to your district Democratic leader and talk to him about it."

Well, what would a congregation think of their pastor if the best he could do was to tell them: "You are all a bunch of sinners, and nothing can make you do right. There is no good in you and I know it. So, brothers and sisters, just put your contributions on the collection plate, go home and leave your salvation to me."

No, a leader should encourage, not discourage; he should rally the people, not disperse them. A wet blanket can never be the banner of freedom.

Of course there must be negotiations made in behalf of our rights, but unless the negotiators are backed by an aroused and militant people, their earnest pleas will be of little avail. For Negro action to be effective—to be decisive, as I think it can be—it must be *mass* action. The power of the ballot can be useful only if the masses of voters are united on a common program; obviously, if half the Negro people vote one way and the other half the opposite way, not much can be achieved. The individual votes are cast and counted, but the group power is cast away and discounted.

Mass action—in political life and elsewhere—is Negro power in motion; and it is the way to win.

An urgent task which faces us today is an all-out struggle to defeat the efforts of the White Supremacists to suppress the N.A.A.C.P. in the South. As in South Africa, where the notorious "Suppression of Communism Act" is used to attack the liberation movement, the enemies of Negro freedom in our country have accused the N.A.A.C.P. of being a "subversive conspiracy" and the organization has been outlawed in Louisiana, Texas and Alabama, and legally restricted in Georgia, Virginia, South Carolina and Mississippi. City ordinances, as in Little Rock, are also used for this purpose.

The indifference with which various other organizations viewed the suppression in 1955 of the Council on African Affairs, which was falsely labeled a "Communist front," should not be repeated now by any group in the case of the N.A.A.C.P. The Red-baiting charges against that organization are utterly untrue, as the makers of such charges know full well; and those elements in Negro leadership who have in the past resorted to Red-baiting as a "smart" tactic should realize that such methods serve no one but our people's worst enemies.

Throughout the South—in Little Rock, in Montgomery and elsewhere—the state and local leaders of the N.A.A.C.P. have set a heroic and inspiring example for Negro leadership everywhere. All of us—the Negro people of the entire country—must rally now to sustain and defend them.

In presenting these ideas on the power of Negro action, the sources of that power and the character of leadership necessary to direct that power most effectively, I offer them for consideration and debate at this time when the challenge of events calls for clarity of vision and unity of action. No one, obviously, has all the answers, and the charting of our course must be done collectively. There must be a spirit of give and take, and clashing viewpoints must find a common ground. Partisan interests must be subordinated to Negro interests—by each of us. Somehow we must find the way to set aside all that divides us and come together, Negroes all. Our unity will strengthen our friends and win many more to our side; and our unity will weaken our foes who already can see the handwriting on the wall.

To be free—to walk the good American earth as equal citizens, to live without fear, to enjoy the fruits of our toil, to give our children every opportunity in life—that dream which we have held so long in our hearts is today the destiny that we hold in our hands.

Society and Politics

Declaration and Resolutions of the First Conference of Independent African States

Accra, April 15–22, 1958

DECLARATION

We, the African States assembled here in Accra, in this our first Conference, conscious of our responsibilities to humanity and especially to the peoples of Africa, and desiring to assert our African Personality on the side of peace, hereby proclaim and solemnly reaffirm our unswerving loyalty to the Charter of the United Nations, the Universal Declaration of Human Rights and the Declaration of the Asian-African Conference held at Bandung.

We further assert and proclaim the unity among ourselves and our solidarity with the dependent peoples of Africa as well as our friendship with all nations. We resolve to preserve the unity of purpose and action in international affairs which we have forged among ourselves in this historic Conference; to safeguard our hard-won independence, sovereignty and territorial integrity; and to preserve among ourselves the fundamental unity of outlook on foreign policy so that a distinctive African Personality will play its part in co-operation with other peace-loving nations to further the cause of peace.

We pledge ourselves to apply all our endeavours to avoid being committed to any action which might entangle our countries to the detriment of our interests and freedom; to recognise the right of the African peoples to independence and self-determination and to take appropriate steps to hasten the realisation of this right; to affirm the right of the Algerian people to independence and self-determination and to exert all possible effort to hasten the realisation of their independence; to uproot forever the evil of racial discrimination in all its forms wherever it may be found; to persuade the Great Powers to discontinue the production and testing of nuclear and thermo-nuclear weapons; and to reduce conventional weapons.

Furthermore, mindful of the urgent need to raise the living standards of our peoples by developing to the fullest possible advantage the great and varied resources of our lands, We hereby pledge ourselves to coordinate our economic planning through a joint economic effort and study the economic potentialities, the technical possibilities and related problems existing in our respective States; to promote co-ordinated industrial planning either through our own individual efforts and/or through co-operation with Specialised Agencies of the United Nations; to take measures to increase trade among our countries by improving communications between our respective countries; and to encourage the investment of foreign capital and skills provided they do not compromise the independence, sovereignty and territorial integrity of our States.

Desirous of mobilising the human resources of our respective countries in furtherance of our social and cultural aspirations, We will endeavour to promote and facilitate the exchange of teachers, professors, students, exhibitions, educational, cultural and scientific material which will improve cultural relations between the African States and inculcate greater knowledge amongst us through such efforts as joint youth festivals, sporting events, etc.; We will encourage and strengthen studies of African culture, history and geography in the institutions of learning in the African States; and We will take all measures in our respective countries to ensure that such studies are correctly oriented.

We have charged our Permanent Representatives at the United Nations to be the permanent machinery for co-ordinating all matters of common concern to our States; for examining and making recommendations on concrete practical steps for implementing our decisions; and for preparing the grounds for future Conferences.

Faithful to the obligations and responsibilities which history has thrown upon us as the vanguard of the complete emancipation of Africa, we do hereby affirm our dedication to the causes which we have proclaimed.

RESOLUTIONS

1. Exchange of Views on Foreign Policy

The Conference of Independent African States,
    Having made the widest exchange of views on all aspects of foreign policy,
    Having achieved a unanimity on fundamental aims and principles,
    Desiring to pursue a common foreign policy with a view to safeguarding the hard-won independence, sovereignty and territorial integrity of the Participating States,
    Deploring the division of the greater part of the world into two antagonistic blocs,
    1. Affirms the following fundamental principles:
    A. Unswerving loyalty to and support of the Charter of the United Nations and respect for decisions of the United Nations;
    B. Adherence to the principles enunciated at the Bandung Conference, namely:
        (i) Respect for the fundamental human rights and for the purposes and principles of the Charter of the United Nations.
        (ii) Respect for the sovereignty and territorial integrity of all nations.
        (iii) Recognition of the equality of all races and of the equality of all nations, large and small.
        (iv) Abstention from intervention or interference in the internal affairs of another country.
        (v) Respect for the right of each nation to defend itself singly or collectively in conformity with the Charter of the United Nations.
        (vi) Abstention from the use of arrangements of collective defence to serve the particular interests of any of the big Powers. Abstention by any country from exerting pressure on other countries.
        (vii) Refraining from acts or threats of aggression or the use of force against the territorial integrity or political independence of any country.
        (viii) Settlement of all international disputes by peaceful means such as negotiation, conciliation, arbitration or judicial settlement, as well as other peaceful

means of the parties' own choice in conformity with the Charter of the United Nations.

    (ix) Promotion of mutual interest and co-operation.

    (x) Respect for justice and international obligations.

2. Affirms its convictions that all Participating Governments shall avoid being committed to any action which might entangle them to the detriment of their interest and freedom;

3. Believes that as long as the fundamental unity of outlook on foreign policy is preserved, the Independent African States will be able to assert a distinctive African Personality which will speak with a concerted voice in the cause of Peace in co-operation with other peace-loving nations at the United Nations and other international forums.

2. The Future of the Dependent Territories in Africa

The Conference of Independent African States,

Recognising that the existence of colonialism in any shape or form is a threat to the security and independence of the African States and to world peace,

Considering that the problems and the future of dependent territories in Africa are not the exclusive concern of the Colonial Powers but the responsibility of all members of the United Nations and in particular of the Independent African States,

Condemning categorically all colonial systems still enforced in our Continent and which impose arbitrary rule and repression on the people of Africa,

Convinced that a definite date should be set for the attainment of independence by each of the Colonial Territories in accordance with the will of the people of the territories and the provisions of the Charter of the United Nations,

1. Calls upon the Administering Powers to respect the Charter of the United States in this regard, and to take rapid steps to implement the provisions of the Charter and the political aspirations of the people, namely self-determination and independence, according to the will of the people;

2. Calls upon the Administering Powers to refrain from repression and arbitrary rule in these territories and to respect all human rights as provided for in the Charter of the United Nations and the Universal Declaration of Human Rights;

3. Calls upon the Administering Powers to bring to an end immediately every form of discrimination in these territories;

4. Recommends that all Participating Governments should give all possible assistance to the dependent peoples in their struggle to achieve self-determination and independence;

5. Recommends that the Independent African States assembled here should offer facilities for training and educating peoples of the dependent territories;

6. Decides that the 15th April of every year be celebrated as Africa Freedom Day.

3. The Question of Algeria

The Conference of Independent African States,

Deeply concerned by the continuance of war in Algeria and the denial by France to the Algerian people of the right of independence and self-determination despite various

United Nations resolutions and appeals urging a peaceful settlement, notably the offer of good offices made by the Moroccan and Tunisian Heads of State,

Considering that the present situation in Algeria constitutes a threat to international peace and the security of Africa in particular,

1. Recognises the right of the Algerian people to independence and self-determination;

2. Deplores the grave extent of hostilities and bloodshed resulting from the continuance of the war in Algeria;

3. Urges France

(a) to recognise the right of the people of Algeria to independence and self-determination;

(b) to put an end to the hostilities and to withdraw all her troops from Algeria;

(c) to enter into immediate peaceful negotiation with the Algerian Liberation Front with a view to reaching a final and just settlement;

4. Appeals to all peace-loving nations to exercise pressure on France to adopt a policy which is in conformity with the principles of the Charter of the United Nations;

5. Appeals to the friends and allies of France to refrain from helping France, whether directly or indirectly, in her military operations in Algeria;

6. Affirms its determination to make every possible effort to help the Algerian people towards the attainment of independence;

7. Recommends that the representatives of the Independent African States at the United Nations be instructed by their various Governments to consult each other constantly and acquaint members of the United Nations with true states of affairs in Algeria and solicit their support for a just and peaceful settlement and to recommend to the Independent African States measures which may from time to time become necessary to be taken and in particular find ways and means whereby the Independent African States may enlighten world opinion on the Algerian situation including the appointment of a mission as soon as possible to tour the capitals of the world to enlist world support of Governments.

4. Racialism

The Conference of Independent African States,

Considering that the practice of racial discrimination and segregation is evil and inhuman,

Deeply convinced that racialism is a negation of the basic principles of human rights and dignity to the extent where it is becoming an element of such explosiveness which is spreading its poisonous influence more and more widely in some parts of Africa that it may well engulf our Continent in violence and bloodshed,

Noting with abhorrence the recent statement made by the head of the South African Government on his re-election to the effect that he will pursue a more relentless policy of discrimination and persecution of the coloured people in South Africa,

1. Condemns the practice of racial discrimination and segregation in all its aspects all over the world, especially in the Union of South Africa, in the Central African Federation, Kenya and in other parts of Africa;

2. Appeals to the religious bodies and spiritual leaders of the world to support all efforts directed towards the eradication of racialism and segregation;

3. Calls upon all members of the United Nations and all peoples of the world to associate themselves with the Resolutions passed by the United Nations and the Bandung Conference condemning this inhuman practice;

4. Calls upon all members of the United Nations to intensify their efforts to combat and eradicate this degrading form of injustice;

5. Recommends that all Participating Governments should take vigorous measures to eradicate where they arise vestiges of racial discrimination in their respective countries.

5. Steps to Be Taken to Safeguard the Independence, Sovereignty and the Territorial Integrity of the Independent African States

The Conference of Independent African States,

Determined to safeguard the hard-won independence, sovereignty and territorial integrity of each of its members,

Believing that the getting together and consulting among Independent African States, as in the present Conference of Accra, is essential for the effectiveness of their contribution to world peace,

1. Declares the determination of all Participating Governments

    (a) to respect the independence, sovereignty and territorial integrity of one another,

    (b) to co-operate with one another to safeguard their independence, sovereignty and territorial integrity,

    (c) to co-operate in their economic, technical and scientific developments and in raising the standard of living of their respective peoples,

    (d) to resort to direct negotiations to settle differences among themselves and if necessary to conciliation or mediation by other African Independent States;

2. Condemns all forms of outside interference directed against the independence, sovereignty and territorial integrity of the Independent African States.

6. Togoland Under French Administration

The Conference of Independent African States,

Having examined the memorandum on the situation in Togoland under French Administration submitted by the Juvento Party, and the statement made by the Representative of this Party during the hearing granted to him in the Conference,

Bearing in mind the objectives of the International Trusteeship System and the objectives proclaimed by the Bandung Conference,

Having regard to the extremely important responsibilities laid upon the Legislative Assembly to be elected on 27th April, 1958, as to the future of the territory by paragraphs 7 and 8 of the operative part of the United Nations Resolution of 29th November, 1957,

1. Expresses grave concern regarding the present electoral laws and system of the Territory;

2. Strongly urges that the Administering Authority will co-operate fully with the United Nations Commissioner in order to ensure fair and democratic elections in the Territory.

7. Cameroons Under French Administration

The Conference of Independent African States,

Having examined the Memorandum on the situation in the Cameroons under French Administration submitted by the Union of the Populations of Cameroons, and the statement made by the Representative of this Party during the hearing granted to him in the Conference,

Bearing in mind the objectives of the International Trusteeship System and the objectives proclaimed by the Bandung Conference,

1. Condemns the use of military force against the unarmed people in the Trust Territory of the Cameroons under French Administration as contrary to the spirit of the United Nations;

2. Calls upon the Administrating Powers to comply with the Charter of the United Nations and satisfy the legitimate aspirations of the people concerned by opening direct negotiations with their representatives;

3. Appeals to the United Nations to intensify its efforts in helping the people of the Cameroons to achieve their legitimate political aspirations.

8. Examination of Ways and Means of Promoting Economic Co-Operation Between the African States, Based on the Exchange of Technical, Scientific and Educational Information, with Special Regard to Industrial Planning and Agricultural Development

The Conference of Independent African States,

Having discussed the economic and social conditions in their respective countries,

Considering that these countries have great and various economic resources, mineral, agriculture and animal,

Considering that there are now possibilities for commercial exchange between Independent African States and that these possibilities should be greatly encouraged,

Considering that steps should be taken to bring about economic emancipation in these countries,

Considering that hitherto non-African forces have arbitrarily divided the African Continent into economic regions, and that the Conference does not recognise this division,

Considering further that Africa could be developed as an economic unit,

Noting that the incorporation of dependent African territories in the economic systems of Colonial Powers is not in the best interests of these peoples,

Recommends to the Participating African States:

1. The establishment within each Independent African State of an Economic Research Committee to survey the economic conditions and to study the economic and technical problems within the State;

2. The establishment of a Joint Economic Research Commission

(a) to co-ordinate information and exchange of views on economic and technical matters of the various Independent African States;

(b) to find measures whereby trade among African countries could be developed and encouraged;

(c) to make proper and detailed investigation as to the possibilities of co-ordinating the economic planning in each State towards the achievement of an all-African economic co-operation;

(d) to find ways and means for common industrial planning within the African States and the possibilities of making available mineral resources and other African products among the African States;

(e) to lay down proposals by which Independent African States can receive foreign capital and employ foreign experts, and to encourage co-operation with other countries in such manner as not to affect their independence, sovereignty and unity;

3. To take steps in order to collect and exchange knowledge and technological information among themselves;

4. To establish joint African enterprises;

5. To hold economic conferences and African exhibitions;

6. To strengthen their co-operation with the Specialised Agencies of the United Nations and especially with the newly proposed Economic Commission for Africa;

7. To make joint efforts as far as practicable to construct means of communications between African States;

8. To investigate the possibility of eventual establishing of an African common market;

9. To provide facilities for exchange of labour and labour information and to encourage co-operation among national trade union organisations;

10. To strengthen the co-operation with the International Labour Organisation;

11. To take joint action for the prevention of disease among human beings, in agriculture and in animal husbandry, and to act against the ravages of locusts;

12. To ensure the establishment of equitable social and economic policies which will provide national prosperity and social security for all citizens.

9. On the Cultural Level, the Formulation of Concrete Proposals for the Exchange of Visiting Missions Between the Various Countries, Both Government and Non-Government, Which May Lead to First-Hand Knowledge of One Country to Another, and to a Mutual Appreciation of Their Respective Cultures

The Conference of Independent African States,

Having made the wide exchange of views on all aspects of the cultures of all Participating Countries,

Desiring to promote the widest dissemination of the cultures of all Participating Countries,

A. Upholds the principles of the Charter of the United Nations and reaffirms the principles approved by the Bandung Conference of April, 1955, concerning Cultural co-operation, and accordingly;

1. States that colonialism is prejudicial to national culture and as such hinders any possible cultural co-operation;

2. Calls for the development of Cultural Co-operation among African States in the larger context of world co-operation and in the spirit of the United Nations Educational, Scientific and Cultural Organisation;

B. Recommends to all Participating Members:

1. To promote and facilitate the exchange of teachers and professors;

2. To encourage the establishment of cultural centres in each other's country on the approval of the country in which such a centre may be established and in conformity with its laws, regulations and practices;

3. To encourage and facilitate the exchange of their students, each providing a certain number of scholarships for students from other African countries;

4. To facilitate the exchange of exhibitions, educational, scientific and cultural material including books, periodicals, bulletins, audio visual aids and other cultural and educational material;

5. To ensure that syllabi of history and geography applied in the schools and educational institutions of each include such material as may help to give each student an accurate information of the way of life and culture in the other African countries;

6. To spare no efforts to revise history and geography, text books and syllabi used in their schools with the view to removing any incorrect information due to colonial or other foreign influences;

7. To co-ordinate their school systems at all levels and to recognise the certificates, diplomas and degrees awarded by their educational institutions and universities of equivalent status;

8. To encourage reciprocal visits by their different organisations of youths, teachers, Press, labour, women, artists, sports, etc., granting them all possible facilities;

9. To strive to include principal African languages in the curriculum of the secondary school and colleges with the view to facilitating the cultural co-operation envisaged;

10. To hold inter-African periodic and *ad hoc* conferences for their educators, scientists, men of letters, journalists, etc., with the view to discussing common problems and to extend all possible facilities for such purposes;

11. To conclude mutual cultural agreements among them for the promotion of cultural co-operation;

12. To encourage in their universities and institutes of higher learning research on African culture and civilisation creating fellowships for this purpose;

13. To encourage the establishment of African publishing centres and to make concerted efforts to publish an African journal edited and contributed to by Africans introducing Africa's culture, civilisation and development to the world and to the various African countries;

14. To set an annual prize for works which promote closer solidarity among the African States, the ideas of liberty, friendship and peace and which disseminate knowledge about African civilisation and culture;

15. To encourage the translation of books dealing with African culture and civilisation into their principal languages, e.g. creating fellowships for this purpose;

16. To establish an annual inter-African sports meeting and an annual youth festival;

17. To set up, each in its respective country, a local organisation whose functions will be the promotion and development of cultural co-operation among African countries.

10. Consideration of the Problem of International Peace and Conformity with the Charter of the United Nations and the Reaffirmation of the Principles of the Bandung Conference

The Conference of Independent African States,

Alarmed at the prospect of nuclear and thermo-nuclear energy being used by the Great Powers for military purposes,

Desiring to strengthen their contribution to world peace and security,

Realising that world peace is a prerequisite for the progress and prosperity of all peoples,

Taking into account the fact that no African nation is at present represented in the international bodies concerned with the problems of disarmament,

1. Calls upon the Great Powers to discontinue the production of nuclear and thermo-nuclear weapons and to suspend all such tests not only in the interest of world peace but as a symbol of their avowed devotion to the rights of man;

2. Views with grave alarm and strongly condemns all atomic tests in any part of the world and in particular the intention to carry out such tests in the Sahara;

3. Appeals to the Great Powers to use atomic, nuclear and thermo-nuclear energy exclusively for peaceful purposes;

4. Affirms the view that the reduction of conventional armaments is essential in the interest of international peace and security and appeals to the Great Powers to make every possible effort to reach a settlement of this important matter;

5. Condemns the policy of using the sale of arms as a means of exerting pressure on Governments and interfering in the internal affairs of other countries;

6. Urges the United Nations to ensure that the African nations are represented equitably on all international bodies concerned with the problems of disarmament;

7. Considers that meeting and consultation on international affairs should not be limited to the big Powers;

8. Expresses its deep concern over the non-compliance with United Nations resolutions, calls upon the Member States to respect such resolutions, and urges a just solution of the outstanding international problems;

9. Expresses its deep concern over the question of Palestine which is a disturbing factor of World Peace and Security, and urges a just solution of the Palestine question;

10. Expresses its deep concern over the South-West African and similar questions which are disturbing factors of World Peace and Security, and urges a just solution to them.

11. The Setting Up of a Permanent Machinery After the Conference

The Conference of Independent African States,

Firmly convinced that a machinery for consultation and co-operation is essential,

1. Decides to constitute the Permanent Representatives of the Participating Governments at the United Nations as the informal permanent machinery,

(a) for co-ordinating all matters of common concern to the African States,

(b) for examining and making recommendations on concrete practical steps which may be taken to implement the decisions of this and similar future conferences, and

(c) for making preparatory arrangements for future conferences of Independent African States;

2. Agrees that meetings of Foreign Ministers, other Ministers or experts be convened from time to time as and when necessary to study and deal with particular problems of common concern to the African States;

3. Agrees that the Conference of the Independent African States should be held at least once every two years;

4. Agrees that the next Conference shall be held within the next two years and accepts the kind invitation of the Government of Ethiopia to hold the next Conference in Addis Ababa.

Maulana Karenga
(b.\1941, United States)

The Nguzo Saba (The Seven Principles):
Their Meaning and Message

The Nguzo Saba are a fundamental communitarian value system which serves as both a central part of Kawaida philosophy and the core of the African American and Pan-African holiday of Kwanzaa. They are posed as the matrix and minimum set of values African Americans need to rescue and reconstruct their lives in their own image and interest and build and sustain an Afrocentric family, community and culture. They were selected in terms of both tradition and reason. Selected from the African communitarian tradition, the Nguzo Saba were also chosen with an appreciation for where we are now as a people and what challenges we face and must deal with successfully as a people. Our most definitive condition is that we are a community in struggle and our values should reflect and lend support to this struggle. The struggle is none other than the struggle to rescue and reconstruct our history and culture, shape them in our own image and interest, and self-consciously contribute to the forward flow of human history.

Thus, although there are many other communitarian values which could have been chosen, these seven core values, the Nguzo Saba, were selected for four basic reasons. First, they were selected because of their prevalence and recurrence in communitarian African societies, therefore reflecting a Pan-African character. Secondly, these particular values were selected because of their perceived relevance to the liberational project of African Americans, i.e., their struggle for freedom, rebuilding community and contributing to a new history of humankind. Thirdly, the seven core principles were chosen because of the cultural and spiritual significance of seven in African culture. And finally, these seven core values were selected because of the manageability of the number seven in terms of teaching, memorization, learning and core emphasis.

What was necessary, then, was to make a selective analysis of continental African cultural values and choose and establish the ones which would best serve the interests and aspirations of the African American family, community and culture. In terms of the interest and aspirations of African American people, the Nguzo Saba were developed and offered as an Afrocentric value system which would serve the following basic functions: (1) organize and enrich our relations with each other on the personal and community level; (2) establish standards, commitments and priorities that would tend to enhance our human possibilities as persons and a people; (3) aid in the recovery and reconstruction of lost historical memory and cultural legacy in the development of an Afrocentric paradigm of life and achievement; (4) serve as a contribution to a core system of communitarian ethical values for the moral guidance and instruction of the community, especially for children; and (5) contribute to an ongoing and expanding use of Afrocentric communitarian values which would aid in bringing into being a new man, woman and child who self-consciously participate in the ethical project of starting a new history of African people and humankind. With these observations in mind, we can now turn to the rich meaning and message of the Nguzo Saba themselves, both in the context of Kwanzaa and daily life.

UMOJA (UNITY)

To strive for and maintain unity in the family, community, nation and race.

This is the First and foundational Principle of the Nguzo Saba, for without it, all the other Principles suffer. Unity is both a principle and practice of togetherness in all things good and of mutual benefit. It is a principled and harmonious togetherness not simply a being together. This is why value-rootedness is so important, even indispensable. Unity as principled and harmonious togetherness is a cardinal virtue of both classical and general African societies. In ancient Egypt, harmony was a cardinal virtue of Maat, i.e., righteousness, rightness. In fact, one of the ways to translate Maat is to define it as harmony—harmony on the natural, cosmic and social level. Likewise, *ceing* among the Dinka means both morality and harmonious living together. Thus in both ancient Egyptian and Dinka society, one cannot live a moral life without living in harmony with other members of the community.

If unity is in essence a Principle, it is no less a practice as are all the other Principles. For practice is central to African ethics and all claims to ethical living and commitment to moral principles are tested and proved or disproved in relations with others. Relations, then, are the hinge on which morality turns, the ground on which it rises or falls. In this regard, we can refer back to the discussion on character development through ethical instruction. Character development is not simply to create a good person abstracted from community, but rather a person in positive interaction, a person whose quality of relations with others is defined first of all by a *principled* and *harmonious* togetherness, i.e., a real and practiced unity.

Another way of discussing unity is to see it as active solidarity. This essentially means a firm dependable togetherness that is born, based and sustained in action. It is usually applied to groups, organizations, classes, peoples and expresses itself as building and acting together in mutual benefit. The key here is again practice. In the end practice proves everything. No matter how many books one reads on swimming, sooner or later s/he must get into the water and swim. This may be called, on this level, the priority of practice. Finally, unity means a oneness, a similarity and sameness that gives us an identity as a people, an African people. And inherent in this identity as a people is the ethical and political imperative to self-consciously unite in order to define, defend and develop our interests.

Unity as principle and practice begins in the family but presupposes value-orientation of each member. Adults and children must respect and approach unity as a moral principle of family and community not simply a political slogan. As principle and practice, this means principled and harmonious living with brothers and sisters, mothers and fathers—sharing and acting in unison. It means avoidance of conflict and quick, willing and principled resolution when it occurs. It means a yielding and gentleness of exchange as taught in the *Sacred Husia* (33). The family must reject harshness and practice gentleness, stress cooperation and avoid conflict, and be very attentive to things that would divide or create differences negative to togetherness.

Especially important is the unity of the father and mother, for they are the models for the children and the foundation for the family in every sense of the word. Here the African concept of complementarity of male and female as distinct from and opposed to the concept of conflict of the genders is instructive and of value. As Anna J. Cooper, educator and social theorist, taught "there is a feminine as well as masculine side to truth (and) these are related not as inferior and superior, not as better or worse, not as weaker or stronger, but as complements—complements in one necessary and symmetric whole" (34). The recognition of this truth and responding creatively to it is necessary, she says, to give balance to the individual, and to save the nation from its extremes. It also is a shield against sexism, i.e., the social practice of using gender to establish and/or justify exploitation, oppression or unequal relations.

In African complementarity, three principles internal to it are necessary and reinforcing of both the concept and practice: (1) equality; (2) reciprocity; and (3) friendship. One starts from the assumption of human equality and cultivates social equality as its logical and necessary complement. Reciprocity among equals is morally and socially compelling. And friendship is the fruit and expected outcome of a mutually-respectful and mutually-beneficial relationship which is tested and tempered through time and is rooted in mutual investment in each other's happiness, well-being and development.

Finally the family must be, as in African culture, the focal point of unity not simply of siblings and of genders, but also of generations. One of the most important expressions of family unity is the respect and collective concern and care for the elders. Respect for elders as Amadi points out is a "cardinal article of the code of behavior" of African society (35). One who does not respect his/her elders is seen as immoral and uncultured. Elders are respected, like the ancestors they will become, for their long life of service to the community, for their achievement, for providing an ethical model and for the richness of their experience and the wisdom this had produced. Thus, elders are seen as judges and reconcilers. It is they who hear cases of conflict and problems and offer solutions. One of the most important aspects of African respect for elders is that it makes them useful and active in the community, unlike the worst of European society which deprives them of meaningful roles and placed them to the side, leaving them with only failing memories.

Also, the active participation and involvement of elders in the daily life of the family not only benefits them but the younger people. For it teaches them to understand and appreciate the process of growing old, gives them access to seasoned knowledge and experience and helps prevent the so-called generation gap so evident and advertised in European society. Key to this linking of young and old is the concept of lineage which links all the living, the departed and the yet unborn. This is translated in practice into the extended family and the protocol, ritual, reciprocity and remembrance this involves and requires. Early in life continental African children are taught to memorize and recite their family tree as far back as any ancestor is known. This keeps historical memory alive and reaffirms respect for those living and departed who contributed to their coming into being and cultural molding.

Now, if one starts with the family when discussing unity, the community becomes of necessity the next level of the concern and practice of unity. The family, as it is written, is the smallest example of how the nation (or national community) works. For the relations, values and practice one has in the family are a reflection and evidence of what one will find in the community, then, begins in the family but it extends to organizational affilia-tion and then the unity of organizations, i.e., African American united fronts. Malcolm X taught that community unity first depended on everyone's belonging to an organization, then all organizations uniting on the basis of common interests and aspirations. He posed community unity—in its two-level form—as morally compelling. It was for him irresponsi-ble and self-destructive not to unite around common interests and instead glory in differ-ences and even differences of religion and unite around their common identity as Africans, and their common interests, especially the interests of liberation (36).

Unity of the nation is unity of the national community as distinct from the local com-munity. The above applies in equal measure to the national community. In terms of "ra-cial" unity, when one says race, one means the world African community. Thus, when Garvey says "Up you mighty race; you can accomplish what you will," he is talking to the world African community. The form of unity this takes is Pan-Africanism, i.e., the struggle to unite all Africans everywhere around the common interests and make African cultural and political presence on the world stage both powerful and permanent. Pan-Africanism requires and urges that we see ourselves and act in history as an African people, belonging to a world community of African peoples. In this way, we self-consciously share in both the glory and burden of our history. And in that knowledge and context act to honor, preserve and expand that history in the struggle for liberation and ever higher levels of human life.

KUJICHAGULIA (SELF-DETERMINATION)

To define ourselves, name ourselves, create for ourselves and speak for ourselves instead of being defined, named, created for and spoken for by others.

The Second Principle of the Nguzo Saba is self-determination. This too expresses itself as both commitment and practice. It demands that we as an African people define, defend and develop ourselves instead of allowing or encouraging others to do this. It requires that we recover lost memory and once again shape our world in our own image and interest. And it is a call to recover and speak our own special truth to the world and raise images above the earth that reflect our capacity for human greatness and progress.

The first act of a free people is to shape its world in its own image and interest. And it is a statement about their conception of self and their commitment to self-determination. Fanon has said each person must ask him or herself three basic questions: "Who am I, am I really who I am and am I all I ought to be?" (37). These are questions of history and culture, not simply queries or questions of personal identity. More profoundly they are questions of collective identity based and borne out in historical and cultural practice. And the essential quality of that practice must be the quality of self-determination.

To answer the question of "Who am I?" correctly, then, is to know and live one's history and practice one's culture. To answer the question of "Am I really who I am?" is to have and employ a cultural criteria of authenticity, i.e., criteria of what is real and unreal, what is appearance and essence, what is culturally-rooted and foreign. And to answer the question of "Am I all I ought to be?" is to self-consciously possess and use ethical and cultural standards which measure men, women and children in terms of the quality of their thought and practice in the context of who they are and must become—in both an African and human sense.

The principle and practice of self-determination carry within them the assumption that we have both the right and responsibility to exist as a people and make our own unique contribution to the forward flow of human history. This principle shelters the assumption that as fathers and mothers of humanity and human civilization in the Nile Valley, we have no business playing the cultural children of the world. So it reminds us of the fact that African people created and introduced the basic disciplines of human knowledge— science, technology, geometry, math, medicine, ethics, advanced architecture, etc. And it urges us as a people not to surrender our historical and cultural identity to fit into the culture of another. Openness to exchange is a given, but it presupposes that one has kept enough of one's culture to engage in exchange, rather than slavishly follow another's lead.

The principle and practice of self-determination expresses and supports the concept and practice of Afrocentricity. Afrocentricity is a quality of thought and practice which is rooted in the cultural image and human interests of African people (38). To say that a perspective or approach is in an African cultural image is to say it's rooted in an African value system and worldview, especially in the historical and cultural sense. And to say that an approach or perspective is in the human interests of African people is to say it is supportive of the just claims African people have and share with other humans, i.e., freedom from want, toil and domination, and freedom to fully realize themselves in their human and African fullness.

It is clearly important to distinguish Afrocentricity from Eurocentricity with its racist and structured denial and deformation of the history and humanity of Third World people. Afrocentricity does not seek to deny or deform others' history and humanity, but to affirm, rescue and reconstruct its own after the Holocaust of Enslavement and various other forms of European oppression. Afrocentricity at its cultural best is an ongoing quest for historical and cultural anchor, a foundation on which we raise our cultural future, ground our cultural production and measure their authenticity and value.

Moreover, Afrocentricity is an ongoing critical reconstruction directed toward restoring lost and missing parts of our historical self-formation or development as a people. It is furthermore a self-conscious posing of the African experience—both classical and general—as an instructive and useful paradigm for human liberation and a higher level of human life. Finally, Afrocentricity, as recovery and reconstruction of a classical African paradigm, is a counter to one of the greatest problems of our time—the progressive Europeanization of human consciousness. That is to say, it is a wall and ongoing world against the European peoples' attempt to impose their culture as the universal and only serious option for humanity; and against the tendency of Third World peoples, i.e., peoples of color, to emulate Europe, and reject or mutilate themselves and their culture in various ways.

Afrocentricity self-consciously assumes the position that to be more than an "obscene caricature" of Europe—to use Fanon's phrase—is to violate historical memory and dishonor the rich and historically significant African cultural legacy. Moreover, such dehumanizing behavior would unquestionably undermine the possibilities inherent in the African experience and leave African people seriously limited in their ability to speak their special truth to the world and join other oppressed and progressive people in the struggle for a new history of humankind. Thus, Afrocentricity as the core and fundamental quality of our self-determination reaffirms our right and responsibility to exist as a people, to speak our own special truth to the world and to make our own contribution to the forward flow of human history. To do the opposite is immoral and suicidal. To do less is dishonorable and ultimately self-destructive.

Ujima (Collective Work and Responsibility)

To build and maintain our community together and make our sister's and brother's problems our problems and to solve them together.

The Third Principle is Ujima (Collective Work and Responsibility) which is a commitment to active and informed togetherness on matters of common interest. It is also recognition and respect of the fact that without collective work and struggle, progress is impossible and liberation unthinkable. Moreover, the principle of Ujima supports the fundamental assumption that African is not just an identity, but also a destiny and duty, i.e., a responsibility. In other words, our collective identity in the long run is a collective future. Thus, there is a need and obligation for us as self-conscious and committed people to shape our future with our own minds and hands and share its hardships and benefits together.

Ujima, as principle and practice, also means that we accept the fact that we are collectively responsible for our failures and setbacks as well as our victories and achievements. And this holds true not only on the national level, but also on the level of family and organization or smaller units. Such a commitment implies and encourages a vigorous capacity for self-criticism and self-correction which is indispensable to our strength, defense and development as a people.

The principle of collective work and responsibility also points to the fact that African freedom is indivisible. It shelters the assumption that as long as any African anywhere is oppressed, exploited, enslaved or wounded in any way in her or his humanity, all African people are. It thus, rejects the possibility or desirability of individual freedom in any unfree context; instead it poses the need for struggle to create a context in which all can be free. Moreover, Ujima rejects escapist and abstract humanism and supports the humanism that begins with commitment to and concern for the humans among whom we live and to whom we owe our existence, i.e., our own people. In a word, real humanism begins with accepting one's own humanity in the particular form in which it expresses itself and then initiating and sustaining exchanges with others in the context of our common humanity. It also posits that the liberation struggle to rescue and reconstruct African history and humanity is a significant contribution to overall struggle for human liberation.

In the context of a communitarian social order, cooperation is another key aspect of Ujima. It is based on the assumption that what one does to benefit others is at the same time a benefit to him/her. Likewise, "one who injures others in the end injures him/herself" as the Yoruba proverb states. In the Lovedu community in South Africa, children are taught not to be aggressive or competitive but to be cooperative and share responsibility (39). Even their language reflects the cooperative thrust. For even when no one has just been given something "give me also". Likewise, their prayer is never just for themselves but for all's health, blessing, prosperity. In fact, to ask for the personal without at the same time asking for the collective is both improper and immoral.

The lesson of the Lovedu is that harmonious living, as with the Dinka, is of paramount importance. Thus, being quarrelsome or contentious is one of the worst offenses. And striving for uncoerced or free and willing agreement is the model of behavior. Reconciliation of conflict is patient and never coercive, and always done keeping the person in mind. And the fundamental objective in conflict is not to mechanically apply the rule but to reconcile the people. For they believe that "if people do not agree, there can be no relationship" (40). And if they have to be coerced, there cannot be genuine agreement. In such a context collective work and responsibility is facilitated and sustained.

Finally, collective work and responsibility can be seen in terms of the challenge of culture and history. Work—both personal and collective—is truly at the center of history and culture. It is the fundamental activity by which we create ourselves, define and develop ourselves and confirm ourselves in the process as both persons and a people. And it is the way we create culture and make history. It is for this reason, among others, that the Holocaust of Enslavement was so devastating. For not only did it destroy tens of millions of lives, which is morally monstrous in itself, but it also destroyed great cultural achievements, created technological and cultural arrest and thus eroded and limited the human possibility Africa offered the world. In fact, the effects of this Holocaust are present even today both in terms of the problems of the Continent and those of the Diaspora.

The challenge of history and culture then is through collective work and responsibility, to restore that which was damaged or destroyed and to raise up and reconstruct that which was in ruins as the ancient Egyptians taught. It is also to remember we are each cultural representatives of our people and have no right to misrepresent them or willfully do less than is demanded of us by our history and current situation as a community-in-struggle. We must accept and live the principle of shared or collective work and responsibility in all things good, right and beneficial to the community.

Ujamaa (Cooperative Economics)

To build and maintain our own stores, shops and other businesses and to profit from them together.

The Fourth Principle is Ujamaa (Cooperative Economics) and is essentially a commitment to the practice of shared social wealth and the work necessary to achieve it. It grows out of the fundamental communal concept that social wealth belongs to the masses of people who created it and that no one should have such an unequal amount of wealth that it gives him/her the capacity to impose unequal, exploitative or oppressive relations on others (41). Sharing wealth is another form of communitarian exchange, i.e., sharing and cooperating in general. But it is essential because without the principle and practice of shared wealth, the social conditions for exploitation, oppression and inequality as well as deprivation and suffering are increased.

Thus, as President Julius Nyerere of Tanzania in his discussion of Ujamaa says, Ujamaa is "based on the assumption of human equality, on the belief that it is wrong for one (person) to dominate or exploit another, and on the knowledge that every individual hopes to live in a society as a free (person) able to lead a decent life, in conditions of peace with his (her) neighbor" (42). Ujamaa, Nyerere tells us, is above all human centered—concerned foremost with the well-being, happiness and development of the human person. And the assumption is that the conditions for such well-being, happiness and development is best achieved in a contest of shared social wealth.

Thus, Pres. Nyerere states, Ujamaa rejects the idea of wealth for wealth's sake as opposed to well-being for all. And he notes that Ujamaa is "a commitment to the belief that there are more important things in life than the amassing of riches, and that if the pursuit of wealth clashes with things like human dignity and social equality, then the latter will be given priority." In the context of improving and insuring the well-being of the people, "the creation of wealth is a good thing and something we shall have to increase." But he concludes that "it will cease to be good the moment wealth ceases to serve (humans) and begins to be served by (humans)".

Ujamaa also stresses self-reliance in the building, strengthening and controlling of the economics of our own community. President Nyerere has said self-reliance in Ujamaa means "first and foremost . . . that for our development we have to depend upon ourselves and our own resources" (43). The assumption here is that we must seize and maintain the initiative in all that is ours, and that we must harness our resources and put them to the best possible use in the service of the community. This, he says, does not mean denying all assistance from or work with others but of controlling policy and shouldering the essential responsibility for our own future.

Closely related to this concept of self-reliance and the responsibility it requires is the respect for the dignity and obligation of work. To respect work is to appreciate its value, reject its exploitation and engage in it cooperatively for the common good of the community. Also, inherent in Ujamaa is the stress and obligation of generosity especially to the poor and vulnerable. In the Book of Ani, we are taught that generosity is its own reciprocal reward. "Small gifts return greater and what is replaced brings abundance" (44). And in the Book of Ptah-Hotep we are taught "Be generous as long as you live. What goes into the storehouse should come out. For bread is made to be shared."

Moreover, Ptah-Hotep informs us, "Generosity is a memorial for those who show it, long after they have departed" (45). This, of course, is the ancient African ethic of care and responsibility which informs the concepts of generosity and shared social wealth. Such an ethic is expressed in one of its earliest forms in the Book of Coming Forth By Day which defines the righteous on one level as one who has "given bread to the hungry, water to the thirsty, clothes to the naked and a boat to those without one" (46). In fact, throughout the sacred teachings of ancient Egypt in particular and Africa in general, the ethic of care and responsibility is expressed in the concept of shared social wealth and service to the most disadvantaged. This, of course, finds its modern philosophical expression in our social thought and struggles, as a people, around and for social justice. And this struggle is not simply to be generous to the poor and vulnerable but ultimately to end their poverty and vulnerability, so that they too can live a decent, undeprived and meaningful life. For only in such a context will they be able to pursue the truly human without the limitation imposed by poverty, deprivation or the debilitating struggle for just life's basic necessities. To share wealth and work, then, is to share concern, care and responsibility for a new, more human and fulfilling future.

NIA (PURPOSE)

To make our collective vocation the building and developing of our community in order to restore our people to their traditional greatness.

The Fifth Principle of the Nguzo Saba is Nia (Purpose) which is essentially a commitment to the collective vocation of building, developing and defending our national community, its culture and history in order to regain our historical initiative and greatness as a people. The assumption here is that our role in human history has been and remains a key one, that we as an African people share in the great human legacy Africa has given the world. That legacy is one of having not only been the fathers and mothers of humanity, but also the fathers and mothers of human civilization, i.e., having introduced in the Nile Valley civilizations the basic disciplines of human knowledge. It is this identity which gives us an overriding cultural purpose and suggests a direction. This is what we mean when we say we who are the fathers and mothers of human civilization have no business playing

Society and Politics

the cultural children of the world. The principle of Nia then makes us conscious of our purpose in light of our historical and cultural identity.

This again reminds us of Mary McLeod Bethune's point concerning our current status as heirs and custodians of a great civilization. She said, "We, as (African Americans) must recognize that we are the custodians as well as heirs of a great civilization. We have," she continues, "given something to the world as a race and for this we are proud and fully conscious of our place in the total picture of (humankind's) development" (47). As noted above, Bethune is concerned that our purpose is derived from three basic facts. The first two are that we are both *heirs* and *custodians* of a great legacy. This means first that we must not simply receive the legacy as a formal historical and cultural transmission, but recognize and respect its importance. Secondly, it means that far from being simple heirs we are also custodians. And this implies an even greater obligation.

To inherit is to receive as legacy, place adequate value on and make a part of one's life. But to be a custodian of a great legacy is to guard, preserve, expand and promote it. It is to honor it by building on and expanding it and in turn, leaving it as an enriched legacy for future generations. Finally, Bethune asks us to recognize and respect our legacy in terms of where it places us in "the total picture of (humankind's) development." It is a call for us to see ourselves not as simple ghetto dwellers or newly arrived captives of the suburbs, but more definitively as a world historical people who have made and must continue to make a significant contribution to the forward flow of human history.

Inherent in this discussion of deriving purpose from cultural and historical identity is a necessary reference to and focus on generational responsibility. Fanon has posed this responsibility in compelling terms. He says, "each generation must, out of relative obscurity, discover its mission, (and then) fulfill it or betray it" (48). The mission he suggests is always framed within the larger context of the needs, hopes and aspirations of the people. And each of us is morally and culturally obligated to participate in creating a context of maximum freedom and development of the people.

Finally, Nia suggests that personal and social purpose are not only non-antagonistic but complementary in the true communitarian sense of the word. In fact, it suggests that the highest form of personal purpose is in the final analysis, social purpose, i.e., personal purpose that translates itself into a vocation and commitment which involves and benefits the community. As we have noted elsewhere, such level and quality of purpose not only benefits the collective whole, but also gives fullness and meaning to a person's life in a way individualistic and isolated pursuits cannot.

For true greatness and growth never occur in isolation and at others' expense. On the contrary, as African philosophy teaches, we are first and foremost social beings whose reality and relevance are rooted in the quality and kinds of relations we have with each other. And a cooperative communal vocation is an excellent context and encouragement for quality social relations. Thus, DuBois' stress on education for social contribution and rejection of vulgar careerism rooted in the lone and passionate pursuit of money is especially relevant. For again our purpose is not to simply create money makers, but to cultivate men and women capable of social and human exchange on a larger more meaningful scale, men and women of culture and social conscience, of vision and values which expand the human project of freedom and development rather than diminish and deform it.

KUUMBA (CREATIVITY)

To do always as much as we can, in the way we can, in order to leave our community more beautiful and beneficial than we inherited it.

The Sixth Principle is Kuumba (Creativity) and logically follows from and is required by the Principle of Nia. It is a commitment to being creative within the context of the national community vocation of restoring our people to their traditional greatness and thus leaving our community more beneficial and beautiful then we, i.e., each generation, inherited it. The Principle has both a social and spiritual dimension and is deeply rooted both in social and sacred teachings of African societies.

Nowhere is this principle more clearly expressed than in the literature and culture of ancient Egypt. Creativity here is both an original act or imitation of the Creator and a restorative act also reflective of the Creator constantly pushing back the currents of chaos and decay and revitalizing and restoring the natural, spiritual and cosmic energy of the world. In ancient Egypt, there was a spiritual and ethical commitment and obligation to constantly renew and restore and great works, the legacy of the ancestors, and the creative energy of the leader and nation. This was considered doing Maat, i.e., reaffirming and restoring truth, justice and righteousness, harmony, balance, order, rightness, etc. Each pharaoh saw his or her reign, then, as one of restoration of Maat, i.e., the reaffirmation, reestablishment and renewal of the Good, the Beautiful and the Right.

Therefore, Queen Hatshepsut says of her reign, "I have restored that which was in ruins; I have raised up that which was destroyed when the Aamu were in the midst of Kemet, overthrowing that which had been made, as they ruled in ignorance of Ra (God)." And King Shabaka found a great work of the ancestors in ruins, the Memphite text on creation and he restored it "so that it was more beautiful than before" (49). This latter contention of restoring the work "so that it was more beautiful than before" is also central to the concept of restoration and was a regular claim of the king, queen, priests and leaders. These concepts of *restoration* and *progressive perfection* which are key concepts in the philosophy of Kawaida and which reflected a fundamental cultural thrust of the 1960's, informed the conception and development of Kwanzaa. And of course, they became a goal and value of Kwanzaa in the principle and practice of Kuumba (Creativity) which again is defined as "to do always as much as we can, in the way we can, in order to leave our community more beautiful and beneficial than we inherited it." Also, *restoration* as principle and practice is central to the Fifth Principle of Nia whose essential thrust is "to restore our people to their traditional greatness." Thus, one has an interrelatedness and interlocking of principles and therefore a similar relationship in the practice of them.

It is interesting to note here that my creation of Kwanzaa falls within the restorative conception of creativity. For when I say I created Kwanzaa, the term "created" does not imply or mean "made out of nothing," for it is clearly not the case as the above discussion on the Continental African origins of Kwanzaa shows. What one has, then, is rather a *creative restoration* in the African spirit of cultural restoration and renewal in both the ancient Egyptian and African American sense of the practice as used in the 1960's.

It is, in fact, a restoring that which was in ruins or disuse in many parts of Africa, and especially among Africans in America and attempting to make it more beautiful and beneficial than it was before as the Principle of Kuumba (Creativity) requires. This, as stated above, contains the interrelated principles of *restoration* and *progressive perfection*. To restore is what we called in the 60's "to rescue and reconstruct." Progressive perfection is a Kawaida concept that assumes an *ability* and *obligation* to strive always to leave what one inherits (legacy, community, etc.) more beautiful and beneficial than it was before. It is again, in this context and spirit of the cultural project of recovering and reconstructing African first fruit celebrations that Kwanzaa was conceived and constructed.

The stress, then, is on leaving a legacy which builds on and enriches the legacy before you. It is again stress on generational responsibility. Kwanzaa reminds us of the ancient Egyptian teaching that if we wish to live for eternity we must build for eternity, i.e., do great works or serve the community in a real, sustained and meaningful way. This reflects both a social and moral criterion for eternal life and it is interesting to note that this discussion of great works and service surfaces in a discussion by Martin L. King on service. He said that all of us cannot build great works but we all can serve and that in itself can lead to greatness.

Finally, King Sesostris I taught that to do that which is of value is forever. A people called forth by its works do not die for their name is raised and remembered because of it. The lesson here is that creativity is central to the human spirit and human society, that it causes us to grow, restores and revitalizes us and the community and insures our life for eternity. And the Book of Kheti teaches that we should not underestimate the positive or negative, the creative or destructive effects of our thought and action. For it says, "Everyday is a donation to eternity and even one hour is a contribution to the future."

IMANI (FAITH)

To believe with all our heart in our people, our parents, our teachers, our leaders and the righteousness and victory of our struggle.

The Seventh Principle is Faith which is essentially a profound belief in and commitment to all that is of value to us as a family, community, people and culture. In the context of African spirituality, it begins with a belief in the Creator and in the positiveness of the creation and logically leads to a belief in the essential goodness and possibility of the human personality. For in all African spiritual traditions, from Egypt on, it is taught that we are in the image of the Creator and thus capable of ultimate righteousness and creativity through self-mastery and development in the context of positive support. Therefore, faith in ourselves is key here, faith in our capacity as humans to live righteously, self-correct, support, care for and be responsible for each other and eventually create the just and good society.

Faith in ourselves is key, Bethune taught us, saying the greatest faith is faith in the Creator but great also is faith in ourselves. "Without faith," she states, "nothing is possible; with it nothing is impossible." Also, she taught that faith in the masses of our people is central to our progress as a people. "The measure of our progress as a race is in precise relation to the depth of faith in our people held by our leaders," (50) she reminds us. As a community-in-struggle there is no substitute for belief in our people, in their capacity to take control of their destiny and daily lives and shape them in their own image and interests. This is fundamental to any future we dare design and pursue.

Especially we must believe in the value and validity, the righteousness and significance of our struggle for liberation and a higher level of human life. This must be tied to our belief in our capacity to assume and carry out with dignity and decisiveness the role Fanon and history has assigned us. And that role is to set in motion a new history of humankind and in the company of other oppressed and Third World peoples pose a new paradigm of human society and human relations. Fanon says we can do anything as long as we don't do two basic things: (1) try to catch up with Europe (after all where is it going—swinging between spiritual and nuclear annihilation); and (2) imitate them so that we become "obscene caricatures" of them. We must, he says, invent, innovate, reach inside ourselves and dare "set afoot a new man and woman." The world and our people are waiting for something new, more beautiful and beneficial from us than what a past of oppression has offered us. Let us not imitate or be taught by our oppressors. Let us dare struggle, free ourselves politically and culturally and raise images above the earth that reflect our capacity for human progress and greatness. This is the challenge and burden of our history which assumes and requires a solid faith.

We must, then, have faith in ourselves, in our leaders, teachers, parents and in the righteousness and victory of our struggle, faith that through hard work, long struggle and a whole lot of love and understanding, we can again step back on the stage of human history as a free, proud and productive people. It is in this context that we can surely speak our own special truth to the world and make our own unique contribution to the forward flow of human history.

Society and Politics

Julius K. Nyerere
(b. 1922, Tanzania)

One-Party Government

The African concept of democracy is similar to that of the ancient Greeks from whose language the word "democracy" originated. To the Greeks, democracy meant simply "government by discussion among equals." The people discussed and when they reached agreement the result was a "people's decision."

Mr. Guy Blutton Brock writing about Nyasaland described traditional African democracy as: "The elders sit under the big tree and talk until they agree." This "talking until you agree" is the essential of the traditional African concept of democracy.

To minds moulded by Western parliamentary tradition and Western concepts of democratic institutions, the idea of an organized opposition group has become so familiar, that its absence immediately raises the cry of "Dictatorship." It is no good telling them that when a group of 100 equals have sat and talked together until they agreed where to dig a well (and "until they agreed" implies that they will have produced many conflicting arguments before they did eventually agree), they have practised democracy. Proponents of Western parliamentary traditions will consider whether the opposition was organized and therefore automatic, or whether it was spontaneous and therefore free. Only if it was automatic will they concede that here was democracy.

Basically democracy is government by discussion as opposed to government by force, and by discussion between the people or their chosen representatives as opposed to a hereditary clique. Under the tribal system whether there was a chief or not, African society was a society of equals, and it conducted its business by discussion.

It is true that this "pure" democracy—the totally unorganized "talking until you agree" can no longer be adequate; it is too clumsy a way of conducting the affairs of a large modern state. But the need to organize the "government by discussion" does not necessarily imply the need to organize an opposition group as part of the system.

I am not arguing that the two-party system is not democratic. I am only saying it is only one form which democracy happens to have taken in certain countries, and that it is by no means essential. I am sure that even my friends in the Labour Party or the Conservative Party in Britain would admit that if their party could succeed in winning all the seats, they would be perfectly happy to form a one-party government. They, the winning party that is, would not be likely to suspect themselves of having suddenly turned Britain into a dictatorship!

Some of us have been over-ready to swallow unquestioningly the proposition that you cannot have democracy unless you have a second party to oppose the party in power. But, however difficult our friends in Britain and America may find it to accept what to them is a new idea—that democracy can exist where there is not formal opposition—I think we in Africa should think very carefully before we abandon our traditional attitude.

It is often overlooked that the Anglo-Saxon tradition of a two-party system is a reflection of the society in which it evolved. Within that society, there was a struggle between the "haves" and the "have nots"—each of whom organized themselves into political parties, one party associated with wealth and the *status quo* and the other with the masses of the people and change. Thus the existence of distinct classes in a society and the struggle between them resulted in the growth of the two-party system. But need this be accepted as the essential and only pattern of democracy?

With rare exceptions the idea of class is something entirely foreign to Africa. Here, in this continent, the Nationalist Movements are fighting a battle for freedom from foreign domination, not from domination by any ruling class of our own. To us "the other Party" is the Colonial Power. In many parts of Africa this struggle has been won; in others it is still going on. But everywhere the people who fight the battle are not former overlords wanting to re-establish a lost authority; they are not a rich mercantile class whose freedom to exploit the masses is being limited by the colonial powers, they are the common people of Africa.

Thus once the foreign power—"the other party"—has been expelled there is no ready-made division, and it is by no means certain that democracy will adopt the same machinery and symbols as the Anglo-Saxon. Nor indeed is it necessarily desirable that it should do so.

New nations like Tanganyika are emerging into independence as a result of a struggle for freedom from colonialism. It is a patriotic struggle which leaves no room for differences, and which unites all elements in the country; and the Nationalist Movements—having united the people and led them to freedom—must inevitably form the first government of the new states. Once the first free government is formed, its supreme task lies ahead—the building up of the country's economy so as to raise the living standards of the people, the eradication of disease and the banishment of ignorance and superstition. This, no less than the struggle against colonialism, calls for the maximum united effort by the whole country if it is to succeed. *There can be no room for difference or division.*

In Western democracies it is an accepted practice that in times of emergency opposition parties sink their differences and join together in forming a national government. *This is our time of emergency,* and until our war against poverty, ignorance and disease has been won—we should not let our unity be destroyed by a desire to follow somebody else's "book of rules."

If these then are the forms of democracy, what are the essentials?

First, the freedom and the well-being of the individual. Freedom alone is not enough; there can be a freedom which is merely the freedom to starve. True freedom must be freedom not only from bondage, from discrimination and from indignity, but also freedom from all those things that hamper a people's progress. It is the responsibility of the government in a democratic country to lead the fight against all these enemies of freedom. To do this the government, once freely elected, must also be free to govern in the best interests of the people, and without fear of sabotage. It is, therefore, also the duty of the government to safeguard the unity of the country from irresponsible or vicious attempts to divide and weaken it, for without unity the fight against the enemies of freedom cannot be won.

When, then, you have the freedom and wellbeing of the individual; who has the right freely and regularly to join with his fellows in choosing the government of his country; and where the affairs of the country are conducted by free discussion, you have democracy.

True democracy depends far more on the attitude of mind which respects and defends the individual than on the forms it takes. The form is useless without the attitude of the mind of which the form is an external expression. As with individuals, so with organized groups, this question of attitude is all-important. It is not enough to ask what attitude will an African government adopt towards an opposition, without also asking what attitude an opposition will adopt towards a popularly elected government.

In the past all that was required of government was merely to maintain law and order within the country, and to protect it from external aggression. Today the responsibilities of governments, whether "communist" or "free," are infinitely wide. However nearly its requirements of money and men may be met, no government today finds it easy to fulfill all its responsibilities to the people.

These common problems of a modern state are no less formidable in young and under-developed countries. The very success of the nationalist movements in raising the expectations of the people, the modern means of communication which put the American and the British worker in almost daily contact with the African worker, the twentieth-century upsurge of the ordinary man and woman—all these deprive the new African governments of those advantages of time and ignorance which alleviated the growing pains of modern society for the governments of older countries.

We must listen to the demands of the common man in Africa, intensified as they are by the vivid contrast between his own lot and that of others in more developed countries, and the lack of means at the disposal of the African governments to meet these demands, the lack of men, the lack of money, above all the lack of time. To all this add the very nature of the new countries themselves. They are usually countries without natural unity. Their "boundaries" enclose those artificial units carved out of Africa by grabbing colonial powers without any consideration of ethnic groups or geographical realities, so that these countries now include within their borders tribal groups which, until the coming of the European Powers, have never been under one government. To those, in the case of East and Central Africa, you must add the new tribes from Asia, the Middle East and Europe. Here are divisions enough to pose a truly formidable task in nation-building.

As if the natural challenge was not enough, with the raising of each new flag come the intrigues of the international diplomacy of rivalry and all that goes with it; the cynical and the criminal attempts by powerful foreign governments to weaken the unity of any country whose government pursues policies which they do not like. Who does not know that foreign nations have again and again poured in money to back up any stooge who will dance to their political tune? As their sole purpose is to confuse the people and weaken the legal government for their own ends, they are quite indifferent to the fact that their chosen puppets have no following at all in the country itself.

It should be obvious, then, why the governments of these new countries must treat the situation as one of national emergency, comparable almost to that of a country at war.

In the early days of nation-building as in time of war the opposition, if any, must act even more responsibly than an opposition in a more developed and more stable, a more unified and a better equipped country in times of peace. Given such a responsible opposition I would be the first person to defend its right. But where is it? Too often the only voices to be heard in "opposition" are those of a few irresponsible individuals who exploit the very privileges of democracy—freedom of the press, freedom of association, freedom to criticize—in order to deflect the government from its responsibilities to the people by creating problems of law and order.

The admitted function of any political opposition is to try and persuade the electorate to reject the existing government at the next election. This is "reasonable" in the case of a responsible opposition with a definite alternative policy in which its members sincerely believe; but that sort of mature opposition is rare indeed in a newly independent state. Usually the irresponsible individuals I have mentioned have neither sincerity, conviction, nor any policy at all save that of self-aggrandizement. They merely employ the catch-phrases copied from the political language of older, stable countries, in order to engage the sympathy of the unthinking for their destructive tactics. Nor are the tactics they use those of a responsible democratic opposition. In such circumstances the government must deal firmly and promptly with the trouble makers. The country cannot afford, during these vital early years of its life, to treat such people with the same degree of tolerance which may be safely allowed in a long-established democracy.

This does not mean, however, that a genuine and responsible opposition cannot arise in time, nor that an opposition of that kind would be less welcome in Africa than it is in Europe or America. For myself, as I have said, I would be the first to defend its rights. But whether it does or does not arise depends entirely on the will of the people themselves and makes no difference at all to the freedom of discussion and the equality in freedom which together make democracy.

To those who wonder if democracy can survive in Africa my own answer then would be that far from it being an alien idea, democracy has long been familiar to the African. There is nothing in our traditional attitude to discussion, and current dedication to human rights, to justify the claim that democracy is in danger in Africa. I see exactly the opposite: the principles of our nationalist struggle for human dignity, augmented as it were by our traditional attitude to discussion, should augur well for democracy in Africa.

Kwame Nkrumah

(1909–1972, Ghana)

The Need for a Union Government for Africa

Speech at Cairo Summit Conference, Organization of African Unity, July 19, 1964

Mr Chairman,

In the year that has passed since we met at Addis Ababa and established the Organization of African Unity, I have had no reason to change my mind about the concrete proposals which I made to you then, or about the reasons I gave for my conviction that only a Union Government can guarantee our survival. On the contrary, every hour since then, both in the world at large and on our own Continent, has brought events to prove that our problems as individual states are insoluble except in the context of African Unity, that our security as individual states is indivisible from the security of the whole Continent, that the freedom of our compatriots still in foreign chains and under colonial rule awaits the redeeming might of an African Continental Government.

We took a monumental decision at the Summit Meeting in Addis Ababa last year. No amount of disappointment or impatience with the pace at which our Charter has been implemented, can detract from the epoch-making and irrevocable nature of our decision to affirm the unity of our Continent.

It was an act of faith, a recognition of reality. We forged the Organization of African Unity fully conscious of all the difficulties facing our various States in committing themselves to common obligations. We have passed through the first year victorious over trials on our loyalty, and over hostile forces seeking to disrupt our unity.

Wherever and whenever the subsidiary bodies set up by the Addis Ababa Charter have met, the spirit of unity, of co-operation and goodwill have prevailed. On that score, none of us can complain; none of us have cause to doubt the strength and permanence of the spirit of unity which found its expression in our Charter.

Yet, even more than last year, I must urge that the historical conditions in which African independence has emerged and the concrete manifestations of our weaknesses and difficulties, call for immense radical and urgent measures which the Addis Ababa Conference did not fulfil. Measures which would have been accounted adequate for dealing with our problems a few years ago, cannot now meet the exigencies of the African revolution.

It is not single States or single Continents which are undergoing de-colonialization, but the greater portion of the world. It is not one empire which is expiring, but the whole system of imperialism which is at bay. It is not individual communities, but the whole of humanity which is demanding a different and better way of life for the world's growing millions.

Great positive and social revolutions have created mighty nations and empires, and the waves of those revolutions lap our shores no less than they do those of other continents. Great technological and industrial revolutions have transformed the economies of large portions of the world, and the waves of those revolutions will not stop short on the Continent of Africa. A revolution in communications brings knowledge of every change in the world to the remotest corners of our continent. The world will not wait—nor will it move step by step, however much we may wish this.

It is against this background of great political, social, cultural, scientific and technological revolutions that the emergence of African independence and the development of Africa must be viewed. None of us imagines that we can keep our own pace, immune from interference, isolated from the world's upsurges and revolutions. What differences there are between us arise from a difference in appreciation of the sense of urgency, not in the understanding we have of our tasks and responsibilities.

Time, indeed, is the crucial factor, for time acts for those who use it with purpose, and not for those who let it slip by. Those who do not use time as their agent, give the advantage to those who do.

When we met last year we were at the beginning of an era of peaceful co-existence. The risk of a World War was abating, and the prospect of peaceful co-operation between the Great Powers appeared to bring to an end the struggle of foreign influences in Africa. We embraced non-alignment in order to escape involving ourselves in the prevailing cold war politics. Instead, we have witnessed the menacing upsurge of imperialism and a revival of colonialism itself in Africa, and foreign interference and subversion in the internal affairs of our African States.

The one essential factor which united us at Addis Ababa—the over-riding factor which made all differences and difficulties seem trivial and irrelevant—was the need to free that part of our continent which is still in the grip of imperialism. In spite of our Charter, in spite of our common front at the United Nations and in other international gatherings, what have we witnessed?

Far from deterring the imperialists and neo-colonialists from giving support to the apartheid regime in South Africa and to the fascist regime in Portugal, the NATO Powers, on the contrary, have poured and are pouring vast sums of money and vast armaments into the apartheid regime of South Africa and Portugal. Not only is South Africa being assisted to grow stronger economically and militarily, but the cruelty, repression and exploitation of our African brothers have reached new heights.

At this point I must comment on the activities of the Liberation Committee set up under the Organization of African Unity at Addis Ababa last year, on which both we and the Freedom Fighters pinned so much hope. It is with great regret that I raise the matter at all, but I would be failing in my duty to the Freedom Fighters and to the cause of African Liberation if I remain silent about the general dissatisfaction which exists regarding the functioning of this Committee.

The frequent and persistent reports from Freedom Fighters about the shortcomings of the aid and facilities for training offered to them, make it impossible for the Government of Ghana to turn over its contribution to this Committee until a reorganization has taken place for more effective and positive action.

This is not a situation in which individuals or individual governments can be held to blame. It is our first essay in a task of stupendous magnitude and with stupendous difficulties. But some of the failures of the Committee are inexcusable because they were so unnecessary.

It failed, for instance, to make the best use of our resources since some Military specialists have been excluded on ideological grounds.

If the Liberation Committee had made effective use of the military experience of Egypt and of Algeria, where neo-colonialist interference and espionage have been frustrated and held at bay, we would have given Freedom Fighters the necessary help in their liberation struggle.

The choice of the Congo (Leopoldville) as a training base for Freedom Fighters was a logical one, and there was every reason to accept the offer of the Congolese Government to provide offices and accommodation for the representatives of the Liberation Movements.

Africa's Freedom Fighters should not, however, have been exposed to the espionage, intrigues, frustrations and disappointments which they have experienced in the last eight months.

What could be the result of entrusting the training of Freedom Fighters against imperialism into the hands of an imperialist agent? Under the Liberation Committee set up at Addis Ababa, the Freedom Fighters had no real security, and were not provided with instruments for their struggle, nor were food, clothing and medicine given for the men in training. Thus, their training scheme collapsed within two months under the eyes of the Liberation Committee, and the Freedom Fighters became disappointed, disgruntled and frustrated.

I am giving you no more than the bare bones of the complaints of the Freedom Fighters. It will not avail us to have a lengthy post-mortem over past failures. But these failures must be understood and acknowledged. The disappointment and frustration of the Freedom Fighters must not be dismissed as unreal or unreasonable. Not only the Liberation Committee, but all of us are to blame, for the way in which we allowed the Liberation Committee to let down the Freedom Fighters.

We dare not say that they could have done their work better until we have all done better. The enormous task of liberating our continent cannot be undertaken in a spirit of compromise and surrender.

By raising a threat at Addis Ababa and not being able to take effective action against apartheid and colonialism, we have worsened the plight of our kinsmen in Angola, Mozambique, Southern Rhodesia and South Africa. We have frightened the imperialists sufficiently to strengthen their defences and repression in Southern Africa, but we have not frightened them enough to abandon apartheid supremacy to its ill-fated doom.

It must be said that by merely making resolutions on African Unity, and not achieving our goal of a Union Government of Africa, we have made our task of freeing the rest of the African Continent harder and not easier.

The North Atlantic Treaty Organization Powers have not been deterred one whit from sending all the arms needed by the Salazar regime to keep down our kinsmen in its colonies. The Portuguese fascist regime has not made a single move to negotiate with the United Nations or with the nationalist forces. It has become more insolent, more mendacious and more repressive since our Conference in Addis Ababa.

WHAT HAS GONE WRONG?

The imperialists regard our Charter of Unity as token unity; they will not respect it until it assumes the form of a Union Government. It is incredible that they will defy a united

Continent. But it is easy to understand that they do not believe that we will be able to accomplish the next stage—to organize and centralize our economic and military and political forces to wage a real struggle against apartheid, Portuguese fascism and those who support these evils with trade, investments and arms.

We have not yet made the imperialists to believe that we can set our continent in order as a mighty economic force, capable of standing together as a united and progressive people.

Serious border disputes have broken out and disturbed our Continent, since our last meeting. Fortunately, good sense and African solidarity have prevailed in all those instances. But the disputes have been smothered, not settled. The artificial divisions of African States are too numerous and irrational for real permanent and harmonious settlements to be reached, except within the framework of a Continental Union.

How, for example, can we prevent the people of Western Somalia, whose whole livelihood is cattle-grazing, from continuing to look for fresh fields for grazing by travelling beyond traditional barriers without bringing them into clashes with their compatriots in Ethiopia?

And yet, in a united Africa, Ethiopian land and Somalian land, even though they may be separately sovereign within the framework of a Union Government of Africa, will belong to a common pool which would assist the general development of cattle-rearing in that part of our Continent, because there would be no artificial barriers to such development. The benefit of the development will be for the benefit of both Ethiopia and Somalia.

I said a little while ago, and I repeat, that the real border disputes will grow with the economic development and national strengthening of the African States as separate balkanized governmental units. That was the historical process of independent states in other continents. We cannot expect Africa, with its legacy of artificial borders, to follow any other course, unless we make a positive effort to arrest that danger now; and we can do so only under a Union Government. In other words, the careers and ambitions of political leaders, on the one hand, and balkanized nationalism on the other, if allowed to grow and become entrenched, could constitute a brake on the unification of African States. The Balkan States of Europe are a lesson for us.

History has shown that where the Great Powers cannot colonize, they balkanize. This is what they did to the Austro-Hungarian Empire and this is what they have done and are doing in Africa. If we allow ourselves to be balkanized, we shall be re-colonized and be picked off one after the other.

Now is the time for Africa's political and economic unification.

By far the greatest wrong which the departing colonialists inflicted on us, and which we now continue to inflict on ourselves in our present state of disunity, was to leave us divided into economically unviable States which bear no possibility of real development. As long as the chief consideration of the industrial Nations was our raw materials at their own prices, this policy made sense for them, if not for us.

Now that their technological impetus is such that they need Africa even more as a market for their manufactured goods than as a source of raw materials, our economic backwardness no longer makes sense for them any more than for us. The output of their great industrial complexes is no longer the primitive and simple implements like hoes and shovels. They now need vaster and more prosperous markets for heavy agricultural tractors and electronic machines. They wish to sell to us, not Ford motors propelled by magnetos or turbo-prop transport aircraft, but the latest in supersonic jets and atomic-powered merchant vessels. Which of us, trading separately in these highly developed market areas, can survive more than a year or two without remaining either economically backward, indebted, bankrupt or re-colonized?

There is much re-thinking on this score among the industrially-advanced countries, although their outlook is obscured because their economies are still geared to monopolistic devices for getting hold of our oil and gas deposits, uranium, gold, diamonds and other raw materials, cheap, and selling their manufactured goods back to us at exorbitant prices.

The poverty of the developing world has become a blot on the ethics and commonsense of the industrial nations. The recent United Nations Conference on Trade and Development was not organized by accident or solely by pressure from the developing nations. The growing economic gap between the two worlds spells misery for the developing countries, but it also threatens the industrialized nations with unemployment and with dangerous recessions and economic explosion.

We have reason to think that the imperialists themselves are in divided councils about the Unity of Africa. They must remain ambivalent, however, as long as they retain direct control over Southern Africa and neo-colonialist control of the Congo. The vast mineral wealth of those territories represents profits which they cannot willingly give up, even for greater markets in the rest of Africa.

But a Union Government of Africa would end the dilemma of the industrialized nations, because inevitably that wealth will be converted into capital for the development of Africa.

The fact that imperialism and neo-colonialism are in that dilemma should be for us the clearest indication of the course we must follow. We must unite for economic viability, first of all, and then to recover our mineral wealth in Southern Africa, so that our vast resources and capacity for development will bring prosperity for us and additional benefits for the rest of the world. That is why I have written elsewhere that the emancipation of Africa could be the emancipation of Man.

Is there any need to point out again that we are potentially the world's richest continent, not only in mineral wealth, but also in hydro-electric power? The wealth of the Sahara is yet untapped; the waters and rivers of Tanganyika and Ethiopia are yet unharnessed. All the capital we need for the development of these regions flows out of Africa today in gold, diamonds, copper, uranium and other minerals from Southern Africa, Northern Rhodesia, the Congo and other parts of the Continent. Every year in the Sahara and in other parts of Africa, new stores of mineral, chemical and petroleum wealth are discovered.

What is lacking for us in Africa, but the will and the courage to unite a divided but compact continent?

Today, in countless ways, our people learn that their poverty is not a curse from the gods or a burden imposed by the imperialists, but a political defect of our independence. The general realization grows that independence is not enough without the unity of Africa, for that is the only road towards the economic emancipation and development of our continent.

We in Africa are living in the most momentous era of our history. In a little less than one decade the majority of the territories in our continent have emerged from colonialism into sovereignty and independence. In a few years from now, we can envisage that all Africa will be free from colonial rule. Nothing can stem our onward march to independence and freedom.

While we have cause to rejoice in this achievement, our central problem as Independent States is the fragmentation of our territories into little independent States and of our policies and programmes into a patchwork of conflicting objectives and unco-ordinated development and plans.

While the post-war years have seen a phenomenal rise in the prices of manufactured goods which we need to sustain progress and development in our States, the prices of the raw materials which we export to these countries have shown an alarmingly steady decline. So the disparity between the "haves" or the highly developed nations and the "have-nots" or developing nations, becomes inevitably wider and wider as our needs grow greater and greater. How can we resolve this tragic paradox, except by uniting our forces and working together in Africa as a team?

Let us look further back on the year that has just passed since we first met at Addis Ababa last year. Think of the unfortunate clashes between Algeria and Morocco, between Somalia and Ethiopia and between Somalia and Kenya which nearly damaged and disrupted our new spirit of understanding and unity. If we had lived within a continental federal government in which the fortunes and fate of one were the fortunes and fate of all, could we have been drawn into such bloodshed with needless loss of precious African lives?

What shall I say of the military upheavals and mutinies in our sister States of Tanganyika, Uganda and Kenya? While no one among us here can tolerate indiscipline and mutiny in our armies, which of us was happy to learn that in their hour of need, our brothers were compelled to resort to the use of foreign troops—the troops of a former colonial power, at that—to bring these disturbances under control.

Before the damage was completely done, our brothers were able to send away these foreign troops and, in one case, called for the assistance of troops from a Sister African State.

Surely, these events have a clear lesson for us all! How can we maintain the safety and security of our respective States as our responsibilities increase and our problems become more complex, except through a united defence arrangement which will invest us with the effective and powerful means for joint action at short notice?

Last year at Addis Ababa I gave the warning that if we did not come together as speedily as possible under a Union Government, there would be border clashes and our people, in their desperation to get the good things of life, would revolt against authority. Subsequent events have fully endorsed that warning.

Look at events in the Congo. Why did they remain so confused, so frustrating and even so tragic for so long? If we had all been jointly responsible for bringing our brothers in the Congo the assistance they needed in their hour of travail, who would have dared to interfere from outside Africa in Congolese affairs? Instead of this, what did we see in the Congo?

On the one hand, internal disagreements and discord, endless manoeuvring for positions among the political leaders, and even the tragedy of fratricidal strife. On the other hand, foreign intervention and pressures, intrigues and coercion, subversion and cajolery.

In all this confusion, the power of imperialism has a fertile ground. It even dares to use openly certain African States to promote its selfish plans for the exploitation and degradation of the Congo. We are unable to hold back foreign intrigues, because we are divided among ourselves. None of us is free and none of us can be safe, while there is frustration and instability in any part of this continent.

I do not need to go on citing specific instances of our common problems and difficulties to prove the urgency and the need for united action on a continental basis in Africa today. There is not one of us here now who does not suffer from the handicaps of our colonial past. Let us therefore move forward together in unity and in strength, confident in the knowledge that with such immense national and human resources as we possess in our continent, we cannot fail to make Africa one of the happiest, most prosperous and progressive areas of the world.

Two years ago we were exposed to the ridicule of the world because they saw us as a divided Africa. They called us names which helped to widen the apparent breach among us: the "radical" Casablanca Powers, the "moderate" Monrovia Group, and the "pro-French" Brazzaville States. There was no justification for these labels, but to the imperialists they were a very convenient means of giving the dog a bad name and hanging him!

It is to our eternal credit that last year at Addis Ababa we put our enemies to shame by forging a common Charter from these groupings and emerging as the Organization of African Unity. Let it be said that at Cairo we put them to greater shame by agreeing to the establishment of a Union Government of Africa. Have you noticed, Brother Presidents and Prime Ministers, that so soon as we achieved this measure of agreement at Addis Ababa, the neo-colonialists and their agents proceeded to sow new seeds of disruption and dissension among us?

They became particularly active and vocal in preaching the new and dangerous doctrine of the "step by step" course towards unity. If we take one step at a time, when they are in a position to take six steps for every single one of ours, our weakness will, of course, be emphasized and exaggerated for their benefit. One step now, two steps later, then all will be fine in Africa for imperialism and neo-colonialism. To say that a Union Government for Africa is premature is to sacrifice Africa on the altar of neo-colonialism. Let us move forward together to the wider fields of our heritage, strong in our unity, where our common aspirations and hopes find abundant expression in the power of our united endeavours.

All over Africa the essential economic pattern developed under colonialism remains. Not one of us, despite our political independence, has yet succeeded in breaking, in any substantial measure, our economic subservience to economic systems external to Africa. It is the purpose of neo-colonialism to maintain this economic relationship.

The developed countries need the raw materials of Africa to maintain their own industries and they are anxious to find markets in Africa for their manufactured goods. But there can be no market for these manufactured goods unless the people of Africa have the money with which to buy them. Therefore I say that the developed countries have a vested interest in Africa's prosperity.

In many cases our most valuable raw materials—such as minerals—are owned and exploited by foreign companies. Large parts of the wealth of Africa, which could be used for the economic development of Africa, are drained out of the continent in this way to bolster the economies of the developed nations.

It is true that the whole world is poised at a delicate economic balance and that economic collapse in any one part of the world would have grave repercussions on us. Our situation in Africa is so weak that we are bound to be the first and the worst sufferers if economic difficulties should set in in Europe or America, and the effect upon us would be absolute and catastrophic. We have nothing to fall back on. We have become so utterly dependent upon these outside economic systems that we have no means of resistance to external economic fluctuations. We have no economic resilience whatsoever within our own continent.

We are so cut off from one another that in many cases the road systems in each of our countries peter out into bush as they approach the frontier of our neighbour. How can we trade amongst ourselves when we do not even have proper means of physical communication? It is now possible to travel by air from Accra to London in six hours. I can fly from Accra to Nairobi or from Accra to Cairo in half a day. It is easy for us to get together to talk. But on the ground over which we fly with such ease and nonchalance, it is frequently impossible to engage in the most elementary trade simply because there are no proper roads, and because we are artificially divided and balkanized.

Our few and negligible roads and railways always lead, ultimately, to some port. In a sense they have become symbols of our economic subservience and our dependence on trade outside the African Continent.

We have inherited from colonialism an economic pattern from which it is difficult to escape. Great forces are arrayed to block our escape. When individually we try to find some economic independence, pressures are brought against us that are often irresistible owing to our disunity.

I am not arguing that we should cut off all economic relationships with countries outside Africa. I am not saying that we should spurn foreign trade and reject foreign investment. What I am saying is that we should get together, think together, plan together and organize our African economy as a unit, and negotiate our overseas economic relations as part of our general continental economic planning. Only in this way can we negotiate economic arrangements on terms fair to ourselves.

The Organization of African Unity was a declaration of intention to unite. It was an optimistic beginning. But we need more than this. We must unite NOW under a Union Government if this intention is to have any meaning and relevance.

Talk is worthless if it does not lead to action. And so far as Africa is concerned, action will be impossible if it is any further delayed. Those forces which endanger our continent do not stand still. They are not moving step by step. They are marching in double step against us.

Every day we delay the establishment of a Union Government of Africa, we subject ourselves to outside economic domination. And our political independence as separate States becomes more and more meaningless.

Brother Presidents and Prime Ministers: as I said a few minutes ago, this decade is Africa's finest hour. Great things are in store for us if we would but take our courage in our hands and reach out towards them. How would South Africa dare to sentence Nelson Mandela and his seven brave colleagues against protests of a United Africa? How could Portugal dare think of continuing the violation of the sovereignty of Angola and Mozambique or so-called "Portuguese Guinea," if these formed part of a United Government of Africa? How could a white settler minority Government in Southern Rhodesia dare to lock up Nkomo and Sithole?

We have gone to Geneva to seek a major victory in our quest for fair play and justice in international trade. There were no less than seventy-five of us in one group set against the few of the great industrialized communities of Europe and the United States. And yet how weak was our bargaining power because of our political and economic disunity and divisions.

How much more effective would our efforts have been if we had spoken with the one voice of Africa's millions. With all our minerals and waterpower and fertile lands, is it not a cause for shame that we remain poor and content to plead for aid from the very people who have robbed us of our riches in the past? How can Egypt, strategically situated as it is, combat the imperialism and neo-colonialism and solve the pressing and urgent problems of the Middle East unless it has the backing of a Union Government of Africa? Only a Union Government can assist effectively in the solution of the problems of the Middle East, including the Palestinian question.

Mr Chairman,

Let us remember, Brother Presidents and Prime Ministers, the Sahara no longer divides us. We do not see ourselves merely as Arab Africa, Black Africa, English Africa or French Africa. We are one people, one Continent with one destiny.

I see no way out of our present predicament except through the force and power of a Union Government of Africa. By this I do not mean the abrogation of any sovereignty. I seek no regional unions as a basis for unity. Indeed, the more Independent States there are within our Union Government, the stronger will be our unity, and the freer will be each sovereign State within the Union to attend to its specific and exclusive problems.

The specific fields of common action I have in mind are: Defence, Foreign Policy and Economic Development (including a common currency for Africa).

In this way, instead of a Charter which operates on the basis of peripatetic or widely-separated commissions under the control of an administrative secretariat without political direction, we shall have a government for joint action in three fields of our governmental activity.

It has been suggested from this rostrum, and it is on our agenda also, that we should decide at this Conference as to the location of the Permanent Headquarters of the Organization of African Unity and appoint a permanent Secretary-General. If, as I hope, we agree in principle, at this Conference to move on to the establishment of a Union Government of Africa, we shall require quite a different set of criteria for selecting the Headquarters of the Organization and its permanent officials. We should also be careful to avoid being drawn into discussions at this stage which could lead to a clash of interests as to which country should have the Headquarters or provide a Secretary-General. This could harm the very unity which we are trying now to establish. I feel very strongly that the status quo should remain.

I see no objection, however, to the proposal that we should appoint a Secretary-General, provided it is agreed that the appointment is made on a provisional basis only. I feel that Addis Ababa should continue as the Provisional Headquarters of our Organization.

Mr Chairman,

I would like to express on behalf of Ghana our sincere thanks to His Imperial Majesty Haile Selassie I and to the Ethiopian Government for maintaining the Provisional Secretariat up to now. I feel, however, that before we rise we should make appropriate contributions from our various States for the upkeep of this our Organization. The burden should not be Ethiopia's alone.

I would like to state in this connection that Ghana is not interested in either the Headquarters or the Secretary-Generalship of the Organization.

Mr Chairman,

Two-hundred-and-eighty million people in strength with a common destiny and a common goal could give progress and development in Africa a new momentum and an impetus which go beyond our wildest dreams. Do not let us speak and act as if we are not aware of the revolutionary forces surging through Africa today. Even the industrialized nations outside Africa recognize this now.

Today, there may be frustration, doubt and distrust in every part of our Continent, but tomorrow will see a new hope and a new march to glory, under a United Government capable of speaking with one voice for all Africa.

Mr Chairman,

For a few moments, please permit me to refer to the pattern of economic structure which we inherited from the colonialists in Africa. All of us, under colonial rule, were encouraged to produce a limited number of primary commodities, mainly agricultural and mineral, for export overseas. Capital for development was owned by foreigners and profits were vigorously transferred abroad.

A trade pattern of this sort stagnated the rest of our national economy, and our resources remained undeveloped. In consequence, indigenous capital formation was negligible, leaving all our countries in a state of abject poverty.

Since independence, we have been making energetic efforts to reverse and overhaul these unsatisfactory features in our economy. In some of the Independent African States great efforts have been made to relax traditional economic links with the ex-colonial Powers, but none of us can say that we have succeeded in breaking those dangerous links completely.

Another handicap which we suffered from colonialism was the restriction of our economies which has hampered economic development in many ways. The very fact that all the Independent African States produce and maintain development plans is an indication of our deep concern for realizing nationalist aspirations and improving the conditions of living of our people.

But however deep our concern, however strong our determination, these development plans will avail us nothing if the necessary capital is not available. This capital, as we all know, is everywhere desperately short. The men with the know-how are few and scattered. It is by our coming together and pooling our resources that we can find a solution to this problem. In other words, only by unified economic planning on a continental basis with a central political direction within a Union Government can we hope to meet the economic challenge of our time.

It takes millions of pounds to build the basic industries, irrigation and power plants which will enable us to escape from our present economic stagnation. Our various individual, separate, balkanized States cannot mobilize the enormous amounts of money required for these major projects and industrial complexes. We cannot bargain effectively for the essential funds from foreign sources on the best possible terms. What we are doing now is to compete between ourselves for the little capital available from foreign sources. In our scramble to get this capital we grant foreign firms extensive and lucrative concessions for the exploitation of our natural resources. These Concessions to secure this capital exacerbate the colonial pattern of our economy. We invest more in raw materials output than in industrial development, and the continued drain abroad of profits which should have been re-invested in economic development retards the progress of our industrialization plans.

In a continental federal union, we can easily mobilize the amount of capital available to the African States by the establishment of a Central Monetary Development Finance Bank. Already our various States have agreed to form an African Development Bank. This, however, cannot succeed without a continental economic plan and without the necessary political direction which only a Union Government of Africa can provide.

An African Monetary Development Bank of the kind I envisage will enable us to formulate continental agreements concerning the terms of loans and investments by foreign interests. Together, we can bargain far more effectively with foreign firms and governments for investments and loans for the kinds of industries we desire and not those they desire. We can bargain on the terms of these loans and we can ensure that the increased savings which will arise from continental development of Africa's huge resources will enable us to develop even more rapidly. The unnecessary competition amongst us for capital would cease and moreover we can work up continental tariff policies designed to protect newly developing African industries. The great risks involved in investing in our individual countries will be reduced, for in an African economic union our development projects would be backed by all the African States together. But even this healthy sign of development is in grave danger of driving us against one another. As the general conditions of our economy are similar in all the Independent African States, and as our national development plans are not being co-ordinated, this can only lead to a concomitant expansion of our separate productive capacities in excess of the quantity which can be profitably marketed either internally or abroad. The result of this is obviously the certainty of establishing cut-throat competition among us with heavy financial losses to our respective economies.

The problem of African Unity must therefore be examined against the background of the economic position of the Independent African States, our aspirations for rapid development and the difficulties with which we are confronted in our separate existence. If we examine these problems carefully, we cannot evade the conclusion that the movement towards African political unity will substantially and immediately contribute to the solution of the economic problems of the Independent African States.

Indeed, I will make bold to state that African Unity based on a Continental Union Government is the only, I repeat only, possible framework within which the economic difficulties of Africa can be successfully and satisfactorily settled. The appeal for a Union Government of Africa is therefore not being made merely to satisfy a political end. It is absolutely indispensable for our economic survival in this modern world of ours.

We must remember that just as we had to obtain political independence from colonial rule as a necessary pre-requisite for establishing new and progressive communities for our respective States, so we cannot achieve economic stability in Africa as a whole without the pre-requisite of a continental Union Government.

Indeed, we cannot hope to sustain the economic development of Africa without first accepting the necessity for a continental division of labour to ensure that particular States specialized in their respective fields for which geographical, economic and social factors make them the most suitable, can develop to their fullest capacity with the best interest of the Continent as a whole in mind.

Take, for example, the steel industry. This could be developed to the highest possible limit in Nigeria, Egypt or Mauretania, or Liberia or Ghana, to mention only a few instances. If we do not unite under a federal government, it is clear that each of the States mentioned will wish in their own national interests to pursue the possibility of establishing and expanding its own steel mill.

Indeed, this is being done already by some of us to the benefit, profit and gain of foreign concerns.

If, however, our resources were combined to set up steel mills on a continental basis, at strategically chosen points in Africa, we would be in a position to make the greatest possible contribution to the industrial progress of the whole continent. Without a conscious effort based on a common governmental programme, we cannot hope to achieve this end. We might even find ourselves using the resources of one area of Africa to retard the progress and development of one or more other areas by cut-throat competition.

How then, at this moment of history, shall we meet this great challenge?

Certainly, we cannot blink at the harsh facts of life which are all too tragically familiar to us. This is especially true when we consider the economic development of Africa, on which all our other aspirations depend.

The most casual glance at our continent should convince anyone that the price of our disunity is continued exploitation from abroad and foreign interference in our internal matters. No matter where we look in the continent, we will find that, to a greater or lesser degree, the same pattern of exploitation persists.

For example: the economy of the Congo (Leopoldville) is still dominated by three foreign groups which represent Belgian, French, British and American interests. Herein lies the woe and tragedy of our beloved Congo. Two foreign firms—the Rhodesian Anglo-American Corporation and the Rhodesian Selection Trust—control the mining output of Zambia. Copper makes up eighty to ninety per cent of Zambia's exports, yet profits and interest shipped abroad annually often mount to as high as *half* of Zambia's total export earnings!

Thus you can see that despite political independence, nearly all of us here today are unable to exploit our agricultural and mineral resources in our own interests. Under a strong union government we would have the material resources for rapid industrialization, whereby all of us—big or small—would be benefited. But so long as we are divided, we will, to this extent, remain colonies in an economic sense. We shall remain puppets and agents of neo-colonialism.

The truth of this is even more evident when we examine monetary zones and customs unions. Most African States are still in monetary zones linked to the former colonial power. One-fourth of these States are in the sterling zone and one-half are in the franc zone. Owing to this currency arrangement, trade between the Independent African States is restricted and hampered. Indeed, trade is practically impossible within this financial environment.

An example of our present economic limitations as separate independent Governments, may be cited from our experience in our economic relations with our brothers from Upper Volta and Togo. Two years ago, in furtherance of our natural desire for closer collaboration in all fields of development with our Sister States, we performed a historic ceremony by breaking down the physical barriers established between Ghana and Upper Volta. The two Governments signed a long-term Trade and Payments Agreement under which each Government agreed to grant a non-interest bearing "swing" credit of about two-hundred-and-fifty-thousand pounds sterling. The Bank of Ghana on behalf of the Government of Ghana was appointed as the technical Agent to operate the Payments Agreement. In the case of the Upper Volta Government, the Banque de l'Afrique Occidental was nominated by the Upper Volta Government as its Agent. To this day, the Banque de l'Afrique Occidental in Ouagadougou [has] refused to execute the banking arrangements drawn up by the bank of Ghana to implement the Agreement. Payment instructions issued by the Bank of Ghana to the Banque de l'Afrique Occidental have so far not been honoured.

On the other hand, the Bank of Ghana has been requested by the Banque de l'Afrique Occidental to transfer sterling in their favour before the Payments instructions will be carried out, in spite of the fact that it is expressly laid down in the Agreement that all payments to or from either country should be effected through the Clearing Account to be maintained by the two banks.

If the Agreement instituted between Ghana and Upper Volta had worked successfully, the operation of the French currency arrangements, which are the medium of commercial undertakings in Upper Volta, would have been seriously undermined. Is it therefore any wonder that the Banque de l'Afrique Occidental made the operation of an Agreement signed between two Sister African States with the best of intentions unworkable and inoperative? Our difficulties with the Republic of Togo arise from the same limitations.

It will be clear from these examples that until we in Africa are able to establish our own independent currency and financial institutions, we shall continue to be at the mercy of the financial arrangements imposed by foreign Governments in their own, and not in our, interest.

As long as the States of Africa remain divided, as long as we are forced to compete for foreign capital and to accept economic ties to foreign powers because in our separate entities we are too small, weak and unviable to "go it alone," we will be unable to break the economic pattern of exploitation established in the days of outright colonialism.

Only if we can unite and carry out co-ordinated economic planning within the framework of African political unity, will it be possible for us to break the bonds of neo-colonialism and reconstruct our economies for the purpose of achieving real economic independence and higher living standards for all our African States, big or small.

Mr Chairman,

After all these arguments that have been advanced, can it still be maintained that a Union Government for Africa is premature? Have we not got the men? Have we not got the resources? Have we not got the will? What else are we waiting for? I know, and some of you know, that we can, right now, if we have the will and determination to do so. Mere resolutions cannot help us. Not even another Charter. The Ghana-Guinea Union, Casablanca Charter, Monrovia Charter and others, have long completed this Resolution and Charter-writing exercise.

Mr Chairman,

It is therefore with great honour and privilege that I now propose to you, Your Majesties, Brother Presidents and Prime Ministers, the framework for a Union Government of Africa.

This Union Government shall consist of an Assembly of Heads of State and Government headed by a President elected from among the Heads of State and Government of the Independent African States. The Executive of the Union Government will be a Cabinet or Council of Ministers with a Chancellor or Prime Minister as its head, and a Federal House consisting of two Chambers—The Senate and a House of Representatives. If you agree, we can appoint our Foreign Ministers, assisted by experts, to work out a constitution for a Union Government of Africa.

Brother Presidents and Prime Ministers: with our common suffering and aspirations, we should be one and a united people. Our Continent, surrounded on all sides by oceans, is one of the most compact land masses in the world. Nature has endowed us with the richest and the best of natural resources. Circumstances and our common experience in history have made all of us a people with one destiny. Let us not betray the great promise of our future or disappoint the great hopes of the masses of our people by taking the wrong turning in this critical and momentous hour of decision.

We cannot save ourselves except through the unity of our continent based on common action through a Continental Union Government. Only a united Africa under a Union Government can cure us of our economic ills and lift us out of our despair and frustration.

I make this sincere and serious appeal in the interest of our common progress, our security and our future well-being. I hope that all of us will accept this appeal with equal sincerity. But I know that, for various reasons, some of us may not be ready or prepared to take this historic and momentous decision now.

Nevertheless, I charge those of us who are ready to do so now—even if we are only a few (and how I wish it could be all of us)—firstly, to come away from Cairo having agreed to the establishment of a Union Government of Africa.

Secondly, those of us who subscribe to this solemn agreement must designate our Foreign Ministers to constitute a Working Committee to draft the Constitution for the Federal Union Government of Africa.

Thirdly, those who subscribe to this agreement should, within six months, meet at a place to be agreed upon, to adopt and proclaim to the world the Federal Union Government of Africa.

Mr Chairman, Brother Presidents and Prime Ministers: It has been said that "great things from little causes spring." How true this saying is, can be judged from the beginnings of some of the world's Great Powers of today. The United States started within thirteen weak economically non-viable colonies exposed to serious political and economic hardships. Yet today, the United States of America is a world power with not less than fifty constituent states.

The Soviet Union, whose scientists have astounded the world with their interplanetary exploits, began their Union amid untold hardships and difficulties with but three States. Today, the Soviet Union is composed of sixteen federated States!

We cannot wait, we dare not wait, until we are encompassed by our doom for failing to seize this grand opportunity rising to the call of Africa's finest hour.

This is the challenge which history has thrust upon us. This is the mandate we have received from our people, that we set about to create a Union Government for Africa now; and this is also the challenge which Providence and destiny has thrust upon us. We cannot, we must not, we dare not fail or falter.

C. L. R. James
(1901–1989, Trinidad)

The Rise and Fall of Nkrumah

The fall of Dr. Kwame Nkrumah is one of the greatest catastrophes that has befallen the minds of Africans in Africa, of people of African descent, and all who are interested in the development and progress of independent Africa.

His dramatic collapse is a thing that many people will find it hard to understand and to place within the context of what is happening in the underdeveloped countries. It will be difficult for people who are genuinely uninstructed about Africa, like the people of the Caribbean (for example, the people of Trinidad and Tobago). But those of us who have been following the developments of Africa and the criticisms of Africans in the European and American press have long been astonished at the confusion and the utter inability to understand of would-be experts on Africa.

Nkrumah's fall is a catastrophe. But it should have been foreseen. In fact it was foreseen, and I shall make that abundantly clear. What must not be lost sight of is that he was one of the greatest leaders of African struggles whom Africa has produced, especially during the last 20 years, the last crucial 20 years. He was not a rogue or a betrayer, or one who lost his head amid the temptations of power.

He was a splendid person, but he was overwhelmed by the economic and political problems which weigh so heavily upon the newly independent countries, particularly the independent countries of Africa. My association with Nkrumah is not only political but it has been personal, although with him, as with me, a personal relation was always governed by political beliefs and perspectives. I met him first in New York about 1941. He saw a great deal of my friends and political associates, and we became very intimately associated. Then in 1943, he said he was going to England to study law, whereupon I wrote a letter that I believe still exists among the archives of George Padmore, and which has become quite famous among us.

[George] Padmore was the leader of an organisation (chiefly of West Indians) devoted to propagating and organising for the emancipation of Africa. Padmore had accumulated an enormous amount of knowledge, a great library of books and papers and a wide international acquaintance of people who were devoted to the emancipation of Africa, and, in fact, of the whole colonial world. I therefore wrote to Padmore telling him about Francis (Nkrumah's English name). This letter said that Nkrumah, a young African, was coming to live in England. I said that he was not very bright but that he was determined to throw the imperialists out of Africa. I asked Padmore to see him and do his best for him, in other words, educate him politically as much as possible.

I am not in the least bothered at having written that Nkrumah was "not very bright." At the time he used to talk a great deal about Imperialism, Leninism and similar data, with which my friends and I were very familiar. Nkrumah used to talk a lot of nonsense about these matters. As a matter of fact, he knew nothing about them.

But as far as I know, Padmore met him at a London railway station. The two of them began to collaborate closely, and about a year later I read an address by Nkrumah on Imperialism which was a masterpiece. In one year he had learnt what had taken us so many years to learn and prepare. But he not only learned. He contributed a great deal of independent knowledge and constructive ideas to Padmore's organisation. And when he left London to go to work in Accra, it would have been difficult to tell of any serious distinction between the two.

How Nkrumah went to the Gold Coast must be remembered for when we come to estimate the cause of his fall this will play a not unimportant role. A body of middle-class Africans of the Gold Coast, lawyers, doctors, retired civil servants, some chiefs, had formed a political organisation called the Convention Party. They aimed at independence, or to be more precise, self-government. They might have been hazy about the name, but they knew what they wanted; to substitute themselves for the British colonial officials wherever possible. This was not an ignoble ambition, but the organisers of this party were too busy with their own affairs to devote themselves to the wearisome task of building the party. So hearing that Nkrumah had taken good degrees in American universities and was actively propagating ideas of freedom and independence for Africa in London, they sent to him and asked him to come and organise their party for them.

Like Caesar, Nkrumah came and saw and conquered, but the first persons he conquered were the people who had employed him. He organised a Youth Party, built a following among the masses, then organised a leadership among the trade unionists and the lower middle class. By the time the educated middle class knew what was happening he had the majority of the country behind him, and organised his own party—The Convention People's Party.

The struggle became extremely bitter between the educated African middle classes whom Nkrumah and his party denounced as stooges of the British Government, and Nkrumah's band of leaders who were derisively labelled "verandah boys." They had no houses of their own and were compelled, so ran the propaganda, to sleep in open verandahs.

Having conquered the middle classes, Nkrumah went on to win independence. It was most brilliantly done and deserves an honoured place in the history of human emancipation.

But you cannot govern a backward country without the co-operation or at least benevolent neutrality of a part of the middle classes. As I heard in London some weeks ago, the middle classes had regained power in the economic and social life of the country. Nkrumah had been balancing now to right and now to left. But as I heard it, he had become more and more dependent upon the leadership of a now huge bureaucracy. In his frantic attempt to modernise Ghana he had been compelled to concentrate more and more power into local hands. I believe that the army has acted on behalf of these.

This, I hasten to say, is *not* similar to what has happened in Nigeria. There the "verandah boys" have never been near to power. The army revolt in Nigeria was aimed at an all-powerful bureaucracy.

But for the time being, and until further evidence comes to hand, we can exercise our minds on the theory that after many years in the darkness and half-light, the middle classes in Ghana are grasping at the power. That is the best we can say now. A journalist so far from the scene cannot *know* anything.

Nkrumah has committed colossal blunders and committed the final blunder of leaving his country in a state where it has to begin all over again to work out an established government. But at a time like this, the one thing observers must never forget is the tremendous political achievements of Nkrumah. If you do not bear those constantly in mind, you will never be able to understand why his government in Ghana lasted so long (fifteen years), created such a great reputation for itself, for Nkrumah, and for Africa; and has now so ignominiously and shockingly collapsed. Nkrumah did three things: He led a great revolution. He raised the status of Africa and Africans to a pitch higher than it had ever reached before. Be prepared for a shock now, Ghana's economic policies were the most dynamic and successful of the new states in Africa.

Let us take them in order. Nkrumah did not win the independence of the Gold Coast by carrying on negotiations with the Colonial Office. He mobilised the population of Ghana and hurled them at the British colonial government. He paralysed the whole working of the state, brought everything to a standstill. This negation of normal life Nkrumah called "positive action" and his main demand was not self-government. Every politician in Ghana was for self-government. What distinguished Nkrumah's politics was the addition of a single word: "now." Thus he agitated for "self-government now" and took drastic steps to force it home. Nobody in Africa has hurled a whole population at an imperialist government.

The Gold Coast government also took a very positive action. They put Nkrumah and his body of leaders in jail. But the government was too late to halt events. Leading his movement secretly from jail, Nkrumah showed his power by an overwhelming victory of his party in elections over one-third of Ghana. He himself from jail ran for Accra and won. By this time his fearlessness, his political courage and political skill, the challenge of this minute David to the huge Goliath, had caught the attention of the world. Journalists from Europe had poured into Ghana. George Padmore, Nkrumah's official agent in London, wrote articles and books, made speeches, ceaselessly informing the world of Nkrumah's policies and events in Ghana. The British pressmen on the spot made it clear that Nkrumah had the mass of the population behind him. And here I write what I have hitherto only said from platforms. The government in Britain was completely baffled by this new apparition of an embattled and revolutionary African population.

It anxiously debated what to do. Some proposed to send force and beat the movement down. Mr. Nehru let it be known that if force were used, India would leave the Commonwealth immediately. Whereupon the British government accepted the inevitable and put in power a government headed by Nkrumah. When things began to go wrong in Ghana, some of us stuck by the Ghana government of Nkrumah almost to the very end. It was not friendship nor sentimentality. We knew what had been done and the man who had done it.

This is what Nkrumah now went on to do. It took him six years to win independence by 1957. He could have gone on to independence in 1951. He preferred to wait. But one day he told me that he didn't know whether he was right to wait, or if he should have gone forward in 1951 as George Padmore and Dorothy Padmore were urging him to do. I did not know what to think at the time, but today I am of the opinion that he should have gone straight ahead. That six-year delay was one cause of the deterioration of his party and government. A revolution cannot mark time for six years.

Nkrumah followed Nehru (a great friend of his) and declared Ghana a republic, setting a pattern followed by nearly all the African states. He sent for George Padmore and Padmore organised the first International Conference of African Independent States. He also organised the first Conference of African fighters. Banda, Nyerere, Tom Mboya, Lumumba, all were there. When Sekou Touré of Guinea defied De Gaulle and refused to be part of the new French community, Nkrumah came to his assistance, lent him money and united the state of Ghana to the state of Guinea. He declared that only a United Independent Africa could save Africa from a new colonialism. He wrote in the constitution of Ghana that the Ghana government would subordinate its sovereignty to the government of a United Africa. But more than that, by magnificent speeches and dramatic actions he made the world see Africa and Africans as contenders for liberty, equality and if not fraternity, respect.

Nkrumah is one of the great men of our day. What then went wrong? *He attempted to do too much, particularly in his drive to make Ghana a country of an advanced economy.* That we shall go into most carefully for it brings out two things: the difficulties of all newly independent states; and the vast difference between Africa and the Caribbean.

For many years no political collapse has unloosed among our people—and many others—the dismay that the fall of Nkrumah has caused. A sense of politics being an insoluble mystery has increased and that is bad for democracy; above all, people must understand. We all accept, I hope, that Nkrumah was no commonplace, incompetent person, a grabber at the profits and prerequisites of power, his personal degeneration at last discovered and exposed. No. His fall is deserved. He had become a disease in the blood of Ghana and of Africa. For us in the Caribbean to understand and learn the lesson of his fall we have to appreciate the immense differences between the territory and the population of Ghana and the territory and population of Trinidad and Tobago. Walk about in Accra, the capital of Ghana. A modern city, fine, concrete, American-style structures. The buildings where the trade union is housed; the party headquarters built by Nkrumah are among the finest in formerly colonial Africa. Motorcars of various styles shoot about the streets. Everywhere, activity, modernism. Outside Accra, a university; at Kumasi (inland), a scientific technological institute planned for the highest standards. Much of this was built by Nkrumah or his government.

But drive five miles from the centre of Accra. Get out and walk around. There is a mud-walled village, houses of a type that could have been there 500 years ago, an elementary school in the process of being constructed by the villagers themselves. Go on for 50 miles. You meet small villages of a few score houses. After 150 miles, mainly of thick forest, with small concentrations of people living African lives and for the most part speaking one of a few tribal languages, you come to Kumasi. Kumasi is quite a modern town. But it is the capital of the Ashanti, a people different from the Africans of the coast in language, religion, tribal practices, and outlook, *and very conscious of these differences.* We are not finished yet.

On our journey we have often seen walking on the road a few dozen cattle, with some cattlemen walking behind them. They are on their way to Accra, where the cattle, thin and exhausted, will be fattened up for beef. Men and beasts have come hundreds of miles from the third area of Ghana, the Mohammedan North with its centre, Tamale. When I was in Ghana in 1957 many of them went without clothes. In 1960 I enquired about them. Elementary education was fighting hard against a primitive past, bad roads, remote villages.

And the famous cocoa industry? The cocoa plantations were deep inside the forests, often miles from each other. To sum up: in a Caribbean island, "All o'we is one." In an African state, and Ghana, by and large, is the most advanced of them, "All o'we is many."

That was what Nkrumah faced. In the struggle for "self-government now" the Convention People's Party had knit the population closer together into one people than even before. *Now, however, in Nkrumah's drive to build a modern economy and create a sense of nationhood, he found himself splitting the new nation into far more intractable divisions than the ancient tribalism.* Let us state the problems as they developed and have finally overwhelmed him.

The first problem was a state, a government. To begin with, he had no independent African government. Like all these new African rulers, he had inherited a British colonial government organised for purposes quite different from his own. Further, in a new government, it is people, personnel, who are an urgent priority. Nkrumah had to find people to create a modern economy and run a modern government.

This put a premium on education so that the educated in every area began rapidly to develop into a aristocracy, or to use a contemporary term, a meritocracy. In this drive for modernisation, the only sure source of discipline and loyalty to the regime was the party. The party gradually acquired enormous power and control. But, try as he would, Nkrumah could not prevent the party becoming the party of the new bureaucracy and no longer the party of the masses as in the days of the struggle for "self-government now." Sharp and persistent conflicts and grave corruption develop in *all* (I repeat, *all*) new and growing bureaucracies. Nkrumah found himself more and more having to decide between honest and dishonest; between groups and individuals fighting often with inter-tribal weapons.

In spite of himself, he had personally to assume dictatorial powers, or to give such powers to individuals whom he could trust or thought he could. In 1960 I warned him of the imminent crisis. By that time he could not understand. He had at the same time, amid these troubles, to battle with the decline in the price of tropical commodities such as cocoa. These prices had dropped fantastically all over the world. But the prices of the manufactured goods these tropical areas had to buy had risen. This was felt acutely by Ghana, dependent on the sale of cocoa, and frantically buying modern goods to modernise itself. It is within these objective practical realities that Nkrumah had to govern, to build a new state. He developed many personal weaknesses (I know quite a few).

But I know that unless you are acutely aware of the economic and social milieu in which a politician is functioning, you get mixed up resignedly in the speculation and analysis of pure personality, and end by shaking your head on the weakness of human, especially political, nature. We can now see Nkrumah the man, fighting with those problems and breaking politically (and personally) under them. As we watch him, we are seeing not merely an individual but a continent, the continent of Africa.

Nkrumah over the years committed what we can now call blunder after blunder. They may not have been clearly [seen] as blunders at the time, but the way in which his enemies have got rid of him shows that there had been accumulating in various sections of the population a great deal of antagonism to him. Unless people are certain that the minds of the population have turned against the political leadership, they do not plot and act in the way they have acted in Nigeria and Ghana. First of all Nkrumah had the greatest contempt for what in democratic countries is known as the parliamentary opposition. A parliamentary opposition, he said, was a luxury which only wealthy and advanced countries could afford. What is needed in Ghana was that everybody should devote himself to developing the country and building the new nation. Nkrumah used to say this openly, and it was a conception of government entirely and utterly false.

Where you have around you only a lot of yes-men, the first victim is yourself. You have no means of judging and testing the information that you get and, most important of all, no means of judging the state of mind of the population. It is perfectly clear that Nkrumah hadn't the faintest idea of what was going on in the minds of the people and in the heads of his chief officials. The first victim of a dictatorship is usually the dictator himself. He cannot govern properly and ensures only the disorder attendant on his removal. Elections were a farce. He ended with a one-party state.

Nkrumah's best known opponents were Danquah, Busia and Appiah. Busia fled. Danquah and Appiah were in and out of jail without trial. The argument that Nkrumah and his supporters used was that Danquah was in reality a city intellectual who, purely for political purposes, had formed an alliance with some of the most reactionary elements in the country, chiefly the rulers of Ashanti. So that when Appiah returned from England he became a leader of the opposition, strongly Ashanti, and was frequently in jail without trial.

Nkrumah's greatest political error was this. He believed that the question of democracy was a matter between him and Danquah and Busia and Appiah and such. He never understood that democracy was a matter in which the official leaders and an opposition were on trial before the mass of the population. It is not a question of conflict between rivals for power, as so many who shout "democracy" believe.

In reality, the concept and practice of democracy is very difficult for people who are just starting it. The new rulers believe that as long as they have a majority in Parliament they can do anything. In Britain and other countries where there is a long tradition of democracy, the politicians know that they cannot overstep certain boundaries without bringing the whole of government into discredit and unloosening dangerous currents among the people. Nkrumah was very energetic. He was not one who could point only to some roads, some schools and some foreign investments. Nkrumah was busy with his truly magnificent Volta scheme for the production of aluminium locally, with building and developing a new town, Tema. But, overwhelmed with work, Nkrumah depended more and more upon the party and less and less upon Parliament. But here his shallow concept of democracy found him out.

When I was in Ghana in 1960 he was engaged in building a special school for the training of party members. The year before he had declared that the party was the real ruler of the country. But having destroyed democracy in Parliament, if even he wanted to, he could not establish democracy in the party. He had made the Parliament into a body of stooges and the party also became the same, a body of stooges. This dual degeneration of the Parliament and of the party had one terrible result. The ablest, the most qualified and the intellectuals of finest character turned their backs on Nkrumah. Some of them, an astonishing number, went abroad and took jobs elsewhere. Those who stayed at home either devoted themselves to their professions, such as law and medicine, or did their work in the government, drew their pay and let Nkrumah govern or misgovern as he pleased. This abandonment of their own government and their own people by gifted, trained intellectuals of high character is a feature of modern underdeveloped countries. Canadian, British, French, even the United States businesses will take them once their degrees and qualifications are good enough. It is a commonplace that nowhere has a country suffered from the disaffection of its ablest intellectuals as Ghana has suffered.

One strong current of opinion is that they refuse to be governed by "the party." All sorts of ignoramuses, gangster-types, only had to prove their loyalty to the regime, i.e., to Nkrumah, and they could go places in the party and in the country. A notoriously ignorant and even more flagrantly corrupt minister had to be fired. But he had influence among the Ashanti. The Ashanti were restless and he was brought back, to the scandal of the whole country.

A false policy persisted in causing a brilliant politician to deteriorate personally. Nkrumah had himself called "Osagyefo" or Saviour. He bought planes, small warships, wasted public money on prestige building, and on prestige diplomacy. He became the advocate of the policy of a United Africa, a profound and far-seeing policy, but he advocated it crudely and with an intolerance that labelled all who disagreed with him as fools or cranks. Posing as an authority on all sorts of historical and philosophical subjects, he began to publish book after book. Years ago I ceased to read them. The drive towards economic expansion continued but now with a huge and self-seeking bureaucracy and the inevitable heavy taxation of the mass of the population. Ghana began to go bankrupt.

At such times all who are not sharing in the spoils begin to draw near each other and to think in terms of a new regime. Nkrumah was shot at two or three times. I wrote to him hinting that where a head of state is threatened so often with assassination something is vitally wrong with his regime; it is the ruler's business to find out what is wrong and correct it. I told him what to do. Nkrumah replied that he was a revolutionary and had to expect that his life was in constant danger. When I read that, I knew that he was no longer the dynamic, sensitive politician of the old days.

Soon he had publicly to accuse the secretary of his party of plotting to murder him, an accusation which discredited him as much as it discredits the accused. Any politician could now divine that there was surely building up in the country a secret opposition. Then came the dismissal of the Chief Justice, for giving a decision Nkrumah did not approve of. I learnt that he was now compelled to lean heavily on heads of the civil service, police and army. They were not only in charge of government departments. They were seeping back into the party. The party, led by the "verandah boys," and then by those whom I call the party gangsters, was coming to an end. With its end has come Nkrumah's end. He says he will return. Maybe. I doubt it. If he does the mess will be bloody.

When he dismissed the Chief Minister, I wrote to him at once and when he did not reply I publicly broke off the relations of twenty-five years. You can poison a Chief Justice, you cannot dismiss him for a decision from the Bench. You destroy the concept of law and order. I knew then that his regime was doomed. I sat down and prepared a book which I called *Nkrumah Then and Now* (published later as *Nkrumah and the Ghana Revolution*). In it I did at length what I am doing here briefly: I showed the former grandeur and present decadence of Nkrumah. I not only prophesied the end of his regime but showed the necessity for bringing it to an end.

What exactly is happening there today I don't know and can't know. Nkrumah studied, thought and knew a lot. But one thing he never mastered: that democracy is not a matter of the rights of an opposition, but in some way or other must involve the population. Africa will find that road or continue to crash from precipice to precipice.

The Rise and Fall of Nkrumah

James Baldwin

(1924–1987, United States)

My Dungeon Shook

Letter to My Nephew
on the One Hundredth Anniversary
of the Emancipation

Dear James:

I have begun this letter five times and torn it up five times. I keep seeing your face, which is also the face of your father and my brother. Like him, you are tough, dark, vulnerable, moody—with a very definite tendency to sound truculent because you want no one to think you are soft. You may be like your grandfather in this, I don't know, but certainly both you and your father resemble him very much physically. Well, he is dead, he never saw you, and he had a terrible life; he was defeated long before he died because, at the bottom of his heart, he really believed what white people said about him. This is one of the reasons that he became so holy. I am sure that your father has told you something about all that. Neither you nor your father exhibit any tendency towards holiness: you really *are* of another era, part of what happened when the Negro left the land and came into what the late E. Franklin Frazier called "the cities of destruction." You can only be destroyed by believing that you really are what the white world calls a *nigger*. I tell you this because I love you, and please don't you ever forget it.

I have known both of you all your lives, have carried your Daddy in my arms and on my shoulders, kissed and spanked him and watched him learn to walk. I don't know if you've known anybody from that far back; if you've loved anybody that long, first as an infant, then as a child, then as a man, you gain a strange perspective on time and human pain and effort. Other people cannot see what I see whenever I look into your father's face, for behind your father's face as it is today are all those other faces which were his. Let him laugh and I see a cellar your father does not remember and a house he does not remember and I hear in his present laughter his laughter as a child. Let him curse and I remember him falling down the cellar steps, and howling, and I remember, with pain, his tears, which my hand or your grandmother's so easily wiped away. But no one's hand can wipe away those tears he sheds invisibly today, which one hears in his laughter and in his speech and in his songs. I know what the world has done to my brother and how narrowly he has survived it. And I know, which is much worse, and this is the crime of which I accuse my country and my countrymen, and for which neither I nor time nor history will ever forgive them, that they have destroyed and are destroying hundreds of thousands of lives and do not know it and do not want to know it. One can be, indeed one must strive to become, tough and philosophical concerning destruction and death, for this is what most of mankind has been best at since we have heard of man. (But remember: *most* of mankind is not *all* of mankind.) But it is not permissible that the authors of devastation should also be innocent. It is the innocence which constitutes the crime.

Now, my dear namesake, these innocent and well-meaning people, your countrymen, have caused you to be born under conditions not very far removed from those described for us by Charles Dickens in the London of more than a hundred years ago. (I hear the chorus of the innocents screaming, "No! This is not true! How *bitter* you are!"—but I am writing this letter to *you*, to try to tell you something about how to handle *them*, for most of them do not yet really know that you exist. I *know* the conditions under which you were born, for I was there. Your countrymen were *not* there, and haven't made it yet. Your grandmother was also there, and no one has ever accused her of being bitter. I suggest that the innocents check with her. She isn't hard to find. Your countrymen don't know that *she* exists, either, though she has been working for them all their lives.)

Well, you were born, here you came, something like fifteen years ago; and though your father and mother and grandmother, looking about the streets through which they were carrying you, staring at the walls into which they brought you, had every reason to be heavyhearted, yet they were not. For here you were, Big James, named for me—you were a big baby, I was not—here you were: to be loved. To be loved, baby, hard, at once, and forever, to strengthen you against the loveless world. Remember that: I know how black it looks today, for you. It looked bad that day, too, yes, we were trembling. We have not stopped trembling yet, but if we had not loved each other none of us would have survived. And now you must survive because we love you, and for the sake of your children and your children's children.

This innocent country set you down in a ghetto in which, in fact, it intended that you should perish. Let me spell out precisely what I mean by that, for the heart of the matter is here, and the root of my dispute with my country. You were born where you were born and faced the future that you faced because you were black and *for no other reason*. The limits of your ambition were, thus, expected to be set forever. You were born into a society which spelled out with brutal clarity, and in as many ways as possible, that you were a worthless human being. You were not expected to aspire to excellence: you were expected to make peace with mediocrity. Wherever you have turned, James, in your short time on this earth, you have been told where you could go and what you could do (and *how* you could do it) and where you could live and whom you could marry. I know your country-men do not agree with me about this, and I hear them saying, "You exaggerate." They do not know Harlem, and I do. So do you. Take no one's word for anything, including mine—but trust your experience. Know whence you came. If you know whence you came, there is really no limit to where you can go. The details and symbols of your life have been deliberately constructed to make you believe what white people say about you. Please try to remember that what they believe, as well as what they do and cause you to endure, does not testify to your inferiority but to their inhumanity and fear. Please try to be clear, dear James, through the storm which rages about your youthful head today, about the reality which lies behind the words *acceptance* and *integration*. There is no reason for you to try to become like white people and there is no basis whatever for their impertinent assumption that *they* must accept *you*. The really terrible thing, old buddy, is that *you* must accept *them*. And I mean that very seriously. You must accept them and accept them with love. For these innocent people have no other hope. They are, in effect, still trapped in a history which they do not understand; and until they understand it, they cannot be released from it. They have had to believe for many years, and for innumerable reasons, that black men are inferior to white men. Many of them, indeed, know better, but, as you will discover, people find it very difficult to act on what they know. To act is to be committed, and to be committed is to be in danger. In this case, the danger, in the minds of most white Americans, is the loss of their identity. Try to imagine how you would feel if you woke up one morning to find the sun shining and all the stars aflame. You would be frightened because it is out of the order of nature. Any upheaval in the universe is terrifying because it so profoundly attacks one's sense of one's own reality. Well, the black man has functioned in the white man's world as a fixed star, as an immovable pillar: and as he moves out of his place, heaven and earth are shaken to their foundations. You, don't be afraid. I said that it was intended that you should perish in the ghetto, perish by never being allowed to go behind the white man's definitions, by never being allowed to spell your proper name. You have, and many of us have, defeated this intention; and, by a terrible law, a terrible paradox, those innocents who believed that your imprisonment made them safe are losing their grasp of reality. But these men are your brothers—your lost, younger brothers. And if the word *integration* means anything, this is what it means: that we, with love, shall force our brothers to see themselves as they are, to cease fleeing from reality and begin to change it. For this is your home, my friend, do not be driven from it; great men have done great things here, and will again, and we can make America what America must become. It will be hard, James, but you come from sturdy, peasant stock, men who picked cotton and dammed rivers and built railroads, and, in the teeth of the most terrifying odds, achieved an unassailable and monumental dignity. You come from a long line of great poets, some of the greatest poets since Homer. One of them said, *The very time I though I was lost, My dungeon shook and my chains fell off.*

You know, and I know, that the country is celebrating one hundred years of freedom one hundred years too soon. We cannot be free until they are free. God bless you, James, and Godspeed.

Your uncle,
James

Cornel West
(b. 1953, United States)

W. E. B. Du Bois: The Jamesian Organic Intellectual

The career of W. E. B. Du Bois serves as a unique response to the crisis of American pragmatism in the twentieth century. Although he was born nine years after John Dewey (and about a hundred miles away) and died one year after Mills, Du Bois already saw the contours of the "Fourth Epoch," a period fundamentally shaped by the decolonization of the third world. As an American intellectual of African descent—the greatest one produced in this country—Du Bois looks at the United States through a different lens from those of Emerson, Peirce, James, Dewey, Hook, and Mills. As one grounded in and nourished by American pragmatism, Du Bois—both by personal choice and by social treatment—allies himself in word and deed with the wretched of the earth. In the United States, this principally takes the form of performing intellectual work within the institutions, organizations, and movements of Afro-Americans or those that focus on their plight.

A New Englander by birth and rearing, Du Bois did not undergo the usual racial discrimination and depreciation during his childhood. He was the only black child in his secondary schools and attended an all-white Congregational church. His family, headed by his mother, was poor, yet not as poor or socially ostracized as the Irish immigrant mill workers in his town. Upon graduation from high school, Du Bois wanted to attend Harvard College, but the poor academic quality of his high school and some white discouragement (though white financial support ultimately allowed him to go) made him settle for Fisk University—the black Yale, as it were. Admitted as a sophomore owing to his excellent record, Du Bois experienced segregation and encountered Afro-American culture for the first time. Unacquainted with the kinetic orality, emotional physicality, and combative spirituality of black music, language, and customs, Du Bois harbored ambiguous attitudes toward this culture. In his graduating class of five in 1888, Du Bois gave a commencement address on his hero, Bismarck, who "had made a nation out of a mass of bickering peoples."[1] As he notes in one of his autobiographies: "I was blithely European and imperialist in outlook; democratic as democracy was conceived in America."[2]

From Fisk, Du Bois matriculated to Harvard College, entering as a junior owing to the "lower standards" at Fisk. Despite having no social life at Harvard, including a rejection from the glee club, Du Bois thrived there intellectually. Emotionally sustained by his involvement in the black community, Du Bois was most impressed at Harvard by William James—and his pragmatism.

> I was in Harvard for education and not for high marks, except as marks would insure my staying ... above all I wanted to study philosophy! I wanted to get hold of the basis

of knowledge, and explore foundations and beginnings. I chose, therefore, Palmer's course in ethics, but he being on Sabbatical for the year, William James replaced him, and I became a devoted follower of James at the time he was developing his pragmatic philosophy.[3]

Du Bois seems to have been attracted to pragmatism owing to its Emersonian evasion of epistemology-centered philosophy, and his sense of pragmatism's relevance to the Afro-American predicament.

> I hoped to pursue philosophy as my life career, with teaching for support . . . My salvation here was the type of teacher I met rather than the content of the courses. William James guided me out of the sterilities of scholastic philosophy to realist pragmatism . . .
>
> I revelled in the keen analysis of William James, Josiah Royce and young George Santayana. But it was James with his pragmatism and Albert Bushnell Hart with his research method, that turned me back from the lovely but sterile land of philosophic speculation, to the social sciences as the field for gathering and interpreting that body of fact which would apply to my program for the Negro . . .
>
> I knew by this time that practically my sole chance of earning a living combined with study was to teach, and after my work with Hart in United States history, I conceived the idea of applying philosophy to an historical interpretation of race relations.[4]

Du Bois never spelled out what he meant by the "sterilities of scholastic philosophy," but given what we know of James's pragmatism, it surely had something to do with sidestepping the Cartesian epistemological puzzles of modern philosophy. Yet, unlike James and more like Dewey, Du Bois took a turn toward history and the social sciences. In 1890, Du Bois received his Harvard cum laude bachelor's degree in philosophy. Du Bois' move toward history and the social sciences, reinforced by James's candid advice (untinged with racial bias) that there is "not much change for anyone earning a living as a philosopher," resulted in his receiving a fellowship to stay at Harvard for graduate work. Since sociology as a discipline did not yet exist at Harvard, Du Bois studied in the history and political science departments. Moreover, the fact that Du Bois "came to the study of sociology by way of philosophy and history"[5]—that is, primarily James's pragmatism and Hart's documentary approach—put him on the cutting edge of new intellectual developments in late-nineteenth-century America.

Upon the encouragement of his supervisor, Hart, Du Bois spent two years (1892–94) at the University of Berlin. In Germany, Du Bois studied economics, history, and sociology in the seminars of Gustav von Schmoller and Adolf Wagner (both "socialists of the chair"); and he heard Max Weber lecture as a visiting professor. Yet the heroic romantic nationalism of Heinrich von Treitschke, the famous Prussian historian and political theorist, impressed Du Bois most. Though Du Bois had come far from his uncritical praise of Bismarck, he still was attracted to Treitschke's notion that history was made by the powerful wills of great men who unify and guide their own peoples. Needless to say, Du Bois saw this role for himself in regard to black Americans. On his twenty-fifth birthday he dedicated "himself as the Moses of his people."[6]

Du Bois' stay in Europe had a tremendous impact on his view of himself and America. On the one hand, it gave him a way "of looking at the world as a man and not simply from a narrow racial and provincial outlook."[7] On the other hand, it provided him with an outlet for his hostility toward America and insight into its provinciality.

> I found to my gratification that they, with me, did not regard America as the last word in civilization. Indeed, I derived a certain satisfaction in learning that the University of

Berlin did not recognize a degree even from Harvard University, no more than Harvard did from Fisk . . . All agreed that Americans could make money and did not care how they made it. And the like. Sometimes their criticism got under even my anti-American skin, but it was refreshing on the whole to hear voiced my own attitude toward so much that America had meant to me.[8]

In June 1894, Du Bois arrived back in "nigger-hating" America.[9] Sailing aboard a ship full of European immigrants, he noted as it arrived in New York harbor:

I know not what multitude of emotions surged in others, but I had to recall that mischievous little French girl whose eyes twinkled as she said: "Oh yes the Statue of Liberty! With its back toward America, and its face toward France!"[10]

Since teaching in white universities was unthinkable, Du Bois accepted a job teaching Greek and Latin at a black parochial school in Xenia, Ohio—Wilberforce University. Having shed his dogmatic religious beliefs under James, Du Bois found it difficult to cope with the deeply pietistic atmosphere at the school. For instance, at one gathering it was announced

that "Professor Du Bois will lead us in prayer." I simply answered "No, he won't," and as a result nearly lost my new job.[11]

Du Bois quite understandably felt constrained at Wilberforce, though he did complete his Harvard dissertation there on the suppression of the African slave trade. In 1896, it was published as the first volume of the Harvard Historical Studies. As Arnold Rampersad has noted, this work, though full of original and ground-breaking research, is essentially "a chapter of the moral history of his country"—ethical motives and national conscience are stressed.[12]

Du Bois stayed at Wilberforce for only two years, thanks to an offer to study the black community in Philadelphia (then the largest black community in the North). This offer was a grand opportunity not just to leave Wilberforce with his new wife but also to test his scientific skills and narrow Enlightenment outlook on race relations.

The Negro problem was in my mind a matter of systematic investigation and intelligent understanding. The world was thinking wrong about race, because it did not know. The ultimate evil was stupidity. The cure for it was knowledge based on scientific investigation.[13]

This outlook guided not only his pioneering study *The Philadelphia Negro* (1899), but also the *Atlanta University Publications* (1896–1914) he directed during his thirteen years as professor of economics at Atlanta University. At the first stage of Du Bois' career, he worked diligently as a social scientist and professor gathering the first empirical data on the social conditions of black Americans. Yet as the institutionalized terrorism escalated in the South with tighter Jim Crow laws and more lynchings. Du Bois' moral idealism along with the scholarly strategy of disclosing the facts and revealing the truth of black oppression became less credible.

Two considerations thereafter broke in upon my work and eventually disrupted it: first, one could not be a calm, cool and detached scientist while Negroes were lynched, murdered and starved; and secondly, there was no such definite demand for scientific work of the sort that I was doing, as I had confidently assumed there would be easily forthcoming. I regarded it as axiomatic that the world wanted to learn the truth and if the truth were sought with even approximate accuracy and painstaking devotion, the world would gladly support the effort.[14]

Du Bois became more and more convinced not only that "most Americans answer all questions regarding the Negro *a priori*,"[15] but also that issues of power, interests, and status played more important roles than he had realized. This recognition led him to put less faith in scientific research as a weapon of social change and to focus more on middlebrow journalism and writing for a general literate public. His American classic, *The Souls of Black Folk* (1903), consisted of eight revised essays already published in leading magazines (mostly *Atlantic Monthly*) and five new pieces. Like Emerson, Du Bois always viewed himself as a poet in the broad nineteenth-century sense; that is, one who creates new visions and vocabularies for the moral enhancement of humanity. This poetic sensibility is manifest in his several poems and five novels. Yet it is seen most clearly in *The Souls of Black Folk*.

Du Bois' classic text can be viewed as being in the Emersonian grain, yet it conveys insights ignored by most of white America. Du Bois attempts to turn the Emersonian theodicy inside out by not simply affirming the capacity of human powers to overcome problems, but, more important, raising the question "How does it feel to be a problem?"[16] in America—a problem America neither admits it has nor is interested in solving. The aim of his text is to convey and enact "the strange experience" of "being a problem:—that is, being an American of African descent."

> The Negro is a sort of seventh son, born with a veil, and gifted with second-sight in this American world—a world which yields him no true self-consciousness, but only lets him see himself through the revelation of the other world. It is a peculiar sensation, this double-consciousness, this sense of always looking at one's self through the eyes of others, of measuring one's soul by the tape of a world that looks on in amused contempt and pity. One ever feels his twoness—an American, a Negro; two souls, two thoughts, two unreconciled strivings; two warring ideals in one dark body, whose dogged strength alone keeps it from being torn asunder.[17]

Du Bois is writing about "the experience of being a problem" at a time in which discernible signs of the awakening third world appear, such as the defeat of Russia by Japan (1904), the Persian revolt (1905), and the Mexican revolution (1911). And as America emerges as a world power, much of the credibility of its rhetoric of freedom and democracy is threatened by the oppression of black Americans.

Emerson had grappled with the "double-consciousness" of being an American, of having a European culture in an un-European environment. Yet, for him, being an American was not a problem but rather a unique occasion to exercise human powers to solve problems. Du Bois' "double-consciousness" views this unique occasion as the *cause* of a problem, a problem resulting precisely from the exercise of white human powers celebrated by Emerson. In short, Du Bois subverts the Emersonian theodicy by situating it within an imperialist and ethnocentric rhetorical and political context.

But, ironically, Du Bois' subversion is aided by his own revision of the Emersonian theodicy. This revision principally consists of exercising his own powers in order to overcome the blindnesses, silences, and exclusions of earlier Emersonian theodicies. The aim remains self-creation and individuality, though with a more colorful diversity; the end is still a culture in which human powers, provoked by problems, are expanded for the sake of moral development of human personalities.

> The history of the American Negro is the history of this strife—this longing to attain self-conscious manhood, to merge his double self into a better and truer self. In this merging he wishes neither of the older selves to be lost. He would not Africanize America, for America has too much to teach the world and Africa. He would not bleach

his Negro soul in a flood of white Americanism, for he knows that Negro blood has a message for the world. He simply wishes to make it possible for a man to be both a Negro and an American, without being cursed and spit upon by his fellows, without having the doors of opportunity closed roughly in his face.

This, then, is the end of his striving: to be a co-worker in the kingdom of culture, to escape both death and isolation, to husband and use his best powers and his latent genius.[18]

Following his mentor Hart's racialist view of history in which each "race" possesses certain gifts and endowments, Du Bois holds that those of the Negro consist of story and song, sweat and brawn and the spirit.[19] Du Bois claims that these gifts of black folk have given America its only indigenous music, the material foundations of its empire, and ethical critiques to remind America of its own moral limits. The music expresses the protean improvisational character of America itself, always responding to, adapting, and experimenting with new challenges. Slavery, the foundation of America's power, exemplifies the tragic and usually overlooked costs concealed by American prosperity. Black ethical critiques, themselves often based on American-style Protestantism and U.S. political ideals, expose the hypocrisy of the American rhetoric of freedom and democracy.

As a highly educated Western black intellectual, Du Bois himself often scorns the "barbarisms" (sometimes confused with Africanisms) shot through Afro-American culture. In fact, I count eighteen allusions to the "backwardness" of black folk.[20] He even goes as far as to support a form of paternalism that leads toward black self-determination.

I should be the last one to deny the patent weaknesses and shortcomings of the Negro people . . . I freely acknowledge that it is possible, and sometimes best, that a partially undeveloped people should be ruled by the best of their stronger and better neighbors for their own good, until such time as they can start and fight the world's battles alone.[21]

This paternalism fits well with his early doctrine of the talented tenth—the educated, cultured, and refined like himself leading the benighted, ignorant, and coarse black masses out of the wilderness into the promised land. Yet, even in this first stage of his career, Du Bois acknowledges and accents the creative powers of the black masses in the cultural sphere, especially in their music.

Du Bois' stress on black music is significant in that here he sees black agency at work. Like Emerson and other pragmatists, Du Bois posits culture making as the prime instance of history making. He does this not only because for Afro-Americans all other spaces were closed, but also because in every society, no matter how oppressive, human creativity can be discerned in culture making. In good Emersonian fashion, Du Bois' democratic mores are grounded in the detection of human creative powers at the level of everyday life.

Du Bois' departure from Atlanta University and his acceptance of the editorship of the *Crisis,* organ of the newly formed National Association for the Advancement of Colored People, inaugurated a second stage in his career. In the eyes of some black figures like Walker Trotter, the NAACP was too interracialist; in the view of those like William James, it was too militant for the times. Yet Du Bois along with other black and white activists, including John Dewey, pushed on for social reform and civil rights by means of public agitation and political pressure. As director of publications and research, Du Bois was the only black national officer in the organization. The first issue of the *Crisis* was published in November 1910 and consisted of a thousand copies; by 1918 a hundred thousand copies were being printed. He held this position for twenty-four years.

Like Dewey, Du Bois supported Woodrow Wilson in 1912 and American entrance into

World War I. Both figures later regretted these decisions and became more radical as a consequence. Du Bois' radicalism principally took the form of an international perspective focused on the decolonization of Africa. As an organic intellectual directly linked to black social agency—and possible insurgency—Du Bois was put at the center of ideological and political debates in America and abroad. He organized the second Pan-African Congress in February 1919 in Paris in order "to have Africa in some way voice its complaints to the world during the Peace Congress at Versailles."[22] Still under the sway of a talented-tenth doctrine, Du Bois drew up an elitist, neocolonial platform for "semi-civilized peoples" in Africa; still influenced by a moral idealism with an insufficient grasp of the role of economic and political power, he had great hopes that the League of Nations would curb American and European racism. Regarding the Pan-African Congress, he wrote:

> We got, in fact, the ear of the civilized world and if it had been possible to stay longer and organize more thoroughly and spread the truth—what might not have been accomplished? . . .
> The world-fight for Black rights is on![23]

The Red Summer of 1919 dampened Du Bois' hopes. Southern black migration into northern industries spurred racial competition between black and white workers, and the decoration of many black soldiers back from the war generated white resentment. During that year seventy-seven blacks were lynched, including a woman and eleven soldiers; there also were race riots in twenty-six cities.

With the collapse of the League of Nations, and debilitating ideological strife in the Pan-African movement, Du Bois found himself loyal to a cause with no organization. The tumultuous rise of Marcus Garvey, the brouhaha over the Harlem "Renaissance," and white racist entrenchment forced Du Bois—now in his late fifties—to reexamine his gradualist perspective. More important, the Russian Revolution, initially held at arms' length by Du Bois, challenged him in a fundamental way. He had considered himself a democratic socialist—a "socialist of the path"—since 1907 and, in fact, joined the Socialist party for a while. In response to left critiques by socialists such as Claude McKay, A. Phillip Randolph, and Chauncey Owens in 1921, Du Bois replied:

> The editor of *The Crisis* considers himself a Socialist but he does not believe that German State Socialism or the dictatorship of the proletariat are perfect panaceas. He believes with most thinking men that the present method of creating, controlling and distributing wealth is desperately wrong; that there must come and is coming a social control of wealth; but he does not know just what form that control is going to take, and he is not prepared to dogmatize with Marx or Lenin.[24]

Du Bois' basic concern is the specific predicament of Afro-Americans as victims of white capitalist exploitation at the workplace and of white capitalists and workers in the political system and cultural mores of the country.

The major impact of the Russian Revolution on Du Bois was to compel him to take seriously the challenge of Marxism as a mode of intellectual inquiry. Marxist historical and social analysis forced Du Bois to go beyond his moralistic democratic socialism, with its primary stress on "light, more light, clear thought, accurate knowledge, careful distinctions."[25] Marxism indeed contained a commitment to scientific knowledge, a crucial requirement for a social scientist with Du Bois' training; but it also highlighted the realities of power struggles in which moral suasion played a minor role, to say the least. In this way, the Russian Revolution for Du Bois was less a historical event and more an intellectual beckoning to Marxist thought, a school of thought that made him see that

> beyond my conception of ignorance and deliberate illwill as causes of race prejudice, there must be other and stronger and more threatening forces, forming the founding stones of race antagonisms, which we had only begun to attack or perhaps in reality had not attacked at all. Moreover, the attack upon these hidden and partially concealed causes of race hate, must be led by Negroes in a program which was not merely negative in the sense of calling on white folk to desist from certain practices and give up certain beliefs, but direct in the sense that Negroes must proceed constructively in new and comprehensive plans of their own. I think it was the Russian Revolution which first illuminated and made clear this change in my basic thought.[26]

On his first visit to Russia in 1926, Du Bois' utopian energies were rekindled. He considered Russia "the most hopeful land in the modern world."[27] But he still unequivocally rejected the strategies of the Communist party in the United States. Even after acknowledging the realities of power in America, Du Bois insisted that revolution would be a "slow, reasoned development" informed by "the most intelligent body of American thought."[28]

The most significant product of Du Bois' encounter with Marxist thought was his seminal book *Black Reconstruction: An Essay Toward a History of the Part Which Black Folk Played in the Attempt to Reconstruct Democracy In America, 1860–1880* (1935). This text is seminal not simply because it focused on the postemancipation struggle over the control of black and white labor rather than on the obfuscating racist mythologies of the leading Reconstruction historians, John W. Burgess and William A. Dunning, nor because the book represented ground-breaking research, for it relied exclusively on secondary sources. Rather Du Bois' *Black Reconstruction* is a seminal work because it examines the ways in which the struggle for democracy was stifled at a critical period in American history from the vantage point of the victims (including both black and white laborers).

In *Black Reconstruction,* Du Bois is still exploring "the strange experience of being a problem," but this exploration has taken a structural socioeconomic and political form. Unlike any of the other pragmatists, Du Bois provides an account of the means by which industrial America imposed severe constraints upon an emerging or at least potential creative democracy. The economic power of northern capitalists and southern planters, the racist attitudes of white workers and politicians and the struggles of black freed persons conjoined in a complex way to give initial hope for but ultimately defeat creative democracy in America. And the defeat of any effective movements for radical democracy is inseparable from the lack of even formal democracy for most black Americans.

Du Bois' analysis illustrates the blindnesses and silences in American pragmatist reflections on individuality and democracy. Although none of the pragmatists were fervent racists themselves—and most of them took public stands against racist practices—not one viewed racism as contributing greatly to the impediments for both individuality and democracy. More specifically, neither Dewey, Hook, nor Mills grappled in a serious way, in essay or texts, with how racism impeded the development of an Emersonian culture of creative democracy. By "racism" here I mean not merely discrimination and devaluation based on race but, more important, the strategic role black people have played in the development of the capitalist economy, political system, and cultural apparatuses in America. To what degree have the demands of blacks fostered and expanded American democracy? In which way is democracy dependent on these demands, given their spin-off effects in demands made by larger ethnic groups, women, gays, lesbians, and the elderly? Du Bois' *Black Reconstruction* implicitly raises these questions in a serious and urgent manner. In graphic and hyperbolic language he writes:

> America thus stepped forward in the first blossoming of the modern age and added to the art of beauty, gift of the Renaissance, and to freedom of belief, gift of Martin Luther and Leo X, a vision of democratic self-government: the domination of political life by the intelligent decision of free and self-sustaining men. What an idea and what an area for its realization—endless land of richest fertility, natural resources such as earth seldom exhibited before, a population infinite in variety, of universal gift, burned in the fires of poverty and caste, yearning toward the Unknown God; and self-reliant pioneers, unafraid of man or devil. It was the Supreme Adventure, in the last Great Battle of the West, for that human freedom which would release the human spirit from lower lust for mere meat, and set it free to dream and sing.
>
> And then some unjust god leaned, laughing, over the ramparts of heaven and dropped a black man in their midst.
>
> It transformed the world. It turned democracy back to Roman imperialism and fascism; it restored caste and oligarchy; it replaced freedom with slavery and withdrew the name of humanity from the vast majority of human beings.
>
> But not without struggle . . .
>
> Then came this battle called Civil War . . . The slave went free; stood a brief moment in the sun; then moved back again toward slavery. The whole weight of America was thrown to color caste. The colored world went down before England, France, Germany, Russia, Italy and America. A new slavery arose. The upward moving of white labor was betrayed into wars for profit based on color caste. Democracy died save in the hearts of Black folk.[29]

Du Bois provides American pragmatism with what it sorely lacks: an international perspective on the impetus and impediments to individuality and radical democracy, a perspective that highlights the plight of the wretched of the earth, namely, the majority of humanity who own no property or wealth, participate in no democratic arrangements, and whose individualities are crushed by hard labor and harsh living conditions. James possessed the ingredients for such a view, but he did not see social structures, only individuals. Dewey indeed saw social structures and individuals yet primarily through an American lens. Hook too adopts a cosmopolitan viewpoint, but his cold war sentiments give a tunnel vision of the third world as a playground for the two superpowers. Mills comes closer than the others, yet, for him, postmodern historical agency resides almost exclusively in the Western (or Westernized) intelligentsia. Du Bois goes beyond them all in the scope and depth of his vision: creative powers reside among the wretched of the earth even in their subjugation, and the fragile structures of democracy in the world depend, in large part, on how these powers are ultimately exercised.

Convinced "that the whole set of the white world in America, in Europe, and in the world was too determinedly against racial equality, to give power and persuasiveness to our agitation,"[30] Du Bois advocated a program of voluntary segregation based on institution building and a separate cooperative economy. This ideological break from the liberal integrationist reformism of the NAACP led to his resignation in 1934. He returned to Atlanta University as head of the Department of Sociology. There he founded and edited *Phylon* and set up a series of conferences on programs to alleviate the economic condition of black people after the war. Yet, unexpectedly, Du Bois was retired by the trustees of the university. Even more surprising, he was asked to return to the NAACP. But after four years of bickering with the NAACP leadership, especially over his support of Henry Wallace in 1948, Du Bois was dismissed.

With the Pan-African movement rejuvenated in 1945 and the peace movement escalating, Du Bois' preoccupation with decolonization found him more and more drawn into the cold war, not only as interlocutor but also as target. In *Color and Democracy: Colonies and Peace* (1945) he excoriated cold warriors as handmaidens of the American imperial empire. The Marshall Plan was the tool of a new postwar colonialism; the containment strategy, a threat to world peace. In 1950, he ran on the Labor party ticket for U.S. Senate, a sure sign of his closer relations with the Communist party. The following February, Du Bois' peace information center, which had disbanded four months earlier, was indicted by a grand jury in Washington, D.C., for "failure to register as agent for a foreign principal." At the age of eighty-three and after over half a century in pursuit of individuality and democracy in America and abroad, Du Bois was an indicted criminal, handcuffed and facing a maximum sentence of five years in prison.

> I have faced during my life many unpleasant experiences; the growl of a mob; the personal threat of murder; the scowling distaste of an audience. But nothing has cowed me as that day, November 8, 1951, when I took my seat in a Washington courtroom as an indicted criminal.[31]

The widespread vilification of Du Bois as a Russian agent in the press—both white and black—left him virtually alone with leftist friends and some black loyal supporters in McCarthyite America. But support overflowed from overseas. And although the government could not prove "subversion" against him (or his colleagues at the peace center), the stigma stuck for the general populace. He was refused the right to travel abroad and to speak on university campuses (and at local NAACP branches!), his manuscripts were turned down by reputable publishers, and his mail was tampered with.

> It was a bitter experience and I bowed before the storm. But I did not break . . . I found new friends and lived in a wider world than ever before—a world with no color line. I lost my leadership of my race . . . the colored children ceased to hear my name.[32]

Six years later Du Bois' request for a passport was finally granted (owing to a Supreme Court ruling). He traveled abroad for nearly a year to China, France, England, Sweden, Germany, Russia, and Czechoslovakia. In 1961, Kwame Nkrumah invited Du Bois to Ghana to begin work on the Encyclopedia Africana, a project Du Bois had proposed in 1909. Du Bois accepted, but before he left for Ghana he joined the Communist Party, U.S.A. Locked into the narrow options of American political culture, Du Bois ultimately preferred a repressive communism that resisted European and American imperialism to a racist America that promoted the subjugation of peoples of color. A few weeks before he departed for Ghana, Du Bois wrote to a friend:

> I just cannot take any more of this country's treatment. We leave for Ghana October 5th and I set no date for return . . . Chin up, and fight on, but realize that American Negroes can't win.[33]

After two years of working on the encyclopedia, Du Bois became a Ghanaian citizen. In that same year, 1963, he died—the very day that 250,000 people gathered in Washington, D.C., to hear Martin Luther King, Jr., immortalize the black Emersonian quest for the American dream. Like Malcolm X and later even King himself, Du Bois concluded that this dream was more a nightmare for those whose measuring rod is the plight of most black Americans. For him, an Emersonian culture of creative democracy had become a mere chimera: a racist, sexist, and multinational capitalist America had no potential whatsoever to realize the pragmatist ideals of individuality and radical democracy. Yet Du Bois still encouraged struggle. About a month before leaving America, Du Bois attended a banquet for Henry Winston, a leading and courageous black communist released from prison after losing his sight owing to jail neglect. In words that aptly describe his own life and work, Du Bois quoted from Emerson's "Sacrifice":

> Though love repine and reason chafe,
>   There came a voice without reply
> 'Tis Man's perdition to be safe
>   When for the truth he ought to die[34]

And though Du Bois may have lost his own ideological "sight" owing greatly to national neglect and limited political options, there is no doubt that what he did "see" remains a major obstacle for an Emersonian culture of radical democracy in America.

NOTES

1. W. E. B. Du Bois, *The Autobiography of W. E. B. Du Bois: A Soliloquy on Viewing My Life from the Last Decade of Its First Century* (New York: International Publishers, 1968), p. 126.

2. Ibid.

3. Ibid., p. 133.

4. Ibid., pp. 133, 148.

5. Ibid., p. 149.

6. Francis L. Broderick, *W. E. B. Du Bois: Negro Leader in Time of Crisis* (Palo Alto: Stanford University Press, 1959), pp. 27–28; Manning Marable, *W. E. B. Du Bois: Black Radical Democrat* (Boston: Twayne, 1986), pp. 19–20.

7. Du Bois, *Autobiography of W. E. B. Du Bois,* p. 159.

8. Ibid., p. 157.

9. Ibid., p. 183.

10. Ibid., p. 182.

11. Ibid., p. 186.

12. Arnold Rampersad, *The Art and Imagination of W. E. B. Du Bois* (Cambridge: Harvard University Press, 1976), p. 50.

13. W. E. B. Du Bois, *Dusk of Dawn: An Essay toward an Autobiography of a Race Concept* (New York: Harcourt, Brace, 1940), p. 58.

14. Du Bois, *Autobiography of W. E. B. Du Bois,* p. 222.

15. W. E. B. Du Bois, *The Souls of Black Folk: Essays and Sketches* (1903; New York: Fawcett, 1961), p. 81.

16. Ibid., p. 15.

17. Ibid., p. 17.

18. Ibid.

19. Ibid., p. 190.

20. Ibid., pp. 48, 50, 75, 76, 83, 87, 101, 107, 109, 125, 126, 132, 139, 150, 170, 171, 182, 189.

21. Ibid., p. 132.

22. Du Bois, *Dusk of Dawn,* p. 261.

23. W. E. B. Du Bois, "My Mission," *Crisis,* 18, no. 1 (April 1919), 9, in *The Seventh Son: The Thought and Writings of W. E. B. Du Bois,* ed. Julius Lester, Vol. 2 (New York: Vintage Books, 1971), p. 199.

24. W. E. B. Du Bois, "The Negro and Radical Thought," *Crisis,* 22, no. 3 (July 1921), 103, in *Seventh Son,* 2: 264.

25. W. E. B. Du Bois, "The Class Struggle," *Crisis,* 22, no. 4 (August 1921), 151, in *Seventh Son,* 2: 265.

26. Du Bois, *Dusk of Dawn*, p. 284.

27. Ibid., p. 290.

28. Ibid., p. 291.

29. W. E. Burghardt Du Bois, *Black Reconstruction: An Essay toward a History of the Part Which Black Folk Played in the Attempt to Reconstruct Democracy in America, 1860–1880* (New York: Russell and Russell, 1935), pp. 29–30. For the most sophisticated treatment of Reconstruction that builds on and goes beyond Du Bois' classic, see Eric Foner's magisterial *Reconstruction: America's Unfinished Revolution, 1863–1877* (New York: Harper and Row, 1988).

30. Du Bois, *Dusk of Dawn*, p. 295.

31. Du Bois, *Autobiography of W. E. B. Du Bois*, p. 379. For more details on this matter, see Marable, *W. E. B. Du Bois*, pp. 182–89.

32. Du Bois, *Autobiography of W. E. B. Du Bois*, p. 395.

33. Quoted from Gerald Horne, *Black and Red: W. E. B. Du Bois and the Afro-American Response to the Cold War, 1944–1963* (Albany: State University of New York Press, 1986), p. 345.

34. W. E. B. Du Bois, *Against Racism: Unpublished Essays, Papers, Addresses, 1887–1961*, ed. Herbert Aptheker (Amherst: University of Massachusetts Press, 1985), p. 320.

Resistance and Renewal

PART SIX

Overleaf: Adinkra symbol for *akofena,* gallantry

The works in this section reflect the continuing human drama of the struggle against domination, invasion, colonialism, and hegemony. But inevitably they are also documents that confirm the aggression of one neighbor against another, one people against another, and one nation against another. In many ways this genre of materials defines a vast corpus of historical and cultural documents that suggest a wide array of texts dealing with agitation, protest, and war. These texts might be viewed as encompassing the themes of resistance to racism, the meaning of violence in anticolonial struggle, and deliberations on war and peace. Since it was impossible to include every significant document on justice and injustice, war and peace, prejudice and equality, and so forth, we made choices reflecting a range of materials that might be consulted on various issues regarding resistance, war, and renewal.

The continent of Africa itself has been a giant arena of competing nations, ethnic groups, and empires. Since African history opens with the conquest of Lower Egypt by Menes (Narmer) of Upper Egypt, one should expect that the uniting of the Two Lands would involve numerous wars. This unification is commemorated on a palette found in 1898 at the temple of Heru (Horus) at Hieraconpolis. It shows Menes wearing the crown of Upper Egypt as he is smiting a cowering captive chief with a mace head. Above the captive's head is a hieroglyphic statement that reads, "Heru brings captives from Lower Egypt to the king." Another mace head shows Narmer seated under a canopy over which hovers the protective vulture of the armies of Upper Egypt. This ceremonial palette commemorates the oldest known account of warfare. Subsequent kings of the Nile Valley looked to Menes' conquest as their founding spirit. Tuthmose III, considered by some as the greatest conqueror of the ancient world, expanded the influence of Egypt far beyond its natural borders. Ahmuse, Rameses II, Piye, Tarharka, and numerous other kings fought both to preserve and to extend the borders of the kingdom. A history of African warfare has yet to be written, but when it is the exploits of Nubian queens and Axumite kings will join the majestic march of the pharaohs of Kemet.

In 1240 Sundiata Keita, the king of Mali, defeated Sumanguru, the emperor of Ghana, in a major battle at Kirina. From that time the history of the western portion of Africa would resemble the earliest records of military conquest in the Nile Valley, where the names of the great conquering kings and queens ring out in the chambers of history. Of course the names of African conquerors and defenders are legendary: Menelik I, Shaka, Zumbi, Nat Turner, Sundiata, Samory Toure, Sunni Ali Ber, Askia Mohammed, Amina of Zaria, Yenenga, Touissant L'Ouverture, Mzilikazi, Asafoitse-Nettey, General Buddho, and Dan Borno are just a few of them.

Africans were enslaved in the seventeenth century in the English colonies of America. From the beginning the African population was in protest against oppression. One of the best-known examples of protest in the United States was the appeal of David Walker, who was a Boston tailor. Since broadsides, petitions, and appeals were common in the early days of African protests, there is nothing surprising about the existence of Walker's "Appeal to the Colored Citizens," except the fact that it called for violence against the "white Christian Americans." Written in 1829, his "Appeal" was at the time the most powerful document ever offered in defense of the enslaved. It was a militant statement against the evils of oppression and a call to arms for those who had nothing to lose but their chains. An entire style of protest was established by Walker, whose successor in style, Henry Highland Garnet, also urged Africans to rise up against their enslavers.

These captivity or resistance narratives often provide insight into the nature of the humiliations Africans suffered in the Americas. Among the famous memoirs, of course, is that of Frederick Douglass. For the most part, Africans who had been enslaved neither spoke nor wrote about slavery for the record. Most could neither read nor write, and thousands who were alive at the beginning of the twentieth century had no chance to tell their stories.

In some senses the important work of Vincent Bakpetu Thompson and Frantz Fanon has converged to demonstrate the invincibility of the spirit of freedom in the African experiences of the Americas. Captured by circumstances and history, the Africans in the Americas created cultures of resistance such as those of the *quilombos, maroons, and cimarrons* of Brazil, Jamaica, Venezuela, and other regions. Even in the American South the maroon populations shared the Native American (Muskogee) regions of Florida and were able to establish Seminole communities. Whether it was Zumbi in Brazil, Yanga in Mexico, or Nana in Jamaica, the presence of charismatic leaders, men and women, in the African resistance made tradition.

If W. E. B. Du Bois can be called the great interpreter of race and Cheikh Anta Diop the great interpreter of culture, then Frantz Fanon is the great interpreter of wars of resistance and anticolonialism. Fanon used the Algerian War between France and the Algerians as the locus of his philosophizing about the nature of warfare. Had he looked deeper into African history, he would have found experiences from Kemetic, Nubianic, and Ghanaian wars that would suggest the same sort of expressive relief and renewal he found in the Algerian War. But one cannot be accused of not doing what could have been done, only of doing what one did, and Fanon gave us brilliant insight into the nature of violence, including redemptive violence, such as occurs when the slave overturns the master. In Brazil, Louisa Mahin and her son Luis Mahin, stand beside the greatest names in African history for their resistance to oppression. Like Malcolm X, Harriet Tubman, and Nat Turner of the United States and Marcus Garvey and Nana of Jamaica, they are symbols and sources of inspiration in the African intellectual heritage. While we cannot include all of the documents of resistance, the inspiration of the heroic ancestors is found in every African community.

Serious challenges to African interests have always produced great leadership, as shown by Queen Mother Yaa Asantewaa's role during the Asante Wars with the British, the Almoravids' challenge in Ghana in 1076 for control of the salt mines, and King Ajaja of Dahomey's conflicts with the British in the 1700s over the slave raids along his coast.

We have included a number of memorials in this section that commemorate moments of military victory and challenge. This is not a glorification of warfare but an attempt to provide the reader with sources that are difficult to find detailing and documenting martial movements and campaigns. The pieces that we have chosen offer an opportunity to appreciate the ways in which Africans have responded to military experiences.

This is not so far from our initial idea that commemoration and deliberation on both war and peace be included in this section as sources of African ideas. To this end, we have seen the connecting link between the resistance to national invasions and intrusions from without as similar to the idea of resisting racism, colonialism, and enslavement within. But with any resistance or aggression, something novel is always developing and becomes a symbol of the battles that are lost and the victories that are won.

Thus, a series of documents suggesting resistance and renewal has brought the African communities throughout the world to the point of self-actualization in political and social terms. Hence the Million Man March/Day of Absence on October 16, 1995, recognized the importance of African people standing together for common interests. The mission statement written essentially by Maulana Karenga grows out of the collective sentiment of the Executive Council of the Million Man March/Day of Absence. At this juncture it represents the thrust toward renewal that had been anticipated by numerous authors.

Ah-mose

(EIGHTEENTH DYNASTY, 1550–1305 B.C., Kemet)

The Expulsion of the Hyksos

The commander of a crew, Ah-mose, son of Eben, the triumphant, says:

I speak to you, all mankind, that I may let you know the favors which have come to me. I have been awarded gold seven times in the presence of the entire land, and male and female slaves in like manner, and I have been vested with very many fields. The reputation of a valiant man is from what he has done, not being destroyed in this land forever.

He speaks thus:

I had my upbringing in the town of el-Kab, my father being a soldier of the King of Upper and Lower Egypt: Seqnen-Ra, the triumphant, his name being Bebe, the son of the woman Ro-onet. Then I served as soldier in his place in the ship, "The Wild Bull," in the time of the Lord of the Two Lands: Neb-pehti-Ra, the triumphant, when I was still a boy, before I had taken a wife, but while I was still sleeping in a net hammock.

But after I had set up a household, then I was taken on the ship, "Northern," because I was valiant. Thus I used to accompany the Sovereign—life, prosperity, health!—on foot, following his excursions in his chariot. When the town of Avaris was besieged, then I showed valor on foot in the presence of his majesty. Thereupon I was appointed to the ship, "Appearing in Memphis." Then there was fighting on the water in the canal Pa-Djedku of Avaris. Thereupon I made a capture, and I carried away a hand. It was reported to the king's herald. Then the Gold of Valor was given to me. Thereupon there was fighting again in his palace. Then I made a capture again there and brought away a hand. Then the Gold of Valor was given to me over again.

Then there was fighting in the Egypt which is south of this town. Thereupon I carried off a man as living prisoner. I went down into the water—now he was taken captive on the side of the town—and crossed over the water carrying him. Report was made to the king's herald. Thereupon I was awarded gold another time.

Then Avaris was despoiled. Then I carried off spoil from there: one man, three women, a total of four persons. Then his majesty gave them to me to be slaves.

Then Sharuhen was besieged for three years. Then his majesty despoiled it. Thereupon I carried off spoil from there: two women and a hand. Then the Gold of Valor was given to me, *and* my spoil was given to me to be slaves.

Now after his majesty had killed the Asiatics, then he sailed southward to Khenti-hen-nefer, to destroy the Nubian nomads. . . .

After this Thut-mose I went forth to Retenu, to assuage his heart throughout the foreign countries. His majesty reached Naharin, and his majesty—life, prosperity, health!—

found that enemy while he was marshaling the battle array. Then his majesty made a great slaughter among them. There was no number to the living prisoners whom his majesty carried off by his victory. Now I was in the van of our army, and his majesty saw how valiant I was. I carried off a chariot, its horse, and him who was in it as a living prisoner. They were presented to his majesty. Then I was awarded gold another time.

The Commemorative Stone of Thutmose III

Speech of Amen-Ra, Lord of Thrones-of-the-Two-Lands:
You are joyous at seeing my beauty,
My son, my champion, Menkheperre, eternal!
I shine for love of you, my heart rejoices
At your good entry to my temple.
My hands have endowed your body with safety and life,
How pleasant to my breast is your grace!
I placed you in my temple and wrote signs for you,
I gave you valor and victory over all lands.
I set your might, your fear in every country,
The dread of you as far as heaven's four supports.
I magnified your awe in every body,
I made your person's fame traverse the Nine Bows.
The princes of all lands are gathered in your grasp,
I stretched my own hands out and bound them for you.
I fettered Nubia's Bowmen by ten thousand thousands,
The northerners a hundred thousand captives.
I made your enemies succumb beneath your feet,
So that you crushed the rebels and the traitors.
For I bestowed on you the earth, its length and breadth,
Westerners and easterners are under your command.
You conquered all foreign lands with joyful heart,
None could approach your majesty's vicinity,
But you, with me your guide, attained them.
You crossed the water of Nahrin's Euphrates,
In might and victory ordained by me,
Hearing your battle cry they hid in holes.
I robbed their nostrils of the breath of life,
And made the dread of you pervade their hearts.
My serpent on your brow consumed them,
She made quick booty of the evildoers.

The lowlanders she swallowed by her flame,
Asiatic heads she severed, none escaped,
The foes were tottering before her might.
I let your valor course through every land,
The gleaming diadem protected you,
I all that heaven circles none defy you.
They came bearing their tribute on their backs,
Bowed down before your majesty as I decreed.
The foes who came toward you I made weak,
Their hearts aflame, their bodies trembled.

THE POEM

I came to let you tread on Djahi's chiefs,
    I spread them under your feet throughout their lands;
I let them see your majesty as lord of light,
    so that you shone before them in my likeness.

I came to let you tread on those of Asia,
    to smite the Asians' heads in Retjenu;
I let them see your majesty clad in your panoply,
    when you displayed your weapons on your chariot.

I came to let you tread on eastern lands,
    to crush the dwellers in the realm of god's land;
I let them see your majesty as shooting star,
    that scatters fire as it sheds its flame.

I came to let you tread on western lands,
    Keftiu, Isy are in awe of you;
I let them see your majesty as youthful bull,
    firm-hearted, sharp of horns, invincible.

I came to let you tread on lowlanders,
    Mitanni's regions cringe in fear of you;
I let them see your majesty as crocodile,
    master of terror in the water, unapproached.

I came to let you tread on islanders,
    the sea-borne people hear your battle cry;
I let them see your majesty as the avenger,
    standing in triumph on his victim's back.

I came to let you tread on Tjehenu,
    the Utjentiu isles are in your power;
I let them see your majesty as fearsome lion,
    as you made corpses of them in their valleys.

I came to let you tread on earth's limits,
    what Ocean circles is enfolded in your fist;
I let them see your majesty as falcon-winged,
    who grasps what he espies as he desires.

I came to let you tread on border people,
    to bind as captives those upon the sand;
I let them see your majesty as southern jackal,
    the racer, runner, roving the Two Lands.

I came to let you tread on Nubians;
    as far as Shat you hold them in your grasp;
I let them see your majesty as your Two Brothers,
    whose hands I joined for you in victory.

EPILOGUE

I placed your sisters behind you as guard,
My majesty's arms are raised to crush evil,
I give you protection, my son, my beloved,
Heru, Strong-Bull-arisen-in-Thebes,
Whom I begot in my divine body, Thutmose, everliving,
Who does for me all that my *ka* desires.
You have built my temple as a work of eternity,
Made longer and wider than it had been,
With its great gateway "Menkheperre-feasts-Amen-Ra,"
Your monuments surpass those of all former kings.
I commanded you to make them,
I am satisfied with them;
I have placed you on the Heru-throne of millions of years,
That you may lead the living forever.

Resistance and Renewal

Thutmose III

(EIGHTEENTH DYNASTY, 1550–1305 B.C., Kemet)

Annals

THE FIRST CAMPAIGN: THE BATTLE OF MEGIDDO

Heru: Strong-Bull-arisen-in-Thebes; Two Ladies: Enduring-in-kingship-like-Ra-in-heaven; Gold-Heru: Mighty-in-strength, Majestic-in-appearance; the King of Upper and Lower Egypt, Lord of the Two Lands: *Menkheperre;* the Son of Ra, of his body: *Thutmose,* given life forever.

His majesty was commanded to record the victories that his father Amen had given him by an inscription in the temple which his majesty had made for his father Amen, so as to record each campaign, together with the booty which his majesty had brought from it, and the tribute of every foreign land that his father Ra had given him.

Year 22, fourth month of winter, day 25, his majesty passed the fortress of Sile on the first campaign of victory to smite those who attacked the borders of Egypt, in valor, strength, might, and right. For a long period of years there was plunder, with every man serving his majesty. For it had happened in the time of other kings that the garrison there was only in Sharuhen, while from Yerdj to the ends of the earth there was rebellion against his majesty.

Year 23, first month of summer, day 4, the day of the feast of the King's Coronation, arriving at the town of "Conquest-of-the-Ruler," the Syrian name of which is Gaza. Year 23, first month of summer, day 5, departure from this place in valor, strength, might, and right, to overthrow that wretched enemy, to extend the borders of Egypt, his father, mighty and victorious Amen, having commanded that he conquer.

Year 23, first month of summer, day 16, arrival at the town of Yehem. His majesty ordered a consultation with his valiant army, saying: "That wretched foe of Kadesh has come and entered into Megiddo and is there at this moment. He had gathered to him the princes of all the foreign lands that had been loyal to Egypt, as well as those from as far as Nahrin, consisting of Khor and Kedy, their horses, their armies, their people. And he says—it is reported—'I shall wait and fight his majesty here in Megiddo.' Now tell me what you think."

They said to his majesty: "How will it be to go on this road which becomes narrow, when it is reported that the enemies are waiting there beyond and they are numerous? Will not horse go behind horse and soldiers and people too? Shall our vanguard be fighting while the rearguard waits here in Aruna, unable to fight? There are two other roads here. One of the roads is to our east and comes out at Taanach. The other is on the north side of Djefti, so that we come out to the north of Megiddo. May our valiant lord proceed on whichever of these seems best to him. Do not make us go on that difficult road!"

The speech of the majesty of the palace: "I swear, as Ra loves me, as my father Amen favors me, as my nostrils are refreshed with life and dominion, my majesty shall proceed on this Aruna road! Let him of you who wishes go on those roads you spoke of. Let him of you who wishes come in my majesty's following. Or they will say, those foes whom Ra abhors: 'Has his majesty gone on another road because he is afraid of us?' So they will say."

They said to his majesty: "May your father Amen, Lord of Thrones-of-the-Two-Lands, who presides over Ipet-isut, do as you wish! We are followers of your majesty wherever your majesty goes! A servant follows his lord."

His majesty ordered to tell the whole army: "Your valiant lord will guide your steps on this road which becomes narrow." For his majesty had taken an oath, saying: "I shall not let my valiant army go before me from this place!" Thus his majesty resolved that he himself should go before his army. Every man was informed of his order of march, horse followed horse, with his majesty at the head of his army.

Year 23, first month of summer, day 19, awakening in life in the royal tent at the town of Aruna. Northward journey by my majesty with my father Amen-Ra, Lord of Thrones-of-the-Two-Lands, that he might open the ways before me, Harakhti fortifying the heart of my valiant army, my father Amen strengthening my majesty's arm, and protecting my majesty.

Coming out of the pass by his majesty at the head of his army, grouped in many battalions, without meeting a single enemy. Their southern wing was at Taanach, and their northern wing on the north side of the Qina valley. Then his majesty called to them: "They are fallen! The wretched enemy. Amen, give praise to him, extol the might of his majesty, for his strength is greater than ———. He has protected the rearguard of his majesty's army in Aruna." Now while the rearguard of his majesty's valiant army was still at Aruna, the vanguard had come out into the Qina valley, and they filled the opening of the valley.

Then they said to his majesty: "Lo, his majesty has come out with his valiant troops and they fill the valley. May our valiant lord listen to us this time. May our lord watch for us the rearguard of his army with its people. When the rearguard has come out to us in the open, then we shall fight against those foreigners; then we shall not be concerned about the rearguard of our army!" His majesty halted in the open. He sat down there to watch the rearguard of his valiant army. Now when the last of the lead-troops had come out from this road, the shadow turned.

His majesty arrived at the south of Megiddo, on the shore of the Qina brook, when the seventh hour was in its course of day. A camp was laid out for his majesty, and the whole army was told: "Prepare yourselves! Make your weapons ready! For one will engage in combat with that wretched foe in the morning." Resting in the royal camp. Giving provisions to the officers, rations to the attendants. Posting the watch of the army; saying to them: "Steadfast, steadfast! Vigilant, vigilant!" Awakening in life in the royal tent. One came to tell his majesty: "The region is safe, and so are the troops of the south and the north."

The Battle

Year 23, first month of summer, day 21, the exact day of the feast of the new moon. Appearance of the King at dawn. An order was given to the whole army to pass. His majesty set out on a chariot of fine gold, decked in his shining armor like strong-armed Heru, lord of action, like Mont of Thebes, his father Amen strengthening his arm. The southern wing of his majesty's army was at a hill south of the Qina brook, and the northern wing to the northwest of Megiddo, while his majesty was in their center, Amen protecting his person in the melee, and the strength of Seth pervading his limbs.

Then his majesty overwhelmed them at the head of his army. When they saw his majesty overwhelming them, they fled headlong to Megiddo with faces of fear, abandoning their horses, their chariots of gold and silver, so as to be hoisted up into the town by pulling at their garments. For the people had shut the town behind them, and they now lowered garments to hoist them up into the town. Now if his majesty's troops had not set their hearts of plundering the possessions of the enemies, they would have captured Megiddo at this moment, when the wretched foe of Kadesh and the wretched foe of this town were being pulled up hurriedly so as to admit them into their town. For the fear of his majesty had entered their bodies, and their arms sank as his diadem overwhelmed them.

Their horses were captured, and their chariots of gold and silver became an easy target. Their ranks were lying stretched out on their backs like fish in the bight of a net, while his majesty's valiant army counted their possessions. Captured was the tent of that wretched fore. Then the entire army jubilated and gave praise to Amen for the victory he had given to his son on that day. They lauded his majesty and extolled his victory and presented the plunder they had taken: hands, living prisoners, horses, chariots of gold and silver and of painted work.

Siege and Surrender of Megiddo

Then his majesty commanded his army, saying: "Grasp well, grasp well, my valiant army! Lo, all the foreign lands are placed in this town by the will of Ra on this day. Inasmuch as every prince of every northern land is shut up within it, the capture of Megiddo is the capture of a thousand towns! Grasp firmly, firmly!" Orders were given to the troop-commanders to provide for their soldiers and to let every man know his place. They measured the town, surrounded it with a ditch, and walled it up with fresh timber from all their fruit trees. His majesty himself was on the fort east of the town, guarding it day and night. It was given the name "Menkheperre-Encircler-of-Asiatics." Guards were placed at the camp of his majesty and were told: "Steadfast, steadfast! Vigilant, vigilant!" No one of them was permitted to come out beyond this wall, except for a coming out to knock at the gate of their fortress.

Now all that his majesty did to this town and to the wretched foe and his wretched army was recorded on its day by the name of the sortie and by the name of the troop-commander. They are recorded on a roll of leather in the temple of Amen to this day.

Now the princes of this foreign land came on their bellies to kiss the ground to the might of his majesty, and to beg breath for their nostrils, because of the greatness of his strength and the extent of the power of Amen over all foreign lands. All the princes captured by his majesty's might bore their tribute of silver, gold, lapis lazuli, and turquoise, and carried grain, wine, and large and small cattle for his majesty's army; one group among them bore tribute on the journey south. Then his majesty appointed the new rulers for every town.

List of the booty which his majesty's army brought from the town of Megiddo. Living prisoners: 340. Hands: 83. Horses: 2,041. Foals: 191. Stallions: 6. Colts: ———. One chariot of that foe worked in gold, with a pole of gold. One fine chariot of the prince of Megiddo, worked in gold. Chariots of the allied princes: 30. Chariots of his wretched army: 892. Total: 924. One fine bronze coat of mail belonging to that enemy. One fine bronze coat of mail belonging to the prince of Megiddo. Leather coats of mail belonging to his wretched army: 200. Bows: 502. Poles of *mry*-wood worked with silver from the tent of that enemy: 7. And the army of his majesty had captured cattle belonging to this town ———: 387. Cows: 1,929. Goats: 2,000. Sheep: 20,500.

List of what was carried off afterward by the King from the household goods of the enemy of Yanoam, Inuges, and Herenkeru, together with the property of the towns that had been loyal to him which were captured by the might of his majesty ———. *Maryan*-warriors belonging to them: 38. Children of that enemy and of the princes with him: 84. *Maryan*-warriors belonging to them: 5. Male and female servants and their children: 1,796. Pardoned persons who had come out from that enemy because of hunger: 103. Total: 2,503. In addition, bowls of costly stone and gold, and various vessels ———. One large jar of Syrian workmanship. Jars, bowls, plates, various drinking vessels, large kettles, knives: [*x+*]17, making 1,784 *deben*. Gold in disks skillfully crafted, and many silver disks, making 966 *deben* and 1 *kite*. A silver statue with a head of gold. Walking sticks with human heads. 3: Carrying chairs of that enemy of ivory, ebony, and *ssndm*-wood worked with gold: 6. Footstools belong to them: 6. Large tables of ivory and *ssndm*-wood: 6. One bed of *ssndm*-wood worked with gold and all costly stones in the manner of a *krkr*, belonging to that enemy, worked with gold throughout. A statue of ebony of that enemy worked with gold with a head of lapis lazuli, bronze vessels, and much clothing of that enemy.

The fields were made into plots and assigned to royal inspectors in order to reap their harvest. List of the harvest which his majesty brought from the fields of Megiddo. Sacks of wheat: 207,300, apart from what was cut as forage by his majesty's army.

Pharaoh Piye and the Victory over North

Year 21, first month of the first season, under the majesty of the King of Upper and Lower Egypt, *Piye beloved-of-Amen*, ever living. Command spoken by my majesty:

> "Hear what I did, exceeding the ancestors,
> I the King, image of god,
> Living likeness of Atum!
> Who left the womb marked as ruler,
> Feared by those greater than he!
> His father knew, his mother perceived:
> He would be ruler from the egg,
> The Good God, beloved of gods,
> The Son of Ra, who acts with his arms,
> *Piye beloved-of-Amen*."

TEFNAKHT'S ADVANCE

One came to say to his majesty: "The Chief of the West, the count and grandee in Netjer, Tefnakht, is in the nome of —, in the nome of Xois, in Hapy, in —, in Ayn, in Pernub, and in the nome of Memphis. He has conquered the entire West from the coastal marshes to Itj-tawy, sailing south with a numerous army, with the Two Lands united behind him, and the counts and rulers of domains are as dogs at his feet.

"No stronghold has closed its gates in the nomes of Upper Egypt. Mer-Atum, Per-Sekhemkheperre, Hut-Sobk, Permedjed, Tjeknesh, all towns of the West have opened the gates for fear of him. When he turned around to the nomes of the East they opened to him also: Hut-benu, Teudjoi, Hut-nesut, Per-nebtepih.

"Now he is besieging Hnes. He has encircled it completely, not letting goers go, not letting entrants enter, and fighting every day. He has measured it in its whole circuit. Every count knows his wall. He has made every man besiege his portion, to wit the counts and rulers of domains." His majesty heard it with delight, laughing joyously.

Then those chiefs, the counts and generals who were in their towns, sent to his majesty daily, saying: "Have you been silent in order to forget the Southland, the nomes of Upper Egypt, while Tefnakht conquers all before him and finds no resistance? *Namart*, ruler of

Hermopolis, count of Hutweret, has demolished the wall of Nefrusi. He has thrown down his own town out of fear of him who would seize it for himself in order to besiege another town. Now he had gone to be at his (Tefnakht's) feet; he has rejected the water of his majesty. He stays with him like one of his men in the nome of Oxyrhynchos. He (Tefnakht) gives him gifts to his heart's content of everything he has found."

PIYE ORDERS HIS TROOPS IN EGYPT TO ATTACK AND SENDS REINFORCEMENTS

His majesty wrote to the counts and generals who were in Egypt, the commander Purem, and the commander Lemersekny, and every commander of his majesty who was in Egypt: "Enter combat, engage in battle; surround ————, capture its people, its cattle, its ships on the river! Let not the farmers go to the field, let not the plowmen plow. Beset the Hare nome; fight against it daily!" Then they did so.

Then his majesty sent an army to Egypt and charged them strictly: "Do not attack by night in the manner of draughts-playing; fight when one can see. Challenge him to battle from afar. If he proposes to await the infantry and chariotry of another town, then sit still until his troops come. Fight when he proposes. Also if he has allies in another town, let them be awaited. The counts whom he brings to help him, and any trusted Libyan troops, let them be challenged to battle in advance, saying: 'You whose name we do not know, who musters the troops! Harness the best steeds of your stable, form your battle line, and know that Amen is the god who sent us!'

"When you have reached Thebes at Ipet-sut, go into the water. Cleanse yourselves in the river; wear the best linen. Rest the bow; loosen the arrow. Boast not to the lord of might, for the brave has no might without him. He makes the weak-armed strong-armed, so that the many flee before the few, and a single one conquers a thousand men! Sprinkle yourselves with water of his altars; kiss the earth before his face. Say to him:

> 'Give us the way,
> May we fight in the shade of your arm!
> The troop you sent, when it charges,
> May the many tremble before it!' "

Then they placed themselves on their bellies before his majesty:

> "It is your name that makes our strength,
> Your counsel brings your army into port;
> Your bread is in our bellies on every way,
> Your beer quenches our thirst.
>
> It is your valor that gives us strength,
> There is dread when your name is recalled;
> No army wins with a cowardly leader,
> Who is your equal there?
>
> You are the mighty King who acts with his arms,
> The chief of the work of war!"

Resistance and Renewal

They sailed north and arrived at Thebes; they did as his majesty had said.

Sailing north on the river they met many ships going south with soldiers and sailors, all kinds of fighting troops from Lower Egypt, equipped with weapons of warfare, to fight against his majesty's army. Then a great slaughter was made of them, whose number is unknown. Their troops and ships were captured, and taken as prisoners to where his majesty was.

BATTLE AT HERACLEOPOLIS

They proceeded toward Hnes and challenged to battle. List of the counts and kings of Lower Egypt:

> King *Namart* and King *Iuput.*
>
> Chief of the Ma, Sheshonq of Per-Usirnebdjedu.
>
> And Great Chief of the Ma, Djedamenefankh of Per-Banebdjedet.
>
> And his eldest son, the commander of Per-Thoth-weprehwy.
>
> The troops of Prince Bakennefi and his eldest son, the Count and Chief of the Ma, Nesnaisu of Hesbu. Every plume-wearing chief of Lower Egypt.
>
> And King *Osorkon* of Perbast and the district of Ranofer.

All the counts, all the rulers of domains in the west, in the east, and in the isles of the midst were united in their allegiance at the feet of the great Chief of the West, the Ruler of the domains of Lower Egypt, the prophet of Neith, mistress of Sais, the *setem*-priest of Ptah, Tefnakht.

They went forth against them; they made a great slaughter of them, exceedingly great. Their ships on the river were captured. The remnant made a crossing and landed on the west side in the vicinity of Perpeg. At dawn of the next day the troops of his majesty crossed over against them and troops mingled with troops. They slew many of their men and countless horses. Terror befell the remnant and they fled to Lower Egypt from the blow that was great and exceedingly painful.

List of the slaughter made of them. Men: ———.

King *Namart* fled upstream southward when he was told, "Khmun is faced with war from the troops of his majesty; its people and its cattle are being captured." He entered into Un, while his majesty's army was on the river and on the riverbanks of the Hare nome. They heard it and surrounded the Hare nome on its four sides, not letting goers go, not letting entrants enter.

PIYE RESOLVES TO GO TO EGYPT

They wrote to report to the majesty of the King of Upper and Lower Egypt, *Piye beloved-of-Amen,* given life, on every attack they had made, on every victory of his majesty. His majesty raged about it like a panther: "Have they let a remnant of the army of Lower Egypt, so as to let some of them escape to report the campaign, instead of killing and destroying the last of them? I swear, as Ra loves me, as my father Amen favors me, I shall go north myself! I shall tear down his works. I shall make him abandon fighting forever!

"When the rites of New Year are performed, and I offer to my father Amen at his beautiful feast, when he makes his beautiful appearance of the New Year, he shall send me in peace to view Amen at his beautiful feast of Ipet. I shall convey him in his processional bark to Southern Ipet at his beautiful feast of 'Night of Ipet,' and the feast of 'Abiding in Thebes,' which Ra made for him in the beginning. I shall convey him to his house, to rest on his throne, on the day of 'Bringing in the God,' in the third month of the inundation, second day. And I shall let Lower Egypt taste the taste of my fingers!"

Then the army that was here in Egypt heard of the anger his majesty held against them. They fought against Permedjed of the Oxyrhynchite nome; they captured it like a cloudburst. They wrote to his majesty—his heart was not appeased by it.

Then they fought against "the Crag Great-of-Victories." They found it filled with troops, all kinds of fighters of Lower Egypt. A siege tower was made against it; its wall was overthrown. A great slaughter was made of them, countless numbers, including a son of the Chief of the Ma, Tefnakht. They wrote of it to his majesty—his heart was not appeased by it.

Then they fought against Hut-benu; its interior was opened; his majesty's troops entered it. They wrote to his majesty—his heart was not appeased by it.

PIYE GOES TO EGYPT AND BESIEGES HERMOPOLIS

First month of the first season, day 9, his majesty went north to Thebes. He performed the feast of Amen at the feast of Ipet. His majesty sailed north to the harbor of the Hare nome. His majesty came out of the cabin of the ship. The horses were yoked, the chariot was mounted, while the grandeur of his majesty attained the Asiatics and every heart trembled before him.

His majesty burst out to revile his troops, raging at them like a panther: "Are you continuing to fight while delaying my orders? It is the year for making an end, for putting fear of me in Lower Egypt, and inflicting on them a great and severe beating!"

He set up camp on the southwest of Khmun. He pressed against it every day. An embankment was made to enclose the wall. A siege tower was set up to elevate the archers as they shot, and the slingers as they hurled stones and killed people there each day.

Days passed, and Un was a stench to the nose, for lack of air to breathe. Then Un threw itself on its belly, to plead before the king. Messengers came and went with all kinds of things beautiful to behold: gold, precious stones, clothes in a chest, the diadem from his head, the uraeus that cast his power, without ceasing for many days to implore his crown.

Then they sent his wife, the royal wife and royal daughter, Nestent, to implore the royal wives, the royal concubines, the royal daughters, and the royal sisters. She threw herself on her belly in the women's house before the royal women: "Come to me, royal wives, royal daughters, royal sisters, that you may appease Heru, lord of the palace, great of power, great of triumph! Grant ———.

"Lo, who guides you, who guides you? Who then guides you, who guides you? You have abandoned the way of life! Was it the case that heaven rained arrows? I was content that Southerners bowed down and Northerners said, 'Place us in your shade!' Was it bad that ——— with his gifts? The heart is the rudder. It capsizes its owner through that which comes from the wrath of god. It sees fires as coolness ———. He is not grown old who is seen with his father. Your nomes are full of children."

He threw himself on his belly before his majesty, saying: "Be appeased, Heru, lord of the palace! It is your power that has done it to me. I am one of the King's servants who

Resistance and Renewal

pays taxes into the treasury. ——— their taxes. I have done for you more than they."
Then he presented silver, gold, lapis lazuli, turquoise, copper, and all kinds of precious
stones. The treasury was filled with this tribute. He brought a horse with his right hand,
and in his left hand a sistrum of gold and lapis lazuli.

His majesty arose in splendor from his palace and proceeded to the temple of Thoth,
lord of Khmun. He sacrificed oxen, shorthorns, and fowl to his father Thoth, lord of
Khmun, and the Ogdoad in the temple of the Ogdoad. And the troops of the Hare nome
shouted and sang, saying:

> "How good is Heru at peace in his town,
> The Son of Ra, *Piye*!
> You make for us a jubilee,
> As you protect the Hare nome!"

.   .   .

CAPTURE OF MEMPHIS

His majesty proceeded to Memphis. He sent to them, saying: "Do not close, do not fight,
O home of Shu since the beginning! Let the entrant enter, the goer go; those who would
leave shall not be hindered! I shall offer an oblation to Ptah and the gods of Memphis. I
shall sacrifice to Sokar in Shetit. I shall see South-of-his-Wall. And I shall sail north in
peace! ———. The people of Memphis will be safe and sound; one will not weep over
children. Look to the nomes of the South! No one was slain there, except the rebels who
had blasphemed god; the traitors were executed.

They closed their fort. They sent out troops against some of his majesty's troops, consisting of artisans, builders, and sailors who had entered the harbor of Memphis. And the
Chief of Sais arrived in Memphis by night to charge his soldiers, his sailors, all the best of
his army, consisting of 8,000 men, charging them firmly:

"Look, Memphis is filled with troops of all the best of Lower Egypt, with barley, emmer,
and all kinds of grain, the granaries overflowing; with weapons of war of all kinds. A
rampart surrounds it. A great battlement has been built, a work of skilled craftsmanship.
The river surrounds its east side; one cannot fight there. The stables here are filled with
oxen; the storehouse is furnished with everything: silver, gold, copper, clothing, incense,
honey, resin. I shall go to give gifts to the chiefs of Lower Egypt. I shall open their nomes
to them. I shall be ———, in a few days I shall return. He mounted a horse for he did not
trust his chariot, and he went north in fear of his majesty.

At dawn of the next day his majesty arrived at Memphis. When he had moored on its
north, he found the water risen to the walls and ships moored at the houses of Memphis.
His majesty saw that it was strong, the walls were high with new construction, and the
battlements manned in strength. No way of attacking it was found. Every man of his majesty's army had his say about some plan of attack. Some said: "Let us blockade ———, for
its troops are numerous." Others said: "Make a causeway to it, so that we raise the ground
to its wall. Let us construct a siege tower, setting up masts and using sails as walls for it.
You should divide it thus on each of its sides with ramparts and a causeway on its north,
so as to raise the ground to its wall, so that we find a way for our feet."

Then his majesty raged against them like panther, saying: "I swear, as Ra loves me, as my father Amen favors me, . . . according to the command of Amen! This is what people say: '———— and the nomes of the South opened to him from afar, though Amen had not put it in their hearts, and they did not know what he had commanded. He (Amen) made him in order to show his might, to let his grandeur be seen.' I shall seize it like a cloudburst, for Amen-Ra has commanded me!"

Then he sent his fleet and his troops to attack the harbor of Memphis. They brought him every ship, every ferry, every *shry*-boat, all the many ships that were moored in the harbor of Memphis, with the bow rope fastened to its houses. There was not a common soldier who wept among all the troops of his majesty. His majesty himself came to line up the many ships.

His majesty commanded his troops: "Forward against it! Mount the walls! Enter the houses over the river! When one of you enters the wall, no one shall stand in his vicinity, no troops shall repulse you! To pause is vile. We have sealed Upper Egypt; we shall bring Lower Egypt to port. We shall sit down in Balance-of-the Two-Lands!"

Then Memphis was seized as by a cloudburst. Many people were slain in it, or brought as captives to where his majesty was.

Now when it dawned on the next day his majesty sent people into it to protect the temples of god for him. The arm was raised over the holy of holies of the gods. Offerings were made to the Council of the gods of Memphis. Memphis was cleansed with natron and incense. The priests were set in their places.

His majesty proceeded to the house of Ptah. His purification was performed in the robing room. There was performed for him every rite that is performed for a king when he enters the temple. A great offering was made to his father Ptah South-of-his-Wall of oxen, shorthorns, fowl, and all good things. Then his majesty went to his house.

Then all the districts in the region of Memphis heard it. Herypedemy, Peninewe, Tower-of-Byu, Village-of-Byt, they opened the gates and fled in flight, and it was not known where they had gone.

Three Rulers Surrender

Then came King *Iuput,* and the Chief of the Ma, Akanosh, and Prince Pediese, and all counts of Lower Egypt, bearing their tribute, to see the beauty of his majesty.

Then the treasuries and granaries of Memphis were allocated as endowment to Amen, to Ptah, and to the Ennead in Memphis.

PIYE VISITS THE SANCTUARIES OF HELIOPOLIS

At dawn of the next day his majesty proceeded to the East. An offering was made to Atum in Kheraha, the Ennead in Per-Pesdjet, and the cavern of the gods in it, consisting of oxen, shorthorns, and fowl, that they might give life-prosperity-health to the King of Upper and Lower Egypt, *Piye* ever living.

His majesty proceeded to On over that mountain of Kheraha on the road of Sep to Kheraha. His majesty went to the camp on the west of Iti. His purification was done: he was cleansed in the pool of Kebeh; his face was bathed in the river of Nun, in which Ra bathes his face. He proceeded to the High Sand in On. A great oblation was made on the

High Sand in On before the face of Ra at his rising, consisting of white oxen, milk, myrrh, incense, and all kinds of sweet-smelling plants.

Going in procession to the temple of Ra. Entering the temple with adorations. The chief lector-priest's praising god and repulsing the rebels from the king. Performing the ritual of the robing room; putting on the *sdb*-garment; cleansing him with incense and cold water; presenting him the garlands of the Pyramidion House; bringing him the amulets.

Mounting the stairs to the great window to view Ra in the Pyramidion House. The king stood by himself alone. Breaking the seals of the bolts, opening the doors; viewing his father Ra in the holy Pyramidion House; adorning the morning-bark of Ra and the evening-bark of Atum. Closing the doors, applying the clay, sealing with the king's own seal, and instructing the priests: "I have inspected the seal. No other king who may arise shall enter here." They placed themselves on their bellies before his majesty, saying: "Abide forever without end, Heru beloved of On!"

Entering the temple of Atum. Worshipping the image of his father Atum-Khepri, Great one of On.

Then came King *Osorkon* to see the beauty of his majesty.

PIYE HOLDS COURT AT ATHRIBIS

At dawn of the next day his majesty proceeded to the harbor at the head of his ships. He crossed over to the harbor of Kemwer. The camp of his majesty was set up on the south of Keheny, in the east of Kemwer.

Then came those kings and counts of Lower Egypt, all the plume-wearing chiefs, all viziers, chiefs, king's friends from the west, the east, and the isles in their midst, to see the beauty of his majesty. Prince Pediese threw himself on his belly before his majesty, saying: "Come to Athribis, that you may see Khentikhety, that Khuyet may protect you, that you may offer an oblation to Heru in his house, of oxen, shorthorns, and fowl. When you enter my house, my treasury will be open to you. I shall present you with my father's possessions. I shall give you gold as much as you wish, turquoise heaped before you, and many horses of the best of the stable, the choicest of the stall."

His majesty proceeded to the house of Heru Khentikhety. An offering of oxen, shorthorns, and fowl was made to his father Heru Khentikhety, lord of Athribis. His majesty went to the house of Prince Pediese. He (Pediese) presented him with silver, gold, lapis lazuli, and turquoise, a great quantity of everything, and clothing of royal linen of every number, couches laid with fine linen, myrrh and ointment in jars, and stallions and mares, all the best of his stable.

He purified himself by a divine oath before these kings and great chiefs of Lower Egypt: "Anyone who hides his horses and conceals his wealth shall die the death of his father! I have said this in order that you bear out your servant with all that you know of me. Tell if I have concealed from his majesty anything of my father's house: gold bars, precious stones, vessels of all kinds, armlets, bracelets of gold, necklaces, collars wrought with precious stones, amulets for every limb, headbands, earrings, all royal adornments, all vessels for the king's purification of gold and precious stones. All these I have presented to the King, and garments of royal linen by the thousands of the very best of my house. I know you will be satisfied with it. Proceed to the stable, choose what you wish, all the horses you desire!" Then his majesty did so.

Then said these kings and counts to his majesty: "Let us go to our towns to open our treasuries, that we may choose according to what your heart may desire, and bring to you the best of our stables, the finest of our horses." Then his majesty did so.

LIST OF THE NORTHERN RULERS

List of their names:

> King *Osorkon* in Perbast and the district of Ranofer,
>
> King *Iuput* in Tentremu and Taan,
>
> Count Djedamenefankh in Per-Banebdjedet and Granary-of-Ra,
>
> His eldest son, the general in Per-Thoth-weprehwy, Ankh-hor,
>
> Count Akanosh in Tjeb-neter, Per-hebut, and Sema-behdet,
>
> Count and Chief of the Ma, Patjenfi in Per-Sopd and Granary-of-Memphis,
>
> Count and Chief of the Ma, Pemai in Per-Usirnebdjedu,
>
> Count and Chief of the Ma, Nesnaisu in Hesbu,
>
> Count and Chief of the Ma, Nekhthor-neshnu in Per-gerer,
>
> Chief of the Ma, Pentweret,
>
> Chief of the Ma, Pentbekhent,
>
> Prophet of Heru, lord of Khem, Pedihorsomtus,
>
> Count Herbes in Per-Sakhmet-nebetsat and in Per-Sakhmet-nebetrehsa,
>
> Count Djedkhiu in Khentnefer,
>
> Count Pebes in Kheraha and Per-Hapy,

with all their good tribute of gold, silver, [precious stones], couches laid with fine linen, myrrh in jars, ——— of good value, horses ———.

——— after this one came to tell his majesty: "——— the wall ———. He has set fire to his treasury and to the ships on the river. He had garrisoned Mesed with soldiers ———." Then his majesty sent soldiers of his to see what was happening there, he being the protector of Prince Pediese. They returned to report to his majesty, saying: "We have slain every man we found there." Then his majesty gave it (the town) to Prince Pediese as a gift.

TEFNAKHT ANNOUNCES HIS SUBMISSION

The Chief of the Ma, Tefnakht, heard it, and a messenger was sent to where his majesty was with cajoling words, saying: "Be gracious! I cannot see your face in the days of shame; I cannot stand before your flame; I dread your grandeur! For you are Nubti, foremost of the Southland, and Mont, the mighty bull! Whatever town you turn your face to, you will not be able to find your servant there, until I have reached the islands of the sea! For I fear your wrath on account of those fiery words which are hostile to me!

"Is your majesty's heart not cooled by the things you did to me? While I am under a just reproach, you did not smite me in accordance with my crime. Weigh in the balance, count by weight, and multiply it against me threefold! But leave the seed, that you may gather it in time. Do not cut down the grove to its roots! Have mercy! Dread of you is in my body; fear of you is in my bones!

"I sit not at the beer feast; the harp is not brought for me. I eat the bread of the hungry; I drink the water of the thirsty, since the day you heard my name! Illness is in my bones, my head is bald, my clothes are rags, till Neith is appeased toward me! Long is the course you led against me, and your face is against me yet! It is a year that has purged my *ka* and cleansed your servant of his fault! Let my goods be received into the treasury: gold and all precious stones, the best of the horses, and payment of every kind. Send me a messenger quickly, to drive the fear from my heart! Let me go to the temple in his presence, to cleanse myself by a divine oath!"

His majesty sent the chief lector-priest Pediamen-nest-tawy and the commander Purem. He (Tefnakht) presented him with silver and gold, clothing and all precious stones. He went to the temple; he praised god; he cleansed himself by a divine oath, saying: "I will not disobey the King's command. I will not thrust aside his majesty's words. I will not do wrong to a count without your knowledge. I will only do what the King said. I will not disobey what he has commanded." Then his majesty's heart was satisfied with it.

FINAL SURRENDERS, PIYE RETURNS TO NUBIA

One came to say to his majesty: "Hut-Sobk has opened its gate; Meten has thrown itself on its belly. No nome is shut against his majesty, of the nomes of the south and the north. The west, the east, and the islands in the midst are on their bellies in fear of him, and are sending their goods to where his majesty is, like the subjects of the palace."

At dawn of the next day there came the two rulers of Upper Egypt and the two rulers of Lower Egypt, the uraeus wearers, to kiss the ground to the might of his majesty. Now the kings and counts of Lower Egypt who came to see his majesty's beauty, their legs were the legs of women. They could not enter the palace because they were uncircumcised and were eaters of fish, which is an abomination to the palace. But King *Namart* entered the palace because he was clean and did not eat fish. The three stood there while the one entered the palace.

Then the ships were loaded with silver, gold, copper, and clothing; everything of Lower Egypt, every product of Syria, and all plants of god's land. His majesty sailed south, his heart joyful, and all those near him shouting. West and East took up the announcement, shouting around his majesty. This was their song of jubilation:

> "O mighty ruler, O mighty ruler,
> Piye, mighty ruler!
> You return having taken Lower Egypt,
> You made bulls into women!
> Joyful is the mother who bore you,
> The man who begot you!
> The valley dwellers worship her,
> The cow that bore the bull!
> You are eternal,
> Your might abides,
> O ruler loved of Thebes!"

King Kwame Ansa

The Portuguese Fortress at El Mina

January 19, 1482, Ghana

I am not insensible to the high honour which your great master the Chief of Portugal has this day conferred upon me. His friendship I have always endeavored to merit by the strictness of my dealings with the Portuguese and by my constant exertions to procure an immediate lading for the vessels. But never until this day did I observe such a difference in the appearance of his subjects; they have hitherto been meanly attired: were easily contented with the commodity they received; and so far from wishing to continue in this country, were never happy until they could complete their landing and return. Now I remark a strange difference. A great number, richly dressed, are anxious to be allowed to build houses, and to continue among us Men of such eminence, conducted by a commander who from his own account seems to have descended from the God who made day and night, can never bring themselves to endure the hardships of this climate; nor would they here be able to procure any of the luxuries that abound in their own country. The passions that are common to us all men will therefore inevitably bring on disputes; and it is far preferable that both our nations should continue on the same footing as they have hitherto done, allowing your ships to come and go as usual; the desire for seeing each other occasionally will preserve peace between us. The sea and the land being always neighbors are continually at variance, and contending who shall give way: the sea with great violence attempting to subdue the land, and the land with equal obstinacy resolving to oppose the sea.

A Shona Song

TAKE UP ARMS AND LIBERATE YOURSELVES

Our ancestor Nehanda died with these words on her lips,
"I'm dying for this country."
She left us one word of advice
"Take up arms and liberate yourselves."

Aren't you coming with us to fight?
Aren't you really?
We are running about carrying sub-machine guns
We carry anti-air missiles
"Take up arms and liberate yourselves."

Chitepo died with these words on his lips
"I'm dying for the fatherland."
He left us one word of advice,
"Take up arms and liberate yourselves."

Father Chitepo died in the thick of the struggle,
Saying, "Now I'm dying for the fatherland."
His last words for us were,
"Take up arms and liberate Zimbabwe."

Hence we are going to the war front,
We hit the enemy and run carrying sub-machine guns,
We brandish anti-air missiles.
"Take up arms and liberate yourselves."

Now we are in the thick of it,
Running up and down with our guns,
Our anti-airs too.
"Take up arms and liberate your fatherland."

Narrative

Sir,—You have asked me to give a history of the motives which induced me to undertake the late insurrection, as you call it—To do so I must go back to the days of my infancy, and even before I was born. I was thirty-one years of age the 2nd of October last, and born the property of Benj. Turner, of this county [Southampton, Virginia]. In my childhood a circumstance occurred which made an indelible impression on my mind, and laid the ground work of that enthusiasm, which has terminated so fatally to many, both white and black, and for which I am about to atone at the gallows. It is here necessary to relate the circumstance—trifling as it may seem, it was the commencement of that belief which has grown with time, and even now, sir, in this dungeon, helpless and forsaken as I am, I cannot divest myself of. Being at play with other children, when three or four years old, I was telling them something, which my mother overhearing, said it had happened before I was born—I stuck to my story, however, and related somethings which went, in her opinion, to confirm it—others being called on were greatly astonished, knowing that these things had happened, and caused them to say in my hearing, I surely would be a prophet, as the Lord had shewn me things that had happened before my birth. And my father and mother strengthened me in this my first impression, saying in my presence, I was intended for some great purpose, which they had always thought from certain marks on my head and breast—a parcel of excrescences which I believe are not at all uncommon, particularly among negroes, as I have seen several with the same. In this case he has either cut them off or they have nearly disappeared—My grandmother, who was very religious, and to whom I was much attached—my master, who belonged to the church, and other religious persons who visited the house, and whom I often saw at prayers, noticing the singularity of my manners, I suppose, and my uncommon intelligence for a child, remarked I had too much sense to be raised, and if I was, I would never be of any service to any one as a slave—To a mind like mine, restless, inquisitive and observant of every thing that was passing, it is easy to suppose that religion was the subject to which it would be directed, and although this subject principally occupied my thoughts—there was nothing that I saw or heard of to which my attention was not directed—The manner in which I learned to read and write, not only had great influence on my own mind, as I acquired it with the most perfect ease, so much so, that I have no recollection whatever of learning the alphabet—but to the astonishment of the family, one day, when a book was shewn to me to keep me from crying, I began spelling the names of different objects—this was a source of wonder to all in the neighborhood, particularly the blacks—and this learning was constantly improved at all opportunities—when I got large enough to go to work, while employed, I was reflecting on many things that would present themselves to my imagination, and whenever an opportunity occurred of looking at a book, when the school children were getting their lessons, I would find many things that the fertility of my own imagination had depicted to me before; all my time, not devoted to my master's service, was spent either in prayer, or in making experiments in casting different things in moulds made of earth, in attempting to make paper, gun-powder, and many other experiments, that although I could not perfect, yet convinced me of its practicability if I had the means. I was not addicted to stealing in my youth, nor have ever been—Yet such was the confidence of the negroes in the neighborhood, even at this early period of my life, in my superior judgment, that they would often carry me with them when they were going on any roguery, to plan for them. Growing up among them, with this confidence in my superior judgment, and when this, in their opinions, was perfected by Divine inspiration, from the circumstances already alluded to in my infancy, and which belief was ever afterwards zealously inculcated by the austerity of my life and manners, which became the subject of remark by white and black.—Having soon discovered to be great, I must appear so, and therefore studiously avoided mixing in society, and wrapped myself in mystery, devoting my time to fasting and prayer—by this time, having arrived to man's estate, and hearing the scriptures commented on at meetings, I was struck with that particular passage which says: "Seek ye the kingdom of Heaven and all things shall be added unto you." I reflected much on this passage, and prayed daily for light on this subject—As I was praying one day at my plough, the spirit spoke to me, saying "Seek ye the kingdom of Heaven and all things shall be added unto you." *Question*—what do you mean by the Spirit? *Ans.* The Spirit that spoke to the prophets in former days—and I was greatly astonished, and for two years prayed continually, whenever my duty would permit—and then again I had the same revelation, which fully confirmed me in the impression that I was ordained for some great purpose in the hands of the Almighty. Several years rolled round, in which many events occurred to strengthen me in this my belief. At this time I reverted in my mind to the remarks made of me in my childhood, and the things that had been shewn me—and as it had been said of me in my childhood by those by whom I had been taught to pray, both white and black, and in whom I had the greatest confidence, that I had too much sense to be raised, and if I was, I would never be of any use to any one as a slave. Now finding I had arrived to man's estate, and was a slave, and these revelations being made known to me, I began to direct my attention to this great object, to fulfill the purpose for which, by this time, I felt assured I was intended. Knowing the influence I had obtained over the minds of my fellow servants, (not by the means of conjuring and such like tricks—for to them I always spoke of such things with contempt) but by the communion of the Spirit whose revelations I often communicated to them, and they believed and said my wisdom came from God. I now began to prepare them for my purpose, by telling them something was about to happen that would terminate in fulfilling the great promise that had been made to me—About this time I was placed under an overseer, from whom I ran away—and after remaining in the woods thirty days, I returned, to the astonishment of the negroes on the plantation, who thought I had made my escape to some other part of the country, as my father had done before. But the reason of my return was, that the Spirit appeared to me and said I had my wishes directed to the things of this world, and not to the kingdom of Heaven, and that I should return to the service of my earthly master—"For he who knoweth his Master's will, and doeth it not, shall be beaten with many stripes, and thus have I chastened you." And the negroes found fault, and murmured against me, saying that if they had my sense they would not serve any master in the world. And about this time I had a vision—and I saw white spirits and black spirits engaged in battle, and the sun was darkened—the thunder rolled in the Heavens, and blood flowed in streams—and I heard a voice saying, "Such is your luck, such you are called to see, and let it come rough or smooth, you must surely bare it." I now withdrew myself as much as my situation would permit, from the intercourse of my fellow servants, for the avowed purpose of serving the Spirit more fully—and it appeared to me, and reminded me of the things it had already shown me, and that it would then reveal to me the knowledge of the elements, the revolution of the planets, the operation of tides, and changes of the seasons. After this revelation in the year of 1825, and the knowledge of the elements being made known to me, I sought more than ever to obtain true holiness before the great day of judgment should appear, and then I began to receive the true knowledge of faith. And from the first steps of righteousness until the last, was I made perfect; and the Holy Ghost was with me, and said, "Behold me as I stand in the Heavens"—and I looked and saw the forms of men in different attitudes—and there were lights in the sky to which the children of darkness gave other names than what they really were—for they were the lights of the Savior's hands, stretched forth from east to west, even as they were extended on the cross on Calvary for the redemption of sinners. And I wondered greatly at these miracles, and prayed to be informed of a certainty of the meaning thereof—and shortly afterwards, while laboring in the field, I discovered drops of blood on the corn as though it were dew from heaven—and I communicated it to many, both white and black, in the neighborhood—and I then found on the leaves in the woods hieroglyphic characters, and numbers, with the forms of men in different attitudes, portrayed in blood, and representing the figures I had seen before in the heavens. And now the Holy Ghost had revealed itself to me, and made plain the miracles it had shown me—For as the blood of Christ had been shed on this earth, and had ascended to heaven for the salvation of sinners, and was not returning to earth again in the form of dew—and as the leaves on the trees bore the impression of the figures I had seen in the heavens, it was plain to me that the Savior was about to lay down the yoke he had borne for the sins of men, and the great day of judgment was at hand. About this time I told these things to a white man, (Etheldred T. Brantley) on whom it had a wonderful effect—and he ceased from his wickedness, and was attacked immediately with a cutaneous eruption, and blood oozed from the pores of his skin, and after praying and fasting nine days, he was healed, and the Spirit appeared to me again, and said, as the Savior had been baptised so should we be also—and when the white people would not let us be baptised by the church, we went down into the water together, in the sight of many who reviled us, and were baptised by the Spirit—After this I rejoiced greatly, and gave thanks to God. And on the 12th of May, 1828, I heard a loud noise in the heavens, and the Spirit instantly appeared to me and said the Serpent was loosened, and Christ had laid down the yoke he had borne for the sins of men, and that I should take it on and fight against the Serpent, for the time was fast approaching when the first should be last and the last should be first. *Ques.* Do you not find yourself mistaken now? *Ans.* Was not Christ crucified? And by signs in the heavens that it would make known to me when I should commence the great work—and until the first sign appeared, I should conceal it from the knowledge of men—And on the appearance of the sign, (the eclipse of the sun last February) I should arise and prepare myself, and slay my enemies with their own weapons. And immediately on the sign appearing in the heavens, the seal was removed from my lips, and I communicated the great work laid out for me to do, to four in whom I had the greatest confidence, (Henry, Hark, Nelson, and Sam)—It was intended by us to have begun the work of death on the 4th July last—Many were the plans formed and rejected by us, and it affected my mind to such a degree, that I fell sick, and the time passed without our coming to any determination how to commence—Still forming new schemes and rejecting them, when the sign appeared again, which determined me not to wait longer.

Since the commencement of 1830, I had been living with Mr. Joseph Travis, who was to me a kind master, and placed the greatest confidence in me; in fact, I had no cause to complain of his treatment to me. On Saturday evening, the 20th of August, it was agreed between Henry, Hark and Myself, to prepare a dinner the next day for the men we expected, and then to concert a plan, as we had not yet determined on any. Hark, on the following morning, brought a pig, and Henry brandy, and being joined by Sam, Nelson, Will and Jack, they prepared in the woods a dinner, where, about three o'clock, I joined them.

Q. Why were you so backward in joining them?
A. The same reason that had caused me not to mix with them for years before.

I saluted them on coming up, and asked Will how came he there, he answered, his life was worth no more than others, and his liberty as dear to him. I asked him if he thought to obtain it? He said he would, or lose his life. This was enough to put him in full confidence. Jack, I knew, was only a tool in the hands of Hark, it was quickly agreed we should commence at home (Mr. J. Travis') on that night, and until we had armed and equipped ourselves, and gathered sufficient force, neither age nor sex was to be spared, (which was invariably adhered to). We remained at the feast, until about two hours in the night, when we went to the house and found Austin; they all went to the cider press and drank, except myself. On returning to the house, Hark went to the door with an axe, for the purpose of breaking it open, as we knew we were strong enough to murder the family, if they were awakened by the noise; but reflecting that it might create an alarm in the neighborhood, we determined to enter the house secretly, and murder them whilst sleeping. Hark got a ladder and set it against the chimney, on which I ascended, and hoisting a window, entered and came down stairs, unbarred the door, and removed the guns from their places. It was then observed that I must spill the first blood. On which, armed with a hatchet, and accompanied by Will, I entered my master's chamber, it being dark, I could not give a death blow, the hatchet blanced from his head, he sprang from the bed and called his wife, it was his last word, Will laid him dead, with a blow of his axe, and Mrs. Travis shared the same fate, as she lay in bed. The murder of this family, five in number, was the work of a moment, not one of them awoke; there was a little infant sleeping in a cradle, that was forgotten, until we had left the house and gone some distance, when Henry and Will returned and killed it; we got here, four guns that would shoot, and several old muskets, with a pound or two of powder. We remained some time at the barn, where we paraded; I formed them in a line as soldiers, and after them through all the manoeuvers I was master of marched them off to Mr. Salathul Francis', about six hundred yards distant. Sam and Will went to the door and knocked. Mr. Francis asked who was there, Sam replied it was him, and he had a letter for him on which he got up and came to the door; they immediately seized him, and dragging him out a little from the door, he was dispatched by repeated blows on the head; there was no other white person in the family. We started from there for Mrs. Reese's, maintaining the most perfect silence on our march, where finding the door unlocked, we entered, and murdered Mrs. Reese in her bed, while sleeping; her son awoke, but it was only to sleep the sleep of death, he had only time to say who is that, and he was no more. From Mrs. Reese's we went to Mrs. Turner's, a mile distant, which

Narrative

we reached about sunrise, on Monday morning. Henry, Austin, and Sam, went to the still, where, finding Mr. Peebles, Austin shot him, and the rest of us went to the house; as we approached, the family discovered us, and shut the door. Vain hope! Will, with one stroke of his axe, opened it, and we entered and found Mrs. Turner and Mrs. Newsome in the middle of a room, almost frightened to death. Will immediately killed Mrs. Turner, with one blow of his axe. I took Mrs. Newsome by the hand, and with the sword I had when I was apprehended, I struck her several blows over the head, but not being able to kill her, as the sword was dull. Will turning around and discovering it, despatched her also. A general destruction of property and search for money and ammunition, always succeeded the murders. By this time my company amounted to fifteen, and nine men mounted, who started for Mrs. Whitehead's, (the other six were to go through a by way to Mr. Bryant's, and rejoin us at Mrs. Whitehead's), as we approached the house we discovered Mr. Richard Whitehead standing in the cotton patch, near the lane fence; we called him over into the lane, and Will, the executioner, was near at hand, with his fatal axe, to send him to an untimely grave. As we pushed on to the house, I discovered some one run round the garden, and thinking it was some of the white family, I pursued them, but finding it was a servant girl belonging to the house, I returned to commence the work of death, but they whom I left, had not been idle; all the family were already murdered, but Mrs. Whitehead and her daughter Margaret. As I came round to the door I saw Will pulling Mrs. Whitehead out of the house, and at the step he nearly severed her head from her body, with his broad axe. Miss Margaret, when I discovered her, had concealed herself in the corner, formed by the projection of cellar cap from the house; on my approach she fled, but was soon overtaken, and after repeated blows with a sword, I killed her by a blow on the head, with a fence rail. By this time, the six who had gone by Mr. Bryant's, rejoined us, and informed me they had done the work of death assigned them. We again divided, part going to Mr. Richard Porter's, and from then to Nathaniel Francis', the others to Mr. Howell Harris', and Mr. T. Doyles. On my reaching Mr. Porter's, he had escaped with his family. I understood there, that the alarm has already spread, and I immediately returned to bring up those sent to Mr. Doyles, and Mr. Howell Harris'; the party I left going on to Mr. Francis', having told them I would join them in that neighborhood. I met theses sent to Mr. Doyles' and Mr. Harris' returning, having met Mr. Doyle on the road and killed him; and learning from some who joined them, that Mr. Harris was from home, I immediately pursued the course taken by the party gone on before; but knowing they would complete the work of death and pillage, at Mr. Francis' before I could get there, I went to Mr. Peter Edwards', expecting to find them there, but they had been here also. I then went to Mr. John T. Barrow's, they had been here and murdered him. I pursued on their track to Capt. Newit Harris', where I found the greater part mounted, and ready to start; the men now amounting to about forty, shouted and hurraed as I rode up, some were in the yard, loading their guns, others drinking. They said Captain Harris and his family had escaped, the property in the house they destroyed, robbing him of money and other valuables. I ordered them to mount and march instantly, this was about nine or ten o'clock, Monday morning. I proceeded to Mr. Levi Waller's, two or three miles distant. I took my station in the rear, and as it was my object to carry terror and devastation wherever we went, I placed fifteen or twenty of the best armed and most relied on, in front, who generally approached the houses as fast as their horses could run; this was for two purposes, to prevent escape and strike terror to the inhabitants—on this account I never got to the houses, after leaving Mrs. Whitehead's, until the murders were committed, except in one case. I sometimes got in sight in time to see the work of death completed, viewed the mangled bodies as they lay, in silent satisfaction, and immediately started in quest of other victims—Having murdered Mrs. Waller and ten children, we started for Mr. William Williams'—having killed him and two little boys that were there; while engaged in this, Mrs. Williams fled and got some distance from the house, but she was pursued, overtaken, and compelled to get up behind one of the company, who brought her back, and after showing her the mangled body of her lifeless husband, she was told to get down and lay by his side, where she was shot dead. I then started for Mr. Jacob Williams, where the family were murdered—Here he found a young man named Drury, who had come on business with Mr. Williams—he was pursued, overtaken and shot. Mrs. Vaughan was the next place we visited—and after murdering the family here, I determined on starting for Jerusalem—Our number amounted now to fifty or sixty, all mounted and armed with guns, axes, swords and clubs—On reaching Mr. James W. Parker's gate, immediately on the road leading to Jerusalem, and about three miles distant, it was proposed to me to call there, but I objected, as I knew he was gone to Jerusalem, and my object was to reach there as soon as possible; but some of the men having relations at Mr. Parker's it was agreed that they might call and get his people. I remained at the gate on the road, with seven or eight; the others going across the field to the house, about half a mile off. After waiting some time for them, I became impatient, and started to the house for them, and on our return we were met by a party of white men, who had pursued our blood-stained track, and who had fired on those at the gate, and dispersed them, which I knew nothing of, not having been at that time rejoined by any of them—Immediately on discovering the whites, I ordered my men to halt and form, as they appeared to be alarmed—The white men, eighteen in number, approached us in about one hundred yards, when one of them fired, (this was against the positive orders of Captain Alexander P. Peete, who commanded, and who had directed the men to reserve their fire until within thirty paces)—And I discovered about half of them retreating, I then ordered my men to fire and rush on them; the few remaining stood their ground until we approached within fifty yards, when they fired and retreated. We pursued and overtook some of them who we thought we left dead; (they were not killed) after pursuing them about two hundred yards, and rising a little hill, I discovered they were met by another party, and had halted, and were reloading their guns, (this was a small party from Jerusalem who knew the negroes were in the field, and had just tied their horses to await their return to the road, knowing that Mr. Parker and family were in Jerusalem, but knew nothing of the party that had gone in with Captain Peete; on hearing the firing they immediately rushed to the spot and arrived just in time to arrest the progress of the barbarous villains, and save the lives of their friends and fellow citizens). Thinking that those who retreated first, and the party who fired on us at fifty or sixty yards distant, had all fallen back to meet others with ammunition. As I saw them reloading their guns, and more coming up than I saw at first, and several of my bravest men being wounded, the others became panick struck and squandered over the field; the white men pursued and fired on us several times. Hark had his horse shot under him, and I caught another for him as it was running by me; five or six of my men were wounded, but none left on the field; finding myself defeated here I instantly determined to go through a private way, and cross the Nottoway river at the Cypress Bridge, three miles below Jerusalem, and attack that place in the rear, as I expected they would look for me on the other road, and I had a great desire to get there to procure arms and ammunition. After going a short distance in this private way, accompanied by about twenty men, I overtook two or three who told me the others were dispersed in every direction. After trying in vain to collect a sufficient force to proceed to Jerusalem,

I determined to return, as I was sure they would make back to their old neighborhood, where they would rejoin me, make new recruits, and come down again. On my way back, I called at Mrs. Thomas's, Mrs. Spencer's, and several other places, the white families having fled, we found no more victims to gratify our thirst for blood, we stopped at Maj. Ridley's quarter for the night, and being joined by four of his men, with the recruits made since my defeat, we mustered now about forty strong. After placing out sentinels, I laid down to sleep, but was quickly roused by a great racket; starting up, I found some mounted, and others in great confusion; one of the sentinels having given the alarm that we were about to be attacked, I ordered some to ride round and reconnoitre, and on their return the others being more alarmed, not knowing who they were, fled in different ways, so that I was reduced to about twenty again; with this I determined to attempt to recruit, and proceed on to rally in the neighborhood, I had left. Dr. Blunt's was the nearest house, which we reached just before day; on riding up the yard, Hark fired a gun. We expected Dr. Blunt and his family were at Maj. Ridley's, as I knew there was a company of men there; the gun was fired to ascertain if any of the family were at home; we were immediately fired upon and retreated, leaving several of my men. I do not know what became of them, as I never saw them afterwards. Pursuing our course back and coming in sight of Captain Harris', where we had been the day before, we discovered a party of white men at the house, on which all deserted me by two, (Jacob and Nat), we concealed ourselves in the woods until near night, when I sent them in search of Henry, Sam, Nelson, and Hark, and directed them to rally all they could, at the place we had had our dinner the Sunday before, where they would find me, and I accordingly returned there as soon as it was dark and remained until Wednesday evening, when discovering white men riding around the place as though they were looking for some one, and none of my men joining me, I concluded Jacob and Nat had been taken, and compelled to betray me. On this I gave up all hope for the present, and on Thursday night after having supplied myself with provisions from Mr. Travis's, I scratched a hole under a pile of fence rails in a field, where I concealed myself for six weeks, never leaving my hiding place but for a few minutes in the dead of night to get water which was very near; thinking by this time I could venture out, I began to go about in the night and eaves drop the houses in the neighborhood; pursuing this course for about a fortnight and gathering little or no intelligence, afraid of speaking to any human being, and returning every morning to my cave before the dawn of day. I know not how long I might have led this life, if accident had not betrayed me, a dog in the neighborhood passing by my hiding place one night while I was out, was attracted by some mat I have in my cave, and crawled in and stole it, and was coming out just as I returned. A few nights after, two negroes having started to go hunting with the same dog, and passed that way, the dog came again to the place, and having just gone out to walk about, discovered me and barked, on which thinking myself discovered, I spoke to them to beg concealment. On making myself known they fled from me. Knowing then they would betray me, I immediately left my hiding place, and was pursued almost incessantly until I was taken a fortnight afterwards by Mr. Benjamin Phipps, in a little hole I had dug out with my sword, for the purpose of concealment, under the top of a fallen tree. On Mr. Phipps' discovering the place of my concealment, he cocked his gun and aimed at me. I requested him not to shoot and I would give up, upon which he demanded my sword. I delivered it to him, and he brought me to prison. During the time I was pursued, I had many hair breadth escapes, which your time will not permit you to relate. I am here loaded with chains, and willing to suffer the fate that awaits me.

David Walker

(1785–1830, United States)

Appeal to the Coloured Citizens of the World: Our Wretchedness in Consequence of Slavery

1829

My dearly beloved Brethren and Fellow Citizens.

Having travelled over a considerable portion of these United States, and having, in the course of my travels, taken the most accurate observations of things as they exist—the result of my observations has warranted the full and unshaken conviction, that we, (coloured people of these United States,) are the most degraded, wretched, and abject set of beings that ever lived since the world began; and I pray God that none like us ever may live again until time shall be no more. They tell us of the Israelites in Egypt, the Helots in Sparta, and of the Roman Slaves, which last were made up from almost every nation under heaven, whose sufferings under those ancient and heathen nations, were, in comparison with ours, under this enlightened and Christian nation, no more than a cypher—or, in other words, those nations of antiquity, had but little more among them than the name and form of slavery; while wretchedness and endless miseries were reserved, apparently in a phial, to be poured out upon our fathers, ourselves and our children, by *Christian Americans!*

These positions I shall endeavour, by the help of the Lord, to demonstrate in the course of the APPEAL, to the satisfaction of the most incredulous mind—and may God Almighty who is the Father of our Lord Jesus Christ, open your hearts to understand and believe the truth.

The *causes*, my brethren, which produce our wretchedness and miseries, are so very numerous and aggravating, that I believe the pen only of a Josephus or a Plutarch, can well enumerate and explain them. Upon subjects, then, of such incomprehensible magnitude, so impenetrable, and so notorious, I shall be obliged to omit a large class of, and content myself with giving you an exposition of a few of those, which do indeed rage to such an alarming pitch, that they cannot but be a perpetual source of terror and dismay to every reflecting mind.

I am fully aware, in making this appeal to my much afflicted and suffering brethren, that I shall not only be assailed by those whose greatest earthly desires are, to keep us in abject ignorance and wretchedness, and who are of the firm conviction that Heaven has designed us and our children to be slaves and *beasts of burden* to them and their children.

I say, I do not only expect to be held up to the public as an ignorant, impudent and restless disturber of the public peace, by such avaricious creatures, as well as a mover of insubordination—and perhaps put in prison or to death, for giving a superficial exposition of our miseries, and exposing tyrants. But I am persuaded, that many of my brethren, particularly those who are ignorantly in league with slave-holders or tyrants, who acquire their daily bread by the blood and sweat of their more ignorant brethren—and not a few of those too, who are too ignorant to see an inch beyond their noses, will rise up and call me cursed—Yea, the jealous ones among us will perhaps use more abject subtlety, by affirming that this work is not worth perusing, that we are well situated, and there is no use in trying to better our condition, for we cannot. I will ask one question here.—Can our condition be any worse?—Can it be more mean and abject? If there are any changes, will they not be for the better, though they may appear for the worst at first? Can they get us any lower? Where can they get us? They are afraid to treat us worse, for they know well, the day they do it they are gone. But against all accusations which may or can be preferred against me, I appeal to Heaven for my motive in writing—who knows that my object is, if possible, to awaken in the breasts of my afflicted, degraded and slumbering brethren, a spirit of inquiry and investigation respecting our miseries and wretchedness in this RE-PUBLICAN LAND OF LIBERTY!!!!!!

The sources from which our miseries are derived, and on which I shall comment, I shall not combine in one, but shall put them under distinct heads and expose them in their turn; in doing which, keeping truth on my side, and not departing from the strictest rules of morality. I shall endeavour to penetrate, search out and lay them open for your inspection. If you cannot or will not profit by them, I shall have done *my* duty to you, my country and my God.

And as the inhuman system of *slavery,* is the *source* from which most of our miseries proceed, I shall begin with that *curse to nations,* which has spread terror and devastation through so many nations of antiquity, and which is raging to such a pitch at the present day in Spain and Portugal. It had one tug in England, in France and in the United States of America; yet the inhabitants thereof, do not learn wisdom, and erase it entirely from their dwellings and from all with whom they have to do. The fact is, the labour of slaves comes too cheap to the avaricious usurpers, and is (as they think) of such great utility to the country where is exists, that those who are actuated by sordid avarice only, overlook the evils, which will as sure as the Lord lives, follow after the good. In fact, they are so happy to keep in ignorance and degradation, and to receive the homage and the labour of the slaves, they forget that God rules in the armies of heaven and among the inhabitants of the earth, having his ears continually open to the cries, tears and groans of his oppressed people; and being a just and holy Being will at one day appear fully in behalf of the oppressed, and arrest the progress of the avaricious oppressors; for although the destruction of the oppressors God may not be effected by the oppressed, yet the Lord our God will bring other destructions upon them—for not unfrequently will he cause them to rise up against another, to be split and divided, and to oppress each other, and sometimes to open hostilities with sword in hand.

Some may ask, what is the matter with this united and happy people?—Some say it is the cause of political usurpers, tyrants, oppressors, &c. But has not the Lord an oppressed and suffering people among them? Does the Lord condescend to hear their cries and see their tears in consequence of oppression? Will he let the oppressors rest comfortably and happy always? Will he not cause the very children of the oppressors to rise up against them, and ofttimes put them to death? "God works in many ways his wonders to perform."

I will not here speak of the destruction which the Lord brought upon Egypt, in consequence of the oppression and consequent groans of the oppressed—of the hundreds and thousands of Egyptians whom God hurled into the Red Sea for afflicting his people in their land—of the Lord's suffering people in Sparta or Lacedemon, the land of the truly famous Lycurgus—nor have I time to comment upon the cause which produced the fierceness with which Sylla usurped the title, and absolutely acted as dictator of the Roman people—the conspiracy of Cataline—the conspiracy against, and murder of Caesar in the Senate house—the spirit with which Marc Antony made himself master of the commonwealth—his associating Octavius and Lipidus with himself in power—their dividing the provinces of Rome among themselves—their attack and defeat, on the plains of Philippi, of the last defenders of their liberty, (Brutus and Cassius)—the tyranny of Tiberius, and from him to the final overthrow of Constantinople by the Turkish Sultan, Mahomed II. A.D. 1453.

I say, I shall not take up time to speak of the *causes* which produced so much wretchedness and massacre among those heathen nations, for I am aware that you know too well, that God is just, as well as merciful!—I shall call your attention a few moments to that *Christian* nation, the Spaniards—while I shall leave almost unnoticed, that avaricious and cruel people, the Portuguese, among whom all true hearted Christians and lovers of Jesus Christ, must evidently see the judgments of God displayed. To show the judgments of God upon the Spaniards, I shall occupy but a little time, leaving a plenty of room for the candid and unprejudiced to reflect.

All persons who are acquainted with history, and particularly the Bible, who are not blinded by the God of this world, and are not actuated solely by avarice—who are able to lay aside prejudice long enough to view candidly and impartially, things as they were, are, and probably will be—who are willing to admit that God made man to serve Him *alone,* and that man should have no other Lord or Lords but Himself—that God Almighty is the *sole proprietor* or *master* of the WHOLE human family, and will not on any consideration admit of a colleague, being unwilling to divide his glory with another—and who can dispense with prejudice long enough to admit that we are *men,* notwithstanding our *improminent noses* and *woolly heads,* and believe that we feel for our fathers, mothers, wives and children, as well as the whites do for theirs.—I say, all who are permitted to see and believe these things, can easily recognize the judgments of God among the Spaniards. Though others may lay the cause of the fierceness with which they cut each other's throats, to some other circumstances, yet they who believe that God is a God of justice, will believe that SLAVERY *is the principal cause.*

While the Spaniards are running about upon the field of battle cutting each other's throats, has not the Lord an afflicted and suffering people in the midst of them, whose cries and groans in consequence of oppression are continually pouring into the ears of the God of justice? Would they not cease to cut each other's throats, if they could? But how can they? The very support which they draw from government to aid them in perpetrating such enormities, does it not arise in a great degree from the wretched victims of oppression among them? And yet they are calling for PEACE!—PEACE!! Will any peace be given unto them? Their destruction may indeed be procrastinated awhile, but can it continue long, while they are oppressing the Lord's people? Has He not the hearts of all men in His hand? Will he suffer one part of his creatures to go on oppressing another like brutes always, with impunity? And yet, those avaricious wretches are calling for PEACE!!!! I declare, it does appear to me, as though some nations think God is asleep, or that he made the Africans for nothing else but to dig their mines and work their farms, or they cannot believe history, sacred or profane.

I ask every man who has a heart, and is blessed with the privilege of believing—Is not God a God of justice to *all* his creatures? Do you say he is? Then if he gives peace and tranquillity to tyrants, and permits them to keep our fathers, our mothers, ou selves and our children in eternal ignorance and wretchedness, to support them and their families, would he be to us a God of *justice?* I ask, O ye *Christians!!!* who hold us and our children in the most abject ignorance and degradation, that ever a people were afflicted with since the world began—I say, if God gives you peace and tranquillity, and suffers you thus to go on afflicting us, and our children, who have never given you the least provocation—would he be to us *a God of justice?* If you will allow that we are MEN, who feel for each other, does not the blood of our fathers and of us their children, cry aloud to the Lord of Sabaoth against you, for the cruelties and murders with which you have, and do continue to afflict us. But it is time for me to close my remarks on the suburbs, just to enter more fully into the interior of this system of cruelty and oppression.

ARTICLE I

Our Wretchedness in Consequence of Slavery

MY BELOVED BRETHREN:—The Indians of North and of South America—the Greeks—the Irish, subjected under the king of Great Britain—the Jews, that ancient people of the Lord—the inhabitants of the islands of the sea—in fine, all the inhabitants of the earth, (except however, the sons of Africa) are called *men,* and of course are, and ought to be free. But we, (coloured people) and our children are *brutes!!* and of course are, and *ought to be* SLAVES to the American people and their children forever!! to dig their mines and work their farms; and thus go on enriching them, from one generation to another with our *blood* and our *tears!!!!*

I promised in a preceding page to demonstrate to the satisfaction of the most incredulous, that we, (coloured people of these United States of America) are the *most wretched, degraded* and *abject* set of beings that *ever lived* since the world began, and that the white Americans having reduced us to the wretched state of *slavery,* treat us in that condition *more cruel* (they being an enlightened and Christian people,) than any heathen nation did any people whom it had reduced to our condition. These affirmations are so well confirmed in the minds of all unprejudiced men, who have taken the trouble to read histories, that they need no elucidation from me. But to put them beyond all doubt, I refer you in the first place to the children of Jacob, or of Israel in Egypt, under Pharaoh and his people. Some of my brethren do not know who Pharaoh and the Egyptians were—I know it to be a fact, that some of them take the Egyptians to have been a gang of *devils,* not knowing any better, and that they (Egyptians) having got possession of the Lord's people, treated them *nearly* as cruel as *Christian Americans* do us, at the present day. For the information of such, I would only mention that the Egyptians, were Africans or coloured people, such as we are—some of them yellow and others dark—a mixture of Ethiopians and the natives of Egypt—about the same as you see the coloured people of the United States at the present day—I say, I call your attention then, to the children of Jacob, while I point out particularly to you his son Joseph, among the rest, in Egypt.

"And Pharaoh, said unto Joseph, thou shalt be over my house, and according unto thy word shall all my people be ruled: only in the throne will I be greater than thou."

"And Pharaoh said unto Joseph, see, I have set thee over all the land of Egypt."

"And Pharaoh said unto Joseph, I am Pharaoh, and without thee shall no man lift up his hand or foot in all the land of Egypt."

Now I appeal to heaven and to earth, and particularly to the American people themselves, who cease not to declare that our condition is not *hard,* and that we are comparatively satisfied to rest in wretchedness and misery, under them and their children. Not, indeed, to show me a coloured President, a Governor, a Legislator, a Senator, a Mayor, or an Attorney at the Bar.—But to show me a man of colour, who holds the low office of a Constable, or one who sits in a Juror Box, even on a case of one of his wretched brethren, throughout this great Republic!!—But let us pass Joseph the son of Israel a little farther in review, as he existed with that heathen nation.

"And Pharaoh called Joseph's name Zaphnathpaaneah; and he gave him to wife Asenath the daughter of Potipherah priest of On. And Joseph went out over all the land of Egypt."

Compare the above, with the American institutions. Do they not institute laws to prohibit us from marrying among the whites? I would wish, candidly, however, before the Lord, to be understood, that I would not give a *pinch of snuff* to be married to any white person I ever saw in all the days of my life. And I do say it, that the black man, or man of colour, who will leave his own colour (provided he can get one who is good for nay thing) and marry a white woman, to be a double slave to her, just because she is *white,* ought to be treated by her as he surely will be, viz: as a NIGER!!!! It is not, indeed, what I care about inter-marriage with the whites, which induced me to pass this subject in review; for the Lord knows, that there is a day coming when they will be glad enough to get into the company of the blacks, notwithstanding, we are, in this generation, levelled by them, almost on a level with the brute creation: and some of us they treat even worse than they do the brutes that perish. I only made this extract to show how much lower we are held, and how much more cruel we are treated by the Americans, than were the children of Jacob, by the Egyptians.—We will notice the sufferings of Israel some further, under *heathen Pharaoh,* compared with our under the *enlightened Christians of America.*

"And Pharaoh spake unto Joseph, saying, thy father and thy brethren are come unto thee:"

"The land of Egypt is before thee: in the best of the land make thy father and brethren to dwell; in the land of Goshen let them dwell: and if thou knowest any men of activity among them, then make them rulers over my cattle."

I ask those people who treat us so *well,* Oh! I ask them, where is the most barren spot of land which they have given unto us? Israel had the most fertile land in all Egypt. Need I mention the very notorious fact, that I have known a poor man of colour, who laboured night and day, to acquire a little money, and having acquired it, he vested it in a small piece of land, and got him a house erected thereon, and having paid for the whole, he moved his family into it, where he was suffered to remain but nine months, when he was cheated out of his property by a white man, and driven out of door! And is not this the case generally? Can a man of colour buy a piece of land and keep it peaceably? Will not some white man try to get it from him, even if it is in a *mud hole?* I need not comment any farther on a subject, which all, both black and white, will readily admit. But I must, really, observe that in this very city, when a man of colour dies, if he owned any real estate it most generally falls into the hands of some white person. The wife and children of the deceased may weep and lament if they please, but the estate will be kept snug enough by its white possessor.

But to prove farther that the condition of the Israelites was better under the Egyptians than ours is under the whites, I call upon the professing Christians, I call upon the philanthropist, I call upon the very tyrant himself, to show me a page of history, either sacred or profane, on which a verse can be found, which maintains, that the Egyptians heaped the *insupportable insult* upon the children of Israel, by telling them that they were not of the *human family.* Can the whites deny this charge? Have they not, after having reduced us to the deplorable condition of slaves under their feet, held us up as descending originally from the tribes of *Monkeys* or *Orang-Outangs?* O! my God! I appeal to every man of feeling—is not this insupportable? Is it not heaping the most gross insult upon our miseries, because they have got us under their feet and we cannot help ourselves? Oh! pity us we pray thee, Lord Jesus, Master.—Has Mr. Jefferson declared to the world, that we are inferior to the whites, both in the endowments of our bodies and of minds? It is indeed surprising, that a man of such great learning, combined with such excellent natural parts, should speak so of a set of men in chains. I do not know what to compare it to, unless, like putting one wild deer in an iron cage, where it will be secured, and hold another by the side of the same, then let it go, and expect the one in the cage to run as fast as the one at liberty. So far, my brethren, were the Egyptians from heaping these insults upon their slaves, that Pharaoh's daughter took Moses, a son of Israel, for her own, as will appear by the following.

> "And Pharaoh's daughter said unto her, [Moses' mother] take this child away, and nurse it for me, and I will pay thee thy wages. And the woman took the child [Moses] and nursed it.
> "And the child grew, and she brought him unto Pharaoh's daughter and he became her son. And she called his name Moses: and she said because I drew him out of the water."

In all probability, Moses would have become Prince Regent to the throne, and no doubt, in process of time but he would have been seated on the throne of Egypt. But he had rather suffer shame, with the people of God, than to enjoy pleasures with that wicked people for a season. O! that the coloured people were long since of Moses' excellent disposition, instead of courting favour with, and telling news and lies to our *natural enemies,* against each other—aiding them to keep their hellish chains of slavery upon us. Would we not long before this time, have been respectable men, instead of such wretched victims of oppression as we are? Would they be able to drag our mothers, our fathers, our wives, our children and ourselves, around the world in chains and hand-cuffs as they do, to dig up gold and silver for them and theirs? This question, my brethren, I leave for you to digest; and may God Almighty force it home to your hearts. Remember that unless you are united, keeping your tongues within your teeth, you will be afraid to trust your secrets to each other, and thus perpetuate our miseries under the *Christians!!!!!* Addition.— Remember, also to lay humble at the feet of our Lord and Master Jesus Christ, with prayers and fasting. Let our enemies go on with their butcheries, and at once fill up their cup. Never make an attempt to gain our freedom or *natural right,* from under our cruel oppressors, and murderers, until you see your way clear—when that hour arrives and you move, be not afraid or dismayed; for be you assured that Jesus Christ the King of heaven and of earth who is the God of justice and of armies, will surely go before you. And those enemies who have for hundreds of years stolen our *rights*, and kept us ignorant of Him and His divine worship, he will remove. Millions of whom, are this day, so ignorant and avaricious, that they cannot conceive how God can have an attribute of justice, and show mercy to us because it pleased Him to make us black—which colour, Mr. Jefferson calls unfortunate!!!!!! As though we are not as thankful to our God, for having made us as it pleased himself, as they (the whites,) are for having made them white. They think because they hold us in their infernal chains of slavery, that we wish to be white, or of their colour—but they are dreadfully deceived—we wish to be just as it pleased our Creator to have made us, and no avaricious and unmerciful wretches, have any business to make slaves of, or hold us is slavery. How would they like for us to make slaves of, and hold them in cruel slavery, and murder them as they do us?—But is Mr. Jefferson's assertion true? viz. "that it is unfortunate for us that our Creator has been pleased to make us *black*." We will not take his say so, for the fact. The world will have an opportunity to see whether it is unfortunate for us, that our Creator *has made us* darker than the *whites*.

Fear not the number of education of our *enemies*, against whom we shall have to contend for our lawful right; guaranteed to us by our Maker; for why would we be afraid, when God is, and will continue, (if we continue humble) to be on our side?

The man who would not fight under our Lord and Master Jesus Christ, in the glorious and heavenly cause of freedom and of God—to be delivered from the most wretched, abject and servile slavery, that ever a people was afflicted with since the foundation of the world, to the present day—ought to be kept with all of his children or family, in slavery, or in chains to be butchered by his *cruel enemies*.

I saw a paragraph, a few years since, in a South Carolina paper, which, speaking of the barbarity of the Turks, it said: "The Turks are the most barbarous people in the world—they treat the Greeks more like *brutes* than human beings." And in the same paper was an advertisement, which said: "Eight well built Virginia and Maryland *Negro fellows* and four *wenches* will positively be *sold* this day, *to the highest bidder!*" And what astonished me still more was, to see in this same *humane* paper!! the cuts of three men, with clubs and budgets on their backs, and an advertisement offering a considerable sum of money for their apprehension and delivery. I declare, it is really so amusing to hear the Southerners and Westerners of this country talk about *barbarity*, that it is positively enough to make a man *smile*.

The sufferings of the Helots among the Spartans, were somewhat severe, it is true, but to say that theirs, were as severe as ours among the Americans, I do most strenuously deny—for instance, can any man show me an article on a page of ancient history which specifies, that, the Spartans chained, and hand-cuffed the Helots, and dragged them from their wives and children, children from their parents, mothers from their suckling babes, wives from their husbands, driving them from one end of the country to the other? Notice the Spartans were heathens, who lived long before our Divine Master made his appearance in the flesh.

Can Christian Americans deny these barbarous cruelties? Have you not, Americans, having subjected us under you, added to these miseries, by insulting us in telling us to our face, because we are helpless, that we are not of the human family? I ask you, O! Americans, I ask you, in the name of the Lord, can you deny these charges? Some perhaps may deny, by saying, that they never thought or said that we were not men. But do not actions speak louder than *words*?—have they not made provisions for the Greeks, and Irish? Nations who have never done the least thing for them, while *we*, who have enriched their country with our blood and tears—have dug up gold and silver for them and their children, from generation to generation, and are in more miseries than any other people under heaven, are not seen, but by comparatively, a handful of the American people? There are indeed, more ways to kill a dog, besides choking it to death with butter. Further—The Spartans or Lacemonians, had some frivolous pretext, for enslaving the Helots, for they (Helots) while being free inhabitants of Sparta, stirred up an intestine commotion, and were, by the Spartans subdued, and made prisoners of war. Consequently they and their children were condemned to perpetual slavery.

I have been for years troubling the pages of historians, to find out what our fathers have done to the *white Christians of America,* to merit such condign punishment as they have inflicted on them, and do continue to inflict on us their children. But I must aver, that my researches have hitherto been to no effect. I have therefore, come to the immovable conclusion, that they (Americans) have, and do continue to punish us for nothing else, but for enriching them and their country. For I cannot conceive of any thing else. Nor will I ever believe otherwise, until the Lord shall convince me.

The world knows, that slavery as it existed among the Romans, (which was the primary cause of their destruction) was, comparatively speaking, no more than a *cypher,* when compared with ours under the Americans. Indeed I should not have noticed the Roman slaves, had not the very learned and penetrating Mr. Jefferson said, "when a master was murdered, all his slaves in the same house, or within hearing, were condemned to death."—Here let me ask Mr. Jefferson, (but he is gone to answer at the bar of God, for the deeds done in his body while living,) I therefore ask the whole American people, had I not rather die, or be put to death, than to be a slave to any tyrant, who takes not only my own, but my wife and children's lives by the inches? Yea, would I meet death with avidity far! Far!! in preference to such *servile submission* to the murderous hands of tyrants. Mr. Jefferson's very severe remarks on us have been so extensively argued upon by men whose attainments in literature, I shall never be able to reach, that I would not have meddled with it, were it not to solicit each of my brethren, who has the spirit of a man, to buy a copy of Mr. Jefferson's "Notes on Virginia," and put it in the hand of his son. For let no one of us suppose that the refutations which have been written by our white friends are enough—they are *whites*—we are *blacks.*

We, and the world wish to see the charges of Mr. Jefferson refuted by the blacks *themselves,* according to their chance; for we must remember that what the whites have written respecting this subject, is other men's labours, and did not emanate from the blacks. I know well, that there are some talents and learning among the coloured people of this country, which we have not a chance to develop, in consequence of oppression; but our oppression ought not to hinder us from acquiring all we can. For we will have a chance to develop them by and by. God will not suffer us, always to be oppressed. Our suffering will come to an *end,* in spite of all the Americans this side of *eternity.* Then we will want all the learning and talents among ourselves, and perhaps more, to govern ourselves.—"Every dog must have its day," the American's is coming to an end.

But let us review Mr. Jefferson's remarks respecting us some further. Comparing our miserable fathers, with the learned philosophers of Greece, he says: 'Yet notwithstanding these and other discouraging circumstances among the Romans, their slaves were their rarest artists. They excelled too, in science, insomuch as to be usually employed as tutors to their master's children; Epictetus, Terence and Phaedrus, were slaves,—but they were of the race of whites. It is not their *conditions* then, but *nature,* which has produced the distinction." See this, my brethren!! Do you believe that this assertion is swallowed by millions of whites? Do you know that Mr. Jefferson was one of as great characters as ever lived among the whites? See his writings for the world, and public labours from the United States of America. Do you believe that the assertions of such a man, will pass away into oblivion unobserved by this people and the world? If you do you are much mistaken—See how the American people treat us—have we souls in our bodies? Are we men who have any spirits at all? I know that there are many *swell-bellied* fellows among us, whose greatest object is to fill their stomachs. Such I do not mean—I am after those who know and feel, that we are MEN, as well as other people; to them, I say, that unless we try to refute Mr. Jefferson's arguments respecting us, we will only establish them.

But the slaves among the Romans. Every body who has read history, knows, that as soon as a slave among the Romans obtained his freedom, he could rise to the greatest eminence in the State, and there was no law instituted to hinder a slave from buying his freedom. Have not the Americans instituted laws to hinder us from obtaining our freedom? Do any deny this charge? Read the laws of Virginia, North Carolina, &c. Further: have not the Americans instituted laws to prohibit a man of colour from obtaining and holding any office whatever, under the government of the United States of America? Now, Mr. Jefferson tells us, that our condition is not so hard, as the slaves were under the Romans!!!!!!

It is time for me to bring this article to a close. But before I close it, I must observe to my brethren that at the close of the first Revolution in this country, with Great Britain, there were but thirteen States in the Union, now there are twenty-four, most of which are slave-holding States, and the whites are dragging us around in chains and in handcuffs, to their new States and Territories to work their mines and farms, to enrich them and their children—and millions of them believing firmly that we being a little darker than they were made by our Creator to be an inheritance to them and their children for ever—the same as a parcel of *brutes*.

Are we MEN!!—I ask you, O my brethren! are we MEN? Did our Creator make us to be slaves to dust and ashes like ourselves? Are they not dying worms as well as we? Have they not to make their appearance before the tribunal of Heaven, to answer for the deeds done in the body, as well as we? Have we any other Master but Jesus Christ alone? Is he not their Master as well as ours?—What right then, have we to obey and call any other Master, but Himself? How we could be so *submissive* to a gang of men, whom we cannot tell whether they are *as good* as ourselves or not, I never could conceive. However, this is shut up with the Lord, and we cannot precisely tell—but I declare, we judge men by their works.

The whites have always been an unjust, jealous, unmerciful, avaricious and blood-thirsty set of beings, always seeking after power and authority.—We view them all over the confederacy of Greece, where they were first known to be any thing, (in consequence of education) we see them there, cutting each other's throats—trying to subject each other to wretchedness and misery—to effect which, they used all kinds of deceitful, unfair and unmerciful means. We view them next in Rome, where the spirit of tyranny and deceit raged still higher. We view them in Gaul, Spain, and in Britain.—In fine, we view them all over Europe, together with what were scattered about in Asia and Africa, as heathens, and we see them acting more like devils than accountable men. But some may ask, did not the blacks of Africa, and the mulattoes of Asia, go on in the same way as did the whites of Europe. I answer, no—they never were half so avaricious, deceitful and unmerciful as the whites, according to their knowledge.

But we will leave the whites or Europeans as heathens, and take a view of them as Christians, in which capacity we see them as cruel, if not more so than ever. In fact, take them as a body, they are ten times more cruel, avaricious and unmerciful than ever they were; for while they were heathens, they were bad enough it is true, but it is positively a fact that they were not quite so audacious as to go and take vessel loads of men, women and children, and in cold blood, and through devilishness, throw them into the sea, and murder them in all kind of ways. While they were heathens, they were too ignorant for such barbarity. But being Christians, enlightened and sensible, they are completely prepared for such hellish cruelties.

Now suppose God were to give them more sense, what would they do? If it were possible, would they not *dethrone* Jehovah and seat themselves upon his throne? I therefore, in the name and fear of the Lord God of Heaven and of earth, divested of prejudice either on the side of my colour or that of the whites, advance my suspicion of them, whether they are *as good by nature* as we are or not. Their actions, since they were known as a people, have been the reverse, I do indeed suspect them, but this, as I before observed, is shut up with the Lord, we cannot exactly tell, it will be proved in succeeding generations.—The whites have had the essence of the gospel as it was preached by my master and his apostles—the Ethiopians have not, who are to have it in its meridian splendor—the Lord will give it to them to their satisfaction. I hope and pray my God, that they will make good use of it, that it may be well with them.

Frederick Douglass
(1817–1895, United States)

Fourth of July Oration

Rochester, 1852

Fellow-citizens, pardon me, allow me to ask, why am I called upon to speak here today? What have I, or those I represent, to do with your national independence? Are the great principles of political freedom and of natural justice, embodied in that Declaration of Independence, extended to us? And am I, therefore, called upon to bring our humble offering to the national altar, and to confess the benefits and express devout gratitude for the blessings resulting from your independence to us?

Would to God, both for your sakes and ours, that an affirmative answer could be truthfully returned to these questions! Then would my task be light, and my burden easy and delightful. For who is there so cold, that a nation's sympathy could not warm him? Who so obdurate and dead to the claims of gratitude, that would not thankfully acknowledge such priceless benefits? Who so stolid and selfish, that would not give his voice to swell the hallelujahs of a nation's jubilee when the chains of servitude had been torn from his limbs? I am not that man. In a case like that, the dumb might eloquently speak, and the "lame man leap as an hart."

But such is not the state of the case. I say it with a sad sense of the disparity between us. I am not included within the pale of this glorious anniversary! Your high independence only reveals the immeasurable distance between us. The blessings in which you, this day, rejoice, are not enjoyed in common. The rich inheritance of justice, liberty, prosperity, and independence, bequeathed by your fathers, is shared by you, not by me. The sunlight that brought light and healing to you has brought stripes and death to me. This Fourth of July is yours, not mine. You may rejoice, I must mourn. To drag a man in fetters into the grand illuminated temple of liberty, and call upon him to join you in joyous anthems, were inhuman mockery and sacrilegious irony. Do you mean, citizens, to mock me, by asking me to speak today? If so, there is a parallel to your conduct. And let me warn you that it is dangerous to copy the example of a nation whose crimes, towering up to heaven, were thrown down by the breath of the Almighty, burying that nation in irrevocable ruin! I can today take up the plaintive lament of a peeled and woe-smitten people!

"By the rivers of Babylon, there we sat down. Yea! we wept when we remembered Zion. We hanged our harps upon the willows in the midst thereof. For there, they that carried us away captive, required of us a song; and they who wasted us required of us mirth, saying, sing us one of the songs of Zion. How can we sing the Lord's song in a strange land? If I forget thee, O Jerusalem, let my right hand forget her cunning. If I do not remember thee, let my tongue cleave to the roof of my mouth."

Fellow-citizens, above your national, tumultuous joy, I hear the mournful wail of millions, whose chains, heavy and grievous yesterday, are today rendered more intolerable by the jubilee shouts that reach them. If I do forget, if I do not faithfully remember those bleeding children of sorrow this day, "may my right hand forget her cunning, and may my tongue cleave to the roof of my mouth!" To forget them, to pass lightly over their wrongs, and to chime in with the popular theme, would be treason most scandalous and shocking, and would make me a reproach before God and the world.

My subject, then, fellow-citizens, is American Slavery. I shall see this day and its popular characteristics from the slave's point of view. Standing here identified with the American bondman, making his wrongs mine, I do not hesitate to declare, with all my soul, that the character and conduct of this nation never looked blacker to me than on this Fourth of July! Whether we turn to the declarations of the past, or to the professions of the present, the conduct of the nation seems equally hideous and revolting. America is false to the past, false to the present, and solemnly binds herself to be false to the future. Standing with God and the crushed and bleeding slave on this occasion, I will, in the name of humanity which is outraged, in the name of liberty which is fettered, in the name of the Constitution and the Bible which are disregarded and trampled upon, dare to call in question and to denounce, with all the emphasis I can command, everything that serves to perpetuate slavery—the great sin and shame of America! "I will not equivocate; I will not excuse," I will use the severest language I can command; and yet not one word shall escape me that any man, whose judgment is not blinded by prejudice, or who is not at heart a slaveholder, shall not confess to be right and just.

But I fancy I hear some one of my audience say, "It is just in this circumstance that you and your brother abolitionists fail to make a favorable impression on the public mind. Would you argue more, and denounce less; would you persuade more, and rebuke less; your cause would be much more likely to succeed." But, I submit, where all is plain there is nothing to be argued. What point in the anti-slavery creed would you have me argue? On what branch of the subject do the people of this country need light? Must I undertake to prove that the slave is a man? That point is conceded already. Nobody doubts it. The slaveholders themselves acknowledge it in the enactment of laws for their government. They acknowledge it when they punish disobedience on the part of the slave. There are seventy-two crimes in the State of Virginia which, if committed by a black man (no matter how ignorant he be), subject him to the punishment of death; while only two of the same crimes will subject a white man to the like punishment. What is this but the acknowledgment that the slave is a moral, intellectual, and responsible being?

The manhood of the slave is conceded. It is admitted in the fact that Southern statute books are covered with enactments forbidding, under severe fines and penalties, the teaching of the slave to read or to write. When you can point to any such laws in reference to the beasts of the field, then I may consent to argue the manhood of the slave. When the dogs in your streets, when the fowls of the air, when the cattle on your hills, when the fish of the sea, and the reptiles that crawl, shall be unable to distinguish the slave from a brute, then will I argue with you that the slave is a man!

For the present, it is enough to affirm the equal manhood of the Negro race. Is it not astonishing that, while we are ploughing, planting, and reaping, using all kinds of mechanical tools, erecting houses, constructing bridges, building ships, working in metals of brass, iron, copper, silver, and gold; that, while we are reading, writing, and ciphering, acting as clerks, merchants, and secretaries, having among us lawyers, doctors, ministers, poets, authors, editors, orators, and teachers; that, while we are engaged in all manner of enterprises common to other men, digging gold in California, capturing the whale in the Pacific, feeding sheep and cattle on the hillside, living, moving, acting, thinking, planning, living in families as husbands, wives, and children, and, above all, confessing and worshipping the Christian's God, and looking hopefully for life and immortality beyond the grave, we are called upon to prove that we are men?

Would you have me argue that man is entitled to liberty? That he is the rightful owner of his own body? You have already declared it. Must I argue the wrongfulness of slavery? Is that a question for Republicans? Is it to be settled by the rules of logic and argumentation, as a matter beset with great difficulty, involving a doubtful application of the principle of justice, hard to be understood? How should I look today, in the presence of Americans, dividing and subdividing a discourse, to show that men have a natural right to freedom, speaking of it relatively and positively, negatively and affirmatively? To do so would be to make myself ridiculous, and to offer an insult to your understanding. There is not a man beneath the canopy of heaven that does not know that slavery is wrong for him.

What, am I to argue that it is wrong to make men brutes, to rob them of their liberty, to work them without wages, to keep them ignorant of their relations to their fellow men, to beat them with sticks, to flay their flesh with the lash, to load their limbs with irons, to hunt them with dogs, to sell them at auction, to sunder their families, to knock out their teeth, to burn their flesh, to starve them into obedience and submission to their masters? Must I argue that a system thus marked with blood, and stained with pollution, is wrong? No! I will not. I have better employment for my time and strength than such arguments would imply.

What, then, remains to be argued? Is it that slavery is not divine; that God did not establish it; that our doctors of divinity are mistaken? There is blasphemy in the thought. That which is inhuman cannot be divine! Who can reason on such a proposition? They that can, may; I cannot. The time for such argument has passed.

At a time like this, scorching irony, not convincing argument, is needed. O! had I the ability, and could I reach the nation's ear, I would, today, pour out a fiery stream of biting ridicule, blasting reproach, withering sarcasm, and stern rebuke. For it is not light that is needed, but fire; it is not the gentle shower, but thunder. We need the storm, the whirlwind, and the earthquake. The feeling of the nation must be quickened; the conscience of the nation must be roused; the propriety of the nation must be startled; the hyprocrisy of the nation must be exposed; and its crimes against God and man must be proclaimed and denounced.

What, to the American slave, is your Fourth of July? I answer: a day that reveals to him, more than all other days in the year, the gross injustice and cruelty of which he is the constant victim. To him, your celebration is a sham; your boasted liberty, an unholy license; your national greatness, swelling vanity. Your sounds of rejoicing are empty and heartless; your denunciation of tyrants, brass-fronted impudence; your shouts of liberty and equality, hollow mockery; your prayers and hymns, your sermons and thanksgivings, with all your religious parade and solemnity, are, to him, mere bombast, fraud, deception, piety, and hypocrisy—a thin veil to cover up crimes which would disgrace a nation of savages. There is not a nation on the earth guilty of practices more shocking and bloody than are the people of the United States, at this very hour.

Go where you may, search where you will, roam through all the monarchies and despotisms of the Old World, travel through South America, search out every abuse, and when you have found the last, lay your facts by the side of the everyday practices of this nation, and you will say with me that, for revolting barbarity and shameless hypocrisy, America reigns without a rival.

Frances Ellen Watkins Harper

(1825–1911, United States)

We Are All Bound Up Together

I feel I am something of a novice upon this platform. Born of a race whose inheritance has been outrage and wrong, most of my life had been spent in battling against those wrongs. But I did not feel as keenly as others, that I had these rights, in common with other women, which are now demanded. About two years ago, I stood within the shadows of my home. A great sorrow had fallen upon my life. My husband had died suddenly, leaving me a widow, with four children, one my own, and the others stepchildren. I tried to keep my children together. But my husband died in debt; and before he had been in his grave three months, the administration had swept the very milk-crocks and wash tubs from my hands. I was a farmer's wife and made butter for the Columbus market; but what could I do, when they had swept all away? They left me one thing—and that was a looking-glass! Had I died instead of my husband, how different would have been the result! By this time he would have had another wife, it is likely; and no administrator would have gone into his house, broken up his home, and sold his bed, and taken away his means of support.

I took my children in my arms, and went out to seek my living. While I was gone, a neighbor to whom I had once lent five dollars, went before a magistrate and swore that he believed I was a non-resident, and laid an attachment on my very bed. And I went back to Ohio with my orphan children in my arms, without a single feather bed in this wide world, that was not in the custody of the law. I say, then, that justice is not fulfilled so long as woman is unequal before the law.

We are all bound up together in one great bundle of humanity, and society cannot trample on the weakest and feeblest of its members without receiving the curse in its own soul. You tried that in the case of the negro. You pressed him down for two centuries; and in so doing you crippled the moral strength and paralyzed the spiritual energies of the white men of the country. When the hands of the black were fettered, white men were deprived of the liberty of speech and the freedom of the press. Society cannot afford to neglect the enlightenment of any class of its members. At the South, the legislation of the country was in behalf of the rich slaveholders, while the poor white man was neglected. What is the consequence to-day? From that very class of neglected poor white men, comes the man who stands to-day with his hand upon the helm of the nation. He fails to catch the watchword of the hour, and throws himself, the incarnation of meanness, across the pathway of the nation. My objection to Andrew Johnson is not that he has been a poor white man; my objection is that he keeps "poor whites" all the way through. (Applause.) That is the trouble with him.

This grand and glorious revolution which has commenced, will fail to reach its climax of success, until throughout the length and brea[d]th of the American Republic, the nation shall be so color-blind, as to know no man by the color of his skin or the curl of his hair. It will then have no privileged class, trampling upon and outraging the unprivileged classes, but will be then one great privileged nation, whose privilege will be to produce the loftiest manhood and womanhood that humanity can attain.

I do not believe that giving the woman the ballot is immediately going to cure all the ills of life. I do not believe that white women are dewdrops just exhaled from the skies. I think that like men they may be divided into three classes, the good, the bad, and the indifferent. The good would vote according to their convictions and principles; the bad, as dictated by preju[d]ice or malice; and the indifferent will vote on the strongest side of the question, with the winning party.

You white women speak here of rights. I speak of wrongs. I, as a colored woman, have had in this country an education which has made me feel as if I were in the situation of Ishmael, my hand against every man, and every man's hand against me. Let me go to-morrow morning and take my seat in one of your street cars—I do not know that they will do it in New York, but they will in Philadelphia—and the conductor will put up his hand and stop the car rather than let me ride.

A Lady—They will not do that here.

Mrs. Harper—They do in Philadelphia. Going from Washington to Baltimore this Spring, they put me in the smoking car. (Loud Voices—"Shame.") Aye, in the capital of the nation, where the black man consecrated himself to the nation's defence, faithful when the white man was faithless, they put me in the smoking car! They did it once; but the next time they tried it, they failed; for I would not go in. I felt the fight in me; but I don't want to have to fight all the time. To-day I am puzzled where to make my home. I would like to make it Philadelphia, near my own friends and relations. But if I want to ride in the streets of Philadelphia, they send me to ride on the platform with the driver. (Cries of "Shame.") Have women nothing to do with this? Not long since, a colored woman took her seat in an Eleventh Street car in Philadelphia, and the conductor stopped the car, and told the rest of the passengers to get out, and left the car with her in it alone, when they took it back to the station. One day I took my seat in a car, and the conductor came to me and told me to take another seat. I just screamed "murder." The man said if I was black I ought to behave myself. I knew that if he was white he was not behaving himself. Are there not wrongs to be righted?

Anna Julia Cooper
(1858–1964, United States)

Womanhood: A Vital Element in the Regeneration and Progress of a Race

The two sources from which, perhaps, modern civilization has derived its noble and enno-bling ideal of woman are Christianity and the Feudal System.[1]

In Oriental countries woman has been uniformly devoted to a life of ignorance, infamy, and complete stagnation. The Chinese shoe of to-day does not more entirely dwarf, cramp, and destroy her physical powers, than have the customs, laws, and social instincts, which from remotest ages have governed our Sister of the East, enervated and blighted her mental and moral life.

Mahomet makes no account of woman whatever in his polity. The Koran, which, unlike our Bible, was a product and not a growth, tried to address itself to the needs of Arabian civilization as Mahomet with his circumscribed powers saw them. The Arab was a nomad. Home to him meant his present camping place. That deity who, according to our western ideals, makes and sanctifies the home, was to him a transient bauble to be toyed with so long as it gave pleasure and then to be thrown aside for a new one. As a personality, an individual soul, capable of eternal growth and unlimited development, and destined to mould and shape the civilization of the future to an incalculable extent, Mahomet did not know woman. There was no hereafter, no paradise for her. The heaven of the Mussulman is peopled and made gladsome not by the departed wife, or sister, or mother, but by houri—a figment of Mahomet's brain, partaking of the ethereal qualities of angels, yet imbued with all the vices and inanity of Oriental women. The harem here, and—"dust to dust" hereafter, this was the hope, the inspiration, the *summum bonum* of the Eastern woman's life! . . .

And here let me say parenthetically that our satisfaction in American institutions rests not on the fruition we now enjoy, but springs rather from the possibilities and promise that are inherent in the system, though as yet, perhaps, far in the future. . . .

Now let us see on what basis this hope for our country primarily and fundamentally rests. Can any one doubt that it is chiefly on the homelife and on the influence of good women in those homes? Says Macaulay: "You may judge a nation's rank in the scale of civilization from the way they treat their women." And Emerson, "I have thought that a sufficient measure of civilization is the influence of good women." Now this high regard for woman, this germ of a prolific idea which in our own day is bearing such rich and varied fruit, was ingrafted into European civilization, we have said, from two sources, the

Christian Church and the Feudal System. For although the Feudal System can in no sense be said to have originated the idea, yet there can be no doubt that the habits of life and modes of thought to which Feudalism gave rise, materially fostered and developed it; for they gave us chivalry, than which no institution has more sensibly magnified and elevated woman's position in society.

Tacitus dwells on the tender regard for woman entertained by these rugged barbarians before they left their northern homes to overrun Europe. Old Norse legends too, and primitive poems, all breathe the same spirit of love of home and veneration for the pure and noble influence there presiding—the wife, the sister, the mother.

And when later on we see the settled life of the Middle Ages "oozing out," as M. Guizot expresses it, from the plundering and pillaging life of barbarism and crystallizing into the Feudal System, the tiger of the field is brought once more within the charmed circle of the goddesses of his castle, and his imagination weaves around them a halo whose reflection possibly has not yet altogether vanished.

It is true the spirit of Christianity had not yet put the seal of catholicity on this sentiment. Chivalry, according to Bascom, was but the toning down and softening of a rough and lawless period. It gave a roseate glow to a bitter winter's day. Those who looked out from castle windows revelled in its "amethyst tints." But God's poor, the weak, the unlovely, the commonplace were still freezing and starving none the less in unpitied, unrelieved loneliness.

Respect for woman, the much lauded chivalry of the Middle Ages, meant what I fear it still means to some men in our own day—respect for the elect few among whom they expect to consort.

The idea of the radical amelioration of womankind, reverence for woman as woman regardless of rank, wealth, or culture, was to come from that rich and bounteous fountain from which flow all our liberal and universal ideas—the Gospel of Jesus Christ.

And yet the Christian Church at the time of which we have been speaking would seem to have been doing even less to protect and elevate woman than the little done by secular society. The Church as an organization committed a double offense against woman in the Middle Ages. Making of marriage a sacrament and at the same time insisting on the celibacy of the clergy and other religious orders, she gave an inferior if not an impure character to the marriage relation, especially fitted to reflect discredit on woman. Would this were all or the worst! but the Church by the licentiousness of its chosen servants invaded the household and established too often as vicious connections those relations which it forbade to assume openly and in good faith. "Thus," to use the words of our authority, "the religious corps became as numerous, as searching, and as unclean as the frogs of Egypt, which penetrated into all quarters, into the ovens and kneading troughs, leaving their filthy trail wherever they went." Says Chaucer with characteristic satire, speaking of the Friars:

> Women may now go safely up and doun,
> In every bush, and under every tree,
> Ther is non other incubus but he,
> And he ne will don hem no dishonour.

Henry, Bishop of Liege, could unblushingly boast the birth of twenty-two children in fourteen years.[2]

. . . However much then the facts of any particular period of history may seem to deny it, I for one do not doubt that the source of the vitalizing principle of woman's development and amelioration is the Christian Church, so far as that church is coincident with Christianity.

Christ gave ideals not formulae. The Gospel is a germ requiring millennia for its growth and ripening. It needs and at the same time helps to form around itself a soil enriched in civilization, and perfected in culture and insight without which the embryo can neither be unfolded or comprehended. With all the strides our civilization has made from the first to the nineteenth century, we can boast not an idea, not a principle of action, not a progressive social force but was already mutely foreshadowed, or directly enjoined in that simple tale of a meek and lowly life. The quiet face of the Nazarene is ever seen a little way ahead, never too far to come down to and touch the life of the lowest in days the darkest, yet ever leading onward, still onward, the tottering childish feet of our strangely boastful civilization.

By laying down for woman the same code of morality, the same standard of purity, as for man; by refusing to countenance the shameless and equally guilty monsters who were gloating over her fall,—graciously stooping in all the majesty of his own spotlessness to wipe away the filth and grime of her guilty past and bid her to in peace and sin no more; and again in the moments of his own careworn and footsore dejection, turning trustfully and lovingly, away from the heartless snubbing and sneers, away from the cruel malignity of mobs and prelates in the dusty marts of Jerusalem to the ready sympathy, loving appreciation and unfaltering friendship of that quiet home at Bethany; and even at the last, by his dying bequest to the disciple whom he loved, signifying the protection and tender regard to be extended to that sorrowing mother and ever afterward to the sex she represented;—throughout his life and in his death he has given to men a rule and guide for the estimation of woman as an equal, as a helper, as a friend, and as a sacred charge to be sheltered and cared for with a brother's love and sympathy, lessons which nineteen centuries' gigantic strides in knowledge, arts, and sciences, in social and ethical principles have not been able to probe to their depth or to exhaust in practice.

It seems not too much to say then of the vitalizing, regenerating, and progressive influence of womanhood on the civilization of to-day, that, while it was foreshadowed among Germanic nations in the far away dawn of their history as a narrow, sickly and stunted growth, it yet owes its catholicity and power, the deepening of its roots and broadening of its branches to Christianity.

[She recounts the peaceful spread of Catholicism through diplomatic strategy.]

•   •   •

The result was [the Church] carried her point. Once more Rome laid her ambitious hand on the temporal power, and allied with Charlemagne, aspired to rule the world through a civilization dominated by Christianity and permeated by the traditions and instincts of those sturdy barbarians.

Here was the confluence of the two streams we have been tracing, which, united now, stretch before us as a broad majestic river. In regard to woman it was the meeting of two noble and ennobling forces, two kindred ideas the resultant of which, we doubt not, is destined to be a potent force in the betterment of the world.

Now after our appeal to history comparing nations destitute of this force and so destitute also of the principle of progress, with other nations among whom the influence of woman is prominent coupled with a brisk, progressive, satisfying civilization,—if in addition we find this strong presumptive evidence corroborated by reason and experience, we may conclude that these two equally varying concomitants are linked as cause and effect; in other words, that the position of woman in society determines the vital elements of its regeneration and progress.

Now that this is so on *a priori* grounds all must admit. And this not because woman is better or stronger or wiser than man, but from the nature of the case, because it is she who must first form the man by directing the earliest impulses of his character. . . .

Woman, Mother,—your responsibility is one that might make angels tremble and fear to take hold! To trifle with it, to ignore or misuse it, is to treat lightly the most sacred and solemn trust ever confided by God to human kind. The training of children is a task on which an infinity of weal or woe depends. Who does not covet it? Yet who does not stand awe-struck before its momentous issues! It is a matter of small moment, it seems to me, whether that lovely girl in whose accomplishments you take such pride and delight, can enter the gay and crowded salon with the ease and elegance of this or that French or English gentlewoman, compared with the decision as to whether her individuality is going to reinforce the good or the evil elements of the world. The lace and the diamonds, the dance and the theater, gain a new significance when scanned in their bearings on such issues. Their influence on the individual personality, and through her on the society and civilization which she vitalizes and inspires—all this and more must be weighed in the balance before the jury can return a just and intelligent verdict as to the innocence or banefulness of these apparently simple amusements.

Now the fact of woman's influence on society being granted, what are its practical bearings on the work which brought together this conference of colored clergy and lay-men in Washington? "We come not here to talk." Life is too busy, too pregnant with meaning and far reaching consequences to allow you to come this far for mere intellectual entertainment.

The vital agency of womanhood in the regeneration and progress of a race, as a general question, is conceded almost before it is fairly stated. I confess one of the difficulties for me in the subject assigned lay in its obviousness. The plea is taken away by the opposite attorney's granting the whole question.

"Woman's influence on social progress"—who in Christiandom doubts or questions it? One may as well be called on to prove that the sun is the source of light and heat and energy to this many-sided little world.

Nor, on the other hand, could it have been intended that I should apply the position when taken and proven, to the needs and responsibilities of the women of our race in the South. For is it not written, "Cursed is he that cometh after the king?" and has not the King already preceded me in "The Black Woman of the South"?[3]

They have had both Moses and the Prophets in Dr. Crummell and if they hear not him, neither would they be persuaded though one came up from the South.

I would beg, however, with the Doctor's permission, to add my plea for the *Colored Girls* of the South:—that large, bright, promising fatally beautiful class that stand shivering like a delicate plantlet before the fury of tempestuous elements, so full of promise and possibilities, yet so sure of destruction; often without a father to whom they dare apply the loving term, often without a stronger brother to espouse their cause and defend their honor with his life's blood; in the midst of pitfalls and snares, waylaid by the lower classes of white men, with no shelter, no protection nearer than the great blue vault above, which half conceals and half reveals the one Care-Taker they know so little of. Oh, save them, help them, shield, train, develop, teach, inspire them! Snatch them, in God's name, as brands from the burning! There is material in them well worth your while, the hope in germ of a staunch, helpful, regenerating womanhood on which, primarily, rests the foundation stones of our future as a race.

It is absurd to quote statistics showing the Negro's bank account and rent rolls, to point to the hundreds of newspapers edited by colored men and lists of lawyers, doctors, professors, D. D's, LL D's, etc., etc., etc., while the source from which the life-blood of the race is to flow is subject to taint and corruption in the enemy's camp.

True progress is never made by spasms. Real progress is growth. It must begin in the seed. Then, "first the blade, then the ear, after that the full corn in the ear." There is something to encourage and inspire us in the advancement of individuals since their emancipation from slavery. It at least proves that there is nothing irretrievably wrong in the shape of the black man's skull, and that under given circumstances his development, downward or upward, will be similar to that of other average human beings.

But there is no time to be wasted in mere felicitation. That the Negro has his niche in the infinite purposes of the Eternal, no one who has studied the history of the last fifty years in America will deny. That much depends on his own right comprehension of his responsibility and rising to the demands of the hour, it will be good for him to see; and how best to use his present so that the structure of the future shall be stronger and higher and brighter and nobler and holier than that of the past, is a question to be decided each day by every one of us.

The race is just twenty-one years removed from the conception and experience of a chattel, just at the age of ruddy manhood. It is well enough to pause a moment for retrospection, introspection, and prospection. We look back, not to become inflated with conceit because of the depths from which we have arisen, but that we may learn wisdom from experience. We look within that we may gather together once more our forces, and, by improved and more practical methods, address ourselves to the tasks before us. We look forward with hope and trust that the same God whose guiding hand led our fathers through and out of the gall and bitterness of oppression, will still lead and direct their children, to the honor of His name, and for their ultimate salvation. . . .

We are the heirs of a past which was not our fathers' moulding. "Every man the arbiter of his own destiny" was not true for the American Negro of the past: and it is no fault of his that he finds himself to-day the inheritor of a manhood and womanhood impoverished and debased by two centuries and more of compression and degradation.

But weaknesses and malformations, which to-day are attributable to a vicious schoolmaster and a pernicious system, will a century hence be rightly regarded as proofs of innate corruptness and radical incurability. . . .

A race cannot be purified from without. Preachers and teachers are helps, and stimulants and conditions as necessary as the gracious rain and sunshine are to plant growth. But what are rain and dew and sunshine and cloud if there be no life in the plant germ? We must go to the root and see that that is sound and healthy and vigorous; and not deceive ourselves with waxen flowers and painted leaves of mock chlorophyll.

We too often mistake individuals' honor for race development and so are ready to substitute pretty accomplishments for sound sense and earnest purpose.

A stream cannot rise higher than its source. The atmosphere of homes is no rarer and purer and sweeter than are the mothers in those homes. A race is but a total of families. The nation is the aggregate of its homes. As the whole is sum of all its parts, so the character of the parts will determine the characteristics of the whole. These are all axioms and so evident that it seems gratuitous to remark it; and yet, unless I am greatly mistaken, most of the unsatisfaction from our past results arises from just such a radical and palpable error, as much almost on our own part as on that of our benevolent white friends.

The Negro is constitutionally hopeful and proverbially irrepressible; and naturally stands in danger of being dazzled by the shimmer and tinsel of superficials. We often mistake foliage for fruit and overestimate or wrongly estimate brilliant results.

The late Martin R. Delany, who was an unadulterated black man, used to say when honors of state fell upon him, that when he entered the council of kings the black race entered with him; meaning, I suppose, that there was no discounting his race identity and attributing his achievements to some admixture of Saxon blood. But our present record of eminent men, when placed beside the actual status of the race in America to-day, proves that no man can represent the race. Whatever the attainments of the individual may be, unless his home has moved on *pari passu*, he can never be regarded as identical with or representative of the whole.

Not by pointing to sun-bathed mountain tops do we prove that Phœbus warms the valleys. We must point to homes, average homes, homes of the rank and file of horny handed toiling men and women of the South (where the masses are) lighted and cheered by the good, the beautiful, and the true,—then and not till then will the whole plateau be lifted into the sunlight.

Only the BLACK WOMAN can say "when and where I enter, in the quiet, undisputed dignity of my womanhood, without violence and without suing or special patronage, then and there the whole *Negro race enters with me.*" Is it not evident then that as individual workers for this race we must address ourselves with no half-hearted zeal to this feature of our mission. The need is felt and must be recognized by all. There is a call for workers, for missionaries, for men and women with the double consecration of a fundamental love of humanity and a desire for its melioration through the Gospel; but superadded to this we demand an intelligent and sympathetic comprehension of the interests and special needs of the Negro.

I see not why there should not be an organized effort for the protection and elevation of our girls such as the White Cross League in England. English women are strengthened and protected by more than twelve centuries of Christian influences, freedom, and civilization; English girls are dispirited and crushed down by no such all-levelling prejudice as that supercilious caste spirit in America which cynically assumes "A Negro woman cannot be a lady." English womanhood is beset by no such snares and traps as betray the unprotected, untrained colored girl of the South, whose only crime and dire destruction often is her unconscious and marvelous beauty. Surely then if English indignation is aroused and English manhood thrilled under the leadership of a Bishop of the English church to build up bulwarks around their wronged sisters, Negro sentiment cannot remain callous and Negro effort nerveless in view of the imminent peril of the mothers of the next generation. *"I am my Sister's keeper!"* should be the hearty response of every man and woman of the race, and this conviction should purify and exalt the narrow, selfish and petty personal aims of life into a noble and sacred purpose.

We need men who can let their interest and gallantry extend outside the circle of their æsthetic appreciation; men who can be a father, a brother, a friend to every weak, struggling unshielded girl. We need women who are so sure of their own social footing that they need not fear leaning to lend a hand to a fallen or falling sister. We need men and women who do not exhaust their genius splitting hairs on aristocratic distinctions and thanking God they are not as others; but earnest, unselfish souls, who can go into the highways and byways, lifting up and leading, advising and encouraging with the truly catholic benevolence of the Gospel of Christ.

.   .   .

The institution of the Church in the South to which she mainly looks for the training of her colored clergy and for the help of the "Black Woman" and "Colored Girl" of the South, has graduated since the year 1868, when the school was founded, *five young women*,[4] and while yearly numerous young men have been kept and trained for the ministry by the charities of the Church, the number of indigent females who have here been supported, sheltered and trained, is phenomenally small. Indeed, to my mind, the attitude of the Church toward this feature of her work is as if the solution of the problem of Negro missions depended solely on sending a quota of deacons and priests into the field, girls being a sort of *tertium quid* whose development may be promoted if they can pay their way and fall in with the plans mapped out for the training of the other sex. Now I would ask in all earnestness, does not this force potential deserve by education and stimulus to be made dynamic? Is it not a solemn duty incumbent on all colored churchmen to make it so? Will not the aid of the Church be given to prepare our girls in head, heart, and hand for the duties and responsibilities that await the intelligent wife, the Christian mother, the earnest, virtuous, helpful woman, at once both the lever and the fulcrum for uplifting the race.

As Negroes and churchmen we cannot be indifferent to these questions. They touch us most vitally on both sides. We believe in the Holy Catholic Church. We believe that however gigantic and apparently remote the consummation, the Church will go on conquering and to conquer till the kingdoms of this world, not excepting the black man and the black woman of the South, shall have become the kingdoms of the Lord and of his Christ.

That past work in this direction has been unsatisfactory we must admit. That without a change of policy results in the future will be as meagre, we greatly fear. Our life as a race is at stake. The dearest interests of our hearts are in the scales. We must either break away from dear old landmarks and plunge out in any line and every line that enables us to meet the pressing need of our people, or we must ask the Church to allow and help us, untrammelled by the prejudices and theories of individuals, to work aggressively under her direction as we alone can, with God's help, for the salvation of our people.

The time is ripe for action. Self-seeking and ambition must be laid on the altar. The battle is one of sacrifice and hardship, but our duty is plain. We have been recipients of missionary bounty in some sort for twenty-one years. Not even the senseless vegetable is content to be a mere reservoir. Receiving without giving is an anomaly in nature. Nature's cells are all little workshops for manufacturing sunbeams, the product to be *given out* to earth's inhabitants in warmth, energy, thought, action. Inanimate creation always pays back an equivalent.

Now, *How much owest thou my Lord?* Will his account be overdrawn if he call for singleness of purpose and self-sacrificing labor for your brethren? Having passed through your drill school, will you refuse a general's commission even if it entail responsibility, risk, and anxiety, with possibly some adverse criticism? Is it too much to ask you to step forward and direct the work of your race along those lines which you know to be of first and vital importance?

Will you allow these words of Ralph Waldo Emerson? "In ordinary," says he, "we have a snappish criticism which watches and contradicts the opposite party. We want the will which advances and dictates [acts]. Nature has made up her mind that what cannot defend itself, shall not be defended. Complaining never so loud and with never so much reason, is of no use. What cannot stand must fall; *and the measure of our sincerity and therefore of the respect of men is the amount of health and wealth we will hazard in the defense of our right.*"

NOTES

1. [This essay was] read before the convocation of colored clergy of the Protestant Episcopal Church at Washington, D.C., 1886.
2. Bascom.
3. Pamphlet published by Dr. Alex. Crummell.
4. Five have been graduated since '86, two in '91, two in '92.

Ida B. Wells-Barnett
(1862–1931, United States)

Lynch Law in All Its Phases

I am before the American people to-day through no inclination of my own, but because of a deep-seated conviction that the country at large does not know the extent to which lynch law prevails in parts of the Republic, nor the conditions which force into exile those who speak the truth. I cannot believe that the apathy and indifference which so largely obtains regarding mob rule is other than the result of ignorance of the true situation. And yet, the observing and thoughtful must know that one section, at least, of our common country, a government of the people, by the people and for the people, means a government by the mob; where the land of the free and home of the brave means a land of lawlessness, murder and outrage; and where liberty of speech means the license of might to destroy the business [of] and drive from home those who exercise this privilege contrary to the will of the mob. Repeated attacks on the life, liberty and happiness of any citizen or class of citizens are attacks on distinctive American institutions; such attacks imperiling as they do the foundation of government, law and order, merit the thoughtful consideration of far-sighted Americans; not from a standpoint of sentiment, not even so much from a standpoint of justice to a weak race, as from a desire to preserve our institutions.

The race problem or negro question, as it has been called, has been omnipresent and all-pervading since long before the Afro-American was raised from the degradation of the slave to the dignity of the citizen. It has never been settled because the right methods have not been employed in the solution. It is the Banquo's ghost of politics, religion and sociology which will not lie down at the bidding of those who are tormented with its ubiquitous appearance on every occasion. Times without number, since invested with citizenship, the race had been indicted for ignorance, immorality and general worthlessness—declared guilty and executed by its self-constituted judges. The operations of law do not dispose of negroes fast enough, and lynching bees have become the favorite pastime of the South. As excuse for the same, a new cry, as false as it is foul, is raised in an effort to blast race character, a cry which has proclaimed to the world that virtue and innocence are violated by Afro-Americans who must be killed like wild beasts to protect womanhood and childhood.

Born and reared in the South, I had never expected to live elsewhere. Until this past year I was one among those who believe the condition of the masses gave large excuse for the humiliations and proscriptions under which we labored; that when wealth, education and character became more general among us,—the cause being removed—the effect would cease, and justice be accorded to all alike. I shared the general belief that good newspapers entering regularly the homes of our people in every state could do more to bring about this result than any agency. Preaching the doctrine of self-help, thrift and economy every week, they would be the teachers to those who had been deprived of school advantages, yet were making history every day—and train to think for themselves our mental children of a larger growth. And so, three years ago last June, I became editor and part owner of the *Memphis Free Speech*. As editor, I had occasion to criticize the city School Board's employment of inefficient teachers and poor school-buildings for Afro-American children. I was in the employ of that board at the time, and at the close of that school-term one year ago, was not re-elected to a position I had held in the city schools for seven years. Accepting the decision of the Board of Education, I set out to make a race newspaper pay—a thing which older and wiser heads said could not be done. But there were enough of our people in Memphis and surrounding territory to support a paper, and I believed they would do so. With nine months hard work the circulation increased from 1,500 to 3,500; in twelve months it was on a good paying basis. Throughout the Mississippi Valley in Arkansas, Tennessee and Mississippi—on plantation and in towns, the demand for and interest in the paper increased among the masses. The newsboys who would not sell it on the trains, voluntarily testified that they had never known colored people to demand a paper so eagerly.

To make the paper a paying business I became advertising agent, solicitor, as well as editor, and was continually on the go. Wherever I went among the people, I gave them in church, school, public gatherings and home, the benefit of my honest convictions that maintenance of character, money getting and education would finally solve our problems and that it depended on us to say how soon this would be brought about. This sentiment bore good fruit in Memphis. We had nice homes, representatives in almost every branch of business and profession, and refined society. We had learned that helping each other helped all, and every well-conducted business by Afro-Americans prospered. With all our proscription in theaters, hotels and on railroads, we had never had a lynching and did not believe we could have one. There had been lynchings and brutal outrages of all sorts in our own state and those adjoining us, but we had confidence and pride in our city and the majesty of its laws. So far in advance of other Southern cities was ours, we were content to endure the evils we had, to labor and to wait.

But there was a rude awakening. On the morning of March 9, the bodies of three of our best young men were found in an old field horribly shot to pieces. These young men had owned and operated the "People's Grocery," situated at what was known as the Curve—a suburb made up almost entirely of colored people—about a mile from city limits. Thomas Moss, one of the oldest letter-carriers in the city, was president of the company, Calvin McDowell was manager and Will Stewart was a clerk. There were about ten other stockholders, all colored men. The young men were well known and popular and their business flourished. This is a case of a special law officer and that of Barrett, a white grocer who kept store there before the "People's Grocery" who inquired for a colored man who lived in the neighborhood, and for whom the officer had a warrant. Barrett went with him and when McDowell said he knew nothing as to the whereabouts of the man for whom they were searching, Barrett, not the officer, then accused McDowell of harboring the man, and McDowell gave the lie. Barrett drew his pistol and struck McDowell with it; thereupon McDowell, who was a tall, fine-looking six-footer, took Barrett's pistol from him, knocked him down and gave him a good thrashing, while Will Stewart, the clerk, kept the special officer at bay. Barrett went to town, swore out a warrant for their arrest on a charge of assault and battery. McDowell went before the Criminal Court, immediately gave bond and returned to his store. Barrett then threatened (to use his own words) that he was going to clean out the whole store. Knowing how anxious he was to destroy their business, these young men consulted a lawyer who told them they were justified in defending themselves if attacked, as they were a mile beyond city limits and police protection. They accordingly armed several of their friends—not to assail, but to resist the threatened Saturday night attack.

When they saw Barrett enter the front door and a half dozen men at the rear door at 11 o'clock that night, they supposed the attack was on and immediately fired into the crowd, wounding three men. These men, dressed in citizen's clothes, turned out to be deputies who claimed to be hunting another man for whom they had a warrant, and whom any one of them could have arrested without trouble. When these men found they had fired upon officers of the law, they threw away their firearms and submitted to arrest, confident they should establish their innocence of intent to fire upon officers of the law. The daily papers in flaming headlines roused the evil passions of the whites, denounced these poor boys in unmeasured terms, nor permitted them a word in their own defense.

The neighborhood of the Curve was searched next day, and about thirty persons were thrown into jail, charged with conspiracy. No communication was to be had with friends any of the three days these men were in jail; bail was refused and Thomas Moss was not allowed to eat the food his wife prepared for him. The judge is reported to have said, "Any one can see them after three days." They were seen after three days, but they were no longer able to respond to the greetings of friends. On Tuesday following the shooting at the grocery, the papers which had made much of the sufferings of the wounded deputies, and promised it would go hard with those who did the shooting, if they died, announced that the officers were all out of danger, and would recover. The friends of the prisoners breathed more easily and relaxed their vigilance. They felt that as the officers would not die, there was no danger that in the heat of passion the prisoners would meet violent death at the hands of the mob. Besides, we had such confidence in the law. But the law did not provide capital punishment for shooting which did not kill. So the mob did what the law could not be made to do, as a lesson to the Afro-American that he must not shoot a white man,—no matter what the provocation. The same night after the announcement was made in the papers that the officers would get well, the mob, in obedience to a plan known to every prominent white man in the city, went to the jail between two and three o'clock in the morning, dragged out these young men, hatless and shoeless, put them on the yard engine of the railroad which was in waiting just behind the jail, carried them a mile north of the city limits and horribly shot them to death while the locomotive at a given signal let off steam and blew the whistle to deaden the sound of the firing.

"It was done by unknown men," said the jury, yet the *Appeal-Avalanche*, which goes to press at 3 A.M., had a two-column account of the lynching. The papers also told how McDowell got hold of the guns of the mob, and as his grasp could not be loosened, his hand was shattered with a pistol ball and all the lower part of his face was torn away. There were four pools of blood found and only three bodies. It was whispered that he, McDowell, killed one of the lynchers with his gun, and it is well known that a policeman who was seen on the street a few days previous to the lynching, died very suddenly the next day after.

"It was done by unknown parties," said the jury, yet the papers told how Tom Moss begged for his life, for the sake of his wife, his little daughter and his unborn infant. They also told us that his last words were, "If you will kill us, turn our faces to the West."

All this we learned too late to save these men, even if the law had not been in the hands of their murderers. When the colored people realized that the flower of our young manhood had been stolen away at night and murdered, there was a rush for firearms to avenge the wrong, but no house would sell a colored man a gun; the armory of the Tennessee Rifles, our only colored military company, and of which McDowell was a member, was broken into by order of the Criminal Court judge, and its guns taken. One hundred men and irresponsible boys from fifteen years and up were armed by order of the authorities and rushed out to the Curve, where it was reported that the colored people were massing, and at point of the bayonet dispersed these men who could do nothing but talk. The cigars, wines, etc., of the grocery stock were freely used by the mob, who possessed the place on pretence of dispersing the conspiracy. The money drawer was broken into and contents taken. The trunk of Calvin McDowell, who had a room in the store, was broken open, and his clothing, which was not good enough to take away, was thrown out and trampled on the floor.

These men were murdered, their stock was attached by creditors and sold for less than one-eighth of its cost to that same man Barrett, who is to-day running his grocery in the same place. He had indeed kept his word, and by aid of the authorities destroyed the People's Grocery Company root and branch. The relatives of Will Stewart and Calvin McDowell are bereft of their protectors. The baby daughter of Tom Moss, too young to express how she misses her father, toddles to the wardrobe, seizes the legs of the trousers of his letter-carrier uniform, hugs and kisses them with evident delight and stretches up her little hands to be taken up into the arms which will nevermore clasp his daughter's form. His wife holds Thomas Moss, Jr., in her arms, upon whose unconscious baby face the tears fall thick and fast when she is thinking of the sad fate of the father he will never see, and of the two helpless children who cling to her for the support she cannot give. Although these men were peaceable, law-abiding citizens of this country, we are told there can be no punishment for their murderers nor indemnity for their relatives.

I have no power to describe the feeling of horror that possessed every member of the race in Memphis when the truth dawned upon us that the protection of the law which we had so long enjoyed was no longer ours; all this had been destroyed in a night, and the barriers of the law had been thrown down, and the guardians of the public peace and confidence scoffed away into the shadows, and all authority given into the hands of the mob, and innocent men cut down as if they were brutes—the first feeling was one of utter dismay, then intense indignation. Vengeance was whispered from ear to ear, but sober reflection brought the conviction that it would be extreme folly to seek vengeance when each action meant certain death for the men, and horrible slaughter for the women and children, as one of the evening papers took care to remind us. The power of the State, country and city, the civil authorities and the strong arm of the military power were all on the side of the mob and of lawlessness. Few of our men possessed firearms, our only company's guns were confiscated, and the only white man who would sell a colored man a gun, was himself jailed, and his store closed. We were helpless in our great strength. It was our first object lesson in the doctrine of white supremacy; an illustration of the South's cardinal principle that no matter what the attainments, character or standing of an Afro-American, the laws of the South will not protect him against a white man.

There was only one thing we could do, and a great determination seized upon the people to follow the advice of the martyred Moss, and "turn our faces to the West," whose laws protect all alike. The *Free Speech* supported by our ministers and leading business men advised the people to leave a community whose laws did not protect them. Hundreds left on foot to walk four hundred miles between Memphis and Oklahoma. A Baptist minister went to the territory, built a church and took his entire congregation out in less than a month. Another minister sold his church and took his flock to California, and still another has settled in Kansas. In two months, six thousand persons had left the city and every branch of business began to feel this silent resentment of the outrage, and failure of the authorities to punish the lynchers. There were a number of business failures and blocks of houses for rent. The superintendent and treasurer of the street railway company called at the office of the *Free Speech,* to have us urge the colored people to ride again on the street cars. A real estate dealer said to a colored man who returned some property he had been buying on the installment plan: "I don't see what you 'niggers' are cutting up about. You got off light. We first intended to kill every one of those thirty-one 'niggers' in jail, but concluded to let all go but the 'leaders.' " They did let all go to the penitentiary. These so-called rioters have since been tried in the Criminal Court for the conspiracy of defending their property, and are now serving terms of three, eight and fifteen years each in the Tennessee State prison.

To restore the equilibrium and put a stop to the great financial loss, the next move was to get rid of the *Free Speech,*—the disturbing element which kept the waters troubled; which would not let the people forget, and in obedience to whose advice nearly six thousand persons had left the city. In casting about for an excuse, the mob found it in the following editorial which appeared in the *Memphis Free Speech,*—May 21, 1892: "Eight negroes lynched in one week. Since last issue of the *Free Speech* one was lynched at Little Rock, Ark., where the citizens broke into the penitentiary and got their man; three near Anniston, Ala., and one in New Orleans, all on the same charge, the new alarm of assaulting white women—and three near Clarksville, Ga., for killing a white man. The same program of hanging—then shooting bullets into the lifeless bodies was carried out to the letter. Nobody in this section of the country believes the old threadbare lie that negro men rape white women. If Southern white men are not careful they will overreach themselves, and public sentiment will have a reaction. A conclusion will then be reached which will be very damaging to the moral reputation of their women." Commenting on this, *The Daily Commercial* of Wednesday following said: "Those negroes who are attempting to make lynching of individuals of their race a means for arousing the worst passions of their kind, are playing with a dangerous sentiment. The negroes may as well understand that there is no mercy for the negro rapist, and little patience with his defenders. A negro organ printed in this city in a recent issue published the following atrocious paragraph: 'Nobody in this section believes the old threadbare lie that negro men rape white women. If Southern white men are not careful they will overreach themselves and public sentiment will have a reaction. A conclusion will be reached which will be very damaging to the moral reputation of their women.' The fact that a black scoundrel is allowed to live and utter such loathsome and repulsive calumnies is a volume of evidence as to the wonderful patience of Southern whites. There are some things the Southern white man will not tolerate, and the obscene intimidation of the foregoing has brought the writer to the very uttermost limit of public patience. We hope to have said enough."

Carter G. Woodson
(1875–1950, United States)

The Mis-Education of the Negro

THE SEAT OF THE TROUBLE

The "educated Negroes" have the attitude of contempt toward their own people because in their own as well as in their mixed schools Negroes are taught to admire the Hebrew, the Greek, the Latin, and the Teuton and to despise the African. Of the hundreds of Negro high schools recently examined by an expert in the United States Bureau of Education only eighteen offer a course taking up the history of the Negro, and in most of the Negro colleges and universities where the Negro is thought of, the race is studied only as a problem or dismissed as of little consequence. For example, an officer of a Negro university, thinking that an additional course on the Negro should be given there, called upon a Negro Doctor of Philosophy of the faculty to offer such work. He promptly informed the officer that he knew nothing about the Negro. He did not go to school to waste his time that way. He went to be educated in a system which dismissed the Negro as a nonentity.

At a Negro summer school two years ago, a white instructor gave a course on the Negro, using for his text a work which teaches that whites are superior to the blacks. When asked by one of the students why he used such a textbook the instructor replied that he wanted them to get that point of view. Even schools for Negroes, then, are places where they must be convinced of their inferiority.

The thought of the inferiority of the Negro is drilled into him in almost every class he enters and in almost every book he studies. If he happens to leave school after he masters the fundamentals, before he finishes high school or reaches college, he will naturally escape some of this bias and may recover in time to be of service to his people.

Practically all of the successful Negroes in this country are of the uneducated type or of that type of Negroes who have had no formal education at all. The large majority of the Negroes who have put on the finishing touches of our best colleges are all but worthless in the development of their people. If after leaving school they have the opportunity to give out to Negroes what traducers of the race would like to have it learn such persons may thereby earn a living at teaching or preaching what they have been taught but they never become a constructive force in the development of the race. The so-called school, then, becomes a questionable factor in the life of this despised people.

As another has well said, to handicap a student by teaching him that his black face is a curse and that his struggle to change his condition is hopeless is the worst sort of lynching.

It kills one's aspirations and dooms him to vagabondage and crime. It is strange, then, that the friends of truth and the promoters of freedom have not risen up against the present propaganda in the schools and crushed it. This crusade is much more important than the anti-lynching movement, because there would no lynching if it did not start in the schoolroom. Why not exploit, enslave, or exterminate a class that everybody is taught to regard as inferior?

To be more explicit we may go to the seat of the trouble. Our most widely known scholars have been trained in universities outside of the South. Northern and Western institutions, however, have had no time to deal with matters which concern the Negro especially. They must direct their attention to the problems of the majority of their constituents, and too often they have stimulated their prejudices by referring to the Negro as unworthy of consideration. Most of what these universities have offered as language, mathematics, and science may have served a good purpose, but much of what they have taught as economics, history, literature, religion, and philosophy is propaganda and cant that involved a waste of time and misdirected the Negroes thus trained.

And even in the certitude of science or mathematics it has been unfortunate that the approach to the Negro has been borrowed from a "foreign" method. For example, the teaching of arithmetic in the fifth grade in a backward county in Mississippi should mean one thing in the Negro school and a decidedly different thing in the white school. The Negro children, as a rule, come from the homes of tenants and peons who have to migrate annually from plantation to plantation, looking for light which they have never seen. The children from the homes of white planters and merchants live permanently in the midst of calculations, family budgets, and the like, which enable them sometimes to learn more by contact than the Negro can acquire in school. Instead of teaching such Negro children less arithmetic, they should be taught much more of it than the white children, for the latter attend a graded school consolidated by free transportation when the Negroes go to one-room rented hovels to be taught without equipment and by incompetent teachers educated scarcely beyond the eighth grade.

In schools of theology Negroes are taught the interpretation of the Bible worked out by those who have justified segregation and winked at the economic debasement of the Negro sometimes almost to the point of starvation. Deriving their sense of right from this teaching, graduates of such schools can have no message to grip the people whom they have been ill trained to serve. Most of such mis-educated ministers, therefore, preach to benches while illiterate Negro preachers do the best they can in supplying the spiritual needs of the masses.

In the schools of business administration Negroes are trained exclusively in the psychology and economics of Wall Street and are, therefore, made to despise the opportunities to run ice wagons, push banana carts, and sell peanuts among their own people. Foreigners, who have not studied economics but have studied Negroes, take up this business and grow rich.

In schools of journalism Negroes are being taught how to edit such metropolitan dailies as the *Chicago Tribune* and the *New York Times,* which would hardly hire a Negro as a janitor; and when these graduates come to the Negro weeklies for employment they are not prepared to function in such establishments, which, to be successful, must be built upon accurate knowledge of the psychology and philosophy of the Negro.

When a Negro has finished his education in our schools, then, he has been equipped to begin the life of an Americanized or Europeanized white man, but before the steps from the threshold of his alma mater he is told by his teachers that he must go back to his own people from whom he has been estranged by a vision of ideals which in his disillusionment he will realize that he cannot attain. He goes forth to play his part in life, but he must be both social and bisocial at the same time. While he is a part of the body politic, he is in addition to this a member of a particular race to which he must restrict himself in all matters social. While serving his country he must serve within a special group. While being a good American, he must above all things be a "good Negro"; and to perform this definite function he must learn to stay in a "Negro's place."

For the arduous task of serving a race thus handicapped, however, the Negro graduate has had little or no training at all. The people whom he has been ordered to serve have been belittled by his teachers to the extent that he can hardly find delight in undertaking what his education has led him to think is impossible. Considering his race as blank in achievement, then, he sets out to stimulate their imitation of others. The performance is kept up a while; but, like any other effort at meaningless imitation, it results in failure.

Facing this undesirable result, the highly educated Negro often grows sour. He becomes too pessimistic to be a constructive force and usually develops into a chronic fault-finder or a complainant at the bar of public opinion. Often when he sees that the fault lies at the door of the white oppressor whom he is afraid to attack, he turns upon the pioneering Negro who is at work doing the best he can to extricate himself from an uncomfortable predicament.

In this effort to imitate, however, these "educated people" are sincere. They hope to make the Negro conform quickly to the standard of the whites and thus remove the pretext for the barriers between the races. They do not realize, however, that even if the Negroes do successfully imitate the whites, nothing new has thereby been accomplished. You simply have a larger number of persons doing what others have been doing. The unusual gifts of the race have not thereby been developed, and an unwilling world, therefore, continues to wonder what the Negro is good for.

These "educated" people, however, decry any such thing as race consciousness; and in some respects they are right. They do not like to hear such expressions as "Negro literature," "Negro poetry," "African art," or "thinking black"; and, roughly speaking, we must concede that such things do not exist. These things did not figure in the courses which they pursued in school, and why should they? "Aren't we all Americans? Then, whatever is American is as much the heritage of the Negro as of any other group in this country."

The "highly educated" contend, however, that when the Negro emphasizes these things he invites racial discrimination by recognizing such differentness of the races. The thought that the Negro is one thing and the white man another is the stock-in-trade argument of the Caucasian to justify segregation. Why, then, should the Negro blame the white man for doing what he himself does?

These "highly educated" Negroes, however, fail to see that it is not the Negro who takes this position. The white man forces him to it, and to extricate himself therefrom the Negro leader must so deal with the situation as to develop in the segregated group the power with which they can elevate themselves. The differentness of races, moreover, is no evidence of superiority or of inferiority. This merely indicates that each race has certain gifts which the others do not possess. It is by the development of these gifts that every race must justify its right to exist.

How We Missed the Mark

How we have arrived at the present state of affairs can be understood only by studying the forces effective in the development of Negro education since it was systematically undertaken immediately after Emancipation. To point out merely the defects as they appear today will be of little benefit to the present and future generations. These things must be viewed in their historic setting. The conditions of today have been determined by what has taken place in the past, and in a careful study of this history we may see more clearly the great theatre of events in which the Negro has played a part. We may understand better what his role has been and how well he has functioned in it.

The idea of educating the Negroes after the Civil War was largely a prompting of philanthropy. Their white neighbors failed to assume this responsibility. These black people had been liberated as a result of a sectional conflict out of which their former owners had emerged as victims. From this class, then, the freedmen could not expect much sympathy or cooperation in the effort to prepare themselves to figure as citizens of a modern republic.

From functionaries of the United States Government itself and from those who participated in the conquest of the secessionists early came the plan of teaching these freedmen the simple duties of life as worked out by the Freedmen's Bureau and philanthropic agencies. When systematized this effort became a program for the organization of churches and schools and the direction of them along lines which had been considered most conducive to the progress of people otherwise circumstanced. Here and there some variation was made in this program in view of the fact that the status of the freedmen in no way paralleled that of their friends and teachers, but such thought was not general. When the Negroes in some way would learn to perform the duties which other elements of the population had prepared themselves to discharge they would be duly qualified, it was believed, to function as citizens of the country.

Inasmuch as most Negroes lived in the agricultural South, moreover, and only a few of them at first acquired small farms there was little in their life which any one of thought could not have easily understood. The poverty which afflicted them for a generation after Emancipation held them down to the lowest order of society, nominally free but economically enslaved. The participation of the freedmen in government for a few years during the period known as the Reconstruction had little bearing on their situation except that they did join with the uneducated poor whites in bringing about certain much-desired social reforms, especially in giving the South its first plan of democratic education in providing for a school system at public expense.

Neither this inadequately supported school system nor the struggling higher institutions of a classical order established about the same time, however, connected the Negroes very closely with life as it was. These institutions were concerned rather with life as they hoped to make it. When the Negro found himself deprived of influence in politics, therefore, and at the same time unprepared to participate in the higher functions in the industrial development which this country began to undergo, it soon became evident to him that he was losing ground in the basic things of life. He was spending his time studying about the things which had been or might be, but he was learning little to help him to do better the tasks at hand. Since the Negroes believed that the causes of this untoward condition lay without the race, migration was attempted, and emigration to Africa was again urged. At this psychological moment came the wave of industrial education which swept the country by storm. The educational authorities in the cities and States throughout the Black Belt began to change the course of study to make the training of the Negro conform to this policy.

The missionary teachers from the North in defense of their idea of more liberal training, however, fearlessly attacked this new educational policy; and the Negroes participating in the same dispute arrayed themselves respectively on one side or the other. For a generation thereafter the quarrel as to whether the Negro should be given a classical or a practical education was the dominant topic in Negro schools and churches throughout the United States. Labor was the most important thing of life, it was argued; practical education counted in reaching that end; and the Negro worker must be taught to solve this problem of efficiency before directing attention to other things.

Others more narrow-minded than the advocates of industrial education, seized upon the idea, feeling that, although the Negro must have some semblance of education, it would be a fine stroke to be able to make a distinction between the training given the Negro and that provided for the whites. Inasmuch as the industrial educational idea rapidly gained ground, too, many Negroes for political purposes began to espouse it; and schools and colleges hoping thereby to obtain money worked out accordingly makeshift provisions for such instruction, although they could not satisfactorily offer it. A few real industrial schools actually equipped themselves for this work and turned out a number of graduates with such preparation.

Unfortunately, however, the affair developed into a sort of battle of words, for in spite of all they said and did the majority of the Negroes, those who did make some effort to obtain an education, did not actually receive either the industrial or the classical education. Negroes attended industrial schools, took such training as was prescribed, and received their diplomas; but few of them developed adequate efficiency to be able to do what they were supposedly trained to do. The schools in which they were educated could not provide for all the experience with machinery which white apprentices trained in factories had. Such industrial education as these Negroes received, then, was merely to master a technique already discarded in progressive centres; and even in less complicated operations of industry these schools had no such facilities as to parallel the numerous processes of factories conducted on the plan of the division of labor. Except what value such training might have in the development of the mind by making practical applications of mathematics and science, then, it was a failure.

The majority of Negro graduates of industrial schools, therefore, have gone into other avenues, and too often into those for which they have had no preparation whatever. Some few who actually prepared for the industrial sphere by self-improvement likewise sought other occupations for the reason that Negroes were generally barred from higher pursuits by trades unions; and, being unable to develop captains of industry to increase the demand for persons in these lines, the Negroes have not opened up many such opportunities for themselves.

During these years, too, the schools for the classical education for Negroes have not done any better. They have proceeded on the basis that every ambitious person needs a liberal education when as a matter of fact this does not necessarily follow. The Negro trained in the advanced phases of literature, philosophy, and politics had been unable to develop far in using his knowledge because of having to function in the lower spheres of the social order. Advanced knowledge of science, mathematics, and languages, moreover, has not been much more useful except for mental disciplines because of the dearth of opportunity to apply such knowledge among people who were largely common laborers in towns or peons on the plantations. The extent to which such higher education has been successful in leading the Negro to think, which above all is the chief purpose of education, has merely made him more of a malcontent when he can sense the drift of things and appreciate the impossibility of success in visioning conditions as they really are.

It is very clear, therefore, that we do not have in the life of the Negro today a large number of persons who have been benefited by either of the systems about which we have quarreled so long. The number of Negro mechanics and artisans have comparatively declined during the last two generations. The Negroes do not proportionately represent as many skilled laborers as they did before the Civil War. If the practical education which the Negroes received helped to improve the situation so that it is today no worse than what it is, certainly it did not solve the problem as was expected of it.

·　　·　　·

The description of the various parts of the world was worked out according to the same plan. The parts inhabited by the Caucasian were treated in detail. Less attention was given to the yellow people, still less to the red, very little to the brown, and practically none to the black race. Those people who are far removed from the physical characteristics of the Caucasians or who do not materially assist them in the domination or exploitation of others were not mentioned except to be belittled or decried.

From the teaching of science the Negro was likewise eliminated. The beginnings of science in various parts of the Orient were mentioned, but the Africans' early advancement in this field was omitted. Students were not told that ancient Africans of the interior knew sufficient science to concoct poisons for arrowheads, to mix durable colors for paintings, to extract metals from nature and refine them for development in the industrial arts. Very little was said about the chemistry in the method of Egyptian embalming which was the product of the mixed breeds of Northern Africa, now known in the modern world as "colored people."

In the study of language in school pupils were made to scoff at the Negro dialect as some peculiar possession of the Negro which they should despise rather than directed to study the background of this language as a broken-down African tongue—in short to understand their own linguistic history, which is certainly more important for them than the study of French Phonetics or Historical Spanish Grammar. To the African language as such no attention was given except in case of the preparation of traders, missionaries, and public functionaries to exploit the natives. This number of persons thus trained, of course, constituted a small fraction hardly deserving attention.

From literature the African was excluded altogether. He was not supposed to have expressed any thought worth knowing. The philosophy in the African proverbs and in the rich folklore of that continent was ignored to give preference to that developed on the distant shores of the Mediterranean. Most missionary teachers of the freedmen, like most men of our time, had never read the interesting books of travel in Africa, and had never heard of the *Tarikh Es-Soudan*.

In the teaching of fine arts these instructors usually started with Greece by showing how that art was influenced from without, but they omitted the African influence which scientists now regard as significant and dominant in early Hellas. They failed to teach the student the Mediterranean Melting Pot with the Negroes from Africa bringing their wares, their ideas, and their blood therein to influence the history of Greece, Carthage, and Rome. Making desire father to the thought, our teachers either ignored these influences or endeavored to belittle them by working out theories to the contrary.

The bias did not stop at this point, for it invaded the teaching of the professions. Negro law students were told that they belonged to the most criminal element in the country; and an effort was made to justify the procedure in the seats of injustice where law was interpreted as being one thing for the white man and a different thing for the Negro. In constitutional law the spinelessness of the United States Supreme Court in permitting the judicial nullification of the Fourteenth and Fifteenth Amendments was and still is boldly upheld in our few law schools.

In medical schools Negroes were likewise convinced of their inferiority in being reminded of their role as germ carriers. The prevalence of syphilis and tuberculosis among Negroes was especially emphasized without showing that these maladies are more deadly among the Negroes for the reason that they are Caucasian diseases; and since these plagues are new to Negroes, these sufferers have not had time to develop against them the immunity which time has permitted in the Caucasian. Other diseases to which Negroes easily fall prey were mentioned to point out the race as an undesirable element when this condition was due to the Negroes' economic and social status. Little emphasis was placed upon the immunity of the Negro from diseases like yellow fever and influenza which are so disastrous to whites. Yet, the whites were not considered inferior because of this differential resistance to these plagues.

In history, of course, the Negro had no place in this curriculum. He was pictured as a human being of the lower order, unable to subject passion to reason, and therefore useful only when made the hewer of wood and the drawer of water for others. No thought was given to the history of Africa except so far as it had been a field of exploitation for the Caucasian. You might study the history as it was offered in our system from the elementary school throughout the university, and you would never hear Africa mentioned except in the negative. You would never thereby learn that Africans first domesticated the sheep, goat, and cow, developed the idea of trial by jury, produced the first stringed instruments, and gave the world its greatest boon in the discovery of iron. You would never know that prior to the Mohammedan invasion about 1000 A.D. these natives in the heart of Africa had developed powerful kingdoms which were later organized as the Songhay Empire on the order of that of the Romans and boasting of similar grandeur.

Unlike other people, then, the Negro, according to this point of view, was an exception to the natural plan of things, and he had no such mission as that of an outstanding contribution to culture. The status of the Negro, then, was justly fixed as that of an inferior. Teachers of Negroes in their first schools after Emancipation did not proclaim any such doctrine, but the content of their curricula justified these inferences.

An observer from outside of the situation naturally inquires why the Negroes, many of whom serve their race as teachers, have not changed this program. These teachers, however, are powerless. Negroes have no control over their education and have little voice in their other affairs pertaining thereto. In a few cases Negroes have been chosen as members of public boards of education, and some have been appointed members of private boards, but these Negroes are always such a small minority that they do not figure in the final working out of the educational program. The education of the Negroes, then, the most important thing in the uplift of the Negroes, is almost entirely in the hands of those who have enslaved them and now segregate them.

With "mis-educated Negroes" in control themselves, however, it is doubtful that the system would be very much different from what it is or that it would rapidly undergo change. The Negroes thus placed in charge would be the products of the same system and would show no more conception of the task at hand than do the whites who have educated them and shaped their minds as they would have them function. Negro educators of today may have more sympathy and interest in the race than the whites now exploiting Negro institutions as educators, but the former have no more vision than their competitors. Taught from books of the same bias, trained by Caucasians of the same prejudices or by Negroes of enslaved minds, one generation of Negro teachers after another have served for no higher purpose than to do what they are told to do. In other words, a Negro teacher instructing Negro children is in many respects a white teacher thus engaged, for the program in each case is about the same.

There can be no reasonable objection to the Negro's doing what the white man tells him to do, if the white man tells him to do what is right; but right is pure relative. The present system under the control of the whites trains the Negro to be white and at the same time convinces him of the impropriety or the impossibility of his becoming white. It compels the Negro to become a good Negro for the performance of which his education is ill-suited. For the white man's exploitation of the Negro through economic restriction and segregation the present system is sound and will doubtless continue until this gives place to the saner policy of actual interracial cooperation—not the present farce of racial manipulation in which the Negro is a figurehead. History does not furnish a case of the elevation of a people by ignoring the thought and aspiration of the people thus served.

This is slightly dangerous ground here, however, for the Negro's mind has been all but perfectly enslaved in that he has been trained to think what is desired of him. The "highly educated" Negroes do not like to hear anything uttered against this procedure because they make their living in this way, and they feel that they must defend the system. Few mis-educated Negroes ever act otherwise; and, if they so express themselves, they are easily crushed by the large majority to the contrary so that the procession may move on without interruption.

The result, then, is that the Negroes thus mis-educated are of no service to themselves and none to the white man. The white man does not need the Negroes' professional, commercial, or industrial assistance; and as a result of the multiplication of mechanical appliances he no longer needs them in drudgery or menial service. The "highly educated" Negroes, moreover, do not need the Negro professional or commercial classes because Negroes have been taught that whites can serve them more efficiently in these spheres. Reduced, then, to teaching and preaching, the Negroes will have no outlet but to go down a blind alley, if the sort of education which they are now receiving is to enable them to find the way out of their present difficulties.

Emperor Haile Selassie

(1892–1975, Ethiopia)

Address to the League of Nations

Geneva, June 30, 1936

I, Haile Selassie I, emperor of Ethiopia, am here today to claim that justice which is due to my people, and the assistance promised to it eight months ago, when fifty nations asserted that aggression had been committed in violation of international treaties.

There is no precedent for a head of state himself speaking in this Assembly. But there is also no precedent for a people being victim of such injustice, and being at present threatened by abandonment to its aggressor. Also, there has never before been an example by any government proceeding to the systematic extermination of a nation by barbarous means in violation of the most solemn promises made by the nations of the earth that there should not be used against innocent human beings the terrible poison of harmful gases. It is to defend a people struggling for its age-old independence that the head of the Ethiopian empire has come to Geneva to fulfill this supreme duty, after having himself fought at the head of his armies.

I pray to Almighty God that He may spare nations the terrible sufferings that have just been inflicted on my people and of which the chiefs who accompany me here have been the horrified witnesses. It is my duty to inform the governments assembled in Geneva, responsible as they are for the lives of millions of men, women, and children, of the deadly peril which threatens them, by describing to them the fate which has been suffered by Ethiopia.

It is not only upon warriors that the Italian government has made war. It has above all attacked populations far removed from hostilities, in order to terrorize and exterminate them.

At the beginning, towards the end of 1935, Italian aircraft hurled upon my armies bombs of tear-gas. Their effects were but slight. The soldiers learned to scatter, waiting until the wind had rapidly dispersed the poisonous gases. The Italian aircraft then resorted to mustard gas. Barrels of liquid were hurled upon armed groups. But this means also was not effective. The liquid affected only a few soldiers and barrels upon the ground were themselves a warning to troops and to the population of the danger.

It was at the time when the operations for the encircling of Makalle [in northern Ethiopia] were taking place that the Italian command, fearing a rout, followed the procedure which it is now my duty to denounce to the world. Special sprayers were installed on board aircraft so that they could vaporize, over vast areas of territory, a fine, death-dealing rain. Groups of 9, 15, 18 aircraft followed one another so that the fog issuing from them formed a continuous sheet. It was thus that, as from the end of January 1936, soldiers, women, children, cattle, rivers, lakes, and pastures were drenched continually with this deadly rain. In order to kill off systematically all living creatures, in order the more surely to poison waters and pastures, the Italian command made its aircraft pass over and over again. That was its chief method of warfare.

The very refinement of barbarism consisted of carrying ravage and terror into the most densely populated parts of the territory, the points farthest removed from the scene of hostilities. The object was to scatter fear and death over a great part of the Ethiopian territory.

These fearful tactics succeeded. Men and animals succumbed. The deadly rain that fell from the aircraft made all those whom it touched fly shrieking with pain. All those who drank the poisoned water or ate the infected food also succumbed in dreadful suffering. In tens of thousands, the victims of the Italian mustard gas fell. It is in order to denounce to the civilized world the tortures inflicted upon the Ethiopian people that I resolved to come to Geneva.

None other than myself and my brave companions in arms could bring the League of Nations the undeniable proof. The appeals of my delegates addressed to the League of Nations had remained without any answer; my delegates had not been witnesses. That is why I decided to come myself to bear witness against the crime perpetrated against my people and give Europe a warning of the doom that awaits it, if it should bow before the accomplished fact.

Is it necessary to remind the Assembly of the various stages of the Ethiopian drama? For 20 years past either as heir apparent, regent of the empire, or as emperor, I have never ceased to use all my efforts to bring my country the benefits of civilization, and in particular to establish relations of good neighborliness with adjacent powers. In particular I succeeded in concluding with Italy the Treaty of Friendship of 1928, which absolutely prohibited the resort, under any pretext whatsoever, to force of arms, substituting for force and pressure the conciliation and arbitration on which civilized nations have based international order.

In its report of October 5, 1935, the Committee of 13 [of the League] recognized my effort and the results that I achieved. The governments thought that the entry of Ethiopia into the League, whilst giving that country a new guarantee for the maintenance of her territorial integrity and independence, would help her to reach a higher level of civilization. It does not seem that in Ethiopia today there is more disorder and insecurity than in 1923. On the contrary, the country is more united and the central power is better obeyed.

I should have procured still greater results for my people if obstacles of every kind had not been put in the way by the Italian government, the government which stirred up revolt and armed the rebels. Indeed the Rome government, as it has today openly proclaimed, has never ceased to prepare for the conquest of Ethiopia. The treaties of friendship it signed with me were not sincere; their only object was to hide its real intention from me. The Italian government asserts that for fourteen years it has been preparing for its present conquest. It therefore recognizes today that when it supported the admission of Ethiopia to the League of Nations in 1923, when it concluded the Treaty of Friendship in 1928, when it signed the pact of Paris outlawing war, it was deceiving the whole world.

The Ethiopian government was, in these solemn treaties, given additional guarantees of security which would enable it to achieve further progress along the pacific path of reform on which it has set its feet and to which it was devoting all its strength and all its heart.

The Walwal incident, in December 1934, came as a thunderbolt to me. The Italian provocation was obvious, and I did not hesitate to appeal to the League of Nations. I invoked the provisions of the treaty of 1928, the principles of the covenant [of the League]; I urged the procedure of conciliation and arbitration.

Unhappily for Ethiopia, this was the time when a certain government considered that the European situation made it imperative at all costs to obtain the friendship of Italy. The price paid was the abandonment of Ethiopian independence to the greed of the Italian government. This secret agreement [of January 1935, between Britain and Italy, recognizing Italian influence over Ethiopia], contrary to the obligations of the covenant, has exerted a great influence over the course of events. Ethiopia and the whole world have suffered and are still suffering today its disastrous consequences.

This first violation of the covenant was followed by many others. Feeling itself encouraged in its policy against Ethiopia, the Rome government feverishly made war preparations thinking that the concerted pressure which was beginning to be exerted on the Ethiopian government might perhaps not overcome the resistance of my people to Italian domination.

The time had to come, thus all sorts of difficulties were placed in the way with a view to breaking up the procedure of conciliation and arbitration. All kinds of obstacles were placed in the way of that procedure. Governments tried to prevent the Ethiopian government from finding arbitrators amongst their nationals: when once the arbitral tribunal was set upon, pressure was exercised so that an award favorable to Italy should be given. All this was in vain: the arbitrators—two of whom were Italian officials—were forced to recognize unanimously that in the Walwal incident, as in the subsequent incidents, no international responsibility was to be attributed to Ethiopia.

Following on this award, the Ethiopian government sincerely thought that an era of friendly relations might be opened with Italy. I loyally offered my hand to the Rome government.

The Assembly was informed by the report of the Committee of Thirteen, dated October 5, 1935, of the details of the events which occurred after the month of December 1934 and up to October 3, 1935. It will be sufficient if I quote a few of the conclusions of that report (Nos. 24, 25, and 26): The Italian memorandum (containing the complaints made by Italy) was laid on the Council table on September 4, 1935, whereas Ethiopia's first appeal to the Council had been made on December 14, 1934. In the interval between these two dates, the Italian government opposed the consideration of the question by the Council on the ground that the only appropriate procedure was that provided for in the Italo-Ethiopian Treaty of 1928. Throughout the whole of that period, moreover, the dispatch of Italian troops to East Africa was proceeding. These shipments of troops were represented to the Council by the Italian government as necessary for the defense of its colonies menaced by Ethiopia's preparations. Ethiopia, on the contrary, drew attention to the official pronouncements made in Italy which, in its opinion, left no doubt "as to the hostile intentions of the Italian government."

From the outset of the dispute, the Ethiopian government has sought a settlement by peaceful means. It has appealed to the procedures of the covenant. The Italian government desiring to keep strictly to the procedures of the Italo-Ethiopian Treaty of 1928, the Ethiopian government assented. It invariably states that it would faithfully carry out the arbitral award even if the decision went against it. It agreed that the question of the ownership of Walwal should not be dealt with by the arbitrators, because the Italian government would not agree to such a course. It asked the Council to dispatch neutral observers and offered to lend itself to any inquiries upon which the Council might decide.

Once the Walwal dispute had been settled by arbitration, however, the Italian government submitted its detailed memorandum to the Council in support of its claim to liberty of action. It asserted that a case like that of Ethiopia cannot be settled by the means provided by the covenant. It stated that, "since this question affects vital interests and is of primary importance to Italian security and civilization," it "would be failing in its most elementary duty, did it not cease once and for all to place any confidence in Ethiopia reserving full liberty to adopt any measures that may become necessary to ensure the safety of its colonies and to safeguard its own interests."

Those are the terms of the report of the Committee of Thirteen. The Council and the Assembly unanimously adopted the conclusion that the Italian government had violated the covenant and was in a state of aggression.

I did not hesitate to declare that I did not wish for war, that it was imposed upon me, and I should struggle solely for the independence and integrity of my people, and that in that struggle I was the defender of the cause of all small states exposed to the greed of a powerful neighbor.

In October 1935, the fifty-two nations who are listening to me today gave me an assurance that the aggressor would not triumph, that the resources of the covenant would be employed in order to ensure the reign of right and the failure of violence. I ask the fifty-two nations not to forget today the policy upon which they embarked eight months ago, and on faith of which I directed the resistance of my people against the aggressor whom they had denounced to the world. Despite the inferiority of my weapons, the complete lack of aircraft, artillery, munitions, [and] hospital services, my confidence in the League was absolute. I thought it to be impossible that fifty-two nations, including the most powerful in the world, should be successfully opposed by a single aggressor. Counting on the faith due to treaties, I had made no preparation for war, and that is the case with certain small countries in Europe.

When the danger became more urgent, being aware of my responsibilities towards my people, during the first six months of 1935 I tried to acquire armaments. Many governments proclaimed an embargo to prevent my doing so, whereas the Italian government, through the Suez Canal, was given all facilities for transporting, without cessation and without protest, troops, arms, and munitions.

On October 3, 1935, the Italian troops invaded my territory. A few hours later only I decreed general mobilization. In my desire to maintain peace I had, following the example of a great country in Europe on the eve of the Great War, caused my troops to withdraw 30 kilometers so as to remove any pretext of provocation.

War then took place in the atrocious conditions which I have laid before the Assembly. In that unequal struggle between a government commanding more than 42 million inhabitants, having at its disposal financial, industrial, and technical means which enabled it to create unlimited quantities of the most death-dealing weapons, and, on the other hand, a small people of 12 million inhabitants, without arms, without resources, having on its side only the justice of its own cause and the promise of the League of Nations, what real assistance was given to Ethiopia by the fifty-two nations who have declared the Rome government guilty of a breach of the covenant and had undertaken to prevent the triumph of the aggressor? Has each of the states members, as it was its duty to do in virtue of its signature appended to Article 15 of the covenant, considered the aggressor as having committed an act of war personally directed against itself? I had placed all my hopes in the execution of these undertakings. My confidence had been confirmed by the repeated declarations made in Council to the effect that aggression must not be rewarded, and that force would end by being compelled to bow before right.

In December 1935 the Council made it quite clear that its feelings were in harmony with those of hundreds of millions of people who, in all parts of the world, had protested against the proposals to dismember Ethiopia. It was constantly repeated that there was not merely a conflict between the Italian government and the League of Nations, and that is why I personally refused all proposals to my personal advantage made to me by the Italian government, if only I would betray my people and the covenant of the League of Nations. I was defending the cause of all small peoples who are threatened with aggression.

What have become of the promises made to me as long ago as October 1935? I noted with grief, but without surprise, that three powers considered their undertakings under the covenant as absolutely of no value. Their connections with Italy impelled them to refuse to take any measures whatsoever in order to stop Italian aggression. On the contrary, it was a profound disappointment to me to learn the attitude of a certain government which, whilst ever protesting its scrupulous attachment to the covenant, has tirelessly used all its efforts to prevent its observance. As soon as any measure which was likely to be rapidly effective was proposed, various pretexts were devised in order to postpone even consideration of the measure. Did the secret agreements of January 1935 provide for this tireless obstruction?

The Ethiopian government never expected other governments to shed their soldiers' blood to defend the covenant when their own immediately personal interests were not at stake. Ethiopian warriors asked only for means to defend themselves. On many occasions I have asked for financial assistance for the purchase of arms. That assistance had been constantly refused me. What, then, in practice, is the meaning of Article 16 of the covenant and of collective security?

The Ethiopian government's use of the railway from Djibouti to Addis Ababa was in practice hampered as regards transport of arms intended for the Ethiopian forces. At the present moment this is the chief, if not the only, means of supply of the Italian armies of occupation. The rules of neutrality should have prohibited transports intended for Italian forces, but there is not even neutrality since Article 16 lays upon every state member of the League the duty not to remain a neutral but to come to the aid not of the aggressor but of the victim of aggression. Has the covenant been respected? Is it today being respected?

Finally a statement has just been made in their parliaments by the governments of certain powers, amongst them the most influential members of the League of Nations, that since the aggressor has succeeded in occupying a large part of Ethiopian territory, they propose not to continue the application of any economic and financial measures that may have been decided upon against the Italian government.

These are the circumstances in which, at the request of the Argentine government, the Assembly of the League of Nations meets to consider the situation created by Italian aggression.

I assert that the problem submitted to the Assembly today is a much wider one. It is not merely a question of the settlement of Italian aggression. It is collective security: it is the very existence of the League of Nations. It is the confidence that each state is to place in international treaties. It is the value of promises made to small states that their integrity and their independence shall be respected and ensured. It is the principle of the equality of states on the one hand, or otherwise the obligation laid upon small powers to accept the bonds of vassalship. In a word, it is international morality that is at stake. Have the signatures appended to a treaty value only in so far as the signatory powers have a personal, direct, and immediate interest involved?

No subtlety can change the problem or shift the grounds of the discussion. It is in all sincerity that I submit these considerations to the Assembly. At the time when my people are threatened with extermination, when the support of the League may ward off the final blow, may I be allowed to speak with complete frankness, without reticence, in all directness such as is demanded by the rule of equality as between all states members of the League?

Apart from the Kingdom of the Lord, there is not on this earth any nation that is superior to any other. Should it happen that a strong government finds it may with impunity destroy a weak people, then the hour strikes for that weak people to appeal to the League of Nations to give its judgment in all freedom. God and history will remember your judgment.

I have heard it asserted that the inadequate sanctions already applied have not achieved their object. At no time, and under no circumstances, could sanctions that were intentionally inadequate, intentionally badly applied, stop an aggressor. This is not a case of the impossibility of stopping an aggressor, but of the refusal to stop an aggressor. When Ethiopia requested and requests that she should be given financial assistance, was that a measure which it was impossible to apply whereas financial assistance of the League has been granted, even in times of peace, to two countries and exactly to two countries who have refused to apply sanctions against the aggressor?

Faced by numerous violations by the Italian government of all international treaties that prohibit resort to arms and the use of barbarous methods of warfare, it is my painful duty to note that the initiative has today been taken with a view to raising sanctions. Does this initiative not mean in practice the abandonment of Ethiopia to the aggressor? On the very eve of the day when I was about to attempt a supreme effort in the defense of my people before this Assembly, does not this initiative deprive Ethiopia of one of her last chances to succeed in obtaining the support and guarantee of states members? Is that the guidance the League of Nations and each of the states members are entitled to expect from the great powers when they assert their right and their duty to guide the action of the League?

Placed by the aggressor face to face with the accomplished fact, are states going to set up the terrible precedent of bowing before force?

Your Assembly will doubtless have laid before it proposals for the reform of the covenant and for rendering more effective the guarantee of collective security. Is it the covenant that needs reform? What undertakings can have any value if the will to keep them is lacking? Is it international morality which is at stake and not the articles of the covenant?

On behalf of the Ethiopian people, a member of the League of Nations, I request the Assembly to take all measures proper to ensure respect for the covenant. I renew my protest against the violations of treaties of which the Ethiopian people have been the victim. I declare in the face of the whole world that the emperor, the government, and the people of Ethiopia will not bow before force; that they maintain their claims that they will use all means in their power to ensure the triumph of right and the respect of the covenant.

I ask the fifty-two nations, who have given the Ethiopian people a promise to help them in their resistance to the aggressor, what are they willing to do for Ethiopia? And the great powers who have promised the guarantee of collective security to small states on whom weighs the threat that they may one day suffer the fate of Ethiopia, I ask what measures do you intend to take?

Representatives of the world, I have come to Geneva to discharge in your midst the most painful of the duties of the head of a state. What reply shall I have to take back to my people?

Mary McLeod Bethune
(1875–1955, United States)

My Last Will and Testament

I leave you love. Love builds. It is positive and helpful. It is more beneficial than hate. Injuries quickly forgotten quickly pass away. Personally and racially, our enemies must be forgiven. Our aim must be to create a world of fellowship and justice where no man's skin, color, or religion, is held against him. "Love thy neighbor" is a precept which could transform the world if it were universally practiced. It connotes brotherhood and, to me, brotherhood of man is the noblest concept in all human relations. Loving your neighbor means being interracial, interreligious and international.

I leave you hope. The Negro's growth will be great in the years to come. Yesterday, our ancestors endured the degradation of slavery, yet they retained their dignity. Today, we direct our economic and political strength. toward winning a more abundant and secure life. Tomorrow, a new Negro, unhindered by race taboos and shackles, will benefit from more than 330 years of ceaseless striving and struggle. Theirs will be a better world. This I believe with all my heart.

I leave you the challenge of developing confidence in one another. As long as Negroes are hemmed into racial blocs by prejudice and pressure, it will be necessary for them to band together for economic betterment. Negro banks, insurance companies and other businesses are examples of successful, racial economic enterprises. These institutions were made possible by vision and mutual aid. Confidence was vital in getting them started and keeping them going. Negroes have got to demonstrate still more confidence in each other in business. This kind of confidence will aid the economic rise of the race by bringing together the pennies and dollars of our people and ploughing them into useful channels. Economic separatism cannot be tolerated in this enlightened age, and it is not practicable. We must spread out as far and as fast as we can, but we must also help each other as we go.

I leave you a thirst for education. Knowledge is the prime need of the hour. More and more, Negroes are taking full advantage of hard-won opportunities for learning, and the education level of the Negro population is at its highest point in history. We are making greater use of the privileges inherent in living in a democracy. If we continue in this trend, we will be able to rear increasing numbers of strong, purposeful men and women, equipped with vision, mental clarity, health and education.

I leave you a respect for the uses of power. We live in a world which respects power above all things. Power, intelligently directed, can lead to more freedom. Unwisely directed, it can be a dreadful, destructive force. During my lifetime I have seen the power of the Negro grow enormously. It has always been my first concern that this power should be placed on the side of human justice.

Now that the barriers are crumbling everywhere, the Negro in America must be ever vigilant less his forces be marshalled behind wrong causes and undemocratic movements. He must not lend his support to any group that seeks to subvert democracy. That is why we must select leaders who are wise, courageous, and of great moral stature and ability. We have great leaders among us today: Ralph Bunche, Channing Tobias, Mordecai Johnson, Walter White and Mary Church Terrell. (The latter two are now deceased.) We have had other great men and women in the past: Frederick Douglass, Booker T. Washington, Harriet Tubman, Sojourner Truth. We must produce more qualified people like them, who will work not for themselves, but for others.

I leave you faith. Faith is the first factor in a life devoted to service. Without faith, nothing is possible. With it, nothing is impossible. Faith in God is the greatest power, but great, too, is faith in oneself. In 50 years the faith of the American Negro in himself had grown immensely and is still increasing. The measure of our progress as a race is in precise relation to the depth of the faith in our people held by our leaders. Frederick Douglass, genius though he was, was spurred by a deep conviction that his people would heed his counsel and follow him to freedom. Our greatest Negro figures have been imbued with faith. Our forefathers struggled for liberty in conditions far more onerous than those we now face, but they never lost the faith. Their perseverance paid rich dividends. We must never forget their sufferings and their sacrifices, for they were the foundations of the progress of our people.

I leave you racial dignity. I want Negroes to maintain their human dignity at all costs. We, as Negroes, must recognize that we are the custodians as well as the heirs of a great civilization. We have given something to the world as a race and for this we are proud and fully conscious of our place in the total picture of mankind's development. We must learn also to share and win with all men. We must make an effort to be less race conscious and more conscious of individuals and human values. I have never been sensitive about my complexion. My color has never destroyed my self respect nor has it ever caused me to conduct myself in such a manner as to merit the disrespect of any person. I have not let my color handicap me. Despite many crushing burdens and handicaps, I have risen from the cotton fields of South Carolina to found a college, administer it during its years of growth, become a public servant in the government of our country and a leader of women. I would not exchange my color for all the wealth in the world, for had I been born white I might not have been able to do all that I have done or yet hope to do.

I leave you a desire to live harmoniously with your fellow men. The problem of color is world-wide. It is found in Africa and Asia, Europe and South America. I appeal to American Negroes—North, South, East and West—to recognize their common problems and unite to solve them.

I pray that we will learn to live harmoniously with the white race. So often, our difficulties have made us hyper-sensitive and truculent. I want to see my people conduct themselves naturally in all relationships—fully conscious of their manly responsibilities and deeply aware of their heritage. I want them to learn to understand whites and influence them for good, for it is advisable and sensible for us to do so. We are a minority of 15 million living side by side with a white majority. We must learn to deal with these people positively and on an individual basis.

I leave you finally a responsibility to our young people. The world around us really belongs to youth for youth will take over its future management. Our children must never lose their zeal for building a better world. They must not be discouraged from aspiring toward greatness, for they are to be the leaders of tomorrow. Nor must they forget that the masses of our people are still underprivileged, ill-housed, impoverished and victimized by discrimination. We have a powerful potential in our youth, and we must have the courage to change old ideas and practices so that we may direct their power toward good ends.

Faith, courage, brotherhood, dignity, ambition, responsibility—these are needed today as never before. We must cultivate them and use them as tools for our task of completing the establishment of equality for the Negro. We must sharpen these tools in the struggle that faces us and find new ways of using them. The Freedom Gates are half a-jar. We must pry them fully open.

If I have a legacy to leave my people, it is my philosophy of living and serving. As I face tomorrow, I am content, for I think I have spent my life well. I pray now that my philosophy may be helpful to those who share my vision of a world of Peace, Progress, Brotherhood and Love.

Martin Luther King, Jr.
(1929–1968, United States)

I Have a Dream

Washington, D.C., August 28, 1963

Five score years ago, a great American, in whose symbolic shadow we stand today, signed the Emancipation Proclamation. This momentous decree came as a great beacon of light of hope to millions of Negro slaves who had been seared in the flames of withering injustice. It came as a joyous daybreak to end the long night of their captivity.

But one hundred years later, the Negro still is not free. One hundred years later, the life of the Negro is still sadly crippled by the manacles of segregation and the chains of discrimination.

One hundred years later, the Negro lives on a lonely island of poverty in the midst of a vast ocean of material prosperity. One hundred years later, the Negro is still languished in the corners of American society and finds himself an exile in his own land. So we have come here today to dramatize a shameful condition.

In a sense we have come to our nation's capital to cash a check. When the architects of our republic wrote the magnificent words of the Constitution and the Declaration of Independence, they were signing a promissory note to which every American was to fall heir. This note was a promise that all men, yes, black men as well as white men, would be granted the unalienable rights of life, liberty, and the pursuit of happiness.

It is obvious today that America has defaulted on this promissory note insofar as her citizens of color are concerned. Instead of honoring this sacred obligation, America has given the Negro people a bad check, which has come back marked "insufficient funds."

But we refuse to believe that the bank of justice is bankrupt. We refuse to believe that there are insufficient funds in the great vaults of opportunity of this nation. So we have come to cash this check—a check that will give us upon demand the riches of freedom and the security of justice.

We have also come to this hallowed spot to remind America of the fierce urgency of now. This is no time to engage in the luxury of cooling off or to take the tranquilizing drug of gradualism. Now is the time to make real the promises of democracy. Now is the time to rise from the dark and desolate valley of segregation to the sunlit path of racial justice. Now is the time to lift our nation from the quicksands of racial injustice to the solid rock of brotherhood. Now is the time to make justice a reality for all of God's children.

It would be fatal for the nation to overlook the urgency of the movement and to underestimate the determination of the Negro. This sweltering summer of the Negro's legitimate discontent will not pass until there is an invigorating autumn of freedom and equality. 1963 is not an end but a beginning. Those who hope that the Negro needed to blow off steam and will now be content will have a rude awakening if the nation returns to business as usual.

There will be neither rest nor tranquility in America until the Negro is granted his citizenship rights. The whirlwinds of revolt will continue to shake the foundations of our nation until the bright day of justice emerges.

But there is something that I must say to my people who stand on the warm threshold which leads into the palace of justice. In the process of gaining our rightful place we must not be guilty of wrongful deeds.

Let us not seek to satisfy our thirst for freedom by drinking from the cup of bitterness and hatred. We must forever conduct our struggle on the high plane of dignity and discipline. We must not allow our creative protest to degenerate into physical violence. Again and again we must rise to the majestic heights of meeting physical force with soul force.

The marvelous new militancy which has engulfed the Negro community must not lead us to a distrust of all white people, for many of our white brothers, as evidenced by their presence here today, have come to realize that their destiny is tied with our destiny and they have come to realize that their freedom is inextricably bound to our freedom. This offense we share, mounted to storm the battlements of injustice, must be carried forth by a bi-racial army. We cannot walk alone.

And as we walk, we must make the pledge that we shall always march ahead. We cannot turn back. There are those who are asking the devotees of civil rights, "When will you be satisfied?" We can never be satisfied as long as the Negro is the victim of the unspeakable horrors of police brutality.

We can never be satisfied as long as our bodies, heavy with the fatigue of travel, cannot gain lodging in the motels of the highways and the hotels of the cities. We cannot be satisfied as long as the Negro's basic mobility is from a smaller ghetto to a larger one.

We can never be satisfied as long as our children are stripped of their selfhood and robbed of their dignity by signs stating "for whites only." We cannot be satisfied as long as a Negro in Mississippi cannot vote and a Negro in New York believes he has nothing for which to vote. No, we are not satisfied, and we will not be satisfied until justice rolls down like waters and righteousness like a mighty stream.

I am not unmindful that some of you have come here out of excessive trials and tribulation. Some of you have come fresh from narrow jail cells. Some of you have come from areas where your quest for freedom left you battered by the storms of persecution and staggered by the winds of police brutality. You have been the veterans of creative suffering. Continue to work with the faith that unearned suffering is redemptive.

Go back to Mississippi; go back to Alabama; go back to South Carolina; go back to Georgia; go back to Louisiana; go back to the slums and ghettos of the Northern cities, knowing that somehow this situation can, and will be changed. Let us not wallow in the valley of despair.

So I say to you, my friends, that even though we must face the difficulties of today and tomorrow, I still have a dream. It is a dream deeply rooted in the American dream that one day this nation will rise up and live out the true meaning of its creed—we hold these truths to be self evident, that all men are created equal.

I have a dream that one day on the red hills of Georgia, sons of former slaves and sons of former slave-owners will be able to sit down together at the table of brotherhood.

I have a dream that one day, even the state of Mississippi, a state sweltering with the heat of injustice, sweltering with the heat of oppression, will be transformed into an oasis of freedom and justice.

I have a dream that my four little children will one day live in a nation where they will not be judged by the color of their skin but by the content of their character. I have a dream today!

I have a dream that one day, down in Alabama, with its vicious racists, with its governor having his lips dripping with the words of interposition and nullification, that one day, right there in Alabama, little black boys and black girls will be able to join hands with little white boys and white girls as sisters and brothers. I have a dream today!

I have a dream that one day every valley shall be exalted, every hill and mountain shall be made low, the rough places shall be made plain, and the crooked places shall be made straight and the glory of the Lord will be revealed and all flesh shall see it together.

This is our hope. This is the faith that I go back to the South with.

With this faith we will be able to hew out of the mountain of despair a stone of hope. With this faith we will be able to transform the jangling discords of our nation into a beautiful symphony of brotherhood.

With this faith we will be able to work together, to pray together, to struggle together, to go to jail together, to stand up for freedom together, knowing that we will be free one day. This will be the day when all of God's children will be able to sing with new meaning—"my country 'tis of thee; sweet land of liberty; of thee I sing; land where my fathers died, land of the pilgrim's pride; from every mountain side, let freedom ring"—and if America is to be a great nation, this must become true.

So let freedom ring from the prodigious hilltops of New Hampshire.

Let freedom ring from the mighty mountains of New York.

Let freedom ring from the heightening Alleghanies of Pennsylvania.

Let freedom ring from the snow-capped Rockies of Colorado.

Let freedom ring from the curvaceous slopes of California.

But not only that.

Let freedom ring from Stone Mountain of Georgia.

Let freedom ring from Lookout Mountain of Tennessee.

Let freedom ring from every hill and molehill of Mississippi, from every mountainside, let freedom ring.

And when we allow freedom to ring, when we let it ring from every village and hamlet, from every state and city, we will be able to speed up that day when all of God's children—black men and white men, Jews and Gentiles, Catholics and Protestants—will be able to join hands and to sing in the words of the old Negro spiritual: "Free at last, free at last; thank God Almighty, we are free at last."

Frantz Fanon
(1925–1961, Martinique)

Colonial War and Mental Disorders

But the war goes on; and we will have to bind up for years to come the many, sometimes ineffaceable, wounds that the colonialist onslaught has inflicted on our people.

That imperialism which today is fighting against a true liberation of mankind leaves in its wake here and there tinctures of decay which we must search out and mercilessly expel from our land and our spirits.

We shall deal here with the problem of mental disorders which arise from the war of national liberation which the Algerian people are carrying on.

Perhaps these notes on psychiatry will be found ill-timed and singularly out of place in such a book; but we can do nothing about that.

We cannot be held responsible that in this war psychiatric phenomena entailing disorders affecting behavior and thought have taken on importance where those who carry out the "pacification" are concerned, or that these same disorders are notable among the "pacified" population. The truth is that colonialism in its essence was already taking on the aspect of a fertile purveyor for psychiatric hospitals. We have since 1954 in various scientific works drawn the attention of both French and international psychiatrists to the difficulties that arise when seeking to "cure" a native properly, that is to say, when seeking to make him thoroughly a part of a social background of the colonial type.

Because it is a systematic negation of the other person and a furious determination to deny the other person all attributes of humanity, colonialism forces the people it dominates to ask themselves the question constantly: "In reality, who am I?"

The defensive attitudes created by this violent bringing together of the colonized man and the colonial system form themselves into a structure which then reveals the colonized personality. This "sensitivity" is easily understood if we simply study and are alive to the number and depth of the injuries inflicted upon a native during a single day spent amidst the colonial regime. It must in any case be remembered that a colonized people is not only simply a dominated people. Under the German occupation the French remained men; under the French occupation, the Germans remained men. In Algeria there is not simply the domination but the decision to the letter not to occupy anything more than the sum total of the land. The Algerians, the veiled women, the palm trees, and the camels make up the landscape, the *natural* background to the human presence of the French.

Hostile nature, obstinate and fundamentally rebellious, is in fact represented in the colonies by the bush, by mosquitoes, natives, and fever, and colonization is a success when all this indocile nature has finally been tamed. Railways across the bush, the draining of swamps, and a native population which is non-existent politically and economically are in fact one and the same thing.

In the period of colonization when it is not contested by armed resistance, when the sum total of harmful nervous stimuli overstep a certain threshold, the defensive attitudes of the natives give way and they then find themselves crowding the mental hospitals. There is thus during this calm period of successful colonization a regular and important mental pathology which is the direct product of oppression.

Today the war of national liberation which has been carried on by the Algerian people for the last seven years has become a favorable breeding ground for mental disorders, because so far as the Algerians are concerned it is a total war. We shall mention here some Algerian cases which have been attended by us and who seem to us to be particularly eloquent. We need hardly say that we are not concerned with producing a scientific work. We avoid all arguments over semiology, nosology, or therapeutics. The few technical terms used serve merely as references. We must, however, insist on two points. Firstly, as a general rule, clinical psychiatry classifies the different disturbances shown by our patients under the heading "reactionary psychoses." In doing this, prominence is given to the event which has given rise to the disorder, although in some cases mention is made of the previous history of the case (the psychological, affective, and biological condition of the patient) and of the type of background from whence he comes. It seems to us that in the cases here chosen the events giving rise to the disorder are chiefly the bloodthirsty and pitiless atmosphere, the generalization of inhuman practices, and the firm impression that people have of being caught up in a veritable Apocalypse.[1]

Case No. 2 of Series A is a typical reactionary psychosis, but [other cases] give evidence of a much more widely spread causality although we cannot really speak of one particular event giving rise to the disorders. These are reactionary psychoses, if we want to use a ready-made label; but here we must give particular priority to the war: a war which in whole and in part is a colonial war. After the two great world wars, there is no lack of publications on the mental pathology of soldiers taking part in action and civilians who are victims of evacuations and bombardments. The hitherto unemphasized characteristics of certain psychiatric descriptions here given confirm, if confirmation were necessary, that this colonial war is singular even in the pathology that it gives rise to.

Another idea which is strongly held needs in our opinion to be re-examined; this is the notion of the relative harmlessness of these reactional disorders. It is true that others have described, but always as exceptional cases, certain secondary psychoses, that is to say cases where the whole of the personality is disrupted definitively. It seems to us that here the rule is rather the frequent malignancy of these pathological processes. These are disorders which persist for months on end, making a mass attack against the ego, and practically always leaving as their sequel a weakness which is almost visible to the naked eye. According to all available evidence, the future of such patients is mortgaged. An example will best illustrate our point of view.

In one of the African countries which have been independent for several years we had occasion to receive a visit from a patriot who had been in the resistance. This man in his thirties came to ask us for advice and help, for around a certain date each year he suffered from prolonged insomnia, accompanied by anxiety and suicidal obsessions. The critical date was that when on instructions from his organization he had placed a bomb somewhere. Ten people had been killed as a result.[2]

This militant, who never for a single moment thought of repudiating his past action, realized very clearly the manner in which he himself had to pay the price of national independence. It is border-line cases such as his which raise the question of responsibility within the revolutionary framework.

The observations noted here cover the period running from 1954–59. Certain patients were examined in Algeria, either in hospital centers or as private patients. The others were cared for by the health divisions of the Army of National Liberation [ALN].

Series A

Five cases are cited here. They are cases of Algerians or Europeans who had very clear symptoms of mental disorders of the reactionary type.

Case No. 1: Impotence in an Algerian Following the Rape of His Wife.

B——— is a man twenty-six years old. He came to see us on the advice of the Health Service of the FLN [Front of National Liberation] for treatment of insomnia and persistent headaches. A former taxi-driver, he had worked in the nationalist parties since he was eighteen. Since 1955 he had been a member of a branch of the FLN. He had several times used his taxi for the transport of political pamphlets and also political personnel. When the repression increased in ferocity, the FLN decided to bring the war into the urban centers. B——— thus came to have the task of driving commandos to the vicinity of attacking points, and quite often waited for them at those points to bring them back.

One day however, in the middle of the European part of the town, after fairly considerable fighting a very large number of arrests forced him to abandon his taxi, and the commando unit broke up and scattered. B———, who managed to escape through the enemy lines, took refuge at a friend's house. Some days later, without having been able to get back to his home, on the orders of his superiors he joined the nearest band of Maquis.

For several months he was without news of his wife and his little girl of a year and eight months. On the other hand he learned that the police spent several weeks on end searching the town. After two years spent in the Maquis he received a message from his wife in which she asked him to forget her, for she had been dishonored and he ought not to think of taking up their life together again. He was extremely anxious and asked his commander's leave to go home secretly. This was refused him, but on the other hand measures were taken for a member of the FLN to make contact with B———'s wife and parents.

Two weeks later a detailed report reached the commander of B———'s unit.

His abandoned taxi had been discovered with two machine-gun magazines in it. Immediately afterward French soldiers accompanied by policemen went to his house. Finding he was absent, they took his wife away and kept her for over a week.

She was questioned about the company her husband kept and beaten fairly brutally for two days. But the third day a French soldier (she was not able to say whether he was an officer) made the others leave the room and then raped her. Some time later a second soldier, this time with others present, raped her, saying to her, "If ever you see your filthy husband again don't forget to tell him what we did to you." She remained another week without undergoing any fresh questioning. After this she was escorted back to her dwelling. When she told her story to her mother, the latter persuaded her to tell B——— everything. Thus as soon as contact was re-established with her husband, she confessed her dishonor to him. Once the first shock had passed, and since moreover every minute of his time was filled by activity, B——— was able to overcome his feelings. For several months he had heard many stories of Algerian women who had been raped or tortured, and he had occasion to see the husbands of these violated women; thus his personal misfortunes and his dignity as an injured husband remained in the background.

In 1958, he was entrusted with a mission abroad. When it was time to rejoin his unit, certain fits of absence of mind and sleeplessness made his comrades and superiors anxious about him. His departure was postponed and it was decided he should have a medical examination. This was when we saw him. He seemed at once easy to get to know; a mobile face: perhaps a bit too mobile. Smiles slightly exaggerated; surface well-being: "I'm really very well, very well indeed. I'm feeling better now. Give me a tonic or two, a few vitamins, and I'll build myself up a bit." A basic anxiety came up to break the surface. He was at once sent to the hospital.

From the second day on, the screen of optimism melted away, and what we saw in front of us was a thoughtful, depressed man, suffering from loss of appetite, who kept to his bed. He avoided political discussion and showed a marked lack of interest in everything to do with the national struggle. He avoided listening to any news which had a bearing on the war of liberation. Any approach to his difficulties was extremely long, but at the end of several days we were able to reconstruct his story.

During his stay abroad, he tried to carry through a sexual affair which was unsuccessful. Thinking that this was due to fatigue, a normal result of forced marches and periods of undernourishment, he again tried two weeks later. Fresh failure. Talked about it to a friend who advised him to try vitamin B-12. Took this in form of pills; another attempt, another failure. Moreover, a few seconds before the act, he had an irresistible impulse to tear up a photo of his little girl. Such a symbolic liaison might have caused us to think that unconscious impulsions of an incestuous nature were present. However, several interviews and a dream, in which the patient saw the rapid rotting away of a little cat accompanied by unbearably evil smells, led us to take quite another course. "That girl," he said to us one day, speaking of his little daughter, "has something rotten about her." From this period on, his insomnia became extremely marked, and in spite of fairly large doses of neuroleptics, a state of anxiety excitation was remarked which the Service found rather worrying. Then he spoke to us for the first time about his wife, laughing and saying to us: "She's tasted the French." It was at that moment that we reconstructed the whole story. The weaving of events to form a pattern was made explicit. He told us that before every sexual attempt, he thought of his wife. All his confidences appeared to us to be of fundamental interest.

> I married this girl although I loved my cousin. But my cousin's parents had arranged a match for their daughter with somebody else. So I accepted the first wife my parents found for me. She was nice, but I didn't love her. I used always to say to myself: "You're young yet; wait a bit and when you've found the right girl, you'll get a divorce and you'll make a happy marriage." So you see I wasn't very attached to my wife. And with the troubles, I got further apart than ever. In the end, I used to come and eat my meals and sleep almost without speaking to her.
>
> In the Maquis, when I heard that she'd been raped by the French, I first of all felt angry with the swine. Then I said "Oh, well, there's not much harm done; she wasn't killed. She can start her life over again." And then a few weeks later I came to realize that they'd raped her *because they were looking for me.* In fact, it was to punish her for keeping silence that she'd been violated. She could have very well told them at least the name of one of the chaps in the movement, and from that they could have searched

out the whole network, destroyed it, and maybe even arrested me. That wasn't a simple rape, for want of something better to do, or for sadistic reasons like those I've had occasion to see in the villages; it was the rape of an obstinate woman, who was ready to put up with everything rather than sell her husband. And the husband in question, *it was me*. This woman had saved my life and had protected the organization. It was because of me that she had been dishonored. And yet she didn't say to me: "Look at all I've had to bear for you." On the contrary, she said: "Forget about me; begin your life over again, for I have been dishonored."

It was from that moment on that I made my own decision to take back my wife after the war; for it must be said that I've seen peasants drying the tears of their wives after having seen them raped under their very eyes. This left me very much shaken; I must admit moreover that at the beginning I couldn't understand their attitude. But we increasingly came to intervene in such circumstances in order to explain matters to the civilians. I've seen civilians willing proposing marriage to a girl who was violated by the French soldiers, and who was with child by them. All this led me to reconsider the problem of my wife.

So I decided to take her back; but I didn't know at all how I'd behave when I saw her. And often, while I was looking at the photo of my daughter, I used to think that she too was dishonored, like as if everything that had to do with my wife was rotten. If they'd tortured her or knocked out all her teeth or broken an arm I wouldn't have minded. But that thing—how can you forget a thing like that? And why did she have to tell me about it all?

He then asked me if his "sexual failing" was in my opinion caused by his worries.

I replied: "It is not impossible."

Then he sat up in bed.

"What would you do if all this had happened to you?"

"I don't know."

"Would you take back your wife?"

"I think I would . . . "

"Ah, there you are, you see. You're not quite sure . . . "

He held his head in his hands and after a few seconds left the room.

From that day on, he was progressively more willing to listen to political discussions and at the same time the headaches and lack of appetite lessened considerably.

After two weeks he went back to his unit. Before he left he told me:

"When independence comes, I'll take my wife back. If it doesn't work out between us, I'll come and see you in Algiers."

Case No. 2: Undifferentiated Homicidal Impulsions Found in a Survivor of a Mass Murder.

S———, thirty-seven years old, a *fellah*. Comes from a village in the country around Constantine. Never took any part in politics. From the outset of the war, his district was the scene of fierce battles between the Algerian forces and the French army. S——— thus had occasion to see dead and wounded. But he continued to keep out of things. From time to time however, in common with the people as a whole, the peasantry of his village used to come to the aid of Algerian fighting men who were passing through. But one day, early in 1958, a deadly ambush was laid not far from the village. After this the enemy forces went into operation and besieged the village, which in fact had no soldiers in it. All the inhabitants were summoned and questioned; nobody replied. A few hours after, a French officer arrived by helicopter and said: "There's been too much talk about this village. Destroy it." The soldiers began to set fire to the houses while the women who were trying to get a few clothes together or save some provisions were driven away by blows with rifle-butts. Some peasants took advantage of the general confusion to run away. The officer gave the order to bring together the men who remained and had them brought out to near a watercourse where the killing began. Twenty-nine men were shot at point-blank range. S——— was wounded by two bullets which went through his right thigh and his left arm respectively; the arm injury gave rise to a fracture of the humerus.

S——— fainted and came to to find himself in the midst of a group of ALN. He was treated by the Health Service and evacuated as soon as it was possible to move him. While on the way, his behavior became more and more abnormal, and worried his escort continually. He demanded a gun, although he was helpless and a civilian, and refused to walk in front of anybody, no matter who they were. He refused to have anyone behind him. One night he got hold of a soldier's gun and awkwardly tried to fire on the sleeping soldiers. He was disarmed rather roughly. From then on they tied his hands together, and it was thus that he arrived at the Center.

He began by telling us that he wasn't dead yet and that he had played a good trick on the others. Bit by bit, we managed to reconstruct his story of the assassination he had attempted. S——— was not anxious, he was in fact rather overexcited, with violent phases of agitation, accompanied by screaming. He did not break anything much, but tired everybody out by his incessant chatter, and the whole Service was permanently on the alert on account of his declared intention of "killing everybody." During his stay in the hospital he attacked about eight patients with makeshift weapons. Nurses and doctors were not spared either. We almost wondered whether we were not witnessing one of those masked forms of epilepsy which is characterized by a wholesale aggressivity which is nearly always present.

Deep sleep treatment was then tried. From the third day on, a daily interview made it possible for us to better understand the moving force of the pathological process. The patient's intellectual confusion progressively toned down. Here are some extracts from his statements:

> God is with me . . . but he certainly isn't with those who are dead. . . . I've had hellish good luck. . . . In life you've got to kill so as not to be killed. . . . When I think that I knew nothing at all about all that business. . . . There are Frenchmen in our midst. They disguise themselves as Arabs. They've all got to be killed. Give me a machine-gun. All these so-called Algerians are really Frenchmen . . . and they won't leave me alone. As soon as I want to go to sleep they come into my room. But now I know all about them. Everyone wants to kill me. But I'll defend myself. I'll kill them all, every single one of them. I'll cut their throats one after the other, and yours with them. You all want to kill me but you should set about it differently. I'd kill you all as soon as look at you, big ones and little ones, women, children, dogs, birds, donkeys . . . everyone will be dead. And afterward I'll be able to sleep in peace. . . .

All this was said in jerks; the patient's attitude remained hostile, suspicious, and aloof.

After three weeks, his state of excitement had disappeared, but a certain reticence and a tendency to seek solitude gave us grounds for fearing a more serious evolution of his disorder. However after a month he asked to be let out in order to learn a trade that would be compatible with his disability. He was then entrusted to the care of the Social Service of the FLN. We saw him six months after, and he was going on well.

Case No. 3: Marked Anxiety Psychosis of the Depersonalization Type After the Murder of a Woman While Temporarily Insane.

Dj————, a former student, a soldier in the ALN, nineteen years old. His illness already dated from some months back by the time he came to the Center. His appearance was characteristic: he seemed very depressed, his hands were constantly moist and his lips were dry; his chest was lifted by continual sighs. Pernicious insomnia; two attempts at suicide since the trouble started. During the conversation, he struck hallucinatory attitudes while listening. Sometimes his glance fixed itself for a few seconds on a point in space, while his face lit up, giving the impression to observers that the patient was witnessing a play. Thoughts woolly. Certain phenomena known in psychiatry by the name of blocking: a gesture or phrase is begun and then suddenly interrupted without apparent reason. But in particular one element aroused our particular attention: the patient talked of his blood being spilt, of his arteries which were being emptied and of his heart which kept missing a beat. He implored us to stop the hemorrhage and not to let him be "sucked by a vampire" within the very precincts of the hospital. Sometimes he could not speak any more, and asked us for a pencil. Wrote: "I have lost my voice; my whole life is ebbing away." This living depersonalization gave us reason to believe that the illness had reached a serious stage of development.

Several times during the course of our conversations, the patient spoke to us of a woman who when night fell came to persecute him. Having learnt beforehand that his mother whom he had been very fond of was dead, and that nothing had been able to console him for her loss (his voice had considerably sunk as he spoke of her, and he shed some tears), I directed the investigation toward the maternal image. When I asked him to describe the woman who obsessed him, I might even say persecuted him, he declared that she was not an unknown person, that he knew her very well, and that it was he who had killed her. It was thus a matter of finding out whether we had to deal with an unconscious guilt complex following on the death of the mother, as Freud has described in *Mourning and Melancholia*. We asked the patient to talk to us about this woman in greater detail, since he had known her so well, and since it was he who had killed her. Thus we were able to reconstruct the following story:

> I left the town where I had been a student to join the Maquis. After some months, I had news of my people. I learnt that my mother had been killed point-blank by a French soldier and two of my sisters had been taken to the soldiers' quarters. Up to now, I have had no news of what happened to them. I was terribly shaken by the death of my mother. Since my father had died some years before, I was the only man in the family, and my sole ambition had always been to manage to do something to make life easier for my mother and my sisters. One day we went to an estate belonging to settlers, where the agent, who was an active colonialist, had already killed two Algerian civilians. We came to his house, at night, but he wasn't there. Only his wife was at home. When she saw us, she started to cry and implored us not to kill her: "I know you've come for my husband," she said, "but he isn't here. I've told him again and again not to have anything to do with politics." We decided to wait for her husband. But as far as I was concerned, when I looked at that woman I thought of my mother. She was sitting in an armchair and her thoughts seemed to be elsewhere. I wondered why we didn't kill her; then all of a sudden she noticed I was looking at her. She flung herself upon me screaming "Please, please don't kill me . . . I have children." A moment after she was dead; I'd killed her with my knife. My commander disarmed me and ordered me to

leave. I was questioned by the platoon commander a few days later. I thought I was going to be shot, but I didn't give a damn.[3] And then I started vomiting after every meal, and I slept badly. After that this woman started coming every night and asking for my blood. But my mother's blood—where's that?

At nightfall that evening, as soon as the patient went to bed, the room was "invaded by women" in spite of everything. It was a manifold repetition of the same woman. Every one of them had an open wound in her stomach. They were bloodless, pale, and terribly thin. They tormented the young patient and insisted that he should give them back their spilt blood. At this moment the sound of running water filled the room and grew so loud that it seemed like a thundering waterfall, and the young patient saw the parquet of his room drenched with blood—his blood—while the women slowly got their color back, and their wounds began to close up. The patient awoke, bathed with sweat and in deep distress, and remained in a state of nervous excitement until the dawn.

The young patient was treated for several weeks, after which time the oneiroid symptoms (nightmares) had practically disappeared. However, a serious deficiency remained in his personality. When he started thinking of his mother, the disemboweled woman rose up before him in redoubled horror. Though it may appear unscientific, in our opinion time alone can bring some improvement to the disrupted personality of this young man.

Case No. 4: A European Policeman in a Depressed State Meets While Under Hospital Treatment One of His Victims, an Algerian Patriot Who Is Suffering from Stupor.

A——, twenty-eight years old, no children. We learnt that for several years both he and his wife underwent treatment, unfortunately with no success, in order to have children. He was sent to us by his superiors because he had behavior disturbances.

Immediate contact seemed fairly good. The patient spoke to us spontaneously about his difficulties. Satisfactory relations with his wife and parents-in-law. His trouble was that at night he heard screams which prevented him from sleeping. In fact, he told us that for the last few weeks before going to bed he shut the shutters and stopped up all the windows (it was summer) to the complete despair of his wife, who was stifled by the heat. Moreover, he stuffed his ears with cotton wool in order to make the screams seem less piercing. He sometimes even in the middle of the night turned on the wireless or put on some music in order not to hear this nocturnal uproar. He consequently explained to us at full length the whole story that was troubling him.

A few months before, he had been transferred to an anti-FLN brigade. At the beginning, he was entrusted with surveying certain shops or cafés; but after some weeks he used to work almost exclusively at the police headquarters. Here he came to deal with interrogations; and these never occurred without some "knocking about." "The thing was that they never would own up to anything." He explained:

> Sometimes we almost wanted to tell them that if they had a bit of consideration for us they'd speak out without forcing us to spend hours tearing information word by word out of them. But you might as well talk to the wall. To all the questions we asked they'd only say "I don't know." Even when we asked them what their name was. If we asked them where they lived, they'd say "I don't know." So of course, we have to go through with it. But they scream too much. At the beginning that made me laugh. But afterward I was a bit shaken. Nowadays as soon as I hear someone shouting I can tell you exactly at what stage of the questioning we've got to. The chap who's had two blows of the fist

and a belt of the baton behind his ear has a certain way of speaking, of shouting, and of saying he's innocent. After he's been left two hours strung up by his wrists he has another kind of voice. After the bath, still another. And so on. But above all it's after the electricity that it becomes really too much. You'd say that the chap was going to die any minute. Of course there are some that don't scream; those are the tough ones. But they think they're going to be killed right away. But we're not interested in killing them. What we want is information. When we're dealing with those tough ones, the first thing we do is make them squeal; and sooner or later we manage it. That's already a victory. Afterward we go on. Mind you, we'd like to avoid that. But they don't make things easy for us. Now I've come so as I hear their screams even when I'm at home. Especially the screams of the ones who died at the police headquarters. Doctor, I'm fed up with this job. And if you manage to cure me, I'll ask to be transferred to France. If they refuse, I'll resign.

Faced with such a picture, I prescribed sick leave. As the patient in question refused to go to the hospital, I treated him privately. One day, shortly before the therapeutic treatment was due to begin, I had an urgent call from my department. When A——— reached my house, my wife asked him to wait for me, but he preferred to go for a walk in the hospital grounds, and then come back to meet me. A few minutes later as I was going home I passed him on the way. He was leaning against a tree, looking overcome, trembling and drenched with sweat: in fact having an anxiety crisis. I took him into my car and drove him to my house. Once he was lying on the sofa, he told me he had met one of my patients in the hospital who had been questioned in the police barracks (he was an Algerian patriot) and who was under treatment for "disorders of a stuporous nature following on shock." I then learnt that the policeman had taken an active part in inflicting torture on my patient. I administered some sedatives which calmed A———'s anxiety. After he had gone, I went to the house in the hospital where the patriot was being cared for. The personnel had noticed nothing; but the patient could not be found. Finally we managed to discover him in a toilet where he was trying to commit suicide: he on his side had recognized the policeman and thought that he had come to look for him and take him back again to the barracks.

Afterward, A——— came back to see me several times, and after a very definite improvement in his condition, managed to get back to France on account of his health. As for the Algerian patriot, the personnel spent a long time convincing him that the whole thing was an illusion, that policemen were not allowed inside the hospital, that he was very tired, that he was there to be looked after, etc.

Case No. 5: A European Police Inspector Who Tortured His Wife and Children.

R———, thirty years old. Came of his own accord to consult us. He was a police inspector and stated that for several weeks "things weren't working out." Married, had three children. He smoked a lot: five packets of cigarettes a day. He had lost his appetite and his sleep was frequently disturbed by nightmares. These nightmares had no special distinguishing features. What bothered him most were what he called "fits of madness." In the first place, he disliked being contradicted:

> Can you give me an explanation for this, doctor: as soon as someone goes against me I want to hit him. Even outside my job, I feel I want to settle the fellows who get in my way, even for nothing at all. Look here, for example, suppose I go to the kiosk to buy

the papers. There's a lot of people. Of course you have to wait. I hold out my hand (the chap who keeps the kiosk is a pal of mine) to take the papers. Someone in the line gives me a challenging look and says "Wait your turn." Well, I feel I want to beat him up and I say to myself, "If I had you for a few hours my fine fellow you wouldn't look so clever afterwards."

The patient dislikes noise. At home he wants to hit everybody all the time. In fact, he does hit his children, even the baby of twenty months, with unaccustomed savagery.

But what really frightened him was one evening when his wife had criticized him particularly for hitting his children too much. (She had even said to him, "My word, anyone'd think you were going mad.") He threw himself upon her, beat her, and tied her to a chair, saying to himself "I'll teach her once and for all that I'm master in this house."

Fortunately his children began roaring and crying. He then realized the full gravity of his behavior, untied his wife and the next day decided to consult a doctor, "a nerve special-ist." He stated that "before, he wasn't like that"; he said that he very rarely punished his children and at all events never fought with his wife. The present phenomena had ap-peared "since the troubles." "The fact is" he said:

nowadays we have to work like troopers. Last week, for example, we operated like as if we belonged to the army. Those gentlemen in the government say there's no war in Algeria and that the arm of the law, that's to say the police, ought to restore order. But there *is* a war going on in Algeria, and when they wake up to it it'll be too late. The thing that kills me most is the torture. You don't know what that is, do you? Sometimes I torture people for ten hours at a stretch. . . .

"What happens to you when you are torturing?"

You may not realize, but it's very tiring. . . . It's true we take it in turns, but the question is to know when to let the next chap have a go. Each one thinks he's going to get the information at any minute and takes good care not to let the bird go to the next chap after he's softened him up nicely, when of course the other chap would get the honor and glory of it. So sometimes we let them go; and sometimes we don't.

Sometimes we even offer the chap money, money out of our own pockets, to try to get him to talk. Our problem is as follows: are you able to make this fellow talk? It's a question of personal success. You see, you're competing with the others. In the end your fists are ruined. So you call in the Senegalese. But either they hit too hard and destroy the creature or else they don't hit hard enough and it's no good. In fact, you have to be intelligent to make a success of that sort of work. You have to know when to lay it on and when to lay it off. You have to have a flair for it. When the chap is softened up, it's not worth your while going on hitting him. That's why you have to do the work yourself; you can judge better how you're getting on. I'm against the ones that have the chap dealt with by others and simply come to see every hour or so what state he's in. Above all, what you mustn't do is to give the chap the impression that he won't get away alive from you. Because then he wonders what's the use of talking if that won't save his life. In that case you'll have no chance at all of getting anything out of him. He must go on hoping; hope's the thing that'll make him talk.

But the thing that worries me most is this affair with my wife. It's certain that there's something wrong with me. You've got to cure me, doctor.

His superiors refused to give him sick leave, and since moreover the patient did not wish to have a psychiatrist's certificate, we tried to give him treatment "while working full time." The weaknesses of such a procedure may easily be imagined. This man knew per-fectly well that his disorders were directly caused by the kind of activity that went on inside the rooms where interrogations were carried out, even though he tried to throw the responsibility totally upon "present troubles." As he could not see his way to stopping torturing people (that made nonsense to him for in that case he would have to resign) he asked me without beating about the bush to help him to go on torturing Algerian patriots without any prickings of conscience, without any behavior problems, and with complete equanimity.[4]

SERIES B

We have here brought together certain cases or groups of cases in which the event giving rise to the illness is in the first place the atmosphere of total war which reigns in Algeria.

Case No. 1: The Murder by Two Young Algerians, Thirteen and Fourteen Years Old Respectively, of Their European Playmate.

We had been asked to give expert medical advice in a legal matter. Two young Algerians thirteen and fourteen years old, pupils in a primary school, were accused of having killed one of their European schoolmates. They admitted having done it. The crime was reconstructed, and photos were added to the record. Here one of the children could be seen holding the victim while the other struck at him with a knife. The little defendants did not go back on their declarations. We had long conversations with them. We here reproduce the most characteristic of their remarks:

a) The Boy Thirteen Years Old:

"We weren't a bit cross with him. Every Thursday we used to go and play with catapults together, on the hill above the village. He was a good friend of ours. He usn't to go to school any more because he wanted to be a mason like his father. One day we decided to kill him, because the Europeans want to kill all the Arabs. We can't kill big people. But we could kill ones like him, because he was the same age as us. We didn't know how to kill him. We wanted to throw him into a ditch, but he'd only have been hurt. So we got the knife from home and we killed him."

"But why did you pick on him?"

"Because he used to play with us. Another boy wouldn't have gone up the hill with us."

"And yet you were pals?"

"Well then, why do they want to kill us? His father is in the militia and he said we ought to have our throats cut."

"But he didn't say anything to you?"

"Him? No."

"You know he is dead now."

"Yes."

"What does being dead mean?"

"When it's all finished, you go to heaven."

"Was it you that killed him?"

"Yes."

"Does having killed somebody worry you?"

"No, since they want to kill us, so . . . "

"Do you mind being in prison?"

"No."

b) The Boy Fourteen Years Old:

This young defendant was in marked contrast to his schoolfellow. He was already almost a man, and an adult in his muscular control, his appearance, and the content of his replies. He did not deny having killed either. Why had he killed? He did not reply to the question but asked me had I ever seen a European in prison. Had there ever been a European arrested and sent to prison after the murder of an Algerian? I replied that in fact I had never seen any Europeans in prison.

NOTES

1. In the unpublished introduction to the first two editions of *L'an V de la Révolution Algérienne*, we have already pointed out that a whole generation of Algerians, steeped in wanton, generalized homicide with all the psycho-affective consequences that this entails, will be the human legacy of France in Algeria. Frenchmen who condemn the torture in Algeria constantly adopt a point of view which is strictly French. We do not reproach them for this; we merely point it out: they wish to protect the consciences of the actual torturers who today have full power to carry on their work; they wish at the same time to try to avoid the moral contamination of the young people of France. As far as we are concerned we are totally in accord with this attitude. Certain notes here brought together, especially in Cases 4 and 5 in Series A, are sad illustrations and justifications for this obsession which haunts French believers in democracy. But our purpose is in any case to show that torture, as might well be expected, upsets most profoundly the personality of the person who is tortured.

2. The circumstances surrounding the appearance of these disorders are interesting for several reasons. Some months after his country's independence was declared, he had made the acquaintance of certain nationals of the former colonial power, and he had found them very likeable. These men and women greeted the new independent state warmly and paid tribute to the courage of the patriots who had fought in the struggle for national freedom. The former militant therefore had what might be called an attack of vertigo. He wondered with a feeling of anguish whether among the victims of the bomb there had been people like his new acquaintants. It was true that the café that it was aimed at was a meeting place for notorious racists; but there was nothing to prevent a quite ordinary passer-by from going in and having a drink. From the first day that he suffered from vertigo the man tried to avoid thinking of these former occurrences. But paradoxically, a few days before the crucial date, the first symptoms made their appearance. After that, they reappeared with great regularity.

In other words, we are forever pursued by our actions. Their ordering, their circumstances, and their motivation may perfectly well come to be profoundly modified *a posteriori*. This is merely one of the snares that history and its various influences sets for us. But can we escape becoming dizzy? And who can affirm that vertigo does not haunt the whole of existence?

3. After considering the medico-legal experts' report which emphasized the pathological character of the action, the legal proceedings which had been set in motion by the General Staff were closed.

4. With these observations we find ourselves in the presence of a coherent system which leaves nothing intact. The executioner who loves birds and enjoys the peace of listening to a symphony or a sonata is simply one stage in the process. Further on in it we may well find a whole existence which enters into complete and absolute sadism.

Amiri Baraka

(b. 1934, United States)

Revolutionary Culture and the Future of Pan African Culture

The definitions of culture that we find most useful are firstly Maulana Karenga's, that culture is a people's way of life, values, and the institutions created to perpetuate these values and that way of life. Culture, then, is how we live, but also what that means to us, and what are the objective and subjective *results* of that life.

It also seems true that culture is produced by society, i.e., by . . . people coming together and how and what they produce as a result of that, materially and spiritually. There is, as [Amilcar] Cabral said, ". . . the strong dependent and reciprocal relationship existing between the *cultural situation* and the *economic* (and political) *situation* in the behaviour of human societies. In fact, culture is always in the life of a society (open or closed) the more or less conscious result of the economic and political activities of that society, the more or less dynamic expression of the kinds of relationships which prevail in that society, on the one hand between man (considered individually or collectively) and nature, and on the other hand, among individuals, groups of individuals, social strata or classes."

Culture is important to discussions we hold here because we are talking in actuality about the liberation of African people throughout the world, and by that projection the liberation of the toiling, struggling masses of people throughout the world. Because, make no mistake, we cannot really be talking about one without the other! . . .

Talk of culture is relevant to this international struggle only in the sense that we understand that a culture can be progressive or reactionary. Culture is directly characterized, to paraphrase Cabral, "by the mode of production and the level of productive forces," i.e., the social utilization of the people, the means of production and stage of development of the society; its control of its environment and relationship to nature, as well as the relationship between people, and other material relationships. The national liberation movements, for instance, are the political expression of the culture whose values are mobilized in a revolutionary fashion. But Africans worldwide suffer under the yoke of the monopoly capitalist mode of production, as the victims of imperialism in one of its forms or another. Our cultures, therefore, are usually characterized as colonized, semi-colonized, neo-colonized, bureaucratic capitalist, comprador capitalist, etc. Either we are oppressed directly by the existence of these forms of imperialism as the mode of production, and the material and spiritual reality created by this mode, or else we are victimized by the internationally-developing native and pseudo-bourgeoisie. This bourgeoisie is part of the exploiting element of black parasites victimizing African people, in clear collaboration with imperialism, which exists in various degrees and forms in almost every African state or community in the world.

In such societies, one aspect of African culture (and sometimes it dominates all others) is reactionary, insofar as it actually collaborates or forms reactionary alliances with the enemies of the masses of the earth's peoples. However . . . in culture are to be found "the seeds of resistance," meaning that the consciousness, memory or will to maintain indigenous ways of life, values and institutions dissimilar to the forms put forward by colonialism or neo-colonialism are in themselves the kernel of potential new life, alternative forms and content in contrast to the culture of imperialism. . . .

The culture of imperialism must either eliminate the colonized or assimilate them in order to more thoroughly exploit them economically. Cultural aggression is a weapon for the destruction of the seeds of resistance and new (revolutionary) culture. Cultural aggression is more dangerous than most other forms of aggression by imperialism since in most cases the people do not even recognize it as aggression. It simply puts negative values and institutions in our societies—values and institutions committed to the exploitation of Africans.

The mode of production and the level of productive forces establish . . . the form a culture will take regardless of nation and race though nation and race are reflected directly in the total cultural existence of a society. Feudalism breeds and develops one kind of culture; capitalism, another. Colonialism and neo-colonialism will project the specific identity of a capitalist subculture, the perverted growth patterns of societies whose productive forces are blunted by foreign domination or continuing domination by international finance capital. . . .

Cabral had pointed out that, "Culture is a dynamic synthesis of the material and spiritual conditions of the society and expresses relationship both between man and nature and between the different classes within a society." The material reality of imperialism— both its economic base, and its ideated and institutional superstructure—is a culture, a way of life, values and institutions. The imposition of this culture at one level as an economic phenomenon, on another level as political aggression, on another as cultural aggression, reduces the people upon whom the aggression is perpetuated to a state of cultural and national underdevelopment.

This lack of development is the result of, and should be called, *exploitation*, created by a culture of the exploiters and resulting in a culture of the exploited. To exist in the culture of the exploited is to be deprived of history, repressed in the present, and uncertain of the future. To be of the culture of the exploited is to regard exploitation in too many instances as normality, or as an act of metaphysical significance, the will of some elemental, anti-African, non-material force that we cannot locate and destroy. In fact we might even worship that force even though it is obviously as anti-African as it is said to be invisible, and yet ultimately that force is material and locatable as the economic and political designs of imperialism.

Exploitation also shapes itself as a set of values, a way of life and institutions which perpetuate that exploitation. In the culture of the exploited, our religion, history, social organization, political organization, economic organization, creative motif and ethos are not only exploited but are themselves forms of exploitation. Our religion and mythology include deities that cannot defeat our enemies. Our history no longer exists or is merely a record of various times we have helped our enemies. Our social organization in reality is a reflection of the exploitative division of labour created by capitalism as well as the deadly capitalist ideology called racism. Our economic organization is as the host of an international parasite, our ethos too often is to either accept our oppression or collaborate actively with our oppressors and call it pragmatism.

The act of foreign domination was not the beginning of all backwardness and reaction in all aspects of our culture. There were backward aspects to African culture simply by virtue of our own historical development, but those aspects did not predominate. Foreign domination was the paralyzing of that culture and the active cultivation of that culture's most reactionary aspects. But foreign domination is also the beginning of *resistance,* so that even the culture of the exploited can develop a form to express the reactive and responsive energy of the oppressed to that oppression. If a man is beaten, there is pain, physical, mental, spiritual agony, depending on the severity of the beating. But what will the beaten man do as a result of the beating? Will he simply bleed and swell up or will he whimper on confusedly, stumble, curse, maybe try to make a deal, perhaps pretend he wasn't even assaulted? Or maybe he will fight!

The revolutionary's task is to transform his culture from an exploited culture to a militant, fighting one. It is this view that we believe is reflected when Comrade Cabral said:

> The more one realizes that the chief goal of the liberation movement goes beyond the achievement of political independence to the superior level of complete liberation of the productive forces and the construction of economic, social and cultural progress of a people, the more evident is the necessity of undertaking a selective analysis of the values of the culture within the framework of the struggle for liberation. The need for such an analysis of cultural values becomes more acute when, in order to face colonial violence, the liberation movement must mobilize and organize the people under the direction of a strong and disciplined political organization, in order to resort to violence in the cause of freedom—the armed struggle for national liberation!

The repression and destruction of our productive forces by imperialism in the era of neo-colonialism [are] only made possible through the collaboration of native agents. That such native agents abound in the African world is one sure indication of the reactionary nature of some aspects of our culture.

> The elements of democratic and socialist culture are present, if only in rudimentary form, in *every* national culture, since in *every* nation there are toiling and exploited masses whose conditions of life inevitably give rise to the ideology of democracy and socialism. But every nation also possesses a bourgeois culture, and most nations a reactionary and clerical culture as well. (Lenin, *Critical Remarks on the National Question.*)

In order to transform African culture . . . it will be necessary to mobilize the positive, democratic, socialist values of our people and to help eradicate the feudalistic, backward, defeatist, or opportunistic values. This requires self-criticism and criticism of our organizations of struggle and our communities at large. It requires self-discipline and relentless reviews of "the prospects for the struggle," i.e., evaluations of ourselves and our enemies, merciless objectivity and the undaunted construction of systems and institutions that objectify the values and ideology of revolution and socialism.

A revolutionary culture is simply the people, their way of life, their values and institutions consciously developed as a force for positive social transformation—the objective of cultural revolution, which is intense struggle to transform the values and life of the masses of people. Cultural revolution in China, progressive Africa and Southeast Asia has not only brought focus to conflict between the two world systems (capitalism and socialism) over the years, but even in the fortress of world imperialism, the USA, the Black Cultural Revolution of the 1960s, the Black Power Movement, led directly to a political reawakening to Africa. This Movement led to the understanding that Africans all over the world must be dedicated to the liberation and unification of the African continent under socialism, as well as to the self-determination, self-respect, and self-defence of Africans everywhere. . . .

Since identity is cultural, a cultural revolution is necessary to wrest that identity from reaction and thrust it toward progressive growth. One aspect of the identity revolution of African people has been nationalism. As Walter Rodney says, "The insistence on an African identity is a worthwhile corrective not only to bourgeois cultural imperialism but also to dogmatic expositions by self-styled Marxists or scientific socialists. . . ."

But nationalism is only an initial step and ultimately if nationalism is not merely a form of preparation for true national liberation struggle, leading directly to socialist construction or socialist revolution, then nationalism, black or yellow, becomes as reactionary as the European variety, and in direct or indirect partnership with it.

In such cases, nationalism becomes the last refuge of rascals and new capitalists yearning only for control of their national market which political liberation of superficial national liberation has made possible.

Nationalism as an aspect of revolutionary culture is necessary, so that anti-imperialist struggles are also clearly struggles to end all forms of foreign domination, including social imperialism. But political liberation and superficial national liberation struggles have created an international class of native agents directly related to imperialism, which is also international. For instance, the pseudo-powerful American black bourgeoisie and petty bourgeoisie could, objectively, be the new agents of yet another scramble for Africa, by saying "Black is Beautiful" or "We are an African people," yet representing the values and designs of U.S. imperialism.

There is a reactionary aspect to the Civil Rights movement (which corresponded to the political independence movement on the continent) and the Black Cultural Revolution that followed in the U.S. It is that the superficial aspects of these movements were co-opted, so that Black power pimps and African nationalist-capitalists abound. The return to the source that Cabral speaks of has become in many instances a display of irrelevance and opportunism, not a re-affirmation of struggle. The signal that the black petty bourgeoisie was ready to struggle on the side of Africa has been distorted too often to either politically-ineffective cults talking nonsense about atavistic, feudalistic Africa in the most modern technological state in the world and confusing that with revolutionary culture or it has been distorted to plain opportunism and neo-capitalist collaboration with imperialism. . . .

The cultural revolution is the result of political struggle or it is conceived as a method of raising the level of political struggle. But if it is authentic a cultural revolution is just that: radicalizing of the superstructure to better perceive the need to transform the material base, forcing the consciousness of the masses to awareness of their own needs. Both these nations that have had cultural revolutions and begun the rapid construction of socialism, and those nations that didn't have cultural revolutions but instead had political counterrevolutions, have proven that cultural revolution, the radical transformation of the ideas, values, institutions and way of life of the masses, is absolutely critical to continued positive national development.

It is also proven that these mass value transformations are a necessary part of the revolutionary program of any progressive nation seriously committed to raising the material and spiritual level of the people. It perhaps should be added that would-be revolutionary formations, revolutionary parties and other formations of struggle also need their own cultural revolutions, ranging from the purging of reactionaries and opportunists to the redefining of ideology and goals in the crucible of practice and in the act of struggle itself, if they are to remain pertinent to the changing realities of life and revolution.

But in creating a revolutionary culture we should try to institutionalize the process of cultural revolution, just as we institutionalize *unity-criticism-unity* within revolutionary formations as a mode of theoretical and practical movement. We shall institutionalize the self-criticism and criticism of African life and culture for the end of positive motion and constructing within the culture the forms and system that promote revolutionary dynamism as opposed to reactionary stagnation. Such stagnation is usually caused by opportunism and subjectivism, and the eradication of these should be our constant goal.

The fact that the political independence movement of the 1960s in Africa and in the West Indies (which was linked directly to the Civil Rights and Black Power Movements in the United States) has in most cases been spent or co-opted and drained of its revolutionary motion should mean that, for progressive Africans world-wide, we should be insisting on some form of values transformation to restore the revolutionary dynamism to our struggle that existed during that earlier period. Obviously the national Liberation Movements in Guinea-Bissau, Angola, Mozambique, Zimbabwe, Namibia, Azania and elsewhere in the African world provide the impetus of a great part of the present revolutionary dynamic of African culture—so much so that sometimes the bodies that represent the established governments of African nation-states on the continent and the West Indies find themselves at variance with the Liberation Movements about the degree of commitment to total liberation and self-reliance to which these governments should pledge themselves.

The revolutionary stance of the political independence movements which led to the gradual end of colonialism in Africa has become, in too many cases, the accommodating posture of the "pragmatic" semi-collaborator with imperialism, even to the extent, in some extreme cases, where African governments do not even want to struggle directly with the blatant colonialists Portugal, South Africa and Rhodesia. Of course, direct struggle with the manipulators of international finance capital situated in the United States, Western Europe and Japan is completely out of the question.

The nations in question, the structures in question, are desperately in need of cultural revolutions, because since the political independence movement begun in the late 1950s in too many cases the internal contradictions of those movements have always been characterized by sectors of African society which simply wanted the colonialists to leave so that African ruling elites could spring into reaction, in open collaboration with world imperialism, no matter their nationalist rhetoric. This is true all over the African world, not merely on the continent. The radical transformation of the values, way of life and institutions of these societies is what is necessary, leading toward socialist construction.

It is reactionary to pretend that there is no class formation and resultant strife, i.e., class struggle, throughout the African world. To say otherwise at this point in history is to be innocent of reality or mischievous for profit. The culture of Africa circa 1960 and the culture of the 1970s is radically changed. The principal struggle is not against colonialism, despite the continued existence of minority white regimes and Portuguese colonialism. The principal struggle in this era is against neo-colonialism. . . .

Unfortunately, in some cases we are obstructed from development by a nationalist mystification of governments because for so long we were subjected to colonial ones, so that the very existence of African governments sometimes moves us to such rapture we cannot be objective and therefore supportive of the social transformation needed by the masses of Africans worldwide.

A neo-colonial relationship to imperialism by African governments is the shaper of the culture which these governments politically express. Alternatively, Liberation Movements, by the act of their revolutionary struggle against racism and imperialism, give to their culture a revolutionary dynamic which is the positive values of the culture mobilized for struggle. . . .

We must be wary of constructions such as the OAU [Organization of African Unity] which represent in one sense, institutionalizing of the political gains of the 50s and 60s without the necessary reshaping that would result from adapting to the new dimensions of oppression brought on by the neo-colonial 1970s and the continued success of imperialism. Most African governments are at least in need of cultural revolutions so that they begin to value radical social transformation, rather than consolidation of economic and political dependency relations with monopoly capitalism.

The fact that revolutionary movements within the West Indies have been almost totally prevented from attending this Sixth Pan African Congress by neo-colonialism is screeching testimony to the existence and strength of such dependency relations, and to how reactionary Black government relations with radical political sectors move. It is ironic that the Fifth Pan African Congress was banished to Manchester, England, because of colonialism, which the participants of that historic meeting pledged to help eliminate; but with the elimination of colonialism, now the Sixth Pan African Congress is distorted by neo-colonialism which will not allow its severest critics to point out its negativity to the entire African World, and to oppressed people everywhere. So even though most of Africa is "independent," some of its sons and daughters in the diaspora cannot be welcomed back because of the mystification of governments above people, and the determination of neo-colonialism not to be criticized, and thence given the possibility of self-criticism and self-transformation. But as one goal of the Fifth Pan African Congress was the destruction of colonialism, one goal of the Sixth Pan African Congress should be the elimination of neo-colonialism, and the total unity and independence of Africa.

Pan Africanism is meaningless without it being conceived as socialist construction, as well as a means of heightening the struggle for world socialism, the literal reorganization of world society and redistribution of the world's wealth. [Kwame] Nkrumah wrote, "At the core of the concept of African unity lies socialism and the socialist definition of the new African society." Unified Independent Africa, struggling for socialist reconstruction, would be an ultimate weapon for the destruction of capitalism and the advent of socialism, internationally. Why? Because we know that one of the important supports for the Liberation Movements, which at their most progressive are socialist revolutions, has been the existence of socialist states. China benefited by the existence of the Soviet Union, whereas the Soviet Union was surrounded completely by capitalist and pre-capitalist states. North Korea, Cuba, North Viet Nam, as well as Guinea, Tanzania, Somalia, Congo, have all benefited by the existence of socialist states. In fact, if we consider not only the subjectivism of the governments, but the needs of the masses as well, all Africa has benefited by the existence of socialist states. The existence of socialist states has transformed world culture and taken one third of the world's peoples away from imperialism already!

A Pan African culture would mean that the values, way of life and institutions of Africa would first be mobilized and then be organized and politicized to promote a unified, independent, socialist, continental African state, which would, by its creation, intensify the struggle for black self-determination, self-respect and self-defence everywhere Africans are. This Pan African culture would do so first by consciously proposing to create changes and also by being a "socialist liberation movement in power," continentally mobilized to defeat capitalism and imperialism and build socialism.

The OAU was conceived in 1963 as a Pan Africanist institution, but in a decade the contradiction of nation-statism has often transformed this continent-wide African body into a protector of the national hegemony of a developing African petty-bourgeoisie. Moreover, to be truly Pan African, Africans in the diaspora, the populations of North America, the West Indies, South and Central America, and the Pacific Islands must be considered as needed members of that body, so that Pan Africanism means world African unity as well.

It is only in progressive African states and the Liberation Movements that one even hears a great deal about Pan Africanism. In many of the nation-states, talk of Pan African- ism is considered at best naive and idealistic—almost as naive and idealistic as talk about socialism. The reactionary nationalist culture that has sprung up can only *talk*, when it does, about the needs of the masses. But the African masses can only be truly provided for by a continental African state, struggling to build socialism internally and internationally, and to defeat capitalism and imperialism.

The failure to understand the integral nature of Africans in the diaspora not only in the struggle to liberate Africa, but also in the struggle to liberate all oppressed people, is finally simply reactionary and means not understanding, for example, that U.S. imperial- ism is in charge of all imperialism. Pierre Jalee, writing in *Imperialism in the 70's*, points out that the gross national product of the United States "all by itself is greater than GNP of all the other capitalist countries combined." Jalee posits that the Black Liberation Move- ment in the U.S. and in the West Indies, harmonized with progressive action on the conti- nent in opposition to new systems of imperialism, could produce vanguard anti-racist, anti-imperialist organizations of revolutionaries struggling within the heart of the chief fortress of imperialism. These organizations would make one of their chief strategic thrusts the liberation of Africa and the resolution of the antagonistic contradiction be- tween the people and imperialism.

If the principal contradiction in the world today is between imperialism and the peo- ple, the most intense or most antagonistic manifestation of that contradiction is between imperialism and the Third World. This is primarily because, as Jalee says . . . "The domina- tion and exploitation of the Third World [is] the basic material condition for the survival of imperialism," but also because the cultural clash that has always existed and intensified between the way of life of the exploiters and the way of life, values, etc., of the exploited [is] therein most sharply drawn.

We know that where cultures are most dissimilar is where imperialism has the hardest time absorbing the people. This is one of the intensifying factors in the contradiction between imperialism and the Third World. We should be most sensitive to that contradic- tion, that vicious conflict between Africans on the continent, in the West Indies, the Pacific Islands or North America, and imperialism, because we share a common heritage, though it is variously reconstructed by our specific experience and history, spread as we are throughout the world.

Oppression has singled us out and generalized our condition, and therefore brought a general description to our various African sub-cultures, as the wretched of the earth. Nkrumah was fond of saying that imperialism will find its grave in Africa. We would like to add that imperialism will be driven to that grave in the struggle with African people all over the world. The 30 to 40 million Africans in the United States alone, that part of the

Third World that capitalism stole from Africa to build North America's industrial magnitude, share the general culture of oppression to which most Africans on this planet are heir, though there is new, swiftly-consolidating class formation in that community and a Black, native, pseudo and petty-bourgeoisie who are the objective servants of imperialism. While we know that our struggle to liberate ourselves in North America cannot be separated from the struggle for liberation to which all other dependent and powerless nations on that continent must commit themselves, we are also connected to Africa by race, history, culture, politics and emotion. There can be no true Pan Africanist thrust without a deep reflection and understanding as to the actual nature of the struggles in the West Indies, North America, South America and the Pacific Islands, and their relationship to the liberation of the continent of Africa, and also an understanding of the continent of Africa's relationship to those Black communities' liberation.

They are inextricably bound together because Africans are potentially the most severe critics, the most extreme battlers against imperialism. Africans in the United States, the chief fortress of imperialism, mobilized in anti-racist and anti-imperialism formation, developing revolutionary value systems that will allow them to utilize the technological advance of North American society without being subjugated by its anti-human philosophies and culture, must play an important role in defeating imperialism. But this role can only be completely fulfilled in concert with the struggle of the Third World, especially the struggle of African people everywhere. It is this kind of Third World and Pan African integration that will help formulate values of international struggle for the communities in the diaspora and the continent, rather than narrow nationalist, or opportunist, or assimilated values and culture.

The true Pan African culture will be African people, institutions, values and way of life, our productive forces, our material and spiritual reality mobilized, organized and politicized (the creation of revolutionary political culture) to struggle on a worldwide basis to defeat colonialism, racial oppression, neo-colonialism, capitalism and imperialism. To create such a culture, meetings like the Sixth Pan African Congress are critical, but we can see that even their healthy existence as complete reflectors of the contradictions and integrity of the struggle can only be the result of a constant battle against opportunism and neo-colonialism.

True Pan African institutions—historical, social, political, economic, creative and ethical—are almost non-existent. The OAU is a nationalist institution of continental proportion, but it is not Pan Africanist or socialist. This Sixth Pan African Congress should help create serious, functioning, efficient, Pan African systems and institutions that raise our level of struggle to a more intense category internationally. It should not just create tourist arrangements with Blacks in the diaspora, or neo-capitalist proposals offering Africa "consumer power" in exchange for African "land and resources." Such ideas are odious whether they come from Europeans or Africans.

The conscious determination to struggle demands the conscious creation of systems of struggle. . . . Africans, oppressed and struggling in various parts of the world, must be integrated into a truly Pan African, anti-imperialist system—one that utilizes the democratic and socialist elements of each society, the revolutionary, anti-bourgeois quality of each of these African communities, the national cultures linked together to struggle, as *an international, anti-imperialist culture.*

We can only build an actual Pan African culture by defeating petty bourgeois statism and neo-colonialism and the rule of imperialist borders and treaties, by creating systems and institutions based on revolutionary ideology, incorporating revolutionary nationalism,

Pan Africanism and truly scientific socialism. This means socialism
our own social structures, though utilizing the universally applic
and international revolutionary experiences. We cannot, as Walt
nationalism to deprive ourselves of the revolutionary aspects of
create an actual Pan African culture by creating revolutionary sys
practice self-criticism and criticism, by creating systems that '
the defeat of capitalism throughout the African world. But we
Africanism is just another stage in our development. As we m'
unity and consciousness, this dramatic liberation of our productive ...
closer to the system of world social, political and economic organization that ...
are ultimately looking for.

There can be no true Pan African culture without the socialist revolution, for instance,
that made possible by the advanced armed national liberation struggles, or the intensification of socialist construction in the already politically independent states. In fact the
commitment to build "true Pan African culture" seems to us basically one part of a commitment to build socialism for African people worldwide, and to take on the struggle
against imperialism everywhere. In short, Pan Africanism and the creation of a Pan African culture is a commitment to struggle for socialism for the world.

Charter of the Organization of African Unity

Addis Ababa, May 25, 1963

We, the Heads of the African and Malagasy States and Governments assembled in the city of Addis Ababa, Ethiopia;

Convinced that it is the inalienable right of all people to control their own destiny;

Conscious of the fact that freedom, equality, justice and dignity are essential objectives for the achievement of the legitimate aspirations of the African peoples;

Conscious of our responsibility to harness the natural and human resources of our continent for the total advancement of our peoples in spheres of human endeavour;

Inspired by a common determination to promote understanding and collaboration among our States in response to the aspirations of our peoples for brotherhood and solidarity, in a larger unity transcending ethnic and national differences;

Convinced that, in order to translate this determination into a dynamic force in the cause of human progress, conditions for peace and security must be established and maintained;

Determined to safeguard and consolidate the hard-won independence as well as the sovereignty and territorial integrity of our States, and to resist neo-colonialism in all its forms;

Dedicated to the general progress of Africa;

Persuaded that the Charter of the United Nations and the Universal Declaration of Human Rights, to the principles of which we reaffirm our adherence, provide a solid foundation for peaceful and positive cooperation among States;

Desirous that all African and Malagasy States should henceforth unify so that the welfare and well-being of their peoples can be assured;

Resolved to reinforce the links between our States by establishing and strengthening common institutions;

Have agreed to the present Charter.

ESTABLISHMENT

Article I

The High Contracting Parties do by the present Charter establish an Organization to be known as the "Organization of African and Malagasy States."

PURPOSES

Article II

1. The Organization shall have the following purposes:
   a. To promote the unity and solidarity of the African and Malagasy States.
   b. To co-ordinate and intensify their collaboration and efforts to achieve a better life for the peoples of Africa.
   c. To defend their sovereignty, their territorial integrity and independence.
   d. To eradicate all forms of colonialism from the continent of Africa; and
   e. To promote international co-operation, having due regard to the Charter of the United Nations and the Universal Declaration of Human Rights.
2. To these ends, the Member States shall co-ordinate and harmonise their general policies, especially in the following fields:
   a. Political and diplomatic co-operation.
   b. Economic co-operation, including transport and communications.
   c. Educational and cultural co-operation.
   d. Health, sanitation and nutritional co-operation.
   e. Scientific and technical co-operation.
   f. Co-operation for defence and security.

PRINCIPLES

Article III

The Member States, in pursuit of the purposes stated in Article II, solemnly affirm, and declare their adherence to the following principles:
1. The sovereign equality of all African and Malagasy States.
2. Non-interference in the internal affairs of States.
3. Respect for the sovereignty and territorial integrity of each State and for its inalienable right to independent existence.
4. Peaceful settlement of disputes by negotiations, mediation, conciliation or arbitration.
5. Unreserved condemnation, in all its forms, of political assassination as well as subversive activities on the part of neighboring States or any other States.
6. Absolute dedication to the whole emancipation of the African territories which are still dependent.
7. Affirmation of a policy of non-alignment with regard to all blocs.

MEMBERSHIP

Article IV

Each independent sovereign African and Malagasy State shall be entitled to become a Member of the Organization.

Rights and Duties of Member States

Article V

All Member States shall enjoy equal rights and have equal duties.

Article VI

The Member States pledge themselves to observe scrupulously the principles enumerated in Article III of the present Charter.

Institutions

Article VII

The Organization shall accomplish its purposes through the following principal institutions:
1. The Assembly of Heads of State and Government.
2. The Council of Ministers.
3. The General Secretariat.
4. The Commission of Mediation, Conciliation and Arbitration.

The Assembly of Heads of State and Government

Article VIII

The Assembly of Heads of State and Government shall be the supreme organ of the Organization. It shall, subject to the provisions of this Charter, discuss matters of common concern to all Member States with a view to co-ordinating and harmonising the general policy of the Organization. It may in addition review the structure, functions and acts of all the organs and any specialized agencies which may be created in accordance with the present Charter.

Article IX

The Assembly shall be composed of the Heads of State and Government or their duly accredited representatives and it shall meet at least once a year (every other year). At the request of any Member State, and with the approval by the majority of the Member States, the Assembly shall meet in extraordinary session.

Article X

1. Each Member State shall have one vote.
2. All resolutions shall be determined by a two-thirds majority of those present and voting.

3. Questions of procedure shall require a simply majority. Whether or not a question is one of procedure shall be determined by a simple majority of all Member States present and voting.

4. Two-thirds of the total membership of the Organization shall form a quorum at any meeting of the Assembly.

Article XI

The Assembly shall have the power to determine its own rules of procedure.

THE COUNCIL OF MINISTERS

Article XII

The Council of Ministers shall consist of Foreign Ministers or such other Ministers as are designated by the Governments of Member States.

The Council of Ministers shall meet at least twice a year. When requested by any Member State and approved by two-thirds of all Member States, it shall meet in extraordinary session.

Article XIII

The Council of Ministers shall be responsible to the Assembly of Heads of State and Government. It shall be entrusted with the responsibility of preparing conferences of the Assembly.

It shall take cognisance of any matter referred to it by the Assembly. It shall be entrusted with the implementation of the decisions of the Assembly of Heads of State. It shall co-ordinate inter-African co-operation in accordance with the instructions of the Assembly and in conformity with Article II (2) of the present Charter.

Article XIV

1. Each Member State shall have one vote.

2. All resolutions shall be determined by a two-thirds majority of those members present and voting.

3. Questions of procedure shall require a simple majority. Whether or not a question is one of procedure shall be determined by a simple majority of all Member States present and voting.

4. Two-thirds of the total membership of the Council shall form a quorum for any meeting of the Council.

Article XV

The Council shall have the power to determine its own rules of procedure.

GENERAL SECRETARIAT

Article XVI

There shall be an Administrative Secretary-General of the Organization, who shall be appointed by the Assembly of Heads of State and Government, on the recommendation of the Council of Ministers. The Administrative Secretary-General shall direct the affairs of the Secretariat.

Article XVII

There shall be one or more Assistant Secretaries-General of the Organization, who shall be appointed by the Council of Ministers.

Article XVIII

The functions and conditions of services of the Secretary-General, of the Assistant Secretaries-General and other employees of the Secretariat shall be governed by the provisions of this Charter and the regulations approved by the Council of Ministers.

　1. In the performance of their duties the Administrative Secretary-General and his staff shall not seek or receive instructions from any government or from any other authority external to the Organization. They shall refrain from any action which might reflect on their position as international officials responsible only to the Organization.

　2. Each member of the Organization undertakes to respect the exclusive character of the responsibilities of the Administrative Secretary-General and the Staff and not seek to influence them in the discharge of their responsibilities.

COMMISSION OF MEDIATION, CONCILIATION AND ARBITRATION

Article XIX

Member States pledge to settle all disputes among themselves by peaceful means and, to this end, agree to conclude a separate treaty establishing a Commission of Mediation, Conciliation and Arbitration. Said treaty shall be regarded as forming an integral part of the present Charter [done July 21, 1964, in Cairo].

SPECIALIZED COMMISSIONS

Article XX

The Assembly shall establish such Specialized Commissions as it may deem necessary, including the following:

1. Economic and Social Commission.
2. Educational and Cultural Commission.
3. Health, Sanitation and Nutrition Commission.
4. Defence Commission.
5. Scientific, Technical and Research Commission.

Article XXI

Each Specialized Commission referred to in Article XX shall be composed of the Ministers concerned or other Ministers or Plenipotentiaries designated by the Governments of the Member States.

Article XXII

The functions of the Specialized Commissions shall be carried out in accordance with the provisions of the present Charter and of the regulations approved by the Council of Ministers.

THE BUDGET

Article XXIII

The budget of the Organization prepared by the Administrative Secretary-General shall be approved by the Council of Ministers. The budget shall be provided by contributions from Member States in accordance with the scale of assessment of the United Nations; provided, however, that no Member State shall be assessed an amount exceeding twenty per cent of the yearly regular budget of the Organization. The Member States agree to pay their respective contributions regularly.

SIGNATURE AND RATIFICATION OF CHARTER

Article XXIV

This Charter shall be open for signature to all independent sovereign African and Malagasy States and shall be ratified by the signatory States in accordance with their respective constitutional processes.

The original instrument, done in English and French, both texts being equally authentic, shall be deposited with the Government of Ethiopia which shall transmit certified copies thereof to all independent sovereign African and Malagasy States.

Instruments of ratification shall be deposited with the Government of Ethiopia, which shall notify all signatories of each such deposit.

Entry into Force

Article XXV

The Charter shall enter into force immediately upon receipt by the Government of Ethiopia of the instruments of ratification from two-thirds of the signatory States.

Registration of the Charter

Article XXVI

This Charter shall, after due ratification, be registered with the Secretariat of the United Nations through the Government of Ethiopia in conformity with Article 102 of the Charter of the United Nations.

Interpretation of the Charter

Article XXVII

Any question which may arise concerning the interpretation of this Charter shall be decided by a vote of two-thirds of the Assembly of Heads of State and Government, present and voting.

Adhesion and Accession

Article XXVIII

1. Any independent sovereign African State may at any time notify the Administrative Secretary-General of its intention to adhere or accede to this Charter.
2. The Administrative Secretary-General shall, on receipt of such notification, communicate a copy of it to all the Member States. Admission shall be decided by a simple majority of the Member States. The decision of each Member State shall be transmitted to the Administrative Secretary-General, who shall, upon receipt of the required number of votes, communicate the decision to the State concerned.

Miscellaneous

Article XXIX

The working languages of the Organization and all its institutions shall be English and French.

Article XXX

The Administrative Secretary-General may accept on behalf of the Organization gifts, bequests and other donations made to the Organization, provided that this is approved by the Council of Ministers.

Article XXXI

The Council of Ministers shall decide on the privileges and immunities to be accorded to the personnel of the Secretariat in the respective territories of the Member States.

CESSATION OF MEMBERSHIP

Article XXXII

Any State which desires to renounce its membership shall forward a written notification to the Administrative Secretary-General. At the end of one year from the date of such notification, the Charter shall cease to apply with respect to the renouncing State, which shall thereby cease to belong to the Organization.

AMENDMENT TO THE CHARTER

Article XXXIII

This Charter may be amended or revised if any Member State makes a written request to the Administrative Secretary-General to that effect; provided, however, that the proposed amendment is not submitted to the Assembly for consideration until all the Member States have been duly notified of it and a period of one year has elapsed. Such an amendment shall not be effective unless approved by at least two-thirds of all the Member States.

In faith whereof, We, the Heads of African and Malagasy States and Governments, have signed this Charter.

Walter Rodney
(1942–1980, Guyana)

How Africa Developed before the Coming of the Europeans—Up to the Fifteenth Century

> Before even the British came into relations with our
> people, we were a developed people, having our own
> institutions, having our own ideas of government.
> —J. E. Caseley-Hayford, 1922
> African (Gold Coast) Nationalist

A General Overview

It has been shown that, using comparative standards, Africa today is underdeveloped in relation to Western Europe and a few other parts of the world; and that the present position has been arrived at, not by the separate evolution of Africa on the one hand and Europe on the other, but through exploitation. As is well known, Africa has had prolonged and extensive contact with Europe, and one has to bear in mind that contact between different societies changes their respective rates of development. To set the record straight, four operations are required:

(1) Reconstruction of the nature of development in Africa before the coming of Europeans.

(2) Reconstruction of the nature of development which took place in Europe before expansion abroad.

(3) Analysis of Africa's contribution to Europe's present "developed" state.

(4) Analysis of Europe's contribution to Africa's present "underdeveloped" state.

The second task has already been extensively carried out in European literature, and only passing references need be made; but the others are all deserving of further attention.

The African continent reveals very fully the workings of the law of uneven development of societies. There are marked contrasts between the Ethiopian empire and the hunting groups of pygmies in the Congo forest or between the empires of the Western Sudan and the Khoisan hunter-gatherers of the Kalahari Desert. Indeed, there were striking contrasts within any given geographical area. The Ethiopian empire embraced literate feudal Amharic noblemen as well as simple Kaffa cultivators and Galla pastoralists. The empires of the Western Sudan had sophisticated, educated Mandinga townsmen, small communities of Bozo fishermen, and nomadic Fulani herdsmen. Even among clans and lineages that appear roughly similar, there were considerable differences. However, it is possible to distinguish between what was uniquely "African" and what was universal in the sense of being characteristic of all human societies at a given stage of development. It is also essential to recognize the process of dialectical evolution from lower to higher forms of social organization; and, in looking at the most advanced social formations, one would appreciate the potential of the continent as a whole and the direction of change.

The moment that the topic of the pre-European African past is raised, many individuals are concerned for various reasons to know about the existence of African "civilizations." Mainly, this stems from a desire to make comparisons with European "civilizations." This is not the context in which to evaluate the so-called civilizations of Europe. It is enough to note the behavior of European capitalists from the epoch of slavery through colonialism, fascism, and genocidal wars in Asia and Africa. Such barbarism causes suspicion to attach to the use of the word "civilization" to describe Western Europe and North America. As far as Africa is concerned during the period of early development, it is preferable to speak in terms of "cultures" rather than civilizations.

A culture is a total way of life. It embraces what people ate and what they wore; the way they walked and the way they talked; the manner in which they treated death and greeted the newborn. Obviously, unique features came into existence in virtually every locality with regard to all social details. In addition, the continent of Africa south of the great Sahara desert formed a broad community where resemblances were clearly discernible. For example, music and dance had key roles in "uncontaminated" African society. They were ever present at birth, initiation, marriage, death, as well as at times of recreation. Africa is the continent of drums and percussion. African peoples reached the pinnacle of achievement in that sphere.

Because of the impact of colonialism and cultural imperialism . . . , Europeans and Africans themselves in the colonial period lacked due regard for the unique features of African culture. Those features have a value of their own that cannot be eclipsed by European culture either in the comparable period before 1500 or in the subsequent centuries. They cannot be eclipsed because they are not really comparable phenomena. Who in this world is competent to judge whether an Austrian waltz is better than a Makonde Ngoma? Furthermore, even in those spheres of culture that are more readily comparable, such as "the fine arts," it is known that African achievements of the pre-European period stand as contributions to man's heritage of beautiful creations. The art of Egypt, the Sudan, and Ethiopia was known to the rest of the world at an early date. That of the rest of Africa is still being "discovered" and rediscovered by Europeans and present-day Africans. The verdict of art historians on the Ife and Benin bronzes is well known. Since they date from the fourteenth and fifteenth centuries, they are very relevant to any discussion of African development in the epoch before the contacts with Europe. Nor should they be regarded as unusual, except with regard to the material in which the sculptures were executed. The same skill and feeling obviously went into sculpture and art-work in non-durable materials, especially wood.

African dance and art were almost invariably linked with a religious world-outlook in one way or another. As is well known, traditional African religious practices exist in great variety, and it should also be remembered that both Islam and Christianity found homes on the African continent almost from their very inception. The features of the traditional African religions help to set African cultures apart from those in other continents; but in this present context it is more important to note how much African religion had in common with religion elsewhere and how this can be used as an index to the level of development in Africa before European impact in the fifteenth century.

Religion is an aspect of the superstructure of a society, deriving ultimately from the degree of control and understanding of the material world. However, when man thinks in religious terms, he starts from the ideal rather than with the material world (which is beyond his comprehension). This creates a non-scientific and metaphysical way of viewing the world, which often conflicts with the scientific materialist outlook and with the development of society. African ancestral religions were no better or worse than other religions as such. But by the end of feudalism, Europeans began to narrow the area of human life in which religion and the church played a part. Religion ceased to dominate politics, geography, medicine. To free those things from religious restraints, it had to be argued that religion had its own sphere and the things of this world had their own secular sphere. This secularization of life speeded up the development of capitalism and later socialism. In contrast, in the period before the coming of the whites, religion pervaded African life just as it pervaded life in other pre-feudal societies, such as those of the Maoris of Australia or the Afghans of Afghanistan or the Vikings of Scandinavia.

Religion can play both a positive and a negative role as an aspect of the superstructure. In most instances in early Africa, religious beliefs were associated with the mobilization and discipline of large numbers of people to form states. In a few instances, religion also provided concepts in the struggle for social justice. The negative aspects usually arose out of the tendency of religion to persist unchanged for extremely long periods, especially when the technology of earning a living changes very slowly. This was the case in African societies, as in all other pre-capitalist societies. At the same time, the religious beliefs themselves react upon the mode of production, further slowing up progress in that respect. For instance, belief in prayer and in the intervention of ancestors and various gods could easily be a substitute for innovations designed to control the impact of weather and environment.

The same kind of two-sided relationship also exists between the means of earning a living and the social patterns that arise in the process of work. In Africa, before the fifteenth century, the predominant principle of social relations was that of family and kinship associated with communalism. Every member of an African society had his position defined in terms of relatives on his mother's side and on his father's side. Some societies placed greater importance on matrilineal ties and others on patrilineal ties. Those things were crucial to the daily existence of a member of an African society, because land (the major means of production) was owned by groups such as the family or clan—the head of which were parents and those yet unborn. In theory, this pattern was explained by saying that the residents in any community were all direct descendants of the first person who settled the land. When a new group arrived, they often made a pretense that they too had ancestry dating back to the settling of the land or else they insured that members of the earliest kin groups continued to perform the ceremonies related to the land and water of the region.

Similarly, the labor that worked the land was generally recruited on a family basis. A single family or household would till its own plots and it would also be available to share certain joint farming activities with other members of the extended family or clan. Annual hunts and river fishing were also organized by a whole extended family or village community. In a matrilineal society such as that of the Bemba (Zambia), the bridegroom spent a number of years working for the father of his bride; and many young men who had married daughters of the same household often formed work teams to help each other. In Dahomey, a young man did not go to live with his wife's family, but the *dokpwe*, or work team, allowed a son to participate in carrying out a task of some magnitude for the father of his wife. In both of those examples, the right of the father-in-law to acquire labor and the obligations of the son-in-law to give labor were based on kinship. This can be contrasted with capitalism where money buys labor, and with feudalism where the serf provides labor in order to have access to a portion of land which belongs to the landlord.

Having been produced on land that was family property and through family labor, the resultant crops and other goods were distributed on the basis of kinship ties. If a man's crops were destroyed by some sudden calamity, relatives in his own village helped him. If the whole community was in distress, people moved to live with their kinsmen in another area where food was not scarce. In Akan country (Ghana), the clan system was highly organized, so that a man from Brong could visit Fante many hundreds of miles away and receive food and hospitality from a complete stranger who happened to be of his own clan.

Numerous examples could be brought forward to show the dominance of the family principle in the communal phase of African development. It affected the two principal factors of production—land and labor—as well as the system of distributing goods. European anthropologists who have studied African societies have done so mainly from a very prejudiced and racist position, but their researchers can nevertheless provide abundant facts relating to family homesteads and compounds, to the extended family (including affinal members who join by association rather than by birth), and to lineages and clans which carried the principles of kinship alliances over large areas. However, while the exact details might have differed, similar social institutions were to be found among the Gauls of eleventh-century France, among the Viet of Indochina at the same date, and virtually everywhere else in the world at one time or another—because communalism is one phase through which all human society passed.

In all African societies during the early epoch, the individual at every stage of life had a series of duties and obligations to others in the society as well as a set of rights: namely, things that he or she could expect or demand from other individuals. Age was a most important factor determining the extent of rights and obligations. The oldest members of the society were highly respected and usually in authority; and the idea of seniority through age was reflected in the presence of age-grades and age-sets in a great many African societies. Circumcision meant initiation into the society and into adulthood. From that moment, a man was placed with others in his own age-group and a woman likewise. Usually, there were at least three age-grades, corresponding roughly to the young, the middle-aged, and the old.

In large parts of Europe, when communalism broke down it gave way to widespread slavery as the new form in which labor was mobilized. This slavery continued throughout the European Middle Ages, with the Crusades between Christians and Moslems giving an added excuse for enslaving people. Slavery in turn gave way to serfdom, whereby the laborer was tied to the land and could no longer be sold and transported. Because it took many years for the transition from slavery to feudalism to take place in Europe, it was common to find that feudal society still retained numbers of slaves. Parts of China, Burma, and India also had considerable numbers of slaves as the society moved away from elementary communalism, but there was never any time-span when slavery was the dominant mode of production in Asia. In Africa, there were few slaves and certainly no epoch of slavery. Most of the slaves were in North African and other Moslem societies, and in those instances a man and his family could have the same slave status for generations, within the overall feudal structure of the society. Elsewhere in Africa, communal societies were introduced to the concept of owning alien human beings when they took captives in war. At first, those captives were in a very disadvantaged position, comparable to that of slaves, but very rapidly captives or their offspring became ordinary members of the society, because there was no scope for the perpetual exploitation of man by man in a context that was neither feudal nor capitalist.

Both Marxists and non-Marxists alike (with different motivations) have pointed out that the sequence of modes of production noted in Europe were not reproduced in Africa. In Africa, after the communal stage there was no epoch of slavery arising out of internal evolution. Nor was there a mode of production which was the replica of European feudalism. Marx himself recognized that the stages of development in Asia had produced a form of society which could not easily be fitted into a European slot. That he called "the Asian mode of production." Following along those lines, a number of Marxists have recently been discussing whether Africa was in the same category as Asia or whether Africa had its own "African mode of production." The implications of the arguments are very progressive, because they are concerned with the concrete conditions of Africa rather than with preconceptions brought from Europe. But the scholars concerned seem to be bent on finding a single term to cover a variety of social formations which were existing in Africa from about the fifth century A.D. to the coming of colonialism. The assumption that will underlie this study is that most African societies before 1500 were in a transitional stage between the practice of agriculture (plus fishing and herding) in family communities and the practice of the same activities within states and societies comparable to feudalism.

In a sense, all history is transition from one stage to another, but some historical situations along the line have more clearly distinguishable characteristics than others. Thus under communalism there were no classes, and there was equal access to land, and equality in distribution—at a low level of technology and production. Feudalism involved great inequality in distribution of land and social products. The landlord class and its bureaucracy controlled the state and used it as an instrument for oppressing peasants, serfs, slaves, and even craftsmen and merchants. The movement from communalism to feudalism in every continent took several centuries, and in some instances the interruption of internal evolution never allowed the process to mature. In Africa, there is no doubt that the societies which eventually reached feudalism were extremely few. So long as the feudal state was still in the making, elements that were communal coexisted with elements that were feudal and with some peculiarities due to African conditions. The transition was also characterized by a variety of social formations: There were pastoralists and cultivators, fishing societies and trading societies, raiders and nomads. They were all being progressively drawn into a relationship with the land, with each other, and with the state, through the expansion of productive forces and the network of distribution.

In feudal societies, there were clashes between the landlord and peasant classes and later on between the landlord and merchant classes. Under capitalism, the principal class contradiction inside Europe was between the proletariat and the bourgeoisie. Those hostile class relations provided the motive force within the respective societies. African communal societies had differences such as age-grades and differences between ordinary members and religious leaders such as rainmakers. However, those were not exploitative or antagonistic relations. The concept of class as a motive force in social development had not yet come about; and in the communal phase one must look at the fundamental forces of production to understand the process of change.

Resistance and Renewal

Using a number of methods and concepts, it is possible to reconstruct the most likely manner in which isolated family living was broken down and production increased. For instance, the rise of age-grades can be seen as responding to the need for greater solidarity, because age-grades included and cut across many families. Similarly, communal labor was entered into by cross sections of the community to make work more efficient. The *dokpwe* work group of Dahomey mentioned above had a wider application in serving the whole community to perform such heavy tasks as clearing land and housebuilding. With the offer of some food and beer or palm wine, a work team or "work bee" could be mobilized in a short time in most African communities, including those of the light-skinned Berbers of North Africa.

Of course, while the organization of labor might have helped to produce more, the principal change in the productive forces was that which comprised new techniques—using the word in its broadest sense to include both tools and skills in dealing with the environment and new plant and animal species. The first prerequisite for mastery of the environment is knowledge of that environment. By the fifteenth century, Africans everywhere had arrived at a considerable understanding of the total ecology—of the soils, climate, animals, plants, and their multiple interrelationships. The practical application of this lay in the need to trap animals, to build houses, to make utensils, to find medicines, and above all to devise systems of agriculture.

In the centuries before the contact with Europeans, the overwhelmingly dominant activity in Africa was agriculture. In all the settled agricultural communities, people observed the peculiarities of their own environment and tried to find techniques for dealing with it in a rational manner. Advanced methods were used in some areas, such as terracing, crop rotation, green manuring, mixed farming, and regulated swamp farming. The single most important technological change underlying African agricultural development was the introduction of iron tools, notably the ax and the hoe, replacing wooden and stone tools. It was on the basis of the iron tools that new skills were elaborated in agriculture as well as in other spheres of economic activity.

The coming of iron, the rise of cereal growing, and the making of pottery were all closely related phenomena. In most parts of Africa, it was in the period after the birth of Christ that those things came about. The rate of change over a few centuries was quite impressive. Millet and rice had been domesticated from wild grasses just as yams were made to evolve from selected wild roots. Most African societies raised the cultivation of their own particular staple to a fine art. Even the widespread resort to shifting cultivation with burning and light hoeing was not as childish as the first European colonialists supposed. That simple form of agriculture was based on a correct evaluation of the soil potential, which was not as great as initially appears from the heavy vegetation; and when the colonialists started upsetting the thin topsoil the result was disastrous.

The above remarks show that when an outsider comes into a new ecological system, even if he is more skilled he does not necessarily function as effectively as those who have familiarized themselves with the environment over centuries; and the newcomer is likely to look more ridiculous if he is too arrogant to realize that he has something to learn from the "natives." However, it is not being suggested that African agriculture in the early period was superior to that of other continents. On the contrary, African standards of husbandry on the land and with livestock were not as high as those independently evolved in most parts of Asia and Europe. The weakness in Africa seemed to have been the lack of a professional interest in acquiring more scientific knowledge and in devising tools to lighten the load of labor as well as to transform hostile environments into areas suitable for human activity. As far as agriculture in Europe was concerned, this professionalism was undertaken by the class with a vested interest in the land—namely, the feudalist landowners and later the capitalist farmers.

It has previously been stated that development is very much determined by the social relations of production (i.e., those which have to do with people's functions in producing wealth). Where a few people owned the land and the majority were tenants, this injustice at a particular stage of history allowed the few to concentrate on improving their land. In contrast, under communalism every African was assured of sufficient land to meet his own needs by virtue of being a member of a family or community. For that reason, and because land was relatively abundant, there were few social pressures or incentives for technical changes to increase productivity.

In Asia, where much of the land was communally owned, there were tremendous advances in some types of farming, especially irrigated farming. This was because the state in India, China, Ceylon, and other places intervened and engaged in irrigation and other hydraulic works on a large scale. This was also true of North Africa, which in most respects followed a pattern of evolution similar to that of Asia. The African land tenure pattern was closer to that of Asia than to that of Europe, but even the most politically developed African states did not play the role of initiators and supervisors of agricultural development. One reason may have been the lack of population pressure and hence the scattered nature of settlements. Another may have been state concentration on trading non-agricultural products to the exclusion of other things. Certainly, when African societies became linked up with other social systems outside the continent on the basis of trade, little attention was paid to agriculture.

When it comes to the question of manufacturing in Africa before the time of the white man, it is also essential to recognize where achievements have been underestimated. African manufacturers have been contemptuously treated or overlooked by European writers, because the modern conception of the word brings to mind factories and machines. However, "manufactures" means literally "things made by hand," and African manufacture in this sense had advanced appreciably. Most African societies fulfilled their own needs for a wide range of articles of domestic use, as well as for farming tools and weapons.

One way of judging the level of economic development in Africa five centuries ago is through the quality of the products. Here a few examples will be given of articles which came to the notice of the outside world. Through North Africa, Europeans became familiar with a superior brand of red leather from Africa which was termed "Moroccan leather." In fact, it was tanned and dyed by Hausa and Mandinga specialists in northern Nigeria and Mali. When direct contact was established between Europeans and Africans on the East and West coasts, many more impressive items were displayed. As soon as the Portuguese reached the old kingdom of Kongo, they sent back word on the superb local cloths made from bark and palm fiber—and having a finish comparable to velvet. The Baganda were also expert barkcloth makers. Yet, Africa had even better to offer in the form of cotton cloth, which was widely manufactured before the coming of the Europeans. Well into the present century, local cottons from the Guinea coast were stronger than Manchester cottons. Once European products reached Africa, Africans too were in a position to make comparisons between their commodities and those from outside. In Katanga and Zambia, the local copper continued to be preferred to the imported items, while the same held true for iron in a place like Sierra Leone.

It was at the level of scale that African manufactures had not made a breakthrough. That is to say, the cotton looms were small, the iron smelters were small, the pottery was

Resistance and Renewal

turned slowly by hand and not on a wheel. Yet some changes were taking place in this context. Under communalism, each household met its own needs by making its own clothes, pots, mats, and such. That was true of every continent. However, economic expansion from there on was associated with specialization and localization of industry—people's needs being met by exchange. This trend was displayed in the principal African manufactures, and notably in the cloth industry. Cotton fiber had to be ginned (separated from the seed), then carded and spun into yarn, before being woven. Either the yarn or the woven cloth had to be dyed, and the making of the dye itself was a complex process. There was a time when all these stages would be performed by a single family or rather by the women in a single family, as in Yoruba-land. But economic development was reflected in the separation of dyeing from cloth-making, and the separation of spinning from weaving. Each separation marked greater specialization and quantitative and qualitative changes in output.

European industry has been intensively studied, and it is generally recognized that in addition to new machinery a most decisive factor in the growth of industry was the change-over from domestic production to the factory system, with the guild marking an intermediary stage. The guild was an association of specialists, passing on their skills by training apprentices and working in buildings set aside for that purpose. Africa, too, had elements of the guild system. At Timbuktu, there were tailoring guilds, while in Benin guilds of a very restricted caste type controlled the famous brass and bronze industry. In Nupe (now northern Nigeria) the glass and bead industry operated on a guild basis. Each Nupe guild had a common workshop and a master. The master obtained contracts, financed the guild, and disposed of the product. Both his own relatives as well as strangers were free to enter the guild and learn the various specialized tasks within the glass industry. What this amounted to was simply that there was increasing specialization and division of labor.

Traditional African economies are usually called "subsistence" economies. Often, small villages farmed, hunted, fished, and looked after themselves independently with little reference to the rest of the continent. Yet, at the same time, the vast majority of African communities fulfilled at least a few of their needs by trade. Africa was a continent of innumerable trade routes. Some extended for long distances, like the routes across the Sahara or the routes connected with Katanga copper. But in the main, it was trade between neighboring or not too far distant societies. Such trade was always a function of production. Various communities were producing surpluses of given commodities which could be exchanged for items which they lacked. In that way, the salt industry of one locality would be stimulated while the iron industry would be encouraged in another. In a coastal, lake, or river area, dried fish could become profitable, while yams and millet would be grown in abundance elsewhere to provide a basis for exchange. The trade so readily distinguishable in every part of the continent between the tenth and fifteenth centuries was an excellent indicator of economic expansion and other forms of development which accompanied increasing mastery over the environment.

As part of the extension of trade, it was noticeable that barter was giving way to some forms of money exchange. Barter was generally practiced when the volume of trade was small and when only a few commodities were involved. However, as trade became more complicated, some items began to be used as the standards for measuring other goods. Those items could be kept as a form of wealth easily transformed into other commodities when the need arose. For example, salt, cloth, iron hoes, and cowry shells were popular forms of money in Africa—apart from gold and copper, which were much rarer and therefore restricted to measuring things of great value. In a few places, such as North Africa,

Ethiopia, and the Kongo, the monetary systems were quite sophisticated, indicating that the economy was far removed from simple barter and subsistence.

There were many other changes of a socio-political nature accompanying the expansion of the productive forces. Indeed, things such as agricultural practices, industry, trade, money, and political structures were inseparable—each interacting with the others. The most developed areas of Africa were those where all the elements converged, and the two sociopolitical features which were the outstanding indices to development were the increase of stratification and the consolidation of states.

The principles of family and deferment to age were slowly breaking down throughout the centuries preceding the arrival of Europeans in their sailing ships. Changes in technology and in the division of labor made that inevitable. The introduction of iron, for example, gave economic and military strength to those who could make and acquire it. Better tools meant more food and a greater population, but the latter tended to outrun the supplies of material goods, and the possibilities of wealth opened up by the possession of iron were seized upon by a few to their own advantage. Skilled workers in iron, cloth, pottery, leather, or salt-making tended to pass on their skills in closed groups known as castes. That insured that the division of labor operated in their favor, because their position was privileged and strategic. Ironworkers were particularly favored in some African societies in which they either became the ruling groups or were very close to the top of the social hierarchy. The division of labor also carried over into non-material spheres, producing professional minstrels and historians. They too had certain special rights and privileges, notably the ability to criticize freely without fear of reprisal. In some circumstances, skilled castes were reduced to very low status. But that was rare, and in any case it does not contradict the general assertion that the tendency was for communalism to give rise to more and more stratification.

Social stratification was the basis for the rise of classes and for social antagonisms. To some extent, this was a logical follow-up of the previous non-antagonistic differences in communal society. For instance, old men could use their control over land allocation, over bride-price, and over other traditional exchanges to try to establish themselves as a privileged economic stratum. Secret societies arose in the area that is now Liberia, Sierra Leone, and Guinea, and they permitted knowledge, power, and wealth to pass into the hands of the elders and ultimately to the elders of particular lineages.

The contradiction between young men and their elders was not the type that caused violent revolution. But young men clearly had reasons for resenting their dependence on elders, especially when it came to such vital personal matters as the acquisition of wives. When disgruntled, they could either leave their communities and set up for themselves or they could challenge the principles within the society. In either case, the trend was that some individuals and families were more successful than others, and those families established themselves as permanent rulers. Then age ceased to matter as much because even a junior could succeed to his father, once the notion of royal blood or royal lineage was established.

In the period of transition, while African society retained many features that were undisputably communal, it also accepted the principle that some families or clans or lineages were destined to rule and others were not. This was true not only of cultivators but of pastoralists as well. In fact, livestock became unevenly distributed much more readily than land; and those families with the largest herds became socially and politically dominant.

An even more important aspect of the process of social stratification was that brought about by contact between different social formations. Fishermen had to relate to cultivators and the latter to pastoralists. There were even social formations such as bands of hunters and food-gatherers who had not yet entered the phase of communal cooperation. Often the relationship was peaceful. In many parts of the African continent, there arose what is known as "symbiosis" between groups earning their living in different ways—which really means that they agreed to exchange goods and coexist to their mutual advantage. However, there was also room for considerable conflict; and when one group imposed itself by force on another, the result was invariably the rise of social classes with the conquerors on top and the conquered at the bottom.

The most common clashes between different social formations were those between pastoralists and cultivators. In some instances, the cultivators had the upper hand, as for instance in West Africa where cultivators like the Mandinga and Hausa were the overlords of the Rulani cattlemen right up to the eighteenth and nineteenth centuries. The reverse situation was found in the Horn of Africa and most of East Africa. Another type of clash was that in which raiding peoples took power over agriculturalists, as happened in Angola and in and around the Sahara, where the Moors and Tuareg exacted tribute from and even enslaved more peaceful and sedentary peoples. The result in each case was that a relatively small faction held control of the land and (where relevant) cattle, mines, and long-distance trade. It meant also that the minority group could make demands on the labor of their subjects—not on the basis of kinship but because a relationship of domination and subordination existed.

In truly communal societies, the leadership was based on religion and family ties. The senior members of the society shared the work with others and received more or less the same share of the total product. Certainly, no one starved while others stuffed themselves and threw away the excess. However, once African societies began to expand by internal evolution, conquest, or trade, the style of life of the ruling group became noticeably different. They consumed the most and the best that the society offered. Yet, they were least directly involved in the production of wealth by farming, cattle herding, or fishing. The ruling class and the kings in particular had the right to call upon the labor of the common man for certain projects and for a given number of days per year. This is known as *corvée* labor, from a similar procedure followed in feudal France. Such a system meant greater exploitation and at the same time greater development of productive resources.

Social stratification as outlined above went hand in hand with the rise of the state. The notion of royal lineages and commoner clans could not have any meaning except in a political state with a concrete geographical existence. It is significant that the great dynasties of the world ruled over feudal states. To the European or European-trained ear, the names of the Tudors, Bourbons, Hohenzollerns, and Romanovs would already be familiar. Japan had its Kamakuras and its Tokugawas; China had its T'ang and its Ming; India had its Guptas and its Marathas; and so on. All of those were feudal dynasties existing in a period some centuries after the birth of Christ, but in addition there were dynasties which ruled in each of those countries before feudal land tenure and class relations had fully crystalized. It means that the transition to feudalism in Europe* and Asia saw the rise of ruling groups and the state as interdependent parts of the same process. In that respect, Africa was no different.

From a political perspective, the period of transition from communalism to feudalism in Africa was one of state formation. At the beginning (and for many centuries), the state

*In Europe, communalism gave way to slavery, and therefore dynasties and strong states were present on the eve of the slavery epoch.

remained weak and immature. It acquired definite territorial boundaries, but inside those boundaries subjects lived in their own communities with scarcely any contact with the ruling class until the time came to pay an annual tax or tribute. Only when a group within the state refused to pay the tribute did the early African states mobilize their repressive machinery in the form of an army to demand what it considered as its rights from subjects. Slowly, various states acquired greater power over their many communities of citizens. They exacted *corvée* labor, they enlisted soldiers, and they appointed regular tax collectors and local administrators. The areas of Africa in which labor relations were breaking out of communal restrictions corresponded to areas in which sophisticated political states were emerging. The rise of states was itself a form of development, which increased the scale of African politics and merged small ethnic groups into wider identities suggestive of nations.

In some ways, too much importance is attached to the growth of political states. It was in Europe that the nation-state reached an advanced stage, and Europeans tended to use the presence or absence of well-organized polities as a measure of "civilization." That is not entirely justified, because in Africa there were small political units which had relatively advanced material and non-material cultures. For instance, neither the Ibo people of Nigeria nor the Kikuyu of Kenya ever produced large centralized governments in their traditional setting. But both had sophisticated systems of political rule based on clans and (in the case of the Ibo) on religious oracles and "Secret Societies." Both of them were efficient agriculturalists and ironworkers, and the Ibo had been manufacturing brass and bronze items ever since the ninth century A.D., if not earlier.

However, after making the above qualification, it can be conceded that on the whole the larger states in Africa had the most effective political structures and greater capacity for producing food, clothing, minerals, and other material artifacts. It can readily be understood that those societies which had ruling classes were concerned with acquiring luxury and prestige items. The privileged groups in control of the state were keen to stimulate manufactures as well as to acquire them through trade. They were the ones that mobilized labor to produce a greater surplus above subsistence needs, and in the process they encouraged specialization and the division of labor.

Scholars often distinguish between groups in Africa which had states and those which were "stateless." Sometimes, the word "stateless" is carelessly or even abusively used; but it does describe those peoples who had no machinery of government coercion and no concept of a political unit wider than the family or the village. After all, if there is no class stratification in a society, it follows that there is no state, because the state arose as an instrument to be used by a particular class to control the rest of society in its own interests. Generally speaking, one can consider the stateless societies as among the older forms of socio-political organization in Africa, while the large stages represented an evolution away from communalism—sometimes to the point of feudalism.

Again, it must be emphasized that a survey of the scene in Africa before the coming of Europeans would reveal considerable unevenness of development. There were social formations representing hunting bands, communalism, feudalism, and many positions intermediate between the last two. The remainder of this section will be devoted to a review of the principal features of several of the most developed societies and states of Africa in the last thousand years or so before Africa came into permanent contact with Europe. The areas to be considered are Egypt, Ethiopia, [and] Nubia. . . . Each serves as an example of what development meant in early Africa and what the direction of social movement was. To a greater or lesser extent, each was also a leading force on the continent in the sense of carrying neighbors along the same path, either by absorbing them or influencing them more indirectly.

SOME CONCRETE EXAMPLES

Egypt

It is logical to start with Egypt as the oldest culture in Africa which rose to eminence. The glories of Egypt under the Pharaohs are well known and do not need recounting. At one time, it used to be said or assumed that ancient Egypt was not "African"—a curious view which is no longer seriously propounded. However, for the present purposes, it is more relevant to refer to Egypt under Arab and Turkish rule from the seventh century onwards. During that latter period, the ruling class was foreign, and that meant that Egypt's internal development was tied up with other countries, notably Arabia and Turkey. Colonized Egypt sent abroad great amounts of wealth in the form of food and revenue, and that was a very negative factor. But the tendency was for the ruling foreigners to break with their own imperial masters and to act simply as a ruling elite within Egypt, which became an independent feudal state.

One of the first features of feudalism to arrive in Egypt was the military aspect. The Arab, Turk, and Circassian invaders were all militarily inclined. This was particularly true of the Mameluks who held power from the thirteenth century onwards. Political power in Egypt from the seventh century lay in the hands of a military oligarchy which delegated the actual government to bureaucrats, thereby creating a situation similar to that in places like China and Indochina. Even more fundamental was the fact that land tenure relations were undergoing change in such a way that a true feudal class came on the scene. All the conquerors made land grants to their followers and military captains. Initially, the land in Egypt was the property of the state to be rented out to cultivators. The state then had the right to reappropriate the land and allocate it once more, somewhat like the head of a village community acting as the guardian of the lands of related families. However, the ruling military elements also became a new class of landowners. By the fifteenth century, most of the land in Egypt was the property of the sultan and his military lords.

If there was a small class which monopolized most of the land, it followed that there was a large class of landless. Peasant cultivators were soon converted into mere agricultural laborers, tied to the soil as tenants or vassals of the feudal landlords. These peasants with little or no land were known as the *fellahin*. In Europe, there are legends about the exploitation and suffering of the Russian serfs, or *muzhik*, under feudalism. In Egypt, the exploitation of the *fellahin* was carried out even more thoroughly. The feudalists had no interest in the *fellahin* beyond seeing that they produced revenue. Most of what the peasants produced was taken from them in the form of tax, and the tax collectors were asked to perform the miracle of taking from the peasants even that which they did not have! When their demands were not met, the peasants were brutalized.

The antagonistic nature of the contradiction between the feudal warrior landlords and the *fellahin* was revealed by a number of peasant revolts, notably in the early part of the eighth century. In no continent was feudalism an epoch of romance for the laboring classes, but the elements of development were seen in the technology and the increase in productive capacity. Under the patronage of the Fatimid dynasty (969 A.D. to 1170 A.D.), science flourished and industry reached a new level in Egypt. Windmills and waterwheels were introduced from Persia in the tenth century. New industries were introduced—papermaking, sugar refining, porcelain, and the distillation of gasoline. The older industries of textiles, leather, and metal were improved upon. The succeeding dynasties of the Ayyubids and the Mameluks also achieved a great deal, especially in the building of canals, dams, bridges, and aqueducts, and in stimulating commerce with Europe. Egypt at that time was still able to teach Europe many things and was flexible enough to receive new techniques in return.

Although feudalism was based on the land, it usually developed towns at the expense of the countryside. The high points of Egyptian feudal culture were associated with the towns. The Fatimids founded the city of Cairo, which became one of the most famous and most cultured in the world. At the same time, they established the Azhar University, which exists today as one of the oldest in the world. The feudalists and the rich merchants were the ones who benefited most, but the craftsmen and other city dwellers of Cairo and Alexandria were able to participate to some extent in the leisured lives of the towns.

Ethiopia

Ethiopia, too, at the start of its history as a great power was ruled over by foreigners. The kingdom of Axum was one of the most important of the nuclei around which feudal Ethiopia eventually emerged, and Axum was founded near the Red Sea coast by a dynasty of Sabean origin from the other side of the Red Sea. But the kings of Axum were never agents of foreign powers, and they became completely Africanized. The founding of Axum goes back to the first century A.D. and its ruling class was Christianized within a few centuries. After that they moved inland and participated in the development of the Christian feudal Ethiopian state.

The Ethiopian, Tigrean, and Amharic ruling class was a proud one, tracing its descent to Solomon. As a state which incorporated several other smaller states and kingdoms, it was an empire in the same sense as feudal Austria or Prussia. The emperor of Ethiopia was addressed as "Conquering Lion of the Tribe of Judah, Elect of God, Emperor of Ethiopia, King of Kings." In practice, however, the "Solomonic" line was not unbroken. Most of the consolidation of the inland Ethiopian plateau was carried out in the twelfth century by an intruding dynasty, the Zagwe, who made claims to descent from Moses. The Zagwe kings distinguished themselves by building several churches cut out of solid rock. The architectural achievements attest to the level of skill reached by Ethiopians as well as the capacity of the state to mobilize labor on a huge scale. Such tasks could not have been achieved by voluntary family labor but only through the labor of an exploited class.

A great deal is known of the superstructure of the Ethiopian empire, especially its Christianity and its literate culture. History was written to glorify the king and the nobility, especially under the restored "Solomonic" dynasty which replaced the Zagwe in 1270 A.D. Fine illuminated books and manuscripts became a prominent element of Amharic culture. Equally fine garments and jewelry were produced for the ruling class and for the church. The top ecclesiastics were part of the nobility, and the institution of the monastery grew to great proportions in Ethiopia. The association of organized religion with the state was implicit in communal societies, where the distinction between politics, economics, religion, medicine, was scarcely drawn. Under feudalism everywhere, church and state were in close alliance. The Buddhists were pre-eminent in feudal Vietnam, Burma, Japan, and to a lesser extent in China. In India, a limited Buddhist influence was overwhelmed by that of the Hindus and Moslems; and of course in feudal Europe it was the Catholic church which played the role paralleled by the Orthodox church in Ethiopia.

The wealth of Ethiopia rested on an agricultural base. The fertile uplands supported cereal growing and there was considerable livestock raising, including the rearing of horses. Craft skills were developed in a number of spheres, and foreign craftsmen were encouraged. For instance, early in the fifteenth century, Turkish artisans settled in the country and made coats of mail and weapons for the Ethiopian army. Coptics from Egypt were also introduced to help run the financial administration. No one denies that the word "feudal" can be applied to Ethiopia in those centuries, because there existed a clear-cut class contradiction between the landlords and the peasants. Those relations grew out of the communalism that had characterized Ethiopia, like other parts of Africa, much earlier.

Feudal Ethiopia included lands that were communally owned by village and ethnic communities as well as lands belonging directly to the crown; but in addition large territories were conferred by the conquering Amharic dynasties on members of the royal family and on soldiers and priests. Those who received huge areas of land became *Ras*, or provincial princes, and they had judges appointed by the emperor attached to them. The peasants in their domain were reduced to tenants who could earn their living only by offering produce to the landlord and taxes to the state (also in produce). The landlords exempted themselves from tax—a typical situation in feudal societies, and one which fed the fires of revolution in Europe when the bourgeois class grew powerful enough to challenge the fact that the feudalists were using political power to tax everyone but themselves. Ethiopia, of course, never reached that stage of transition to capitalism. What is clear is that the transition to feudalism had been made.

Nubia

Nubia was another Christian region in Africa, but one which is not so famous as Ethiopia. In the sixth century A.D., Christianity was introduced into the middle Nile in the districts once ruled by the famous state of Kush, or Meroë. In the period before the birth of Christ, Kush was a rival to Egypt in splendor, and it ruled Egypt for a number of years. Its decline in the fourth century A.D. was completed by attacks from the then expanding Axum. The three small Nubian states which arose some time afterwards were to some extent the heirs of Kush, although after their conversion to Christianity it was this religion which dominated Nubian culture.

The Nubian states (which had consolidated to two by about the eighth century) achieved most from the ninth to the eleventh centuries, in spite of great pressures from Arab and Islamic enemies; and they did not finally succumb until the fourteenth century. Scholarly interest in Nubia has focused on the ruins of large red-brick churches and monasteries which had murals and frescoes of fine quality. Several conclusions can be drawn from the material evidence. In the first place, a great deal of labor was required to build those churches along with the stone fortifications which often surrounded them. As with the pyramids of Egypt or the feudal castles of Europe, the common builders were intensely exploited and probably coerced. Secondly, skilled labor was involved in the making of the bricks and in the architecture. The paintings indicate that the skills surpassed mere manual dexterity, and the same artistic merit is noticeable in fragments of painted pottery recovered from Nubia.

It has already been indicated that the churches and monasteries played a major role in Ethiopia, and this is worth elaborating on with respect to Nubia. The monastery was a major unit of production. Numerous peasant huts were clustered around each monastery, which functioned very much as did the manor of a feudal lord. The wealth that accumulated inside the churches was alienated from the peasants, while the finest aspects of the non-material culture, such as books, were accessible only to a small minority. Not only were the peasants illiterate, but in many cases they were non-Christians or only nominally Christian—judging from the better known Ethiopian example of the same date. When the Christian ruling class of Nubia was eliminated by the Moslems, very little of the achievements of the old state remained in the fabric of the people's daily lives. Such reversals in the historical process are not uncommon throughout human experience. Ultimately, the dialectic of development asserts itself, but some ebbing and flowing is inevitable. The Nubian states were not in existence in the fifteenth century, but they constitute a legitimate example of the potentialities of African development.

One can go further and discern that Kush was still contributing to African development long after the kingdom had declined and given way to Christian Nubia. It is clear that Kush was a center from which many positive cultural elements diffused to the rest of Africa. Brasswork of striking similarity to that of Meroë was reproduced in West Africa, and the technique by which West Africans cast their brass is generally held to have originated in Egypt and to have been passed on by way of Kush. Above all, Kush was one of the earliest and most vigorous centers of iron mining and smelting in Africa, and it was certainly one of the sources from which this crucial aspect of technology passed to the rest of the continent. That is why the middle Nile was a leading force in the social, economic, and political development of Africa as a whole.

Message to the Grassroots

Detroit, 1964

We want to have just an off-the-cuff chat between you and me, us. We want to talk right down to earth in a language that everybody here can easily understand. We all agree tonight, all of the speakers have agreed, that America has a very serious problem. Not only does America have a very serious problem, but our people have a very serious problem. America's problem is us. We're her problem. The only reason she has a problem is she doesn't want us here. And every time you look at yourself, be you black, brown, red or yellow, a so-called Negro, you represent a person who poses such a serious problem for America because you're not wanted. Once you face this as a fact, then you can start plotting a course that will make you appear intelligent, instead of unintelligent.

What you and I need to do is learn to forget our differences. When we come together, we don't come together as Baptists or Methodists. You don't catch hell because you're a Baptist, and you don't catch hell because you're a Methodist. You don't catch hell because you're a Methodist or Baptist, you don't catch hell because you're a Democrat or a Republican, you don't catch hell because you're a Mason or an Elk, and you sure don't catch hell because you're an American; because if you were an American, you wouldn't catch hell. You catch hell because you're a black man. You catch hell, all of us catch hell, for the same reason.

So we're all black people, so-called Negroes, second-class citizens, ex-slaves. You're nothing but an ex-slave. You don't like to be told that. But what else are you? You are ex-slaves. You didn't come here on the "Mayflower." You came here on a slave ship. In chains, like a horse, or a cow, or a chicken. And you were brought here by the people who came here on the "Mayflower," you were brought here by the so-called Pilgrims, or Founding Fathers. They were the ones who brought you here.

We have a common enemy. We have this in common: We have a common oppressor, a common exploiter, and a common discriminator. But once we all realize that we have a common enemy, then we unite—on the basis of what we have in common. And what we have foremost in common is that enemy—the white man. He's an enemy to all of us. I know some of you all think that some of them aren't enemies. Time will tell.

In Bandung back in, I think, 1954, was the first unity meeting in centuries of black people. And once you study what happened at the Bandung conference, and the results of the Bandung conference, it actually serves as a model for the same procedure you and

I can use to get our problems solved. At Bandung all the nations came together, the dark nations from Africa and Asia. Some of them were Buddhists, some of them were Muslims, some of them were Christians, some were Confucianists, some were atheists. Despite their religious differences, they came together. Some were communists, some were socialists, some were capitalists—despite their economic and political differences, they came together. All of them were black, brown, red or yellow.

The number-one thing that was not allowed to attend the Bandung conference was the white man. He couldn't come. Once they excluded the white man, they found that they could get together. Once they kept him out, everybody else fell right in and fell in line. This is the thing that you and I have to understand. And these people who came together didn't have nuclear weapons, they didn't have jet planes, they didn't have all of the heavy armaments that the white man has. But they had unity.

They were able to submerge their little petty differences and agree on one thing: That there one African came from Kenya and was being colonized by the Englishman, and another African came from the Congo and was being colonized by the Belgian, and another African came from Guinea and was being colonized by the French, and another came from Angola and was being colonized by the Portuguese. When they came to the Bandung conference, they looked at the Portuguese, and at the Frenchman, and at the Englishman, and at the Dutchman, and learned or realized the one thing that all of them had in common—they were all from Europe, they were all Europeans, blond, blue-eyed and white skins. They began to recognize who their enemy was. The same man that was colonizing our people in Kenya was colonizing our people in the Congo. The same one in the Congo was colonizing our people in South Africa, and in Southern Rhodesia, and in Burma, and in India, and in Afghanistan, and in Pakistan. They realized all over the world where the dark man was being oppressed, he was being oppressed by the white man; where the dark man was being exploited, he was being exploited by the white man. So they got together on this basis—that they had a common enemy.

And when you and I here in Detroit and in Michigan and in America who have been awakened today look around us, we too realize here in America we all have a common enemy, whether he's in Georgia or Michigan, whether he's in California or New York. He's the same man—blue eyes and blond hair and pale skin—the same man. So what we have to do is what they did. They agreed to stop quarreling among themselves. Any little spat that they had, they'd settle it among themselves, go into a huddle—don't let the enemy know that you've got a disagreement.

Instead of airing our differences in public, we have to realize we're all the same family. And when you have a family squabble, you don't get out on the sidewalk. If you do, everybody calls you uncouth, unrefined, uncivilized, savage. If you don't make it at home, you settle it at home; you get in the closet, argue it out behind closed doors, and then when you come out on the street, you pose a common front, a united front. And this is what we need to do in the community, and in the city, and in the state. We need to stop airing our differences in front of the white man, put the white man out of our meetings, and then sit down and talk shop with each other. That's what we've got to do.

I would like to make a few comments concerning the difference between the black revolution and the Negro revolution. Are they both the same? And if they're not, what is the difference? What is the difference between a black revolution and a Negro revolution? First, what is a revolution? Sometimes I'm inclined to believe that many of our people are using this word "revolution" loosely, without taking careful consideration of what this word actually means, and what its historic characteristics are. When you study the historic nature of revolution, the motive of a revolution, the objective of a revolution, the result of a revolution, and the methods used in a revolution, you may change words. You may devise another program, you may change your goal and you may change your mind.

Look at the American Revolution in 1776. That revolution was for what? For land. Why did they want land? Independence. How was it carried out? Bloodshed. Number one, it was based on land, the basis of independence. And the only way they could get it was bloodshed. The French Revolution—what was it based on? The landless against the land-lord. What was it for? Land. How did they get it? Bloodshed. Was no love lost, was no compromise, was no negotiation. I'm telling you—you don't know what a revolution is. Because when you find out what it is, you'll get back in the alley, you'll get out of the way.

The Russian Revolution—what was it based on? Land; the landless against the landlord. How did they bring it about? Bloodshed. You haven't got a revolution that doesn't involve bloodshed. And you're afraid to bleed. I said, you're afraid to bleed.

As long as the white man sent you to Korea, you bled. He sent you to Germany, you bled. He sent you to the South Pacific to fight the Japanese, you bled. You bleed for white people, but when it comes to seeing your own churches being bombed and little black girls murdered, you haven't got any blood. You bleed when the white man says bleed; you bite when the white man says bite; and you bark when the white man says bark. I hate to say this about us, but it's true. How are you going to be nonviolent in Mississippi, as violent as you were in Korea? How can you justify being nonviolent in Mississippi and Alabama, when your churches are being bombed, and your little girls are being murdered, and at the same time you are going to get violent with Hitler, and Tojo, and somebody else you don't even know?

If violence is wrong in America, violence is wrong abroad. If it is wrong to be violent defending black women and black children and black babies and black men, then it is wrong for America to draft us and make us violent abroad in defense of her. And if it is right for America to draft us, and teach us how to be violent in defense of her, then it is right for you and me to do whatever is necessary to defend our own people right here in this country.

The Chinese Revolution—they wanted land. They threw the British out, along with the Uncle Tom Chinese. Yes, they did. They set a good example. When I was in prison, I read an article—don't be shocked when I say that I was in prison. You're still in prison. That's what America means: prison. When I was in prison, I read an article in *Life* magazine showing a little Chinese girl, nine years old; her father was on his hands and knees and she was pulling the trigger because he was an Uncle Tom Chinaman. When they had the revolution over there, they took a whole generation of Uncle Toms and just wiped them out. And within ten years that little girl became a full-grown woman. No more Toms in China. And today it's one of the toughest, roughest, most feared countries on this earth—by the white man. Because there are no Uncle Toms over there.

Of all our studies, history is best qualified to reward our research. And when you see that you've got problems, all you have to do is examine the historic method used all over the world by others who have problems similar to yours. Once you see how they got theirs straight, then you know how you can get yours straight. There's been a revolution, a black revolution, going on in Africa. In Kenya, the Mau Mau were revolutionary; they were the ones who brought the word "Uhuru" to the fore. The Mau Mau, they were revolutionary, they believed in scorched earth, they knocked everything aside that got in their way, and their revolution also was based on land, a desire for land. In Algeria, the northern part of Africa, a revolution took place. The Algerians were revolutionists, they wanted land.

France offered to let them be integrated into France. They told France, to hell with France, they wanted some land, not some France. And they engaged in a bloody battle.

So I cite these various revolutions, brothers and sisters, to show you that you don't have a peaceful revolution. You don't have a turn-the-other-cheek revolution. There's no such thing as a nonviolent revolution. The only kind of revolution that is nonviolent is the Negro revolution. The only revolution in which the goal is loving your enemy is the Negro revolution. It's the only revolution in which the goal is a desegregated lunch counter, a desegregated theater, a desegregated park, and a desegregated public toilet; you can sit down next to white folks—on the toilet. That's no revolution. Revolution is based on land. Land is the basis of all independence. Land is the basis of freedom, justice, and equality.

The white man knows what a revolution is. He knows that the black revolution is worldwide in scope and in nature. The black revolution is sweeping Asia, is sweeping Africa, is rearing its head in Latin America. The Cuban Revolution—that's a revolution. They overturned the system. Revolution is in Asia, revolution is in Africa, and the white man is screaming because he sees revolution in Latin America. How do you think he'll react to you when you learn what a real revolution is? You don't know what a revolution is. If you did, you wouldn't use that word.

Revolution is bloody, revolution is hostile, revolution knows no compromise, revolution overturns and destroys everything that gets in its way. And you, sitting around here like a knot on the wall, saying, "I'm going to love these folks no matter how much they hate me." No, you need a revolution. Whoever heard of a revolution where they lock arms, as Rev. Cleage was pointing out beautifully, singing "We Shall Overcome"? You don't do that in a revolution. You don't do any singing; you're too busy swinging. It's based on land. A revolutionary wants land so he can set up his own nation, an independent nation. These Negroes aren't asking for any nation—they're trying to crawl back on the plantation.

When you want a nation, that's called nationalism. When the white man became involved in a revolution in this country against England, what was it for? He wanted this land so he could set up another white nation. That's white nationalism. The American Revolution was white nationalism. The French Revolution was white nationalism. The Russian Revolution too—yes, it was—white nationalism. You don't think so? Why do you think Khrushchev and Mao can't get their heads together? White nationalism. All the revolutions that are going on in Asia and Africa today are based on what?—black nationalism. A revolutionary is a black nationalist. He wants a nation. I was reading some beautiful words by Rev. Cleage, pointing out why he couldn't get together with someone else in the city because all of them were afraid of being identified with black nationalism. If you're afraid of black nationalism, you're afraid of revolution. And if you love revolution, you love black nationalism.

To understand this, you have to go back to what the young brother here referred to as the house Negro and the field Negro back during slavery. There were two kinds of slaves, the house Negro and the field Negro. The house Negroes—they lived in the house with master, they dressed pretty good, they ate good because they ate his food—what he left. They lived in the attic or the basement, but still they lived near the master; and they loved the master more than the master loved himself. They would give their life to save the master's house—quicker than the master would. If the master said, "We got a good house here," the house Negro would say, "Yeah, we got a good house here." Whenever the master said "we," he said "we." That's how you can tell a house Negro.

If the master's house caught on fire, the house Negro would fight harder to put the blaze out than the master would. If the master got sick, the house Negro would say, "What's the matter, boss, *we* sick?" *We* sick! He identified himself with his master, more than his master identified with himself. And if you came to the house Negro and said, "Let's run away, let's escape, let's separate," the house Negro would look at you and say, "Man, you crazy. What you mean, separate? Where is there a better house than this? Where can I wear better clothes than this? Where can I eat better food than this?" That was that house Negro. In those days he was called a "house nigger." And that's what we call them today, because we've still got some house niggers running around here.

This modern house Negro loves his master. He wants to live near him. He'll pay three times as much as the house is worth just to live near this master, and then brag about "I'm the only Negro out here." "I'm the only one on my job." "I'm the only one in this school." You're nothing but a house Negro. And if someone comes to you right now and says, "Let's separate," you say the same thing that the house Negro said on the plantation. "What you mean, separate? From America, this good white man? Where you going to get a better job than you get here?" I mean, this is what you say. "I ain't left nothing in Africa," that's what you say. Why, you left your mind in Africa.

On that same plantation, there was the field Negro. The field Negroes—those were the masses. There were always more Negroes in the field than there were Negroes in the house. The Negro in the field caught hell. He ate leftovers. In the house they ate high up on the hog. The Negro in the field didn't get anything but what was left of the insides of the hog. They call it "chitt'lings" nowadays. In those days they called them what they were—guts. That's what you were—gut-eaters. And some of you are still gut-eaters.

The field Negro was beaten from morning to night; he lived in a shack, in a hut; he wore old, castoff clothes. He hated his master. I say he hated his master. He was intelligent. That house Negro loved his master, but that field Negro—remember, they were in the majority, and they hated the master. When the house caught on fire, he didn't try to put it out; that field Negro prayed for a wind, for a breeze. When the master got sick, the field Negro prayed that he'd die. If someone came to the field Negro and said, "Let's separate, let's run," he didn't say, "Where we going?" He'd say, "Any place is better than here." You've got field Negroes in America today. I'm a field Negro. The masses are the field Negroes. When they see this man's house on fire, you don't hear the little Negroes talking about "*our* government is in trouble." They say, "*The* government is in trouble." Imagine a Negro: "*Our* government"! I even heard one say "*our* astronauts." They won't even let him near the plant—and "*our* astronauts"! "*Our* Navy"—that's a Negro that is out of his mind, a Negro that is out of his mind.

Just as the slavemaster of that day used Tom, the house Negro, to keep the field Negroes in check, the same old slavemaster today has Negroes who are nothing but modern Uncle Toms, twentieth-century Uncle Toms, to keep you and me in check, to keep us under control, keep us passive and peaceful and nonviolent. That's Tom making you nonviolent. It's like when you go to the dentist, and the man's going to take your tooth. You're going to fight him when he starts pulling. So he squirts some stuff in your jaw called novocaine, to make you think they're not doing anything to you. So you sit there and because you've got all of that novocaine in your jaw, you suffer—peacefully. Blood running all down your jaw, and you don't know what's happening. Because someone has taught you to suffer—peacefully.

The white man does the same thing to you in the street, when he want to put knots on your head and take advantage of you and not have to be afraid of your fighting back. To keep you from fighting back, he gets these old religious Uncle Toms to teach you and me, just like novocaine, to suffer peacefully. Don't stop suffering—just suffer peacefully. As Rev. Cleage pointed out, they say you should let your blood flow in the streets. This is a shame. You know he's a Christian preacher. If it's a shame to him, you know what it is to me.

There is nothing in our book, the Koran, that teaches us to suffer peacefully. Our religion teaches us to be intelligent. Be peaceful, be courteous, obey the law, respect everyone; but if someone puts his hand on you, send him to the cemetery. That's a good religion. In fact, that's that old-time religion. That's the one that Ma and Pa used to talk about: an eye for an eye, and a tooth for a tooth, and a head for a head, and a life for a life. That's a good religion. And nobody resents that kind of religion being taught but a wolf, who intends to make you his meal.

This is the way it is with the white man in America. He's a wolf—and you're sheep. Any time a shepherd, a pastor, teaches you and me not to run from the white man and, at the same time, teaches us not to fight the white man, he's a traitor to you and me. Don't lay down a life all by itself. No, preserve your life, it's the best thing you've got. And if you've got to give it up, let it be even-steven.

The slavemaster took Tom and dressed him well, fed him well, and even gave him a little education—a *little* education; gave him a long coat and a top hat and made all the other slaves look up to him. Then he used Tom to control them. The same strategy that was used in those days is used today, by the same white man. He takes a Negro, a so-called Negro, and makes him prominent, builds him up, publicizes him, makes him a celebrity. And then he becomes a spokesman for Negroes—and a Negro leader.

I would like to mention just one other thing quickly, and that is the method that the white man uses, how the white man uses the "big guns," or Negro leaders, against the Negro revolution. They are not a part of the Negro revolution. They are used against the Negro revolution.

When Martin Luther King failed to desegregate Albany, Georgia, the civil-rights struggle in America reached its low point. King became bankrupt almost, as a leader. The Southern Christian Leadership Conference was in financial trouble; and it was in trouble, period, with the people when they failed to desegregate Albany, Georgia. Other Negro civil-rights leaders of so-called national stature became fallen idols. As they became fallen idols, began to lose their prestige and influence, local Negro leaders began to stir up the masses. In Cambridge, Maryland, Gloria Richardson; in Danville, Virginia, and other parts of the country, local leaders began to stir up our people at the grassroots level. This was never done by these Negroes of national stature. They control you, but they have never incited you or excited you. They control you, they contain you, they have kept you on the plantation.

As soon as King failed in Birmingham, Negroes took to the streets. King went out to California to a big rally and raised I don't know many thousands of dollars. He came to Detroit and had a march and raised some more thousands of dollars. And recall, right after that Roy Wilkins attacked King. He accused King and CORE [Congress of Racial Equality] of starting trouble everywhere and then making the NAACP [National Association for the Advancement of Colored People] get them out of jail and spend a lot of money; they accused King and CORE of raising all the money and not paying it back. This happened; I've got it in documented evidence in the newspaper. Roy started attacking King, and King started attacking Roy, and [James] Farmer started attacking both of them. And as these Negroes of national stature began to attack each other, they began to lose their control of the Negro masses.

The Negroes were out there in the streets. They were talking about how they were going to march on Washington. Right at that time Birmingham had exploded, and the Negroes in Birmingham—remember, they also exploded. They began to stab the crackers in the back and bust them up 'side their head—yes, they did. That's when [President] Kennedy got on the television and said "this is a moral issue." That's when he said he was going to put out a civil-rights bill. And when he mentioned civil-rights bill and the Southern crackers started talking about how they were going to boycott or filibuster it, then the Negroes started talking—about what? That they were going to march on Washington, march on the Senate, march on the White House, march on the Congress, and tie it up, bring it to a halt, not let the government proceed. They even said they were going out to the airport and lay down on the runway and not let any airplanes land. I'm telling you what they said. That was revolution. That was revolution. That was the black revolution.

It was the grassroots out there in the street. It scared the white man to death, scared the white power structure in Washington, D.C., to death; I was here. When they found out that this black steamroller was going to come down on the capital, they called in Wilkins, they called in [A. Philip] Randolph, they called in these national Negro leaders that you respect and told them, "Call it off." Kennedy said, "Look, you all are letting this thing go too far." And Old Tom said, "Boss, I can't stop it, because I didn't start it." I'm telling you what they said. They said, "I'm not even in it, much less at the head of it." They said, "These Negroes are doing things on their own. They're running ahead of us." And that old shrewd fox, he said, "If you all aren't in it, I'll put you in it. I'll put you at the head of it. I'll endorse it. I'll welcome it. I'll help it. I'll join it."

A matter of hours went by. They had a meeting at the Carlyle Hotel in New York City. The Carlyle Hotel is owned by the Kennedy family; that's the hotel Kennedy spent the night at, two nights ago; it belongs to his family. A philanthropic society headed by a white man named Stephen Currier called all the top civil-rights leaders together at the Carlyle Hotel. And he told them, "By you all fighting each other, you are destroying the civil-rights movement. And since you're fighting over money from white liberals, let us set up what is known as the Council for United Civil Rights Leadership. Let's form this council, and all the civil-rights organizations will belong to it, and we'll use it for fund-raising purposes." Let me show you how tricky the white man is. As soon as they got it formed, they elected Whitney Young as its chairman, and who do you think became the co-chairman? Stephen Currier, the white man, a millionaire. [Adam Clayton] Powell was talking about it down at Cobo Hall today. This is what he was talking about. Powell knows it happened. Randolph knows it happened. Wilkins knows it happened. King knows it happened. Every one of the Big Six—they know it happened.

Once they formed it, with the white man over it, he promised them and gave them $800,000 to split up among the Big Six; and told them that after the march was over they'd give them $700,000 more. A million and a half dollars—split up between leaders that you have been following, going to jail for, crying crocodile tears for. And they're nothing but Frank James and Jesse James and the what-do-you-call-'em brothers.

As soon as they got the setup organized, the white man made available to them top public-relations experts; opened the news media across the country at their disposal, which then began to project these Big Six as the leaders of the march. Originally they weren't even in the march. You were talking this march talk on Hastings Street, you were talking march talk on Lenox Avenue, and on Fillmore Street, and on Central Avenue, and 32nd Street and 63rd Street. That's where the march talk was being talked. But the white man put the Big Six at the head of it; made them the march. They became the march.

Message to the Grassroots   727

They took it over. And the first move they made after they took it over, they invited Walter Reuther, a white man; they invited a priest, a rabbi, and an old white preacher, yes, an old white preacher. The same white element that put Kennedy into power—labor, the Catholics, the Jews, and liberal Protestants; the same clique that put Kennedy in power, joined the march on Washington.

It's just like when you've got some coffee that's too black, which means it's too strong. What do you do? You integrate it with cream, you make it weak. But if you pour too much cream in it, you won't even know you ever had coffee. It used to be hot, it becomes cool. It used to be strong, it becomes weak. It used to wake you up, now it puts you to sleep. This is what they did with the march on Washington. They joined it. They didn't integrate it, they infiltrated it. They joined it, became a part of it, took it over. And as they took it over, it lost its militancy. It ceased to be angry, it ceased to be hot, it ceased to be uncompromising. Why, it even ceased to be a march. It became a picnic, a circus. Nothing but a circus, with clowns and all. You had one right here in Detroit—I saw it on television—with clowns leading it, white clowns and black clowns. I know you don't like what I'm saying, but I'm going to tell you anyway. Because I can prove what I'm saying. If you think I'm telling you wrong, you bring me Martin Luther King and A. Philip Randolph and James Farmer and those other three, and see if they'll deny it over a microphone.

No, it was a sellout. It was a takeover. When James Baldwin came in from Paris, they wouldn't let him talk, because they couldn't make him go by the script. Burt Lancaster read the speech that Baldwin was supposed to make; they wouldn't let Baldwin get up there, because they know Baldwin is liable to say anything. They controlled it so tight, they told those Negroes what time to hit town, how to come, where to stop, what signs to carry, what song to sing, what speech they could make, and what speech they couldn't make; and then told them to get out of town by sundown. And every one of those Toms was out of town by sundown. Now I know you don't like my saying this. But I can back it up. It was a circus, a performance that beat anything Hollywood could ever do, the performance of the year. Reuther and those other three devils should get an Academy Award for the best actors because they acted like they really loved Negroes and fooled a whole lot of Negroes. And the six Negro leaders should get an award too, for the best supporting cast.

Walter Rodney

(1942–1980, Guyana)

Towards the Sixth Pan African Congress:
Aspects of the International Class Struggle
in Africa, the Caribbean, and America

1974, Dar es Salaam, Tanzania

Political conferences of the oppressed invariably attract a variety of responses, varying from cynical conviction that they are an utter waste of time to naive optimism that they will change the face of the world. In actuality, popular struggle continues from day to day at many different and more profound levels; its intensity at any given time primarily determines the relevance and utility of the conference as a technique of coordination. The Sixth Pan African Congress consciously aims at being heir to a tradition of conferences which grew out of the response of Africans to their oppression in the first half of this century. Therefore, its rationale must be sought through a careful determination of the coordinates of the contemporary endeavours of African people everywhere.

Since the Fifth Pan African Congress held in Manchester in 1945, the political geography of Africa has been transformed by the rise of some forty-two constitutionally independent political units presided over by Africans. This is to state the obvious. Yet, following in the wake of the great pageant of the regaining of political independence, there has come the recognition on the part of many that the struggle of the African people has intensified rather than abated, and that it is being expressed not merely as a contradiction between African producers and European capitalists but also as a conflict between the majority of the black working masses and a small African possessing class. This, admittedly, is to state the contentious; but the Sixth Pan African Congress will surely have to walk the tightrope of this point of contention.

Any "Pan" concept is an exercise in self-definition by a people, aimed at establishing a broader redefinition of themselves than that which had so far been permitted by those in power. Invariably, however, the exercise is undertaken by a specific social group or class which speaks on behalf of the population as a whole. This is always the case with respect to national movements. Consequently, certain questions must be placed on the agenda:

1. Which class leads the national movements?
2. How capable is this class of carrying out the historical tasks of national liberation?

3. Which are the silent classes on whose behalf "national" claims are being articulated?

The significance of the above questions emerges clearly in the classic case of Pan Slavic nationalism. The Pan Slavic ideology of the late nineteenth century and the turn of this century offered the Slav peoples of Eastern Europe a unified vision of themselves, aiming to transcend the fragmentation which was a consequence of the powerful waves of imperial expansion which had struck the shores of the Adriatic and the Black Seas. The Slav intelligentsia who advocated Pan Slavism were spokesmen of emergent bourgeois forces in the clash against feudalism, and their position also reflected some sympathy for the oppressed peasantry since it was in the interests of capitalism that serfdom be removed. But their hopes were frustrated because they failed to unseat indigenous and external feudal oppressors, including their Slav "brothers" who formed the ruling class in tsarist Russia. Subsequently, the local Balkan bourgeoisie were unable or unwilling to confront capitalist/imperialist partition, and their region gave rise to the term "balkanisation," as the supreme expression of failure to carry out the task of national liberation and unification. It was left to the Balkan masses under working class leadership, albeit under conditions of war, to tackle effectively the problems of nationalism and of broader eastern European unity in the period after the Second World War. Significantly enough, they did so within the context of socialist reconstruction, a task which was beyond groups benefiting from capitalist exploitation.

Pan Africanism in the post-independence era is internationalist in so far as it seeks the unity of peoples living in a large number of juridically independent states. But it is simultaneously a brand of nationalism, and one must therefore penetrate its nationalist form to appreciate its class content. This exercise is made easier by the fact that the nationalist movements in Africa which led to the regaining of independence in more than three dozen states constitute a phenomenon which has already received considerable attention. These movements were essentially political fronts or class alliances in which the grievances of all social groups were expressed as "national" grievances against the colonisers. However, while the workers and peasants formed the overwhelming numerical majority, the leadership was almost exclusively petty bourgeois. Understandably, this leadership placed to the fore those "national" aims which contributed most directly to the promotion of their own class interests; but they voiced sentiments which were historically progressive, partly because of their own confrontation with the colonialists and partly because of pressure from the masses.

Pan Africanism was one of these progressive sentiments, which served as a platform for that sector of the African or black petty bourgeois leadership which was most uncompromising in its struggle against colonialism at any given time during the colonial period.

Virtually all leaders of African independence movements paid at least lip service to the idea that regional freedom was only a step towards the freedom and unity of the whole continent, and the most advanced nationalists were usually the most explicit on the issue of Pan African solidarity. Nkrumah and Kenyatta were both at Manchester, while Nyerere, Kaunda, and Mboya were the driving forces behind the Pan African Movement for East and Central Africa (PAFMECA). Within the Francophone sphere, several leaders took Pan Africanist positions in one form or another. The radical Union des Populations de Cameroun refused to accept colonial boundaries in Africa; Senghor espoused a culturally oriented doctrine of black internationalism, comparable to Pan Africanism; and even Houphouet-Boigny was initially associated with a political party which was Pan Africanist in thrust, the Rasemblement Démocratique, which addressed itself to the whole of French

West Africa. Pan African solidarity also manifested itself with regard to the war of independence in Algeria, an episode which united not merely North Africa but also helped forge alliances between progressive nationalists on both sides of the Sahara. Similarly, the rise of national liberation movements dedicated to achieving freedom by any means necessary served to underscore the reality of Pan Africanism. All African leaders had to concede that freedom in Southern Africa was vital to guarantee freedom of any given sort in Africa, and the test of practice showed that commitment was greatest in the case of the most forward-looking of the petty bourgeois governments: Ghana (under Nkrumah), Egypt (under Nasser), Algeria, Tanzania, Zambia and Guinea.

It would be unhistorical to deny the progressive character of the African petty bourgeoisie at a particular moment in time. Owing to the low level of development of the productive forces in colonised Africa, it fell to the lot of the small, privileged, educated group to give expression to a mass of grievances against racial discrimination, low wages, low prices for cash crops, colonial bureaucratic commandism and the indignity of alien rule. But the petty bourgeoisie were reformers and not revolutionaries. Their class limitations were stamped upon the character of the independence which they negotiated with the colonial master. In the very process of demanding constitutional independence, they reneged on a cardinal principle of Pan Africanism: namely, the unity and indivisibility of the African continent.

The first Pan Africanists to engage in the political mobilisation of the African masses on African soil had a continental outlook. The African National Congress, which was formed in the Union of South Africa in 1912, aimed at being "African" and not merely "South African" and it was renamed in 1923 to emphasise this fact. Significantly, organisations of the same name extended into what is now Zimbabwe, Malawi, Zambia and Tanzania. It is also significant that dynamic African spokesmen of the 1930s like Nnamdi Azikiwe and Wallace Johnson were African first, rather than Nigerian or Sierra Leonean.

But the lawyers and place-seekers who eventually took the independence movement in hand were incapable of transcending the territorial boundaries of the colonial administrations. Imperialism defined the context in which constitutional power was to be handed over, so as to guard against the transfer of economic power or genuine political power. The African petty bourgeoisie accepted this, with only a small amount of dissent and disquiet being manifested by the progressive elements such as Nkrumah, Nyerere and Sekou Toure. Areas of West and Central Africa which experienced unipartite French colonial rule witnessed the shameless dismantling of those colonial polities which had a large territorial base. Whereas the French had maintained unity for exploitation, the African petty bourgeoisie lacked the capacity to demand both unity and freedom. So they accepted the balkanisation which led to fragments called Ivory Coast, Upper Volta, Niger, Chad, Central African Republic and so on. Since independence, little or no progress has been registered with respect to reversing this balkanisation.

It is a striking historical fact that the bourgeoisie proper have been the spearheads of national unity in the areas in which capitalism was first engendered. They sought political unity to guarantee the integration of production and distribution, giving rise to what were then relatively large nation states in Britain, France and Germany as compared to the numerous feudal chiefs which previously existed. The North American continent provides the most formidable example of the identification of bourgeois interests with federal unity and with the building of an infrastructure which rolled across a whole continent without regard to the cost in blood, especially since the blood spilt was principally African and Native American (Indian).

The petty bourgeoisie of Asia, Africa and Latin America are a different breed. They cannot be described as "entrepreneurs," "pioneers," "captains of industry," "robber barons" or in any of the swash-buckling terms coined to glorify the primary accumulation of capital. Frantz Fanon flays them unmercifully but truthfully when he points to the shoddy, imitative, lack-lustre character of the African petty bourgeoisie. Their role in the international capitalist system has always been that of compradors. Their capital outlay might often be greater than that of a factory owner during the industrial revolution in England during the early nineteenth century, but in the present era of monopoly capitalism it suffices mainly for chicken-farms. In any event, most of the African petty bourgeoisie is not directly involved in economic enterprises, their real sphere being the professions, the administration and the military/police hierarchy. They lack both the vision and the objective base to essay the leap towards continental unity.

A close scrutiny further reveals that the failure of the African ruling class to effect meaningful unity is not merely due to weakness. Recalling once more the dismantling process which took place in Francophone Africa at the time of negotiated independence, it can be seen that the pusillanimity of the African petty bourgeoisie in the face of the deliberate creation of non-viable, dependent mini-states by France attests not merely to the strength of the colonisers but also to fear on the part of the presumptive African rulers that larger territorial units might have negated their narrow class welfare. Throughout the continent, none of the successful independence movements denied the basic validity of the boundaries created a few decades ago by imperialism. To have done so would have been to issue a challenge so profound as to rule out the preservation of petty bourgeoisie interests in a compromise "independence" worked out in conjunction with international capital.

If the weakness of the present petty bourgeois leadership of Africa were the only problem then they could be dismissed as passive by-standers, who cannot make operational the potential of Pan Africanism as an ideology of liberation. However, they maintain themselves as a class by fomenting internal divisions and by dependence on external capitalist powers. These policies are antithetical to Pan Africanism. The record since independence confirms that the interests of the African petty bourgeoisie are as irreconcilable with genuine Pan Africanism as Pan Africanism is irreconcilable with the interests of international capitalism.

Most African mini-states are engaged in consolidating their territorial frontiers, in preserving the social relations prevailing inside these frontiers, and in protecting imperialism in the form of the monopolies and their respective states. The capitalist super powers, directly and indirectly, individually and collectively, guarantee the existence of the African petty bourgeoisie as a ruling class and use them to penetrate and manipulate African society. This has been done so crudely and openly that one does not have to be especially informed or specially aware in order to perceive what has been occurring. Ex-ambassadors of the U.S. have a way of reminiscing on how they cynically manoeuvred the Reds and the Blacks; local representatives of American, British and French security forces are so entrenched that they dispense with all cover; and the African petty bourgeoisie itself is so gauche that it rushes openly to the defence of an international monopoly such as Lonrho, when even the metropolitan political rulers are too embarrassed to do so.

All the activities of international capital aim at perpetuating the division of the continent which they initiated at the time of the Partition. The petty bourgeoisie is also showing that it seeks to maintain division of the African masses since the anti-colonial alliance with all other classes has gained its objective of formal independence. The only alliance which the African ruling class now vigorously defends is that with imperialism against the African people. Most decidedly, this power structure does not want to allow the masses either the consciousness or the reality of unity.

Pan Africanism has been so flouted by the present government that the concept of "African" is dead for all practical purposes such as travel and employment. The "Africanisation" that was aimed against the European colonial administrator soon gave way to restrictive employment and immigration practices by Ivory Coast, Ghana (under Busia), Zaire, Tanzania, Uganda, Zambia and others—aimed against Dahomeans, Nigerians, Burundi nationals, Malawians, Kenyans and all Africans who were guilty of believing that Africa was for the Africans. Of course it was said that unemployment among citizens of any given country forced the government to take such extreme steps. This is a pitiable excuse, which tries to hide the fact that unemployment is the responsibility of the neo-colonial regimes, which can do nothing better than preside over dependent economies with little growth and no development. In many respects, one African has been further shut off from another during the present neo-colonial phase than was the case during raw colonialism. Even within the context of the existing African nation states, the African ruling class has seldom sought to build anything other than tribal power bases, which means that they seek division and not unity at all levels of political activity, be it national, continental, or international.

The dominant mode of thinking of Africa today is inherited from the colonial masters and is given currency by the state apparatus. Not surprisingly, therefore, the very concept of class is ignored or mystified. The petty bourgeoisie get very upset at being called "petty bourgeois," and strenuously deny that there are any class differences between themselves on the one hand and the workers and peasants on the other hand. It is not surprising that socialism has been enemy number one for so many African states. African leaders fight the bogey of Communist threat rather than the reality of capitalist/imperialist oppression. Even the more progressive of this ruling class harbour and protect local reactionaries while neutralising or eliminating Marxist and other left wing elements. In ten, twelve, or fifteen years of constitutional independence, the various parts of Africa have scored no victories in ending exploitation and inequality. On the contrary, social differentials have increased rapidly and the same applies to the amount of surplus extracted by foreign monopoly capital. In the spheres of production and technology, the so-called "development decade" of the sixties offers the spectacle of decreasing agricultural production, a declining share of world trade and the proliferation of dependency structures because of the further penetration of multi-national corporations. All of these matters are highly relevant to a discussion of Pan Africanism.

The transformation of the African environment, the transformation of social and production relations, the break with imperialism, and the forging of African political and economic unity are all dialectically inter-related. This complex of historical tasks can be carried out only under the banner of Socialism and through the leadership of the working classes. The African petty bourgeoisie as a ruling class use their state power against Socialist ideology, against the material interests of the working class and against the political unity of the African masses.

Of course, the rhetoric of the African ruling class is something else. Only a Banda has the temerity to openly abuse the concept of African unity, and only a few others would openly espouse capitalism and imperialism as decent and just. Otherwise, the petty bourgeoisie prefers the technique of paying lip service to progressive ideas, seeking the defeat of these ideas through a process of trivialisation and vulgarisation. Both Socialism and Pan Africanism are of the utmost importance with respect to this technique. In one sense, the unwillingness of the petty bourgeoisie to manifest overt hostility to Socialism and Pan Africanism is a testimony to the development of mass consciousness and to the level of confrontation between progressive and reactionary forces on the world stage. But it is also very invidious in so far as pseudo-revolutionary positions tend to pre-empt genuinely revolutionary positions. For instance, the existing African regimes have helped create the illusion that the OAU [Organization of African Unity] represents the concretisation of Pan African unity. The OAU is the principal instrument which legitimises the forty-odd mini-states visited upon us by colonialism.

It is a tribute to the momentum of Pan Africanism that the OAU had to be formed. The idea of Pan African political unity had taken deep roots, and it had to be given expression if only in the form of a consultative international assembly. This indicates a higher level of continental political coordination than was to be found in Latin America during the period when the old colonial regimes there were demolished. It is also true that no imperialist power is a voting member of the organisation, in the way that the United States of America is entrenched within the Organisation of American States. Nevertheless, the OAU does far more to frustrate than the realise the concept of African unity.

The degree of its penetration by imperialist powers had been evidenced on numerous occasions, the most striking being those which have arisen around the Unilateral Declaration of Independence by the white minority in Zimbabwe, around the issue of "dialogue" with the white racist South African regime and over the persistence of the French in selling arms to the Republic of Southern Africa.

At best, the OAU regulates a few internal conflicts between the petty bourgeoisie from different parts of the continent. Beyond this, it is committed to maintain the separation of African peoples implicit in the present territorial boundaries, so as to buttress the exploitative social systems which prevail on the continent in this neo-colonial epoch.

When Lumumba was waging his heroic battle against imperialism in the Congo, it seemed for a brief while that there would be an alignment of progressive *versus* reactionary African forces. The masses of Africa were only too anxious to join their Congolese brothers in the fight against white and black mercenaries. Indeed, the lines were drawn so clearly that international revolutionary solidarity was forthcoming from many parts of the world. However, the continent suffered a setback in the Congo. Affairs in the Congo were "normalised" to the point of changing the country's name to Zaire. Meanwhile, one of the most important principles accepted by African governments in the wake of the defeat of the Congolese was that no popular dissident movement in an independent African country can be supported by any group or government in another independent African country. In constitutional terms, this is expressed in the fine-sounding phrase "non-interference in the internal affairs of a member state." In practical terms, this is how the most reactionary elements of the petty bourgeoisie tie the hands of the masses of Africa.

One of the cardinal principles of Pan Africanism is that the people of one part of Africa are responsible for the freedom of their brothers in other parts of Africa; indeed, black people everywhere were to accept the same responsibility. The OAU denies this, apart from areas still under formal colonial rule. By so doing, they are implying that the objective conditions which impelled the African masses to fight the colonialists have since been transformed, which is a blatant falsehood. Any exploitative, oppressive and autocratic African state is cordoned off against fellow African intervention or criticism, even when the most elementary civil and human rights are trampled down. Meanwhile, the more progressive states are not really protected against intrigues and various forms of aggression arranged by imperialism through the agency of the adjacent neo-colonial African states; and, in any event, Socialism cannot be built in any one African country, so that the few initiatives towards Socialist transformation on the continent are bound to be stifled by the continued division of Africa into artificial states.

The questions posed at the outset of this analysis in relation to the class content of nationalism suggested that one identifies the leading class, assesses its revolutionary capacity and evaluates the manner in which the subordinate classes are handled. Our conclusions at this point are that the African petty bourgeois leadership since independence has been an obstacle to the further development of the African revolution. A final illustration to this effect is the way in which the very vanguard of the Pan Africanist movement (as it emerged from the Fifth Congress) lost its direction and wallowed in bourgeois theory and practice. Like other African leaders, they too propagated the false antithesis between Pan Africanism and Communism, and intellectual activity spearheaded by no less a person than George Padmore.

Understandably, his practical politics suffered a corresponding decline; in spite of once having stood in the ranks of the international working class movement, Padmore found himself intervening in Guyana in the mid-1950's on the side of that section of the local leadership which was supported by the British and American governments, by local and foreign capitalists and by the CIA-infiltrated trade union, the AFL-CIO. At the same time, Nkrumah was engaging in ideological mystification under new facades such as "consciencism," while doing little to break the control of the international bourgeoisie or the Ghanaian petty bourgeoisie over the state. He had already eliminated the genuine working class leadership from the CPP [Convention People's Party] during the first years of power, and it was only after his overthrow by a reactionary petty bourgeois coup d'état that Nkrumah became convinced that there was a class struggle in Africa and that the national and Pan African movements required leadership loyal to its mass base of workers and peasants.

Obfuscation of the notion of class in post-independence Africa has made Pan Africanism a toothless slogan as far as imperialism is concerned, and it has actually been adopted by African chauvinists and reactionaries, marking a distinct departure from the earlier years of this century when the proponents of Pan Africanism stood on the left flank of their respective national movements on both sides of the Atlantic. The recapture of the revolutionary initiative should clearly be one of the foremost tasks of the Sixth Pan African Congress.

Although New World black representation predominated at all Pan African Congresses and Conferences in the past, the agenda were usually devoted almost exclusively to the affairs of the African continent. It can be assumed that the Sixth Pan African Congress will not be substantially different, but the creation of independent Caribbean nation-states does introduce a new dimension with regard to the participation of this part of the black world.

Having sketched the main outlines of the petty bourgeois position in Africa, it is unnecessary to elaborate on the Caribbean scene because of the numerous and basic similarities. It is to be noted, however, that which appears as tragedy against the vast back-cloth of Africa reappears as comedy in the Caribbean. Early this year, the people of the then-colony of Grenada took to the streets to express in uncompromising terms their opposition to the exploitative and oppressive system of Anglo-American colonialism, which is manned locally by a certain petty bourgeois clique. At the same time, the British government carried on, regardless, in its plans to grant independence to the said petty bourgeois clique, expressing reservations only on the point of whether or not it was safe to send a member of the Royal Family to preside over the independence ceremony. As it was, militant striking workers deprived the independence celebrations of telephone services, port services and electricity, but the petty bourgeois regime managed to find some fireworks to mark the auspicious occasion. What term other than "comedy" can describe such a situation?

The ruling class in each given British Caribbean territory usually takes pains to create a "national" identity, which amounts to little more than glorifying the fact that some Africans were sent to slave plantations in Jamaica or Trinidad rather than Barbados or Antigua, as the case may be. On the basis of this "nationalism," the petty bourgeoisie can continue the former British colonial policy of preventing trade unionists and progressives from moving freely amongst the people of the Caribbean. Another antic which is common on the part of the West Indian regimes is that they operate against (unarmed) national liberation movements inside the Caribbean while loudly proclaiming support of African liberation movements in Southern Africa.

This latter posture, along with other pro-African rhetoric, was forced on several West Indian leaders because of popular sympathy for the African cause at the mass level. The posturing and the rhetoric are extremely useful on jaunts to Africa in their quest for class alliances with the African petty bourgeoisie.

Yet, the realities of state power have predetermined that when the Sixth Pan African Congress meets in Dar es Salaam in June 1974 it will be attended mainly by spokesmen of African and Caribbean states which in so many ways represent the negation of Pan Africanism. One immediate consequence of the rise of constitutionally independent African and West Indian states is that for the first time such a gathering will be held on African soil and will be sponsored and directed by a black government, rather than being sponsored by blacks intellectuals as such and attended mainly by small black protest organisations, as was the case up to the Fifth Congress in Manchester. Already it is clear that states will be represented as states and that the OAU will play some role.

When a few individuals began to contemplate this Congress some three years ago, it was felt that it should be a coming together of black political movements, as distinct from governments. One school of thought envisaged that it would be select conferences of the most progressive elements in the black world. To a large extent, this was the significance of the All African People's Conference held in Accra in 1958. However, plans for a similar meeting in the 1970s would be hopelessly idealist. The African radicals of 1958 are by and large the incumbents in office today. The radicals of today lead at best an uncomfortable existence within African states, while some languish in prison or in exile. The present petty bourgeois regimes would look with disfavour at any organised programme which purported to be Pan African without their sanction and participation.

None of the progressive African regimes, which are already isolated and exposed to internal and external reaction, would dare to host a Congress which brought together only those who aggressively urge a unity of the African working masses and the building of a Socialist society. Such a Congress would have to be held in a metropolitan center, and would thus condemn itself to serve primarily as a forum for alienated intellectuals.

In the light of the above considerations, any African committed to freedom, Socialism and development would need to look long and hard at the political implications of participation in the Sixth Pan African Congress. The purists might be tempted to eschew any association whatsoever; but revolutionary praxis demands that one should contend against class enemies in theory and in practice, by seizing every opportunity to utilise all of the contradictions within imperialism as a global system; in this instance, contradictions born of economic exploitation and racist oppression.

Without falling into the trap of imagining that the present states of Africa and the

Caribbean will liberate the African masses from the tyranny of man and nature, it still remains an open political question as to how far they can be pressured to take steps which lessen the immediate impact of imperialist exploitation and which perhaps grant a respite to the producers and progressive forces. Southern Africa provides excellent illustrations to this effect. Our brothers in the South are striking blows which include attacks on enemy bases in Angola, the destruction of rail links in Mozambique, the disruption of production through strikes in Namibia and South Africa, and the intensification of politico-military offensives in Zimbabwe. The leadership even in the most reactionary African states have found it difficult to avoid responding in some positive manner to these activities; just as liberal organisations and governments of the capitalist world are now finding it prudent to join Socialists and radicals in giving international support to African liberation movements. It would be naive to abstain from participation in forums where the above processes are taking place, because a committed presence is essential both to accelerate, as well as to control, contributions which could otherwise cease to be merely opportunist and become actively counter-revolutionary.

Turning to the economic policy of African regimes, one also perceives that the dilemma of increasing underdevelopment places the petty bourgeoisie on the defensive. Whether within the OAU or in a wider non-aligned context, they can be propelled to consider new marketing arrangements, new forms of African and Third World cooperation and some devices to moderately restrain foreign exploitation. The agreement between oil producers has been the most striking in recent times. African governments have been understandably ambivalent in their attitude towards the manoeuvres of North African oil states and other producers in the Middle East, but the fact that so many members of the OAU broke diplomatic relations with Israel was no insignificant achievement in the face of Zionist and imperialist propaganda and penetration in Africa. Clearly, the system of neo-colonialism is not closed to elementary progressive steps by the present leadership. Strictly speaking, such steps derive from the restlessness of the workers and peasants and not merely from the perceived class interests of the petty bourgeoisie. For this reason, it is crucial that within a Pan African forum a principled and analytical position should be advanced for the adoption of increasingly revolutionary strategies for African economic and political liberation. The petty bourgeoisie must either be pushed forward or further exposed.

As stated at the outset, popular struggle is carried on in many ways and at many different levels. The struggle to participate is the opening round of the series of inter-connected battles likely to emerge out of the proposed Sixth Pan African Congress.

Queries have been raised with the Temporary Secretariat of the Congress concerning fears that anti-governmental organisations in the Caribbean would be excluded from participation, owing to the involvement of at least two (English-speaking) Caribbean governments in financing and in offering venues for preparatory meetings. . . .

In spite of re-assurances, it will undoubtedly require vigilance, mobilisation and perhaps confrontation within the Caribbean on the part of the left movements to confirm their right to attend, albeit alongside of representatives of governments and pro-government organisations. The apparent restriction of delegations to the English-speaking Caribbean is another negative feature. The seemingly superficial difference of language has always sharply divided the international black movement into an Anglophone sector and a Latin culture zone. French-speaking (and Spanish-speaking) blacks joined their brothers in French-ruled Africa in elaborating the initially anti-colonialist and anti-racist doctrine of *Negritude*. But, like Pan Africanism, *Negritude* in the hand of petty bourgeois black states became a sterile formulation of black chauvinism, incapable of challenging capitalism and imperialism. *Negritude* in Senegal buttresses neo-colonialism, while in Haiti it is used to gloss over an even more desperate situation of exploitation and suppression of the black masses.

It is important to break through the language barrier and it is crucial to recognise the existence of opposed tendencies within the international black world. The Congress organisers must be asked to take steps to reach the known nationalist and Socialist opponents of French colonial rule in places like Martinique and French Guyana; and they cannot be allowed to side-step the existence of a large black population in Cuba who have already accumulated rich experience in the liquidation of racism through Socialist transformation. But of course these are not tasks to be left solely to the Secretariat and the host country of Tanzania. Any Pan Africanists committed to Socialist revolution will first strive to ensure that the Congress and the future of Pan Africanism are not left to the tender mercies of the black petty bourgeoisie.

It is still not clear which governments will or will not participate in the proposed Sixth Pan African Congress. . . . The more conservative African governments may well view the whole idea with scepticism if not hostility. For them the OAU is quite enough for the realisation of Pan Africanism. . . .

The Congress must be asked to adopt the position that Liberation Movements should at all times be allowed to speak for themselves. The demand should be that, both inside and outside Africa, Liberation Movements should have unshakable credentials, instead of being excluded when their interests are being discussed, or instead of having to fight anew on each occasion to determine whether they should have the status of observers or second-class participants. It is for the Movements to indicate their own priorities and necessities at the Congress, and in response other delegates would contemplate the practical support which can be mobilised. It should also be made clear that the most positive support is the advancement of popular anti-imperialist power everywhere on the continent and in the Pan African world.

Vying with liberation in importance in the estimation of the authors of *The Call* is the question of science and technology. *The Call* asserts rightly that *"if we do not control the means of survival and protection in the context of the twentieth century we will continue to be colonised."* (Emphasis in the original.) Consequently, it proposes the establishment of a Pan African Centre of Science and Technology geared towards such priorities as the development of a viable, self-supporting agricultural system in Africa.

On the issue of technology, one is again faced with the fact that, superficially, universal agreement can be obtained. No one would deny the necessity for mobilising maximum resources in science and technology to fight the war against ignorance, disease and poverty. No one can remain indifferent to the chronic malnutrition or to the acute suffering brought on by widespread drought and famine. The danger is that a discussion of technology tends to become "technocratic" in the worst sense of the word. Drought and famine, for instance, are not merely "natural phenomena" arising out of the failure of precipitation from on high. The incapacity to prevent or deal with drought and famine and the fantastic hardship which ensues are all related to the socio-economic structures of neo-colonial Africa and to the way that our economies are located within the international imperialist system. It requires certain *political* decisions to change these structures and the system. Whether or not Africa will make scientific progress, whether or not the technology will be relevant and adequate, whether or not the mass of the people will benefit from scientific/technological innovations are all questions which can be resolved only within specific socio-economic contexts and questions which are therefore ultimately political and ideological.

It is precisely in the politico-ideological sphere that *The Call* is most deficient. It confines itself to the broad distinction between colonised blacks and European colonisers. It says nothing about the existence of capitalist and Socialist systems or of struggle within the capitalist/imperialist world. It comes out against the fact that Africans allow finance capital to dominate and direct their economic and social life; but this leaves room for the national bourgeois interpretation that this domination can be remedied while still remaining within the capitalist fold. Indeed, most African governments are at the moment screaming to become more deeply involved in the European Common Market. With regard to indigenous exploitation, the authors of *The Call* are prepared to *"stand with those who are avowed and open enemies of the elite who wish to lead a life of privilege among our people"*— which is fine but hardly sufficiently analytical and explicit.

•   •   •

Whatever may emerge from the Sixth Pan African Congress, it is necessary that some participants should be identified with a platform which recognises that:

1. The principal enemies of the African people are the capitalist class in the USA, Western Europe and Japan.

2. African liberation and unity will be realised only through struggle against the African allies of international capital.

3. African freedom and development require disengagement from international monopoly capital.

4. Exploitation of Africans can be terminated only through the construction of a Socialist society, and technology must be related to this goal.

5. Contemporary African state boundaries must be removed to make way for genuine politico-economic unity of the continent.

6. The Liberation Movements of Southern Africa are revolutionary and anti-imperialist and must therefore be defended against petty bourgeois state hegemony.

7. The unity of Africa requires the unity of progressive groups, organisations and institutions rather than merely being the preserve of states.

8. Pan Africanism must be an internationalist, anti-imperialist and Socialist weapon.

Martin Luther King, Jr.
(1929–1968, United States)

Letter from a Birmingham Jail

April 12, 1963

My dear Fellow Clergymen,

While confined here in the Birmingham [Alabama] city jail, I came across your recent statement calling our present activities "unwise and untimely." Seldom, if ever, do I pause to answer criticism of my work and ideas. If I sought to answer all of the criticisms that cross my desk, my secretaries would be engaged in little else in the course of the day, and I would have no time for constructive work. But since I feel that you are men of genuine good will and your criticisms are sincerely set forth, I would like to answer your statement in what I hope will be patient and reasonable terms.

I think I should give the reason for my being in Birmingham, since you have been influenced by the argument of "outsiders coming in." I have the honor of serving as president of the Southern Christian Leadership Conference, an organization operating in every southern state, with headquarters in Atlanta, Georgia. We have some eighty-five affiliate organizations all across the South—one being the Alabama Christian Movement for Human Rights. Whenever necessary and possible we share staff, educational and financial resources with our affiliates. Several months ago our local affiliate here in Birmingham invited us to be on call to engage in a nonviolent direct-action program if such were deemed necessary. We readily consented and when the hour came we lived up to our promises. So I am here, along with several members of my staff, because we were invited here. I am here because I have basic organizational ties here.

Beyond this, I am in Birmingham because injustice is here. Just as the eighth century prophets left their little villages and carried their "thus saith the Lord" far beyond the boundaries of their hometowns; and just as the Apostle Paul left his little village of Tarsus and carried the gospel of Jesus Christ to practically every hamlet and city of the Graeco-Roman world, I too am compelled to carry the gospel of freedom beyond my particular hometown. Like Paul, I must constantly respond to the Macedonian call for aid.

Moreover, I am cognizant of the interrelatedness of all communities and states. I cannot sit idly by in Atlanta and not be concerned about what happens in Birmingham. Injustice anywhere is a threat to justice everywhere. We are caught in an inescapable network of mutuality, tied in a single garment of destiny. Whatever affects one directly affects all indirectly. Never again can we afford to live with the narrow, provincial "outside agitator" idea. Anyone who lives in the United States can never be considered an outsider anywhere in this country.

You deplore the demonstrations that are presently taking place in Birmingham. But I am sorry that your statement did not express a similar concern for the conditions that brought the demonstrations into being. I am sure that each of you would want to go beyond the superficial social analyst who looks merely at effects, and does not grapple with underlying causes. I would not hesitate to say that it is unfortunate that so-called demonstrations are taking place in Birmingham at this time, but I would say in more emphatic terms that it is even more unfortunate that the white power structure of this city left the Negro community with no other alternative.

In any nonviolent campaign there are four basic steps: (1) collection of the facts to determine whether injustices are alive, (2) negotiation, (3) self-purification, and (4) direct action. We have gone through all of these steps in Birmingham. There can be no gainsaying of the fact that racial injustice engulfs this community.

Birmingham is probably the most thoroughly segregated city in the United States. Its ugly record of police brutality is known in every section of this country. Its injust treatment of Negroes in the courts is a notorious reality. There have been more unsolved bombings of Negro homes and churches in Birmingham than any city in this nation. These are the hard, brutal and unbelievable facts. On the basis of these conditions Negro leaders sought to negotiate with the city fathers. But the political leaders consistently refused to engage in good faith negotiations.

Then came the opportunity last September to talk with some of the leaders of the economic community. In these negotiating sessions certain promises were made by the merchants—such as the promise to remove the humiliating racial signs from the stores. On the basis of these promises Rev. Shuttlesworth and the leaders of the Alabama Christian Movement for Human Rights agreed to call a moratorium on any type of demonstrations. As the weeks and months unfolded we realized that we were the victims of a broken promise. The signs remained. Like so many experiences of the past we were confronted with blasted hopes, and the dark shadow of a deep disappointment settled upon us. So we had no alternative except that of preparing for direct action, whereby we would present our very bodies as a means of laying our case before the conscience of the local and national community. We were not unmindful of the difficulties involved. So we decided to go through a process of self-purification. We started having workshops on nonviolence and repeatedly asked ourselves the questions, "Are you able to accept blows without retaliating?" "Are you able to endure the ordeals of jail?" We decided to set our direct-action program around the Easter season, realizing that with the exception of Christmas, this was the largest shopping period of the year. Knowing that a strong economic withdrawal program would be the by-product of direct action, we felt that this was the best time to bring pressure on the merchants for the needed changes. Then it occurred to us that the March election was ahead and so we speedily decided to postpone action until after election day. When we discovered that Mr. Connor was in the run-off, we decided again to postpone action so that the demonstrations could not be used to cloud the issues. At this time we agreed to begin our nonviolent witness the day after the run-off.

This reveals that we did not move irresponsibly into direct action. We too wanted to see Mr. Connor defeated; so we went through postponement after postponement to aid in this community need. After this we felt that direct action could be delayed no longer.

You may well ask, "Why direct action? Why sit-ins, marches, etc.? Isn't negotiation a better path?" You are exactly right in your call for negotiation. Indeed, this is the purpose of direct action. Nonviolent direct action seeks to create such a crisis and establish such creative tension that a community that has constantly refused to negotiate is forced to confront the issue. It seeks so to dramatize the issue that it can no longer be ignored. I just referred to the creation of tension as a part of the work of the nonviolent resister. This may sound rather shocking. But I must confess that I am not afraid of the word tension. I have earnestly worked and preached against violent tension, but there is a type of constructive nonviolent tension that is necessary for growth. Just as Socrates felt that it was necessary to create a tension in the mind so that individuals could rise from the bondage of myths and half-truths to the unfettered realm of creative analysis and objective appraisal, we must see the need of having nonviolent gadflies to create the kind of tension in society that will help men to rise from the dark depths of prejudice and racism to the majestic heights of understanding and brotherhood. So the purpose of the direct action is to create a situation so crisis-packed that it will inevitably open the door to negotiation. We, therefore, concur with you in your call for negotiation. Too long has our beloved Southland been bogged down in the tragic attempt to live in monologue rather than dialogue.

One of the basic points in your statement is that our acts are untimely. Some have asked, "Why didn't you give the new administration time to act?" The only answer that I can give to this inquiry is that the new administration must be prodded about as much as the outgoing one before it acts. We will be sadly mistaken if we feel that the election of Mr. Boutwell will bring the millennium to Birmingham. While Mr. Boutwell is much more articulate and gentle than Mr. Connor, they are both segregationists, dedicated to the task of maintaining the status quo. The hope I see in Mr. Boutwell is that he will be reasonable enough to see the futility of massive resistance to desegregation. But he will not see this without pressure from the devotees of civil rights. My friends, I must say to you that we have not made a single gain in civil rights without determined legal and nonviolent pressure. History is the long and tragic story of the fact that privileged groups seldom give up their privileges voluntarily. Individuals may see the moral light and voluntarily give up their unjust posture; but as Reinhold Niebuhr has reminded us, groups are more immoral than individuals.

We know through painful experience that freedom is never voluntarily given by the oppressor; it must be demanded by the oppressed. Frankly, I have never yet engaged in a direct action movement that was "well-timed," according to the timetable of those who have not suffered unduly from the disease of segregation. For years now I have heard the word "Wait!" It rings in the ear of every Negro with a piercing familiarity. This "Wait" has almost always meant "Never." It has been a tranquilizing thalidomide, relieving the emotional stress for a moment, only to give birth to an ill-formed infant of frustration. We must come to see with the distinguished jurist of yesterday that "justice too long delayed is justice denied." We have waited for more than 340 years for our constitutional and God-given rights. The nations of Asia and Africa are moving with jetlike speed toward the goal of political independence, and we still creep at horse and buggy pace toward the gaining of a cup of coffee at a lunch counter. I guess it is easy for those who have never felt the stinging darts of segregation to say, "Wait." But when you have seen vicious mobs lynch your mothers and fathers at will and drown your sisters and brothers at whim; when you have seen hate-filled policemen curse, kick, brutalize and even kill your black brothers and sisters with impunity; when you see that vast majority of your twenty million Negro brothers smothering in an airtight cage of poverty in the midst of an affluent society; when you suddenly find your tongue twisted and your speech stammering as you seek to explain to your six-year-old daughter why she can't go to the public amusement park that has just been advertised on television, and see tears welling up in her little eyes when she is told that Funtown is closed to colored children, and see the depressing clouds of inferiority begin to form in her little mental sky, and see her begin to distort her little personality by unconsciously developing a bitterness toward white people; when you have to concoct an answer for a five-year-old son asking in agonizing pathos: "Daddy, why do white people treat colored people so mean?"; when you take a cross-country drive and find it necessary to sleep night after night in the uncomfortable corners of your automobile because no motel will accept you; when you are humiliated day in and day out by nagging signs reading "white" and "colored"; when your first name becomes "nigger" and your middle name becomes "boy" (however old you are) and your last name becomes "John," and when your wife and mother are never given the respected title "Mrs."; when you are harried by day and haunted by night by the fact that you are a Negro, living constantly at tiptoe stance never quite knowing what to expect next, and plagued with inner fears and outer resentments; when you are forever fighting a degenerating sense of "nobodiness"; then you will understand why we find it difficult to wait. There comes a time when the cup of endurance runs over, and men are no longer willing to be plunged into a abyss of injustice where they experience the blackness of corroding despair. I hope, sirs, you can understand our legitimate and unavoidable impatience.

You express a great deal of anxiety over our willingness to break laws. This is certainly a legitimate concern. Since we so diligently urge people to obey the Supreme Court's decision of 1954 outlawing segregation in the public schools, it is rather strange and paradoxical to find us consciously breaking laws. One may well ask, "How can you advocate breaking some laws and obeying others?" The answer is found in the fact that there are two types of laws: there are *just* and there are *unjust* laws. I would agree with Saint Augustine that "An unjust law is no law at all."

Now what is the difference between the two? How does one determine when a law is just or unjust? A just law is a man-made code that squares with the moral law or the law of God. An unjust law is a code that is out of harmony with the moral law. To put it in the terms of Saint Thomas Aquinas, an unjust law is a human law that is not rooted in eternal and natural law. Any law that uplifts human personality is just. Any law that degrades human personality is unjust. All segregation statutes are unjust because segregation distorts the soul and damages the personality. It gives the segregator a false sense of superiority, and the segregated a false sense of inferiority. To use the words of Martin Buber, the great Jewish philosopher, segregation substitutes an "I-it" relationship for the "I-thou" relationship, and ends up relegating persons to the status of things. So segregation is not only politically, economically and sociologically unsound, but it is morally wrong and sinful. Paul Tillich has said that sin is separation. Isn't segregation an existential expression of man's tragic separation, an expression of his awful estrangement, his terrible sinfulness? So I can urge men to disobey segregation ordinances because they are morally wrong.

Let us turn to a more concrete example of just and unjust laws. An unjust law is a code that a majority inflicts on a minority that is not binding on itself. This is difference made legal. On the other hand a just law is a code that a majority compels a minority to follow that it is willing to follow itself. This is sameness made legal.

Let me give another explanation. An unjust law is a code inflicted upon a minority which that minority had no part in enacting or creating because they did not have the unhampered right to vote. Who can say that the legislature of Alabama which set up the segregation laws was democratically elected? Throughout the state of Alabama all types of conniving methods are used to prevent Negroes from becoming registered voters and there are some counties without a single Negro registered to vote despite the fact that the

Negro constitutes a majority of the population. Can any law set up in such a state be considered democratically structured?

These are just a few examples of unjust and just laws. There are some instances when a law is just on its face and unjust in its application. For instance, I was arrested Friday on a charge of parading without a permit. Now there is nothing wrong with an ordinance which requires a permit for a parade, but when the ordinance is used to preserve segregation and to deny citizens the First Amendment privilege of peaceful assembly and peaceful protest, then it becomes unjust.

I hope you can see the distinction I am trying to point out. In no sense do I advocate evading or defying the law as the rabid segregationist would do. This would lead to anarchy. One who breaks an unjust law must do it *openly, lovingly* (not hatefully as the white mothers did in New Orleans when they were seen on television screaming, "nigger, nigger, nigger"), and with a willingness to accept the penalty. I submit that an individual who breaks a law that conscience tells him is unjust, and willingly accepts the penalty by staying in jail to arouse the conscience of the community over its injustice, is in reality expressing the very highest respect for law.

Of course, there is nothing new about this kind of civil disobedience. It was seen sublimely in the refusal of Shadrach, Meshach and Abednego to obey the laws of Nebuchadnezzar because a higher moral law was involved. It was practiced superbly by the early Christians who were willing to face hungry lions and the excruciating pain of chopping blocks, before submitting to certain unjust laws of the Roman Empire. To a degree academic freedom is a reality today because Socrates practiced civil disobedience.

We can never forget that everything Hitler did in Germany was "legal" and everything the Hungarian freedom fighters did in Hungary was "illegal." It was "illegal" to aid and comfort a Jew in Hitler's Germany. But I am sure that if I lived in Germany during that time I would have aided and comforted my Jewish brothers even though it was illegal. If I lived in a Communist country today where certain principles dear to the Christian faith are suppressed, I believe I would openly advocate disobeying these anti-religious laws. I must make two honest confessions to you, my Christian and Jewish brothers. First, I must confess that over the last few years I have been gravely disappointed with the white moderate. I have almost reached the regrettable conclusion that the Negro's great stumbling block in the stride toward freedom is not the White Citizen's Counciler or the Ku Klux Klanner, but the white moderate who is more devoted to "order" than to justice; who prefers a negative peace which is the absence of tension to a positive peace which is the presence of justice; who constantly says, "I agree with you in the goal you seek, but I can't agree with your methods of direct action"; who paternalistically feels that he can set the timetable for another man's freedom; who lives by the myth of time and who constantly advises the Negro to wait until a "more convenient season." Shallow understanding from people of good will is more frustrating than absolute misunderstanding from people of ill will. Lukewarm acceptance is much more bewildering than outright rejection.

I had hoped that the white moderate would understand that law and order exist for the purpose of establishing justice, and that when they fail to do this they become dangerously structured dams that block the flow of social progress. I had hoped that the white moderate would understand that the present tension of the South is merely a necessary phase of the transition from an obnoxious negative peace, where the Negro passively accepted his unjust plight, to a substance-filled positive peace, where all men will respect the dignity and worth of human personality. Actually, we who engage in nonviolent direct action are not the creators of tension. We merely bring to the surface the hidden tension that is already alive. We bring it out in the open where it can be seen and dealt with. Like a boil that can never be cured as long as it is covered up but must be opened with all its pus-flowing ugliness to the natural medicines of air and light, injustice must likewise be exposed, with all of the tension its exposing creates, to the light of human conscience and the air of national opinion before it can be cured.

In your statement you asserted that our actions, even though peaceful, must be condemned because they precipitate violence. But can this assertion be logically made? Isn't this like condemning the robbed man because his possession of money precipitated the evil act of robbery? Isn't this like condemning Socrates because his unswerving commitment to truth and his philosophical delvings precipitated the misguided popular mind to make him drink the hemlock? Isn't this like condemning Jesus because His unique God-consciousness and never-ceasing devotion to His will precipitated the evil act of crucifixion? We must come to see, as federal courts have consistently affirmed, that it is immoral to urge an individual to withdraw his efforts to gain his basic constitutional rights because the quest precipitates violence. Society must protect the robbed and punish the robber.

I had also hoped that the white moderate would reject the myth of time. I received a letter this morning from a white brother in Texas which said: "All Christians know that the colored people will receive equal rights eventually, but it is possible that you are in too great of a religious hurry. It has taken Christianity almost two thousand years to accomplish what it has. The teachings of Christ take time to come to earth." All that is said here grows out of a tragic misconception of time. It is the strangely irrational notion that there is something in the very flow of time that will inevitably cure all ills. Actually time is neutral. It can be used either destructively or constructively. I am coming to feel that the people of ill will have used time much more effectively than the people of good will. We will have to repent in this generation not merely for the vitriolic words and actions of the bad people, but for the appalling silence of the good people. We must come to see that human progress never rolls in on wheels of inevitability. It comes through the tireless efforts and persistent work of men willing to be co-workers with God, and without this hard work time itself becomes an ally of the forces of social stagnation. We must use time creatively, and forever realize that the time is always ripe to do right. Now is the time to make real the promise of democracy, and transform our pending national elegy into a creative psalm of brotherhood. Now is the time to lift our national policy from the quicksand of racial injustice to the solid rock of human dignity.

You spoke of our activity in Birmingham as extreme. At first I was rather disappointed that fellow clergymen would see my nonviolent efforts as those of the extremist. I started thinking about the fact that I stand in the middle of two opposing forces in the Negro community. One is a force of complacency made up of Negroes who, as a result of long years of oppression, have been so completely drained of self-respect and a sense of "somebodiness" that they have adjusted to segregation, and, of a few Negroes in the middle class who, because of a degree of academic and economic security, and because at points they profit by segregation, have unconsciously become insensitive to the problems of the masses. The other force is one of bitterness and hatred, and comes perilously close to advocating violence. It is expressed in the various black nationalist groups that are springing up over the nation, the largest and best known being Elijah Muhammad's Muslim movement. This movement is nourished by the contemporary frustration over the continued existence of racial discrimination. It is made up of people who have lost faith in America, who have absolutely repudiated Christianity, and who have concluded that the white man is an incurable "devil." I have tried to stand between these two forces, saying that we need not follow the "do-nothingism" of the complacent or the hatred and despair of the black nationalist. There is the more excellent way of love and nonviolent protest. I'm grateful to God that, through the Negro church, the dimension of nonviolence entered our struggle. If this philosophy had not emerged, I am convinced that by now many streets of the South would be flowing with floods of blood. And I am further convinced that if our white brothers dismiss us as "rabble-rousers" and "outside agitators" those of us who are working through the channels of nonviolent direct action and refuse to support our nonviolent efforts, millions of Negroes, out of frustration and despair, will seek solace and security in black nationalist ideologies, a development that will lead inevitably to a frightening racial nightmare.

Oppressed people cannot remain oppressed forever. The urge for freedom will eventually come. This is what happened to the American Negro. Something within has reminded him of his birthright of freedom; something without has reminded him that he can gain it. Consciously and unconsciously, he has been swept in by what the Germans call the *Zeitgeist,* and with his black brothers of Africa, and his brown and yellow brothers of Asia, South America and the Caribbean, he is moving with a sense of cosmic urgency toward the promised land of racial justice. Recognizing this vital urge that has engulfed the Negro community, one should readily understand public demonstrations. The Negro has many pent-up resentments and latent frustrations. He has to get them out. So let him march sometime; let him have his prayer pilgrimages to the city hall; understand why he must have sit-ins and freedom rides. If his repressed emotions do not come out in these nonviolent ways, they will come out in ominous expressions of violence. This is not a threat; it is a fact of history. So I have not said to my people "get rid of your discontent." But I have tried to say that this normal and healthy discontent can be channelized through the creative outlet of nonviolent direct action. Now this approach is being dismissed as extremist. I must admit that I was initially disappointed in being so categorized.

But as I continued to think about the matter I gradually gained a bit of satisfaction from being considered an extremist. Was not Jesus an extremist in love—"Love your enemies, bless them that curse you, pray for them that despitefully use you." Was not Amos an extremist for justice—"Let justice roll down like waters and righteousness like a mighty stream." Was not Paul an extremist for the gospel of Jesus Christ—"I bear in my body the marks of the Lord Jesus." Was not Martin Luther an extremist—"Here I stand; I can do none other so help me God." Was not John Bunyan an extremist—"I will stay in jail to the end of my days before I make a butchery of my conscience." Was not Abraham Lincoln an extremist—"This nation cannot survive half slave and half free." Was not Thomas Jefferson an extremist—"We hold these truths to be self-evident, that all men are created equal." So the question is not whether we will be extremist but what kind of extremist will we be. Will we be extremists for hate or will we be extremists for love? Will we be extremists for the preservation of injustice—or will we be extremists for the cause of justice? In that dramatic scene on Calvary's hill, three men were crucified. We must not forget that all three were crucified for the same crime—the crime of extremism. Two were extremists for immorality, and thusly fell below their environment. The other, Jesus Christ, was an extremist for love, truth and goodness, and thereby rose above his environment. So, after all, maybe the South, the nation and the world are in dire need of creative extremists.

I had hoped that the white moderate would see this. Maybe I was too optimistic. Maybe I expected too much. I guess I should have realized that few members of a race that has oppressed another race can understand or appreciate the deep groans and passionate yearnings of those that have been oppressed and still fewer have the vision to see that injustice must be rooted out by strong, persistent and determined action. I am thankful, however, that some of our white brothers have grasped the meaning of this social revolution and committed themselves to it. They are still all too small in quantity, but they are big in quality. Some like Ralph McGill, Lillian Smith, Harry Golden and James Dabbs have written about our struggle in eloquent, prophetic and understanding terms. Others have marched with us down nameless streets of the South. They have languished in filthy roach-infested jails, suffering the abuse and brutality of angry policemen who see them as "dirty nigger-lovers." They, unlike so many of their moderate brothers and sisters, have recognized the urgency of the moment and sensed the need for powerful "action" antidotes to combat the disease of segregation.

Let me rush on to mention my other disappointment. I have been so greatly disappointed with the white church and its leadership. Of course, there are some notable exceptions. I am not unmindful of the fact that each of you has taken some significant stands on this issue. I commend you, Rev. Stallings, for your Christian stance on this past Sunday, in welcoming Negroes to your worship service on a non-segregated basis. I commend the Catholic leaders of this state for integrating Springhill College several years ago.

But despite these notable exceptions I must honestly reiterate that I have been disappointed with the church. I do not say that as one of the negative critics who can always find something wrong with the church. I say it as a minister of the gospel, who loves the church; who was nurtured in its bosom; who has been sustained by its spiritual blessings and who will remain true to it as long as the cord of life shall lengthen.

I had the strange feeling when I was suddenly catapulted into the leadership of the bus protest in Montgomery several days ago that we would have the support of the white church. I felt that the white ministers, priests and rabbis of the South would be some of our strongest allies. Instead, some have been outright opponents, refusing to understand the freedom movement and misrepresenting its leaders; all too many others have been more cautious than courageous and have remained silent behind the anesthetizing security of the stained-glass windows.

In spite of my shattered dreams of the past, I came to Birmingham with the hope that the white religious leadership of this community would see the justice of our case, and with deep moral concern, serve as the channel through which our just grievances would get to the power structure. I had hoped that each of you would understand. But again I have been disappointed. I have heard numerous religious leaders of the South call upon their worshippers to comply with a desegregation decision because it is the *law*, but I have longed to hear white ministers say, "Follow this decree because integration is morally *right* and the Negro is your brother." In the midst of blatant injustices inflicted upon the Negro, I have watched white churches stand on the sideline and merely mouth pious irrelevancies and sanctimonious trivialities. In the midst of a mighty struggle to rid our nation of racial and economic injustice, I have heard so many ministers say, "Those are social issues with which the gospel has no real concern," and I have watched so many churches commit themselves to a completely otherworldly religion which made a strange distinction between body and soul, the sacred and the secular.

So here we are moving toward the exit of the twentieth century with a religious community largely adjusted to the status quo, standing as a taillight behind other community agencies rather than a headlight leading men to higher levels of justice.

I have traveled the length and breadth of Alabama, Mississippi and all the other southern states. On sweltering summer days and crisp autumn mornings I have looked at her beautiful churches with their lofty spires pointing heavenward. I have beheld the impressive outlay of her massive religious education buildings. Over and over again I have found myself asking: "What kind of people worship here? Who is their God? Where were their voices when the lips of Governor Barnett dripped with words of interposition and nullification? Where were they when Governor Wallace gave the clarion call for defiance and hatred? Where were their voices of support when tired, bruised and weary Negro men and women decided to rise from the dark dungeons of complacency to the bright hills of creative protest?"

Yes, these questions are still in my mind. In deep disappointment, I have wept over the laxity of the church. But be assured that my tears have been tears of love. There can be no deep disappointment where there is not deep love. Yes, I love the church; I love her sacred walls. How could I do otherwise? I am in the rather unique position of being the son, the grandson and the great-grandson of preachers. Yes, I see the church as the body of Christ. But, oh! How we have blemished and scarred that body through social neglect and fear of being nonconformists.

There was a time when the church was very powerful. It was during that period when the early Christians rejoiced when they were deemed worthy to suffer for what they believed. In those days the church was not merely a thermometer that recorded the ideas and principles of popular opinion; it was a thermostat that transformed the mores of society. Wherever the early Christians entered a town the power structure got disturbed and immediately sought to convict them for being "disturbers of the peace" and "outside agitators." But they went on with the conviction that they were "a colony of heaven," and had to obey God rather than man. They were small in number but big in commitment. They were too God-intoxicated to be "astronomically intimidated." They brought an end to such ancient evils as infanticide and gladiatorial contest.

Things are different now. The contemporary church is often a weak, ineffectual choice with an uncertain sound. It is so often the arch-supporter of the status quo. Far from being disturbed by the presence of the church, the power structure of the average community is consoled by the church's silent and often vocal sanction of things as they are.

But the judgment of God is upon the church as never before. If the church of today does not recapture the sacrificial spirit of the early church, it will lose its authentic ring, forfeit the loyalty of millions, and be dismissed as an irrelevant social club with no meaning for the twentieth century. I am meeting young people every day whose disappointment with the church has risen to outright disgust.

Maybe again, I have been too optimistic. Is organized religion too inextricably bound to the status quo to save our nation and the world? Maybe I must turn my faith to the inner spiritual church, the church within the church, as the true *ecclesia* and the hope of the world. But again I am thankful to God that some noble souls from the ranks of organized religion have broken loose from the paralyzing chains of conformity and joined us as active partners in the struggle for freedom. They have left their secure congregations and walked the streets of Albany, Georgia, with us. They have gone through the highways of the South on tortuous rides for freedom. Yes, they have gone to jail with us. Some have been kicked out of their churches, and lost support of their bishops and fellow ministers. But they have gone with the faith that right defeated is stronger than evil triumphant. These men have been the leaven in the lump of the race. Their witness has been the spiritual salt that has preserved the true meaning of the gospel in these troubled times. They have carved a tunnel of hope through the dark mountain of disappointment.

I hope the church as a whole will meet the challenge of this decisive hour. But even if the church does not come to the aid of justice, I have no despair about the future. I have no fear about the outcome of our struggle in Birmingham, even if our motives are presently misunderstood. We will reach the goal of freedom in Birmingham and all over the nation, because the goal of America is freedom. Abused and scorned though we may be, our destiny is tied up with the destiny of America. Before the Pilgrims landed at Plymouth we were here. Before the pen of Jefferson etched across the pages of history the majestic words of the Declaration of Independence, we were here. For more than two centuries our foreparents labored in this country without wages; they made cotton king; and they built the homes of their masters in the midst of brutal injustice and shameful humiliation—and yet out of a bottomless vitality they continued to thrive and develop. If the inexpressible cruelties of slavery could not stop us, the opposition we now face will surely fail. We will win our freedom because the sacred heritage of our nation and the eternal will of God are embodied in our echoing demands.

I must close now. But before closing I am impelled to mention one other point in your statement that troubled me profoundly. You warmly commended the Birmingham police force for keeping "order" and "preventing violence." I don't believe you would have so warmly commended the police force if you had seen its angry violent dogs literally biting six unarmed, nonviolent Negroes. I don't believe you would so quickly commend the policemen if you would observe their ugly and inhuman treatment of Negroes here in the city jail; if you would watch them push and curse old Negro women and young Negro girls; if you would see them slap and kick old Negro men and young boys; if you would observe them, as they did on two occasions, refuse to give us food because we wanted to sing our grace together. I'm sorry that I can't join you in your praise for the police department.

It is true that they have been rather disciplined in their public handling of the demonstrators. In this sense they have been rather publicly "nonviolent." But for what purpose? To preserve the evil system of segregation. Over the last few years I have consistently preached that nonviolence demands that the means we use must be as pure as the ends we seek. So I have tried to make it clear that it is wrong to use immoral means to attain moral ends. But now I must affirm that it is just as wrong, or even more so, to use moral means to preserve immoral ends. Maybe Mr. Connor and his policemen have been rather publicly nonviolent, as Chief Pritchett was in Albany, Georgia, but they have used the moral means of nonviolence to maintain the immoral end of flagrant racial injustice. T. S. Eliot has said that there is no greater treason than to do the right deed for the wrong reason.

I wish you had commended the Negro sit-inners and demonstrators of Birmingham for their sublime courage, their willingness to suffer and their amazing discipline in the midst of the most inhuman provocation. One day the South will recognize its real heroes. They will be the James Merediths, courageously and with a majestic sense of purpose facing jeering and hostile mobs and the agonizing loneliness that characterizes the life of the pioneer. They will be old, oppressed, battered Negro women, symbolized in a seventy-two-year-old woman of Montgomery, Alabama, who rose up with a sense of dignity and with her people decided not to ride the segregated buses, and responded to one who inquired about her tiredness with ungrammatical profundity: "My feet is tired, but my soul is rested." They will be the young high school and college students, young ministers of the gospel and a host of their elders courageously and nonviolently sitting-in at lunch counters and willingly going to jail for conscience's sake. One day the South will know that when these disinherited children of God sat down at lunch counters they were in reality standing up for the best in the American dream and the most sacred values in our Judeo-Christian heritage, and thusly, carrying our whole nation back to those great wells of democracy which were dug deep by the Founding Fathers in the formulation of the Constitution and the Declaration of Independence.

Never before have I written a letter this long (or should I say a book?). I'm afraid that it is much too long to take your precious time. I can assure you that it would have been much shorter if I had been writing from a comfortable desk, but what else is there to do when you are alone for days in the dull monotony of a narrow jail cell other than write long letters, think strange thoughts and pray long prayers?

If I have said anything in this letter that is an overstatement of the truth and is indicative of an unreasonable impatience, I beg you to forgive me. If I have said anything in this letter that is an understatement of the truth and is indicative of my having a patience that makes me patient with anything less than brotherhood, I beg God to forgive me.

I hope this letter finds you strong in the faith. I also hope that circumstances will soon make it possible for me to meet each of you, not as an integrationist or a civil rights leader, but as a fellow clergyman and a Christian brother. Let us all hope that the dark clouds of racial prejudice will soon pass away and the deep fog of misunderstanding will be lifted from our fear-drenched communities and in some not too distant tomorrow the radiant stars of love and brotherhood will shine over our great nation with all of their scintillating beauty.

Yours for the cause of Peace and Brotherhood,
Martin Luther King, Jr.

Martin Luther King, Jr.
(1929–1968, United States)

Negroes Are Not Moving Too Fast

America is fortunate that the strength and militancy of Negro protest have been tempered by a sense of responsibility. This advantage can be dissipated if some current myths are not eliminated. The first such myth is that the Negro is going ahead too far, too fast. Another popular, erroneous idea is that the Negro will happily take whatever he can get, no matter how little. There also are dangerous myths about the "white backlash," which was so much talked about in the campaign just finished. And then there are myths about how the Negro riots occurred last summer. The white leadership—the power structure—must face up to the fact that its sins of omission and commission have challenged our policy of nonviolence.

Among many white Americans who have recently achieved middle-class status or regard themselves close to it, there is a prevailing belief that Negroes are moving too fast and that their speed imperils the security of whites. Those who feel this way refer to their own experience and conclude that while they waited long for their chance, the Negro is expecting special advantages from the government.

It is true that many white Americans struggle to attain security. It is also a hard fact that none had the experience of Negroes. No one else endured chattel slavery on American soil. No one else suffered discrimination so intensely or so long as the Negroes. In one or two generations the conditions of life for white Americans altered radically. For Negroes, after three centuries, wretchedness and misery still afflict the majority.

Anatole France once said, "The law, in its majestic equality, forbids all men to sleep under bridges—the rich as well as the poor." There could scarcely be a better statement of the dilemma of the Negro today. After a decade of bitter struggle, multiple laws have been enacted proclaiming his equality. He should feel exhilaration as his goal comes into sight. But the ordinary black man knows that Anatole France's sardonic jest expresses a very bitter truth. Despite new laws, little has changed in his life in the ghettos. The Negro is still the poorest American—walled in by color and poverty. The law pronounces him equal, abstractly, but his conditions of life are still far from equal to those of other Americans.

More important than all of these facts is that the gap between Negroes and whites is not narrowing as so many believe. It is growing wider. The technological revolution expressed in automation and cybernetics is edging the Negro and certain poor whites into a socially superfluous role, into permanent uselessness and hopeless impoverishment.

In 1964, the nation's production has hit historic heights. Yet U.S. government statistics reveal that the unemployment rate of Negro youth averages thirty-three percent. In some of the northern ghettos the rate of unemployment of youth is fifty percent. These figures of unemployment dwarf even those of the depression of the 1930s, and they shed some light on why there was such a high proportion of young people in last summer's riots. Despair made them active participants.

Charges that Negroes are going "too fast" are both cruel and dangerous. The Negro is not going nearly fast enough, and claims to the contrary only play into the hands of those who believe that violence is the only means by which the Negro will get anywhere.

Another, more enduring myth is that the Negro has waited so long that any improvement will satisfy him. A beginning sincerely made is one thing, but a token beginning that is an end in itself is quite another thing, and Negroes will not be deluded into accepting one for the other. The tragedy of the present is that many newly prosperous Americans contemplate that the unemployable Negro shall live out his life in rural and urban slums, silently and apathetically. This thinking is wrong. Walter Lippmann has summed up the facts behind the folly in these words: "The Negro minority is too large to be subdued. . . . Negro grievances are too real, their cause too just, to allow the great white majority to acquiesce in the kind of terrorism and brutality that would be needed to silence them."

Federal, state and municipal governments toy with meager and inadequate solutions while the alarm and militancy of the Negro rises. A section of the white population, perceiving Negro pressure for change, misconstrues it as a demand for privileges rather than as a desperate quest for existence. The ensuing white backlash intimidates government officials who are already too timorous, and, when the crisis demands vigorous measures, a paralysis ensues.

And this exposes the folly of so much that has been said about the white backlash itself.

The most popular explanation for the backlash is that it is a response to Negro "aggressiveness" and "excessive demands." It is further attributed to an overzealous government which is charged with so favoring Negro demands that it has stimulated them beyond reason.

These are largely half-truths and, as such, whole lies. A multitude of polls conducted during the past two years reveals that even during the buildup of the white backlash, a majority of Americans approved the reforms Negroes have sought. The high point of white support occurred at the time of the historic march on Washington in 1963. Significantly, there was no white backlash then. Instead, there was respect and sympathy which resulted in substantial white participation in the Washington march. It is therefore demonstrable that militancy is not the basis for white resentment on a mass scale. Something happened after the summer of 1963 which must explain the backlash. It is here that Negro acts of commission and omission contributed to the ugly result in various communities.

Whites must bear the heaviest guilt for the present situation, but it would be both unwise and unjust to gloss over Negro culpability. In the first place, it must be admitted that the principal Negro leadership in effect abruptly abdicated, though not intentionally. For many years Negro actions had a sporadic quality, and as a result, the leadership neither planned ahead nor maintained itself at the helm at all times. All leaders, including myself, continued to work vigorously, but we failed to assert the leadership the movement needed. Into this vacuum there flowed less-experienced and frequently irresponsible elements. For month after month the initiative was held by these people, and the response of the main leadership was either a negative reaction or disdain.

The irresponsibles were free to initiate a new, distorted form of action. The principal distortion was the substitution of small, unrepresentative forces for the huge, mass, total-community movements we had always organized. Our reliance on mass demonstrations, intended to isolate and expose the evildoer by the mass presence of his victims, was a key element in our tactics. It showed to the white majority that Negroes in large numbers were committed and united. We also designed in each case a concrete program which was expressed in clear terms so that it might stand examination.

In contrast, the sporadic, fragmentary forays of the new groups had no perceptible objectives except to disrupt the lives of both Negroes and whites, including whites who were our friends and allies. When a mere handful of well-intentioned but tragically misguided young people blocked the doorways to New York City's Board of Education, or threatened to stop traffic to the World's Fair, or charged into the streets to spread garbage, and to halt traffic on bridges, they were reducing the imposing grandeur of the movement to cheap chaos. The mass movement of millions was overnight exposed to ridicule and debasement.

On reflection, it was insufficient, at the time, for the principal leadership merely to withhold support of such conduct and perversion of our aims and methods. We were under a duty to attack it boldly and vigorously. Action is not in itself a virtue; its goals and its forms determine its value.

In a period of turbulence, mistakes, which under other circumstances might have been contained, are frequently made worse by unexpected developments. This occurred when some elements who had never been a part of the civil rights movement erupted in violence in the subways and on the streets in New York and other cities. The headlines of a sensation-seeking press enlarged essentially small events to the level of catastrophes.

These exaggerations obscured the fact that crime lives in the heart of all large cities. The irritating deeds of certain irresponsible civil rights forces, and the senseless violence in which the perpetrators were Negro, merged in the minds of many people. For a large section of the population, Negroes became a menace. The physical safety of people who must use the streets and subways is closer to them than the abstract questions of justice for a minority, however appalling its grievances. Civil rights leaders cannot control crime. They can control the demonstrations they initiate,however. They have a responsibility to maintain discipline and guidance that no one is able to confuse constructive protest with criminal acts, which all condemn.

The ghetto has hidden many things from whites, and not the least of these is the rampant racketeering that has a sanctuary in the slums and corrupts the ghetto's already miserable life. The mayors of troubled cities who look only into Negro excesses for the causes of unrest would do well to look critically into their own law enforcement agencies.

In 1963, at the time of the Washington march, the whole nation talked of Negro freedom and the Negro began to believe in its reality. Then shattered dreams and the persistence of grinding poverty drove a small but desperate group of Negroes into the swamp of senseless violence. Riots solved nothing, but they stunned the nation. One of the questions they evoked was doubt about the Negro's attachment to the doctrine of nonviolence.

Ironically, many important civic leaders began to lecture Negroes to adhere to nonviolence. It is important to recall that *Negroes* created the theory of nonviolence as it applies to American conditions. For years they fought within their own ranks to achieve its acceptance. They had to overcome the accusation that nonviolence counseled love for murderers. Only after dozens of Birminghams, large and small, was it acknowledged that it took more courage to employ nonviolent direct action than impetuous force.

Yet a distorted understanding of nonviolence began to emerge among white leaders.

They failed to perceive that nonviolence can exist only in a context of justice. When the white power structure calls upon the Negro to reject violence but does not impose upon itself the task of creating necessary social change, it is in fact asking for submission to injustice. Nothing in the theory of nonviolence counsels this suicidal course.

The simple fact is that there cannot be nonviolence and tranquility, without significant reforms of the evils that endangered the peace in the first place. It is the effort of the power structure to benefit from nonviolence without yielding meaningful change that is responsible for the rise of elements who would discredit it.

Is the dilemma impossible for resolution? The best course for the Negro happens to be the best course for whites as well and for the nation as a whole.

There must be a grand alliance of Negro and white. This alliance must consist of the vast majorities of each group. It must have the objective of eradicating social evils which oppress both white and Negro. The unemployment which afflicts one third of Negro youth also affects over twelve and one-half percent of white youth. It is not only more moral for both races to work together but more logical.

One argument against a grand alliance holds that the shortage of jobs creates a natural climate of competition which tends to divide, not unify. If those who need jobs regard them as bones thrown to hungry animals, a destructive competition would seem inevitable. However, Negroes certainly do not want nor could they find the path to freedom by taking jobs from the white man. Instead, they want the white man to collaborate with them in making new jobs. This is the key point. Our economy, our resources are well able to provide full employment.

It has also been argued that while alliances for economic advancement can be achieved, several "subjective questions" such as housing and schools will be more stubborn. But these questions are based upon myth, not reality. Just as Negroes would be foolish to seek to overcome ninety percent of the population by organizing their ten percent in hostile combat, whites would be equally foolish to think that the Negroes' ten percent is capable of crowding the schools and neighborhoods of ninety percent.

The majority of Negroes want an alliance with white Americans to tackle the social injustices that afflict *both* of them. If a few Negro extremists and white extremists manage to divide their people, the tragic result will be the ascendancy of extreme reaction which exploits all people. For some Americans deluded by myths, the [presidential] candidacy of a [Barry] Goldwater seemed a solution for their ills. Essentially he identified big government, radicalism and bureaucracy as the cause of all evils. Civil rights legislation, in his view, is not a social necessity—it is merely oppressive big government. He ignored the towering presence of discrimination and segregation, but vividly exaggerated crime in the streets. The poverty of the Negroes, he implied, is due to want of ambition and industry. The picture that emerged to delight the racist was that of undeserving, shiftless, criminally dangerous radicals who have manipulated government for their selfish ends, but whose grievances are largely fanciful, and will wither away if left to the states.

Our nation has absorbed many minorities from all nations of the world. In the beginning of this century, in a single decade, almost nine million immigrants were drawn into our society. Many reforms were necessary—labor laws and social welfare measures—to achieve this result. We accomplished these changes in the past because there was a will to do it, and because the nation became greater and stronger in the process. Our country has the need and capacity for further growth, and today there are enough Americans, Negro and white, with faith in the future, with compassion, and will to repeat the bright experience of our past.

Abdias do Nascimento

(b. 1915, Brazil)

Cultural Revolution and the Future of the Pan African Culture

Address at Sixth Pan African Congress,

Dar es Salaam, Tanzania, 1974

> . . . a true racial democratic revolution, in our era, can only happen under one condition: the black man and ·the mulatto must become the *anti-white man* to embody the purest democratic radicalism and show to the white men the true sense of the democratic revolution of personality, of society and of culture.
>
> Florestan Fernandes

The contemporary aspirations of Pan Africanism were a reality for our forefathers. They lived in a land which was their own, having their own cultures, languages, life-styles and civilizations; they and only they enjoyed the fruits of their labour. This harmony—man, labour and culture—on the continent was disrupted by exploitation and a colonialistic invasion.

This Sixth Pan African Congress is realized in the spirit which shone and still shines over the entire Pan African struggle. This is the Congress of a ruptured unity, which not only the peoples of Africa but also all of the black peoples of the world wish to recuperate and enrich.

These are the historical circumstances of Africa and of the international scenario which preside over and make meaningful the Sixth Pan African Congress. We have traversed a long and arduous road since the first of these Congresses, even up until the one in which we are now participating.

We all know of the visible and hidden means utilized by colonialism to impede, hinder and prevent the struggle of Africans and Blacks against oppression, exploitation and racism. Dividing, separating and undermining physical strength and spiritual resistance have been some of the continual actions directed against our unity and our strength. In the system of barriers, language has played a salient and efficient role. Above and beyond these barriers we must realize the fatiguing forcefulness of the fact that we mutually understand one another using the language of the oppressor. The principal reason for the Black Brazilian's absence from previous Pan African Congresses lies in a language problem also. Physical absence, however, does not indicate neglectfulness during this period of incessant struggle, of battles and of suffering.

In the beginning, an awareness of the tragedy of the African peoples came about, and now progress toward that which today confirms and reveals the Pan African liberation process; from being invaded and violated, the African soil occupied and her sons valued only for their usefulness, her natural and cultural resources diverted from their rightful destination in the name of the accumulation of the material wealth in the West—from this we now march towards its opposite: that situation which gestates self-government and promotes sovereignty. What was a human being in Africa has been *reified* by capitalism, or *nativized* in his own homeland.

The restitution to the African man of that which was originally his, in the historic moment when the crisis of capitalism takes place, necessarily has an *ecumenical* function.

Once again the redemption of the oppressed, full of their historic consciousness, comes to liberate the oppressor from the prisons to which he was led by the illusion of conquest.

CULTURE: A CREATIVE UNITY

Western culture has reached the point of historic exhaustion. Her validity has extinguished itself and produced the crossroads at which humanity must confront itself. An empire is perplexed. It seems as though those societies which are most deeply westernized are less able to deter this growing process of deterioration. In this way a not only important, but urgent, role is opened to the creative potential of all men and nations. It is when there arises in one place—in another place, something—perhaps an historic mystery: the culture of a specific area, until now marginalized, projects itself toward the area of ecumenical expansion.

We are speaking of the African and Black cultures which lend support to a Pan African culture.

The enrichment of Pan Africanism in this Sixth Pan African Congress is not united in terms of its details, but it is the meaning of African unity which is essential here. For what is culture if not the creative unity of forces which would merely be dispersed in their singularity?

Tanzania understands our historic times. She is absorbed in self-questioning, interrogating the future; but, in a simultaneous movement, she incorporates her past experiences. Her culture becomes significant. Her global perspective of society; for example, *Ujamaa* is a symbol upon which international attention converges. And from my perspective, the notion of self-reliance finds its support in mythic poetry; the land as well as artistic creativity—but, as President Nyerere has stated, divine gifts—are instruments of similar importance in the Pan African Revolution.

Let us put forth our goals. It is not a matter of introducing a new and unstudied knowledge, but of renewing, criticizing and amplifying an already existent knowledge.

Let us try to visualize those elements necessary for a Pan African cultural revolution. One is the promotion of the liberation of the human personality while an historic being. Equally important is to tell and demonstrate to men that they are capable of transforming the circumstances in which they live; that from a led people, they may lead themselves; that they maintain sovereignty over their own history; that they must liberate themselves from that in the past which had an impact on them which was foreign to them; that they must forcefully reject all forms of oppression and exploitation.

Resistance and Renewal

On the one hand, it is necessary to reaffirm our traditional integrity, the egalitarian values of our Pan African society, cooperation and creativity. Simultaneously, it is imperative that we transform our tradition into an active being, criticize its anachronistic elements, actualize it. The actualization of African and Black cultures in a Pan African nation is a goal of our vision.

THE EXAMPLE OF PALMARES

. . . In early 1630, some of the enslaved Africans in Brazil broke the shackles of slavery and fled toward the jungle lying between the states of Pernambuco and Alagoas. Initially it was only a small group. Little by little . . . though, this group grew until it became a community of nearly thirty thousand "arisen" Africans. They established the first government of free Africans in the New World, a truly African State, known as the Republic of Palmares.

At more or less the same time it happened that, in a place very close to here, in Angola, Rainha Ginga valiantly resisted the invasion of his territories by the Portuguese.

The Republic of Palmares, with an immense population in terms of the beginning of colonization of Brazil, dominated a territorial area more or less one third the metropolitan area of Portugal. This land was the property of all. The results of collective labour were the property of all. The free Africans planted, harvested and bartered products with their white neighbours. They also organized, both socially and politically, and became skilled in the art of war.

Palmares put into question the entire colonial structure, the army, the large estates and the Church. It waged some twenty-seven wars of destruction. It resisted for more than half of a century: from 1643 to 1694. Palmares confronted both the Portuguese and the Dutch colonial structures established in the state of Pernambuco.

Zumbi, the last chief of Palmares, is celebrated in the Black-African experience of Brazil as the first hero of Pan Africanism. . . .

CHICO-REI: A REALITY WHICH HAS BECOME LEGEND

Quilombo is a word which means "group or community of free Africans evading slavery." Throughout the great expanse of the country of Brazil there was this type of resistance, similar to that of Palmares. Another form or style of struggle was waged by an African king enslaved with his family and his tribe. In the middle of the Atlantic Ocean his wife and one of his two sons died. The slaveholders baptized him with the Christian name "Francisco." He and his tribe were sold to a gold mine owner in the Town of Vila Rica, today called Ouro Preto, in the state of Minas Gerais.

All of the slaves considered of excellent stock and behavior were given one day per week in which they were allowed to work for their own benefit. Francisco took full advantage of the opportunity. He laboured during these free days, dearly saving what he earned, until he had enough to buy the liberty of his son. He continued to work and save his earnings, now with the help of his free son. In a short while the time arrived to purchase the liberty of Francisco himself. They continued the arduous struggle, both working and liberating more members of their tribe. These then joined Francisco and his son, freeing more and more until they had freed the entire tribe.

Francisco, above and beyond being an indefatigable worker, proved himself to also have exceptional political talents. They were thus able to gather enough money to purchase one of the gold mines—the mine of Encardideira—which had belonged to their old slave owner. The Encardideira mine prospered. It was property of the entire tribe. Francisco remarried and also managed a Catholic Church for his people. Catholicism was the official religion of the State. The prestige and power of Francisco grew, and he became something of a Chief of State within the state of Minas Gerais, which was known then as Chico-Rei. It attained the greatest splendor that the Gold Age was capable of producing, until it was completely destroyed. Few documents remain to tell of its fabulous existence. Chico-Rei attained the legendary immortality of mythic poetry. This occurred in the 18th Century.

From Slave to Black Man

Although there is no precise date, slavery began soon after the arrival of Pedro Alvares Cabral on the coast of Brazil. The history of Brazil records his name as the "discoverer" of a land which had been inhabited for centuries, and even millennia, by the Indians. Fifteen hundred is recorded as the year of "discovery"; then the Africans began to plant the sugar cane and to run the mills by the strength in their backs. After a cycle of mining, there began the "coffee culture." On all these various levels of economic development of the nation, the African was always the only labourer. He built a nation for others: the white man. The native Indians of Brazil may not be included in the concept of "others," though, as they were rapidly disappearing, either as the result of direct violence against them by the white man, or by the grace and action of the "civilizing force" of the western culture. The structure of race relations in Brazil is so well established that it has been possible for it to have remained unaffected throughout all of the political and social changes of the nation.

The formal abolition of slavery took place in 1888. The enslaved African became a "citizen" as stated under the law, however he also became a black man pursued on all sides. If slavery had been a crime, a more monstrous and cruel crime was the manner in which the African was "liberated." As has been stated: abolition was a business transaction by whites, for whites.

Nearly a century prior to the abolition of slavery, in 1789, a group of blacks, mulattoes and whites held a meeting in Bahia. They intended to begin a revolutionary movement to not only abolish the regime of slavery, but to also propose many other social reforms inspired by the French Revolution. Four blacks participating in what has been called the Revolt of the Tailors (Revolta dos Alfaiates) were condemned to death; they were hanged and quartered, and their bodies were hung on public posts as an example to the public citizenry.

Several decades after the Revolt of the Tailors, there occurred an extraordinary historical event: the son of the Portuguese King, Dom João VI, Prince Dom Pedro, in collusion with the rural oligarchy of Brazil, declared Brazil independent. This, called the Cry of Ipiranga, occurred in 1822, and might be considered something of a paradox did it not so clearly reveal the roots of Portuguese neo-colonialism. Even with the independence of Brazil, there still remained the same enslavement of Africans. This historic experience ought to serve to warn our African brothers of Mozambique, Angola and Guinea-Bissau. But it does not. Because my brothers know—in their very flesh, with guns in their hands— much better than we ourselves, of the *seas always navigated,* of the greed, violence, hypocrisy and cruelty of the Portuguese colonialism. As a result of these "virtues" and "discoveries," Portugal succeeded in becoming the colonialist paradigm: being the last European country to give up her African spoils, after having been the first to invade the African lands, to violate the African woman and to serve as the instrument of the nascent imperialist capitalism of England.

Let us resume the thread of history. We have spoken of the abolition of slavery on the 13th of May, 1888, as a modification of the situation of the ex-slave, in one way only: from labour force, he then became a true pariah.

In the following year, 1889, a marshall proclaimed Brazil a Republic and Emperor Pedro II was sent into exile. Through all of this the conditions of the ex-slave remained the same, and indeed, after the *legal* liberation the foundations of their existence deteriorated ceaselessly. They lacked employment, for the most part because of a large influx of European immigrants, free labourers who supplied all the necessary labour. There inevitably followed a time of starvation, disease, prostitution and black criminality. Racial discrimination and prejudice arose as yet one more barrier to a necessary reorganization of the black personality, family and continued existence.

HEROIC BLACK MEN

It was during the campaign to abolish slavery in Brazil that two black men distinguished themselves—one, Jose do Patrocinio, son of a white Catholic priest by a black woman, born in Campos, a town in the State of Rio de Janeiro. Later he went to the former capital of the entire nation, Rio de Janeiro. It was in this town that his journalistic and oratorical battles took place. The other black man was Lūiz Gama, son of a free African woman and a Portuguese aristocrat who sold his son as a slave in Bahia. As a slave, Lūiz Gama was sent to São Paulo; in spite of his condition, he studied and became a brilliant lawyer, his oratory confronting pretentious slave-owners of the rural aristocracy. The money which he earned defending cases was destined to purchase the liberty of his black brothers. He also wrote poetry satirizing mulattoes who called themselves white men, and singing of the beauty of the black woman. He was a model of dignity, generosity, integrity and greatness.

These seeds of non-conformity and revolt, of persistence in the struggle for freedom, bore fruit between 1920 and 1937. A protest movement began in São Paulo. The black press transmitted dissatisfaction, condemning discrimination in the opportunities for employment for Blacks and the racism which prohibited Blacks from entering certain commercial establishments, schools, housing, hotels, military organizations, diplomatic circles, etc. Meanwhile we must note that Brazil, to combat the legal government of Solano Lopez of Paraguay, formed its first regular army. And who were the soldiers? The African slaves. They were herded together and forced to fight a war which was not even theirs to fight.

The black man, however, always distinguished himself in the military activities of Brazil. The history of the nation registers several prominent names: Henrique Dias in the battle against the Dutch invasion of Pernambuco; the sailors Marcilio Dias and João Candido, the latter being the leader of the *Revolta da Chibata* (Revolt of the Whip).

This protest movement which began in São Paulo, an industrial centre in the south of Brazil, and spread to all of the principal urban centers of the nation, such as Rio de Janeiro, Pernambuco, Porto Alegre, Bahia, Belo Horizonte, etc., took the form of a mass movement under the name *Frente Negra Brasileira*, or the Black Brazilian Front. Just as it truly began to grow and evolve into a meaningful movement, the Front was eradicated by the dictatorship of the *Estado Novo* (New State) in 1937.

THE BLACK EXPERIMENTAL THEATRE

Thus black protest through the Black Brazilian Front was quieted in 1937. Nothing resulted from the resistance of some leaders, exemplified in the case of Jose Correa Leite. When, in 1944, we founded the Black Experimental Theatre in Rio de Janeiro, the battle for freedom once again regained its force. What was this "Black Experimental Theatre"? In purpose, a quite complex organization. It existed, fundamentally, as a project designed to rescue black African values, oppressed and inferior within the Brazilian culture—a laboratory of artistic and cultural experimentation. The Black Experimental Theatre was conceived as an instrument to oppose the domination and supremacy of the white-European culture, and as a systematic unmasking of racial ideology ruling the nation. There was, and still is, a philosophy of race relations which underlies Brazilian society. Paradoxically, it is called "racial democracy," while in reality this merely supports the privileges of the white strata of society at the expense of African descendants. Marginalization of the black community accompanied the abolition of slavery, while miserable living conditions made the black man a "declassified" citizen. All non-black workers benefited from this precarious state of existence. Some of these non-black workers became members of the middle class, while others even aspired to the national bourgeoisie, their upward social ladder based firmly on the disgrace of the black man.

Racial democracy in Brazil has meant up until now the oppression of Blacks, the degradation and proscription of their cultural values, and insensitive and cruel exploitation by all white classes, rich and poor alike. The country thus developed a culture base on racist values, institutionalizing a situation which may be called the "pathology of normality." Sociologically, this politics of race relations represents a form of genocide.

As a consequence of the immobility of the structure of black and white relationships, all black efforts towards changing their condition and attaining a suitable level of existence have been futile. All of the black man's efforts to develop a consuetudinary and effective racial democracy have only earned him the white man's domination of the country, the disinterest or disdain of whites, and even threats and violence. The white man has been arbitrarily dictating what Christianity, justice, beauty and civilization have meant since the beginning of time. Monopolizing economic and political powers, the white man is driving the black man to extinction, after having made him impotent. The population of Brazil exceeds 110 million inhabitants. Forty to fifty percent of this figure is black—including both the very dark and those considered lighter. This is the second largest black country in the world. Meanwhile, blacks do not even pose a threat to the system, only potentially, which is a long way from actuality. The majority of blacks continue to be semi-slaves, hardly able to survive, incapable of developing the critical consciousness *then* necessary to perceive their condition, and the context molding their existence. They are completely plundered, both in body and in spirit.

The Black Experimental Theatre, fulfilling its revolutionary purpose, introduced the black hero and his formidable dramatic and lyric potential to the Brazilian stage. The Black Experimental Theatre transformed the typical black woman, performing domestic duties with humility, and the black labourer—some illiterate—into actors and interpreters of the highest quality. The existence of black interpretation demonstrated the artistic precariousness of the practice of painting the white man black to play the roles of artistic responsibility. It also made the traditional image of the black man as a caricature or domesticated man obsolete. A dramatic literature and an esthetic of performance, founded on the values of an African culture in Brazil, emerged as a result of the scrutiny, reflection, criticism and realizations of TEN (Black Experimental Theatre). By providing national conferences and congresses which gave blacks the chance to analyze, discuss and exchange information and experience, the TEN promoted the revision of Black Studies, denouncing as totally unreal the purely descriptive historical or ethnographic focus of many research studies conducted by whites who had used blacks as objectives of pseudoscientific studies.

SELF-RELIANCE OF PAN AFRICAN CULTURE

Isolated efforts such as the one just described occurred in almost all African nations and among blacks from non-African countries. Our isolation has been a burden imposed upon us by colonialism, imperialism and racism. But the dream of Pan African Unity was still alive in all of us wherever we may be. The national independence of so many Africans appears as the first victory of the dream and of the struggle. If each nationality was and still is a necessary step in the dismantling of colonialism, then this represents a "tactic of necessity." New steps must be resolutely taken towards this strategy of advancement and complete liberation, taking into consideration the objectives of the communion between our brotherly peoples.

All strategy, whatever struggle, presupposes a very clear ideology, so that any action resulting from this, that is the unity of the dream, is not destroyed along the arduous road to reality, permitting struggle among brothers. The presence of the government which supports this political, economic and Pan African cultural unity, and representatives of black communities from all over the world gives us hope that conflicting positions between actual sovereign units are being solved rapidly.

It is clear, then, that the construction of transcultural mechanism in the heart of the Pan African community is the fundamental instrument which guarantees the realization of Pan Africanism. Future steps, taking the pragmatic path, ought to try to find the means to emphasize and develop the Pan African culture, more than to merely promote the black Brazilian, Yoruba, Haitian, etc., cultures.

This notion of self-reliance is implicit in the development of this process. This goal of necessary unity requires us to traverse the long road of self-emancipation of our singular capacities. We must immediately begin to recognize our dependency upon ourselves, to explore our potential force, to know our own circumstances, to control our energies and resources—these are the ways in which we will be able to systematically build our own unity.

The terms we have referred to, a cultural policy, should be close to the concrete reality of each unity—be it individual, partisan or national—but should not exhaust itself in the practice of its own singular experience. In this dialectic of vocation for self-reliance and reciprocal cooperation, long-sought unity will be consolidated. Autonomy and self-reliance cannot be synonyms of isolation. The example, on the continental scale, of the OAU (Organization of African Unity), has been demonstrating on several levels the efficiency of this strategy. It is an obligation of the efforts of this Congress that we develop new aspects, new perspectives towards the concretization of these ends. In this unity, the

Pan African movement will consolidate and amplify its potential, obtaining in this manner the conditions necessary in the fulfillment of its historic destiny on the international level.

Concerning Science and Technology

The same opinion applies with respect to technology and science. The same principles should prevail. The initial appeal is for the encouragement of investigation, the consecration of autochthonous knowledge, in the sense of building a national being, spiritually and materially. We believe in a pedagogy which frees the technology of our actual tendency to enslave the human being. To the contrary, this technology ought to exist as a support to the consecration of man/woman on their condition of being. Self-reliance in the building up of technology and in scientific development occurs simultaneously with the development of nationalities, with functional adjustments to reality. This is because in the structure of the present phase of "technical aid," the advanced forms of the technology of industrial capitalism not only do not cooperate in, but also promote the alienation of, national self-knowledge. This technical and scientific cooperation will only be able to acquire a sense of liberation when the values which rule and regulate their mechanism are *not used* to deter the consciousness of the people and national independence. As stated by the late President [Kwame] Nkrumah, capitalist technology is the producer of "noble servants" colonized by the structure of colonial knowledge.

One consequence of our reasoning is that nationalities first must develop their own conceptual, organizational and technological apparatus, and then they may also realize their technological liberation. Secondly, techno-scientific cooperation has a pedagogical significance: a productive efficacy, an administrative "economicity" with its own practices, easy and convenient to utilize in the social sense.

The transmission of technology should not constitute a means of accentuating the gap between the producer and the consumer, but something which respects the structures as well as the customs of each national unit. Scientific and technical cooperation also implies a system of values ought to be articulated in the realization of the objectives of Pan African unity. To promote unity as a value is to give it a sense of liberation, rather than one of dependency. And scientific and technological dependency, equivalent to strangulation, is created by systems oppressive because they are based on the value of the ambition for profit. Or, as stated by President Nyerere, the system where money is king. For us, the king is the principle of sovereignty-consciousness, knowledge, technological projections, all interwoven, travelling directly toward the emancipation of our culture.

A cultural revolution, based on technological and scientific autonomy, is not only the foundation of social justice and human dignity, but also a prerequisite for the economic progress of mankind and international political sovereignty.

There exists a need for scientific and technological cooperation in order to accelerate and promote the global development of our culture. However this necessity must not allow the acceptance of "aid" with colonialist or imperialist motivations. Aid should not be a synonym for exploitation; aid implies a free association between he who offers and he who receives, as long as it is a catalyst of collective efforts.

Capitalism versus Communitarianism

We have attempted to say, up until now, that capitalism is in direct contradiction to the traditional communitarianism of the African cultures and that the mechanical notions which have been proposed to understand Africa and Pan Africanism under criteria which apply to capitalism can lead to grave errors. We must understand, radically, the novelty of the African experience on the actual level.

Arriving directly from colonialism, we are a people in reflection. In a certain sense we are the "weakest link" of the iron chain of capitalism; meanwhile, we hold the conviction that it is through Pan African communitarianism that this iron chain will be made forever unable to mend itself. We enter the construction of our own road with the purest of heart and hands. We are open beings in the face of unexpected events.

We must view as enemies all those who, even without knowing it, clamour for a modernity which has already passed: We are contemporary beings ready for a new life.

The span of our project demands a permanent Cultural Revolution. We all know that a revolution cannot consist of substituting one person for another, or even in the exchange of one system for another. At best, to the contrary, a revolution creates persons and systems. The system of values is the backbone of all cultures. Values impregnate our creative spirit, this forming the complexity of inaugural myths, the mythic-poetry.

As paradigmatic images of experience, these myths constitute a matrix which reproduces our daily actions. They embody the most original aspects of our ontology.

Our historic being is of mythic origin. It is a lesson in our art. Our art, contrary to that of the West, is, for us, a most natural and creative experience.

Only in the nourishment of beliefs and values do we realize that art is a most powerful instrument in our social communication, and in dialogue with our deepest roots.

In the African cultures art is the grasp on all life experiences and because of this the black man is integrated in his rhythm, in his mystery. Neither European rationalism, nor North American mechanics, art is that other *eye of Ifa* which inspires, organizes and gives meaning to our daily lives.

The Pan African Culture is the form and the exegesis of mythic-poetry.

The mythic-poet's adventure is concomitant with our existence while at the same time much older than it, part of the subject and part of the object. It is capable of inducing and being reflected. Our reason is poetic as well as forged—an instrument to detect our prospective visions.

One of the basic supports of the Pan African revolution is the capacity for struggle in the black woman. We in Brazil celebrate the name Luiza Mahim, mother of Luiz Gama. Between 1825 and 1835, during the various revolts and uprisings, Luiza Mahim combated slavery without respite. She was finally thrown into jail. Yamanja, goddess of the waters, mother of gods and men, heroine of African history and martyr of the history of the West, the black woman does not have to revindicate: she conquered the right to exercise the responsibility of all levels of life a long time ago. Thus through force and suffering, the race has survived. Embodied in the black woman, mythic-poetry maintains itself and becomes permanent as a rite of love continually renewed.

In 1938, six blacks, young men between the ages of 18 and 25, got together and organised an Afro-Campineiro Congress in the city of Campinas, in the state of São Paulo.

It was realized in a private session, where they swore to one day return to Africa to help in the struggle for the liberation of blacks and of the African continent. Life separated them in the immense geography of the nation. Meanwhile, it happened that the first of them was able to fulfill the oath. For the first time I walked the ground of my ancestors, the free land of Tanzania. And this happened in an exceptional moment. I have the happy opportunity to testify to something marvelous. This has to do with prophets.

Once upon a time a prophet isolated himself on the peak of a mountain and remained there for some time, preaching and meditating. When the prophet descended from the hills, he carried in his hands a tablet of laws needed to lead his people to salvation.

An inverse movement is now taking place. The prophet, *and his people,* are climbing the mountain *together.* He carries in his heart a lit candle which is planted on the top of Mount Kilimanjaro; it is the light of Pan Africanism. This light irradiates all over Africa and even reaches beyond to the rest of the world. It illuminates all people and all races, bringing to all "hope where there was despair, love where there was hate and dignity where before there was only humiliation. . . ."

Evocation to the Absent, the Silenced and the Imprisoned

We all know why, in actuality, Blacks in Brazil remain silent. Yet yesterday all of us here heard the Representative of Tanzania, the Honorable Joseph Rwegasira, insisting very adequately on the expression "black man." There seems to have been established throughout the world a new category of crime: the crime of being black. The black race has suffered, and suffers, merely by reason of his epidemic condition, all sorts of aggression. Not only physical injury, but also attacks upon his spirit and upon his intelligence. This is why we wish to evoke, in this historic Congress, the voices which were silenced. At this time we call forth the Blacks which were intimidated and threatened, those who have been thwarted from being present here, to those who are now in prison because of their militancy towards a black culture. We vehemently condemn anti-black intolerance, including not only capitalist-style governments and military dictatorship, but also, principally, the countries whose socialism *ought* to constitute an effective guarantee for the exercise of our integral and full realization as human beings.

Resistance and Renewal

Angela Y. Davis
(b. 1944, United States)

Black Women and Music:
A Historical Legacy of Struggle

Throughout the history of the African presence in America, song and dance have informed the collective consciousness of the Black community in vital and enduring ways. Music has long permeated the daily life of most African-Americans; it has played a central role in the normal socialization process; and during moments characterized by intense movements for social change, it has helped to shape the necessary political consciousness. Any attempt, therefore, to understand in depth the evolution of women's consciousness within the Black community requires a serious examination of the music which has influenced them—particularly that which they themselves have created.

Social consciousness does not occur spontaneously. As Marx and Engels pointed out, it arises on the basis of concrete conditions of human life in society. "It is not the consciousness of men [and women!—AYD] that determines their being, but, on the contrary, their social being that determines their consciousness."[1] If it is true that music in general reflects social consciousness and that African-American music is an especially formative element of Black people's consciousness in America, the roots of the music in our concrete historical conditions must be acknowledged. For Black women in particular, music has simultaneously expressed and shaped our collective consciousness.

African-American women who have had the most enduring impact on popular culture have been deeply rooted in the ethnic musical traditions of our community, traditions forged originally on the continent of Africa, then reshaped and honed by the conditions of slavery, the Reconstruction years, and the two world wars. And indeed, precisely because Black music resides on a cultural continuum which has remained closest to the ethnic and socio-historical heritage of African-Americans, it has been our central aesthetic expression, influencing all the remaining arts. Black music, writes James Cone,

> unites the joy and the sorrow, the love and the hate and the despair of black people and it moves the people toward the direction of total liberation. It shapes and defines black being and creates cultural structures for black expression. Black music is unifying because it confronts the individual with the truth of black existence and affirms that black being is possible only in a communal context.[2]

In this essay I will first examine some of the critical moments in the history of Black music before the "Classic Blues" era, initiated by Gertrude "Ma" Rainey, emerged. My emphasis will be on the roles women played in shaping that history. I then will explore the musical contributions of Rainey, a seminal female figure in the Black music tradition, while analyzing and evaluating her catalytic role in awakening collective social consciousness about the African-American predicament. This analysis will attempt to single out some of the specific ways her music gave expression to the emotional dimensions of Black women's lives during the first decades of this century—their consciousness of self, their grasp of the dynamics of male-female bonds as well as female-centered relationships, and the link between these processes and the objective factors conditioning Black women's lives.

W. E. B. Du Bois wrote that Black music is "the most beautiful expression of human experience born this side of the seas. . . . It remains as the singular spiritual heritage of the nation and the greatest gift of the Negro people."[3] During the period of slavery, music alone escaped the devastating cultural genocide wrought by the slaveocracy on the lives of Africans who were involuntarily and forcibly transported from their homeland to the shores of North America. While Black people were denied the right to speak in their native tongues, to engage in their traditional religious practices, to build their traditional families and communities, they were able to sing as they toiled in the fields and as they practiced their newfound Christian religion. Through the vehicle of song, they were able to preserve their ethnic heritage, even as they were generations removed from their original homeland and perhaps even unaware that their songs bore witness to and affirmed their African cultural roots. If they were permitted to sing, it was only because the slaveocracy's ethnocentric naiveté prevented them from comprehending the social function of African music, or indeed of music in general. Interpreting the slave songs as amusement or, at best, as a phenomenon facilitating work or the Christian religious indoctrination they hoped would result in the collective internalization of social inferiority on the part of the slaves, the slaveholders either acquiesced in or actively encouraged the slaves to sing their work songs and their spirituals.

Traditional West African music was never merely amusement or entertainment; it was always functional and was a central ingredient of every facet of community life. Always inextricably linked to economic activity, communal interrelationships, and spiritual pursuits, all of which were themselves interrelated, music as an aesthetic abstraction from the activities of daily life was unknown to the African ancestors of slaves in the United States. Ernest Borneman has enumerated eight different kinds of song which functioned in a basic way to regulate the community's cultural patterns. Among these are the songs associated with young men whose purpose was to influence young women: "songs of courtship, songs of challenge, songs of scorn."[4] One can't help but speculate that the author's failure to acknowledge the possibility that young women also sang songs to influence the men is an omission that must be attributed to the influence of sexism on his scholarship, for the societies to which he makes reference had distinct female courtship customs. Borneman further enumerates mothers' educational and calming songs: play songs, game songs, and lullabies. Again he discusses the songs older men used in the preparation of boys for manhood, but fails to recognize the corresponding songs used for the passage from girlhood to womanhood. Among the remaining types of songs he acknowledges are those "used by workers to make their tasks easier: work songs to stress the rhythm of labor, group songs to synchronize collectively executed work, team songs sung by one team to challenge and satirize the other."[5] West African music was functional in the deeper sense that it was more than an external tool, utilized to facilitate a given human activity. Rather it was always considered to be a part of the activity itself. Thus music was not employed as an aesthetic instrumentality, external to work but facilitating its execution; rather work songs were inseparable from the very activity of work itself. Janheinz Jahn has referred to the West African philosophical concept of *Nommo*—"the magic power of the word"—as being the very basis of music. According to the world-view of West African culture—if such a generalization is permitted—the life force is actualized by the power of the word. "According to African philosophy man has, by the force of his word, dominion over 'things.' He can change them, make them work for him and command them."[6]

Song is the practice of *Nommo*. As an African proverb affirms, "the spirit cannot descend without song." This song is not rigorously differentiated from everyday speech as came to be the case with European music, for most West African languages incorporate several of the basic structural elements of music: pitch, timbre, and timing.[7] A word uttered at a certain pitch may have a different meaning from the same word spoken at another pitch. The same dynamic applies to timbre and timing.

A further factor differentiating African from European music is the structural emphasis on rhythm as opposed to the emphasis on melody and harmony in European music. Rhythm's central role derives from its part in the process of *naming*, of imbuing things with the life force, in short, of humanizing the environment. There is a striking parallel to be drawn between the West African notion of *Nommo* and Karl Marx's definition of labor as "the living, shaping fire."[8] It can be argued, in fact, that the process of "naming" is something of a spiritual transmutation of the labor process—an ideological expression of what human labor can accomplish in society.

Throughout the history of Black music in the United States, *Nommo* was destined to remain the very essence of Black music making. African-American women musicians would rely on the power of *Nommo*, which would permit them to incorporate in their music and to impart to others by means of their music a collective consciousness and a very specific communal yearning for freedom. *Nommo* would moreover assist them in shaping through song an expression of the special meaning of Black womanhood, its realities, its limitations, its socio-historical legacy, and its collective potential with respect to the forging of a new society, based on economic, racial, and sexual equality.

Once Africans were forcibly planted in North America, they began to practice music-making in conjunction with the economic activity imposed on them by the conditions of slavery. The work songs they sang were "more than simply a means to ease hard physical labor."[9] They provided opportunities for commentary on the oppressiveness of slave work.

> Well, captain, captain, you mus' be blin'
> Look at you watch! See ain't it quittin' time?
> Well captain, captain, how can it be?
> Whistles keep a-blowin' you keep a-working me.[10]

The slaves sang in the old African tradition, but injected a new content into their music, a content that quite specifically reflected the conditions of their oppression and their desire to transform their collective predicament. But there were often references to the African past.

> The Negro work song became another example of the Negro's attempt to make the agonies of slavery bearable by integrating them with the images of his African past. There was no getting away from the miseries of plantation labor, so the work was in-

fused with the songs of better days and soon the songs were to influence the music of the slaves and their descendants.[11]

Aside from lullabies sung by slave women to white babies (and indeed those sung to their own as well) and possibly other songs related to specifically female domestic tasks, one discovers few gender distinctions in the great body of work songs of the slaves. This is not surprising, since there was a distinct lack of a sexual division of labor in the chattel slave system. Economically, the women were called upon to perform the same tasks as the men and while sexual abuse and the violation of women's reproductive rights, for example, constituted a special form of oppression for women, the overall predicament was not qualitatively differentiated from that of their brothers, fathers, sons, and husbands. Like the work songs, the spirituals place little or no emphasis on the specificity of women's experiences within their commentary on the collective experience of oppression. The historical and spiritual transcendance of the religious slave songs did not, however, establish a male supremacist vision of the slave experience. On the contrary, the aesthetic community forged by means of the spiritual was one which was based in the concrete participation of the individual slaves, men and women alike.

> The spirituals are historical songs which speak about the rupture of black lives; they tell us about a people in the land of bondage and what they did to hold themselves together and to fight back. We are told that the people of Israel could not sing the Lord's song in a strange land. But, for Blacks, their *being* depended upon a song. Through song they built new structures for existence in an alien land. The spirituals enabled blacks to retain a measure of African identity, while living in the midst of African slavery, providing both the substance and the rhythm to cope with human servitude.[12]

The incorporation of concrete historical conditions related to the slaves' desire to live free, human lives, into religious songs which, on their face, transcended concrete historical realities, can be clearly illustrated by the songs employed by the woman who became the most prominent conductor on the Underground Railroad—Harriet Tubman. In his 1942 article entitled "General Tubman, Composer of Spirituals," Earl Conrad argued that Harriet Tubman made abundant use of spirituals to facilitate the process of leading masses of people to their freedom. Although "Old Chariot" may have had an obvious eschatological meaning, its worldly dimension involved a public proclamation of the preparations under way for the trek northwards. Harriet herself, in fact, was also known as "Old Chariot"—a name that rhymed with her own.[13]

> When the old chariot comes,
> I'm going to leave you.
> I'm bound for the promised land.
> I'm going to leave you.

Conrad gives an account of one of Harriet Tubman's trips during which she was compelled to leave a party of fugitive slaves in order to find food for them:

> She dared not go back to them til night, for fear of being watched. . . . They listen eagerly for the words she sings, for by them they are to be warned of danger or informed of safety. Nearer and nearer comes the unseen singer, and the words are wafted to their ears.

Hail, oh hail, ye happy spirits,
Death no more shall make you fear,
Grief nor sorrow, pain nor anguish
Shall no more distress you there.

Around him are ten thousand angels,
Around him are ten thousand angels.
They are always hovering around you
Till you reach the heavenly land.

Jesus, Jesus will go with you;
He will lead you to his throne;
He who died has gone before you
Trod the winepress all alone.

He whose thunders shake creation;
He who bids the planets roll;
He who rides upon the tempest
And his sceptre sways the whole.

Dark and thorny is the desert
Where the pilgrim makes his ways.
Yet beyond this vale of sorrow
Lies the field of endless days.

This spiritual served as a sign that the slaves should listen for a further song-signal. If she sang this one a second time, they knew that they could leave their hiding places, but if she sang a verse of "Go Down Moses," this was an indication that there was danger and they should remain hidden.[14] Other verses of "Go Down Moses" were used to summon together those who would be accompanying Harriet Tubman on the long journey to freedom, and "Wade in the Water" warned the fugitive slaves that bloodhounds were on their track and if they walked in the shallow waters of rivers and streams, the dogs would lose their scent.[15]

Tubman's spirituals were functional not only in the sense that they provided concrete information about the struggle for liberation, they also were functional in the sense that they assisted in the forging of a collective social consciousness—indeed of both an aesthetic and a socio-historical community of individuals who had a very basic need to be free. Collective consciousness of freedom does not automatically accompany oppression. That consciousness must be actively created. For Black people in the United States during the era of slavery, the spiritual played a fundamental role in communicating the ingredients of that collective consciousness to masses of slaves. Freedom was named—literally and metaphorically—in accordance with the West African tradition of *Nommo*.

Oh Freedom, oh Freedom!
Oh Freedom, I love thee!
And before I'll be a slave,
I'll be buried in my grave,
And go home to my Lord and be free.

Another outstanding Black woman of the slave era also used song to make her point about freedom. Sojourner Truth used religious hymns to convey her message of freedom and she even composed her own verses, such as the following ones, which were sung at an abolitionist meeting.

> I am pleading for my people,
> A poor downtrodden race,
> Who dwell in freedom's boasted land,
> With no abiding place.
>
> I am pleading that my people,
> May have their rights restored;
> For they have long been toiling,
> And yet have no reward.
>
> They are forced the crops to culture,
> But not for them they yield,
> Although both late and early
> They labor in the field.
>
> Whilst I bear upon my body
> The scars of many a gash,
> I am pleading for my people
> Who groan beneath the lash.[16]

W. E. B. Du Bois described the coming of freedom for Black slaves in the South as the rising of a new song:

> There was joy in the South. It rose like perfume—like a prayer. Men stood quivering. Slim dark girls, wild and beautiful with wrinkled hair, wept silently; young women, black, tawny, white and golden, lifted shivering hands and old and broken mothers, black and gray, raised great voices and shouted to God across the field, and up the rocks and the mountains.
>
> A great song arose, the loveliest thing born this side the seas. It was a new song. It did not come from Africa, though the dark throb and beat of that Ancient of Days was in it and through it. It did not come from white America—never from so pale and hard and thin a thing, however deep these vulgar tones had driven. Not the Indies nor the hot South, the cold East or heavy West made that music. It was a new song and its deep and plaintive beauty, its great cadences and wild appeal wailed, throbbed and thundered on the world's ears with a message seldom voiced by man. It swelled and blossomed like incense, improvised and born anew out of an age long past, and weaving into its texture the old and new melodies in word and thought.[17]

However, the new-found freedom was to present a whole host of new problems for the former slaves, indeed, entirely new modes of oppression emanating from a transitional socio-economic system which had left slavery behind and would rapidly move in the direction of industrial capitalism. A new song was indeed eventually consolidated, but it was not the song of freedom, corresponding to the goal so passionately sought in the spirituals of slavery times. It was a song called the blues, which enumerated, again in the West African tradition of *Nommo*, the new troubles Black people faced in a world that still re-

Resistance and Renewal

fused to accept them as equals, a society that thrived on the systematic exploitation and discrimination meted out to the former slaves. The blues also incorporated a new consciousness about private love relationships, which had been denied to Black people, except in a rudimentary way, as long as they were slaves. In many ways, in fact, interpersonal relationships functioned as metaphors for the freedom they sought: trouble in the relationship was trouble in the overall social universe. The happiness they sought in their relationships indicated by the expression of a need for "a good woman" or for "a man who won't treat me mean" symbolized their search for a life which would be free of the countless brutal realities encountered in postslavery America. If there was a hidden meaning behind the religious language of the spirituals, there was also a hidden meaning behind the sexual language of the blues. As the spirituals consolidated a collective social consciousness of the need to fight for freedom under slavery, the blues also forged a communal consciousness, one that was based on the communication and sharing of African-Americans' individual suffering and the expression of the possibility of prevailing over the most intransigent problems.

Gertrude "Ma" Rainey was called the "Mother of the Blues" because she was the first widely known black entertainer who used blues as the basis of her repertoire. The first blues singers, who were predominantly male, were not formal entertainers, but rather individuals who engaged in the same economic activity as their peers, but who were most capable of incorporating the group's personal as well as social experiences into song. Ma Rainey, on the other hand, performed in circuses, tent shows, minstrel and medicine shows, singing all the same about the Black predicament and establishing the basis in song for the sharing of experiences and the forging of a community capable of persevering through private tribulations and even of articulating new hopes and aspirations. Ma Rainey's most essential social accomplishment was to keep poor Black people grounded in the Southern tradition of unity and struggle, even when they had migrated to the North and Midwest in search of economic security. As Sandra Lieb has pointed out,

> For her audience, whether listening to her records in a small Mississippi town or watching her perform in Chicago, she was a reminder, a witness, an affirmation of Southern black culture as positive, resilient, and life-affirming, even as great numbers of people were being up-rooted and displaced from that culture by migration to the North.[18]

The most vivid account of Ma Rainey's impact on her audience is contained in a poem by Sterling Brown. He describes the audience as consisting of people who had come from all around on mules and on trains, from the river settlements, from lumber camps and from "blackbottom cornrows." He continues, in the third and fourth verses:

Ma Rainey,
Sing yo' song:
Now you's back
Whah you belong.
Git way inside us,
Keep us strong . . .
Sing us 'bout de hard luck
'Roun' our do';
Sing us 'bout de lonesome road
We mus' go . . .

I talked to a fellow, an' the fellow say,
"She jes' catch hold of us, somekindaway.
She sang 'Backwater Blues' one day . . .
An' de folks, dey natchally bowed dey heads an' cried,
Bowed dey heavy heads, shet dey moufs up tight an' cried,
An' Ma lef' de stage, an' followed some de folks outside,"
Dere wasn't much more de fellow say;
She jes' gets hold of us dataway.[19]

The vast majority of Ma Rainey's blues revolve around problems emanating from personal relationships. However, the meaning of sexual love for the former slaves and their descendants was far more central than it might have been if their lives had offered more options for creative expression. Because of the objective limitations imposed by the economic circumstances surrounding them—Black people in the South during that period were by and large sharecroppers or tenant farmers and those in the North who found work were miserably exploited and always risked being the first fired—their only immediate hopes for happiness resided in the possibility of establishing a love relationship that would provide them with personal fulfillment. Moreover, the language of sexual love in Ma Rainey's blues metaphorically reveals and expresses a range of economic, social, and psychological difficulties which Black people suffered during the post–Civil War era. And the desire to find a good man symbolizes the desperate desire to create a life free of poverty, discrimination, and all the other material causes of the blues. It is most often the case that Ma Rainey's songs do not explicitly point to the causes of Black people's misery; they are generally referred to simply as the "blues." And indeed, in the West African tradition of *Nommo*, she often simply names the blues. Consider the text of "Blues Oh Blues":

Oh blues, oh blues, oh blues, oh blues, blues, oh blues.
I'm so blue, so blue, I don't know what to do.
Oh blues, oh blues, oh blues.

I'm going away, I'm going to stay; I'm going away, I'm going to stay
I'm going away, oh mama's going to stay.
I'm going to find the man I love some sweet day.

Oh blues, oh blues, oh blues, oh blues, blues, oh blues.
I'm so blue, so blue, oh mama don't know what to do.
Oh blues, I'm blue, oh blues.[20]

In this song, Rainey calls the name of the blues over twenty times, thus conjuring up all the various causes of her miserable predicament and at the same time using the power of the word to magically assert control over circumstances otherwise far beyond her reach. This magical, aesthetic assertion of control over the blues is an implicit expression of the real need to transform the objective conditions that are at the root of these blues: a camouflaged dream of a new social order. This is the powerful utopian function of the blues. The language in which this dream is expressed is the language of sexual love, thus "I'm going to find the man I love some sweet day." If Ma Rainey's audience was as deeply

Resistance and Renewal

moved as Sterling Brown's poem indicates, they must have sensed the deeper meaning of her words.

A characteristic dynamic of Ma Rainey's music is the public communication of private troubles. This dynamic contains an implicit recognition of the social nature of Black people's individual situations and at the same time it allows for the development of a collective social consciousness within the Black population. The consciousness of the social character of Black people's suffering is the precondition for the creation of a political protest movement—and, indeed, by the 1920s, such movements had begun to crystallize.

"Bad Luck Blues" begins by alerting the audience of the singer's intention to publicize her own situation: "Hey, people, listen while I spread my news *(Repeat)* / I want to tell you people all about my bad luck blues." She continues by asking the audience to acknowledge the commonality of her problem and theirs, for implied in the question of the second stanza is that they have certainly experienced something similar to the episode which has caused her to be afflicted with the blues.

> Did you ever wake up just at the break of day,
> Did you ever break up just at the wake of day,
> With your arm around the pillow just where your daddy used to lay?

While her words refer to a concrete situation—the loss of a love partner—the deeper meaning of this language has to do with need or desire in general. Certainly every Black person who listened to Ma Rainey sing was in need of something critically important in her or his life. Sharing and communicating need was a central feature of the blues, and the process of developing an awareness of the collective nature of the experience of need was very much related to the ability of the African-American people to survive when all odds were against them.

During the historical era leading up to the 1920s, the Jim Crow system of segregation was consolidated, Black people were systematically disenfranchised, and the Ku Klux Klan and other terrorist groups were responsible for untold thousands of lynchings. The economic predicament of Black people in the South caused many to travel northwards in search of jobs, and there they discovered that racism was often just as devastating as in the South. During the summer months of 1919, there were so many bloody riots directed against African-American people, that this season came to be known as the Red Summer of 1919. Certainly Ma Rainey's fans perceived the deeper meaning of songs like "Bad Luck Blues." A few of Ma Rainey's songs directly attacked the issue of Black people's economic misery, and some of them, such as "Ma and Pa's Poorhouse Blues," use humor to soften the cutting edge of oppression. This blues was recorded together with "Papa" Charlie Jackson and is introduced by a dialogue between them about the hard times they are both experiencing. The dialogue concludes:

> *Ma:* Charlie, you know I'm broke?
> *Charlie:* Ma, don't you know I'm broke too? What we gonna do?
> *Ma:* Let's both go to the poorhouse together.
> *Charlie:* All right, let's go together.

At the end of this blues, they both sing: "We better go to the poorhouse, try to live anyhow." The comic dimension of this particular song, unambiguously conveyed by the duo's performance, reveals and simultaneously encourages the African-American community's resilience and its powers of perseverance. Its message is clear: unity is the community's saving grace.

In other songs, Ma Rainey calls upon Black people who have traveled North to look back to their Southern homeland for consolation and inspiration. "South Bound Blues" specifically evokes the situation of a woman who has accompanied her man to the North, only to have him leave her in that alien world:

> Yes I'm mad, my heart's sad,
> The man I love treated me so bad;
> He brought me out of my home town,
> Took me to New York and threw me down.

> Without a cent to pay my rent,
> I'm left alone, without a home;
> I told him I would leave him and my time ain't long.
> My folks done sent the money, and I'm Dixie bound.

Her decision to return home gives her the strength to consider the eventuality of challenging the man who is responsible for her troubles: "I told him I'd see him, honey, some of these days, / And I'm going to tell him 'bout his low down dirty ways." The last verse is celebratory and optimistic:

> Done bought my ticket, Lord, and my trunk is packed,
> Going back to Georgia, folks, I sure ain't coming back.
> My train is in the station, I done sent my folks the news,
> You can tell the world I've got those Southbound blues.

The message of this song clearly indicates that African-American culture rooted in the Southern experience is the source of Black people's creative energy and of their ability to survive as a people. As in most of Ma Rainey's songs, the focal point is an interpersonal relationship, and the man in the relationship is evoked in an accusatory fashion. However, the adversities attributed to male behavior within a love relationship can also be interpreted as the material hindrances of racism. What is needed to survive these difficulties is the inspiration that comes from knowing that Black people in the South have survived the Middle Passage from Africa and at least two centuries of slavery, as well as the horrendous racism in the aftermath of slavery. The actual return by train to Georgia described in "South Bound Blues" is also a spiritual identification with the Black ethos of the South. That ethos incorporates the cumulative struggles Black people have collectively waged over the centuries, struggles that alone have insured our survival.

"South Bound Blues" also evokes the special problems encountered by Black women— since its protagonist is a woman who finds herself betrayed and mistreated by a man whom she has accompanied to an alien and hostile world. The spiritual identification encouraged with the Black culture of the South is with a culture that necessarily produced a standard of womanhood based on self-reliance and independence. In other words, "South Bound Blues" also appeals to women to summon up within themselves the courage and independence of their foremothers.

Several of Ma Rainey's songs are direct exhortations to Black women to develop a spirit of self-reliance that directly contradicts the ideological notion of womanhood prevalent in the larger society. "Trust No Man" advises women not to depend on their men if they do not wish to be deceived.

> I want all you women to listen to me,
> Don't trust no man no further than your eyes can see;
> I trusted mine with my best friend,
> But that was the bad part in the end.
>
> Trust no man, trust no man, no further than your eyes can see.
> I said, trust no man, no further than your eyes can see.
>
> He'll tell you that he loves you and swear it's true,
> The very next minute, he's going to trifle on you;
> Ah—trust no man, no further than your eyes can see.

While on its face, this song might appear to be utterly, though perhaps only temporarily, antimale, its deeper meaning might have less to do with the proclamation of Black men's negative traits than with the need for Black women to develop economic and psychological independence. W. E. B. Du Bois's essay, "The Damnation of Women" describes the development of economic independence among Black women during the postslavery era and argues that African-American women's experiences demonstrated to the larger society that women could not be imprisoned in the home and that they could not be required "on pain of death to be nurses and housekeepers."[21] "Trust No Man" implies that women should not be compelled to be appendages to men, blindly following their lead, but rather should carry forth the historical legacy of independence forged throughout the history of Black women's presence in North America.

Another song that directly addresses women, "Prove It on Me Blues" has most frequently been interpreted simply as a bold affirmation of lesbianism. Of course Ma Rainey's emotional and sexual ties with women have been documented and it has been speculated that she and Bessie Smith engaged at one time in relations with each other. On the surface, "Prove It on Me Blues" is a flaunting song about women-identified emotional and sexual relations, but it is also about the affirmative emotional links between Black women, whatever their sexual identification might be.

> I went out last night with a crowd of my friends,
> They must have been women, 'cause I don't like no men.
> Wear my clothes just like a fan,
> Talk to the gals just like any old man;
> 'Cause they say I do it, ain't nobody caught me,
> Sure got to prove it on me.

Certainly close emotional relationships between Black women—as family members, as workers, or as political activists—have been an important source of female independence. These relationships have so often been denied by those who would portray Black women as chronically competitive personalities, especially where men are concerned.

Gertrude "Ma" Rainey made an inestimable contribution both to the musical culture of the Black community and to the development of a collective social consciousness related to the specificity of the African-American predicament. Until very recently, her cultural value had been virtually ignored. Derrick Stewart-Baxter's *Ma Rainey and the Classic Blues Singers* was the only book-length study devoted to the blueswomen of Ma Rainey's era, and only a few pages in that short book were actually dedicated to Ma Rainey herself. In 1981, Sandra Lieb published her pioneering book, *Mother of the Blues: A Study of Ma Rainey.* Her book is an extremely valuable scholarly contribution, although it does not explore the entire spectrum of meaning in Ma Rainey's songs. A further study should evaluate the texts of Ma Rainey's blues, relating them to the general socio-historical context in which they were created and performed, which includes not only the objective conditions of her time, but also the music's cultural continuum, a continuum that reaches back to Harriet Tubman's spirituals, to slave women's work songs, and indeed to the original West African musical tradition of *Nommo.* Only then will we be in a position to accurately evaluate the part played by Ma Rainey's music in the forging of Black social consciousness and ultimately in the creation of a vital mass movement for Black equality.

Bessie Smith's music, much of it recorded simultaneously with Ma Rainey's—and, indeed, some of it prior to her elder's first recordings—was created in the same tradition as that of the "Mother of the Blues." The women's blues tradition also directly influenced the work of Billie Holiday. While it is not possible here to examine the body of these two women's work, an appropriate conclusion of this essay might be the texts of the most revealing political songs of these two artists. For Bessie Smith, it is "Poor Man's Blues":

> Mr. rich man, rich man, open up your heart and mind *(Repeat)*
> Give the poor man a chance, help stop these hard, hard times.
>
> While you're living in your mansion, you don't know what hard times mean
>   *(Repeat)*
> Poor working man's wife is starving, your wife is living like a queen.
>
> Please listen to my pleadin', 'cause I can't stand these hard times long *(Repeat)*
> They'll make an honest man do things that you know is wrong.
>
> Now the war is over; poor man must live the same as you *(Repeat)*
> If it wasn't for the poor man, mister rich man, what would you do?

For Billie Holiday, it is, of course, "Strange Fruit":

> Southern trees bear a strange fruit
> Blood on the leaves, blood on the root
> Black bodies swinging in the Southern breeze
> Strange fruit hanging from the poplar trees
> Pastoral scene of the gallant South
> The bulging eyes and the twisted mouth
> Scent of magnolia sweet and fresh
> Then the sudden smell of burning flesh
> Here is a fruit for the crows to pluck
> For the rain to gather, for the wind to suck
> For the sun to rot, for the tree to drop
> Here is a strange and bitter crop.

NOTES

1. Karl Marx and Frederick Engels, *Marx and Engels on Literature and Art* (Moscow: Progress Publishers, 1976), p. 41.

2. James Cone, *The Spirituals and the Blues* (New York: The Seabury Press, 1972), p. 5.

3. W. E. B. Du Bois, *The Souls of Black Folk* (New York: New American Library, 1969), p. 265.

4. Ernest Borneman, "The Roots of Jazz," in *Jazz,* ed. Nat Hentoff and Albert J. McCarthy (New York: Da Capo Press, 1975), p. 3.

5. Ibid., p. 4.

6. Janheinz Jahn, *Muntu, The New African Culture* (New York: Grove Press, 1961), p. 135.

7. Borneman, "Roots," p. 6.

8. Karl Marx, *Grundrisse der Kritik der Politischen Oekonomie* (Berlin: Dietz Verlag, 1953), p. 266.

9. Giles Oakley, *The Devil's Music, A History of the Blues* (New York: Harcourt Brace Jovanovich, 1976), p. 39.

10. Ibid., p. 39.

11. Borneman, "Roots," p. 14.

12. Cone, *Spirituals and the Blues,* pp. 32–33.

13. Earl Conrad, "General Tubman, Composer of Spirituals: An Amazing Figure in American Folk Music," *The Etude* (May 1942), p. 305.

14. Ibid., p. 305.

15. John Lovell, Jr., *Black Song: The Forge and the Flame* (New York: The Macmillan Company, 1972), p. 196.

16. Jacqueline Bernard, *Journey Toward Freedom, The Story of Sojourner Truth* (New York: W. W. Norton and Company, 1967), pp. 149–150.

17. W. E. B. Du Bois, *Black Reconstruction in America* (New York: Meridian Books, 1964), p. 124.

18. Sandra Lieb, *Mother of the Blues: A Study of Ma Rainey* (Amherst: The University of Massachusetts Press, 1981), p. 79.

19. Ibid., pp. 14–15.

20. This text and the remaining texts of Ma Rainey's, Bessie Smith's, and Billie Holiday's songs are based on my own transcriptions.

21. W. E. B. Du Bois, *Darkwater, Voices from Within the Veil* (New York: Harcourt, Brace and Howe, 1920), p. 18.

Awa Thiam
(b. 1936, Mali)

Black Sisters, Speak Out

The problems that beset Black women are manifold. Whether she is from the West Indies, America or Africa, the plight of the Black woman is very different from that of her White or Yellow sisters, although in the long run the problems faced by all women tend to overlap. Their common condition is one of exploitation and oppression by the same phallocratic system, whether it be Black, White or Yellow. In Africa as in Europe, it is not unusual to find battered wives; in Europe as in Africa there are polygamous husbands. Whether polygamy is institutionalized or illegal, it is imposed on women by external forces. Women are still, in our own day, considered as objects, as sub-human. Everyone behaves as if women had no human sensitivities. The most convincing example of this is when little girls are married or betrothed as soon as they are born. In a country like Mali, and particularly in the Segu region, families can be found in which all the daughters are betrothed very young, some having been promised in marriage at birth. The reason given—true or false—is the wide-spread practice of polygamy, which would soon make for a shortage of wives. But this is only a hypothesis. If this partially explains the custom of child brides, it by no means justifies it. Among certain ethnic groups, the Tukolor and Fulani for instance, it is frequently accepted as a tradition.

Sometimes, these marriages may be contracted for reasons of social prestige. When a man marries a girl of "good family," he acquires greater social consideration, more respect. So, as soon as a son is born, some men hasten to ask for the hand of a girl for their son, sometimes before she is even conceived.

Polygamy seems to be rampant in every country in Black Africa. In the Republic of Guinea, which claims to be progressive, and whose first president, Ahmed Sékou Touré, opted for a socialist state, women are faced by the same problem as their Senegalese, Malian, Ghanaian or Nigerian sisters.

Polygamy continues to exist there, in spite of measures taken, not to forbid it, but to limit the number of people who practise it. So we read the words of the then President of Guinea, Sékou Touré, in Pierre Hanry's *Erotisme Africain* (p. 74):

> Guinean women must not be instruments of production in the economic life of the nation, nor domestic instruments in the life of the family. They must be workers, aware of the economic improvement of the nation and equal partners in the home.
>
> Young people of Guinea, polygamy is in your hands: you can maintain it or see that it disappears, according to the quality of your education and your strength of will in building a new Africa which will be permanently rid of the inferiority and oppression of women.

Hanry then goes on to say,

> Unfortunately as in all areas where it was exercised in 1965, the revolutionary action of the Secretary-General of the PDG (Parti Démocratique Guinéen) seems in this matter to have scarcely gone beyond the stage of words. (p. 75, *op. cit.*).

Polygamy certainly still exists in Guinea at the present time, but Pierre Hanry's point of view in this matter is not necessarily the correct one. To present the problem in this way is to blind ourselves, consciously or not, to the real issues. Arbitrary measures that the masses, especially women—the principal people concerned—cannot understand, will not help us arrive at equality of rights and duties, which still have to be defined. It is only by unremitting struggle that women will succeed in forcing action to be taken whereby they can obtain little scraps of equality, and in the end an equality that is imposed on everyone and observed by everyone.

The countries of Black Africa must certainly overhaul their economies, but social reform is also necessary. A close look must be taken at customs since, if women are to be liberated, the prerequisite must be a change in people's mental attitudes. In fact, there would have to be a total upheaval in the colonial and neo-colonial structures that still exist in Black Africa, and by this we mean a radical revolution. To conceive of the liberation of Black African women on any other footing is to delude ourselves. We deliberately speak of "liberation" of women, in preference to the term "emancipation," as the latter word suggests *a priori* the idea of a typical infantile character of women. It reduces a woman to the status of a minor, a child whom it would be necessary to emancipate. Is this not in fact what a large number of people think? And perhaps this is how we must understand the subjection of women.

We had to wait until the sixteenth century before women were acknowledged to have souls. How much longer must we wait before it is conceded that Black folk, and more especially Black women, also possess this attribute?

On the practical level, irrespective of all religious considerations, what is the situation respecting polygamy nowadays? In any European country, when a husband goes in for that form of semi-condoned polygamy that consists of taking a mistress—or several—the wife can have recourse to the law by instituting action for divorce, or at least obtain support for better treatment from him. Such a course of action is not possible for a Muslim woman, who grows up in a system of institutionalized polygamy, where this is not permitted. What is more, such action would appear aberrant in a Black African context, in which marriage is generally religious, not civil. This difference between the situation of Black and White women is found at practically all levels. And this is the main basis for our claim that the Black woman's struggle is of a different nature from that of her White sister. The majority of European women do not lack essentials, whereas Black women are fighting for survival as much in the field of institutions as in the manner of her daily existence. In other words, European women can gain much more advantage from their struggles—even if these don't lead to a radical revolution and a total upheaval of social structures. Where Black women have to combat colonialism and neo-colonialism, capitalism and the patriarchal system, European women only have to fight against capitalism and patriarchy.

Maulana Karenga
(b. 1941, United States)

The Million Man March/Day of Absence
Mission Statement

October 16, 1995

PREFACE

This Mission Statement is on one hand the product of the ongoing concern and conversation in the African American community about who we are as a people, where we stand and what we are compelled to do in view of our self-understanding and the conditions confronting us. But more specifically, it evolves out of a wide-ranging vigorous and many-sided discussion that was initiated by the call of Minister Louis Farrakhan last year for a Million Man March in Washington, D.C. Immediately, questions were raised about the priority-focus on men, the call for a day of atonement as a component part of the March proposal, the relevance of the March, its goals, its possible results and a host of related concerns. Moreover, the discussion is focused and expanded by Min. Farrakhan's invitation to a broad spectrum of scholars, activists and religious, political, business and civic leaders in May 1995 to gather and help shape the March in the most inclusive and effective form.

From this meeting local organizing committees were established in over 318 cities and conversations continued about the meaning, goals and possibilities of the March. Moreover, a National Organizing Committee was established to coordinate the continuously expanding circle of participants. The inclusive and diverse character of the National Organizing Committee and the numerous local organizing committees allowed discussions to draw on a wide-ranging source of knowledge, experience and differing views. Our frequent meetings were marked by lengthy debates over critical issues and a series of fraternal and sororal disagreements as well as agreements. However, by the end of this lengthy process, an impressive agreement on common ground had developed. The Statement thus reflects a document and project shaped in exchange. As more and more people embraced the idea of the March, the idea expanded to reflect new and varied concerns without compromise of principle. And thus, it is out of this inclusive and diverse gathering and process that the context and content of the Mission Statement were developed.

The Statement, then, reflects the common ground in principle and the operational unity in practice forged over a long period of vigorous and expansive exchanges. It represents our consciousness of the critical juncture of history at which we live and the challenges it poses for us, our profound concern for increasing racism, deteriorating social and environmental conditions and the urgent need for a transformative and progressive leadership in such a context. The Statement also reaffirms our commitment to the ongoing struggle for a free and empowered community, a just and good society, a better world and the self-determination, sacrifice and hard work this requires.

Finally, the Mission Statement reaffirms the best values of our social justice tradition which require respect for the dignity and rights of the human person, economic justice, meaningful political participation, shared power, cultural integrity, mutual respect for all peoples and uncompromising resistance to social forces and structures which deny or limit these.

The document is collective in both conception and completion. For all of the members of the Executive Council brought their own summaries and understanding of the exchanges on the local and national level and gave critical input into the shaping of the document. Those members include: Dr. Benjamin Chavis, Executive Director, NMMM/DOA Organizing Committee; Mr. Ron Daniels, Campaign for a New Tomorrow; Minister Louis Farrakhan, Nation of Islam; Dr. Maulana Karenga, The Organization Us; Ms. Mawina Kouyate, All African People's Revolutionary Party; Mr. Bob Law, Million Man March Citywide Coordinating Council; Mr. Haki Madhubuti, Third World Press; Mr. Leonard Muhammad, Nation of Islam; Dr. Imari Obadele, Republic of New Africa; Rev. Dr. Frank Reid, Bethel African Methodist Episcopal Church; Rev. Willie Wilson, Union Temple Baptist Church; and Dr. Conrad Worrill, National Black United Front.

We acknowledge with deep appreciation Min. Louis Farrakhan's development of the initial idea of the March and his willingness to share it with us, and invite us all to participate in it and help shape its form and content for the common good of our people. And it is in this spirit of openness and cooperation for the common good that we seek to put forth in this document a vision of possibility that will advance the struggle for an empowered community, a just society and a better world.

I. INTRODUCTION

We, the Black men and women, the organizations and persons, participating in this historic Million Man March and Day of Absence held in Washington, D.C., on October 16, 1995, on the eve of the 21st century, and supported by parallel activities in cities and towns throughout the country:

conscious of the critical juncture of history in which we live and the challenges it poses for us;

concerned about increasing racism and the continuing commitment to white supremacy in this country; deteriorating social conditions, degradation of the environment and the impact of these on our community, the larger society and the world;

committed to the ongoing struggle for a free and empowered community, a just society and a better world;

recognizing that the country and government have made a dangerous and regressive turn to the right and are producing policies with negative impact on people of color, the poor and the vulnerable;

realizing that every man and woman and our community have both the right and responsibility to resist evil and contribute meaningfully to the creation of a just and good society;

reaffirming the best values of our social justice tradition which require respect for the dignity and rights of the human person, economic justice, meaningful political participation, shared power, cultural integrity, mutual respect for all peoples and uncompromising resistance to social forces and structures which deny or limit these;

declare our commitment to assume a new and expanded responsibility in the struggle to build and sustain a free and empowered community, a just society and a better world. We are aware that we make this commitment in an era in which this is needed as never before and in which we cannot morally choose otherwise.

In doing this, we self-consciously emphasize the **priority need** of Black men to stand up and assume this new and expanded responsibility without denying or minimizing the equal rights, role and responsibility of Black women in the life and struggle of our people.

Our priority call to Black men to stand up and assume this new and expanded sense of responsibility is based on the realization that the strength and resourcefulness of the family and the liberation of the people require it;

that some of the most acute problems facing the Black community within are those posed by Black males who have not stood up; that the caring and responsible father in the home; the responsible and future-focused male youth; security in and of the community; the quality of male/female relations; and the family's capacity to avoid poverty and push the lives of its members forward all depend on Black men's standing up;

that in the context of a real and principled brotherhood, those of us who have stood up, must challenge others to stand also; and that unless and until Black men **stand up,** Black men and women cannot **stand together** and accomplish the awesome tasks before us.

II. The Historical Significance of the Project

The Million Man March, forming a joint project with its companion activity, The Day of Absence, speaks to who we are, where we stand and what we are compelled to do in this hour of meeting and posing challenges. Its significance lies in the fact that:

1. It is a timely and necessary statement of challenge both to ourselves and the country in a time of increasing racism, attacks on hard won gains, and continually deteriorating conditions for the poor and vulnerable and thus an urgent time for transformative and progressive leadership;

2. It is a declaration of the resolve of Black men in particular and the Black community in general, to mobilize and struggle to maintain hard won gains, resist evil and wrong wherever we find it and to continue to push our lives and history forward;

3. It is a reaffirmation of our self-understanding as a people that we are our own liberators, that no matter how numerous or sincere our allies are, the greatest burdens to be borne and the most severe sacrifices to be made for liberation are essentially our own;

4. It is an effective way to refocus and expand discussion on critical issues confronting our people, this country and the world and put forth our positions on them;

5. It is both an example and encouragement of operational unity, unity in diversity, unity without uniformity and unity on principle and in practice for the greater good;

Resistance and Renewal

6. It is a galvanizing and mobilizing process to raise consciousness, cultivate commitment and lay the groundwork for increased positive social, political and economic activity;

7. And finally, it is a necessary continuation of our ancient and living moral tradition of speaking truth to power and seeking power for the vulnerable, justice for the injured, right for the wronged and liberation for the oppressed.

III. THE CHALLENGE TO OURSELVES

1. The Million Man March and Day of Absence are posed first in challenge to ourselves. We understand that the challenge to ourselves is the greatest challenge. For it is only by making demands on ourselves that we can make successful demands on society. In this regard we have raised three basic themes: **Atonement, Reconciliation** and **Responsibility.** For it is through being at one with the Creator, each other and creation, and reconciling our differences with each other, that we can stand up and together in unity, strength and dignity and accept and bear the responsibility heaven and history have placed on us at this critical juncture in the life and struggle of our people.

Atonement

2. For us, atonement in the best spiritual and ethical sense is to recognize wrongs done and make amends, to be self-critical and self-corrective. It means turning inward and assessing the right and the wrong, recognizing shortcomings and committing oneself to correct them.

3. Atonement means being always concerned about standing worthy before the Creator, before others and before the creation, being humble enough to admit mistakes and wrongs and hold enough to correct them.

4. We call then for a Holy Day of Atonement on this October 16, 1995, a day to meditate on and seek right relationships with the Creator, with each other and with nature.

5. We call also for a special remembering of the ancestors on this day and honoring them by a renewed commitment to speak truth, do justice, resist evil and always choose the good, as they taught us through word and deed.

6. To the extent that we have failed to do all we can in the way we can to make ourselves and our community the best of what it means to be African and human, we ask forgiveness from the Creator and each other. And therefore, we dare to atone:

    a. for all our offenses, intentional and unintentional, against the Creator, others and the creation, especially those offenses caused by our accepting the worst and weakest conceptions of ourselves;

    b. for not always following the best teachings of our spiritual and ethical traditions of Islam, Christianity, Judaism (Hebrewism), Maat, Yoruba, Akan, Kawaida and all others; and sacrificing and ignoring the spiritual and ethical in pursuit of material things;

    c. for over-focusing on the personal at the expense of the collective needs of our families and our people;

    d. for collaborating in our own oppression by embracing ideas, institutions and practices which deny our human dignity, limit our freedom and dim or disguise the spark of divinity in all of us;

e. for failing to contribute in a sustained and meaningful way to the struggle of our people for freedom and justice, and to the building of the moral community in which we all want to live;

f. for failing to do as much as we can to protect and preserve the environment through practicing and struggling for environmentally friendly patterns of consumption and production;

g. for any time we have turned a blind eye to injustice, a deaf ear to truth or an uncaring heart away from the suffering and pain around us;

h. for not resisting as much as we can sexist ideas and practices in society and in our own relations and failing to uphold the principle of equal rights, partnership and responsibility of men and women in life, love and struggle;

i. for lacking the moral consideration and human sensitivity towards others that we want for ourselves; and

j. for not always practicing the Seven Principles: unity, self-determination, collective work and responsibility, cooperative economics, purpose, creativity and faith.

7. And thus we commit and recommit ourselves on this day and afterwards to constantly strive to be better persons, live fuller and more meaningful lives, build strong, loving and egalitarian families, and struggle to make our community, society and the world a better place in which to live.

Reconciliation

8. We call also for reconciliation which is a companion practice of atonement. For it means, for us, to bring oneself into harmony with the Creator, others and creation.

9. This means we call for all of us to settle disputes, overcome conflicts, put aside grudges and hatreds in our personal and social relationships and in and between our organizations and institutions in the spirit of brotherhood and sisterhood, to reject and oppose communal, family and personal violence, and to strive to build and sustain loving, mutually respectful and reciprocal relations; in a word, to seek the good, find it, embrace it and build on it.

10. Reconciliation also means that we must strive for and achieve a principled and active unity for the common good. This we call **operational unity,** a unity in diversity, a unity without uniformity, a unity **on principle** and **in practice.**

11. We therefore commit and recommit ourselves to the principle and practice of reconciliation. For it is in and through reconciliation that we can embrace, stand together, organize our community and solve the problems in it, harness its energies for maximum development and struggle to end injustice and create the just and good society.

Responsibility

12. Finally, we challenge each Black man, in particular, and the Black community in general to renew and expand our commitment to responsibility in personal conduct, in family relations and in obligations to the community and to the struggle for a just society and a better world. And for us, to be responsible is to willingly and readily assume obligations and duties; to be accountable and dependable.

13. It means to stand up, stand together and stand in practice; to stand up in consciousness and commitment; to stand together in harmony and unity as men, as brothers, as women and sisters, as partners, as family and as community; and to stand in the practice of struggle, dedication, discipline, sacrifice and achievement; always building, doing good, resisting evil and constantly creating and embracing possibilities for fuller and more meaningful lives.

We thus commit and recommit ourselves to take personal and collective responsibility for our lives and the welfare and future of our families and our community. And we commit ourselves to stand up in knowledge and resolve, to stand together in principled and active unity and to stand in moral and liberating practice.

14. In raising the challenge of a new, renewed and expanded assumption of responsibility, we call on those Black men and women with greater means to shoulder greater responsibility; to invest in the community and transform it; and to avoid imitating the established order in its disdain for and blame of the poor and the vulnerable.

15. Our obligation is to remember the ancient moral teaching that we should give food to the hungry, water to the thirsty, clothes to the naked and a boat to the boatless, that we should be a father for the orphan, a mother to the timid, a shelter for the battered, a staff of support for the aged, a companion and comforter of the ill, an aid to the poor, strength for the weak, a raft for the drowning and a ladder for those trapped in the pit of despair. In a word, we must love justice, hate wrongdoing, resist evil and always do the good.

IV. The Challenge to the Government

16. Central to our practice of responsibility is holding responsible those in power who have oppressed and wronged us through various challenges. At the core of the practice of speaking truth to power is the moral challenge to it to be responsible, to cease its abuse, exploitation and oppression, and to observe its basic role as a structure instituted to secure human rights, not to violate them or assist in their violation. And where it has violated its trust, it must be compelled to change.

17. Historically, the U.S. government has participated in one of the greatest holocausts of human history, the Holocaust of African Enslavement. It sanctioned with law and gun the genocidal process that destroyed millions of human lives, human culture, and the human possibility inherent in African life and culture. It has yet to acknowledge this horrific destruction or to take steps to make amends for it.

18. Moreover, even after the Holocaust, racist suppression continued, destroying lives, communities and possibilities. And even now, members of the government are pushing the country in a regressive right-wing direction, reversing hard won gains, blaming the victims, punishing the vulnerable and pandering to the worst of human emotions.

19. We thus call on the government of the United States to atone for the historical and current wrongs it has committed against African people and other people of color. Especially, do we call on the government of this country to address the morally compelling issue of the Holocaust of African Enslavement. To do this, the government must:

    a. publicly admit its role and the role of the country in the Holocaust;

    b. publicly apologize for it;

    c. publicly recognize its moral meaning to us and humanity through establishing institutions and educational processes which preserve memory of it, teach the lessons and horror of its history and stress the dangers and destructiveness of denying human dignity and human freedom;

d. pay reparations; and

e. discontinue any and all practices which continue its effects or threaten its repetition.

20. We call on the government to also atone for its role in criminalizing a whole people, for its policies of destroying, discrediting, disrupting, and otherwise neutralizing Black leadership, for spending more money on imprisonment than education, and on weapons of war than social development; for dismantling regulations that restrained corporations in their degradation of the environment and failing to check a deadly environmental racism that encourages placement of toxic waste in communities of color. And of course, we call for a halt to all of this.

21. Furthermore, we call on the government to stop undoing hard won gains such as affirmative action, voting rights and districting favorable to maximum Black political participation; to provide universal, full and affordable health care; to provide and support programs for affordable housing; to pass the Conyers Reparations Bill; to repeal the Omnibus Crime Bill; to halt disinvestment in social development and stop penalizing the urban and welfare poor and using them as scapegoats; to adopt an economic bill of rights including a plan to rebuild the wasting cities; to craft and institute policies to preserve and protect the environment; and to halt the privatization of public wealth, space and responsibility.

22. In addition, we call on the government of the U.S. to stop blaming people of color for problems created by ineffective government and corporate greed and irresponsibility; to honor the treaties signed with Native Peoples of the U.S., and to respect their just claims and interests; to increase and expand efforts to eliminate race, class and gender discrimination, and to stop pandering to white fears and white supremacy hatreds and illusions and help create a new vision of human and societal possibilities.

23. We also are compelled to call on the government of this country to craft a sensible and moral foreign policy that provides for equal treatment of African, Caribbean and other Third World refugees and countries; that forgives foreign debt to former colonies; that fosters a just and equitable peace and recognizes the right of self-determination of peoples in the Middle East, in the Caribbean and around the world; that rejects embargoes which penalizes whole peoples; that supports the just and rightful claims and interests of Native Peoples, and that supports all Third World countries in their efforts to achieve and maintain democracy and sustainable economic and social development.

24. Finally, we call on the government and the country to recognize and respond positively to the fact that U.S. society is not a finished white product, but an **unfinished** and **ongoing multicultural project** and that each people has both the right and responsibility to speak their own special cultural truth and to make their own unique contribution to how this society is reconceived and reconstructed.

V. THE CHALLENGE TO THE CORPORATIONS

25. We begin our challenge to corporations by rejecting the widespread notion among them, that corporations have no social responsibility except to maximize profit within the rules of an open and competitive market, through cutting costs, maximizing benefits and constantly increasing technological efficiency. Our position is that no human conduct is immune from the demands of moral responsibility or exempt from moral assessment. The weight of corporations in modern life is overwhelming and their commitment to

maximizing profit and technological efficiency can and often [does] lead to tremendous social costs such as deteriorating and dangerous working conditions, massive layoffs, harmful products projected as beneficial, environmental degradation, deindustrialization, corporate relocation, and disinvestment in social structures and development.

26. We thus call on corporations to practice a corporate responsibility that requires and encourages efforts to minimize and eventually eliminate harmful consequences which persons, communities and the environment sustain as a result of productive and consumptive practices.

27. We also call on corporations to respect the dignity and interest of the worker in this country and abroad, to maintain safe and adequate working conditions for workers, provide adequate benefits, prohibit and penalize racial and gender discrimination, halt displacement and dislocation of workers, encourage organization and meaningful participation in decision-making by workers, and halt disinvestment in the social structure, deindustrialization and corporate relocation.

28. Moreover, we call on corporations to reinvest profits back into the communities from which [they] extract . . . profits, to increase support for Black charities, contribute more to Black education in public schools and traditional Black universities and colleges, and to Black education in predominantly white colleges and universities; to open facilities to the community for cultural and recreational use and to contribute to the building of community institutions and other projects to reinvest in the social structure and development of the Black community.

29. In further consideration of profit made from Black consumers, we call on corporate America to provide expanded investment opportunities for Black people; engage in partnership with Black businesses and business persons; increase employment of Black managers and general employees; conduct massive job training among Blacks for work in the 21st century; and aid in the development of programs to halt and reverse urban decay.

30. Finally, we call on corporations to show appropriate care and responsibility for the environment; to minimize and halt pollution, deforestation and depletion of natural resources, and the destruction of plants, animals, birds, fish, reptiles and insects and their natural habitats; and to rebuild wasted and damaged areas and expand the number, size and kinds of areas preserved.

VI. THE DAY OF ABSENCE

31. We call on those who do not come to Washington, especially, Black women, to mobilize and organize the community in support of the Million Man March and its goals. The Day of Absence is a parallel activity to the Million Man March and a component part of one joint and cooperative project: the standing up and assumption of a new and expanded responsibility by the Black man in particular and the Black community in general.

32. Women are in the leadership of the Day of Absence without exclusion of men as men are in the leadership of the Million Man March without exclusion of women. And both activities are equally essential.

33. The Day of Absence is a **sacred day, a holy day,** a day of atonement, reconciliation and responsibility. It thus has activities to reflect this. To observe this sacred day, we call on all Black people to stay away from work, from school, from businesses, and from places of entertainment and sports and to turn inward and focus on the themes of atonement, reconciliation and responsibility in our lives and struggle.

34. We call on those who choose prayer and meditation as essential ways of observation

to do this in groups of family and friends at home or in larger groups at mosques, churches, synagogues, temples and other places of worship.

35. Also, we call for teach-ins at homes and in community gatherings on:

a. the meaning of this day and the juncture of history at which we are as people;

b. the meaning of the Million Man March, the Day of Atonement, Reconciliation and Responsibility, and the Day of Absence and the goals of this joint project as set forth in the Mission Statement;

c. the importance and requirements of our struggle for liberation and justice;

d. the indispensability of spiritual and ethical grounding in our families, our communities and our struggle; and

e. the glory and burdens of our history as fathers and mothers of human civilization, sons and daughters of the Holocaust of African Enslavement and authors and heirs of the reaffirmation of our Africanness and our recommitment to liberation in the 60's.

36. Furthermore, we call on this day for massive voter registration as an essential act of responsibility for being politically active and morally engaged persons profoundly committed to the improvement of the quality of life in the community and larger society.

37. And finally, we call on all to contribute to the establishment of a Black Economic Development Fund as also an essential act of responsibility for the economic development of the community and to embrace the ancient and excellent teaching that small things given return in abundance and the good we do for others is actually done for ourselves. For it helps build and strengthen the moral community we all want to live in.

VII. CONTINUING PRACTICE AND PROJECTS

38. The Million Man March and Day of Absence can only have lasting value if we continue to work and struggle beyond this day. Thus, our challenge is to take the spirit of this day, the process of mobilization and the possibilities of organization and turn them into ongoing structures and practices directed toward our liberation and flourishing as a people.

39. Central to sustaining and institutionalizing this process is:

a. the follow-up development of an expanded Black political agenda and the holding of a Black Political Convention to forge this agenda for progressive political change;

b. a massive and ongoing voter registration of Black people as independents; using our vote to insist and insure that candidates address the Black agenda; and creating and sustaining a progressive independent political movement;

c. the building and strengthening of Black united fronts and collective leadership structures like the National African American Leadership Summit to practice and benefit from operational unity in our addressing local, national and international issues;

d. the establishment of a Black Economic Development Fund to enhance economic development, cultivate economic discipline and cooperative practices and achieve economic self-determination;

e. the reaffirmation and strengthening of family through quality male/female relations based on principles of equality, complementarity, mutual respect and shared responsibility in love, life and struggle; and through loving and responsible parenthood that insists on discipline and achievement, provides spiritual, moral and cultural grounding and through expanding rites of passage programs, mentorships and increasing adoptions;

f. the ongoing struggle for reparations in the fullest sense, that is to say: public admission, apology and recognition of the Holocaust of African Enslavement and appropriate compensation by the government; and support for the Conyers Reparations Bill on the Holocaust;

g. the continuing struggle against police abuse, government suppression, violations of civil and human rights and the industrialization of prisons; and in support of the freedom of all political prisoners, prisoners' rights and their efforts to transform themselves into worthy members of the community;

h. the critical task of organizing the community as a solid wall in the struggle against drugs, crime and violence in the community which we see as interrelated and which must be joined with the struggle to reduce and end poverty, increase employment, strengthen fatherhood, motherhood and family, support parents, provide education and prevention programs; and expose and reject those who deal in death for the community.

None of this denies external sources of drugs nor stops us from demanding uniform sentencing and penalties for those involved in the drug trade on the local, national and international level, but it compels us to stand up and take responsibility for the life we must live in spite of external impositions;

i. continuing and expanding our support for African-centered independent schools through joining their boards, enrolling our children, being concerned and active parents, donating time, services and monies to them and working in various other ways to insure that they provide the highest level of culturally-rooted education; and intensifying and broadening the struggle for quality public education through heightened parental concern and involvement and social activism which insist on a responsible administration, professional and committed teachers, continuing faculty and staff development; safe, pleasant, encouraging and fully-equipped campuses and an inclusive and culture-respecting curriculum which stresses mastery of knowledge as well as critical thinking, academic excellence, social responsibility and an expanded sense of human possibility;

j. continuing and reinforced efforts to reduce and eliminate negative media approaches to and portrayals of Black life and culture; to organize a sustained and effective support for positive models, messages and works; to achieve adequate and dignified representation of Blacks in various media and in various positions in these media; to expand support for and development of independent Black media; and to challenge successful and notable African Americans in various media to support all these efforts.

k. strengthening and supporting organizations and institutions of the Black community concerned with the uplifting and liberation of our people by joining as families and persons, volunteering service, giving donations and providing and insisting on the best leadership possible;

l. building appropriate alliances with other peoples of color, supporting their liberation struggles and just demands and engaging in mutually supportive and mutually beneficial activities to create and sustain a just and good society;

m. standing in solidarity with other African peoples and other Third World peoples in their struggles to free themselves, harness their human and material resources and live full and meaningful lives;

n. reaffirming in the most positive ways the value and indispensability of the spiritual and ethical grounding of our people in accomplishing the historical tasks confronting us by freeing and renewing our minds and reaffirming our commitment to the good, the proper and the beneficial, by joining as families and persons the faith communities of our choice, supporting them, living the best of our traditions ourselves and challenging other members and the leadership to do likewise and constantly insisting that our faith communities give the best of what we have to offer to build the moral community and just society we struggle for as a people;

o. and finally, embracing and practicing a common set of principles that reaffirm and strengthen family, community and culture, The Nguzo Saba (The Seven Principles); Umoja (Unity); Kujichagulia (Self-Determination); Ujima (Collective Work and Responsibility); Ujamaa (Cooperative Economics); Nia (Purpose); Kuumba (Creativity), and Imani (Faith).

VIII. CONCLUSION

We stand in Washington conscious that it's a pivotal point from which to speak to the country and the world. And we come bringing the most central views and values of our faith communities, our deepest commitments to our social justice tradition and the struggle it requires, the most instructive lessons of our history, and a profoundly urgent sense of the need for positive and productive action. In standing up and assuming responsibility in a new, renewed and expanded sense, we honor our ancestors, enrich our lives and give promise to our descendants. Moreover, through this historic work and struggle we strive to always know and introduce ourselves to history and humanity as a people who are spiritually and ethically grounded; who speak truth, do justice, respect our ancestors and elders, cherish, support and challenge our children, care for the vulnerable, relate rightfully to the environment, struggle for what is right and resist what is wrong, honor our past, willingly engage our present and self-consciously plan for and welcome our future.

Glossary of Names and Terms

This glossary is intended to assist the reader in discovering pathways we have used in our own exploration of the African intellectual heritage. Therefore, we have included names from the selections as well as others that might be useful in the study of concepts, philosophies, and movements that are pertinent to the readings in our book.

ABIMBOLA, WANDE (Nigeria, b. 1938). The most important contemporary Yoruba philosopher of Ifa, Abimbola has spent his life studying the traditions and nuances of the Yoruba culture. His work is the standard for numerous other writings by Cuban, Puerto Rican, Brazilian, Haitian, English, and American authors. He has served as president of the University of Ife and of the Nigerian Senate.

ABRAHAM, WILLIAM E. (Ghana, b. 1934). One of his country's finest philosophers and teachers. In 1957 he was the first African and the third non-European to become a fellow of All Souls College in Oxford University, England. Named the chair of philosophy and pro-vice chancellor at the University of Ghana. Currently teaches philosophy at the University of California at Santa Cruz.

ABUBAKARI II (Mali, early fourteenth century). Leader of the Mali Empire who is said to have sent 200 long fishing boats across the Atlantic Ocean toward Mexico in 1311–12.

ABYDOS. Sacred city of Ausar (Osiris) in Upper Egypt.

ACHEBE, CHINUA (Ogidi, Nigeria, b. 1930). The first modern African novelist to have a wide readership outside of Africa. His book *Things Fall Apart* (1954) gave him international stature.

AFRICAN METHODIST EPISCOPAL CHURCH. One of the oldest African institutions in the United States, tracing its history back to Richard Allen of Philadelphia, who started the church in 1787 as a protest against white supremacy in religion.

AFRICANISMS. Cultural elements that have been retained by transplanted Africans, specifically in the Americas and Caribbean.

AFROCENTRICITY. Late-twentieth-century intellectual idea based on the works of Molefi Kete Asante. Using the concept of location, Asante and his colleagues interpret phenomena from the standpoint of African agency.

AH-MOSE (Kemet). First king (1550–1526 B.C.) of the Eighteenth Dynasty.

AKAN. A language group comprised of several related languages (including Asante, Fante, Brong-Ahafo, Akyem, and Akuapim). Called Twi in the West African country of Ghana.

AKHENATEN (Kemet). King of the late Eighteenth Dynasty (c. 1550–1305 B.C.) who established Aten as the supreme deity and moved the capital of Kemet to Tell El Amarna (1365–1349 B.C.).

AMEN. The great sun deity of the city of Thebes in Upper (Southern) Egypt.

AMENEMOPE (Kemet). King during the Twelfth Dynasty (c. 1990–1785 B.C.).

AMENEMOPE (Kemet). The high priest of the temple of Amen-Ra at Thebes during the Nineteenth Dynasty (1305–1195 B.C.).

AMERICAN ANTI-SLAVERY SOCIETY. Organized in Philadelphia on December 4, 1833, by a group of African and European Americans, the society eventually had chapters in every major city in the northern United States.

AMERICAN COLONIZATION SOCIETY. Organized by prominent whites in 1816 to send Africans back to Africa, the society persuaded the U.S. Congress to appropriate $10,000 to establish Liberia as refuge for Africans from the Americas. Liberia was founded in 1822, and nearly 13,000 Africans from the United States had gone there by 1860.

AMO, ANTON WILHELM (Ghana, eighteenth century). A philosopher who lived and taught in Germany.

ANI (Kemet). Theban scribe believed to belong to the Eighteenth Dynasty (c. 1468–1438 B.C.), but it is not known whom he served. His papyrus is undated and includes chapters of the Theban Rescension of the Book of the Dead, hymns to Ra and Ausar, and descriptions of scenes such as the great judgment in the hall of the goddess Ma'at.

ANSA, KWAME (Fante, late fifteenth century). The king of the Fante nation in what is now Ghana when the Portuguese fought his people to establish a foothold on the African coast in 1482.

ASANTE. A major ethnic group of the Akan-speaking people of Ghana and Cote d'Ivoire, who date their origins to the historical appearance of the priest Okomfo Anokye and the young king of Kumasi, Osei Tutu, and the miraculous Golden Stool in the seventeenth century.

ATEN. Deity of the sun disk and the main deity during the reign of Akhenaten in Kemet in the Eighteenth Dynasty (c. 1365–1349 B.C.).

ATLANTA COMPROMISE. A doctrine expounded by Booker T. Washington in a speech given to the Cotton States Exposition in Atlanta in September 1895.

ATUM. Supreme deity of Heliopolis.

AUSAR (Osiris). Egyptian deity of the resurrection; brother to Auset, Set, and Nebhet.

AUSET (Kemet). The wife and sister of Ausar and the mother of Heru (Horus).

AY (Kemet). Member of Akhenaten's court and later an Eighteenth Dynasty king (c. 1369–1349 B.C.).

BA. In ancient Kemet, an aspect of the soul with a separate existence from a person in the afterlife.

BABA, AHMED (Songhay, sixteenth century). Noted professor and scholar at the University of Sankore in Timbuktu in the late 1500s.

BAKER, HOUSTON A. (United States, b. 1942). Literary scholar and theorist.

BALDWIN, JAMES (United States, 1924–1987). Outstanding novelist and essayist who challenged racism during the 1960s with eloquent appeals to justice.

BARAKA, AMIRI, formerly Leroi Jones (United States, b. 1934). Poet, playwright, and essayist; widely regarded as the leading activist playwright of the Black Arts Movement of the 1960s and 1970s.

BAROZVI. A southern African people located in Zambia and Zimbabwe, whose language is related to that of the Sotho of South Africa. Also often called the Lozi.

BETHUNE, MARY MCLEOD (United States, 1875–1955). One of the leading political figures in the United States in the 1930s, and the only woman in the "shadow cabinet" set up by President Franklin Roosevelt; the founder of the Bethune-Cookman College in Daytona Beach, Florida.

BHAKUZA (South Africa, nineteenth century). Son of Senzangakhona, king of the Zulu people.

BHUZA (South Africa, nineteenth century). General of the Mthetwa regiment of iziChwe, to which Shaka, as a young soldier, also belonged.

BLYDEN, EDWARD WILMOT (Saint Thomas, 1832–1912). A scholar and diplomat who was born in the Virgin Islands, studied in the United States, mastered several languages, traveled extensively, undertook diplomatic assignments, and became the president of Liberia College in 1881.

CABRAL, AMILCAR (Guinea-Bissau, 1921–1973). Revolutionary philosopher and political figure.

CÉSAIRE, AIMÉ FERNAND (Martinique, b. 1913). Poet, philosopher, and a founder of the Negritude Movement.

CINQUE, JOSEPH (West Africa, nineteenth century). A Mandinka prince who led a mutiny on board the *Amistad* in 1839.

CLARK-BEKEDEREMO, J. P. (Nigeria, b. 1935). A major playwright and poet concentrating on the values of African traditions and customs; former professor and chair of English at the University of Lagos.

CLARKE, JOHN HENRIK (United States, b. 1915). Editor and author best known as a critic and anthologist who has published short stories, poetry, and historical essays. He was a co-founder of *Harlem Quarterly* and the organizer of the African Heritage Studies Association in 1969.

COOPER, ANNA JULIA (United States, 1858–1964). An educator and author, she graduated from Oberlin College and earned a doctorate from the Sorbonne in Paris in 1895. She was a teacher and administrator with the M Street School in Washington, D.C., for nearly 50 years.

CRUMMELL, ALEXANDER (United States, 1819–1898). An American clergyman, Crummel worked in Africa from 1852 to 1873 as an agent of the American Colonization Society, thus effectively missing the American Civil War. He founded the Saint Luke Protestant Episcopal Church in Washington, D.C., after his return to the United States in 1873.

DAVIS, ANGELA YVONNE (United States, b. 1944). Teacher and political activist associated with the California prison inmate George Jackson in 1970, the American Communist Party as a political candidate, and the women's movement. Davis's first book, *If They Come in the Morning* (1972), launched her career as a scholar-activist.

DELANY, MARTIN ROBINSON (United States, 1812–1885). Scholar and public official who became the first African American to hold the rank of field officer in the Civil War, in which Delany served as a medical officer in the Union Army. An early advocate of African American nationalism, he became famous for his scientific scholarship. He negotiated treaties with the Abeokuta chiefs for land and settlers from the United States.

DINGISWAYO (South Africa, d. 1818). King and founder of the Mtethwa Empire in southern Africa. Shaka Zulu served a military apprenticeship under him.

DIOP, CHEIKH ANTA (Senegal, 1923–1986). One of the greatest African intellectuals of the twentieth century, whose book *The African Origin of Civilization* (1976) altered the historiography of Africa. His work has influenced scholarship in history, anthropology, Egyptology, physics, sociology, and politics.

DOGON. West African ethnic group located in Mali near the central bend of the Niger River, known for their astronomical observations made without the use of technology and their intense, metaphysical sculptures.

DOUGLASS, FREDERICK (United States, 1817–1895). Abolitionist, orator, and government official who was the preeminent African American spokesperson of the nineteenth century. Each of his several autobiographies outlined the horrors of enslavement. He led distinguished campaigns for African and women's rights.

DU BOIS, W. E. B. (United States, 1868–1963). The most prominent African American scholar, whose corpus includes more than 2,000 publications—articles, monographs, and books. DuBois regarded Kwame Nkrumah's Ghana as a beacon for African liberation. In response to Nkrumah's invitation, he became a citizen of that country late in his life, and his tomb has become one of Ghana's national shrines.

ENOCH, BOOK OF. Ethiopian sacred book that is compared with many spiritual writings in other cultures. Sometimes called the Book of Henok, it is thought to have been written soon after the time of Jesus Christ.

EQUIANO, OLAUDAH (Nigeria, 1745–1797). The first enslaved African to write a treatise about his capture and the culture of his native Ibo Country.

ESU-ELEGBARA. The Yoruba *orisha* (divinity) responsible for mischief, variation, and transformation.

FANON, FRANTZ (Martinique, 1925–1961). Author of several influential books during the 1960s that dealt with psychology and revolution. The most famous, *The Wretched of the Earth* (1963), discusses the Algerian Revolution and the impact of African revolutions in general on the new elites.

GA. A Kwa-speaking people who inhabit a series of coastal towns and inland villages in southeastern Ghana, including Accra, the capital. They trace their origin from ancient Egypt through the Benin kingdom (present-day Nigeria).

GARVEY, AMY JACQUES (Jamaica, 1896–1973). Activist and journalist, who published two volumes of the philosophy of her husband (Marcus Garvey) as well as a biography of him.

GARVEY, MARCUS MOZIAH (Jamaica, 1887–1940). One of the greatest mass leaders in the history of the African people, he united millions of Africans in the Diaspora and on the continent of Africa. The advocate of a "back-to-Africa" philosophy, Garvey founded the Universal Negro Improvement Association and the African Communities League, which attracted millions of dues-paying members during the first quarter of the twentieth century.

GATES, HENRY LOUIS, JR. (United States, b. 1947). Literary scholar and cultural commentator. Gates is a professor of English and African American Studies at Harvard University.

GIKUYU. An ethnic group of the Kenyan highlands (also spelled Kikuyu).

GUGUANO, OTTOBAH (Ghana, eighteenth century). He was captured by the British from Ghana and enslaved in Grenada. He was then taken by Lord Hoth to England, where he worked as a painter. Guguano played an active role in the antislavery movement.

GYEKYE, KWAME (Ghana, b. 1934). An expert on West African philosophy whose engagement in the debate over the question of philosophy in Africa has established him as a major figure in the field.

HAILE SELASSIE (Ethiopia, 1892–1975). The emperor of Ethiopia for more than half a century.

HAREMHAB (Kemet). Army commander under Tutankhamun who became the last king of the Eighteenth Dynasty (c. 1300 B.C.).

HARKHUF (Kemet). Governor of Upper Egypt during the reigns of Mernere and Pepi II in the Sixth Dynasty (c. 2300–2150 B.C.), who succeeded Weni; his accounts of the four expeditions he led to Nubia provide invaluable information about the relations between the two nations during this time.

HARLEM RENAISSANCE. An era of self-conscious creativity centered in the New York City community of Harlem and corresponding roughly to the years 1920–40.

HARPER, FRANCES ELLEN WATKINS (United States, 1825–1911). Campaigner for equal justice and liberty for African Americans. A writer of significant skill and passion, she wrote essays and poems in protest against the injustices she observed.

HATHOR. Kemet's patron goddess of love, usually represented by a cow.

HATSHEPSUT (Kemet). Daughter of Thutmose I and widow of Thutmose II, who became queen in the mid-Eighteenth Dynasty; one of the great leaders in Kemet's history, she sent expeditions to other parts of Africa and built obelisks and great temples.

HAYFORD, J. Caseley (Ghana, 1866–1933). A founder of West African nationalism and pan-Africanism.

HELIOPOLIS. City of the deity Atum in Lower Egypt (Kemet).

HORTON, DR. JAMES AFRICANUS BEALE (Freetown, Sierra Leone, 1835–1883). Of Igo origins, he was first educated at the Church Missionary Society School, Freetown, and Fourah Bay Institution, and then studied medicine at King's College, London, and the University of Edinburgh. After graduation in 1859, he entered the British Army Service Corps where he had a distinguished career, mostly in Ghana. Horton also established a bank, probably the first by an African, to help the West African business community. He also wrote seven books and several monographs.

HOTEP-HER-AKHET (Kemet). A noble of the Fifth Dynasty (c. 2450–2300 B.C.).

HUGHES, (JAMES) LANGSTON (United States, 1902–1967). Poet and writer of fiction associated with the Harlem Renaissance.

IGBO. Ethnic group living mainly in southeastern Nigeria.

JAMES, C(YRIL) L(IONEL) R(OBERT) (Trinidad, 1901–1989). Writer of numerous works on politics and colonialism, especially in the West Indies.

JOHNSON, JAMES WELDON (United States, 1871–1938). A leader of the NAACP, poet, and composer of spirituals as well as the African American anthem, "Lift Every Voice and Sing," Johnson was recognized as an ardent advocate for justice.

KA. Ancient Egyptian term corresponding to spirit or personality.

KARENGA, MAULANA NDABEZITHA (United States, b. 1941). A philosopher, scholar, and political organizer. As the founder of the holiday Kwanzaa and of US, an African American political and social organization committed to the redemption of the African people, he has influenced millions of contemporary Africans.

KAWAIDA. A philosophical and social movement initiated by Maulana Ndabezitha Karenga in the 1960s to reconstruct African values. Kawaida, a Kiswahili word, is translated as "traditions."

KEMET. The ancient civilization renamed Egypt (*Agyptos,* or house of Ptah) by the Greeks.

KENYATTA, JOMO (Kenya, 1891–1978). Champion of political rights for Africans and first president of the Republic of Kenya.

KHNUM. One of the oldest gods of Kemet, worshiped since predynastic times in Nubia and Kemet. His cult center was at Abu, capital of the First Nome of Upper Egypt. Usually appearing as a ram or a ram-headed man, Khnum was most famous as the potter god who modeled the *ka* of the queen or king on his potter's wheel.

KHOI. Ethnic group derived from the earlier Khoisan nomadic hunting and gathering society of ancient South Africa. By the fifteenth century, the Khoi had developed into a pastoralist society, distinct from the related San of the Kalahari.

KIKUYU. See GIKUYU.

KING, MARTIN LUTHER, JR. (United States, 1929–1968). Baptist minister and key figure in the U.S. civil rights movement; influenced by Gandhi, he was a proponent of nonviolent political protest. The leader of numerous demonstrations against discrimination, King delivered his famous "I Have a Dream" speech in 1963 at the Lincoln Memorial in Washington, D.C.

KUNENE, MAZISI (South Africa, b. 1930). The leading contemporary Zulu poet and critic, who has written and translated many traditional Zulu oral praise-songs and poems for Western audiences.

LOCKE, ALAIN L. (United States, 1886–1954). Scholar and critic who was the first African American Rhodes Scholar. He was internationally acclaimed as an interpreter of the contributions of Africans to the American culture.

LUO. Kenya's second largest ethnic group whose roots are in Nyanza province; believed to have migrated into Kenya from the southern Sudan near the end of the fifteenth century.

LUYIA. Ethnic group in western Kenya.

MAAFA. The great holocaust of colonization, enslavement, and oppression initiated by the European conquest of Africa. The term was first applied by the philosopher Marimba Ani.

MA'AT. The ancient Kemetic term for righteousness, justice, harmony, and balance; the fundamental basis of all human and spiritual relationships.

MALCOLM X (United States, 1925–1965). A charismatic religious and revolutionary leader who was the foremost spokesperson for black nationalism during the early 1960s. Starting principally as a leader of the Nation of Islam, he became an international symbol of the militancy of the African American movement.

MARTIN, TONY (Trinidad, b. 1942). The leading authority on the works of Marcus Garvey.

MAZRUI, ALI A. (Kenya, b. 1933). The leading political theorist of Africa; the second African to give Reich Lectures on the B.B.C. Currently Albert Schweitzer Professor in the Humanities at SUNY-Binghamton.

MBITI, JOHN (Kenya, b. 1931). A leading writer on African religion. Former Makerere University professor and director of the Ecumenical Institute in Basel, Switzerland.

MDU NTR. Ancient Egyptian language rendered as sacred words.

MEMPHIS. The ancient city of Ptah, on the west bank of the Nile.

MKHABI (Zulu, nineteenth century). Mother of Bhakuza and Senzangakhona's favorite wife.

MPHAHLELE, ESKIA (EZEKIEL) (South Africa, b.1919). Scholar, author, and political activist who founded the Mbari cultural movement in Nigeria and became the director of the Congress for Cultural Freedom in Paris and the director of the Chemchemi Cultural Center in Nairobi. He studied and taught in the United States and returned to South Africa in the late 1970s.

NANDI (Zulu, nineteenth century). Mother of Shaka and wife of Senzangakhona. She became a political force and strategist for her son during his rise to power in the nineteenth century.

NASCIMENTO, ABDIAS DO (Brazil, b. 1915). The most prominent African intellectual in twentieth-century Brazil. A playwright, professor, poet, politician, and painter as well as the leading campaigner for African political representation in Brazil.

NEAL, LAWRENCE (P.) (United States, 1937–1981). Poet and leader of the Black Arts Movement in the 1970s. A cultural philosopher whose boldness and creativity became the embodiment of the African American aesthetic.

NEBHET (Nephthys). Egyptian deity who was the sister of Auset (Isis) and the consort of Set.

NEFER-SESHEM-RA (Sheshi) (Kemet). Noble of the Sixth Dynasty (c. 2300–2150 B.C.).

NEGRITUDE. Intellectual and artistic movement of the 1930s and 1940s associated with the writings of Léopold Sédar Senghor, Aimé Césaire, and Leon Damas, who sought to advance the idea of an African aesthetic that was different from what they had discovered in Europe.

NEPHTHYS. *See* Nebhet.

NI-SEDJER-KAI (Kemet). Princess of the early Fifth Dynasty (c. 2450–2300 B.C.).

NKRUMAH, DR. F. NWIA KOFIE KWAME (Ghana, 1909–1972). A philosopher, political leader, scholar, and educator, Nkrumah served as prime minister of the Gold Coast (1952–60) and as president of the independent country of Ghana (1960–66). He was removed from office in a military coup and died in exile in Guinea.

NUN (Kemet). The primordial waters out of which the world emerged; the celestial sea.

NYERERE, JULIUS K(AMBARAGE) (Tanzania, b. 1922). A philosopher of African socialism, he was the first president of Tanzania.

OBENGA, THÉOPHILE (Brazzaville, Congo, b. 1936). The leading African Egyptologist and the author of more than twenty books on African civilizations, particularly the science and culture of Kemet. An important teacher of the ancient Kemetic language Mdu Neter, which he has introduced to thousands of people.

OGUN. The Yoruba god of iron and forging and therefore of all who use metal tools—blacksmiths, goldsmiths, butchers, hunters, and soldiers. Also regarded as the Yoruba god of warfare, wealth, and prosperity, as well as the protector of work at the beginning of the day. One tradition holds that Ogun made an ax and hatchet to cut a path through a thick forest so that the gods could settle on earth. Another holds that Ogun helped his father (Oduduwa) fight their enemies and was rewarded with the Kingdom of Ire; his sanctuary stands on the spot where he is said to have sunk into the ground with his sword, telling citizens in need to call on him for aid. In Nigeria, the kings of Ire claim to be Ogun's descendants.

OKPEWHO, ISIDORE (Nigeria, b. 1941). Scholar and novelist whose best-known works deal with African myths and epics.

OZIDI. The epic saga of the Ijo people of southeastern Nigeria that in its dramatic form takes seven days to perform.

PAHERI (Kemet). Grandson of King Ah-mose of the Eighteenth Dynasty, mayor of two towns, and scribe of the grain accounts.

P'BITEK, OKOT (Uganda, 1931–1982). Poet whose commentary on the influence of colonialism on African societies made him the leading voice for cultural nationalism in the 1960s and 1970s. After living in Kenya and Nigeria for many years, he returned to his homeland late in his life.

PEPI I (Kemet). Succeeded Teti to become the most powerful ruler of the Sixth Dynasty (c. 2300–2150 B.C.), having sufficient authority to hold Kemet's partially independent governors well in hand. Pepi I had a vigorous foreign policy and conquered the Nubians, conscripting them into his own army. He rebuilt the temple at Dendera; built his pyramid at Saqqara, inscribing its walls with texts; and is responsible for many monuments throughout Egypt.

PIYE PIANKHI (Kemet). The first king of the Twenty-Fifth Dynasty (c. 753–656 B.C.); credited with leading a revolution in arts and culture by restoring the temples and monuments. After he united the Nile Valley civilizations, he moved the capital city from Tebes to his native Napata.

PTAH. Supreme deity of ancient Kemet; the Greeks are said to have named Kemet *"Agyptos,"* or "house of Ptah," after seeing the many temples dedicated to the god.

PTAH-HOTEP (Kemet). Vizier during the reign of King Isesi in the Fifth Dynasty (c. 2450–2300 B.C.).

RA (RE). Egyptian sun deity, a supreme deity and equal to Ptah, Amen, and Atum, all considered to be creator deities.

REKHMIRE (Kemet). Vizier to the great conquering king Thutmose III during the Eighteenth Dynasty (c. 1550–1305 B.C.). His tomb in Thebes is one of the best preserved of this period.

ROBESON, PAUL (United States, 1898–1976). One of the greatest actors in African American history. He distinguished himself as a singer, intellectual, lawyer, athlete, and internationalist, bringing recognition to the artistic and intellectual genius of the African people.

RODNEY, WALTER (Guyana, 1942–1980). Activist, political philosopher, and educator; an eloquent spokesperson for African identity and activism during the 1970s. He was murdered in Guyana.

SAN. Nomadic society living around the Kalahari Desert who held onto their ancient hunting-and-gathering way of life; once ranging from Ethiopia south to the Cape of Good Hope, they left a record of their society in cave and rock paintings.

SARBAH, JOHN MENSAH (Ghana, 1864–1910). A lawyer, scholar, and nationalist whose works had considerable influence on such scholars as J. B. Danquah, J. Caseley Hayford, R. S. Rattray, and Eva Meyerowitz. The son of a wealthy, civic-minded merchant who served on the Gold Coast Legislative Council, Mensah Sarbah studied law at Lincoln's Inn, London, and was called to the bar in 1887 at the age of 23, thereby becoming the youngest West African barrister.

SARPONG, BISHOP PETER AKWASI (Ghana, b. 1933). Born in Kumasi, the capital of the Ashanti region of Ghana, Sarpong was ordained as a Catholic priest in 1959. He earned a Ph.D. at Oxford University in the mid-1960s and was named Bishop of Kumasi in 1970.

SEALE, BOBBY (United States, b. 1937). Founder, along with Huey P. Newton, of the Black Panther Party in Oakland, California, in October 1966.

SENGHOR, LÉOPOLD SÉDAR (Senegal, b. 1906). Poet, scholar, and political leader. First African and black to be made a member of the French Academy. Founding member of the Negritude Movement. President of Senegal from 1960 to 1980.

SENZANGAKHONA (South Africa, nineteenth century). King of the Zulu people and father of Shaka and Bhakuza.

SHAKA (South Africa, 1795–1828). Founder and emperor of the Zulu nation. The most memorable and fearsome foe of European imperialism in the nineteenth century, Shaka achieved legendary status because of his innovations in military strategies and weapons.

SHONA. Ethnic group in Zimbabwe comprised of several related peoples, such as the Kore-Kore, Manyika, and Karanga.

SIGNIFYING MONKEY. A mythical character in African American culture usually responsible for initiating conflict.

SINUHE (Kemet). Kemetic governor over Asian lands and a confidant of King Senusert I during the Twelfth Dynasty (1990–1785 B.C.).

Soyinka, Wole (Nigeria, b. 1934). Nobel laureate in drama and poet whose work synthesizes African and Western cultural traditions.

Spirituals. A body of poetry produced by Africans in America during the period of enslavement and sung in an elegant, classical style. The songs employ the pentatonic scale and notes foreign to most conventional Western major and minor sequences. They are choral expressions of communal experiences in the American society.

Stewart, Maria W. (United States, 1803–1879). The first African American woman to give a public speech when she delivered an address in Boston in 1834.

Sundiata. Legendary king of Mali who defeated the Ghana Empire in 1242 at the Battle of Kirina.

Teti (Kemet). King and founder of the Sixth Dynasty (c. 2300–2150 B.C.) during Egypt's Old Kingdom. Probably he had been a powerful local governor who was able to ascend to the throne. The hieroglyphic inscription on his pyramid at Saqqara says, "The pyramid which is enduring of places." The interior walls were inscribed with texts.

Thiam, Awa (b. 1936, Mali). An outspoken politician; her first book, *La parole aux Negresses* (1978), was translated by Dorothy Blair as *Black Sisters, Speak Out: Feminism and Oppression in Black Africa* (1986).

Thurman, Howard (United States, b. 1900). Great religious mystic known for his spiritual books that suggest that the engagement in the real world, where social and ethical issues are worked out, is the true engagement of the moral life.

Thutmose III (Kemet). Perhaps the greatest military conqueror of the ancient world and one of Kemet's most ambitious pharaohs. He reigned during the middle of the Eighteenth Dynasty (c. 1468–1438 B.C.) He led sixteen military campaigns against the rebellious Asiatics under Kadesh and destroyed the Hyksos Empire.

Trotter, Monroe (United States, 1872–1934). Educated at Harvard, he was the first African American elected into Phi Beta Kappa. A campaigner for human rights and an outstanding journalist, this passionate debater spent time in jail for disrupting a speech by Booker T. Washington and got into a shouting match with President Woodrow Wilson at the White House.

Turner, Bishop Henry McNeal (United States, 1833–1915). The first African chaplain in the U.S. Army and a leader of the African Methodist Episcopal Church. Prior to becoming an AME bishop, he had participated in the Reconstructed Negro Church. Turner served as a state senator from Bibb County, Georgia, from 1868 to 1870.

Turner, Nat (United States, 1800–1831). A principal African American hero who led an uprising against the slavocracy in 1831.

Umfundalai. An aesthetic philosophy developed by the Afrocentric philosopher Kariamu Welsh Asante in the 1970s and 1980s, growing out of her work with African dance in Buffalo, New York, Philadelphia, and Harare, Zimbabwe. Umfundalai seeks to explain the unique aesthetic dimensions of the African world.

Unas (Kemet). Last king of the Fifth Dynasty (c. 2450–2300 B.C.), whose funerary temple is located at the Saqqara Pyramid in Kemet.

Vizier. The title of the head of the bureaucracy of ancient Egypt (Kemet).

Walker, David (United States, nineteenth century). A revolutionary agitator from Boston who called for the abolition of slavery and the uprising of Africans in the pamphlet *Appeal to the Coloured Citizens of the World* in 1829–30.

Washington, Booker T(aliaferro) (United States, 1856–1915). Educator and founder of Tuskegee Institute; became the chief spokesperson for African Americans after the death of Frederick Douglass. Famous for his search for accommodation with whites, Washington's pragmatism often created controversy among African Americans who sought social and political rights in addition to economic advancement.

Wells-Barnett, Ida B. (United States, 1862–1931). Known for her anti-lynching crusade and journalism during the latter nineteenth century. A diligent participant in social and community affairs, she was the most widely known African American woman of her generation to campaign for justice.

WELSING, FRANCES CRESS (United States, b. 1935). Psychiatrist and educator who specializes in analyzing white racial supremacy doctrines and their effect on whites and Africans.

WEN-AMON (Kemet). A high priest of the temple of Amen in Thebes during the Twenty-First Dynasty (1070–945 B.C.).

WENI (Kemet). Magistrate and then governor of Upper Kemet (Egypt), whose long career spanned the reigns of Teti, Pepi I, and Mernere in the Sixth Dynasty (c. 2300–2150 B.C.). He recorded Kemet's military campaigns in his time.

WEST, CORNEL (United States, b. 1953). Major twentieth-century African American philosopher and ethicist. Credited with turning attention to the discussion of racial relations in a period of nihilism with the publication of his book *Race Matters* in 1992, West has become a leading interpreter of the contemporary United States. He is professor of Religion and African American Studies at Harvard University.

WOODSON, CARTER G. (United States, 1875–1950). A major African American historian who founded Black History Month, the *Journal of Negro History,* and the Association for the Study of African American Life and History.

WRIGHT, RICHARD (United States, 1908–1960). A writer and political essayist, Wright was born in Mississippi and moved to Chicago as a young man. He distinguished himself as a writer, becoming famous after the publication of *Native Son* (1940).

YORUBA. Major ethnic group living in southwestern Nigeria and parts of Benin; known for their art, philosophy, and religion, the Yoruba were spread throughout the Americas during the European slave trade.

ZULU. Major ethnic group living in South Africa, known for their cultural rituals, dance, poetry, and epics.

ZWIDE (South Africa, nineteenth century). One of the most powerful kings of the Ndwandwe. His armies were overrun by the army of Shaka in a dramatic battle for dominance in southern Africa.

Suggestions for Further Reading

Abraham, W. E. *The Mind of Africa*. Chicago: University of Chicago Press, 1966.

Achebe, Chinua. *Morning Yet on Creation Day: Essays*. London: Heinemann, 1975.

Alexis, Stephen. *Black Liberator: The Life of Toussaint L'Ouverture*. New York: 1949.

Amadiume, Ifi. *Afrikan Matriarchal Foundations*. London: Karnak House, 1987.

Ani, Marimba. *Yurugu: An Africa-Centered Analysis of European Thought and Behavior*. Trenton: Africa World Press, 1994.

Anyanwu, K. C., and Ruch, E. A. *African Philosophy: An Introduction to the Main Philosophical Trends in Contemporary Africa*. Rome: Catholic Book Agency, 1984.

Aptheker, Herbert. *American Negro Slave Revolts*. New York: International Press Publishers, 1963.

Asante, Molefi Kete. *The Afrocentric Idea*. Philadelphia: Temple University Press, 1987.

———. *Afrocentricity*. Trenton: Africa World Press, 1988.

———. *Kemet, Afrocentricity, and Knowledge*. Trenton: Africa World Press, 1990.

———. *Classical Africa*. Maywood, NJ: Peoples Publishing Group, 1993.

———. *Malcolm X as Cultural Hero and Other Afrocentric Essays*. Trenton: Africa World Press, 1993.

Asante, Molefi Kete, and Asante, K. W. (Eds.). *African Culture: The Rhythms of Unity*. Trenton: Africa World Press, 1990.

Asante, Molefi Kete, and Mattson, Mark A. *Historical and Cultural Atlas of African Americans*. New York: Macmillan, 1992.

Azikiwe, Nnamdi. *Renascent Africa*. London: Cass, 1969.

Baker, E., Houston, A., Jr. *The Journey Back: Issues in Black Literature and Criticism*. Chicago: University of Chicago Press, 1990.

———. *Long Black Song: Essays in Black American Literature and Culture*. Charlottesville: University of Virginia Press, 1990.

Baldwin, James. *Go Tell It on the Mountain*. New York: Grove, 1953.

———. *Notes of a Native Son*. Boston: Beacon Hill Press, 1957.

Ball, Charles. *Fifty Years in Chains*. New York: Dover Publications, 1970.

Baraka, Amiri. *Dutchman and the Slave*. New York: Morrow, 1964.

———. *Selected Plays and Prose of Amiri Baraka*. New York: Morrow, 1979.

Barrett, Leonard. *Soul-Force: African Heritage in Afro-American Religion*. Garden City, NY: Doubleday, 1974.

Ben-Jochannon, Y. *African Origins of Major "Western Religions."* New York: Alkebulan Books, 1973.

———. *Black Man of the Nile*. Trenton: Africa World Press, 1990.

Bennett, Lerone. *Before the Mayflower*. Chicago: Johnson Publishing Company, 1990.

Bernal, M. *Black Athena*. New Brunswick: Rutgers University Press, 1987.

Betts, Raymond F. (Ed.). *The Ideology of Blackness*. Lexington, MA: D. C. Heath, 1971.

Blackshire, C. Aisha (Ed.). *Language and Literature in the African American Imagination*. Westport, CT: Greenwood Press, 1992.

Blassingame, John. *The Slave Community: Plantation Life in the Antebellum South*. New York: Oxford University Press, 1972.

Blyden, Edward W. *Christianity, Islam, and the African Race*. San Francisco: First African Arabian Press, 1992.

———. *The Negro in Ancient History*. Washington, DC: 1869.

———. *Christianity, Islam, and the Negro Race*. Baltimore: Black Classic Press, 1994.

Bradford, Sarah H. *Harriet, The Moses of Her People*. Auburn, AL: Auburn University Press, 1987.

Brawley, Benjamin. *The Negro Genius*. New York: 1937.

Breasted, J. H. *Ancient Records of Egypt*. 5 vols. Chicago: University of Chicago Press, 1906–7.

Broderick, Francis L. *W. E. B. DuBois: Negro Leader in a Time of Crisis*. Stanford: Stanford University Press, 1959.

Browder, Tony. *Nile Valley Contributions to Civilization*. Washington, DC: Karmaic Institute, 1991.

Budge, E. A. Wallis. *The Book of the Dead*. New York: Dover Publications, 1967.

Busby, Margaret (Ed.). *Daughters of Africa: An International Anthology of Words and Writing by Women of African Descent from the Ancient Egyptians to the Present*. New York: Pantheon, 1993.

Butcher, Margaret Just. *The Negro in American Culture*. New York: Knopf, 1956.

Cabral, Amilcar. *Revolution in Guinea: Selected Texts*. Translated and edited by Richard Handyside. New York: Monthly Review Press, 1969.

———. *Return to the Source: Selected Speeches*. Edited by Africa Information Service. New York: Monthly Review Press, 1973.

Carmichael, Stokely, and Hamilton, Charles. *Black Power*. New York: Vintage, 1967.

Cartey, Wilfred, and Kilson, Martin (Eds.). *The African Reader*. 2 vols. New York: Random House, 1970.

Césaire, Aimé. *Discourse on Colonialism*. Translated by Joan Pinkham. New York: Monthly Review Press, 1972.

———. *Notes on a Return to the Native Land*. Berkeley: University of California Press, 1991.

Chinweizu. *The West and the Rest of Us*. Lagos: Nok Publishers, 1978.

———. *Decolonising the African Mind*. London and Lagos: Pero, 1987.

Chrisman, Robert, and Hare, Nathan (Eds.). *Contemporary Black Thought: The Best from the Black Scholar*. Indianapolis: Bobbs-Merrill, 1973.

Clarke, John Henrik. *African World Revolution*. Trenton: Africa World Press, 1991.

——— (Ed.). *Marcus Garvey and the Vision of Africa*. New York: 1963.

Cooper, Anna Julia. *A Voice from the South*. New York: Oxford University Press, 1988.

Cronon, Edmund. *Black Moses*. Madison: University of Wisconsin Press, 1968.

Crummell, Alexander. *Africa and America: Addresses and Discourses*. New York: Negro Universities Press, 1969.

———. *The Future of Africa, Being Addresses, Sermons, etc., Delivered in the Republic of Liberia*. New York: Negro Universities Press, 1969.

———. *Destiny and Race: Selected Writings, 1840–1898*. Edited by Wilson J. Moses. Amherst: University of Massachusetts Press, 1992.

Cruse, Harold. *The Crisis of the Negro Intellectual*. New York: William Morrow, 1967.

Davidson, Basil. *The Lost Cities of Africa*. Boston: Little, Brown, 1959.

Davis, Angela Y. *Women, Race, and Class*. New York: Random House, 1981.

———. *Women, Culture, and Politics*. New York: Random House, 1989.

Davis, David Brion. *The Problem of Slavery in Western Culture*. Ithaca, NY: Cornell University Press, 1966.

Delany, Martin. *The Condition, Elevation, Emigration, and Destiny of the Colored People*. Salem, NH: Ayer Co., 1968.

Diodorus, Siculus. *Diodorus of Sicily in Twelve Volumes*. Cambridge, MA: Harvard University Press, 1970–89.

Diop, Cheikh Anta. *The African Origin of Civilization: Myth or Reality*. New York: Lawrence Hill, 1974.

————. *Black Africa: The Economic and Cultural Basis for a Federated State.* Translated by Harold Salemson. Westport, CT: Lawrence Hill, 1978.

————. *The Cultural Unity of Black Africa.* Chicago: Third World Press, 1978.

————. *Precolonial Black Africa.* New York: Lawrence Hill, 1987.

————. *Civilization or Barbarism: An Authentic Anthropology.* Translated by Yaa-Lengi Meema Ngemi. Edited by Harold J. Salemson and Marjolin de Jager. New York: Lawrence Hill Books, 1991.

Douglass, Frederick. *The Life and Writings of Frederick Douglass.* Edited by Phillip S. Foner. 4 vols. New York: International, 1965.

————. *Frederick Douglass on Women's Rights.* Edited by Phillip S. Foner. New York: Da Capo Press, 1992.

Drake, St. Clair. *Black Folk Here and There: An Essay in History and Anthropology.* Vol. 1. Los Angeles: Center for Afro-American Studies, 1987.

Drake, St. Clair, and Clayton, Horace. *Black Metropolis.* New York: Harcourt, Brace and Co., 1945.

DuBois, W. E. B. *Black Titan: W. E. B. DuBois.* Edited by John H. Clark et al. Boston: Beacon Press, 1970.

————. *The Seventh Son: The Thought and Writings W. E. B. DuBois.* Edited and with an introduction by Julius Lester. 2 vols. New York: Random House, 1971.

————. *Darkwater: Voices from within the Veil.* Introduction by Herbert Aptheker. Millwood, NY: Krause-Thomson Organization, 1975.

————. *Against Racism: Unpublished Essays, Papers, Addresses, 1887–1961.* Edited by Herbert Aptheker. Amherst: University of Massachusetts Press, 1985.

————. *The Souls of Black Folk.* New York: Bantam Books, 1989.

————. *Black Reconstruction in America.* Introduction by David Levering Lewis. New York: Atheneum, 1992.

————. *Dusk of Dawn: An Essay toward an Autobiography of a Race Concept.* Introduction by Irene Diggs. New Brunswick: Transaction Books, 1992.

————. *The World and Africa.* New York: International Publishers, 1995.

Ellison, Ralph. *Invisible Man.* New York: Vintage International, 1947.

Erman, A. *The Literature of the Ancient Egyptians.* Translated by A. M. Blackman. London: 1927.

Fanon, Frantz. *Black Skin, White Masks.* Translated by Charles Lam Markmann. New York: Grove Press, 1967.

————. *A Dying Colonialism.* Translated by Haakon Chevalier. New York: Grove Press, 1967.

————. *The Wretched of the Earth.* Translated by Constance Farrington. Preface by Jean-Paul Sartre. New York: Grove Press, 1968.

————. *Toward the African Revolution: Political Essays.* Translated by Haakon Chevalier. New York: Grove Press, 1969.

Faulkner, R. O. *The Ancient Egyptian Pyramid Texts.* 2 vols. Oxford: Oxford University Press, 1969.

Fauset, Arthur Huff. *Sojourner Truth: God's Faithful Pilgrim.* Chapel Hill: University of North Carolina Press, 1938.

Fernandes, Florestan. *The Negro in Brazilian Society.* New York: Columbia University Press, 1969.

Fisher, Miles Mark. *Negro Slave Songs in the United States.* Ithaca: Cornell University Press for the American Historical Association, 1953.

Forbes, Jack D. *Africans and Native Americans.* Urbana: University of Illinois Press, 1993.

Foster, Frances Smith (Ed.). *A Brighter Coming Day.* New York: Feminist Press, 1990.

Frankfort, H. *The African Foundation of Ancient Egyptian Civilization.* Florence, Naples, and Rome: Atti del I Congresso Internazionade di Preistoria et Protoistoria Mediterranea, 1950.

Franklin, John Hope. *Emancipation Proclamation.* Garden City, NY: Doubleday, 1963.

Gardiner, A. H. *Ancient Egyptian Onomastica.* 3 vols. Oxford: Clarendon Press, 1947.

Garvey, Marcus. *Philosophy and Opinions of Marcus Garvey.* Edited by Amy Jacques Garvey. Preface by Hollis R. Lynch. 2 vols. in 1. New York: Atheneum, 1969.

Gates, Henry Louis, Jr. *The Signifying Monkey: A Theory of African American Literary Criticism.* New York: Oxford University Press, 1988.

Gbadegesin, Segun. *African Philosophy: Traditional Yoruba Philosophy and Contemporary African Realities*. New York: P. Lang, 1991.

Grimshaw, Anna (Ed.). *C. L. R. James Reader*. Cambridge, MA: Blackwell Publishers, 1992.

Gyekye, Kwame. *An Essay on African Philosophical Thought: The Akan Conceptual Scheme*. Rev. ed. Philadelphia: Temple University Press, 1995.

Harding, Vincent. *There Is a River*. New York: Harcourt Brace Jovanovich, 1981.

Harlan, Louis. *Booker T. Washington*. New York: Oxford University Press, 1972.

Harris, Joseph E. (Ed.). *Global Dimensions of the African Diaspora*. Washington, DC: Howard University, 1982.

Harris, Leonard (Ed.). *Philosophy Born of Struggle: An Anthology of Afro-American Philosophy from 1017*. Dubuque, IA: Kendall/Hunt, 1983.

Herodotus. *The Histories*. Translated by Aubrey de Selencourt. Revised edition with introduction and notes by A. R. Burn. Harmondsworth, Eng.: Penguin, 1954, 1972.

Higgins, Chester. *Feeling the Spirit*. New York: Bantam, 1995.

Hilliard, Asa. *The Maroon within Us*. Trenton, NJ: Africa World Press, 1995.

Hodges, Norman. *Breaking the Chains of Bondage*. New York: Simon and Schuster, 1972.

Holloway, Joseph E., and Vass, Winifred K. *The African Heritage of American English*. Bloomington: Indiana University Press, 1993.

Hooks, Bell. *Talking Back: Thinking Feminist, Thinking Black*. Boston: South End Press, 1989.

———. *Black Looks: Race and Representation*. Boston: South End Press, 1992.

———. *Sisters of the Yam: Black Women and Self-Recovery*. Boston: South End Press, 1993.

———. *Outlaw Culture: Resisting Representations*. New York: Routledge, 1994.

Hountondji, Paulin J. *African Philosophy: Myth and Reality*. Translated by Henry Evans with Jonathan Ree. Introduction by Abiola Irele. Bloomington: Indiana University Press, 1983.

Hughes, Langston. *I Wonder as I Wander*. New York: Rinehart and Co., 1956.

Hurston, Zora Neale. *Their Eyes Were Watching God*. Philadelphia: J. B. Lippincott, 1937.

Idowu, E. B. *Olodumare: God in Yoruba Belief*. London: Longmans, 1962.

Jackson, John G. *Man, God, and Civilization*. New Hyde Park, NY: University Books, 1972.

———. *Christianity before Christ*. Austin, TX: American Atheist Press, 1985.

James, C. L. R. *Notes on Dialectics: Hegel, Marx, Lenin*. London: Allison and Busby, 1980.

———. *Spheres of Existence: Selected Writings*. London: Allison and Busby, 1980.

———. *At the Rendezvous of Victory: Selected Writings*. London: Allison and Busby, 1984.

———. *The Black Jacobins: Toussaint L'Ouverture and the San Domingo Revolution*. 2nd ed., rev. New York: Vintage Books, 1989.

———. *American Civilization*. Edited and with an introduction by Anna Grimshaw and Keith Hart. Afterword by Robert A. Hill. Oxford: Blackwell, 1993.

———. *Beyond a Boundary*. Introduction by Robert Lipsyte. Durham: Duke University Press, 1993.

James, George. *Stolen Legacy*. New York: Philosophical Library, 1954.

Jean, Clinton M. *Behind Eurocentric Veils: The Search for African Realities*. Amherst: University of Massachusetts Press, 1991.

Kagame, Alexis. *La Philosophie Bantu-Rwandaise de l'être*. Brussels: Arsom, 1956.

Kambon, Kobi. *The African Personality in America: An African-Centered Framework*. Tallahassee, FL: Nubia Nation Publications, 1992.

Karenga, Maulana. *The African-American Holiday of Kwanzaa: A Celebration of Family, Community, and Culture*. Los Angeles: University of Sankore Press, 1966.

———. *Essays on Struggle: Positions and Analysis*. San Diego: Kawaida Publications, 1978.

———. *Kawaida Theory*. Inglewood, CA: Kawaida Publications, 1980.

———. *Introduction to Black Studies*. 2nd ed. Los Angeles: University of Sankore Press, 1993.

——— (Ed. and trans.). *The Husia*. Los Angeles: Kawaida, 1984.

Karenga, Maulana, and Carruthers, Jacob H. (Eds.). *Kemet and the African Worldview: Research, Rescue, and Restoration—Selected Papers of the Proceedings of the First and Second Conferences of the Association for the Study of Classical African Civilizations*. Los Angeles: University of Sankore Press, 1986.

Kenyatta, Jomo. *Facing Mt. Kenya*. New York: Vintage, 1965.

Keto, C. T. *The Africa-Centered Perspective of History*. Trenton, NJ: C and A Publishers, 1992.

King, Martin Luther, Jr. *Stride toward Freedom*. New York: Harper and Row, 1958.

———. *Why We Can't Wait*. New York: Harper and Row, 1964.

———. *Where Do We Go from Here: Chaos or Community?* Boston: Beacon Press, 1967.

———. *The Trumpet of Conscience*. New York: Harper and Row, 1968.

———. *A Testament of Hope: The Essential Writings and Speeches of Martin Luther King, Jr.* Edited by James Melvin Washington. New York: Harper Collins, 1991.

King, Woodie, and Anthony, Earl (Eds.). *Black Poets and Prophets: The Theory, Practice, and Esthetics of the Pan-Africanist Revolution*. New York: New American Library, 1972.

Knibb, Michael. *Ethiopian Book of Enoch*. New York: Oxford University Press, 1978.

Kunene, Mazisi. *Emperor Shaka the Great! A Zulu Epic*. London: Heinemann, 1979.

Levine, Lawrence. *Black Culture and Black Consciousness*. New York: Oxford University Press, 1977.

Lichtheim, Miriam (Ed.). *Ancient Egyptian Literature*. 3 vols. Berkeley: University of California Press, 1980.

Locke, Alain. *The Philosophy of Alain Locke: The Harlem Renaissance and Beyond*. Edited by Leonard Harris. Philadelphia: Temple University Press, 1989.

——— (Ed.). *The New Negro: An Interpretation*. Introduction by Arnold Rampersad. New York: Atheneum, 1992.

Logan, Rayford. *The Betrayal of the Negro*. New York: L'Ouverture, 1949.

Luthuli, Albert, et al. *Africa's Freedom*. New York: Barnes and Noble, 1964.

Malcolm X. *The Autobiography of Malcolm X*. Edited by Alex Haley. New York: 1964.

Mandela, Nelson. *I Am Prepared to Die*. London: International Defense and Aid Fund for Southern Africa, 1984.

———. *No Easy Walk to Freedom*. London: Heinemann, 1990.

———. *The Struggle Is My Life: His Speeches and Writings Brought Together with Historical Documents. An Account of Mandela in Prison by Fellow Prisoners*. Rev. ed. New York: Pathfinder Press, 1990.

Marable, Manning. *African and Caribbean Politics: From Kwame Nkrumah to Maurice Bishop*. London: Verso, 1987.

Martin, Tony. *Race First: The Ideological and Organizational Struggles of Marcus Garvey and the Universal Negro Improvement Association*. Westport, CT: Greenwood Press, 1976.

Masolo, D. A. *Africa Philosophy in Search of an Identity*. Bloomington: Indiana University Press, 1994.

Mazrui, Ali. *The Africans: A Triple Heritage*. London: BBC Press, 1986.

Mbiti, John. *African Religions and Philosophies*. New York: Doubleday, 1970.

Meier, August, Rudwick, Elliott, and Broderick, Francis L. (Eds.). *Black Protest Thought in the Twentieth Century*. 2nd ed. New York: Macmillan, 1985.

Moore, Carlos. *Castro, the Blacks, and Cuba*. Los Angeles: Center of Afro American Studies, UCLA, 1988.

Mudimbe, V. Y. *The Invention of Africa: Gnosis, Philosophy, and the Order of Knowledge*. Bloomington: Indiana University Press, 1988.

———. *Parables and Fables: Exegesis, Textuality, and Politics in Central Africa*. Madison: University of Wisconsin Press, 1991.

———. *The Idea of Africa*. Bloomington: Indiana University Press, 1994.

Myers, Linda James. *Understanding the Afrocentric Worldview*. Dubuque, IA: Kendall-Hunt, 1988.

Nascimento, Abdias do. *Racial Democracy in Brazil: Myth or Reality*. Ibadan: Sketch Publishing, 1977.

———. *Brazil: Mixture or Massacre?—Essays in the Genocide of a Black People*. Translated by Elisa Larkin Nascimento. 2nd rev. ed. Dover, MA: Majority Press, 1989.

Nascimento, Elisa Larkin. *Pan-Africanism and South America: Emergence of a Black Rebellion*. Buffalo: Afrodiaspora, 1980.

Nell, William. *The Colored Patriots of the American Revolution*. Boston: R. F. Wallcut, 1855.

Ngubane, Jordan. *Conflicts of Minds.* New York: Books in Focus, 1989.

Ngugi wa Thiong'o. *Petals of Blood.* New York: Dutton, 1978.

———. *Decolonising the Mind.* London: Heinemann, 1986.

———. *Moving the Centre: The Struggle for Cultural Freedoms.* London: Curry/Heinemann, 1993.

Niane, D. T. *Sundiata: An Epic of Old Mali.* Translated by A. D. Pickett. New York: Longman, 1986.

Nkrumah, Kwame. *Consciencism: Philosophy and Ideology for Decolonization.* London: Heinemann, 1964.

———. *Africa Must Unite.* New York: International, 1970.

———. *The Class Struggle in Africa.* New York: International, 1970.

———. *Revolutionary Path.* New York: International, 1973.

Nobles, Wade. *Afrikan Psychology.* Oakland: Institute for the Advanced Study of the Black Family.

Nyerere, Julius. *Freedom and Unity: Uhuru na Umoja—A Selection from Writings and Speeches, 1952–1965.* London: Oxford University Press, 1967.

———. *Ujamaa: Essays on Socialism.* London: Oxford University Press, 1968.

———. *Freedom and Development: Uhuru na Maendeleo—A Selection from Writings and Speeches, 1968–1973.* New York: Oxford University Press, 1973.

———. *Essays on Socialism.* London: Oxford University Press, 1974.

Obenga, Théophile. *Ancient Egypt and Black Africa.* Chicago: Karnak House, 1990.

———. *A Lost Tradition: African Philosophy in World History.* Philadelphia: Source Editions, 1995.

Okolo, Chukwudum B. *Racism: A Philosophic Probe.* Jericho, NY: Exposition Press, 1974.

Okpewho, Isidore. *The Epic in Africa.* New York: Oxford University Press, 1979.

Olela, Henry. *From Ancient Africa to Ancient Greece: An Introduction to the History of Philosophy.* Edited by Edward F. Collins and Alveda King Beal. Atlanta: Black Heritage, 1981.

Onyewuenyi, Innocent. *The African Origin of Greek Philosophy: An Exercise in Afrocentrism.* Nsukka: University of Nigeria Press, 1993.

Oruka, H. Odera. *The Philosophy of Liberty: An Essay on Political Philosophy.* Nairobi: Standard Textbooks, 1991.

——— (Ed.). *Sage Philosophy: Indigenous Thinkers and Modern Debate on African Philosophy.* Leiden: E. J. Brill, 1990.

Osei, G. K. *The African Philosophy of Life.* 2nd ed. London: African Publication Society, 1971.

P'bitek, Okot. *Africa's Cultural Revolution.* Nairobi: Macmillion, 1973.

Pritchard, J. B. (Ed.). *Ancient Near Eastern Texts Related to the Old Testament.* Princeton: Princeton University Press, 1955.

Quarles, Benjamin. *Frederick Douglass.* Washington, DC: Associated Publishing, 1948.

———. *The Negro in the Making of America.* New York: 1964.

Raboteau, Albert. *Slave Religion.* New York: Oxford University Press, 1981.

Redding, J. Saunders. *They Came in Chains: Americans from Africa.* New York: Doubleday, 1950.

Redkey, Edwin. *Black Exodus.* New Haven: Yale University Press, 1969.

Robeson, Paul. *Here I Stand.* Boston: Beacon, 1971.

Rodney, Walter. *The Grounding with My Brothers.* Introduction by Richard Small. London: Bogle L'Ouverture, 1969.

———. *How Europe Underdeveloped Africa.* Washington, DC: Howard University Press, 1986.

———. *Walter Rodney Speaks: The Making of an African Intellectual.* Introduction by Robert Hill. Foreword by Howard Dodson. Trenton: Africa World Press, 1990.

Rogers, J. A. *Sex and Race.* 3 vols. New York: J. A. Rogers Publishing, 1940–44.

Sarpong, Peter. *Sacred Stools of the Akan.* Tema: Ghana Publishing Corporation, 1974.

Senghor, Leopold Sedar. *Prose and Poetry.* Selected and translated by John Reed and Clive Wake. London: Oxford University Press, 1965.

———. *The Foundations of "Africanite" or "Negritude" and "Arabite."* Translated by Mercer Cook. Paris: Presence Africaine, 1971.

Sertima, Ivan Van. *They Came before Columbus.* New York: Random House, 1976.

Snowden, Frank, Jr. *Blacks in Antiquity: Ethiopians in the Greco-Roman Experience.* Cambridge, MA: Belknap Press of Harvard University Press, 1970.

Soyinka, Wole. *Art, Dialogue, and Outrage: Essays on Literature and Culture*. New York: Pantheon Books, 1993.

Sproul, Barbara C. *Primal Myths*. New York: HarperCollins, 1979.

Stewart, Maria W. *Maria W. Stewart: America's First Black Woman Political Writer*. Edited by Marilyn Richardson. Bloomington: Indiana University Press, 1987.

Stuckey, Sterling. *Slave Culture*. New York: Oxford University Press, 1987.

Tempels, Placide. *Bantu Philosophy*. Paris: Presence Africaine, 1969.

Thiam, Awa. *Speak Out, Black Sisters: Feminism and Oppression*. Translated by Dorothy Blair. London: Pluto, 1986.

Thompson, Vincent B. *Africa and Unity: The Evolution of Pan Africanism*. London: Longman, 1969.

———. *The Making of the African Diaspora*. New York: Longman, 1987.

Walker, David. *One Continual Cry: David Walker's Appeal, Its Setting, and Its Meaning*. Edited by Herbert Aptheker, with the full text of the 3rd and last edition of the Appeal. New York: Published for A.I.M.S. by Humanities Press, 1965.

Walters, Ronald. *Pan-Africanism in the African Diaspora: An Analysis of Modern Afrocentric Political Movements*. Detroit: Wayne State University Press, 1993.

Washington, Booker T. *Up from Slavery*. New York: Magnum, 1968.

Wells-Barnett, Ida B. *Ida B. Wells-Barnett: An Exploratory Study of an American Black Woman, 1893–1930*. Edited by Mildred Thompson. Brooklyn: Carlson Publishers, 1990.

Welsh-Asante, Kariamu (Ed.). *The African Aesthetic: Keeper of the Traditions*. Westport, CT: Greenwood Press, 1993.

Wesley, Charles H. *Prince Hall: Life and Legacy*. Washington, DC: United Supreme Council, Southern Jurisdiction, Prince Hall Affiliation, 1977.

West, Cornel. *Race Matters*. Boston: Beacon Press, 1992.

White, Charles. *A Man Called White: The Autobiography of Walter White*. New York: Viking Press, 1948.

Williams, Chancellor. *The Destruction of Black Civilization*. Chicago: Third World Press, 1988.

Williams, Eric. *Capitalism and Slavery*. New York: Russell and Russell, 1961.

Willmore, Gayraud. *Black Religion and Black Radicalism*. Garden City, NY: Doubleday, 1972.

Wilson, Willam Julius. *The Declining Significance of Race: Blacks and Changing American Institutions*, 2nd ed. Chicago: University of Chicago Press, 1978.

Wood, Peter H. *Black Majority: Negroes in Colonial South Carolina from 1670 through the Stono Rebellion*. New York: Knopf, 1974.

Woodson, Carter G. *The Mis-Education of the Negro*. Trenton: Africa World Press, 1990.

Wright, Richard. *Native Son*. New York: Harper and Row, 1966.

Sources and Credits

In many instances, the editors have used the first published versions of these documents. For the convenience of readers who would pursue topics in more depth, recent editions are listed here and in the Suggestions for Further Reading.

PART ONE   The Creation of the Universe

"The Heliopolis Creation Narrative": Translation by the editors from the Pyramid Texts, which were collected from the walls of the pyramids by several authors. A recent version is found in Raymond O. Faulkner, *The Ancient Egyptian Pyramid Texts* (Oxford: Clarendon Press, 1969).

"The Memphite Declaration of the Deities": Translation by the editors from the Shabaka Stone, a basalt stele now in the British Museum. Cf. James Pritchard, ed., *Ancient Near Eastern Texts Related to the Old Testament* (Princeton: Princeton University Press, 1955).

Pharaoh Unas, "Vision of the Universe": Editors' translation; the original text was found in the sarcophagus chamber on the south wall. Other versions appear in A. Plankoff, *The Pyramid of Unas* (Princeton: Bollingen series, 40:5, 1968), and S. A. B. Mercer, *The Pyramid Texts in Translation and Commentary*, 4 vols. (New York, 1952).

Pharaoh Teti, "Vision of the Universe": Original from the walls of the pyramid of Teti; a translation may be found in S. A. B. Mercer, *The Pyramid Texts in Translation and Commentary*, 4 vols. (New York, 1952).

Pharaoh Pepi, "Vision of the Universe": Original from the walls of the pyramid of Pepi I; a translation may be found in S. A. B. Mercer, *The Pyramid Texts in Translation and Commentary*, 4 vols. (New York, 1952).

Princess Ni-sedjer-kai, "Tomb Inscription": From *Ancient Egyptian Literature*, vol. I, *The Old and Middle Kingdoms*, by Miriam Lichtheim. Berkeley: University of California Press. Copyright © 1973 The Regents of the University of California. Used by permission.

Hotep-her-akhet, "Tomb Inscription": Original inscription carved on his tomb. Translation by J. H. Breasted, *Ancient Records of Egypt*, vol. I (Chicago, 1906).

Nefer-seshem-ra, "Tomb Inscription": Inscription carved on his tomb, translated by Breasted, vol. I.

Ni-hebsed-Pepi, "Memorial Stone": From H. G. Fischer, *Inscriptions from the Coptite Nome Dynasties VI–XI*, Analecta Orientalia 40 (Rome, 1964). See also Lichtheim, vol. I.

"The San Creation Narrative": From *Primal Myths* by Barbara C. Sproul. Copyright 1979 by Barbara C. Sproul. Reprinted by permission of HarperCollins Publishers, Inc.

"The Khoi Creation Narrative": From *Primal Myths* by Barbara C. Sproul. Copyright 1979 by Barbara C. Sproul. Reprinted by permission of HarperCollins Publishers, Inc.

"The Barozvi Creation Narrative": From *Primal Myths* by Barbara C. Sproul. Copyright 1979 by Barbara C. Sproul. Reprinted by permission of HarperCollins Publishers, Inc.

"The Dogon Creation Narrative": From *Conversations with Ogotemmeli: An Introduction to Dogon Religious Ideas* by Marcel Griaule, with an introduction by Germaine Dieterlin. London and New York: Published for the International African Institute by the Oxford University Press, 1970; © 1965. Used by permission.

"The Yoruba Creation Narrative": From *Tales of Yoruba Gods and Heroes* by Harold Courlander. Copyright © 1973 by Harold Courlander. Used by permission of the author.

"The Asante Tower to Heaven": From "The Ashanti of the Gold Coast" by K. A. Busia, in *Africa Worlds*, ed. Daryll Forde. Copyright 1952 Oxford University Press. Reprinted by permission of Oxford University Press.

"The Asante Concept of the Creation of the Lesser Gods": From *Ashanti Proverbs* by R. S. Rattray (Oxford: Oxford University Press/Clarendon Books, 1916).

James Weldon Johnson, "The Creation": From *God's Trombones: Seven Negro Sermons in Verse* by James Weldon Johnson (New York: Viking Press, 1927).

PART TWO   Religious Ideas

Nefer-rohu, "The Prophecy": From *Ancient Near Eastern Texts Related to the Old Testament*, ed. James Pritchard. Copyright © Princeton University Press, 1969. Third edition. Reprinted with permission by Princeton University Press.

Paheri, "Tomb Prayers": From *Topographical Bibliography of Ancient Egyptian Hieroglyphic Texts, Reliefs, and Paintings*, by B. Porter and R. L. B. Moss. vol. 5 (Oxford, 1927–51).

"Selections from the Papyrus of Ani": From *The Book of the Dead: The Hieroglyphic Transcript of the Papyrus of Ani* translated by E. A. Wallis Budge (Avenal, NJ: Gramercy Books, 1895).

Akhenaten, "Hymns to Aten": Editors' translation; cf. Miriam Lichtheim, *Ancient Egyptian Literature*, vol. II, *The New Kingdom*.

Haremhab, "Prayer and Hymn": From H. E. Winlock, *The Journal of Egyptian Archaeology*, vol. 10 (1924), pp. 1–5.

"Penitential Hymns": From translation by B. Gunn in *The Journal of Egyptian Archaeology*, vol. 3 (1916), pp. 83–89. Cf. Lichtheim, vol. II.

"Selections from the Book of Henok (Enoch)": Copyright © Oxford University Press 1978. Reprinted from *The Ethiopian Book of Enoch*, edited by Michael Knibb and Edward Ullendorff, vol. 2 (1978), by permission of Oxford University Press.

Jomo Kenyatta, "Religion and Ancestor Veneration": From *Facing Mount Kenya: The Tribal Life of the Gikuyu* with an introduction by B. Malinowski. Copyright 1978 AMS Press. Reprinted with permission.

"Asante Praise Poems to Tano River and the Earth": From *Ashanti Proverbs* by R. S. Rattray (Oxford: Oxford University Press/Clarendon Books, 1916).

"A Lodagaa Libation to the Ancestors": From *The Myth of the Bagre* by Jack Goody. Copyright 1972 by Oxford University Press (Oxford). Reprinted by permission of Oxford University Press.

Abu Shardow Abarry, "Recurrent Themes in Ga Libation (Mpai) Oratory": From "Mpai: Libation Oratory" by Abu S. Abarry, in *The African Aesthetic: Keeper of the Traditions*, Kariamu Welsh Asante, ed. Westport, CT: Greenwood Press, 1993. Reprinted by permission of Greenwood Press, an imprint of Greenwood Publishing Group, Inc., Westport, CT.

"Igbo Invocations": From *Poetic Heritage: Igbo Traditional Verse*, Romanus Egudu and Donatus Nwoga, eds. UNESCO Language Translation series. Enugu, Nigeria: Nwankwo-Ifejika & Co.

Wande Abimbola, "Wapele: The Concept of Good Character in Ifá Literary Corpus": From *The Yoruba Ifá Divination System: An Exposition of Ifá Literary Corpus* by Wande Abimbola. Copyright 1976 Oxford University Press (New York). Reprinted by permission of University Press Plc.

Mensah Sarbah, "Akan Religion": From *Fanti National Constitution: A Short Treatise on the Constitution and Government of the Fanti, Ashanti, and Other Akan Tribes of West Africa, Together with an Account of the Discovery of the Gold Coast by Portuguese Navigators, a Short Narration of Early English Voyages, and a Study of the Rise of British Gold Coast Jurisdiction* by John Mensah Sarbah (London: William Clowes, 1906).

Wole Soyinka, "African Classical Concepts of Tragedy": Reprinted from *Myth, Literature and
African World*. Copyright 1990, Cambridge University Press (New York). Reprinted with permission of Cambridge University Press.

Peter Sarpong, "The Akan Blackened Stool and the *Odwira* Festival": From *Sacred Stools of
in* by Peter Sarpong. Tema: Ghana Publishing Corp. [no date]. Reprinted by permission.

A Shardow Abarry, "The Ga Homowo (Hunger-Hooting) Cultural Festival": Used with
permission of the author.

J. Africanus B. Horton, "Africa as the Nursery of Science and Literature": From *West African
Countries and Peoples and A Vindication of the African Race* by J. A. B. Horton. London: W. J.
Johnson, 1868.

Molefi Kete Asante, "The Principal Issues in Afrocentric Inquiry": From *Kemet, Afrocentricity,
and Knowledge* by Molefi Kete Asante. Lawrenceville, NJ: Africa World Press, 1991. Reprinted
with permission of Africa World Press.

Théophile Obenga, "Genetic Linguistic Connections of Ancient Egypt and the Rest of Africa": From *A Lost Tradition: African Philosophy in World History*. Philadelphia: The Source Editions, 1995. Reprinted with permission of the author.

PART FOUR   Philosophy and Morality

John Mbiti, "The Study of African Religions and Philosophy": From *African Religions and
Philosophy* by John Mbiti. Copyright 1969, London: Heinemann Publishers (Oxford) Limited.
Reprinted with permission.

Kwame Gyekye, "The Idea of African Philosophy": From *An Essay on African Philosophical
Thought: The Akan Conceptual Scheme*, revised edition (Philadelphia: Temple University Press,
1995). Copyright 1995 Kwame Gyekye. Reprinted by permission of the author.

Ptah-hotep, "Moral Teachings": From Papyrus Prisse of the Bibliothèque Nationale. One
translation was provided by B. Gunn in *The Instruction of Ptah-hotep and the Instruction of Ke'gemni:
The Oldest Books in the World* (London and New York, 1909). Many other versions of this text
have been published; see, for example, *The Teachings of Ptahhotep*, edited by Asa Hilliard, Larry
Williams, and Nia Dimali (Atlanta: Blackwood Press, 1987). To avoid burdening the text, the
editors have not indicated their departures from previous translations.

Sinuhe, "My Victory over Circumstances": Many versions of this story exist. There are five
major papyri and seventeen ostraca. For the present version the editors have used sections of
the translations by A. H. Gardiner, *Notes of the Story of Sinuhe* (Paris, 1916), and A. M. Blackman,
The Story of Sinuhe, Bibliotheca Aegyptiaca, II (Brussels, 1932). Other publications include J. W.
B. Barns, *The Ashmolean Ostracan of Sinuhe* (London, 1952); John A. Wilson, "The Story of
Sinuhe," in Pritchard; and Lichtheim, vol. II.

Amenemope, "Instructions for Well-Being": The editors' translation relies on E. A. W.
Budge, *The Teaching of Amen-em-apt, Son of Kanekht* (London, 1924), and F. Ll. Griffith, *Journal
of Egyptian Archaeology*, 12 (1926), 191–231.

"The Pharoah's Speech at the Installation of Rekhmire as Prime Minister": From an inscription on the walls of Rekhmire's tomb in the Valley of the Nobles, found in Breasted, vol. II.

"The Doomed Prince": From a translation by T. E. Peet in *Journal of Egyptian Archaeology*,
vol. II (1925), 227–229. Cf. Lichtheim, vol. II.

"The Story of the Two Brothers": From *Ancient Egyptian Literature*, vol. I, *The Old and Middle
Kingdoms*, by Miriam Lichtheim. Copyright © 1973, by the Regents of the University of California. Used by permission of the University of California Press.

Wen-Amon, "My Journey to Asia": From A. Erman, *The Literature of the Ancient Egyptians*,
translated by A. M. Blackman (London, 1927). Cf. Lichtheim, vol. II.

"The Lion in Search of Man": From the Leiden Demotic Papyrus, I, 384. Translated into
German by W. Erichsen, *Demotische Lesestücke* (Leipzig, 1937), and from the German into English by Dr. C. A. Blackshire-Belay, 1994.

Léopold Sédar Senghor, "African Socialism": From *African Socialism: A Report to the Constitu-*

tive Conference of the Party of African Federation. Translated and edited by Mercer Cook. Published by the American Society of African Culture (New York, 1959).

Kwame Nkrumah, "Consciencism": From "Consciencism: Philosophy and the Ideology for Decolonization" in *Consciencism.* Copyright © 1970, Monthly Review Press. Reprinted by permission of Monthly Review Foundation.

"The Zulu Personal Declaration": From various oral sources. It was recited to Molefi Kete Asante by the late Jordan Ngubane in Washington, DC, in 1978; subsequently a published version appeared in his book, *Conflicts of Minds* (New York: Books in Focus, 1978), now out of print.

Chinua Achebe, "The African Writer and the English Language": From *Morning Yet on Creation Day* (London: Heinemann, 1975). Reprinted with permission of David Bolt, London.

"Igbo Proverbs": Common proverbs contributed to this volume by various colleagues, including Dr. Victor Okafor of Eastern Michigan University.

"Luyia Proverbs": Common proverbs contributed to this volume by various colleagues, including Dr. Ndiika Mutere, Alexandria, Virginia.

"African American Spirituals": Traditional.

Maria W. Stewart, "On African Rights and Liberty": From an address delivered at the African Masonic Hall, Boston, February 27, 1833. First published in *Productions of Mrs. Maria Stewart* (New York, 1835). For a recent edition of Stewart's essays and speeches, see *Maria W. Stewart: America's First Black Woman Political Writer,* edited by Marilyn Richardson (Bloomington: Indiana University Press, 1987).

Marcus Garvey, "Philosophy and Opinions": From *Philosophy and Opinions of Marcus Garvey,* compiled by Amy Jacques Garvey, with a new introduction by E. U. Essien-Udom, 2nd edition (London: Frank Cass, 1967). Reprinted by permission of Frank Cass & Co. Ltd., 890–900 Eastern Avenue, Ilford IG2 7HH, Essex, England.

W. E. B. Du Bois, "The Concept of Race": From *Dusk of Dawn: An Essay Toward an Autobiography of a Race Concept* by W. E. Burghardt Du Bois (New York: Harcourt Brace and Co., 1940). Recently reprinted with a new introduction by Irene Diggs (New Brunswick, NJ: Transaction Books, 1992).

Alain Locke, "The Ethics of Culture": From *Howard University Record,* 17 (1923), 178–185. Reprinted with the permission of Moorland-Springarn Research Center, Alain Locke Collection, Howard University.

William E. Abraham, "The Life and Times of Anton Wilhelm Amo, the First African (Black) Philosopher in Europe": From *The Transactions of the Historical Society of Ghana,* vol. 2, no. 1 (Accra, 1963).

PART FIVE   Society and Politics

Weni, "Autobiography": From Breasted, vol. I.

Harkhuf, "Autobiography": From Breasted, vol. I.

William E. Abraham, "Theory of Human Society": From *The Mind of Africa.* Chicago: The University of Chicago Press, 1962. Reprinted with permission of The University of Chicago Press and Weidenfeld & Nicolson.

Mensah Sarbah, "On the Fante National Constitution": From *Fanti National Constitution: A Short Treatise on the Constitution and Government of the Fanti, Ashanti, and Other Akan Tribes of West Africa, Together with an Account of the Discovery of the Gold Coast by Portuguese Navigators, a Short Narration of Early English Voyages, and a Study of the Rise of British Gold Coast Jurisdiction* by John Mensah Sarbah (London: William Clowes, 1906).

Edward Wilmot Blyden, "Mohammedanism and the Negro Race": From *Christianity, Islam, and the Negro Race* by Edward Wilmot Blyden, with an introduction by Samuel Lewis (London: W. B. Whittingham, 1887). A recent edition (1994) is available from Black Classic Press in Baltimore.

Edward Wilmot Blyden, "Christianity and the Negro Race": From *Christianity, Islam, and the*

Negro Race by Edward Wilmot Blyden, with an introduction by Samuel Lewis (London: W. B. Whittingham, 1887). A recent edition (1994) is available from Black Classic Press in Baltimore.

Booker T. Washington, "Racial Accommodation": Reprinted with permission of the Booker T. Washington Collections, Tuskegee University Archives.

Booker T. Washington, "The Atlanta Exposition Address": Reprinted with permission of the Booker T. Washington Collections, Tuskegee University Archives.

W. E. B. Du Bois, "Of Mr. Booker T. Washington and Others": From *The Souls of Black Folk* by W. E. Burghardt Du Bois. First published in 1903, the book has been reprinted many times. See, for example, the Penguin USA edition (New York, 1969).

Monroe Trotter, "A Critique of Booker T. Washington's Plan": From a newspaper article that appeared in the *Boston Guardian*, 1901.

Amy Jacques Garvey, "Women as Leaders": From an editorial in *Negro World*, October 24, 1925.

Abdias do Nascimento, "Brazilian *Quilombismo*": From a speech presented at the Sixth Pan-African Congress, Dar-es-Salaam, 1974. Translated from the Portuguese by Elisa Larkin Nascimento. Used with permission of the author.

"Pan-African Congress Resolution (1919)": Resolution adopted by the Congress in Paris, 1919.

"Pan-African Congress Resolution (1945)": Resolution adopted by the Congress in Manchester, England, 1945.

Paul Robeson, "The Power of Negro Action": From *Here I Stand* (Boston: Beacon Press, 1971). Copyright © 1958 by Paul Robeson. Reprinted by permission of Beacon Press.

"Declaration and Resolutions of the First Conference of Independent African States (1958)": Adopted by the Conference in Accra, Ghana, April 15–22, 1958.

Maulana Karenga, "The Nguzo Saba (The Seven Principles): Their Meaning and Message": From *The African American Holiday of Kwanzaa: A Celebration of Family, Community, and Culture* by Maulana Karenga. Los Angeles: University of Sankore Press, 1989. Used by permission of the University of Sankore Press.

Julius K. Nyerere, "One-Party Government": From *Transition: A Journal of Arts, Culture and Society*, vol. I, no. 2, Kampala, Uganda: December 1961.

Kwame Nkrumah, "The Need for a Union Government for Africa": From *Two Hundred Years of English in Africa*, ed. LaLage Brown. London: Heinemann Educational Books, 1973. Reprinted by permission of the publisher.

C. L. R. James, "The Rise and Fall of Nkrumah": From Grimshaw, Anna, ed., *The C. L. R. James Reader*. Cambridge, MA: Blackwell, 1992. Reprinted with permission of the publisher.

James Baldwin, "My Dungeon Shook: Letter to My Nephew on the One Hundredth Anniversary of the Emancipation": Originally published in *The Progressive*, © 1962 by James Baldwin. Copyright renewed. Collected in *The Fire Next Time*, published by Vintage Books. Reprinted with the permission of the James Baldwin Estate.

Cornel West, "W. E. B. Du Bois: The Jamesian Organic Intellectual": From *The American Evasion of Philosophy: A Genealogy of Pragmatism* by Cornel West. Madison: University of Wisconsin Press. Copyright © 1989. Reprinted with permission of the University of Wisconsin Press.

PART SIX   Resistance and Renewal

Ah-mose, "The Expulsion of the Hyksos": From Breasted, vol. II; B. Gunn and A. H. Gardiner, *The Journal of Egyptian Archaeology*, 5 (1918).

"The Commemorative Stone of Thutmose III": From Breasted, vol. II.

Thutmose III, "Annals": The editors' translations rely on Breasted, vol. II; R. O. Faulkner, *The Journal of Egyptian Archaeology*, 28 (1942), 2–15; H. H. Nelson, *The Battle of Megiddo* (Chicago, 1913); and Lichtheim, vol. II.

"Pharaoh Piye and the Victory over North": From Breasted, vol. IV.

King Kwame Ansa, "The Portuguese Fortress at El Mina": From *A History of the Gold Coast and Ashanti: From the Earliest Times to the Commencement of the Twentieth Century* by W. Walton

Claridge; originally published in 1915. A more recent edition is available with an introduction by W. E. F. Ward (New York: Barnes and Noble, 1964).

"A Shona Song": "Take Up Arms and Liberate Yourselves," a popular martial song sung by Zimbabwean soldiers during the Second Chimurenga War, the war of liberation from Rhodesia.

Nat Turner, "Narrative": From *Confessions of Nat Turner.* Virginia: Southhampton Institute, 1831.

David Walker, "Appeal to the Coloured Citizens of the World: Our Wretchedness in Consequence of Slavery": From *An Appeal to the Coloured Citizens of the World,* a series of four articles that originally appeared in 1829–1830. See also *One Continual Cry: David Walker's Appeal, Its Setting and Its Meaning* by Herbert Aptheker, with the full text of the third and last edition of the Appeal (New York: Published for A.I.M.S. by Humanities Press, 1965).

Frederick Douglass, "Fourth of July Oration": From various sources; see, for example, Arthur L. Smith and Steven Robb, *The Voice of Black Rhetoric* (New York: Harper and Row, 1970).

Frances Ellen Watkins Harper, "We Are All Bound Up Together": From *A Brighter Coming Day: A Frances Ellen Watkins Harper Reader,* edited by Frances Smith Foster (New York: The Feminist Press of the City University of New York, 1990), pp. 217–218. Used by permission.

Anna Julia Cooper, "Womanhood: A Vital Element in the Regeneration and Progress of a Race": From *A Voice from the South, by a Black Woman of the South.* Xenia, OH: Aldine Printing House, 1892.

Ida B. Wells-Barnett, "Lynch Law in All Its Phases": From *Ida B. Wells-Barnett: An Exploratory Study of an American Black Woman, 1893–1930,* Mildred Thompson, ed. Brooklyn: Carlson Publishers, 1990.

Carter G. Woodson, "The Mis-Education of the Negro": From *The Mis-Education of the Negro* by Carter Goodwin Woodson. Washington, DC: Associated Publishers, DC, 1933.

Emperor Haile Selassie, "Address to the League of Nations": From the Archives of the League of Nations housed in the Dag Hammarskjöld Library of the United Nations.

Mary McLeod Bethune, "My Last Will and Testament": From the collection of Bethune's papers at the Amistad Research Center at Tulane University, New Orleans. Reprinted by permission.

Martin Luther King, Jr., "I Have a Dream": From *Martin Luther King, Jr.: A Documentary* by Flip Shulke. Copyright 1963 by Martin Luther King, Jr., copyright renewed 1991 by Coretta Scott King. Reprinted by arrangement with the Heirs to the Estate of Martin Luther King, Jr., c/o Joan Daves as agent for the proprietor.

Frantz Fanon, "Colonial War and Mental Disorders": From *The Wretched of the Earth* by Frantz Fanon (New York: Grove, 1963). Copyright © 1963 by Présence Africaine. Used by permission of Grove Atlantic.

Amiri Baraka, "Revolutionary Culture and the Future of Pan African Culture": From *Proceedings of the Sixth Pan African Congress,* Dar-es-Salaam, 1974.

"Charter of the Organization of African Unity": Adopted in Addis Ababa, Ethiopia, May 25, 1963.

Walter Rodney, "How Africa Developed before the Coming of the Europeans—Up to the Fifteenth Century": From *How Europe Underdeveloped Africa* by Walter Rodney. Copyright © 1972 by Howard University Press. Reprinted with permission of Howard University Press.

Malcolm X, "Message to the Grassroots": From *Malcolm X Speaks,* ed. George Breitman. Copyright © 1965, 1989 by Betty Shabazz and Pathfinder Press. Reprinted by permission.

Walter Rodney, "Towards the Sixth Pan African Congress: Aspects of the International Class Struggle in Africa, the Caribbean, and America": From *Proceedings of the Sixth Pan African Congress,* Dar-es-Salaam, 1974.

Martin Luther King, Jr., "Letter from a Birmingham Jail": From *Martin Luther King, Jr.: A Documentary* by Flip Shulke. Copyright 1963 by Martin Luther King, Jr., copyright renewed 1991 by Coretta Scott King. Reprinted by arrangement with the Heirs to the Estate of Martin Luther King, Jr., c/o Joan Daves as agent for the proprietor.

Martin Luther King, Jr., "Negroes Are Not Moving Too Fast": From *A Testament of Hope: The Essential Writings of Martin Luther King, Jr.* Copyright 1964 by Martin Luther King, Jr., copyright

Index

A l'Echelle humaine, 342
aárùún (Yoruba sacrifice materials), 99
Abaluyia ethnic group, 297–98
Abarry, Abu Shardow: Ga Homowo cultural festival, 254; Ga libation oratory, 92–95
Abay River Complex (Nile Valley), 12
Abraham, William E., on career of A. W. Amo, 424–38; theory of human society, 452–61
Abrahams, Peter, 379
Abusua (Akan clan concept), 455
Achebe, Chinua, 211–12, 286, 379–84
Achenwall, Gottfried, 437, 440n.35
Adae festival, 251
aesthetics, Afrocentricity and, 258
African Americans: Africa for the Africans movement, 402–408; Afrocentricity and, 256–57, 260–61; blues music and cultural identity in, 763–76; concern for African rights and liberty, 388–96; creation myths of, 13, 53–55; educational experiences of, 656–63; emergence of African national culture and, 240–42; employment and social conditions of, 189–92; King's critique of civil rights movement, 674–76, 740–54; literature of, 218–26, 381–82; Pan-African movement and, 735–39; politics of, 444; pre-Columbian presence of, 509; race relations and, 483–88; religious ties to Africa among, 292; Robeson's call for activism among, 522–32; syncretic religions of, 62
African antiquity, origin of world and, 207–209; sources on, 1–2
African Communities League, 445
African Cultural Society, 240
African Lodge, 221
"African Morality, An," 298
African Origin of Civilization, The, 507
African Political Systems, 296, 303n.11
African Religions and Philosophy, 294–95, 303n.1
African Systems of Kinship and Marriage, 296
African Traditional Religion, 291, 303n.12
African Worlds, 296, 303n.8
Afro-Asiatic (journal), 266
Afro-Asiatic linguistic group, 266–81
Afro-Brazilians. *See* Brazil

Afrocentricity: aesthetic of, 258; axiological issues, 258; contextualized definition and, 260–61; cosmological issues, 256–57; epistemological issues, 257–58; geographic issues, 259, 261; Karenga's seven principles and, 547; principle issues, 256–61; research issues, 258–61; theory and ideology of, 113
Afro-Cuban mythology, signifying monkey in, 167–70
Agbèrù (Yoruba deity), 99
agene (kene-kene-koro) dance, in *Ozidi* saga, 146
agriculture in Africa: in early Ethiopia, 719; economic planning and, 347–52; Ga agricultural rites, 92–95; in precolonial Africa, 711–12
Ah-mose (Kemet king), 600–601
Ahuman, Attoh (Reverend), 425, 438n.3
àjẹ́ (Yoruba witches), 99
ajogun (Yoruba warriors against man), 99
Akan (language and ethnic group): bard-musicians of, 120–21, 128, 146–47; cultural and religious influences of, 297; Egyptian connections to, 276–81; Fante National Constitution and, 461–69; geographic spread of, 297; *Odwira* festival and, 251–53; psychological theory among, 452; religious principles, 107–108; sacred script of, 2; theory of State among, 455–56
Akan Doctrine of God, The, 292
Akhenaten, hymns to Aten, 60–61, 75–78
Alade, Modupe, 102
alcohol consumption, patterns of, in Africa, 216
Alexander, J. Addison, 471
Alexander, the Great, 5
Algeria, impact of French occupation on, 688n.1
Al-Hajj Omaru (Sheikh), 474
Allen, Richard, 190
Along This Way, 223
alphabets, in African languages, 213–14
Amado, Jorge, 381–82
Amenemope, writings of, 285, 312–25
Amenhotep IV. *See* Akhenaten
Amen-Ra, hymn to, 82–83
American Colonization Society, 190
American Stuff, 225
Americanization, African cultural identity and, 215–17

Bueno, Salvador, 168
burial texts, of Egyptians, 4–5
Busia, K. A., 297–98, 301–302, 303nn.14–15,
    304n.26

Cabral, Amilcar, 113, 243–47, 689–90
Cabrera, Lydia, 167
Call, The, 738–39
Camara, Seydou, 124–25, 127, 129n.4
Cambyses, 207
Candeia, João, 512–13
Candido, João, 759
Candomble religion, African sources of, 62
Cane, 161, 222
Capital, 344
capitalism: vs. communitarianism, in African culture,
    762–64; impact of, on African politics, 215–16;
    role of, in economic conditions, 348–53
Capitein, John Jacob Eliza, 425–26, 438
Carter, Jimmy, 215
Carthage, 5
causation, in African philosophy, 299–300
Césaire, Aimé Fernand, 113, 202–206, 353
Chadwick, H. M. and N. K., 124, 129n.21
Chama Cha Mapinduzi (CCM) political party, 214
Champollion, Jean-François, 2, 508
Chesnutt, Charles W., 222, 225
Chico-Rei, 757–58
Chinweizu, 6, 286
Christianity: African religions and, 291, 300–301; in
    early Ethiopia, 718–19; influence in Africa of,
    444, 477–82
"chthonic realm" of Yoruba tragedy, 249
churches, importance of, to African Americans, 199
Cissé, Alioune, 347, 353n.14
"City of Refuge, The," 223
clan structure, in Akan society, 454–56
Clark-Bekederemo, J. P., 127, 130n.35, 136–49, 380,
    383
Clarke, John Henrik, 218–26
class structure: absence of, in African religion, 59; Af-
    rocentricity and, 257; in ancient Egypt, 717–18;
    consciencism and, 362–70; cultural identity and,
    245–47; Du Bois's concept of, 195–97; Pan-Afri-
    can movement and, 720–39; in precolonial Af-
    rica, 710–11, 714–15; role of, in African
    economic planning, 347–53
Clay, Henry, 190
Cohen, Marcel, 266
Colin, Roland, 344
college education, Du Bois on importance of, 194
colonialism: African democracy and, 556–58; con-
    sciencism and, 365–68; Fanon's analysis of,
    677–88; impact on African intellectualism,
    218–26; impact on African literature, 380–81;
    Pan-African cultural identity and, 236–42, 690–
    97. *See also* imperialism
colonization movement, 190, 197
Color and Democracy: Colonies and Peace, 591
Come Away My Love, 381
communism: African attitudes regarding, 342; im-
    pact of, on African Americans, 588–89, 591
communitarian tradition: African concept of, 59–60;
    capitalism vs., 762–74; *Nguzo Saba* (Seven Princi-

ples) of, 543–54; in precolonial Africa, 708–709,
    714–15; Robeson on power of, among African
    Americans, 522–32
Community's Fund of Aid and Cooperation (F.A.C.),
    348–49
comparative linguistics: defined, 263–65; genetic
    connection between Egyptian and African lan-
    guages, 265–81
Cone, James, 765, 777n.2
Congress of Negro Writers and Artists: First Congress
    (1956), 227–28; Second Congress (1959),
    229–35
Conjure Woman, The, 222
Conrad, Earl, 768–69, 777n.13
Conrad, Joseph, 379
consciencism, 286, 354–70
Cooper, Anna Julia, 643–50
Coptic Egyptian language, linguistic connections to
    African languages, 264–81
Cornish, Samuel, 221
corruption, cultural transition in Africa and, 211–13
Crane, 161, 172
creation narratives: African American narrative, 13,
    53–55; African American response to, 13; Asante
    narrative, 13, 50–52; Barozvi (Barotse or Balozi)
    narrative, 39–40; Dogon narrative, 13, 41–44;
    Hotep-her-akhet text, 13, 32; Khoi narrative, 38;
    Nefer-seshem-ra (Sheshi) text, 13, 33; Ni-hebsed-
    Pepi text, 13, 34; Ni-sedjer-kai text, 13, 31; Pepi
    pyramid text, 13, 27–30; pyramid inscriptions of,
    13; sacred idiom in, 11–13; San narrative, 35–37;
    Teti pyramid text, 13, 24–26; Unas pyramid text,
    13, 17–23; Yoruba narrative, 13, 45–49
Crisis magazine, 200, 222–25, 587
Cruse, Harold, 193
Cry of Ipiranga, 758–59
Cullen, Countee, 200, 416–17
cultural identity: African American educational expe-
    rience and, 656–63; African American literature
    and, 218–26; of African Americans, 160–72,
    189–92; Afrocentricity and, 256–58; context of
    struggle for, 243–47; Du Bois's Negro intellec-
    tual, 193–200; ethics and, 418–23; Europeaniza-
    tion vs. Americanization, 215–17; integration of,
    in Africa, 210–11; language and culture change,
    213–15; national culture and, 236–42; oral epic
    and, 119–28; overview of sources, 112–13; Pan-
    African cultural revolution and, 689–97, 755–64;
    pluralism of, in Africa, 295–98; precolonial Af-
    rica and, 706–720; socialism in Africa and,
    344–53; tripartite synthesis in twentieth-century
    Africa, 210–17 culture, defined, 193
Culture and Anarchy, 196
Cush society, 3
Cyrenaica, 5

Dahomey, religious concepts in, 300–301
Dammann, E., 291
Dan people, griot among, 122, 128, 129n.15
dance: Afrocentricity and, 257–58; in *Ozidi* saga,
    144–47; in precolonial Africa, 707–708
Danqua, J. B., 292
Dantu (Ga deity), 92–93, 94n.4
Dark Princess, 200

Index   819

Hilliard, Asa, 5, 7
Hima Diki (Ghanian king), 185–86
Himes, Chester B., 225
Hincks, E., 266
historiography, of early African civilizations, 207–209
History of the Intellectual Development of Europe, 471
Hittites, Egyptian struggle against, 60
Holiday, Billie, 776
Home to Harlem, 200, 223
Homer, African bards compared with, 122, 125–28
Homowo (Ga traditional New Year), 92, 95n.4, 254
Hope of Liberty, The, 221
Horemhab, prayer and hymn of, 60–61, 79–81
Horton, George Moses, 221
Horton, James Africanus Beale, 113, 255
Hotep-her-akhet, 13, 32
Houessou-Adin, Thomas, 286
Howard University Bibliography of African and Afro-American Religious Studies with Locations in American Libraries, 292
Hughes, (James) Langston, 200, 222, 240
Hume, David, 364–65
hunger-hooting festival, among Ga, 254
Hurston, Zora Neale, 172, 222–23
Husia, The, 7, 12
Huso Husovic, Cor (guslar), 125
hymns: Akhenaten's hymns to Aten, 60–61, 75–78; Horemhab's prayer and hymn, 60–61, 79–81; penitential hymns of Kemet, 60, 82–85

Ibo (ethnic group), 211–12. *See also* Igbo people
íbọ (Yoruba divinities), 99
Identity of Meaning Principle, 355
Idowu, E. Bolaji, 292, 297, 303n.17
If He Hollers Let Him Go, 225
Ifá (deity and sacred texts), 98–106, 163–66, 171–72
Igbo people: Asaba, 129n.24; invocations of, 96–97; proverbs of, 286, 385–86
ijala (Yoruba heroic chants), 121–23, 127–28
Ijo peoples: dialects of, 141–44; festivals and religious occasions of, 147–49; mother's status among, 148–49; *Ozidi* saga among, 136, 139
Ikenga-Metuh, E., 292
Iliad, 121
Image of God Among the Sotho-Tswana, The, 292
Imani (faith), 553–54
Imhotep, 285
imperialism, cultural identity and, 243–47, 694–97, 706–720
Imperialism in the 70's, 695
In Old Plantation Days, 222
Independent African States, Declaration and Resolution of First Conference (1958), 533–42
indeterminacy, in African American narrative, 172
Indo-European languages, development of, 262–64
Infants of the Spring, 200
Innes, Gordon, 129n.15
Instructions for Well-Being (Amenemope), 312–25
intellectuals: Du Bois and Negro intellectual movement, 193–94, 223–24, 587–93; national culture and, 237–42; role of, in precolonial Africa, 218–26. *See also* Harlem Renaissance
Interesting Narrative of the Life of Gustavas Vassa, 219–20

interpretation, Yoruba myth of origins of, 164–65
Invisible Man, 200
Islam, African attitudes regarding, 355–70, 444, 470–76
Iwà (Yoruba deity), 99–106
Iwàpèlé (good character), 98–100

Jackson, Michael, 217
Jahn, Janheinz, 290–91, 767, 777n.6
Jalee, Pierre, 695
James, Cyril Lionel Robert, 445, 573–79
James, William, 587
Jeffers, Lance, 225
Johnson, Charles S., 200
Johnson, James Weldon, 200, 223; on African American creation myths, 13, 53–55
Jones, Henry B., 225
Jones, LeRoi. *See* Baraka, Amiri
journalist literature, 221
Junker, H., 12, 13n.2

Kabo-Kunbowei clans, 141
Kagame, Alexis, 290, 292–93
Kagemni, 285
kainga (drum), in *Ozidi* saga, 146
Kaiser, Ernest, 199–200
Kambili epic, bards in, 123–25
Kant, Immanuel, 364–65
Kanute, Banna, 129n.17
Kanute, Dembo, 129n.17
Karenga, Maulana Ndabezitha, 7, 12, 445, 543–54, 599, 689; Million Man March/Day of Absence statement, 599, 780–90
Karisi (Nyanga deity), 127
Kariuki, Joseph, 381
Kawaida theory, 445
Kebra Nagast, 61
Keita, Modibo, 345
Kelly, William Melvin, 226
Kemet (ancient civilization): creation myths in, 11–13; origins of, 5–6; penitential hymns of, 60, 82–85; role of, in Africalogy, 259–61, 597–98. *See also* Egypt
Kenya, Kiswahili language in, 214
Kenyatta, Jomo: decrees Kiswahili as official language of Kenya, 214; Negritude Movement and, 240; writings of, 60–61, 88–89
Khoi ethnic group: creation myths of, 13; creation narrative, 38
Khunanup, 285
KiKongo people, *nganga* concept of, 169, 174n.24
Kikuyu, 61
"kile" (ululation), Ijo use of, 140, 142–43
Killens, John O., 225
kindoki, concept of, 174n.24
King, Martin Luther, Jr., 591, 674–76, 740–54
kings, stooling and destooling of, in Ghana, 185–88
kinship obligations: of Akan clans, 455–56; cultural transition in Africa and, 211–12. *See also* family structure
Kintu concept, in African religion, 290
Kirima, N., 293
Kiswahili: alphabet for, 213; as primary language of discourse in Africa, 214

Index   823

"primitive" religions, 288
Principle of Sufficient Reason, 436
Principles of Sociology, 288–89
Pritchard, James B., 12
Problems de Linguistique Générale, 263
"Promised Land, The," 223
protection invocation, 96
proverbs, African reliance on, 286
psychology: African attitudes toward, 452–61; colonialism and reactionary psychosis to, 678–88, 688n.2
Ptah (Kemet deity), 11; hymn to, 84–85
Ptah-hotep (Kemet official), 5, 285–86, 306–307, 550
Ptolemy, 2, 5
Ptolemy V Epiphanes, 2–3
pyramid texts, 5, 12–13

quantum theory, African philosophy and, 355–56, 360
Quarcoopome, T. N. O., 293
quilombismo, 445, 505–16, 757–58

Ra (Ra-Atum) (deity), 11
Ra (Re) (Egyptian deity), 12; popularity of, 61
race and racism: Africalogy and, 256, 261; Brazilian *quilombismo* and, 509–14; cultural identity and, 112–13; Du Bois on concept of, 409–17, 589–93; Washington's commentary on racial accommodation, 483–88
"Race Traits and Tendencies," 410
Radillo, Teofilo, 168–69, 174n.22
Rainey, Gertrude ("Ma"), 765–66, 771–76
Rameses II, 60
Rampersad, Arnold, 585, 592n.12
Randall, Dudley, 197–98
Reagan, Ronald, 215
Reddick, Lawrence D., 225
Redding, Saunders, 200n.4
redemptive religions, 288
Rekhmire (Kemet prime minister), 326–28
religion: metaphysics in African, 298–302; overview of African, 287–93; in precolonial Africa, 707–708, 718–20; role of, in African society, 444
Religion of the Yorubas, The, 508
religious war, African concept of, 60, 443
republican society: in Akan Gold Coast communities, 467–69; role of bard in, 128
research methodology: in Africalogy, 258–61; African religious studies and, 290–93; genetic linguistics, 262–81
resurrection, as theme in Teti pyramid text, 13
retributive justice, absence of, in African religion, 59
Revolt of the Tailors (*Revolta dos Alfaiates*), 758
Rise of Shaka, The, 151–59
Risher, Rudolph, 200
rituals: in African American culture, 162; of Ga people, 92–95; of *Odwira* festival, 251–53
Robert, Shabaan, 380–81
Robeson, Paul, 445, 522–32
Robinson, John H., Jr., 226
Rodney, Walter, 706–720, 729–739
Roman Empire, Africa during, 5
Roman-Carthaginian War, 5

Rosetta Stone, 2–3
Ruch, E. A., 293
Rurede, Shekarisi, 122
Russian Revolution, and African Americans, 588–89
Russwurm, John B., 220–21
Rwanda, religious concepts in, 300–302

sacred and religious texts, as source material, 1–2
sacred idiom, in African creation documents, 11
saman-twen-twen (Akan ghost), 454
San nomadic society: creation myths of, 13; creation narrative of, 35–37
Sankore, University of, 218–19
Santeria, African sources of, 62
Sarbah, John Mensah, 61, 107–109, 462–69
Sarpong, Peter, 113, 251–53
Schmoller, Gustav, 199
Schnee, Heinrich, 402–403
Schuh, Russell G., 266
Schuyler, George S., 224
science: African American educational experience and, 661–63; African philosophy and, 356–70; Africans' historical role in, 113, 255; American influence on, in Africa, 216; Pan-African culture and, 762; in precolonial Egypt, 717–18
Scott, Walter (Sir), 129n.10
secret societies: scripts of, 2; in United States, 221
Sékou Touré, Ahmed, 778–79
Seleucus I, 5
self-praise, bard's songs of, 121, 127–28, 129n.9
self-reliance: *Kujichagulia* (self-determination concept), 546–47; Pan-African culture of, 761–62; spirit of, in African American blues music, 774–76
Semitic languages, list of, 266
Senegal: conquest of, 208; economic conditions in, 348–49; government study groups in, 344–45
Senghor, Léopold Sédar, 240, 286, 342–53
Serbian guslars, African bards compared with, 120, 122, 124–25
Sertima, Ivan Van, 509
Sethe, K., 12
Setiloane, G. M., 292
Shabaka (King), 12
Shaka (Zulu founder and emperor), 151–59
Shango religion, African sources of, 62
Shehu Shagari, Al'Hajji, 215
Shilluk ethnic group, 297, 300, 302
Shona ethnic group, song of, 619
Siculús, Diodorus, 3
signatures, of an *Odu,* 164
Signifying Monkey: *guije (jigue)* (Afro-Cuban monkey analogue), 167–70, 174nn.22–23; origins of, 164–67
Sinuhe, 285, 308–11
slave narratives: emergence of, 219–22, 598; Nat Turner's story, 620–26; Olaudah Equiano's narrative, 176–84
slavery: absence of, in precolonial Africa, 709–710; African slave traders, 425–26, 438n.7, 439n.9; in Akan society, 461; Brazilian *quilombismo* concept and, 509–14, 758–59; Christianity and, 479–82; cross-cultural exchange through, 161; Douglass's oration against, 637–40; impact of, on African

American literature, 219–26; music influenced by, 767–68; role of, in Africalogy, 260; slave rebellions, 494–94, 620–26, 758–59; Walker's appeal regarding, 627–36

Slavic bards, African bards compared with, 127

Smith, Bessie, 776–77

Smith, Bosworth, 471, 473–75

Smith, Edwin, 296

Smith, John Caswell, Jr., 226

Snowden, Frank, Jr., 4

social conditions: in Akan society, 452–61; in ancient Africa, 443–45; of Brazilian Africans, 510–11; and polygamy in African countries, 778–79; in precolonial Africa, 708–714

socialism: in Africa, 342–53, 369–70; Du Bois's embrace of, 588; Pan-African culture and, 696–97

soft drinks, African consumption patterns, 216

Somalia, development of alphabet in, 213

Sonchis, 285

Song of Igor's Campaign, The, 127

"Song of the Jigue," 168–70

Songhay Empire, 207–208; intellectual life of precolonial era, 218–19

soul, African religious concept of, 300–301

Souls of Black Folk, The, 193–200, 586

Sourkata (Mandingo deity), 127–28

South America, Africalogy studies of, 259–60

Soyinka, Wole, 113, 248–50

Spencer, Herbert, 288–89

spiritual intervention, African tradition of, 59–62

spirituals, of African Americans, 388–96; intellectual roots of, 219; women's influence on, 767–69

Sport of the Gods, The, 222

Sproul, B., 12

Spunk, 223

State, Akan theory of, 455–56

Stewart, Maria W., 286, 397–401

Stewart-Baxter, Derrick, 776

stooling and destooling of kings and leaders: Akan government structure and constitution, 466–69; case studies of, in Ghana, 185–88; *Odwira* festival and, 112, 251–53

Story Magazine, 225

"Story of Osetua, The," 163

"Story of the Two Brothers, The," 286, 332–34

Strength of Gideon, The, 222

structural linguistics, and Egyptian connections to African languages, 265

Studies on Slavery in Easy Lessons, 481

Suchier, Wolfram, 425, 431–32, 436, 438nn.5–6

Sudan, government study groups in, 344–45

Suicide ou Survie de l'Occident, 347

Sumanguru (King), 121

Sumner, Charles, 481

Sundermeier, Theo, 291

Sundiata (Mali legendary king): conquests of, 597–98; Kouroukan Fougan (Division of the World), 131–35

Sunjata, 120–22, 124–26

sunsum (Akan concept), 452–53

Survey Graphic, 224

Sùúrù (Yoruba deity), 105

Swahili culture: early civilizations, 208; poetry in, 214

synchronic linguistics, defined, 262

syncretic religions, African sources of, 62

Tafawa Balewa, Al'Hajii, 215

Tanzania, Kiswahili language in, 214

Tarakiri Clan: dialect of, 141; *Ozidi* saga and, 136, 141–44, 149

Tarikh es-Sudan, 207

Taylor, John V., 291, 297, 303n.16

Teachings of Ptahhotep, 5

technology, American dominance of, in Africa, 216

Tempels, Placide, 290, 344

temptation and fall as theme in *Ozidi* epic, 138

Temugedege (mythical figure in *Ozidi* epic), 138, 145

Teti (Kemetic king), pyramid text, 13, 24–26

Their Eyes Were Watching God, 172

Theogony, 122, 126–27

They Came Before Columbus, 509

Thiam, Awa, 778–79

Thiong'o, Ngugi wa, 286

Thomasius, Christian, 429, 431–32

Thompkins, Grace W., 225

Thompson, Vincent Bakpetu, 598

Thomsen, Christian, 260–61

Thurman, Wallace, 200, 224

Thutmose I, 112; commemorative stone of, 602–604

Thutmose II, 112

Thutmose III, 597, 605–608

Timbuktu, 218–19

Timbuktu the Mysterious, 218–19

time, African concept of, 295

tofo (Akan ghost), 454

tomb inscriptions, 2, 5, 13; Hotep-her-akhet, 32; Nefer-seshem-ra (Sheshi), 33; Princess Ni-sedjer-kai, 31

tomb prayers, of Paheri, 60, 66–70

Toomer, Jean, 161, 172, 222

totemism, African religions and, 289

Towards Colonial Freedom, 365–66, 369

Tower to Heaven (Asante), 50

tragedy, African concept of, 113, 248–50

"Tragedy at Three Forks, The," 222

Transactions of the Faculty of Philosophy of Halle, 436

Transactions of the Historical Society of Ghana, 427

Treitschke, Heinrich von, 409–10

trickster topos, 161–72

Tropic Death, 223

Trotter, Monroe, 500–502

Trotter, Walker, 587

Truth, Sojourner, 770

Tubman, Harriet, 768–69, 776

Turner, Nat, 620–26

Tutola, Amos, 383

Tylor, E. B., 288

Uglijanin, Salih, 122, 125, 127

Ujamaa (cooperative economics), 549–50

Ujima (collective work and responsibility principle), 548–49

Ulric, Anton (Duke), 424–27

Umbanda religion, African sources of, 62

Umoja (unity concept), 544–46

Unas (Kemetic king), pyramid text, 13, 17–23

unborn, in African religions, 59–60
Uncle Tom's Children, 225
Unified Black Movement Against Racism and Racial
  Discrimination (Brazil), 512
Unilateral Declaration of Independence (Zimbabwe), 734
Universal Negro Improvement Association, 402–408,
  445

Vai people: religion of, 61; secret society, 2
Vashona people, religious concepts of, 302
Vassa, Gustavas. *See* Equiano, Olaudah
Verification Principle (Nkrumah), 355
vernacular tradition of African Americans, signifying
  ritual and, 161–62, 172, 173n.5
visions of the universe: Pepi text, 27–30; Teti text,
  24–26
"vital force" theory, African religions and, 290
Voodoo, African sources of, 62
Vroman, Mary E., 226

Wali, Obi, 382–83
Walker, David, 221, 598, 627–36
Walrond, Eric, 223
Ward, Samuel Ringgold, 221
Washington, Booker T., 195, 197–99, 223, 529; Atlanta Exposition address of, 489–91; Du Bois's
  evaluation of, 492–99; on racial accommodation,
  444–45, 483–88; Trotter's critique of, 500–502
Ways of White Folks, The, 222
Wells-Barnett, Ida B., 651–55
Wen-Amon, Asian journey of, 286, 335–39
Weni (Kemet magistrate), 444, 446–48
Wennofer, 285
West, Cornel, 445, 583–93
West Africa: economic development programs for,
  345–52; intellectual life of precolonial era,
  218–19; prehistory of, 207–208
West African Celebrities, 425
Westerlond, D., 293
Western culture: African attitudes regarding,
  355–70; African cultural identity and, 215–17,
  241–42, 706–720; attitudes toward African religion and philosophy, 287–92, 506–508; impact
  on African American educational experience of,
  656–63
Wheatley, Phillis, 219–20
White, Walter, 200n.4, 224
"Why Monkey Did Not Become Man," 167
Wife of His Youth and Other Stories of the Color Line, The,
  222

Wilde, Oscar, 193–94
Wilkins, Roy, 201n.4
Williams, Ethel L., 292
Williams, Larry, 5
Williams, Raymond, 193, 200n.2
Williamson, Kay (Dr.), 141–42, 149n.6
Wilson, Daniel, 261
Wilson, Godfrey, 298, 304n.23
Wilson, John, 7
Wilson, Monica, 300
Winston, Henry, 592
Wiredu, K., 293
wisdom statements, in Akan society, 459–61
Wolff, Christian, 431–32, 436
Wolff, Moses Abraham, 435–36
women: African American women, experiences of,
  503–504, 530, 641–50; in Akan society, 458; ancient African sources by, 6–7; assertion of power
  by, Queen Hatshepsut as symbol of, 112; Ijo people's taboos regarding, 148–49; leadership by, in
  African liberation movement, 445; need for political activism among, 778–79; role of, in black
  music, 765–76; in Yoruba religion and folklore,
  101–106
Woodson, G. Carter, 656–63
worship, *Ozidi* saga and, 147–48
Wright, Richard, 200, 225–26, 240
writing: African writers and the English language,
  286, 379–84; ancient Africans' awe of, 2; role of,
  in Yoruba Ifa texts, 164–65, 171–72, 174n.13

Yaa Asantewaa (Queen), 7, 599
Yerby, Frank, 225
Yoruba ethnic group: Brazilian Africans linked to,
  508; concept of good in, 61; concept of person
  in, 300; creation myths of, 13, 45–49; cultural
  and religious influence of, 297; cultural clashes
  with Ibo, 211–12; Esu-Elegbara (trickster figure)
  of, 161–72; geographic spread of, 297; Ifá sacred
  texts of, 98–106, 163–64; *ijala* (heroic chants) of,
  121–23, 127–28; linguistic connections to Egyptian language, 265; *Odu Ifa* divination verses, 162;
  origins of signifying monkey with, 167; *Oriki Esu*
  narrative, 162; tragedy as concept in, 248–50
"Yoruba praises to Ogun," 112, 117–18
Young, Whitney, 201n.4

Zagwe (Ethiopian dynasty), 718–19
Zemp, Hugo, 122, 129n.15
Zimbabwe, ancient civilization of, 207
Zogic, Demail, 122
Zulu Personal Declaration, 286, 371–78